THE REPOSE OF THE SPIRITS

SUNY SERIES IN ISLAM

Seyyed Hossein Nasr, editor

THE REPOSE OF THE SPIRITS

A SUFI COMMENTARY ON THE DIVINE NAMES

AḤMAD SAMʿĀNĪ

TRANSLATED AND WITH AN INTRODUCTION BY
William C. Chittick

SUNY
PRESS

Published by State University of New York Press, Albany

Printed in the United States of America

For information, contact State University of New York Press, Albany, NY
www.sunypress.edu

Library of Congress Cataloging-in-Publication Data

Names: Samʿānī, Aḥmad ibn Manṣūr, 1094–1140, author. | Chittick, William C., translator, writer of introduction.
Title: The repose of the spirits : a sufi commentary on the divine names / Aḥmad Samʿānī ; translated and with an introduction by William C. Chittick.
Other titles: Rawḥ al-arwāḥ fī sharḥ asmāʾ al-malik al-fattāḥ. English
Description: Albany : State University of New York, [2019] | Series: Suny series in islam | Includes bibliographical references and index.
Identifiers: LCCN 2018019233 | ISBN 9781438473338 (hardcover : alk. paper) | ISBN 9781438473352 (e-book) | ISBN 9781438473345 (pbk : alk. paper)
Subjects: LCSH: God (Islam)—Name—Early works to 1800. | Sufism—Early works to 1800.
Classification: LCC BP166.2 .S34513 2019 | DDC 297.2/112—dc23
LC record available at https://lccn.loc.gov/2018019233

10 9 8 7 6 5 4 3 2 1

CONTENTS

Acknowledgments, ix

Introduction, xi

The Samʿānīs, xiii

Sufism in Aḥmad's Khorasan, xxviii

The Keys to the Unseen, xlviii

The Text and Translation, lxviii

Notes, lxix

The Repose of the Spirits: Explaining the Names of the All-Opening King, 1

1. *Hū:* He, 3

2. *Allāh:* God, 4

3. *Alladhī Lā Ilāha Illā Hū:* There is no god but He, 6

4–5. *al-Raḥmān al-Raḥīm:* the All-Merciful, the Ever-Merciful, 7

6. *al-Malik:* the King, 9

7. *al-Quddūs:* the Holy, 11

8. *al-Salām:* the Peace, 14

9. *al-Muʾmin:* the Faithful, 19

10. *al-Muhaymin:* the Overseer, 26

11. *al-ʿAzīz:* the Exalted, 32

12. *al-Jabbār:* the All-Compelling, 38

13. *al-Mutakabbir:* the Proud, 43

14. *al-Khāliq:* the Creator, 48

15. *al-Bāriʾ:* the Maker, 52

16. *al-Muṣawwir:* the Form-Giver, 57

17. *al-Ghaffār:* the All-Forgiving, 63

18. *al-Qahhār:* the Severe, 67

19. *al-Wahhāb:* the Bestower, 72

20. *al-Razzāq:* the Provider, 78

21. *al-Fattāḥ:* the All-Opening, 84
22. *al-ʿAlīm:* the Knower, 90
23–24. *al-Qābiḍ al-Bāsiṭ:* the Contractor, the Expander, 107
25–26. *al-Khāfiḍ al-Rāfiʿ:* the Downletter, the Uplifter, 120
27–28. *al-Muʿizz al-Mudhill:* the Exalter, the Abaser, 138
29–30. *al-Samīʿ al-Baṣīr:* the Hearing, the Seeing, 148
31–32*: al-Ḥakam al-ʿAdl:* the Ruler, the Just, 167
33. *al-Laṭīf:* the Gentle, 186
34. *al-Khabīr:* the Aware, 201
35. *al-Ḥalīm:* the Forbearing, 220
36. *al-ʿAẓīm:* the Tremendous, 239
37–38. *al-Ghafūr al-Shakūr:* the Forgiving, the Grateful, 258
39–40. *al-ʿAlī al-Kabīr:* the High, the Great, 264
41. *al-Ḥafīẓ:* the Guardian, 270
42. *al-Muqīt:* the Nourisher, 274
43. *al-Ḥasīb:* the Reckoner/the Sufficer, 281
44–45. *al-Jalīl al-Jamīl:* the Majestic, the Beautiful, 285
46. *al-Karīm:* the Generous, 290
47. *al-Raqīb:* the Watcher, 297
48. *al-Mujīb:* the Responder, 302
49. *al-Wāsiʿ:* the Embracing, 308
50. *al-Ḥakīm:* the Wise, 315
51. *al-Wadūd:* the Loving/the Beloved, 323
52. *al-Majīd:* the Splendorous, 328
53. *al-Bāʿith:* the Upraiser, 334
54. *al-Shahīd:* the Witness, 339
55–56. *al-Ḥaqq al-Mubīn:* the Real, the Clarifier, 345
57–58. *al-Wakīl al-Qawī:* the Trustee, the Strong, 352
59. *al-Matīn:* the Firm, 357
60. *al-Walī:* the Friend, 362
61. *al-Ḥamīd:* the Praiser/the Praised, 368
62. *al-Muḥṣī:* the Enumerator, 371
63–64. *al-Mubdiʾ al-Muʿīd:* the Originator, the Returner, 375
65–66. *al-Muḥyī al-Mumīt:* the Life-Giver, the Death-Giver, 380
67–68. *al-Ḥayy al-Qayyūm:* the Alive, the Self-Standing, 385
69. *al-Wājid:* the Finder, 390

70–71. *al-Wāḥid al-Aḥad:* the One, the Unique, 394

72. *al-Ṣamad:* the Self-Sufficient, 398

73–74. *al-Qādir al-Muqtadir:* the Powerful, the Potent, 403

75–76. *al-Muqaddim al-Mu'akhkhir:* the Forward-Setter, the Behind-Keeper, 408

77–80. *al-Awwal al-Ākhir al-Ẓāhir al-Bāṭin:* the First, the Last, the Outward, the Inward, 415

81. *al-Barr:* the Kind, 421

82. *al-Tawwāb:* the Ever-Turning, 428

83. *al-Muntaqim:* the Avenger, 433

84. *al-'Afū:* the Pardoner, 439

85–89. *al-Ra'ūf Mālik al-Mulk Dhu'l-Jalāl wa'l-Ikrām al-Wālī al-Muta'ālī:* the Clement, the Owner of the Kingdom, the Possessor of Majesty and Generous Giving, the Protector, the Transcendent, 444

90–91. *al-Muqsiṭ al-Jāmi':* the Impartial, the Gathering, 444

92–93. *al-Ghanī al-Mughnī:* the Unneedy, the Need-Lifter, 449

94–95. *al-Ḍārr al-Nāfi':* the Harmer, the Benefiter, 454

96. *al-Nūr:* the Light, 458

97. *al-Hādī:* the Guide, 464

98. *al-Badī':* the Innovating, 471

99–100. *al-Bāqī al-Wārith:* the Subsistent, the Inheritor, 477

101. *al-Rashīd:* the Director, 484

102. *al-Ṣabūr:* the Patient, 491

Notes, 495

Works Cited, 541

Index of Quranic Verses, 557

Index of Hadiths and Arabic Sayings, 571

Index and Glossary of Terms, 585

ACKNOWLEDGMENTS

I owe a great debt of gratitude to the prolific reviver of ancient texts Najib Mayel Heravi, who published the book translated here, *Rawḥ al-arwāḥ*, thirty years ago and sent me a copy at that time. When I looked it over, I realized that it was an extraordinary discovery, and I soon wrote an article trying to suggest its riches. I also made good use of it in my recent study *Divine Love*. Various people exposed to translated excerpts have asked me why I did not translate the whole text—a question I often asked myself. Finally, in 2013, I proposed a translation to the John Simon Guggenheim Foundation and was awarded a generous fellowship for the academic year 2014–15. Without the fifteen months of concentrated study that the fellowship made possible, this book would still be a dream, so I am deeply indebted to the Guggenheim Foundation.

INTRODUCTION

The full name of the book translated here is *The Repose of the Spirits: Explaining the Names of the All-Opening King* (*Rawḥ al-arwāḥ fī sharḥ asmāʾ al-malik al-fattāḥ*). It is the first and one of the longest commentaries on the divine names in the Persian language. It was written by Aḥmad Samʿānī, who belonged to a prominent scholarly family from Merv in Central Asia and died at the young age of forty-six in the year 1140. It is a remarkable expression of Islamic spirituality and one of the most accessible books on the inner meanings of the Quran ever written.

Commentary on the divine names was a common genre in Arabic, but Samʿānī did not write in imitation of earlier scholars, who were mainly lexicologists and theologians. He avoided their abstract analyses and arid exactitude, highlighting instead the divine love that permeates all of existence. His book prefigures the poetical tradition that was to bloom with ʿAṭṭār (d. ca. 1221), Rūmī (d. 1273), and Saʿdī (d. 1292). Recent research has even shown that Ḥāfiẓ (d. 1390), typically considered the greatest of all Persian poets, composed scores of verses that follow *The Repose of the Spirits* almost verbatim.[1] *Repose* offers a clear depiction of the worldview underlying the work of the poets and celebrates love with the same sensitivity to beautiful language. In contrast to the poets, however, Samʿānī grounds his text explicitly in the names of God that are the archetypes of all that exists.

It seems that no one else before Ibn ʿArabī (d. 1240)—who was born sixteen years after Samʿānī died—was able to plumb the depths of divine love and mercy with such insight. Ibn ʿArabī, however, wrote for the intellectual elite. He produced several thousand pages of highly sophisticated and erudite prose and a good deal of poetry. His opus was accessible only to those familiar with the whole range of Islamic sciences—Quran, Hadith, Arabic grammar, jurisprudence, Kalam, Sufism, and philosophy. In contrast, Samʿānī wrote in the spoken Persian of Khorasan (which is practically identical with today's literary Persian in Iran, Afghanistan, and Central Asia), and he addressed the general populace. He exposed the underlying message of the Islamic tradition with exceptional clarity and extraordinary subtlety.

Samʿānī's name was almost forgotten in later times, but *The Repose of the Spirits* was certainly being read. One of the few later scholars who did provide the author's name along with the title of his book was the Ottoman bibliophile Kātip Çelebi, also known as Ḥājjī Khalīfa (d. 1657), though he said nothing about the book's content.[2] The first text on which *Repose* left a noticeable impression was the ten-volume Persian commentary on the Quran, *Kashf al-asrār* (*The Unveiling of the Mysteries*) by Rashīd al-Dīn Maybudī, who lived in Maybud near Yazd in central Iran. Maybudī says that he started writing his book in the year 1126, when Samʿānī would have been thirty-two.

He shows no sign of having read *Repose* until the beginning of volume six, when he suddenly starts making wholesale use of it, without ever mentioning his source. Nowadays we would call this plagiarism, but in both Persian and Arabic it was common practice at the time. In his introduction Maybudī says that he based his book on a Quran commentary by the famous Hanbali jurist and Sufi ʿAbdallāh Anṣārī (d. 1088), though no such work is known to have existed. Maybudī often quotes Anṣārī, but the second half of his book depends much more on Samʿānī.[3]

One of the few explicit references to *The Repose of the Spirits* in the later literature is found in *Fawāʾid al-fuʾād* (Benefits of the Heart), the Persian conversations of Niẓām al-Dīn Awliyāʾ (d. 1325), the patron saint of Delhi (translated into English by Bruce Lawrence). The compiler, Amīr Ḥasan Sijzī, says that he visited Niẓām al-Dīn on June 8, 1312 with a certain book in hand. Noticing the book, Niẓām al-Dīn said, "Among the books the shaykhs have written, *The Repose of the Spirits* has much comfort.... Qāḍī Ḥamīd al-Dīn Nāgawrī learned it and spoke about it a great deal from the pulpit. Among the books written by the former masters, *Nourishment of the Hearts* is a beautiful book in Arabic, and *The Repose of the Spirits* in Persian."[4] Given that *Nourishment of the Hearts* (*Qūt al-qulūb*) by Abū Ṭālib Makkī (d. 996) is one of the most important books of early Sufism, Niẓām al-Dīn's high opinion of it is not surprising. His mention of *The Repose of the Spirits*, however, shows that it also was being recognized as an outstanding presentation of Sufi teachings.

As for Qāḍī Ḥamīd al-Dīn Nāgawrī (d. 1246), he was a major disciple of Muʿīn al-Dīn Chishtī (d. 1235), the eponym of the Chishtī Order, and wrote several books. One of these, a short Persian work on love called *Lawāʾiḥ*, was published sixty years ago in Iran but ascribed wrongly to ʿAyn al-Quḍāt Hamadānī. It is the only printed text I have seen that quotes *Repose* by name, though he does not mention its author.[5] He also wrote an unpublished Persian commentary on the divine names called *Ṭawāliʿ al-shumūs* (Rising suns), a scan of which was acquired for me by my friend Seyed Amir Hossein Asghari. At 1,040 pages of twenty-two lines each, the manuscript is about fifty percent longer than *The Repose of the Spirits*. It is a fresh and original interpretation of 103 divine names addressed to practitioners of Sufism, with constant reference to Quran and Hadith. It focuses on love much more than *Repose*, which itself stands apart from its Arabic predecessors because of the same focus. Nāgawrī rarely quotes from other authors, but he does include about thirty short passages, mostly in Arabic, from *The Repose of the Spirits* and often mentions that "Samʿānī" was the author of the book.[6]

It is not clear why *The Repose of the Spirits* escaped the notice of historians of Persian literature and Sufism for most of the twentieth century. Copies are found in various libraries, so the reason is probably not the scarcity of manuscripts. Perhaps it was overlooked because it appears at first glance to be a typical commentary on the divine names. Its title suggests that it would be of interest only to specialists in theology, which has never been a favorite topic among modern scholars of Persian literature. A second reason may be that from the thirteenth century onward the formulation of Sufi teachings came to be dominated by the much more theoretical and philosophical approach of Ibn ʿArabī. Thus, for example, commentators on Rūmī's *Mathnawī* typically drew from Ibn ʿArabī's perspective. If instead they had drawn from Samʿānī, the result would have been much closer to Rūmī's own mode of presentation.

Repose was first brought to the attention of specialists by the indefatigable manuscript-reader Muḥammad-Taqī Dānishpazhūh (d. 1996), who published an article in 1968 describing seven manuscripts that he had seen in various libraries. Only three of these manuscripts mention the author's name, two in corrupted form. Dānishpazhūh wrote that the book was a precious example of early Persian prose, full of stories in the style of homilists and Sufi teachers and adorned with Persian and Arabic poetry. "The prose," he said, "is fluent, eloquent, heart-pleasing, and ancient, so much so that you never become tired of reading it and you want to keep on reading to the end."[7] In the following year the unsurpassed Rūmī expert Badīʿ al-Zamān Furūzānfar (d. 1970) confirmed Dānishpazhūh's evaluation of the book in his commentary on Rūmī's *Mathnawī*. He also pointed out that Rūmī's tale of the nomad and the caliph (in book 1, vv. 2244ff.) is based on an Arabic passage from *Repose* (288).[8] Furūzānfar then devoted two pages to describing the book, since it was still almost unknown in the secondary literature. He mentioned the beauty of the prose, the great variety of anecdotes about the Prophet, the Companions, and other saintly figures, and went on to agree with Dānishpazhūh, on the basis of various historical sources, that the author must be Abu'l-Qāsim Aḥmad ibn Manṣūr Samʿānī.

I will have more to say about the specific characteristics of Samʿānī's book, but something first needs to be said about the author and the milieu of Islamic learning in which he flourished.

The Samʿānīs

Aḥmad Samʿānī's birthplace, the oasis city of Merv, is now a UNESCO heritage site near the modern city of Mary in Turkmenistan. In Achaemenid times it was the capital of the province of Margiana. After Alexander's invasion, it was known for a time as Alexandria. It remained the capital of the province during the empires that followed, and the last Sassanid emperor, Yazdegerd III, was killed near the city in the year 651 while fleeing Arab invaders. It then became the capital, or one of the capitals, of Khorasan, a region that embraced the eastern part of present-day Iran, most of Afghanistan, and a good deal of Central Asia. In 1037 Merv was conquered by the Seljuq Turks, under whom it continued to flourish. It soon became one of the largest cities in the world, certainly a rival to Baghdad, the seat of the Abbasid caliphate. It was during this period that the Samʿānīs came to prominence. The city's decline began with its pillage by the Ghuzz nomads in 1153, thirteen years after Aḥmad Samʿānī's death. In 1221 the Mongols under Tolui, a son of Genghis Khan, destroyed Merv and massacred the entire population.

Merv was known as a great center of learning. The famous geographer Yāqūt Ḥamawī (d. 1229) spent three years in Merv in his search for knowledge, leaving in 1219. He wrote that he would have stayed until the end of his life if not for the impending invasion. Its people were good-natured, and the city had ten libraries endowed with excellent books. These were of such easy access that he would sometimes take out over two hundred volumes at once. Indeed, he says, "I collected most of the details for this and my other books from those libraries." Two of the ten libraries belonged to madrasas with which the Samʿānīs were involved—the Niẓāmiyya and the ʿAmīdiyya—and two to the Samʿānī family itself.[9]

Other important cities of Khorasan at the time included Herat, the home of ʿAbdallāh Anṣārī, about two hundred miles south of Merv; Nishapur, a great center of learning and the birthplace of ʿAṭṭār, about two hundred miles southwest; and Bukhara, the home of the famous Hadith scholar Bukhārī, 225 miles northeast. Juwayn, the birthplace of the theologian Imām al-Ḥaramayn Juwaynī (d. 1085), a teacher of Samʿānī's father Manṣūr, lies 120 miles southwest of Merv. Tus, the birthplace of Juwaynī's best-known student, Abū Ḥāmid Ghazālī (d. 1111), is about thirty miles southwest of Juwayn. Balkh, the area from which Rūmī hailed, lies about two hundred miles east-southeast of Merv. Ghazna, the seat of the Ghaznavid Empire (977–1163) and the home of Sanāʾī (d. 1135), the first great Sufi poet, is about 450 miles southeast. As for the largest city in the area today, Mashhad, "the place of martyrdom"—that is, the martyrdom of the eighth Shi'ite Imam, ʿAlī ibn Mūsā Riḍā (d. 818)—it is located about 150 miles southwest of Merv; at the time it was still a small town outside of Tus known as Nawqān, famous as a place of pilgrimage to the tomb of the Imam and also as the location of the grave of the Abbasid caliph Hārūn al-Rashīd (d. 809).[10] I mention the proximity of these cities because today they belong to four different countries and might be imagined to pertain to distinct areas rather than the same cultural environment. As for more distant cities of the Islamic world, Isfahan is about seven hundred miles southwest of Merv, Baghdad about 1,100 miles west, and Mecca about 1,800 miles southwest. These distances are straight lines, so travel between any of these cities would entail much more hardship than the mileage suggests.

The only known contemporary account of Aḥmad Samʿānī is by his nephew, Abū Saʿd ʿAbd al-Karīm Samʿānī (d. 1166), a well-known scholar who wrote about one hundred books and treatises, most of which were dedicated to Hadith and Hadith-transmitters. The bulk of his corpus, which included a history of Merv—the longest of his books—seems to have disappeared with the destruction of the city. Two of his biographical works have survived. One is the five-volume *Ascriptions* (*al-Ansāb*), which provides accounts of hundreds of scholars according to their *nisba*, that is, their "ascription" to tribe, family, region, or whatever. The other is an account of his own teachers, abridged by an unknown author, called *The Abridgement of the Lexicon of the Shaykhs* (*al-Muntakhab min Muʿjam al-shuyūkh*), providing details on 1,446 of those who transmitted Hadith and other learning to him.[11] Another work, his addendum to the history of Baghdad by Khaṭīb Baghdādī (d. 1071), was somewhat longer than *Ascriptions* and widely used in the later biographical literature, but it seems to be lost. ʿAbd al-Karīm's fame as an inveterate traveler and collector of shaykhs is suggested by the historian Ibn al-Najjār (d. 1245), who said that he heard Hadith from seven thousand scholars.[12]

To understand ʿAbd al-Karīm Samʿānī's status in the tradition, we need to recall that for centuries one of the primary occupations of Muslim scholars was preserving the basic teachings of the religion by transmitting Hadith. It was never considered sufficient to read a hadith in a book. One needed to "hear" (*samāʿ*) the text from a teacher. The teacher in turn must have heard it from a teacher, who had heard it from a teacher, and so on back to the Prophet. Part of the process of hearing was to hear the chain of transmission, the *isnād*. The importance of the science of *rijāl*, "the men," arises from here: It was always fair to ask if the scholars who transmitted a hadith were reliable transmitters. Ad hominem criticism was the rule. If any link of the *isnād* was unreliable, one could not be sure that the saying had come from the Prophet.

One of the many criteria for judging a hadith's reliability was the length of the chain—the shorter, the better. This meant that seekers of Hadith often exerted great effort to find scholars who had received hadiths with short *isnāds*, even if these were the same hadiths that they had heard from other teachers. One of 'Abd al-Karīm's claims to fame is that he heard hadiths from many scholars with "high" (*'ālī*) rather than "low" (*nāzil*) chains, that is, short rather than long.

The extent to which scholars dedicated themselves to collecting hadiths is hard for us to imagine today and, I think, for many of their contemporaries. Abū Ḥāmid Ghazālī, for example, thought that it was much more important to put one's efforts into actualizing the fullness of intelligence (*'aql*). However this may be, there is an extensive biographical literature on transmitters of Hadith, and these works have provided historians with one of their main sources of information on individuals. 'Abd al-Karīm's works are among the earliest in this genre.

It is important to understand that 'Abd al-Karīm wrote both *Ascriptions* and *Abridgement* with the aim of describing *'ulamā'*, "scholars," a word that means literally "knowers." He typically uses this word in a narrow sense to mean those who transmitted Hadith. He often says that so-and-so was "one of the folk (*ahl*) of the Quran and of knowledge," meaning that the individual was learned both in the Holy Book and in Hadith. If the person happened to have other qualifications, he specifies this by saying that he was also a jurist, a Sufi, a Quran-reciter, and so on.

That 'Abd al-Karīm should use the generic word "knowledge" to mean knowledge of Hadith shows his limited standpoint in searching for knowledge and in providing accounts of individuals in his books. For example, he does not have a listing for the word "Ghazālī" in *Ascriptions*, even though he was well informed about Abū Ḥāmid Ghazālī and his younger brother Aḥmad (d. 1126), author of a short Persian classic on love. If he did not feel that their name was worthy of a separate entry, it is surely because they were not transmitters of "knowledge," that is, Hadith. Tāj al-Dīn Subkī (d. 1370), author of the well-known biographical tome *Ṭabaqāt al-Shāfi'iyya* (The Generations of the Shafi'is), quotes 'Abd al-Karīm as saying about Abū Ḥāmid Ghazālī, "I do not think that he transmitted any hadiths, or if he did, only a few, for no hadith has been narrated from him." [13]

In *Ascriptions* 'Abd al-Karīm dedicates the heading "Sam'ānī" to an account of his family. In *Abridgement* he describes several of his relatives individually, sometimes adding details not given in *Ascriptions*.[14] He explains that the word Sam'ānī refers to Sam'ān, a subdivision of Banū Tamīm, one of the major tribes of Arabia. The patriarch of the Sam'ānīs in Merv was the learned and pious judge (*qāḍī*) and imam Abū Manṣūr Muḥammad ibn 'Abd al-Jabbār (d. 1058), who wrote useful works in Arabic grammar and lexicology and was the first of the family to transmit Hadith. Among the handful of books that 'Abd al-Karīm attributes to him, one has been published, the four-volume *Majmū' gharā'ib al-aḥādīth* (A Compilation of Rarities in the Hadith), a dictionary of unusual words employed by the Prophet.[15]

MANṢŪR IBN MUḤAMMAD

Muḥammad ibn 'Abd al-Jabbār had two sons, Abu'l-Muẓaffar Manṣūr (1035–96) and Abu'l-Qāsim 'Alī. The latter was a scholar who traveled to Kerman, married into the family of the local king's vizier, and continued to teach and transmit Hadith. When he learned that his brother had changed his *madhhab* (school of jurisprudence) from Hanafi to Shafi'i, he wrote to him and criticized him for leaving the path of their father. Manṣūr replied that he had not changed their father's creed (*'aqīda*), only his *madhhab*, because the Hanafis in Merv no longer had proper beliefs. They had all become Qadarīs, that is, "free-willers" (an attribute often attributed to Mu'tazilite theologians), which is to say that they believed people are rewarded or punished in the next world strictly on the basis of their choices in this world (Sam'ānī offers critiques of this position in *Repose*). Eventually the two brothers were reconciled, and 'Alī sent his son Abu'l-'Alā' 'Alī to study with Manṣūr. After several years, the younger 'Alī returned to Kirman, and when his father died he took over the family madrasa and the rearing of his siblings. This branch of the family does not seem to have received any further notice by historians.[16]

'Abd al-Karīm calls his grandfather Manṣūr "the undisputed imam of his era, without equal in his field." His words are not simply family pride. Subkī relates that Imām al-Ḥaramayn Juwaynī, with whom Manṣūr studied as a young man, said about him, "Were jurisprudence a fine garment, Abu'l-Muẓaffar ibn Sam'ānī would be its embroidery."[17]

Manṣūr wrote ten books, three of which have been published: a six-volume commentary on the Quran; a five-volume tome on the philosophy of law called *Qawāṭi' al-adilla fī uṣūl al-fiqh* (The Definitive Proofs in the Principles of Jurisprudence); and a four-volume explication of the differences between Shafi'i and Hanafi jurisprudence, *al-Iṣṭilām fi'l-khilāf bayn imāmayn al-Shāfi'ī wa Abī Ḥanīfa* (The Extirpation: On the Disagreements between the Two Imams, Shāfi'ī and Abū Ḥanīfa). One of his lost books was a collection of one thousand hadiths, ten transmitted from each of one hundred scholars.[18]

Manṣūr set off for the hajj in 1069, three years after his father's death. He was accompanied by his good friend Ḥusayn ibn Ḥasan Ṣūfī, who said that when they arrived at the first waystation, three farsakhs (about twelve miles) from Merv, Manṣūr spent all of his money—five dirhams—on their needs for the day, so they relied on God's bounty for the rest of the trip.[19] Another companion on this pilgrimage, Ḥasan ibn Aḥmad Marwazī, said that whenever they reached a village, they would stay with the Sufis (who commonly put up travelers in their lodges) and Manṣūr would search out scholars of Hadith.[20] The pilgrims spent a good deal of time in Baghdad, where Manṣūr interacted with many scholars of Hadith and jurisprudence. In Mecca he became the companion of Sa'd Zanjānī (d. 1078), under whose influence he changed his *madhhab* from Hanafi to Shafi'i in the year 1070. He studied Hadith with numerous scholars in Mecca without any thought of returning to Merv, but his father appeared to him in a dream and told him to go back. He consulted with Zanjānī, who told him to obey his father, so he returned to Merv in the year 1075.[21]

When Manṣūr arrived back in Merv and announced that he had changed his *madhhab*, the Hanafis were dismayed, and this led to rioting in the city. The Shafi'i mosque was shut down, and Manṣūr was expelled by the local governor. He was welcomed in Tus and Nishapur and settled down in the latter. The famous scholar and vizier Niẓām al-Mulk, who held office as the virtual ruler of the Seljuq kingdom from 1064 until his murder in 1092, sent him robes of honor and money. He was given a teaching post at the Niẓāmiyya Madrasa, one of many universities established by Niẓām al-Mulk throughout the kingdom. Only in 1086 did he return to Merv, where he taught in a Shafi'i madrasa.[22]

A book on the history of Nishapur by ʿAbd al-Ghāfir Fārisī (d. 1135) provides a relatively long account of Manṣūr, in whose sessions the author used to recite the Quran. Indeed Fārisī remarks proudly that Manṣūr "loved my recitation of the Quran more than his own."[23] He says that Manṣūr was unique in his time "in erudition, *ṭarīqa*, renunciation (*zuhd*), and scrupulosity (*waraʿ*); and he belonged to a family of knowledge and renunciation."[24] Renunciation, mentioned twice here in a single sentence, was commonly ascribed to those engaged in the devotional practices of Sufism, so much so that some historians have suggested that there was a gradual evolution within Islamic religiosity from renunciation (or "asceticism" as it is more commonly translated) to "mysticism," that is, Sufism (*taṣawwuf*). It is probably more accurate to say, as Alexander Knysh has recently argued, that the words renunciation and Sufism were used interchangeably.[25]

As for the word *ṭarīqa* or "path," it was commonly used to designate the path to God that Sufis were striving to follow, in which case I use the anglicized form Tariqah. It is possible that in this passage Fārisī is using the word generically to mean Manṣūr's way of doing things, but it is more likely that he is alluding to an affiliation with Sufism, where the word is understood to mean emulation of the inner life of the Prophet. In this meaning Tariqah is contrasted with "Shariah" (Islamic law), which is based on imitating the Prophet's outward activity. As Samʿānī says in *Repose*, "The master of the whole world in the Shariah and the Tariqah was Muḥammad" (405). Shariah and Tariqah are frequently discussed along with Haqiqah (*ḥaqīqa*), the "Reality," a word that can designate God inasmuch as He lies beyond all things, or the realm of metaphysical things as contrasted with outward and inward practices. Thus Samʿānī describes the Prophet as "the peacock in the orchard of the Haqiqah, the nightingale in the garden of the Tariqah, and the phoenix in the house of the Shariah" (343). Fārisī uses all three terms while describing the famous Sufi master Abu'l-Qāsim Qushayrī (d. 1072): "He combined the two learnings of the Shariah and the Haqiqah and he explained the principles of the Tariqah with the most beautiful explanation."[26]

In his account of Manṣūr Samʿānī, Fārisī says that he came to Nishapur in his youth and attended the sessions of Imām al-Ḥaramayn Juwaynī, who praised him highly. After he returned from the hajj and was expelled from Merv, he and his retinue were welcomed in Nishapur and given an honored place of residence by order of Niẓām al-Mulk. Then he proceeded to hold regular sessions of *tadhkīr*, "reminder," in which "he was an ocean. He had memorized many stories, fine points, and poems, and he was accepted by the elect and the common."[27]

The word *tadhkīr* is derived from *dhikr*, which means to remember and mention. The Quran designates *tadhkīr* as the role of the prophets and their scriptures, and it constantly encourages its readers to practice *dhikr Allāh*, the remembrance and mention of God. *Tadhkīr* came to designate a form of preaching aimed at a wide audience and encouraging *dhikr*, the practice of which is shared by all forms of Sufism. This helps explain why one modern scholar, having quoted Fārisī to the effect that Ghazālī attended sessions of *tadhkīr* held by Abū ʿAlī Fārmadī (d. 1084), translates the word *tadhkīr* as "mystical practices."[28] What Fārisī says about Fārmadī is similar to what he says about Manṣūr: he was "the shaykh of the shaykhs of his era, unique in his *ṭarīqa* of *tadhkīr*. His *ṭarīqa* had no precedent in expression, refinement, beauty of presentation, sweetness of metaphor, fineness of allusions, and subtleness of elegant words, nor in the impression his speech left in hearts."[29]

Notice that Fārisī says Manṣūr Samʿānī was accepted by the elect (*khāṣṣ*), that is, the scholars, and the common (*ʿāmm*), that is, those not well versed in the Quran and Hadith. This probably means that he was speaking Persian, given that only well-trained scholars would be able to follow lectures in Arabic. A good preacher speaks to his audience at the level of their understanding. A lecture delivered in a madrasa to a group of Hadith-transmitters would be different from a sermon delivered in a mosque with its doors open to the general public. A scholar who transmitted Hadith to fellow scholars could keep them glued to his words by providing *isnāds* more "elevated" than what they had. A homilist busy with reminder, however, could not simply cite scripture and list the names of dead scholars unless he wanted to lose his listeners. His job was to bring out the meaning of the transmitted learning in a language that his listeners could understand—all the more so when they were not native speakers of Arabic. Manṣūr's skill at speaking both to the elect and to the common with "stories, fine points, and poems" suggests that his son Aḥmad was continuing a family tradition. The goal of *The Repose of the Spirits* is not to add to the store of the readers' learning, but rather to open up their hearts to the remembrance of God.

If we look at Manṣūr's three published books, there is little to suggest that he was a master of homily and *tadhkīr*. The most explicit suggestions of his involvement with Sufism come in *Repose*, where Aḥmad quotes him fourteen times. In almost every case the words sound like an aphorism of a Sufi shaykh. Given that Manṣūr died when Aḥmad was two years old, he must have heard these sayings from his brothers or other students of his father. It does not seem possible that he could be quoting him directly, even if his nephew ʿAbd al-Karīm says that Aḥmad was recounting (*yunbiʾu*) from his father at the age of two.[30]

I did notice one exception to Manṣūr's neglect of the Sufi dimension of Islam in his printed works. This is a short supplication in the introductory paragraph of *al-Iṣṭilām*, his study of the differences between Hanafi and Shafiʿi jurisprudence. The manner in which he brings together contrasting divine and human attributes is thoroughly reminiscent of Sufi rhetoric generally and *The Repose of the Spirits* specifically:

> O God, make my breast the storehouse of Your *tawḥīd*, make my tongue the key to Your magnification, and make my limbs the sanctuary of Your obedience, for there is no exaltation except in abasement to You, no wealth except in poverty toward You, no security except in fear of You, no settledness except in disquiet with You, no repose except in grief for Your face, no ease except in approving of Your apportionment, and no delight except in the neighborhood of those brought near to You.[31]

Manṣūr had five children, two of whom died in infancy and three of whom became scholars. The eldest of the surviving sons was ʿAbd al-Karīm's father Abū Bakr Muḥammad, the middle Abū Muḥammad Ḥasan, and the youngest Abu'l-Qāsim Aḥmad, the author of *Repose*.

MUḤAMMAD IBN MANṢŪR

Abū Bakr Muḥammad ibn Manṣūr (1074–1116) continued in his father's footsteps as imam, jurist, and scholar of Hadith. According to ʿAbd al-Karīm, Manṣūr used to say in his public sessions that his son Muḥammad was more learned and more excellent than himself. An anecdote provided by Subkī suggests the sort of learning in which Muḥammad excelled. Subkī cites as his source ʿAbd al-Karīm, who heard the account from one of his father's students.

> In the sessions of his homilies he used to dictate hadiths with their *isnāds*. One of the contenders protested and said, "Muḥammad Samʿānī goes up on the pulpit and lists names that we do not recognize. Perhaps he is just making them up as he goes along." He wrote these words on a piece of paper, and it was given to him.
>
> After ascending the pulpit, he looked at the paper. Then he narrated the hadith, "If someone lies about me intentionally, let him prepare to take up his seat in the Fire," giving it by ninety-some routes [of transmission]. Then he said, "If no one in this land knows Hadith, then I seek refuge in God from dwelling in a land where someone does know Hadith. And if someone does know, let him write out ten hadiths with their *isnāds*, leave out a name or two from each *isnād*, and mix up some of the *isnāds*. If I do not discern this and put every name in its place, then he is as he claims." They did this as a test, and he returned each name to its proper place. The Quran reciters who were reciting in the session that day asked for something, and the attendees gave them one thousand dinars.[32]

TABLE 1. **The Samʿanis**

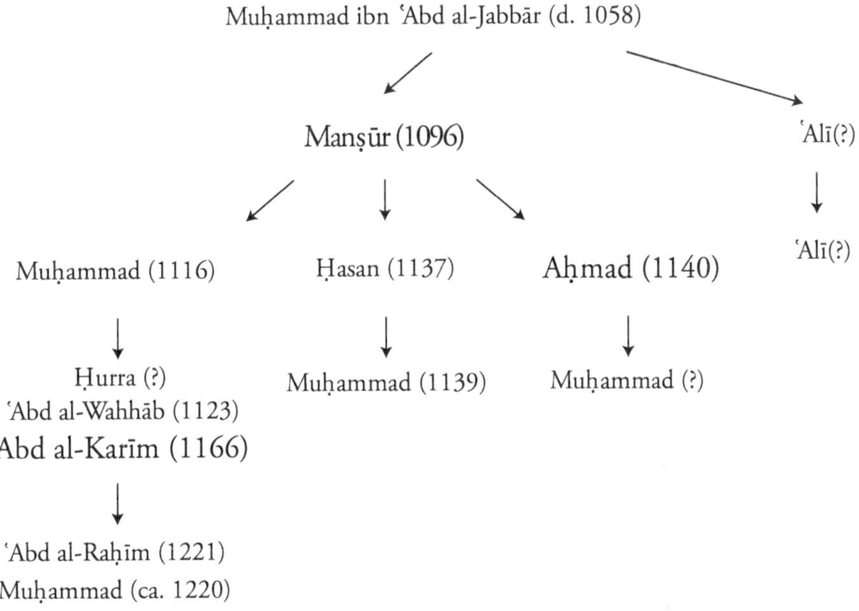

The biographer Ibn Khallikān (d. 1282) quotes ʿAbd al-Karīm as saying that his father performed the hajj in the year 1104, lectured at the Niẓāmiyya Madrasa in Baghdad on his way back, and then went to Isfahan to collect Hadith.[33] ʿAbd al-Karīm writes that his father dictated 140 sessions in Hadith, "and anyone who studies them will recognize that no one preceded him in anything like that." He had a wide knowledge of literature and composed poems in both Arabic and Persian, though he destroyed the poems ("washed away the ink") before he died, perhaps because he considered poetry too frivolous to be the legacy of a scholar. When he passed away at the age of forty-three, his son ʿAbd al-Karīm was three and a half years old.[34]

In an account of a shaykh by the name of Aḥmad the Sufi, who lived in the village of Fāz outside Tus, ʿAbd al-Karīm cites an Arabic poem of his father that escaped the destruction of his notebooks. Aḥmad the Sufi heard him recite the poem while he was passing through Fāz on his way back from the hajj:

> I dismounted at a village called Fāz
> that was sweeter than reaching safety.
> I compared all the lands to its earth
> and saw them as metaphors for its reality.[35]

Muḥammad seems to have had two wives. We know nothing about the first other than that she would have been the mother of Amatallāh Ḥurra, who was born in 1098, fifteen years before ʿAbd al-Karīm. Of Ḥurra he says, "My sister was a worthy, chaste woman who studied the Quran a great deal. She was always fasting and was eager in good and in deeds of piety. My father attained for her a license [*ijāza*, i.e., written permission to transmit what one had learned] from Abū Ghālib Muḥammad ibn Ḥasan Bāqillānī of Baghdad. With her I studied hadiths and stories, and from her I received a license in them."[36]

ʿAbd al-Karīm's own mother was Fāṭima bint Ḥasan Zandakhānī (ca. 1088–1138). He provides a brief account of her in a list of eighty-two of his female shaykhs. She was born into a prominent family in the village of Zandakhān near Sarakhs, a town located about halfway between Merv and Nishapur. Her father became the *raʾīs* or "headman" of Merv, though the exact function of the headman is unknown.[37] She was eager in the good and did much that was honorable and beautiful toward the people.[38] Her younger brother Muḥammad studied jurisprudence with her husband Muḥammad, but then he occupied himself with other affairs; he was tortured and killed by the Ghuzz when they pillaged Sarakhs in the year 1155.[39] ʿAbd al-Karīm thinks that she was born after 1088, that is, less than ten years before the birth of his sister Ḥurra.

Fāṭima gave birth to her first son, ʿAbd al-Wahhāb, in 1111. ʿAbd al-Karīm provides an account of him as one of his own shaykhs in *Abridgement*. Clearly, he uses the word *shaykh* rather loosely. Literally it means an old man, someone whose white hair demands respect, but it was also used to mean teacher, with the connotation of elderliness. Shaykh ʿAbd al-Wahhāb, however, died at the age of twelve. ʿAbd al-Karīm writes, "My father transmitted Hadith to my elder brother and me in Nishapur. My brother busied himself with literature [*adab*] and read its important books, but death carried him away before he reached puberty. In Nishapur he heard from ʿAbd al-Ghaffār Shīruwī and ʿUbayd Qushayrī; and in Merv from Muḥammad Kurāʿī and others. From him I heard a bit of poetry."[40]

In another account he tells how his brother's first shaykh, ʿAbd al-Ghaffār Shīruwī, also came to be his own shaykh. The passage highlights the importance of "hearing," given that ʿAbd al-Karīm was not yet old enough for kindergarten. In a glowing and relatively long passage he says that Shīruwī was a prominent merchant in Nishapur and Isfahan. After retiring from travel, he proceeded to transmit Hadith for forty years, dying at the age of ninety-six (lunar) in the year 1117, a few months after ʿAbd al-Karīm heard Hadith from him. After mentioning some of Shīruwī's numerous teachers and students, ʿAbd al-Karīm tells of his own attendance at his sessions, and then goes on to list six texts that he himself had "heard" from him. Given that he mentions Shīruwī as one of his uncle Aḥmad's shaykhs, it is almost certain that Aḥmad (who would have been twenty-three at the time) was also present at this meeting.

> My father took me to Nishapur, and this shaykh came to be present with him in the Abū Naṣr ibn Abi'l-Khayr Madrasa. He brought me and my brother to the session. We heard much from him, and I was a child of three and a half years. Most of the things we heard were written down in the hand of my father. In the *samāʿ* [certificate of hearing] he would write his own name and then write, "And present was his son Abu'l-Muẓaffar ʿAbd al-Wahhāb," that is, my brother, "who brought along his brother Abū Saʿd ʿAbd al-Karīm." Between me and my brother were twenty months.[41]

Ibn Khallikān quotes ʿAbd al-Karīm as saying that his father died shortly after returning to Merv from Nishapur.[42] He was buried next to his own father in Sinjidhān, one of the cemeteries of Merv.

In *Ṭabaqāt al-Shāfiʿiyya* Subkī provides a relatively long account of Muḥammad ibn Manṣūr, adding a few details to those given by ʿAbd al-Karīm. Like him, he lists various scholars from whom he heard Hadith, though the lists are different. The first he mentions is Abū Saʿīd ʿAbd al-Wāḥid Qushayrī (d. 1101), a son and successor of the famous Abu'l-Qāsim Qushayrī.

In a brief note on the word Qushayrī in *Ascriptions*, ʿAbd al-Karīm tells us that Abu'l-Qāsim Qushayrī was known for his virtue, knowledge, and renunciation and that he had six sons who transmitted Hadith. He does not mention any of his books, saying only that he had a prominent position in "knowledge" and that he himself had heard Hadith from him by fifteen different intermediaries and from all of his sons by many more intermediaries.[43] The specific son who was Muḥammad ibn Manṣūr's teacher, ʿAbd al-Wāḥid, became the head of the Qushayrī family after his father's death and took over the post of *khaṭīb* in the Manīʿī mosque in Nishapur from Imām al-Ḥaramayn Juwaynī. He served in this post—that is, the person who delivers the *khuṭba* or Friday sermon—for fifteen years. It is said that his father gave him the *kunya* Abū Saʿīd because the famous Sufi teacher Abū Saʿīd ibn Abi'l-Khayr (d. 1049) asked that the infant be named after him.[44] The fact that ʿAbd al-Wāḥid was one of the teachers of Muḥammad Samʿānī, who in turn was the primary teacher of his brother Aḥmad, suggests one of the many routes by which Sufism was transmitted to the author of *Repose*.

ʿAbd al-Karīm himself had two sons, one of whom, Abu'l-Muẓaffar ʿAbd al-Raḥīm, was born in the year 1143 and became a leading Shafiʿi scholar of his generation. He was killed during the Mongol invasion around the turn of the year 1221. The other son, Abū Zayd Muḥammad, seems to have been an official in the court of the king of Khwarazm, since he was sent by him as a messenger to the caliph in Baghdad, presumably seeking aid against the Mongols. The aid was not forthcoming, of course, and Khwarazm fell in 1219–21.[45]

ḤASAN IBN MANṢŪR

Aḥmad Samʿānī's second brother, Abū Muḥammad Ḥasan ibn Manṣūr (1076–1137), was learned in jurisprudence and stood next in line to his elder brother in their father's scholarly legacy, but he had a reclusive nature. The attributes that ʿAbd al-Karīm applies to him tell us that he was engaged in the practices of Sufism: renunciation, scrupulosity, constancy in worship and night vigils, cleanliness, luminosity, elegance in old age, and keeping himself away from the people. He barely left his house except for the required congregational prayers. He heard Hadith from a variety of scholars both in Merv and in Nishapur, including ʿAbd al-Wāḥid Qushayrī and Niẓām al-Mulk the vizier. His life was cut short when he was strangled by burglars, who had come to steal a valuable trust that had been left with his wife by an official of the Turks. Thus, says ʿAbd al-Karīm, he was granted the "death as a martyr" for which he used to pray.

ʿAbd al-Karīm heard a great deal from Ḥasan and mentions among other things two lists of books, including all of his grandfather Manṣūr's lectures and his collection of one thousand hadiths.[46] Subkī's account of Ḥasan in *Ṭabaqāt al-Shāfiʿiyya* simply summarizes ʿAbd al-Karīm's account in *Ascriptions*. Subkī concludes by saying that Ḥasan's students were ʿAbd al-Karīm "and others," which is no doubt true, but either the others were not prominent enough to be mentioned in the biographies, or Ḥasan's role in their education was not especially significant.[47]

In *Abridgement* ʿAbd al-Karīm concludes his description of Ḥasan by quoting two texts that he had heard from him, a hadith and a short Arabic poem, while reminding us that an almost identical hadith is found in both Bukhārī and Muslim: "The most astute of words are those spoken by the poet Labīd: 'Is not everything other than God unreal?' And Ibn Abi'l-Ṣalt was almost a Muslim."[48] The quote from Labīd is a half line of poetry. Aḥmad cites it three times in *Repose*, not least because it sums up a major theme of his book.

The poem that ʿAbd al-Karīm received from Ḥasan is given an *isnād* going back to the Sufi teacher Aḥmad ibn ʿAṭāʾ Rūdhbārī (d. 980), who introduced it by saying that he thought it was composed by his maternal uncle, that is, Abū ʿAlī Aḥmad ibn Muḥammad Rūdhbārī (d. 933), a student of Junayd and other prominent Sufi shaykhs.[49]

When you become a companion of the Men, be a chevalier
    as if you are a slave to every friend.
Be sweet and cool for every comrade,
    like water for a burning liver.[50]

In Sufism "Men" (*rijāl*) is a term for perfected human beings, and "chevalier" (*fatā*)—which means literally "young man"—connotes perfect generosity and self-sacrifice.[51] In *The Repose of the Spirits* Aḥmad repeatedly uses the standard Persian translation of chevalier (*jawān-mard*) to address his readers. Like the word dervish or "poor man," which he uses in the same way, chevalier suggests the character traits that one needs to cultivate in the path to God.

'Abd al-Karīm also provides two accounts of Ḥasan's son, Abū Manṣūr Muḥammad (ca. 1100–39). In *Abridgement* he speaks of him with the deference one would expect toward a teacher: "He was an erudite youth, a knower of lexicography, prose, and poetry; delicate in nature, quick to compose poetry, with beautiful poetry in the two tongues, Arabic and Persian, a rare individual. He heard from his father and a group of shaykhs the like of whom has not been seen." These shaykhs included his uncle Muḥammad, Muḥammad Sawsaqānī,[52] and the brothers Faḍl and Khalaf Kākū'ī.[53] The Kākū'ī brothers seem to have been family friends; 'Abd al-Karīm says that his father Muḥammad heard a great deal from Faḍl Kākū'ī and that he himself received much from him by way of Faḍl's son and two daughters and his uncle Aḥmad.[54] He goes on to say that in conversations with his cousin he wrote down some of his poetry and the poetry of others. In his account of his own family in *Ascriptions*, he praises his cousin's knowledge of literature but adds an apology: "He busied himself with something that his forebears did not, namely sitting with youths and girls in their pastimes and conforming with them in what they were doing. May God overlook us and him!"[55] One suspects that Muḥammad was on good terms with his uncle Aḥmad, since the two shared a love for literature.

AḤMAD IBN MANṢŪR

This brings us to Abu'l-Qāsim Aḥmad (1094–1140), author of *The Repose of the Spirits*. When his father died in 1096, Aḥmad was two. He was adopted by his brother Muḥammad, who was twenty-three at the time and soon became his teacher in Hadith and jurisprudence. Muḥammad's daughter Ḥurra was born two years later, so she would have been a sister to Aḥmad. His two nephews, 'Abd al-Wahhāb and 'Abd al-Karīm, joined the family thirteen and fifteen years later, so both he and Ḥurra would have been involved in their education.

In describing his uncle, 'Abd al-Karīm says that he was an imam, a scholar (that is, of Hadith), a debater (*munāẓir*), a Quran commentator (*mufassir*), a mufti, a protector of the Shafi'i school, a composer of beautiful poetry in both Arabic and Persian, and a homilist (*wā'iẓ*) whose elegant homilies were full of benefits and fine points. He was dignified, sedate, modest, generous, firm, forbearing, patient, and unblemished in soul. He spent all of his time gaining knowledge and imparting knowledge. When his brother Muḥammad died, Aḥmad was twenty-three. He took over from him in all that he had delegated to him, by which 'Abd al-Karīm presumably means teaching in the madrasa and leading prayers in the mosque.[56] As we will see later, the madrasa in question seems to have been the Niẓāmiyya.

Aḥmad heard Hadith from various teachers besides his brother Muḥammad. 'Abd al-Karīm lists Muḥammad Māhānī, Kāmkār the litterateur (*adīb*), and the brothers Ismā'īl Nāqidī (d. ca. 1100) and 'Abd al-Jabbār Nāqidī (d. 1114). In *Abridgement* 'Abd al-Karīm mentions only one of these scholars as his own shaykh, namely, ʿAbd al-Jabbār Nāqidī. He received a license from him, however, in December 1113 when he was about ten months old; it was procured for him by Muḥammad Daqqāq (d. 1122), who is mentioned as having acquired licenses for him from a number of other shaykhs when he was an infant.[57] In *Ascriptions* ʿAbd al-Karīm provides brief accounts of both Nāqidīs, adding that his uncle Aḥmad narrated to him from Ismāʿīl.[58] As for Muḥammad Māhānī, ʿAbd al-Karīm mentions him in *Abridgement* as a transmitter of Hadith to several of his own shaykhs, usually along with his father Muḥammad and/or Daqqāq, suggesting that these three were on close terms. He mentions several times that Kāmkār was the teacher in a *maktab* (a grammar school). In his history of Nishapur, Fārisī has a section on Kāmkār in which he says that he was one of the scholars who accompanied Manṣūr when he was exiled from Merv and who returned along with him.[59]

ʿAbd al-Karīm tells us that Aḥmad traveled with his brother Muḥammad to Nishapur and heard Hadith from ʿAbd al-Ghaffār Shīruwī and others.[60] The mention of a trip with his brother to see Shīruwī most likely means that Aḥmad was present with his two nephews in the session of 1116, shortly before the deaths of Shīruwī and Muḥammad. It also suggests that the others from whom he heard in Nishapur included ʿUbayd Qushayrī (d. 1118), the second person mentioned as having imparted Hadith to his nephews in that city. The biographies mention that ʿUbayd, like Shīruwī, was a merchant who transmitted Hadith (with no connection to the famous Qushayrī family).[61]

When Muḥammad died, the welfare of his two young sons was put in the hands of Ibrāhīm ʿAṭāʾī (d. 1141), who had been a student of his father Manṣūr. After listing some of the scholars from whom Ibrāhīm heard Hadith, ʿAbd al-Karīm adds, "I heard a great deal from him. Before his death my father delegated watching over my best interests and those of my brother to him, making him the executor of his will. Ibrāhīm did that beautifully and arranged our affairs in the most beautiful arrangement."[62] At the same time, ʿAbd al-Karīm's primary teacher in jurisprudence was his uncle Aḥmad, from whom he also heard Hadith, took notes on issues in disputation (*khilāf*), and learned the Shafiʿi school. He traveled with him to Sarakhs, perhaps to visit relatives of his mother.[63] In 1135, when Aḥmad was forty-two and ʿAbd al-Karīm twenty-three, they traveled together to Nishapur. ʿAbd al-Karīm refers to this journey as the reason for ending his studies with his guardian Ibrāhīm. As he puts it, "An affair of importance came up for me with my uncle the imam," that is, this trip.[64]

ʿAbd al-Karīm tells us that he initiated the trip to Nishapur with the aim of hearing two important books in Hadith, the *Ṣaḥīḥ* of Muslim from Muḥammad Furāwī (d. 1136) and the *Kitāb al-tawakkul* of Ibn Khuzayma from Hibatallāh Sayyidī (d. 1138). He and Aḥmad were accompanied by Maḥmūd Dabbūsī, who had been ʿAbd al-Karīm's schoolmate from childhood. Together the two had studied jurisprudence with Aḥmad and heard Hadith from, among others, the famous Sufi teacher Yūsuf Hamadānī (d. 1140). In Nishapur they attended the sessions of Furāwī, Sayyidī, and ʿAbd al-Munʿim Qushayrī (d. 1138), the youngest son of Abu'l-Qāsim. Dabbūsī, however, became ill and could not continue in the company of ʿAbd al-Karīm, so he returned to Merv.[65]

The biographical literature accords Muḥammad Furāwī an honored place among Hadith-transmitters. Subkī gives him a relatively long notice in *Ṭabaqāt al-Shāfiʿiyya*, saying among other things that he was raised among Sufis and was unique in his time for the *Ṣaḥīḥ* of Muslim, meaning that his *isnād* was the "most elevated" to be found. He would have been about eighty-five years of age when Aḥmad and ʿAbd al-Karīm attended his sessions. Subkī quotes several statements about him from ʿAbd al-Karīm, including this: "He was an imam, a mufti, a debater, and a homilist. He had beautiful character traits and good manners. He often smiled, and he honored strangers. I did not see his like among my shaykhs."[66]

Although ʿAbd al-Karīm does not provide a notice for Furāwī in either of his two published books, he does have a notice for Furāwī's daughter Sharīfa (d. 1141–42), for whom he lists many teachers. It is not unlikely that he attended her sessions along with Aḥmad. He wrote a number of texts at her dictation, including *al-Arbaʿūn* (Forty [Hadiths]) by Abū ʿAbd al-Raḥmān Sulamī (d. 1021). Sulamī was the author of *Ṭabaqāt al-ṣūfiyya* (The Generations of the Sufis), one of the earliest works on the biographies of Sufis, as well as one of the earliest explicitly Sufi commentaries on the Quran, *Ḥaqāʾiq al-tafsīr* (The Realities of Exegesis).[67]

In *Abridgement* ʿAbd al-Karīm tells us that the other teacher he wanted to hear in Nishapur, Hibatallāh Sayyidī, was the son-in-law of Imām al-Ḥaramayn Juwaynī. He was learned and pious, but he was hard in character, always scowling, and did not like Hadith-transmitters. ʿAbd al-Karīm goes on to say that he thinks no one heard as much as he did from him and then provides a rather long list of books on Hadith and biography.[68]

When ʿAbd al-Karīm went to Nishapur with Aḥmad in 1135, it seems that he had no intention of returning with him to Merv, but it was not easy to convince his uncle to let him stay. Most likely a great deal of give-and-take lies behind this statement of ʿAbd al-Karīm: "My uncle aimed to return to Merv, but I stayed behind in hiding so that I might reside in Nishapur after he left. He waited until I appeared, and I returned with him as far as Tus. Then he gave me permission to return to Nishapur, and he himself went back to Merv." ʿAbd al-Karīm remained in Nishapur for a year and then went on to Isfahan and from there to Baghdad, where he was informed that Aḥmad had died in the town of Idrīqād on 17 Shawwāl 534 (5 June 1140). He was carried back to Merv and buried next to his father.[69] It was also in Baghdad that ʿAbd al-Karīm heard that his guardian Ibrāhīm had been killed during a raid on Merv by forces from Khwarazm.[70]

ʿAbd al-Karīm mentions Aḥmad in passing in a few accounts of other shaykhs. For example, he tells us that the scholar Ḥusayn Lāmishī, who was known for his knowledge of disputation and Kalam, came to Merv and stayed in the Ribāṭ al-Sulṭān. "I was taken to him along with my brother ʿAbd al-Wahhāb. At the time I was nine years old. He acted humbly toward us and honored us greatly. We listened along with him as my uncle Aḥmad read a copy of the hadiths of Abū Makīs Dīnār ibn ʿAbdallāh narrated from Anas ibn Mālik."[71] This would have been in the year 1122, so Aḥmad would have been twenty-eight.

ʿAbd al-Karīm describes another meeting in the year 1133 or 1134, when he was twenty-two and Aḥmad forty-one. He says that ʿUmar Basṭāmī came to Merv and sat in the Khān al-Barāzīn to give a homily. During the talk he mentioned the name Abū Sulaymān Dārāʾī, a well-known Sufi teacher. Aḥmad corrected him by saying "Dārānī." Then ʿAbd al-Karīm recounts, "Right in front of them I said, 'Both this and that are correct, for when a word's *alif* in the last place is *maqṣūra*, one may choose in making the ascription to add the *nūn* or leave it out. Thus we have Dārānī and Dārāʾī, and we have Ṣanʿānī and Ṣanʿāʾī.' My uncle stayed silent and said nothing."[72] Clearly, ʿAbd al-Karīm was proud of his youthful prowess in Arabic grammar.

ʿAbd al-Karīm refers to Aḥmad several times in *Abridgement* as "my uncle the imam." We can be sure that he means Aḥmad and not Ḥasan because, in the smaller number of instances where he mentions Ḥasan, he refers to him either by name or with the title *shahīd*, "the martyr." In one of these accounts, he mentions that Aḥmad taught at the Niẓāmiyya Madrasa and that he himself would repeat the lessons for those who needed help. The account pertains to one Fakhrāwar Rāzī, for whom ʿAbd al-Karīm provides no dates other than that they met in 1134, that is, the year before he left with Aḥmad for Nishapur. He writes, "He was an erudite jurist who came to Merv and dwelt with us in the Niẓāmiyya Madrasa. During the lessons of my uncle the imam, he and I used to repeat [the lessons for other students]." ʿAbd al-Karīm then tells us that Fakhrāwar had heard the book *Ḥilyat al-awliyāʾ* (The Adornment of the Friends) by Abū Nuʿaym Iṣfahānī (d. 1038) from Ḥasan Ḥaddād in Isfahan (who had heard the book from Abū Nuʿaym himself), and that he read with him one or two of its folios.[73] *Ḥilyat al-awliyāʾ* is a ten-volume account of the friends of God, beginning with the Prophet and his Companions and coming down to recent times. It is one of the main sources of information on teachers who were known as or came to be seen as Sufis in retrospect. Abū Nuʿaym was a prolific author of books on Hadith. *Ḥilyat al-awliyāʾ* is one of only two books that Aḥmad mentions by name in *The Repose of the Spirits*, the other being the *Ṣaḥīḥ* of Bukhārī.

In an account of Qāḍī Ḥassān Ṭūsī (b. ca. 1068), ʿAbd al-Karīm again mentions Aḥmad and shows a sense of humor. He says that Qāḍī Ḥassān studied jurisprudence in Merv with his grandfather Manṣūr, who took to him and kept him near. ʿAbd al-Karīm met him first in Tus, then in Nishapur, and then studied with him in Jāgharq (a village located between Tus and Nishapur), hearing from him three or four sessions of his grandfather's lectures. The two became close: "Among him, me, and my uncle the imam were kinship and great intimacy, like what he had with my grandfather." Then, he says:

> One day in Tus a group of us were going to a gathering and banquet. I said to my uncle the imam—God have mercy on him—"Let us first visit the graves of the shaykhs, then we will take in the gathering," and he concurred. So we went on and as we were passing the house of the host, Qāḍī Ḥassān said, "Masters, let us first enter this house and eat what we have been invited to, for it will disappear, but visiting will not disappear, for the dead do not depart from their graves." The whole group laughed, and we did what he said.[74]

Another of ʿAbd al-Karīm's teachers was ʿAbd al-Raḥmān Bārnābādhī, an erudite jurist and debater who was scrupulous in practice and much devoted to Quran recitation and prayer. "For a time he took over the Friday sermons as the deputy for my uncle the imam. He had studied jurisprudence with my grandfather the imam Manṣūr. Then he went to Bukhara and saw the imams there. He went on to Tus and stayed for a time with Muḥammad Ghazālī, and then for a time with Ḥusayn Baghawī.... I wrote a little from him before I left on my journey."[75] Baghawī (d. 1122) was the author of several books, the best known of which is his commentary on the Quran, *Maʿālim al-tanzīl*.

ʿAbd al-Karīm makes another reference to his trip to Nishapur with his uncle in an account of Aḥmad Masjidī. He writes, "He was the first shaykh from whom I heard Hadith in Nishapur.

I recall that when we entered Nishapur, he came to greet my uncle the imam and introduced himself by saying, 'I am the son of Sahl Masjidī.' "[76]

Apparently the only other mentions of Aḥmad by someone who actually met him are found in two books by Ibn ʿAsākir, the author of the huge *Taʾrīkh madīna Dimashq* (History of the City of Damascus). Born in Damascus in 1106, Ibn ʿAsākir studied at the Niẓāmiyya Madrasa in Baghdad, left for the East around 1133, became a friend and traveling companion of ʿAbd al-Karīm, and returned to Damascus in 1139. Concerning him ʿAbd al-Karīm writes, "My dear friend and comrade, Abu'l-Qāsim ʿAlī ibn Ḥasan ibn Hibatallāh, the hafiz and Shafi'i from Damascus, collected the city's history in keeping with the stipulations of the Hadith-transmitters."[77] In at least fourteen instances in *History of the City of Damascus*, Ibn ʿAsākir mentions that he received a hadith from Aḥmad ibn Manṣūr Samʿānī, to whom he gives the title "jurist" in the first mention.[78] In practically all of these instances, Aḥmad's role was to narrate hadiths from the already mentioned ʿAbd al-Ghaffār Shīruwī. Aḥmad would have heard these when he visited Nishapur along with his brother Muḥammad and his two nephews in the year 1116.

Ibn ʿAsākir begins each passage in which Aḥmad is mentioned by saying that Shīruwī "wrote" the hadith "to me" (*kataba ilayya*), which might be understood to mean that he wrote out a license specifically for him, but he also says that Aḥmad Samʿānī "reported" (*akhbara*) the hadith from Shīruwī, which would mean that Aḥmad recited the hadith from a written document, presumably the license that he himself received from Shīruwī. Ibn ʿAsākir could not have received the hadiths directly from Shīruwī because Shīruwī died when he was eleven years old, long before he set out on his travels. In all of these hadiths, the *isnād* goes by way of Abū Bakr ibn Ḥasan Ḥīrī (d. 1030), a well-known Shafi'i judge in Nishapur and one of Shīruwī's teachers. ʿAbd al-Karīm mentions that Shīruwī was the last living person to have a direct link to Ḥīrī.[79]

None of the hadiths that Ibn ʿAsākir heard from Aḥmad are mentioned in *The Repose of the Spirits*, nor is their content in any way suggestive of Aḥmad's specific concerns in his book. In this respect they are in marked contrast to a single hadith Ibn ʿAsākir narrates from him in his *Muʿjam al-shuyūkh* (Lexicon of Shaykhs), which enumerates 1,621 individuals. Unlike ʿAbd al-Karīm in his lexicon of shaykhs, Ibn ʿAsākir provides no information about his teachers other than their names. In each case he mentions one hadith (with *isnād*) that he heard from the shaykh in question. One can surmise that each hadith reflects the personality or specific concerns of the shaykh. It certainly does so in the case of Aḥmad. After providing Aḥmad's full name followed by the title "jurist," Ibn ʿAsākir cites the following hadith, which Aḥmad received from Abū ʿAbdallāh Muḥammad ibn Abī Jaʿfar Ḥammāmī in Merv: The Companion Abū Mūsā said, "O Messenger of God, a man loves people and joining with them." The Prophet replied, "A man will be with those he loves."[80] We will see that Ibn ʿAsākir also associates ʿAbd al-Karīm specifically with love.

The later biographical literature takes little notice of Aḥmad. This is not surprising in books about Hadith-transmitters and jurists, given that, on the evidence of *The Repose of the Spirits*, Aḥmad's primary concern was not transmitting Hadith or teaching jurisprudence but rather opening up students to the inner dimension of Islamic learning. As for why his name was not remembered in Sufi circles, this remains a puzzle; no doubt it has something to do with the failure of his book to be widely disseminated, perhaps because of the Mongol invasion. It may also be connected to the dominance of Shi'ism in Iran from the sixteenth century onward, when books by Sunni scholars were often ignored.

Subkī's account of Aḥmad in *Ṭabaqāt al-Shāfiʿiyya* adds nothing to what ʿAbd al-Karīm says in *Ascriptions*.[81] We do learn from him, however, that Aḥmad had a son by the name of Abū Bakr Muḥammad, to whom Subkī dedicates a separate entry. He takes his information from *Taʾrīkh Khwārazm* by Maḥmūd Khwārazmī (d. 1173), who was the author of a book called *al-Kāfī* in jurisprudence. Khwārazmī's account of Muḥammad ibn Aḥmad suggests that he followed in his father's footsteps as a propagator of the religion of love. Given that this is apparently the only mention of Aḥmad's son in the literature, it is likely that he, like the sons of ʿAbd al-Karīm, perished in the Mongol invasion. Notice that Muḥammad was outstanding in "reminder," like his father and grandfather:

> Said the author of *al-Kāfī* in *Taʾrīkh Khwārazm*, "He was a youth of elevated rank among the leading men of Khorasan. He was among those unique at the time in subtlety of exposition and eloquence of tongue, and he had no equal in reminder. He came to Khwārazm twice, narrating Hadith on the authority of his father. He was the son of ʿAbd al-Karīm's paternal uncle.
>
> "I heard him say from the pulpit, 'Guard your oaths just as you guard the turban on your head! Do not let your turbans be more exalted in your sight than your oaths!' Or something like that, for he mentioned it in Persian and I have translated it.
>
> "He also composed a poem [in Arabic] while on the pulpit, saying,
>
> Once a modest maid from Iraq
> stopped for a moment at Bāb al-Ṭāq,[82]
> A girl of thirteen or fourteen,
> the death of this enthralled yearner.
> I said, "Who are you, O captivator?" She said,
> "I come from the Creator's gentle art.
> "Be not forward with me, for my fingers
> are stained with my lovers' blood."[83]

Those familiar with Sufi literature will hardly be shocked by this imagery. The goal of lovers is to achieve "union" with their Beloved. Given that two can never be one, the Beloved must "shed the lover's blood" to erase the duality. Aḥmad frequently speaks of being killed by the Beloved, as in this Persian line: "No matter how You kill me, I come to life! // But don't kill me with separation—anything but that" (6).

Sufism in Aḥmad's Khorasan

"Sufism" is a difficult if not impossible word to define. Some historians take an easy way out and say that it is mysticism and then continue on as if they had explained something. But what exactly is mysticism? And why exactly are Sufis mystics? What are the precise characteristics that make one person a mystic and another a jurist, one a Sufi and another a sociologist? And if mysticism can be defined as modern-day scholars define it, how could that definition have been in the minds of those who talked about Sufism one thousand years ago? Other possible translations, such as "esotericism" or "spirituality," run into similar problems. In fact the primary texts are not clear as to what the words Sufi and Sufism mean, nor is there much evidence that those who used the words at various times and places had a single meaning in mind.[84]

The general picture that one might get from studying Western accounts (and many Muslim accounts as well) is that whatever the word Sufism designates, the phenomenon itself is inconsistent with—perhaps even hostile to—mainstream, "orthodox" Islam. When we look at criticism of Sufism in the primary literature, disagreements on religious issues often turn out to be driven by political and social factors of a local sort, as historians are wont to explain when they do in fact investigate actual situations.[85] My own attempt to understand the religious and social environment in which Aḥmad Samʿānī lived has led me to believe that his family represents a case study in one of the major themes of Ahmet Karamustafa's book *Sufism: The Formative Period*. As he puts it in one passage, "In the eyes of many traditionalists," that is, Hadith-transmitters, "irrespective of their pietistic orientation, Sufism was utterly mainstream."[86]

Given that it is not clear how the term Sufism was understood during Samʿānī's time (or any other time), I need to clarify my own frequent mentions of the word. I use it first because the texts employ it. If I am not translating or commenting on a specific passage where the word is used, I use it to designate a broad trend among Muslims, clearly present in the Quran, the Prophet, and some of his Companions, to stress the inner meaning over the outward form, to insist that every act should be done while keeping God foremost in mind, and to hold that outward adherence to doctrine and ritual is not efficacious unless it is accompanied by the intention to purify oneself from everything of which God disapproves. In this broad sense Sufism has no necessary connection with "mysticism." It simply designates the general contours of *iḥsān* or "beautiful-doing" as this term is employed in the Quran and the Hadith, especially in the famous Hadith of Gabriel, where *iḥsān* is contrasted with *islām* ("submission" through outward acts) and *īmān* ("faith" through understanding and conviction).[87] This description of Sufism is broad enough to embrace what the Samʿānīs and their contemporaries meant when they used the word, but it is not specific enough to describe exactly what they had in mind in any given instance.

It bears repeating that there is no generally accepted definition of Sufism offered by the classical authorities or modern scholars. In books by authors whom Aḥmad Samʿānī certainly read—like Qushayrī and Abū Nuʿaym Iṣfahānī—the word is given a variety of interpretations. In general it designates an advanced station on the path to God or an exalted state of mind achieved by travelers on the path. Numerous aphorisms are cited to describe it, but none of them is anything like a definition. Rather, each needs to be taken as an "allusion" (*ishāra*) to a state of mind and heart. The teachers who uttered these sayings were attempting to help their students escape from the limitations of habit and blind belief so that they could see things for themselves.

Aḥmad himself rarely mentions the words Sufi or Sufism. To be precise, he does so in eleven instances, nine of which are quotations. Nonetheless, it seems fair to call *The Repose of the Spirits* a Sufi text inasmuch as it focuses on the inner life of Muslims rather than the outward forms of their beliefs and practices. As Aḥmad puts it in one of the two mentions of Sufism that is not a quotation, "Have you seen a lotus flower? You must learn Sufism from it. It has a radiant outwardness and an inwardness in the cape of humbleness. It has the blue coat of grief on the inside and green on the outside. A dervish must be like that. He must wear the tattered cloak on his heart, not his body" (179). "The tattered cloak," *khirqa*, was a garb adopted by certain Sufis or "dervishes"—that is, followers of the path of spiritual poverty—as a sign of their detachment from the worldly aims of society. But the cloak per se meant nothing if not accompanied by detachment from everything that pulls away from God. In the same way, the turbans and robes of the scholars tell us nothing about the learning and intentions of those who wear them.

Although he rarely uses the word Sufism, Aḥmad often talks about the Islamic tradition in terms of Shariah and Tariqah (and/or Haqiqah). In discussing the significance of the divine name Aware (*khabīr*), for example, he says that the seeker who knows that God is aware of all things will assign watchfulness (*murāqaba*) to his own states. "He will not take one breath without the permission of the Shariah and the Tariqah. He will weigh his outwardness in the scales of the Shariah and pull his inwardness into the playing field of the Haqiqah." The seeker does not stop there, however, since those who truly follow in the Prophet's footsteps will detach themselves from everything other than God. This is why, the shaykhs maintain, "The felicitous person is he who has an outwardness conforming to the Shariah, an inwardness following the Haqiqah, and a secret core quit of relying on his Shariah and his Haqiqah" (201).

The word Tariqah is well known in the secondary literature because Sufis have commonly been understood as members of specific organizations called by this name. In this context the word is usually translated as "order" rather than path (on the model of monastic orders). Historians acknowledge that clearly demarcated Tariqahs did not appear until around the sixth/twelfth century, even though there were numerous individuals before that time who were recognized as Sufi teachers. What may have differentiated these early Sufi teachers from shaykhs in other fields of learning like Hadith and jurisprudence was that some of their close students were "disciples" (*murīd*) who had entered into a compact of allegiance with them on the model of "the compact of God's approval" (*bayʿat al-riḍwān*), which was made with the Prophet by the Companions at Ḥudaybiyya (referred to in Quran 48:10 and 48:18). The Sufi shaykh, often called the master (*ustādh*), had the duty of training (*tarbiya*) disciples by guiding them on the path to God, and the disciples had the duty of obeying the master's instructions. Books like Qushayrī's *Treatise* provide a good deal of information on specific teachers who came to be known as Sufis, along with the instructions that they gave to their disciples and their descriptions of the path leading to the divine presence. But as Qushayrī often reminds us, each of these teachers spoke from his own standpoint. As he says in discussing the important technical term *maʿrifa*, "recognition" (usually translated as "gnosis"), "Each of the shaykhs spoke about what occurred for himself and alluded to what he found in his own present moment [*waqt*]."[88]

At the time of Aḥmad Samʿānī, Sufism in the sense of instruction in the Tariqah and the Haqiqah could be found everywhere in society, not least in teaching institutions such as mosques and madrasas. It was simply a standard part of mainstream learning.[89] It is enough to read through ʿAbd al-Karīm's mentions of the teachers whom he designates as Sufis to see that they were often jurists, imams, and Quran-reciters as well. Nonetheless, some institutions were associated specifically with Sufism. These were typically called khanaqahs or ribats, two words that are more or less synonymous. Both designate lodges for the poor and centers for teaching Sufism.[90] As we have seen, Aḥmad's father Manṣūr was able to walk to Mecca staying every night in Sufi lodges, which is to say that they were omnipresent. They were open to the public like mosques, so anyone could go in and expect to be provided with room and board, at least temporarily. At the same time they were singled out for the "poor" (Ar. *faqīr*, P. *darwīsh*). These "fakirs" and "dervishes" were not only those without means but also Sufi masters and their disciples. They called themselves poor not least because the Quran makes poverty the most basic of human attributes: *"God is the Unneedy, and you are the poor"* (47:38).

So, was Aḥmad Samʿānī a "Sufi"? It depends on what you mean by the word. If you mean, as I do, someone who undertakes a serious, personal engagement with transforming the soul on the basis of following the Sunnah of the Prophet, then the evidence of his book is that Aḥmad was an eminent Sufi practitioner and teacher. *Repose* shares attributes and qualities with hundreds of books written before and after that are classified as Sufi texts. But if you mean a person who formally swore allegiance to a Sufi shaykh and became his disciple, we simply do not know, since neither he nor anyone else provided explicit evidence to this effect. Nonetheless, on the basis of his book and environment, I would guess that he was affiliated with the line of transmission represented by the Qushayrīs (as were many other scholars of the time, such as the Ghazālī brothers, who were linked to Abu'l-Qāsim Qushayrī by the intermediary of Abū ʿAlī Fārmadī). *Repose*, it seems safe to say, is the first major exposition of Qushayrī's teachings in the Persian language.

But let us come back to our main source of information on the Samʿānī family, ʿAbd al-Karīm. He never says that Aḥmad or anyone else in his family was a "Sufi," though he identifies 120 of his own shaykhs as Sufis. Many of these Sufis were also jurists and imams, and ʿAbd al-Karīm clearly saw no contradiction between expertise in the Shariah and accomplishment in the Tariqah.

In a few passages ʿAbd al-Karīm alludes to some of the reasons for the tensions that often existed between Hadith-transmitters and Sufis. For example, in his description of Shaykh Abū Saʿīd ibn Khalīfa (d. 1149) from Nishapur, he points out that Abū Saʿīd narrated Hadith, but he did not do so according to the rules. ʿAbd al-Karīm himself held these rules in great esteem, so much so that one of his few surviving books is dedicated to the proper comportment of Hadith-transmitters and students. Called *Adab al-imlāʾ waʾl-istimlāʾ* (The Courtesy of Dictating and Taking Dictation), it is a collection of hadiths and scholarly sayings—most of the text consisting of *isnāds*—setting down rules for narrating Hadith and attending sessions of narration. If this book represents ʿAbd al-Karīm's notion of the proper behavior of "scholars," it is not difficult to understand why he was taken aback by the comportment of Abū Saʿīd ibn Khalīfa:

> He was a Quran-reciter, a jurist, a homilist, a Sufi, graceful, gentle in nature, much in memorization and benefits, beautiful with company, loving toward the people. . . . I heard from him in the first journey. Then, when I was returning from Iraq, I happened to meet him when he was dictating. I borrowed some of his dictations from one of the scholars,

> and I saw hadiths both elevated and low. It was as if he did not know the stipulation of narrating hadiths. Then he came to us in Merv after I had returned there from Nishapur. A session was held in my place, and he did it beautifully, and all of those present wept. I heard that the imam Muḥammad Ghazālī used to say, "If anyone wants to look at the face of Sufism, let him look at Abū Saʿīd ibn Khalīfa."[91]

ʿAbd al-Karīm devoted his life to *ʿilm*, knowledge or learning, and practically everyone he mentions in his books was an *ʿālim*, a knower, a learned person, a scholar. But again, we need to remember that when he says "scholar" he means learned in Hadith and involved in its transmission. Becoming a scholar demanded a long period of dedicated study and, once this rank was achieved, it was often a lifetime occupation. Moreover, as Richard Bulliet reminds us, scholars were drawn from society's elite, no matter how their families may have attained that status—trade, government or military service, scholarship itself.[92]

Among those known as Sufis, some, like the Qushayrī family, were unquestionably scholars and members of the social elite, but many were not. Sufis called themselves "dervishes" primarily because of the spiritual significance of poverty, but often they were poor in the worldly sense as well, whether by choice or circumstance. Many of them thought that poverty, far from the trappings of books and turbans, was the ideal mode of life. Lack of formal education or failure to come from an important family was never considered a barrier in the path to God. ʿAbd al-Karīm's account of Junayd Qāʾinī, who studied jurisprudence with his grandfather Manṣūr and several other "folk of knowledge," suggests that Sufism was often associated with a mode of life completely outside the circles of the learned. He writes,

> He was an imam, erudite, godwary, scrupulous, a scholar, a doer of what he knew, much in worship, and constant in night vigils and Quran recitation. . . . For forty years he was the shaykh and *muqaddam* [leader and teacher] of the Sufis in the ribat of Fīrūzābād outside of Herat, but none of them recognized him for who he was, since he did not put himself ahead of them. He lived amicably with them as one of them. He did not single himself out for anything that they did not have. As a matter of course he did not let it be apparent that he knew anything of knowledge, so those who saw him thought he was one of the Sufis. He was humble, generous of soul, and honored strangers.

Notice here a common criticism of Sufis by jurists and Hadith experts: "They did not know anything of knowledge," meaning of course Hadith and other forms of book learning. But we also see here a criticism of the scholarly class: They were proud of their learning and kept themselves apart from the masses. And, when they did mix with them, they made sure that they were treated with the deference that they deserved.

ʿAbd al-Karīm goes on to insist that Junayd was not just a Sufi and that he did in fact "know something of knowledge." He lists twenty of his teachers in Hadith, including Niẓām al-Mulk the vizier. He tells us that when he himself went to Herat, he would stay with Junayd one or two nights a week, and he mentions fifteen books that he heard from him. He also quotes from him, rather out of character, a long anecdote about a wise madman and a poem by Abū Nuwās about wine-drinking.[93]

In *Repose* Aḥmad narrates a saying from his father Manṣūr that may throw some light on the contrasting paths of Hadith-transmitters and Sufis—inasmuch as either group considered its own path the exclusive way to serve God: "For thirty years a Sufi and a scholar were put into the same pot. Fire was lit, and the water boiled. When they were brought out, both were still raw" (51). Becoming cooked in the path to God was not a matter of choosing one path over another, but rather of coming out of oneself "like a snake from its skin" (471). Or to use the common image already mentioned, it was to be killed by the Beloved.

In another passage Aḥmad contrasts the Shari'ite expertise of the jurists with the vision of the Haqiqah achieved by those who have shucked off their mortal nature:

> Whenever something comes to hand with the Shariah, the sultan of the Haqiqah charges forth and plunders it. The preacher of the Shariah calls out from the pulpit of bounty, "Have faith and declare *tawḥīd* lest you be deprived of paradise!" Then the sultan of majesty comes into the field of exaltation on the steed of the Haqiqah and shouts out to the whole world, "No one but He loves Him, no one but He recognizes Him, and no one but He seeks Him. *They measure not God with the rightful due of His measure* [6:91]. *They encompass Him not in knowledge* [20:110]. What do the creatures have to do with the Haqiqah? What do water and clay have to do with talk of the Lord of the Worlds?" (140)

SUFISM AMONG ʿABD AL-KARĪM'S TEACHERS

We have seen that ʿAbd al-Karīm's father took him to hear shaykhs when he was three years old. There was nothing unusual about this. Given the stress on having short chains of transmission, children were often taken to hear old men to help them achieve this goal.[94] ʿAbd al-Karīm even mentions that his father obtained a written license for him from Khalaf Kākūʾī in November 1112, that is, three months before he was born.[95] His accounts make clear that he saw several of his teachers when he was an infant. Given that his father died before his fourth birthday, his uncles Ḥasan and Aḥmad and his guardian Ibrāhīm must have continued taking him to hear Hadith-transmitters, a good number of whom were also Sufis. Among them were the following. Remember that ʿAbd al-Karīm was born in February 1113.

Ismāʿīl ibn ʿAlī ibn Sahl from Nishapur: "He was from a family of Sufi shaykhs and was one of the realizers [*muḥaqqiqūn*]—that is, those who abide by the stipulations of the Sufis and Sufism." He had heard from Abu'l-Qāsim Qushayrī and, "in the year 1115–16, he wrote for me a license in all of his *masmūʿāt* [the narrations heard from his teachers]." He died in 1124 and was buried in his khanaqah.[96]

Ismāʿīl ibn ʿAlī ibn Muḥammad from Tus: "An eminent renunciant, he was one of the Sufis, and I think he was their *muqaddam*. . . . In June 1117 he wrote for me a license to transmit all of the *masmūʿāt* he had from Isfahan."[97]

Ḥamza ibn Ḥusayn from Ghazna: "He was a shaykh, wholesome [*ṣāliḥ*], a scholar, a Sufi, straight in conduct, one of the folk of knowledge and the Quran." Ḥamza heard from many shaykhs and gave ʿAbd al-Karīm a license to transmit all of his *masmūʿāt* in Rajab October 1119, that is, when he was about eighty-three and ʿAbd al-Karīm six and a half.[98]

Aḥmad ibn Ismāʿīl Jawharī: "I think he was from Nishapur, though he resided in Ghazna. . . . He heard from the imam Abu'l-Qāsim Qushayrī. He wrote for me a license in all that he had heard and all that he had gathered. He said, 'Especially, from what I have heard, the *Risālat al-ṣūfiyya* composed by Qushayrī, according to how I heard it from him.' He wrote out a license for me in his own hand in March 1120. He died a year later."[99] In other words, ʿAbd al-Karīm received a license to transmit the foremost textbook of Sufism from a student of the author when he was seven years old.

Nāṣir ibn Aḥmad Sarakhsī (d. 1120): "He was a shaykh, a jurist, a Sufi, a scholar, a homilist, truthful in friendship, a reliable knower of Hadith and literature. He heard a great deal of Hadith when both young and old, and he was a companion of the folk of knowledge and Sufism. He wrote some compositions toward the end of his life, adorned with his useful and firm poems; I heard these from him in recitation and dictation." Among Sarakhsī's many shaykhs was ʿAbd al-Karīm's grandfather Manṣūr. His father Muḥammad heard a great deal from Sarakhsī, as did many of the scholars of Khorasan, who then passed it all on to ʿAbd al-Karīm, for whom Sarakhsī "wrote a license in all of his *masmūʿāt.*"[100]

One of the more interesting examples of the importance given to the transmission of knowledge at a young age comes in connection with Ḥasan Ḥaddād (d. 1122), to whom ʿAbd al-Karīm dedicates the longest entry in *Abridgement.* He tells us that when Ḥaddād was a child, his father, on his way to work, would drop him off every morning at the mosque of Abū Nuʿaym Iṣfahānī, the author of the ten-volume *Ḥilyat al-awliyāʾ* as well as numerous collections of Hadith, some of which are explicitly about Sufism. In Ḥaddād's old age, students came to him from all over the world to hear Abū Nuʿaym's books and treatises. ʿAbd al-Karīm tells us proudly that Ḥaddād gave him a written license to transmit all of his *masmūʿāt* on two occasions. About him he says, "He was the greatest of the shaykhs who licensed me among those whose chains of transmission were short and who had many narrations."[101] He does not remind us, however, that he would have been nine years old when Ḥaddād died, which is to say that the two licenses were procured for him, since he did not go to Isfahan until he was in his twenties.[102] Probably his guardian or one of his uncles had asked friends going to Isfahan to have Ḥaddād write out a license for the boy, and two of them came back with letters. In any case ʿAbd al-Karīm lists among many other books for which he had a license from Ḥaddād sixty-nine by Abū Nuʿaym. This is not to say that he never in fact "heard" these books. Elsewhere he tells us that he heard the whole text of *Ḥilyat al-awliyāʾ* from ʿAlī Filakī and parts of it from three other shaykhs, all four of whom had heard it from Ḥaddād.[103] In other notices he mentions hearing many of the other books by Abū Nuʿaym for which he had received Ḥaddād's license.

Another prominent Sufi teacher whose works ʿAbd al-Karīm often heard from his teachers was Abū ʿAbd al-Raḥmān Sulamī from Nishapur. ʿAbd al-Karīm mentions fifteen of Sulamī's compositions that he heard from various teachers, including *Ṭabaqāt al-ṣūfiyya* (from three shaykhs) and *Ḥaqāʾiq al-tafsīr* (from two). As noted, *Ṭabaqāt* is the first book dedicated specifically to the lives of the Sufis, and *Ḥaqāʾiq* is one of the earliest Sufi commentaries on the Quran.[104]

One of the more famous Sufi teachers of the generation before ʿAbd al-Karīm is the aforementioned Aḥmad Ghazālī, younger brother of Abū Ḥāmid Ghazālī and author of the short Persian classic *Sawāniḥ*. ʿAbd al-Karīm makes his only reference to him in his printed books while describing Ḥamza Hamadānī.[105] Concerning Ḥamza he writes, "He was a staunch Sufi, accepted by them. He made the hajj several times and transmitted Hadith. He heard from Aḥmad Ghazālī. I met him in Isfahan where he was staying with us in the khanaqah of Banū Manda. He had sweet songs and a beautiful voice. I wrote from him lines of poetry and I parted from him in the year 1136–37." ʿAbd al-Karīm goes on to cite two poems that Ḥamza narrated from "Aḥmad Ghazālī the homilist, in Baghdad." The very fact that ʿAbd al-Karīm feels that these verses are worth quoting—despite seldom quoting poetry—suggests that he was proud to have heard something from Aḥmad Ghazālī, even if only indirectly. I quote the verses because they are similar in style to many Arabic verses cited by Aḥmad in *The Repose of the Spirits*. The manner in which the two poems reached ʿAbd al-Karīm suggests how those verses may have reached his uncle.

By the sacred union that we had
    though you did not come back to it,
Kill me that I may be at ease from your chastisement,
    for separation from you is worse than death.

*

My friend, the red wine was sweet,
    so I've returned after piety—that's more to be praised.
Give me the wine in the shirt of its glass,
    like a ruby burning inside a pearl.[106]

As for the more famous Ghazālī brother, Abū Ḥāmid Muḥammad, ʿAbd al-Karīm mentions him on twenty occasions in his two books, but almost always as a teacher of jurisprudence (sometimes along with his grandfather Manṣūr, since he and Ghazālī often taught the same students). He certainly recognized Ghazālī's exceptional status, calling him, for example, an imam of the world, but he did not consider him worthy of being mentioned as one of the "scholars," since he was only a jurist. And rarely does ʿAbd al-Karīm even allude to Kalam or philosophy, two other fields in which Ghazālī excelled.[107] The only time he mentions Ghazālī explicitly in connection with Sufism is in his already cited words, "If anyone wants to look at the face of Sufism, let him look at Abū Saʿīd ibn Khalīfa." On another occasion ʿAbd al-Karīm alludes to Ghazālī's role as a theologian, philosopher, and Sufi by mentioning, for the only time, his famous book *Iḥyāʾ ʿulūm al-dīn*. This is found in an account of a fellow student, Naṣr Ṣaffār, who worked in the brass bazaar in Merv. ʿAbd al-Karīm describes him as a pious and chaste young man who studied jurisprudence, "but then he occupied himself with renunciation and copying the *Iḥyāʾ al-ʿulūm* of Ghazālī."[108] Clearly renunciation/Sufism went hand-in-hand with Ghazālī's writings.

On one occasion ʿAbd al-Karīm also mentions Ghazālī as a transmitter of Hadith rather than a jurist. This is in connection with the aforementioned Abū ʿAlī Fārmadī, who was a disciple of several prominent shaykhs, not least Abu'l-Qāsim Qushayrī. In saying that Ghazālī transmitted

Hadith to Fārmadī, ʿAbd al-Karīm does not mention a fact made clear by other sources, namely, that Fārmadī was Ghazālī's first teacher in Sufism.[109]

In speaking about Fārmadī and his three sons, ʿAbd al-Karīm shows his love for the Sufi path, even though he does not use the words Sufi or Sufism in the accounts. About Abū ʿAlī he writes, "He was the tongue and shaykh of Khorasan, the possessor of a beautiful Tariqah in the training of disciples and companions. According to what I have heard, the sessions of his homilies were like a garden with many sorts of flower and fruit."

ʿAbd al-Karīm received Hadith from Fārmadī by way of his son ʿAbd al-Wāḥid, concerning whom he says, "I met him and read some booklets before him, and he honored me. Then when I entered Tus for the second time, he had become an invalid and was staying in his house, and the people did not go to see him. I went to greet him and met him while he was sitting in his prayer corner unable to move. I wept and sat with him for an hour, and then I returned to Nishapur. He died in 1135."[110] This second visit to Tus would have been when he obtained permission from his uncle Aḥmad to return to Nishapur rather than go back with him to Merv.

Before Fārmadī became a disciple of Qushayrī, he was a disciple of Abū Saʿīd ibn Abi'l-Khayr, whose life is famously told in the Persian classic *Asrār al-tawḥīd* (The Secrets of *Tawḥīd*), which was written in 1179 by Ibn Munawwar, a fifth-generation descendant of the shaykh. ʿAbd al-Karīm heard Hadith from six of Abū Saʿīd's grandsons, all of whom he calls by the title Sufi.[111] He also heard Hadith from several of the Qushayrī grandchildren, including Hibat al-Raḥmān (d. 1152), the son of ʿAbd al-Wāḥid and the *muqaddam* of the Qushayrīs in Nishapur. Hibat al-Raḥmān narrated from the sessions of both his grandfather and his grandmother Fāṭima, who was the daughter of Qushayrī's master, Abū ʿAlī Daqqāq (d. 1015). ʿAbd al-Karīm tells us that he attended Hibat al-Raḥmān's sessions when he went to Nishapur with his uncle Aḥmad in 530/1135–36 as well as in 534/1139–40 and 537/1142–43. He heard a great deal from him, including dictations and treatises by Qushayrī and several books by Sulamī. Other sources suggest that Hibat al-Raḥmān was uniquely qualified among the Qushayrī grandchildren as *murshid* or spiritual director.[112]

One of the most famous Sufi teachers of this period is the aforementioned ʿAbdallāh Anṣārī, whose rank as a Hadith-transmitter, jurist, and theologian was such that, as Richard Bulliet remarks, he was one of the rare scholars to be called "Shaykh al-Islām" at the time.[113] Anṣārī is the author of the classic text in Arabic on the stages of the path to God, *Manāzil al-sāʾirīn* (The Waystations of the Travelers) as well as a similar Persian work, *Ṣad maydān* (One Hundred Fields). Among Persian speakers he is most famous for his *munājāt* or "whispered prayers," written in simple and exquisite prose. He (or his circle) is also the author of the book *Ṭabaqāt al-ṣūfiyya* (Generations of the Sufis), the most important Persian precursor of ʿAṭṭār's famous *Tadhkirat al-awliyāʾ* (Memorial of the Friends).

In *Abridgement* ʿAbd al-Karīm mentions more than thirty of his own teachers who had received Hadith or dictation from Anṣārī, many of whom he visited in Herat. Among them was Anṣārī's son Jābir, from whom ʿAbd al-Karīm had a license, but whom he apparently never saw. His account of Jābir provides a good example of how Sufism could be contrasted with the book learning of the jurists. ʿAbd al-Karīm says that he was "empty of erudition" (*khālī min al-faḍl*), but "his father's disciples believed in him." Having said this, he might be expected to go on and debunk this unlearned Sufi, but in fact he shows respect for him. He writes, "He saw from them a complete acceptance such as was seen by no one in his era. His affairs went forth in propriety and uprightness. He used to hold sessions on Tuesdays in the three months of Rajab, Sha'ban, and Ramadan in his father's place in Herat's congregational mosque, and countless people attended his sessions. He had a sound reputation and a shining visage. He wrote for me a license in all of his *masmū ʿāt*; it was acquired for me by Muḥammad Ashhabī the hafiz. Many people narrated to me from him."[114]

ʿAbd al-Karīm seems to have had a better opinion of Jābir's son, ʿAbdallāh. Although he lists him in his lexicon of shaykhs, he does not mention having heard anything from him. He simply says that he was "the nearest of ʿAbdallāh Anṣārī's children to him and the one accepted by most of his grandfather's disciples."[115] ʿAbd al-Karīm also tells us that he received a license to narrate all of the *masmū ʿāt* of a second Anṣārī grandson, ʿAbd al-Bāqī ibn ʿĀmir, who was an outstanding homilist, having a beautiful delivery and a clear and logical structure of presentation. He used to take turns with his grandfather in sessions of reminder and became his deputy, remaining so for many years.[116]

Among the Sufis with whom the Sam ʿānī family had close personal connections was Muḥammad Kushmīhanī (d. 1153), who was linked by marriage to ʿAbd al-Karīm's grandfather Manṣūr and from whom ʿAbd al-Karīm heard a number of books. He writes:

> In his era he was the shaykh of Merv and the *muqaddam* of the Sufis. He studied jurisprudence with my grandfather the imam, frequented him for a time, and married him to the daughter of his sister. He was a scholar, intelligent, scrupulous, clever in affairs, astute and bright, and exceedingly careful in serving the Sufis. He would not accept any donations from the folk of the army. He served the Sufis and travelers for nearly fifty years. He was generous of soul, observant of the rights of the people, and tender toward them. I never saw his like among the shaykhs of the Sufis. He was like a father to me, tender in firm affection and in the rights of the companionship that he had with my father the imam in both travel and at home.[117]

The fact that Kushmīhanī was a scholar as a well as a Sufi was clear to Ibn ʿAsākir, who mentions having heard Hadith from him in Merv in about forty-five instances, three times as often as he mentions having heard from ʿAbd al-Karīm. He often calls Kushmīhanī by the title *khaṭīb* and on two occasions *ṣūfī*.[118]

In a number of passages ʿAbd al-Karīm refers to shaykhs who were "special friends" (*mukhtaṣṣ*) of his grandfather Manṣūr or his father Muḥammad. The context suggests that they were disciples, though he does not use the word *murīd*. Take, for example, Maḥmūd ibn ʿAbd al-Raḥmān from Shiraz: "One of the staunch Sufis, he was a special friend of my grandfather the imam, and he served him and was his companion for a long period." Maḥmūd had heard from both Qushayrī and his wife Fāṭima. When Maḥmūd died, he was buried in the graveyard of the great teacher Abū Bakr Wāsiṭī (d. 932).[119] About Wāsiṭī Aḥmad says in *Repose*, "No one in the Tariqah has spoken words of more purity" (416).

In the case of another prominent Sufi shaykh, Yūsuf Hamadānī (d. 1140), ʿAbd al-Karīm seems to have been a devotee if not formally a disciple. Like Ghazālī, Hamadānī was a student of Abū ʿAlī Fārmadī. He came to be looked back upon as the first in a line of seven founding *khwājagān* or masters of the Naqshbandī Order, the seventh of whom was Bahāʾ al-Dīn Naqshband (d. 1389), after whom the order is named. In *Ascriptions* ʿAbd al-Karīm speaks about Hamadānī in glowing terms, though he has no entry for him in *Abridgement*. Notice also that he does not call him a Sufi, even though, with hindsight, only a handful of those mentioned in his books might be more deserving of this label.

> "Būzanjirdī" is an ascription to Būzanjird, a village of Hamadan in the direction of Sāwa. From it came Abū Yaʿqūb Yūsuf ibn Ayyūb Hamadānī Būzanjirdī. He was an imam, scrupulous, one who acted in keeping with his knowledge. He was an argument against the Muslims, a possessor of manifest states and stations, and he had the ability to speak about [people's] thoughts. To him went back the nurturing of truthful disciples in Merv. The wholesome and the scholars gathered together with him in his ribat such that they gathered nowhere else. From childhood to the time of his death he clung to the straight path, worship, seclusion, and occupation with knowledge and practice.

Notice that ʿAbd al-Karīm says that Hamadānī was a possessor of "states and stations" (*aḥwāl wa maqāmāt*), two technical terms that are often discussed together in Sufi literature, such as Qushayrī's *Risāla*. The terms are used to designate the ascending stages of the path to God. ʿAbd al-Karīm does not ascribe them to any other of the numerous shaykhs and Sufis mentioned in his two books. In his account he also lists several shaykhs with whom Hamadānī studied jurisprudence and from whom he heard Hadith. Then he writes, "I heard from him a great deal and copied from him in my own hand more than twenty booklets."[120] Hamadānī died in the year 1140, five months after Aḥmad Samʿānī and long before ʿAbd al-Karīm had returned to Merv from Baghdad. Hence his time as Hamadānī's student pertains to the years prior to his leaving Merv at the age of twenty-three in 1135; as noted, he used to attend Hamadānī's sessions along with his childhood friend Maḥmūd Dabbūsī.

ʿAbd al-Karīm hints that the rest of his family members were close to Hamadānī. He tells us, for example, that the scholar Sahl Kammūnī from Sarakhs, who was the son of his grandfather Manṣūr's sister, was buried in Sinjidhān cemetery within the enclosure (*ḥaẓīra*) around the grave of Hamadānī.[121] He also describes a woman by the name of Karīma Kūfānī (d. 1160), who "resided in our house in Merv" and who learned to read the Quran at an old age. Presumably, she was a servant of some sort, perhaps in a religious capacity, for ʿAbd al-Karīm mentions her among his female shaykhs because of "the rights of her service" (*ḥuqūq khidmatihā*). She heard from Yūsuf Hamadānī and other shaykhs and was buried within his enclosure.[122] A third account tells of Muḥammad Īlāqī from Farghana, a wholesome jurist of beautiful conduct, exceedingly observant of the rights of his friends. "Between him and me there was a firm affection, and I was his companion in Nishapur in the year 530," that is, on the trip with his uncle Aḥmad. With Īlāqī ʿAbd al-Karīm heard many hadiths from Furāwī and the last surviving Qushayrī son, ʿAbd al-Munʿim. "When I returned from Iraq in the year 538, Īlāqī took up residence with me in the ʿAmīdiyya Madrasa until he died in 539/1144." He was buried within the enclosure of Hamadānī.[123]

ʿAbd al-Karīm also provides an account of one of Hamadānī's well-known disciples, Ḥasan Andāqī of Bukhara (d. 1157). The account suggests both ʿAbd al-Karīm's attachment to Sufi teachers and the manner in which Hamadānī's influence was spreading. According to ʿAlī Kāshifī (d. ca. 1532), author of the Persian *Rashaḥāt ʿayn al-ḥayāt* (Trickles from the Fountain of Life), which is the earliest description of the Naqshbandī Tariqah, Andāqī was one of four successors (*khalīfa*) appointed by Hamadānī. Kāshifī bases much of what he says about both Hamadānī and Andāqī on passages translated from ʿAbd al-Karīm, though he seems to have had more in hand than what we have today.[124] In *Abridgement* ʿAbd al-Karīm says about Andāqī, "He was the shaykh of his era without opposition, the owner of miracles and signs [*karāmāt wa āyāt*]. He was one of the earliest disciples of our shaykh Yūsuf Hamadānī and traveled with him for a time and served him. Yūsuf used to honor him and respect him; he placed him before many of the disciples and companions affiliated with him. Ḥasan spoke words about the Tariqah as beautiful as could be, and many of the folk of his time took benefit from him, so his blessing [*baraka*] appeared to them. I met him in Bukhara and visited him more than once, benefiting from him and his words."[125]

Only on two other occasions does ʿAbd al-Karīm mention shaykhs who had "miracles and signs." Both accounts show that he considered extraordinary phenomena marks of nearness to God. He does not call either of these scholars a Sufi, but in both cases he mentions renunciation and worship (*ʿibāda*). Worship, like renunciation, was closely associated with Sufism. The first is Muḥammad Juwaynī (d. 1135), who was "one of those famous and often mentioned for renunciation, wholesomeness, erudition, knowledge, and training disciples [*tarbiyat al-murīdīn*]. He followed the most beautiful Tariqah and the most comely conduct [*sīra*]. He was the possessor of miracles and signs, and he used up his life in searching for knowledge, worshiping, and benefiting the people." ʿAbd al-Karīm then mentions some of the teachers from whom Juwaynī had received licenses, including Abu'l-Qāsim Qushayrī. Juwaynī wrote out a license for ʿAbd al-Karīm in all of his *masmūʿāt* but, as becomes clear, without ever having met him. He says that on his way to Nishapur with his uncle Aḥmad in 1135, he stopped in Tus, where ʿAbd al-Wāḥid Fārmadī, the son of Abū ʿAlī, invited him to stay for a few days because Muḥammad Juwaynī would soon be coming to the city. But he was eager to continue on in order to meet Furāwī and Sayyidī—both of whom were quite elderly. Later he decided to go to Juwayn to meet Juwaynī, but before he could do so, he received news of Juwaynī's death.[126]

In the case of the third shaykh to whom ʿAbd al-Karīm attributes miracles and signs, ʿUthmān Nawqānī (d. 1145), he speaks from his own observations. He mentions having visited him twice. Concerning his first visit, he writes,

> He was a shaykh, a Quran-reciter, erudite, a renunciant, much in worship, a possessor of miracles and signs. He did not leave his sitting place except at the times of prayer. It happened one day that we went to him in his mosque after the afternoon prayer. Some of us said the two cycles of prayer for the mosque, and some did not. We conferred among ourselves about that in keeping with the habits and disagreements of the jurists. Then we

> sat in silence waiting for the shaykh to come. He entered after a time and I thought to myself, "It would be fitting if the shaykh would speak about the topic of our contention."
>
> When he entered, he prayed two cycles. Then he turned to us and said, "The scholars have disagreed concerning the permissibility of the two cycles after the afternoon prayer. The preferred opinion is that it is permissible, for this prayer has a cause, which is entering the mosque." This is what I witnessed from him.

In describing his second meeting with ʿUthmān, he says that he went to visit him with Fakhr Juwaynī (d. 1138–39), a great-grandson of Imām al-Ḥaramayn Juwaynī. The two had become close friends while studying with Fakhr's grandfather, Hibatallāh Sayyidī, during ʿAbd al-Karīm's visit to Nishapur with his uncle Aḥmad. He says that Fakhr was "the *muqaddam* of the companions in Nishapur for a time," the context implying that he was the leader of ʿAbd al-Karīm's scholarly circle because of his "erudition, cleverness, and astuteness" and his mastery of debate and reminder. They traveled together to Nawqan (Mashhad) to make a pilgrimage to the tomb of ʿAlī ibn Mūsā Riḍāʾ.[127] It must have been on this occasion that he met ʿUthmān for the second time.

> It also happened that I came to Nawqan with Fakhr Abu'l-Qāsim Juwaynī, the *muqaddam* of our companions in Nishapur, and we went to visit him. We sat in the shaykh's mosque and began to talk. Before that I had often been saying to Fakhr, "Why don't you shave your head? The Prophet prohibited tufts of hair." I thought to myself that it would be good if the shaykh spoke about this. As soon as this entered my mind, he put his hand to his temple and said, "My son, what are you doing with so much hair? Cut it off!" He was a shaykh famous among the people of the town for miracles and speaking about unseen things.[128]

These are a few of the many teachers whom ʿAbd al-Karīm associates with Sufism. Most of these shaykhs are simply unknown in the later literature, or they are given brief accounts that add nothing to ʿAbd al-Karīm's words. This should not make us assume, however, that they were insignificant. As shaykhs, they were teachers who not only transmitted Hadith but who also taught the Shariah and the Tariqah to their students. Many may well have written books in various fields of learning that were subsequently lost or lie moldering in libraries or private collections. Take, for example, Muʾammal Khumrakī, concerning whom there seems to be no contemporary record other than ʿAbd al-Karīm's mentions of him in both *Ascriptions* and *Abridgement.* He tells us that Khumrakī studied jurisprudence first in Bukhara and then in Shash (modern Tashkent). Then he came to Merv and settled in the ribat of Yaʿqūb the Sufi, where he lived until his death in about 1123, when ʿAbd al-Karīm would have been ten or eleven. "He was a graceful and delicate imam, a scrupulous Sufi; the companion of imams, scholars, and the folk of the religion and the good. After studying jurisprudence, he occupied himself with worship, struggle, practice, and training disciples and companions linked to him." Having listed various teachers from whom Khumrakī received Hadith, including his grandfather Manṣūr, ʿAbd al-Karīm says, "I met him more than once and I was present in his ribat, though I do not know whether or not I heard Hadith from him. I think I saw his license to me in his handwriting."[129]

If not for a single manuscript containing what are apparently Khumrakī's dictations, this would have been the sum total of what is known about him. This manuscript, published forty years ago as a 250-page book with the title *Rawḍat al-farīqayn* (The Garden of the Two Groups), is a Persian disquisition on the ritual prayer. The "two groups" mentioned in the title seem to be the jurists and the Sufis, that is, the folk of the Shariah and the folk of the Tariqah. The book would have been written thirty or forty years before *The Repose of the Spirits*, making it a relatively rare example of early Persian prose. It fits into a genre that is often called *asrār al- ʿibādāt*, "the secrets of the acts of worship." It describes the daily prayer with juridical precision, introducing the topic with an explanation of the essential role of knowledge, purification, and intention. With each description of a specific ritual act, Khumrakī clarifies the significance and symbolism, citing well-known Sufi teachers. The prose is simple and straightforward, reminiscent of *Repose* in some respects, but hardly of the same elegance and beauty. The book illustrates the typical manner in which scholars saw the Tariqah and the Shariah as complementary. Jurisprudence delineated the proper way of doing things, and Sufism instructed practitioners in the meaning of the ritual activity and its impact on the soul. *Rawḍat al-farīqayn* has been largely ignored by historians of Sufism, perhaps because so much of it is devoted to jurisprudence rather than "mysticism."

Finally, let me mention one additional piece of evidence suggesting that ʿAbd al-Karīm's involvement with Sufism was more than simply theoretical, namely, Ibn ʿAsākir's entry on him in *History of the City of Damascus*. After listing some of ʿAbd al-Karīm's teachers, Ibn ʿAsākir writes, "I was together with him in Nishapur, Baghdad, and Damascus. He heard my reading, and I heard his reading; he wrote from me, and I wrote from him. He was *mutaṣawwif*, chaste, beautiful in character traits."[130] The word *mutaṣawwif*, active participle of *taṣawwuf* or "Sufism," means one who is engaged with the practices of Sufism, though it does not imply the same explicit espousal of the Tariqah that the word *ṣūfī* does. In place of *mutaṣawwif*, however, the printed text of *History of the City of Damascus* has *mutaṣawwin* (self-guarding, or honor-preserving; one who is careful about his reputation). *Mutaṣawwif* and *mutaṣawwin* can easily be confused in handwriting. In a footnote the editor says that his manuscript has *mutaṣawwif*, but he prefers to follow the text as quoted by Dhahabī in *Siyar aʿlām al-nubalāʾ*. Dhahabī was writing two hundred years after Ibn ʿAsākir, when many jurists and Hadith-transmitters were becoming more critical of Sufism. Given ʿAbd al-Karīm's prominence as a Shafiʿi scholar, Dhahabī would have had an incentive to obscure his connections to Sufism, even if "self-guarding" is a word rarely found in the texts and hardly appropriate as praise for a close friend.[131]

One more point about Ibn ʿAsākir's account of ʿAbd al-Karīm seems significant. Toward the end of it he cites a single hadith that he heard from ʿAbd al-Karīm. The *isnād* tells us that ʿAbd al-Karīm had heard the hadith from Shīruwī, that is, during his visit to Nishapur in 1116, a few months prior to Shīruwī's death; presumably, his father or his uncle Aḥmad had written it down. It is another version of the hadith that Ibn ʿAsākir says he heard from Aḥmad in his lexicon of shaykhs. This seems to indicate that Ibn ʿAsākir saw ʿAbd al-Karīm and his uncle Aḥmad as having the same understanding of the importance of love. The hadith is this:

> A man said, "O Messenger of God, when will the Hour come?"
> He replied, "And what have you made ready for it?"
> The man did not mention much except that he loved God and His Messenger.
> The Prophet said, "You will be with those whom you love."[132]

The Repose of the Spirits

Whether or not ʿAbd al-Karīm would have called himself a Sufi, his accounts of his teachers make clear that he and his family had numerous ties with Sufis, some of whom are well known and some unremembered. These Sufi teachers were typically members of the community of scholars and occupied with transmitting Hadith, acting as imams for mosques, and teaching jurisprudence in the madrasas. Aḥmad Samʿānī fit neatly into this environment. His *Repose* shows him as widely learned not only in Hadith but also in Quran commentary, Sufi lore, jurisprudence, and Arabic and Persian literature. He has special strength and originality in his interpretations of Quranic verses.[133] ʿAbd al-Karīm recognized this in *Abridgement* by beginning the description of his uncle with the words *imām mufassir*, "an imam, a Quran commentator." He names less than ten of his 1,446 teachers in *Abridgement* as Quran commentators, which is to say that it was an unusual qualification—in contrast, for example, to jurist.

In his printed books ʿAbd al-Karīm offers a perfect example of an approach to learning that Sufi teachers often criticized, whether or not his extant books represent the full range of his accomplishments. Transmitted learning—the Quran, the Hadith, the words of the Companions, the opinions of the scholars, and so on—forms the basis of the religion, no doubt, but the goal of knowledge cannot be simply to compile it. The role of knowledge is rather to provide the basis for walking on the path to God and, in short, to open up the soul to the divine presence. Four times Aḥmad quotes a saying of the Sufi teacher Muḥammad ibn al-Faḍl Balkhī (d. 931): "Recognition"—*maʿrifa*, that is, true knowledge of self and God, "is the heart's life with God." Ghazālī makes this abundantly clear in *Iḥyāʾ ʿulūm al-dīn* (Giving Life to the Sciences of the Religion), and even more so in his Persian reconfiguration of that work, *Kīmiyā-yi saʿādat* (The Alchemy of Felicity). The titles of these two books—not to mention their content—remind the reader that transmitted knowledge is dead unless one can bring it to life by tracing it back to the inner meaning that gave rise to it in the first place. The process of bringing knowledge to life will not be fully accomplished until the base metal of the soul is transmuted into pure gold. Only then will the seeker reach the spirit's repose.

At first sight it may seem odd that ʿAbd al-Karīm never mentions that his uncle wrote a book on the divine names. It is possible, though unlikely, that he did not even know that he wrote it, for Aḥmad probably composed it toward the end of his life while ʿAbd al-Karīm was traveling. But given ʿAbd al-Karīm's dedication to learning, it is hard to imagine that he was unaware of it. Why then did he not mention it? Perhaps for the simple reason that he never mentions Persian books.[134]

Even if ʿAbd al-Karīm had wanted to mention his uncle's book, he may have refrained because it was not a book of "knowledge," that is, a book on Hadith. Nor was it the sort of book that any of his 1,446 shaykhs would have transmitted to him, even if it had been in Arabic. The Sufi texts that ʿAbd al-Karīm received from his teachers pertain largely to the genre of transmitted learning, whether Hadith or the sayings of the Companions and other great Muslims. To take the most famous among them, the *Risāla* of Qushayrī is mostly a collection of sayings by Sufi shaykhs arranged according to theme. The style is that of Hadith-transmitters, even if there is a good deal of interspersed explanatory material. Moreover, ʿAbd al-Karīm makes no mention of having heard two other well-known books of Qushayrī, both of which were put to good use by Aḥmad. These are *Sharḥ asmāʾ Allāh al-ḥusnā* (Explanation of God's Most Beautiful Names), and *Laṭāʾif al-ishārāt* (Subtle Allusions), a commentary on the Quran. These texts provide many explanations by Qushayrī himself, even if the latter is structured as a collection of transmitted sayings on Quranic verses; the style of Hadith-transmission lingers, but the actual content is given over to explaining the hidden meanings of the Quran and the Hadith in light of the soul's need to undergo alchemical transformation.

ʿAbd al-Karīm may also have ignored his uncle's book because he took it to be a mere collection of homilies. It would certainly appear so if he were judging it on the basis of the one commentary on the divine names that we know he received from a teacher. That is *al-Asmāʾ waʾl-ṣifāt* (The Names and Attributes) by the well-known scholar Abū Bakr Bayhaqī (d. 1066), an Ash'arite theologian and close friend of Abu'l-Qāsim Qushayrī. ʿAbd al-Karīm mentions that he heard Hadith from ten of Bayhaqī's companions and that he had a written license from Bayhaqī's son, Ismāʿīl Bayhaqī, to transmit all of his *masmūʿāt* (which presumably included all of his father's books).[135] He mentions the names of thirteen of Bayhaqī's books that he had heard from various teachers, including not only *The Names and Attributes* but also *al-Iʿtiqād* (The Belief), a shorter book that addresses the divine names in some detail.[136] Both of these are written in the style of Hadith-transmitters and, to the extent that they provide explanation, illustrate the abstract theological thinking that preoccupied numerous scholars at the time. If ʿAbd al-Karīm took Bayhaqī's books as the proper, "scholarly" way to discuss the divine names, he certainly would have looked upon *The Repose of the Spirits* as homilies for the common people, mere sessions of "reminder" for Persian speakers who did not have sufficient learning to hear Hadith and who needed to be instructed with anecdotes and poetry.

The often conversational style of *Repose* and its lack of systematic structure suggest that the text was originally presented as oral lectures. The fact that Samʿānī constantly addresses his readers with the words "O dervish" and "O chevalier" implies that his listeners were engaged in Sufi practices. He probably delivered these talks in the Niẓāmiyya Madrasa in Merv. It is unlikely that they were delivered in a more public place, given that the text includes a great deal of Arabic that would have been difficult to understand for those unfamiliar with scholarly discourse. Of course he could have translated the Arabic passages into Persian during the oral presentation, but the final version of the text does so only occasionally. Moreover, Aḥmad often put a great deal of artistry into complex Persian sentences, making them difficult to decipher, so it is hard to imagine that he presented the text as it stands to the general public. The complicated nature of some of the prose led Maybudī to abridge and simplify it when using it in *Kashf al-asrār*.

Aḥmad himself offers little help in determining what sort of audience he had in mind. The book has practically no introduction, which would be the normal place to mention the audience to whom a book is addressed. It begins with the words "Hereby opens up the explanation of the names of the Lord in Persian for the benefit of the Muslims," which does not help us determine which Muslims he meant other than Persian speakers. The introduction is also the normal place for an author to explain why he gave the book its name, but Aḥmad does not do so. Nonetheless, it is not difficult to understand what he had in mind when we look at the manner in which he uses the words of the title in the text.[137]

Rawḥ, "repose," derives from the same root and is written the same way as *rūḥ*, "spirit," which helps explain why many speakers of both Persian and Arabic instinctively read the title as "the spirit of the spirits." *Rawḥ* can also mean breeze (like Latin *spiritus*), so it can designate a breath of fresh air that gives comfort and ease. The Quran uses the word in three instances. The first two occur in Jacob's counsel to his sons when he sent them to Egypt in search of Joseph: *"Despair not of the repose of God; no man despairs of God's repose except the people of the unbelievers"* (12:87). The third occurs in reference to paradise: *"But if he should be of those brought near to the Throne, then repose and ease, and a Garden of Delight"* (56:88–89). As for *rūḥ*, the Quran uses the word about twenty times. Perhaps the most significant instances for our purposes are three verses about the creation of Adam. After molding Adam's clay, God blew into him of His spirit (15:29, 32:9, 38:72). It is this spiritual essence of man that ties him directly to his Creator. Spirit in this meaning is often contrasted with soul (*nafs*), which is generally understood as individual awareness inasmuch as it is forgetful, clouded, and immersed in the world of the senses. By overcoming the soul's forgetfulness, one can regain the spirit's awareness, clarity, and freedom. At that point the soul itself is transmuted such that it achieves ease with God. This, in short, is the goal of the Tariqah, as Samʿānī suggests when he puts these words into God's mouth:

> O exalted spirit, you are the quarry of subtleness and the source of repose and comfort! It is We who sent you away from your homeland as a stranger, made you the companion of the tumult-inciting soul, and imprisoned you in this dustbin. The goal was to call you back to Our Presence at the end of the work with a hundred thousand gentle robes, kindly gifts, and secret bestowals: *O serene soul, return to thy Lord, approving, approved!* [89:28]. (67)

In another passage Samʿānī explains the qualities that are needed by those who want to travel on the Tariqah, ending with the sentence, "It wants a spirit in whose truthful earth grows the fragrant herb of repose while it contemplates spiritual affairs and luminous forms, having struck fire into the corporeal senses and mortal imaginings" (212–13). Having traveled the path, the spirit may be opened up to the world of repose and ease. "When the sorrowful body is burned by the fire of tribulations and its eyes are sewn shut to observation, the spirit will spread its arms in the world of repose and see face-to-face all that was hidden from it, without the talk and chatter, the questions and answers, of the doorkeepers of the Shariah" (263–64), that is, the quibbling of the jurists.

In a few passages Samʿānī uses the expression "repose of the spirit" in the singular. In one he says that he will now offer "an intimation that will increase the repose of the spirit for the lovers" (407). In the only poem of the book that he ascribes to himself, he makes the spirit's repose the goal of the lover's quest: "Around the repose of the spirit circles His lovers' aspiration" (119). In still another passage he describes the Prophet's excellent qualities and says that his Companions found their comfort and ease in his very person: "He was seated at the forefront on the cushion of tremendousness and majesty and adorned with the adornment of prophethood and messengerhood. He was the eye of the aeons and the ages, the repose of the spirit for the Emigrants and Helpers" (45).

One might ask why Samʿānī chose two specific divine names, King (*malik*) and All-Opening (*fattāḥ*) for the subtitle: "Explaining the Names of the All-Opening King." For one thing, *fattāḥ* rhymes with *arwāḥ*, spirits, and a title can always use a rhyme. For another, the two names have a certain affinity because *malik* is mentioned in the Fātiḥa, the "opening" or first chapter of the Quran. But Samʿānī did not necessarily choose the title before the subtitle. He may well have decided to mention the All-Opening at the outset in order to highlight God's role as the opener of doors and the sole source of understanding, wisdom, and advancement on the Tariqah. Another word from the same root, *futūḥ* ("opening"), is used by Sufi teachers in a technical sense to mean the opening up of the soul to the divine presence. It is this meaning that Ibn ʿArabī had in mind when he named his great book *The Meccan Openings* (*al-Futūḥāt al-makkiyya*).

Samʿānī shows his awareness of the technical meaning of the word *futūḥ* by using it in several passages, typically in connection with the spirit. Thus he speaks of *futūḥ-i rūḥ*, "the opening of the spirit," in the sense of receptivity to the spirit's light. In some passages he associates opening with the spirit blown into Adam at his creation: "Before the opening of the spirit reached Adam—the chosen, the limpid, the first wayfarer, the rising place of the sun of good fortune—he had a shirt of clay" (314). He compares the human heart to a falcon that has flown from the "nest of mystery," in its beak "the heaviness of dust" and in its claws "the opening of the spirit" (470). One of the qualifications of someone who wants to enter the Tariqah is that he "keeps his spirit waiting for opening" (253). True life will be reached only when the spirit inside the clay joins with the spirit that comes from God: "Here you have an exalted state—the opening of the spirit is poured down on the head of your secret core. In short, until you come alive, you will not reach the Alive" (180).

SOURCES OF THE TEXT

Samʿānī uses a wide variety of sources, such as Hadith, Quran commentary, and works on Sufism in both Arabic and Persian. Though he cites Hadith constantly, only on three occasions does he adopt the stance of a Hadith-transmitter by providing the *isnād*. On the first occasion (129) he mentions that he received the hadith from the imam and renunciant Abu'l-Faḍl ʿAbdallāh ibn Aḥmad Naysābūrī, about whom nothing is known other than that he transmitted Hadith in Merv.[138] On the second occasion (200) he says that he received the text from Muḥammad ibn Manṣūr Samʿānī, that is, his eldest brother and first teacher. On the third occasion (487) he received it from "the imam, the crown of Islam," by whom he may mean his brother. The only other person he mentions as having transmitted knowledge to him is his father. As noted, however, these quotations must have come by way of his brothers or other students of his father.

Aḥmad often quotes Sufi sayings, though he does not always mention their authors. These are mainly in Arabic, rarely in Persian. He quotes Arabic poetry from more than seventy-five individuals, though only on three occasions does he name the author (twice Ḥallāj and once Shāfiʿī). I was often able to trace the poems in earlier literature, though I do not mean to imply that he was using the specific works I mention. Given the manner in which knowledge was transmitted from scholar to scholar, it is likely that he heard most of the poems orally from his shaykhs and is simply quoting them without *isnād.*

Aḥmad made use of several books, though he almost never mentions the fact. Many of the sayings he quotes and some of the Arabic poetry are found in Qushayrī's *Treatise.* He frequently borrows passages from Qushayrī's Quran commentary, *Subtle Allusions*, sometimes in the original Arabic and sometimes in Persian translation or paraphrase. On one occasion, he introduces a sentence from it with the words "The master Abu'l-Qāsim Qushayrī said" (123). When quoting another sentence (297), he remarks that these are the words of "the Master Imam" (*ustād-i imām*), a title by which Qushayrī was commonly known (as, for example, in the many anecdotes about him in Ibn Munawwar's *Asrār al-tawḥīd*). The only other scholar whom he calls by the title Master—in all ten instances in which he mentions his name—is Qushayrī's teacher Abū ʿAlī Daqqāq (again, this was a title by which he was well known). Aḥmad was also familiar with Qushayrī's commentary on the divine names, though he makes relatively little use of it, contrary to what might be expected. He also used two of Qushayrī's minor works, *Manthūr al-khiṭāb* and *al-Mukhtaṣar fi'l-tawba.*

Aḥmad borrowed brief passages from the Quran commentaries of Abu'l-Layth Samarqandī (d. 983) and Māwardī (d. 1058). He does not use the commentary of his father Manṣūr, which is not too surprising, given that it is a rather standard summary of earlier works. Other Arabic sources include Ghazālī's *Iḥyā' ʿulūm al-dīn* (two brief quotes). He translates a few short passages from the treatises of the ninth-century philosophers, the Ikhwān al-Ṣafāʾ. This may seem odd, given that Hadith-transmitters, jurists, and theologians generally took scant notice of philosophers and tended to criticize them if given the chance. Ghazālī and many other Sufi teachers, however, benefited from their writings. The passages that Aḥmad translates pertain to the human microcosm; in some of his remarks on this topic, he must have had in view Ghazālī's *Kīmiyā-yi saʿādat*, which itself has an eye to the Ikhwān.

By far the most important Persian source of *Repose* is the earliest Persian book on Sufism, *Sharḥ al-taʿarruf*, a four-volume commentary on a short Arabic book by Abū Bakr Kalābādhī (d. ca. 994), *al-Taʿarruf li-madhhab al-taṣawwuf* (Introduction to the School of Sufism). Kalābādhī's treatise was translated by A. J. Arberry as *The Doctrine of the Sufis* and is one of the key works in early Sufism. ʿAbd al-Karīm knew of Kalābādhī as a Hadith-transmitter, since he mentions hearing his *Maʿānī al-akhbār* (The Meanings of the Reports)—a collection of eighty hadiths pertaining mostly to the inner life—from two different teachers.[139] As for his *Taʿarruf*, it is a compilation of Sufi sayings arranged according to prominent themes in Kalam and Sufism, especially the "states and stations" on the path to God. Kalābādhī was from Bukhara, and the book's commentary was written by his townsman Ismāʿīl Mustamlī (d. 1043).

Sharḥ al-taʿarruf has largely been ignored by modern scholars, even though it was first published (in India) over a hundred years ago. It is written in simple and eloquent Persian and provides copious explanation of the sayings cited by Kalābādhī. Its length, however, is enough to deter most would-be readers. In *Ascriptions* ʿAbd al-Karīm provides a brief account of Mustamlī, though he does not seem to have been familiar with his book or even know that it was written in Persian. He simply quotes the entry from *Muʿjam al-shuyūkh* of ʿAbd al-ʿAzīz

Nakhshabī (d. ca. 1064), one of the books upon which he modeled his lexicon of shaykhs.[140] He writes, "In the principles Ismāʿīl Mustamlī inclined toward the school of the Kalam experts [*mutakallimūn*]. He commented on the book *Introduction to the School of Sufism* by Abū Bakr Kalābādhī and mentioned there the heresies [*bidaʿ*] that he mentioned."[141] For many of the Hadith-transmitters, Kalam was by definition full of heresy, so there is nothing strange about Nakhshabī's remark. ʿAbd al-Karīm probably had no idea that his uncle made use of the book.

There is one more important Persian source for *Repose*, namely, the poetry of Sanāʾī of Ghazna, the first in a long line of outstanding Sufi poets. Aḥmad quotes his poetry frequently, though he never mentions his name. He also quotes verses attributed to about ten other Persian poets, including ʿUmar Khayyām, Abū Saʿīd ibn Abi'l-Khayr, Rūdakī, and Muʿizzī. He seems to cite a good deal of his own poetry as well, though he makes this explicit only once. In introducing a ten-verse ghazal (119), he says, "Once these verses occurred to my mind," thus confirming his nephew's statement that he wrote poetry in Persian. On the basis of the style of this ghazal, I would guess that he also composed another fifteen ghazals and short poems found in the book.[142]

As for the numerous Persian quatrains in the text, some were surely composed by Aḥmad, but given the omnipresence of quatrains in Persian literature and the relative ease with which they can be composed, they are the most difficult sort of poetry to ascribe to an author with confidence. For example, nine of the quatrains that Samʿānī mentions are also found in the *Dīwān* of Rūmī (thus adding to an already significant list of quatrains that are wrongly ascribed to him); they could easily have been composed by Aḥmad. Seven more are ascribed to Abū Saʿīd in Ibn Munawwar's *Asrār al-Tawḥīd*, but this book is a hagiography composed with a good deal of poetic license forty years after Samʿānī's death. Given that Abū Saʿīd himself claimed not to have composed any poetry, it is plausible that some of the poems ascribed to him are by our author.[143] ʿAbd al-Karīm says that his uncle also wrote poetry in Arabic, so it is likely that he composed some of the Arabic verses the authors of which I was unable to trace.

Among Persian books that might be expected to have influenced Samʿānī, the most obvious is the aforementioned classic, *Sawāniḥ* by Aḥmad Ghazālī, the text of which is not more than five percent the length of *Repose*. Modern scholarship generally assumes that this little book must have influenced anyone who wrote about love in Persian from the twelfth century onward. This assumption, however, became the received wisdom before *Repose* was published. Certainly *Repose* and *Sawāniḥ* have parallel discussions, but this is simply because the topic of love necessarily calls forth similar issues. The actual language of the texts does not suggest that Samʿānī had read Ghazālī's book. What is more likely is that both authors were drawing from oral and written teachings prevalent in Khurasan, especially in the circles connected with the Qushayrīs.

A second well-known Persian text on Sufism that Samʿānī might have read is *Kashf al-maḥjūb* (The Unveiling of the Veiled) by Hujwīrī (d. 1073), translated by R. A. Nicholson in 1911, but again there is no evidence (other than a shared saying or two) that he made use of it. Like Qushayrī in his *Risāla*, Hujwīrī provides biographies of Sufi shaykhs and summarizes their teachings, largely in the relatively dry style of Hadith-transmitters. The book was famous among Muslims in the subcontinent, so much so that anyone looking for a spiritual director was told to pray for guidance, visit the tombs of saints (especially Hujwīrī's in Lahore), and read *Kashf al-maḥjūb*.[144]

I should also make clear that by mentioning all these sources I am not implying that *The Repose of the Spirits* is a compilation of quotations, far from it. It is not at all like *Kashf al-asrār*, the Quran commentary by Maybudī, who frequently borrowed passages from *Repose* (and numerous other books). Although Maybudī carefully integrated the borrowed passages into the tapestry of his text, he showed little sign of creative thought. Samʿānī borrows proportionately far less than Maybudī and shows himself as a powerful and original thinker.

The Keys to the Unseen

Uniquely among the world's scriptures, the Quran highlights its own role as a revealed book, the very speech of God. It calls its content *āyāt*, "signs"—a word usually translated as "verses." It also designates the phenomena of the universe and the human self as *āyāt*. It presents its revealed signs as the keys to understanding the signs in the self and the world, but only for those *"who have faith in the Unseen"* (2:3).

Basing themselves on the Quranic symbolism of language, authors like Ibn ʿArabī developed the notion of three great books, each of which discloses the fullness of divine wisdom, the totality of God's signs/verses. These are (1) the universe in its entirety (including not only all space and time but also the spiritual and angelic dimensions); (2) the human being in full, multidimensional reality, as exemplified by "the perfect human being" (*al-insān al-kāmil*), the supreme instance of whom is Muḥammad; and (3) revealed scripture, which employs human language to articulate all of reality, whether transcendent or immanent, absent or present. In other words, the three great books are the universe as macrocosm, the human being as microcosm, and the Quran.

Given the Quran's theocentric vision and the linguistic homologies that it posits among all things, one can say that it designates "the most beautiful names" (*al-asmāʾ al-ḥusnā*)—an expression it uses in four verses—as keys to the relationships among all that exists. Ibn ʿArabī often says that the divine names are the roots (*uṣūl*) of the cosmos and the soul, the sources of every articulation in the macrocosm and the microcosm. As for the Divine Reality in Itself—often called the "Essence" (*dhāt*)—It is plain, nameless, and unknowable in the simplicity of Its *wujūd*.

The word *wujūd* came to be used in Islamic thought from the time of Avicenna (d. 1037) to designate existence or being, though its linguistic and Quranic sense is finding and perceiving. Before Avicenna, theologians had already discussed two divine names derived from the same root, the active participle *al-wājid*, "the Finder," and the passive participle *al-mawjūd*, "the Found." [145] When *wujūd* is used for the general notion of existence, the names Finder and Found can be understood to mean that God is He who finds and is found eternally, who knows and is known forever, who exists without beginning and end. In contrast, everything other than God is mostly out of touch with reality, so its finding and being found—its awareness and existence—are contingent on Real *Wujūd*. Inasmuch as anything other than God exists, it is simply a sign of *Wujūd*, a pointer in Its direction.

When people find and know things, they name them. As for God, He *"knows all things,"* as the Quran says in thirty verses. In other words, God knows everything eternally and timelessly, for as creator of time and place He is unaffected by temporality. His beginningless knowledge delineates the eternal names of things, for to know a thing is to recognize it as this thing rather than that thing. God's precise knowledge of each thing is its eternal name, known to Him forever. When His knowledge of a thing tells Him that it will be found in the universe, He issues the creative command: *"His only command when He desires a thing is to say to it 'Be!,' so it comes to be"* (36:82). Once the thing comes into being, its apparent existence is nothing more than that—apparent and not real, for it remains in bondage to the Real *Wujūd*. As Samʿānī puts it:

> After coming into existence the creatures are just as captive to power as they were before existence. When they were nonexistent, they were captive to power. If He wanted, He brought them into existence, and if He did not want, He did not. Now that they are existent, they are still captive to power. If He wants to keep them, He does, and if He does not want, He does not. After existence they will be exactly what they were in the state of nonexistence. And He, after bestowing existence, is exactly what He was before bestowing existence. So the existence of the creatures right now is similar to nonexistence. (329)

Muslim philosophers often debated whether God has knowledge of the particulars (*juzʾiyyāt*) along with knowledge of the universals (*kulliyyāt*). Some of Ibn ʿArabī's followers picked up on this language and referred to the infinite things known eternally to God as His particular names. Each individual thing names God inasmuch as it is a sign designating qualities and attributes that derive from Him. All particular names are then signs and traces of universal names, which designate the general qualities presupposed by the existence of things. From this standpoint, God's particular names are the specific things found in the cosmos, and His universal names are the modalities of existence discussed by theologians, philosophers, and scientists. Inasmuch as these universal names are specified by the Quran, they are God's "most beautiful names."

The Quran says that God created the human being as His vicegerent (*khalīfa*) or representative in the earth. The picture it draws of Adam, the primordial human being, makes clear that the human role in the universe has everything to do with knowledge of the names. As Samʿānī says, "The Exalted Lord wanted to clothe this speck of dust in the shirt of existence-giving, sit him on the chair of vicegerency, bind the collar of finding [*wujūd*] on the neck of his eminence with His munificence, and string the gemstone of knowledge on the necklace of his felicity: *And He taught Adam the names, all of them* [2:31]" (172).

As knower of both the universal and the particular names, Adam found and knew all things. His children, the Adamites (*ādamiyān*), have the potential to know all the names taught to their father. But they are left with a dilemma: Given the infinity of the names and their own brief life spans, which names should they strive to know and understand?

Religion and philosophy have generally opted for the universal names, which designate the broad modalities in which reality appears to us. Such names allow us to grasp the big picture and address big questions like "What is the meaning of life? Why are we here? What is our telos? Where does salvation lie?" Modern-day schools and universities typically stress the particular names, because they help us engage with the nitty-gritty of engineering and commerce and discourage us from asking the big questions, which appear unanswerable if not absurd to most modern sensibilities.

For Muslim theologians and thinkers, the most beautiful names of God designate the attributes that govern the cosmos and determine the nature of everything that exists. Without knowing these names and their significance, people will know nothing of lasting import about the world and themselves, for the names delineate the very warp and weft of existence. The attributes they designate—life, knowledge, desire, power, making, form-giving—establish reality as we actually find it. They differentiate and specify the modalities of the Real *Wujūd's* manifestation, whether in the outside world or within ourselves. Moreover, the attributes designated by the most beautiful names appear as the character traits of truly human and humane individuals—mercy, love, forgiveness, gentleness, wisdom, justice. The divine qualities that structure and animate the universe are the same qualities that enliven human souls and allow for the actualization of the fullness of morality, ethics, and spirituality. The fact that all attributes and qualities have a common source suggests some of the dangers of dividing the domains of human endeavor into categories like objective and subjective, physical and spiritual, material and mental, scientific and artistic. When Adamites forget the names they were taught at their creation, they fall into endless differentiation, dispersion, and chaos.

That the divine names and attributes are the roots of all that exists is taken for granted in much of Islamic literature, not least in the great Persian poetical tradition that was getting under way during Samʿānī's lifetime. Among the Sufi poets, Rūmī describes the connection between worldly phenomena and divine noumena in especially explicit terms, as in these verses:

Know that the creatures are like pure and limpid water,
    within which shine the attributes of the Majestic.
Their knowledge, their justice, their gentleness,
    are heaven's stars in running water.
Kings manifest the Real's kingship,
    the learned mirror the Real's awareness.
Generations have passed, and this is a new generation;
    this moon is that moon, but this water is not that water.
Justice is the same justice, learning the same learning,
    but generations and nations have changed.
Generations upon generations have passed, O friend,
    but the Meanings are constant and steady. . . .
Know that the attributes are like stars of Meaning,
    sitting on the heaven of Meanings.
Beautiful faces are the mirror of His beauty,
    love for them the reflection of seeking Him.
Cheek and mole will go back to their root—
    how can images remain in water forever?
All forms are reflections in the water of the stream;
    when you rub your eyes, all are He.[146]

INTERPRETATION OF THE NAMES

An essay in *The Economist* describes theories of contemporary scientists and philosophers on the topic of "Animal Minds." Twentieth-century behaviorism, it says, has largely been discarded, and now the prevailing view is that "no animals have all the attributes of human minds; but almost all the attributes of human minds are found in some animal or other."[147] For those schooled in Islamic meditation on the divine names, this is to say that all animals display the signs of certain specific divine names, but human beings alone are able to display the full range of the names and attributes, for they alone were taught all of them.

In other terms, man alone was created in the image of God. The saying of Muḥammad that reiterates this biblical theme uses the word *ṣūra*, which can be translated better as "form" than as image. The Quran designates God as *al-muṣawwir*, "the Form-Giver" (no. 16 in Samʿānī's list), which is the active participle of the verb *taṣwīr*. It uses this verb in several passages, such as the verse, *"God is He who made for you the earth a settledness and heaven a building; and He formed you, so He made your forms beautiful"* (40:64). What makes human forms beautiful is that God created them in His own form and, as the famous hadith has it, "God is beautiful, and He loves beauty." And given that God's knowledge of human beauty is eternal, His love for their beautiful forms is also eternal and unqualified—a point that Samʿānī often highlights.

The Economist goes on to say that language is the one exception to the rule that all human attributes are found in animal minds, so language "can still be claimed as uniquely human."[148] In Islamic terms, this is to say that Adamites alone have the potential to know all the names, so they alone have the ability to say anything at all, to express linguistically anything that may possibly exist in any mode whatsoever, even if only in our imagination. In contrast, animals know only snippets of names, so they are able to grasp certain aspects of reality but never the whole picture. Language is the sign that human beings carry this innate knowledge of all things and the ability to articulate all the forms created by the Form-Giver.

Knowing is never completely distinct from existence, that is, from finding and being found—a point that is implicit in the use of the word *wujūd*. To find and be found is to know and be known. Hence the fact of knowing the names implicit in Adamic nature implies finding the very existence of what is designated by the universal and particular names. Samʿānī dedicates a good bit of space—inspired by the Ikhwān al-Ṣafāʾ and Ghazālī—to explaining why the human microcosm has the potential to find within itself everything in the macrocosm. He writes, for example, "There is no animal or plant, nothing silent or speaking, no sphere, planet, constellation or any other existent thing whose specific characteristic or likeness is not found again in this speck of dust. This is why the great ones have said that everything is found once again in the Adamite, but the Adamite is not found again in anything" (136).

The notion that language is a uniquely human gift is of course an ancient theme, appearing for example in the Aristotelian concept of man as a "rational animal." This expression was translated into Arabic as *ḥayawān nāṭiq*, "talking animal." Rationality has everything to do with the ability to articulate and express meaning through language. Islamic thought considers this ability the key to our relationship with reality. It is knowledge of the names that gives Adamites their superiority over the angels and justifies the divine command for the angels to prostrate themselves before this speck of dust. Satan's refusal to obey God's command sets up the backdrop for the perennial conflict between good and evil, not to mention the mystery of human free will despite God's eternal omniscience and omnipotence. If Samʿānī constantly returns to the drama of Adam's creation, it is precisely because knowledge of the names is the key to both our existential plight and our salvation.

When the original human being learned the names, he knew precisely what they meant, for his teacher was the Omniscient. This God-given knowledge is the human *fiṭra*, the primordial created nature that gives people the instinctive recognition of unity and the potential to know all that is knowable. All Adamites have the same potential. Their destinies are then shaped by the names that they do in fact come to know, for their understanding of the names determines their worldview and ethos.

We should not forget that there is nothing odd about the notion that man can know everything. Putting aside resonances with other traditional worldviews, the implicit if not explicit pillar of modern civilization is potential omniscience. The science on which our world is built has long been attempting to uncover the real names of all things so that they can be manipulated and controlled. The magical power of names is of course well known in mythic lore. Islamic texts sometimes talk of the "greatest name of God," which, when uttered, bestows the answer to every prayer (Samʿānī alludes to this magical power several times by mentioning Balaam Beor, a biblical character whose story is referred to in the Quran). In the ethos of modernity the ability to gain this power has been turned over to quantum physicists, neurobiologists, and computer engineers.

Given the frequency with which the Quran mentions various divine names in all sorts of contexts, it is not surprising that explanation (*sharḥ*) of the names became a relatively common genre in lexicology, Kalam, and Sufism. The issues addressed, however, were by no means ignored by scholars writing in other genres. Much of the complex history of the various schools of Kalam, philosophy, and Sufism has to do with debates over delineating and understanding the names that are applied to existent and nonexistent things.

The Quran mentions names of God singly, in pairs, and in set phrases like *"He is powerful over everything."* Sometimes it offers short lists (the longest of which is found in 59:22–24). The Hadith literature provides many more examples. The famous notion that God has ninety-nine names derives from a hadith found in Bukhārī, Muslim, and other canonical sources: "Surely God has ninety-nine names, one hundred less one. Whoever enumerates them will enter the Garden." In some of these sources, the text goes on to list the ninety-nine names, but Hadith experts agree that the list cannot be traced back to the Prophet. Unsurprisingly, the word enumerate (*iḥṣāʾ*) was given a variety of interpretations.

No one took the number ninety-nine as definitive or limiting. It was understood to mean that God discloses Himself in scripture, the world, and the human soul in many namable ways. If we ask how many names the Quran ascribes to God, the answer will depend on how we define the word name. Although the Quran frequently talks about names, it does not specify what counts as a name, so this is left to the reader. However we define the word, we will not end up with ninety-nine if we count them as they occur in the text. For example, in his commentary on the divine names ʿAfīf al-Dīn Tilimsānī (d. 1291) goes through the Quran chapter by chapter and comes up with a total of 146 distinct names.

The best historical survey of the wide range of questions that Muslims asked and answered while investigating the divine names is Daniel Gimaret's *Les noms divins en Islam*. He describes twenty-three Arabic commentaries on the names down to Ghazālī and mentions another fifteen written during the following two centuries, while acknowledging that many more were produced. Among the later books that he does not mention is the long *Sharḥ al-asmāʾ* by the nineteenth-century philosopher Mullā Hādī Sabziwārī (d. 1873), unusual in that it comments on a list of 1,001 divine names found in *al-Jawshan al-kabīr* (The Great Chainmail), a supplication that Shi'ite sources trace back to the Prophet.

Gimaret says that the authors he studied generally took one of three approaches: lexicology (etymology and literal meaning), theology (the names' meanings in the context of a general theory of naming God), and spirituality (meditation on the names as a means of gaining nearness to God). Many authors combined these approaches, though Gimaret focuses on the first two. In choosing which names to include in their works, most scholars followed one of the transmitted lists of ninety-nine (of which there are five; only forty-four names are mentioned in all five lists). Others preferred to analyze words used to designate God in the Quran and Hadith and to decide on the basis of various criteria which names can appropriately be ascribed to Him. Gimaret mentions about 275 names discussed by his authors and attempts a thematic analysis of two hundred.

In reading Gimaret's book one might conclude that he has provided a relatively comprehensive study of the divine names in early Islamic thought. But that would be to forget that he gives only lip service to the spiritual approach. It would also ignore the fact that all God-talk employs names and attributes. Both Kalam and Sufism tend to be as God-centered as the Quran itself, which means that the divine names and their implications are discussed frequently in these two fields—and not infrequently by philosophers. To take an extreme example of how Gimaret's approach might mislead the reader, he states without going into detail that Ibn ʿArabī addresses the divine names in chapter 558 of *al-Futūḥāt al-makkiyya* as well as in one other book. Ibn ʿArabī wrote several hundred books and treatises, and chapter 558 of the *Futūḥāt*, if it were published separately, would be a book of perhaps one thousand pages, making it one of the longest studies of the theological and spiritual significance of names in Islamic literature. This chapter, however, is only a small part of the massive *Futūḥāt*, every page of which talks directly or indirectly about the divine names, as does every other book and treatise written by Ibn ʿArabī. Thirty-five years ago when I began research for my first book-length study of Ibn ʿArabī, I assumed that most of my effort would be focused on the notion of *waḥdat al-wujūd*, "the oneness of existence," given that the secondary literature agreed at the time that this was the key theme of his writings. Once I had read a thousand pages of the *Futūḥāt*, however, I realized not only that there is no such technical term in his works, but also that the divine names provide the backdrop to everything he says.

In short, one should not think that the genre of explaining the divine names is in any way unusual; on the contrary, every discussion of God in this enormously God-centered religion is rooted in the notion that people have no choice but to speak of God in terms of specific names and attributes with specific meanings, despite God's essential namelessness.

After dealing with the relatively minor issue of which divine names should be discussed, scholars who wrote commentaries dedicated most of their effort to explaining what exactly each name designates and how exactly it does so. The divine names pertain to human language, so they need to be understood in human terms. All the most beautiful names, with the one exception of *God* itself (and according to many, *All-Merciful*), can also be applied to created things. To explain what exactly a name means when applied to human or nonhuman beings can be a complicated task. What does it mean, for example, to say that something is "alive" (*ḥayy*, one of the divine names)? Biologists are still stumped by this question. To bring out what the same name means when applied to God—the Infinite and Ultimate Reality—cannot be quite so simple.

In the broad context of Islamic thought, the names need to be understood because they represent the core message of the prophets, whose role in history has been to "rectify the names," to use the famous expression of Confucius (*Analects* 13:3). Though Adam was taught all the names, his descendants are plagued by forgetfulness. They need to remember the true names of things, a process that demands reorientation of thought, change of mind, *metanoia*. To use Quranic language, the first step in recovering the names as taught to Adam is *tawba*, "turning." This word is usually translated as "repentance" because it designates turning away from self-oriented thinking and turning toward God-oriented thinking. But "turning" is not simply a human attribute. Several times the Quran calls God *tawwāb*, "Ever-Turning" (no. 82), an emphatic form of *tawba's* active participle. People turn toward God because He has turned toward them: *"Then He turned toward them so that they would turn; surely He is the Ever-Turning, the Ever-Merciful"* (9:118). Theologians see here a universal principle, often voiced by Ghazālī in the form "There is no actor but God" (*lā fā ʿila illa'llāh*).

Ghazālī's sentence is a version of "the formula voicing *tawḥīd,*" that is, the words "(There is) no god but God" found in the first testimony of faith, the Shahadah. When we look at the manner in which Muslim scholars interpret the theological significance of the names, we can see that they typically have this formula in mind. Even if they do not voice it explicitly, it lurks beneath the surface and provides the key to how they understand the meaning of any name that can properly be applied to God. If He is the Actor, then no one acts but God. If He is the Merciful, then no one is merciful but God. If He is the Knowing, then no one knows but God. If He is the Ever-Turning, then no one turns but God.

Reflection on the implications of *tawḥīd* typically leads in either one or both of two directions, often called *tanzīh* and *tashbīh*. *Tanzīh* is the assertion of God's incomparability and transcendence, the fact that, as the Quran puts it, *"Nothing is as His likeness"* (42:11). *Tashbīh* is the assertion of God's similarity and immanence, the fact that *"He is with you wherever you are"* (57:4). The contrasting perspectives represented by *tanzīh* and *tashbīh* play major roles in theological thinking, even if this specific pairing of terms did not come into prominence before Ibn ʿArabī.[149]

In terms of *tanzīh*, *tawḥīd* alerts us to the fact that God is the only ultimate reality, the only thing that can properly be called real (*ḥaqq*); nothing is comparable with Him because nothing else is truly real. It follows that everything other than God is unreal (*bāṭil*). The verse *"The Real has come, and the unreal has vanished away"* (17:81), appears then as a statement of how to perceive things correctly. Next to the Real, all things are evanescent: *"Everything is perishing but His face"* (28:88). That these verses bring out the stark reality of *tawḥīd's* basic significance is suggested by the already cited hadith: "The most astute of words are those spoken by Labīd: 'Is not everything other than God unreal?' "

But *tashbīh* must also be taken into account. If God were incomparable in every respect—if He were simply the God of negative theology—there would be no common measure between the Real and the unreal, a heretical position that theologians called *ta'ṭīl*, or "divesting" God of His names and attributes (Deism is a modern version of *ta'ṭīl*). But the Real expresses Itself in human language, declaring Its own names and employing the same names to speak of the created realm. God is alive, people are alive. God is knowing, people know. God is powerful, people have power. God is desiring, people desire. God is speaking, people speak. And so on down the list. All names of the Real leave marks and traces in the universe and the human soul. Every individual thing, even if it is only a vestige and a sign, partakes of reality in some way or other, and this partaking is necessarily denoted by the names that designate the very modalities of the Real *Wujūd* in Its self-disclosure.

FOUR COMMENTARIES ON THE NAMES

It was noted that Gimaret discerns three basic approaches to explaining the divine names. The lexicological approach analyzes the meanings of the words in the context of the Arabic language. The theological approach attempts to explain which words can justifiably be called divine names and what exactly these words tell us about God. The spiritual approach builds on the first two in order to tell us how to live our lives in harmony with what the names denote.

Discussion of the spiritual significance plays an important role in the approaches of many scholars. Their books address how we relate to the names both in terms of *tanzīh*, our utter difference from God, and *tashbīh*, the presence of the divine attributes within our human configuration. In terms of *tanzīh*, the divine names designate qualities that pertain exclusively to God, so the human task is to understand our situation vis-à-vis the transcendent God and act accordingly. If God is Lord, then people are servants who must do as the Lord commands. If God is Creator, then people are created things that are utterly subservient to His creative power. *Tanzīh* sets up the difference between human beings and God, reminding them of their unreality in the face of His reality.

From the standpoint of *tashbīh*, the names designate qualities that are innate to human souls because God created them in His form. This notion was often conceptualized in terms of *khuluq*, character or character trait, the plural of which, *akhlāq*, is typically translated as "ethics." Hadiths mention that God has a certain number of character traits—often three hundred—and that anyone who actualizes even one of them will enter paradise. Some of these sayings use the expression *al-takhalluq bi-akhlāq Allāh*, "becoming characterized by God's character traits," and this phrase is often mentioned in discussions of the names. Sam'ānī does not use it, but he refers to the principle. On one occasion, for example, he cites a famous saying of the Prophet's wife 'Ā'isha concerning her husband: "His character was the Quran." Sam'ānī then remarks, "He arrived where he arrived through the attributes of the Real" (159). In another passage he makes the same point by quoting the Quranic verse addressed to Muḥammad, *"Surely thou hast a tremendous character"* (68:4): "By means of revelation the character of mortal nature was removed and the character of the Quran put in its place" (189). Needless to say, the "character of the Quran" is that of the eternal Word, the divine self-expression designating God in Himself, a self-expression that can be summarized by listing the most beautiful names.

Sam'ānī's manner of explaining the spiritual significance of the names can usefully be compared with those of three other scholars, some of whose students he would have known personally: Bayhaqī (d. 1066), author of *The Names and Attributes*; Qushayrī (d. 1072), author of *Explanation of God's Most Beautiful Names*; and Ghazālī (d. 1111), author of *The Highest Goal* (*al-Maqṣad al-asnā*).

Bayhaqī is famous as an Ash'arite theologian but is mainly a Hadith-transmitter. In *The Names and Attributes* he arranges his topics in the systematic manner of the theologians, but most of his text is taken up by the citation of hadiths with *isnāds*. Gimaret points out that the early part of *The Names and Attributes*, which is dedicated specifically to the definition and classification of the divine names in the manner of the Kalam experts, is derived almost verbatim from two earlier works on Kalam.[150] In the latter part of the book, Bayhaqī discusses many Quranic verses that speak of God's attributes—including those that mention, for example, God's Throne, face, and hands—and cites hadiths concerning their meaning. In short, Bayhaqī's commentary is the sort of work that would have pleased 'Abd al-Karīm Sam'ānī, since it consists mainly of narrating the words of the Prophet and the early authorities. As for how the names impinge on the very reality of the human soul and how people must respond, these are questions left to the reader's interpretation of the transmitted sayings.

Qushayrī's *Explanation* offers a much more sophisticated approach to the names while bringing out their implications for the spiritual life, which is to say that he points explicitly to their impact on the soul. He devotes about twenty percent of his 250-page book to the theoretical background of discussing the names in a manner that reflects his training in Ash'arite Kalam. He then proceeds to comment on each of the names, following with slight variation the most commonly cited list, which is that traced back to the Companion Abū Hurayra by Tirmidhī in his *Sunan*. Ghazālī and Sam'ānī follow the same list (see table 2). It begins by mentioning the names found in the longest enumeration in the Quran: *"He is God; there is no god but He... the All-Merciful, the Ever-Merciful... the King, the Holy, the Peace, the Faithful, the Overseer, the Exalted, the Compeller, the Proud... the Creator, the Maker, the Form-Giver"* (59:22–24). Ghazālī counts fourteen names in this passage, so he understands Abū Hurayra's list to have exactly ninety-nine names. Both Sam'ānī and Qushayrī count sixteen names, because they consider *He* and *There is no god but He* as individual names. Both also make minor adjustments to the list, so Sam'ānī ends up with 102 names and Qushayrī with ninety-six. Although Bayhaqī quotes Abū Hurayra's list, he also discusses many other names mentioned in the Quran and Hadith.

Table 2. The Divine Names

Abū Hurayra	Samʿānī	Qushayrī	Ghazālī
1. Hū	1	3	—
2. Allāh	2	1	1
3. Alladhī Lā Ilāha Illā Hū	3	2	—
4. al-Raḥmān	4	—	2
5. al-Raḥīm	5	—	3
6. al-Malik	6	4	4
7. al-Quddūs	7	5	5
8. al-Salām	8	6	6
9. al-Muʾmin	9	7	7
10. al-Muhaymin	10	8	8
11. al-ʿAzīz	11	9	9
12. al-Jabbār	12	10	10
13. al-Mutakabbir	13	11	11
14. al-Khāliq	14	12	12
15. al-Bāriʾ	15	13	13
16. al-Muṣawwir	16	14	14
17. al-Ghaffār	17	15	15
18. al-Qahhār	18	16	16
19. al-Wahhāb	19	17	17
20. al-Razzāq	20	18	18
21. al-Fattāḥ	21	19	19
22. al-ʿAlīm	22	20	20
23. al-Qābiḍ	23	21	21
24. al-Bāsiṭ	24	22	22
25. al-Khāfiḍ	25	23	23
26. al-Rāfiʿ	26	24	24
27. al-Muʿizz	27	25	25
28. al-Mudhill	28	26	26
29. al-Samīʿ	29	27	27
30. al-Baṣīr	30	28	28
31. al-Ḥakam	31	29	29

continued on next page

Table 2 (cont'd)

Abū Hurayra	Samʿānī	Qushayrī	Ghazālī
32. al-ʿAdl	32	30	30
33. al-Laṭīf	33	31	31
34. al-Khabīr	34	32	32
35. al-Ḥalīm	35	33	33
36. al-ʿAẓīm	36	34	34
37. al-Ghafūr	37	35	35
38. al-Shakūr	38	36	36
39. al-ʿAlī	39	37	37
40. al-Kabīr	40	38	38
41. al-Ḥafīẓ	41	39	39
42. al-Muqīt	42	40	40
43. al-Ḥasīb	43	41	41
44. al-Jalīl	44	42	42
—	45. al-Jamīl	43	—
45. al-Karīm	46	44	43
46. al-Raqīb	47	45	44
47. al-Mujīb	48	46	45
48. al-Wāsiʿ	49	47	46
49. al-Ḥakīm	50	48	47
50. al-Wadūd	51	49	48
51. al-Majīd	52	50	49
52. al-Bāʿith	53	51	50
53. al-Shahīd	54	52	51
54. al-Ḥaqq	55	53	52
—	56. al-Mubīn	54	—
55. al-Wakīl	57	55	53
56. al-Qawī	58	56	54
57. al-Matīn	59	57	55
58. al-Walī	60	58	56
59. al-Ḥamīd	61	59	57
60. al-Muḥṣī	62	60	58
61. al-Mubdiʾ	63	61	59

continued on next page

Table 2 (cont'd)

Abū Hurayra	Samʿānī	Qushayrī	Ghazālī
62. al-Muʿīd	64	62	60
63. al-Muḥyī	65	63	61
64. al-Mumīt	66	64	62
65. al-Ḥayy	67	65	63
66. al-Qayyūm	68	66	64
67. al-Wājid	69	67	65
68. al-Mājid	—	—	66
69. al-Wāḥid	70	68	67
—	71. al-Aḥad	—	—
70. al-Ṣamad	72	69	68
71. al-Qādir	73	70	69
72. al-Muqtadir	74	71	70
73. al-Muqaddim	75	72	71
74. al-Muʾakhkhir	76	73	72
75. al-Awwal	77	74	73
76. al-Ākhir	78	75	74
77. al-Ẓāhir	79	76	75
78. al-Bāṭin	80	77	76
79. al-Barr	81	78	79
80. al-Tawwāb	82	79	80
81. al-Muntaqim	83	80	81
82. al-ʿAfū	84	81	82
83. al-Raʾūf	85	82	83
84. Mālik al-Mulk	86	—	84
85. Dhu'l-Jalāl wa'l-Ikrām	87	83	85
86. al-Wālī	88	—	77
87. al-Mutaʿālī	89	—	78
88. al-Muqsiṭ	90	84	86
89. al-Jāmiʿ	91	85	87
90. al-Ghanī	92	—	88
91. al-Mughnī	93	86	89
92. al-Māniʿ	—	87	90

continued on next page

Table 2 (cont'd)

Abū Hurayra	Samʿānī	Qushayrī	Ghazālī
93. al-Ḍārr	94	88	91
94. al-Nāfiʿ	95	89	92
95. al-Nūr	96	90	93
96. al-Hādī	97	91	94
97. al-Badīʿ	98	91	95
98. al-Bāqī	99	93	96
99. al-Wārith	100	94	97
100. al-Rashīd	101	95	98
101. al-Ṣabūr	102	96	99

In his commentary Qushayrī begins each name by explaining its meaning in the manner of lexicologists and theologians. Then he quotes sayings of various Sufi shaykhs about the qualities designated by the names and their pertinence to the human situation. Both he and Bayhaqī stress the importance of remembrance (*dhikr*), that is, mentioning the names in prayer and supplication. Bayhaqī does so by citing the encouragements of the tradition and Qushayrī by adding theological and spiritual justifications, often in the aphoristic style that is characteristic of his Quran commentary. His introduction is taken up mainly by explaining the significance of various Quranic verses that point to the human implications of the names. For example, he writes:

> The Real knows that you have no approved names, so He says, "*To God belong the most beautiful names, so call Him by them!*" [7:180]. If you call the names of your Lord, that is better for you than to call your own names. When you are with yourself, you are with that which does not subsist, but when you are with Him, you are with that which has always been. What a difference between this attribute and that attribute![151]

Ghazālī's *Highest Goal* consists of two hundred pages divided into ten chapters. Nine of the chapters—about half of the book—are devoted to linguistic and theological issues of names and naming. The fifth and longest chapter provides a brief explanation of the meaning of each of the ninety-nine names. In keeping with his theological and philosophical approach, Ghazālī gives a relatively high profile to *al-takhalluq bi-akhlāq Allāh*, a topic to which he devotes one of his introductory chapters. He calls this chapter: "Explaining that the servant's perfection and felicity lie in becoming characterized by God's character traits and being adorned by the meanings of His attributes and names in the measure conceivable in his case."

In this chapter Ghazālī explains that servants who achieve nearness to God have a share (*ḥaẓẓ*) of the names in two respects. First they attain recognition (*maʿrifa*) of the true meanings of the names by way of unveiling (*mukāshafa*) and contemplation (*mushāhada*), that is, by way of unmediated knowledge. This is a knowledge that does not come merely by way of imitation (*taqlīd*) and transmission (*naql*), in contrast to knowledge received by memorizing the Quran, Hadith, and sayings, or studying Kalam. The servant comes to recognize the reality (*ḥaqīqa*) of the names in the same unmediated manner that he recognizes his own inner qualities, that is, "by inner contemplation, not outward sense perception. How greatly this differs from belief held by imitating one's parents and teachers, even when one is convinced of it by way of the dialectical proofs of Kalam!" The servants' second share of the names is reverence toward the meanings received through unveiling such that their yearning (*shawq*) to become qualified (*ittiṣāf*) by God's attributes increases and their love (*ʿishq*) for Him intensifies.[152] When Ghazālī turns to the specific meaning of each name, he devotes about half of each discussion to how the servant should become qualified by a share of the name.

In sum, Bayhaqī's book on the names is based mainly on hadiths and sayings quoted from earlier authorities, without neglecting the *isnāds*. Qushayrī's book explains the meaning of each name and then describes how the servant should interact with it, both by understanding God's exclusive possession of the attribute and by becoming characterized by its meaning; most of his text is taken up by sayings or anecdotes of Sufi teachers without *isnāds*. Ghazālī keeps his discussion almost purely theoretical, with few quotations or anecdotes, while stressing the need to undergo spiritual transformation by escaping from reliance on transmitted learning and achieving the realization (*taḥqīq*) of the truth of things and the actualization of one's own innate intelligence.

Samʿānī's approach is similar to that of Qushayrī in that he provides relatively brief definitions of the names, followed by sayings and anecdotes. Not more than five percent of the text, however, is dedicated explicitly to discussing the names and the proper manner of interacting with them. Compared to other books on the names, the stated topic seems to be a pretext for delving into the mysteries of the divine love that permeates the universe.

Samʿānī gives his book no clear structure other than the sequence of the names. This is shown among other things by the amount of space he devotes to each name. Both Ghazālī and Qushayrī wrote careful compositions that dedicate one to three or four pages to each name, whereas Samʿānī makes no attempt to be consistent in the length of his discussions. Most of his seventy-four sections explain one name, but a number are dedicated to two or more. In dealing with the first seven names, he provides short discussions, three pages or less. From the eighth to the twenty-first name, he doubles the length of his expositions. In the next ten sections, which deal with a total of fifteen names, he enters into much more detail, so the length of each section is two or three times the length of the second group. Then, at the beginning of the discussion of names 37 and 38, he writes, "From here on I will speak briefly in fear of boring the hearts of those who love the Possessor of Majesty," and the sections remain relatively short, similar to the second group of names.

Samʿānī also differs markedly from Qushayrī and Ghazālī in his failure to discuss the theoretical issue of naming God, preferring instead to offer concise explanations of the meaning of each name and then to address the manner of living one's life with God in mind. Rare remarks on the general significance of the names appear in passing. In one place, for example, he quotes (or perhaps composes) an Arabic aphorism: "The greatest of God's blessings on His servants are two things: His teaching them His name and His making Himself recognized to them" (329). Only in one place does he step back to suggest the role played by the divine names in the human situation. He offers these remarks as God's own explanation of a Quranic verse that refers to His love for human beings as contrasted with His relationship with the angels:

> *God is the friend of those who have faith* [2:257]: "I am your friend. I did not disclose an iota of the realities of My secrets before bringing you into existence. What can be disclosed to a multitude of slaves [angels]? And what can be hidden from friends?
>
> "In the state of union friends have beauty, and in the state of separation they have the specter of imagination. Although I am pure of imagination, the waves of yearning began to clash in the state of separation, so I made a necklace of the ninety-nine names with the name *God* as its centerpiece. Then I sent it to you on the hand of the Seal of the Prophets, who is the white falcon of the world of mystery, so that it might be a sample of perfect beauty and majesty." (433)

The final words of this passage, beauty and majesty, refer of course to the two basic categories of names. Names of beauty stress *tashbīh*, and names of majesty stress *tanzīh*. Notice also the reference here to "imagination" (*khayāl*). Ibn ʿArabī often reminds his readers that imagination is the key to their proper relationship with God. The Prophet makes this clear, he says, in the Hadith of Gabriel, where he describes *iḥsān* or beautiful-doing as "to worship God as if you see Him, for even if you do not see Him, He sees you." The words "as if" (*ka ʾanna*) indicate that seekers must train their imagination to gaze upon God; otherwise, they will never learn how to love Him. This is no small matter, given that without the intervention of love, separation between lover and Beloved, servant and Lord, creature and Creator, will be drawn out forever. As Samʿānī puts it, "It is love that carries a man to the Beloved—all else is a thief on the road" (364). Imaginal understanding must be employed to supplement and actualize the rational understanding that comes by way of theology and philosophy. Ibn ʿArabī explains:

> By God, were it not for the Shariah that came with the divine report-giving, no one would recognize God! Had we remained with our rational proofs—which, in the opinion of the rational thinkers, demonstrate the knowledge that God's Essence is "not like this" and "not like that"—no created thing would ever have loved Him. But, the divine reports have come in the tongues of the Shariahs, saying that "He is like this" and "He is like that" and mentioning things whose outward meanings are contradicted by rational proofs. . . .
>
> We recognize God only by means of what He has reported about Himself: His love for us, His mercy toward us, His clemency, His tenderness, His loving-kindness, His descent into limitation so that we may conceive of Him in images and place Him before our eyes in our hearts, our kiblah, and our imagination "as if" we see Him. Or rather, we do indeed see Him within ourselves, for we have come to recognize Him by His making Himself recognized, not by our own rational consideration.[153]

It is the central role given to imagination, I think, that separates Samʿānī's *Repose of the Spirits* from earlier commentaries on the divine names. Such works were typically written by scholars trained in academic methodologies. In keeping with the rational tools of their disciplines, they placed special stress on God's incomparability and tended to explain away scriptural passages telling us that "He is like this" and "He is like that." Samʿānī does not ignore the usefulness of rational proofs, but he employs the language of image, symbol, and poetry to bring out the fact that the concrete, imaginal representations of God in scripture and *"in the signs on the horizons and your souls"* (42:53) convey far more of God's reality than the abstract arguments of systematic theologians.

DIVINE COMPLEMENTARITY

In discussing *tawḥīd* and the fact that, as the Quran puts it, *"Everything is perishing but His face"* (28:88), Samʿānī often employs the standard pair "reality" (*ḥaqīqa*) and "metaphor" (*majāz*). The complementary meanings of these two terms are highlighted in the well-known proverb "The metaphor is the bridge to the reality." One basic interpretation of *tawḥīd* is simply that we and the universe are metaphors, not reality itself. A metaphor is a sign, a verse, a linguistic expression, a configuration of names and attributes signifying the Unseen. People need to understand that they live in the realm of metaphor. Otherwise they will never grasp the peril of their situation. "It is clear what realities can be unveiled in the world of metaphor. It is obvious what sort of pictures can be painted on a gnat's wing" (478).

Despite their unreality, metaphors provide the bridge to the Real *Wujūd*, which is the Necessary Existence that underlies all, the Essence named by all the names. Rūmī often reminds his readers of the importance of understanding metaphors, especially when he contrasts real love (love for the Real) with metaphorical love (love for anything other than God). Human love should be celebrated precisely because it is a metaphor that provides a bridge to the Reality, the Haqiqah. Through it we eventually come to understand that wholeness will be found only in love for the Real. As he puts it in one passage, giving solace to jilted lovers:

> Consider it His solicitude that you lost in the street of love.
> Put aside metaphorical love, for the end is love for the Real.
> The soldier gives his son a wooden sword
> for him to become a master and take a sword into battle.
> Love for a human being is that wooden sword.
> Once the trial ends, the love will be for the All-Merciful.[154]

Samʿānī devotes much of his explanation of the divine name the Praiser/the Praised (no. 61) to commenting on the Surah of Praise, that is, the Fātiḥa or Opening of the Quran, which, after the *basmalah*, begins with the words *"The praise belongs to God, the Lord of the worlds."* It is clear that creatures should praise their Creator, but why does God begin His Book by praising Himself? Samʿānī has God answer like this:

> The praise that is worthy of Me is what I bring for Myself, not what you bring for Me. You are a creature and newly arrived [*muḥdath*], and your praise is your attribute. The attribute of a creature is a metaphor, and the attribute of a newly arrived thing is a trace. Moreover, your praise is caused by requesting. How can something with a cause be worthy of Me? My majestic Presence is incomparable with causes, hallowed beyond defects, and purified of slips. The praise worthy of Me is the reality, and that is My praise, for I am the Real and My attributes are the reality. Hence I brought a real praise worthy of Myself. Now that this reality has become apparent by virtue of generosity, you also bring a praise in keeping with the utmost limit and final end of your possibility [*imkān*]. Thus your metaphor will follow the reality, and its ruling property will become the reality's ruling property. (368)

This is the essential message of *The Repose of the Spirits*: Human beings must bring their metaphorical existence into conformity with Real Existence. That can happen only when they become qualified by the attributes that designate the reality of the Real, as summarized by the Most Beautiful Names.

Samʿānī commonly highlights the contrasting perspectives of *tanzīh* and *tashbīh* by describing the opposite effects of the names Severe (*qahhār*) and Gentle (*laṭīf*), or Majestic (*jalīl*) and Beautiful (*jamīl*). Inasmuch as God is severe, majestic, wrathful, transcendent, incomparable, unknown, and inaccessible, His absolute reality nullifies creation. Inasmuch as He is gentle, beautiful, merciful, immanent, similar, known, and accessible, His infinite reality affirms creation. Like many other theologians and philosophers, Samʿānī sees the entire created realm as governed by these complementary qualities, a standpoint that Sachiko Murata calls "the Tao of Islam."[155] Specifically, however, it is the human reality—created in the all-encompassing form of God Himself—that experiences the conflicting demands of severity and gentleness, majesty and beauty, transcendence and immanence. In one of his many accounts of Adam's creation, Samʿānī puts these words into God's mouth: "O angels, you move over to the side and watch from a distance. It is the Adamites who will taste the blows of Our severity and be caressed by Our gentleness. Sometimes We will slice them up with the sword of severity, and sometimes We will anoint them with the gaze of gentleness" (230).

The activity of severity and gentleness drives creatures in diverse directions. "His majesty displays His exaltedness, and His beauty discloses His gentleness. His majesty makes all speakers dumb, and His beauty brings all the dumb into speech" (416). In one passage Samʿānī sees the divergent energy of the divine names reflected in the activities of the "imams," meaning the prayer-leaders and teachers of the religion. Some are vocal, and others stay silent. "The eyes of one imam fall on the severity of the divinity, those of another imam on the perfect gentleness of all-mercifulness. Severity stamps a seal on the lips of one imam, and mercy puts another imam on the carpet of bold expansiveness" (332).

The differing standpoints of the two imams correlate with the two formulas of the Shahadah, one of which highlights majesty and the other beauty. Inasmuch as people look at God Himself and acknowledge that there is nothing real but the Reality, their own reality is utterly effaced by majesty and transcendence. Inasmuch as they look at God's prophets and friends, recognizing them as messengers and spokesmen, their created reality is embraced by gentleness and kindness. "You can also say that the eyes of one imam fall on the severity of the divinity, and the eyes of the other imam fall on the character of prophethood. The awesomeness of the Sultan silences speakers, but it is not surprising that in the presence of Muḥammad's character, a stone should glorify God, or a cup and a lizard should praise Him" (332), the last two clauses referring to miraculous events recounted in the Prophet's biographies.

When talking about the absolute reality of the Real and the unreality of everything else, Samʿānī frequently takes the position of the silent imam, since human expression and existence have no independent worth. Nonetheless he always comes back to the standpoint of the speaking imam, for he continually stresses the priority of beauty and gentleness and the importance of following Muḥammad in order to live in the divine presence. Once people have recognized the fact of *tawḥīd*, they need to harness their limited freedom in order to live up to what they have come to know. Their silence should turn into speech. They must call out to the divine gentleness and compassion, which was revealed to them in the form of the prophets generally and Muḥammad specifically.

Like the vocal imams who undertook *tadhkīr*, Samʿānī devotes much of his effort to explaining why people should follow the prophets on the path to God. His most original contribution to Islamic thought may indeed lie in his interpretations of the prophets' function in the human cosmos. He has a special, perhaps unparalleled, gift for clarifying the multilayered Quranic message found in the prophetic tales. Here his prowess as a Quran interpreter—noted by his nephew ʿAbd al-Karīm—comes to the fore. Discussion of God per se as exemplified by the disquisitions of the Kalam experts tends to remain abstract and distant from everyday concerns, but the prophets were mortal human beings like us. The Quran repeatedly tells their stories, and Samʿānī interprets these in a variety of ways to show their relevance not simply to events in the past but also to our own situation at the present moment. He sums up the importance of God's storytelling and his own *tadhkīr* like this:

> What wisdom is there in His speaking to you of Adam, Noah, Abraham, Moses, and Jesus? He is warming up the place of your hopes in Him and fanning the fire in the chamber of your patience. When someone sits down in front of a hungry man and eats delicious food, his mouth starts to water. "O friend, though My goods are expensive and the poor can't buy them, well, there's no law against hoping." (101)

In some ways Samʿānī's depiction of the prophets anticipates what Ibn ʿArabī was to do in his famous *Fuṣūṣ al-ḥikam* and other works, though he does not explain their role with anything like Ibn ʿArabī's theoretical abstruseness and systematic rigor. Samʿānī describes the prophets as human embodiments of proper engagement with the divine names. In each case, prophetic words and conduct provide guidance to the human soul in becoming characterized by the divine character traits. Samʿānī's approach is also reminiscent of Ibn ʿArabī's in the prominence that he gives to our common ancestor, to whom Ibn ʿArabī dedicates the first chapter of the *Fuṣūṣ*. Samʿānī sees the Quran's depiction of Adam as an explication of an eternal love affair between

God and man: "In the Beginningless He first talked about you to Himself, then He talked about you to you" (119). The Beginningless is the realm of God's eternal knowledge, the realm in which He loved us before we existed.

> What beautiful-doing is beyond the fact that you were in the concealment of nonexistence, and He was taking care of your work with bounty and generosity? You were in the concealment of nonexistence, and He chose you out from the whole world. You were in the concealment of nonexistence, and He was taking care of your work without any previous intercession, without any subsequent benefit, without your taking any trouble in the present state, and without any rightful due made incumbent in the future. He was tossing the secret hook of *He loves them* into the ocean of *they love Him* [5:54]. (186)

God's beginningless love, *"He loves them,"* is the seed of our endless love, *"they love Him."* God makes us suffer separation's pain so that we may come to understand who it is that we really love. The goal of metaphorical existence is to pave the way to real existence. Trial and tribulation should be welcomed as gifts of the Beautiful-doer. As Rūmī explains:

> Pain renews old medicines and lops off
> every branch of indifference.
> Pain is an alchemy that makes everything new.
> Where is indifference when pain intervenes?
> Beware, do not sigh coldly in indifference—
> seek pain, seek pain, pain, pain.[156]

Theologians before and after Samʿānī contrasted the standpoints of the two formulas of the Shahadah by speaking of two commands (*amr*): the engendering (*takwīnī*) or creative (*khalqī*) command, and the prescriptive (*taklīfī*) or religious (*dīnī*) command. The creative command is the divine word "Be!" (*kun*), which is the source of the realm of being (*kawn*). The prescriptive command takes the form of the rules and guidelines of right conduct, that is, religion generally, or the Shariah and the Tariqah. Those who follow the religious command do so because the creative command instills conformity with it into them. Those who reject the religious command cannot fail to follow the creative command. Samʿānī calls the creative command the "decree" (*ḥukm*) and often contrasts it with the "command," meaning the religious command. He writes, for example:

> The commanded is one thing, the decreed something else.... What was commanded in the case of Abū Jahl, Abū Lahab, Pharaoh, and Nimrod was one thing, but what was decreed was something else. The command was coming, striking with the whip of the invitation, and the decree was coming, pulling back the reins. It is permitted for the servant's act to be different from what is commanded, but it is not permitted for it to be different from what is decreed. (51–52)

In one passage Samʿānī contrasts Islam with Guebrism (*gabrī*), a word that denotes Zoroastrianism specifically and dualistic beliefs or "associationism" (*shirk*) generally, that is, associating other realities with the Real. He traces *tawḥīd* and its rejection back to the two commands:

> Beautifully done O Perfect Exaltedness! A hundred thousand people were stirred up to exalt the rites of Islam, lest His command fall to the ground. A thousand thousand others were stirred up to take the sash of Guebrism to heart, lest His decree go to waste. By the decree of His majesty, a group remained in deprivation, and by the decree of His beauty, a group took benefit. (398)

The decree expresses God's eternal knowledge of things, for it bestows existence on what He has known forever. Talk of the divine decree is one way to express the well-known doctrine of *taqdīr* or "predetermination," the understanding that all things are measured out and apportioned in God's unchanging knowledge. Predetermination is a straightforward corollary of the fact that "there is no creator but God." Faced with the decree, the imams remain silent.

> O chevalier, when the scales of majestic Unity and perfect Divinity are brought forth, created nature does not weigh a jot, nor half a jot. Know that in reality, "No one carries the Real but the Real." You were wanted so you could be a spectator. (420)

As for the religious command, it addresses people's ability, limited though it may be, to shape their own destinies. To deny predetermination is to reject *tawḥīd*, and to deny free will is to nullify the teachings of the prophets and turn all human aspirations into illusions. Samʿānī points to the desired balance of perspectives in the following passage (among others):

> O chevalier, our position is neither compulsion nor free will. The free-willers want to take away *No god but God*. The compulsionists want to quarrel with *Muḥammad is God's Messenger*. *No god but God* negates the creed of free will. *Muḥammad is God's Messenger* erases the slate of compulsion. (52)

Ibn ʿArabī often points out that the religious command is a concomitant of the creative command, which is to say that the reality of prophethood follows necessarily upon God's Unity. This is because the religious command provides people with real principles of right action and ethics, principles known fully only to the Creator. Once obedience to the religious command is an option, various modalities of existence become possible that would otherwise have had no raison d'être. People have no choice but to accept responsibility for the decisions they make in their lives. As Ghazālī, Ibn ʿArabī, and others maintained, they are "compelled to be free" (*majbūr ʿalā ikhtiyārihim*). It is their free choices that make them worthy of paradise or deserving of hell. These are two real worlds that become actualized as the karmic repercussions of human freedom—or, in theological terms, as realms of reward and punishment. It follows that human freedom (or the freedom of analogous beings in other worlds) brings about realms of being that have no other reason to exist. In effect people are cocreators of their own destinies, even though, in the last analysis, all creativity goes back to the One Real. Thus the religious command is not simply a "moral imperative." It is an inescapable, ontological necessity.

Samʿānī does not shy away from drawing the logical conclusion of this line of thinking. After all, the Prophet said, "If you did not sin, God would bring a people who did sin, and then He would forgive them." Throughout *The Repose of the Spirits*, he comes back to the fact that human forgetfulness and sinfulness are built into the very fabric of existence and demanded by God's unqualified love, a love that is proven by the fact that there is absolutely nothing people can do to deserve it. As Samʿānī puts it in one passage, "He completed His bounty on this community in order to drive you into great boldness, impudence, sinfulness, and offense. Then, when the lights of love become apparent, that will be without any precedent service or mediating obedience" (369).

The Text and Translation

The editor of the Persian text, Najib Mayel Heravi, learned about the book's existence in 1981 when he came across a copy while cataloging manuscripts in the library of the shrine of Imam Riḍā in Mashhad (Āstāna-yi Quds-i Raḍawī). The more he studied the manuscript, the more he was impressed by its beauty and profundity, and he soon decided to publish it. Having acquired copies of four more manuscripts, he began the task of collation and was finally able to publish an edited text along with a detailed introduction in 1989.

When I was working on the second draft of my translation in early 2015, I contacted Dr. Heravi in the hope that he would be able to help me solve various difficulties I was having with a number of passages. He informed me that he was aware that the printed version had many typographical errors and other shortcomings (not unrelated to the troubled times during which he published the book). He also told me that he was working on a revised edition that, however, was far from complete. Nonetheless, he generously provided me with a PDF file of the partially corrected text; where appropriate, I have incorporated his revisions into my translation.

The majority of Dr. Heravi's changes pertain to orthography and grammatical issues that have no effect on the meaning. Nonetheless, I made several hundred minor changes on the basis of his revised text, not to mention many other changes in the sections of the book that he has not yet revised. Often these were corrections of typographical errors, sometimes fairly obvious, or words or phrases dropped from the printed edition. Given that Dr. Heravi's revision is a work in progress and given that I would like to move on to other projects while I still can, I decided to publish this translation without waiting for his revised edition.

In making the translation I also made use of a complete manuscript of the text from the Majlis library in Tehran (no. 2739), a copy of which was kindly acquired for me by Ali Karjoo-Ravary. Although Dr. Heravi used this manuscript in his first edition, he seems not to have made a careful collation at that time, so it was helpful in correcting a number of errors in the text and in deciphering some obscure passages.

In translating the book I have attempted to be as literal as possible. On occasion this leads to awkward English, but the meaning is typically clear from the context. Samʿānī conveys his points by means of the imagery and symbolism favored by poets much more than by theoretical elaboration. I prefer to maintain the flavor of his sometimes ornate style, with its profusion of metaphors (sometimes mixed), rather than try to decipher exactly what he has in mind. Translators, especially of prose, often strive to turn a figurative expression into an abstract idea, but given the central role that Sam'ānī gives to imagination (not only in the literary but also in the theological sense), preserving his imagery is a much better way to appreciate his understanding of the Islamic tradition.

Several of the books from which Sam'ānī quotes have been translated into English, such as Qushayrī's *Treatise.* I may mention these translations in my notes, but I do not follow them. Anyone who compares passages translated in other sources with those translated here will sometimes find significant differences, of which I am well aware. One reason for these is my consistency in employing technical terminology and the fact that other translators may use different terms or simply do not recognize the technical nature of the discussion. On occasion the context of Sam'ānī's discussion makes the meaning of rather obscure sayings or poems clear, and other translators may not have had the advantage of that context. Another reason for discrepancies is that Sam'ānī may provide a different reading of the text. Variants are common in manuscripts, and the printed editions do not always represent the best choice of wording, so I follow Sam'ānī's reading unless it represents a clear copyist error.

About ten percent of the text is in Arabic, more often than not in the form of quotations or borrowings. I have italicized these passages. Sam'ānī sometimes translates the Arabic into Persian, and in these cases I usually translate both the Arabic and the Persian, except in rare instances when the Persian text is a word-for-word rendering of the Arabic. In many passages of the book the interspersed Arabic and Persian produces a patchwork of italicized and roman characters, but this is a faithful representation of the feel of the original text.

My notes aim to provide sources for the sayings, poetry, and quotations that dot the text and to illustrate the manner in which the author made use of earlier works. With few exceptions I have refrained from explaining or elaborating upon what he is saying, not least because that task could go on indefinitely. The index along with glossary provides page references for important terms as well as the original Persian and Arabic words.

Notes

1. Faryāmanish, "Rawḥ al-arwāḥ." I demonstrated in "Rūmī and Waḥdat al-Wujūd" that in every instance in which R. A. Nicholson, the translator of Rūmī's *Mathnawī*, claims that Rūmī must have been influenced by the teachings of Ibn 'Arabī, *The Repose of the Spirits* was a far more likely source.

2. *Kashf al-ẓunūn* 1:915. The Süleymaniye Library in Istanbul has a beautifully written but thoroughly abridged and revised version of *Rawḥ al-arwāḥ* (Ayasofya 1864), with the correct title but without the name of the author. It belonged to a library endowed by the Ottoman sultan Mahmud II (r. 1808–39).

3. See the introduction to my partial translation of *Kashf al-asrār*.

4. Sijzī, *Fawā'id* 103. In the English translation (*Morals* 176), the translator missed the reference to *Repose*, no doubt because the book was still practically unknown to the scholarly community.

5. Nāgawrī, *Lawā'iḥ* 31. On Nāgawrī's books, see Lawrence, "The Lawa'ih."

6. Nāgawrī quotes less often from two well-known Arabic commentaries on the divine names, *al-Taḥbīr* by Abu'l-Qāsim Qushayrī and *al-Maqṣad al-asnā* by Muḥammad Ghazālī, about both of which more will be said later.

7. Dānishpazhūh, "Rawḥ al-arwāḥ" 303.

8. Furūzānfar, *Sharḥ* 915–17. Heravi summarizes the reports of these two scholars in his introduction (*Rawḥ* xv–xxii).

9. Yāqūt, *Muʿjam* 5:114.

10. *Ḥudūd al-ʿālam*, trans. Minorsky, 103.

11. The published work of ʿAbd al-Karīm called *al-Taḥbīr* is an abbreviated and defective version of *Muʿjam al-shuyūkh* (see the introduction to *Muntakhab*). A brief published work by him in the same genre collects sayings about Damascus.

12. Dhahabī, *Siyar* 20:462. For a good summary of the picture of ʿAbd al-Karīm drawn by the later literature, see the introduction to *Muntakhab*, which includes a list of his writings with mention of their length.

13. Subkī, *Ṭabaqāt* 6:215. The sentence is taken from ʿAbd al-Karīm's account of Ghazālī in his lost *Dhayl ʿalā taʾrīkh Baghdād* (Griffel, *Ghazālī* 292, n. 21).

14. The accounts of the Samʿānīs found in the later biographical literature are drawn almost entirely from ʿAbd al-Karīm's works, even if some of the biographers provide details not found in ʿAbd al-Karīm's extant books. These accounts typically ignore his uncle Aḥmad. See, for example, Ibn Khallikān, *Wafayāt* 3:209–12 (*Dictionary* 2:156–59).

15. *Ansāb* 3:298.

16. *Ansāb* 3:298–99. ʿAbd al-Karīm mentions Manṣūr's brother ʿAlī in one other place, an account of a scholar who studied jurisprudence with Manṣūr and received from him a letter of introduction to his brother before going to Kirman (*Muntakhab* 688). Subkī (*Ṭabaqāt* 5:341) provides a more detailed account of the split between the two brothers.

17. Subkī, *Ṭabaqāt* 5:342.

18. *Ansāb* 3:298–300.

19. Subkī, *Ṭabaqāt* 4:337. This is probably Abū Muḥammad Ḥusayn ibn Ḥasan Ṣāʾigh, mentioned by ʿAbd al-Karīm as his father's companion on the hajj (*Muntakhab* 703).

20. Subkī, *Ṭabaqāt* 4:338.

21. *Ansāb* 3:299.

22. *Ansāb* 3:299. See also the introduction to Manṣūr's *Qawāṭiʿ al-adilla*, which provides more information on Manṣūr's teachers, students, juridical standpoints, and influence. Subkī (*Ṭabaqāt* 5:335–46) provides a relatively long notice on him.

23. Fārisī, *Siyāq* 443.

24. Fārisī, *Siyāq* 442.

25. For the idea that there was an evolution from renunciation to Sufism, see for example, Bulliet, *Patricians* 41; Knysh, *Islamic Mysticism* 5ff.; Karamustafa, *Sufism* 1ff. In a more recent study, *Sufism*, Knysh argues cogently that *taṣawwuf* or Sufism, which he translates as "mysticism," and *zuhd* or renunciation and asceticism, are, "essentially, conterminous and complementary" (*Sufism* 12). He still thinks that a meaningful distinction can be drawn between the

two words. I would agree, but how can we be sure that it is the same distinction that exists in early sources?

26. Fārisī, *Siyāq* 334.
27. Fārisī, *Siyāq* 443.
28. Griffel, *Ghazālī* 52.
29. Fārisī, *Siyāq* 413.
30. *Muntakhab* 307.
31. *Iṣṭilām* 1:39.
32. Subkī, *Ṭabaqāt* 7:7.
33. Ibn Khallikān, *Wafayāt* 3:210 (*Dictionary* 2:157). In *Muntakhab* 703, ʿAbd al-Karīm mentions the date of his father's pilgrimage as 498/1105 instead of 497/1104.
34. *Ansāb* 3:300.
35. *Muntakhab* 190.
36. *Ansāb* 3:301. In his account of Bāqillānī, Dhahabī (*Siyar* 19:236) mentions that he transmitted Hadith to Muḥammad ibn Manṣūr.
37. Bulliet (*Patricians* 66–68) suggests the range of functions fulfilled by the *raʾīs* in Nishapur.
38. *Muntakhab* 1907.
39. *Ansāb* 3:171 (under Zandakhānī); *Muntakhab* 1419–20.
40. *Muntakhab* 1146.
41. *Muntakhab* 1089–94.
42. Ibn Khallikān, *Wafayāt* 3:210 (*Dictionary* 2:157).
43. *Ansāb* 4:503.
44. Chiabotti, "ʿAbd al-Karīm" 280–82; see also Bulliet, *Patricians* 154; Ṣafadī, *Wāfī* 19:172.
45. Dhahabī, *Siyar* 22:107–9.
46. *Ansāb* 300–1; *Muntakhab* 671–77.
47. Subkī, *Ṭabaqāt* 7:69.
48. Labīd ibn Rābiʿa was a poet who became a Companion and died approximately 660; Umayya ibn Abi'l-Ṣalt (d. ca. 625) was a poet mentioned in a number of hadiths that suggest the Prophet appreciated his poetry.
49. Qushayrī gives accounts of both Rūdhbārīs in his *Risāla* (*Epistle* 62–63, 73–74).
50. *Muntakhab* 676–77.
51. On the important role of "chivalry" (*futuwwa*) in Sufi ethics, see Zargar, *Polished Mirror* chapter 8; Ridgeon, *Morals and Mysticism*.
52. For a brief mention of this scholar, from whom ʿAbd al-Karīm received a license to transmit his *masmūʿāt*, see *Ansāb* 3:334–35.
53. On Faḍl Kākūʾī, see *Ansāb* 5:20–21; on Khalaf, see *Muntakhab* 776.
54. *Ansāb* 5:21.
55. *Ansāb* 3:301; *Muntakhab* 1428.
56. *Ansāb* 3:301; *Muntakhab* 307.
57. *Muntakhab* 1043; also 264, 488, 1548. On the practice of licensing infants and unborn children, see Shahrazūrī, *Introduction* 113ff.

58. *Ansāb* 5:448–49.

59. Fārisī, *Siyāq* 428.

60. *Ansāb* 3:301; *Muntakhab* 306–8.

61. For sources on ʿUbayd Qushayrī (d. 1118), also a merchant by profession, see *Muntakhab* 996, n. 1.

62. *Muntakhab* 333–34. See also *Ansāb* 3:397 (under Falkhārī) and 5:262–63 (under Marwaʾl-Rūdhī).

63. *Ansāb* 3:301; *Muntakhab* 307–8.

64. *Muntakhab* 335.

65. *Muntakhab* 1706–8; *Ansāb* 2:455.

66. *Ṭabaqāt* 6:166–70.

67. *Muntakhab* 1890–91.

68. *Muntakhab* 1809–13.

69. *Ansāb* 3:301; *Muntakhab* 306–8.

70. *Muntakhab* 335.

71. *Muntakhab* 718–19. Abū Makīs Ḥabashī, who apparently died in the 840s, claimed to be a servant of the longest-lived Companion, Mālik ibn Anas (d. ca. 710) and narrated a number of prophetic hadiths from him. Shahrazuri cites him as an example of a fabricator of Hadith (*Introduction* 184n.).

72. *Ansāb* 2:436–37.

73. *Muntakhab* 1333.

74. *Muntakhab* 739–40.

75. *Muntakhab* 1003–4.

76. *Muntakhab* 175–76. ʿAbd al-Karīm also provides an account of Aḥmad's father, Sahl ibn Ibrāhīm, from whom he received several texts by way of his own father Muḥammad (*Muntakhab* 864–67).

77. *Ansāb* 2:492.

78. *Taʾrīkh* 7:223, 9:380, 25:472, 31:261, 33:21, 36:235, 40:410, 46:62, 51:240, 55:341, 61:278, 61:440, 65:369, 67:334.

79. *Ansāb* 2:298.

80. *Muʿjam* 127–28. The hadith is found with slightly different wording in both Bukhārī and Muslim. In *Taʾrīkh* 25:222 Ibn ʿAsākir says that he received the same hadith in writing from Shīruwī and heard it from ʿAbd al-Karīm and others (though he does not mention Aḥmad).

81. Subkī, *Ṭabaqāt* 6:65–66. The well-known Hanbali scholar Ibn al-Jawzī (d. 1201) considers him significant enough to mention his name (*Muntaẓam* 18:5), but he provides no information other than the year of his death. In effect he was acknowledging his scholarly importance despite his antipathy toward his nephew ʿAbd al-Karīm (on which see Yazigi, "Claim").

82. Bāb al-Ṭāq is still a neighborhood in Baghdad.

83. *Ṭabaqāt* 6:87 (no. 612).

84. The papers collected by Lloyd Ridgeon, *The Cambridge Companion to Sufism*, illustrate the diversity of opinion among historians and provide a good survey of the academic literature. On the basis of a typology offered by Max Weber, Christopher Melchert holds that "it is entirely just to

describe Sufism as 'Islamic mysticism'" (14). Eric Ohlander thinks that "mystico-ascetic religiosity" (53) is appropriate, while acknowledging that these are foreign categories. The editor of the volume explores some of the problems connected with using the word mysticism indiscriminately (chapter 6). For some of my thoughts on the issue, see Chittick, *Sufism.*

85. A good place to get a sense of the complicated issues connected with defining Sufism in its historical actuality is the tome edited by de Jong and Radtke, *Islamic Mysticism Contested.*

86. Karamustafa, *Sufism* 93.

87. See Murata and Chittick, *Vision of Islam*, a book based on the Hadith of Gabriel.

88. Qushayrī, *Risāla* on *maʿrifa* (*Epistle* 320)

89. A point belabored by Karamustafa in *Sufism*, especially chapter 4.

90. For a good summary of their role, see Karamustafa, *Sufism* 125–27.

91. *Muntakhab* 1600.

92. Bulliet describes the sorts of circles in which scholars ran in *Patricians.*

93. *Muntakhab* 551–60.

94. See Bulliet's remarks on the practice in *Patricians* 59–60.

95. *Muntakhab* 776.

96. *Muntakhab* 410.

97. *Muntakhab* 408.

98. *Muntakhab* 759–60.

99. *Muntakhab* 135.

100. *Muntakhab* 1777–78.

101. *Muntakhab* 578–601.

102. I do not mean to suggest that he was hiding this fact; it is obvious from the dates, which he provides assiduously for practically every scholar. Moreover, he often mentions that he did not meet a specific shaykh but rather received a written license by means of an intermediary. For example, in three different accounts he says that the scholar Muḥammad Daqqāq obtained for him written licenses for the *masmūʿat* of shaykhs from Bukhara in 1115, when he was just past his second birthday (*Muntakhab* 264, 488, 1548). In at least twenty instances he mentions that his friend Ibn ʿAsākir obtained a license for him from a shaykh (*Muntakhab* 686, 773, 777, 800, 813, 878, 900, 916, 967, 1050, 1146, 1334, 1403, 1539, 1721, 1745, 1853, 1870, 1874, 1898, 1919).

103. *Muntakhab* 1250–51, 1303, 1333, 1339.

104. For *Ṭabaqāt*, see *Muntakhab* 534, 1038, 1346; for *Ḥaqāʾiq*, see *Muntakhab* 1712, 1749. For other treatises, see *Muntakhab* 127, 232, 248, 354, 394, 534, 978, 1108, 1138, 1418, 1598, 1677, 1698, 1769, 1829–30, 1891.

105. In his lost addendum to Khaṭīb's history of Baghdad, ʿAbd al-Karīm seems to have given a detailed account of Aḥmad, since a good deal of what we know about him from later authors is attributed to this source (see Lumbard, *Ahmad al-Ghazali* 32).

106. *Muntakhab* 760–61. The second poem is by Ibn al-Muʿtazz (Ṣūlī, *Ashʿār* 186–87).

107. In an account of Imām al-Ḥaramayn Juwaynī (*Ansāb* 2:129), ʿAbd al-Karīm writes that God blessed Juwaynī with students that became the imams of the world, namely, Khwāfī, Ghazālī, Kiyāʾ Harāsī, and ʿUmar Nawqānī.

108. *Muntakhab* 1793–94.
109. For example, Griffel, *Ghazālī* 9, 52.
110. *Ansāb* 4:335.
111. *Muntakhab* 825, 1326, 1342.
112. *Muntakhab* 1827–31. On Hibat al-Raḥmān's status among the Qushayrī grandchildren, see Chiabotti, " 'Abd al-Karīm" 283–86.
113. *Patricians* 51–52.
114. *Muntakhab* 528.
115. *Muntakhab* 935.
116. *Muntakhab* 1030.
117. *Muntakhab* 1487–89.
118. Mentions of him as *khaṭīb*: *Taʾrīkh* 1:281, 17:160, 19:81, 26:231, 33:164, 33:247, 44:379, 44:386; as *ṣūfī*: 36:35, 36:453. Subkī (*Ṭabaqāt* 6:124–25) calls him both *khaṭīb* and *shaykh al-ṣūfiyya*.
119. *Muntakhab* 1696–97.
120. *Ansāb* 1:412.
121. *Muntakhab* 872–73.
122. *Muntakhab* 1917–18.
123. *Muntakhab* 1453–54.
124. *Rashaḥāt* 15–17.
125. *Muntakhab* 612–13.
126. *Muntakhab* 1448–49.
127. *Muntakhab* 1127.
128. *Muntakhab* 1208–9.
129. *Muntakhab* 1775; see also *Ansāb* 2:397.
130. *Taʾrīkh* 36:447.
131. *Mutaṣawwin* is typically used with a negative particle to designate someone who does not guard his behavior (i.e., religiously speaking). ʿAbd al-Karīm never uses the word in *Ansāb* or *Muntakhab*, but he uses *mutaṣawwif* about fifteen times.
132. *Taʾrīkh* 36:448.
133. See, for example, his interpretation of 2:30 under the name Wise (no. 50), after he has quoted Māwardī's commentary, which is fairly typical of the genre.
134. In eight instances he mentions that his teachers composed Persian poetry; three of the eight pertain to his own family (his father Muḥammad, his uncle Aḥmad, and his cousin Muḥammad ibn Ḥasan). For the other five, see *Muntakhab* 768, 1139, 1270, 1447, 1725.
135. *Muntakhab* 372–75.
136. *Ansāb* 1:438–39.
137. It is worth noting that Ibn al-Jawzī also wrote a book called *Rawḥ al-arwāḥ* (in Arabic), a 100-page collection of anecdotes about Sufi shaykhs interspersed with a great deal of poetry. There is no similarity with Aḥmad's book except in the focus on the Sufi dimension of the tradition.

138. ʿAbd al-Karīm mentions him as having transmitted hadiths to three of his own teachers (*Muntakhab* 1438, 1483, 1726).

139. *Muntakhab* 491, 1205. According to Arberry, who cites manuscripts not used in the printed edition, there are 222 hadiths in the book (Kalābādhī, *Doctrine* xi)

140. *Muntakhab* 113.

141. *Ansāb* 5:289.

142. For the fifteen poems, see 17 (Though), 30 (O captive), 42 (O You), 139 (Anyone), 141 (Oh, the), 201 (It's best), 218 and 232 (Rise), 228 (Though), 244 (The road), 267 (Rise), 289 (When I), 340 (Don't think), 341 (As long as), 417 (I cannot), 474 (The king). Heravi thinks that Samʿānī uses the word *rahī* ("servant") in several quatrains and other Persian lines as his signature (*takhalluṣ*); this is plausible, though far from certain. He mentions specifically these lines (where I translate *rahī* as "I" or "my"): 7 (Lean back), 29 (The moment), 30 (I said), 105 (My heart's), 110 (Ever since), 341 (As long as), 498 (Forever).

143. On the poetry ascribed to Abū Saʿīd, see Shafīʿī's introduction to Abū Rawḥ, *Ḥālāt*.

144. Ernst, "Shaykh ʿAlī Hujwīrī."

145. See Gimaret, *Noms* 133–36, 226–28.

146. Rūmī, *Mathnawī* 6:3172–83

147. "Animal Minds," *The Economist* (Dec. 19, 2015–Jan. 1 2016): 72.

148. "Animal Minds" 74.

149. Ibn ʿArabī takes the equilibrium of *tanzīh* and *tashbīh* as the core of true understanding and spiritual realization (see Chittick, *Sufi Path of Knowledge*, passim). See also Murata and Chittick, *Vision*, part 2.

150. Gimaret, *Noms* 21–22.

151. *Sharḥ* 23.

152. *Maqṣad* 42 (*Ninety-Nine Names* 31).

153. Ibn ʿArabī, *Futūḥāt* 2:326, line 12. For more on his depiction of the relationship between rational thought and imagination, see Chittick, *Sufi Path of Knowledge*, especially chapter 11.

154. Rūmī, *Dīwān*, vv. 336–38.

155. See her book by this title, which provides numerous examples of complementarism in Islamic thought.

156. Rūmī, *Mathnawī* 6:4302–4.

THE REPOSE OF THE SPIRITS

Explaining the Names of the All-Opening King

In the name of God, the All-Merciful, the Ever-Merciful

My Lord, make easy and seal with the good![1]

Hereby opens up the explanation of the names of the Lord in Persian for the benefit of the Muslims—*and God is the giver of success!* First *He* will be discussed. Then an allusion will be made briefly and succinctly to each name in order, *God willing.*

1. *Hū:* He

The meaning of *hū* is *ū* [he/she/it]. Among the common people, as long as you do not define *he* as God, the speaker's meaning will not be understood. As for the elect and the folk of election, the men of the playing field of the religion, and the lords of the eye of certainty—those who have limpid hearts, high aspirations, and empty breasts—when *he* passes over the speaker's tongue, from this word they understand nothing but the Real.

In reality you must have a heart made limpid of caprice, a breast adorned with guidance, and an inwardness prepared to receive the Real before the reality of the he-ness is unveiled to you and you come to be described as perceiving its mystery.

They say that an exalted man was walking along, and a dervish came before him and said, "Whence are you coming?"

He said, "He."

He said, "Where are you going?"

He said, "He."

He said, "What is your goal?"

He said, "He."

No matter what he asked, he received the reply "He."[2]

> My eyes are so fixed on Your image
> whatever I see I fancy is You.[3]

When the word *He* comes forth from within the breast of a man who possesses the present moment, nothing will veil him. If the Throne or the Footstool should come before him, he will burn it in the fire of love. This is why that exalted one of the age said, *"Were the Throne to intrude upon me, I would destroy it."* If the lofty Throne were to come into my present moment, I would lay it low.[4]

A dervish's eyes fell on a moonlike beauty, and his heart followed in the tracks of his eyes. He said, "I like this house—I'll stay here." The hand of love's tumult gave the harvest of his patience to the wind, his capacity was bent in two, and the moon of his restraint waned. He put his aspiration to work to turn away from his goal. It was said to him, "Is what you are doing what is done to friends?"

He said, *"But who is He that He should offer himself to my heart?"* Who is He that He should circle around my heart's pavilion?

One of their sayings is this: *"Nothing is worthy of the heart's attention but He."* No one is worthy of the heart's clinging but He.

They have also said that when a work charges forth to you, look at your heart's kiblah. What is it? Is it a creature or the Real? Your heart's kiblah at the first onslaught and blow of the work is the object of your worship, for it is your goal and object of witnessing.

In verified truth *He* is the most specific of all the names.

Hū is one letter, and that is *h*. *Ū* is for the breath to become established. The proof that *Hū* is one letter is that when you make it dual, you say *humā*, not *hūmā*. So this is the name of the Solitary, denoting solitariness.

O chevalier, every mentioned name and attribute except *He* goes by way of the tip of the tongue, but it comes forth from the depth of the spirit. The tongue has nothing to do with this name. Whenever you pass a name over the tongue, you move your lips. But tongue and lips, which are the trustees and doorkeepers of the heart, have nothing to do with *He*. It comes forth not from the tip of the tongue but from the depth of the spirit, the bottom of the heart, and the core of the breast.

He must climb up from the bottom of the heart with a pure breath—from a pure soul, a pure heart, a pure secret core, a pure mind, and a pure inwardness—aiming for the pure Threshold, passing on, running forth, and cutting, like a strike of lightning and a blast of wind, nothing clinging to it, and it clinging to nothing.

2. *Allāh:* God

For the folk of learning and the lords of realization, the meaning of *God* is *"He who has divinity. And divinity is the power to innovate and devise."*[5]

God is He who has divinity, and divinity is the power to create and make appear. This is the attribute of the Real—*majestic is His majesty!*—for He is powerful over existence-giving, devising, configuring, and innovating. His power has no laxity, and His strength no incapacity. If He wants, He will create a thousand thousand Adams and worlds in an instant and choose a thousand thousand like the Beloved [Muḥammad] and the Bosom Friend [Abraham].

His act has no instrument, His artisanry no cause, His doing no contrivance. He created the lofty Throne and made it the crown on the head of being's realm. He brought the insignificant dust mote into the world of existence-giving and concealed it from the eyes. But in reality, the Throne is like a dust mote, and the dust mote is like a Throne. The Throne is like a dust mote in respect of power, and the dust mote like a Throne in respect of wisdom.

If you gaze on the world of power, the Throne will appear to you like a dust mote, but if you look at the world of wisdom, the dust mote will appear to you like a Throne. In power the lofty Throne is the same as the paltry dust mote, and in wisdom the two are alike. With the tongue of its state the paltry dust mote says to the great Throne, "Whether me or you—the Real has power to perfection, unity without cease, and wisdom without change."

Power demands existence-giving and creation, unity requires taking to nonexistence, and wisdom demands bringing back. The wisdom in bringing back is to realize the two attributes of wretchedness and felicity.

Existence-giving at the first is demanded by power, taking to nonexistence in the middle is demanded by unity, and bringing back is demanded by wisdom.

With power He scatters the seeds of creation in the earth of wisdom. Various sorts of plants sprout forth, some of them sweet-smelling roses, others liver-scraping thorns. Then the wind of jealousy will come forth from the World of Unity, and the simoom of severity will blow, clothing the world in the garment of nonexistence. With the hand of severity He will remove the collar of existence from the neck of the existent things and creatures. The sultan of wisdom will charge forth from the top of the playing field of majesty and exaltation, for there is no stipulation to disregard. *Surely God grants respite, but He does not disregard.*[6] It will be said to Seraphiel, the executioner of the covenant, "Blow the trumpet," which is the curtain of power, "for the yearning of dust has reached its limit, and My lover has tasted the poison of separation. Let this handful of dust be made present in the desert of the covenant and the open space of the decree."

After that, all existent things and creatures will once again place their heads on the pillow of nonexistence, except the Adamites. They are the counterpart of the perfection of prosperity, the majesticness of the state, and the height of good fortune, so they are the vinegar and greens on the table of existence. The All-Compelling will address this handful of dust from the world of severity with these words: *"I remain and you remain*—it's Me and you."

Then the end of being, which is called "death," will be brought forth in the form of a salt-colored ram and slaughtered with the sword of severity. What is this? True retaliation. *Surely you have life in retaliation* [2:179]. Then the waistcoat of endless subsistence and the robe of the everlasting kingdom will be thrown over the neck of the felicitous. They will be made to sit on the cushion of prosperity contemplating the Majestic King—constant cups of union and continuous robes of prosperity, at every moment a caress and a reception, at every instant a bestowal and an arrival. And the garment of disgrace, castigation, banishment, abasement, rejection, veil, impediment, and punishment will be thrown over the neck of the wretched—at every moment a regret and a grief, at every instant a portion of the harvest of abandonment. Their asking will have no response and their share will be nothing but punishment. The preacher of the lordly decree on the pulpit of the Glorified's loftiness will give out this call: *"O folk of the Garden, everlastingness, and no death! O folk of the Fire, everlastingness, and no death!"*[7]

How sweetly did he speak who said, *"There is no alienation with God, and no ease with other than God."*[8] To be with the Friend with nothing is sweet, but to be without the Friend with everything is not sweet. Everyone veiled from the Friend dwells in affliction itself, even if he has the key to the kingdom's treasuries in his sleeve. Everyone attracted to the Friend's gentleness dwells in bestowal itself, even if he does not have his evening bread. This is why Sarī Saqaṭī said, *"O God, however You chastise me, chastise me not with the abasement of the veil!"*[9] Lord God, chastise me with whatever You want, but do not chastise me with the veil, for I have no capacity for the chastisement of the veil.

No matter how You kill me, I come to life!
But don't kill me with separation—anything but that.

Since the Lord has said about the unbelievers, *"No indeed, but on that day they shall be veiled from their Lord"* [83:15], this is manifest evidence that the faithful will have no veil. Their only reckoning will be rebuke.

They say paradise has a host—
there's no host without seeing.
If both enemy and friend were veiled,
how would they be different?

Know that in reality, even if God were to send union's tent and proximity's dome into hell, the friends of the Garden of the Beginningless, who became drunk on the song of the nightingales of the unseen attraction, would make hellfire into their eyes' collyrium. And if for one instant in the Highest Firdaws, the Garden of Eden, and the Abode of Settledness they were to be afflicted with the abasement of the veil, they would lament so loudly that the denizens of hell would have mercy on them.

Riḍwān, bliss, and black-eyed houris—
I will never ever want them without Your face.

3. *Alladhī Lā Ilāha Illā Hū:* There is no god but He

Talk of *No god but He* will be made briefly and succinctly, *God willing*. In plain Persian this statement means "There is no god [*khudāy*] but God [*khudāy*]"—*majestic is His majesty!*

This *no god* is the policeman of negation's severity, seated on the steed of awe, in its hand a sword of the Lord's jealousy [*ghayra*]. Wherever there is some other [*ghayr*], it lops off its head with jealousy's sword so that the sultan of *but God* may sit on the royal seat of the heart's kingdom and issue commands to the serving boys, which are the limbs. Then, when someone places his head on the line of the command and binds his waist with the belt of acquiescence, it will place the embroidery of exaltation on the garment of his secret core. But when someone twists his head away from the collar of servanthood, it will place the brand of loss on his face and put the collar of imprecation, expulsion, and rejection around his neck.

O chevalier, when a sultan is about to dismount at a dwelling, the first stipulation is for the chamberlain to come and sweep the dwelling, take away the refuse and rubbish, and put down the sultan's royal seat. When the sultan arrives, the work will be finished and the dwelling ready.

In the same way, when the exalted sultan of *but God* is about to dismount in a breast, the chamberlain of *no god* goes ahead. It sweeps the courtyard of the breast with the broom of disengagement and solitariness and eliminates the rubbish and refuse of mortality, Adamic nature, satanity, and human nature. It sprinkles the water of approval, spreads the carpet of loyalty, lights up the sandalwood of limpidness, and puts down the royal throne of felicity and the seat of chieftainship. Then, when the sultan of *but God* arrives, He leans back on the cushion of the secret core in the cradle of the Covenant.

> Lean back on my spirit—may it be Your sacrifice!
> Why lean back in a corner of the Creator's house?

There is another secret more exalted than this. It is that this *No* is like a gallows at the crossroads of the All-Compelling's desire. He appointed the swordsman of His will so that if the meddlesome intellect does not pull back its feet in the measure of the gelim—as they say, *"Extend your feet in the measure of your cloak"*—it will be hung by the hand of severity from the gallows of *No* as a lesson for the eyes and an occasion for the wakefulness of the breast. *So take heed, O you who have eyes!* [59:2].

O dervish, anyone who aims for the Presence of *but God* must pass over the bridge of *no god*, which is severity's mouth, open like a crocodile's. This crocodile of severity must swallow down all of his attributes, whether disobedient or obedient. Then he will arrive at the auspicious presence of *but God*, solitary and disengaged—no dust on the heart, no burden on the back, no reckoning with anyone, no harm in the breast, nothing to do with any created thing. *He will be effaced in God, a faithful friend at God.* He will have erased the dust of the others from the tablet of the heart, made his makeup taste the poison of severity, and taken his aspiration beyond the peak of the Throne. He will have fled from the realm of being and found rest with the Friend, thrown the ball of revelry into the playing field of seeking, drawn the sword of severity from the scabbard of manliness, made do with the Friend from the depth of the spirit, thrown the die of the heart on the board of love, cast the hook of seeking into the ocean of good fortune, overthrown the whole family of mortal nature, cleansed the tablet of caprice, and torn the cloak of disloyalty.

4–5. *al-Raḥmān al-Raḥīm:* the All-Merciful, the Ever-Merciful

In the view of the folk of the meanings it is correct that *the All-Merciful is He who has mercy.*[10] The interpretation of mercy is *the desire to bless.* The All-Merciful is He who possesses and has the attribute of mercy, and mercy is the desire to bless.

It is also correct that there is no difference between *raḥmān* and *raḥīm* in respect of meaning, just as *nadmān* and *nadīm* have one meaning. These two words are combined for emphasis. In the same way, they say, *"So-and-so is exerting, striving"* [*jādd mujidd*].

Now words will be spoken about this name to the extent possible in respect of the secret, the reality, the meaning, and the Tariqah:

God reports of the Real's power to innovate. *The All-Merciful, the Ever-Merciful* reports of the help He gives as gratuitous gift. Through His power the object of His desire exists, and through His help His servants voice *tawḥīd.*

Another mystery: Hearing *God* with these words brings about awe, and awe is the cause of annihilation and absence. Hearing *the All-Merciful, the Ever-Merciful* brings about presence with the Presence, and presence is the cause of subsistence and nearness. Anyone who hears *God* is confounded by the unveiling of majesty, and anyone who hears *the All-Merciful, the Ever-Merciful* is stunned by the expanse of beauty.[11]

Another mystery: Hearing this phrase is a wine poured into the cup of joy and placed in the goblet of intimacy, a wine that the Real Himself gives to His lovers without intermediary. *When they drink, they seek; when they seek, they rejoice; when they rejoice, they fly; when they fly, they arrive; when they arrive, they depart; when they depart, they join; when they join, they acquire. So their intellects are drowned in His gentleness, and their hearts are consumed by His unveiling.*[12]

When God's friends drink the wine of yearning in the garden of gentleness, on the lawn of the covenant, and in the company of the lovers, they begin to seek. When they seek, they rejoice. When they rejoice, they fly beyond the cage of the two worlds. When they fly, they arrive. When they arrive, they reach themselves. In this state their intellects are drowned in gentleness and their hearts consumed by unveiling. Having lost themselves, they find Him. The sun of beginningless gentleness shines on the garden of their hearts and the narcissus of intimacy blooms in that holy garden. The jasmine of the covenant sprouts up, the lily of loyalty and the rose of limpidness show their heads, and the nightingales of generous gifts sing on the sweet herbs of allusion.

Another secret: He unveiled Himself to His servants with *God*, but the name *God* is mixed with severity, so they did not have the capacity to listen to this word. He placed the salve of mercy on their hearts with the name *All-Merciful*, so they gained subsistence. Otherwise they would have become nonexistent because of awe before the word *God*, and neither their names nor their marks would have remained.

O chevalier, were it not that forgetfulness, absence, incapacity, and deficiency are the state of dust and clay, He would not have brought the hearts back to talk of mercy after the word *God*. But since man does not have the capacity to carry the burden of *God*, He spoke of mercy, thereby mixing His rightful due with your share so that man would not flee. Otherwise, in respect of the rightful due of His lordhood and divine majesty, why would He bring up talk of mercy? But the Adamite—*except as God wills*—moves only in keeping with his own shares. Talk of mercy is linked to your seeking. It is not linked to the perfect majesty of the Real.

Another mystery: He is the All-Merciful by refreshing, the Ever-Merciful by intimating; the All-Merciful with kindly acts, the Ever-Merciful with lights; the All-Merciful by benefiting, the Ever-Merciful by repelling; the All-Merciful by disclosing Himself, the Ever-Merciful by taking charge; the All-Merciful by blessing, the Ever-Merciful by protecting; the All-Merciful by deploying blessings generally, the Ever-Merciful by unveiling generosity both specifically and generally; the All-Merciful by making acts of worship easy, the Ever-Merciful by verifying *the most beautiful and an increase* [10:26].

He gave them unveiling through His word God, *which gives news of His power. Then He followed that with the name* All-Merciful, *because it nourishes them with His blessings. Then He said,* "Ever-Merciful," *because it forgives them in the end through His mercy. It is as if He let them know that He created them with His power, provided for them with His blessings, and will forgive and free them through His mercy.*

First He said *God*, and this word gave news of utmost power. Then He said *All-Merciful*, which alludes to feeding, nurturing, and strengthening with blessings. Then He said, *Ever-Merciful*, which lets us know of mercy ad infinitum.

It is as if He addressed His servants like this: "I created you with My power, I have nurtured you with My blessings, and I will forgive you with My mercy. At the beginning is My power, in the middle My blessings, and at the end My mercy."

When the beginningless ocean of power, the endless ocean of mercy, and the present ocean of blessings are brought together, how can the opacity of a handful of dust appear?

This explains why that exalted one of the age said, *"When the ocean of mercy bubbles up, every slip comes to nothing, for the slip was not, and the mercy always was. How can that which was not, then was, stand up to that which has always been and will always be?"*[13] When the ocean of mercy surges with generosity and forgiveness, all slips and acts of disobedience go back to nonexistence and nothingness, for the slip *was not*, and mercy *always is*. How can *was not* stand up to *always is*?

6. *al-Malik:* the King

He is the King, the Owner [*mālik*], the Owner of the Kingdom, and the Possessor of the Kingdom. The kingdom [*mulk*] and the property [*milk*] belong to Him in reality, and He is the absolute owner.

For the folk of the Sunnah and the lords of the meanings, the reality of kingship is the power to configure, innovate, and create; this is the attribute of the Real.[14]

The Persian for *malik* is *pādshāh*. The true king is he whose kingship has no removal, whose seriousness has no levity, whose exaltation has no abasement, whose decree has no rejection, who himself has no peer, and from whom there is no escape. Thus He revealed to Moses, *"I cling to you inescapably, so cling to the inescapable."*[15] O Moses, I am unavoidable to you. Everything can be avoided, but there is no avoiding Me. You have a remedy for everything, but you have no remedy for Me.

When the certain, truthful, loving, loyal, and limpid person of faith comes to know that the king, owner, and possessor in reality is the Real—*glory be to Him!*—he must break the tablet of claims, pluck out the eyes of pride and I-ness, roll up the carpet of folly, empty the head of egoism's delusions, pull back his skirt from the two worlds, break the bond of attribution, and surrender possessions and kingship to the Absolute Owner. He must consider His desire prior to his own desire and know that in reality this King does not hold His kingdom with an army. No one is the King of kings but He, and He is not exalted through drums, banners, servitors, and retinue.

The sultans of the world display their armies, mount up their servitors and retinue, and show their horses and chattel. Then they lift up their heads and boast of kingship and possessions, blessings and enjoyments, cavalry and infantry, royal court and audience hall. But He will strike the fire of unneediness into the vestiges and traces of being and turn the world into *scattered dust* [25:23]. With the sword of severity He will strike the celestial spheres, and with the sickle of *Curse not the aeon, for God is the aeon,*[16] He will slice off the head of the aeonists. He will turn everyone's makeup into motes and shake the dust of the others off the skirt of power, putting the bridle of taking to nonexistence on the fast-paced steed of existence. He will call out, *"Whose is the kingdom today?"* Who will have the gall to come forth in response to this address? Then the very majesty of unity will give out the answer to the beauty of self-sufficiency, and the exaltedness of holiness will respond to the perfection of glorifiedness: *"God's, the One, the Severe"* [40:16].

When the believing person of faith believes with certitude and verification that the kingdom and the possessions belong to the Real, then in reality he will disdain to abase himself before any created thing or to bend his upright neck for a grain, a draft, or a mouthful.

He who aims for the ocean has no need for rivulets.[17]

When a diver has a high aspiration, trades with his own life in the all-encompassing ocean, and acquires in exchange the night-brightening pearl, how will he bend his body before the smoke of a tiny lamp?

That exalted one spoke beautifully: *"He who recognizes God will not put up with the coquetry of the creatures."*[18] Whoever knows the Real's majesty will not incline toward the creatures' coquetry. His destination will be God's threshold, his truthfulness's hand will be kept back from the two worlds, his passion's feet will always be in the road, his heart will be in the grasp of the King's exaltation, and his spirit will be caught in the net of love for the King of kings. Ecstasy, finding, unveiling, and witnessing will be his companions on the road. For him the bottom of the well will be a balcony. He will be aware of the fine realities of the notebooks of love and affection, and his secret core will be the quarry for the secret of the Possessor of Majesty. He will have the mark of prosperity on his forehead, the light of learning the lessons of God's acts in the eye of his certainty, the rose of bounty on his religion's cheek, and fragrant gusts from the meadow of union in his nostrils. He will have a bouquet of sweet herbs from the garden of love in his hand, the sandals of limpidness and good fortune on his feet, the crown of dignity on his head, the robe of poverty on his back, the cape of servanthood on his outside, and the ornament of gazing on the mysteries of Lordhood on his inside. By day he will be in secret whispering, by night in joy. His morning draft will be the wine of purity, his evening draft the fine wine of realized delight. His breakfast will be struggle, his supper contemplation. He will walk forth in accordance with pleasure and always stay in this snare. People stay with bread and name, but he will have no bread or name. He will be a dust mote in the wind of power, a ball on the playing field of creation, a grain under the millstone of the Will. He will be a nightingale in the garden of At-ness, a falcon of the mystery of Unity, a peacock in the rose garden of the Holy, and a swimmer in the majestic sea of the Glorified.

O dervish, there is a sunlight called the sunlight of solicitude, shining endlessly from the constellation of the Beginningless. Whenever it falls into someone's breast, he becomes a source of splendor, a pearl without price, a quarry of eminence, and the Mount Sinai of love. Like Moses at the *appointed time* of unsettledness, he will shout out, *"Show me."* From the sweet Beloved he will hear the meanings of the response *"thou shalt not see Me"* [7:143]. The mountain of the dust-dwelling soul will be struck by the tumult-inciting bandit of *crumbling to dust* [89:21].[19]

7. *al-Quddūs:* the Holy

The meaning of holy is that the Lord—*majestic is His majesty!*—is pure of all defects. *He is hallowed and incomparable.* His majesty and beauty do not come from the hallowing of the hallowers or the glorification of the glorifiers.

"If you do the beautiful," the beauty of it will belong to you, "and if you do the ugly" [17:7], *the bane of it will go against you, but the reality of the Self-Sufficient is incomparable, holy, and purified of your beauty and your bane.* If you bind the collar of attestation to the neck of *tawḥīd*, that will be the beauty of your times and the boastful title of your days. If your heart's foot is pierced by the thorn of associating others with Him, that will be the castigation of your times and the stain on your states. The reality of self-sufficiency and the secret of *tawḥīd* are incomparable with and hallowed beyond the *tawḥīd* of the *tawḥīd*-voicers and the association of the associators.

A bird sat on a mountain peak and flew away.
  Look what the mountain gained and what it lost.[20]

When the basis of judging the world is the lordly unneediness and the perfection of the kingly beauty, then in reality the existence of creation is a useless bother. However, *He created us so that we would benefit from Him, not so that He would benefit from us.*[21] He brought us into existence for the sake of our portion and share, even though His exalted and majestic Presence is pure of portions and shares. The attribute of bounty rose up seeking the obedient, the attribute of severity rose up seeking the disobedient, and the attributes of majesty and beauty rose up seeking lovers.

O chevalier, it is incumbent on a rich man to give alms to the poor. If we suppose that the deserving man does not sit and ask at the door of the rich man's house, then it is incumbent on the rich man to take alms to the door of the poor man's hut. The unneedy in reality is the Real, and the poor in reality are we.

Alms are of two sorts: secret alms and open alms. Openly He sends the alms of invitation on the hand of the prophets, and secretly He sends the alms of guidance to secret cores.

O dervish, He had a gentleness and a severity to perfection, a majesty and a beauty to perfection. He wanted to distribute these treasures. On one person's head He placed the crown of gentleness in the garden of bounty. On another person's liver He placed the brand of severity in the prison of justice. He melted one in the fire of majesty; He caressed another in the light of beauty. He lit up the candle of invitation on the bench of access, for *God invites to the abode of peace* [10:25]. A thousand thousand of the helpless and suffering threw themselves on the candle like moths and were burned, but not a speck was diminished from or added to the candle.

I ache for Him who aches not for me,
  I obey Him who obeys not me.
I buy His iniquity and disloyalty with a hundred spirits,
  but He buys not my love and loyalty for a barleycorn.[22]

O chevalier, *he who seeks nearness to the King by sitting in the corner of his room doing his prayers is mocking himself.* The unfortunate fellow who stands or sits in the hut of his own misfortune and thinks that because of his standing and sitting, he is doing the King of the Age a favor, heads up the world's madmen. All the obedient acts, worshipful doings, deeds, acts, words, and states of the children of Adam from the beginning of existence to the end of the age, placed next to the perfection of the divine beauty, are the noise of an old woman's spindle. Beware, do not think you are doing Him any favors!

Had He in His generosity and bounty not invited this handful of dust-dwelling, rascally dust to the court of His eternity and spread out the carpet of bold expansiveness in the house of guidance, how could this woebegone of existence, this speck of impure dust, have the gall to put his foot on the edge of the carpet of the King of kings? *But there is no consultation in love.*[23]

We've come in shame at our own existence,
we've come without root or worth to the world.
In the realm of the gelim of misfortune,
we've come black instead of colored.

Some perform acts of obedience and desire the reward, others disobey and sketch the line of asking pardon in the tablet of the heart. Still others don't have the gall to lift up their heads, ashamed of their own existence.

The stories tell of an afflicted man who was walking along the road when a very beautiful woman passed by. His eyes fell on her perfect beauty, and his heart became her prey. He set off in her tracks. When she reached the door of her house, she turned back and saw the afflicted man behind her. She said, "What do you want?"

He said, "The ruling power of your beauty has exercised its authority over my feeble makeup and pulled it by the harness of its severity. My claim is that I want to make love to you, and this claim is no metaphor."

That woman had the adornment of perfect intellect on the dress of beauty. She said, "I will answer you tomorrow and solve your problem."

The next day the afflicted man was sitting in wait, his eyes open. When would the perfect beauty of his goal appear? When would what had happened to him be resolved? The woman came, behind her a maid holding a mirror. She said, "Maid, hold the mirror before him. With that head and face, does he want to make love to me? Does he desire to reach union with me?"

You want to have a hidden secret with me?
You find in yourself a need for me?
In truth, black crow, you're a fine bird—
you want to mate with a white falcon!

O chevalier, when a penniless beggar claims to love the sultan, his claim is nothing but loss. He will stay in the house of sorrows, the pit of abasement, and the shirt of contempt. But if in generosity and gentleness the sultan takes the poor man's hand, caresses him with gentleness, attends to his business with generosity, places the crown of prosperity on his head, dresses him in the robe of good fortune, and says, "I love you," then he will be the comrade of good fortune and exaltation, living in ease and dwelling in comfort.

A thousand thousand brilliant pearls were inside the oysters of the various sorts of glorification and calling holy. A thousand thousand celestial figures were swimming in the sea of glorification and traveling in the world of hallowing on top of this tall world, this bright garden, this high arch, this brocade canopy, this blue disk. Their morning draft was *we glorify Thy praise* and their evening draft was *we call Thee holy* [2:30]. But the falcon of love's mystery aimed for a sparrow of small dignity. This state was expressed in the tongue of good news with these words: *"I am yours, whether you wish it or refuse, and you are Mine, whether you wish it or refuse."* You are mine, whether or not you want it so, and I am yours, whether or not you want it so.

Yes, the glorifiers, *tawḥīd*-reciters, and hallowers of the palisades of holiness and the meadows of intimacy were tipsy with the wine of we-ness. A subtlety was needed to break that tipsiness and clarify for them the tenor of the word *we*. He brought into existence a person from *molded mud* [15:26], dressed in a garment of remorse and destitution, on his head the turban of not-finding, around his waist the belt of disappointment, and evident to the world his names *great wrongdoer* and *deeply ignorant* [33:72]. Then all at once He sent those 700,000-year-old elders, tipsy with the wine of calling holy, to welcome the prosperity of this man walking by himself. He issued the command "When he arrives at the city of being, scatter your prostrations—which are the gist of deeds and the mystery of states—over his good fortune. Then you will know that the majesty of My existence does not need the beauty of your prostration."

When the sun of Adam's good fortune rose from the constellation of prosperity, the world took on rays of light. That accursed one, that bat of the era, was rubbing his eyes so that perhaps he might see the beauty of the era's sultan. But how could a miserable bat find the means? His eyes did not get along with the sun's beauty.

And what about the dust mote? What did it do as soon as the beauty of the sultan-sun placed its hand on the neck of the era? As long as the sultan-sun was not sitting on the emerald throne, no one perceived the dust mote, but when the sun sat like Jamshid on the throne of good fortune, the bewildered and tiny dust mote turned its face to contemplating the sun's perfect beauty and began to dance despite its own defects.

What did the miserable bat do? As long as night did not tie down its tent, making the whole world a cup of tar and pitch, it did not have the gall to put its head outside the hole of its own misery.

Two men, one sewing, one weaving,
sit face-to-face on the first heaven—
One never stops weaving the cloak of misery,
one keeps on sewing the dress of prosperity.[24]

*

Two craftsmen sit on top of the sphere,
one stitching, one weaving.

One sews caps for kings,
 the other weaves black gelims.[25]

Have you ever seen the sun-worshiper, which is the animal the Arabs call the chameleon, in the great desert during summer's midday heat—*a heat like the heart of ardor, melting the lizard's brain*, a heat bringing the brain to boil and cooking stones? Whenever the sun puts forth its luminous head and puts on its golden mask, the chameleon comes out of its tiny house and goes to the top of a twig. It puts down its two hands and assigns its eyes to the sun's beauty. The brighter the sun's rays, the more its eyes stick to that beauty. This animal stays on top of the twig until the sun turns its face toward setting. When the sultan of the sun puts on the garment of setting, it goes back bewildered to the corner of its sorrows.

God set up three furnaces of trial in the road of the angels. The first furnace was the trial of the secrets. He said, *"I am setting in the earth a vicegerent"* [2:30] in order to see what secret would show itself from them. The next furnace was the trial of knowledge. He said, *"Tell Me the names of these if you are truthful"* [2:31]. Last was the trial of deeds. He said, *"Prostrate yourselves before Adam"* [2:34]. The divine secret and lordly goal in setting up these furnaces was to bring out the impurities in the hard cash of the spirits. The Exalted Presence wanted to clear away all the unworthy from the Threshold. He let down a hundred thousand curtains to conceal the veiled virgin of beginningless knowledge, keep her away from the eyes of the others, and convey her to the court of the endless decree.

8. *al-Salām:* the Peace

The folk of meanings have spoken about this name. Some have said, *"The meaning of peace is the possessor of safety [salāma]."* This is to say, in Persian, that the Lord is pure of all defects and blights. So *Peace* means *Holy*, a name that has already been discussed.

Others have said that the meaning of *Peace* is *"He who greets His friends with 'peace.'"*[26] *God says, "Their greeting on the day that they encounter Him will be 'peace'"* [33:44]. Tomorrow the Lord will say "peace" to His friends without any intermediary or spokesman and without anyone else's words.

On the day You say "peace" to us,
 the spheres will be our slave boys.
I don't expect You to ask after us—
 Your thought will be enough.

Here you have an exalted state—the striver reaches the Goal, the seeker the Sought, the worshiper the Worshiped, the desirer the Desired! The breeze of union blows from the side of prosperity, the friend reaches the Friend, the sigil of exaltedness is written on the edict of good fortune, the ball of anticipation is thrown to the far side of the field of the Endless, the banner of arrival and acceptance is unfurled, the rose of union blooms, the messenger of the Goal comes forth, the days of separation end, and the Friend enters with the stipulation of love.

It is said that when the faithful see the Real, the Real will begin by saying "peace" to them. Concerning this several meanings have been mentioned. The most beautiful of these is that when two friends come together after a long separation, the one that says "peace" first is the one who has more yearning. In certain reports has come, *"Surely the yearning of the pious to encounter Me has become protracted, but surely I yearn to encounter them even more."*[27] My friends' yearning to see Me has become drawn out, but I have more yearning to see them.

No one has patience without his beloved
for more than the blink of an eye.
Long have I been patient without you—
that is not how lovers act![28]

Tomorrow He will address His exalted ones: *"My servants, have you been yearning for Me?"* My servants, have you been wishing for Me at all?

An exalted one has said, *"The hearts of the yearners are illumined by God's light. When their yearning moves, the light brightens everything between heaven and earth. God presents them to the angels and says, 'These are the ones who yearn for Me. I bear witness to you that I yearn for them even more.'"*[29] The hearts of those who yearn for the majesty and beauty of the Real are illuminated by the divine light. When the fire of their yearning starts to send up flames and begins to blaze, the light of their yearning brightens heaven and earth, the Throne and the Footstool. The Real addresses the proximate ones of the Presence, "They are yearning for My majesty and beauty. I testify to you that My yearning for them is more than their yearning for Me."

In certain reports it has come that the Lord revealed to David, *"Say to the young men of Israel, 'Why are you busy with other than Me when I yearn for you? What is this disloyalty?'"*[30] Why do you degrade yourselves with those of no worth? Why do you go to the threshold of this and that? You attach your hearts to ʿAmr and Zayd while I yearn for you. What sort of disloyalty is this?

Act with beauty toward me, Umm ʿAmr—
may God increase your beauty!
Don't sell me cheaply!
The likes of me are bought at high price.[31]

*

I, a sincere lover; you, a fickle beloved—
I'll try some other way, you're so shameless.
Let's not recall the past, let's start all over—
today's for good fortune, now's the time for peace.

"O you who claimed yearning but did not put yearning right! You claimed truthfulness but did not put it right! You claimed love but did not put it right! You claimed recognition but did not put it right! *What do you have to do with yearning, when the collar of love for this world is around your neck? What do you have to do with love, when you fall prey to a barley corn?"*

It is written in the Torah, "We filled you with yearning, but you did not yearn; We filled you with fear, but you did not fear."[32]

"I displayed a hundred thousand varieties of gentleness, sorts of blessings, and kinds of bounty and generosity. I adorned the eight paradises and I promised endless subsistence, the everlasting kingdom, the cushion of perfection, and the shirt of beauty. The verified truth is that the original goal and the universal desire was that you would yearn to contemplate Me, but that did not make you wish for Me.

"Like an executioner I brought burning hell into the world of unneediness and sent a hundred thousand threats and warnings. The goal was to make you fear, but you had not a speck of fear for Me. *Beautifully done,* O disloyal Adamite—*O bag of defects and quarry of sins, small in body and great in offenses, a corpse by night and idle by day, a hand of frivolity in a bodily frame of associationism, bound by the sash of self-admiration!*"

"The mark of yearning is to wish for death while on the carpet of well-being."[33]

"The mark of yearning is to wish for death in the midst of ease."[34]

The mark of the soundness of yearning is that when things accord with your desire, when the days are favorable, the companions agreeable, the work taken care of, and the bazaar set right, you wish to go to the Presence. When Joseph was thrown into the well, he did not say *"Receive me."* When they auctioned him off and he was sold for eighteen dirhams, he did not say, *"Receive me."* But when the kingdom of Egypt came to belong solely to him, when good fortune was set in order, and when his brothers were face down on the ground before his throne, he said, *"Receive me as a submitter* [12:101]. Now bring me to Thy Presence!"[35]

We have the most perfect joy, but
the joy's not complete without you.
The defect of what we have, O worthy of love,
is that you are absent and we are present.[36]

A great work has fallen upon us. We want to yearn, but we do not give yearning its due. We want to be friends, but we do not give friendship its due. We want to be familiars, but we do not stay loyal to familiarity. We want to be lovers, but we have been routed by cold wind and breath.

If you're a lover, you must be low—
otherwise stay away from the road of love.

*

O you who lament so much in the ruins,
not for the ruins but for those within,
The custom of lovers is one—
when you're in love, you're miserable.[37]

Wanting the station of the great ones, the standing of the truthful, and the placement of the lovers, you have not undertaken their perils. *He who does not put up with perils will not reach the goal.*

Wanting the breath of Adam, the answered prayers of Noah, the station of Abraham, and the pain of Muḥammad, you have not taken one step outside your own desires, you have not taken one breath except in your own appetites. Have you not heard these heart-melting words? *"The religion is not gained with wishfulness and self-adornment."*[38]

If you desire the stations of the Substitutes,[39] *you must transform your states.* After all, is it permissible for a garbage dump, which is the nest of crows, to be the bench of kings? But there are intermediaries in the midst. If you want to reach someplace and become someone, you must rise up from where you are—your existence and your distracted, tainted, worn-out makeup. You must make a crown from the Shariah and a belt from the Haqiqah, and you must put a stop to your own talk, narrative, and tales.

A story: Once Shaykh Abū Saʿid ibn Abi'l-Khayr set out to have a session in his khanaqah. A tremendous gathering came. There was crowding, and the place was narrow. He came out and went up on the pulpit. His first words were these: "Exert some effort and rise up a bit from where you are." He said this, passed his hands over his face, and came down from the pulpit.

O dervish, He began His secret with this handful of dust in friendship, so the bold expansiveness of dust passed the limit. Had He not given Moses the cup of speech without intermediary at the top of Mount Sinai, how could he have had the gall to stand on the carpet of bold expansiveness and say *"Show me!"* [7:143]? *But do not give the child one lest he ask for a second.*

This is a marvelous business. At the door to Shuʿayb's house, Moses said, *"Surely I am poor toward any good Thou sendest down upon me"* [28:24]. Yes, at Shuʿayb's door, all he could ask for was bread. When he came to the Presence of Majesty and drank cups of speech's wine one after another, he became drunk with the speech and began the uproar of *show me!*

This is a marvelous business. There he wanted bread, here he wanted vision. The asker asks what he asks for in the measure of aspiration. *Every place has its words, and every deed its men.*

O chevalier, He is the munificent in reality, so what was *thou shalt not see Me* [7:143]? Indeed, though the ocean is munificent, and men of munificence are compared to it, the pearl is exalted. As long as a man does not put forth his own life and dive upside-down into the man-eating ocean, he will not bring to hand the night-brightening pearl.

His munificence is the description of His act, but exaltedness is the attribute of His Essence. Tomorrow He will bestow a vision of Himself on His friends, but He will do so at the request of His own beauty. As for insignificant mortals, how could they have the gall to come forth with such a request?

This is a marvelous business: So that His beauty and comeliness not be seen by the eyes of others, jealousy adds mask upon mask, but beauty's perfection lifts up the curtains!

> Though the Friend flees from me and jumps away,
> He's my eyes and light, my spirit and world.
> Though He's always hidden behind the curtain,
> the light of His face appears on every horizon.
> It's no wonder that He finds no rest with me—
> the gazelle always flees from the hunter.

The fact that tomorrow's vision will be at the request of beauty is indicated by the sound report from Muṣṭafā, related by Ṣuhayb ibn Sinān: *"When the folk of the Garden enter the Garden, a call will come to them, 'O folk of the Garden, you have an appointment with God that He desires to fulfill.'*

"They will say, 'And what is that? Have You not whitened our faces?'

He said: "So He—exalted and majestic is He!—will remove the veil, and they will gaze upon Him." Then he said, "By God, God will never give them anything more beloved to them than that."[40] *Then he recited, "Those who do the beautiful shall have the most beautiful and an increase"* [10:26].

When the folk of paradise come into paradise and take up residence in the goodly dwellings, the exquisite chambers, and the decorated palaces, a call will come, "O friends of the Real! The Real has given you a promise. Come and be present, for the Real will realize that promise through His bounty."

They will say, "What promise is that?" How lovely are the promises of friends, even if broken! What then if a promise is truthfulness itself? It is not that they do not know what they were promised. Someone asked Shāfiʿī, *"Who is the intelligent man?"*

He replied, "The clever man who pretends to be heedless."[41] He shows forth his knowledge as ignorance.

So He removes the veil. As soon as the veils are lifted, they will see the Lord without how and why. Moreover, vision will appear tomorrow such that everyone will fancy that he alone sees. If they were to suppose that others also see, the pleasure would not outweigh the pain.

> *I compared her beauty to her acts,*
> *but her loveliness did not outweigh her sins,*
> *Nor, by God, did her words, though she is*
> *like the full moon, or the sun, or the spheres.*[42]

Even though someone is beautiful, when she belongs to everyone, her beauty will not outweigh her offenses. Yes, eating meals along with your brothers makes you happy, but seeing your friend along with someone else does not.

It has been reported that once Shiblī was overpowered by ecstasy. He said, "Lord God, raise up everyone blind tomorrow so that no one but I will see You!"

Another time he supplicated, "Lord God, raise up Shiblī blind, for it would be a shame for someone like me to see You!"

The first words were jealousy for beauty against the eyes of others, and the second jealousy for beauty against his own eyes. The second step is more complete.

Another exalted man said, "If tomorrow the call comes, 'Go, you are not worthy of Me!,' I will say to Him, 'Yes, it would be a shame for such beauty to belong to me.' "

> In my jealousy for You, I'll pull out heart and eyes
> lest the eyes see You or the heart know more of You.

O dervish, you will not see Him tomorrow until He sees Himself through you. *By God the tremendous*, if tomorrow you want to see, you must have pure vision. Pure vision is that He sees Himself through you. *Tawḥīd* in this world is like vision in that world. If today you bring *tawḥīd*, you are you. If tomorrow you want to see, you are you. This is why that exalted man of the era, Sahl ibn ʿAbdallāh Tustarī said, *"O God, show gratitude to You through me, for my gratitude will not live up to Your rightful due."* Lord God, I do not have the capacity to render thanks for Your blessings. In Your generosity, You Yourself give thanks on my behalf!

Tomorrow, when the exalted ones of the Real, yearning for majesty and drowned in the ocean of beauty, reach the contemplation of the Possessor of Majesty, do not suppose that their yearning will diminish in the slightest. There is a heat in the liver of the fish that will not settle down one iota even if you gather together all the world's oceans.

> Even if You give me a thousand drinks of union,
> love will lift its voice and say, *"Is there any more?"* [50:30].[43]

Today a heart that is a heart is at work, and tomorrow also it will be at work. Today it is in yearning itself, and tomorrow it will be in tasting itself along with burning and yearning.

> *Though I'm enraptured by ecstasy for her in constant union,*
> *her words are beautiful and keep on coming.*

O chevalier, *As long as love remains, yearning will remain. There is no way to perfect union even in the marks that bear witness to proximity.* Even if the heart-burnt yearner is in the midst of the marks bearing witness to proximity and the loci of contemplating union, he will have no road to union's perfection. When He bestows on you vision of Himself, He will give it in the measure of your eyes' capacity, not in the measure of His majesty and beauty. This is why it has been said, *"He spoke to Moses in respect of Moses. Had He spoken to Moses in respect of His tremendousness, Moses would have melted."* When He spoke to Moses, He spoke in the measure of his hearing's capacity. Had He made manifest a speck of the world of His own majesty and tremendousness, Moses would have melted.

Those who are the lords of sorrow will wake up tomorrow and look into their own breasts. If they find a speck of their sorrow missing, they will lament, and the eight paradises will not have the courage to wander around that sorrow. If they were to suppose that the Garden of the Refuge, the Uppermost Everlastingness, and the black-eyed houris were striking a blow against their sorrow, they would never allow their eyes to gaze again on paradise. Indeed, they go there so that they may walk in endless sorrow on the endless road.

> *As soon as the glance turns away from seeing Him*
> *the heart comes back in yearning for Him.*[44]

9. *al-Mu'min:* the Faithful

The meaning of *mu'min* is truth-confirming. The Real calls Himself the truth-confirmer.

This is His knowledge that He is truthful.[45] The meaning of this word in describing Him is that He has knowledge that He is truthful. It can also be that the word is confirming the truthfulness of the faithful servants; it is His knowledge that they are truthful.[46]

It can also be that the meaning of *mu'min* is giver of security [*amān*]: The Real is He who gives security to the faithful. And it can also be that the meaning of *mu'min* is He who confirms the truthfulness of the promise.[47]

When a man makes himself appear with the trait of being faithful, when he binds the jewel of faith's attribute to the neck of his days, and when he grabs hold of the *firmest handle* [2:256] of *tawḥīd*, then the stipulation is that he should convey truth-confirming to the utmost realization, stroll in the orchards of the realities of faith on the feet of truthfulness and certainty, keep his steps firmly fixed on the avenue of the Straight Path, daub the collyrium of repentance and penitence on the eye of his religion, place the earring of humbleness and humility on the ear of certainty, attach the collar of *tawḥīd* to the neck of disengagement, bind the belt of hitting the mark on the waist of solitariness, drink the wine of love from the hand of the cupbearer of truthfulness, draw the sword of aspiration from the scabbard of passion, pluck the roses of the recognitions from the garden of the subtleties, strike off the evil head of caprice's tumult with the sword of guidance, remain courteous on the carpet of expansion, stay still and settled in the grip of contraction, settle down in the *Abode of Settlement* [40:39] of attesting to the Real's unity, run between the Safa of limpidness and the Marwah of manliness, dress the center-point of the heart in the shirt of poverty, hold the rose of trust to the nose of surrender, walk forth in intoxication and sobriety along with affirmation and effacement, and overturn the worlds of the high and the low.

Once he comes to embrace the realities of faith and the subtleties of *tawḥīd* and beautiful-doing, then, when you ask him, *"Do you have faith?"* he will say, *"I have faith truly, God willing."* Thus he will give faith its just due and pull back his feet from the street of making claims.

Some have voiced an absurdity and said, " *'God willing' is doubt." How far they have gone from the religion!* Here *"God willing"* is the heart's fear of hidden deprivation.

They say a man was walking down the road with several dirhams in his sleeve and a defect in his belief. Someone said to him, "Where are you going?"

He said, "I have a few dirhams, and I am going to the silk merchants to buy some silk."

He said, "You should say, *'God willing.'* "

He said, "Why is *'God willing'* required? The gold is in my sleeve and the silk in the bazaar." He went on. In the road a cutpurse ran into him and took the gold by trickery.

When the man became aware that the gold had been taken, he returned in embarrassment. As it happened, the same man ran into him. He said, "Hey, did you buy the silk?"

He replied, "They stole the gold, *God willing.*"

He said, "You've got it all wrong. You should say *'God willing'* when it will do some good."

How many a prayerful old man has spent seventy years in obedience to the extent of his capacity! He made the night a strainer for the warm water of his eyes and the day a cup for cold wind. The rosary of glorification in hand, he was drunk with the wine of hallowing and reciting *tawḥīd*. When the thread of his life was running thin and the day of his hopes darkening, *there appeared to them from God that with which they had never reckoned* [39:47]. And how many a young tavern-goer rubbed the dregs of Satan's defilement in his face, planted the tree of his days on the garbage dump of appetite, and grew up with wine, music, and gambling! Suddenly, by way of opening, the messenger of acceptance and reconciliation came down and said,

The Friend greets you and says,
"I have some words with you."

O you who have faith, if any of you turns away from your religion, God will bring a people whom He loves and who love Him [5:54].

It is told that there was a muezzin who gave the call to prayer in a mosque for several years. One day he went up on the minaret to give the call to prayer. His gaze happened to fall on a Christian woman, and he was caught up with her. When he came down from the minaret, as much as he wrestled with himself, he could not win. He went to the door of the woman's house and told her the story. The woman said, "If you speak truly in your claim, the stipulation is conformity. Bind your waist with the Christian sash!"

He bound the sash and—refuge in God!—he drank wine. When he became drunk, he tried for the woman. She fled and went into the house. That miserable fellow went up on the roof so as to throw himself into the house by trickery. The beginningless deprivation charged forth and he fell from the roof, perishing after having turned away from his religion. For many years he had been a muezzin and had observed the laws of Islam, but in the end he died having turned away and did not reach the goal.[48]

It is also told that a poor man was walking in the bazaar of Baghdad. His eyes fell on a beautiful face, and he lost his heart.

O heart! O heart! O ill-starred!
You're my trial, so whom do I blame?
You desire this, you add that—
two will not stay in one heart.

Bewildered, thirsty, and naked, he returned to the corner of his sorrows, his heart no longer in his breast, nothing to show but pain in his liver. He made a pen with his eyelashes, ink with his liver's blood, paper with his cheeks, and penmanship with his tears. Sending troops of sighs to the sky, he spent the night like someone bitten by a serpent, the rose of his face stained by his heart's blood. Then, before the chief of the planets had placed embellishment's saddle on heaven's mount, he set out for the bazaar, his heart seared by the brand of love. When he reached the bazaar, the person who was the sum of beauty and the sign of perfection appeared. Love increased, and distraction and bewilderment reached their utmost limit.

He vied patiently with patience, so patience asked for help.
The lover said to patience, "Patience!"[49]

He asked everyone who that was, and he was told that it was a Christian youth. In the end he went to the door of that comely person's shop and told him about the reality of his own situation. That heart-thief said, "If you are truthful, you must bind your waist with the sash in conformity, for the reality of love lies in conformity."

The man said, "That can be done." He went back to the cottage of his sorrows. He had a close friend, so he told the story to his friend. The friend said, "When you go to the bazaar, buy two sashes."

The man went to the bazaar and bought two sashes, just as his friend had said, and then he went to the shop of his goal. He said, "What are these two sashes?" He told him the story. That youth said, "Since you have such conformity, it would not be beautiful to ambush you. Accept me into Islam."

If someone's work falls into the hands of the All-Compelling, how can he find a place to settle down? He is the one on the skirt of whose justice one mote of wrongdoing would not sit even if He were to turn paradise into hell and hell into paradise, bring forth black water from the midst of the Kaabah and turn an idol temple into the Kaabah, remove the angelic garment from the angels of the Dominion and drape it over the satans, blacken the face of the sun and moon, and make Jerusalem into an idol temple and a tavern; or if He were to bind Muḥammad, who is the pearl in the ocean of messengerhood, and Jesus, who is the head of the register of purity and the Trust, and John, who was a prophet and the son of a prophet and who never sinned or thought of sin, on one chain and keep them forever and ever in hell.

One day Gabriel came into the presence of Muḥammad. The Messenger asked, "How is your state in the precinct of holiness?"

Gabriel replied, "From the day when that one [Iblis] was taken from our midst, no angel has sat in his corner in security and stillness."

He avoids sins and then has fear of them—
as if all his beautiful deeds were sins.[50]

Sarī Saqaṭī said, "Several times a day I look at my nose fearing that my face has been turned black by the Lord's punishment."[51]

Junayd said, *"Fear is to expect punishment with every passing breath."*[52] Fear is that, breath by breath, instant by instant, you fear and tremble lest the hand of causeless rejection should appear from behind the curtain of the Unseen, be placed against your forehead, and drag you away forsaken.

He has a gentleness without cause and a severity without cause. Gentleness seeks out the tainted, washing them with the rain of solicitude so that it will be apparent that His gentleness is pure of causes. Severity seeks out the pure and worshipful, blackening their faces with the smoke of separation so that it will be obvious that the ruling power of His severity is undefiled by causes.

You'll be an estranged servant at the bottom of separation's street
if you don't seek a familiar at the top of union's street.
A familiar with the Prophet, what a stranger was Abū Lahab!
Coming from Abyssinia, how familiar was Bilāl![53]

He made a haystack of a thousand thousand seeking spirits in the world of causeless desire, but with the five fingers of exaltedness He tossed them to the wind of unneediness. He incinerated a thousand thousand spirits of the burnt lovers in the fire of the heart and drowned them in the water of the eyes, but He did not show them a single hair of the tresses of their Goal. He made a thousand thousand hearts into kabobs, He filled a thousand thousand eyes with water, He destroyed a thousand thousand worlds, and all the while this call was coming from the world of exaltedness: "Your existence is like nonexistence, your nonexistence like existence. *If He wants, He will take you away and bring a new creation—that is no great matter for God* [14:19]."

"Sometimes I inscribe felicity for an ʿUmar, who had made an idol his kiblah, and sometimes I inscribe wretchedness for an Iblis, who had made the Throne his kiblah. Sometimes I bring the dog of the Companions of the Cave into the row of the friends' good fortune, putting it on display in My eternal Quran and caressing it with My noble speech: *And their dog was extending its paws at the doorstep* [18:18]. Sometimes I bind Balaam Beor to a kennel and drive him from the threshold with the whip of rejection and banishment: *So his likeness is the likeness of a dog* [7:176].[54] Sometimes I bring a prophet out from under the skirt of a wretch, and sometimes a wretch out from under the skirt of a prophet.[55] Sometimes I pass over a mountain, and sometimes I take to task for a straw."

Many things came into existence from Joseph's brothers such that, had one of them come into existence from anyone else, he would have seen what he saw and received what he received. But when He is going to accept, He will not reject for anything, and when He is going to reject, He will not accept for anything. *One group sought Him, and He abandoned them; one group fled from Him, and He seized them.* One group kept to seeking, hardship, and exertion, but they were addressed by beginningless exaltedness: *"The seeking is rejected, the road blocked."*[56] Another group turned their faces away from the road and walked in the playing fields of heedlessness, but the urger and despatcher of exaltedness followed in their tracks: *"I am yours, whether you wish it or refuse, and you are Mine, whether you wish it or refuse."*

He drives one from the monastery and calls him a stranger;
He brings another from the idol temple and says he's a familiar.

They saw someone running in the desert without supplies or camel. They said to him, "You're not required to make the hajj."

He replied, "I know, but the keeper is sitting in the house and He won't let me settle down."

A child fled from grammar school. The teacher sent the children after him to bring him back unwillingly. An old man saw this and was amused. He said, "He's taking him with severity so that he may teach him his attributes."

Intellects and sciences do not arrive at His perfection, understandings and imaginations fall short of His majesty, eyes are dazzled by His beauty, spirits reach the brink of death in the world of His unqualified love, and livers are torn to pieces by the bend of His will's mallet. He drives the precedent as He wants, He sets down the conclusion as He knows.

The Sultan of the will places the signet of the bitter decree on the edict of desire, desire puts its head back on the pillow of nonexistence, and He keeps the world of knowledge hidden from the eyes. He brings a hundred thousand creatures into the road. They come but know not whence they came. They go but know not where they go. *The servant is bewildered, the served one proud.*

A world is hunting for marks, but nowhere is there any mark; a world is seeking, but nowhere is there any road. A world is talking and chattering, but no one has anything in hand but fancy; a world is seeking and searching, but no one finds anything but cold sighs and pale cheeks. A world has set up exalted sessions, planted the sweet herbs of hope, built beautiful sites of seclusion, poured the fire of love into the braziers of the spirit, sat for fifty years in anticipation, and found no share but pain and deprivation.

Oh pain, Oh deprivation! All that rising and sitting has left me
with dust on my head and wind in my hand.[57]

*

A careful friend and companion,
upright in traits, was seized by the drinking of wine.
I came upon him, night's curtain hanging down,
buried among the herbs in the shadows.
I said, "Take." He said, "My hand will not obey me."
I said, "Stand." He said, "My feet will not let me.
I was heedless of the cupbearer, but he it is who made me
what you see, bereft of intellect and religion."[58]

Abū Yazīd Basṭāmī said, *"I went to the Throne and found it thirstier for Him than I was."* He is saying that he heard the verse, *"The All-Merciful sat on the Throne"* [20:5], so he charged up to the Throne to see its state, but he found it thirstier than himself.

What a marvelous business! He attached suspicion to the skirt of the Throne and Footstool, but He made the Exalted Presence incomparable with location, throwing a hundred thousand intellects into the whirlpool of bewilderment!

I'm accused of love for a moonlike cheek—
I don't have the cheek to say a thing.

*

Tell me, son, what is there outside bewilderment?
Tell me, who's aware of the work of the world?
Tell me, has anyone lived a night happily
and not wept bitterly the next day? Tell me.[59]

*

Nearness to You is like distance from You,
so when will I be at ease?[60]

*

My plight with You is that from me You have
a thousand ways to escape, but I have none from You.[61]

A man struck by tribulation went down a street. His eyes fell on a heart-stealing beauty and he was caught in the trap of love. That moon-cheeked maiden knew he had fallen for her. She laughed and concealed her face.

You approached me until you caught me
with words that undo bonds and smooth the sand.
Then you went from me when I had no escape
and left my breast with what you left.[62]

*

First you caressed me with a thousand endearments;
then you melted me with a thousand pains.
You played with me like a marvelous die
and tossed me afar when I was totally yours.

For a long time that poor man went to her street and heard nothing about the one he sought, nor did he see a trace. There was a little dog in that quarter, so he said to himself, "I'll become familiar with the dog." As much as he followed the dog around, it would not become familiar with him. Every day he would buy some bread and meat for the dog, but the dog paid him no attention. As soon as it saw the man from a distance, it would start barking and making a racket.

Sometime later he saw the one he sought and began complaining of love, reciting painful tales of heartache and shedding agate tears on his amber face.

A poverty like the poverty of the prophets—an exile
and an ardor that have never been anyone's trial![63]

She said to him, "Go, watch out for yourself, for I have many suitors. You don't want them to shed your blood."

She said, "Don't pass by my street drunk
lest you be killed, for my suitor is jealous."[64]

"I had come that day looking for someone else, but your throat was caught on the hook of my love."

The afflicted man said, "Then why did you laugh?"

She said, "I was laughing at you, not with you."

Would that someone could see your notebook
and count those killed at your doorstep.
You've got no prey or food but spirits and livers,
so not every head has the head for you.

The kings and sultans of this world decorate their thresholds and courts with spears and shields, but He decorates the threshold of majesty, the gate of magnificence, and the court of exaltedness with the spirits and livers of the sincerely truthful and the prophets. In every corner is someone He's killed, in every nook someone He's burned. Which body has not been melted by His severity? Which heart has not been caressed by His gentleness? Which spirit has not been clutched by the falcon claws of His exaltedness? Which head has not been drunk with the wine of His love? If you go to the corner of the dervishes—burning for Him. If you go to the street of the tavern-goers—the pain of not having found Him. If you go to the church of the Christians, all are on the carpet of seeking Him. If you go to the synagogue of the Jews, all are yearning for His beauty. If you go to the fire temple of the Guebres, all are burned by His majesty. If you look at His familiars, all are wounded by His tipsy eyes and His coquettish beauty. If you look at those estranged from Him, all are tied back by the bonds of His exaltation and majesty.

A thousand lovers came wanting My companionship,
tossing their hearts and eyes before My servants.
All were wounded by separation's grief and sorrow,
for none had ever seen or known a mark of Me.

The same thing happened to the suspicion-tainted Throne. When suspicion's rosy color was pulled across its yellow face—for *the All-merciful sat on the Throne* [20:5]—in its ecstasy it let out this painful cry of destitution:

I'm like incense on fire from the bad-speaker's words—
it's me who's burning while others catch the scent.

10. *al-Muhaymin:* the Overseer

The meaning of *muhaymin* is witness [*shahīd*], and the witness is the knower. Some have said that the meaning of *muhaymin* is watcher, and a watcher [*raqīb*] is a watchman [*nigahbān*]. When the servant knows that the Real is watcher of his states and near to him, he must don the clothing of shame and be ashamed before the place of the Real's awareness.

One of the exalted ones was asked, *"What is the mark that you have recognized Him?"*

He said, *"Whenever I consider opposing Him, a caller calls to me from inside my heart: 'Are you not ashamed before Him?' "*[65] The thought of opposing Him never enters my breast without a preacher saying from inside my heart, "Have you no shame before your Lord?"

It is as if one of Your watchers watches over my thoughts
and another over my gaze and my tongue.
After You when my eyes look at anything
ugly to You, I say, "Those two are looking at me."
After You when my mouth voices joy
in other than You, those two pull back on my reins.
The talk of truthful brothers tires me
and from them I hold back my gaze and my tongue.
It is not renunciation that diverts me from them—
I have found You witnessed in every place.[66]

In one of the revealed books the Lord says, *"My servant, when you have shame before Me, I will make people forget your faults, I will make the regions of the earth forget your sins, I will efface your slips from the Mother of the Book, and I will not interrogate you at the accounting on the Day of Resurrection."*[67] My servant, as soon as you wear the garb of shame and sit on the steed of loyalty, I will conceal every fault of yours from the creatures; I will make the regions in which you sinned forget your sins so that tomorrow they will not bear witness against your disobedience; I will erase your slips from the Guarded Tablet; and when I call to account tomorrow, I will walk the path of leniency and mildness.

They say that it was revealed to Jesus, *"Counsel yourself! If you heed the counsel, then counsel the people. Otherwise, have shame before Me in counseling the people."*[68] O Jesus, first give advice to yourself. If your makeup can take advice, then advise others. If there is anything other than this, be ashamed for advising others but not taking the advice yourself.

Know that shame is of several kinds.[69] There is a shame because of slips, like the shame of Adam. When the predetermined things appeared from the ambush of the Unseen and Adam brought the wheat to hand, his crown and garb flew off and he went into every corner in embarrassment. The call came, *"Are you fleeing from Me?"*

He said, "No, but I am ashamed before You."[70]

There is shame in venerating the majesty of the Real that belongs to the angels. *Seraphiel would cover his head with his wings because of the Real's awesomeness and majesty.*

I yearned for Him and when He appeared,
I bowed in veneration
Not in fear but in awe
and to protect His beauty.
I shunned Him to shelter myself,
hoping for the specter of His image,
For death is for Him to turn His back
and life that He turn this way.[71]

There is shame because of generosity, like the shame of Muḥammad. *He was ashamed before his community to say, "Go outside!" So God said,* "[*When you are invited for a meal, disperse,*] *not lingering for talk;* [*that is hurtful to the Prophet, and he is ashamed before you, but God is not ashamed before the truth*]" [33:53].

There is shame because of respect, like the shame of ʿAlī, who was ashamed to ask Muṣṭafā the rule about seminal leakage during foreplay, because Fāṭima was under his decree. He requested from Miqdād Aswad that he ask Muṣṭafā about it.[72]

There is shame because of considering something trivial, like the shame of Moses, who said in whispered prayer, "O Lord, sometimes I need something trivial, but I am ashamed to ask You for it." The call came, *"Ask of Me—even the salt for your dough and the fodder for your sheep."*[73]

There is shame because of the curtain, and that is the shame of Shuʿayb's daughter, who came from her father to invite Moses. The Quran says, [*"Then came one of the two women to him*] *walking with shame"* [28:25]. She was ashamed before Moses, because he was a stranger, so she went to him while stamping her feet.

There is shame belonging to servants called "the shame of servanthood." God's Messenger said, *"Have shame before God as is the rightful due of His shame!"*[74] He said that you should have shame before God just as you have shame before the lords.

There is shame called "the shame of generosity," and that is the shame of the Exalted Threshold. God's Messenger said, *"Surely God has shame and is generous; because of His shame, 'He forbade indecencies'* [7:33]."[75]

There is shame that is the shame of the Real. When the servant passes over the Narrow Path, He will give him a sealed letter, within which is this: *"You did what you did, and I am ashamed to make it manifest to you. Go, for I have forgiven you."*[76] In that letter it is written that you did what you did, but My generosity does not allow Me to make it appear. Go, for I have forgiven you and erased the pages of your crimes and the scrolls of your slips.

> One gaze of the Friend, and a hundred thousand felicities!
> I'm waiting for that gaze to come.

There is shame that is the shame of the obedient because of their obedience. Abū Bakr Warrāq said, *"Sometimes I pray two cycles for God, then turn away, and my shame is like someone who has turned away after stealing."*[77] It sometimes happens that I perform two cycles of prayer, and when I say the greeting and finish, I am embarrassed and ashamed of this obedience of mine, as if I had stolen something. As long as a man does not arrive at this station, the pleasure of obedience will not reach the taste buds of his faith.

Sufyān Thawrī was sitting in a howdah having set off for the Kaabah. With him in the howdah was a friend. Sufyān kept weeping and scattering the water of his eyes' ocean on the shores of his cheeks. His friend said, "O Sufyān, do you weep in fear of sins?"

Sufyān reached out and picked up a piece of straw. He said, "I have many sins, but for me my sins do not have the measure of this piece of straw. I fear this: Is this *tawḥīd* I have real *tawḥīd?"*

Those were people who had, but they showed themselves as not having. You do not have, but you show yourselves as having. They were the rich who fancied themselves indigent, the preceders with the remorse of those who fall short. Now, the situation has been reversed, and men have become obstinate in irreligion. They are indigent but fancy themselves rich. They fall short but claim to be preceders. Are you a man—you who hope for nobility? The will must be your will, the want your want, and the desire your desire. *But this is an affair that will not be completed with associationism.*

A tried and afflicted man, his spirit at the brink of death, had fallen beneath a thorn bush, attacked by a hundred thousand trials, troubles, adversities, and hardships. All at once this call rose up from him: "For one moment at least give me back to myself so that I may recover my own thread."

He heard a call, *"This is an affair that will not be completed with associationism."* This is a work that will not be set straight in partnership. *"Either Me or you."*

Don't think about this talk, put on the shroud
and clap your hands like a man.
Say, "Either You or me in the city"—
a realm with two heads is in turmoil.

The ship must be broken and the man drowned, leaving only you and the Goal, the Goal and you.

In my love for Buthayna I desired
that we two be alone on a raft in the ocean.[78]

He is saying, "O Buthayna, I have one wish. It is that you and I be sitting in a ship when suddenly waves come and smash the ship. All the people drown, and you and I are on a raft. I and you, you and I."

Break the name of everything other than the Friend,
lose the name of everything other than love![79]

Everything other than the Goal is a crowd on the road to the Goal. The veiled lady of this talk is jealous. She will not show her beautiful face in the midst of a crowd of others. She will not lift off the mask of exaltedness.

That dust mote in the sun of the world of love will not show its face if the sun fills the world. It wants a place of seclusion without the crowding of others before it will take off the mask of jealousy.

The master Abū ʿAlī Daqqāq said, *"The Garden has no business with me, and the Fire has no access to me, for there is nothing in my heart but happiness with my Lord."* Paradise has no business with me, and hell has nothing to do with me, for there is nothing in my heart but joy in the Real's subsistence.

The moment I became happy in Your subsistence
I drew the line of annihilation around myself.

Those who step into this road do not do so for any cause, only for love. The exactor of the debt does not come from the door but from within the breast. *Love for my Lord extracts from me what nothing else extracts.*[80] They put paradise and hell into nonexistence and then walk on the road.

Expecting compensation for obedient acts is a fatal poison.[81] Expecting compensation in the road of obedience is a fatal poison. If you were to walk on this road for a thousand years and your obedience was not accepted, and then it occurred to your mind that it should have been accepted, you will have been a status-seeker, not a road-seeker. You will not be a realizer in this road until you abandon your status with both the Real and the creatures.

Someone will say, "I don't want status with the creatures, I want it at the threshold of the Real." Do not seek status for yourself, whether here or there! Bind up your waist like a man and find a broom of solitariness and disengagement. Sweep your own alienated existence away from this threshold a thousand times every day. If it happens that you stay at this threshold for a thousand years and then it is said to you, "Go, for you are not worthy of Us," you will have been given your just due.

O captive of the monastery, that is not the road.
  The only road is aspiration for the Threshold.
First become pure of the two worlds—
  if you're not pure, there's no road.
Don't think to mix status with the road—
  status is found only in severity's pit.
How long will you say, "Where is a companion?"
  Son, there's no companion in this road.
If blood drips from your throat on the polo field, say,
  "No one has the ball but the king."
You keep on claiming truthfulness in love—
  why then is your heart not single, your face not pale?

In a past community there was a man who had spent many years in obedience, worship. exertion, and effort. He had undergone various sorts of discipline and deprivation and seen great hunger. Revelation came to the prophet of the time: "Tell that man, 'Don't give yourself so much trouble, for you are one of the folk of hell.' "

I said, "Have mercy on me, for I'm a poor man."
  He said, "I have more than a thousand slave boys."
I said, "Separation from You has filled my heart with wounds."
  He said, "You're complaining to Me about your lot."

The prophet delivered the revelation to the worshiper. The man increased his obedience and the people were surprised. They said, "What is this? It has been revealed to the prophet of the time that you are one of the folk of hell, and every day you increase your exertion and effort in obedience."

He said, "I had fancied that I did not have the worth of a straw in His empire. Now I am worthy for hell, which is lit up by the attribute of His wrath. What good fortune lies beyond that?"

This removes all doubt that I am Wāmiq:
  I cling to your door while you shun me.[82]

⋆

I did not want what they wanted—their want
  came, and I abandoned my own want.[83]

⋆

O You who put me in poverty's garb, no harm has touched me from You:
  abuse from You is praise, and others' praise is bitter.

By the rightful due of the Real! Suppose you obey for a thousand years; you mix together the eye's water, the liver's blood, and the heart's pain and make them into love's threesome, and then you burn in the monastery of your own tribulation. Then, if there is talk of you in that Presence, whether in rejection or acceptance, that is more than enough compensation for a thousand thousand years of obedience.

Muṣṭafā said to Ubayy ibn Kaʿb, "O Ubayy, the Lord of Lords said to me that I should recite the Quran for Ubayy."

He said, *"O Messenger of God, was I mentioned there?"*[84] Was there indeed talk of someone like me in that Presence?

Don't think I'm in love with your face—
I'm the dirt on the paws of the dogs in your street.

This verse was recited before Shiblī: *"Slink you into it, and do not talk to Me"* [23:108]. He said, "How happy for them!"[85]

When the folk of hell go into hell, for seven thousand years they will ask Mālik to offer the tale of their pain to the Presence, but Mālik will remain silent. After seven thousand years, he will be told to respond, *"You will surely tarry* [43:77]. You have no way to come out. You must surrender to that."

When they despair of Mālik, they will turn their faces to the Threshold and request from the Real. They will begin to weep: "Lord God, *bring us forth out of it* [23:107]. O Lord, we took our request to Mālik but did not receive a healing response. Now we ask from You. We offer our tale's sorrow to Your threshold."

For seven thousand more years they will ask, and after that the response will come: *"Slink you into it, and do not talk to Me."* This is the way dogs are addressed: "O rejected by My Presence and separated from My threshold, keep silent!"

When Shiblī heard this, he said, "How happy for them that the Maker spoke to them after seven thousand years!" Shiblī did not look at what He said. He looked at who said it.

A word from you, did you but know,
is honey the bees gather from camel's milk.[86]

*

I don't know from whom to seek my heart's ease.
This work just happened—I don't know whom to tell.
My beloved killed me—she had no fear.
Despite her fearlessness, I'm in love with her.

*

Say a word to me and after that
kill me if you want—you're the king.

That exalted man said, *"Approve of me as a lover! If You do not approve of me as a lover, approve of me as a servant! If You do not approve of me as a servant, approve of me as a dog!"*

I approve though He does not
for I'm content.[87]

It seems to me that in these words the speaker is saying, "Take me as a dog, for that has compensation."

They say that someone said, "O God, take me as Your dog!" He was walking along a road, and a dog began to speak to him. It said, "You've put yourself in a magnificent position. No hair of mine has ever moved in opposition to Him. You want to have my station?"

The lover is destitute and the Beloved disdainful and proud. What can he do but counter His disdain with abasement and come forth to His arrogance with graciousness and to His overburdening with tolerance?

I'm disposed to romance and not consoled—
I'm always amorous, then amorous.
In every tribe I've met, I have a spirit,
in every group I've left, I have a heart.
Sometimes I'm accepted, sometimes driven out—
such is the custom of love: distance and nearness.

*

Whether You're at war or peace You're lovely,
You've got no match in beauty and comeliness.
You keep on making war because
with war You increase love's beauty.

11. *al-ʿAzīz:* the Exalted

ʿAzīz has several meanings. Some have said that the name's meaning is someone who dominates and over whom no one dominates, someone severe toward whom no one acts severely. The Arabs say, *"He became exalted," when someone dominates over someone toward whom he turns simply by raising his eyes.*

Some have said that the meaning of exalted is powerful. Some have said that its meaning is exalter [*muʿizz*], just as the meaning of *alīm* [painful] is *muʾlim* [pain-giver]. Some have said that the exalted is he who has no likeness. The Arabs say, *"It became exalted" when something becomes peerless.*

Some have said that the meaning of exalted is inaccessible, or that its meaning is impregnable. The Arabs say "impregnable" and "exalted" when something cannot be reached. That which cannot be reached is called exalted. And when something cannot be reached because it has no limits, it is even more appropriate to call it exalted.[88]

This is a concise allusion to the meaning of this word in terms of lexicology. As for the reality, *the Exalted is He who is not grasped by seekers and not disabled by fleers.*[89] The Exalted is He whom the seeker has no way to grasp and the fleer has no way to make incapable.

If a *tawḥīd*-voicing, believing, loving, truthful man should recite a hundred thousand surahs of unity, turn everything that has been transmitted into hard cash, bind to himself everything that intellect has shown, and dive into the oceans of the transmitted and the intellectual, the principles and the ramifications, stringing the pearls and gems of brilliant minds on the thread of learning—when he looks closely, he will see that the result of his expended effort is but a report and a trace. *Before the Unseen are curtains, and behind the curtains are secrets concealed from the eyes of the others.*

Since I won't be given what I've come for,
 I've come to the world to look around.

So glory be to Him, the Exalted within the oceans of whose tremendousness intellects are misled, short of perceiving whose blessings minds become bewildered, and beneath the full praise of whose majesty and the full description of whose beauty tongues become dumb!"[90]

Whoever outstrips in depicting Him
 is ascribed to incapacity.
Whoever surpasses in describing Him
 is forgotten in the midst.[91]

Here we have Muḥammad—God's Messenger, the most eloquent of those who have lived and died, the most elegant of those who have come and gone. After he had gone to great lengths in praising His majesty and describing His beauty, he said, "I do not number Thy laudations—Thou art as Thou hast lauded Thyself."[92]

The eyes of intellects are dazzled in the perception of His majesty, the shining faces of the self-exalted turn dull before the shine of His beauty, the minds of the mindful are bewildered in the perception of His depiction, and the thoughts of the possessors of sciences come to nothing at the margins of His exaltedness. The lords of sight, insight, cleverness, astuteness, piercing thought, and wisdom are drowned in a drop from the oceans of His magnificence, and the secret cores of the pious are incinerated by the fire of intimacy with His majesty.

Hands placed on their burning hearts—you'd say
 all lovers have torches in their hands.

The tongues of the folk of eloquence stay shamefully dumb in lauding His majesty and describing His beauty—in every corner a thousand thousand are thrown down, wounded, martyred, and slain.

Do you see time as easing encounter,
 bringing yearner together with yearner?
Time's turnings are many, the hardest of which
 is coming together on the day that separation's decreed.
O eye, why did you offer yourself to love?
 Did you not see the slaughter grounds of the lovers?[93]

Here we have Muḥammad, God's Messenger, the title page of whose covenant's edict was eloquence, gracefulness, openhandedness, and forbearance. His fingers were the udder of the spring clouds in generosity, and his tongue was the vicegerent of an Indian sword in sharpness. He subjugated the ignorance of the ignorant and let the courtyards of the erudite flourish. His glances were the beauty of the breasts, and his words the healing of the breasts. He lit the aloes wood of the call in the incense-burner of generosity, sewed up the eyes of the religion's enemies with the arrows of severity, taught liberality to the clouds of spring, and kindled the fire of love in the community's breasts. The falcon of his aspiration rose beyond the pinnacles of eminence, and his essence was the night-brightening pearl of which the world was the oyster. Surpassing in eloquence, he won the race, spread out the carpet of union, and rolled up the cloth of separation. Such was he that he received the exalted address, *"I created what I created only for thee."*[94] When I strung the pearl of day and the agate of night on the string of power and fastened it to the neck of the turning wheel, when I threw the die of the sun on the turquoise cloth and placed the kinglike moon on the emerald board, when I bound the pearls, necklaces, and jewels—the sparkling planets—to the neck of the circling wheel, when I brought the blue depths and the dusty circle from the curtain of concealment to the desert of *"Be!" so it comes to be* [2:117]—all of it was for you.

Then with the tip of his tongue—upon which flowed the sweetness of the spirits—Muḥammad voiced a thousand thousand chapters in praise of the Lord and the bounty of the All-Merciful. On the final page, like Moses, he threw down the tablets of eloquence—*he threw down the tablets* [7:150]. He put on the garment of destitution and incapacity and burned the harvest of *"I am the most eloquent of the Arabs"*[95] in the fire of unneediness: *"Thou art as Thou hast lauded Thyself."*

> I wrote a hundred tablets and learned them by heart,
> but love for You took me back to the first tablet.

This is a rare business. He brought these hapless ones into existence from *feeble water* [77:20] and *molded mud* [15:26]—*the weak from the weak from the weak, dust from dust from dust, the bewildered from the bewildered from the bewildered, the incapable from the incapable from the incapable, the indigent from the indigent from the indigent.* Then He took them by the collar and placed them without hope in the battlefield of the brave—a battlefield in which the command pulls in one direction and the decree in another. The beauty of the Threshold calls out, "O friend, pass over My road," and from the pavilion of exaltedness the beginningless majesty addresses them: "Hapless ones—*beware, beware!*"

> She said, "Don't pass by my street drunk
> lest you be killed, for my suitor is jealous."
> I said some strange words, but I have an excuse—
> "Better killed in your street than far from your face."[96]

The moth has a mad fervor for union with the candle, so all its circling round the fire's tongue is in hope of union, for lovers give drink to the mad fervor of the heart's core with the cup of "perhaps" and "maybe." But when the sultan of the fire's beauty draws the severe blade of majesty and unneediness, the spirits of a hundred thousand moths aren't worth a barleycorn.

Who am I that my spirit should carry the bags of loyalty to You,
  or my eyes be porters for the burden of Your cruelty?
Death's angel—Your cruelty—will not take my spirit
  so long as I carry the Seraphiel of loyalty to You.
What does the Throne do that it should not carry my saddlecloth?
  My spirit carries the saddlecloth of Your ruling and decree.
I travel only on air when I long for You,
  I see only loyalty when I carry Your cruelty.
By God, if You aim for my awareness and intelligence,
  I'll take them both by the ear and carry them to Your house.
If You issue the decree to my heart, spirit, and body,
  I'll carry all three dancing to Your love.[97]

O chevalier, how can a weak-bodied ant come face to face with the strength of a crocodile having the form of a serpent?

Oh, Your locks are a serpent and my lonely heart an ant.
  How will it keep its head against a serpent on the day of battle?
My miserable ant aimed for Your black serpent
  and Your serpent swallowed it down.

O chevalier, if that ant with its weak makeup, tiny composition, and contemptible shape should suddenly want to rise up to the spheres, that would be absurd. By the rightful due of the Real, your incapacity in the face of His majesty is more than that ant's incapacity in the face of the serpent's strength!

Some have turned their faces toward stones, others toward clods of dirt. Some have turned toward the East, others toward the West. Some are rushing and running, others seeking and searching. One group is talking and chatting, another shouting and yelling. *But the Real is exalted, the path long, the steed weak. Proximity is distance and union separation. The realities are well guarded, the meanings protected by the Unseen, the secrets stored away in the Unseen's storehouses, and the creatures have nothing but talk and blabber.*[98]

If I become nothing in heartache for You, there's no shame—
  a hundred spirits in Your scales have no worth.
In seeking You I've nothing of Your color—
  if an ant fails to reach the spheres, there's no quarrel.

*

To wish for Suʿdā is chastisement—as if
  she would give you a cold drink in your thirst.
If a wish turns real, that would be the most beautiful wish—
  otherwise we'll live easily with it for a time.[99]

Abu'l-Ḥusayn Nūrī said, *"In what we are busy with the nearest nearness is the farthest farness."*[100]

A man looks in a mirror and sees his own form before his eyes. In respect of the outward state, he says, "I'll lift up my hand and grab this form in my grasp." But when he looks, this nearness is distance itself. If he were to rise up seeking that form in mad fervor, his life would come to an end without his becoming aware of a mote of that form's existence.

In love for You a hundred thousand lives have ended—
they went without finding a trace of union.

*

Your union is separation, your love hate,
your nearness distance, your peace war.
In you—God's is the praise!—is hardness
and your every docile steed is unruly.[101]

Proximity to the Essence is in fact impossible. If there were "proximity" to the Essence, then direction, measure, approach, conjoining, and disjoining would appear, but the Real is incomparable with all of these.

Proximity to the attributes gives rise to thirst and unsettledness, not satiation and stillness. A man looks into his heart and sees that the heart's sorrowful corner is empty of the object of his desire, even though he keeps on hearing the exalted address, *"And He is with you wherever you are"* [57:4].

Every day the Throne says several times to the Footstool, *"Have you any news?"* The Footstool says to the Throne, *"Have you any trace?"* Heaven says to earth, *"Has any seeker passed you by?"* Earth says to heaven, *"Has any lover dismounted in your courtyard?"*

He pulled a pearl from the ocean of unneediness, strung it on the necklace of beginningless knowledge, and fastened it to the neck of the Throne. The Throne says, "I have what's happening. Ask me, and I'll tell you about my state."

I'm worn out by accusations of loving You
even though I've never reached union with You.
People rebuke me for a fool—
a wolf with empty stomach and bloody mouth.

He has kept the whole world pleased with rushing and running, talking and chatting, never having given anyone a drop from the draft in His exaltation's cup.

By your life, if you knew anything of what I have,
you'd give me to drink only with a dropper.
Enough for me that there's a vineyard on my block—
when I pass its door, I nearly fall down drunk.[102]

A man in love with wine came to the door of a wine-merchant and asked him for a bit of wine. He said, "The vat's empty."

The man said, "Take me by the hand to the top of the vat so that I may sniff it. I become more drunk with its smell than others do with several overflowing cups."

In the Shariahs of past communities, wine was permitted, but in this community it is forbidden, for wine is the stuff of revelry, and past people needed wine to bring about revelry. When the turn of this community came, so many cups of the spirits' joy flew down from the tavern of the Unseen that there was no need for drops coming by way of new arrival.

With our wine the tribe's lame man began to walk,
and the blind—we gave him three cups and he saw.
The dumb man hadn't spoken for thirty seasons—
the day we passed him the cup he began to shout.[103]

When a man places a vast desert before his eyes and falls into the dragon-mouth of its heat, thirst dominates over him and his whole self becomes busy with it. Wherever he looks, he sees water, *like a mirage in a spacious plain* [24:39]. He fancies that the mirage is drink, and he thinks that dust is pure water. When he arrives, he puts sorrow's hand on bewilderment's chin and recites the chapter of hopelessness from the book of embarrassment. In the same way, the experienced lover, his heart given to the wind, steps out on the road and devotes his whole self to seeking, driven by the overpowering force of yearning, the heat of ecstasy's flames, and the burning fire of love. Wherever he looks he sees nothing but the object of his search, he knows nothing but his goal, and it alone appears as the object of his desire. He inscribes the figure of reality across the face of imagination, but from the quarter of the divine majesty a wind blows that turns all his fancies into *scattered dust* [25:23].

Despairing of approach,
I'm eager in great distance—
I hope for death in loving you,
for my heart is struggling.[104]

They say that there was a merchant coming along the road with a basket of glassware. When he reached the gate of the city, he sat on a wall to rest. He put down the basket and nurtured his delusions.

With wishes you will pass the night in bliss—
surely wishes are the capital of the destitute.[105]

He said, "I'll take this glass to the city and sell it for so much. With its price I'll buy sheep, and those sheep will reproduce. I'll sell the sheep and buy camels. Then, when I've gathered a great amount of wealth, I'll buy a castle and ask for a wife. She'll have a boy, and I will turn him over to a teacher to make him well mannered. If he shows ill manners, I'll teach him manners," and he kicked out heedlessly. The basket of glass fell from the wall and broke.

Someone was sitting behind the wall and heard his imaginings. He said, "All the work would have been set right if you hadn't become angry this one time."

12. *al-Jabbār:* the All-Compelling

Lexicologists have discussed this name. Some say that it is derived from *a* jabbār *palm-tree, that is, one that passes beyond the hands.*[106] When a palm-tree is tall and hands fail to reach it, the Arabs call it a *jabbār* palm-tree. So, describing the Lord as "all-compelling" means that understandings, imaginations, intellects, and sciences do not reach the core of the majesty and beauty of His lordhood and kingship.

If the Lord shows all-compellingness, the attribute is praised, but if a servant does so, the attribute is blamed. For Him all-compellingness means that He does not come under anyone's rule, but for the servant it means denying the Real and abandoning humility toward the command.

Some say that *jabbār* comes from *jabartu al-amr, "I restored the affair,"* which is to say that its meaning is to bring the work to wholesomeness. The Real is He who brings about the wholesomeness of the servants' work.

Some say that it comes from *jabartuhu 'ala'l-amr, "I forced the affair upon him,"* that is, to coerce someone into doing something.

In reality, whoever becomes aware of the secret of this word must know that *there is no path to Him and no escape from Him. What belongs to the servant today is recognizing Him, and what belongs to him tomorrow is His forgiveness, pardon, and approval. As for the reality of His self-sufficiency, that is incomparable with and hallowed beyond perception.*[107] There is no road to Him and no escape from Him. Today the servant has recognition, and tomorrow pardon and forgiveness. As for the reality of self-sufficiency and the perfection of unity, that is incomparable with the perception of mortal man and the grasp of his puny intellect.

O chevalier, there is a recognition necessitated by the command, and a recognition necessitated by the rightful due; there is a recognition by the command, and a recognition by the measure. When He calls you to account, He does so in keeping with what is necessitated by the command so that He may pardon your deeds. If He were to take you to task in keeping with what is necessitated by the rightful due, a thousand years of obedience would have the same color as a thousand years of disobedience. If all the prophets and the friends, the rational and the mad, the wholesome and the ungodly, came together in one circle, none would have the capacity to undertake His rightful due or answer to His rightful due.

There is a decree, a rightful due, and a command. Whenever you take something to the assayer of the decree, it comes out genuine; whenever you take something to the assayer of the rightful due, it comes out counterfeit; and whenever you take something to the assayer of the command, some of it comes out genuine and some counterfeit. You should constantly say in supplication, "Lord God, do not send our deeds to the assayer of the command or the rightful due! Send them to the assayer of the decree!"

The decree accepts everything, the rightful due rejects everything, and the command accepts some and rejects some. The decree is sheer bounty, the rightful due is sheer justice, and the command is bounty in one respect and justice in another. If you send the deeds of the one hundred twenty-some thousand pearls of sinlessness to the assayer of the rightful due, they will come out counterfeit. If you send the deeds of the tavern-goers to the assayer of the decree, you should know that it will be the opposite of that.

Moreover, the command is finite but the rightful due is infinite, for the command subsists as long as the prescription of the Law subsists. Prescription takes place in the abode of prescription, which is this world. The rightful due subsists with the subsistence of the Essence, and the Essence is infinite, so the subsistence of the rightful due is infinite.

That exalted man of the age said, "What is necessary by the command will disappear, but what is necessary by the rightful due will never disappear. This world will pass away and the turn of the command will pass away along with it. But the turn of the rightful due will never pass away."

Today when someone looks into the mirror of the command, a delusion falls into his head—" I'm coming from someplace." But tomorrow when he looks into the mirror of the rightful due, he will see his own incapacity, helplessness, and destitution. Today the prophets and messengers look at their own prophethood and messengerhood; the angels look at their own obedience and worship; and the *tawḥīd*-voicers, strugglers, faithful, and sincere look at their own *tawḥīd*-voicing, struggle, faith, and sincerity. Tomorrow, when the pavilions of the lordly rightful due are thrown open, the prophets will come forth in the perfection of their majesty and the elevation of their state, but they will put away talk of their own knowledge: *"We have no knowledge—surely Thou art the Knower of unseen things* [5:109]." The angels of the Dominion will come forth and strike fire into the monasteries of worship; they will toss the harvest of their hallowing and glorifying to the wind of unneediness and say, *"We have not worshiped Thee with the rightful due of Thy worship!"* The recognizers and *tawḥīd*-voicers will come forth dancing—"*We have not recognized Thee with the rightful due of Thy recognition!*"[108]

Intelligence wanted to go forward in the road of His divinity and fell short. The light of intellect wanted to come near His majesty and became *scattered dust* [25:23]. The heart's awareness wanted to know the measure of His perfection but was dazzled. Recognition wanted to encompass the presence of asserting His holiness and solitariness but was incapable.

> On the day they stamped a seal on the work of all the low,
> they stamped a different seal on the gold of love.
> Your intellect will never grasp how they sealed it—
> the gold they stamped lies outside its house.[109]

O You whom it is absurd to seek and baneful to express! Since You are with me, how can I seek You? Since You are not like anything, how can I express You? There's no way with You and no way without You.

> Without You my heart's desire has no bazaar,
> nor do I incline toward any friend.

Without You no one has any patience, and with You no one has any rest. No one can be without You, and no one can flee from You. *There is no capacity to be with You and no ease in other than You, so help is sought from You against You.*[110]

When I said, "Separation bestows on me the robe of cruelty,"
she said, "Love without separation would not be pleasant."
When I said, "My distress is constant," she said,
"Those alone are counted as lovers who are always distressed."
When I said, "I did not sin," she said in reply,
"Your life is a sin to which no sin can compare."[111]

*

Nearness brings chastisement, distance remorse,
and both are nothing but hard for me.
O grief of my heart, you've brought me to the edge!
O tears of my eyes, none of you are left![112]

O You whose exaltedness has placed the attribute of lowliness in all exalted things, O You whose majesty has put the brand of tininess on all majestic things, O You whose perfection has written the script of deficiency on every perfection, O You whose divinity has placed the robe of servanthood on all the world! O You whose Essence has no "where," O You whose attributes have no "how," O You whose grasping has no limbs, O You whose gazing has no eye, O You whose love has no seizing! O You whose attributes bewilder intellects; O You whose Essence distracts spirits; O You whose desire, will, decree, and ruling are pure of the defilement of creaturely imaginings; O You whose attributes of eternity are exempt from perception by the notions, thoughts, and minds of water and clay! O You for whom all the world have put their spirits to love's auction and gained nothing but sorrow, O You the porch of whose radiant majesty is taken as the goal by all the passionate without reaching anything but despair, O You whose road all roasted-heart lovers have taken, giving their possessions, position, family, and nobility to the wind and bringing to hand nothing but wind!

I've given my whole life to your work,
but you're busy with your own work, and I'm in the wind.
Though in the work of love I'm a master, sweetheart,
I've fallen hard in your trap.

*

Even when approval's repose does not reach me,
even when anger's days do not pass,
I love Him whether His deed is ugly or beautiful,
and for His sake I decree for myself what He decrees.[113]

With the sieve of free choice they sifted the wherewithal of the Adamites, but not one iota of reality came to the surface. They searched all the corners of mortal man, but not a needle's point of purity showed itself. Shiblī said, *"No one says, 'No god but God,' for whoever says it, says it as his own share. How can realities be perceived by shares?"*[114]

O chevalier, it is said concerning Adam that he was the stone on the seal-ring of the world, the pearl on the crown of power, and the garb on the secret of creation: *And We made covenant with Adam before, [but he forgot, and We found in him no resoluteness]* [20:115]. They sifted the dust of Adam, but not a speck of exaltedness came to the top. *When the first of the jug is dregs, what do you think its last will be?*[115] Since the first drink of that vat was dregs, what else could the last of it be?

It was He who brought forth habit and metaphor in order to sprinkle dust on the reality. He gave hypocrisy existence so that it would fight against sincerity. He made ignorance appear so that it would struggle against the sultan of knowledge. He brought forth doubt so that it would scratch the face of certainty's mirror. He stirred up ambiguity so that it would slash the cheek of argument. He brought forth associationism so that it would travel the path of quarreling with *tawḥīd*. For every friend He created a hundred thousand enemies. For everyone sincerely truthful He created and brought forth a hundred thousand heretics. Wherever there is a mosque, He built a church next door. Wherever there is a monastery, there is a tavern, wherever a turban, a sash. Wherever there is attestation, there is denial; wherever a friend an enemy, wherever a worshipper a refuser, wherever a truthful lover an ungodly heretic. He filled the space from East to West with adornments and blessings, and beneath each blessing He put the trappings of tribulation and trial. The great ones have said, *"Part of this world's trouble is the harm of almonds and the benefit of myrobalan."*[116]

Part of this world's trouble for the free man is that
he has no escape from being friendly toward enemies.[117]

He gave existence to an individual who is mad when hungry, drunk when full, a corpse when asleep, and bewildered and without wherewithal when awake. In no state and no station can you put your finger on a purity that belongs to him. Incapacity is his comrade and weakness his requisite attribute. If he circles around recognition, it is said, *"They measure not God with the rightful due of His measure"* [6:91]. If he circles around worship, it is said, *"They were commanded only to worship God, making the religion sincerely His"* [98:5]. If he pulls back his feet from both, he is addressed with the words *"Surely thy Lord's assault is terrible"* [85:12]. If he seeks someone to intercede, the call comes, *"Who is there to intercede with Him save by His leave?"* [2:255]. If he wants to reach somewhere with his own wherewithal, this sword of severity is drawn from the sheath of exaltedness: *"We shall advance upon what deeds they have done and make them scattered dust"* [25:23]. If he seeks for a likeness, it is said, *"Nothing is as His likeness"* [42:11]. If he wishes for Him in a place, majesty will brand him with *"Eyesights perceive Him not"* [6:103]. If his gaze falls on himself, he will be struck with the whip of *"If thou takest associates, thy deeds will surely fail"* [39:65]. If he wants to search for exaltation, this address will come: *"Surely the exaltation, all of it, belongs to God"* [4:139]. *Magnificence is My cloak and tremendousness My shawl; if anyone contends with Me in either, I will chastise him.*[118] If he wants to slip away into a corner, this call comes: *"He is the First and the Last and the Outward and the Inward"* [57:3]. If he wants to talk to himself in his fervor, watchers and guards have been set out: *"He utters not a word but by him is a ready watcher"* [50:18]. If he wants to pull his face back from outward things, keep himself busy in a corner of his heart, and drink down his own folly, the address will come: *"He knows the secret and the most hidden"* [20:7]. If he seeks a hiding place and a crevice, it will be said, *"To Him is the homecoming"* [5:18]. If he wants to say something, it will be said, *"He will not be asked about what He does"* [21:23].

He does all this, but in fear
a man has not the gall to sigh,
for the face is like a mirror,
and sighs will mar a mirror.

*

Why do they keep on striving to destroy themselves
when they see You "morning and evening" [33:42]*?*
Were they to gaze with the eyes of their love,
they would gaze upon You while reciting tawḥīd.
O You who wear the robes of beautiful traits,
in love for You I've donned talk and chatter.

O you who have remained in your trial while the world keeps on trying you! To Muṣṭafā He said, *"I sent you to try you and to try by means of you."*[119] O Muḥammad, I have sent you to throw you into trial and to throw the creatures into trial by means of you. Take up the sword! Receive and strike like a man! Sometimes the Day of Badr, sometimes the Day of Uhud; sometimes a thousand robes of honor and gifts, sometimes tripe on the neck.

O Muḥammad, you say, *"Three things of this world of yours were made beloved to me: perfume, women, and the delight of my eyes was put in the prayer."*[120] You say, "I love sweet aromas"—here, take tripe. You say, "I love women"—here, take this calumny about ʿĀʾisha. See what His exaltation and majesty do to the spirits of this hapless handful!

O You whose trial has imprisoned
all who talk of loving You.
The world's lovers are all distraught
in Your exaltedness and magnificence.
Stamp on the tale of those who love You
the signet of Your "yes" or "no."
May my head be lopped off if I lay it not down
in the spot marked by Your foot.
If You give me poison, it will be like honey,
not in my view, O Idol, but in Yours.
You will always be happy with my annihilation,
and I will always be happy with Your subsistence.
Though You are cruel toward my spirit,
I will always be loyal to You.

May my spirit and a hundred spirits like mine
be Your sacrifice, O Youth!
Other than spirit, heart, and liver,
what else is found in Your turning mill?

Yes, come into this road and see the remorse of Adam, hear the cries of Noah, see the disappointment of Abraham, hear the talk of Jacob's affliction, see the moonlike Joseph's well and prison, observe the saw on Zachariah's head and the blade on John's neck, and see the burnt liver and roasted heart of Muḥammad. A wound this severe, a love this sharp—the Beloved disdainful and inaccessible. Each moment He is more unneedy and more jealous of His own majesty and beauty. The more His burnt ones are docile, the more refractory is He. The more His lovers are abased, the more He kills them. The tamer are His yearning seekers, the more He thirsts for their blood.

Those drunken, tipsy eyes
keep filling my eyes with blood.
I'm amazed—how can that moon's eyes
be drunk without taking wine?
How can she shoot arrows into the heart
without hand, bow, fist, or thumb?
She's taken the hearts of the world's lovers
and twisted them on the hooks of her two tresses.
When she knew that trouble had come,
she hid herself and sat in the house.
A whole city is grieving for her—
that's not surprising, it can happen.
Their feet are bound by her irons,
her hand is on their heads.[121]

13. *al-Mutakabbir:* the Proud

This name is said to have three meanings, *and God knows better.*

First is that pride, magnificence, elevation, and highness give news that God deserves descriptions of perfection and attributes of majesty and that His Essence is hallowed beyond and incomparable with imperfections and blights.[122]

The next meaning is that the Real in Himself stands proudly beyond the attributes of imperfection and the descriptions of new arrival ascribed to Him by the unbelievers, the lost, the deniers, and the obstinate.

The third meaning is that proud means the same as king, a name that has already been discussed.

It has been related that Ḥasan Baṣrī said, "It has reached us that Moses said in his whispered prayer, *'O God, what is Your shawl?'*

"God replied, *'Tremendousness.'*

"He said, 'And what is Your cloak?'

"He said, *'Magnificence.'*

"He said, *'And what is Your gown?'*

"He said, *'O son of 'Imrān, you have asked Me about a tremendous affair. My gown is My mercy. Whenever someone hopes for it, I will dress him in it.'* "[123]

When faithful servants believe that pride is the attribute of the Real, they must don the shirt of humility, the garment of reverence, and the dress of meek servanthood, for no garment is more appropriate for the stature of dust than the garment of humility and meekness.

O chevalier, *someone who has twice traveled the urinary canal should not be proud.*[124] Someone who has twice gone by the passageway of urine can never lift up pride's head or heedlessly build up a market for himself!

There is nothing more beautiful for servitors in the presence of lords than humility. In the presence of kings and sultans, servitors and servants have no ornament more comely than humility.

> In the presence of kings, it's best to seek well-being.
> When looking at emperors, it's best to look from afar.
> Why make the story long? It's best to be short:
> in a jungle with raging lions, it's best to be a fox.

Anas ibn Mālik narrated as follows: *"God's Messenger would visit the ill, escort caskets, ride donkeys, and respond to the call of slaves. On the day of Qurayẓa and Naḍīr, he sat on a donkey haltered with a rope of palm-fiber and a saddle of palm-fiber."*[125] On the sleeve of his perfection Muṣṭafā wore the edict of priority over the two worlds, and on the cheek of his beauty he had the mole of prosperity. The one hundred twenty-some thousand center-points of prophecy ran before his flashing Burāq, shouting, *"Make way, make way!"* Because of his great humility and meekness in the world of servanthood, he used to sit on a tiny little donkey, and, if a slave-boy called to him, he would answer. On the day of Qurayẓa and Naḍīr, he sat on a donkey, and the donkey's harness and saddle were made of palm-fiber.

What a marvelous business! At one time he was mounted on Burāq, a beast of burden from paradise whose pace reached as far as its gaze, and at another time on a tiny little donkey. Yes, the steeds were different, but in each case the rider had one attribute, one aspiration, and one desire. If he was on Burāq, no arrogance was in his head. If he was on a donkey, the dust of abasement did not fall on the face of his prophethood's exaltedness. When the pen of desire has drawn this sigil of chieftainship on a man's edict of felicity—*To God belongs the exaltation, and to the Messenger* [63:8]—the dust of abasement will not settle on the pedestal of his adorned forehead's secrets.

Concerning the attributes of Muṣṭafā, the following has been narrated from Abū Sa'īd Khudrī: *"He used to feed the camels, sweep the house, repair shoes, patch garments, milk the sheep, eat with the servitor, and grind flour with him when he became tired. Shame never prevented him from carrying his goods from the market to his family. He shook hands with the rich and the poor and was the first to say salaam. He never looked down on what he was invited to, even if it was the poorest of dates. He was radiant in face. He would smile without laughing and sorrow without frowning. He was humble without abasement, munificent without extravagance, tender in heart, ever-merciful toward every submitter. He never belched in satiation nor extended his hand in covetousness."*[126]

What was intended from these words is *"humble without abasement."* He had meekness in servanthood, but creatures from first to last have swept up the elixir of perfect exaltedness from his good fortune's doorstep.

Having come down in humility and risen up in loftiness,
you have the rank of descent and elevation,
Like the sun that cannot be surpassed
when it sends down brightness and radiance.[127]

The caesar of the planets and king of the stars lifts its head from the constellation of eminence. If the folk of the world combined their aspirations aiming to grasp an iota of its light, they could not do so. Nonetheless, by virtue of its humility and generosity, it shines on the miserable shacks of beggars and the sorrowful nooks of the poor just as it shines on the palaces of sultans and lords. Muḥammad the Messenger of God was the sun of felicity's sphere, the moon of chieftainship's heaven, the Jupiter of the world of knowledge, the pearl of the oyster of eminence, and the embroidery on the cape of existence.

On the day of the conquest of Mecca, two men were brought before him, their bodies trembling. He looked up and said, *"Be at ease, for I am the son of a woman of Quraysh who used to eat jerky."*[128]

Yes, as long as a man's makeup does not become dust in his own eyes, the dust of his feet will not be made into the eyes' collyrium. Do you not see that the chieftain of the apostles, Muḥammad the Messenger of God, possessed the banner of majesty, the sign of perfection, the limit of good fortune, and the extremity of beauty? He was seated at the forefront on the cushion of tremendousness and majesty and adorned with the adornment of prophethood and messengerhood. He was the eye of the aeons and the ages, the repose of the spirit for the Emigrants and Helpers. He was enthroned, made eminent, given proximity, honored, and authenticated with the crown of exaltedness. He was the key to the door of integrity and the lamp in the house of propriety, having poured the dust of humility and abasement on the head of aspiration. Both realms of being were disclosed to him, but he did not cling to them. On the night of the *mi'rāj* the Lord sat him down on the dome of the proximity of *two-bows' length away* [53:9] and scattered a hundred thousand coins of gentleness on the head of his good fortune, making the two worlds the dust beneath his feet and bringing the celestial realm and the terrestrial center under the banner of his rulership. The wisdom in this was for him to be expansive on the carpet of intercession: "O Muḥammad, if tomorrow you ask Us for the two realms of being and the two worlds, you will have asked for the dust beneath your feet. If with the gentleness of eternity We make the dust beneath your feet your servitors in the work of serving, that is not far-fetched for Our perfect generosity."

The collyrium of insight was daubed on the narcissus eyes of that paragon's prophethood—*upon insight, I and whosoever follows me* [12:108]. He knew that dust should be tame, not headstrong. Tameness belongs to dust, not headstrongness.

Moreover, when the sultan picks up a penniless beggar from the midst of the road, puts him next to the throne of his realm, places the crown of special favor and proximity on his head, binds the belt of priority and nobility around his waist, dresses him in a robe of elevation, sits him down at the court of his favorites, and says to him, "You are I, and I am you," then the stipulation for the beggar is not to forget himself. He must always think of his tattered rags and his lack of honor before the people. *May God have mercy on the man who recognizes his own worth!*

They say that it reached the ears of the Commander of the Faithful, ʿUmar ibn ʿAbd al-ʿAzīz, that his son had a ring made for himself and placed a stone bought for one thousand dirhams on the ring. He wrote a letter to him: "My son, I hear that you have made a ring and that you bought a stone worth one thousand dirhams and placed it on the ring. If you want my approval, sell the stone, feed a thousand hungry people, and make a ring for yourself from a piece of silver. Engrave it with the words *'May God have mercy on the man who recognizes his own worth!'* "[129]

The sultan of power picked up a handful of dust from the earth: *"Surely God created Adam from a handful that He took from all the earth."*[130] He molded him with the beautiful-doing of giving him form: *Surely We created man in the most beautiful stature* [95:4]. He brought him into the fermentation of bringing to be: *"He fermented Adam's clay in His hand for forty mornings."*[131] He sat the spirit-king on the royal seat of his makeup: *And I blew into him of My spirit* [15:29]. In the kingdom of the Beginningless He read the edict of his vicegerency and sultanate: *"I am setting in the earth a vicegerent"* [2:30]. He recorded the names of all existent things with the pen of eternal gentleness on the tablet of his spirit. He commanded the glorifiers and hallowers of the palisades of holiness and the gardens of intimacy to prostrate themselves before the throne of his good fortune: *"And when We said to the angels, 'Prostrate yourselves before Adam!'"* [2:34]. With one abandonment He hung the teacher of the angels on the gallows of admonition in front of Adam's magnificent throne and bound the collar of the curse and rejection around his neck: *"Upon thee shall be My curse until the Day of Doom!"* [38:78].

Having grabbed a handful of dust with His will, He made the lights of chosenness and the traces of artisanry appear within him. He adorned his round head—which is the pavilion of the intellect-king and the palace of the vizier of knowledge—with all sorts of expression, and from it He brought into existence the monastery of the senses.

It is said that when this composite makeup and hollow individual gained measure and worth, he gained it through intellect and knowledge. The Adamite's worth lies in intellect and his beauty in knowledge.

"When God created the intellect, He said to it, 'Stand,' so it stood. Then He said, 'Sit,' so it sat. Then He said, 'Turn back,' so it turned back. Then He said, 'Turn forward,' so it turned forward. Then He said, 'By My exaltation and majesty, I have not created a creature more beloved to Me or

more honored by Me than you. With you shall be taken, with you shall be given, and with you shall I be recognized. Through you will be the reward and by you will be the punishment."[132]

He created this individual's forehead like a bar of pure silver. He strung his two bow-like eyebrows with pure musk. He deposited two dots of light into two figures of darkness. He made a hundred thousand red roses grow up in the meadow of his two cheeks' garden. He concealed thirty-two pearls in the oyster of his mouth, which He sealed with glistening agate. He created twenty-eight mansions from the beginning of his lips to the end of his throat, and in each He composed a star from among the letters. From his heart He brought a sultan into existence, from his breast a parade ground, from his aspiration a fleet-footed mount, from his thoughts a swift messenger. He created two taking hands and two running feet. He made apparent a hundred thousand fine points of wisdom and realities of artisanry. At the top of the register of his creation He wrote, *"So blessed is God, the most beautiful of creators!"* [23:14].

What is meant by these auspicious expressions and flashing allusions is that the Adamite is a handful of dust; everything beyond that is the Lord's gentleness. He bestows upon you because of His generosity, not your merit. He gives because of His munificence, not your prostration. He gives because of His bounty, not your intellect. He gives because of His Godhood, not because you are the housemaster. *Solicitude comes before water and clay.*

The Real created the whole cosmos, but He gazed on no creature with love, He sent no messenger to any existent thing, and He gave no message to any created thing. When it was the turn of the Adamites—who were pulled up by gentleness, caressed by bounty, and made quarries of lights and secrets—the gentleness of the Possessor of Majesty made them the locus of His gaze and sent 124,000 prophets to them. Night and day, He set over them the angels of the Dominion as watchers and couriers and He commanded them to protect them breath-by-breath, moment-by-moment, instant-by-instant, movement-by-movement. He put burning in their breasts and love in their hearts. One after another He sent incitements to yearning and motivations to desire. He conveyed pure revelation from the pure Unseen to their secret cores without the intermediary of mortal man.

Although the messengerhood of the prophets was sealed by Muḥammad, the awareness of hearts is the effect of the messengers' messengerhood. Although the carpet of the messengers' invitation was rolled up, burning in the breasts is the vicegerent of the prophets' invitation. To the outer realms He talks with the intermediary of the messengers, and to the inner realms without intermediary. He has no secrets with any created thing in the universe, whether Throne, Footstool, angels, or spheres, because all of them are servants. He does have secrets with the Adamites, because they are friends. The secret enters the heart when the heart is pure, for it receives food from the Exalted Presence Itself, not taking nourishment from strangers. If it goes, it travels by the command, and if it eats, it eats by the command.

A weak bee that travels by the command and eats by the command becomes the locus of revelation: *Thy Lord revealed to the bee* [16:68]. Muṣṭafā said, *"You should partake of the two healings: honey and the Quran."*[133] Look at the degree given to the leftover of a fly's food, the vomit of a bee's nature! Outward selves are healed by honey, and inward selves are healed by the Clear Quran. The bee with its tiny makeup has the high aspiration to come down only in pure places. Seek its aspiration as your companion!

He said that you should give your hands over to conformity and companionship with the Eternal Quran. This lowly bee traveled by the command and took nourishment by the command; it ate the pure and put down the pure. Once the produce of its makeup separated from it, it became the healing of the ill. In the same way, when a thought comes forth from the heart's secret core to a sincerely truthful man of realization, and when that man has gone forth according to the command and received the nourishment of the heart from a pure place while confining his aspiration to purity, then the pure thought that comes forth from him will be the cause of the healing of those ill on the road and the guide of those bewildered at the Threshold.

Abraham, the All-Merciful's bosom friend, breathed a breath from a penitent heart and said, *"The praise belongs to God before anyone else."* The seven heavens, the seven earths, and everything in between became the container of this one sentence. Then he said, *"The praise belongs to God after anyone else."* In calculating the wage for this sentence, the angels of the celestial and terrestrial dominions took pens into their generous hands and wrote for a few thousand years, but its wage was still more. Then he said, *"The praise belongs to God in every state."*

They said, "O God, what do You command concerning this sentence? What should we do and what should we write?"

The command came, "Creation is drowned in it. Nothing but My majestic bounty and My perfect knowledge can encompass this sentence. Go back to your hallowing and magnifying, for I know what must be done with this sentence and Abraham's heart." [134]

O genuine man of *the creed* of *your father Abraham* [22:78]. He is the father of your religion. Your heart should be like his heart, for you dwell on a branch of his submission. Then, when this sentence appears from you, it will be both healing for pain and loyalty to the covenant.

14. *al-Khāliq:* the Creator

The meaning of creator is the one who makes appear from nonexistence and who brings into being from nonbeing. Some say it means form-giver. What is correct is that to create means to devise [*ikhtirāʿ*], and other meanings are metaphorical.[135]

When the faithful servant believes that the Creator is the Lord, that perfect power belongs to Him, and that mortal nature is the locus of incapacity and the wherewithal of weakness, he will pull back his skirt from created things, tear his heart away from known and delineated things, and trust in the Lord of Lords. The truthfulness of servanthood will then become apparent in the annihilation of looking at mortal nature and in the severance of settling down with creatures. The servant's intimate will be God and his session will be at God's threshold. He will have no road to anyone, nor will anyone have a road to him. At all times he will be in the place of seclusion, his head in prostration, his secret core in witnessing, his heart in finding, and his spirit on the carpet of munificence contemplating the Object of worship.

I confided to You in my heart,
while sitting with my companion.
My body's my companion's intimate,
my heart is my Beloved's.[136]

So also when the faithful servant knows that the Real is the Creator and that he himself is the created, he must acquiesce to the Creator's decree and surrender to His command, for the created thing has no protest against the Creator, nor any way to turn away from Him.

An exalted man was asked, *"What is servanthood?"*

He said, *"Turning away from protest"*[137]—putting aside protest, bringing forth approval of the decree, chewing the poison of the decree with the teeth of surrender, and not bringing any knots to the brow.

I love you, O sun and full moon of time,
even if dull and bright stars blame me for that,
For your excellence is dazzling,
not that living with you is easy.[138]

O chevalier, being a servant is a tremendous work! That accursed one had servanthood for seven hundred thousand years, but he was not able to be a servant for one instant.

"Servanthood is to abandon free choice in all the apportionings that appear."[139]

"Servanthood is to abandon self-governance and to witness predetermination."[140]

"Servanthood is to be His servant in every state, just as He is your Lord in every state."[141]

"Servanthood is to witness lordhood."[142]

"Servanthood lies in four traits: loyalty to covenants, preserving limits, approval of what exists, and patience in what has been lost."[143]

"Servanthood is to throw away the seeing of one's worshipfulness in the contemplation of the Worshiped."[144]

"Servanthood is to abandon occupations and to be occupied with the occupation that is the root of detachment."[145]

"Servanthood is complying beautifully and abandoning demands."[146]

"Servanthood is to do what you must do and to give thanks for all that you have."[147]

"Servanthood is extinction by abandoning free choice in the decree's flow and the apportionings' alterations."

Thus has it been said,

His turnings flow over you
while He looks askance at your concerns.[148]

*

If you want, kill me, or drive me away, or keep me.
All my reckoning with You is of one sort.

Another exalted man said,

I have no share in other than You,
so test me as You wish.[149]

In the flow of the apportionings you must pull the thorn of free choice from your traveling feet. To reach the station of servanthood, you must lop off the head of the portion-seeking soul's evil, be extinguished beneath the millwheel of the troubling flow of the decrees, and wash your hands of mortal governance in the midst of the alterations of the Lord's predetermination. In certitude and verification, His servant is he who is pure of portions and quit of free choice and desire.

My paragon, Shaykh al-Islām[150]—God hallow his spirit—used to say, "In this world there are a hundred thousand servants of the All-Provider, servants of the Bestower, and servants of the Ever-Merciful, but you will never see one servant of God [*ʿabdallāh*]." He did not mean that you will see no one named ʿAbdallāh, for there are many ʿAbdallāhs. But, in reality, the servant is he who is pure of portions. When someone worships Him for the portion, he is a servant of the portion, not a servant of God.

It was also my paragon who used to say—and indeed, these are the words of Pir Bū ʿAlī Siyāh—"If you are asked, 'Do you want paradise, or two cycles of prayer?' do not choose paradise. Choose the two cycles of prayer, for paradise is your portion, and prayer is His rightful due. Whenever your portion is in the midst—even if it is a generous bestowal upon you—it may become a deceiving ambush. Your own portion is full of deception and mischief, but performance of the rightful due has no mischief or deception."

When Moses—the speaking companion of the Presence, the honored at the Exalted Threshold—came to the Mount, in his hand he had a staff, a piece of wood without deception or mischief. As soon as He was addressed by the All-Compelling, *"And what is that in thy right hand, O Moses?"* [20:17], he said, *"It is my staff"* [20:18]. As soon as it became evident that he claimed a portion, the staff became a serpent and turned its face toward him. Thus you may know that whenever you claim to have a portion of something, your claim will bring forth discord, turmoil, tumult, and trial.

In the same way at the time of Noah the whole world was safe in outward appearance, without turmoil or agitation. As soon as Noah appeared while making claims—*"Surely my son is one of my folk"* [11:45]—the world was thrown into turmoil: black water was brought up from the world and the storm was sent. What was that? It was the blight of laying claim to his own child. As soon as Noah's child was destroyed, as reported by the text of the Book—*"And the waves came between the two"* [11:43]—the address came, *"O earth, swallow thy water, and O heaven, hold back!"* [11:44]. O heaven, hold back the water, and O earth, drink down the water, for taking care of the Lord's secret is complete.

In the same way, the Bosom Friend gazed at Ishmael. The command came, "Kill Ishmael!" When the Bosom Friend detached his heart, took the knife in hand, and laid Ishmael out like a sheep, a call arrived from the Unseen, and what was intended was achieved.

So also when Moses came close to Khiḍr, he protested twice, first on behalf of the boy and second because of the breaking of the ship. Since no portion was in the midst, Khiḍr showed patience. But when Moses was moved by his own portion—*"Had you wanted, you could have taken a wage for it"* [18:77]—he said, *"This is separation between me and you* [18:78]. Now that your own portion has moved you, there is no way for me to continue as your companion."

When Moses protested because of the breaking of the ship, he was not moved because of his own portion. He did not fear the river, for at the beginning of the work he was thrown into the river so as to become familiar with it. "O Moses, today become familiar with the river so that tomorrow, when you reach the edge of the sea, the sea will give you a road into itself. Of its own makeup it will build a playing field for you so that within that field you may bring Pharaoh's prideful head into the curve of severity's mallet."

It was said to Moses's mother, *"If you fear for him, cast him into the river* [28:7]. When you fear for him because of the enemies, throw him into the river."

Well done, O cure of fear! "When you throw him into the river, We will command the river to be his nursemaid."

What a marvelous business! "A mother preserves her child from water and fire, but by Our command Moses's mother sometimes nurtured Moses in water and sometimes in fire: for *We revealed to Moses's mother, 'Suckle him, but if you fear for him, cast him into the river.'* Yes, when a sword is needed to take off the heads of enemies, sometimes it is passed over fire and sometimes over water. Being Pharaoh is a bad road, for it is to make the claim *'I am your lord the most high'* [79:24]. We made a sword from Moses's makeup and struck off the head of his claim."

The point is that when Moses protested [about the ship], he was not making reference to his own portion, nor when he protested about killing the boy. But in the third state, he came out for his own portion, so it was said to him, "There is no way to continue the companionship."

What a marvelous business! The deed of Khiḍr accorded with the rightful due, and the protest of Moses accorded with the rightful due: *"You have done a terrible thing"* [18:71]. What was that deed of Khiḍr, and what was that protest of Moses? Yes, Moses was acting by choice, but Khiḍr was acted upon. The drinking place of the former was one thing, and the drinking place of the latter another. The station of the former was one thing, and the station of the latter another. To the former was sent the Torah, adorned with commands and prohibitions, and in front of the latter was placed the Guarded Tablet of the unseen decrees. Moses was possessor of the Shariah, but Khiḍr was possessor of the Haqiqah. Moses gave news of the command, and Khiḍr gave marks of the decree. Their companionship did not turn out right, for the lords of the rules cannot put up with the lords of the unveilings.

Shaykh al-Islām used to say, "For thirty years a Sufi and a scholar were put into the same pot. Fire was lit, and the water boiled. When they were brought out, both were still raw."

The owners of the outward affairs do not recognize the owners of the inward affairs, but the owners of the inward affairs recognize the owners of the outward affairs. Moses did not recognize Khiḍr, so he asked to be his companion. Khiḍr recognized Moses, so he said, *"Surely you will not be able to bear patiently with me"* [18:67].

O chevalier, the commanded is one thing, the decreed something else. The position of the Folk of the Sunnah and Congregation is that it is indeed permitted for the commanded to be one thing and the decreed something else. What was commanded in the case of Abū Jahl, Abū Lahab, Pharaoh, and Nimrod was one thing, but what was decreed was something else. The command was coming, striking with the whip of the invitation, and the decree was coming, pulling back the reins. It is permitted for the servant's act to be different from what is commanded, but it is not permitted for it to be different from what is decreed.

All arguments rise up from the world of the command, and all excuses rise up from the world of the decree. When someone will be shown bounty, the command's tongue is silenced and the decree is allowed to speak. When someone will be shown justice, the decree's tongue is silenced and the command is allowed to speak. When you hear talk of mercy, that is nothing but His instructions to the army of His decree's authority. When you hear talk of punishment, that is nothing but His instructions to the army of the command.

When He wanted to raise Adam and put the crown of chosenness on his head, He brought His decree into words. When He wanted to blacken the face of Iblis with the smoke of the curse, He let His command do the talking: *"What prevented thee from prostrating thyself before him whom I created with My own two hands?"* [38:75]. Adam had not yet slipped when the tailor of gentleness sewed the waistcoat of repentance. Iblis had not yet disobeyed when the physician of severity mixed the draft of poison: *Upon thee shall be My curse* [38:78].

O chevalier, our position is neither compulsion nor free will. The free-willers want to take away *No god but God.* The compulsionists want to quarrel with *Muḥammad is God's Messenger. No god but God* negates the creed of free will, and *Muḥammad is God's Messenger* erases the slate of compulsion.

Faith is not put right through destiny and decree; it is put right through attestation, speech, acquisition, and act. Then, when something goes back to lordhood, we accept it with veneration; when something goes back to servanthood, we confess our own incapacity.

Jaʿfar Ṣādiq was asked, *"Does God compel the servants in their acts?"*

He said, "He is more just than that He would compel them, then punish them."

It was said, "Then does He disregard them?"

He said, "He is more wise than that He would disregard them."[151]

His justice comes and gives the wherewithal of the compulsionists to the wind. His exaltedness, power, tremendousness, knowledge, and wisdom come and strike fire into the harvest of the madness of the folk of free will. The free-willers do not know the measure of His power and become deluded by their own selves. The compulsionists do not reach the end of His decree and become heedless of His justice.

The compulsionists say, "He does all of it." The free-willers say, "We do all of it." The folk of the Sunnah say, "What He does, we do not do, and what we do, He does not do. He is greater than that He should do what we do, and we are more incapable than that we should do what He does."

15. *al-Bāriʾ:* the Maker

The meaning of maker is creator, about which has been spoken.

When the faithful *tawḥīd*-voicer believes that the Creator is the Lord, he gains deliverance from the pit of eye-service and escapes from the dark veil of self-admiration, for it is absurd to serve the eyes of others with deeds. The servant has acquisition,[152] but it is created by the Lord. How can a man serve eyes when he has wind in his hands?

When the wayfaring man rolls back the carpet of eye-service and lifts up the veil of self-admiration, he reaches the garden of sincerity and the orchard of the Haqiqah. For as they say, *"Sincerity is to be wary of glancing at creatures [and truthfulness is to be cleansed of observing the soul], so the sincere man has no eye-service and the truthful man has no self-admiration."*[153] Sincerity is to remove the creatures from the road, and truthfulness is to lift yourself out from the midst.

Once you have reached this station, traversed these two man-eating deserts, and flown with the wings of struggle and hardship in the space of contemplation and unveiling, eye-service will have no shine with you and self-admiration no worth. When you lift up the veil of self-admiration and raise the banner of truthfulness in the world of love, no veil will remain for you at the Threshold. *Unveiling upon unveiling, contemplation upon contemplation, gentleness upon gentleness, beholding upon beholding, presence upon presence, delight upon delight, light upon light, joy upon joy, prosperity upon prosperity, union upon union, bestowal upon bestowal, bounteousness upon bounteousness, veneration upon veneration*—all of this will become evident.

The veil belongs to the non-privy. When someone becomes privy, the veil is removed. Someone is privy when he washes the pollution of outsiderness from his makeup. So long as you do not totally wash the pollution of outsiderness from your own makeup, you will not reach the world of proximity, for your proximity with Him lies in your distance from you. In this station the least mark of realizing proximity and truthfulness is continuity in self-guarding and self-watching.

It is told in the stories that a shaykh singled out one of his disciples by welcoming and caressing him. The other disciples asked about this, and the pir wanted to answer them in practice. He placed a bird in the hand of each and said, "Kill this bird where no one will see you." They went to secluded places, killed the birds, and brought them back to him. The youth who had been singled out for the pir's welcome brought back the bird alive. He said, "Why did you not kill it like your companions?"

The youth said, "You commanded me to kill the bird where no one saw. I did not find a place outside the gaze and sight of the Real."

The pir said, "The cause of his priority and being singled out is that you are dominated by talk of creation, but he is dominated by talk of the Real."[154]

Then, when a man reaches proximity, if his gaze falls on proximity in the midst of proximity itself, he will immediately be tried by distance, for *"Seeing proximity is a veil of proximity."*[155] Seeing is itself the veil of proximity. This is why the exalted ones have said, *"May God alienate you from your own proximity!"*[156] May God alienate you from your proximity—that is, your seeing and gazing upon proximity—and give you aversion to it.

In reality whenever a traveler affirms and sees for himself that he has one iota of status, level, place, and rank, he has fallen into deception and dwells in the world of distance. Do you not see that the angels of the Dominion and the residents of the Holy Palisades looked upon their own deeds with the eyes of approval and pleasure? They said, *"We glorify Thy praise and call Thee holy"* [2:30]. The ruling power of the command came from the World of the Desire and said, *"Prostrate yourselves before Adam!"* [2:34]. Prostrate yourselves before this handful of clay so that the worth of prostration may disappear from your eyes.

What a marvelous business! He commanded the angels to turn their faces toward dust, and He said to the Adamites, "Turn your faces toward a stone!" What is this? This is to show the worth and level of deeds.

He said to Moses, *"But look at the mountain"* [7:143]. Look at the mountain, for *the mountain is a stone, and you are a clod.* Stones are worthy of clods, and clods are worthy of stones.

When He gives vision tomorrow, He will give it as a bestowal, not because of worthiness. No eye is worthy of seeing Him, no ear is worthy of hearing His speech, no intellect is worthy of recognizing Him, and no foot is worthy of His road.

My eyes want only Your vision;
 my ears want only Your speech—
Both have high aspiration,
 but neither is worthy of You.[157]

*

Where in the earth can I seek union with You?
 You are a king for whom no one can aim.[158]

No matter who may be seeking Him, until he gauges his own weightlessness in the scales of worthlessness, his seeking will not be put right. They have said, *"None are suited for this Tariqah but a people with whose spirits God sweeps the garbage dumps."*[159] They have also said, *"The spirits of this group were presented to the dogs of the garbage dumps, but no dog looked at them."*[160]

Shiblī said, *"My abasement has suspended the abasement of the Jews."*[161] My lowliness has left no lowliness for Jews.

Abū Sulaymān Dārānī said, *"Anyone who sees worth in himself will not taste the sweetness of service."*[162] If someone sees worth in his own deeds, states, and words, the sweetness of obedience will never reach the taste buds of his present moment.

Shuʿayb ibn Ḥarb said, "I was in the place of circumambulation when someone came from behind me and pulled me back. I looked and saw Fuḍayl ibn ʿIyāḍ. He said to me, *'O Abū Ṣāliḥ, if you suppose that this season has witnessed anyone worse than me and you, how bad is your supposition!'* "[163]

It is also Fuḍayl who said, "Were it not for the inauspiciousness of my presence, one could hope that the folk of the standing place would be forgiven." [164]

There's no one more worthless than I in the city—
 no mother gave birth to a son more lowly.[165]

Whenever anyone reaches the edge of the carpet of the Lord's exaltedness, his claims all come to an end, his wherewithal falls apart, his beautiful deeds all take on the color of slips and ugly deeds, and his obedient acts all become no different from disobedient acts. Even if he is the most eloquent man in the world, he becomes dumb. Even if he is the most knowledgeable man in the world, he becomes ignorant. Even if he is a traveling wayfarer, he becomes lame.

In the World of Unneediness the ruling power of His majesty conveys this call to the hearing of the elect and the common: "In My tremendousness your existence is like nonexistence! In My power your nonexistence is like existence! When you gaze on My tremendousness and exaltedness, you will ascribe all existent things to nonexistence. When you cast your eyes on My power, strength, innovating, and devising, you will consider all nonexistent things to be existent. Nothing was added to My power when I gave you existence, and nothing will be taken away from My tremendousness if I take you to nonexistence. If I want, in an instant I will create a hundred thousand like Muḥammad, and at each of their breaths I will take them to the station of *two-bows' length away* [53:9], and not one iota will be added to My majesty. If I want, in one moment I will create a hundred thousand like Pharaoh so that they may claim, *'I am your lord the most high'* [79:24] and quit themselves of servanthood to Me, and not one iota will be diminished from My perfection and beauty. If everyone on the face of the earth were a denying, obstinate unbeliever and I were to drown them in the ocean of My mercy and make their refuge the garden of paradise, not one iota would be diminished from the attribute of My severity. And if I were to pull every prophet, friend, and sincerely truthful person in the world by the chain of severity and keep them in painful chastisement forever and ever, that would not cause one iota of loss to the attribute of My mercy.

"There where the mark of My power shows forth and the banner of My tremendousness is raised and the elevated flag of My all-compellingness flies, what weight have the things given being, the formed things, the predetermined things, the created things, the existent things? O Seraphiel, take the Trumpet in your mouth and busy yourself with the forms! O Michael, take care of the storehouses of provision! O Gabriel, convey the gifts and bestowals of the secrets to the prophets and messengers! O Azrael, seize the spirits, for I have made a sown field appear in the meadow of this world and placed a scythe of severity and a cup of poison in your hand. With this scythe of severity harvest every plant that lifts up its head in this meadow!

"O Riḍwān, adorn the garden of gentleness! O Mālik, polish the mirror of the house of severity! O sun, go from East to West! O moon, stroll across this bright rose garden! O Adamites, look sometimes at heaven, sometimes at earth—*Have they not gazed on the dominion of the heavens and the earth?* [7:185]—sometimes at the Kaabah, sometimes at Jerusalem, sometimes at Moses, sometimes at Jesus, and sometimes at Muḥammad!"

The Real is solitary in His majesty, without end and without beginning. All this busyness comes from His exaltedness. If He needed anything at all, He would not have made each tiny thing busy with other tiny things. He is showing you that whether or not you come, it's the same.

Her face had itself as a moon;
her eye had itself as collyrium.[166]

He said to the angels, "Circle around the Throne, ask forgiveness, say the rosary of glorification, and recite *tawḥīd*. Say *'Glory be to God and the praise belongs to God.'* "

He said to the Adamites, "Circumambulate the Kaabah: *Circumambulate the Ancient House* [22:29]. Run between Safa and Marwah: *Surely Safa and Marwah are among the rites of God* [2:158]."

He tied each thing back to what is fitting, but in the place that is fitting for the Real, all things turn into nothing.

The aeon is but alteration and apportionment.
Pull back your reins—there's no one in the house.

A man sent his child to grammar school. When he came back at night, his father asked him what the teacher had taught him. He said, "He taught us that *alif* has nothing at all." [167]

This talk appeared in the attribute of exaltedness from the World of the Unseen Unity. It will stay seven thousand years[168] in the world of exile, and it will go back again in the cape of exaltedness without anyone ever having done it justice.

The master Abū ʿAlī was asked, *"What is servanthood?"*

He said, "A debtor whose debt will never be paid and an exile whose rightful due will never be performed."

O dervish, the perfection of the beauty of sultans is their own majesty. *No one carries the loads of kings but the steeds of kings, and no one carries the Real but the Real.*

Bring what pulls together the hearts of the friends!
Like a crocodile let it pull sorrow from my heart!
Bring the son of the Magi, turn him over to the Magian elder,
for only Rostam's Rakhsh can carry Rostam.[169]

A mouthful has come that is not fit for your craw. The mouthful is that of elephants, and the craw that of sparrows. You have been brought into a tremendous road. The whole world is bewildered because of the command, "Seek Me!"

Man is so incapable that the Quran says, *"If a fly steals something from them, they cannot retrieve it"* [22:73]. If a man cannot bring to hand something snatched away by a fly, how can he bring to hand the majesty of the Beginningless? Nonetheless, in the measure of your capacity and strength, expend your effort, and He, from His world, will straighten your work.

Know that in reality this world and that world are both for the sake of seeking. If someone says that the next world is not a world of seeking, that is absurd. True, there will be no prayer and no fasting, but there will be seeking. Tomorrow all the shariahs will be scratched out by the pen of abrogation, but two things will remain forever and without end: *love for God and praise for God.* These will have no severance, dissolution, or elapsing. It is fitting for prayer, fasting, hajj, and struggle to come to an end, but it is not fitting for seeking to come to an end. It is permissible for prayer and fasting to be abrogated, but it is not fitting for the pact of love and the covenant of passion to be abrogated.

O dervish, in reality, you should believe that if you go to paradise, every passing day will open you up to a world of recognizing the Real that was not there before. This is a work that will never come to an end, and may it never come to an end!

As long as I live, this will be my craft and work,
this will be my ease, settledness, and dispeller of grief.
This will be my day, this will be my time—
I will be seeking the prey, and this will be my hunt.[170]

The seeking of these Men has no cause that it might disappear by a cause. If seeking, yearning, and love disappeared through contemplation, they would have a cause. If they had a cause, they would lie within a veil, and if they were veiled, they would be rejected.

This seeking was put there by Him at first and will be given by Him at last. You are put into the midst of the journey and given by Him. The beginningless is what He put, and the endless is what He gives. You are one of the travelers put by Him and given by Him. First you were put there without a cause, and last He will give to you without a cause.

What is my stratagem? The apportionings do as commanded,
the people between lost and righteous.[171]

*

When they drove him into the desert of causes,
they took care of his work without cause.
They threw in today as a pretext—
they set up tomorrow yesterday.[172]

16. *al-Muṣawwir:* the Form-Giver

The Persian for form-giver is maker of forms. *God says, "And He formed you, so He made your forms beautiful"* [40:64]. The Lord says, "I painted your form, and I painted it beautifully."

May no man's evil eye reach your days!
May the evil eye stay far away, for you are very beautiful.

O chevalier, He raised up the seven green domes, spread out the seven dusty circles, and set up the unshakable mountains. From the concealment of nonexistence He brought a hundred thousand marvels of artisanry into the world of existence. He made the world-adorning sun a sphere, He formed the heaven-traversing moon, and He illumined the realm of being with their beauty. But He did not address any existent thing with the words *"He made your forms beautiful,"* nor did He bestow its eminence on any created thing except this handful of dust. Yes, *the solicitude of the judge is better than two just witnesses.*[173]

He who compared your eye to a narcissus fell short in description. Who ever saw a seeing narcissus? He who compared your eyebrow to a bow knew nothing. Who ever saw an arrow whose bow was an eyebrow? He who compared your tresses and face to jet and ivory was ignorant. Who ever saw heart-stealing jet and tumult-inciting ivory? He who compared your eyelashes to arrows was mistaken. Who ever saw a blood-drinking arrow? He who compared your stature to a cypress was not thinking. Who ever saw a strolling cypress? He who compared your cheek to the moon was in error. Who ever saw a moon in heaven like your face?[174]

Put aside talk of love and be straight with me—
is it not unbelief to describe someone like that like this?[175]

"Surely We created man in the most beautiful stature" [95:4]. *"So blessed is God, the most beautiful of creators!"* [23:14].

O chevalier, many there are who paint forms, but no one can paint pictures on water, wind, dust, and fire!

O dervish, all of this generosity lies in your creation's robe. At the root of creation everyone is the same as you. Do not bind your heart to saying that the eminence of this creation is here one day, gone the next—do not believe that. Think carefully about the gentle gifts of compassion that He explains in these words: *"He loves them and they love Him"* [5:54]. *"God is the friend of those who have faith"* [2:257]. *"Their Lord will give them to drink"* [76:21]. Did He give any proximate angel or any composite form such bestowals of eminence? Did He confer this robe of honor on any of them? No. This is the garb on the stature of Adam's worth—that lion-livered, foe-smashing, firm-footed man.

> One city and everyone talks of that beautiful face—
> all the world's hearts are captive to her.
> I try hard and others try too—
> whose hand will she take, whose friend will she be?

*

> *God clothed him in the garb of elevation—*
> *not too long and not too short.*[176]

*

> Of all the beauties and lovelies of the army,
> you alone are fit for belt and cap.

Yes, the angels are proximate, sinless, pure, hallowing, glorifying, and spiritual, but the work of water and clay is something else.

> *Not every water is like the first that flows forth,*
> *nor is every planting good for pasture.*[177]

The Shaykh al-Islam my father said, "In the hand of this handful of dust He put a bow that could not be strung by Gabriel and Michael. Wherever the shadow of the Adamite's good fortune falls, no one dares to claim priority. *Kings, when they enter a town, work corruption there* [27:34]."

There were luminous individuals and celestial figures in the meadow of hallowing, grazing on the jasmine of glorification and flying with the wings of prosperity in the space of bounteousness. When the sun of Adam's majesty lifted its head in the constellation of beauty, the angels of the Dominion were commanded to prostrate themselves before the chair of his leadership. When they lifted their heads, they saw that their own teacher had been deformed and the bond of his obedience abolished: "O accursed and tempted one, it is not that the beauty of Adam's days had any need for your prostration. Rather your refusal itself is My argument for driving you from the threshold of My generosity."

The angels were the exalted ones of the Presence. Each was wearing a shirt of sinlessness with a girdle of obedience, performing acts of worship without blight. *They do not disobey God in what He commands them* [66:6]. When the turn of Adam's good fortune arrived and the drum of exaltedness was beaten with the strap of his sultanate's majesty, a quaking fell into their spirits and they called out from their obedience, *"What, wilt Thou set therein one who will work corruption there?"* [2:30]. Yes, they were looking at the outward things, and the Real was looking at the secrets. They were looking at the opacity, and the Real was looking at the gentleness of the lordhood. They were looking at the outer defilement, and the Real was looking at the inner adornment.

He answered them by saying, *"Surely I know what you do not know* [2:30]. I know what I know in your midst, and I also know what is in their midst. In your midst there is someone like Iblis, who has pulled the mask of scheming over his face and is wearing the tunic of thieves, on top of which he has put on the patched cloak of the renunciants. In their midst there is someone like Muḥammad, who in the world of acceptance is like Iblis in the world of rejection. Wherever there are prayers of blessing, they are for Muḥammad, and wherever there are curses, they are for Iblis."

Yes, when that accursed fellow's life span was extended to the outskirts of the resurrection, it was not to bestow eminence on him. The divine goal was that every child who lifted up a stone would throw a curse at his head.

O chevalier, when the angels said, *"What, wilt Thou set therein?"* the Real did not say that they would not work corruption. He said, *"Surely I know what you do not know.* You have no awareness of the secrets of Our divinity, and you have no cognizance of the gentle gifts of Our lordhood toward Adam and the Adamites."

The slanderers do not diminish your rank
with me, nor do the backbiters harm you.
It's as if they praise you unwittingly
with all the faults that they find.[178]

"Surely I know what you do not know. If they are unworthy, I will make them worthy. If they are far, I will bring them near. If they are abased, I will make them exalted. You see their outward disloyalty, but I see their inward loyalty. You gaze on the opposition of their limbs and bodily parts, but I gaze on the conformity of their hearts and ribs. You wear the waistcoat of obedience, but they have donned the shirt of union. You have the robe of worship, but they have the cap of forgiveness. You have extended your hands in sinlessness, but they have extended their hands to My mercy. What weight has your sinlessness if I do not accept it? What harm has their disobedience if I pardon it?[179]

"Surely I know what you do not know. I know what you do not know, and what you know, I know even better. As for them, they are lifted up by beginningless gentleness and caressed by endless bounty. *Slips do not intrude upon the Endless."*

It is said that one day Abū Yazīd Basṭāmī was walking on a road when he heard the sound of a group of people. Wanting to know the state, he went forward and saw a child fallen into black mud, the people standing there watching. All of a sudden the child's mother ran out from a corner and threw herself into the mud. Pulling back the child, she went away. Abū Yazīd saw that and became happy. Shouting out he stood there and said, "Tenderness comes and takes away defilement! Love comes and takes away disobedience!"

Your excuses with Me are many,
and sins from the likes of you are ignored.
What displeases is not a man's acts—
everything he brings is displeasing.[180]

O chevalier, what is left that He did not do for us? Which robe of honor did He not bestow upon us? Which eminence did He not confer upon us? Which gentleness did He not record in our name in the register of generosity? Which exaltedness did He not send down to us? Which proximate angel did He not employ in our work? Which noble prophet did He not send to our corner? Which allusion did He not make for us? Which good news did He not give to us?

We are those caressed by His gentleness and pulled up by His compassion. We are recognizers because He gives us recognition, eminent by His bestowal of eminence, arrivers by His making us arrive, and joyful at union with Him. We are the narcissus of the meadow of munificence, the cypress in the garden of existence, the jewel box for the pearls of wisdom, and the blossom in the orchard of the World of Power, the light in its eye.

We are created things without likeness and peer, just as He is the Creator without likeness and peer. It is not allowed for us to have a likeness, nor for Him. *Nothing is as His likeness, and He is the Hearing, the Seeing* [42:11]. It is allowed for us to have likeness in respect of power, but not in respect of love's jealousy. Creating a hundred thousand like us in respect of power is allowed, but creating someone like us in respect of love is never allowed.

On the day He drew the circle of bringing to be around this person of clay, He made this address: "I will create someone the like of whom I have never created." It is not that He did not have the power to do so, but jealousy had taken hold of the reins of power. This was expressed like this: *"He fastened to them the word of godwariness, to which they have more right and of which they are worthy"* [48:26].

If someone says, "What right do you have at this threshold?" you should reply, "How is this the place for 'right'? Here there is talk of *more right.*"

"At every instant I can compound, arrange, form, and determine a thousand thousand like you, but I will not do so, for the mystery of unqualified love belongs specifically to you."

A man had a son whom he loved. They said to him, "How much do you love your son?"

He said, "Because of the love I have for him, I do not want another child, lest he have a partner in love."

The master Abū ʿAlī said, "God said about Adam, '*Surely God chose Adam and Noah*' [3:33]. He said about Abraham, *'God took Abraham as a bosom friend'* [4:125]. He said to Moses, *'I chose thee for Myself'* [20:41]. Then He said about this handful of dust, *'He loves them and they love Him'* [5:54]. *'God is the friend of those who have faith'* [2:257]. *'Their Lord will give them to drink of a pure wine'* [76:21]."

It was you who first drew the lot of love.[181]

Heaven and earth, the Throne and the Footstool, paradise and hell, the Tablet and the Pen—all are freeloaders on your existence.

"Every night God descends to the nearest heaven and says, 'Is there any supplicator?' "[182]

"He planted the tree of Ṭūbā with His hand."[183]

"He built the Garden of Eden with His hand."[184]

A hadith says: *"The All-Compelling will place His foot on the Fire and it will say, 'Enough! Enough!' "*[185]

"Curse not the aeon, for God is the aeon."[186]

The All-merciful sat on the Throne [20:5].

In the midst of all this, there is no declaration of likeness, resemblance, or similarity.

What was intended by these robes of honor was not in fact heaven and earth, the Throne and the Footstool, paradise and hell. Rather, the eternal decree had already been issued that you would be passing by these waystations and casting your glance on these places and stages. "In each waystation, We have placed a token of Our gentleness so that, when Our friends reach there, they will take their share and portion."

O chevaliers, grab hold of His beginningless solicitude—His precedent gentleness that always was, long before dust and clay. "O dust and clay, O you whose breast is the howdah for the veiled virgin of lights! O *molded mud* [15:26], O you whose friendship with Me increases every day! O *dried clay, like pottery* [55:14], O you the secret core of whose heart is the place for the covenant of union! O feeble sperm drop, O stone on the ring of love! O molded mud, O stuffed with the perfume of recognition! O made exalted, O both friend and servant! You should not suppose that Our work with you pertains to today or Our talk with you pertains to now. There was no world and no Adam, no substances and no accidents, no Throne and no Footstool, no paradise and no hell, no Tablet and no Pen—and I was talking to you without you."

> *How blessed were the days when we were in nonexistence itself*
> *and He was saying in His generosity, "O My servants!"* [39:53].

*

> *How blessed was the time of Your covenant, without which*
> *my heart would have had no place for ardor!*[187]

*

> *I offer myself as ransom to You, or rather, may all the days of my life*
> *be ransom for the days when I recognized You.*[188]

May a thousand thousand exalted spirits be sacrificed to that heart-caressing moment when we had a place of seclusion without us! For us He opened the door to boundless gentle gifts and conveyed His pure address to ears that had no control over listening. He asked questions on the part of Knowledge and answered on the part of Will. He made Knowledge like a questioner and Will the respondent. In the chamber of assembly He fed us the milk of chosenness, in the cradle of the covenant before exertion and effort He provided the food of gentle gifts, in the bond of the compact He took care of and attended to our work, and in the pure desert of listening He made us hear *"Am I not your Lord?"* [7:172]. It was He who asked and He who dictated the answer.

Suppose He had said, "Who am I?" All would have been mute and obliterated. They would have been bewildered in the station of stopping. Because of His beginningless gentleness, He said, *"Am I not your Lord?"* so that half would be the question, and half the dictation of the answer.

O dervish, we gain access to Him only through His eternal beautiful-doing.

Ḥasan ibn Sahl was the vizier of Ma'mūn. One day a man came to him whom he did not recognize. Turning to him Ḥasan said, "Who are you?"

He said, *"I am the one toward whom you acted beautifully in such and such a year."*

Ḥasan said, *"Welcome to the one who gained access to me through my acting beautifully!"* Then he commanded that the man be presented with gifts and caressed.[189]

The dervishes who seek the means of access to Him seek it by way of the eternal beautiful-doing.

Surely the beginning of kindness is a precedent splendor,
but the most splendorous splendor lies in completion.
The beauty of the crescent delights the eyes
but not like the beauty of the moon when it is full.[190]

They speak to Him like this: "O Nurturer, You planted the seed of guidance in our hearts with beginningless solicitude, You watered it with the messengerhood of the prophets, You made it grow with the help of success-giving, and You brought it to fruition with the gaze of Your own beautiful-doing. Now we request that You keep the drought of exaltedness away from it, You rouse not the simoom of severity against it, You blow not the winds of justice across it, and You assist the seed planted by beginningless solicitude with endless kind favor! Our fear is of You, and our hope is in You."

Sahl ibn ʿAbdallāh Tustarī said, *"Fear is masculine and hope is feminine, and from the two are born the realities of faith."* Fear and hope are mates. When they come together in companionship, the beauty of faith will show itself, for hope has the attribute of femininity and fear the attribute of masculinity. This is because the domination of hope gives rise to laziness and softness, attributes of the female; the domination of fear gives rise to briskness and toughness, attributes of the male; and faith subsists through the subsistence of these two meanings. When these two meanings disappear, the result will be either security or despair, both of which are attributes of unbelievers. People feel secure from those who are incapable, but to believe that He has the attribute of incapability is unbelief. People despair of the vile, but to believe that He has the attribute of vileness is associationism. One must prepare a confection and make an electuary combining hope and fear.

Indeed, when a lamp has no oil, it gives off no brightness. When there is oil but no fire, it gives off no illumination. When it has oil and fire but no wick to sacrifice its being to the fire's burning, the work will have no luster.

Fear is like the burning fire, hope like the replenishing oil, faith acts like a wick, and the heart has the shape of a lamp holder. If there is only fear, that is like a lamp that has fire but no oil. If there is only hope, that is like a lamp that has oil but no fire. When fear and hope come together, a lamp appears that has both the oil that is the aid of subsistence and the fire that is the stuff of illumination. When faith takes help from both—subsistence from the one and illumination from the other—the person of faith will travel with the escort of illumination and stride forth with the aid of subsistence.

17. *al-Ghaffār:* the All-Forgiving

The Lord is the All-Forgiving, the Forgiver [*ghāfir*], and the Forgiving [*ghafūr*]. *Ghaffār* is an intensive, like *ʿallām* [all-knowing].

To forgive means to cover. The Arabs call a helmet a *mighfar* because it covers the head. The Lord's forgiveness of His servants is that He covers them, curtains their sins, and pardons them. This curtaining and pardoning is through an excellence of God, not an excellence of the servants. Moreover, in verified truth, just as your disobedient acts need curtaining, so also your obedient acts need curtaining. If the blights of your obedient acts were brought forth, you would fear obedience more than disobedience.

Muṣṭafā said, *"Surely I ask forgiveness from God one hundred times a day."*[191] The skirt of prophecy was far too pure for the dust of disobedience and the dirt of slips to settle on it, so he asked forgiveness for his obedience.

Rābiʿa ʿAdawiyya often used to say, *"I ask forgiveness from God for my lack of sincerity in saying, 'I ask forgiveness from God.'"*[192]

ʿĀʾisha the sincerely truthful related as follows: "I asked Muḥammad the meaning of the verse *'Those who give what they give, their hearts quaking'* [23:60]. *Are they the ones who fornicate, steal, drink wine, and fear?*

"He said, 'No, they are the ones who pray, fast, give alms, and fear that these will not be accepted from them.'"[193]

O chevalier, there are two curtains. One has been lifted—and may it never be let down! The other has been let down—and may it never be lifted! The curtain that has been lifted is the veil of disavowal from the hearts of the *tawḥīd*-voicers and the breasts of the faithful. The curtain that has been let down is the curtain of generosity before the acts and deeds of the disobedient, the obedient, the sincerely truthful, the godwary, and the sincere.

O dervish, by the decree of the eternal severity, the curtain of generosity was lifted from the obedience of Iblis, and it all became disobedience. His knowledge was made deaf and dumb, and God's beginningless knowledge began to speak. By the decree of sheer gentleness, the curtain of pardon was let down before Adam's slip, and the decree of intercession loosed its tongue: *"But he forgot, and We found in him no resoluteness"* [20:115].

O dervish, it is because of His curtain that we say salaam to each other and pass our days together. *Refuge in God!* If He were to lift this curtain, fathers would first cut themselves off from their sons and mothers from their children.

> Were the curtain lifted from our work,
>   I fear they would not let us into the taverns.

I wonder at the empty-headed Quran-reciter who makes two cycles of prayer at night and the next day throws the knot of self-seeing on his forehead and lays the favor of his own being on heaven and earth. All the motes of existence say to him, "What a simpleton you are!"

It is here that they make a Kaabah into an idol temple, turn a 700,000-year worshiper into the forever accursed Satan, and bind Balaam son of Beor—who had God's greatest name in his breast and whose every prayer was answered—in a kennel for dogs.

> O clueless of the work of this passing world,
> you little drunkard—you know nothing of Me!

What is needed is a realizing man, not an unmanly Quran-reciter. Anyone who speaks about his own deeds and looks at them for a single day will not achieve what we are talking about. The unmanly Quran-reciter is he who performs two cycles of prayer at night and the next day wants the whole world to hear about it. As for the man of realization, he fills the East and the West with prostrations of sincerity and throws them into the water of unneediness.

An exalted man said, "I examined all my days, and in my whole life I had not committed more than forty sins. I repented of each sin three hundred thousand times, but I still walk in danger."

If you could attach nothing to yourself, that would be a beautiful deed.

Abu'l-Ḥasan Kharaqānī has some magnificent words. He said, "If tomorrow He raises me from the earth and makes all the creatures present in that standing place, I will go to the Ocean of Unity and dive in so that the One may be, and Abu'l-Ḥasan may not be."[194]

Strive to be angry with yourself for one day from morning to night and see what that day will bring! The men who came into this path fought a war against themselves, a war that had no way to peace, for they found that the soul is the opposite of the religion. How can a man of the religion make peace with its opposite?

Sometimes they described the soul as a dumb beast, sometimes as a serpent, sometimes as a dog, sometimes as a pig. Every picture they painted was correct—except the picture of the religion.

> O vile soul, lost and deluded—
> whatever touchstone I use, you come up false.

You must see all your obedient acts in the color of disobedience and count all your own meanings as empty claims. You must make your own spirit a broom for the garbage dumps and see mangy dogs as better than yourself. You must sweep the doorstep of the Guebres with your beautiful traits and walk a thousand thousand deserts of disappointment to the end. Otherwise you are simply a knocker on the door.

Dust must belong to dust and stay pure of all claims. God has men who, from the first day of their existence, placed their heads on the threshold of nonexistence with the attribute of poverty and indigence. They never lifted their heads from that threshold. They will rise up from the earth, come to the resurrection, pass over the Narrow Path, and go on to paradise without ever having lifted their heads.

O chevalier, in the daytime someone puts on clothes and comes to the market, and at night he goes back home and takes them off. But what can he do with his skin? If they put a thousand kingly crowns on your head and a thousand royal belts on your waist, what will you do with your own beggarly face and poverty-stricken color?

Tomorrow, the exalted ones who had news of these words will be made present in the private chamber of the elect. They will be given flagons of lordly gentleness one after another, and the breeze of union will blow against them from the direction of prosperity. But these exalted ones will be saying, "I am the same beggar I was on the first day."

O dervish, poverty, indigence, abasement, and lowliness are the root attributes of dust and clay. It is true that dust sits on the face and can be washed away with water, but water cannot take away the color of your face.

Yaḥyā Muʿādh Rāzī said, *"My proof is my need, my provision my indigence."*[195]

No gaze causes greater loss than one that rises up from you and falls back on you. Such a gaze is the foundation of all blights. As for the gaze that goes far from you, that is the foundation of every opening.

Sahl ibn ʿAbdallāh Tustarī said, *"I looked at this affair and saw no path nearer to God than poverty and no veil thicker than making claims."*[196] I looked at this affair, turning the eye of insight toward the realities, and found no road closer than need and no veil thicker than making claims.

Look at the road of Iblis and see nothing but claims. Look at the road of Adam and see nothing but need. O Iblis, what do you say? *"I am better than he"* [38:76]. O Adam, what do you say? *"Our Lord, we have wronged ourselves"* [7:23].

He brought all the existent things from the concealment of nonexistence into the space of the decree, but the plant of need grew only in dust. When this handful of dust was molded, it was molded with the water of need. It had everything, but it also had to have need so that it would never stop weeping at the Threshold.

Adam's makeup was molded with need, and he received help from need. He was made the object of the angels' prostration and placed on the throne of kingship and vicegerency. The proximate ones were made to stand before him, but his need did not decrease by one iota. He was taken to paradise, and this proclamation was given out: *"Eat thereof easefully, you two, wherever you want* [2:35]. The eight paradises belong to you; wander freely as you wish." But his poverty did not disappear.

By God the Tremendous, it was Adam's hand in which was placed the worth of paradise! Among all the existent things, there was no bride more comely than paradise, with her face so beautiful and her adornment so perfect. All at once the sultan of Adam's aspiration came down from the world of the unseen jealousy and placed her worth in the scales and her splendor in the pan. Paradise began to shout, "I cannot put up with this brazen man!"

O chevalier, if tomorrow you go to paradise and look at paradise from the corner of your heart's eye, in truth, in truth, you will have fallen short in the aspiration of Adamic nature. Something your father sold for one grain of wheat—why would you settle down there?

Adam said, "O Lord, what You have said—*'I am setting in the earth a vicegerent'* [2:30]—is correct. This great eminence derives from Your bounty. But our rightful due is this: *Our Lord, we have wronged ourselves* [7:23]. The royal seat of vicegerency is Your gift, but the just due of our makeup is *Our Lord, we have wronged ourselves."*

"O Adam, of all the blessings, why did you choose the grain of wheat?"

He replied, "Because I found the scent of need in it."

Adam was molded with need, and the wheat had the scent of need. He who was molded of need was brought together with the scent of need. This is why the stalk of wheat grew up in front of Adam's throne wherever it was placed—it had an affinity with his molding.

Wherever Adam went, need went along with him. Everlastingness, blessings, kingship, and good fortune came from paradise, but the station of chosenness, election, pain, and remorse came from the grain of wheat. The lovers' enjoyment of remorse is sweeter than kings' enjoyment of good fortune.

In paradise Adam was an exile, and that grain of wheat was also an exile. An exile gets along only with an exile.

You've given me refuge, for we're exiles here,
and every exile is kin to an exile.[197]

*

Mercy on the exile in the land!
A far traveler can do nothing for himself.
Having parted from his friends and gone,
they have no pleasure in him, and he none in them.[198]

O dervish, do you fancy that the unbelievers drove Muṣṭafā out of Mecca? No, it was this talk that brought him out. He was a man sitting safely in his homeland. Then the talk of exile came, took his hand, and drew him out of his homeland and lodging, giving him the attribute of an exile.

I'm an exile among the people of Bust,
though my clan and family live here.
It's not distance from home that exiles a man, by God,
it's failure to find someone of his own kind.[199]

Adam had two existences—the first existence and the second existence.

The first existence belonged to this world, not to paradise, and the second belonged to paradise. "O Adam, come out of paradise and go into this world. Lose your crown, belt, and hat in the road of love! Put up with pain and tribulation. Then tomorrow We will bring you back to this exalted homeland and this lodging place of subsistence with a hundred thousand robes of gentleness and every sort of honor in front of witnesses and in the assembly of the one hundred twenty-some thousand center-points of prophethood, the possessors of purity and sources of limpidness. Then the creatures will come to know that, just as We can take you out with the attribute of severity, so also We can bring you back with the attribute of gentleness."

Tomorrow Adam will go into paradise with his offspring. A cry will rise up from every speck of paradise because of the crowding. The angels of the Dominion will look with wonder and say, "Is this that solitary man who moved out of paradise a few days ago, penniless and empty-handed?"

"O Adam, bringing you out of paradise was a curtain over the work and a veil over the mysteries, for the loins of your good fortune were the ocean of the one hundred twenty-some thousand pearls of prophethood. Suffer a bit of trouble, then in a few days, take the treasure!"

"O Muḥammad, when We put the Meccans in charge of throwing you out of Mecca, We also commanded you to emigrate to Medina, put on the garment of exile, and go into the corner of remorse with Abū Ayyūb Anṣārī.[200] All this was making ready. The root goal was to bring you back to Mecca on the Day of the Conquest along with ten thousand sword-wielding, spear-throwing, armored warriors, *of whom only their eyes were seen*,[201] while the stalwarts of Quraysh and the headmen of the unbelievers stood by in wonder: 'Is this that man who fled?' "

God has a secret in your elevation—
your enemies' words are ravings.[202]

"O exalted spirit, you are the quarry of subtleness and the source of repose and comfort! It is We who sent you away from your homeland as an exile, made you the companion of the tumult-inciting soul, and imprisoned you in this dustbin. The goal was to call you back to Our Presence at the end of the work with a hundred thousand gentle robes, kindly gifts, and secret bestowals: *O serene soul, return to thy Lord, approving, approved!* [89:27–28].

"O Adam, though We sent you out of paradise in the company of the serpent and Iblis, We brought you back in the company of forgiveness and mercy and with the escort of good fortune and prosperity.

"O Muḥammad, though We brought you out of Mecca with the attribute of abasement, made you the witness of struggle, and kept you in the company of ʿAbdallāh ibn Ubayy ibn Salūl and the other unbelievers and hypocrites, We brought you back to Mecca in the company of conquest, victory, and triumph.

"O exalted spirit, though We have afflicted you for a few days with this dustbin, this domicile of grief, this house of separation's sorrows; and though We have kept you for a time in the company of this vile soul, in the end We will bring you back to the neighborhood of generous bestowal in the company of Our approval and with the escort of the exalted address, *'Return!'* "

18. *al-Qahhār:* the Severe

The Real is both *qāhir* and *qahhār. God says, "And He is the Severe* [*qāhir*] *over His servants"* [6:18]. *And He says, "the One, the Severe* [*qahhār*]*"* [12:39].

The meaning of severe is all-compelling, for He knows what He desires and wills, and He looks at no one's approval or anger.

I've been abased—how lovely the Abaser
who makes shedding my blood lawful!
When He exalts himself, I accept Him
with abasement—the effort of the destitute.[203]

He is severe toward whomsoever He wants, howsoever He wants.

It is told that one of the Abbasid caliphs had a slave who was the head of the army, and this slave had five thousand mercenaries. When the time for the caliph's death approached and the thread of his life was frayed, the days of his hope became dark. He commanded the pillars of the state and the great men of the court to come into his presence so as to swear allegiance to one of his sons. That slave was the leader of the army and stood by his head, while the caliph and the whole group were on a balcony. It so happened that the caliph looked at the slave, and the slave fancied that he had brought a sin into existence and that the gaze was a gaze of anger. In awe before that gaze he stepped back and fell off the balcony. He broke his neck and died, and at the same moment the caliph died. They put him in the house. When they came back, they saw that a rat had come and pulled out the eye with which he had gazed on that slave. *So glory be to Him who is severe to His servants with any of His creatures that He wants!*[204]

"O accursed Nimrod, O rejected and wretched! You filled the world with the trial of your recalcitrance, obstinacy, refusal, denial, and pride. Behold: We have sent a lame gnat to place your worth before you.

"O Pharaoh, O recalcitrant, obstinate, rebellious, defiant, full of claims, headstrong, self-seeing! You shout out, '*I am your lord the most high*' [79:24], and claim godhood. Behold: We have sent a piece of wood from Our Presence so that it may place the worth of your height and recalcitrance before you.

"O Bilqīs, you had a tremendous throne, boasted of your horse and chattel, lifted up the head of pride and haughtiness, and delighted in your kingdom and possessions! Behold: We sent a stinking, tiny hoopoe to recite the tablet of your incapacity and weakness.

"O kings of the world, you sit on the steed of boasting, drive the tent pegs of your all-compellingness into the eyes of the sun, the moon, and the Pleiades, and bring land and sea, sky and planets, under your severity! We assign a weak fly to you so that it may recite, with the tongue of its state, the edict of your incapacity, helplessness, and penury: *If a fly steals something from them, they cannot retrieve it. Feeble are the seeker and the sought!* [22:73].

"O Abraha, you aimed for Our House with your army on the back of mountainous, undulating animals, and you depended on your number, provisions, weapons, and instruments! We sent weak little birds from the treasury of severity to wreak havoc on you and set you afire: *And He sent against them birds in swarms, throwing at them stones of baked clay, and He made them like eaten husks* [105:3–5].

"O stalwarts of Quraysh and headmen of unbelief, you aimed for Our beloved, drove him from your homeland, and came after him with the thought of killing him, while Our friend went into the cave of jealousy with Abū Bakr! We sent a spider to be his policeman, to shut the hand of claims and falsities, and to drive against you the harshness of the Lord's severity."

What a marvelous business and rare story! "Sometimes We make a weak fly prey of a spider, and sometimes We bring Muḥammad—God's Messenger, the chieftain of the envoys and Seal of the Prophets—under a spider's protection. Yes, in Our road a spider engages in warfare, a gnat leads an army, a pigeon turns into a doorman, a lizard preaches, a wolf leads, an ant reminds, a stone glorifies, a dog becomes a passionate lover, a cave keeps secrets, a staff in the desert turns into a dragon, a river obeys commands, a fire becomes an intimate friend, and a living tree holds a torch."

O chevalier, the paragon was commanded to emigrate, and on the road he was concealed from the eyes of others in the cave of jealousy. God's messenger Muḥammad was the sun in the sphere of felicity and the Jupiter in the heaven of leadership. On occasion the sun undergoes eclipse, for *"The* [evil] *eye is real."*[205] With the hand of power, He binds a black mask over the face of the sun as a talisman.[206] Although the paragon's concealment in the cave had the form of an eclipse [*kusūf*], its meaning was unveilings [*kushūf*] upon unveilings.

"O paragon of the two worlds, the cave of jealousy must be honored by your feet, and that weak little animal must take rest in your beauty.

"And there is a burnt man who has been kept in the collar of slavery and the bonds of servitude. For two hundred years he has wandered in the synagogues and gone to the churches, hot and cold reaching his head, putting up with much suffering and tasting many poisons. His name is Salmān. That truthful Muslim will be at rest in your moonlike face and lunar form."

The point is that first statement: "The paragon was commanded to emigrate." Emigration has a form and a meaning, a shell and a kernel, an outwardness and an inwardness. The outwardness of emigration is departure, transferal, and exile from the homeland. The inwardness of emigration is to bid farewell to and repudiate all beings.

His outward emigration was temporary, but his inward emigration was constant. In the outward emigration the companion was Abū Bakr; in the inward emigration the companion was assent. In the outward emigration, the supplies were food and drink; in the inward emigration the nourishment was the gentleness of the Lord of Lords. In the outward emigration, the domicile was the cave; in the inward emigration the domicile was abandoning free choice and negating others. In the outward emigration the protector was a spider; in the inward emigration the protector was constancy and fixity. The outward emigration was from Mecca to Medina; the inward emigration was from the agitation of the tumult-inciting soul to the tranquility of the breast. The outward emigration was migrating away from homelands; the inward emigration was migrating away from the world of *"Be! and it was."* In the outward emigration there was the victory [*fatḥ*] at Badr; in the inward emigration there was the opening [*futūḥ*] of the breast. In the outward emigration there was the Battle of Uhud; in the inward emigration there was peace with the One [*aḥad*]. In the outward emigration there was the conquest of Khaybar; in the inward emigration there was the conquest of the greatest adversary's castle. In the outward emigration there was seeing Abū Ayyūb; in the inward emigration there was the elation and expansion of hearts. In the outward emigration the intimate was Anas; in the inward emigration the intimate was the Holy Presence. In the outward emigration the steed was a camel; in the inward emigration the steed was poverty and want. In the outward emigration there was seeing the folk of hypocrisy;

in the inward emigration there was stepping into the world of conformity. The outward emigration was for the Companions; the inward emigration was for all the troops of the lovers. The outward emigration was the mark of faith; the inward emigration was the indicator of security.

Where is a man alone, solitary, disengaged, one in aspiration, one in striding forth, one in thought?

Isolated from friends in every land—
the greater the sought, the fewer the helpers.[207]

Being's realm put on the garment of war with him and drew the sword of judgment. He put the chainmail of stoutheartedness on his breast and the helmet of manliness on his head. In safety he packed his bags from the homeland of free choice and left Mecca, which was *the first earth whose dust touched my skin.*[208]

Camels, despite their thick livers, yearn for their watering holes, and birds traverse the breadth of the earth to their places.[209]

He left his domicile and homeland and, like a paragon, sat on the camel of poverty and indigence in the company of [Abū Bakr,] the sincerely truthful in assent, the kind companion of success-giving, and the friend of realization, aiming for the cave of jealousy, the domicile of bewilderment, the fount of limpidness, the dome of proximity, and the pavilion of exaltedness. This call was conveyed without mortal intermediary from the World of the Unseen to the ear of his love's togetherness: *"He is with you wherever you are"* [57:4].

There is no whispering among three but that He is the fourth of them, nor among five, but that He is the sixth of them [58:7]. O chevalier, look at the bestowal of eminence in the case of Muṣṭafā's community. In the story of the Companions of the Cave He said, *"The sixth of them was their dog"* [18:22]. In the case of this community, He said, *"The sixth of them* is their Lord."

O gentleness that has no end and O generosity that has no limit!

It has been narrated that the Lord gave existence to the Pen so that it would be the housemaster of the endless mystery, the exegete of the beginningless secret, and the auditor of the decree's ruling power. Yes, O chevalier, this is a marvelous reed! It brought its head up from the earth, raised the hands of its leaves in prayerful need, put on the robe of the wide-eyed houris, and bound its waist in ten places, *tube above tube, as if it were about to melt in its love.* O reed, what are all these waists? With the tongue of its state it sings this lover's song from the pulpit of *tawḥīd*:

Your command came and I jumped from my place—
You kept on commanding and I kept on girding my waist.

This is the rightful due of His command when it comes to us. One must go forth in this way to the command of the sultan.

That wonderful reed poked up its head from the earth in the robe of brides. For a time it stayed in the freshness of beginning, the robe of green, the adornment of the gentleness of the Presence. Breezes of the wind [*rīḥ*]—which is the friend of the spirit [*rūḥ*]—blew from every side. The north wind made amorous glances. The morning breeze—the boon companion of the folk of youthful fervor—leaped against it. Finally the simoom of severity began to charge forth from the world of the Unseen Majesty, tearing that green robe from its sides, throwing that lovely crown from its head, and cutting it off from its roots with severity's sword.

At dawn morning separates us—
which bliss is not darkened by time?[210]

For a time it is thrown down in the summer sun so that it will dry and leave behind being's dampness and wetness. After that, the scribe wants to make manifest the secrets of consciousness hidden behind the curtains of thought. He takes a sharp knife and cuts off the reed's head. He strikes the unhesitating knife on its crown and cuts it into two halves, making of it a courier without burden. At each moment he puts it into the inkwell, within which is the remedy of wounded hearts, and he blackens its face. With the tongue of its state it says, "Though I'm miserable, ill, wounded, and at work night and day, it may be that when they first write with me, they will write the name of the Friend: *'In the name of God, the All-Merciful, the Ever-Merciful.'* "

The only profit I take now is my eyes' tears,
my life worn down by emigration's grief.

The point is this: When the Pen passed over the Tablet and recorded the secrets of the Beginningless, it wrote down the acts of obedience and disobedience of the communities. When the work reached the deeds of this community, the Pen recorded so many offenses, faults, sins, and slips that it broke in shame. The address came, "O Pen, write: *'A sinful community and a forgiving Lord!'* "[211]

If you do a beautiful deed, that's in your hand.
A hundred hearts are in your two idol-worshiping tresses!

We return to our first discussion: Outwardly Muṣṭafā had two emigrations, and inwardly he had a thousand thousand emigrations. Of the outward emigrations, one was to Medina and the other was to heaven.

In that emigration, his kind companion was [Abū Bakr] the Sincerely Truthful, and in this emigration his kind companion was Gabriel. In that emigration, the steed was one of the faultless beasts of paradise, and in this emigration it was the Burāq of yearning for the Unseen. In that emigration he made the folk of Medina the prey of his beauty; in this emigration he made the folk of the Holy Palisades the prey of his perfection. In that emigration Medina was the final end; in this emigration *surely unto thy Lord is the final end* [53:42]. In that emigration he gave the creatures their just due; in this emigration he asked for the just due of his own aspiration. In that emigration he came down at the little corner of Abū Ayyūb; in this emigration he did not look back at Gabriel's holy palisades. In that emigration the spider came forth; in this emigration the peacock of the angels spoke these words: *"Were I to draw closer by a finger's breadth, I would be incinerated."*[212]

It seems to me that Muṣṭafā's joy in emigrating to Medina was beyond his joy in emigrating to heaven. This is because the Real's exaltedness was in the former emigration, and the Real's bounteousness in the latter emigration. The delight of the elect in His exaltedness is greater than the delight of the common people in His bounty.

> My heart is such that if it had no sorrow for a moment,
> it would go to the sorrowful and take sorrow on loan.

19. *al-Wahhāb:* the Bestower

The meaning of *wahhāb* is bestower and giver. The Real is the giver and the forgiver.

When the *tawḥīd*-voicer with certainty and faith believes that the Real is the Bestower, he must present all of his needs in all of his states only to the Presence and know that he has no shelter and no recourse but the Threshold. Whether in little or much he must always refer to the sufficiency of the Lord. They say, *"It is not beautiful for the desiring, free man to abase himself before the servants when he will find what he desires from his Patron."*[213] It is not beautiful for a man to make himself the plaything of the wants of just anyone when the Real Himself has given him the assurance of what he needs and more.

It has been narrated that Bishr Ḥāfī said, "I saw the Commander of the Faithful Alī ibn Abī Ṭālib in a dream and asked him for advice. He said, *'How beautiful it is for the rich to show compassion to the poor in seeking God's reward! And more beautiful is for the poor to be haughty toward the rich by relying on God.'* "[214] How beautiful it is for the rich to show tenderness toward the poor in order to seek the reward. More beautiful is for the poor to show pride toward the rich because of their extreme confidence in the Real's generosity.

They have also said, *"Recognition is to scorn all measures save His measure and to efface all remembrances save His remembrance."*[215] Recognition is to look with the eye of scorn on all measures save the Real's measure and to erase all remembrances save the Real's remembrance.

This also is one of their sayings: *"When the Lord is tremendous in the heart, the creatures will be small in the eye."*[216] When the majesty and tremendousness of the Real settle down in the breast, the mark is that the worth of the creatures packs its bags.

Muṣṭafā said, *"If someone humbles himself before a wealthy man because of his wealth, two-thirds of his religion will have left him."*[217] What is meant by this report is that a man is three things: heart, tongue, and body. If he humbles himself with his tongue and body, two-thirds of his religion will leave him. If he believes in his heart what he brings to his tongue and body, the whole of his religion will leave him.[218] *Refuge in God!*

This also is among their sayings: *"A created thing seeking aid from a created thing is like a prisoner seeking aid from a prisoner."*[219] You must understand this secret and become aware of this reality. Then you will no longer let your heart be bound by the others, you will pass your days only at the Threshold, and you will bind your heart only to His bounty.

A nomad came before Sayf al-Dawla and recited these two verses:

> *You are ʿAlī and this is Aleppo,*
> *my supplies are exhausted, my search at its end.*

Time your servant has driven me to you,
fleeing from your servant's iniquity.[220]

The nomad had a feedbag with him. Sayf al-Dawla commanded that the feedbag be filled with gold and given to the nomad. The nomad came before Sayf al-Dawla and scattered the gold on his head and said, "Your largesse is from your storehouse."

With the beauty of your face I need gold?

Bukhārī narrates in the *Ṣaḥīḥ* from Ibn ʿAbbās that the Real commanded Abraham to take Ishmael and Hagar to Mecca and put them in that barren valley. Abraham set off with Ishmael and Hagar in keeping with the command, Ishmael a suckling infant and Hagar a weak woman. He brought them to Mecca and put them down in the place of Zamzam, where there was still no house. Then he turned to go away. As soon as he turned away, Hagar said to him, "Are you leaving us in this place? Who commanded you to bring us here?"

Abraham said, "God."

Hagar said, "Then go, for He will not let us go to waste."

Ibn ʿAbbās said that he left Hagar and went back where he came from.

Consider this story carefully, for it has many secrets. Perhaps you will reach the place where you will cut off hope from creatures.

What a marvelous business! He took them to the valley of Mecca, where there was no intimate or sitting companion, then he turned away and went. Hagar came to Ishmael and used the few dates and the bit of water in the goatskin until there were no more dates and the water was finished—and the heat was the heat of Mecca. In that valley there was neither crop nor udder, and the infant was twisting on the ground because of extreme heat. Hagar's heart was in pain. She ran up on Safa to see if there was any water, but she did not see any. She ran down and then ran up on Marwah to see if somewhere there was an intimate, but she did not see anyone. Her heart was with the infant. She came back and saw him still twisting in himself. Again she went up on Safa but saw no one, and again she went up on Marwah while lifting up the edge of her dress. She saw no water anywhere and saw no one. She went seven times back and forth, and from that time onward—when that old woman ran there seven times because of her burning—the Real made this part of the Shariah, so that everyone who goes there will run seven times from Safa to Marwah and Marwah to Safa.

Yes, one day someone stricken by pain lifted a few steps in that place; someone burned let out a few sighs. Conforming with the pain-stricken brings about many things. Here you have the exaltedness of the seekers' feet because of pain: an old woman lifted up a few steps, and this was made part of the Shariah and one of the pillars of the hajj. When she had run up seven times and was standing at the top of Marwah, she let out a cry in extreme pain: "Help!" A curtain was lifted from her hearing; she heard the sound of the wings of Gabriel's victory. He was coming to place his wing near the feet of Ishmael, and he struck it against a stone. Water boiled up. Hagar came and put stones and dust around the water so that it would not go to waste.

The Messenger said, "If Hagar had not done that, Zamzam would be a flowing stream." Thus you may know what sort of bond Adamic eagerness is.[221]

What a marvelous business! Hagar set out seeking water and with exertion and effort ran from this hill to that hill. But clear water bubbled up from beneath the feet of a suckling infant without seeking or acquisition. Thus you may know that seeking is not a cause, nor is finding by stratagem.

The master Abū ʿAlī Daqqāq said, *"In your view you have no escape from your daily provision, but in my view your daily provision has no escape from you."* You believe that you have no escape from your daily portion, but I believe that your daily portion has no escape from you.

Where is a dervish, the turban of disengagement tied, the cloak of solitariness donned, his breast swept of the dust of all others, everything less than God bid farewell, and the tent of love set up between the Safa of limpidness and the Marwah of loyalty? Quit of being, he will take as his friend the Being-Bestower. By the decree of eternal gentleness the fountain of life will bubble up from beneath the feet of his togetherness, and he will take up spirit-increasing drafts from the fountain and drink them to the vision of the Friend.

O chevalier, the head of the aspiration of these men never comes down for any other. Heaven and earth, Throne and Footstool, paradise and hell, do not carry the burden of their work. The aspiration of these men has a place around which it circumambulates. It wants a pure space in order to fly, a vast desert without rubbish and refuse. No space is purer than the space of lordhood, and no desert has less intrusion than the desert of unity. Sometimes their aspiration goes from the desert of unity to the space of lordhood, and sometimes it goes from the space of lordhood to the desert of unity.

O chevalier, aspiration does not circumambulate the Kaabah or Jerusalem, heaven or earth, for it has a Kaabah beyond all Kaabahs. A Kaabah was built for the secret cores, and a Kaabah was built for the outward things. The secret cores are not at ease with the Kaabah of the outward things, and the outward things do not reach the Kaabah of the secret cores. What a marvelous business! A man is sitting, his feet pulled beneath his cloak, and his secret core is circumambulating.

Yes, in the world of *no god but God* there is a Kaabah, compared to which the form of *no god but God* is like the form of that world compared to the Kaabah. When the secret cores circumambulate, they turn around that Kaabah.

The secret core of the world of form is the Sanctuary, the secret core of the Sanctuary is Mecca, and the secret core of Mecca is the Kaabah. The secret core of the World of the Haqiqah is the Quran, the secret core of the Quran is the sentence of *tawḥīd*, and the secret core of the sentence of *tawḥīd* is God. You must traverse the playing field of *no god* and go to the desert of *but*. You must traverse this desert with yearning until you reach the Kaabah of God. Then, like someone disengaged, you must circumambulate in hope and fear and bring your soul to the Mina of your own present moment, and then sacrifice it.

In this road, a man must have the attribute of a fish, which takes nourishment only from the source of life and gets along only with the water of life. When a man takes on this attribute, death will never circle around his true life. Muṣṭafā said, *"The ocean's water is pure, its carrion permitted."*[222] The carrion of the world is forbidden, but the carrion of the ocean is permitted.

The fish were asked, "How is it that it is forbidden to use a knife on you?"

They said, "Because we are the companions of the ocean and nurtured by the water of life."

"O fish, how is it that you do not become the plaything of the butcher and no one drives a knife across your throat?"

They said, "When we turn back, we turn back to the oyster with the pearl. When we look up, we see an umbrella of the ocean's waves. When the ocean's waves fall, they fall on our heads. When the night-brightening pearl rises up, it rises up beneath our feet. When pearls are born from beneath someone's feet and waves rise up from above his head, what does he have to do with a butcher? We have established a lineage with the water of life. Our grazing place is the water of purity and the source of light. Water has two attributes: the attribute of life and the attribute of purity. If we look to the right, we see the attribute of life, and if we look to the left, we see the attribute of purity. How can impurity rise up from the midst of life and purity?"

He is the ocean no matter how you come to him,
his depth liberality, his shore munificence.
Had he nothing in hand but his spirit,
he would be munificent—so let his asker be wary of God.[223]

This is one of their sayings: *"Be the neighbor of an ocean or a king."*[224] Do not be a man of puny aspiration. Either live in the shadow of a surging ocean or as the neighbor of a severe king.

Once a bedouin set off on the ocean. Waves rose up, the ship was smashed, and he was left on a plank. After many hardships and much suffering, he fell to the shore. Sometime later he came to the edge of the ocean and saw it still and calm. He said, *"Do not delude me with your forbearance, for I have seen wonders from your vehemence."*[225] Do not deceive me with your forbearance, penitence, and stillness, for I have seen wonders from your vehemence and wrath.

O chevalier, the only person who can become the companion of the ocean is he who has detached his heart from life. Yes, the encompassing ocean has sent messengers to the sides: "Where is someone who has detached his heart from life? Only someone like that is worthy of companionship with Me. *Surely God has bought from the faithful their souls and their possessions* [9:111]."

Though I be killed by arrows in battle with you,
in fear of your torment I will not breathe a sigh.
Wounded by your blood-drinking eyelashes,
I will die laughing like a rose when I see you.[226]

What a marvelous business! For a few days the fish was a companion of water and became entranced by it. It had no patience without water. When it was lifted out of the water and thrown on the dust, it gave up its spirit in the pain of separation from its beloved's beauty. It finished its life in sorrow at separation from water's companionship. Then the secret of water's life and the center-point of its purity came forth with loyalty. The water said, "As long as the fish was alive, it was loyal to my life. Now that it has given up the spirit in the pain of separation from me, I will give it the loyalty of purity."

O dervish, as long as you still have the attribute of being, everything will be consigned to you. For a moment, become nonbeing so that the doors of consignment may be shut. When you close your eyes, loyalty will come from the Unseen. Today strive to be loyal for a while to the Unseen. Then, when you close your eyes, the Unseen will be loyal to you forever and without end. He has brought you into the world for a few days and commanded you to be loyal to the Unseen—*who have faith in the Unseen* [2:3]—and He has made the Unseen gaze upon you. He has let you wander in the measure of your capacity in this playing field, sometimes with head hung down, sometimes covered with dust; in one state asleep, in another awake. Then at last severity's hand will come forth from the world of unneediness and lift away the head of your being—the Unseen will be commanded to be loyal to you.

What a marvelous business! Faith in the Unseen is an attribute, and attributes abide through that to which they are attributed. But that to which they are attributed becomes dust, while faith in the Unseen abides. What is this? The loyalty of the Unseen.

O chevalier, a fish lives only in water. There alone will it be at ease and there alone will it settle down. But a lizard is at ease in dry dust and will not settle down anywhere else. If you take a fish to the house of a lizard, it will be finished, and if you take a lizard to the house of a fish, it will be destroyed. In the same way, there is a group who take delight only in His gentleness, and a group whose life lies in His severity. There is a group who live in what they desire and a group who live in what He desires. There are people who are at ease in their shares, and people who are at ease in the Real. There is a group who, it is feared, would bind the sash of unbelief and apostasy if a needle should appear to them from the world of severity. There is another group who would fill the world with wails of longing and burning if the nourishment of trial and the food of affliction were cut off from them for an instant.

Love is trial but I'm not one to avoid trial.
  When love is asleep, I stir up misfortune.
My friends say, "Avoid trial."
  Trial is my heart. How can I avoid my heart?
I keep on nurturing love's tree in my heart.
  When it needs water, I pour it from my eyes.[227]

O chevalier, He placed the burden of His severity only on a handful of dust. *"Neither the heavens nor the earth embraces Me, but the heart of My faithful servant does embrace Me."*[228] The Throne cannot support the gaze of My majesty, and the Footstool cannot carry My welcome. It is the secret core of the heart of Adam and the Adamites that carries the burden of contemplating Me.

"The heart was named qalb *because of its fluctuation [taqallub]."*[229] The attribute of the heart is to be without rest. Why does it keep on fluctuating? Because the brand of severity's ruling

power has been placed upon it. It is impossible to put a fiery brand on an unbroken colt and command it to be still. Yes, spirits are in ease itself, but hearts have the attribute of motion. He placed bonds on the spirit so that it would stay still, but He let the heart move.

The butcher throws down the sheep and ties up its two front legs along with one back leg, leaving one leg free. He says, "It would be wrong to bind all four. Putting the blade on the throat and not letting the sheep move would be a great wrongdoing, for then it would taste the wound of the blade while being still. Nothing is lost by letting it move."

Tying together the three legs is the butcher's severity, and leaving one leg free is his gentleness—a gentleness in severity, a severity in gentleness. The latter does not remove the former, nor the former the latter.

This is one of their sayings: *"Sufism is agitation without stillness."*[230] Sufism is movement without any settledness, for if water settles down, it begins to stink: *"When water lingers for a time, its vileness appears, and when its surface is still, its odor begins to move."*[231]

Thou shalt see the mountains, which thou reckoned as solid, passing by like clouds [27:88]. It is permissible for a man to be settled down in his own little corner while his secret core is busy circumambulating and wandering.

Once Junayd did not get up for the *samāʿ*. They asked him why he did not get up. He recited this verse—*"Thou shalt see the mountains, which thou reckoned as solid, passing by like clouds."*[232] Yes, when the going becomes fast, vision turns into its contrary. Do you not see that, when the mill wheel reaches its utmost speed, it tells the eyesight of form that it is standing still?

"O Pir, why didn't you get up for the *samāʿ*?"

He said, "You did not see my going. When going reaches the extreme, it does not enter into vision." The beginning of going can be seen, but going's end cannot be seen.

The dawn breeze passes by such that no one is aware. What are you doing with the wind that comes and shakes doors and walls? The dawn breeze comes and brings news of the Friend such that your own collar is unaware.

And as the caravan departed, their father said, "Surely I find the fragrance of Joseph" [12:94]. Their father said,

> The water of Muliyan River keeps on coming,
> the scent of that kind friend keeps on coming.
> In delight for reunion with the friend, my steed
> crosses the Jayhun while the water keeps on coming to its waist.[233]

As for him who was burning for Joseph—the folk of the caravan had no news of that marvelous scent, that strange breeze, that masterful wind, nor were his brothers aware. But at a distance of eighty farsakhs its pull fell into Jacob's spirit and heart.

> *Morning breeze, when you visit the earth of my beloved,*
> *single her out for my greetings.*
> *Convey to her that I am a pawn to ardor,*
> *that my debt is beyond all debts:*

"I would be pleased by the coming of your image
were my eyes given the comfort of sleep.
"I would have no concern for gardens or flames
had I a station in that land."[234]

20. *al-Razzāq:* the Provider

The Provider is one of the names of God. The reality of provision is what prepares and assists the reception of benefit.

Provision is divided into permitted and forbidden.[235] This is one of the issues in the principles, and disagreement in this issue is well known.

When someone believes that in reality the Provider is the Lord, his mark is that his heart trusts totally in Him and he cuts himself off from others. The Lord in His gentleness will take care of his work and caress him at every moment with various sorts of generosity.

A man came to Ḥātim Aṣamm and asked him, "How are you able to you pass your days, for you have no income, no expenditures, no belongings, and no estates."

He said, "From His storehouse."

He said, "Does He throw bread to you from heaven?"

He said, "Had He not the earth, He would throw bread to me from heaven."

Then the man said, "You're just talking words."

He said, "Because nothing descends from heaven but words."

He said, "I have no strength to dispute with you."

He said, "Because falsehood has no strength against truth."[236]

It was also Ḥātim who one day was leaving his family. He said, "I have the thought to travel. How much should I leave for your expenditure?"

His wife said, "Leave expenditure in the measure that I have life remaining to me."

Ḥātim said, "You have brought forth a difficult question. How should I know how long you will live?"

She said, "Entrust it to Him who knows."

When Ḥātim went, the group of women who were her neighbors came to her to share her grief: "Ḥātim is gone and he has left you with nothing."

The old woman said, "Unburden your hearts, *for he was someone who ate provisions—he was not a provider."*[237]

It is said that a man came to Shiblī and complained about his many family members and tight livelihood. Shiblī said, "Go back to your house and throw out anyone whose daily provision is not God's to give."[238]

It is said that a group entered in upon Junayd and said, *"Should we seek our provision?"*

He said, "If you know where it is, seek it."

They said, "We will ask it from God."

He said, "If you suspect He has forgotten you, ask."

They said, "We'll go home, close the doors, and have trust."

He said, *"Putting to the test is dangerous."*

They said, "So what is the stratagem?"

He said, "The stratagem is to abandon stratagems." It is to leave aside stratagems and detach the heart from others.[239]

It has been reported that Abū Ya'qūb Aqṭa' Baṣrī said, "Once I was in the Sanctuary. For ten days I suffered want and found nothing. Weakness appeared in me. I got up and wandered around the valley so that perhaps I might find something. From afar I saw a discarded turnip. I went and picked it up, but it was rotten and stank; as much as I wanted to use it, I could not. It was as if someone was saying to me, *'You were hungry for ten days, and you have received a rotten turnip.'*

"I threw it away, went into the Sanctuary, and sat down. While I was there, a Persian man entered the Sanctuary, sat down before me, put down a sugar-pot, and said, 'This belongs to you.'

"I said, 'Why is it that you have made this belong to me?'

"He said, 'We were on the ocean for ten days. The waves were rising, the sea was agitated, and there was fear that the ship would sink. Each of us made a vow. I vowed that if God delivered me, I would give this sugar-pot as alms to the first person I saw at the Sanctuary, and you are the first person.'

"I said, 'Open the pot.' He opened it, and inside I saw Egyptian crackers, candied walnuts, and fine sugar. I took a handful of each and said, 'Now take the rest and give it to your children—let it be my gift to you.' Then I said to myself, *'Your provision has been traveling toward you for ten days, but you sought it from the valley.'* For ten days your provision was being brought to you, but you were wandering here and there looking for it."[240]

It is said that in a past community a man was traveling with one loaf. Whenever he wanted to eat the loaf, he would say, "I must not, for if I eat it, I will not find any more and will die." The Lord had entrusted an angel to him, saying, "If he eats the loaf, give him another." He finally did not eat it because of fear, and he died.[241]

Ibrāhīm Khawwāṣ said, "I was traveling in the desert of the Children of Israel. I saw a young man traveling without supplies or camel. I said, 'Where are you going?'

"He said, 'To Mecca.'

"I said, 'Without supplies and camel?'

"He said, *'O weak in certainty, is He who can carry the heavens and the earth without pillars not able to convey me to Mecca without encumbrances?'* He said this and set off walking, and I did not see him again until Mecca. When I arrived I saw him circumambulating and reciting this verse:

> *O eye, weep forever! O soul, die in grief!*
> *Love no one but the Majestic, the Self-Sufficient!*

"I went forward and greeted him. He answered and said, *'Are you still weak in certainty?'* O Shaykh, how is your illness?"[242]

O chevalier, there is no illness worse than weak certainty! Establish your certainty in the Real, and the game is yours.

There is the name of certainty, the knowledge of certainty, the eye of certainty, the truth of certainty, and the reality of the truth of certainty. The name of certainty belongs to the common people, the knowledge of certainty to the elect, the eye of certainty to God's friends, the truth of certainty to the prophets, and the reality of the truth of certainty to Muṣṭafā.

The foundation of the work lies in certainty. A man who becomes a man becomes so through certainty. Certainty must reach the tongue for him to be a speaker, the eye for him to be a seer, the ear for him to be a hearer, the hand for him to be taker, the foot for him to be a traveler.

Muṣṭafā said, "Jesus walked on water. Had his certainty increased, he would have walked on air." The master Abū ʿAlī Daqqāq said, "He alluded to himself, meaning, 'When I walked on air on the night of the *miʿrāj*, that was because of perfect certainty.' "[243]

One of their sayings is this: *"Have mercy on the rich for the paucity of their gratitude, have mercy on the poor for the paucity of their patience, and have mercy on everyone for the paucity of their certainty."*[244] Forgive the rich for their lack of gratitude, forgive the poor for their lack of patience, and forgive everyone for their lack of certainty.

Sahl ibn ʿAbdallāh Tustarī said, *"It is forbidden for a heart to catch a whiff of certainty so long as it has settled down with other than God."*[245] Whenever the heart has an iota of looking at others, it is forbidden for it to catch a whiff of the sweet herb of certainty.

"When the servant reaches the realities of certainty, trial becomes a blessing for him, and ease an affliction."[246] When a man reaches the reality of certainty, tribulation becomes a blessing for him, and blessing a tribulation.

People say that when Job said, *"Harm has touched me"* [21:83], he suffered and moaned because of trial. As for the realizers, they say that he suffered because of the removal of the trial. God had revealed to him, *"O Job, seventy prophets before you chose this trial, but I chose it only for you." So when God desired to remove it, he said, "Harm has touched me."*[247] O Job, seventy prophets asked Me for this trial with pleading and weeping, but I kept it stored in the unseen storehouses specifically for you. When these words reached the ears of Job's love, he came to know that he was singled out. When the Real wanted to remove the trial, Job was jealous for the trial's secret and said, *"Harm has touched me,"* because of the removal of the trial, not because of the trial itself.

The sorcerers of Pharaoh had sworn an oath by Pharaoh's exaltedness and displayed their deceiving ropes, corrupt illusions, and deceitful staffs. When the sun of divine gentleness rose from the mansion of No Place and shone forth in the house of their secret cores, that work took place and the falcon of the unitary mystery took the finch of their folly in the claws of its severity. They let out the cry, *"We have faith"* [20:70]. They tore the dress of disloyalty with the hands of loyalty and washed their registers of their offenses. Pharaoh the unaided shouted, *"I will surely cut off your hands and your feet alternately, and I will surely crucify you on the trunks of palm trees"* [20:71]. I will cut off your hands and your feet and crucify you. They were saying, *"So decree what you will decree!"* [20:72]. Do whatever you like, O simpleton! You are giving us good news—you are not threatening us. Our greater adversary is ourselves. Our wish is that we reach the shelter of the Real's pure gaze before our own suspicious gaze falls on ourselves.

How can he fear the adversary at the top of the street
when he's lost his gelim at the bottom?

This is one of their sayings: *"Approval is to welcome the decrees with joy."*[248] Approval is to welcome the sultan of the decree on the Burāq of joy.

Muṣʿab was one of the Followers.[249] One day he was wearing a white garment. He looked down at the garment and said, "How beautiful when the liver's blood runs down in streams on a white garment." When he said these words, all at once the call to war sounded. He bound up his waist for war and went forth with seriousness and love. An arrow came and struck his shoulder and the blood ran down in streams. He looked at the wound, but it was small. He said, *"Surely this is small, but God blesses the small."* This wound is small, but God gives blessings to the small so that they may become great. What heart he had!

When plague appeared on the hand of Muʿādh, he rubbed his hand on his face and kissed it. When he fell into the agonies of death and the intensity of the soul's extraction appeared, he was saying, *"Strangle me with Your strangling, for by Your exaltedness I love You."*[250] Strangle me without kindness, for I love You.

> O Lamp of the world, I am Your slave boy.
> Do whatever You want, the time is Yours.
> Wherever You see me, draw back Your bow—
> my heart and spirit are Your target.

An exalted man said, "I went to visit a sick dervish and said, 'No one is truthful in love for Him if he has no patience with His blows.'

"The man lifted up his head and said, 'You have it wrong. *No one is truthful in love for Him if he takes no pleasure in His blows.*' "[251]

The shaykhs of Iraq said, *"No man becomes a recognizer until withholding and bestowal are equal for him."*[252]

Shiblī denied that and said, "No, rather, no one is a recognizer unless withholding is more beloved to him than bestowal, for withholding is the Real's desire, and bestowal is the servant's desire. The true recognizer is he who sacrifices his own desire to His desire." Shiblī said, "That is wrong. A man becomes a recognizer when withholding outweighs bestowal for him, for withholding is the Real's desire specifically, but bestowal is the servant's desire. The true recognizer is he who sacrifices his desire to the desire of the Desired."

It is told that once a king awakened to the path of the religion. His grief's clouds rained down so many drops of regret on the earth of his face that his eyes went blind. They asked him, "All this effort and striving that you have—what has the Real given you for this struggle?"

He said, "He has given me everything, for He has stripped me of what I desired and replaced it with desire only for what He desires." He said, "He has given me everything, for He took my desire away from me and replaced it with the fact that I want nothing but what He wants."

> As long as my desire follows every desire,
> take all my desires as unmet.
> If any desire of mine is not Your desire,
> let it be destroyed in my mouth.

Abū Dharr said, *"How beloved are the three disliked things—illness, poverty, and death!"*[253]

They knew that the Real desired for them not to reach their desires, so they threw away their desires in His desire. They said, "Let it all be what He wants, and let none of it be what we want."

The short of it is that the blood of the friends' livers was mixed with the tears of their eyes to make the mortar for the bricks of love's castle. Then the crier of unneediness was sent to the top of the castle to convey this call to the ears of the lovers: *"This is nothing but throwing away the spirit. Otherwise, do not busy yourself with the nonsense of the Sufis."*[254]

This is the road of need, not the road of kindness. The first thing He did with Muṣṭafā was to take away his father and mother so that he would not see a mother's kindness or sit at the feet of a father's tenderness.

Surely We shall cast upon thee a heavy word [73:5]: "O Muḥammad, you have come to the cave of Ḥirā and made it your place of seclusion, but there is a steep climb ahead of you. You must go to the door of Abū Jahl, be joyful beneath camel tripe, give your teeth to the stones of the stone-hearted, and strike your face against the blood of your own upright heart. You must take from Us and convey to the people, keeping an upright character in the midst. This is a marvelous business for you: companionship with the people along with disengagement from the people. All of them will be seizing your skirt, but your heart must pay regard to no one."

O chevalier, the one who keeps his heart with God without the companionship of people is not like him who keeps his heart with God along with their companionship. He who keeps his heart with God in the mosque is not like him who keeps his heart with God in the bazaar.

It is said that one of the men of the road went into the desert and hunted a lion. He sat on its back, took a viper in his hand and made it into a whip, and then came back into town. He reached the door of a bakery and the baker said to him, "Hey, you! What is this business? The work of a man is to sit between the two pans of a scale and make his heart one with God. The Lord loves the strong-hearted person of faith."

O dervish, there is a tremendous principle of the road: No one is allowed to open his eyes toward the creatures if he stops seeing the Real when he sees the creatures. If someone loses sight of the Real when he sees the creatures, he is not allowed to look at them.

The burden of messengerhood is a heavy burden—passing the days with creatures while being pure of them. Muḥammad came to the cave of Ḥirā without any burdens, his back straight. He returned with his back bent, his body trembling.

> You keep on doing what takes away my heart,
> I keep on doing the work of patience and supplication.

When Muḥammad returned from the mountain, he said to Khadīja, *"Wrap me up! Wrap me up!"* He drew up the blanket and pulled it over his bowed head. At once Gabriel came from the Presence of Majesty and said, *"O thou enwrapped one*! [73:1]: O you who have pulled your head under the blanket, you cannot be so fragile and delicate in My road!"[255]

> They purified the blood of the sincerely truthful and made it into a road—
> if you don't give up your life for this road, you won't take a single step.[256]

This is the work of the bold. O chevalier, until you throw down the shield from your side and turn your breast toward the arrows, you will not gain the name "courageous." As long as a man has a shield in hand, he has not detached his heart from life. When he throws down his shield, hamstrings his horse, draws his sword, and fixes his feet on the ground, then you will know that he has detached his heart from life.

There is no elevation but in a spear,
blade driven, drinking from the killed,
Edges red from hunting gazelles,
herds of horse, anklets bloody,
The fire of splendor on the cutting blades,
the light of exaltedness on the horse's forelocks.

It is said that the pure-born John wept so much that the skin on his face came off, pits appearing in his cheeks. He was weeping constantly and blood came forth instead of tears.

I wonder at my tears and eyes
before and after separation.
I used to have eyes without tears,
and now I have tears without eyes.[257]

In pain Zachariah looked at his son from afar. He would clean the blood from his eyes with a piece of cotton, which he would squeeze, the blood dripping from the cotton. One day he said, "Lord God, have mercy on this poor soul, for he has no ease or rest!"

The address came, "O Zachariah, keep your tenderness at a distance. You should not be so fragile at My threshold."

O dervish, there is a secret here. *By God the tremendous*, suppose there were none of these pains, trials, and tribulations and you were brought into existence, taken by the hand, and put into paradise. You would not find an iota of pleasure. This is why Adam went and found no pleasure.

On the day you sit on the seat of good fortune in the highest paradise, you will cross your legs, take the tweezers of gentleness, and one by one pull the thorns from your feet. You will say, "What a pity that these thorns went into my feet instead of my spirit!"

The travelers will find pleasure when they reach the *seat of truthfulness* [54:55] and the place of gentleness, where He Himself will call out, "O My friends, your little bits of suffering have arrived. *The burdens undertaken by the emburdened for My sake are esteemed by Me. The burdens you undertook are exalted for Me.* I saw the bits of suffering that reached you."

Then He will say to David, *"Stand up and declare My splendor with your soft voice!"*[258] Entertain My friends for a while with your sweet voice in the scented garden of gentleness at the table of the All-Merciful. Such a feast, such hospitality, such music, such acceptance! The canticles of intimacy in the compartments of holiness with assertions of praise and declarations of splendor!

The desirer will have reached the Desired—the water gone back to the reservoir, the bird hastened to its nest, the smoke gone, the dust settled. The work will have come back to this: *the servant and the Lord, the Lord and the servant.*

21. *al-Fattāḥ:* the All-Opening

This is one of the names of God. One of the meanings of *fatḥ* in lexicology is judgment. The Arabs call a judge "the all-opening" because he unravels disputes with his judgment. The Real is the All-Opening in the sense that He is the judge. He is also the All-Opening in the sense that He opens the doors to provisions and good things. The Arabs say, *"He opened for them the gate of good,"* and *"He opened against them the gate of evil."*[259]

When the servant with faith believes that the Lord of Lords is the All-Opening of doors, he will close the doors of his own fear, hope, want, and dread toward the creatures. With the feet of abandoning his own desire and free choice, he will stand in the station of beautiful anticipation inside the flow of the apportionings. He will become a devotee at the mosque of togetherness in the prayer-niche of solitariness, acknowledging his own incapacity, shortcoming, helplessness, and taintedness. He will become watchful toward finding the divine munificence and stay absent from seeking his own portion and share. He will walk only in the playing field of the eternal gentleness and talk about things he cannot escape only with the Friend.

O dervish, whenever the Real's measure descends into a heart, the measure of the whole world packs its bags. When the contemplation of the Real finds a place in the eyes, every other contemplation turns into nothing.

Intimate with Him, I have no other desire—
my only fear is going astray and not seeing Him.[260]

As long as a man has not reached the center of the work and become aware of the secret of the issue, he will grab hold of every branch and become attached to every little thing. Once he reaches the treasury of the secrets and finds the quarry of the realities and the wellspring of gentle gifts, he will fall back on the fountain of life that is the *goodly life* [16:97]. He will see that creation's existence next to the Real's existence is nonexistence, he will know that creation's subsistence next to the Real's subsistence is annihilation, and he will recognize that creation's exaltedness next to the Real's exaltedness is abasement. He will take his little corner far from the homelands of mortal nature, the courtyard of Adamic nature, and the waystations of human nature and put it into the pavilions of majesty. He will know that seeking wealth from poverty is absurd and taking the wherewithal of subsistence from the source of annihilation is ignorance. He will be consumed by contemplation itself and drowned in the ocean of unveiling. He will become like a dust mote before the sun, appearing only when it witnesses the sun's beauty.

O dervish, these stars, high on the dome of the celestial world, each with a ray of light in its mouth, are much more exalted in form than the dust motes in the terrestrial world, for they have light, radiance, splendor, and brilliance, and the motes are simply dust hanging in the air, bewildered in the footsteps of existence and nonexistence. But do not look at the highness, radiance, limpidness, and brilliance of the stars, nor at the dust motes' nonbeing and tininess. Wait until the emperor of the stars and the chief of the planets sticks up its head. You will see all those high in rank and elevated in degree disappear, losing name and mark, but these tiny shapes and insignificant makeups will come out of the confines of tininess into the vast plain of manifestation.

What is the divine wisdom and lordly secret in this? It is that stars, which are the stonings of the satans,[261] are attached to the arrogance of appearance and the self-esteem of manifesting their own light, but the sun's empire does not accept the intrusion of duality. *"Two swords do not come together in one scabbard, nor two lions in one thicket."*[262] When the sultan-sun sits on its steed of light, it charges forth on the field of exaltation. The stars conceal their faces with the veil of despair and the mask of shame. They declare themselves quit of manifesting their own light.

As for the dust mote, it is helpless, nurtured in the cradle of indigence, all imaginings fallen away from it. It is the prisoner of the wind, not grasped by the hand or perceived by the eye. As soon as the world-adorning sun sticks up its head from the horizon of eminence, the mote comes forth to serve the sun in helplessness, lowliness, and abasement. By the decree of generosity, the sun dresses it in a robe of light, and the dust mote discloses itself to the eyes in the robe of the sun's brightness.

Now that this introduction has been made, you should know that in reality His Men are the same in relation to the divine beauty and majesty. Those who imagine themselves to be existent and make self-seeing claims, relying on their own acts and states, are like stars who try to associate themselves with the sun in brightness. When the sun of the divine majesty rises from the constellation of self-sufficiency, they all pull their faces behind the mask of shame and place the finger of bewilderment in the mouth of remorse. They come to know that mortal man has nothing in his hands but wind.

As for those who are pure of appetite for fame, disgusted with every claim, and naked of all self-seeing, like dust motes they have turned their eyes to the beauty of the Presence and sit in anticipation of the breaking dawn of union. When the sun of majesty shows its head from the constellation of beauty, they settle down on the knees of abasement and pleading, needy for the Presence, sorrowful for the Exaltedness, helpless in the road, and fallen before the Threshold. They come forth in the garment of destitution, but the royal generosity and divine munificence bestow on them a robe of pure light, and with this light they appear to the eyes.

> You're the sun; I'm a mote—
> like a mote I'm known through the sun.[263]

Here there is another secret. God says, *"Surely We offered the Trust to the heavens and the earth and the mountains"* [33:72]. The sun of the Trust shone forth from the constellation of the divine offer. For several thousand years the angels of the Dominion had dwelt in the gardens of declaring holy, grazing with the nostrils of acquiescence on the jasmine of glorification, the sweet briar of praise, and the red rose of reciting *tawḥīd*. They were shouting, *"we glorify Thy praise,"* and making the uproar of *"we call Thee holy"* [2:30]. Then they put on the garment of poverty like the stars and confessed their incapacity and brokenness: *"They refused to carry it"* [33:72]. They refused out of apprehension, not pride. But that fearless mote pulled the hand of need from the sleeve of poverty and indigence and took the Trust to his very spirit, with no thought whatsoever of the two worlds.

> Don't think about this talk; put on the shroud
> and clap your hands like a man.
> Say, "Either You or me in the city"—
> a realm with two heads is in turmoil.

O chevalier, don't fancy that when He offered the Trust to the heavens and the earth, He desired that the heavens and the earth would accept it. If we suppose that He desired their acceptance, then they would have accepted it—what He desired would not fall flat. Rather, first He offered it to the unworthy so that the worthy would get up from their places and seize the skirt of the sought.

I mean you, O neighbor, so listen![264]

O dervish, suppose you put many new pieces of cloth next to a few burnt ones and strike the iron to the flint. The fire will catch in the burnt cloth, but not in the new. O fire, what is it with you that you do not catch in the new cloth but aim for the burned? It says: "Indeed, the burned has been tested by me. The stipulation is that when I burn something at the beginning, I will get along with it at the end."

Adam was scorched by the fire of love and burned by the fire of affection. The other existent things were unaware of love's secret. When the flint of the Sultan's command was struck against the iron of the divine decree, the fire of unneediness sprang up and caught only in him who was burned by the Covenant.

I fear that to light up the session
  I'll need to teach the fine points of love.
O unaware of the burned and the burnable,
  love comes—it can't be learned.[265]

The heavens said, "I have the attribute of elevation." The earth said, "I have the robe of expanse." The mountains said, "I'm wearing the robe of fixity and have jewels inside my quarries. We must not suffer any blight, lest we lose these attributes and robes." The handful of dust said, "What can they take from me? When they abase things, they rub them in dust. What can dust be rubbed in?" Like a man the dust came forth to the burden that was not carried by the realms of the spheres, putting it on the shoulders of its own manliness and shouting out, *"Is there any more?"* [50:30].

O dervish, Adam had aspiration in his head. He dealt in his own aspiration. Whenever the Adamites reach something, they reach it with aspiration. Otherwise they would never reach anything with what they have in their own makeup.

When Adam was first brought into existence, he was dressed in the robe of munificence and exaltedness and the cape of anointing, and the angels prostrated themselves before him. The name of kingship and vicegerency was recorded in the edict of his covenant and the eight paradises were given over to his exclusive use: *"O Adam, dwell thou and thy spouse in the Garden* [2:35]. O Adam the chosen, act freely in the House of Subsistence and the Abode of Everlastingness according to your own desire and want, and be ready in the life of ease for the day of the promise!"

Adam's headstrong aspiration placed him like a sultan on the steed of love. He took an arrow of solitariness from the quiver of disengagement, placed it in a warrior's bow, and pulled it all the way back. He shot the adorned peacock of paradise strutting in the Garden of the Refuge, for this is the road of the disengaged. It is the work of those with high aspiration, the threshold of the proximate. Time, place, entity, traces, vestiges, shapes, existent things, known things—all must be totally lifted away from you. If any of these cling to your skirt, the name of freedom will not sit upon you. As long as the name *free* does not sit upon you, your servanthood will never be rectified.

It is said that they reported to Shaykh Abū Saʿīd that in such and such a place there is a master gambler, and they told many stories about him. It came into his heart that they should see this man, for he wanted them to take the secret from wherever their eyes fell. He set off with a group of dervishes and went to the place of the gambler. They saw him with a reed mat wrapped around himself, sitting in ashes. The Shaykh wondered at this state. He said, "Are you the master gambler?"

He said, "So they say."

He said, "How did you gain the name of master?"

He said, "By playing fair and losing all."[266]

Though I hold my head high in deeds
    and have no need for people's knowledge,
I've been thrown down by the dice-throwers—
    I'm dust beneath the feet of those who lose it all.

When a man is going to the Kaabah to make the hajj, they tell him that he must bind the *iḥrām*. He says, "What is the *iḥrām?*"

They say, "It is that you make a full ablution, you abandon your own portions, you take off the turban of nobility, you remove fancy clothing, and you put aside the soul's appetites and pleasures. Then you put on a loincloth and wrap yourself in a mantle. With need and pain you turn your face toward your goal and keep on saying *'Labbayk.'* "[267]

How marvelous! Someone aims for the House and is not allowed to settle down in his own portion. When someone aims for the Real, how can he be allowed to settle down in his own portion?

That is the outward stipulation, attached to *make My house pure!* [22:26]. As for the inward *iḥrām*, it is that you cut yourself off from all others, bind yourself in a loincloth of need, and put on a cloak of loyalty and forbearance. You keep on saying the *labbayk* of love in the world of truthfulness, you turn your face to the desert of solitariness, and in the pain of contemplating unity you shout out,

Though the Kaabah of Your union disdains me
    and the desert of separation keeps me back,
I'll wander everywhere in the desert,
    for you can pray to the Kaabah from afar.

He said to Abraham and Ishmael, "Build for Me a house *in a valley without crops* [14:37], from a handful of stones, an endless land on one side, a boundless sea on the other. On the sleeve of its exaltedness embroider the ascription, 'the House of God.' Then go, O Abraham, to the top of Mount Būqubays and let out a cry for the ears of the seekers on the road of My approval.

Watch My lovers show their love for this house built of stone, though *anyone who has patience without it has a heart harder than stone."*

It is a house built of stone but a magnet of hearts. If it were a house built of precious gems, for example, or of emeralds, carnelians, and rubies; or if it were set in the midst of scented gardens, orchards, meadows, rivers, and trees; and then someone wanted to visit it, that would be no surprise. But it is a handful of stones piled up a thousand farsakhs distant in the midst of an ocean of man-eating desert, with a hundred thousand churlish, hard-hearted nomads sitting on its road. The fire of the lovers' love increases and becomes hotter every day, for the Kaabah is like a candle, and His passionate lovers are like moths. The fire of passion's object has no mercy, and passionate moths have no patience.

The Banū ʿUdhra were one of the Arab tribes, and their passionate love is the stuff of proverbs. Most who fell into love were destroyed. When one of the tribe was asked why this was so, he said, *"Our hearts are tender, and our women chaste."* Tenderness dominates over our hearts, and chastity over our women.

He built a Kaabah in the outward realms and He built a Kaabah in the inward realms. The heart in the breasts is like a Kaabah. The outward Kaabah is made of stones, the inward Kaabah of secrets. That Kaabah is circumambulated by various sorts of people, this Kaabah by the gentle gifts of the Creator. That Kaabah is gazed upon by people, this Kaabah by the Real. That Kaabah is the kiblah of the creatures' hearts, this Kaabah of the Real's acceptance. That Kaabah was built by Abraham, this Kaabah by the gentleness of the Generous. That is the Sacred Mosque, this the mosque of the noble angels. In that place is Arafat, in this place felicitations. In that place is the Sanctuary, in this place generosity. In that place are Marwah and Safa, in this place the varieties of love and loyalty. In that place are rites and waymarks, in this place gifts and good tidings. That House is *a place of visitation for the people* [2:125], this house a place of intimacy. That place is the station of the Bosom Friend, this place the station of the gentleness of the Majestic. In that place are circumambulators, devotees, bowers, and prostraters; in this place are gentle favors, recognitions, traces, and lights of munificence. In that place are *signs, clear signs* [3:97], in this place marks of friendship and felicities. In that place drink is given to the hajjis; in this place sits the king of throne and crown. In that place is the well of Zamzam, in this place cups of gentleness time after time. In that place is the Yemen Pillar, in this place the treasuries of meanings. In that place is the Black Stone, in this place the everlasting black spot in the secret core. In that place are the blessed hajj and the thanked deed, in this place the wellsprings of joy, delight, presence, and light. In that place are Muzdalifa and Mina, in this place proximity, nearness, and election. In that place is Masjid al-Khayf, in this place the waystation of quaking and fear.

This holy Kaabah, garden, and meadow, built in the province of the friends' breast and made ready with gentleness, is not in the Garden of Refuge or the Highest Firdaws. The garden is this garden, the paradise this paradise, the palace this palace, the firdaws this firdaws, the tree this tree, the fruit this fruit. *A goodly word is like a goodly tree, its roots fixed and its branches in heaven* [14:24].

What is the seed of this tree? What then is its root? What is its branch? What is its water? What is its fruit? What flavor does its water have? Who is the planter of this tree? To whom does the tree belong? In which earth does this tree grow?

Anas Mālik narrated from Muṣṭafā that he said, *"The likeness of this religion is a fixed tree. Faith is its trunk, alms tax its branches, fasting its roots, prayer its water, beauty of character its leaves, and keeping back from what God has forbidden its fruit. Just as a tree is not complete without goodly fruit, so faith is not complete without keeping back from what God has forbidden."*[268]

What was just said is the tongue of learning. As for the tongue of the secret core, it is that this is the tree of gentleness: *And God is gentle to His servants* [42:19].

Its trunk is attestation: *God bears witness that there is no god but He* [3:18].

Its branches are the practice of faith: *"Faith is belief in the heart, attestation with the tongue, and deeds with the limbs."*[269]

Its water comes from the effusion of bounty: *Say: "In the bounty of God and His mercy"* [10:58]. *That is God's bounty* [62:4]. *The Lord lets forth the clouds of bounty and the billows of prosperity and sends down the rain of sufficiency on the soul, the rain of guidance on the heart, the rain of subtlety on the tongue, the rain of purity on the limbs, the rain of favor on the secret core, and the rain of blessings on the spirit. From the rain of sufficiency grow obedience and loyalty, from the rain of guidance yearning and limpidness, from the rain of subtlety gratitude and laudation, from the rain of purity remembrance and supplication, from the rain of favor joy and shame, and from the rain of blessings vision and encounter.*

Its leaves are leaflessness. *"Whoever loves Me becomes indigent and whoever seeks Me falls into disquiet."*[270]

Its fruit is *tawḥīd*. "Tawḥīd *is disengagement from the world of the others by solitariness in the world of the secrets: 'And when thou rememberest thy Lord, Him alone, in the Quran'* [17:46]."

Its flavor is recognition. *"Recognition is waves that fall, rise, and encompass."*[271]

"When someone recognizes God, his night will have no morning and his ocean no shore."[272]

A boy faced me, slender and fine,
his like never seen by my eyes.
Then I was thrown separate from him
into an ocean that has no shore.

Who is the planter of this tree? Muṣṭafā.

To whom does the tree belong? God.

These words can be verified in another way: Faith is like a tree that has seven roots, seven branches, seven leaves, and seven fruits. It is watered by seven rains from seven clouds. Its gardener is the body, which tends the tree from seven directions. When the gardener takes the garden's new fruit to the sultan, he receives seven robes of honor from the sultan's presence.

As for the seven roots: certainty, trust, approval, patience, fear, hope, and surrender.

The seven branches: purity, prayer, charity, fasting, struggle, beautiful character, and commanding the honorable.

The seven leaves: limpidness, praise, laudation, sincerity, humility, reverence, and loyalty.

The seven fruits: penitence, shame, disengagement, solitariness, renunciation, love, and yearning.

The seven rains: sufficiency, friendship, guidance, kind favor, proximity, blessings, and solicitude.

The seven clouds: mercy, generosity, munificence, gentleness, beautiful-doing, favor, and forgiveness.

Tending to this tree is through seven things: poverty, indigence, renunciation, hunger, abasement, brokenness, and need.

The robes of honor given by the sultan: recompense, bestowal, blessings, everlastingness, subsistence, approval, and encounter.

22. *al-ʿAlīm:* the Knower

ʿAlīm, *ʿālim* [knowing], and *ʿallām* [all-knowing] are names of the Lord. The knower is he who knows.

The mark that someone knows that the Real's knowledge encompasses his acts, states, and words is that quaking and dread become his watchword, and awe holds up the banner of rulership from his head to his toes. He constantly watches out for the commandments of the Commander and stays patient beneath the hammers of the unseen decrees. He is like a dust mote in yearning for the whip of the divine command and like a mountain in face of the dagger of prohibition's severity, for a dust mote's attribute is movement and a mountain's attribute is stillness. In complying with the commandments he throws dust in the eyes of the moving mote of his makeup, and in desisting from the world of prohibitions he teaches stillness to the mountains.

Know also with certitude and verification that were the command's beauty and the prohibition's perfection to become apparent to the eye of your secret core, there would be no need for so much talk urging and inciting you to discharge the commanded and hold back from the prohibited. What felicity do you have beyond that He should say, "O handful of dust, belong to Me with a pure heart! O feeble sperm drop, choose only Me! O potter's clay, grow in the garden of union with Me with the assistance of My welcome!" What good fortune is there beyond the fact that five times a day, by the decree of bounty, He sends the packhorse of the court of union at the hand of the stirrup-holder of gentleness to the hut of your incapacity and records this exalted sigil on the edict of your good fortune: *"I have divided the prayer into two halves between Me and My servant. When the servant says, 'The praise belongs to God* [1:2],*' God says, 'My servant is praising Me,'" and so on.*[273]

Moses was God's speaking companion and a noble man, a unique pearl in the oyster of prophethood, but He kept him in sheer anticipation for forty days. When the turn of this community arrived, the tablecloth of anticipation was taken away and the cupbearer of gentleness filled the goblet of union time after time, for *"The prayer is the* miʿrāj *of hearts."*[274] This does not make the communities superior to the prophets, but rather *"The weaker someone is, the gentler to him is the Lord."* The Lord of the Worlds takes care of the work of the weak such that all the strong are in wonder. A hundred thousand proximate, holy angels were offering their bowing and prostrating at the Threshold, but no one talks about them. They themselves gave news of their road, but He set up the signpost of *surely I know* [2:30] on the highway of Adam's good fortune. Here we have a penniless beggar who wakes up from sleep and says, "Oh, it's late." In the splendorous scripture the Lord of Lords wrote this inscription of exaltedness on the cape of his secret whispering: *"Their sides shun their couches as they supplicate their Lord in fear and hope"* [32:16].

There is more as well: "A dog took a few steps in the tracks of Our friends, and We made the dust under its feet the collyrium of the eyes of the proximate. In the Splendorous Speech We bound this collar of eminence on the neck of its covenant: *And their dog was extending its paws at the doorstep* [18:18]. We made the shoulders of Our friends the howdah of its exaltedness."

Thus the lords of the Tariqah inscribed this secret of the Haqiqah on the ringstone of gentleness: *"At the beginning [God's friends] were [the dog's] trials, and at the end they became its steeds."*[275]

He does not stop a dog from seeing the moon—
even dogs look at the moon from time to time.

One of the exalted men of the Tariqah always used to say, *"O God, approve of me as a lover! If You do not approve of me as a lover, approve of me as a servant! If You do not approve of me as a servant, approve of me as a dog!"* O Lord, approve of me for Your friendship. If You do not approve of me for Your friendship, approve of me for servanthood. If You do not approve of me for servanthood, approve of me as one of the dogs of Your threshold.

Is this not enough boasting for me? They call me
the dirt at the top of the street of your familiar.[276]

It seems that someone else had this wish, and a dog began to speak with him: "What sort of wish is this that you have made? Not a single hair of mine has ever moved in opposition to Him. How many steps you have taken in opposition!"

O chevalier, always be broken by seeing yourself. Drink down the cups of the sorrow of your own being. Know in reality that if someone becomes helpless in the pain of his own being, he will no longer be concerned with happiness. *By God the Tremendous*, if one iota of the pain of your being should seize you by the skirt, you would mourn from East to West and from the highest to the lowest. No one has any way to be happy with himself.

God's Messenger Muḥammad was the unique pearl of the ocean of messengerhood and the centerpiece on the necklace of evidence, but he used to shout out at the pain of his own being: *"Would that the Lord of Muḥammad had not created Muḥammad!"*[277] Those who were the preceders, the truthful, and the wayfarers on the road paid not an iota of regard to themselves and were not happy with their own being. In the tablet of their own existence they read nothing but the fanciful notions of the commanding, deceiving, cheating, deluding soul.

Wahab ibn Munabbih said, *"One mark of the hypocrite is that he loves praise and hates blame."*[278] The mark of the hypocrite is that he loves lying praise and hates truthful blame.

O chevalier, He opened His book with the words *"The praise belongs to God"* [1:2].

Praise is extolling and lauding. Since the Lord of Lords and the Owner of Kings says, "All praise and laudation belong to Me," what remains for you?

In the Battle of Mu'ta, ʿAbdallāh ibn Rawāḥa addressed himself with these words:

I swear, O soul, that you will go forth—
you will go forth or be forced.
The people are shouting and the clamor intense,
but why do I see you disliking the Garden?
For a long time you have been serene—
are you aught but sperm in a water bag?[279]

How can a bit of stinking water in a bit of tattered skin have the worthiness to extol and laud? The long and the short of it is that *after examination and study the command belongs to God, the decree belongs to God, the creation belongs to God, and the praise belongs to God.*

"You say, *'The praise belongs to God,'* so that We will say, *'The servant belongs to God.'* "

The sincerely truthful lose their nerve at this threshold while those who divest Him [of attributes] pass their days in delusion. A man came to ʿAbdallāh ibn Masʿūd and said, *"Would that I were one of the Companions of the Right Hand!"*

ʿAbdallāh ibn Masʿūd said, *"Would that when I die I would not be raised up again!"*[280] Would that when ʿAbdallāh becomes dust, his name were cleansed from the register of existence so that he would never lift up his head from the dust.

One man acts with obedience and wishes for the reward. Another disobeys and keeps his eyes on pardon. Still another never lifts up his head from the shame of his own existence.

O dervish, detach your heart from life so that all the poisoned swords may come down on your head. Let your honor be trampled under the feet of the dogs of the wastelands so that everyone may ridicule you. Then be happy—your head in prostration, your secret core in finding, your spirit in the contemplation of the Found.

There was a dervish in the time of Naṣrābādī. He prayed all night long, and the next day he came before his shaykh in the hope that he would praise him. He said, "O Shaykh, how do you see me?"

Naṣrābādī said something like, "Today you resemble a Jew."

The dervish got up and began to lament.

O lovers of the world, help me, help!
That stone-heart scorned my heart, scorned!
I see no way other than patience and forbearance.
What's better in love than patience and forbearance?[281]

It is said that one day Junayd was sitting with Ruwaym or some other exalted man of the Tariqah, and Shiblī came in. Shiblī was very kindhearted. When Junayd's words were finished, Ruwaym looked at Junayd and said, "He is a kindhearted man, this Shiblī."

Junayd said, "You are talking about someone who is one of those who have been rejected by the Threshold." When Shiblī heard this, he was broken. He got up in shame and went outside.

Ruwaym said, "Junayd, what were those words you said about Shiblī? You know the purity and truthfulness of his state."

Junayd said, "Yes, Shiblī is one of the exalted ones at the Threshold. But, *when you speak to Shiblī, do not speak to him from beneath the Throne, for His swords spill blood.* Ruwaym, those words of yours concerning his purity were a sword aimed at his days to hamstring the steed of his practice. I made my words into a shield to repel that sword."[282]

Say: "I am a mortal like you" [18:110]. *If thou takest associates, thy deeds will surely fail* [39:65]. *Had We not made thee firm* [17:74]. Yes, lifting up on the day of the *miʿrāj* wanted nothing less than the Day of Uhud, and the crown that is *by thy life* [15:72] had an amulet that was nothing less than broken teeth and a face tainted by the liver's blood.

One day you see us immersed in the sweets;
next day you see us eating stale bread.[283]

On the Day of Badr the army of beauty was sent forth from the world of bestowal and bounteousness in order to build up the gentleness and generosity made ready by the decree of the eternal desire and to overthrow the foundation of associationism and lies. This call was given out in the world: *"Light has become manifest, falsehood has been nullified, and Muḥammad has been recognized with delight."*[284]

On the Day of Uhud the army of majesty was sent forth from the world of perfection to build up what had been made ready by severity and to display the secret of *Doer of what He desires* [11:107]. The secret of the decree of eternity recited this verse from the pulpit of majesty: *"If a wound touches you, a like wound has already touched that people"* [3:140].

O dervish, there is a state that is the state of showing, and there is a state that is the state of snatching away. Sometimes they show a man to himself, and sometimes they snatch him away from himself.

On the night of proximity there was a man whose portion's camel was walking in the desert of seclusion without provision and equipment and whose good fortune's steed was pulled by its reins to a station that had no room for place or time. This was the same man who, on the Day of Uhud, did not have the strength to go to the top of a hill.

There was another man next to whom were placed the perfumed and scented virgins of paradise, and for many long years the same man was called to account for a grain of wheat. Thus it becomes known to the lords of knowledge that *He will not be asked about what He does, but they will be asked* [21:23].

O chevalier, the states of the servant are diverse. A state comes upon a wayfaring man that he takes as associationism, but in another state he does not approve that the Throne and Footstool should be the shoestrings of his aspiration, nor does he pick up the celestial realm and the terrestrial center with the dust under the soles of his feet. In the battle ranks of effacing attributes he cuts the throat of the turning wheel with the sword of his own state's majesty. He does not approve of paradise and hell as servitors of the court of his own elevated rank and lofty distinction. On the carpet of expansiveness he lets out this shout in the midst of exultation and elation: *"Glory be to me! How tremendous is my status!"*[285]

Another state comes upon him in which he sees that the world's pigs and dogs have a higher degree than himself. He recognizes the superiority of Guebres, Magi, and fire-worshipers. He hears all ridicule as about himself; he sees all faults in himself. If someone throws a stone at him, he voices his gratitude; if someone curses him, he supplicates for him; if someone slaps him, he shows loyalty to him.

There's no one more worthless than I in the city—
    no mother gave birth to a son more lowly.
Among the people in the circle of making claims,
    I'm farther away than a knocker on the door.
A Magi among the Guebres has truer obedience than I;
    a dog among the dogs is more congenial in nature than I.
Though I know for sure that in the whole world
    no one has a state more miserable than I,
There's still room for thanks: When standing before majesty,
    he who despairs most will have the most hope.[286]

*

I desire and nothing is given, and what is given I don't desire;
    my knowledge falls short of the unseen things.[287]

Have you not heard that the same man who in the world of solitariness was shouting out while contemplating the beauty of unity, *"Glory be to me, glory be to me!"* was quarreling with himself in the next breath? It was said to him, "O pir of the Tariqah and forerunner in the Haqiqah! What are you doing?"

He said, "I am cutting the sash of my unbelief."

It was also he who at the time of the soul's extraction said, "Tangarī Tangarī," meaning that he was a Turk having newly become a Muslim.[288]

Here you have a marvelous disposition! Sometimes he says things that heaven and earth won't put up with. Sometimes he's such that *his morning is evening, his evening is clouded, his claims are lies, his words falsehood, his wakefulness sleep, his sleep death, his approval imagination, his hope fantasy, his certainty doubt, his doubt calumny, his path envy, his nature covetousness, his perfection defect, his rulership dismissal, his outwardness remorse, and his inwardness bewilderment.*

O dervish, these men were given two eyes so that with one eye they would see the attributes of the soul's blights and with the other the limpidness of God's generous gifts. With one eye they see faults, with the other the gentleness of the Unseen. With one eye they see His bounty; with the other they see their own acts. When they look at the Real's bounty, they boast of it, and when they look at their own incapacity and weakness, they express their poverty. When they see the generosity of Pure Eternity, they become joyful, and when they see the footsteps of dust's nonexistence, they express their need.

That distracted man of Iraq [Shiblī], burned by the fire of separation, used to say, *"Would that I were a furnace-stoker and had never heard this talk!"* Would that I were a furnace-tender or a tavern-goer and had nothing to do with this talk.

Sometimes he would say, "Where are the proximate angels and residents of the Holy Palisades?! Let them spread their carpets before the throne of my good fortune and the chair of my exaltedness!"

Sometimes wounded by separation, sometimes in the garden of union;
sometimes my place is low, sometimes it's high.

*

I'm satin—
I come to be in every color.[289]

*

Sometimes my hand's full of silver, sometimes I'm poor;
sometimes my heart's elated, sometimes wounded;
Sometimes behind the people, sometimes ahead;
I'm the satin of my own days.

That same man who struck the fire of love into the merchandise of the Dominion's angels and took all eight paradises as his exclusive fief was offered a cow. He was told to seek nourishment *with the toil of your right hand and the sweat of your brow.*[290] Here we have a marvelous business—one moment of happiness followed by three hundred years of sorrow and grief!

Love is sweet and its outcome bitter.
The heart's ardor melts the lover.
I commend you to God—leave me
with the days of separation and pouring tears.
I turned away, but yearning called within me,
"Be kind to your heart—what it seeks is precious."[291]

Yes, it's a marvelous business. His trial was from a grain of wheat, but he set out to seek his own trial.

O chevalier, never say that paradise was taken from Adam. Say rather that Adam was taken from paradise.

The wall said to the nail, "Why are you making a hole in me?"

It said, "Ask the one who is hitting me, for the stone that is behind me will not leave me alone."[292]

The wall said to the nail, "Why are you making a hole in me?"

The nail said to the wall, "Ask the stone they're banging on my head."

The world's folk keep on wondering why Adam sold the eight paradises for a grain of wheat. But love's tipsiness in his head would not give him over to paradise, for this road wants a man seeking the Solitary.

The roads are many, but the road of the Real is one.
On His road the wayfarers are solitary.[293]

The elect of majesty's pavilions, the solitaries of beauty's encampments, the men of love's playing field, the drunkards of yearning's garden, the residents of proximity's dome, the divers in the unseen ocean, the tattered cloak-wearers of God's color, the confounded and stunned by God's creativity, the intoxicated by the wine of *show me that I may gaze upon Thee* [7:143], the subjugated by the dice of love in *"Here I am, O God, here I am,"* the deprived on the journey of desire, the privy to the world of felicity on the expansive carpet of *"Glory be to me, glory be to me!"* the brides behind the veils of the divine gentleness, the dregs-drinking limpid, the headstrong with high aspiration, the self-killing warriors, the sultanlike beggars, the wanderers in the desert of the beginning, the swimmers in the limpid ocean of sobriety—all have pulled back the hem of their aspirations and the skirt of their states from this dunghill. In the zawiya of election they have put on the garment of destitution and the cloak of surrender at the hand of the pir of sincerity. In the tavern of effacing attributes, negating blights, and destroying all that undergoes annihilation, they have drunk down the goblet of joy from the hand of the subsistent cupbearer while contemplating the subsistent things: *"Rejoice in Me!"*[294] On the chessboard of cutting attachments and removing barriers they have seen themselves checkmated by the realities. With a quieting knife, an avenging sword, and an unhesitating blade they have cut off the evil head of worthless pride. They will not take a breath without regrets, moans of remorse, and sighs of bewilderment until they step into the garden of eternal gentleness and the meadow of the friends' gathering, begin to breathe in the green field of the lovers' convocation, and hear without intermediary the address *Am I not your Lord* [7:172] in the cradle of the covenant of *Did I not make covenant with you, O children of Adam?* [36:60]. Day and night, they pull the veil of the outward life over their thirst for that wine, and with a thousand blades of severity they kill the spy of the distracted intellect. But wishing for the moment and fearing the bell's clang, they do not have the gall to say a word. This is why that dervish, when asked if he remembered the day when it was said, *"Am I not your Lord?"* said, "Surely that was yesterday."[295]

Yes, my spirit and world, the specks of the offspring, which were in Adam the chosen's hidden jewel box, solid loins, firm waist, and assisted back, were taken out: *When thy Lord took from the children of Adam, from their loins, their offspring and had them bear witness against their own souls* [7:172]. In the orchards of the realities and without the intrusion of attachments and the tugging and pulling of the policeman of impediments, they became drunk, overthrown, and empty-handed with the wine of *Am I not*. Once they became drunk with that wine, they became like dust motes in the sun. In the rush of the sunshine of munificence, they stepped out to the carpet of existence and put the finger of expansiveness on the subtle point of their own difficulty. Blindly drunk in the negation of being, they kept on giving out these shouts of love in the desert of truthful attributes: *"Show me how Thou givest life to the dead"* [2:260], *"Show me, that I may gaze upon Thee"* [7:143]. That distracted man of Basṭām was saying, *"Glory be to me!"* That madman of Iraq was saying, *"I am the Real."*[296] *But don't become proud, lest you be disowned.*

O dervish, listen to an intimation of love: When a sultan drinks goblets of pure wine in the tavern of bragging, then puts on the garment of beauty and walks into the city, he will throw the town into turmoil.

That unbelieving idol threw the town into turmoil
when she came strolling out the tavern door.[297]

At the beginning of the work inside the tavern of effacing attributes, Adam—that wonder of the eternal gentleness with his limpid gait—was given so much of the wine of love and the potion of proximity—that spirit-mixed, turmoil-inducing liquor—that he sent the turban of the chieftainship of *surely God chose Adam* [3:33] to the bazaar of the lost-hearted and pawned it for the appetizer of *Adam disobeyed* [20:121], the mask of *our Lord, we have wronged ourselves* [7:23], and the belt of *surely he was a great wrongdoer, deeply ignorant* [33:72].

If my friend did not spend nights in the tavern,
why would I pass so much time there?
You said, "Don't burden me by coming at night—
I fear the police and their slaps."

The satin of leadership and the shirt of good fortune were placed on that sapling of the prosperous garden of bounties, that sincere diver in the oceans of majesty's secrets. With the hand of *Adam disobeyed* he began to seek and he tore those garments to pieces. In place of that world and this world he bought the patched cloak of "great wrongdoing" and "deep ignorance" with heart and spirit. *Surely God chose* put the crown of the sultanate on his head, but the crown was plundered by *surely he was a great wrongdoer, deeply ignorant.*

These men are at rest only when they are disgraced and hung by the neck from the noose of not reaching desires.

Not finding what we desire is our good fortune.

Abū Dardā said, *"How beloved are the three disliked things: illness, poverty, and death."*[298]

It makes you happy to see my heart sad.
You rejoice when I approve of what you approve.
But when my soul settles down
in what you love, how can I be seen as sad?[299]

Surely God chose Adam [3:33] is the good news of a robe of honor, and *surely he was a great wrongdoer, deeply ignorant* [33:72] alludes to the robe's secret.

Surely God chose Adam was his beautiful face, and *surely he was a great wrongdoer, deeply ignorant* was the mole on his cheek.

O friend, they gave Adam the chosen the majestic cape and beautiful shirt of *surely God chose Adam* along with the patched cloak of *surely he was a great wrongdoer, deeply ignorant* so that, if the angels should wonder at the highness of his station, the loftiness of his steps, the elevation of his days, and the greatness of his name, He would show them the exalted robe and beautiful cape. But if Adam's makeup should lead him into self-admiration, he would be shown the patched cloak of poverty and would hold himself back.

As for the mouthful that stuck in that paragon's throat, that was because of this same secret: The eight paradises were made his fief, and he was allowed to listen to the canticles of intimacy in the compartments of holiness. The crown of teaching, the diadem of priority, the robe of honoring, and the lights of the eternal gentleness's artisanry were scattered over his secret core. Morning and evening the subtle spirits had been drinking down the potations and drafts of worshipful acts, but they were sent to be his students. He said, *"O Adam, tell them their names"* [2:33].

O diadem of the era's beauty,
    O you with whom I'm always happy,
O stone in the seal ring of the king,
    O jewel at the center of the crown!

Then that grain of wheat, its breast wounded by the sword of need, was sent forth on the steed of severity from the concealment of the Unseen. With goblets of poison it attacked the caravan of Adam's majesty and the camels of his beauty. It snatched away the shawl of chosenness and put the cane of *Adam disobeyed* in his hand. It clothed him in the patched cloak of *he forgot, and We found in him no resoluteness* [20:115]. It gave him the deprived and poor man's pot of *our Lord, we have wronged ourselves* [7:23] and put him into the man-eating desert of love.

It is no abasement to travel on the Tariqah, and the heart is the only waystation in the road of the Haqiqah.

In Your road, love's only food is the heart,
    the only waystation the waystation of pain.
No one should recklessly aim for You
    if he's not clay in Your love's shovel.

*

In my love for You I dwell in a waystation
    that bewilders every mind that settles there.[300]

The waystations of the world of seeking are ladders for the feet of imagination and targets for the arrows of understanding. At the beginning of these deserts the phoenix-intellects of both the elect and the common lose the feathers of thought and the wings of deliberation. *So the hearts of the seekers are enraptured and bewildered in the desert of His magnificence. As much as they tremble in striving to reach the goal, the glories of majesty send them back with severity upon severity. When they try to turn away in despair, a call comes from the pavilions of beauty: "Patience, patience!"*[301]

Which master knows this road's secret
    that we may be his students?
We'll soon wear out in this meditation,
    though we be made of iron and steel.

From the era of Adam's good fortune until now, the intellects of the world's intelligentsia have sat on the steeds of consideration and meditation. With the permission of God's decree and apportioning they have deduced proofs and lessons in keeping with their own faculties and measures, trying to provide a summary of the differentiated, tangled, and tumult-inciting locks of the Possessor of Perfect Beauty. Majesty's jealousy charged forth from the world of *I do not care*[302] and gave a twist to the curled, tumult-inciting earlocks, thus tossing all their seeking, talking, and searching to the wind.

They said, "He's near." I said, "What would I do
with the nearness of sunlight, even in my lap?
"I have nothing of Him other than the mind's remembrance,
stirring up the fire of love's yearning in my breast."[303]

*

She is the sun dwelling in heaven,
her beauty's exaltedness exalting the heart.
But you cannot rise up to her,
nor can she come down to you.[304]

*

Night leads travelers with the glowing moon,
but I've lost the trail in the moonlight.

O dervish, the curling locks of the beloveds are the traps of the lovers' hearts, and the obscurity of the attribute of Will is the ambuscade of the wayfarers' hearts. When He wants to shed the blood of the one hundred and twenty-some thousand center-points of sinlessness, He mixes up a marvelous dye and a strange color in the vat of Will.

That moonlike face speaks secrets to the moon,
and her musky locks get along fine with tulips.
By design she made her ablutions with a thousand lovers' blood,
then performed her prayers to spite the religion.

"I sent you to try you and to try by means of you."[305] O Muḥammad, I turned your face toward trial and with you I turned the face of the people toward trial.

"Surely the people most severely tried are the prophets, then the friends, then the next best, then the next best."[306]

When He wants to plunder the hearts and spirits of a thousand thousand truthful friends, He alludes to the ruling power of His unneediness. When He wants to roast the hearts of a thousand thousand lovers and fill their eyes with water, He curls the earlocks of exaltedness on the cheek of the Will.

Who is not drunk with the wine of His Will? Who is not laid flat by the burden of His majesty? Who is not tipsy with the wine of His exaltedness? Which heart is not wounded by the sword of His severity?

You've fallen in love—wash your hands of heart and eyes.
This is but today—wait until tomorrow!

Anyone whose heart desires to be ʿAdhrā's companion
must become Wāmiq from the roots of his thirty-two teeth.

*

Love is intoxication, its tipsiness destruction,
its wilting and emaciation beautiful.
People fault those who persist in pride,
but beauty is embroidered with pridefulness.[307]

Who is not drunk with the scent of the heart-seeking potion of proximity with Him? Who is not bewildered and distracted with the world of His Unseen?

With a hundred thousand caresses and exaltings, He brought [Moses] into the road—that headman of the registry of the truthful, that verse from the ode of the lovers. He sewed the exalted embroidery of *I chose thee for Myself* [20:41] on the cape of his good fortune, He placed the prosperous mole of *I cast upon thee love from Me* [20:39] on the cheek of his limpid beauty, He draped him with the elevated robe of *surely I have chosen thee over the people* [7:144], and He threw the shawl of uncaused beautiful-doing over the shoulders of his innate nature. He sent one hundred twenty-some thousand cups of sealed secrets to his ears in the unmediated speech of the Glorified. He pitched the whole of the earth as the pavilion of his proximity. He conveyed him to a station in which there were God and Moses, Moses and God, but he became confounded when he was addressed in whispered conversation. He became drunk with this wine, so He sent the proximate of the Presence with fans of intimacy to fan him. In the story: "*When he heard God's speech, he fainted, so God sent the angels to fan him with fans of intimacy.*"

Either don't caress the servant or,
if You caress him, don't melt him.
It's not praiseworthy for generous paragons
first to endear, then to attack.

He prepared a banquet at the peak of Mount Sinai and spread the table of *surely I, I am God* [28:30]. He made the candle of that banquet a living tree and secretly placed the gentle morsel of *God spoke* [4:164] into its mouth. As soon as He dressed his hearing in the robe of unmediated speech, his eyesight also began to seek a robe. "*Show me!*" [7:143], he said. From the Unseen World a call came, "*Thou shalt not see Me.* O Moses, you have received your robe, so do not seek the robe of others. I have put the robe of vision in the coffer of jealousy and locked it with exaltedness until the arrival of that solitary man, that bosom friend of majesty, that Joseph of beauty, that Solomon of perfection. It is not that you have no worthiness for this robe, or that I do not have the munificence and generosity to give it. But jealousy for the steps of that man requests from the eternal gentleness that I place the seal of exaltedness on this goblet. Once he drinks it, his bounty will give the leftover to all the lovers and all the ranks of the yearners."

The lovers will put on no garment of love
nor take off any not worn out by me.
They will drink no cup of love, bitter
or sweet, not left over from what I've drunk.[308]

O you who are exalted in the world, give back a mark of this state on the tongue of discourse! *"Do you wonder that bosom friendship belongs to Abraham, speech to Moses, and vision to Muḥammad?"*[309]

How many there are who sought union with me,
but I refused her what she sought.
I sought your approval by making her angry—
your withholding is better than her giving.[310]

Moses was coming drunk with the wine of *God spoke* [4:164], intoxicated by the goblet of *surely I, I am God* [28:30], and busy with the drunkenness of *I cast upon thee love from Me* [20:39]. He said, *"Show me, that I may gaze upon Thee* [7:143]." *I am here, weak, standing before You.*

Anyone whose heart is suffering
seeks what befits the suffering.[311]

*

Everything has an alms tax that must be paid—
beauty's alms tax is mercy on the likes of me.[312]

O dervish, *his Lord spoke to him* [7:143] put Moses on the carpet of expansiveness. But one of their sayings is *"Stand on the carpet and beware of expansiveness! You will not be secure from the striking of whips until you pass over the Narrow Path."*[313]

What has the chosen one to do with free choice? What has the slave to do with ownership? What has the servant to do with sitting at the forefront with kings? "They have no choice. Glory be to Him and high indeed is He above what they associate!" [28:68].

Show me, that I may gaze upon Thee. "O Moses, have you brought along your own eyes that you say *show me*? Now that you have come with eyes, We have made your eyes wellsprings of blood and—by virtue of the uncaused Will that has always been—We will make you gaze on a rock."

O chevalier, why would He show you His always-having-been? Rather, He will show you yourself in your own attribute of never-having-been. As long as a mote of you is left, He will cast upon you the veil of the mountain.

"O My spirit and world, I am yours, and you are Mine!" What wisdom is there in His speaking to you of Adam, Noah, Abraham, Moses, and Jesus? He is warming up the place of your hopes in Him and fanning the fire in the chamber of your patience. When someone sits in front of a hungry man and eats delicious food, his mouth starts to water. "O friend, though My goods are expensive and the poor can't buy them, well, there's no law against hoping."

With wishes you will pass the night in bliss—
surely wishes are the capital of the destitute.[314]

If plants do not grow in a house where they sprinkle water, well, at least the dust will settle down and it will become cool. If you do not have enough water to take to a landed estate, well, drinking is permitted and no one will prevent you from drinking, even if the stream belongs to someone else. Miserable is the cook who takes the trouble, blackens his clothes, and suffers the fire's heat—then someone else eats the food!

Moses said, *"Show me,"* and he was struck by the blade of the severity of *thou shalt not see Me.* Then a piece of rock received this robe of honor: *When his Lord disclosed Himself to the mountain.*

When the vanguards of majesty's blows and the spears of beauty's banners appeared from the world of self-disclosure, the mountain fell to the ground and was effaced in itself, and Moses fell down thunderstruck. When he came back to himself, he said, "Lord God, where did the mountain go?"

The address came: "It was effaced and fell into the concealment of nonexistence. O Moses, if I had given you what you wanted, My beauty would not have been diminished, nor would My majesty have been harmed. But instead of the mountain, you would have been effaced by the world of sorrow, and I have work for you to do."

I will not let you off so easy—
I have work to do with your locks and lips.

What a marvelous business! It was said to Moses, *"Thou shalt not see Me."* Then it was said, *"But look at the mountain!* [7:143], *Go to Pharaoh!"* [22:24]. What His exaltedness does to the spirits of the folk of love!

It is said that when he reached this station and these tales took place, he wanted to go back to his wife and children. The address came, *"You have fallen in, so hold fast."* Now that you have fallen into the trap, given your heart over to My name, and set out on the road, you must dedicate your heart to sorrow and your life to the dangers of the path.

You must dedicate your heart to sorrow and your spirit to danger
when your heart becomes single in its love for the pretty-faced.
How will the lover be severed from his own attributes' incapacity?
Severance from his attributes' incapacity is where love begins.

Two foxes fell into a trap. One said to the other, "When will I see you again?"

He said, *"The day after tomorrow, in the furriers' bazaar."*

Moses said, *"Unloose the knot from my tongue"* [20:27]. Lord God, lift away the knot from my tongue.

The address came, *"Thou hast been given thy request, O Moses!"* [20:36].

He said, "Lord God, now that You have lifted away the knot, *show me!"*

"O Moses, how can this be the place for that talk? The knots and bonds are in the curled tresses of the jealousy of Beauty and Majesty."

Let loose another curl from those two world-burning tresses,
  add another shine to that spirit-brightening face!
Charge once again into the field of intellect and safety
  with the unbelief-stirring, faith-burning wearers of black!
Assign again to the Sufi-natured, limpid-spirited lovers
  those two rows of insolent, heart-taking, spirit-piercing sorcerers![315]

At the beginning of his state Moses was caressed by the breeze of gentleness. At the end he was melted by the simoom of severity. It is said that when he asked for vision and was struck by the blade of not reaching his desire, the angels came, took him by the hair, and pulled him through those mountains, saying, *"O son of menstruating women, you want to see the Exalted Lord?!"*[316]

It is said that this address arrived from the Presence of Majesty: *"My angels, say nothing to Moses."*

O dervish, *"Don't become proud, lest you be disowned."*

Don't talk coldly to My cameleer—
  he likes exile and travel by night.[317]

All that gentleness at the beginning, and all this severity at the end!

Your union is separation, your love hate,
  your nearness distance, your peace war.
In you—God's is the praise!—is hardness
  and your every docile steed is unruly.[318]

*

At first you inclined toward me. Where's that inclination?
  Today you're weary of me. What happened?
By our friendship, O friend, tell me the truth,
  what was that inclination, why this weariness?

The same thing happened to Adam. At the beginning, he was clothed in the robe of generosity and placed on the chair of majesty. The angels had to prostrate themselves before him, and an edict was written for the celebration of his vicegerency. In the second state, the address came, *"Go down!"* [2:36].

The same angels who had prostrated themselves before his chair put their hands on his back, as when someone is evicted and ejected from a house. Adam was biting the fingers of wonder with the teeth of bewilderment: "What's this? What happened?"

Unqualified love was saying, "O lover, seek, and have no fear!"

Last night you carried my burden with heart and eyes;
  today you're not letting me near your presence.
Last year I had a hundred joys in your street;
  this year I'm weeping blood with a hundred needs.

*

O questioner, how will it go for you after me?
I met what was ugly and that made Him happy.
I'd become conceited in union
and began to feel secure from His deception.
His aversion burned me such
that not a speck of what I witnessed remains.[319]

*

You think well of things when the days are beautiful
without fearing the ugliness of the apportioning.
You make peace with the night, deluded by it,
but opacity will come forth in the night's limpidness.[320]

Adam looked with wonder. *From the pulpit of beauty the tongue of majesty called out with the melodies of coquetry, "O Adam, you are in one valley, and We in another. O wonder of creativity, O unprecedented marvel of power, O priceless of the spheres, O object of the angel's prostration, O possessor of crown and robe, O prodigy of differentiation and totality! Did you not know that 'At first love is being duped, and at last it is being killed,'*[321] *at first it is deceit and at last headache, at first acceptance upon acceptance, and at last wilting upon wilting, at first life and at last death, at first proximity and at last flames, at first generosity and at last debts, at first intoxication upon intoxication and at last fire upon fire?"*

O chevalier, this is one of their sayings: "Trial is needed in love like salt in a pot." Any possessor of beauty who does not play the coquette with her passionate lover has not given her beauty its rightful due. By the rightful due of the Real, if tomorrow the address should come, "Gaze upon Me!" you should say, *"Your beauty lies far beyond the gaze of my likes!"*[322]

I yearned for Him and when He appeared,
I bowed in veneration,
Not in fear but in awe
and to protect His beauty.
I shunned Him when He came close
hoping for the specter of His image,
For death is for Him to turn His back
and life that He turn this way.[323]

O dervish, if He had not taken Adam to task for that grain of wheat, His majesty would not have been diminished. If He had shown Moses His vision, His beauty would not have suffered any loss. But the perfection of beauty demands that a thousand thousand lovers wail and moan, captive to the chains of His severity.

Eyes and neck a gazelle's ransom,
his long stature a willow branch,

His locks' chains,
heart-catching nets—
The divan of beauty tells his tale,
the hint of his glance a verse.
When his lovers are presented to him,
I reckon myself to be first in line.

Adam was truthful in his passion and conforming in his love. He happily drank down all he was given—the poisonous drafts of disappointment and the slaps of severity.

If what my envier says makes you happy,
no harm is done when you approve of my pain.[324]

He was saying with the tongue of his state, "If You send me a poisonous draft, I'll welcome it with my spirit, and if You strike me with severity's slap, I'll put up with it from the depths of my heart."

Don't drive me away, but if You burn me, that's fine.
What I want in all this is Your approval.
When a heart is fit for friendship with You
and put in the hottest fire, it won't be harmed.

Don't send me away, but if You put me on the gallows, that's agreeable; don't abandon me, but if You kill me, that's appropriate, for Your love's good fortune subsists forever. I will reap the fruit of spirit and heart when I drink more of Your severity's wine. I will find pleasure in life when I suffer blow after blow from the sword of Your majesty's severity.

If I don't take this love to the end,
I won't reap the fruit of heart and spirit.

*

When someone dies in love—let him die like that.
There's no good in a love without death.[325]

"He who loves, stays chaste, conceals, and dies, dies a martyr."[326]

O dervish, if your head starts to ache one night, serve that ache with head and eyes, for a headache that He gives is not trivial.

It is said that revelation came to Ezra: "O Ezra, if I give you an apricot, thank Me for the apricot. Do not look at the apricot's insignificance. Look at the fact that on the day I was dividing up the provisions, I remembered you."

My heart's name, O pretty one, is in Your book—
I'm happy that I'm part of Your army.
I obey, in short, Your every command—
all my bags ride on Your donkey.

What is this talk? *A disease without remedy, a night without dawn, an ocean without shore, an illness without cure, a wound without surgeon, a trial without healing. "And that He may try the faithful with a beautiful trial"* [8:17]. He sends a trial, and then He says: "Here's a beautiful trial for you." *The trial is beautiful because it is from Him, and the trial is pleasant because He comes along with it.*

At first love appears as a need
that springs up but then events drive
the young man into passion's path
and grown men cannot bear what happens.[327]

On the day they spread love's carpet and set up passion's banner in the world of yearning, they set fire to all the objects of desire. They scattered the seeds of not reaching desires in the ground of the hearts and soaked it with the water of remorse and the flood of bewilderment.

Here we have Adam the chosen, that first wayfarer and first center-point of good fortune. For three hundred years he scattered his liver's blood on his cheeks and, in the khanaqah of the heart, quarreled with the deceiving soul sitting in the corner.

Here we have Noah, chosen and raised up, the verse *surely he is not of thy folk* [11:46] striking against his liver. Satan sat in the ship with him, and a piece of his heart was hung on the gallows.[328]

Here we have Abraham, wearing the robe of bosom friendship and taken to the dome of proximity and the howdah of messengerhood. Then the rebellious Nimrod was put in charge after the seed of enmity toward Abraham was sown in his breast. That miserable man, blameworthy in activity and heavy in eyesight, nurturing delusions and engaging in follies, placed the paragon of the age in the ballista of trial. And he, from the world of realized assent itself, was letting out the cry, *"Of you, no."*[329] In the end the wind of changing fortune blew and a lame, one-winged gnat gave the arrogance of that miserable man to the wind.

Here we have Jacob, who was brought into the House of Sorrows for seventy years, the ruling power of love put in charge on every side of his heart's realm.

Here we have Joseph, who was auctioned off among the ranks of slaves at a crossroads in Egypt and sold for a few bad dirhams. In the end the buyer came banging at the door, though *they had been renouncing him* [12:20].

Here we have Moses, brought into the presence of secret whispering with a thousand endearments and exaltings, then taken to pain and melting.

Here we have Zachariah the sinless, the saw laid on top of his head and pushed down to his feet.

And here we have John the pure, his face in the dust, his head cut off like a sheep.

He does all this, but in fear
a man has not the gall to sigh,
for the face is like a mirror,
and sighs will mar a mirror.

23–24. *al-Qābiḍ al-Bāsiṭ:* the Contractor, the Expander

Some have said that the meaning of these names is that He—*majestic is His majesty!*—takes the spirits to Himself from the bodies at the time of death, and that He expands the spirits within the bodies at the time of bringing to life. Some have said the meaning is contracting alms from the rich—a contracting that is verified by its acceptance—and expanding provisions for the poor, in the sense of bestowing and giving daily portions. Some have said that contracting means constricting and tightening the daily portion, and expanding means making the daily portion vast. Some have said that this is the contraction of hearts; from time to time you see a man tight-hearted without any cause, and from time to time you see him once again happy-hearted without any cause.[330]

Contraction and expansion are the divine decree and royal predetermination. *He will not be asked about what He does, but they will be asked* [21:23]. Sometimes He holds them in the grasp of His contraction so that the ruling power of majesty wreaks havoc on them, and sometimes He places them on the carpet of His expansion so that the ruling power of beauty caresses them with bestowal.

It is stipulated for the possessor of pain that he be in the grasp of power's contraction without protest and on the carpet of love's expansion without turning away. May a thousand thousand lives be sacrificed to the forehead that shows no creases of judgment!

That exalted man of the era said, "*Approval is to welcome the decrees with joy.*"[331] Approval is that you drink down goblets of pure poison without wailing and crying.

That burnt one said,

> *The lovers complain in their ardor—would that*
> *I alone carried what was thrown to them.*
> *Then I would have all love's pleasure*
> *met by no lover before or after me.*[332]

Once the spirits of the elect find the way to the dome of election and the proximity of the Threshold, they sing like nightingales in the morning of felicity on the sweet briar of the nearness and stability of the Presence, enjoying meditation and remembrance. Then they are perfectly jealous for the beauty of love, so much so that whenever the sultan of majestic exaltedness draws a sword from the sheath of the perfect will, they want to send their heart's last breath, stuffed with the sorrows and anxieties of love, on the steed of approval to welcome His acceptance.

> How can I not be happy having bought for one heart
> a love worth a thousand sweet spirits!

*

> *Prison, bonds, yearning, exile,*
> *and distance from the Friend—surely that is terrible.*
> *If a man stays constant in the covenant's compact*
> *when suffering the like of this, surely he is noble.*[333]

O dervish, when *the Fluctuater of Hearts and Eyes*[334] takes the arrow of trial from the quiver of friendship with the hand of the decree, He has no target other than the core of pious hearts.

A dervish came to a khanaqah. The servant came and was pulling off his boots and saying, "Are you well?"

The dervish said, "Quick, give me back my boots and don't talk nonsense. On the day I took up the staff of seeking in this talk, I threw the prayer carpet of the two worlds' well-being into the ocean of trial and set fire to the haystack of safety."

Love for You threw me into the trap with trickery;
 it threw me into the burning fire of the days.
Holding the cup of separation's cruelty in hand,
 it threw my religion, heart, and wholesomeness into the cup.

*

Alas for the lovers, how wretched are their shares
 if what I have is the like of what they have![335]

O chevalier, you need an eye that does not have the squint of attending to causes. You need a heart that has no thorns of judgment so that, whenever a laden caravan comes out of the city of severity, it receives it *with cheerful face and smiling teeth*. My paragon, my father, used to say, "If you see a dervish with a knot on his forehead, know that he has changed his object of worship."

There was an old man the mountain of whose eyes had received rays from the sun of the Gaze along with secrets of the Unseen. Whenever he made a prayer, it was answered. Forty of his children were killed and he spoke not a word. They asked him, "Why don't you complain?"

With smiling face and weeping eyes he said, *"One does not have recourse to kings when they are wrathful."* It is not part of courtesy to talk with kings when they are angry.

Enough for me that You know my heart
 loves You and You recognize all I find.
Between me and my aim I place the recognition
 that time will not cease until the Endless ceases.
I will leave this world with Your love
 between my sides, no one else aware of it.[336]

*

Every heart afflicted by love
 becomes a mine of heartache, tribulation, and trial.
Foreign to the joy of all hearts
 is a stature bent over by love.
Never again will those stand straight
 who are familiar with the heartache of love.

One of them said, *"When someone recognizes God, his sorrows will disappear."* Another said, *"When someone recognizes God, his sorrows will be drawn out."*

When a whiff of this meadow reaches someone's nostrils, a thousand thousand grindstones of trouble and millstones of trial will turn round his heart and liver. If he should say a word, he will be hung on the gallows of his judgment at the crossroads of abandonment. The draft he drinks is not small like those given to the infants of the Tariqah in the cradle of the covenant's beginning. It is an overflowing goblet taken in hand by adults on the road. In sincere truthfulness his every speck will shout out,

My work is your stature, O tall cypress,
but today your tresses are bonds upon bonds.
For a time I ate of the world to my heart's desire,
but today I'm content with the way things are.

*

When it's not as you desire, desire it as it is.

Here you have a manger full of fat without fodder, and there you have the hiss of a frying pan without fat.

Suffering and abandoned, a hundred thousand sorrows piled up in his heart, if he should expose one iota of his complaint and bring it out in the open, love's bile would no longer have the gall to pitch its beauty's tent in the world. He drinks down cups of poison, contemplates the beauty of severity, and shouts out,

What place is His decree for the headstrong? With Him
I'm a candle—happy when its neck is trimmed.[337]

The long and the short of it is that being in love is a watery soup that has none of the salt of kindness.

Love is built on severity—were the
beloved indulgent, that would not be fit.
In the rulebook of love it's not beautiful
for a lover to string out arguments.[338]

*

What should the lover do if not forbear?

*

When you love, serve and obey the one you love—
you won't reach union if your soul doesn't cling to humility.[339]

The helpless, fervent lover—his soul captive in the cottage of the breast, his heart wounded by the blades of a thousand disappointments, the stairways of his sighs firmly shut down! Each time a sigh wants to lift up its head to the balcony of manifestation, His jealousy slaps it in the face. At every moment a thousand special serving boys are sent from the Presence of Election—"Tell that sigh to stay in place, for if the sigh of someone burned were to come out into the open plain, neither this nor that would remain. *One sigh of the lovers would burn up the two worlds and extinguish the two fires."* O hand of jealousy, go and put the bridle of exaltedness on the mouths of the burnt ones. Keep the sigh, which is the precious pearl of the ocean of pain, right there. It must not come out into the open because of love's bile at perfect tribulation, or else the sigh of that empty-handed drunk would flatten the green dome and the dusty circle.

O chevalier, favors are done for Quran-reciters, night-risers, prayer-performers, and fasters, but no favors are done for lovers.

O you who lament so much in the ruins,
not for the ruins but for those within,
The custom of lovers is one—
when you're in love, you're miserable.[340]

*

Ever since the sorrow of your love grabbed my skirt,
suffering and trial have shown their heads from my collar.

*

The mark of a man in love
is humble eyes when he looks.
He conceals what he encounters, mindful of love,
but when love commands, he hears and obeys.

This is one of their sayings: *"The servant will not find the sweetness of faith until trial comes to him from everywhere."*[341] No one will find faith until he becomes the target of trial's arrow.

Unjust and unfair, you deny what you know;
your threats are truthful and your promises broken.
Explain your approval to me, then evade or be gentle.
You've been harsh to the slender gazelle, so its eyes are weeping.

*

Nothing will ever reach
the lover's spirit but suffering.
When he finds the scent of his beloved,
the spheres will not be able to string his bow.

The first lover to write the ABCs of love in the grammar school of existence was Adam. Look what happened to him! No kindness was done to him with that grain of wheat. The sword of *Adam disobeyed* [20:121] was drawn from the sheath of the Eternal Desire, and severity's cup was filled with the drink of poison. The same man who was striking fire into the monasteries of the obedient with the brilliance of his lightning turned his face to this ruined tavern. He heard the call, *"Go down out of it, all of you"* [2:38].

Yesterday that man was talking fine points and fancy words—
today he's pawned his cloak in the tavern.
Now that he's pawned his cloak,
he'd best forget the fine points and fancy words.

O dervish, when a man is a gambler and tavern-goer, the awards of sultans and the bestowals of kings have no luster. When he receives a gift, he takes it to the tavern and gambles it away. But since the sultan loves this tavern-goer, the more he goes to the tavern, the more he bestows on him robes of honor.

Adam the chosen walked into the neighborhood of slips and took as wages the chamber of *Adam disobeyed*, but by virtue of the beginningless solicitude, the King gave him goblets of chosenness one after another and hamstrung the envy of the enviers.

O friend, when the sultan's award bestows luster, it does so for a perfectly judicious possessor of resoluteness. But the saddlecloth of resoluteness was snatched away from the shoulders of this center-point of dust's existence, for *he forgot, and We found in him no resoluteness* [20:115].

Why do you look at the repentance of the judicious possessor of resoluteness? Look rather at the fact that the sultan gave him a robe of honor only once in his lifetime. But this cheerful, ineffectual fellow receives an uninterrupted bestowal of gentleness moment by moment.

O exalted Gabriel, O peacock of the angels! It is now several thousand years that you have been moving the pieces of resoluteness on the chessboard of obedience to the extent of your ability, but in your lifetime you have been given only one robe of honor. The work is done by this carefree scoundrel. The tailor of beginningless gentleness sewed the cape of his exaltedness with the needle of never-ending bounty on the height of his measure and the stature of his gifts, for *He loves them and they love Him* [5:54]. *God is the friend of those who have faith* [2:257].

The splendorous Throne was given one robe of honor: *Then He sat upon the Throne* [7:54]. The elevated heaven was sent one award, the award of "descent"[342]—though similarity and likeness are far from the road. Mount Sinai was given one drink with the hand of love, and that was the drink of self-disclosure.[343] The other existent things were all like this. Those who received robes that acknowledged their dignity kept the robes. When this fearless handful of dust was sent a robe, he took it down to the tavern of mortal nature and gambled it away for the dregs of the pain and the pure wine of love's vat.

Drinking dregs in the tavern is my custom,
being ruined by drunkenness is my creed.
The bigger the cup the better for me—
not finding desires is my good fortune.

O dervish, I will tell you a secret. Once the world's folk hear this secret, they should let their spirit and world be plundered. It is a secret concerning which speech cries out, "It's not my work to tell it." The pen moans, "Love's pounding has already grabbed me—it's not my work to write it down." The ink says, "My black gelim cannot cover the manifestation of its realities." The polo field of the blank page says, "The ball of love has no place here." But I will speak openly if you do not constrict your heart. The secret is this:

In the row of chosenness Adam the chosen was given a cup of love's limpid wine. The cap of his good fortune and the mirror of his greatness were set up from the distant Pleiades to the ends of the earth. The angels of the Dominion were commanded to prostrate themselves before him. But his greatness, honor, eminence, good fortune, rank, and chosenness did not appear in their prostration. It appeared in *Adam disobeyed* [20:121]. In certitude and verification, the summit of these words lies beyond the Splendorous Throne. Why? Because caresses at the time of conformity are no indication of honor. Caresses at the time of opposition indicate honor.

With the crown of prosperity on his head and the robe of bounteousness on his body, the chosen and beautiful Adam sat on the chair of majesty and perfection. The steed of bestowal was at the door, the pillars of his good fortune's seat went higher than the Throne, the parasol of kingship was open above his head, and he himself had raised the exalted banner of knowledge in the world. If the angels and the celestial spheres should kiss the ground beneath his feet, that is no surprise. What is surprising is that he fell into the pit of the slip. His straight stature, which had been pulled up by *surely God chose Adam* [3:33], was bent because *Adam disobeyed*. Then the crown of *He chose him* [20:122] took wing from the heaven of the beginningless gentleness.

O dervish, if God had not wanted to accept him with all his faults, He would not have created him with all those faults.

If you don't cover your eyes for your friend
and pardon what he does, you'll die rebuking him.[344]

*

If you rebuke your friend in everything,
you'll never meet what you don't rebuke.
So live alone, or join with your brother, for
sometimes he yields to sin or avoids it.
If you stop drinking because of impurity,
you'll stay thirsty—whose drinks are limpid?[345]

O dervish, you should not believe that Adam was brought out of paradise for eating the wheat. God wanted to bring him out. Adam did not contradict the decrees, for His decrees remain pure of contradiction. Tomorrow God will bring a thousand thousand people who committed great sins into paradise. Should He take Adam out of paradise for one act of disobedience? *No—the decrees of majesty are far too majestic to be weighed in the scales of the Mu'tazilites.*[346]

If you say that Adam was brought out of paradise because of his disobedience, what then did the Messenger do in *two-bows' length away* [53:9] that he was brought back from there? Rather, he was taken to *two-bows' length away* so that the angels would learn service from his silence and stillness. He was brought back so that the earth-dwellers would learn the Shariah from his speech. There he was saying, *"I do not number Thy laudations."*[347] Here he was saying, *"I am the most eloquent of the Arabs."*[348]

The Messenger said, "One should be a guest for no more than three days. When the fourth day arrives, a man becomes heavy. Seeing the heavy is the fever of the spirit."[349]

Another secret: A man has a wife and companion. He does not know that he loves his wife, for friendship is hidden by companionship. Wait until he divorces her, and then the friendship will appear. Adam was the friend, but his friendship was hidden by the bestowal of paradise, for not everyone who receives a bestowal is a friend—all of Byzantium is gold and silver, but there is not an iota of love anywhere. When the veil of paradise was lifted, the reality of love became apparent.

When Iblis was not yet Iblis—according to the view of those who say he was not an angel—no one knew that he was Iblis. He was a worshiper and prostrator. He had bound the belt of the work, his face washed with the water of conformity. When his foot slipped, it became apparent that he was neither friend nor servant.

When Adam was on the throne of exaltedness and the couch of good fortune, he had the ring of the Real's gentleness in his ear and the shawl of the sultanate over his shoulder; he was the friend, but the secret of love was covered by blessings. When his foot slipped, it became apparent that he was both friend and servant.

The marvelous thing is that He brought Iblis the enemy and Adam the friend together in one place. But a castle that brings things together has both a forefront, where the king sits, and a toilet, which is a place of dread.

That accursed one flew with the back feathers of fear and the fore feathers of priority in the sky of obedient acts, while thinking that he was one of the beautiful-doers. When the eyes of predetermination and the glances of apportioning looked askance at him, his wings were clipped and his cups were filled with the wine of the curse. "And God does what He wills" [14:27], *and "He decrees what He desires"* [5:1].

As for Adam, that possessor of stability, he stretched his hand to the prohibited tree and left nothing in the bow of opposition. But the Real said, "Then his Lord chose him" [20:122]. *This, by my life, is a gift of approval and a fine bestowal!*

He—*majestic is His majesty!*—pulled up this handful of dust with a tremendous pull. *"O folk of the Garden, everlastingness, and no death! O folk of the Fire, everlastingness, and no death!"*[350] He placed a road without end before him, both trial without limit and bestowal without end. "O wild animals, birds, and beasts, become dust and clear the face of the earth! O handful of dust, the work is your work, the friend your friend, the mystery your mystery, the joy your joy! On the day I said *'Am I not your Lord?'* [7:172], I seized your skirt and bound you inside the pavilions of My majestic Presence. As long as you have not paid the just due and I have not paid the just due—the hand of your incapacity and destitution, and the skirt of My majesty and bestowal! I will burn all those with whom you get along, I will strike fire into every homeland where you settle down, and I will send an informant in pursuit wherever you may be.

Day and night, I'll oversee your work—
 if you get along with anyone I'll smash your bazaar.

"When I conveyed talk of Myself to your hearing at the beginning of the work, I conveyed it without intermediary. When I put you into the cradle of gentleness in that era and addressed you with the words *'Am I not your Lord'* without intermediary, where were Gabriel, Michael, Muḥammad, and Abraham? With you I have a work in which intellects become distracted."

How blessed were the days when we were in the concealment of nonexistence and He was calling out to us by virtue of the gentleness of eternity, without any precedent steps: " 'Am I not your Lord' O My servants!"

O dervish, seizing does not happen because of a cause. We do not say that He does not seize anyone, but the request that comes forth from the pavilion of exaltedness to the open plain of favor comes without any cause.

It is said that one day ʿAbd al-Malik Marwān summoned ʿAzza, who was Kuthayyir's beloved, and said, "Lift your mask so that I may see if Kuthayyir is right to be in love with you." She lifted the mask. ʿAbd al-Malik looked closely, but he did not see ʿAzza as very beautiful. He turned to her and said, " 'Azza, I do not know what Kuthayyir saw in you that he became entranced."

ʿAzza looked up at him and said, "O ʿAbd al-Malik, what did the Muslims see in you that they made you their commander?"

When thy Lord took from the children of Adam [7:172]. The pearl-diver of power was sent into the ocean of Adam's loins to bring out the night-brightening pearls and the night-colored beads and to place them on the shore of existence: Pharaoh and Moses, Abraham and Nimrod, firm Muṣṭafā and accursed Abū Jahl. Just as He brought forth the friends, so also He brought forth the enemies. He offered them the drink of the Lord's address, and they all took it with the hand of *Yes indeed*. They drank it down and put the ring of servanthood on their ears. By answering the address of the Lord of Lords, they appeared.

Then, at last, there will come the address of majesty: *"Whose is the kingdom today?"* [40:16]. No one will say a word. At the beginning, there was *talk upon talk*, at the end there will be *silence upon silence*. Yes, beginners have a tongue and a talk, but the advanced have neither tongue nor talk.

At first, they were under the sway of the Shariah. The policeman of the Shariah was behind them, and the Shariah affirms man, so they appeared with *Yes indeed*. But at last they will have the garb of the Haqiqah. The Haqiqah negates man, so they will not speak.

O dervish, you can buy a nightingale, which calls out night and day, for one dirham. But a falcon, which does not call out once in its lifetime, costs a thousand dinars.

At first they were in the road of sobriety and being, so they answered the address. At last they will be in the road of effacement and nonbeing, so He, in the perfection of His gentleness, will make Himself their deputy. He will say, *"God's, the One, the Severe"* [40:16].

This is an exalted secret. If at first He Himself had answered the address and said *"Yes indeed,"* then all the blights would have been lifted from the road. In this world there would be neither synagogue nor church, neither cross nor crucifix. But this world is the house of blights, and the next world is the house without blight. Blights cannot be avoided here, but they cannot take form there.

The first address was the policeman of this world's road, and the last address will be the policeman of the next world's road. Anyone who finds life in this world finds it by virtue of the first address: *"Am I not your Lord?"* Anyone who finds subsistence in the next world will find it by virtue of the last address: *"Whose is the kingdom today?"*

Know that in reality, if He had answered the first address, this world would never undergo annihilation. And if you were to answer the last address, the next world would never subsist. It is the wound of your answer that came across this world and made it susceptible to annihilation. It was the ray of His answer's robe that will shine on the next world and give it the attribute of subsistence.

O chevalier, know that in reality a covenant was made with you on that day to see who would remain with the covenant.

Whom do I have whose heart will stay firm in his love
and who, when he moves on, will not swerve in his covenant?
Oh, the misery of my soul when my brother leaves me
and takes no profit from the beauty of loyalty to his covenant!
He makes his words limpid, not his character,
and his aloes smile is mixed with honey's sweetness.
His tongue gives out the pearls of his contract,
but his heart boils in the pot of his rancor.
He cares not whether I put up with his unruliness.
In Thee I seek refuge from enviers and their trickery![351]

Strive from the depth of your spirit not to lose the ring that you put on your ear with your attestation on the day of the Covenant of Alast. Otherwise you will be hung by the ring of trial's snare. Breaking off from the curly earlocks of the black-moled Beloved, and then, in the end, breaking the Covenant—these are not the marks of manliness. If they cut off your head, if they bring the two worlds out against you, if they put the dagger of antagonism against the throat of your present moment—still, you must be solitary, you must be a man.

Be the man whose feet are on the ground
and whose head aspires to the Pleiades.[352]

On the Day of *am I not your Lord?* [7:172] a table of love was set up. By the decree of gentleness, you were sat down at the table and given a lawful morsel from the covenant of Lordhood's majesty. With the hand of *yes indeed* you placed that morsel in love's mouth. *There is no morsel more appetizing than the morsel of* tawḥīd *in the mouth of love.*

Beware, beware, do not cast away this morsel with dislike! If you do, you will remain forever in the trial [*balāʾ*] of your *yes indeed* [*balā*].

The first sapling that He planted in the garden of your hearing was the sapling of His Lordhood. He watered it with gentleness, and it sent down roots. Then the branch of loyalty grew up: *Those who are loyal to their covenant when they make a covenant* [2:177]. The leaf of approval grew: *God approves of them and they approve Him* [5:119]. The flower of praise and laudation bloomed: *"Those who praise God much in every state."*[353] The fruit of union and encounter took shape: *Faces that day radiant, gazing on their Lord* [75:22–23]. He recorded the book of the Covenant of Lordhood on the tablets of the spirits with the ink of assistance and the pen of eternal gentleness: *Those—He wrote faith in their hearts and confirmed them with a spirit from Him* [58:22].

To the bodies He spoke of Lordhood and to the spirits He spoke of love.

"O bodies, I am God! O hearts, I am the Friend!

"O bodies, you belong to Me! O hearts, I belong to you!

"O bodies, toil, for that is what Lordhood requires from servanthood. O hearts, be joyful—*'Rejoice in Me and take pleasure in remembering Me'*[354]—for that is what unqualified love demands.

"O bodies, yours are the realities of struggle! O hearts, yours are the gardens of contemplation!

"O bodies, yours is the discipline of practice! O hearts, yours is the rose garden of beginningless gentleness!

"O bodies, yours is asking! O hearts, yours is bestowal!

"O bodies, yours is need! O hearts, yours is joy!

"O bodies, yours is doing! O hearts, yours is pain!

"O bodies, do not let go of obedience! O hearts, do not obey the souls!

"O bodies, yours is suffering! O hearts, yours is the treasure!

"O bodies, be like a knocker on the door! O hearts, ascend beyond the Splendorous Throne!

"O bodies, surrender the body on credit! O hearts, deal only in hard cash!"

Do you not see that when there is talk of the body, promises are made? [*But as for him who feared the station of his Lord*] *and prohibited the soul its caprice, surely the Garden shall be the shelter* [79:40–41]. But, when there is talk of the heart, there is talk of hard cash: *"I sit with him who remembers Me."*[355] *"I am with My servant's thoughts of Me."*[356] *And He is with you wherever you are* [57:4].

O dervish, bounty's paradise is found in the paradise of union. But union's paradise is not found in the paradise of bounty.

"O bodies, yours is a pathway! O hearts, yours is a drinking place!

"O bodies, busy yourself with fasting and prayer! O hearts, busy yourself with secret whispering, supplication, pain, and melting!

"O bodies, journey with *Thee alone we worship*! O hearts, gaze with *Thee alone we ask for help*! [1:5]."[357]

"Thee alone we worship" because we belong to Thee, "and Thee alone we ask for help" because we come into being through Thee.

"Thee alone we worship" in loyalty to servanthood, "and Thee alone we ask for help" in gazing on the limpidness of Lordhood.

"Thee alone we worship" because we are servants at Thy door, "and Thee alone we ask for help" because we number among Thy lovers.

"Thee alone we worship" because we are servitors, "and Thee alone we ask for help" because we are passionate lovers—and it is fitting to give a hand to drunken lovers.

"Thee alone we worship," thus negating compulsion, "and Thee alone we ask for help," thus rejecting free will.

"Thee alone we worship" through our effort, "and Thee alone we ask for help" so that Thou wilt preserve us in our covenant.

"Thee alone we worship" is to bind the belt of diligence on the waist of truthfulness, and *"Thee alone we ask for help"* is to ask for the effusive bounty of His munificent Existence. It is a stipulation that you take your diligence to His munificence. Then perhaps the rays of the sun of His munificence will shine on your diligence, and your diligence will become worthy of His Majestic Presence.

"Thee alone we worship" in the majesty of Thy command, "and Thee alone we ask for help" in the perfection of Thy bounty.

"Thee alone we worship" because of the exaltedness of Thy command, "and Thee alone we ask for help" because of the treasury of Thy bounty.

"Thee alone we worship" arises from the street of service, and *"Thee alone we ask for help"* arises from the street of aspiration.

When the servant says, *"Thee alone we worship,"* the Real says, "Accept whatever he has brought." When the servant says, *"And Thee alone we ask for help,"* He says, "Give him whatever he wants."

O dervish, the storehouse of bestowers gains luster from the askers' asking and need. No asker had greater need than dust. It was given heaven and earth, the Throne and the Footstool, but its need did not decrease by one iota. The eight paradises were given over entirely to its work, but need seized its reins, for poverty was the host at the table of its existence: *Surely man was created grasping* [70:19].

A grasping person is someone who never becomes full. He brought Adam into paradise and permitted him its bliss, but He said, "Don't go after that tree." Nonetheless, despite all the blissful things, Adam was seized by the tree. *The forbidden is enticing.* Yes, He forbade it to him, but He did not purify his inwardness of wanting it. Indeed, every serving boy in the world serves his own want.

They say that in the Guarded Tablet it is written, "O Adam, do not eat the wheat." And in the same place it is written that he ate it. *Surely man was created grasping.*

The avarice of the Adamites goes back to the days of Adam himself. Whoever is not avaricious is not an Adamite. As much as a person eats, he needs more. If someone eats something and says "I'm full," he's lying. There is still room for more. The Adamite is never full. *"Nothing will fill up the stomach of Adam's child but dust."*[358]

Someone may ask, "Is what is written about Adam in the Tablet an argument in his favor?"

Indeed it is—in order to silence Moses. In a sound report it has come that Moses said, *"You are the one who made us wretched and weary and brought us out of the Garden."* O Adam, such a fully laden table was placed before you! Why is it that you did not partake of that stew?

Adam said to him, "Have you read in the Torah" up to the place where he says, "Do you blame me for something God wrote for me before I was created?"[359]

Moses said, "Then what was this *'Our Lord, we have wronged ourselves'* [7:23]?"

Adam said, "That was to put the adversary to flight."

The argument is what He wrote, but his means of approach to the Exalted Threshold was *'Our Lord, we have wronged ourselves.'"* Argument will not take anyone to Him.

Someone said to someone, "Does He predetermine us to sin and then punish us?"

He answered, "He's done it, and you can't say a word."

The point is that first statement: This speck of dust is the quarry of need and the mine of poverty and indigence. *"Our poverty is our boast."*[360]

"O Adam, you came into paradise and sat down at the tablecloth of approval. That is indeed beautiful, but what does a traveling man have to do with the tablecloth of approval? You must invite the specks of your children's offspring to the covenant. Then We will spread the tablecloth of the address *'Am I not your Lord?'* [7:172]. We will make the goblets of the wine of *He loves them* [5:54] come one after another. We will put forth the cups of the gentleness of *their Lord will give them to drink* [76:21] again and again."

The Higher Plenum remained in wonder: "Love-making is no surprise from Adam. What is surprising are the specks of his offspring, who are jumping on the ship of trial [*balā'*] and sitting in the boat of *'Yes indeed'* [*balā*; 7:172]."

From the pulpit of bounty the tongue of gentleness said, "Don't be surprised—they're ducklings. It's not necessary to teach ducklings how to swim."

O dervish, no one in the whole realm of creation dared to drink the wine in the cup from which they drank. The cup of the angels, both the elect and the common, was no more than *they are honored servants* [21:26]. In the eighteen thousand worlds no one other than the Adamites drank down the goblet of love's covenant: *He loves them.*

Pour me a big one—I'm big.
Only the small drink from the small.[361]

*

Come, pour for her some Babylonian wine
resembling sunrays, or even better,
For the partridge has sung after silence
and the rose has fulfilled its promise to return.[362]

Yes, this talk is not a wine that just anyone's maw can handle. It is not a hand that takes hold of just anyone, a sultan who kills just anyone, a hat suited for every head, a wind blowing on every garden, a tongue talking to everyone, a beauty lifting her mask for all.

O unbelief, what are you that the Magi should brag of you?
They worship your name but are exempt from you yourself.
Those in Islam who are always splitting hairs
never find access to one hair of yours with their learning.

"He loved you before you loved Him, He sought you before you sought Him, He remembered you before you remembered Him, He bestowed upon you before you asked Him and thanked Him, He responded to you before you supplicated Him, and He desired you before you desired Him."[363]

It had never occurred to the mind of water and clay before it reached the degree of friendship that it had the station of servanthood. In the beginningless He first talked about you to Himself, then He talked about you to you.

Shiblī was once asked, *"What is it toward which the hearts of the folk of recognition incline?"*

He said, "Toward what happened to them at first, in the beginningless, in the Presence when they were absent from it."[364]

Peace be on the covenants that
water my fever and cool it with breeze.
No longer at night am I wary of separation's hardship,
for I take my evening rest in union's ease.
Now my earth dwells in her earth,
its lightning empty of rain and imagination's specter.[365]

Once these verses occurred to my mind:

What was that time when fortune and prosperity were mine,
when love's luster was my feathers and affection my wings?
Those long years in union's world passed like one breath,
but one moment in separation's street is a journey of three hundred years.
When the wind of splendor and gentleness blew in the gardens of ecstasy,
a hundred thousand saints were given ecstasy and states.
Without cause the Lord's bounty and the Bestower's munificence
acted as broker for the pearl of the beginningless ocean of gentleness.
Around the repose of the spirit circles His lovers' aspiration,
night and day, wandering moment by moment.
Therein sessions of intimacy, cups full of joy's wine,
friends gathered together, the Real's gentleness speaking.
In their midst a hundred thousand of the heart's secrets,
concealed by the remembrance of curling locks and mole.
Such is the house of disengagement, the clothing of solitariness,
the morsel of *tawḥīd*, the drink of bounteousness.
Each goblet they drink at the hand of the Unseen
overflows with the wine of prosperity and fortune.
With acceptance, arrival, subsistence, and encounter,
our days are felicitous and our kiblah prosperity.

In one of the revealed books is written, *"I created the whole world for you, and I created you for Me."*[366]

There was a man who had a repulsive face. One day he looked in a mirror and thought in wonder, "What was God's wisdom in creating this ugly face?"

He heard a voice from the midst of the mirror, *"My wisdom in creating you is My love in your heart."* The wisdom in creating you is the love that I kneaded into your secret core. The secret of that love was curtained by the jealousy of the Unseen so that the eyes of others would not fall upon you.

When the shirt of existence was put on this center-point of dust-dwelling dust in keeping with the affair of generosity and munificence, the secret of love appeared: *"I am the King and I invite you to become kings! I am the Alive and I invite you to live!"*[367]

O dervish, if He had not given you kingship, no recognition of Him would have come to you, for no one recognizes a king but a king. Where does the splendorous scripture allude to this good news? *"Then We made you vicegerents"* [10:14]. *"And He made you kings"* [5:20].

He made you a king and He gave you a kingship. This kingship is a concise, subtle expression of the Possessor of Majesty's kingship. A throne of love was built from your spirit and a footstool of truthfulness was set up as your heart. A tent was erected in the desert of your makeup as the dwelling-place for the cavalry of your imagination. Your brain was placed before you as a Guarded Tablet. Your five senses were turned into the angels of your heavenly dominion's makeup. Your intellect was made into a moon and your knowledge a sun, shining on the sphere of your body. Through all of these you were made a king. In the tongue of prophecy, this was expressed in these terms: *"Each of you is a shepherd, and each of you will be asked about his sheep."*[368]

O friends of the Real, be careful not to look at yourselves with contempt, for that is not the place where your dignity's phoenix will fly or your secret core's falcon soar. Your dignity is great and your level tremendous. Although your outwardness is dust-dwelling and your custom audacity, your inwardness comes from the world of purity. Who is equal to you in the two worlds? Though the peacock of your existence did not fly in the meadow of the Beginningless, it will fly in the gardens of the endless approval and reach union with the Friend, forever and ever. Even if at the beginning your inner pearl was mixed with bestial and predatory attributes, once it has been sifted by the sieve of good fortune and struggle, and once the blood of this refractory soul has been spilled and its nature disgraced, it will be worthy of the neighborhood of the Sultan's Presence. It is a heavenly pearl on the face of the earth. What is the expression of this state? *"Recognition is the radiance of lights flashing in the hearts and lifting them away from faults to the unseen things."*[369]

25–26. *al-Khāfiḍ al-Rāfiʿ*: the Downletter, the Uplifter

The Persian of *khāfiḍ* is "he who puts down," and the Persian of *rāfiʿ* is "he who lifts up."

The Real is the Owner of the Kingdom. One person He puts at the front row of exalted measure, and another He stands in the back row of abased castigation. *Each day He is upon some task* [55:29]. *"He lifts up a group and He puts down a group."*[370] He gives a crown to one and lets another be plundered. He puts one group on top of the gallows and another beneath a crown. He puts one on the carpet of gentleness and another beneath the carpet of severity. He pulled up the dust-dwelling Adam from the dust of abasement and put the crown of prosperity on the head of his aspiration by the decree of bounteousness, without bias. He pulled down ʿAzāzīl, who was the teacher of the angels, from the celestial world and hung him on the rack of punishment at the crossroads of the causeless desire, without iniquity. To one group He says, *"So rejoice in your trading!"* [9:111], to another group He says, *"Die in your rage!"* [3:119]. Moses the speaking companion set off seeking the fire of *he observed a fire on the side of the mountain* [28:29]. He was a shepherd without a blanket, and he returned a prophet, a speaking companion. And Balaam Beor knew the Greatest Name, but why do you look at that? He also went up a mountain as a friend in respect of form, but he came back down as a dog in respect of attribute and meaning.

> You'll be an estranged servant at the bottom of separation's street
> if you don't seek a familiar at the top of union's street.
> A familiar with the Prophet—what a stranger was Abū Lahab!
> Coming from Abyssinia, how familiar was Bilāl![371]

Shāfiʿī said,

> *You created the servants as You know them,*
> *both young and old coming forth from Your knowledge,*
> *This one felicitous, that one wretched;*
> *this one ugly, that one beautiful.*
> *What You want comes to be, though I want it not,*
> *and what I want will not be if You do not want it.*[372]

What did the dog of the Companions of the Cave do that the dust under its feet was made into the collyrium for the eyes of the friends and it received the caress of *their dog was extending its paws at the doorstep* [18:18]? And what did the dog of your neighborhood do that this fatwa was issued concerning it? *"A dog is most polluted when washing itself."*[373]

> Many a prayerful pir has fallen from his steed,
> many a tavern-goer has saddled a lion.[374]

What did Adam the chosen do that he was brought into the row of chosenness, with the collar of election and the shawl of limpidness thrown over the neck of his good fortune? What did the miserable Iblis do that the angelic garb was pulled from his head and he was made into the ill-fated of the spheres?

If the cause of Adam's chosenness and rank were the limpidness of his road because of the rushing and running of his feet, then His prohibition—majestic is His majesty!—struck fire into the haystack of this cause, for He brought him into the Garden of Eden by the decree of eternal gentleness at the first step. And if you judge the root of Iblis's rejection to have been disobedience, He destroyed the basis for this judgment when He said to Iblis, "Prostrate yourself," and he did not; and He said to Adam, "Do not eat the wheat," but he did. So what caused the crown of Adam's chosenness to be added to the hat of his election? And what caused that miserable one to be rejected such that he will never have a road to acceptance and never have a standing placc at the Court? *"The decrees of majesty are far too majestic to be weighed in the scales of the Muʿtazilites."*[375] How can the ships of intellect use causes to cross the billowing ocean of the beginningless secrets?

> On the day they stamped a seal on the work of all the low,
> they stamped a different seal on the gold of love.
> Your intellect will never grasp how they sealed it—
> the gold they stamped lies outside its house.[376]

The decree of eternal gentleness daubed the collyrium of realization and the antimony of success on the insightful eyes of the lords of the pure gaze. It sprinkled the elixir of the reposeful spirit on the copper of their souls and made their breaths into the precious pearls of pain's necklace. The heart-grabbing fire of sultanlike love burned away the thorn of boasting about others and shut the eyes of their secret cores against paying regard to the two worlds. With the steps of love they passed beyond the realm of both worlds and raised the banner of truthfulness in the open plain of the heart's limpidness. They removed the dust and clay from the road in the world of the divine decrees. Anyone who talked about this powerless Guebre was fancied to be a Guebre. This state was expressed like this: *"The free-willers are the Magi of this community."*[377]

Know that in verified truth the realm of being is nothing more than an image in the mirror of His majesty. Anyone who consigns something to himself independently is attached to an absurdity. Concerning this station Muḥammad, God's Messenger, reported like this: *"I was sent as an inviter, and nothing of guidance goes back to me. Satan was sent as an embellisher, and nothing of misguidance goes back to him."*[378] O dervish, if that miserable fellow were able to throw anyone into error, he would have kept guidance for himself.

The uninformed lords of intellect's merchandise think that they can gain precedence over the roaring, cold wind by riding on the backs of little goats. They think that with a tiny bit of incapacity-mixed power they can enter the field of disputing with the decrees of majesty and consign the secrets manifest from the curtains of the Unseen to mortal nature. They are like ants, weak in composition and small in makeup, walking across a sheet of paper. Suppose an ant sees a black line appearing on the paper. It will imagine that it is the work of the pen; its aspiration will not reach the knowledge and power of the writer. Those who see the outward causes and shut their eyes to the celestial apportionings have a state like this.

Exalted friend, Adam had not yet eaten the wheat when the hat of chosenness was sewn. Iblis had not yet refused when the arrow of the curse was dipped in the poison of severity.

Iblis says, "Though You commanded me to prostrate myself to Adam and I did not, You commanded Adam not to eat the wheat and he did. One for one!"

"O expelled from the Threshold! Don't you know that the slips of friends are not counted against them?"

> *When the beloved comes with one sin,*
> *his beautiful traits bring a thousand interceders.*[379]

"And that the obedient acts of enemies are not counted for them?"

> *When someone's not suited for union,*
> *all his beautiful-doing is sin.*[380]

Someone may say, "What about the call *'Adam disobeyed'* [20:121]?"

The answer: "Why are you looking at the whip of *Adam disobeyed*? Look rather at the magnificent crown of *his Lord chose him* [20:122]."

O dervish, Adam made a patched cloak from the leaves of the trees of paradise and turned his face toward the journey in dust. It was fitting for him to have a staff. They made a staff for him from *Adam disobeyed*, for it is fitting that a dervish have a patched cloak and a staff.

O chevalier, they made him a cup of poison from *Adam disobeyed* and at once they sent the antidote of gentleness in its tracks: *If guidance comes to you from Me, then whosoever follows My guidance, no fear shall be upon them* [2:38].

With one hand you're stingy, with the other you soothe.[381]

They placed so many bejeweled crowns of leadership on the felicitous head of Adam the dust-dweller that, had they not clothed him in the patched cloak of the severity of *he was a great wrongdoer, deeply ignorant* [33:72] and had they not buttoned it up with *Adam disobeyed*, there would have been fear of many things.

What a marvelous business! He made apparent the secrets of His Lordhood in places where the imaginative wings of intellect's phoenix cannot fly. He took a handful of dust in the grasp of perfect power and kept it for forty years in the sunlight of His gaze until being's dampness left it. Then He commanded the angels of the Dominion, "Go to the gate of this wondrous form, marvelous shape, and subtle guise and kiss the threshold of its majesty, which is beyond these seven heavens. *Fall before him in prostration!* [15:29]."

O dervish, He said to the angels, "Prostrate yourselves before Adam." This level, distinction, rank, and status did not belong to water and clay, but rather to the ruling power of the heart. In the core of Adam's heart was deposited one of the divine subtleties, royal secrets, and unseen meanings, a secret concealed by the curtain of *the spirit is of the command of my Lord* [17:85]. God gave back a mark of this hidden secret on the purified tongue of Muṣṭafā with the words *"He created Adam in His form"*[382]—not by way of asserting likeness and similarity.

When the angels of the Higher Plenum saw his greatness and elevation, they threw their spirits down before this fearless dust. But when the accursed one, that bat of the era, was placed before Adam's sunlight, he rubbed his eyes in utmost misery and saw nothing of good fortune.

Luck has fallen out this way for me:
my share of love is separation.

Adam's essence was the depository of the secrets of the Unseen. Otherwise, how could a handful of dust have such worth that the residents of the precincts of holiness and the preachers on the pulpits of intimacy prostrate themselves before him? Is a handful of barren clay and water given such respect that it should be said to trustworthy Gabriel, unshakeable Michael, and stable Seraphiel, *"Prostrate yourselves before him"*? No, no—that handful of clay had a jewel box in the secret core of its heart.

O chevalier, all the intellectuals of the world have bitten the fingers of wonder with the teeth of bewilderment: "Why is it that He loves this handful of dust and clay?" By the rightful due of the Real! He loves only Himself, for everyone who loves his own artisanry loves himself.

They recited this verse before Shaykh Abū Saʿīd: *"He loves them and they love Him"* [5:54]. *He said, "By the rightful due of 'He loves them,' surely He loves only Himself."*[383]

O dervish, since there are no others in existence, how can you say that He loves anyone else?

The master Abu'l-Qāsim Qushayrī said, *"The others are lost in His existence, and when His rightful due is witnessed, traces and vestiges are effaced."*[384]

Another exalted man said, *"Come quickly to the Exalted Presence, the carpet of generosity, the session of intimacy, the space of the spirit, the courtyard of the divinity, and the very hub of the Lordhood, for everything in being is nonexistent and all within it is but a decree."*[385]

These creatures that you see affirm power and negate jealousy. The sultan of majesty's jealousy will charge forth from the world of exaltedness and perfection and snatch the cap of existence from the head of the world's folk. "How can it be correct for you to be existent and Him to be existent, for you to have being and Him to have being? *God is the Unneedy, and you are the poor* [47:38]."

If you say concerning an existence whose edges are open to nonexistence that it is existent, that is a metaphor. *An existence between two nonexistences is like no existence.*

Recite the verse of your own nonexistence from the tablet of His eternity! Raise the flag of your own nonbeing in the world of His being! From the cup of Sufism's covenant drink the unmixed wine of negating self-determination in the flow of the decrees! Draw the line of erasure across the register of your days! Do not charge the dead donkey of your own miserable *was not* into the same field as the majestic Burāq of *He has no beginning and no end.*

In the world of the command, sit on the steed of existence so that you may perform the commandments! In the world of love, sit on the steed of nonexistence so that you may receive the commandments! When the draft of the address arrives in the cup of the Sunnah and the Book, drink down the wine of the command and become drunk with its beauty! Once you have drunk down the wine of the command and put on the garment of compliance, become confounded in nonexistence by the tipsinesss of love, contemplating the Eternal Witness and unaware of awareness.

In your bowing and prostrating, give being and existence to yourself and become existent in the majestic existence of *He is God* [28:70]. But in reality, tear away the cloak of metaphorical existence and look back to the divine beauty and royal perfection. These creatures that you see are existent through His munificence and nonexistent through His existence. His munificence has tossed the cape of existence on the neck of the existent things, but His existence tosses all existent things back into the concealment of nonexistence.

When I'm with myself, I'm less than nonexistence, less.
    When I'm with You, I'm the whole world.
Buy me from me for nothing,
    even though for free, I'm still expensive.[386]

O chevalier, they collected the existence and being of mortal man and gave it over to the broker of His majesty. No one bought it for a single grain.

All the sincerely truthful of the world wish to dive into the ocean of is-not-ness and never reach the shore of *then he came to be.*

This verse was recited in front of ʿUmar ibn Khaṭṭāb: *"There came upon man a time when he was not a thing remembered"* [76:1]. *ʿUmar said, "Would that it had been finished."*[387] Would that this slate had been finished without the intrusion of our heads and faces.

O chevalier, this is talk of someone who detached his heart from his own head and face and whose heart was detached from his own existence.

O dervish, if the moth had one iota of worth in its own eyes, it would not throw itself like that on the candle. All the lovers of the world wish to be taken as moths or madmen, but it is not about them that people talk.

A man says, "My existence and prostration, my being and health, my life and subsistence, my coming and going, my choice and desire, my stillness and movement, my steps and thoughts." From the Presence of Exaltedness comes the call of intense severity: "Do not make so much mention of the delusions you're nurturing, for one puff of My severity will give a thousand thousand haystacks of delusion to the wind."

"How can I enjoy myself when Seraphiel has put the Trumpet to his lips?"[388]

It was said to Seraphiel, "When the moment arrives, give a puff and take away these delusions with the wind of unneediness. I have planted crops in this world, and I have put the scythe of severity and the cup of poison in your hand. Circumambulate the world and harvest any crop that sticks up its head." This is demanded by the jealousy of *He alone—no associate has He.* O dervish, whatever affirms createdness negates *He alone—no associate has He.*[389]

When something makes gentleness appear, it conceals exaltedness. "O Byzantines, I am the Outward, so the argument will be against you! O faithful, I am the Inward, so you will have an excuse." O First, You have bound tight the hearts of the lovers with the compacts of the Beginningless! O Last, You have hunted the spirits of the truthful with the promises of the Endless! O Outward, You have brought the outward things into the Shariah's bond with Your command! O Inward, You have put the secret cores into the cradle of the Haqiqah's covenant with Your decree!

When a man travels in the attribute of firstness, the attribute of lastness charges out. When he travels in the attribute of outwardness, the attribute of inwardness plunders his wherewithal. The poor wretch will be confounded between the two attributes and senseless between the two names.

O you who ask me to explain my state—
I'm afflicted by every wondrous thing.
I conceal my love, but tears keep coming
when I hide my story with the beloved.
How can I hope for healing when my disease
comes from the cure and my illness from the physician?

*

Bewilderment upon bewilderment, thirst upon thirst,
sometimes supposition is certainty, certainty supposition.
His Presence is Exaltation and Majesty, His carpet unneediness—
a hundred thousand caravans are waylaid in this road.

O dervish, the lightning of this talk flashed in the world and set fire to a thousand thousand helpless hearts. Then the lightning returned to the Unseen and left behind this handful of heart-lost indigents.

Junayd was whispering in prayer and saying, *"My Beloved, who has tried me with You?"* Then he said, *"Increase me in my trial!"*

Yes, my spirit and world, His He-ness demands the bewilderment of the world's folk. Any love that does not bring bewilderment is not love, nor does it have any pleasure. Intellect says, "How?" Mortal nature says, "Why?" And the Presence of Majesty calls out to you: "Without how! Without why!"

One draft of this talk was poured on the breast of that old woman called Bilqīs. She had busied herself with ease in her resting place and stationed the officers and door-keepers at the gate. She became astonished and distracted, and that fire stuck up its head inside her breast. The hoopoe, *the possessor of crown and silk*, was coming, and it threw Solomon's note into her place of seclusion. When she woke up, she rebuked the captains of her court: "Where were you? What are you for? Who brought this stranger into the place in which I had secluded myself?"

They said, "If anything comes by the road, write it against us. But if it comes by air, we have no access to it. No door can be shut firmer than David shut it, and no armor can be made stronger than he made it. But the arrow of predetermination cannot be repelled by the armor of preparation. Given that this is so, at least look at what caused this distraction."

She opened the letter and saw that *it is from Solomon, and it is in the name of God, the All-Merciful, the Ever-Merciful* [27:30]: "O Bilqīs, you have a crown. You must take off the crown, make sandals, and come to the court."

O dervish, a thousand thousand crowns of the pride of chosenness must be replaced by sandals before they will give you a single thread of love's sash.

Love has colored me with the trace of Jewishness—
remembering Him has melted my body with love,
As if my paleness is my yellow badge
and my thinness my Christian sash.[390]

*

With the iniquity of your tall stature and long tresses,
the unbelief in your eyes drunk without wine,
I fear you'll see me in a Christian church,
a bell in one hand, your hand in the other.[391]

Intellects are bewildered in His majesty, intelligences distracted by His beauty, understandings incapable of perceiving His secret, thoughts thrown into turmoil by His command, livers made bloody by His severity, hearts melted by recognizing Him.

If love doesn't make a man throw dirt on his head,
he'll never lift up his head as one of Your lovers.
No man's head and work will appear with You
until he puts his whole head into Your work.

O dervish, come into this road and see the caressing of the servants! Come and see the melting of the lovers! You must dedicate yourself outwardly to the Shariah and inwardly to the

Haqiqah. You must make night and day the two steeds of your deeds and empty the carpet of all others. You must step outside your own pleasures, lest your name be written on ice.

> O partridge with a thousand falcons in your trap!
> O lion-catching gazelle, how much more of this from you?
> How many there are who never joined with you
> though they plunged into heartache and trial for you!

O dervish, that spot of love and speck of affection was wrapped in the jealousy of the Unseen, waiting for this fearless handful of dust to step forth. An uproar fell into heaven and earth, tumult and turmoil appeared in the world. When the desire to give existence to Adam the chosen came forth from the ambuscade of knowledge into the open plain of manifestation, a call was given out that an army would be brought into the world to kill adversaries. The waves of the words of the Possessors of the Stations[392] began to clash. Those who were the wellspring of cleanliness and the essence of purity began to speak: "We, we."

The Sultan of beginningless knowledge was walking in the field of beginningless majesty without attending to anyone's tumult or looking at anyone's words. The beginningless knowledge gave out this call: *"Hey there, 'Surely I know what you do not know!'* [2:30]."

"Is there a work more splendid than this, an occupation with a better arrangement? A whole world in glorification, hallowing, sinlessness, and purity!"

"Surely I know what you do not know! Ah, I have a work on the way of which knowledge is the emissary. Yes, there are glorification and hallowing, but what is needed is a lover who is unitary in essence, someone who will suddenly leap without fear from the abode of subsistence to the abode of trial. Yes, you will go straight and they will go every which way. But behind the curtain of friendship things happen that would be faults outside the curtain, things that are tolerated inside the shelter of friendship."

> *When the beloved comes with one sin,*
> *his beautiful traits bring a thousand interceders.*[393]

"When I wanted to bring them into existence while knowing that they would have faults and slips, I spread the carpet of love so that, no matter what they did, the decree of love would eliminate it from them."

Someone was a companion of someone else for a time. Indeed, it was Ibrāhīm Adham. When the moment came to bid farewell, he apologized and said, "Let not your heart be concerned, for I was your companion because of love, and a friend sees nothing bad from a friend."

Abū Yazīd Basṭāmī said, *"The wonder is not that I love You, for I am a weak servant. The wonder is that You love me, for You are a strong lord."*[394] The wonder is not that I love You, given that a possessor of perfect beauty does not lack for lovers. The wonder is that You love me, given that from head to toe I am all incapacity, weakness, lowliness, and taintedness.

Moon-faced Joseph does not lack for lovers, but a man is wanted to love black-faced, indigent Bilāl.

O chevalier, you are both friend and servant. Outwardly you are a servant in the bonds of the command, but inwardly you are a friend sprinkled with the gentleness of the All-Merciful. How could it ever be permissible for the rose of love to grow from the disposition of your breast's clay? Nonetheless, in the firm text of the revelation He sent this overflowing wine and this cup of prosperity on the hand of the cupbearer of gentleness: *"He loves them and they love Him"* [5:54]. What can the poor lover do to keep from breaking the pen of patience and writing on the heart's core with love's madness?

> Who am I in Your road that in my house
> a rose from Your face should bloom in my clay?
> Is it not enough in my passion for You
> that my heart is adorned with Your love?[395]

Indeed, in verified truth one cannot speak of love in this house. When a house is built of a handful of foam, its roof is a bit of smoke, its light coming from inanimate things, and its life from a drop of water, how can one speak of its having love?

O dervish, love trades only with the heart, and the lover can wrong none but his own spirit. The substance of love stirs up dust from water and brings forth a cold wind from a burning house. The two worlds cannot bear an iota of love. Would that you had an iota of love! But where in the world is an iota of love?

A pir said, "Indeed, no more than an iota of love came out from His Unseen into the open. It traveled around the whole world and saw no one worthy, so it returned to the Unseen."

> Love came sweet and sultanlike from the Unseen's ambush
> and attacked me like fire on reeds.

Abū Yazīd said, "One night I came out of my corner, took a step, and sank into love up to my neck."

What was it with the former pir, and what was it with the latter? It was the majesty of the Presence that appeared to the first pir, and it was the beauty of the Threshold that disclosed itself to the second.

O dervish, know that in reality love has taken away the shine of both worlds. In the world of servanthood, both paradise and hell have worth. In the world of love, neither has any worth at all. They gave the eight paradises to Adam the chosen, but he sold them for a grain of wheat. He put the bags of aspiration on the camel of his lot and came down to the house of sorrows.

It is said that Jesus was passing by three people and saw them outwardly weak and skinny, wilted and emaciated. He asked them the cause of their emaciation and skinniness. They said, *"Fear of the Fire."* He said, *"It is God's responsibility to keep the fearful secure."*

When he passed on, he saw others whose emaciation and wilting were even more. When he asked the cause of their emaciation, they said, *"Yearning for the Garden." He said, "It is God's responsibility to bestow on you what you hope for."*

When he passed them by, he saw three more people whose emaciation and wilting were even more, *as if in their faces were mirrors of light.* He said, *"What is it that has conveyed you to what I see?"*

They said, "Love for God."

He said, "You are the proximate, you are the proximate, you are the proximate!" You are the proximate to the Exalted Threshold; you are the elect of the Lordly Presence.[396]

It is said that the Exalted Lord sent revelation to David: *"O David, My remembrance is for the rememberers, My Garden for the obedient, My visitation for the grateful, and I belong specifically to the lovers."*[397]

In truth, in truth, talk of pardon and forgiveness went down into talk of yearning and love and never came back!

It is said that Mamshād Dīnawarī was in the throes of death. A dervish was standing before him and supplicating: "Lord God, have mercy on him and grant him Your paradise." Mamshād looked at him and shouted, "O heedless man, it is thirty years since the eight paradises with their marvels, chambers, houris, and palaces were disclosed to me, *but I never glanced at them.* Now that I am arriving at the fount of the Haqiqah, you intrude and want paradise and mercy for me?!"[398]

This talk does not fit into your craw. It is called "knowledge of the inward." This knowledge of the inward, which is specific to those men whose breaths are the tested antidote for pain, is one root of Muṣṭafā's Sunnah.

The shaykh, the imam, the renunciant, Abu'l-Faḍl ʿAbdallāh ibn Aḥmad Naysābūrī said as part of what he gave me permission to transmit, "The jurist Abū Ḥāmid Aḥmad ibn Jaʿfar Rādhakī Ṭūsī reported to me from Ḥākim Abu'l-Ḥasan Aḥmad ibn Muḥammad, from the wholesome shaykh Abū Zurʿa Aḥmad ibn Muḥammad ibn Faḍl Ṭabarī in the village of Shīrdara, from Abū Muḥammad ibn ʿAbdallāh ibn Jaʿfar, from Muḥammad ibn Maʿūna, from Abu'l-Faḍl Jaʿfar ibn Muḥammad, from Shādhān ibn ʿAbdallāh Sūsī, from Naṣr ibn ʿAlī Maqdisī, from Aḥmad ibn ʿAṭāʾ. He said, 'I asked Aḥmad ibn Ghassān about knowledge of the inward. He said that he asked ʿAbd al-Wāḥid ibn Zayd about knowledge of the inward. He said that he asked Ḥasan ibn Abi'l-Ḥasan Baṣrī about knowledge of the inward. He said that he asked Ḥudhayfa Yamān about knowledge of the inward. He said that he asked God's Messenger about knowledge of the inward. He said, 'It is a knowledge between God and His friends of which no proximate angel nor any of His creatures is aware.' "[399]

The exalted ones have said, *"Our secrets are virgin, not seized by the imagination of any imaginer."*[400] *"As for the secrets, protect them from the others!"*

> All who catch a scent of this meaning are jealous—
>   you might say they have neither tongue nor speech.
> If they talk, their jealousy for the meaning
>   keeps their words to the tracks and traces of the tents.

The lords of the orchards of the realities and the seekers of the wine of severing attachments have perfect jealousy for the beauty of the exalted meanings, so they bind them in a thousand thousand curtains. Then perhaps they can conceal the virgin brides of meaning behind a veil—namely, the breast of a dregs-drinking possessor of pain—without the intruding accusations of others.

"The breasts of the free are the graves of the secrets."[401]

"He who has no secret is persistent."[402]

"One of the characteristics of the free is keeping secrets from others."[403]

Sometimes they give out this talk as the locks and mole of Laylā, sometimes as the distractedness of Majnūn's state; sometimes as intoxication, sometimes sobriety; sometimes as annihilation, sometimes subsistence; sometimes as ecstasy, sometimes finding. These words, expressions, and letters are the containers for the fine wine of realized meanings. Those in the ranks of the lovers are busy with the wine itself. The unworthy are in bondage to the cup.

The understanding of these Men in the secrets of the Sunnah and the Book has reached an inviolable sanctuary. Around it the imagination of the lords of the outward meanings does not have the gall to circle. From each letter they have a station, from each word a message, from each verse a rulership, from each chapter a burning.

Their share of *alif* is familiarity [*ulfat*] with the secrets and disdain [*anafat*] for the others; of *bā'* kindness [*birr*] and disavowal [*barā'at*]; of *tā'* godwariness [*taqwā*] and recitation [*talāwat*]; and so on to the last of the letters.

In their road threats are promises and promises hard cash. In their road paradise and hell are waystations, and for them everything less than the Real is unreal.

Is not everything other than God unreal?[404]

This world and the next are two miles in the desert of their present moment. Their hearts and spirits travel in the path of love. Day and night are two steeds in their road, and the trailing skirts of their states are pure of the stains of the others. By day they dwell in the lodging place of secret whispering, by night in the howdah of joy. By day they gaze on the artifacts, by night they contemplate the beauty of the Artisan. By day they dwell with the people in good character, by night with the Real in the *foot of truthfulness* [10:2]. By day they are in the work, by night in drunkenness. By day they seek the road, by night they speak of the mysteries.

Your face puts my night in the forenoon sun—
darkness belongs only to the sky.
The people are in the darkness of their night,
but I'm in the brightness of Your face.[405]

They have burned the soul in the crucible of the breath, raised the torch of love in the road of truthfulness, lifted the head of aspiration beyond the spheres, and dumped the caprice of the refractory soul into the pit. They have stirred up their makeup from the sleep of heedlessness and heard the call *"Am I not your Lord?"* [7:172] with the ears of love. They have reached the standing of free men and have not attended to their own rightful due. They have gone down into the Zamzam of holy intimacy and cleansed themselves of the pollution of deep ignorance. On the prayer carpet of the Covenant of the Presence they sit in wait for the call to prayer of *whose is the kingdom today?* [40:16]. They have traveled a long road on the stallion of need, cut the throat of appetite with the blade of truthfulness, escaped from the trap of the two worlds, and achieved release from the dragon of caprice. *In earth they are ascribed to heaven and in heaven to the Lord. Their bodies are earthly, but their hearts pertain to heaven, rather to the Throne, rather to unity, rather to self-sufficiency. They are neither of 'the East nor of the West'* [24:35]*; rather, of majesty, rather of the unseen beauty.*

They have pulled rags over the moons of the secrets. *Patched cloaks are the curtains of pearls.* They have concealed the secret pearl of their headmanship over the realm of being inside the shell of their cloak. *They have impounded a pearl, but the pearl is inside the oyster.*

O my spirit and world, the angels came, wearing the majestic silk of hallowing and the perfect shirt of glorifying: *We are those in rows, we are the glorifiers* [37:165–66]. Adam the dust-dweller came, wearing the patched cloak of deep ignorance and the tattered coat of great wrongdoing. The angels recited the sermon of their own days: *"We are those in rows,"* but God praised this handful of dust by Himself: *"We honored the children of Adam"* [17:70].

We chose them, out of knowledge, above the worlds [44:32] is a secret. We are wounded by our own existence, but we receive bestowals from His subsistence. When we look at our own existence, we see only annihilation, but when we look at His uncaused munificence, we see only subsistence.

O dervish, do not look at the form of the dust [*turbat*]—look at the secret of the nurturing [*tarbiyat*]. When you give a grain to dust, it will give it back many times over, but when you give something to fire, it will burn it away. They gave that grain of wheat—which carries the mystery of nourishment's wherewithal—to the nursemaid dust, so that she would nurture it at her side and breast. Then in a short time she gave back produce many times over, *in every ear a hundred grains* [2:261].

He sprinkled the grain of love and the unique seed of affection on the clay of dust's breast, for *He loves them and they love Him* [5:54]. Then He fermented the clay with the hand of gentleness, for *"He fermented Adam's clay in His hand for forty mornings."*[406] He nurtured it with the right hand of auspiciousness and the left hand of bestowal and assisted it with the limpid water of bounty from the clouds of prosperity, for *He confirmed them with a spirit from Him* [58:22]. In the spring of the secrets the ear of acceptance grew fat and joined with the produce of connection and arrival. *A goodly word is like a goodly tree, its roots fixed and its branches in heaven; it gives its fruit every season by the leave of its Lord* [14:24–25].

The sentence of the Shahadah is a tree growing on the bank of the blessed lake of the heart. Its roots are in the earth of passion, its trunk in the world of yearning, its upper reaches in the world of blessings and beneficent gifts, its irrigation from the Zamzam of gentleness and generosity, its branches in the air of the He-ness, its leaves from the secrets of At-ness, its blossoms from the world of the lights of hearts, its flowers from the gifts of the pavilions of the Unseen Realms, its fruit proximity, its largesse love. Yes, a tree like this grows only in the garden of God and is guarded only by the King's gaze.

Then again, trees give their yield once a year, but this tree gives its yield at every moment, a new fruit at every instant. Its root is at the bottom of the ocean of the hearts of the sincerely truthful. Its shade-giving shadow gives rest to the spirits of the lovers. *"The resting place of the worshipers is beneath the tree of blessedness"*[407]—today the *goodly tree,* tomorrow the tree of blessedness. Its branches are the handhold of the truthful: *Whoever disbelieves in idols and has faith in God has laid hold of the firmest handle* [2:256]. Its leaves are the paper for the words of the yearners, its fruit the pleasure of those burned in whispered prayer.

Adam had such a tree, and from it he picked the fruit of chosenness: [*So they ate from it...*] *Then his Lord chose him, so He turned toward him and guided* [20:121–22]. Noah had a tree from which he picked the fruit of salvation: *Make the ship before Our eyes* [11:37]. Moses had a tree from which he picked the fruit of whispered prayer: *When he came to it, he was called from the right bank of the watercourse, in the blessed hollow, from the tree* [28:30]. Zachariah had a tree from which he picked the fruit of martyrdom. Mary had a tree from which she picked the fruit of fresh dates: *Shake to thyself the trunk of the palm tree* [19:25]. Muṣṭafā had a tree from which he picked the fruit of approval and felicity: *When they swore allegiance to thee beneath the tree* [48:18]. We have a tree from which we pick the fruit of love: *A goodly word is like a goodly tree.*

O chevalier, this is a tree whose roots are in the earth of certainty, whose branches are in the heaven of the religion, whose irrigation is from the clear water of bounteousness and the wellspring of the prosperity of the chieftain of the envoys, whose planter is the Lord of the Worlds, whose keeper is the Seal of the Prophets, whose blossoms are the formulae of remembrance of the leader of *the bright-faced and white-cuffed,*[408] and whose leaves are the traces of the rain of the gaze of the Lord of heaven and earth. Why would it be surprising if its fruit in this world is certainty and in that world seeing without what and without how in the uppermost everlastingness and the highest of the high?

The roots of another tree are in the clay of the breast and its branches in the heaven of faith and tranquility: *He it is who sent down the tranquility into the hearts of the faithful* [48:4]. Its irrigation is from the well of the life of the spirits, its planter is *the Splitter of the dawn* [6:96] *and the Creator of the bodies*, and its leaves are from the gentleness of the Day of the Compact. Why would it be surprising if its fruit in this world is love, affection, and yearning, and in that world the ease of union without intrusive separation?

The roots of another tree are in the earth of good fortune, its branches in the Pleiades of aspiration, its irrigation from the fountain of limpidness, its blossoms from the lights of the Haqiqah, and its leaves from the pages of the Shariah. Why would it be surprising if its fruit in this world is unveiling and contemplation and in that world union and vision?

The roots of another tree are in the earth of sufficiency, its branches in the heaven of kind favor, its irrigation from the wellspring of solicitude, its planter the beginning, its keeper protection, its blossoms from guidance, and its leaves from rulership. Why would it be surprising if its fruit in this world is bearing witness and in the afterworld felicity?

The roots of another tree are in the earth of union, its branches in the heaven of bounty, its irrigation from the wellspring of intimacy, and its blossoms from the world of holiness. Why would it be surprising if its fruit in this world is friendship and in that world subsistence and encounter?

Who knows what deposits have been placed in this dust? It would be a shame for you to leave this world having wasted the passing days while unaware of this weighty merchandise. "*If anyone thinks that God's blessings on him consist of food, drink, clothing, and sex, his knowledge has fallen short and his chastisement made ready.*"[409] You fancy that there is nothing more than the work you are busy with, but "*It was for a reason that Qaṣīr cut off his nose.*"[410]

What is stipulated for you is that you appoint the guards of both the Shariah and the Haqiqah over all your senses and breaths. Do not waste a single breath. Lift up the pickax of struggle and break the stone that veils the wellspring of your heart so as to reach the clear water of contemplation. It is not just any defiled fellow who can enter the battlefield of the Men and strike the sword to acquire permitted spoils.

> Don't color Your sword with the blood of just any defiled fellow.
> You have Rostam's craft, so You'd best strike Rostam.
> The creatures are at ease in the tavern of their own makeup—
> with just one wink throw the creatures into turmoil![411]

If you do not want to be trampled underfoot tomorrow at that tremendous convocation, then don't be heedless today of punishing the inner adversary. Bring the body into the work like a steed. Place the bridle of godwariness on its head, put the saddle of discipline on its back, bind it with the belt of judiciousness, and keep it on the straight path in the playing field of the religion with the whip of resoluteness. Put the heart, which is the king of your makeup, at the center of the empire on the throne of exaltedness and the row of limpidness. Make the faculty of imagination, whose chamber is the front of the brain, its courier. Make memory, whose lodging place is the back of the brain, its treasurer. Make the tongue its spokesman. Make the five senses its spies. Send each of them as an informant to a region—the eyes to the world of colors, the ears to the world of sound, and so on, each to a world. Then these spies will convey reports to the faculty of imagination, which is the courier. The courier will convey them to the faculty of memory, which is the treasurer. After that the faculty of memory will present them to the heart, which is the king.[412] *Have they not gazed on the dominion of the heavens and the earth?* [7:185]. *And in your souls; what, do you not see?* [51:21]. *"Think about the creatures, but think not about the Creator!"*[413]

This ordering of the gaze is an inescapable condition at the beginning. Then, when a traveling, road-going, wayfaring man aims for the road and passes by all the stages of the wayfaring, every moment a secret will appear to him in the World of the Unseen from behind the veil of exaltedness and the curtain of jealousy. With an empty breast and a high aspiration he will swallow down the oceans of being like a raging crocodile. The jasmine of the covenant, the rose of the heart, and the sweet herb of the spirit will grow from the All-Merciful's bounty in the garden of his present moment—*light upon light, joy upon joy, presence upon presence, delight upon delight, union upon union, prosperity upon prosperity, ad infinitum.*

O chevalier, this heart, which is the sultan in the castle of your breast, has soldiers arranged in ranks, some of whom are seen by the eyes and some of whom are not. The soldiers seen by the eyes are the outward bodily members. The proof that these members are the soldiers of the heart is that when the heart commands the eye to look, it looks, and when it says not to look, it does not look. So also are the other members. Just as the angels are subjected to the command of the Exalted Lord, so also these members are subjected to the heart. However, there is one difference, which is that these members are subjected and unaware, and the angels of the Dominion are subjected and aware.[414]

The soldiers not seen by the eyes are like wrath, appetite, knowledge, and wisdom. Appetite is like an ill-mannered slave, deceptive and bad-acting, who presents himself in the form of a sincere advisor. His custom is to quarrel with the vizier, who is intellect. Wrath is like the chief of police, known as the superintendent. The chief of police must observe the stipulations of the

Shariah, but he himself will observe the Shariah's stipulations only when intellect's whip has taught him courtesy.

Once you come to know this, you should also know that all animals share with the Adamites in appetite, wrath, and the outward senses. What is specific to the substance of the Adamic heart is knowledge and recognition, both of which lie beyond the level of sensory things. The tongue of the lords of the heart alludes to this secret like this: *"Knowledge is a light that God throws into the heart of any of His servants that He wills."*[415] They have also said, *"Recognition is the heart's life with God."*[416]

My father used to say that two living things must become companions in order to produce a child. One is the life that comes from the Unseen: *So also We revealed to thee a spirit from Our command* [42:52]. The other is a life that is inborn: *And I blew into him of My spirit* [15:29].[417] When these two lives become companions, another life, called "recognition," is born from the two. This is expressed in these terms: *"Recognition is the heart's life with God."*

Let me offer one more likeness for the heart, and then I will return to the discussion: Hearts are like containers for the fine wine of realized meanings. ʿAlī said, *"God has containers in His earth, and they indeed are the hearts. Of them the most beloved to Him is the most tender, most limpid, and most solid."* Then he said, *"Most solid in the religion, most limpid in certainty, and most tender toward brethren."*[418]

At first this container was clay, suitable for neither food nor drink. It had to be passed over fire to make it into a cup for drink and a bowl for food. The stipulation now is that you pass the heart over the fire of passion so that it will be worthy for the food of proximity and suitable for the drink of love. Then you will be given the drink of good fortune in the cup of the heart. That is expressed like this: *"Their Lord will give them to drink of a pure wine"* [76:21].

O dervish, the heart is like a container, but a container full of water does not have any air. In the same way, when the heart is occupied with other than the Real, talk of the Unseen will not enter into it, for *the occupied are not put to work.*[419]

Let us come back to the first discussion: It is known that the specific characteristic of man's heart is knowledge and wisdom. The perfect state of his clay lies in knowledge and the eminence of his road lies in wisdom. When someone holds back from knowledge and wisdom and steps into the road of ignorance and foolishness, he is a beast in reality, though an Adamite in form.

In a similar way the horse has the specific characteristic of pomp and splendor. It shares with the donkey the strength to carry burdens. If people do not find that pomp and splendor in it, they will make saddle bags for it and bring it down to the rank of a donkey. So also if the Adamite does not put his specific characteristic to work, he will be brought down to the beasts: *They are like cattle. No, they are further astray* [7:179]. This is because the specific characteristic of the human substance does not lie in feeding and procreation, for plants have the same thing. Nor does it lie in the senses and movement, for animals have that too. Nor does it lie in the beautiful form, for the same thing is found on walls. Its specific characteristic is knowledge and recognition.[420]

O dervish, the Adamite was given a weighty place. With one glance he attains to the degree of Gabriel and Michael—rather, he passes beyond it. And with a single thought he becomes a dog or a pig. If he goes forward in accordance with knowledge and in keeping with intellect, then we have a noble angel: *This is no mortal! This is but a noble angel!* [12:31]. If he goes after his appetites and attaches his heart to Satan's doorstep, then we have a worthless beast. He may be avaricious like a pig, fawning like a cat, spiteful like a camel, proud like a panther, sly like a fox, mean like a dog. *His likeness is the likeness of a dog* [7:176].

The Adamite is an all-comprehensive city. His essence is a container for all the meanings of the cosmos. The wisdom in this is as follows: The Exalted Lord wanted to instill the treasuries of all knowledge into this wondrous shape and allow him to witness all the meanings of the cosmos, but the cosmos is too vast and the face of the earth too extensive. There was no way for mortal nature to travel around the entire cosmos, given its short life span and incapacity in affairs. Hence the divine wisdom demanded and requested from power that an abridged transcript be made of the root of the macrocosm and be written out in the microcosm. Then He placed that abridged tablet before the child, intellect, and He made him bear witness to it: *He had them bear witness against their own souls: "Am I not your Lord?" They said, "Yes indeed, we bear witness"* [7:172].[421]

You should know that the composition of your body alludes to the composition of the spheres, constellations, heavens, and their layers. The traveling of your soul's faculties by God's leave—and what is meant by "soul" is the body's form[422]—alludes to the traveling of the various sorts of angels in the layers of the heavens and the earths, from the highest of the high to *the lowest of the low* [95:5].

Just as the seven spheres were arranged, so also were the seven bodily members composed. Since the spheres are divided into twelve constellations—as the Exalted Lord reported in the Splendorous Scroll, *"By heaven, possessor of the constellations!"* [85:1]—there are twelve holes in the structure of your body, like the twelve constellations: two eyes, two ears, two nostrils, two paths, two nipples, mouth, and navel. Six constellations are to the south and six to the north; likewise, six of your body's holes are to the right and six to the left. *That is the predetermination of the Exalted, the Knower* [6:96] *and the governance of the King, the Tremendous.*

When He pulled up the spheres and spread this green carpet, there were seven planets, to whose forelocks—according to some—are tied misfortune and felicity, *but the Unseen is with God.* In the same way, there are seven faculties in your body to which your body's wholesomeness is tied: the faculty of eyesight, the faculty of hearing, taste, smell, touch, speech, and intellect. The root of these branches is in the heart. The allusion to this secret in the prophetic speech is this: *"Surely in the body there is a lump of flesh. When it is wholesome, the rest of the body is also wholesome, and when it is corrupt, the rest of the body is also corrupt; surely it is the heart."*[423]

There are two nodes in a celestial sphere, called the "head" and the "tail." Both are themselves hidden, though their traces appear by the decree of the divine power. In the same way your body has two hidden meanings whose traces are manifest: the soundness of the constitution and the illness of the constitution. The body's movements are like the movements of the planets, its birth like the rising of the planets, its death like the setting of the planets, the straightness of its states like the straightness of the planets, its delay and turning back like the return of the planets, its illnesses and diseases like the blights of the planets, its bewilderment in affairs like the pausing of the planets, its elevation in rank like the elevation of the planets, its decline in rank like the falling of the planets.

This much takes into account the celestial world. When we take into account the structure of the terrestrial world, then the body is like the earth, its bones like the mountains, its marrow like the minerals, its belly like the ocean, and its viscera and veins like rivers. Flesh is like dust, hair like plants, the front like the inhabited parts, the back like the uninhabited parts, before the face like east, behind the back like west, the right hand like south, the left hand like north, breath like wind, speech like thunder, sounds like thunderbolts, laughter like light, sorrow and grief like darkness, weeping like rain, sleep like death, wakefulness like life, the days of childhood like the days of spring, the days of youth like the days of summer, the days of maturity like the days of autumn, and the days of old age like the days of winter.

Know that the long and the short of it is that there is no animal or plant, nothing silent or speaking, no sphere, planet, constellation, or any other existent thing whose specific characteristic or likeness is not found again in this speck of dust.[424] This is why the great ones have said that everything is found once again in the Adamite, but the Adamite is not found again in anything. Sometimes he is courageous like a lion, sometimes timid like a rabbit, stingy like a dog, savage like a leopard, tame like a pigeon, scheming like a fox, simple like a sheep, hurried like a gazelle, heavy like a bear, overbearing like an elephant, docile like a camel, strutting like a peacock, auspicious like a parakeet, inauspicious like an owl, guiding like a grouse, dumb like a fish, talking like a nightingale, changing like a wolf, avaricious like a pig, lost like an ostrich, beneficial like a bee, harmful like a rat, blessed like a phoenix.[425]

O chevalier, when someone claims to recognize things but is ignorant of himself, he is like someone who gives food to others but is himself hungry, or someone who shows others the way but is himself lost.[426] In verified truth, until a man connects with the assistance of the divine success-giving, he will not recognize himself. And in reality, whoever recognizes himself does not get along with himself for one moment.

This body, which is the world of form, is an adorned figure, composed of flesh, skin, veins, fat, and bones. These bodies are tenebrous, earthly, and temporal. But the heart is a substance that is heavenly, spiritual, and luminous. It has no kinship with this dustbin. Night and day it thinks about when it will be delivered from the demanding claws of this rapacious wolf and hurry to the gentle world of *return to thy Lord!* [89:28].

> O happy moment—the morning of union,
> the wind of triumph rising, blowing on the lovers!

The poor bird that falls suddenly into a trap! It aspires only to the open plain. This statement is obvious to the intelligent.

God sent revelation to David: *"O David, be like a cautious bird, neither secure nor settled."* It is a foolish bird that gets along with a narrow cage and detaches its heart from the delightful garden. This is like the spring bird that is taken from the delightful meadow with a deceiving call. It wants union with its heart-enticing mate, but its neck is hung in the noose of the trap.

"O nightingale in the garden of the lovers' hearts, if you had not fastened yourself like a decoy to the trap of the invitation in the springtime of faith's covenant, saying, *'I am a mortal like you'* [18:110], what use would I have had for the narrow cage of the Law's prescription?"

But this decoy is also struck by trial: *"I sent you to try you and to try by means of you."*[427] The hunter wanders around, the trap in hand, looking for a green meadow. Then in the midst of the greenery he sets the trap of deception. The little bird has come to a blooming rosebush and scolds its companion: "Last night at the moment of dawn the morning breeze—called 'the wageless messenger of lovers'—blew on my days, but where were you?"

Oh, a thousand hearts of the bold are slave boys of the nightingale's feathers as it gives back its answers by way of allusion. A hundred thousand calls of gentleness pass between the two mates. They understand the meanings of subtlety, but the hunter tells those hundred thousand stories in ignorance. That little bird comes, sits on the little branch of blossoms, and sings a song of a thousand sorts of brokenness and attachment. A secret is sent forth from the Will so that its friend stays hidden. Then in seeking its friend it is hung by the neck. They take it and put it in a narrow cage, and every day it pecks a few grains. The helpers—who are called the "inner appetites"—say, "You must surrender, for flapping has no benefit."

> I chose patience in Your trap, for the poor prey
> will suffocate in the trap from flapping.
> A dog sleeps in the dust at the end of Your street,
> so I'm the friend of Your street's dog when it bites.
> Now that Your approval has settled on my grieving for You,
> the grieving for You I taste seems like sugar.[428]

The poor prisoner! He is cautious with the grain, but after a few days, he makes do with it. When the hunter first put him in the cage, another bird was singing. He looked on in wonder. "How can I talk in this narrow cage?" After a few days pass, he also begins to talk. The carpet of joyful expansiveness is spread between the two, and he says to the old bird, "Why did you fall in and for whom did you fall in? Why did you become my trap?"

Yes, in the first era the spirits were solitary nightingales in the gardens of gentleness. They sang varieties of glorification and sorts of magnification. Then a hunter came into the meadow whose name was "power." The newly caught bird was Adam, and the decoy was becoming accustomed to the grain of wheat. The singing birds of the spirits were hunted in the meadow of solitariness with the decoy of Adam.

O chevalier, just as they put a little bird in a cage, so also they put the subtle, root spirit in the cage of the dense body. Several times every day and night it puts its head out from the window of each soul: "When will I fly?" Be careful not to pluck its wings! Disobedience is to pluck its wings. If you pluck its feathers and wings today, it will be held back when it has to return to the branch of the beginning. This is why there are levels of traveling on the path. Whenever the wings of someone's wholesome deeds are stronger, his traveling will be stronger. Whenever someone's feathers have been plucked today, then a moth will not fall into a candle the way he will fall into the Fire.

Even though in terms of your eyesight the human structure is tiny, in terms of the meanings, elevated things, treasures, and intimations that are deposited within it, it is the macrocosm. Yes, these planets, which have adorned pageants in the high world; and this moon, which is sitting in the shape of a king on the emerald throne, a green helmet on its head, sometimes appearing in the attribute of lovers, sometimes in the form of the beloved; and this sun, which has set up the flag of light and plundered the garment of darkness—all of them take the light they have from the heart of the person of faith, and the person of faith takes light from the gaze of the Real. *What of him whose breast God has expanded for the submission, and he is upon a light from his Lord?* [39:22].

The Exalted Lord created the Throne and put it on the shoulders of the proximate angels. He created paradise and gave it to Riḍwān. He created hell and gave it to Mālik. When He created the heart of the person of faith, Riḍwān said, "Give it to me, for within it are found the fine wine of intimacy and the drink of holiness."

Mālik said, "Give it to me, for within it are found the flames of yearning and the fire of passionate love."

The proximate angels said, "Give it to us, for it is the elevated throne of love and the wide plain of affection."

Others said, "Give it to us, for it is an adorned heaven, its passing thoughts like shooting stars."

The Exalted Lord dismissed them all and said, *"The hearts are between two fingers of the All-Merciful."*[429] By these are meant bounty and justice. Sometimes the breeze of bounty blows over the heart and makes it joyful. Sometimes the simoom of severity strikes against it and melts it. It is confounded between the two attributes, senseless between the two states.

Sometimes the drink of Your union makes me drunk,
sometimes the blow of separation lays me low.
When I put aside the cash of separation's heartache,
love for You puts more cash in my hand.

27–28. *al-Muʿizz al-Mudhill:* the Exalter, the Abaser

The meaning of exalter is the one who makes exalted, and the meaning of abaser is the one who makes lowly. He puts the robe of elevation on one person, without bias, and He plunders the crown of another, without iniquity.

When the Exalted Lord wants to place the crown of exaltation on the servant's head, He gives him access to the carpet of secret whispering. When He wants to place a brand on his cheek, He drives him from the station of proximity with the whip of vengeance. *And to whomsoever God assigns no light, no light has he* [24:40]. *When God desires ugliness for a people, none can repel it, and apart from Him they have no protector* [13:11].

In fear of this station the hearts and livers of all the exalted ones of the Tariqah have burned. *"Surely a man may do the deeds of the folk of the Garden while in God's eyes he is one of the folk of the Fire, or he may do the deeds of the folk of the Fire while in God's eyes he is one of the folk of the Garden."*[430] He put into effect what preceded as He knew it, and He laid down the outcome as He wanted it. He brought into existence a weak-compositioned arrow of mortal nature, put the arrow into the bow of beginningless knowledge, and fired it at the target of the endless decree. If it goes straight, the laudation and bravo belong to the shooter. If it goes crooked, the curse belongs to the arrow.

Bewilderment upon bewilderment, thirst upon thirst,
sometimes supposition is certainty, certainty supposition.

*

I'm bewildered in Thee, take my hand,
O guide of those bewildered in Thee![431]

Oh how many seclusions of an exalted one He has set on fire, how many haystacks of obedience He has thrown to the wind of unneediness, how many livers of the sincerely truthful He has turned into tiny pieces in the turning grindstone of the decree! Here we have Adam the chosen sent out from paradise with a thousand remorses and pains. Here we have Noah the exalted, the brand of *surely he is not of thy folk* [11:46] placed on his liver. Here we have Abraham the bosom friend, put in the ballista of trial and thrown into the fire. Here we have Jacob the noble kept back for eighty years in the House of Sorrows. Here we have Joseph the sincerely truthful, afflicted with bonds, prison, and the envy of his brothers. Here we have Job the prophet sat down at the tablecloth of the bitter decree, cups of poison poured one after another. Here we have Zachariah the purified, the blanket of severity on his back while he was sawed in two from head to foot. Here we have John the sinless, his throat cut like a sheep at the hands of the depraved adulteress. Here we have Moses the speaking companion, sent from the Presence at Mount Sinai to the door of the prideful court of the rebellious, defiant Pharaoh, having been given the overflowing, poisonous drink of *thou shalt not see Me* [7:143]. And here we have Muḥammad the beloved, his exalted teeth broken and his face tainted with blood. And so on.

Anyone entranced by Your work, O Friend,
must carry Your burden on heart and spirit, O Friend.
There is a new secret in all those entranced by You,
but none has access to Your secrets, O Friend,
As long as Your face and hung-down tresses
are in reality like sun and cross, O Friend,
Lovers will take from Your tresses and face
nothing but pure Guebrism, O Friend.
A city full of Your lovers is heart-burned, each
thrown down by the rule of Your work, O Friend.
They're all at a loss in Your work because
not every corpse has a horse fit for Your road, O Friend.

This is one of their sayings: *"The wonder is not that anyone fails to recognize Him—the wonder is that anyone recognizes Him."* Everything that enters your perception is like you, and everything that fits into your heart has your measure. *No recognizer's recognition perceives the Real, and no knower's knowledge reaches the Real. "Eyesights perceive Him not, and He perceives the eyesights. And He is the Gentle, the Aware"* [6:103]. The ocean enters a cup, the fish falls into a trap.

The Shariah says, "O intelligent adult, shake the chain on the door of recognition!" The Haqiqah says, "O woebegone beggar, take the bags of your misfortune away from the threshold of My majesty."

Whenever something comes to hand with the Shariah, the sultan of the Haqiqah charges forth and plunders it. The preacher of the Shariah calls out from the pulpit of bounty, "Have faith and voice *tawḥīd* lest you be deprived of paradise!" Then the sultan of Majesty comes into the field of exaltation on the steed of the Haqiqah and shouts out to the whole world, *"No one but He loves Him, no one but He recognizes Him, and no one but He seeks Him. 'They measure not God with the rightful due of His measure'* [6:91]. *'They encompass Him not in knowledge'* [20:110]. *What do the creatures have to do with the Haqiqah? What do water and clay have to do with talk of the Lord of the Worlds?"*

My lovely idol has never shown her face—
their talk and chatter is nonsense.
He who praises my idol as she is worthy
has heard nothing of her but a report.[432]

When the Real whispers to you something too fine for understanding, do not turn the judgment over to the defective intellect. A thousand thousand heavy drinks were sent to the presence of the heart's sultan on the hand of the cupbearer of listening, but intellect was a stranger to them all. In the world of bewilderment it was like a prisoner saying, "*Woe is me!*" The eyes gazed but did not reach the how-less attributes. The heart scattered a handful of dust in the eyes, and everyone turned away blind and embarrassed.

The scholars stood up and said, "We know such and such." The astronomers stood up and said, "We measure the spheres degree by degree." The philosophers stood up and said, "We have established the Prime Matter and the First Cause." The merchants stood up and said, "We did this trading and took this much profit. We crossed over those mountains and deserts."

The majesty of exaltedness answers, *"This is an affair that will not be completed with associationism."* O naturalists, look at My power! O Kalam experts, look at My desire! O merchants, look at My apportioning! Power says, "Here is error for you!" Desire says, "Here are mistakes for you!" Apportioning says, "Here is folly for you!"

On the day in the beginningless when they beat the drum for the falcon of mystery, this is how they beat it: "Annihilation for creation, and His subsistence! Nonexistence for creation, and His existence!"

O dervishes, take this advice in His road: Turn all of existence over to Him!

O chevalier, in respect of the divine command, the whole world has seeking, existence, and free choice, but in respect of the lordly power, *there is no inhabitant in the house.* One sliver of the world of Lordhood's severity was made apparent, and those who were the forerunners of the road and the proximate of the Threshold said, *"We have no knowledge"* [5:109].

Do you know what you should take to the Threshold on this long road? An iota of need. What is need? A burning in the heart, a pain in the breast, and dust on the face—such that your aspiration is in the East and your body in the West. When you come back to the work, you will be neither eastern nor western.

Someone came before his master and said, "Lamentations!"

He said, "Against whom?"

He said, "Against God."

He said, "To whom?"

He said, "To God."

Abu'l-Ḥusayn Nūrī said, "For thirty years I was attacked and melted in the furnace of pain. After thirty years the call came, 'O Abu'l-Ḥusayn, where you are, I have no place. And where My unity's majesty is, you have no access.' "

These Men threw the East into the West and the West into the East. Wherever they went, they heard this call: "You have no escape from seeking, but there is no way to find."

All pens broke, all imaginations were bewildered, all understandings were severed. No one knows His secret but He who said, *"Surely I know"* [2:30]. Intellects were bewildered in His majesty, intelligence distracted by His beauty, bodies impotent in giving thanks for His caresses, hearts melted by recognizing Him.

> Oh, the spirits and hearts of all creatures
> are hung from the hooks of Your tresses.
> Blood began to flow from my eyes
> when my heart joined with love for You.
> The pen of well-being was taken away
> as soon as Your sorrow sat in my heart.
> The servant's heart lost in loving You,
> he became drunk in separation from You.
> How long will You keep awareness from the heart-lost?
> How long will You strike the drunk?
> Don't let separation break the back of the servant
> who broke his repentance for You.

When Moses arrived at the Presence, he said, "O Lord, a Threshold so exalted and so empty!"

It was said to him, "O Moses, so exalted is My road that no one has the capacity for Me."

The helpless polo ball in the field! Struck by the mallet, it runs on its own head, sent by the hands and feet of the riders. If it reaches this one—a mallet. If it reaches that one—a mallet. A frail handful of dust was put at the end of the mallet of exalted severity. The ball is driven from the top of the field of the beginningless will to the bottom of the field of the endless desire. At the top of the field, a banner is set up: *"He will not be asked about what He does, but they will be asked"* [21:23]. At the bottom of the field a second banner reads, *"Doer of what He desires"* [11:107].

But a stipulation was made with the ball: "You look at the gaze of the sultan, not the striking of the mallet." Those who looked at the striking of the mallet fled from the burden of the work. *They refused to carry it* [33:72]. Then Adam, with a lion's liver, lifted up the burden, so he reaped the fruit.

After all, they were six-day infants—[*God is He who created the heavens, the earth, and what is between the two*] *in six days* [32:4]. An infant is not up to carrying burdens, but Adam was put in the cradle of the Covenant for forty years, and he was given the milk of friendship from the nipple of kind favor. *"He fermented Adam's clay in His hand for forty mornings."*[433]

Heaven and earth saw today's burden [*bār*], but Adam saw tomorrow's access [*bār*]. He said, "If I do not carry this burden, I will not be given access to the court of majesty tomorrow." He came into the work like a man, so he became the center-point of the compass of secrets.

In truth, in truth, the seven heavens and the earth have not smelt a whiff of this talk. If anyone has an inkling, it is this water and dust. "If not for the pain in your hearts, I would not have mixed the electuary of love, for *'I am with those whose hearts are broken.'*[434] No one was aware of this talk or had any news of this mystery. I began the mystery, I brought forth the omen of union."

For several years Jacob sent his sons to Joseph, but as long as a seeker from Joseph's own makeup had not appeared, the goal was not achieved. *Do you know what you did to Joseph?* [12:89]. He lifted the curtain from his own name and began the talk about himself. Otherwise, how would they have dared to talk about Joseph? When he began with this mystery, they said, *"What, are you indeed Joseph?" He said, "I am Joseph"* [12:90].

He created the whole universe and kept it in the station of awe. No one had the gall to talk about Him or think about Him. He Himself said, *"Am I not your Lord?"* [7:172].

O dervish, when He wants to give, He gives without deliberation. And when He puts deliberation in the midst, you must detach your heart. Do you not see that He said, *"Surely We offered the Trust to the heavens and the earth"* [33:72]? The deliberation was because He did not want to give. But when He brought forth Adam, the center of the work, He did not allow for deliberation and made him no offer. The man himself had fallen into the work. When Adam saw that He was offering it to others, he was moved by jealousy. He fearlessly threw himself forth because of jealousy. He stepped into the field of danger without the offer. Then He said, *"Surely he was a great wrongdoer, deeply ignorant."* This alludes to his lack of fear. He stepped into the world of purity because he was fearless.

When they brought this paragon into the world, he was addressed with the words "The whole of paradise is given over to you. But beware, do not go near that tree." At the same time it was said to the tree, "Do not put yourself anywhere except before Adam's eyes, for We have secrets in this path."

You're a wondrous friend, O Khorasani friend![435]

O dervishes, the wondrousness of the beloveds has come! "O Adam, you have come into paradise and sat down at Riḍwān's tablecloth. This is indeed fine, but you should invite some of your offspring for whom provision has not been stipulated."

Every food he tasted in the highest paradise grabbed his skirt and said, "Be with us!" except wheat. It said, "O paragon, detach your heart from these existent things, for He will not leave you here."

When he came out he said, "I need the nourishment of wheat, because the others just flirted with me. It was wheat that spoke the truth."

The Shariah was saying, *"Do not go near this tree!"* [2:35]. The Tariqah was saying, *"Go down out of it!"* [2:38]. The Shariah was saying, "Keep your hands away!" The Haqiqah was saying, "Strike fire to everything!"

From the day that paragon stepped from that world into this world, the eight paradises have been burning because of separation from his feet.

O dervish, Adam was in paradise, but he caught the scent of something else. He said, "This world is adorned, but I have it in my heart to return one day to the nest of my sorrow."

Oh, the wolves of misfortune; oh, the edge of the forest!
    What am I doing here, a thousand thoughts in my heart?

"Even though the angels said, *'What, wilt Thou set therein one who will work corruption there?'* [2:30], I will go to a place where they will have to follow in my tracks."

The first attribute to shine in Adam's heart was the secret of faith. It said, "O Adam, come into exile, for *'Islam began as an exile, and it will return as it began, an exile.'* "[436]

He said, "Why should I come?"

It said, "To do the work."

He said, "Is there a work to be done better than this work? The eight paradises are under my command, Riḍwān is my servant and slave boy, and the angels of the Dominion are prostrating themselves before the presence of my majesty."

It said, "No, you must exchange the Abode of Peace for the Abode of Blame. You must remove the crown from your head and pour the dust of destitution on your head. You must replace the good name of *surely God chose Adam* [3:33] with the blame of *Adam disobeyed* [20: 121], for the good fortune of love will subsist forever.

[Adam said,] "I will give out the call of *'I do not care'* in the world and open the hand of plunder to the house of vicegerency's good fortune. Perhaps the Sultan of Love will say to me, *'Peace be upon you!'* "

What work can I do better
    than call myself Your servant?
Without thought of people's blame,
    I'll greet You where I see You.
I'll build a new mosque at the end of Your street
    and call it the mosque of the lovers.

On the day Gabriel the Trustworthy came to take a handful of dust, the dust sought help. It said, "Beware! Let me stay hidden just as I am. If you bring me from the cave of jealousy into the open plain of manifestation, tumult will fall into the world."

From the World of Exaltedness a call was coming: "This work will not be put straight with faint-heartedness." Adam the chosen was leaning back on the cushion of leadership at the front of Firdaws, supported by the couch of exaltedness and nobility. He made the proximate of the Higher Plenum and the prostrators of the celestial orb stand in the row of servitors at the threshold of his majesty. With the hand of aspiration he suddenly separated the edict of love's tumult from the scroll of purity and smashed the Higher Plenum's monasteries of *I and no one else*. He let out this call in the world: "I have come to strip the shirt of claiming we-ness from your backs. I will punish the court of majesty with this whip: *Above every possessor of knowledge is one who knows* [12:76]."

O dervish, as long as Adam had not come, the Throne was hungry, the Footstool naked, the Pen thirsty. When Adam came forth, he made everyone happy. He sipped from the goblet of love's covenant, for *We made covenant with Adam before* [20:115]. Drunk with the covenant's wine, he took a dip in the Ocean of At-ness. This was expressed with the words *"in a seat of truthfulness at an Omnipotent King"* [54:55].

"O Gabriel, ʿAzāzīl did not prostrate himself. How is it that you have taken the job of messenger boy?"

He answered, "I see the characteristics of the breast, not the form of clay."

There are many waystations and stages separating the characteristics of the breast from the form of clay. When the angels of the Dominion prostrated themselves before Adam the chosen, they did so because the pearl of the heart had not been placed inside the jewel box of their own existence. Adam, however, had a heart. In reality, all the treasuries of the secrets and the meanings have a road into this drop of blood. *"Deeds are [judged] by intentions"*[437] is an allusion to this secret. As long as this drop in the ocean of your innate disposition does not lift up the saddlecloth of good fortune and lead the way, you will not be taken to the world of contemplation and struggle. It must walk in front of the steed of your aspiration shouting, *"Make way! Make way!"* Beware, do not look at this drop with the eye of contempt, for the robe of forerunning was placed on its shoulders.

In His munificence the Exalted Lord gave existence to this fortified fortress, which is the locus of adornment and beautification. He scattered over it the effusion of bounties from the clouds of tenderness, making it a faultless mortal and well-proportioned body. He sat the spirit-king on this royal seat, for *I blew into him of My spirit* [15:29]. Then He gave all the reins of rulership over this makeup into the hands of the heart, which is the king in the celestial sphere of the body's world: *"Surely in the body there is a lump of flesh. When it is wholesome, the rest of the body is also wholesome, and when it is corrupt, the rest of the body is also corrupt; surely it is the heart."*[438]

When the Maker—exalted is His name!—wanted to lay the foundation of the city of clay and the town of your breast, He brought into existence a finely made little shape from water and clay.[439] Some have spoken about the four humors, the four elements, and the four natures, but the reality is as He said: *"We created man from an extraction of clay"* [23:12]. O water and clay, O worthy of being accepted by the Lord of the Worlds!

Then from this water and clay He gave existence to nine pearls diverse in shape, such as bones, nerves, veins, blood, and so on. These radiant pearls taken from the ocean of power He strung on the string of composition, arrangement, combination, and burdening. He set up this clay city with 240 columns, straight in stature and well-proportioned in creation, which are the bones. He tied this essence together with 720 bonds, which are the nerves. He filled the treasuries with multicolored pearls, such as brain, marrow, heart, spleen, and intestines. He inscribed highways and made paths appear. He opened doors, brought forth fountains and springs, set down rivers, and made 360 streams. In the wall that surrounds it he opened up twelve windows: two ears, two eyes, two nostrils, two paths, two nipples, mouth, and navel. He appointed six servitors over this city to serve it, namely, the faculties of attraction, retention, digestion, repulsion, growth, and alimentation. He put five avaricious guards in charge of protecting it, namely, the five senses.

Then He kept this town upright on top of two pillars and gave it movement with two wings in six directions. Next came the secret of what is at issue in this city. He collected three different groups: a tribe of jinn, a tribe of humans, and a tribe of angels. He set over them a king and taught the king their names, commanding him to guard and protect the city. He said, *"Tell them their names"* [2:33]. Then He commanded them to obey him: *"And when We said to the angels, 'Prostrate yourselves before Adam,' they prostrated themselves, except Iblis"* [2:34], who is caprice.

The two pillars are the two legs, the two wings are the two hands, and the six directions are behind, ahead, right, left, above, and below.

The tribes are like the meanings placed within him and the souls deposited therein: The appetitive soul, which is alluded to with *"Surely the soul commands to ugliness"* [12:53], is like the jinn and the satans. The animal soul, which is the blaming soul, is like humans. The serene soul—which is serene beneath the burdens of the road and is alluded to in the Splendorous Scripture with *"O serene soul!"* [89:27]—is like the angels. The king of all is the heart.

When you consider the state of the body and what it contains—the wonders of the composition of its parts and the various sorts of combination in the joints—you would say that the body is a well-equipped house. When you consider the state of the spirit and the marvels of its exercising control over the body, you would say that the heart is the housemaster who controls his own house. This meaning has already been explained briefly.[440]

In another respect, if you gaze with the eye of insight, you will see that your own body with the diversity of its shapes and parts is like a shop. The heart[441] is like an artisan, and all the parts of the body are like the artisan's tools. With each bodily part the heart displays a deed, just as artisans make deeds apparent with each tool. Carpenters trim with axes, cut with saws, and make holes with drills. In the same way smiths and other artisans work with tools. So also is the state of the heart with the body. It hears with the ears, sees with the eyes, talks with the tongue, tastes with the mouth, feels with the hands, walks with the feet, thinks with the center of the brain, imagines sensory things with the front of the brain, and remembers and records known things with the back of the brain. *So blessed is God, the most beautiful of creators!* [23:14].[442]

In another respect, when you consider the states of the heart and you awaken the eye of intellect from the sleep of heedlessness, you will say that the body is a womb and the heart the embryo, or the body is a cradle and the heart the infant. States and alterations pass over it until it reaches the border of perfection and the witnessing places of majesty and beauty.

If you consider the two in another respect, you will find the body like a ship and the heart like a sailor. Wholesome deeds are like merchandise, this world is like a sea full of crocodiles, death is the shore, the afterworld's house is like a city of merchants, and the Exalted Lord is a dealer buying deeds.[443] *"When someone stores up provisions in this world, it will profit him in the next world."*[444]

When you consider in another respect, you will find the body like a steed and the heart like a rider. This world is the playing field, the doers of deeds and the strugglers are the preceders, and at the head of all the preceders is Muḥammad, just as he said: *"We are the last, the preceders."*[445] *"We are the last" in existence, "the preceders" in generosity and munificence. "We are the last" in respect of our footsteps, "the preceders" by the gentleness of eternity. "We are the last" in calling to account, "the preceders" in being called to account.*

When you consider in another respect, you will find the heart is like a plowman and the body like a field. Deeds are seeds and produce, death is the reaper, and the resurrection is the threshing floor. *A group in the Garden* belongs to those fit for storing, *and a group in the Blaze* [42:7] belongs to those fit for burning.

When you consider in another respect while meditating on the wonders of this structure and seeing how the heart benefits from the various sorts of knowledge by means of the body, you will see the body as a grammar school and the heart like a child in the school. Night and day it acquires knowledge *while seeking arrival at the Presence of the King, the Self-Standing. God says, "No soul knows what delight of the eyes is hidden away for them"* [32:17].[446] The child acquires knowledge through spiritual subtleties beyond the sense faculties. These are the faculties of imagination, thought, memory, speech, and artisanry; they assist one other in perceiving the traces of practices.

The explanation of this is that when the faculty of imagination takes on the traces of the sensory things—in the same way that wax receives the imprint of a seal-ring—it immediately gives them over to the faculty of thought. The work of the faculty of thought is to delve into their realities and to investigate their secrets along with their benefits and harms and then to turn this over to the faculty of memory to preserve it. When it wants to report about those meanings, it composes words from letters with the faculty of speech, whose chamber is the tip of the tongue, and it conveys these to the listener's faculty of hearing.

Here there is another subtle point: The Exalted Lord did not set down the custom for sounds to remain in the air until the listener can take a share, for the pen of form cannot inscribe the imprint of speech on the smooth tablet of air. Hence the divine wisdom required that the meanings of words be delineated by artisanry. Thus the faculty of artisanry, whose place is in the fingers, composed the shapes of the lines with pens and deposited them on tablets, pages, and notebooks, so that knowledge would remain delineated as the benefit left by the forebears for the successors—from those who have gone to those who are coming. This is one of the majestic favors of the Exalted Lord, just as He reported in the Splendorous Scripture: *"Recite, and thy Lord is the most generous, who taught by the pen, taught man what he knew not"* [96:3–5].[447]

As for the fact that our paragon did not know how to write, that was not because of a deficiency of his state. Rather He sent the paragon to whiten the black, not to blacken the white. But this is a form through which allusion is made, and the folk of the reality do not rest with form. In terms of verification, a pen has a tip for taking the secret deposited within it and writing it out on a white page. Muṣṭafā's secret core, however, was too exalted to be perceived by a pen. How is it fitting for a secret core of which no proximate angel or sent prophet was aware to come under the control of the tip of a pen?[448]

Some have said that this Adamic makeup is an epitome of the Guarded Tablet.[449] This is why Shaykh Abū Yazīd, when asked about the Guarded Tablet, said, *"I am the Guarded Tablet."*[450] They offered a simile for this in order to bring it closer to people's understandings. They said that once there was a king who had a share of knowledge and wisdom. He had several beloved and honored children upon whom his heart was gazing. He wanted to discipline his children and teach them courtesy before he brought them into his assembly, for as long as a man is not rectified and courteous, he is not worthy for the carpet of kings. In accordance with his own weighty view and firm resoluteness, he had a castle constructed better and sturdier than any seen before. In that castle he made a sitting place for each child and set up a chamber. He recorded every knowledge that he wanted to teach each of them on the edges and sides of the sitting place, and he imprisoned them in the castle and appointed slaves and servants to take care of them. Then he addressed the children: "Meditate and gaze upon these forms so as to understand their meanings. Once you have understood these meanings, you will have understood the meanings of the scholars, the learned, the wise, and the pious. When you have become like that, I will convey you to the sitting place of intimacy and the presence of the majesty of your king and keep you favored and honored."

The wise king and generous padshah is the Exalted Lord. The small children are an allusion to Adam and the Adamites, who are honored in the Exalted Presence with the address *"He loves them and they love Him"* [5:54]. The raised-up castle is the spheres, and the individual sitting places are the forms of human nature. The acts of courtesy given form are the marvelous compositions and wonderful combinations of this body. The written, inscribed, and recorded sorts of knowledge are the meanings in the heart and the recognitions in the secret core. When these dust-dwelling souls gain these knowledges, they become worthy for the sitting place of intimacy and the palisades of holiness. Such is the allusion made by the Eternal Speech: *"Surely the godwary will be amid gardens and a river, in a seat of truthfulness, at an Omnipotent King"* [54:54–55].

Today your stipulation is discipline [*riyāḍa*] so that tomorrow you may reach the gardens [*riyāḍ*] of gentleness. *"If you desire the stations of the Substitutes, you must transform your states."* Only an exalted person can abandon his own objects of desire. The falcon's nest is taken from the top of the tree to the hand of the king only because the falcon has abandoned its own desires.

A pir said, "Once it happened that I was sitting by the gate of a king, and a great number of people were present. No one dared to go into the king's castle. Every hour a certain black slave would go in and come back out. I said, 'This is marvelous—noblemen and commanders like this are sitting at the gate, and no one dares to go inside. What rank does this black man have that he goes in without a veil?'

"Someone said, 'The reason is that his appetite's instrument has been cut off.' "

The pir said, *"Glory be to Him who after seventy years admonished me with a eunuch! If someone desires entrance without a veil, let him abandon appetite."* If anyone wants to find access to the Presence, tell him to put aside the burden of desire and free choice.[451]

"O falcon, how is it that you have the prey in your talons but do not eat?"

It said, "Yes, the inner boiling tells me to eat, but the courtesy in my breast says, 'Beware, beware, watch out!' The trial is not that I catch a pheasant and then do not lift it to my beak. The trial is that my stomach is empty, and everyone blames me by saying, 'Look at that stupid little bird! He has a fat prey in his talons, his stomach is hungry, and his beak is sharp, but he does not have the gall to eat it.' "

A godwary man puts a permitted morsel before himself and trembles: "What should I do? I must not eat this morsel and then suffer loss tomorrow because of being hungry." Someone else eats forbidden morsels and does not think of the resurrection, nor does he fear God, nor is he ashamed before the Messenger.

The falcon says, "Today you see that all the birds hide under the leaves when they hear my jingling bells. They did not see the day when my eyes were sewn shut with the needle of severity in order to kill the desire within me. On the day the needle of severity was being used, I kept my lips together despite that wound and had patience. Today the result is patience. My tongue is mute, but my talons are eloquent. Come to the hunting grounds to see the eloquence of my practice!"

> I'm a man of aspiration—can a falcon be like this?
> I show want and need to no one.
> I'm happy with myself inside the curtain of mystery,
> sometimes prey, sometimes trap, sometimes joy, sometimes want.[452]

O chevaliers, it is no great work to hunt a tiny sparrow, turn it into a morsel, put it to use, and entrust it to annihilation. The work lies in hunting a falcon, catching it, placing it on the hand of exaltedness, caressing it with gentleness, and putting it to work with such kindliness that it will be taught by you and cling to you, its heart one and straight in its love for you. Then you may remove the bond from its foot and let it fly in the open plain on the wings of courtesy, catch with the beak of honor, and come back to the hand of the covenant because of the pull of loyalty.

O dervish, in reality you are the falcon of mystery. Today is the day in which your eyes are bound and your feet tied. You see but a little and eat but a little. These Shari'ite rules and forms of courtesy that were explained by Muṣṭafā's purified tongue are the discipline of your states so that your breast may become limpid, your heart may be prepared to receive the Real, your eyes may begin to see, your hands may take, and your feet may walk. Then you will be conveyed to the world of subsistence and allowed to fly in the endless plain and everlasting sky. Once your feet are released, your wings spread, your hands given strength, and your eyes allowed to see, and once all the beings of the Unseen, the hidden secrets of bounty, the veiled virgins of gentleness, and the secrets of the road have been made your prey, you will fly on the wings of subsistence in the air of limpidness, arrive at the mysteries of the Haqiqah, and lift up the veils from the unseen wonders. Then at loyalty's invitation you will return to the *seat of truthfulness* [54:55].

29–30. *al-Samīʿ al-Baṣīr:* the Hearing, the Seeing

The Exalted Lord is hearing and seeing, but not with limbs and organs—high indeed is God above that!

When the truthful assenting man of faith believes that the Real is hearing and seeing, he must devote his outwardness to perseverance and keep his inwardness in watchfulness. Outwardly he must persevere with deeds and inwardly he must be watchful over the states of his secret core. There is nothing more surprising in the whole world than that someone should recognize Him and then take a step in opposition to Him. *When someone recognizes Him, he becomes familiar with Him, and when someone is familiar with Him, he disdains opposition to Him.*

Yaḥyā ibn Muʿādh Rāzī said, *"The night is long—do not shorten it with sleep. The day is bright —do not darken it with sin."*[453]

It was said to Bishr Ḥāfī, "Why is it that you do not sleep at night and are unsettled in the daytime?"

He said, "Because I am sought." A seeker is in my tracks.

The same thing was said to someone else. He said, *"The snakebitten does not sleep."*

It is said that one night a guest came to the house of ʿAlī, the Commander of the Faithful. He caressed him and gave him food, and then put out bedclothes for him. The heedless man stayed in the bedclothes until daytime, while that paragon stood on the feet of service and busied himself with obedience to the Lord. When it was daytime, the man said, *"Not once in my life have I had a wakeful and worshipful night like your night."*

ʿAlī said, "Not once in my life have I had a sleep-filled and heedless night like your night."

Your day, deluded one, is neglect and heedlessness;
your night is sleep, your ruin clinging to it.
You're striving for an outcome you'll dislike—
such is the life of beasts in the world.[454]

*

Night has passed, but we're still not awake,
we're still busy with neglect and heedlessness.
The sun of subsistence has reached the top of the wall,
but we're still at the door of fancy's dawn.

Look at the work that has befallen us: no honor in the mosque, no place in the tavern.

O Friend, time passes by with the ascription of forms as You weave together black and white reeds. By the rightful due of loyalty, make it longer! Perhaps in this container I'll be sent an inkling of this talk.

Ashʿath the Covetous was passing by a tray-maker's shop. He said, "Make these trays you're making bigger. Perhaps someone will send me something on one of them."

Here we have your breast full of wishes! Here we have your worthless heart!

It is said that there were 360 idols placed in the Kaabah. If all the accountants in the world came to record the number of idols that you have in your breast, they would not be able to do so.

In our times it is not necessary for Azar to carve idols, for everywhere in the world there's someone with unwashed face, an Azari idol in his breast. *"The soul is the greatest idol."*[455]

In the city a Magian is walking with his cap on his head, and you are walking with the turban of *tawḥīd* on your head and a fanciful notion of *tawḥīd* inside. If turban and robe make someone a Muslim, then bravo, O leader of the sincerely truthful! And if being a Guebre means to attach your heart to two, well, you know what needs to be done.

In short, know that nothing will be given out on the basis of talk!

Abu'l-Qāsim Mudhakkir[456] lived in Nishapur, though he was originally from Merv. He spoke sweetly in reminding. Once he was holding a session and speaking forth fine words. A man stood up and said, *"If the work is completed with talk, you have gone to the place of honor.* But if this pot needs some seasoning, you can't settle down on the basis of words."

There was a singer who used to go to the home of a patrician. Whenever he sang a song, the patrician would say, *"Beautifully done!"* He would sing another song and again he would say, *"Beautifully done!"* The singer was also a poet. One day he said,

Every time I sing you say, "Beautifully done, sing another!"
You can't buy flour with "Beautifully done."[457]

In the bazaar, you can't buy anything with *Beautifully done*! They want pure gold and unalloyed silver.

O respectable man, in this road they want a burnt liver, they want a heart full of pain, they want footsteps with truthfulness, they want a spirit with love, they want togetherness without dispersion. If you have the hard cash, the work is yours.

Indeed, the first trial you face is the trial of your own being. Gather that being and turn it over to the ruling power of *tawḥīd* so that it may be destroyed, for nothing can bring together a dispersed man except *tawḥīd*. "Tawḥīd *is to isolate the Eternal from the newly arrived."*[458] *Tawḥīd* is assaying: throwing away the counterfeit, the newly arrived, and picking out the genuine, the Eternal.

One of them said, *"Tawḥīd*, the *tawḥīd*-voicer, and the One? This makes Him *the third of three* [5:73]."[459]

Everyone in the world is attached to giving one and taking two. These Men are attached to giving all and taking one.

O dervish, sacrifice this world and that world! Then the danger will be whether you are given one iota.

"Embrace poverty, make patience your pillow, treat appetites as the enemy, and implore God in all affairs."[460] Make patience your bed, embrace need, and do not get up until the morning of the resurrection breaks.

Shiblī said, "I have a need that seized my hand and brought me into this road."

They said, "What need do you have?"

He said, "It is a need such that the eight paradises were made into a mouthful and thrown into it, but not a mote of them appeared."

By God the tremendous, Adam knew the worth of paradise when they put it in his hand.

"O Adam, what is paradise worth?"

He said, "When someone fears hell, paradise is worth a thousand lives. But when someone fears You, paradise is not worth a grain."

When Adam reached for that grain of wheat, it was not that he did not know what it was. On the contrary, he knew, but he made his own road short.

What a marvelous business! The wheat was put there in his name and made his nourishment, but it was forbidden to him: *Do not go near this tree*! [2:35]. Love took hold of his bridle.

The forbidden is enticing. He stretched his hand toward the tree. The tree said, "You were commanded not to eat of me." He paid no attention.

The moment the grain of wheat reached his throat, the call rose up all over paradise, *"And Adam disobeyed"* [20:121]. The crown flew from his head, saying, *"Peace be upon you, Adam, for your sorrow will be drawn out."* The throne said, *"Get down from me, for I do not carry anyone who opposes Him."*

O chevalier, the decree was watching and the command severe. The severe command came outwardly, but the watching decree looked at the secret core. *"The worst of men is he who eats alone, beats his servant, and forbids helping him."*[461]

Yes, my spirit and world, the great ones have spoken about this and pierced the pearl of meaning with the diamond of thought. What was the wisdom in ejecting Adam from paradise?

Some say that the Exalted Lord wanted Adam's knowledge of Him to increase. First He brought him into the garden of gentleness and sat him down on the chair of happiness. He gave him goblets of joy, one after another. Then He sent him away weeping, burning, and wailing. Just as he savored the goblet of gentleness at first, so also he tasted the drink of pure, unmixed severity at last—without any cause. O chevalier, God wrapped the edict of loftiness and transcendence in the exalted embroidery of *"I do not care,"*[462] and no one had the gall to protest.

Again, some say that the sapling of good fortune was planted with the hand of gentleness in the orchard of his covenant. It was watered with the effusion of lordly bounty until the tree became fixed: *its roots fixed and its branches in heaven* [14:24]. He was the coffer of the wonders of power, within which were the secret coffers of creativity. Or he was an ocean within which were both gemstone and brick, night-brightening pearl and night-colored bead, truth-speaker and liar, sincere and heretic, enemy and friend, wretched and godwary. Paradise was not the abode of enemies or the home of the wretched, so the lordly wisdom required that he should come into this world in order for the goodly to be separated from the vile: *So that God may distinguish the vile from the goodly* [8:37].

It can also be said that Adam wanted from the tree to stay in paradise forever, but when his eyes fell on the tree, he was told the time had come to pack his bags. *"Do not let the limpidness of the present moments delude you, for in between are the obscurities of blights."*[463] *"Between the favors appear the shadows of the teeth."*

O chevalier, never say that paradise was taken from Adam. Say rather that Adam was taken from paradise. A roasted heart will never be content with roast chicken.

Wahab ibn Munabbih narrated that when the Lord created Adam and brought him into paradise, He decorated him with all sorts of adornments and robes. The form was the form of Adam, but the adornments were the adornments of paradise and the adorner was the Unseen. Then the command came, "O Adam, get up and wander around paradise to see if any form is more beautiful than yours." Adam wandered around paradise and did not see any form more beautiful than his own. Delight and elation appeared in him and he began to strut. His Lord called out to him, *"Be conceited, for it is your right to be conceited. I created you solitary for the Solitary."*

"Then," said Wahab ibn Munabbih, "the delight that appeared in Adam was bequeathed to his children. It comes as arrogance in the ignorant, pride in sultans, and ecstasy in friends and lovers."[464]

O breeze of Najd, when did you leave Najd?
Your blowing has piled ecstasy on ecstasy.[465]

It was the sultan of solitariness and the army of *tawḥīd* that hunted Adam in paradise and snatched him away from all beings. When someone is plundered by the sultan of jealousy, he no longer concerns himself with any others.

Abu'l-Ḥasan Ḥuṣrī was a student of Shiblī. He said, "I saw Shiblī in a dream after his death. I asked him, 'How did your work turn out? What was done with you?' "

O dervish, the whole world has stopped in its place: "What will be done with us?" He created a handful of dust and said, "I have work with you," but He kept the work in the Unseen. This work has not yet been shown to you. Today you have the burden of the work, not the work itself. A man gets a porter from the bazaar and puts a sealed burden on his back. He shows him the road and says, "Lift up this burden and take it." What does the porter know about what is inside the burden? Wait until he reaches the destination and opens it. *Refuge in God* that a serpent should come out from the burden!

Today the burden of servanthood is under the seal of Lordhood. The burden itself is hard cash, but the secrets of the burden are in the Unseen. All the sincerely truthful of the world have turned their livers into water and their hearts into kabobs worrying about what will emerge from this burden. The verified truth is that *when someone has been taken far by the precedents, he will not be brought near by the means of approach.*[466]

So Ḥuṣrī said that he asked Shiblī what happened to him.

Shiblī said, "He brought me into His Presence and said, 'Ask for something.' I said, *'O God, if You put me into the Garden, that is Your justice, and if You make me worthy for union, that is Your bounty.'* "

The expression people use is, "Lord God, if You put me into paradise, that is Your bounty, but if You put me into hell, that is Your justice." Shiblī turned this around and said, "Lord God, if you put me into the Garden of Eden, that is Your justice, but if You make me worthy of union, that is Your bounty."

If separation settled down in the Garden,
the servants' bliss therein would turn into hell.[467]

The exalted ones have said, *"The renunciant is the Real's prey in this world, and the recognizer is the Real's prey in the Garden."*[468]

Therein you shall have whatsoever your souls hunger for [41:31] *and pleases the eyes* [43:71]. *He will unveil one group through His Essence and address another group through His attributes.* He will keep one group busy with paradise, but another group will not be able to put up with this station. One group will have no concern with the realm of being, for beauty will address them and majesty will unveil itself to them.

The oblivious are distracted from You by their business,
but I make all my business You, O final end of my business![469]

His love came and burned away everything else. When His love comes, it strikes jealousy's fire into the haystack of gazing on others.

A naked heart, within it a shining lamp![470] Exalted is the heart that has no room for others!

A body is wanted, tamed by the commandments. A heart is wanted, contemplating the command. A spirit is wanted, drunk with the wine of holiness in the session of intimacy. A secret core is wanted, standing on the carpet of expansiveness and empty of all being. A radiance of the light of gentleness is wanted, shining from the Mount Sinai of unveiling, snatching you away like Moses from all others and setting you down in the station of contemplation and the domicile of struggle. It will remove the *shoes* [20:12] of gazing on the two worlds from your feet, snatch the *staff* [20:18] of disobedience from your hand, and bring you to the *holy valley* [20:12] and the unqualified bush. It will make you drunk with spirit-mingled and repose-inducing wine, and every moment it will call out to the hearing of your secret core, *"Surely I am God* [20:14]. It is I who am I. If anyone says 'I am,' I will break his neck. Even if you are not jealous of your own thoughts, aspiration, and resolution, I in My Lordhood am jealous."

This is one of their sayings: *"Jealousy is two: human jealousy and divine jealousy. Human jealousy is concerned with outward things, and divine jealousy is concerned with conscious thoughts."*[471]

Do you fancy that He has kept these secrets protected by His gaze all this time because of foolishness? Just as He is jealous of His own Unseen, He is jealous of your secret core. This is why He said, *"Surely I know what you do not know"* [2:30]. It is because He is keeping that for this and He is nurturing this for that. What an exalted moment it will be when the curtain is lifted, the secret core gazes on the Unseen, and the Unseen gazes on the secret core! What do you say about that time? Will forgiveness be taken into account?

"We made the whole world the servant of your good fortune's presence. We addressed you and said, 'Do not be the servant of any but Our Threshold: *Do not prostrate yourselves to the sun and the moon, but prostrate yourselves to God, who created them'* [41:37]."

We created you, then We formed you, then We said to the angels, "Prostrate yourselves before Adam" [7:11]. O folk of the world, prostrate yourselves before him! O handful of dust, prostrate yourselves only to Him!

What is this? It is the divine jealousy toward the creation of dust. *"I am jealous and Saʿd is jealous, and God is more jealous than we are. Part of His jealousy is that He 'forbade indecencies'* [7:33]."[472]

He busied every speck of yours with one of His secrets: O hearing, be gathered in listening! *And when the Quran is recited, listen to it* [7:204]. O eyesight, have insight and heedfulness! *So take heed, O you who have eyes* [59:2]. O tongue, remember His beautiful-doing! *So remember God, as you remember your fathers, or with more intense remembrance* [2:200]. O nose, be disdainful of smelling the stench of the others! O hands, be takers of the goblets of gentleness! O feet, be walkers in the gardens of discipline! *Say "God," then leave them* [6:91]. *And devote yourselves to Him devoutly* [73:8]. *So take Him as a trustee* [73:9].

If it were appropriate for one speck of you to belong to another, then what was the mission of the prophets? He sent one hundred twenty-some thousand center-points of messengerhood with limpid states, and the gist of their invitation was this: "O dust and clay, belong to Me from the depths of your spirit and heart! If you turn away from the road by one iota, the whips of punishment are in place. The commandments have been sent. If you turn away from the commandments, the reprimands are in place."

He calls with gentleness, but He brings back with harshness. He has filled the world with dread and blights: thorns with fresh dates, tipsiness with wine, troubles with treasures, tribulation with good fortune. You can never settle down, find intimacy and familiarity, or reach conformity with a single mote. Whether you like it or not, whether by compulsion or free choice, you will go back to the Threshold.

"Command them to the prayer when they are children of seven, and impose it on them when they are children of ten."[473] Muṣṭafā said to command children to pray when they are seven and to strike them for it when they are ten. If they do it by choice, good. Otherwise—the rod and the whip. This is a marvelous business: A frail compound, an insignificant makeup, a defective intellect, inadequate knowledge. Then the command of the Prophet comes: "Command him to pray."

What is this prayer? Its meaning is that an invitation was offered to heaven with its length and breadth, to earth with its expanse and vastness, and to the towering, firm-rooted, lofty mountains, but they all refused. What a marvelous business! If the many-thousand-year-old heaven could not carry this burden, what is the secret here that the command of Majesty comes and places it on the head of a frail child? "Yes, give him a taste of this draft so that he will mix with it and become accustomed to it. Then he will know its flavor."

The long and the short of it is this: "Be seven years old or seventy, the burden of My work will not pass by your door. Whatever color you may have, you must carry My burden. *Swallow the bitters without frowning!* You must take on the job, despite Iblis." What a marvelous business! The sword is drawn, the draft is prepared, and the man is frail.

O dervish, a request came out from the curtain of the Unseen to the open plain of manifestation. It passed by the whole world and paid no attention to anyone. When it reached Adam's dust, it pulled back the reins of Majesty. It lifted the veil from its own heart-snatching beauty and said, *"Peace be upon you!* I have come for you. Are you ready for Me?"

How many have reached out to union with Me
without ever attaining a share![474]

*

No, things do not revolve around service—
they revolve only around the apportioning.
A tattered cloak is of no account—
nothing counts but burning.[475]

*

With heartache I killed a thousand lovers like you
lest My fingers be tainted by blood.

One of the revealed books says, *"I created the whole world for you, and I created you for Me."*[476] I brought everything into existence for you, and you for Myself.

Who knows what things have been made ready inside this clay?! *"I created the hearts of the servants from My approval."* We kneaded the clay of Our friends with the pure water of Our approval. Then We tied the body to the saddle-strap of the heart and sent it into the world of form. Next We sent a policeman after this meddlesome body—the prescription of the Law. We said, "O eyes, you be under the control of the policeman of prescription! O heart, you be the sitting companion of the sultan of Our love!"

O Adam—*surely God chose Adam* [3:33]. O Abraham—*God took Abraham as a bosom friend* [4:125]. O Moses—*I chose thee for Myself* [20:41]. O Muḥammad, *by thy life!* [15:72]. O handful of dust and clay, *He loves them and they love Him* [5:54]. He did not say, *"because of their obedience"* or *"because of their worship." He disengaged love from every cause*: He disengaged and purified love from every cause.

It is said that one day the master Abū ʿAlī Daqqāq was passing this talk over his tongue. One of those present asked, "Do we have the place of friendship?"

The master said, "Ask that from Him." He is saying that everything in the world was written down as a serving boy, but the Adamite was written down as the paragon. The crown of leadership was put on his head, and the world and the world's folk were given over to the hand of his plundering. *He subjected to you whatsoever is in the heavens and whatsoever is in the earth, all together, from Him* [45:13]. From the Throne down to the lowest point, beneath every clod is a treasure. *There is nothing that does not glorify Him in praise* [17:44]. The key to this treasure is in your hand. Whenever you reach this treasure full of pearls, you will open its door with the key of gazing on the treasure. String the pearl of *tawḥīd* and the secret of disengagement on the thread of belief and put it on the neck of loyalty. *And those who are loyal to their covenant when they make a covenant* [2:177].

The mountains have not the capacity for this talk, nor heaven and earth, nor the Throne and the Footstool. When He said, *"If We had sent this Quran down on a mountain, [thou wouldst have seen it humbled, split apart by the fear of God]"* [59:21], He was reporting about the incapacity of the mountains. The figures and forms of bodies and orbs have no weight and are not looked upon. You see an angel who brings the two horizons under its wings, but it does not have the capacity to carry this meaning. And you see a poor wretch, skin stretched over bones, fearlessly quaffing the wine of trial in the goblet of love, drinking it down in remembrance of Him with truthfulness and limpidness, yet no change appears in him. Why is that? Because he is a possessor of the heart,

And the heart carries what camels cannot.[477]

O dervish, when they string a fat pearl along with black beads, it is not because of the meanness and lowliness of the pearl, nor because of its splendor and value. Rather, the goal is to prevent its being struck by the evil eye. In the same way, the Exalted Lord singled out Adam and his children for a hundred thousand characteristics, rarities, subtleties, favors, and varieties of gentle gifts. Then He concealed these marvelous deposits inside the dense body of dust, and He threw the world into doubt about him. The clear revelation gives this report: *"We created man from an extraction of clay, then We placed him as a sperm drop in a firm settledness"* [23:12–13].

"O water and clay, O coffer of the pearl of the pure secret! *Rather it is signs, clear signs, in the breasts of those who have been given knowledge* [29:49]. O water and clay, O you whose heart is the carrier of the ruling power of My love! *He loves them and they love Him* [5:54]. O pottery of dried clay, O worthy of the pavilion of nearness and union! *When My servants ask thee about Me, surely I am near* [2:186]. O extraction of clay, O precious stone in the seal-ring of good fortune, O you who have put the saddle of limpidness on the steed of loyalty, O center-point of time and earth, O singled out for this rank! *So blessed is God, the most beautiful of creators!* [23:14]. O feeble sperm drop, O entrusted with the treasuries of the unseen secrets, O *molded mud* [15:26], O electuary of the water of limpidness and the dust of loyalty! *"He fermented Adam's clay in His hand for forty mornings."*[478]

O dervish, *heed is paid to the graft, not to the root. The graft is nearness, and the root is dust. The root is in respect of the sperm drop and the created disposition; the graft is in respect of nearness and help.*[479]

Tomorrow all will be addressed with the words "Pass by!" but you will be addressed with the words "Come up!"

They said to a dervish, "Who are you?"

He said, *"I am the son of the Beginningless."*

In respect of sonship our lineage goes back to Adam, but in respect of love it goes back to the beginningless gentleness.

God cannot have children, but He can have those whom He loves. *He begets not, nor was He begotten* [112:3] came and cut off every sort of child. *He loves them and they love Him* came and affirmed every sort of love.

The angels were saying, "Such a heavy burden and such a frail body! This body is not fit for the burden, nor is the burden fit for this body. Do they put the morsels of elephants into the craws of sparrows?"

Adam said, "You see the burden, I see the lap."

When Adam lifted the burden of the Trust, it was after eating the wheat. He said, "If it is I who am to set this work right, well, the first fruit of the garden of my existence has already reached the Presence. If it is He who is to set it right, well, 'Once the water is over the head, let it be a hundred feet deep.' "

Insignificance is hidden in the shadow of laziness
and the majesty of the momentous in competition.[480]

Adam was the marvel of creation. When he saw that heaven and earth did not lift the burden of the Trust, he stretched out the hand of need. Yes, the angels looked at the burden's tremendousness and refused it. Adam looked at the generosity of Him who was offering the Trust. He said, "The burden of the Trust of the generous is carried with aspiration, not with strength." When he lifted the burden, he was addressed with the words *"We carried them on land and sea* [17:70]. *Is the recompense of beautiful-doing anything but beautiful-doing?* [55:60]."

There is a likeness for this in the outward realm. When trees have firmer roots and more branches, their fruit is smaller. Those weaker in form have larger fruit, like melon and squash. Here, however, there is a subtle point: When a tree's fruit is larger and the tree does not have the capacity to carry it, they tell it, "Put the burden on top of the earth." Thus the world's folk will know that whenever someone is weak, he is nurtured by the gentleness of the Presence.

This is a marvelous business. When Adam lifted the burden of the Trust, the address came, *"He was a great wrongdoer, deeply ignorant"* [33:72]. But when the angels said, *"What, wilt Thou set therein one who will work corruption there, and shed blood?"* [2:30], He sent a fire that burned several thousand of them. True, friends say things about friends, but they are not content to let outsiders look at them with sharp eyes. *"I'll backbite my brother, but I won't let anyone else backbite him."*[481]

When God brought Adam into existence, He said, *"Surely I am creating a mortal of clay"* [38:71]. The angels were saying, *"What, wilt Thou set therein one who will work corruption there?"* Iblis was saying, *"I am better than he. Thou hast created me of fire, and Thou hast created him of clay"* [38:76]. The Exalted Lord answered them all: *"Surely I know what you do not know"* [2:30]: Don't shut the door on the fortunate or you'll damage your own spirit's wherewithal! O fire, you have force, but earth has good fortune. How can incidental force stand up to merited good fortune?

O dervish, when this talk came, it came to the Adamite, even though the talk's luster shone on all existent things. It would have been a tremendous loss if the other existent things had lived in this talk's luster and the Adamite had been deprived.

You should know that in verified truth the grain of wheat that Adam put in his mouth was the fortress of his days, for mortal nature demands glancing, and whoever looks at himself will not be delivered. This is why the exalted ones have written letters to their brothers saying, *"May God give you no taste of your own self, for if you taste it, you will never be saved."*[482]

That grain of wheat was made Adam's fortress, for every time Adam looked at himself, he looked with embarrassment. He came forward asking forgiveness, not showing pride.

The stipulation of the traveler is that whenever he looks at God's success-giving, he should say, *"The praise belongs to God"* [1:2], and whenever he looks at his own deeds, he should say, *"I ask forgiveness from God."*[483]

The most exalted thing is to manifest incapacity after you have been loyal, on condition of knowledge. The Prophet said, *"I do not number Thy laudations"*[484] *after he had exhausted the means of praise and laudation.*

O dervish, paradise was the place for union and the pavilion for proximity. The enviers set out to upset the bliss and, perhaps, to drive Adam out with trickery. The gentleness of the Presence said, "Wait and see. We will cut the roots of expectations and eliminate the substance of the enviers' envy. We will take Adam the chosen to the world of transactions on the pretext of a slip. Then it will be spread about in the world that he is in prison and bondage, in separation and distance. We will set up the pavilion of secrets, secret core to secret core, without the intrusion of others. We will bring the goblets of gentle gifts one after another and root out the intrusion of the enemies' accusations. We will give his outwardness over to the policeman of *Go down!* [2:36] and bring his inwardness into the exalted encampment of bounty. We will give this goblet of joy to him moment by moment: *If guidance comes to you from Me, then whosoever follows My guidance, no fear shall be upon them* [2:38]."

This is a marvelous story. It was said to Adam, *"Go down!"* It was said to Muṣṭafā, *"Ascend!"*

"O Adam, go to the earth so that the world of dust may settle down in the awesome majesty of your sultanate. O Muḥammad, come up to heaven so that the summit of the spheres may be adorned with the beauty of your contemplation. The secret here is that I said *'Go down!'* to your father so that I could say *'Ascend!'* to you. Sit on the steed of aspiration and take the top of the spheres as the dust on the carpet beneath your blessed feet. Travel away from both the corporeal and the spiritual. Gaze upon Me without yourself. Bring the pure gift of *'The felicitations belong to God, and the prayers and the goodly things'* to the Presence. Then the overflowing goblet of the good fortune of *'The peace be upon thee, O Prophet, and God's mercy and His blessings'*[485] will be sent to you on the hand of the cupbearer of the Covenant. Take it with the fingers of acceptance and drink it down! And, like the noble, pour a draft on the earth of the hearts of the community, for, as the noble have said,

> *We drank and poured a draft on the earth,*
> *for the earth has a share of the nobleman's cup.*[486]

*

> Everyone's spirit is just like his cup;
> everyone's learning suits his intellect.[487]

*

> *The wine of the glance, whose cup intoxicates the mind,*
> *wearies neither its cupbearer nor its drinker.*
> *Your sobriety with my words is all intoxication;*
> *your intoxication with my glance makes drinking lawful.*[488]

A group whose eyes were not anointed with the collyrium of success denied the *mi'rāj* of the paragon. They said that it was a dream, nothing more. Basing themselves on intellect, they considered it absurd that someone could wander around the seven heavens in one or two hours and then come back. As for the folk of the Sunnah—before the nostrils of whose truthfulness is held the sweet herb of love—they agree that Muṣṭafā's *mi'rāj* was real and that it was during wakefulness, not dreaming. If it had been a dream, Muṣṭafā would have had no excellence in this, for it is permissible for a Jew or a Christian to see paradise in a dream or to see hell in a dream. If something is permissible for an unbeliever, how could Muṣṭafā have any excellence in that?[489]

He said, *"Glory be to Him who took His servant by night!"* [17:1]. He said *"took by night"* so that no one would be surprised. He said *"His servant"* so that Muḥammad would not admire himself. *Took by night* means to take. If it were simply a dream, taking would be absurd. When someone dreams, his body is not taken. And He said, *"His servant."* What is meant by this *servant* is the servant's person. Thus in other places He said, *"Surely I am the servant of God* [19:30], *and when the servant of God stood* [72:19], *and the servants of the All-Merciful* [25:63]." There are many similar verses.

In short, know that denying the *miʿrāj* to Jerusalem is unbelief, because the clear text of the Quran speaks of it, and denying the clear text is unbelief. But if someone denies the taking to heaven, he does not become an unbeliever, because this has come in reports from single narrators, and reports from single narrators do not necessitate knowledge. Someone like that, however, is a heretic.

Know that the *miʿrāj* was not built on intellect, for this gold coin was struck outside intellect's house. It was built rather on the divine power and the imperial wisdom: *God does what He wills* [14:27] and *He decrees what He desires* [5:1].

Concerning Moses He said, *"When Moses came to Our appointed time"* [7:143], but concerning Muṣṭafā He said, *"Glory be to Him who took His servant by night!"* He ascribed Moses's name to the sea and to the bush, but He ascribed Muṣṭafā's name to Himself.

O dervish, if the servant had any robe of honor more beautiful than the robe of servanthood, He would have bestowed it upon Muṣṭafā on the night of the *miʿrāj*. Jesus said in the cradle, *"Surely I am the servant of God"* [19:30], but about Muṣṭafā the Real said without intermediary, *"His servant."*

When He mentioned the proximity of Moses, He praised Moses. When He mentioned the proximity of Muṣṭafā, He praised Himself. He said, *"Glory be to Him who took by night."* This indicates that Moses was subsisting in the attributes of Moses and that Muṣṭafā had been annihilated from his own attributes in the attributes of the Real. Thus ʿĀʾisha said, *"His character was the Quran."*[490] He arrived where he arrived through the attributes of the Real.

This is "taking," but not with his own attributes, for that would be "coming." The comer is the seeker and the taken the sought. The comer is the desirer and the taken the desired. The comer is the rememberer and the taken the remembered. The seeker is never like the sought, nor the desirer like the desired.

The comer is absent. Once he comes, he is present. Someone taken is not absent from the taker for one moment.

Coming is a general attribute, and bringing a specific attribute. "Whoever wants Me has no escape from coming. Whomever I want, I Myself bring. Whenever someone comes by himself, he may or may not find the road. Whoever is taken cannot not find the road."

Moses came by himself, so the brand of *thou shalt not see Me* [7:143] was put on his liver. Muṣṭafā was taken, so the crown of *hast thou not seen thy Lord?* [25:45] was placed on his head. In the same way when Moses saw the mountain and the Real's self-disclosure to the mountain, he was thunderstruck, as the Exalted Lord said in the clear text of the revelation: *"And Moses fell down thunderstruck"* [7:143]. This is because coming is the attribute of the comer. Anyone who abides through his own attribute can be overcome by someone else. The attributes of the Real cannot be overcome.

As for Muṣṭafā, he saw all the stations of the prophets. He saw the paradises and gardens, the serving boys and servants, the houris and palaces, the rivers and trees, hell and the varieties of punishment, the Tablet and the Pen, and the decree and its apportioning, but he did not budge in the slightest from his place. This is because he was taken. Taking is the attribute of the Real, and *the Real's attribute is not overcome.* Again, since Moses was abiding through his own attributes, he was overcome, but Muṣṭafā was abiding through the Real's attributes, so he overcame.

What is strange is that Gabriel brought the verse, *"Glory be to Him who took His servant by night."* He came and said, "Get up so that I may take you."

"If you are the taker, then what is *Glory be to Him*? And if He is the taker, what are you doing in the midst? O Gabriel, you were not sent to take me, for the taker, the bringer, and the keeper is the Exalted Lord. Rather, a cape of the spirit's repose was placed on you, but the cape needed an embroidery, for a garment is not complete without an embroidery. Service at the doorstep of my prophethood was made the exalted embroidery on the cape of your existence."

Gabriel said, "Get up so that I may take you."

"If you brought yourself, then take me."

"We descend not save by the command of thy Lord" [19:64].

"Since you have no way to take a step without the command, he who takes me is not you."

In the reports of the story of the *miʿrāj* it has come that Muṣṭafā said, *"I prayed the last prayer of the night with you, I prayed cycles at the House in Jerusalem, and I prayed the* witr *under the Throne."*[491] O you who are asleep, a sleeping person does not pray. This is evidence that it took place in wakefulness, not sleep.

When the unbelievers of Quraysh criticized Muṣṭafā and wanted to call him a liar, they asked him about the marks of the House in Jerusalem. The command came to Gabriel, "Lift up the House in Jerusalem and take it to My friend." This is not strange, for the report has come, *"The earth was brought together for me, and I was shown its eastern parts and its western parts."*[492]

Gabriel beat his wings once, lifted up the House in Jerusalem, and held it in the air in front of Muṣṭafā, but he veiled it from the eyes of the unbelievers. They were asking about the marks, and Muṣṭafā was giving reports to them. They knew that he had never been there, so they were all amazed. *But there is no artifice against rejection and dismissal.*

Guidance is not in respect of striving; guidance comes only in respect of the beginning. Guidance is not through the servant's thoughts and gaze; guidance comes only through the bounty of the Real and the beauty of His gaze.[493]

When Gabriel was taking Muṣṭafā to Syria, a caravan of the Quraysh came toward them on the way from Syria. A man was seated on a camel and felt cold, so he asked his servant for a blanket. Muṣṭafā was thirsty, so he lifted the man's bottle and drank the water. The bottle's owner asked for the bottle but found no water in it. And when the camels of the caravan saw Muṣṭafā's Burāq, they fled, so the caravan busied itself with searching for the camels.

When Muṣṭafā reported to the Meccans about going to the House in Jerusalem, they said to him, "Our caravan is on the road. Where did you pass it?" He mentioned the place, told them about drinking the water, and named the man. He said, "That man felt cold and asked for a blanket from his servant."

O dervish, cold in the land of the Hijaz is strange. That was the breeze of the friend's nearness leaving its trace in the people of the caravan.

They said to him, "If you speak the truth, when will our caravan arrive?"

He said, "If they had not become busy searching for camels, they would have come this morning. But they stayed searching for them and will arrive here at sunrise."

It has been said—*and the responsibility is on the narrator*—that the caravan was still far away. A command came to the angel entrusted to the sun to pull back on the sun's reins for a while. Gabriel was commanded to roll up the earth so that the words of His friend would not fall flat. The folk of Mecca divided into two groups. One group watched for the sun and the other group for the caravan. All at once cries rose up from both groups. One group said, "The caravan has arrived." The other group said, "The sun has risen." The Meccans were bewildered. Nonetheless, this verse is appropriate:

What is my stratagem? The apportionings do as commanded,
the people between lost and righteous.[494]

By the star when it fell! Your companion is not misguided, nor is he astray, nor does he speak from caprice. It is naught but a revelation revealed, taught to him by one intensely strong. Possessor of power, he stood up straight while he was on the highest horizon. Then he drew close, so He came down [53:1–8].

Some have said that this *star* is the Pleiades.

Some have said that this *star* is the stars of the Quran, for the Quran came from heaven as *star after star.*[495]

Some have said that what is meant by this *star* is Muṣṭafā: *"God swears an oath by Muḥammad when he descended from heaven on the night of the* miʿrāj." In this verse He calls him a star, and in another verse he calls him a sun, as He says: *"a light-giving lamp"* [33:46], for this lamp is the sun: *"And He made the sun a lamp"* [71:16]. Thus the Exalted Lord calls Muṣṭafā a lamp and He also calls him a sun. What is the wisdom in this? The wisdom is that when the sun goes down, no trace of its light remains. As for a lamp, other lamps are lit from it. If the first lamp is taken away, the other lamps stay lit. If the Exalted Lord had called him the sun, when he concealed his face within the veil of dust, the lamps of recognition in the hearts of his community would have been extinguished. He called him a lamp so that every lamp that lights up at his invitation will remain lit until the Day of Resurrection, even after he has been removed from the midst.

In another place He calls him the full moon. Thus He says, "Ṭāhā. *We did not send down the Quran upon thee for thee to be wretched"* [20:1–2]. Some have said that *Ṭā* is revelry [*ṭarab*] and *Hā* is lowliness [*hawān*]: *God swears an oath by the revelry of the folk of the Garden in the Garden and by the lowliness of the folk of the Fire in the Fire.* Others have said that according to the numerical value of letters, *Ṭā* is nine and *Hā* is five. Five plus nine is fourteen. It is as if He is addressing him by saying, "O My moon of the fourteenth night, O My shining sun, O My bright moon, O My sparkling star!"

A luminous moon shining forever,
its lovers resurrected before it;
A full moon whose gazers wish
it were walking upon their eyes.

Your companion is not misguided, nor is he astray [53:2]. "O Muḥammad, if the Meccans spoke ill words to you, do not fear, for We have written the tablet of your extolment and laudation with the pen of eternal gentleness. Whenever they read from the slate of ridiculing you, begin the surah of My extolment and laudation. *So glorify the praise of thy Lord!* [110:3]."

Nor does he speak from caprice [53:3]. He does not speak from caprice, for caprice is to seek what is desired, and the lover has no desire. When someone seeks his desire, he is taken to where his desire is not. But when he tramples his desire underfoot, he reaches his desire.

It is naught but a revelation revealed [53:4]. This friend of Mine does not say a word except by My revelation. *Taught to him by one intensely strong* [53:5]. *Some say, "Gabriel taught him,"* and in the stories of the Quran Gabriel's strength is obvious. Others say that this is the attribute of the Real: *The Lord, the Strong taught him*: "I am extremely strong; no one overcomes Me." This is just like what He says elsewhere: *"He taught thee what thou didst not know"* [4:113].

Possessor of power, he stood up straight [53:6]. *This means "possessor of strength."* It is fitting for this to be Gabriel's strength, and it is fitting for it to be the Real's strength.

While he was on the highest horizon [53:7]. *Some say that Gabriel stood up straight while he was on the highest horizon.* They say that this is Gabriel's attribute. He stood up straight in the very createdness and form in which the Real created him on the highest horizon. Others have said that *he stood up straight* is the attribute of Muḥammad, for he stood up straight in his soul through struggle, in his heart through contemplation, in his spirit through unveiling, and in his secret core through gentle gift. He stood up straight: He did not take a step outside of Our command, he did not step into Our prohibition, and he did not say a word without what We desired.

He stood up straight: He stood up straight for the sake of what We desire, and he trampled underfoot every desire of his own. What We desired became what he desired, and We did whatever he wanted. *We will turn thee toward a kiblah that thou wilt approve* [2:144]. *Thy Lord will bestow upon thee, and thou wilt approve* [93:5].

He stood up straight: He stood up straight for Us. In what sense? In the sense that whatever he heard, he heard from Us; wherever he looked, he was seeing Us; however he moved, he was moving for Us; and whatever he thought, he was thinking about Us. And beware lest this seem far-fetched to you, for this is the very attribute of lovers when their love is not ungodly, so this attribute is fitting for a love that is truthful.

He stood up straight: He stood up straight in friendship. What is standing up straight in friendship? Wanting nothing from the Friend but the Friend.

"We have two houses: the house of annihilation and the house of subsistence. We offered the house of annihilation to him and he said, *'What have I to do with this world? With this world I am like a rider who dismounts in the shade of a tree for an hour, takes his rest, and departs.'*[496] His companionship with the house of annihilation was like this, and he left it for the enemies."

The evidence that this is the house of the enemies is the words of Muṣṭafā, *"Surely God will defend His faithful servant from this world just as one of you defends his camel from pastures of destruction."*[497] Muṣṭafā is saying that just as you protect your camels from poisonous plants, the Real defends His friends from this world. Hence it is correct that Muṣṭafā left this world for the enemies. When the work reaches the abode of subsistence, he will leave the abode of subsistence for the friends and pack his own bags from both worlds.

Do you not see that when the house of subsistence becomes apparent, everyone will rush to enter it more quickly? He will be standing on the plain of the resurrection, the shawl of intercession on his shoulders and the ring of love in his ear. "O Muḥammad, are you not going?"

He will say, "I will not go as long as anyone remains."

Tomorrow everyone will be talking on his own behalf. They will be saying, *"my soul, my soul!"* But that paragon of paragons and emperor of the planets of prophethood will not be talking on his own behalf. What he says at that time—*"my community, my community!"*[498]—will not be the cause of the salvation of the community. It will be for the sake of manifesting the purity of his own secret core. It will make apparent to the creatures that this is a servant who never said *"my soul!"* on his own behalf.

He stood up straight: This means that his outwardness stood up straight with his inwardness. His outwardness had no shortcoming in service, and his inwardness had no change in contemplation.

He stood up straight: "He entrusted himself to Us. Anyone who pulls himself back is crooked. Anyone who entrusts himself to Us is straight. He grieved not the slightest at the loss of what he left behind when We took him, and he showed not the slightest happiness at what We put before him where We conveyed him." The Withholder distracted him from the withholding so that he would not remember grief for what was withheld; the Bestower distracted him from the bestowal so that he would not remember happiness for what was bestowed.

He stood up straight: He stood up straight. If he had aspired to a place, he would not have reached the station to which he aspired. He looked neither right nor left. Had he gazed right or left, he would have stayed right there. Wherever he arrived, he held back his eyes. Whatever We brought forth, he walked across. Whoever goes by the straight road will reach the lodging. Whoever goes right or left will not reach the lodging. For the common people, going right or left is in the body, but for the elect it is in the heart. Whoever looks to the right, which is the afterworld, or to the left, which is this world, will not reach the Exalted Presence.

He stood up straight while he was on the highest horizon. His soul stood up straight in conformity with the heart, his heart stood up straight in conformity with the secret core, his secret core stood up straight in conformity with the Real. There is no way to be the companion of the straight except through straightness. "If his soul had not stood up straight with his heart, We would not have given that heart to that soul. If his heart had not stood up straight with his secret core, We would not have given that secret core to that heart. And if his secret core had not stood up straight with Us, We would not have become the companion of that secret core."

Then he drew close, so He came down, so he was two-bows' length away, or closer [53:8–9]. *He drew close with the drawing close of proximity, not that of familiarity; the drawing close of honoring, not that of the body; the drawing close of intimacy, not that of the soul; the drawing close of response, not that of kinship; the drawing close of listening, not that of coming together; the drawing close of union, not that of conjoining; the drawing close of joyful expansiveness, not that of the carpet.*[499]

Jaʿfar Ṣādiq said, "When the beloved neared with utmost nearness, utmost awe overcame him, so his Lord was gentle with the utmost gentleness, for the utmost awe can be endured only with the utmost gentleness."[500]

God says, "God warns you of Himself" [3:30]. *This is a word of awe. Then God says, "And God is clement toward the servants"* [3:30]. *This is a word of gentleness. In the same way He says, "In the name of God," a word of awe, and then at once He says, "the All-Merciful, the Ever-Merciful," which are words of clemency and mercy, giving subsistence to souls and spirits. In the same way, when God said to Moses, "Surely I am thy Lord"* [20:12], *Moses' heart was awestruck, but when He said, "Take off thy shoes"* [20:12], *his spirit relaxed and his mind quieted.*

The paragon reached the waystation of *then he drew close*, stepped onto the carpet of *so He came down* [53:8], went up to the *two-bows' length away* of proximity, and leaned back on the exalted cushion of *or closer* [53:9]. He heard the mystery, tasted the wine, reached contemplation, fled from the two worlds, and took ease with the Friend. *Then He revealed to His servant what He revealed* [53:10].

O dervish, whoever takes along the gift of *the eyesight did not swerve* [53:17] will bring back the bestowal of *He revealed to His servant what He revealed.* In other words, there was what there was, and there happened what happened, but no one is aware of these mysteries. *The breasts of the free are the graves of the secrets.*[501]

No one keeps the secret but a man of dignity—
with a noble man the secret stays hidden.
With me the secret is locked in a room,
its key lost, its gate sealed.[502]

*

He came to me curtained in the shirt of night,
warily coming close to me in my yearning.
There was what there was, what I will not mention,
so think the best and ask not for news.[503]

All intellects and imaginations are dismissed from that. It was a mystery inside the curtain of jealousy, conveyed to the prophetic hearing without the intrusion of others—a soul subjugated, a heart aided, the others far from the pavilion of secrets. *Light upon light, joy upon joy, delight upon delight.*

He told the story to honor him
and He hid the secrets to magnify him.

*

I have a secret with the night, a marvelous secret,
the night knows and I know—I know, and the night.

*

Never, O Candle of Chigil, will I let out Your secret,
even if that's a most difficult task.
The pain I have in loving You,
the heart knows and I know—I know, and the heart.

It was not a proximity in terms of place and location; it was a proximity in terms of stability and possibility. It was not a drawing close in terms of expanse; it was a drawing close in terms of gentleness.

Junayd was asked about nearness to God. He said, "Near not through adherence, far not through separation."[504] It is a nearness not by virtue of joining, and a farness not in terms of breaking off.

Someone may ask what wisdom there is in the fact that on the night of the *miʿrāj*, Moses spoke with Muṣṭafā in order to alleviate the burden of the prayer, but no other prophet spoke of that.[505] I would say that in this world Moses was the possessor of whispered prayer, and he thought that no one's level was higher than his and no one's *miʿrāj* went beyond his *miʿrāj*. It was shown to him that the *miʿrāj* is the *miʿrāj* of Muḥammad, for Moses's *miʿrāj* was to the mountain, but Muḥammad's *miʿrāj* was to the Carpet of Light. Moses was commanded to fast for forty days, and when he was made present in the presence of whispered prayer, some of his requests were granted and some were not. Muḥammad was the unique pearl of the ocean of creativity, and he was taken to the Presence while still stained by sleep. In one moment and one step he asked several times for alleviation of the burden, and all of that was granted to him. This was so that Moses would come to know the eminence of the paragon and ask forgiveness for what he had said: "A young man was made to pass over my head!"

Even higher is that when Moses came forth asking for vision, the sword of the jealousy of *thou shalt not see Me* was drawn from the scabbard of exaltedness, and the eye of his seeking was slaughtered. He was penalized for that question and paid the fine with *I repent to Thee* [7:143]. But the eyes of Muṣṭafā were anointed with the collyrium of *stretch not thine eyes* [15:88] and bound with the band of *the eyesight did not swerve, nor did it trespass* [53:17]. When he was made present to the Presence—not because of himself, but because of intimacy—Majesty and Beauty were unveiled to his eyes.

As for what ʿĀʾisha said, *"If anyone supposes that Muḥammad saw his Lord with the eye of his head, his slander against God is tremendous,"*[506] she meant that if anyone says that Muṣṭafā saw the Real with the eyes alone, *his slander against God is tremendous*. Rather, he saw Him with the eyes and he saw Him with every speck of his eyes; from head to toe all of him became eye.

> *If I remember Him, all of me is heart;*
> *if I look at Him, all of me is eye.*[507]

*

> All my body becomes heart when I whisper with You,
> I see only Your beauty when I open my eyes.
> I consider it forbidden to talk with others—
> talking with You, I draw out my words.[508]

O dervish, seeing the Exalted Lord in paradise is not impossible. *Indeed, Muḥammad saw his Lord, but it was not in a moment of seeing Him in this world. Rather it was as God said: "Indeed he saw Him another time, at the Lote Tree of the Final End"* [53:13–14]*; vision is not impossible in the Garden. "The Lote Tree of the Final End" is the final end of bodies and souls, and "surely unto thy Lord is the final end"* [53:42] *is the final end of spirits and knowledge.*

Again, one of the exalted ones was asked about this difficulty: Did Muṣṭafā see the Real with the eye of the heart, or no, with the eye of the head? He said, *"When the self-disclosure is sound, the eye and the heart are one."* When the majesty of the self-disclosure becomes evident, the eye is the heart, and the heart is the eye.

It has been narrated that Muṣṭafā said to Gabriel, *"Will you part from me in a place like this?"*[509] But when Abraham was put in the ballista, Gabriel came to him and said, *"Have you any need of me?"*[510] He paid him no regard.

What was this unneediness and what was that need? First, look at this secret: Gabriel had the ability to circle around the station of the Bosom Friend, but he did not have the ability to circle around the station of the Beloved, for *"I have a moment with God [embraced by no proximate angel, nor any sent prophet]."*[511] This is why Gabriel said, *"Were I to draw closer by a finger's breadth, I would be incinerated."*[512]

O chevalier, the Bosom Friend was in trial itself, for that was the time of trial. At the time of trial, one is taken to task iota by iota, and kindness is not shown for an instant. This is why he said not a word. But the Beloved was on the carpet of coquetry's bold expansiveness. He was being taken in endearment itself on the carpet of mystery, and whatever a dear child says is overlooked.

There is another secret that is worth a thousand thousand lives. In any case, nod your head—for free. Whenever Gabriel came to the Prophet's presence with a cup of revelation in hand, God's messenger Muḥammad would drink the cup and Gabriel would go back. The Messenger was jealous over Gabriel's state.

Sometimes I wish I were the messenger
so that tomorrow I'd reach my desires and wants.

It passed into the pure secret core of the Prophet to wonder if he would ever have a moment of which Gabriel had no awareness or cognizance. When he reached the Lote Tree and drank the goblet of election in the court of the elect, he stepped beyond the Lote Tree. When Gabriel pulled back his feet and sat down next to the Lote Tree, the paragon turned to him and said, *"Will you part from me in a place like this?"* Why is it that every time you left me in the earth, you charged the horse of aspiration to the top of the *seven firmaments* [78:12], and in this station you have pulled back your feet?

Gabriel answered the Messenger's words with the tongue of his state: "That world is the house of your exile, and in the land of exiles one can show bold expansiveness toward the sultan. But on the king's carpet I do not have the gall to show bold expansiveness."

What a marvelous business! It has been said that when Moses came back from the royal court at the mountain, he brought light as his robe of honor and blinded the eyes of anyone who looked at him. Muṣṭafā stepped beyond his steps, and his state went beyond his state, but the eyes of those who looked at him showed no defects. This is because Moses's light was the light of awesomeness, and Muḥammad's light was the light of intimacy.

Also, the station of Moses's community relative to Moses was like Moses's station in the Presence. His form was branded with the veil because of the wisdom of the Unseen. It was said to him, *"Thou shalt not see Me"* [7:143]. There his portion was the veil, and here his community's portion is the veil. But when Muṣṭafā reached the presence of proximity, the veils were lifted, and when he came back, he lifted the veils. The likeness of this is that when the leader of an army receives a robe of honor from the sultan, he gives robes of honors to his own elect. If he suffers confiscation, he confiscates from his retinue.

Also the community of Moses transgressed the limit. They said, *"Show us God openly"* [4:153]. It was said to them, *"You are not able to bear gazing at the face of Moses. How will you be able to gaze upon Me?"* You do not have the capacity to look at Moses. How will you have the capacity to contemplate My majesty and beauty?

But the community of Muṣṭafā had cut away the thorn of free choice from the garden of their days. They were addressed by these words: *"Faces that day radiant, gazing on their Lord"* [75:22–23].

Moses chose seventy of his people, as the Exalted Lord reports: *"And Moses chose his people, seventy men, for Our appointed time"* [7:155]. Concerning this community the Exalted Lord reports, *"We chose them, out of knowledge, above the worlds"* [44:32]. This community had the strength of faith and with the strength of their faith they stayed in place while seeing Muṣṭafā. But the people of Moses had weak faith and did not have the capacity to see Moses.

31–32. *al-Ḥakam al-ʿAdl:* the Ruler, the Just

Ḥakam and *ḥākim* have the same meaning. *ʿAdl* means the same as *ʿādil* and also means the possessor of justice. In the meaning of *ʿādil* it is one of the attributes that assert similarity and give form.

He ruled what He wanted as He wanted. This is a ruling without bias, a decree without iniquity. He recorded the name of one person in the ledger of the felicitous, accepting him with beginningless solicitude, without any deeds in the midst. He recorded the name of someone else in the register of the wretched, binding the sash of rejection and distance to his waist, driving him from the threshold of acceptance and prosperity, and he does not have the gall to say a word.

> Such does Your love pull that nothing can be said—
> not just anyone can walk in Your street.

It is impossible to remove the shirt sewn by the careful tailor of the beginningless decree with the hand of mortal nature. *With Me the word does not change, nor do I wrong the servants* [50:29]. *One group sought Him, and He abandoned them; one group fled from Him, and He seized them.* One group passed night and day in acts of struggle and discipline, taking nourishment with a few peas and beans, but *"The seeking is rejected, the road blocked"* was recited in their ears. Another group became the devotees of idol temples, taking Lāt and Hubal as the objects of their worship and prostration, but the call of exaltedness kept on coming: *"I am yours, whether you wish it or refuse, and you are Mine, whether you wish it or refuse."* You are Mine and I am yours, whether or not you want it so.

O dervish, if assistance is sent from the Unseen in your name, a warrior will not take a Byzantine prisoner as this gaze will take you, but it will not come for any cause or travel for any reason. When the exalted gaze comes, in one instant it will make a Guebre into a possessor of the breast and a highwayman into a traveler on the path.

You'll be an estranged servant at the bottom of separation's street
if you don't seek a familiar at the top of union's street.
A familiar with the Prophet—what a stranger was Abū Lahab!
Coming from Abyssinia, how familiar was Bilāl![513]

"Yes, Adam's loins were the ocean of Our secrets, and Our power was the diver in that ocean. Sometimes the attribute of Our severity dove down and brought back the likes of Pharaoh, Nimrod, and Haman, putting them on the shore of creation, without any cause in the midst. Sometimes the attribute of gentleness dove down and brought back the likes of Muḥammad, Jesus, and Moses, giving them refuge in the neighborhood of exaltedness, without any cause in the midst."

By the rightful due of the Real! If He were to give out talk of Him because of merit, your share would not be one iota. He took away causes from the midst so that, just as those who are pure will have hope, so also the impure will have a thousand times more.

So remember Me; I will remember you [2:152]. This verse does not place causes in the Lordhood. Rather it affirms servanthood. "Our He-ness first drew the figure of *No* across Our attributes, then across the others. Once Our He-ness consigned the attributes to *neither He nor other than He*,[514] it accepted you."

The Folk of the Sunnah affirm servanthood, but they declare God incomparable with causes. If you want to be a Sunni, then think about affirming servanthood, not about affirming causes in the lordhood. If someone says that God acts for the sake of something, he has tainted lordhood with causes. It is not appropriate for the eternal artisanry to be the effect of a newly arrived cause, for everything newly arrived [*muḥdath*] is a defilement [*ḥadath*]. Flies sit on defilement.

Is not everything other than God unreal
and every bliss inescapably evanescent?[515]

O chevalier, *He fastened to them the word of godwariness* [48:26] came into the world to efface all causes.

Is it they who divide up the mercy of thy Lord? We have divided [43:32]—bit by bit for one person, pot by pot for another.

Two children were arguing over a walnut. An old man arrived and saw them arguing. He said, "Stop arguing and let me divide the walnut between the two of you."

They said, "We approve."

He broke the walnut and it was hollow. He heard a voice, "Old man, if you are the divider, then divide."[516]

His Lordhood has tied everyone's hands, and He runs the kingdom as He desires.

He fielded the ball and broke the opponent's mallet,
taking the ball from side to side as He desired.

Glory be to Him who placed His treasuries between the B *and the* e! *"And when He decrees an affair, He says to it only 'Be!' so it comes to be* [2:117]."[517]

A great man was walking in the hot desert, overcome by thirst. He thought to himself, "With so many billowing oceans in the world, what would it matter if there was a rivulet here?"

It was said to him, "Listen to yourself! Godhood [*khudāʾī*] is Godhood, and housemastery [*kad-khudāʾī*] is housemastery. That which you are thinking is housemastery, and that which has been decreed is Godhood. *God does what He wills* [14:27] and *He decrees what He desires* [5:1]. We bring a thousand thousand of the sincerely truthful into the man-eating desert and destroy them with the sword of the Will so that a few crows may fill their stomachs. If some protestor should open the eyes of protest and look sharply at the ruling authority of the Desire, We will draw this fiery pencil across his eyes: *He will not be asked about what He does* [21:23]. The crow is My crow, and the sincerely truthful man belongs to Me. What have the meddlers to do with the why and the wherefore?"

Oh, the burning of the hearts! Oh, the tumult of the spirits! O Exalted, as soon as You put on the cape of exaltation, all hearts detached their hearts from their hearts! O All-Compelling, as soon as You came from the Majestic Threshold to the poverty-stricken hut of dust, people's eyes began to weep blood. So many hearts in Your trap and so many revelries in Your name!

Seeking Your tresses I'm twisting like Your tresses,
wanting Your eyes I'm drunk like Your eyes.
You're carefree, but I foolishly tell my heart,
"Say something so the Friend may remember me."
Without the shine of Your face, my heart full of pain
knows not head from foot, turban from shoe.
What indeed is my heart that You should approve of it?
What indeed is my body that You should be troubled?
Being apart from You has robbed me of intellect—
accept my excuse for my lack of intelligence!
I belong to You, my body and spirit are Yours,
whether You take me to the pulpit or the gallows.
Like a king, light up a fire of gentleness
and strike it to my house, not to my sins or the sinner.[518]

On the day Adam was brought into existence, he was brought from the door of pain. *Trial for love is like flames for gold.* In this road there are a thousand thousand surging oceans of lovers' blood, but they won't buy a thousand for a barleycorn.

You're staying safe, but I'm entranced by trial—
there's no safety in the path of the bold.

*

God will not relieve me because I hold out my hand—
I ask of Him because He loves to give relief.[519]

*

My heart's caprice reached its furthest limit—
love tore me apart and made me anew.
O you who censure me, if you had tasted love's pain,
you would have found its hardship intense.[520]

The work of the angels is straight because there was no talk of love with them. The ups and downs of the Adamites is because this talk was for them.

Your love made me haunt taverns like this—
otherwise I was safe and orderly.

"O angels of the Dominion, keep the treasuries of glorifying and hallowing filled! Keep on saying *'Glory be to God!'* and *'The praise belongs to God!'* It is the Adamites who will be caressed by Our gentleness and melted by Our severity. Sometimes We will wound them with the sword of uncaused desire; sometimes We will anoint them with a gentle gaze."

The master Abū ʿAlī Daqqāq said, *"When someone recognizes Him who always was and always will be, his night will have no day and his ocean no shore."*

O dervish, when the phoenix of love [محبت] flew from the nest of the Unseen, it reached the Throne and saw tremendousness, it reached the Footstool and saw embracingness, it reached heaven and saw elevation, it reached paradise and saw beneficence, it reached hell and saw punishment, it reached the angels and saw worship, it reached Adam and saw tribulation [محنت], and it settled down with him. They said to it, "Why did you settle down with Adam?"

It said, "The two of us have compatible meanings, secrets, and realities, even though we have been differentiated by a dot."

Wanting to differentiate, the outward man looks at the dot of form, but the verifying man lifts his eyes from the dot and busies his spirit with the work of meaning.

There was a king who had perfect beauty. One day he said to his vizier, "I have this perfect beauty—isn't there anyone burnt who can come into give-and-take with my beauty? *'I was a hidden treasure, so I desired to be recognized.'* "[521]

The vizier said, "O king, many are in love with you, but none is more truthful than a certain dervish, sorrowful in the work of the king's beauty."

Few in this era have your greatness—
hapless is he whose beloved is great!

*

They said, "Hold back your passion, cut it short!"
I said, "Don't blame me for amorousness!"
I sigh and offer no excuse for my weeping—
my heart has melted in her and my soul expired.
I will love my passion all my life, and when I die,
may it alone be my bedfellow in the grave!

O dervish, when heartache and sorrow circumambulate, they circle around the hut of the dervishes. When trial sets off from heaven and they ask it "Where are you going?" it says, "To the hut of the poverty-stricken."

O most just of men except in dealing with me!
In disputes about you, you're both disputant and judge![522]

*

I supplicated You, my Patron, secretly and openly,
the supplication of a heart burning in purest love.
I've been tried by one hard of heart who recognizes no affection,
killing God's creatures with ardent rapture.
If You don't consummate the affection between us,
my heart will never be empty of love for him.
I'll approve of this as long as I live, and when I die,
he'll be enough reward for me in the afterlife, enough.[523]

The king said, "Show us this dervish."

He said, "When you go out to the polo field tomorrow, he will be standing at the bottom of the field gazing at your beauty."

The next day the king got up, adorned his own beauty, and took extra care preparing himself. They said to him, "Why is it that today you take extra care?"

He said, "Well, each day I go hunting for game, but today I go hunting for hearts."

He passed us by, hawk in hand,
marvelous things, he and the hawk;
One hunting birds from above,
one hunting hearts with his eyes.[524]

When the beautiful king strolled into the playing field and brought the ball to the curve of the mallet, he looked from the top of the field and saw the burnt dervish standing at the field's bottom, the fingers of bewilderment in the teeth of longing. The king drove his horse so that it would go near the dervish. *"I am with those whose hearts are broken."*[525] When the king reached him, the dervish lifted up his head to look at his beloved's beauty. The king said, *"Peace be upon you!* Give me the ball." The greeting of his beloved had not yet reached his ears when a sound arose from him and he gave up his spirit along with the ball.[526]

When someone dies in love—let him die like that.
There's no good in a love without death.[527]

*

As soon as I saw your face, O idol,
 I was dizzy with love and lost the road.
One day you'll see them saying, "In the grief of his love
 for you, he's gone—*surely we belong to God* [2:156]."

When the king saw that happen, he came down from the horse and held the dervish's head to his side. *And We are nearer to him than the jugular vein* [50:16]. Then he issued the command, "Bury the dervish at our mausoleum, for it is more beautiful that someone killed by contemplating me should be in my mausoleum, for *'When I kill someone, I am his wergild.'* "[528]

O chevalier, He created all existent things at the request of power, but He created Adam and the Adamites at the request of love. He created other things as the Powerful, but He created you as the Friend. First He began talking of you with Himself in the beginningless. *He mentioned you, then He named you, then He gave you recognition, then He made you appear.* First He mentioned, then He named, then He made familiar, then He brought into the open.

The Exalted Lord wanted to clothe this speck of dust in the shirt of existence-giving, sit him on the chair of vicegerency, bind the collar of finding on the neck of his eminence with His munificence, and string the gemstone of knowledge on the necklace of his felicity: *And He taught Adam the names, all of them* [2:31]. The angels of Dominion said, *"What, wilt Thou set therein one who will work corruption there, and shed blood?"* [2:30].

The preacher of eternal gentleness came to the pulpit of the Will and gave them their answer: *"There is no consultation in love."*[529] Love and deliberation do not come together.

"What weight will your glorification have if I do not accept it? How will their sins harm them if I do not chastise?"[530] What weight will your glorification have if I do not accept it? How will their sins harm them if the cupbearer of gentleness places the goblet of pardon's limpid wine in their hands? *Those—God will change their ugly deeds into beautiful deeds* [25:70]. Why do you look at the fact that they have remained in the opacity of slips? Look at the fact that the limpidness of My pardon belongs to them. *"If you did not sin, God would bring a people who did sin, and then He would forgive them."*[531]

"Suppose all of Adam's offspring put the ring of obedience in their ears, threw the mantle of acquiescence over their shoulders, and swept the filth of opposition from the courtyards of existence with the broom of struggle. If so, I would bring people into existence who sin and blacken their days with the smoke of disobedient acts, and then I would forgive them. This is so that the creatures will know that My mercy comes as a gift, not at a price."

When the Exalted Lord wanted to clothe that essence of the meanings and that center-point of the sublimities in the cape of existence, He put the eternal artisanry in charge of nonexistence. First He commanded that it take the secret and extract the quintessence from every sort of clay. That was then fermented for forty days. The morning breeze of felicity blew on it from the direction of gentleness and desire. The secret in this is that you cannot offer the sultan unleavened bread. Then from this dough was made the electuary of love.

All the angels placed the arrows of imagination in the bows of thought and pulled them back with the hand of consideration and pondering: "Who is this person? If he is to lift his head from the pillow of nonexistence, there should be forty thousand years: *Surely a day with your Lord is like a thousand years as you count* [22:47]." *Their opinions were divided and their thoughts scattered.*

As soon as Adam lifted his head from the pillow of nonexistence, he took the sword of poverty's severity and cut off the heads of the claims of those who were saying *"We glorify Thy praise"* [2:30]. They saw a person whose outwardness was all clay and whose inwardness was all heart. At first they kept on saying, as a question—if we suppose that it was not a protest—*"What, wilt Thou set therein one who will work corruption there, and shed blood?"* At the end, when they saw him, *the angels, all of them, prostrated themselves* [15:30].

The slanderers do not diminish your rank
with me, nor do the backbiters harm you.
It's as if they praise you unwittingly
with all the faults that they find.[532]

O dervish, when the angels said, *"What, wilt Thou set therein one who will work corruption there and shed blood?"* the Exalted Lord did not reply that He would not do that. He said, " '*Surely I know what you do not know,*' namely, My forgiveness of them. *You recognize their disobedience, but I know My forgiveness of them.* In your glorification you make manifest your own activity, but in My forgiveness I make manifest My bounty and generosity. '*Surely I know what you do not know,' namely, My love for them and the limpidness of their belief in loving Me.* Though their outward practice is barefoot, their inward love for Me is limpid. '*Surely I know what you do not know,' namely, My love for them.* However they may be, I love them.[533]

Love's affair is truly strange,
thrown to you without a cause.[534]

"Although I made you felicitous by making you sinless, I grasped them in My mercy.[535] Although your felicity lies in your sinlessness, I desire to show mercy to them. You wear the vest of sinlessness, but they are curtained by mercy. Your conjoining with sinlessness is in the state of existence, but the attachment of My mercy to them was in the beginningless beginning. You show your beauty and act coyly with your own acts of obedient conformity, but they stay broken and shattered by witnessing themselves."

On the day that He created Adam from dust, His generosity made mercy incumbent on Himself. He said, *"Your Lord wrote mercy against Himself"* [6:54]. He wrote Adam's slip with the intermediary of others, but He wrote mercy against Himself without intermediary. After all, dust is the wherewithal of incapacity and weakness. What can be shown to the weak but mercy?

Except those on whom your Lord has mercy, and for that He created them [11:118–19]. A group of the exegetes hold that this means, *"for mercy He created them."*[536] He created you in order to have mercy on you.

Dust in its makeup is humble and submissive, trampled underfoot and looked down upon by everyone, but fire in its makeup is self-elevating and proud, aiming to go up. Water has a certain innate limpidness and connatural humility. Dust does not have the limpidness, but it does have humility.

When Adam was brought into existence, he was brought from dust and water, so the foundation of his work was built on purity and submissiveness. Then this water and dust, which had become *molded mud* [15:26] and *clinging clay* [37:11], was honored with the attribute of the hand. God said, "*What prevented thee from prostrating thyself before him whom I created with My own two hands?*" [38:75]. But fire, which waxed proud, was made the object of severity through the attribute of the foot: "*The All-Compelling will place His foot in the Fire, and it will say, 'Enough, enough.'*"[537]

O chevalier, by "hand" we do not mean the bodily limb, as is meant by those who declare His similarity, nor the hand of power, as the free-willers say. If we were to say that the hand is the bodily limb, like those who have gone astray, then we would be making it permissible for Him to have a newly arrived attribute, and that is unbelief. If we were to say that it is the hand of blessing and power, meaning that He created Adam with His blessing and power, well He also created Iblis with the hand of power. So what difference would there be between Adam and Iblis? The similarity-asserters have no awareness, the divesters have no weight, and the folk of the Sunnah are the pure gazers. The similarity-asserters deserve punishment, the divesters deserve blame, and the folk of the Sunnah deserve honor.

Those who assert similarity do not know His measure, for they have declared Him similar to newly arrived things. Those who interpret do not know their own measure, for they claim to know what is behind the curtains of the Unseen. We in any case know both our own measure and His measure.

He honored dust with the attribute of the hand and then fastened His own speech to it: "*He fastened to them the word of godwariness*" [48:26]. But He showed severity to fire through the attribute of the foot. The attribute of the hand imparts the sense of elevation, and the attribute of the foot imparts the sense of debasement. Dust was debased by its own attribute but elevated by His attribute. Fire was elevated by its own attribute but debased by His attribute. "O dust, O you who are put down by your attribute and lifted up by My attribute! O fire, O you who are lifted up by your attribute and put down by My attribute!"

Iblis performed many acts of obedience and worship, but all of them were accidental. His innate attribute was disobedience, for he was created of fire, and fire possesses the attribute of pride. Pride is the wherewithal of the disobedient.

Adam slipped, and we disobeyed. But the attribute of disobedience is accidental, and the attribute of obedience original. After all, we were created from dust, and the attribute of dust is humility and submissiveness. Humility and submissiveness are the wherewithal of the obedient. God looks at the foundation of the work and the point around which the compass turns; He does not look at uncommon things and accidents.

O dervish, on the day Adam slipped, they beat the drum of good fortune for all the Adamites. God set down a foundation for Adam at the beginning of the work. He gave him wherewithal from His own bounty. The first example of the bounty that He showed Adam was that He placed him in paradise without any merit and without his asking. And the first example that Adam displayed of his own wherewithal was his slip.

God made a contract with Adam at the beginning of the work. The stipulation of the contract was that whenever someone buys something or sells something, he should give a taste. Adam gave a taste of his wherewithal when he disobeyed the command and ate the wheat. God gave a taste of the goblet of bounty when He pardoned that slip.

No sin is greater than the first sin, especially when the person was nourished on beautiful-doing and nurtured by beneficence. The angels had to prostrate themselves before him—the chair of his good fortune was placed on the shoulders of the proximate. He was taken into paradise without any merit and given a home in the neighborhood of His gentleness. Since He pardoned the first slip, this is proof that He will forgive all sins.

After all, we have a thousand times more excuses than Adam had. If we need the darkness of clay, we have it. If we need the frailty of dust, we have it. If we need the impurity of *molded mud* [15:26], we have it. If we need some confused morsels, we have them. If the times should have become dark with injustice and corruption, we have that. If the accursed Iblis has to sit in wait for us, we have him. If caprice and appetite have to dominate over us, we have them. At the first slip, Adam was forgiven without any of these meanings. Since we have all these opacities, why would He not forgive us? In truth, He will forgive us.

O dervish, they robbed the caravan of the Adamites on the day that Adam slipped. *Once the caravan has been waylaid, it is secure.*

A blind man was sitting in the hot sun in the Hijaz eating walnuts and dates. Someone asked him, "Why are you eating two very hot things in this terrible heat?" [538]

He replied, "Well, they waylaid my caravan, and everything I feared has come to pass. Now I'm secure."

When that exalted man came into paradise, he looked around. He said, "My traveling feet cannot be bound by stirrups and my head full of the tipsiness of love's secrets cannot carry the burden of a crown. I was a given a stature like *alif* [ا] and I must be like *alif* in having nothing." [539] He threw the causes, means, and consignments into the fire and kept on shouting *"Here I am"* like a lover. He gambled away the eight paradises on the board of witnessing and contemplation.

> Do you know the first rule of the tavern?
> Quick, gamble away crown, belt, and cap.

*

> *Come and pour me some of that rosy wine,*
> *even if I lose my shirt by drinking it.*
> *My armband, bracelet, whatever I have—*
> *it's all yours. Just don't hold back the wine.*[540]

What a marvelous business! If He wanted to bring Adam out of paradise so quickly, what was the wisdom of putting him into paradise? Yes, my spirit and world, He sold paradise to Adam and the Adamites, but, in the school of Imam Shāfiʿī, selling something absent is not allowed. If it is done, there is still the right to refuse. He took Adam to paradise so that the sale would be correct and he would not have the right of refusal. He took him to paradise to see what was being sold. Then He brought him into this world, which is the grammar school of practice, so that he could pay the price. Even though our merchandise is defective, the buyer is generous.

"Accept me, though I'm adulterated, for the noble man is lenient even when he knows." Though our wherewithal is faulty and not worthy of the Threshold, they take whatever they can get from a destitute debtor. *Take from the bad debtor, even if only a brick.*

When Adam went into paradise, he was on the shoulders of the angels. When he entered the road of seeking, he found nothing to cover his privates. *"May God disgrace a man who approves of being elevated by the appearance of his possessions and beauty! That is the share of only the most despicable men and women. No, by God, let him be elevated by the two greater things, his aspiration and his soul, and the two lesser things, his heart and his tongue."*[541]

"O Adam, your crown is My bitter decree and your robe My causeless will. This is the stipulation for lovers in the road of the Jealous."

God's Messenger saw that Muṣʿab ibn ʿUmayr was approaching, wrapped in a sheepskin. He said, *"Look at this man, whose heart God has illuminated! I saw him when his parents were nurturing him with the best of food and drink. The love of God and the Messenger has called him to what you see."*[542] Look at the tribulation that love has rained down upon him!

> Don't be a lover if you can avoid it
> lest you remain in love's heartache.
> Love is not a matter of choice—
> you should know that much.
> The beloved seeks no one's approval,
> no matter how much blood you shed from your eyes.[543]

You must dedicate yourself outwardly to the Shariah and inwardly to the Haqiqah. You must make night and day the two steeds of your deeds and empty the carpet of all others, lest your name be written on ice.

> You must be solitary in the road of need,
> always the comrade of pain.
> Clinging to union is not manly—
> you must be a man in the days of separation.[544]

O chevalier, supposing there was no talk of dust in the world, then for sure the pure secrets would have remained in the Unseen. But uproar fell into heaven and earth, and tumult appeared in the world. When the desire to give existence to Adam came forth from the ambuscade of knowledge into the open plain of manifestation and when it was said that such an army would be brought into the world to kill adversaries, all at once turmoil stuck up its head from the breasts. Those who were the wellspring of cleanliness and the essence of purity began to speak: "Our acts of obedience and worship!"

The Sultan of beginningless knowledge was walking in the field of beginningless majesty without looking at anyone. He answered, *"Surely I know what you do not know"* [2:30].

"Is any work needed more splendid than what we have? Can there be an empire with a better arrangement? A whole world is taken up with our chants of glorification, hallowing, and reciting *tawḥīd*, and all of us put down our prayer-carpets on the straight road of obedience."

The declaration came, *"Surely I know.* Ah, I have a work on the way of which knowledge is the emissary. Yes, there are glorification and hallowing, but what is needed is a reckless lover who will exchange the Abode of Peace for the Abode of Blame and have no fear. Yes, you will go straight, and they will go every which way. But I want to bring them into existence, so I have spread the carpet of love. If the cheek of their Covenant should be stained by the smoky mole of sin, the musky lock of love will ask pardon for them."

When the beloved comes with one sin,
his beautiful traits bring a thousand interceders.[545]

"Surely I know what you do not know. You see how they deal with Me in their practice, but you do not see how I deal with them in love."

"Do not rely on the affection of someone who loves you only when you are sinless."[546]

"There is no good in a love whose torment cannot be borne and whose water is not drunk when opaque."[547]

Before the existence of Adam, who was the embroidery on the cape of love's secret, the angels kept the rows of worship straight and adorned the ranks of obedience. They did not know that there was a man in the Unseen who, when he put on the garment of dried clay, would upset the rows of their obedient acts when he became drunk with the goblet of union.

As soon as Adam stepped from the concealment of nonexistence into the world of existence and fixed his eyes on the center-point of witnessing, the nightingale of his passion became distraught and the rose of his love blossomed. Then the angels began to shout: "That man of dust has come to set fire to the merchandise of our obedience with his brazenness!"

The address came: "O angels of the Dominion, turn your faces away from the Throne. The chair of Adam's good fortune is now your throne and his essence is your kiblah. All of you, turn toward the presence of his majesty and the courtyard of his good fortune, for he is the knower and you are doers. He is the friend and you are servants."

Nay, they are honored servants [21:26]. When those exalted ones, whose home is this blue cupola and suspended dome, turned their faces to the presence of dust's majesty, they complied with the divine mandate, *"Prostrate yourselves before Adam"* [2:34]. The lordly exaltation charged forth from the world of imperial majesty and put Adam in the wrathful crucible of *Adam disobeyed* [20:121]. It struck him with the fire of trial until the moisture of gazing on the angel's prostration left him. Then he appeared in this shirt of poverty: *"Our Lord, we have wronged ourselves"* [7:23].

In the morning he was carried by the angels, all of whom prostrated themselves before him. On his head was the crown of union, on his waist the belt of proximity, and around his neck the collar of familiarity. No one was higher than he in rank, no individual was like him in elevation, and every instant the call kept coming to him, "O Adam, O Adam!" Evening had not yet arrived when his clothes were taken from him, his intimacy was stripped away from him, and he was harshly expelled by the angels: "Leave without delay!"[548]

I felt secure with Him, and in security He showed me
severity—such is he who feels secure with his beloved.

Every mote of Adam's makeup gave out this cry of love:

I will afflict my spirit with love's heartache,
I will make it the shield for cruelty's arrow.
A lifetime not passed in aching for You—
today I'll offset it with my heart's blood.[549]

The wonder is that until the resurrection children will be reading in the grammar schools, "And Adam disobeyed" [20:121]. *God did not hide this for him as would be required by the necessities of election. Rather, He gave relief to his children's descendants when they are overcome by disobedience and described by absence in the state of being mastered by appetite.*

This is a marvelous business! He clothed Adam in a hundred thousand ornaments of prosperity and robes of bounteousness and tied a thousand thousand sorts of gentle adornment around his neck. Why was it necessary to have the children in the grammar schools recite until the Day of Resurrection, *"And Adam disobeyed"*? The majestic crown of *Prostrate yourselves!* needed the severe blindfold of *And Adam disobeyed* so as to shorten the man's road, for in sum, *trials are in keeping with the heights*. Moreover, not everyone has Adam's breath—a handful of the maimed and marred are in this road. "Send out the poisoned goblet of *Adam disobeyed* on the hand of the cupbearer of the Will! Then, if one of his children does something while in the state of absence and overmastery by appetite, that will be a support for him."

O chevalier, *benevolence is for beginners. As for the advanced, their possessions are free for the taking and their blood may be shed. The road for them is severity upon severity and trial upon trial.*

Here we have Adam, crowned with the crown of majesty, capped with the diadem of beauty, elevated from the depths of mortal nature to the top of the spheres of gentle gifts, settled down such that the intricacies of the attributes were bewildered by the splendors of his majesty, but then the sultan of the Will attacked him from the ambuscade of the Desire. In the morning he was more exalted than the centerpiece of the necklace, and in the evening he was dragging the skirt of abasement, his throat choked with bewilderment.

In love are both exaltation and abasement.[550]

Yes, love is a sultan. There is no way to judge how a sultan's time and a sultan's work will play out. *"Beware of kings! If you become their companion, they will weary you, and if you abandon them, they will abase you. When they punish, they deem beheading a trifle; and when they reward, they deem responding to a request great."*[551]

And here we have Moses: He was given to drink from a brimful cup of Speech, and a tent of exaltedness was erected above his head; he was sat down at the table of affection, and noble serving boys wandered around him. But when he drank a good deal and became drunk, he was clothed in the mantle of contraction. The carpet of expansiveness had been spread in the pavilions of proximity and he was made to drag the mantle of hope in the gardens of expecting encounter. He was saying, "Show me, that I may gaze upon Thee" [7:143].

It was said to him, "O son of menstruating women, you want to see the Exalted Lord?!"[552]

On the day He brought the Adamites into existence He said, "Come and seek, but detach your heart from finding the Sought!" The man will be seeking, but the Sought will be inside the curtain of jealousy. Seeking will not come to an end, nor will the Sought come out into the open.

O dervish, wherever there is beauty, there is coquetry. Wherever there is captivity, there is abasement.

I count heartache for You as revelry
    and accept Your unfairness as justice.
If I become dust in Your road with all this,
    I still won't be worthy of Your feet.

*

You're my heart's light, though You pair me with fire;
    You're my head's crown, though You keep me in dust.
You're my heart's ease, though You unsettle me;
    You're dear like my eyes, though You abase me.

Shiblī said, *"My abasement has suspended the abasement of the Jews."*[553] You have seen how lowly are the Guebres, the Jews, and the Christians in the eyes of the Muslims. In their own eyes the men of this road are a hundred times more lowly. You must sweep the dust at the doorsteps of the Guebres with your own beautiful traits and have no attribute from which comes forth an iota of disdain. If at that moment an iota of chieftainship should grab your skirt, you will still be at the first step. It is the consensus of the folk of the Tariqah that anyone who sees himself better than Pharaoh is worse than Pharaoh.

Fuḍayl ibn ʿIyāḍ said, *"Anyone who sees worth in himself has no humility."*[554]

Putting yourself down in the eyes of people is easy. The man is he who puts himself down in his own eyes. So long as you have not been rejected at every door, become the false coin among all the genuine, and turned into the counterfeit on every scale, do not suppose that you have an iota of humbleness as your share. Humbleness is inner humbleness, not outer humbleness. Do not be deluded by outward humility. Your inwardness must be decorated with the adornment of humbleness, and your outwardness must be radiant and cheerful. Even with no bread in the house, the light of approval must shine on your forehead.

They say that if you see a dervish with eyebrows knotted and forehead creased, you will know that he has changed his object of worship.[555]

Have you seen a lotus flower? You must learn Sufism from it. It has a radiant outwardness and an inwardness caped in humility. It has the blue coat of grief on the inside and green on the outside. A dervish must be like that. He must wear the tattered cloak on his heart, not his body.

Sufism is not that a chevalier meets you
    while you are wearing a tattered cloak.
Sufism is ordinary clothes, within which
    the chevalier is fearful of God and humble.[556]

*

The teeth are laughing and the bowels burning,
the laughter false and contrived.
How many the weepers with no tears in their eyes;
how many the laughers with no shine on their teeth![557]

The lotus, which has thrown its shield into the water like a lover, laughs outwardly and burns inwardly. Its feet are in the water of life and its eyes in the wellspring of the sun. It grows only in clear water and lifts up its head only at seeing the sun. It constantly wants assistance for its life, both from above and below. If you take away its water, it will turn its face to annihilation: "I have no subsistence without the assistance of life." If the sun goes down, it will pull down its head: "I have no existence without seeing the Goal."

O chevalier, if a man becomes great in measure, he does so with his own standing place and seeing place. His standing place must first be pure and sound so that his seeing may become pure and sound, for pure seeing is the fruit of a pure station. As long as a tree does not take root in a goodly place and become established in pure soil, it will not produce goodly fruit.

From roots fixed in the soil rises
a branch to the stars, not reached by the tall.[558]

Since the standing place was *he drew close, so He came down, so he was two-bows' length away, or closer* [53:8–9], the seeing was *the eyesight did not swerve, nor did it trespass* [53:17].

Then again, when someone's standing place is sound, he will be given what he did not ask for. When someone's standing place is not sound, he will not be given even what he asks for. At Mount Sinai Moses asked for seeing. The blight of the veil grew up beneath his standing place, so it was said to him, *"But look at the mountain"* [7:143]. Do you know what this was? He was showing him his standing place: "Moses, look at your standing place. Will the standing place you have give you the fruit of seeing?"

A man must have both standing and seeing. When standing comes together with seeing, a result is born from the midst called "the moment." It was from here that the paragon said, *"I have a moment with God."*[559] His standing came together with his seeing, the two became companions, and from them came forth something new named "the moment."

Our paragon, my father, often used to say that if a dead thing were to be the companion of a living thing for a thousand years, no living thing would appear. A living thing must become the companion of a living thing for a living thing to appear.

This is talk of life. When something is born, it is born between two spirits: a spirit that is inside people, and a spirit that arrives from the Unseen: *So also We revealed to thee a spirit from Our command* [42:52]; *I blew into him of My spirit* [15:29]. Then, when these two spirits become companions, a life appears from the midst. It is this life that this talk is about. Here you have an exalted state—the opening of the spirit is poured down on the head of your secret core. In short, until you come alive, you will not reach the Alive.

O dervish, He who made this Adamite appear made him appear so that he would be "alive, knowing, powerful." He of course is pure of association; these are rather the lights of Adam's robe of honor, not the traces of association. The robe of honor on dust and clay is not something trivial. We are the ones given eminence by His knowledge, pulled up by His remembrance, adorned by His gentleness, made present by His desire, lifted up by His will, made apparent by His artisanry, named by His bounty. He put within us what He put. Our work is not a game, our story not a metaphor—*"It was for a reason that Qaṣīr cut off his nose."*[560] Our work came forth from knowledge, was displayed by predetermination, has the mark of desire, and carries the signet of wisdom.

He created the Throne but sent it no message. He brought the Footstool into existence but sent it no messenger. Then He brought forth a handful of dust, whose drinking place was the limpidness of knowledge and whose food was the kernels of the meanings. He did not come uninvited. Rather, He sent a hundred thousand requests and entreaties to the door of his secret core's nook: *messengers bringing good news and warning* [4:165]. And he, with sweet disdain, took on the amorous glances of the beloveds and the coquetry of the sweethearts.

How much beauty have I seen, but
I chose you among mortals.[561]

There were many existent things and countless artifacts, but the work He has with you He had with no other existent thing. If there were any cause for this, well He had luminous individuals and celestial figures, all of them with the garment of sinlessness, the shirt of reverence, the station of service, and the feet of obedience. *They do not disobey God in what He commands them* [66:6] was the edict of their states. *Nay, they are honored servants* [21:26] was the parasol of their pomp and authority. But not everyone who is worthy for service is also worthy for love. Not everyone worthy for the edge of the carpet is also worthy for the station of expansiveness. Not everyone who is an ornament of the threshold is like the beauty of the forefront. Not everyone who was created not to see Him is like him who was created to see.

"At the beginning of the work, Our knowledge requested that We bring into existence heaven and earth and the Throne and the Footstool. We gave existence to daytime as a white-faced servitor and to night as a black-cheeked maid, and We sent them to serve the house of your interactions. It was the sun of your good fortune that rose over heaven and earth so that We could dress them in the shirt of their existence. We gave forth this overflowing cup: *We offered the Trust to the heavens and the earth and the mountains* [33:72].

"It was the ray of your state's majesty that shone on the Throne so that We could adorn it with the attribute of tremendousness and make it the kiblah for supplication. It was the lightning of your greatness and nobility that struck the Footstool such that We gave it eminence with this declaration: *His Footstool embraces the heavens and the earth* [2:255]. It was the sun of your status that shone on Mount Sinai and dressed it in this robe of elevation: *Then, when his Lord disclosed Himself to the mountain, He made it crumble to dust, and Moses fell down thunderstruck* [7:143]. It was your burning that shone upon a dog and turned it into a saint. It was your pain that shone upon a saint and turned him into a dog.[562]

"It was for the sake of your disobedience that We made apparent the attribute of severity. It was by virtue of your frailty and incapacity that We put bounty to use. It was because of the heat of your desire that We called out, *'He loves them and they love Him'* [5:54]. It was because of Our eternity's bounty toward this handful of dust that We said, *'My mercy takes precedence over*

My wrath.'[563] It was because of Our beginningless kind favor that We said for the sake of this fearless handful, *'Your Lord wrote mercy against Himself'* [6:54]."

O dervish, if you gather a large amount of copper and iron and toss on it a speck of the elixir, it will all turn into pure gold. Copper and iron are such that they have no trace of the mystery of the elixir, but once the elixir has acted upon them, they become pure gold.

You and I were a handful of dust, and Adam was a handful of clay. Adam had not seen the mold of power and had not yet come out from behind the curtain of the subtle artisanry. The secret of knowledge had not yet shone its light upon him, and coming down had not yet become his specific attribute. The oyster of the decree had not yet become the container for the pearl of his secret core, and the sun of majesty had not yet risen over his days from the constellation of beauty. The subtle secret of union and the reality of the meaning of love had not yet shown their faces to him. But once these meanings became manifest and the pearls of these realities were deposited in the coffer of his heart, if you say that Adam is dust, you will have wronged him. If you say that he is *molded mud* [15:26], you will have scorned him.

The elixir is an artifact of creatures. If it is suitable for turning iron into gold, how can it be that love, which is the attribute of the Real, cannot purify dust of its opacity and make it the crown on top of the celestial spheres? If the clay that you knead yields roses, why are you surprised that the clay He kneads yields a heart? Yes, it was dust, but then the Real's gentleness came and made the dust the object of His seeking. Had it been nothing but dust, all of it would have been *Adam disobeyed* [20:121]. Had it been nothing but gentleness, all of it would have been *surely God chose Adam* [3:33].

O chevalier, when a Muslim judge makes a ruling, he does so on the basis of just witnesses and truthful testimony. Dust testifies with the tongue of *Adam disobeyed*. Then the gentleness of the Real comes and testifies with the tongue of *his Lord chose him* [20:122]. What do you say? Which one gives a more just testimony? Dust, which was not and then came to be, or gentleness, which is an attribute of the Real?

"O you who were made apparent by My knowledge in the Beginningless! O you who exist by My command at the moment! O you who are preserved by My decree in the Endless! Knowledge has rulership in the Beginningless, the command has rulership at the moment, and the decree has rulership in the Endless."

When a sultan has special friends, he gives each of them a rulership. There are three rulerships: the rulership of the Beginningless, the rulership of the moment, and the rulership of the Endless.

"O knowledge, you take the side of the Beginningless! O command, you take the road of the moment! O decree, you take the skirt of the Endless!

"I gave you over to three attributes, and in the end I brought you back to Myself. First I gave you to the sultan of knowledge, then I gave you to the king of the command, then I surrendered you to the emperor of the decree. Finally I gave out this call in the world: '*Surely unto thy Lord is the final end*' [53:42]. O knowledge, give to the command! O command, give to the decree! O decree, give to Me!"

Knowledge is all limpidness, the command is all trial, and the decree is all subsistence. Who knows what subtle things have been readied inside this mote of dust!

For seven hundred thousand years the angels of the Dominion circumambulated in their noble stations, circling around the Kaabah of obedient acts and worship. Their kiblah was praise, for *we glorify Thy praise* [2:30]. At the first of his work, Adam the chosen lifted up his head from that center and said, *"The praise belongs to God"* [1:2].

What a marvelous business! All the existent things were made to appear through *"Be!" so it comes to be* [2:117]. But Adam was placed for forty days between Mecca and Taif. He was brought out from the cottage of water and clay, while subtleties were sprinkled on him again and again. The world waited: What was God making? What would He bring into appearance? Clouds of generosity were coming, and droplets of gentleness were raining down. Clouds of severity were coming, and droplets of the liver's blood were raining down. Sometimes the sapling of joy was planted in the garden of union, and sometimes the clay of his heart was kneaded with the blood of remorse at separation. Sometimes there was the fire of love, sometimes the water of gentleness.

O dervish, the two worlds are a box, and the pearl inside the box is the existence of Adam. A box can be carved in an hour, but it takes many years before the precious jewel, which is called the unique pearl, will be put inside. Adam's outwardness was made of clay, and clay needs no respite. That is what the heart needs—not the respite of power, but the respite of greatness. Stars are for the sake of coming up and going down, and so also sun and moon, so their work is finished with *"Be!" so it comes to be.*

"Here a heart is needed to recognize Me, a tongue is needed to praise Me, an eye is needed to see Me, a hand is needed to take the cup of My union, a foot is needed to rush into the garden of My approval. If We were to bring him into existence in an instant, We would be making Our power apparent. But when We bring him into the midst over many years, We display his greatness and magnificence. We would rather make the greatness of Our friends apparent than display Our own power."

That paragon was adorned with all sorts of good fortune and bounteousness and with the lights of perfection and beauty. Then he was sent into paradise. He wandered around, but he found nothing to cling to. He reached the tree known as *the tree of trial* [*balāʾ*], though in fact it was *the tree of friendship* [*walāʾ*]. He saw it, so to speak, as a road-worthy steed. He did not hesitate a moment. When he reached it, he bridled it up. That bad bridling was expressed as *Adam disobeyed* [20:121]. He had sharp eyes and saw within it the secret of a traveling companion. And the tree also—it lifted the veil from its face and showed him: "You cannot travel this road without me."

O dervish, Adam's steed, though road-worthy, came to a stop when it reached the wheat. As for the auspicious steed and majestic packhorse of Muḥammad, God's messenger, it circled around the cosmos without stopping anywhere. That was expressed this way: *"The eyesight did not swerve, nor did it trespass"* [53:17].

The 700,000-year conduct of the Higher Plenum in the world of hallowing and glorifying was turned into the stuffing for the pillow of praise and placed at the top of the good fortune of the chieftain of the envoys. Thus the Eternal Quran reports, *"It may be thy Lord will raise thee up to a praised station"* [17:79]. The praised station is that pillow, which was stuffed by the conduct of the angels. But that paragon did not lie back, for he said, *"Without boasting"*:[564] "If I lie back, my back will not be straight tomorrow at the resurrection."

In terms of form Muḥammad was an Adamite, but in terms of reality Adam was a Muhammadan: "You are surprised that tomorrow at the Resurrection a few of those with unwashed faces will be brought under my work of interceding. When he who was the first foundation in the tablet of gentleness fell into the lowland of the slip, his support was nothing but my name."

The first drink that was given to Adam was the drink of knowledge, and the first drink of beginners is the drink of knowledge. As long as his work was with the angels, he had the garment of knowledge. When he reached the center-point of wisdom, he was clothed in the shirt of forgetfulness. Yes, the beginningless knowledge requires that all knowers throw down the shield of their knowledge and acknowledge their ignorance.

All the hallowers and glorifiers of heaven were thirsty. When the sun of Adam's good fortune shone, those pure ones were given water from the ledger of vicegerency: *O Adam, tell them their names* [2:33]. As for Adam, he was thirstier in his makeup than the angels, but it is a stipulation for the chieftains of the road that they first give to the thirsty, then they drink themselves. *"A people's cupbearer is the last to drink."*[565] Eminence and honor were bestowed on that paragon's essence through blessings and benefits. The vicegerency of the realm of the earth was surrendered to him and the drum of his sultanate was beaten in the spheres. Then all the angels prostrated themselves before him, but he himself had not yet prostrated himself.

Once you placed your hat on the full moon,
I saw the hats of kings lying in the dust of your road.[566]

For many thousands of years the glorifiers and *tawḥīd*-reciters of heaven had been at the Exalted Threshold, standing straight on the feet of obedience to the extent of their capacity. When the top hat of good fortune appeared in Adam's chosenness, they lost themselves in that hat. *And when We said to the angels, "Prostrate yourselves before Adam!"* [2:34]. As for the one who held back, though he had nearly filled the earth with obedience, he became the abandoned one of the Endless.

That paragon was sent into paradise as a requisite of munificence and generosity. He was put on the couch of exaltedness with the whole of paradise placed under his command. He looked it over but did not see a speck of sorrow or of love's reality. He said, *"Oil and water do not mix."*

The stipulation of poverty is disengagement and solitariness. When a fruit ripens in the shade, it has no flavor. "The stipulation of Our road is for your pillow to be tossed aside and your bed to be ashes."

It was said, "O Adam, since this is the state, you must go back to the dustbin where you took the first step."

He said, "I will need an excuse for all these pretty faces."

It was said, "We will call out your excuse." This is expressed in the Quran with the words *"Adam disobeyed"* [20:121].

When he came out of paradise, he saw a black mark on his face. He said, "O Lord, what is this?"

He said, "O Adam, what you have chosen does not come with whiteness of face, for *'Poverty is blackness of face in the two worlds.'*[567] Even though everything in the two realms of being is for your sake, you are more beautiful barefoot."

He created an individual, threw the noose of subjection around the neck of everything in heaven and earth, and put it in his hand. The sun was his torch-holder, the moon his dyer and cook, the mountains his treasurers, heaven his roof, earth his carpet.[568] He subjected to him the exalted angels, with their high degrees and ranks and their brilliant stations and honors. One of them drives the clouds, another brings the rain, a third provides daily bread, a fourth writes down works, a fifth asks forgiveness.

What a marvelous business! Someone sins, and dust sits on the pages of his state. The Shariah gives out a proclamation to the spirits of the animals saying that this man has slipped and disobedience has come into existence from him, but He wants to wash away the stain of that slip: "For his sake We have written an edict to your spirits: 'Sacrifice your lives for him!' "

He created everything for him, but He did not turn him over to anything. He gave him a name, but He did not turn him over to the name. He sat him on a throne and had the angels prostrate themselves before him, but He did not turn him over to that. He brought him into this world and made the whole of this world his kingdom, but He did not turn him over to this world. At first he had the cape of nonexistence, but He did not turn him over to nonexistence. Then he put on the cape of existence, but He did not turn him over to that. He gave him attributes, but he did not let him loose with those attributes. He created him, gave him beauty, and displayed the beauty to the world's inhabitants. A hundred thousand seekers began to seek, but the Exalted Jealousy came out and did not turn him over to anyone. "If you did not want to sell, why did you give him to the broker?" All being took a share of his beauty, but he himself kept the trailing skirts of his state pure of those shares.

Before the existence of Adam, the angels did not see the beauty of the sultan of the command. Before the carpet of Adam's existence was spread out, no command had come from the Unseen. When He drew the compass of bestowing existence on Adam's clay, the beauty of the sultan of the command became apparent.

Yes, Adam was the vicegerent and the one entrusted with a robe of honor. When a paragon is clothed in a robe of honor, his attendants are also given a share. It was said to the angels, *"Prostrate yourselves before Adam!"* [2:34]. Those who received robes of honor were delighted with this command.

Not everyone, however, stayed in place under the Sultan's caress. There were many who fell into error because of it. The pure ones knew that a state would appear from one of them. Gabriel was going to ʿAzāzīl, who today is Iblis, and saying, "If such a state appears, it will be put on my head."

He said, "Write that work for me."

Michael was saying the same thing. All the chief angels made the same request, and he made the guarantee for everyone: "Let your heart be at ease." He had in his own heart that he would be the pivot of this work that was still in the Unseen.

When the sultan of the command charged into the field of exaltedness with the raised sword of the causeless will—*Prostrate yourselves before Adam!*—that accursed one, who had sold himself to them as chieftain, was not able to pull back the reins of chieftainship. He held himself like a tree before the cold wind of the command's severity, and the wind pulled him up by the roots—*as if they were uprooted palm trunks* [54:20]. *"The unbeliever is like a pine tree until he is thrown down all at once."*[569] But Adam was a little shrub before the breeze of the command, so he came forth in surrender.

The same thing happened to that other unfortunate fellow, Pharaoh the unaided. He had sold himself to the people as chieftain. When the splitting of the sea appeared, he knew that the sea had been opened up for him. He wanted to pull back on the reins because of love for life, but passion for chieftainship did not let him do so.

O dervish, if Iblis, who was the enemy, was hung from the gallows of severity, that is no surprise. The surprise is that the burnt Adam wept for three hundred years and no one said to him, "What happened to you?"

Have you not heard about David? After his prostration, the call came, *"Are you hungry that I may feed you? Are you thirsty that I may pour for you?"* O David, are you hungry or thirsty?

Adam's heart and liver were being ground under the mill wheel of the causeless will. He let out a breath with burnt heart. "All the plants have burned." After three hundred years Gabriel came with water and said, "O Adam, purify yourself."

He said, "How should I wash?"

He said, "First wash your face, for its luster was taken away by the slip, and this will bring back its purity."

When he purified himself, his repentance was accepted under the shelter of purity's greatness. *Surely God loves the repenters and He loves those who purify themselves* [2:222].

What a marvelous business! He said to Adam, "Do not go after the wheat," but wherever they put Adam's chair, the wheat was there disclosing itself like a bride. There is a secret in this. Yes, the people consider his greatness to be that he had a chair, hat, crown, and belt, but this is wrong.

"O Adam, beware, beware! Do not go after this tree!" But the decree had gone out, and the decree had the upper hand. As soon as Adam put that morsel into his mouth, the greatness of those ornaments fell away from him. Adam was left naked with only the crown of the chosenness of *surely God chose Adam* [3:33] and the robe of *his Lord chose him* [20:122]. Thus people will know that the root greatness has no need for those trappings.

33. *al-Laṭīf:* the Gentle

Laṭīf means knowing and it also means beautiful-doing.[570] *God says, "God is gentle to His servants"* [42:19]. What beautiful-doing is beyond the fact that you were in the concealment of nonexistence while He was taking care of your work with bounty and generosity? You were in the concealment of nonexistence while He was choosing you out from the whole world. You were in the concealment of nonexistence while He was taking care of your work without any precedent intercession, without any subsequent benefit, without your taking any trouble in the present state, and without any rightful due made incumbent in the future. He was tossing the secret hook of *He loves them* into the ocean of *they love Him* [5:54].

You were not there when I was there for you,
snatching you away from separation's hand.
You don't do all that I've commanded,
but I'll do all that I have shown.

To the worshipers He said, "I am the Gentle," in the sense of knowing so that they would be on guard against the hidden sorts of associationism and the subtle sorts of eye-service. To the disobedient He said, "I am the Gentle," in the sense of beautiful-doing so that they would not despair.

Yaḥyā ibn Muʿādh Rāzī said, *"You were gentle to Your friends, so they recognized You. Had you been gentle to Your enemies, they would not have refused You."*[571] You made the jasmine of Your gentleness, the sweet briar of Your intimacy, and the fragrant herb of Your bounty grow in the garden of Your friends' hearts such that, by means of these gentle gifts, they reached the secret of the recognitions and performed the obligations. If You had done this with the enemies of the road and shown them this beautiful-doing, the Abode of Islam and the Abode of Unbelief would be the same.

A group reaches the spheres, another the pit—
I lament at Your threats to this handful of dust!

Pharaoh's sorcerers were busy with unbelief and sin, and it is said that sorcery will not be effective unless a man is polluted. But when the wind of good fortune blew from the direction of gentleness and generosity, it left neither sorcery nor sorcerer, neither unbelief nor unbeliever. In the morning they were busy with the sin of unbelief and denial, and in the evening they took the side of faith and asking forgiveness.

Shaykh Abū Saʿīd said, "Whoever lifts up a burden from the garden of solicitude will put it down in the playing field of friendship. Whoever suckles milk from the nipple of kind favor will be nurtured in the embrace of protection."

The Master Abū ʿAlī said, "Whoever is given familiarity in the morning can hope for forgiveness in the evening."

Solicitude destroys sins. The long and the short of it is that when someone is caught by the noose of felicity, he will be lifted up from the nest of abasement and set down on the throne of exaltedness.

A whiff of the breeze of this felicity became the share of Adam's dust. Abasement was changed into exaltation, distance into proximity, separation into union, and misfortune into prosperity. Dust, which is the quarry of darkness, became the source of the pure water of subtle secrets, rising suns, and luminous moons. *He was not a thing remembered* [76:1] reached the degree of *their Lord will give them to drink of a pure wine* [76:21].

The whiff passed by the hut of the idol-carver, Azar, and garbed his branch in the garment of bosom friendship and the robe of good fortune. It sat him down on the dome of the revelry of *God took Abraham as a bosom friend* [4:125], bringing him into the banquet of the ascription "God's bosom friend," where he sacrificed his dear child as the party favor for bosom friendship's banquet.

It circled around the chamber of ʿImrān the Israelite and made his son's breast the highway of one hundred twenty-some thousand words without intermediary. It sat him down on the top of the Mount and placed the exalted embroidery of *I chose thee for Myself* [20:41] on the sleeve of his perfect beauty.

It passed by that orphan of Zachariah and concealed in her inwardness a hundred thousand realities of the meanings. It made her womb the oyster for the pearl of *the Word of God*. The womb of all the world's women is the locus of appetite, but her womb was the locus of the Word.

It passed by the earth of Tihama in Hijaz and wrote the inscription of chosenness and election on the tribe of Kināna. Then it sifted Kināna with the fine sieve of exaltedness, and Quraysh came to the top. It put the embroidery of the mystery on the existence of Quraysh. It sifted Quraysh, and Banū Hāshim came to the top, so it struck the high banners of solicitous meanings in the courtyards of their majesty. When it sifted Banū Hāshim, the Seal of the Prophets, the chieftain of the limpid and the world of chieftainship, felicity, and elevation came to the top, his name being Muḥammad, Aḥmad, ʿĀqib, Ḥāshir, and Māḥī.

He derived his name from Himself to magnify him,
for the Owner of the Throne is the Praised [maḥmūd] and he is Muḥammad.[572]

Then the one hundred twenty-some thousand center-points of prophethood put on the garment of eloquence in the royal court of his majestic covenant and said, "O Muḥammad,"

The aeon is a word, and thou art its meaning;
the command is an ocean, and thou art its utmost.[573]

That paragon had no news of what had been prepared in his name by the Unseen. He gave himself over to wage-earning for Khadīja and was content to trade with Syria. All at once a spark jumped from the fire-steel of the Unseen gentleness, found a burnt breast, and caught.

Her love came to me before I knew love—
it came across a carefree heart and took possession.[574]

There was a world full of folly. Children were given the name Muḥammad, but having the same name does not mean belonging to the same kind. The Shaykh al-Islam, my father, used to say, "There are many named Abū Saʿd [father of felicity] and Abu'l-Futūḥ [father of opening], but nowhere is there any felicity or opening."

A world was busy with its own seeking and searching, but this blessed morning rose up in the family of ʿAbd al-Muṭṭalib. The call was given out, *"Light has become manifest, falsehood nullified, and Muḥammad has been recognized with delight."*[575] The dust of abasement sat on the face of the caesar and clothing was stripped from the emperor. The fire of the Guebres, lit many thousand years ago from the radiance of the soles of his feet, died down. *The Real has come, and the unreal has vanished away* [17:81]. Heaven and earth were altered.

Before the banner of messengerhood and the flag of prophethood were raised at the threshold of God's messenger Muḥammad, the devils had gone high in this world. They were listening by stealth and hearing the secrets of the Unseen.[576] As soon as the pillow of his messengerhood's felicity was placed at the forefront of chieftainship, guards were put on watch in the heavens to drive away the satans by stoning and keep them far from awareness of the secrets of good news and warning, so that he would be safe and protected. For him an earth was spread out, a heaven raised up, and piercing flames were brought together.

What was the wisdom in these flames? They were guardians and protectors so that the secrets, which the trustworthy couriers conveyed to his blessed ears by the warrant of Him who has always been, would be guarded from the eyes of others and the intrusion of the satans: *Surely it is We who have sent down the Remembrance, and surely it is We who are its guards* [15:9]. Thus they conveyed the mystery that went forth from the beginningless Presence to the Muhammadan court.

It is the custom that when a king is under a roof, a guard is on top of the roof. Muḥammad, God's messenger, is a king, and the stars are the guards of the secrets of his messengerhood. *Surely we touched heaven, and we found it full of terrible guards and flames* [72:8].

O chevalier, when a sultan sends a carriage to a city with a precious and great preparation and deposit, he sends it on the hands of an elect, but they are merely an escort. From the era of Adam to the dissolution of the world, no secrets came down from heaven to earth like those that came down in the era of the prophethood of Aḥmad the Arab. *All that We recount to thee of the tidings of the messengers is that whereby We make thy heart firm* [11:120]. Exalted pearls from the oceans of the divine secrets were poured into the lap of the covenant of Muḥammad's prophethood. Although the carrier of the revelation was the Trustworthy Spirit, the road was not secure. The highwaymen and robbers were watching the road, so a police force was needed.

Several thousand years before the existence of Adam, this suspended dome and green skiff was adorned and held up by perfect power *without pillars* [13:2]. A thousand thousand shining pearls were attached to its outwardness; lanterns, lamps, and candles were lit.

O dervish, ornament is beautiful, but every ornament has a wisdom. What is the gist of the wisdom? That they be the guards of the Muhammadan secrets. He was a man who came out from under the cloak of ʿAbd al-Muṭṭalib. He passed by mortal wombs and loins, but a word came out from the Unseen and altered his states and words: *Surely thou hast a tremendous character* [68:4]. *Nor does he speak from caprice. It is naught but a revelation revealed* [53:3–4]. By means of revelation the character of mortal nature was removed and the character of the Quran was put in its place. The speech of mortal nature was taken and a speech was given from revelation, and this cry was given out in the world: "*Then We configured him as another creation*" [23:14]. The Lord who can turn a sperm drop into a clot and a clot into a tissue can convey creation from the attribute of opacity to the attribute of limpidness itself. Hence he came speaking with the Shariah, traveling through the Real, moving by the command, and standing still by the decree. On the night of the *miʿrāj* the eight paradises were presented to him, the marvels and the chambers were shown to him, but he paid not an iota of attention to any of them. This embroidery of loyalty was sewn on the cape of his limpidness: *The eyesight did not swerve, nor did it trespass* [53:17].

Then, when he stepped onto the carpet of the whispered secrets of the prayer, he said, "*The delight of my eyes was put in the prayer,*"[577] which is the station of whispered secrets. "*The praying person is whispering with his Lord.*"[578] "*If the praying person knew with whom he was whispering, he would not glance around.*"[579] "*The prayer is the* miʿrāj *of hearts.*"[580]

O dervish, when you want Him to speak to you, recite the Quran. And when you want to speak to Him, come into the sanctuary of the prayer. Know that in reality the five prayers are a souvenir that the paragon brought to you from the world of the purity of *two-bows' length away* [53:9].

O dervish, the measure of your height is very short. You do not reach the *miʿrāj*, nor is your greatness such that Burāq would come to your house. You should put on a cape of purity's eminence and stroll into the splendorous heaven of the mosque. Go in among the faithful like an angel. Come in at first with the attribute of servants, standing on the feet of need, and go out at last with the attribute of friends, sitting on the carpet of whispered secrets.

The Exalted Lord in His gentleness brought together all the Shariʾite pillars in the prayer. In the prayer there is the meaning of fasting and more. Fasting is refraining along with the intention; in the prayer there is the same refraining along with the intention. And there is more, for in fasting you are permitted to sleep, walk, and do other deeds, but in prayer these are not permitted.

In the prayer there is the meaning of the alms tax. There you give five dirhams to someone poor so that he may be at ease. Here you say at the end of the prayer, "*O God, forgive the faithful, men and women,*" so that everyone may be at ease.

In the prayer there is the meaning of the hajj. In the hajj, there is ritual consecration and deconsecration, and in the prayer there is consecrating and bringing the consecration to an end.

In the prayer there is the meaning of jihad. When you have made the ablution, this is like putting on armor. The imam is like a warrior, and the people are like the army. He stands in front of the rows in the *miḥrāb*, which is the place of war [*ḥarb*], and the people line up behind him, their feet firmly fixed to assist and follow him. In jihad, when they triumph and win victory in the struggle, property and spoils are distributed. In prayer, when the imam gives the greeting, the bounty of the Possessor of Majesty is distributed.

It is as if every person of faith who performs the prayer goes on the hajj, even if he is not able to do so; he pays the alms tax, even if he has no property; and he fasts, even if he does not have the strength for it. So beware, do not step into the presence of the prayer like the impure. The one hundred twenty-some thousand pearls of sinlessness, persons of honor, and quarries of greatness and wisdom pulled their heads beneath the mask of dust, seeking and wishing for this robe of honor, since no one had a necklace as precious as that of Aḥmad's community. Or rather, all of them had prayer, but some of them had standing without sitting, some had prostration without standing, and some had the act without the recitation. Then the turn arrived for the good fortune of the source of limpidness, who was the horseman leading the army of the prophets, the light of the eyes of the friends, the blossom in the garden of the limpid. He was a man *whose radiance was borrowed by the sun and whose splendor by the moon.* He was a forerunner *at whose coming the sleeves of hope brought forth blossoms and the moment of reaping the fruit approached.*

The Exalted Lord made a necklace of acts, its pearls of words, and He attached it to the neck of Muḥammad's community with the hand of generosity and munificence. It was this paragon at whose arrival *the morning smiled in face of the frowning shadows and disclosed itself like a polished sword drawn from the scabbard.* In no station did he forget you, whether in Mecca or Medina, in the mosque or in his chamber. In the same way, at the summit of the Throne and on the cushion of *two-bows' length away* [53:9] he had the sweet scent of remembering you. He brought you a foodstuff from every table, a message from every station, and a feast from every waystation.

Yes, the generous paragon is he who does not forget the serving boys. In the cave he said, *"Surely God is with us"* [9:40]. At the forefront of *two-bows' length away* he said, *"The peace be upon us."*[581] Tomorrow he will take the banner of praise in hand and spread the carpet of good fortune at the eminence of the *praised station* [17:79] while saying, *"my community, my community!"*[582] In this world he spread the carpet of the Shariah and in the afterworld he will erect the banner of praise.[583] Wait until tomorrow to see the perfection of his greatness, for he will bind this world's Adam to the saddle-straps of the next world's Adam. The next world's Adam is Muṣṭafā, for he will be the first person to lift up his head from the belly of the earth.

At the beginning of the work the existent things that are now visible and known had no name or mark. *"God was, and there was nothing with Him."*[584] A heaven and an earth were created, one made a carpet and the other a roof. *We made heaven a guarded roof* [21:32]. *God made earth a carpet for you* [71:19]. A sun and a moon were brought into existence, one made your chief cook and the other your dyer. Then the hand of power attached a strand of pearls to the neck of the spheres, and this spread carpet was fixed in place with stones, that is, the mountains. At the first of the work there was neither day nor night, neither light nor darkness. When day and night were created, one was made the field of livelihood, the other the seat of seclusion, and a thousand thousand candles of intimacy were lit.

When this castle was completed, He Himself called out: "O dust-dwelling Adam, wake up from the sleep of nonexistence, for the feet of the one hundred twenty-some thousand prophets are waiting for your good fortune. Put on a garment of destitution, place a turban of love on your head, and bind a belt of pain on your waist. With My bounty and beautiful-doing I will send exaltedness to welcome your need. I will beat this drum of your greatness in East and West: *I am setting in the earth a vicegerent* [2:30]. I will build the base of your throne from the shoulders of the proximate angels of My own Presence. I will keep the Splendorous Throne like a parasol above your head. I will turn the uppermost everlastingness into your home and dwelling. I will make the gardens of Eden your promenade and gazing place. At times I will clothe you in this robe of honor: *Surely God chose Adam* [3:33]. And at times I will place this embroidery on the sleeve of your good fortune: *Then his Lord chose him* [20:122]."

When Adam saw all this rank, he wanted to declare for himself and take the rulership in hand. He heard a call from the World of Exaltedness: "O Adam, watch out for yourself, for there is someone in your road who is jealous. *'I am jealous.'*[585] This blade of jealousy and sword of exaltedness has been drawn: *'Adam and those after him are under my banner.'* "[586]

"O Adam, though in form you are my precursor, in reality you are the child of my good fortune."[587]

O chevalier, why is it surprising that he should be sitting in Medina while the emperor and the caesar fail to settle down in their kingdoms? What is surprising is that several thousand years were needed to bring him into the confines of existence, though the shouts of "Make way" had fallen into the world. *And from before they had been seeking victory over those who disbelieve, but when there came to them what they recognized, they disbelieved in it* [2:89].

"I was aided by terror at a month's journey."[588] How is this the place for one month? Here there were shouts of "Make way" for several thousand years. Heaven and earth, the Throne and the Footstool, were the ornament of his greatness: "We will send a sultan from the court of nonexistence into the city of existence on the packhorse of eternal gentleness as the companion of munificence. It is not beneath Us to set up the ornament of his greatness in the city of power." On every mote He brought into existence from nonexistence He placed the brand of being Muḥammad's servant-boy.

They desire to extinguish God's light with their mouths [9:32]. All the world gathered together and came out in enmity against him. They said, "He must not come to be, and this religion must not become apparent." The Exalted Lord said, *"That He may make it prevail over every religion"* [9:23].

"I was the Seal of the Prophets in the Mother of the Book at God when Adam was still thrown down in his clay."[589] Adam had still not lifted his head from the clay when my name was written in the Mother of the Book as the Seal of the Prophets.

> The edict of your perfect beauty was written:
> "All the world's beauties are ugly before your face."

*

> *All the runners ran with you until they reached*
> *their limit—you ran on while they stood still.*[590]

If an intelligent and aware person should ponder and reflect, conceiving in his breast of the realities and intricacies of the divine gentleness, he will come to know that the goal of giving existence to the existent things and engendering the engendered things, all of which came forth from the hiding places of the Unseen to the open plain of manifestation and walked out from behind the curtain of nonexistence into the world of existence, was to lay down the cradle of Muḥammad's good fortune and to establish his Shariah.

At dawn the sun, which is the king of the spheres and the headman of the planets, raises the banner of light over East and West, smiles in the face of the frowning darknesses, snatches the tar-colored mantle from the shoulders of the sky, and routs the cavalry of the night. At noon, it begins declining down this purple dome and turquoise meadow. At the time of the afternoon prayer, it becomes yellow-faced in fear of separation. At the time of the evening prayer, it pulls up the ropes of its tent of light. At the time of the night prayer, it completely gathers the trailing skirt of brightness. All this descending and departing, this alteration from state to state, is so that the Muhammadan army and troops will know the times of whispered prayer with the Real.

On the first night the moon appears from the West like a nail paring, or a dagger-guard, or a golden horseshoe. On the fourteenth night it reaches fullness and takes up the seat of honor. In the end it is afflicted by the blight of waning. All this is so that Muḥammad's community may determine the fixed times. *They ask thee about the new moons. Say: "They are appointed times for the people, and the hajj"* [2:189].

The stars, which have set up a hall of mirrors before the throne of the kinglike moon, are there to protect the secrets of Muḥammad's presence. If anyone should lose his way in the desert, they will be his guide. Michael pays the wages of Muḥammad's soldiers and Gabriel is the foe-smashing leader of his army. Abraham, who set up the foundation of the Sacred House, set it up with the brilliant lightning of his greatness. Moses at Mount Sinai told the story of yearning for him and in the end slept in the grief of separation from him. Jesus had the flow of breath that brought the dead to life as the escort of the good news of Muḥammad's stepping forth; in the Torah he read the description of his eminence and superiority and in the Gospel he saw him exalted and extolled.

Muṣṭafā said, "When my mother became pregnant with me, she saw in a dream that a light appeared from her that took over the whole world." [591]

O chevalier, in the whole of a sultan's realm the capital is one city, even if his rule, greatness, mantle, and awesomeness have taken over all the empires. "Seven thousand years, which is the time of this world's subsistence, is the empire of our serving boys, but the capital city of our existence is the last five hundred."

It is not that the edict of a sultan who does not go to a place is not put into effect. What a pure Lord, who created a servant, the top hat of whose majestic good fortune rubs against the crown of the north star, the howdah of whose covenant reaches the dome of the proximity of *two-bows' length away*, and the carrier of whose chieftainship and elevation is not lifted by being's camel! On the splendor of his forehead was bound the turban of *by thy life!* [15:72], on the sleeve of his covenant was the exalted embroidery of *Muḥammad is God's messenger* [48:29], and at the door of his secret core's pavilion was raised the flag of the rulership of *We have opened up for thee a clear opening* [48:1]. In the midst of all this greatness and majesty, he did not gaze at himself for the blink of an eye.

On the day of the conquest of Mecca, two men were brought before him, their bodies trembling in awe. He said, *"Be at ease, for I am the son of a woman of Quraysh who used to eat jerky."*[592]

"O Muḥammad, We have tossed many robes of generosity around your neck. Beware, beware, lest you raise your head proudly. All this is the effusion of the bounty of Our self-sufficiency. As for what is yours, it is this: *Did He not find thee an orphan and shelter thee?* [93:6]. *Thou knewest not what the Book was, nor faith* [42:52]." Sometimes he was made to hear this address, and sometimes it was said, *"If not for thee, I would not have created the two worlds."*[593]

Muḥammad is not the father of any of your men, but rather the messenger of God and the seal of the prophets [33:40]. That paragon was given many kinds of drink and sent many sorts of garment. When he came out of the specific chamber of servanthood to the general court of prophethood, the beneficent robe of *by thy life* [15:72] was thrown over the neck of his good fortune. When he returned from the general court of prophethood to the specific chamber of servanthood, the curtain was lifted from his work and he was shown to himself: *Did He not find thee an orphan and shelter thee, find thee misguided and guide thee, find thee in want and free thee of need?* [93:6–8].

O dervish, what is needed behind the curtain is a poison-laced drink and an unhesitating sword such as *surely thou wilt die* [39:30]. Then the beneficent, overflowing drink of *by thy life!* may be sent to a man and he will not become blind drunk.

If We willed, We would send out a warner in every city [25:51]. If We wanted, We would have sent someone like you to every town. *If We willed, We would take away that which We revealed to thee* [17:86]. If We wanted, We would pull up the sapling of revelation that We planted in the garden of your heart with the hand of unneediness.

"O Muḥammad, your prophethood is a pure prophethood, your covenant an exalted covenant, your greatness a tremendous greatness, your affair an immense affair, your exhortation a noble exhortation, but We are that selfsame Lord. We do whatever We want."

O dervish, there was no mark of this talk in the world. As soon as the turn of Adam's good fortune arrived, a cloud of gentleness rose up and drops of love rained down. When the breast of an exalted man was brought forth, a few drops were sprinkled on the garden of his days. When the turn of Muḥammad's good fortune arrived, the drops were taken away and a shoreless ocean placed in the midst, and then the prophets and sincerely truthful were diving into the seas of prophethood and truthfulness. No one came near the steed of the chieftain of the envoys. Day was one of his steeds, and night one of his steeds. In the end these steeds were worn out and that chieftain of chieftains passed on.

"Yes, we put all the horsemen of the empire in front and told them to charge forth to the extent of their capacity and strength, for *we are the last, the preceders.*[594] Since we ourselves warmed up the steed of prophethood, we will pass beyond all."

In prophethood there were few horsemen like Moses, but when the truthfulness of Moses's prophethood put its feet in the stirrups of love, he was able to come only as far as the edge of the paragon's playing field. When Moses saw the fleet-footedness of his own steed, he said, "What feet my steed has for all the fields of the road! Spread the field of that paragon before me so that I may drive the steed of my aspiration into it!"

The call came, "*Take what I have given thee, and be one of the thankful* [7:144]. Be thankful for the field that We have placed before you."

He said, "If I cannot drive my horse into that field, at least give me leave to be a stirrup-holder. *O God, make me one of Muḥammad's community!*"[595]

Whatever generosity He commanded for a messenger, He commanded something more magnificent for our Messenger and made his standing place pass beyond it. Adam was the exalted of the world and was placed on the royal seat of existence. He was the seal ring on the hand of noble qualities, but that accursed one instilled disquiet into him so as to throw him into a slip. But the lightning of our Messenger's greatness flashed out at the devil and put him to work: *"There is none of you who has not been entrusted to a comrade from among the jinn."*

They said, "Not even you, O Messenger of God?"

He said, "'Not even I, but God has aided me against him, so he submitted.'"[596]

O dervish, if it is allowable for an angel to become a devil, it is allowable for a devil to become a truthful disciple. Indeed, the time of Adam was the first fruit of this talk, but he was brought forth by way of the threshold of severity. The shadow of the severity he saw fell on an angel, who became a heretic and a satan. "But I was brought forth by way of the gate of gentleness. The shadow of the gentleness I saw fell on a devil, and he became one of the sincerely truthful. *I was a prophet when Adam was still thrown down in his clay.*[597] Prophethood is the final end of traveling on the Adamites' road, and dust and clay are the beginning of their existence. In my case I had completed the final end of the traveling of the Adamites when others had still not completed the beginning."

Although Noah was given a ship to carry him in the water of the storm, the pure Unseen carried Muḥammad. In the highest Dominion Noah was given a ship [*safīna*] and Muḥammad and his community were given tranquility [*sakīna*]. The ship became the cause of salvation, and the tranquility became the cause of elevation in degrees. Noah said, *"My Lord, leave no disbeliever dwelling on the earth!"* [71:26]. But when Muṣṭafā's teeth had been broken and his blessed cheek stained with his blood, he was saying, *"O God, guide my people, for they do not know!"*[598] Lord God, though they strike stones against my teeth, sprinkle the sugar of acceptance on their heads!

Although today Nimrod's fire was made into *coolness and safety* [21:69] for Abraham, look at tomorrow when the fire of hell will be made *coolness and safety* for Muḥammad's serving boys. The accursed Nimrod lit up a fire for Abraham, and Abraham was the bosom friend of the All-Merciful. It is not surprising that Nimrod's fire should freeze at the feet of the All-Merciful's bosom friend. What is surprising is that a fire kindled by the wrath of the Exalted Lord, a fire in which the fire of this world has been washed seventy times, should become cold at the feet of one of Muḥammad's serving boys and turn into jasmine and roses.

The target of the Bosom Friend's eyesight was made into the place of Muḥammad's feet, nor was he ever turned over to fire. Rather, he was taken on until he was conveyed to this station: *Then he drew close, so He came down, so he was two-bows' length away, or closer* [53:8–9].

So also We were showing Abraham the dominion of the heavens and the earth [6:75]. The dominion of the heavens and the earth was the place of Abraham's vision and also the place where the saddlebags of the feet of Muḥammad's aspiration were put down. Abraham set his eyes on the star, the moon, and the sun, but our Messenger put his feet on the top of the star, the moon, and the sun. In his bosom friendship Abraham gazed on the place that Muḥammad traversed with his feet. Abraham's eyes gazed on the highest Dominion. To Muṣṭafā *while he was on the highest horizon* [53:7] it was said, *"Hast thou not seen thy Lord?"* [25:45]. The final end of Abraham's gaze was made into a playing field so that Muṣṭafā traversed with his feet what Abraham saw with his eyesight. If the beginning of someone's walking is the final end of Abraham's gaze, what then is the final end of that someone's gaze? Abraham said, *"Surely I am going to my Lord"* [37:99]. The Real said, *"Glory be to Him who took His servant by night!"* [17:1].

On the night of the *mi'rāj*, when the paragon reached him, Abraham asked, "Who is this?"

He said, "It is he the nail in the hoof of whose riding beast you saw when We made that the beginning of your road," for the star that was disclosed to the Bosom Friend's eyes was the nail in the hoof of Muḥammad's steed.

When Abraham heard this, he said boastfully, *"Welcome to the wholesome son and wholesome prophet!"* It is not that he was adorning the Messenger as his own child; rather, he was adorning himself as Muṣṭafā's father.

"He made a request from Me: *'Make for me a tongue of truthfulness among the later folk'* [26:84]. And concerning Muṣṭafā I said at the beginning, without his request, *'Did We not raise up thy mention for thee?'* [94:4]."

Although a ram was sent as a sacrifice for the exalted Ishmael so that he was released from being killed, tomorrow a sacrifice will be sent for every one of the riffraff in Muḥammad's community: *"The unbeliever will be brought, and it will be said to the person of faith, 'This is your sacrifice from the Fire.' "*[599] It is not strange that a sheep should have been sent as a sacrifice for Ishmael, the child of the Bosom Friend, so that he would be released from being killed without deserving to be killed. What is strange is that He should send one of His own servants as a sacrifice for a grimy tavern-goer from Muḥammad's community in order to release him from hell, though he is deserving of hell.

Although the knife had no effect on Ishmael's outwardness, poison did not work on Muḥammad's inwardness. Then, when the work reached its end and the journey to the next world came forth, the poison was put to work so that, just as he is the Chieftain of the Prophets, so also he is the Chieftain of the Martyrs. Muḥammad reported about this secret: *"What I ate at Khaybar keeps coming back to me, and this time it will sever my aorta."*[600] This is so the eminence of the station of his martyrdom may be known.

Although Joseph had a beauty in which the world was bewildered and although the women of Egypt cut their hands in contemplating its perfection, this in itself is not surprising. "O Muḥammad, if Joseph showed his face so that the women of Egypt—deficient in intellect and lacking in capacity—cut their hands in contemplating his beauty, you move your index finger so that by your finger's pointing, the moon, to which all the world's beauty is compared, may be split in two."[601]

Muṣṭafā was asked, *"Are you more beautiful, or was Joseph?"*

He said, "He was more comely, but I am more lovely."[602] Even though that comeliness became the cause of cutting fingers, this loveliness became the cause of cutting the sashes of unbelief.

"O David, you have a tremendous standing and a high degree. You were raised up and it was said, *'O David, surely We made thee a vicegerent in the earth'* [38:26]. You are My vicegerent.

"O Muḥammad, give Me a bit of news about your standing and rank!"

The Companions said, *'Will you not appoint a vicegerent over us?'*

"He said, *'God is my vicegerent over you.'* "[603]

I'm sultan of the world—You're my sultan.

*

Stand up, slave, pour the wine,
bring the cup for all the friends.
God knows I love
clinging to you and embracing you.
I call you slave in public,
but I'm your slave in private.[604]

*

Is it not strange that someone like me is humble
before someone like you, though possessions are humble to me?
You disobey me, but you own my obedience.
The possessions of this age are mine though I obey you.

I am proud before kings and the exalted,
but before you fearful and humble.
If not for love, no leader would have led me to you,
but love does what it wants to the free.[605]

Although Solomon said, *"Give me a kingdom"* [38:35], Muḥammad said, *"Let me live in indigence, let me die in indigence, and muster me in the ranks of the indigent!"*[606] What would I do with an empire in which Ṣakhr the jinni could sit in my place? What I want is the empire about which the trustworthy Gabriel will say, *"Were I to take another step, I would be incinerated."*[607]

"Although the wind was subjected to Solomon and the report was given, *'its morning course a month and its evening course a month'* [34:12], I was given a rulership such that in one instant I reached from Mecca *two-bows' length away.*"

Why is it surprising that a devil or a wind be subjected to a prophet? What is surprising is that a rag-wearer, bewildered and confounded, driven from every door and scorned by every eye, should be handed the reins of the unseen decrees, and that Muṣṭafā should report about the majesty of his state like this: *"There is many a disheveled, grimy, possessor of two rags paid no regard by anyone who, were he to swear an oath to God, would see it answered."*[608]

"O Solomon, the wind and the devil are under your command! O rag-wearer of Muḥammad's community, Our pure Unseen is gazing on your instructions!"

Although Moses was given the station of whispered prayer and taken to Mount Sinai, when he was sent back a light was sitting on his face such that no one had the capacity to contemplate his visage without a mask. But when Muḥammad was sent back, there was no trace on his face. This is because he was the beloved, and Moses was the lover. *"When He loves you, He conceals you, but when you love Him, He makes you well known and calls out about you."*[609] Objects of love are preserved behind the curtain, but lovers are announced in the city.

Although Moses came back from the carpet of awe, as has come in his story—*"His Lord disclosed Himself to the mountain"* [7:143]—Muṣṭafā came from the carpet of mercy.

Although Moses had the station of whispered prayer, was taken to Mount Sinai, and was spoken to without intermediary, tomorrow this station will be given to each of Muḥammad's serving boys: *"There is none of you to whom your Lord will not speak face to face, without any spokesman between Him and you."*[610] And there is something even higher than this: Five times in one day and night *"the praying person is whispering with his Lord."*[611]

"Although the ropes and falsities of Pharaoh's magicians came to nothing through Moses's staff, tomorrow on the Day of Resurrection a hundred thousand registers of offense and sin belonging to the disobedient of your community will come to nothing with one word of your intercession."

The address came to Moses, "Take off your shoes and throw down your staff." But Muḥammad was taken to *two-bows' length away* and was not told to take off a thread, for he was disengaged from all others.

When Muṣṭafā reached that exalted station, he did not say, *"Show me, that I may gaze upon Thee"* [7:143]. Rather, it was said to him, *"Hast thou not seen thy Lord?"* [25:45]. For he had seen Moses killed in the road and the spilled blood of one hundred twenty-some thousand center-points of sinlessness.

O dervish, whenever you take away someone's desire, you kill him. That paragon spoke not a word. Everything was put into his embrace without his having asked. *"When remembrance of Me busies someone from asking of Me, I bestow upon him the most excellent of what I bestow on the askers."*[612]

Concerning Moses He says, *"We called to him from the right side of the mountain"* [19:52]. Anyone may hear a call. When there was talk of Muṣṭafā, He reported like this: *"He revealed to His servant what He revealed"* [53:10]. "We said what We said." *This belongs to that of which "no proximate angel, nor any sent prophet"*[613] *becomes aware.*

Although Jesus was taken to heaven and Muṣṭafā was put into the earth, this is not because of any defect he had. Rather, his era was at the end of time, and the famine years of the Muslims were coming. It was said, "[*Whatever you harvest,*] *leave in its ear*" [12:47]. "Muḥammad is the seed and the community is the ear. Leave the seed in the ear, for the famine years of the end of time are before you. The same thing was done in the era of Joseph."

O chevalier, when night comes and the tar-colored veil is thrown over the head of the bride of night, making the world into an ocean of tar and pitch, the stars begin to circumambulate the green depths like limpid pearls. Venus says, "Who has the gall to vie with me in light?" Jupiter says, "Who can take the ring of good fortune from my hand?" Mercury says, "Who can battle with me in the field of light?" The full moon says, "Who can intrude upon me at the forefront?" Wait until the emperor of the planets lifts up its head from the purple dome and puts on the crown of light. Then it will pass beyond the stars' good fortune and force and put all of folly's baggage on the dromedary of decline.

In the same way all the messengers in their own eras were like shining full moons and sparkling stars in the heaven of lordly gentleness, their tongues scattering pearls on the pulpit of the lordly *tawḥīd*. When the auspicious sun of the prophethood of God's messenger Muḥammad rose from the constellation of eminence, they all packed their bags. It was said to the paragon, "Your Shariah has no abrogation, your covenant has no abolition, and your community has no deformation." Is there any eminence beyond the Exalted Lord's words, *"Say: 'If you love God, follow me; God will love you'"* [3:31]? Look at the degree of following Muṣṭafā! The fruit of his friendship is the Real's friendship.

The Bosom Friend with all of his greatness said, *"Then whosoever follows me is of me"* [14:36]. Anyone who goes in my tracks is mine. But the Lord said to Muṣṭafā, "Anyone who goes in Muḥammad's tracks is My friend." The one who went in the tracks of the Bosom Friend became the friend of the Bosom Friend, and the one who went in the tracks of the Prophet became the friend of the majestic Lord.

God says, *"God took Abraham as a bosom friend"* [4:125]. The whole world was in wonder: Is a mortal man indeed given such a robe of honor? When the auspicious carpet of Muḥammad's prophethood was spread—*at the time morning's falcon spread its wings until it folded them on sunset's horizon*—another work, beyond that work, was made apparent: "O Muḥammad, *say: 'If you love God, follow me; God will love you.'* The dust of your pure feet is the elixir of My love."

It was said to Jaʿfar Ṣādiq, "The Lord called Abraham His 'bosom friend' and He called our Messenger His 'beloved.' He spoke plainly about the Bosom Friend in the Quran, but he did not speak of the Beloved. What is the wisdom in this?"

Ja'far said, "Yes, that is so. But the Exalted Lord exposed a secret through which Muḥammad's degree is known. He caressed Abraham with His bosom friendship, but He caressed the serving boys, burnt ones, and servitors with His love. When He bestows the robe of love on the emulator, what indeed is the robe bestowed on the emulated?" [614]

O chevalier, the *mi'rāj* is the *mi'rāj* that belongs to his name. Where does the *mi'rāj* of the body appear in the *mi'rāj* of the name? "[*Did We not*] *raise up thy mention for thee?* [94:4]. '*I will not be mentioned unless you are mentioned along with Me.*'[615] Nowhere in the world will My name be mentioned unless your name and My name are on the same thread. I have paired your name with the formula of *tawḥīd*. I have adorned the celestial orb and the terrestrial center with your stepping forth."

That paragon was a sun whose East was Mecca, whose West was Medina, and whose eclipse was in the cave. But this was an eclipse within which a hundred thousand gentle deposits were unveiled.

There was a world taken over by the darkness of wrongdoing. The waves of misguidance were clashing in the seas of ignorance. The dark pavilions of refusal had encompassed the surrounding world. One of them had raised up an arch as an emperor in order to be even more of a lord. Another was whispering in prayer to Hubal[616] in order to become even more thrown down. All at once the wind of good fortune and the breeze of bounteousness began to blow from the land of Hijaz. The winds of delight sprang up, the lights of the secrets came forth from the sleeves of perfection, a corner of the curtain of the unseen gentleness was lifted, and this call was given out: "*There have come to you from God a light and a clarifying book*" [5:15]. The canopy of that paragon's messengerhood was stretched from East to West and the carpet of his prophethood was spread from Jabulqa to Jabulsa.[617] The banners of the darkness of unbelief were thrown down, the enemies of the religion were made lowly, and the seat of the headman of his secret core was made higher than the Throne. The long and the short of it is that first of all was his aspiration, in the middle was his honor, and last was the burning [in the breasts] of his community.

It was because of his perfect eminence that the Exalted Lord mentioned his bodily parts in the firm text of His Book. He mentioned his face, in which the cheeks of beauty were joined in perfect proportion: "*We have seen thy face turning about in heaven* [2:144]: O Muḥammad, for the sake of your approval We have turned the kiblah away from Jerusalem." He mentioned his eyes, which were the wellspring of life and the narcissus of the garden of approval: "*The eyesight did not swerve, nor did it trespass*" [53:17]. He mentioned his ear, which was the oyster for the pearls of wisdom's secrets: "*Say: 'An ear of good for you'*" [9:61]. He mentioned his heart, which was the scented garden of gentleness: "*His heart did not lie about what it saw* [53:11]. *Brought down upon thy heart by the Faithful Spirit that thou mayest be one of the warners*" [26:193–94]. He mentioned his breast, which was the quarry of brilliance and the source of laudation: "*Did We not expand thy breast for thee?*" [94:1]. He mentioned his tongue, which was a lake full of the blessing of *tawḥīd*: "*For We have made it easy on thy tongue*" [19:97]. He mentioned his hand, which was suited for the seat of sublimities and the bench of meanings: "*Make not thy hand* [*be shackled to thy neck*]" [17:29]. He mentioned his feet, whose two shoes were the crown of the north star: "Ṭāhā. *We did not send down the Quran upon thee for thee to be wretched*" [20:1–2].[618] He mentioned his back, which is the support of all the friends: "*Did We not lift from thee thy burden that weighed down upon thy back?*"

[94:2–3]. He mentioned his character, which was the reservoir of sweet water and the waterhole of pleasing drink: *"Surely thou hast a tremendous character"* [68:4]. He mentioned his life, which is the cause of the flourishing of the lovers' hearts: *"By thy life!"* [15:72].

Ibn ʿAbbās said, *"Surely God bestowed upon Muḥammad the character of Adam, the recognition of Seth, the courage of Noah, the loyalty of Abraham, the approval of Isaac, the strength of Jacob, the beauty of Joseph, the intensity of Moses, the patience of Job, the obedience of Jonah, the voice of David, the eloquence of Ṣāliḥ, the renunciation of John, the sinlessness of Jesus, the dignity of Elias, the struggle of Joshua, and the love of Daniel."*

The most majestic imam, the crown of the submission, the helper of the religion, Abū Bakr Muḥammad ibn Manṣūr ibn Muḥammad ibn ʿAbd al-Jabbār Samʿānī[619] *narrated to us that Abu'l-Qāsim Ismāʿīl ibn Muḥammad ibn Aḥmad*[620] *narrated to him that Abu'l-Fayḍ Aḥmad ibn Muḥammad ibn Isḥāq narrated to him that ʿAlī ibn Ḥajar narrated to him that ʿAlāʾ ibn ʿAbd al-Raḥmān narrated to him from his father, from Abū Hurayra, who said: "God's Messenger said, 'I was given excellence over the prophets with six things: I was given the all-comprehensive words, I was aided by terror, the beasts were made lawful to me, the earth was made a place of prostration and purity for me, I was sent to all people, and the prophets were sealed with me.'"*[621] If the earth carries the burden of my feet, its robe of honor is not less than that its dark dust should be given the rank of pure water.

O dervish, the greatness of a missive lies in its seal. At first Muṣṭafā did not have a seal ring on his hand. He wanted to write a letter to Persia. It was said to him, "When a letter does not have a seal, it will not be read." He commanded that a ring be made on whose seal was written *"Muḥammad God's messenger."*

The edict of prophethood was written for one hundred twenty-some thousand center-points of sinlessness. When the work reached the signet, it was said, "This needs a seal." The name of Muḥammad was made the seal on the edict of the prophets' prophethood.

Another secret: He is called the "seal" because, when kings first look at a letter, they look at the seal. When they finish at last, they finish with the seal. "When We first gazed with mercy, We gazed at you. When We sent at last, We sent you. Thus in both states the prophets will be bound to you, but you will not be bound to anyone."

O chevalier, our paragon is greater than all paragons, and we are more excellent than all communities: *"You are the best community"* [3:110]. In form Muḥammad's community rose up late, but in meaning they rose up early. On the morning of making manifest, Will was sticking up its head: "They have risen up." But the sun of Power's making manifest sat back, for they were tearing at the shirt of nonexistence. They were late-risers in the world of Power but early-risers in the world of the Will. They came afterward in service but went beforehand in the robe of honor.

The Arabs proudly lifted their heads and said, "Muḥammad came in our language."

O Muḥammad, give a report about the love of the Persians! *"Were the religion suspended from the Pleiades, it would be attained by men from Persia."*[622] In the era of Muṣṭafā, the land of the Persians was surging with unbelief and refusal. Muṣṭafā set up the royal seat of prophethood on the couch of chivalry. The love of the Persians was disclosing itself to the pain of the Arabs: Supposing that this religion were on the tip of the Pleiades, lovers would rise up from the dust of Persia to throw the noose of love on the Pleiades and pull the exalted religion to themselves.

The exalted Lord said, *"We sent no messenger save in the tongue of his people"* [14:4]. The Arabs are your people, but the Persians must also be your people, so say a few words in the tongue of Persia. Say to Ḥasan, *"Kakh kakh."*[623] In the hadith about Jābir: *"He has made for us a* sūr [feast]."[624] One day Abū Hurayra was wandering in the mosque. Muṣṭafā said, "O Abū Hurayra, what is it with you? Is it that *shikamat dard* [your stomach is in pain]?"[625] Thus, just as the Arabs are your people, so also the Persians are your people.

34. *al-Khabīr:* the Aware

He who knows the acts and words of the servants. The mark that the watchful servant has come to know that the Real's knowledge encompasses his states is that he assigns watchfulness to his own stillness and movement. He will not take one breath without the permission of the Shariah and the Tariqah. He will weigh his outwardness in the scales of the Shariah and pull his inwardness into the playing field of the Haqiqah. He will keep his root center-point pure of relying upon either of them, for, as they say, *"The felicitous person is he who has an outwardness conforming to the Shariah, an inwardness following the Haqiqah, and a secret core quit of relying on his Shariah and his Haqiqah."* Alas if he should rely on himself one iota! Then we would have sheer Magianism, utter Judaism, unmixed Guebrism, and pure unbelief.

O dervish, if you take everywhere from the highest of the high to *beneath the ground* [20:6] and make it into *the Inhabited House* [52:4], filling it with the obedience of the proximate angels, that would not be like letting go of one iota of what belongs to yourself. As long as you do not consider yourself farthest back in the whole world, you will not be worthy of this road.

"The spirits of this group were presented to the dogs of the garbage dumps, but no dog looked at them."[626] The poor dust mote bewildered in the air! It does not have the weight to come to the earth nor the measure to go higher.

> It's best not to speak of self—
> let's wash our hands of self and its work.
> Our nobodiness and worthlessness
> make our price that of water in a stream.
> We wouldn't fit into the world with our uproar
> if they'd let us smell the stopper of the vat.
> All of us indeed are nothing but faulty,
> so why should we search for others' faults?
> We don't discern the road from the well—
> why do we recklessly take the road of folly?
> Not yet struck by the mallet,
> we're dizzy like the ball in the field.

What a shame that a thousand thousand caravans of meanings and secrets have reached the wayfarers, but your share is not even the sound of a bell.

Who are we? *The smallest of the servants and the least significant among the folk of* tawḥīd: in spelling, the [unpronounced] *wāw* of ʿAmr; in writing, the [unpronounced] connecting *alif*; in grammar the uninflected; in lineage among *those who are unrecognized*; in Persian the dot under *p*;[627] in the vocative the cut-off final syllable; among the beasts *and their dog was extending its paws* [18:18]; among the flyers *scattered moths* [101:4]; among the people the ill fortunate of the spheres, *the miserable Abū So-and-So*. We are content with a little, grateful for a promise, and satiated in our craving with a morsel.

O chevalier, not everything in the ocean is a pearl and not everything in the night is a full moon; there are also crocodiles and lamps. *Not everything in the heaven is shining stars; there are also the stonings of satans. Not every soldier walks on the carpet; rather, some have only name or number, though all are servitors of the king.* Not everyone in the sultan's court is a boon companion; one in a thousand is a boon companion, and the others dwell in the trial of distance.

It was said to Abu'l-Qāsim Naṣrābādī, "Do you have anything of what the past shaykhs had?"

The shaykh said, "I have the pain of not finding it." [628]

In short, you must have a heart in which there is either the pain and affliction of not finding or the happiness and exaltation of finding. Beware of being carefree for the blink of an eye, for *"Surely God hates the healthy and carefree."*[629]

If you say, "I'm working on it," look closely at what your work is. Are you being put to work by Satan, or are you busy with the work of the All-Merciful? Every day you go to the shop in the morning, and at night you come home. Look: don't the Jews and the Guebres do the same thing? You say your prayers so that God will bless the enjoyments you have. You make the hajj so that the people will call you "hajji." If you go to war, there also you go deluded. You are held back by the name and the trappings, while that which is the secret of the work is leaning back like a sultan on the cushion of exaltedness, unseen behind its curtain. It will never come to the hut of someone like this, nor will it ever give him access to itself. Yes, my spirit and world, this is talk of the Men, not the defiled. It is talk of the work of the fallen, not the self-made. It is talk of the yearners, not the circumambulators. It is talk of the heroes, not the idle.

A man must be like Jesus son of Mary, who never settled down anywhere but wandered around the world. When he was asked the reason for this, he said, "It may be that someone sincerely truthful has walked somewhere and I will put down my feet in that dust. Then the dust will intercede for me." If you collect the pain of all the sincerely truthful and the friends, it would not reach the pain of the regretful feet of pure Jesus. Such was his need in the road!

"Our treasuries are full of acts of obedience, so you must have abasement and poverty."[630] Need is the herb that shows its face from the meadow of the existence of Adam and the Adamites. The angels had boasts, for *we glorify Thy praise* [2:30], but dust had need, for *our Lord, we have wronged ourselves* [7:23].

David's son Solomon had land and sea under his command and prohibition, and he put the harness of subjection on the head of the wind. One day when his carpet was coming through the air, an ant was saying to an ant, *"Enter your dwelling places! Do not let Solomon and his soldiers trample you* [27:18]. Solomon's people must not step on you and beat you down underfoot."

Solomon heard a helpless voice and said to the wind, "Put down the carpet of my sultanate right here, for a needy voice has reached my ears." Then he said to the ant, "Why did you say these words? I was traveling in the air."

It said, "We are a community of humility. When my people saw such height and elevation, we were beaten down."

One of the exalted men of the Tariqah said that those ants were garbed in black with girded loins in self-effacement before His command. Solomon knew that the experienced, tiny ant was aware of the secret. He sat for forty days at the door of its nest saying, "All of you go about your work, for I have talk and work with this ant." Solomon was experienced and the ant was experienced, and the experienced must sit next to the experienced, speaking about the grief and happiness of this talk, for both know the worth of the work. As for us, we are a handful of the dead, and the work of the living does not come forth from the dead.

Some will be surprised at this. They will say, "Ants are neither called to account nor rebuked. They are not obligated or addressed by the Law. How can they have anything to do with this talk?"

But here we have the hoopoe of Solomon, and here we have the dog of the Companions of the Cave. These two scatter dust on the intellects of the meddlers. This is not a cup under the ruling power of the intellect, even if intellect drank the cup of honor at the beginning of the work: *"I have created no creature more honored by Me than you."*[631] Nonetheless there are some things to which intellect has no access. Thereby become evident sheer surrender and unmixed consignment, without the intervention of mortal nature.

It is said that one day David was performing his prayers and an ant was walking across his prayer carpet. He threw the ant aside. The ant began to speak to him: "O David, do you fancy that our pain and burning is less than that of others?"

I can say no more than this, for tiny intellects cannot bear it.

There was also that little rock that the Messenger picked up and held in his hand. When the rock saw that it had this robe of honor and elevation, it lifted the mask of silence from the face of the covenant and came forth in the tongue of gratitude. It said, *"Glory be to God!* I was under the veil of muteness, but I have begun to talk in the hand of the paragon." When it was put in the hand of Abū Bakr and ʿUmar, it kept talking like this, but when it was put in the hand of others, it became dumb in its own state, and the secret was concealed.

What a marvelous business! The era of Muṣṭafā was one in which the scent of the heart rose up from stones and clay. Now we have an era in which the scent of stones comes from hearts. *Then your hearts became hardened after that, so they were like stones or even harder* [2:74].

Heaven burns in this talk and earth is seeking this talk. Every day when the sun lifts its head from another constellation it says, "I went into that constellation and said my glorifications to God. Perhaps I will come into this new constellation and find a new robe of honor." The moon grows in hope of a robe of honor. Then it returns to tininess, a burnt seeker.

If you go into the fire temple of the Guebres, the fire will say to you with the tongue of its state, "In my burning I have no concern for these disrespectful people." And if you go into the idol temple of the idol-worshipers, you will find the same sort of thing. When the Messenger came into this world and made a first prostration of thanksgiving, there was a handful of stones in the Kaabah piled on one another, 360 idols. When Muḥammad removed the mask of exaltedness from his holy face, they all fell down in prostration.

> When you showed your beauty, love for idols became foolish.
> Let them go, for among these beauties, it's you and you alone.
> What is spirit next to your face other than a meddler?
> What is intellect next to your lips other than a fool?[632]

The only thing farther back than the Adamite is the Adamite. Heaven and earth, Throne and Footstool, angels and celestial spheres, from the highest of the high to *beneath the ground* [20:6]—whatever can be called a "thing"—all are seeking and searching, rushing and running. It is the Adamite that has the attribute of great wrongdoing and deep ignorance. He is weak, unjust, dust-low, thrown down, least in all the scales, counterfeit among all the hard cash. He sits with the disloyal, gets along with His enemies, and harasses His friends.

If someone asks you who you are, beware, do not talk of Islam! That is an empire adorned, a garden trimmed. Does anyone like us need to be struck by the evil eye?

But if you are a man of good fortune, say a word for our work, put the hand of tenderness on our heads, for the only ones more beggarly than we are we ourselves.

They give charity to the worthy, and we are the worthy. *"Good from us is a slip, and evil is our attribute."*[633] Our father Adam had the cap of election and the crown of chosenness, but he fell prisoner to a grain of wheat. What then is the state of us children who have been left in the church of this world? *"When the first of the jug is dregs, what do you think its last will be?"*[634]

And We made covenant with Adam before [20:115]. What was that covenant? That he not flee from grammar school. *But he forgot* [20:115]. He was still a child, so he was brought into the path of caresses. The path of children is one thing, the furnace of heroes something else. He was taken into paradise on the shoulders of the exalted of the empire. Paradise was made the cradle for his greatness and the pillow for his chieftainship, but he still did not have the capacity for the audience hall of severity.

But he forgot, and We found in him no resoluteness [20:115]. He did not have the resoluteness of the Possessors of Resoluteness. Whenever someone is pulled newly into this talk, he is a child of the road, even if he is a seventy-year-old man.

The one you call Iblis was named ʿAzāzīl. Because of having this name, he wore a garment of fancy, which was called "being led on step by step." He was not able to see Adam's exaltedness and came out with envy. *"The envier is a refuser, because he does not approve of the decree of the One."*[635]

> *If they envy me, I don't blame them.*
> *Learned men before me have also been envied.*
> *What I have and they have will remain for me and for them,*
> *even if most of us die in rage at what we find.*
> *I'm the one they find in their throats,*
> *not rising up from there, nor going down.*[636]

The folk of the empire were commanded to serve Adam, but Iblis did not bow his head. He was struck with a blow. What was that blow? *"Go forth from it; surely thou art an outcast"* [15:34]. When Adam saw that blow, the fear and terror of it sat in his heart.

In the same way, when the teacher disciplines a child in grammar school, the fear of that blow works on the hearts of others. The nobler someone is, the more he fears. It may even be that he cannot bear it and he flees from school or hides behind a wall. His kind father comes seeking him and sees him upset, tears dripping from his eyes. He puts him on his shoulders and takes him back to the school. All the way back he instructs him: "If the teacher asks you where you were, tell him your relatives took you someplace."

He said, *"Have you fled from Us, O Adam?"*[637] He fled because of that blow and wanted to hide, so He sent mercy to take him in its arms and instruct him with an excuse: *But he forgot, and We found in him no resoluteness* [20:115]. He said: "Adam was still a child. He did not have the resoluteness of the possessors of resoluteness."

Then he became an adult and tasted the flavor of this talk. When he found the flavor, he gained access to this talk. The call came, *"Go down!"* [2:36]. Now the two of you must go down to the house of transaction! Grapple and wrestle with each other.

Your father turned out to be stronger, for he had the robes of messengerhood, courage, vicegerency, and prophethood. He threw the accursed one down beneath himself. When Iblis fell down at his hands, he fled from him. Then he said, "I need something from you. I do not say that you should remember me in your supplications or intercede for me, for my work has gone beyond that. My need is for you to apply the balm of your curses on my wounded spirit. Then the embroidery of cursing will be renewed by your good fortune." His wish was to request the sincerely truthful to curse him, for they, because of their abhorrence of self, would not have concerned themselves with cursing him. Moreover, there would be times when he aimed at the Men so that they would talk about him so much that they would say, "that accursed one." He would make that day a festival and put on a new robe of honor.

In the era of Solomon, Iblis sent his children to do service, and in the era of the chieftain of the envoys, he himself came into service. He said, "The world of prophethood has use for a serving boy." The paragon seized him by the throat to destroy him, but then let him go saying, "We are mercy, not torment."

Iblis said, "Concerning you it was said, *'We sent thee only as a mercy to the worlds'* [21:107]. After all, I am one of the world's folk, so look with favor on me."

God said, "You are behind the curtain of reprieve.[638] When that day comes, I will command that a pulpit be set up for you on the courtyards of the resurrection, its legs made of wrath and its top of anger. Then you too can offer your excuse."

And Satan will say, once the affair is decided, [*God surely promised you a true promise, and I promised you, then I failed you . . .*] [14:22]. When someone is heedless and wants to step on the skirt of the religion, the accursed one says, "You do not recognize me. I am the one who taught the courteous acts of glorification to the folk of the first heaven, the courteous acts of reciting *tawḥīd* to the folk of the second heaven, and so also to the folk of the other heavens. The seat of my teaching was set up on the top of the green dome. I gambled away all that good fortune so that the ornament of curses would be placed on my forehead and the collar of wretchedness put on my neck. I was nominated for leading astray at the top of the street of Muṣṭafā's Shariah: *I shall surely lead them all astray, except Thy sincere servants among them* [15:39–40]. Either bring the crown of sincerity and go forth, or make do with my saddle-straps if you are not a man of the religion."

The accursed one does not move from his place for just anyone, for he has tremendous pride. Do you not see that his pride did not let him put his hand in the bowl along with Adam? To those with low aspiration he assigns the fervor of envy, rancor, and avarice. But when someone sincerely truthful appears in the empire, he moves from his place. If he cannot hamstring him, he appears as his serving boy. He says, "O you who are sincerely truthful, I need something from you. I do not say that you should remember me in your supplications or intercede for me, for my work has gone beyond all that. My need is for you to apply a balm of your curses on my wounded spirit so that the embroidery of the curses of your good fortune will watch over His curse."

Just as the prophets boast of their prophethood and sinlessness, the accursed one boasts of his collar of curses, which was placed on his neck without intermediary.

O dervish, Iblis had not yet shown opposition when the arrow of the curse was dipped in the poison of severity. Adam had not yet slipped when the robe of chosenness was sewn.

Jaʿfar Ṣādiq was asked which disobedient act brings the servant closer to the Real and which obedient act takes him farther away. He said, "Whenever the beginning of an obedient act is security and the end of it is self-admiration, it takes the servant farther from the Real. Whenever the beginning of a disobedient act is fear and the end of it is apology, it takes the servant closer to the Real."

Yaḥyā ibn Muʿādh said, "A sin through which I turn in poverty toward Him is more beloved than a deed through which I become bold toward Him."[639]

They have said, "If you encounter Him with the abasement of destitution, that is better than encountering Him with the boldness of sincerity." An obedient person who admires himself is disobedient, and a disobedient person who apologizes is obedient. *Apology, even if a little, is the price of sin, even if much.*

In my view the wergild of sin is apology.[640]

In his obedience Iblis admired himself and said, "I was obedient."

The call came, "I curse you."

When Adam slipped, he said, "Lord God, I did bad."

The call came, "I pardon you."

Thus it was shown to the world's folk that disobedience with apology is better than obedience with self-admiration.

It is said that one day Muʿādh ibn Jabal entered into the presence of the Muhammadan prophethood. He had made his eyebrows a row of pearls from weeping, a flood was running down the sides of the cheeks of his days, and he was tearing the clothes of self-restraint with the hand of misery. That chieftain of chieftains and source of felicities said, "O Muʿādh, what happened to you that you are weeping and roasting like this? Tell me what you have uncovered from the exalted curtains of the lordly predetermination such that the army of impatience has thrown your heart into such turmoil."

He said, "O forefront and full moon of prophethood and pearl in the crown of chivalry! I was coming in the road when I saw a young man, stripped to the waist, his face blossoming like a new rose. He was draining his liver's blood by way of his eyes and staining both cheeks with blood. His stature would have been like a cypress had his back not been bent by the burden of fear. His cheeks would have been like roses had his liver's blood not scattered drops on them. His two narcissus eyes were watery with blood and his moonlike face had a mask of gold plate."

The paragon said, "O Muʿādh, bring him to me so that I may hear the story of his grief. If the water of his eyes is from fear of sin, I will cure it with the good news of forgiveness. If the burning of his heart is from the fire of love, I will place on it the balm of remembering the Friend."

Muʿādh went and brought that heart-burned youth with his thousand moans and miseries to the Muhammadan presence. The paragon said, "O youth, what is the cause of your suffering?"

He said, "O chieftain, why should I not suffer and why should I not weep? The pure heaven of my *tawḥīd* has been darkened by the clouds of mortal nature's caprice, and the eye of my intellect has been dazzled by the smoke of disobedient acts. Adam the chosen was magnifying God in the first row of chosenness, but because of one slip he lamented so much that the angels of the Dominion felt mercy toward him. Because of one misstep David wept and wailed so much that the birds of the sky themselves began to weep.[641] The sinless John, pure-born and prophet-born, never having sinned or thought of sin, wept so many tears of fear that he wounded both cheeks by lamentation and weeping. If this is so, having committed such a crime I am more suited to melt my body with wailing and turn my eyes over to water."

"O youth, even if your sins fill the earth, you have hope of intercession from me."

He said, "O paragon, my sins more than fill the earth."

"O youth, even if your sin is great, in the end it has the stamp of limit. Throw the notebook of your disloyalties into the ocean of the Real's generosity, for the shore of the ocean of the Real's generosity cannot be attained by mortal understanding and its depths cannot be contemplated by any eye."

With the hand of shame the afflicted youth put a saffron mask on both cheeks and loosened his tongue concerning his deeds and words. He said, "O pearl of sinlessness and O figure of mercy! I am someone who for twenty years has been ambushing those who have chosen the road of the next world. When night stamps blackness on the horizons, when darkness raises its banners from the mountains, and when the sky's hand ties the edges of the pitch-black night to the spheres, my wrongdoing and transgression shatter the Real's prison. O Messenger of God, last night, when night had put a black hat on the sky and tainted the world with ambergris, a new, young bride came from the marriage bed to the grave. I heard that news and went to her grave from my own house of misfortune. I lifted the curtain from her face, pulled her to the edge of the grave, removed her shroud, and threw her on the impure ground. When I returned to my house, the face of that new bride's beauty hung in my heart. The courier of Satan's disquiet and the emissary of the soul's caprice came one after another.

My soul's caprice tied the lasso of appetite to my neck: 'Is that it? Come on, why this heedlessness!? *Have you not heard that "the night is more concealed for wailing"?*' The work reached the point that overmastery by this thought threw the garment of protection off my heart and turned my eyes away from the shame of being with that chaste woman. All this wailing and weeping is for this. As soon as the fire of the appetites went out and the fire of caprice died down, the hand of remorse scattered bewilderment on my head. My heart became the storehouse of sorrows, my eyes became clouds raining tears, and my tongue began singing lamentations like a nightingale."

The paragon said, "O ungodly youth, *how close you are to the Fire!*"

When the young man heard these words, he shut the eyes of hope for the world's folk and ceased his aspiration for the Real's mercy. He made the gazelles' grazing ground the garden of his intimacy and the wild asses' playground the resting place of his spirit. He passed his days and nights in those deserts of the times. The gazelles became familiar with him, the predators were at ease with him, and the wild animals gathered around him. Once he had apologized for his own deed with the blood of his heart for forty days and nights, he again found the road to the threshold of pardon. He said, "O Lord, why do I still have the army of grief in my eyes and carry the burden of tribulation with the strength of my heart? Now no dampness remains in my eyes and no strength in my heart. Either caress me with Your pardon or melt me in the crucible of trial so that perhaps, having been melted by the fire of this world, tomorrow I may be caressed by the bliss of paradise. *O God, though I have walked with my own feet into trial, how much I have ground the teeth of regret! O God, my act silences me but my poverty brings me to speech. Though I have been slow in putting on the garment of godwariness, the robe of hope and wishing is not in tatters.*"

He still had not finished with this whispered prayer when there came the sound of the wings of the courier of the Presence. The emissary of the empire came to the Prophet, conveyed the Presence's message, and brought this verse: *"And those who, when they do an indecency or wrong themselves, remember God and ask forgiveness for their sins—and who forgives sins but God?—and do not knowingly persist in the things they did* [3:135]. Those of Our servants who sin and who blacken their ledger with the smoke of disobedient acts—when they awaken and sigh once, I will forgive that sin because of that sigh. O Muḥammad, go to that poor man who has put his face on the ground, and place the crown of pardon on his head."

Muṣṭafā went to find that disloyal, misstepping youth. He saw that he had made the desert's dust the perfume of his cheeks and the collyrium of his eyes. The paragon said, "O youth, lift up your head from the dust."

He said, "O paragon, I have been disobedient, and it is better for the face of the disobedient to be placed in the dust."

"Youth, weep no more!"

He said, "I have sinned, and it is better that water always pour forth from the eyes of sinners."

"Youth, do not make your face yellow!"

"Yes, but a yellow face comes from a heart full of pain."

"Youth, do not fill your heart with pain!"

"Yes, in my heart is the wound of disobedience. As long as there is not the balm of forgiveness, it will not get better."

"Youth, my good news to you is that the register of your offense has been crossed out by the pen of effacement. The page of your apology has been stamped with the seal of acceptance. Your sin has been passed over and your punishment taken away." [642]

In this road, you must have truthful need, hot seeking, and unsettled pain. The first way-station in the road of seeking is need. The great ones of the religion have said that need is the Real's messenger to the servant. Once the kernel of need is planted in the servant's breast, his reins will be pulled to the Presence.

The passing days make the beginners on the road familiar with need. When they take painful steps on the road of need for a time, need turns into aspiration. Earlier they had been the owners of need, and now they are the possessors of aspiration. The pirs of the road agree that when love comes out from the Unseen Pavilion, it finds no home except in the chamber of the disciples' aspiration.

When they travel on the road of aspiration for a time and tramp on the path with footsteps of seriousness, aspiration turns into seeking. Just as the sperm drop becomes a blood clot, the blood clot becomes a lump of flesh, and the lump of flesh is then dressed in human nature, so also need turns into aspiration, aspiration becomes seeking, and seeking is pulled into the highway of the realities of *No god but God.* This drum of good fortune is beaten at the threshold of His sultanate: *"Whoever seeks Me shall find Me."* [643]

The call then goes out, "O everything high, O everything low, O paradise and hell, O Throne and Footstool! Get out of the way of My seekers, for they are My prey, and it is I whom they are seeking and aiming for. If they should tramp on you, nothing of you will remain."

Know that these levels and degrees I have mentioned are a *miʿrāj* in this road. No one takes a step in this road without having a *miʿrāj* in keeping with his desire. The prophets had both an outward *miʿrāj* and an inward *miʿrāj*, and God's friends have a *miʿrāj* inwardly.

Know that in reality Muṣṭafā's *miʿrāj* did not begin in Mecca or Medina. Rather, it began when at the outset of his work they called him "Muḥammad the trustworthy." From being Muḥammad the trustworthy, he was pulled to prophethood, and from prophethood he was pulled to messengerhood. Then he advanced in messengerhood until he reached poverty. Then he was made to advance further in poverty until he reached indigence.

Poverty, want, need, and indigence were the embroidery on the mystery of his prophethood. Had there been a belt in the beginningless and endless house of good fortune more exalted than the belt of poverty and indigence, it would have been sent to Muṣṭafā so that he could bind it on the waist of servanthood's covenant.

When the substance of God's messenger Muḥammad rose up and advanced on these steps, ladders, and degrees, one attraction took him on the path of following from before the gate of the Kaabah to the place of Abraham's prostration, which is the Aqṣā Mosque. From there he was taken with one pull to *two-bows' length away*. Then the Lord's jealousy let down the exalted curtain before the virgin secrets and gave nothing out to the people save this: *"Then He revealed to*

His servant what He revealed" [53:10]. All the fluent and eloquent speakers stayed empty of this story. Only that paragon of the empire knows the flavor of that wine.

> If others fault me because of wine, you should not—
> in my hand is the wine, in their hands the wind.

For seventy thousand years the folk of the heavens were waiting to see when this man would show his head from the hiding place of the secret. What gift would he bring to the Exalted Presence? When the night arrived about which the Splendorous Book says, *"Glory be to Him who took His servant by night!"* [17:1], the proximate angels and the cherubim of the Higher Plenum stuck out their heads from the gazing places of glorification and hallowing: How would that paragon stroll into the Majestic Presence? At his first step into the Threshold, he said, *"I do not number Thy laudations—Thou art as Thou hast lauded Thyself."*[644]

Inescapably those who step onto that paragon's road with the feet of following will have a *mi ʿrāj* in the measure of their own present moments. We said concerning their *mi ʿrāj* that they will reach aspiration by way of need and seeking by way of aspiration. Then, when the aspiring man steps into the world of seeking, he will be addressed like this: "You cannot find Him with your own seeking, but if you do not seek, you will be an associator. And if you say, 'I will seek in order to find,' then too you will be an associator."

In certitude and verification, if the policeman's top hat of beginningless seeking had not appeared from the specific chamber of generosity, everyone in the world would be blowing in the wind of his own fancy. Seeking comes from finding, not finding from seeking.

The master Abū ʿAlī Daqqāq said, *"In your view you have no escape from your daily provision, but in my view your daily provision has no escape from you."*

O dervish, know that in reality nothing is more obligatory for you than seeking. If you go to the shop, seek Him. If you go the mosque, seek Him. If you go to the tavern, seek Him.

> I'm in the tavern, my Friend's in the tavern—
> wine in hand I whisper in prayer.

Even if the angel of death comes to you, be careful not to stop seeking. Say to him, "You do your work, I'll do mine."

> On the day my spirit leaves my breast,
> Your name alone will be my notebook.
> If You have no head for me, O heart-taker,
> Your feet's dust will be my head's crown.

*

> I have bound the belt of loyalty to You and will not undo it.
> If You are cruel, I will come forth in apology.
> If You increase in disloyalty, I will increase in love.
> I indeed am worthy for the ache of Your separation.

*

Other than love for You, may all my loves be forgotten!
May Your pain be in my embrace in place of You!
As long as I have the spirit's pearl in the body's coffer,
may the ring of serving You be on my ear!

You must make a thousand thousand poisoned arrows into a silk scarf for your love's neck before you will be allowed to step into the world of seeking.

I remembered you as the spears passed between us,
their blades having drunk from our blood.
By God I do not know—and surely I am truthful—
if illness stripped me of your love, or sorcery.
If sorcery, then that is my excuse in love;
if some other malady, then the excuse is yours.[645]

Have you not heard this hadith of Muṣṭafā? He had a tooth stick in his mouth and saw Azrael coming with his belt tightened for work. He said, "O prophet of God, what do you command? Shall I go back, or shall I go forward in that for which I came?"

Muṣṭafā did not take the tooth stick out of his mouth and kept on cleaning his teeth. He said, "O Azrael, you do your work, I'll do mine."

Good man, if you are taken down to hell, take care not to stop seeking. Say, "O Mālik, here you have my head, sacrificed to the maces of your severity. Strike the mace of severity on my meddling head and let me dive into the ocean of seeking." Then—wherever the work may take you. And if you are set down in paradise, do not busy yourself with the houris and wide-eyed maidens. Smell the jasmine of seeking's covenant and run into seeking's street, lest you become one of the wasted.

Once a few disciples of Khayr Nassāj had gone to look at a Christian church. When they came back and went into the khanaqah, the shaykh said to them, "Where were you?"

They said, "Looking at the church."

He said, "What have you brought back from the road?"

They said, "What can be brought back from a church?"

He said, "Did you not seek God?"

They said, "O pir, we do not grasp your words."

The shaykh said, "Go back so that I may teach you how to go to a church."

They went back and went into the church with the shaykh. Those strangers had painted the form of Jesus and Mary on the wall and were worshiping them. The shaykh turned to the wall and shouted at the forms: *"Didst thou say to the people, 'Take me and my mother as two gods apart from God'?"* [5:116]. At once the forms fell down from the wall, and this call rose up from the wall's particles: *"No god but God, He alone; no associate has He."*

Because of that pir's awesomeness, belief, and seriousness, thirty of the strangers cut off their sashes and put on patched cloaks. He then turned to the disciples and said, "Do not stop seeking! When you come to a church, come like this."

O chevalier, what use is the assertion that you will seek if contriving to seek has disappeared? Talking with you will be like scattering a handful of millet on an anvil or pouring water in a sieve. What use is an assertion to which you do not assent?

Yaḥyā ibn Muʿādh Rāzī said, *"The affair has three states: abandoning blights, bringing forth obedient acts, and awaiting gifts and generous bestowals."* The reality of the road of Islam has three states: the abandonment of blights, obedience on the basis of sincerity, and waiting for the generous bestowals and gentle gifts of the Lord. It is not just anyone's work to throw his spirit into the battlefield in order to bring lawful plunder to hand.

It was said to Abū Yazīd, "Give a mark of the greatest blow that you struck against your soul in seeking the religion."

He said, *"It cannot be unveiled, for you will not be able to bear it. Should I tell you of the least blow that I struck?"*

They said, "Tell us."

He said, "I invited my soul to some of the obedient acts, but it did not answer, so I forbade it water for a year."[646] I said to myself, since you are lazy in serving the religion, water will be held back from you. Either give up life because of thirst, or give up the body to obedience.

And struggle in God as is the rightful due of His struggle. He chose you [22:78]. Subdue your caprice on the carpet of struggle, keep your heart together in the road of contemplation, cut off your meddling head with the sword of discipline, and slash the belly of your wishes with the blade of vengeance. In your view nothing is more precious than life. If you are ready for talk of God, first kick life in the head.

Be the man whose feet are on the ground
and whose head aspires to the Pleiades.
Pouring out the water of life
is less than pouring out the luster of face.[647]

*

How will color and words allow a piece of straw to reach this road?
It needs curtain-burning pain, a man striding forth.
It takes years for the sun to make a plain stone
into a Badakhshani ruby or a Yemeni carnelian.
With two kiblahs you cannot walk straight on the road of *tawḥīd*—
either the Friend's approval or your own caprice![648]

This road wants a man whose feet are with his heart, whose heart is with his thought, whose thought is with his secret core, whose secret core is with his spirit, and whose spirit is with the Unseen. It wants a body purified of the defect of envy, a soul whose breath conforms with the heart, a heart whose feet are in the stirrups of seeking, and a breast whose goodly clay gives forth the jasmine of *tawḥīd's* covenant. It wants a mind in command of the tumult-inciting makeup, a heart that has abandoned desires, and an inwardness that has settled down in the neighborhood of the Haqiqah. It wants a spirit in whose truthful earth grows the fragrant herb of repose while it contemplates spiritual affairs and luminous forms, having struck fire into the corporeal senses and mortal imaginings—just as has come in the prophetic intimation: *"Surely in the Garden are what no eye has seen, what no ear has heard, and what has never passed into the heart of any mortal."*[649] In the firm text of the Revelation has come this: *"No soul knows what delight of the eyes is hidden away for them as a recompense for what they were doing"* [32:17].

You must have a secret core confounded by the joy of contemplation, stunned in the midst of the attributes of firstness and lastness. If one iota of all the world should enter into your aspiration, you will not be traveling straight in His road. *By God, no one reaches the All save him who cuts himself off from all!*

The belief is that if on the night of the *miʿrāj* that chieftain of chieftains and source of felicities had looked back toward anything whatsoever for the blink of an eye, he would have been kept right there and would not have been conveyed to the dome of proximity of *two-bows' length away*.

A sultan commanded that a slave boy attending his session be given wine. First he told the cupbearer to give him a cup, but he did not take it. He commanded a boon companion, but he still did not take it. He commanded the vizier, but again he did not take it. The sultan himself got to his feet and held the cup before the slave boy. He did not take it. He was asked, "Why didn't you take it?"

He said, "It is because I did not take it that the sultan has stood before me."[650]

In this road there must be a headstrong aspiration, a burden-lifting soul.

A covenant was made with this world: *"O this world, serve anyone who serves Me; if anyone serves you, make him your servant."*[651] When someone busies himself with serving Me, bind the belt of servanthood to him. And when someone is your servitor, place the halter of subjection on his head.

ʿAbd al-Wāḥid ibn Zayd said to Abū ʿĀṣim Baṣrī, "What did you do when Ḥajjāj summoned you?"

He said, "I was sitting in my chamber. When Ḥajjāj's agents entered, the chamber moved and threw me on Mount Būqubays."

He said, "How did you stay there? Where did you find nourishment?"

He said, "Every evening an old woman came at the time of breaking the fast. She brought a loaf or two and gave it to me."

ʿAbd al-Wāḥid said, *"She was this world. God commanded her to serve Abū ʿĀṣim."*[652]

Sarī Saqaṭī was the great man of the world. He had a sister who used to serve him. One day she came into his house and saw that an old woman was sweeping the house. The sister became jealous and went to Aḥmad ibn Ḥanbal to complain. Aḥmad came to Sarī and told him the story. Sarī said, "I have no complaint about my sister, but the old woman she saw was this world. Sometimes she comes and takes the dust of my house to the dump."[653]

Have a high aspiration and place your foot on top of the existent things. Look at nothing, for if you look back at anything at all, you will fall. *Pay no regard, for if you pay regard, you will fall.*

Adam was the exalted of the world, pulled up and chosen. He was taken into paradise and adorned with all sorts of jewels and robes. The angels of the Dominion—whose nourishment was glorifying and hallowing—were commanded to prostrate themselves before the throne of his leadership. But when one grain seized his skirt, it was said, "Let go of the crown, hat, and shawl. Take that grain of wheat in your embrace and go about your business."

O dervish, you cannot attach your aspiration to two things!

As long as you're seeking Me, that is stepping forth,
but every breath without Me is a trap.
A heart in love with the Heart's Ease
also seeking life from the spirit is not yet cooked.[654]

*

O heart, O heart, O ill-starred!
You are my trial, so whom should I blame?
You desire this, you add that—
two will not stay in the heart.

*

When you're with yourself, don't put love's brand on the heart.
Become a moth, then you will know, you and the candle.[655]

Someone came to a pir and said, "Give me some advice."

He said, "Be solitary for the Solitary." Be one for the One.

Someone was sitting there. He said, "O pir, you have driven him away!"

He said, "I measure for all of you as was measured for me."

A villager bought dates. He was eating them along with the pits and suffering because of that. It was said to him, "Throw away the pits."

He said, "This is the way they were weighed against me." They weighed them like this, and I paid the silver.

"Poverty is like the staff of Moses." When the serpent of poverty opens the mouth of aspiration, it swallows down the two worlds with no effect whatsoever. What is the secret of poverty? Being one for the One.

It is said that once a man made a marriage contract with a woman. On the day they were transporting her paraphernalia, he saw a kitten, all adorned. He asked, "What is this?"

They said, "The bride loves it."

He said, "Remove the goods. Take the cat back to her and say, 'You stay right there and love the cat.' "[656]

If you want Me, wash your hands of yourself.
First leave yourself, then seek Me.

If someone aims for the green sea, he should not put down his bags at a tiny rivulet. If someone wants to make a crown from the beginningless gentleness and a throne from the endless bounty, he should not put the reins of his camel into the hands of the two worlds.

Those at the forefront, dwelling in the pavilions of the eye's observations and the stations of the generous bestowals of *two-bows' length away*, are sometimes in the robe of struggle, sometimes in the shirt of contemplation; sometimes in intoxication and gratitude, sometimes in sobriety and effacement. They both are and are not; they are both sober and drunk. Sometimes their hearts are incinerated by the fire of jealousy, sometimes their spirits are drowned in the ocean of bewilderment. They are runners standing still, silent speakers. *Surely they were chevaliers* [18:13] is the embroidery of their garment of splendor. *Thou wouldst have thought them awake, but they were asleep* [18:18] is the title page of the book of their covenant. *And you are the poor* [47:38] is the sigil of their edict. *Desiring His face* [18:28] is the height of their aspiration. *And let not thine eyes turn away from them* [18:28] is the perfection of their greatness. And *"I am hidden in the heart of the person of faith"* alludes to the secret of their proximity.

So they dwell in the perfection of bestowal and the felicity of auspiciousness. Wearing the robes of union and crowned with the crown of proximity, they recline on the couches of repose, smell the sweet herbs of intimacy, strut in the beauty of nearness, and drink from the cup of love.[657]

When I drank one draft of love
I became so drunk that I threw off my veil.
How much I struggled, and then His face appeared,
and with His face I let go of all restraint.[658]

*

A thousand deeds were done in their essences
by the painters of the beginningless workshop.
All became nonbeing before the exalted Being,
holding high the banner of unneediness.
Having drunk a draft to the face of the cupbearer,
they put aside all that becomes annihilated.
They are servants but like shadows of the phoenix;
they are alive but like solid rock.
"We have not worshiped Thee" is their exertion,
"We have not recognized Thee" is their belief.[659]

What a marvelous business! You were reared for these states and stations. The edict of your heart's light was adorned with the exalted sigil of *What of him whose breast God has expanded?* [39:22]. But you put aside this lofty standing and pulled the head of your aspiration down to this house of beggars. If you want to busy yourself with someone, then busy yourself with someone beautiful so that it will be worth the blame. *Love for the ugly is abandonment, and love for the comely is trial.* Anyone entranced by someone beautiful will be afflicted, and anyone entranced by someone ugly will be abandoned.

O dervish, the stipulation for all the world's passionate lovers is to learn truthfulness in love from the breath of Adam. He threw away the eight paradises and made a patched cloak from leaves. *And Adam disobeyed* [20:121] is the stone on the seal ring of love. *He forgot, and We found in him no resoluteness* [20:115] is the embroidery on the cape of gambling away all.

One precondition for the imamate is bravery. The imam must be bold. When Adam was created, he was created for the sultanate, and a sultan cannot be fainthearted. He said, "I accept the brand of great wrongdoing and I will suffer the severity of deep ignorance, but I will not throw Your command to the ground."

O dervish, there is your life and there is the goal. It wants a man to say, "Either I'll die or I'll reach the goal."

This is talk of the night-brightening pearl. The pearl's exaltedness is the fact that its doorman is the ocean's waves. It has a hundred thousand seekers who sacrifice their lives for it, going upside down to the ocean's depths.

Do not look at the beauty of the full moon. Look rather at its abasement because no one is looking for it. And do not look at the emaciation and weakness of the crescent moon. Look rather at its exaltedness because all eyes are seeking its beauty.

The exaltedness of the Adamites is that there are many among them seeking the Presence of the Lord of Lords. He brought the whole world from the concealment of nonexistence to the open space of existence, but He did not send a messenger or a message to anyone. As soon as the turn of this handful of fearless dust arrived, He sent courier after courier and message after message. The dust was a devotee in the monastery of secret whispering, full of need for the Unneedy. It wore the tattered cloak of disengagement and drank down the draft of solitariness because of the heart's yearning, writing *"The decree belongs to God"* [40:12] on the heart's necklace.

In awareness of *God does what He wills* [14:27]
    he put a ring on his ear like a slave.
In the midst of his mind he made
    an arrow from *Say "God" then leave them* [6:91].
Because of poverty and rapture he
    became *no* in the perfection of *but God.*[660]

From the hand of the cupbearer of approval he drank cup after limpid cup full of the wine of loyalty. A hundred thousand center-points of sinlessness, wearing the shirt of honor, were sent to him. God appointed the angels of the Throne to watch over his states, deeds, and words and to act as couriers. He commanded them to record everything of his—breath by breath, moment by moment, movement by movement, instant by instant. He placed burning in breasts, He prepared awareness in hearts, He inserted incitements to yearn and motivations to desire in inwardnesses and secret cores. He watered the gardens of the lovers' wishes with the clear water of good fortune and bounteousness. He rained down drops of generous gifts from the clouds of necessity on the meadows of the lovers' breasts. He brought the nightingales of gentleness into song on the flowers of bounty, the blossoms of secrets, the branches of beautiful-doing, and the leaves of the lovers' hearts.

He—*majestic is His majesty!*—had no secret with any created thing in the universe, for all of them were servants. But He did have secrets with the Adamites, for they are friends, and secrets are told to friends. Then He displayed all the secrets of the divinity from places around which none of the minds of creatures had wandered.

For several thousand years the holy ones of heaven had been smelling the jasmine of glorification and the sweet briar of hallowing, flying in the air of obedience with the wings of ability. They had set up the tent of *me and no one else* and put on the robe of sinlessness at the hand of the sultan of the beginningless decree. All of a sudden the tongue of generosity read out the edict of Adam's kingship over all the world. This pure call was given out from the world of the Unseen Purity: *"I am setting in the earth a vicegerent* [2:30]. I am creating in the expanse of the earth someone trustworthy with whom to adorn the forefront of magnificence."

When this declaration reached the ears of that gathering, which had lit up the candle of sinlessness on the bench of limpidness, they shouted out, *"What, wilt Thou set therein one who will work corruption there?"* [2:30]. This was not by way of protest against predetermination, but rather by way of seeking to understand.

The Lord of Lords said, *"Surely I know what you do not know"* [2:30]. You who are gazers at the highest gazing place, keep on gazing, for I know the secrets of divinity. Has it ever been the case that tiny minds, partial sciences and intellects, defective and newly arrived understandings and insights have had access to the secrets of My divinity?

As soon as this awesome declaration fell on their assemblies and gatherings, they daubed their eyes with the collyrium of anticipating Adam's arrival. The lordly power made the sultanlike Adam appear from a speck of dust. He brought that marvel of the empire from the pavilion of the Will to the vast plain of manifestation, the crown of majesty on his head, the robe of beauty on his body. He daubed the aspiring eyes of all the intelligent with the collyrium of jealousy lest they perceive Adam's perfect good fortune. They all showed their skill on the horses of perspicacity, but that hidden pearl was concealed from the insights of the world's folk in *molded mud* [15:26]. No mind's falcon sat on the branch of his good fortune's tree and no seer's eyes saw his beautiful countenance. Then that paragon was put on the throne of exaltation and magnification, and the proximate ones of the empire were commanded, "Bind the belt of serving him and do not shut the door on the fortunate, lest harm come to the wherewithal of the spirit."

Then it was called out that one of the secrets of *surely I know what you do not know* will be made evident. They all said, "O King, O All-Compelling, what is it?"

The address came, *"Prostrate yourselves before Adam!"* [2:34]. *They imagined that they were superior because of their glorifying and hallowing, so He made them recognize that the carpet of exaltedness is hallowed beyond being beautified by the obedience of someone obedient or being sullied by the slip of an obstinate refuser. He turned them over to prostration before Adam to manifest His unneediness toward any conformity or opposition. Majestic is His measure beyond His creation's declaration of His majesty and exalted is He beyond mortal man's exaltation of His remembrance!*[661]

The Real clarified that He is hallowed by His own majesty, not by their acts. The threshold of eternity has no need for the *scant merchandise* [12:88] of the obeyers' obedience: *If you do the beautiful, you will have done the beautiful for your own souls, and if you do the ugly, it will be against them* [17:7].

Then the call came, "O shaper of shapes, O source of exaltedness and good fortune, O canon of guidance, O quarry of solicitude, O ointment of the eyes of the elevated, O elixir of noble traits and meanings, O foundation of the sacred, O leaven of good fortune, O nest of the falcon of love's secret, come into the playing field of love and see a hundred thousand secrets!"

Rise—let us make our spirits and hearts the path.
The caravan has gone; we too should depart.
Let us go out to the desert of love,
making our feet from Gabriel's wings.
Let us make a torch with the fire of love
and a banner with the hope of union.

That paragon was at rest in the world of comfort and ease. Like a king he was leaning back on the chair of exaltation and nobility, and like a prince he wandered wherever he wished and desired in the orchards of the Highest Paradise. All at once the exactor of passion's debt, love's deputy, was unexpectedly pounding the knocker on the door of his heart: "Get up! Go like a lover into the field of severity, the realm of not reaching your desires! Then the beauty of what you seek will be unveiled to your heart. O Adam, you who are standing still in good fortune, move into the world of passion and love!"

Take the business of the two worlds to the session of the rascals
and disturb and disperse it like forelocks on the faces of the lovely.
In the session of the veiled and the row of the deprived,
drain the cup like Rostam and strike the sword like Rostam.
If you give me wine, give it to me on top of Saturn.
If you play the flute, play it for me in the depths of hell.
Daub the collyrium of *show me, that I may gaze upon Thee* [7:143] on Moses's eyes,
draw the mole of *Adam disobeyed* [20:121] on Adam's cheek![662]

Adam's manliness took him by the skirt and sought its rightful due from him. Severity's army plundered his crown and pulled off his robe. Riḍwān came and said, "Adam, step out of paradise, for this is the house of ease, and there is no ease in the street and quarter of lovers—only trial upon trial. Settle down in the house of tribulation inside the circle of love. Then the sultan of love will take everything that is justly due from you."

At that point the Exalted Lord offered the Trust to heaven and earth. The goal was not that heaven and earth should accept it, but rather that the offer should shake the chain of Adam's love and make him stand up in the station of jealousy.

The exaltedness of Adam's acceptance became manifest because of their refusal and unwillingness, and his courage appeared in their cowardice. If no one in the world was timid and fainthearted, how would the courage of the courageous appear? In the days of security, everyone wears a weapon. The manly man is he who appears on the day of war. How is it that just the other day the angels were saying, "*We glorify Thy praise*" [2:30], and today they put on the belt of apprehension?

O chevalier, the strength of a sword and its blow lies not in the sword's sharpness but in the arm. The sword of ʿAmr Maʿdī Karib was famous among the Arabs. One day someone came and wanted to borrow his sword, so he lent it. The man was not able to use the sword like ʿAmr. He said, " ʿAmr, your sword does not work."

He said, "I lent you my sword, not my arm."

First He offered the Trust to heaven and earth so that they would refuse and Adam's love would appear. Things are offered first to the unworthy so that the worthy will get moving. Adam started to move because of his love.

The address was coming, *"Surely he was a great wrongdoer, deeply ignorant"* [33:72]. What is this? Adam's incense against the evil eye.

At the first waystation the caravan was attacked and his wherewithal taken as plunder. He was sent indigent into this world and shown that if he wanted to reach someplace, he could not do so with his own wherewithal. Once a servant's wherewithal is thrown to the wind, if his lord wants to send him for another transaction, he has to give him new wherewithal.

Know in verified truth that love's foundation came to be firmly established by carrying the burden of the Trust. To carry the Lord's Trust, a man must step outside the malady of mortal nature: *And man carried it* [33:72]. When Adam carried the Trust, the work's foundation was established, for once there is carrying, the foundation is firm.

When a man buys a slave girl from the bazaar, he can sell her whenever he wants. But once he has taken her in companionship and the carrying [of his child] appears, they say, "You are not permitted to sell her, for she has your trust."

On the day Adam carried the Trust, he firmed up the foundation of love. Even if he now brings into existence a hundred thousand betrayals, sins, and acts of disobedience, the foundation will not be destroyed.

In the firm text of the revelation the Exalted Lord says, *"Surely We created man of dried clay"* [15:26]. The ascription is to dust, but the attribute is proximity. When a fire dies down, nothing is left but ashes, which are not good for anything. If clay breaks, it can be fixed with a few drops of water.

Such was the enemy Iblis. When the lamp of obedience shining on him was extinguished, he became useless and could not be repaired. But, when Adam stumbled, he was repaired with the water of solicitude: "Then His Lord chose him" [20:122].

"On the first day, We had a gentleness and a gaze for you. We honored you with that gentleness and gaze. If a slip occurs from you, no one will have the gall to begin talking. *Who is there to intercede with Him save by His leave?* [2:255]. When the sultan of the world rebukes his favorite boon companion in an intimate session, who can say anything to either of them?"

It is the first gaze that must come to intercede and scour away the dust of deeds from the mirror of days with the polish of gentleness. He will call us to the Presence and take us to task, mote by mote, so the knowledge of certainty may become the eye of certainty, for He knows what happened to us. Then He will let that exalted gaze—which He presented to us at first and through which He honored us—intercede. In reality, the only interceder for the sin of the beloveds is their beauty.

When He lets Muḥammad and the other exalted ones intercede, that will be to honor them, but nothing new will happen to you because of their words. He will bring forth the eternal gaze He had for us, pure of any causes, and make it the interceder for offenses and sins. Then He will say, "I brought you into existence with this pure gaze, and there was no cause whatsoever. I forgive you with My own pure gaze, and there is no cause whatsoever." *Peace!*

35. *al-Ḥalīm:* the Forbearing

Forbearance means delay when someone deserves punishment.[663] The Real is forbearing in the sense that His knowledge encompasses the disobedience of the disobedient, but His forbearance delays punishing them. *"No one hurries to punish unless he fears escape."*[664] Someone hurries to punish when he fears that a life will slip from his hand, but the Real is incomparable with any such fear.

It is said that there was a wronged man in the prison of one of the caliphs, having remained there for many years. One night the caliph leaped up from sleep in fright and terror. He commanded that they go to the prison and bring the imprisoned man to him. They went and brought him. He sat him down in front of himself and said, "I saw Muṣṭafā in a dream, and he said to me, 'So-and-so is in your prison. Help him, for he has been wronged.' Tell me truthfully, what was the supplication you used that brought such a quick response?"

The man said, "It is many years that I have been in your prison wrongfully. I had no more patience. In my distress I said to the All-Compelling King, *'O God, surely You are forbearing, but I do not have the patience for Your forbearance.'* O Lord, Your forbearance has no limit, but I no longer have any patience with Your forbearance."

He gave an accursed man kingship for four hundred years without headache. At last He sent Moses and Aaron to the door of his house. He said, *"Speak to him with soft words"* [20:44].

One of the exalted ones of the Tariqah—indeed, it was Mālik Dīnār—said that in his neighborhood there was a young man who was shameless, irresponsible, depraved, and ungodly. Night and day he was busy embarking on indecencies. The neighbors were stuck with his trouble and corruption, and he was stuck in his own trouble and corruption. "One day they came to me, letting loose the tongue of injury and complaint. I sent someone to the youth telling him to come. When he came, I said to him, 'All the neighbors are complaining about you. You must leave the neighborhood.'

"He said, 'The house is my house. I will not leave it.'

"I said, 'Put the house up for sale.'

"He said, 'I will not sell my own property.'

"I said, 'I will complain to the sultan about you.'

"He said, 'The sultan will take care of my side better than yours.'

"I said, 'I will supplicate bad for you.'

"He said, 'God is more merciful toward me than you are.'"

Mālik said, "These words left a trace in my heart and I became upset. That night when I was busy with my prayers and saying my litanies, I supplicated bad for that youth. Then a voice spoke to me, *'Do not supplicate against him, for surely the youth is one of God's friends.'* Beware, beware, do not go after that young man, for he is one of My friends."

"I got up and went to the door of that young man's room and knocked. He came to the door and saw me. He supposed that I had come to throw him out of the neighborhood. He began to speak by way of apology. I said, 'Young man, be aware that I did not come for the sake of what you suppose, but I dreamed such and such.'

"He began to weep. Then he said, 'Now that God's gentleness toward me is such, I repent and return to God at your hands.' The next day he left the city, and after that I did not see him. Then it happened that it came time for me to visit the House of God. When I came to the Sacred Mosque, I saw a circle of people, so I went to see what was there. I saw that youth, who had become wasted and emaciated, weak and frail, overcome by illness. Cries were coming, 'The youth has gone from this world.' "[665]

It is mentioned in the books that in the era of Ḥasan Baṣrī there was a youth who was idle night and day and was not troubled by anyone's blame. He had fallen passionately in love with his own wretchedness and was burning his harvest with his own hands. Then all at once a tremendous illness overcame him, and everyone gave up hope for him. When the pains and sufferings came constantly one after another, he said with an unsteady tongue and a broken and forlorn voice, *"O God, absolve my stumbles and lift me up from my fall, for surely I will not return."*

The Exalted Lord healed him from that illness, and he became worse than he was before. Again he was seized and assaulted and thrown on the bed of sickness and disease. He made the same supplication, and the Lord healed him. When he got up, his tumult and turmoil were even more than before. Once again he was banefully seized and severely assaulted. He made the same supplication, *so God lifted him up from his fall.* When he got up after the illness, he got up a thousand times worse than he had been before. As the decree would have it, one day he passed by Mālik [Dīnār], with whom were Ḥasan, Ayyūb Sakhtiyānī, and Ṣāliḥ Murrī. Ḥasan looked at him and saw his cunning, wickedness, and gaze upon himself. *He said, "Young man, fear God as if you see Him, for if you do not see Him, He sees you!"*

He said, "O Ḥasan, why are you striking cold iron with a hammer? You cannot keep a young man back from enjoying the pleasures of this world."

Ḥasan said, *"By God, it is as if death has descended into the courtyard of this youth to crush him totally."* Not much separates this deluded youth in the house of his delusion from death. Death will soon come and wreak havoc on his days. He said these words and became silent.

Several days later Ḥasan was sitting in his mosque and a young man entered. He said, "O physician of hearts, O friend of spirits, and O placer of balm on breasts! That young man whom you admonished and who did not listen is my brother. Right now he is in the agonies of death. Is there any way, O Ḥasan, that you can step into his hut with your beautiful character? Perhaps something may happen and felicity may come of it."

Ḥasan said, "O companions, get up so that we may gaze on His wonders, marvels, bounty, and severity and be on our guard against this treacherous world."

When Ḥasan reached the door of the youth's house, he knocked. There was a woman in the house, the mother of the two young men. She said, "Son, who are you?"

He said, "Ḥasan Baṣrī."

The old woman said, *"What is the like of you doing at the door of my house when my son has left no sin uncommitted and nothing sacred unviolated?"* O Ḥasan, what does someone like you have to do with my son's house? What do lovers have to do with the house of the ungodly? How can the wholesome be familiar with the corrupt?

He said, "Announce us to him, for surely our Lord accepts stumbles." Old woman, have a happy heart, for there is no way to despair of His mercy.

The mother went and told the ravaged youth that Ḥasan Baṣrī was at the door. The youth said, "Oh, I do not know if he has come to blame me or to visit me. Open the door and let him come in. Perhaps something will come of it."

Ḥasan came and saw that the youth was dying, remorse in his eyes, the agony of death mustering its army. Ḥasan said, "O youth, repent and return to God, for the door of acceptance is open. Supplicate so that God may respond."

The youth said, *"He surely will not."* O pir of the Muslims, I fear that He will not respond.

He said, "Are you describing God as niggardly, when He is the Generous, the Munificent?" With your own tiny capacity you want to turn the green sea of munificence into a rivulet.

The youth told his story from beginning to end. "I became ill four times, and I returned to God in the illness. Then, when I regained health, I broke my repentance and turned away from the Threshold. This time when I sought absolution and presented the story of my pain to the Threshold, *a caller called out from the corner of the house: 'I hear a sound, but I do not see the person. There is no "Here I am," no "at Thy service." We have tested you repeatedly and found you to be a liar. O youth, how long will you keep on lying?'* "

When Ḥasan heard this, he got up and turned to the door, leaving the youth with all his moaning, remorse, tears, and agonies. The youth turned his face to his mother and said, *"My chieftain is 'He who accepts repentance from His servants and pardons the ugly deeds'* [42:25]. Though my outwardness is defiled by disobedient acts, my inwardness is cleansed of associationism's impurity. When the spirit becomes separate from the body and the journey to the next world becomes reality, put this pillow under my head in a corner, place my cheek on the dust, and ask of your Lord for me. Perhaps He will forgive me because of you."

The old woman carried out the testament. She was still not finished with her whispered prayer when a voice called out, *"O woman, surely God has forgiven your child and pardoned his sins for your sake."* Whatever deed came into existence from your son I have taken care of for you.[666]

Yaḥyā ibn Muʿādh Rāzī said, *"Were it not that He much loves to pardon you, He would not have thrown you into so much sin."* Were it not that He loves pardoning so much, He would never scatter the dust of disobedient acts on His servants' skirts.

Let me point to a few of the words of Yaḥyā ibn Muʿādh Rāzī, for the realizers among the folk of *tawḥīd* must spread the wings of victory in hearing them. That exalted man said, *"Were it not that pardon is one of His attributes, the folk of recognition would not disobey Him."* If pardon were not His attribute, the folk of recognition would never go after disobedient acts.

He also said, *"He threw them into sin to make them recognize that they are in want of Him. Then He pardoned them to make them recognize His generosity toward them."*[667] He afflicted the obedient worshipers with slips in order to remove from them the veil of self-admiration and the peril of gazing on self. Then He pardoned the offenses so that they might know the unmixed gentleness, the signs of bounty, and the perfect generosity and munificence of the Presence. First He throws into trial so that they will know that they are needy, then at last He pardons so that they will know that they are the crown on the head of the headmen. *"If He forgives, He is the best of the merciful; and if He chastises, He is not a wrongdoer."*[668]

He also said, *"Were pardon not one of the things most beloved to Him, He would not have inflicted the sin on Adam, the noblest of creatures for Him."*[669] If it were not that pardon is the most exalted of all things for the Real, He would not have afflicted Adam with tasting the tree. He would not have called out concerning him, *"And Adam disobeyed"* [20:121], given that he was possessor of throne and crown and the oyster for the pearl of the possessor of the *miʿrāj*. That slip, however, was the prelude to a hundred thousand subtle secrets.

He forbade him by His command from going near the tree, and He threw him with His severity into what He had prohibited so that after the curtain of His kindness the subtleties of His secret would appear.[670] Oh, what He does to this handful of tested, sorrowful dust!

How low have I fallen in the ache of my love for You!
    With what misery have I fallen into the skirt of Your torment!

*

I said perhaps I'd be wary of Your flirting and love.
    No, no, I said it wrong—I'll put my life in danger.
Every night I aim to call Your name,
    but then I don't and busy myself elsewhere.
You put me in a road where Your flirting
    turns my foolish conduct upside down.

*

O partridge with a thousand falcons in your trap!
    O lion-caching gazelle, how much more of this from you?
How many there are who never joined with you,
    though they plunged into heartache and trial for you!

When Adam was afflicted with that slip and came down to this dark world, everyone who looked at his form thought that he was distant. But in reality a thousand thousand realities of proximity were contained inside that form of distance. When a slave is the sultan's favorite, he stands at the edge of the carpet, and the boon companions and pillars of the realm sit around the throne, but a hundred thousand subtleties found in that favorite servant's distance are not found in the boon companions' proximity. This is not the distance of abasing—it is the distance of coquetry. A hundred thousand secret proximities are prepared in the outward distance, and a hundred thousand secret distances are deposited in the inward proximity. Thus bewilderment piles on bewilderment. You see the branch in the mosque, but the root is in the church. You see the root in the mosque, but the branch is in the church. ʿUmar came with the sword on his belt, and a call came from the Unseen, *"Make way for the servant of the Lord of the Worlds."*[671]

O You who lit a fire on top of the Water of Life
and burned therein the lovers' faith and unbelief!
O You whose perfection has filled the purses of the losers at dice,
O You whose beauty has sewed the sacks of the destitute!
Sometimes Your severity draws swords with those black eyes;
sometimes Your gentleness lights candles with those sweet lips.
In an hour Your love's hand threw into the pit
all the status my intellect gained in one hundred years.[672]

The favorite slave has no veil with the sultan, but the vizier and boon companion have a hundred thousand veils. The favorite slave does not find access with the escort of the usher, but the usher and the doorman find access with the escort of the favorite slave. Thus you should not suppose that on the night of the *miʿrāj*, when Muṣṭafā reached that world, he reached it with the escort of Gabriel. In fact when Gabriel and Michael arrived there, they arrived with his escort.

Know also that in reality, unless all the veils in front of you are lifted, you will not find access to the dome of proximity, the bench of limpidness, the garden of approval, the walled garden of the Haqiqah, and the green field of the lovers' convocation.

Until you strike fire to all that you have
your life's reality will never be sweet.
If you're bold, then bed down in the mountains.
Otherwise leave, don't stretch your legs in My street.[673]

The stipulation of the wayfaring man is to come out of this dark well in which the life of love is the life of this world. Then he will see a world with another color and another hue, its folk like kings, contemplating the gardens of proximity. At the summit of its sky are none but birds trained to the hand. In the depths of its attributes' ocean are nothing but night-brightening pearls. If its folk stroll into the garden of love, they will see the heart's chamberlain spreading the carpet of proximity. If they aim for the Holy Presence, they will see good fortune's horses and steeds charging forth from the Sultan's capital city.

O heart, how long in this waystation, deceived by this and that?
Just once leave this dark well to see the world—
A world where every heart you'll see is king,
a world where every heart you'll see is joyful.
When you don a garment there, you'll find its sleeves are justice.
When you take a house, you'll see its threshold is bounty.
Why do you make the decree into a pretext? Resolve to serve like a man.
Once resolved, what success and power you'll see!
For an hour charge forth in battle like Fereydun
and see Kaveh's flag wherever you go.[674]

If you become a martyr in religion's road a hundred times,
you'll still be a Guebre if you see yourself in the midst.
Here you taint copper with gold and then you boast—what benefit
will that have there when you see the touchstone?
Will you ever have the pain to see yourself without caprice?
Will you ever be the man to see yourself with contempt?
Treat this celestial guest with honor so that on the day
it flies beyond this dome you'll see it as your host.
Adorn this peacock of the Throne with every sort of wisdom
so that outside the cage you'll see the joy of its nest.[675]

The greatest veil in the road is the veil of mortal nature and the blockage of created nature. This blockage must be struck down and this veil lifted so that you may reach the threshold of the Real.

Whatever is less than the Real is creation, whether in this world or the afterworld, whether soul or spirit, obedience or disobedience. As long as you have not removed yourself from this world by not being at ease with it, from the afterworld by not looking at it, from the soul by not following it, from the heart by not seeking wherewithal from it, and from disobedience by not paying attention to it, you will not be given proximity to the Real.

Once you have traversed this path, taken the street of disengagement to its end, and died to yourself before death, the work will still be in peril from the poisonous gaze of mortal nature. If you do all this and then look back at your own deeds for the blink of an eye, a sash of unbelief will be made from that look and fastened to the waist of your days.

O dervish, it is better to be in the station of distance, remorseful at not finding, than to be in the station of proximity, admiring yourself for having found. Self-admiration is the prelude to disappearance, and remorse is the vanguard of bestowal. In short, you must purify the road of self, you must tear apart the clothing of mortal nature, and you must pour dust on your dust-dwelling eyes. In this road, those who display themselves are like catamites.

In the rulings of the Shariah, women have been commanded to conceal and curtain themselves: *Flaunt not your charms like the flaunting in the former ignorance* [33:33]. But in terms of the secrets of the Tariqah and the allusions of the lords of the Haqiqah, manifesting one's own soul is more worthy of criticism. It causes more trouble than bringing naked ladies from behind their veils and auctioning them off before the eyes of others.

There was someone in the era of Adam who spoke of himself. Though he was the teacher and leader of the angels, he made his own self appear and thereby became a catamite and a female on the road. It was said to him, "Go far from Our Presence. Go, for I have given you this world. Go down into the cave of delusion and adorn that garbage dump for the eyes of those who have no aspiration." *I shall adorn for them* [15:39].

What a marvelous business! At first, he claimed aspiration and said, "I will not prostrate myself to dust." In the end, he gave himself over to the lack of aspiration.

I marvel at the arrogance of Iblis
and his ugly intention.

Too proud to bow before Adam,
he became the leader of his offspring.[676]

Part of Adam's greatness is that the accursed one was thrown into a thorn bed of severity and never allowed to smell a rose of gentleness. God gave the respite of forbearance for a thousand thousand ill words about Himself, but when the work reached talk of His friend, He struck fire into the spirits. *He made them talk, then He burned them*: "The curtain of My forbearance conceals a thousand thousand ill words from Adam's era to the dissolution of the world, but the attribute of My love will not let one word about My friend pass on credit, for no respite is given in talk of friends."

If a man steals and his right hand is cut off because of the wrong, two rightful dues have turned toward him: the rightful due of God and the rightful due of the servant. The Exalted Lord commands, "Cut off his right hand for the sake of My servant, for he needs his rightful due, though I do not need Mine. I pardon My rightful due, but I do not pardon the rightful due of friends."

Adam was brought into existence in the name of a friend. The generous are lenient with their own rightful due, but they are not lenient with their friends' rightful due. Leniency in your own rightful due is generosity and mercy, but in the case of your friends' rightful due, it is betrayal.

They said, "These people will be blood-shedders and corruption-workers."

The Real said, *"Surely I know what you do not know* [2:30]."

They said, "If there is a love in the world that has no room for blame, it is our love. Who offers an argument on their behalf?"

"My knowledge. Your eminence is from your deeds, but their eminence is from My knowledge. Sometimes I put the crown of *He taught* [2:31] on their heads; sometimes I nurture them in the cradle of *Surely I know."*

O dervish, He brought severity down on Iblis's head, and He brought it down completely. He showed gentleness to this handful of dust, and He showed it completely. He capped one with a crown and the other He made the crown of the gallows. Just as He rejected Iblis such that He will never accept him, so also He accepted Adam such that He will never reject him. *One group sought Him, and He abandoned them; one group fled from Him, and He seized them.* One group is running and rushing, searching and seeking, with nothing in their hands but wind. Another group has turned away from the road and flees from the Exalted Presence, but love's despatcher and urger is in their tracks.

"O *tawḥīd*-voicers, *'When it is time both for the prayer and for dinner, begin with dinner.'*[677] When the evening prayer and dinner are both present, begin with dinner, for *'I was sent with the easy, easygoing, primordial way,'*[678] without bias. And O Christian who have reduced your food to a few peas, you have nothing to do with Me and have no way to My Presence, without iniquity. *Complete is the word of your Lord in truthfulness and justice* [6:115]."

In his own era Adam's greatness fell so far down that there was no need for Iblis, but He runs things such that every possessor of beauty has a counterpart in blackface. Any palace that does not have a garbage dump is incomplete. A lofty palace must have a garbage dump as its counterpart so that all the trash and filth that gathers in the palace can be thrown there.

In the same way, whenever God sculpted a heart with the light of purity, He made the garbage dump of this vile soul its counterpart. The black spot of deep ignorance flies on the same wings as the pearl of purity. There needs to be a bit of adulteration so that purity can be built upon it. A straight arrow needs a crooked bow. O heart, you be like a straight arrow! O soul, you take the shape of a crooked bow!

They take a bit of copper or iron and add it to silver so that it may receive a seal. If they did not add the impurity to the pure silver, it would not accept the seal. When the heart is clothed in the garb of purity, it is presented with the black spot of great wrongdoing and deep ignorance so that it will not forget itself and will know who it is. When a peacock spreads all of its feathers, it gains a different joy from each feather. But as soon as it looks down at its feet, it becomes upset. That black spot of deep ignorance is the peacock's foot that comes along with you.

One of the kings of this world had many storehouses. His vizier gave the key of each storehouse to one person, but he kept the key of one storehouse for himself. Every morning when he wanted to go to the court, he would open the door to that room and go in, and then he would quickly come out. This was reported to the king. He asked for the key from the vizier in the hope that there would be treasure there. The king went into the room, in which were placed a staff, a bag, and a pair of shoes. He asked the vizier, "What's this?"

The vizier said, "When I came to the city, this is what I had. Every day when I come to the court and see the exalting and the honoring, I forget myself. The next day I open the door to this room and say to myself, 'You are this. Don't forget yourself!' "

How can a bit of stinking water in a bit of tattered skin be proud? Surely our leadership is the evil eye of existence.

> As long as I've been, I've not been happy with my being,
> nor have I ever done a thing that pleases me.
> No matter how hard I think, I cannot recall
> how I fell into my own existence.

When we were born from Adam, we were born on the day of Adam's affliction. When a child is born on a day of affliction, the first sound it hears is lamentation. How will that be? As a matter of course when anyone becomes aware of these words, his gallbladder will burst in fear.

> The lover's heart is never empty of torment—
> you might say his clay was kneaded from torment.
> The man deprived has nothing from deprivation but pain,
> the lover has nothing from love but torment.

Those who have fallen into the bonds of being—even if they have tremendous degrees in friendship, prophethood, truthfulness, and love—are envious of those who have not come from nonexistence into existence, for such existence does not make any intelligent man happy, nor does it brighten his eyes. ʿUmar Khaṭṭāb—who had the elevated robe of the honor of *"Were there a prophet after me, it would be ʿUmar"*[679]—was walking in a road. He reached out his hand, picked up a piece of straw, and said, *"Would that I were this piece of straw."*[680]

ʿImrān ibn Ḥusayn was passing by some ashes when the wind fell on them and took them out into the world. He said, *"Would that I were that."*[681]

O dervish, when an afflicted person reaches the limit in his affliction, he throws dust on his head. He who created you created you from dust itself, so your makeup is affliction itself. Other afflicted things throw dust on their heads because of you. The whole world was paradise as long as you had not come along. The earth was all gardens and orchards before you came. When your blessings came into the world, kind sir, the orchard became a field of brambles, the garden a scar, the roses thorns, and good fortune tribulation. It is you who have made yourself helpless, and it is because of you that the creatures are helpless. You do not know your cure, nor does anyone else know your cure.

My paragon said, "When sultans hold a celebration, it is their custom to bring someone whose face is repellant and dress him in black clothes. It is told that once a prince held a celebration, and someone with an exceedingly repulsive face was brought, dressed in black. A tray of charcoal was put in his hands, and a piece of something dreadful was put on the charcoal. The prince was quick. He said, 'You yourself were not enough? You needed something else?' "

O chevalier, He could have created a subtle person from an exalted substance and begun this mystery with him. Nonetheless, from a bit of stinking water and a handful of dust, he brought into existence a person who had never done anything, never practiced, and never traveled on any road. He threw the robe of unqualified love on the neck of his good fortune. Thus creation would know that all is He, all is in Him, and all is from Him.[682]

O dust and clay, O jewel box for the secret pearl of the heart!

O dervish, what do beggars have to do with love for kings? A beggar who goes forth in a king's work has been cruel to his own spirit.

Where in the earth can I seek union with You?
You are a king for whom no one can aim.[683]

*

I grieve, my friends, but you do not;
each is empty of his comrade's grief.[684]

*

Though love for You has left me with wind in my hands,
I'm happy with You no matter what I have.
In love for You I cut myself off from the road of safety,
in loving you I sat myself down in the street of blame.
In love for You I avoided flirting as much as I could,
but Your love's flirting did not leave me alone.
In the monastery I tore the veil of my love for You,
in the idol-temple I broke repenting of Your cruelty.

In love for you I'm distraught like a moth for a candle,
    in loving you I'm perplexed like a drunken madman.
I gave You my heart's disappointment—if You don't accept,
    I'll bring You my life, for there's nothing else in my hands.

*

O chieftain whose stars have risen in good fortune,
    God knows the measure of my yearning for you.
How many an oath I've sworn and not fulfilled
    though my yearning swears that no, I'll do it.
As much as I've said, "O patron, you wrong me,"
    my ecstasy says to me, "No, you wrong him."
The worst for me is that I'm afflicted with someone
    who wants to kill me wrongfully while I show mercy to him.

Nonetheless, O dervish, there is a subtle secret here. If a dervish claims to love the sultan, he will turn the road into loss for himself. But if on his own the sultan should say, "O penniless beggar, I have some business with you," then his love, not yours, will be the cause of good fortune, honor, and elevation.

It was you who first drew the lot of love—
    you picked the limpid rose in the garden of loyalty.

When He loves someone in the beginningless, He will not reject him because of his slips. When He gazes on you, He gazes in terms of His pure knowledge, not your tainted deeds. *What a wonder that Adam tasted the wheat, but the Real said, "His Lord chose him"* [20:122]; *ʿAzāzīl was worshiping his Lord and prostrating himself, but the Real said, "God humiliated and banished him."*

The decrees of the Lord are far from the judgment of mortal man. Canaan came from Noah's loins but was not given access to the ship, though access was given to the accursed Iblis.[685] It may be that this talk is not told to kings but is told to the guards. It was not told to Pharaoh, but it was told to the old woman in his house.[686]

When Adam stretched out his hand for the grain of wheat, he was pulling down the curtain, not jumping from the road. The avarice of Adam, which was the result of dust, stuck up its head from his breast. It saw that the beauty of chosenness had made dense dust the depository for the subtle spirit. Chosenness was the spirit's share, but the dust was struck with the whip of *surely he was a great wrongdoer, deeply ignorant* [33:72]. When the attribute of dust saw that the beauty of the reposeful spirit was the object of prostration in the row of limpidness and the world of chosenness and purity, it said, "I need to come up with some stratagem to pull Adam from the row of limpidness." It wanted to inflict a more severe wound, but the reins of the beginningless solicitude held it back.

Joseph's brothers said, "Kill Joseph."

Judah said, "Do not kill him, but throw him into the well."[687]

In reality, this world is that same well, and the darkness and dread of the well did not take away Joseph's beauty and status.

"The person of faith is like a pearl: wherever he may be, his light goes along with him."[688] You are a pearl that We have brought out from the ocean of nonexistence with the hand of power and placed on the shore of existence by the decree of generosity and munificence. If you are in paradise, light will be with you; if you are in dust, light will be with you; and if you are at the resurrection, light will be with you: *their light running before them* [57:12].

What a marvelous business! The drop is finite, but the intended goal is infinite. Indeed, the drop is finite, but the drop is being carried by infinite love. The intended goal has infinite gentleness, and the intender has infinite pain.

The position of the Folk of the Sunnah is that the Real's gentle gifts have no end. The world may finish, but no one will reach the core of the Real's gentle gifts toward this handful of dust. The gist of all the gentle gifts is that He created you for subsistence. The rapacious lion and crashing elephant were subjected to you; the meaning of annihilation was subjected to the meaning of subsistence. Although those animals have huge bodies, they are there for annihilation, and you are here for subsistence.

The position of the aeonists is that this world is for subsistence and the creatures for annihilation, but the position of the Folk of the Sunnah is that this world is for annihilation and the creatures for subsistence.

Who are we? We are a pearl brought out from the ocean of power and put into the jewel box of dust. After a few days, the jewel box decays and is thrown away. The pearl is then taken back to the oyster of exaltedness. *"The spirits of the martyrs are in the craws of green birds, flying in the meadows of the Garden."*[689]

Tomorrow all will be mustered and the call will go out, *"Be dust!"*[690] The angels will be addressed, "Gather around the Throne and glorify, recite *tawḥīd*, and declare holy! The robes of Riḍwān and the chains of Mālik have nothing to do with you."

A man in shallow water is one thing, a man in a whirlpool something else. *"What happens to the back of the person being flogged is easy for the observers."*[691]

It is said that once a rooster had a debate with a falcon. The falcon said to the rooster, "You are such a disloyal animal!"

The rooster, "How so?"

He said, "Because the Adamites nurture you and feed you with their own hands. But if they ever come after you, your cries reach the whole world and in no way do you give yourself up. As for me, they catch me in the desert, they sew up my eyes with the needle of severity, and they afflict me with all sorts of trials. I become accustomed to them, get along with them, and mix with them."

The rooster said, "You have an excuse, for you are far from the source. No one has ever seen a falcon on a spit. I have seen plenty of chickens stuck on spits and put into intense fire."

"O angels, you move over to the side and watch from a distance. It is the Adamites who will taste the blows of Our severity and be caressed by Our gentleness. Sometimes We will slice them up with the sword of severity, and sometimes We will anoint them with the gaze of gentleness."

O chevalier, in a place where they celebrate a wedding, people go and watch. In a place where they mete out punishment, they also go and watch: *Let a group of the faithful witness their chastisement* [24:2].

"We have brought a group from the abode of trial and testing into the abode of recompense and favor. We have dressed them in the robe of good fortune and sat them on the chair of joy and elevation. We have pulled another group into the prison of anger and the abode of distance with the shackles of abasement and the chains of contempt. The stipulation is that you watch both groups. O you who are the glorifiers and hallowers in your stations of honor, watch and see what We will do to this handful of dust!"

Dear friends, know that in reality if there were no dust, there would be none of this burning and none of this tumult. If there were no dust, there would be none of this happiness, and if there were no dust, there would be none of this sorrow. If there were no dust, there would be none of this talk and none of this pain.

O chevalier, dust itself expresses the pain and reality of love.

Lovers drink only my leftover—
they set out to love only after me.[692]

Hell with all its chains and punishments is the surplus of the sorrow of dust. Paradise with all its bounties and blessings is the superabundance of the secret caress of dust. Satan's curse is one of the traces of the perfection of the majesty of dust. Seraphiel's trumpet is prepared by the yearning of dust. The resurrection is stirred up by the secrets of dust. The Scales are the result of the straight-seeing of dust. Munkar and Nakīr are deputies in the breast of the love of dust. The reckoning and interrogation are among the lights of the truthful traveling of dust. The Narrow Path is one of the footsteps of dust. Mālik and all the Zabāniya are the sword of the remorse of the lagging of dust. Riḍwān and all the serving boys are the helpers of the joyful union of the feet of dust. Beginningless prosperity is an inscription on dust. The Throne with all its tremendousness is eager for the lodging place of dust. The Footstool with all its elevation wishes to be struck by the footsteps of dust. The Unseen's request was prepared in the name of dust. The divine power is the master of the work of dust. The lordly artisanry is the hairdresser of the beauty of dust. The divine love is the food of the secrets of dust. Severity and exaltation are the policemen of the tumult of dust. Gentleness and mercy are entrusted specifically to the door of dust. The eternal attributes are supplies and provisions for the road of dust. And the pure, holy, transcendent Essence is witnessed by the hearts of dust, *desiring His face* [6:52].

What I am talking about does not pertain to now. There was no dust, but there was gentleness toward this handful of dust.

When they drove him into the desert of causes,
they took care of his work without cause.
They threw in today as a pretext—
they set up tomorrow yesterday.[693]

He loves them is the offering of the pure Unseen to dust, and *they love Him* [5:54] is the gift of dust to the pure Unseen. *He loves them* went out ahead, and *they love Him* came along behind. Supposing that *He loves them* had not gone out before, you would not have found *they love Him.*

Dust had not yet come, but pure gentleness had prepared an offering for dust. There was no mouth, but the wine was ready. There was no head, but the hat was shaped. There was no foot, but the road was paved. There was no heart, but the gaze was steady. There was no sin, but the storehouse was full of mercy. There was no obedience, but paradise was adorned. *Solicitude comes before water and clay.*

O Muslims, come, let us all talk only about the Beginningless! Let us all smell the roses of gentleness in the beginningless meadow! Let us all drink of the beginningless wine! Let us all wear the shirt of the beginningless covenant!

> Rise—let us make our spirits and hearts the path.
> The caravan has gone; we too should depart.
> Let us go out to the desert of love,
> making our feet from Gabriel's wings.
> Let us make a torch with the fire of love
> and a banner with the hope of union.

*

> Fill the measure to overflowing, lift it up, and give it to me.
> Drink a little yourself, cupbearer, and give a lot to me.
> If a big man comes to the tavern in arrogance,
> don't give him access to you—give it to me![694]

Before Adam it was the time of the rich and the possessors of wherewithal. As soon as Adam's turn arrived, the sun of poverty and need stuck up its head and indigence appeared. There was a group of creatures sitting on the treasure of glorification and hallowing, auctioning off their own merchandise: *"We glorify Thy praise"* [2:30]. But Adam was a poor man who came from the hut of need and the corner of secret whispering. He had made his garb from indigence and lack of wherewithal and he used his penury as a means of approach. In remorse he cried out at the Exalted Threshold: *"Our Lord, we have wronged ourselves"* [7:23].

O dervish, they take counterfeit coin from beggars in place of the genuine. They close their eyes to the transaction. But when it comes to the rich, they examine thoroughly and with caution. Yes, the angels of the Dominion had the wherewithal, but they also had a ready self-importance. They had written the label of we-ness on the merchandise of their own obedient acts. Adam had no wherewithal, but his breast was a mine for the jewel of need and an oyster for the pearl of poverty.

Whenever coin is impure, it must be placed in the furnace so that its impurity will go away and it will become pure. Adam was a man who had the burn of seeking. His breast was the fireplace of love, and nothing in the realm of being had the capacity for one spark of that blaze. *A single breath of the yearners incinerates the deeds of men and jinn and extinguishes the fires of the two worlds*. When he put paradise into his work, it was because of the heat of his seeking. The wheat was ready at hand, and the whispering of Iblis was a pretext. Seeking the secrets was his mark.

"O angels of the Dominion, O inhabitants of the precincts of holiness and the gardens of intimacy! All of you have wealth and riches, but Adam is a poor man and sees himself as lowly. Your coin is impure because of attending to and gazing on yourselves. Now take the coin of your deeds to the furnace of Adam's need, for he is the assayer of the Presence: *Prostrate yourselves before Adam!* [2:34]."

The first inscription that poverty wrote on the face of Adam's days was this: *"He was a great wrongdoer, deeply ignorant"* [33:72]. *"Poverty is blackness of face in the two worlds."*[695]

It seems in the eyes of the sweetheart love is unbelief.

O chevalier, aloes has a secret. If you smell it for a thousand years, it will never give off a scent. It needs fire to display its secret. Its face is black and its color dark. Its taste is bitter and its genus wood. It wants a hot fire to display the mystery in its heart.

There was a fire of seeking in Adam's breast, and its sparks looked at all the acts of worship and obedience and all the wherewithal of the angels of the Dominion as nothing. *He was a great wrongdoer, deeply ignorant*. He was an incense that had to be thrown on the fire. From that incense a breeze appeared. What was it? *He loves them and they love Him*.

The chevalier's trials announce his nobility,
like fire that announces the excellence of ambergris.[696]

By God, you come to be in *He loves them*, and by God, you cease to be in *they love Him*! *He loves them* says, "Lift them all up." *They love Him* says, "Put them all aside."

When you say, *"He loves them,"* your own shirt collar says, "You've got nothing over me." When you say, *"they love Him,"* the Throne comes before you and says, "I'm your slave."

They said to a dervish, "Who are you?" He replied, "I'm the sultan. He's my agent."

Stand up, slave, pour the wine,
bring the cup for all the friends.
I call you slave in public
but I'm your slave in private.[697]

Before Adam was brought into existence, there was a world full of existent things, creatures, formed things, determined things—all a tasteless stew. The salt of pain was missing. When that paragon walked out from the concealment of nonexistence into the open space of existence, the star of love began to shine in the heaven of the breast of Adam's clay. The sun of loverhood began to burn in the sky of his secret core.

Suddenly I saw, and the work began.

Who is this? A beginner in the road of creation, advanced in the road of limpidness. Who is this? The utmost in loveliness and beauty. Who is this? The sign of the gentleness of the Possessor of Majesty. Who is this? The one kneaded by the mysteries of Our knowledge and wisdom, the one lifted up by Our choice and will.

When they brought Adam out, they brought him out in this garment. If you pile dust on dust for a million years so that something may come of it, nothing will come. Look what happened to fire, a limpid substance, when His gaze was taken away from it. Since that happened to the subtle substance of fire, what hope can you have in dense dust?

"We lauded the not-yet-created, We gave the empire to the not-yet-brought-into-being. Through his existence We gave the Throne the robe of elevation, We gave the Footstool the attribute of embracingness, We gave heaven the trait of loftiness, We gave earth the attribute of expansion, We gave the mountains the garment of pointing the way."

For forty years Adam was placed between Mecca and Taif as a piece of hollow clay. The Exalted Lord gazed upon him and, with that uncaused gaze, deposited within him the lights and secrets of the Tariqah and the Haqiqah. Then He brought the spirit into him. Just as Adam became Adam through the spirit, so also all existent things came from the domicile of power to the domicile of wisdom through Adam's creation.

Adam was the possessor of beauty in the two worlds, and his beauty needed an amulet to ward off the evil eye. The castigation of Iblis was made the amulet of Adam's beauty.

The amulet of Joseph's beauty was the tumult of his states, since that sort of beauty needed that sort of mole, and that sort of mole needed that sort of beauty.

As for the exalted beauty of *by thy life* [15:72], it had more need for the black mole of *thou wilt die* [39:30] than for spirit and heart.

The mole on your cheek at night
is black upon black upon black.[698]

No matter how a child's mother may keep him while he is in the house, when she wants to send him out into the street, she dresses him up and puts a little blue spot on his cheek as an amulet for his beauty. As long as Adam was in the Unseen, he had no need for a talisman. When it was time to send him out to this land, to spread his covenant's carpet, and to let the eyes of others fall on the jewel box of his secrets, his perfect beauty needed an amulet. It was said, "Castigate deceitful Iblis and let him step before the throne of Adam the chosen's majestic good fortune. Then the castigation of Iblis will be the talisman for Adam's beauty."

O dervish, that Lord who was able to protect Joseph from an indecency could have prevented Adam from tasting the tree. But since the world has to be full of tumult and trial, what could be done?

Those drunken, tipsy eyes
keep on filling my eyes with blood.
I'm astonished—how can that moon's eyes
be drunk if she hasn't tasted wine?
How can she shoot arrows into the heart
without hand, bow, fist, or thumb?

She's taken the hearts of the world's lovers
and twisted them on the hooks of her two tresses.
When she knew that trouble had come,
she hid herself and sat in the house.
A whole city is grieving for her—
that's not surprising, it can happen.
Their feet are bound by her irons,
her hand is on their heads.[699]

Adam was brought into paradise, made to slip, and then brought out. "O Adam, this is not a work that could have been set right by you alone. On the day the angels prostrated themselves, you were not alone. On the day of binding the compact, you were not alone. There was no stipulation that you should be alone in paradise. '*The worst of men is he who eats alone.*'[700] It is not the work of chevaliers to eat alone. Come out into this world, which is the workshop of seeking. The teacher poverty will write out the alphabet of love for you."

At the mountain, Moses asked for vision. It was said, "*Thou shalt not see Me* [7:143]. O Moses, there is no stipulation that you be provided for. A hundred thousand poor wretches, exiled from their homes and families, down on their knees, their hearts roasted and their eyes full of tears, offer up their spirits in yearning for My Presence. There is no stipulation that I leave them in their pain and single out one individual for the goal.

"O Adam, you are the sealed purse of the secrets, the source of love and affection. In the world of your makeup are moonlike Greeks and black Abyssinians. In the jewel box of your existence are shining gems and night-colored beads. In the wallet of your being are fine linen and coarse wool. In the ocean of your makeup are pearls and potsherds.

"I have two houses: In one I spread the dining-cloth of approval, entrusting it to Riḍwān. In the other I light up the fire of wrath, putting it in the hands of Mālik. If I were to leave you in the Garden, My attribute of severity would not approve. So depart from here and go down into the furnace of trial and the crucible of affliction. Then I will display the deposits, artifacts, subtleties, and duties that are inside the coffer of your heart."

O chevalier, it is seven thousand years since the Joseph of beauty and majesty—the caravan of the existence of Adam and the Adamites—was imprisoned at the door of the Egypt of the Will. Do you fancy that this is too much?

One city and everyone talks of that beautiful face—
all the world's hearts are captive to her.
I try hard and others try too—
whose hand will she take, whose friend will she be?

Glory be to God! Many thousand secrets and meanings were prepared in this nimble, sultan-like speck of dust! The first prey hunted by Adam's greatness was Iblis, for he was pulled down from leadership and chieftainship and made to roll in the dust of abasement and lowliness. As soon as he became headstrong, he was hung by the hand of severity on the gallows of the curse. This was done to the master so the students would learn a lesson.

You must fasten heaven and earth to the saddle-straps of your aspiration, catch this world and the next in the lasso of your good fortune, lay low the heads of all those with heads raised high under your own salamanderlike hooves,[701] and step forth into the realities of the attribute of chosenness that was given to you: *I am setting in the earth a vicegerent* [2:30]. Only then will you become one of the Men.

Glory be to God! How many pure subtleties are in this speck of dust! The Adamite is a steed and a rider. The steed is the soul, the rider the spirit. As for the angels, they go without steeds.

Those who have no steeds always go by the road, for they do not have the wherewithal to go by other than the road. The one who is mounted goes sometimes by the road and sometimes by other than the road. The rider always aims for the road, but the steed aspires to the roadless road. *What I want and what the horse wants are different.*

When the aim of the steed overcomes the rider's aim, he takes the roadless road, but when the rider's aim overcomes the steed's aim, he takes the road. When the spirit overcomes the soul, then the jonquil of obedience, the hyacinth of chieftainship, and the sweet grass of felicity grow up, but when the soul overcomes the spirit, only disobedience rises from the salt marsh of its distracted makeup.

In reality the road is out there for the Adamites. The angels are feathered birds, *having wings two, three, and four* [35:1]. As for you, O dervish, do not look at the height of the birds. Look at the wiles of the hunters.

[The angels] *ask forgiveness for those who have faith* [40:7]. They were created from sheer spirit, and human beings from the subtlety of spirit and the heaviness of dust. From these two things God took two praised attributes—subtlety from spirit and heaviness from dust. From these He compounded, arranged, and put together an individual, whom He called Adam. The density remained with the bodies and bodily things, and the lightness with the angels.

O dervish, it was an infinite felicity that you were brought into existence from these two meanings abiding through these two essences. Had He not made you an individual by taking lightness from the spirit and denseness from the dust, you would have been castigated in both worlds.

The Shaykh al-Islām said, "There was a man who had an ugly face and a beautiful disposition. He had a wife with a beautiful face and an ugly disposition. The man said, 'Wife, let us cohabit so that we will have a child with your face and my disposition.' As it happened, a child came out with the father's face and the mother's disposition. About him they said, 'O bad substance, *O you who combine the disgraces of both parents!*' "

O chevalier, you must wait many years for a tree to bear fruit, and then one day you may have some. If you want it to bear earlier and better fruit, you must take a graft from another tree. *Glory be to God!* How many blessings are found in cutting!

Many thousands of years before Adam walked forth, the angels were walking around and performing acts of obedience, but they did not reach the standing, level, degree, and rank that Adam reached at the first step. Yes, they were trees full of fruit, but they did not have a graft from another branch.

On the circle of bringing to be He drew this individual of clay, destined to remain in this world for only a short time. At once the Unseen Presence prepared a subtlety in the spirit and grafted it to the tree of his existence so that in a short time he would reach what others would not reach in a long time. He received no help from his own makeup, but rather from the solicitude of the Teacher. May the evil eye stay far away—for He made him very beautiful!

Once the body cohabited with the spirit, there appeared between the two a heart, called "the point of limpidness." No other created thing has a heart. The heart is not that lump of flesh which, if you threw ten of them to a dog, would not satisfy it. That is simply an outward target so that opinions and understandings may gain some courtesy. The heart's meaning is pure of that.

From the spirit the heart took subtlety and from the dust heaviness. It came to be *praised on both sides and approved by both parties*. Then it became the locus for the gaze of the Unseen. It is neither spirit nor body; or rather, it is both spirit and body. If it is spirit, where does the embodiment come from? If it is body, why is it subtle? It is neither this nor that, but it is both this and that.

When the heart came into existence from these two meanings, the disparity of states and the diversity of steps appeared. The spirit does one work, the soul does another, and the heart is a prisoner between the two, having read from the slate of poverty. If it inclines toward the spiritual base, the deeds of the spirit become manifest. If it leans toward the corporeal base, the deeds of the body appear. This is why the Chieftain of the Two Worlds, the Messenger to the Two Weighty Ones, said in this station, *"The heart is like a feather in the desert; the wind makes it tumble back and forth."*[702]

This speck of dust is the chameleon of power and the marvel of creativity's secret. Sometimes God praises it with a praise whose foot walks on the head of the angels. Sometimes He blames it with a blame of which Iblis would be ashamed. They are *the repenters, the worshipers* [9:112], and so also they are the *ungrateful* [100:6], the *grasping* [70:19], the *impatient* [70:20], the *grudging* [70:21], the *great wrongdoer* [33:72], the *deeply ignorant* [33:72], and the *unthankful* [42:48].

Kings will ever be criticized and praised.[703]

If He praises, He will be showing the majesty of His own power. If He blames, He will be making manifest His incomparability and holiness. Wherever there is a brisk and busy bazaar, the scale of the balance is sometimes full and sometimes empty.

The angels are *honored servants* [21:26], but we are honored friends: *And We honored the children of Adam* [17:70]. Do not fancy that we were stationed in the earth and they at the summit of the spheres because of our lowliness. The wisdom here is that earth is our house, and heaven our ceiling. It is a stipulation that when a king goes into a house, the guards go up on the roof. They were commanded to watch over our states, and the stipulation for watchers is to look down from above.

When you put something in one scale of a balance, it stands on the earth, and the empty scale goes up. The meanings, secrets, and realities in the Adamic essence are not found in any other essence. He went down because of the disparity in the contraposition, not because his state was defective. So be aware and awake!

Were only possessors of positions high,
armies would rise and dust would fall.[704]

The angels are the proximate, the pure, and the exalted, but

you are indeed another, your love something else.[705]

The angels were the exalted ones of the Presence. Each of them wore a shirt of sinlessness and an earring of obedience, worshiping without blight. But as soon as dust had a turn at good fortune, they called out from their own purity, belching in the bazaar of *I, and no one else.* They said, *"We glorify Thy praise"* [2:30].

"O angels of the Dominion, although you have obedience, you have no appetite in your souls or darkness in your makeup. If they disobey, they have appetite in their souls and opacity in their makeup. Your obedience along with all your forcefulness does not weigh a mote before My majesty and tremendousness. Their disobedience along with all their dejection and brokenness does not diminish the perfection of My realm. Although you cling to your sinlessness, they cling to My mercy. With your obedience you display your sinlessness and greatness, but with their disobedience they show forth My bounty and mercy."

O dervish, there was a world at rest. The existent things in their chambers were still and serene, resting their heads on the pillow of the command. One group was in the holy palisades, another in the gardens of intimacy. But Adam was coming, and he was bringing the edict of turmoil.

Elevated eminence will not be safe from torment
until blood pours forth from every side.[706]

By the decree of predetermination the world was like a newly taken city. A newly taken city does not come to rest until the sultan puts punishment into effect. *So take heed, O you who have eyes!* [59:2]. Look at Iblis and pass by!

ʿAbdallāh ibn ʿAbbās said, "The world was a world at peace. The fish at the bottom of the sea were at peace with the vultures in the air. The vultures would come to the shore and the fish would come to the top of the water and they would whisper to each other. As soon as Adam stepped into the world, the vultures said, 'Farewell, for a man has entered the world who will bring us down from the sky and pull you up from the bottom of the sea.' "

Apropos of this is the story that a vulture said to a camel, "How is it that you let a child pull you this way and that?"

The camel said, "You have an excuse, for your work is with the dead, and mine with the living."

O dervish, fear that vulture, for he will step into the field and say, "Let be what will be."

I will attack the lines not knowing
if death awaits me there or somewhere else.[707]

On the Day of Badr, or the Day of Uhud, ʿUmar ibn Khaṭṭāb and his brother Zayd had one set of armor. Zayd said, "Brother, you wear the armor so that if something happens, it will happen to me."

ʿUmar said, "What do you suppose about me? If you must become a martyr, I too must become one." They threw away the armor and entered the battlefield.

This is talk of the burned, not the self-made. Fire wants something already burned in order to catch. That Orb of light, that Illuminator of the dark night, that Host of the speaking companion Moses and that Narcissus of the bosom friend Abraham—He wants the burned!

If you put a thousand precious silks before stone and iron, the fire will not catch, for they have the frivolity of color. If you bring new cloth, that will be of no use, for it has the smell of existence.

Fire comes into the open from the curtain of concealment and throws out sparks. When it does not see any confidant, it pulls back its head. If it does find something already burned, it catches and brightens the world.

In the same way, the fire of love will never catch in any self-seeing wealthy man or refractory sultan. It will catch rather in someone so burned that, if you test him by poking your finger on a spot of his heart, it will fall to pieces.

If the fire is to get going, you need the burned. If you try with Byzantine or Baghdadi silk, that won't do. If you use new cloth, the fire will hardly catch. You need a worn-out patch, halfway between existence and nonexistence—distraught and bewildered between effacement and affirmation.

First the patch is thrown to the edge of nonexistence, but the structure of its parts is kept together. Once it has been chastised by the passing of time and trampled underfoot by the days, you bring it and wash it clean. Then you strike fire to it so that its parts may be put to work and burn. Then you place a heavy burden on it and keep it in a solid cupboard. With the tongue of its state the fire will say, "I have burned it, and a day will come when I will brighten it."

"O luminous fire, this burnt cloth is black and dark. What do you want with it?"

It says, "So it is, but it has my brand."

Today the fire of *He loves them and they love Him* [5:54] has been struck in your heart and you have been burned by love. Just as they put a heavy burden on that burnt cloth, so also they will put the heavy burden of death on your parts and members. Then they will keep you in the cupboard of the grave, contemplating the gentleness of the One. After that, when the light of the King's gaze appears in the world tomorrow, it will catch in you and give you a beauty such that next to you the full moon will be worthless. No longer will the moon have any standing, nor the sun any light. Where is this expressed? *Faces that day radiant, gazing on their Lord* [75:22–23]. *And when you see, you will see bliss and a great kingdom* [76:20].

36. *al-ʿAẓīm:* the Tremendous

The magnificent. This is not the tremendousness of body, for the Real—*majestic is His majesty!*—is incomparable with that. Rather, it is in respect of tremendous power.

One of the shaykhs of the Tariqah was asked about the Real's tremendousness. He said, "What do you say about a Lord who has a servant called Gabriel with six hundred wings, two of which, if he were to spread them, would cover the land, the sea, and all the spheres?" [708]

Glory be to Him! How tremendous is His status! O You in whose tremendousness and majesty intellects are dazzled! O You in the world of whose uncaused will everyone's intelligence is distracted!

No one measures Him, no one encompasses Him, no one perceives Him, and nothing stands up to His tremendousness.

You stand without realms, You continue without terms, You are powerful without stratagems!

The states of creation change, but His state does not change. The proof of His greatness is His very greatness, the evidence of His Being His very Being, and allusions to Him come from Himself. Expressing His greatness is by His permission, remembering Him is by His command, and seeking His bounty is by His pull.

He was Lord before He created how and why. How and why do not reach the majesty of His pure Essence. *He is He, and there is no He but He.* He was solitary before all, He is solitary when He brings all into existence, and He will be solitary when all are gone.

He makes all appear so that they may come to be, and He reduces all to nothing so that He alone may be.

Consider all existent things as nonbeing itself, and count all nonexistent things as being through His power.

He did, spoke, adorned, disclosed, and bestowed robes of honor in the Beginningless, and so it will be in the Endless. He did the deed in the Beginningless, and today He shows you what He did. He spoke the words in the Beginningless, and today He makes you hear the spoken words. He adorned in the Beginningless, and today He discloses what was adorned in the Beginningless. He bestowed robes of honor in the Beginningless, and today He conveys the robes that were bestowed.

Each day He is upon some task [55:29]. *He drives the predetermined things to their appointed times—beings and nonexistent things at known moments through recognized causes. Resistance is frivolity.*

"Today you know Me—I am not of today. Your knowing is newly arrived, but My Being is described by eternity. Your taking belongs to now, but My giving is eternal.

"For some time I have been speaking to you of the mysteries, but you hear now. In the Beginningless, the beginningless hearing was your deputy in listening to the beginningless speech. In the Beginningless, the beginningless knowledge was your deputy in knowing the beginningless attributes.

"When a guardian has a child's property, he has it as the child's deputy. When the infant reaches adulthood, he gives it back to him. You were the infants of nonexistence, and the eternal gentleness took care of your work. What is left that I did not do for you?

"I conveyed the Law's prescription to your hearing, I conveyed the decree to your heart, I spoke of the mysteries to your spirit, I inscribed obedience on your limbs. At every moment I sent a new gift. I made you anticipate arrivals from the Unseen—at every moment a robe of honor, at every instant a gift, at every breath a new bestowal.

"If I were to be gentle because of your merit, I would not be gentle, because you have no merit. If I were to bestow because of your gratitude, I would not bestow, because your gratitude is not worthy of My bestowal. If I were to send gifts because of your seeking, I would not send them, because you have no capacity to seek. O you who await the arrival of My gentleness! O you who look for the marks bearing witness to My Unseen!"

O spirit and world, what place is this for not making do?
It's a place for revelry and showing gratitude!

"Has *'Rejoice in Me!'*[709] not sat on the cushion of your heart? Has the ruling authority of My secret not struck the knocker on your heart's door? Has the messenger of My kindness not conveyed the message of gentleness to your spirit?"

In truth, in truth, whatever He gives, He gives as hard cash. He does not hold back anything, for *"The hearts of the free do not tolerate waiting."*[710] He holds back the form of paradise, but He hurries forth with the reality of paradise. When this talk came, it brought paradise along with it.

The master Abū ʿAlī Daqqāq said, *"The scholars point you to the Garden, and that is real. I point you to a meaning such that, were a whiff of it offered to the heavens and the earth, every single mote of them would become an exalted Garden."*

They have said, "The body surrenders itself for credit, but the heart deals only in hard cash."

Abu'l-Ḥasan Kharaqānī said, "People disagree as to whether or not they will see Him tomorrow. As for Abu'l-Ḥasan, he deals only in hard cash. When a beggar does not have his evening bread, he takes the scarf from his head and offers it at auction. He would never sell it for credit."[711]

"Waiting is the red death."[712] Before Adam heaven and earth were waiting for Adam's arrival, but Adam was not waiting for the existence of anyone. The earlier communities were waiting for our existence, but we are not waiting for the existence of anyone. He brought all of them first, and He brought us last. Why? To tell us their slips and not to tell anyone our secrets. Now that they have gone, they are sitting at the table waiting for us to arrive. He gave them little by little, but He gave us to overflowing. When a group arrives last at a session of wine, it is said to the cupbearer, "Give them overflowing cups so that they may catch up with us."

"My community is like the rain; it is not known if its first is better or its last."[713]

"How could He destroy a community in the first of which I am and in the last of which Jesus will be?"[714]

"My community is a community shown mercy."[715]

"A sinful community and a forgiving Lord!"[716]

"My intercession belongs to the folk of great sins in my community."[717]

When God sent down His words, *"Thy Lord will bestow upon thee, and thou wilt approve"* [93:5], he said, *"Then I will not approve for any of my community to be in the Fire."*[718]

"Do you wonder that tomorrow I will step into the courtyards of the resurrection and intercede for someone who has worked corruption for forty or fifty years and pull him from the depths of Gehenna? The intercession my heart made in this world for the poor of this community will then seem small next to tomorrow's intercession. Because of the tenderness of prophethood in this world, my heart interceded so much for Bilāl that they beat the drum of his good fortune: *'Whosoever hates Bilāl hates God.'*

"Do you wonder that when the scent of Joseph came from his shirt, Jacob said, *'Surely I find the fragrance of Joseph'* [12:94]? I smell the scent of the Josephs of the community from the corners of the churches and idol temples. When someone is descended from mortal loins, his covenant will hold that Joseph is one. But when someone is descended from the loins of the Tariqah, then from Abyssinia there arises for him the Joseph of loveliness, from Persia the Joseph of beauty, from Byzantium the Joseph of good."

O dervish, from the street of the Friend comes the scent of the Friend. The turn of the Friend's face comes after the Friend's scent. Jacob first smelled the scent, then reached contemplation.

It was said to someone, *"What is the best fragrance?"*

He said, "The fragrance of the person you love or the child you raised."[719]

This is a rare business! The shirt was in the hands of Joseph's brothers, but they had no awareness of the work's secret. The attractions of love had fallen into Jacob's heart and spirit. He sent out his yearning in welcome, and Joseph sent his scent to the possessor of awareness. At a distance of eighty farsakhs the scent reached the yearning. The yearning became all scent, and the scent became all yearning. Jacob's cry was heard from the House of Sorrows: *"Surely I find the fragrance of Joseph!"* What a masterful puff of air!

O dervish, first the station of Mount Sinai began seeking Moses, then Moses began to seek. Otherwise, Moses was carefree. First the station of *two-bows' length away* [53:9] began yearning for Muḥammad's feet, then Burāq was sent to Muḥammad. Otherwise, that paragon's work was all set. First Joseph's beauty came looking for Jacob's love, then Jacob bound the belt of love. Otherwise, Jacob had no awareness of that story. First the beginningless request set out to seek us, then we began to seek. Otherwise, we knew nothing of love's secret.

The sought must begin to seek if the seeker's seeking is to be sound. Jacob kept on trying to find Joseph with his own seeking, but until Joseph began to seek, Jacob gained nothing by sending his sons.

It is said that Jacob and Joseph met. Jacob said, "My son, why did you not send me a note? You knew where I was."

Joseph commanded that a coffer be brought, full of sheets of paper. He showed them to his father one by one, the title of each being *"From Joseph to Jacob."* He said, "Every time I aimed to write a letter, Gabriel came from the Exalted Presence and said, 'Put down the pen, for the time has not yet come.' "

You stay alone because You kill so many friends.
Each friend You kill weeps in misery.
I want a hundred spirits so You'll kill me a hundred times,
and You'll kill me also when You kill a friend.

"O sincerely truthful Joseph, you have thousands of means, supplies, and soldiers. Whom will you send to bring Jacob?"

He said, "I will not send a commander or a vizier. I will put a bit of my scent in my shirt and give it into the hand of the east wind—called 'the wageless messenger of lovers'—and send it hunting in the direction of Canaan."

O chevalier, what marvels come from beloveds! The brothers were still in Egypt when the scent reached the possessor of awareness in Canaan.

O breeze of Najd, when did you leave Najd?
Your blowing has piled ecstasy on ecstasy.[720]

O dervish, Joseph's beauty was more jealous over Jacob's love than Jacob's love was jealous over Joseph's beauty. Jacob's gaze fell on Benjamin, and Joseph became jealous because of that gaze. He said, "You have a little brother. Bring him. If you do not bring him next time, I will not give you any food." *Father, the measure was denied to us* [12:63]. This was a diversion—straw was being thrown on the fire.

When I was thirsty for her saliva
I took wine in place of it.
But what is wine next to saliva?
I was diverting an ailing heart.[721]

Jacob said to his children, "What do you want of this old man with his burnt heart? You gave one of my sons to the wind, and now you aim for the other." Then he took oaths from them and told them the story of his grief. But there are wonders in the Unseen, and that goblet was placed in Benjamin's luggage.

O dervish, Joseph did not seize him because of the accusation of taking the goblet. He seized him because of the accusation of receiving Jacob's gaze. Otherwise, what worth has a goblet that someone like Joseph—the generous, son of the generous, son of the generous—should address his brothers, *"You are thieves"* [12:70]?

"Yes, Jacob's gaze has work with Benjamin, but my beauty has work with Jacob's gaze."

Day and night I'll oversee your work—
if you get along with anyone I'll smash your bazaar.

Dear friends, our seeking is our seeking, and His seeking is His seeking. Jacob did not reach Joseph until Joseph sought. How will we reach the Pavilions of Majesty without the escort of His seeking? In truth, in truth, the seekers' seeking is deception itself! The aimers' aiming and the worshipers' wayfaring and worship are simply form. If the peaked cap of seeking's policeman did not appear from generosity's special chamber,

You'd be nothing, nothing, and your empty words, nothing—
you'd take home no morsels with the wind of caprice.[722]

What a marvelous business! Jacob, who was God's Israel, pure and purified, a prophet and born of a prophet, was given over to the hand of love's tumult: *Surely you are in your same old error* [12:95], *that is, your same old love.*

He was remembering Joseph so much that one day when his collar became separated from his shirt and he asked for a tailor, he wanted to say, "Attach the collar here," but what came to his tongue was "Attach Joseph here."[723]

"Love is the malady of the noble."[724]

"Love is a divine madness."[725]

"Love is the Real's net to catch the hearts of the pure."[726]

"At first it is madness and at last death, at first patience and at last the grave."

The road of lovers is full of wonders,
beginning and ending with pain.
How will a meddler find the mark of this road?
How will a fool reach the wondrous?
Love without trial is most absurd—
fresh dates won't be found without thorns.
How long will you turn this way and that like the lazy?
The time has come to start seeking!
You must make *ṭ* and *h* your own hard cash—
flight [*harab*] will give birth to the secret of joy [*ṭarab*].

It is the perfect divine gentleness that causes debris to fall into the eyes of an exalted person's days. Then those left behind will have something to cling to.

Adam fell on his head in the abode of sinlessness. The Exalted Lord predestined a slip at first because this house would be a house of sinners. Then if a frail person falls on his head, he will not lose hope. He will say, "In the house of subsistence, the abode of bestowal, the station of security, and the place of honor, Adam fell on his head, and the Exalted Lord accepted his excuse. In the house of annihilation, the abode of trial, and the world of grief and trouble, it will not be surprising if a frail person falls on his head and the Exalted Lord does not take him to task, but instead accepts his excuse."

O paragon of paragons, give back a report of this state. He said, *"If you did not sin, God would bring a people who did sin, and then He would forgive them."*[727] *"Surely there is no sin too great for God to forgive."*[728]

Who am I with God that when I sin,
He would not forgive me?
I hope for pardon from Adam's children—
why would I not hope for it from my Lord?[729]

Noah was imprisoned by a gaze at his child,[730] for the child is a part of the man, the locus of love, a piece of the liver, and the place for tenderness, and the Adamite is attached to his child. Noah's time was a time of hardness and an era of cleanliness and purity, but there are those who become attached to a gaze and hang on to a talisman. "O Noah, despite your hardness and cleanliness, when you observe My trial and severity at the time of My punishment and anger, gaze back at your child. Then, if an undefiled father should gaze back at a child distracted by the times, he can seize hold of your gaze."

O chieftain of chieftains and O source of exaltedness and generous gifts, say something about this: *"Fāṭima is part of me."*[731] *"Children are a cause of niggardliness, cowardice, and sorrow, and surely they are fragrant herbs from God."*[732]

If not for my daughters and my ugly deeds,
I would hurry to yearn for death.[733]

"O Abraham, you are the shine of the creed, good fortune in the robe of bosom friendship, the essence of immaculateness, the wellspring of sinlessness, and the springhead of greatness. I am going to bring something down on you for the sake of a secret. The tongue has tremendous slips, caprice has a hard overmastery, and man is helpless before his private parts, gullet, and tongue. It is allowed for those who have not reached your station, when they are afflicted by a lie—whether by a misstep, caprice, intention, or boldness—to be helpless before an act of opposition. O tongue of Abraham, in three stations avoid outward truthfulness!"

"Abraham uttered three lies about God."[734] One was when the king aimed for his wife Sarah, and he said that she was his sister. The second was on the day of Nimrod's festival when the people went out on the plain and he was healthy, but he said, *"Surely I am sick"* [37:90]. The third was when they talked to him about breaking the idols after he had broken them, and he said, *"No, it was the large one of them that did it"* [21:63].

"O Abraham, in the garment of bosom friendship you spoke for your own sake a hundred thousand truthful words. Now for My sake speak three words for the offspring of Adam left behind. These words will be an amulet for your days of perfection, a talisman for the robe of your bosom friendship, and a place of reliance for the fallen children of Adam."

O paragon of paragons and O best of Adam's children, stamp the signet on this edict! *"God's Messenger did not give permission to lie except in three cases: war, making peace among people, and a man's talk with his wife."*[735]

Jacob was also thrown into trial, for people's inclination toward people is a tremendous inclination. Beauty has in its makeup a subjugating rulership, and the outward eyes are helpless before the beauty of form. Many in the world will be hung up on people, and lovers cannot be left without a commander-in-chief.

"O Jacob, gaze on Joseph and be hung up on him. Adorn the road of love with your blessed feet and decorate the pathway of form with your beauty. Then, if someone hapless, helpless, and imprisoned by the soul becomes afflicted and distressed by a form and is held back by a creature, two things will not be brought together in him: lost-heartedness and My rejection. He will not be afflicted by two trials: separation from the heart-holder and My anger. You be their commander-in-chief! Then tomorrow, when those fallen into passion and burned by love raise their heads from the dust, they will have a supporter. They will say, 'Lord God, in that world You overlooked the commander-in-chief of the lovers. In this world, overlook Your slave boy.'

"O eyes of Jacob, gaze on Joseph! O beauty of Joseph, place a tie on Jacob's heart! Then We will give out the story of your love in the name of *the most beautiful of stories* [12:3]. We will make your days a mark for the eyes of the lesson-learners. We will make your standing place the antimony of the eyes of the bewildered and burned."

O Seal of the Prophets and leader of the limpid, give a report about this station: *"He who loves, stays chaste, conceals, and dies, dies a martyr."*[736]

I ask forgiveness from God—surely God is all-forgiving,
and there is no sin or shame for a lover.
My people threatened me with the Fire, so I said to them,
"The Fire will have mercy on him in whose heart is fire."

If not for love I would have curtained it from the blamers
when the curtains were rent before them.

"O Zulaykhā, burned by Joseph! Seize Joseph's skirt with the hand of accusation so that I Myself may send the policeman of sinlessness to cut off your accusation-tainted hand from the skirt of prophethood with the sword of harshness and bind that thought to the skirt of the soul: *I do not absolve my soul* [12:53]."

O Chieftain of the Two Worlds, say something about this station! *"God has lifted away from my community what their souls whisper to them."*[737]

"O Moses the speaking companion, even though you have perfect exaltedness in your own tremendousness, when you go before the unaided Pharaoh with the white hand, the garment of prophethood, the shirt of limpidness, and the crown of generosity, first the eyes of that unbeliever will fall on your perfect beauty, but no harm will reach your perfection from his eyes. 'O hand of Moses, intervene in the empire without Moses's wanting it and throw down that Egyptian with a fist.' Then, when you go before Pharaoh on the first day, he will not talk of perfection with you. First he will rebuke you for the mistake, saying, *'You killed a soul'* [20:40]. The mistake that happened was the talisman of your hand's perfection. After you, there will be people who are heedless, ignorant, and mistaken. Because of a mistake one of them may unrightfully shed blood, smashing one of My prisons. Tomorrow everyone will be made present in the station of asking and answering, and I will ask him about what he did. He will lay his eyes on the perfection of Moses and, with the talisman of Moses's mistake, make Moses's days the interceder for his own days."

You, O chieftain of the world, draw your mark across this register! *"Lifted away from my community are mistakes, forgetfulness, and what they are coerced into doing."*[738]

"O Job, I poured a hundred thousand trials on the head of your aspiration. I made you the target for trial's arrow and gave out your name among the people because of your patience. It cannot be that your patience in the face of the decrees was such that you never sighed, for no one has the capacity for that much patience. O tongue of Job, after much patience, moan! Say, *'Harm has touched me'* [21:83]. Then, if I convey a trial in this world to someone weak and incapable of bearing it and he moans because of incapacity and helplessness, he will have the place for an excuse."

O exalted of the days, and O fine point of prophethood's secret, stamp this edict with the signet of your permission! At the end of his work, when he came into the chamber of 'Ā'isha, his head bound and hurting, he was saying, *"Oh my head!"*[739]

I wove a poem from my sorrows and recited it,
for I am an exile, and exiles are sorrowful.
Time has softened me—had I been a stone
I would have softened, for everyone is softened by trial.
Do not wonder at my moans and sighs:
every exile moans in the darkness.[740]

*

The scissors are not aware of the cut gold's heat,
    the falcon of the quail's torn guts;
The long night's not aware of my moaning,
    possessors of blessing are not aware of my need.

"O David, seclude yourself in a corner and ask Me to give you back to yourself for an hour! Despite your greatness I have made you the prisoner of a bird, and despite your prophethood I have made you helpless before a woman.[741] Thus if turmoil should fall on someone burned in a corner, if a traveler's present moment should become opaque for him, if a wayfarer's days should be thrown into tumult, or if a possessor of contemplation should become lax such that he falls from the Real to creation, he will have a handhold."

O beloved of God, say something about his excuse! *"Women are Satan's snares."*[742]

"O Jesus, you came pure and you went pure. You never thought about or made any slips. I have made you a place for making claims. Thus, in this world, someone may be made the mark of a work, and people may look at him and attach their hearts to him. If I question him tomorrow about the truthfulness of his days and ask him about the people's claims, he will seize hold of your skirt and say, 'If the claims they made about Jesus are to be pardoned, those about me should also be pardoned.' "

O Messenger of God, give a report about this secret and acquit yourself of claims! *"Do not lavish praise on me as the Christians lavish praise on Jesus son of Mary. Say rather, 'God's servant and His messenger.' "*[743]

O chevalier, whoever stands up tomorrow will be wearing a patched cloak. *"Surely I ask forgiveness from God a hundred times a day."*[744] To ask forgiveness is to add a patch. He stained everyone with slips so that holiness would be singled out for the Exalted Presence.

This is a sound hadith from Muṣṭafā:

Adam and Moses had a debate. Moses said, "You are the one who brought us out from the Garden and threw us into suffering."

Adam said, "You are Moses upon whom God sent down the Torah."

He said, "Yes."

He said, "How did you find the mention of me in the Torah?"

He said, "I found it was written for you before your creation."

He said, "Do you blame me for something that was determined for me before my creation?"

Then the Prophet said, "So Adam defeated Moses, Adam defeated Moses, Adam defeated Moses!"[745]

"O tree, put up your head next to Adam's throne!

"O appetite for fruit, enter into Adam's heart!

"O accursed one, let loose the reins of your disquiet!

"O Eve, show the way!

"O Adam, don't eat the fruit, be patient!

"O patience, don't circle around Adam!"

Lord God, what is this? "We want to bring Adam down from the throne of disdain to the dust of need. We want to display the secret of love."

"O servant, avoid disobedience and stay away from caprice!

"O caprice, take his reins!

"O this world, disclose yourself to his eyes!

"O servant, be patient!

"O patience, don't circle around him!"

Lord God, what is this? "We want to make the servant plead with Us. We want to uncover Our attribute of forgiveness."

"O Abraham, go to the court of Nimrod and invite him.

"O Nimrod, light up a fire of four square farsakhs and throw Abraham into it!

"O fire, do not burn Abraham!"

Lord God, what is this? "We want to make the fire into a garden and display the trace of bosom friendship."

"O adversary of the disobedient man, seize him at the resurrection!

"O disobedient man, read your book!

"O interceders, say not one word!

"O Zabāniya, take him to the Fire!

"O Mālik, entrust him to the Fire!

"O Fire, do not burn him!"

Lord God, what is this? "Yes, first I drive home the severity of Lordhood, then I uncover the beginningless solicitude."

O dervish, a hundred thousand sins of the constrained will be overlooked, but not one sin of the carefree will be overlooked.

Yaḥyā ibn Muʿādh Rāzī said, "If anything is in my hands tomorrow, I will not chastise lovers, *for their sins are sins of constraint, not free choice.*"[746]

Adam sinned because of constraint, so he was given the goblet of limpidness. Iblis sinned because he was carefree in his self-seeing, so he was expelled and cursed such that he will never have access to acceptance.

The Exalted Lord created paradise and made it the settling place of the prophets and the friends. Paradise lifted up its head and said, "It is I who caress." He brought Adam there and made a slip happen at his hand. Then He created hell and made it the quarry of the enemies. Hell lifted up its head and said, "It is I who burn." He assigned one of His enemies to Abraham. He taught courtesy to paradise with Adam and He taught courtesy to hell with Abraham.

"O paradise, if you are the one who caresses, let me see you caress Adam. O hell, if you are the one who burns, let me see you burn Abraham. O paradise, I have dismissed you from caressing! O hell, I have dismissed you from burning! O knife, I have dismissed you from cutting!" To the world's folk He showed that *To God belongs the command before and after* [30:4]. With Adam He cut off the wanting of those who want paradise, and with Abraham He cut off the fear of those who fear hell.

Ibrāhīm Adham said, "For fifteen years I obeyed while wanting paradise, and for fifteen more years fearing hell. After thirty years I saw in a dream that the resurrection had come, and paradise and hell were put at the right and left hands of the Throne. I said to myself, 'I have found what I sought.' The two of them called out, *'O Ibrāhīm, how long will you circumambulate us? Circumambulate our Creator!'* "

Adam knew that he was reared for another secret. When he reached for the grain of wheat, he made his road short. He said, "I love a single rebuke from the Presence more than all the blessings of paradise." It was because of wishing and yearning for the rebuke of the Presence that he reached for the wheat—so that he could come out of paradise, for paradise was not He. Since he made that slip by constraint, it was overlooked.

When Adam was brought from paradise into this world, it was not because of the slip. Even if we suppose that he had not slipped, he still would have been brought into this world, for the hand of vicegerency and the carpet of the sultanate were waiting for his stepping forth. *Ibn ʿAbbās said, "God had taken him out of the Garden before putting him into it."*

If you say that Adam was brought into this world because he slipped in paradise, what was our Messenger's sin that he was brought back here from *two-bows' length away* [53:9]?

O dervish, He brings about the decree of His Lordhood according to the requisite of His will. He does not look at anyone's talk and chatter. When He took Adam into paradise on the shoulders of the proximate angels with a hundred thousand endearments and exaltings, that was a blessing. When He brought him out naked and hungry, that was jealousy. By giving him paradise, He made Lordhood apparent, and by bringing him out, He made love manifest.

O chevalier, the root of every work is recognizing value. The sultan of Adam's aspiration sat on the steed of his majestic state. It rode into the Garden to determine its value. There is a difference of opinion as to whether or not a person can buy what he has not seen. But all agree that you cannot judge the value of something without having seen it.

"O Adam, what is entering paradise worth to you?"

He replied, "When someone fears hell, paradise is worth a thousand lives. But when someone fears You, paradise is not worth a grain." Hence the wisdom in taking Adam to paradise was to make manifest his aspiration.

In the same way, the wisdom in taking God's messenger Muḥammad on the *miʿrāj* was to make manifest the height of his aspiration. Some of the scholars of the community have alluded to this wisdom.[747] To him was disclosed the empire of the World of Witnessing, which is this world, but he did not open his coquettish eyes toward it. The empire of the World of the Unseen, which is the gardens and paradises, was also presented to him, but he did not open the narcissus-like eyes of prophethood to it. It was said, *"The eyesight did not swerve, nor did it trespass"* [53:17].

When he reached the majestic court of *two-bows' length away*, he lifted up his voice: *"O Lord, in Thee I am."* The call came, *"O Muḥammad, to thee I belong."*

The Exalted Lord commanded the earth to be rolled up and brought before him, just as the paragon said: *"The earth was brought together for me, and I was shown its eastern parts and its western parts."*[748] Then he said, "It was for the sake of this that [Pharaoh] said, *'I am your lord the most high'* [79:24]. He boasted of it and said, *'And these rivers, flowing beneath me'* [43:51], and he shot arrows joyfully at the sky. And [Solomon] asked for it in supplication: *'My Lord... give me a kingdom'* [38:35]. But what weight and measure does it have?" He turned his face away.

The angels of the dominion were surprised at his high aspiration. Something that Solomon asked for was brought before him without his asking, but he turned his face away from it and paid no regard. This is because he knew that what the Friend desired from this display was testing, not giving, for this was not the time of giving.

There is something even more subtle. The paragon said, "I knew that all this belonged to me. Why should I look at what belongs to me? I looked at Him to whom I belong. To look at something is to seek it, but that which belongs to me seeks me, and it would be absurd for me to seek it."

He held back his eyes from the afterworld not because of rejecting the King's gift, but because turning toward something is to turn away from something else. When it was wanted that he turn away from this world, the greatness of the afterworld was presented to him. When it was wanted that he also turn away from the House of Subsistence, the majesty of the exalted presence of the Possessor of Majesty was unveiled to his secret core. *Thus the Being-Bestower distracted him from gazing at the realm of being. "The eyesight did not swerve" to this world, "nor did it trespass" to the afterworld. The meaning is that in this world he did not turn away from the Friend toward this world, and in the afterworld he did not overstep the limit by choosing his own desire rather than the Patron's desire.*

O dervish, *"When someone approves of his station, he is veiled from what is ahead of him."* When Gabriel came and said to the presence of prophethood, "O Muḥammad, get up so that I can take you," the tongue of messengerhood said on the pulpit of his majestic state, "At this time it will become clear if you are taking me, or I am taking you." When they reached *the Lote Tree of the Final End* [53:14], which is the origin of the footsteps of the Muhammadan truthfulness, Gabriel stood still and said, *"O Muḥammad, go forward!"* He answered, "In the earth you were saying, 'Get up so that I can take you.' If you are taking, then you should go and I should stay. Since I am going and you are staying, it has become clear that I was taking you, not you me."

When Muṣṭafā said to Gabriel, "Come along with me," he replied, *"There is none of us but has a known station"* [37:164]. The paragon said, "I fancied that you were the lord of my station, but you are staying in the station." This is the meaning of what was said: *"When someone approves of his station, he is veiled from what is ahead of him."*

In one of the stories it is told that when Gabriel stood still, Muṣṭafā said to him, "Come forward one step." He came forward one step and *"he became like a sparrow."* He shrank. When he became like a sparrow, he said, "Come forward one more step." He took one more step and became like a gnat. Again he said, "Come forward one more step."

Gabriel said, "This is not proximity. If I come forward one more step, I will burn because of proximity."

Muṣṭafā replied, "If I am taken one step back, I will burn because of distance."

At the top of his turmoil a tumultuous one said,

I had a *miʿrāj* in the tavern last night—
He who has less need than I do needed me.
In my hope for union I had possessions and ownership,
in my moment's limpidness I had throne and crown.
My serving boys were Kayqubad, Bahman, and Parviz;
my servitors were the likes of Junayd, Shiblī, and Ḥallāj.
My hand was the cutpurse of bags of gold and silver;
my spirit was Ḥajjāj in the Kaabah of effacement and nonexistence.[749]

When someone seeks this world, the afterworld will elude him. When someone seeks the afterworld, the Patron will elude him. When someone seeks the Patron, he will have both this world and the afterworld, for when someone has the Patron, how can other than the Patron elude him?[750]

In one of the tales it is said that a caliph had a group of goldsmiths sit down and make some jewelry. When many pieces had been gathered, he called his slave girls and poured the jewelry on their heads. Each slave girl took away something, but one of them, who was more clever than the rest, paid no attention to any of it. She came forward and fell at the caliph's feet. He said, "Why aren't you taking something like the others?"

She said, "I'm taking my goal and desire."

You can also say that the wisdom in taking the paragon on the *miʿrāj* was to make manifest the perfection of His love. "By taking him on the *miʿrāj* I showed that no servant is more beloved to Me than he is."

It is the habit of kings that when they want to pull up one of their servants and give him a rank and level that others do not have, they show him their hidden things and treasures. The treasures of the abode of annihilation were shown to the paragon, just as he said: *"The earth was brought together for me, and I was shown its eastern parts and its western parts."*[751] This rolling up of the earth and pulling it together was not for the sake of showing the outwardness of the earth, but rather for showing the treasures of the earth. Once he saw the treasures of the house of annihilation, he was taken to the world of subsistence and shown its treasures, which are the house of chastisement and the house of mercy, the treasures of bounty and justice. The treasures of approval and anger were shown to him because "My approval has no cause, and My anger has no cause. My approval gives rise to conformity—it is not that conformity gives rise to approval. My anger gives rise to opposition—it is not that opposition gives rise to anger."

This showing of the secrets of the treasuries is evidence of love and the perfection of the Trust. As long as love is not confirmed, the secret will not be told, and as long as the Trust is not perfect, the hidden things will not be shown.[752]

You can also say that the wisdom in this was that Muṣṭafā was being trained to see paradise and hell. This has an example in the story of Moses. When he came to the station of whispered prayer, the Exalted Lord said, *"And what is that in thy right hand, O Moses?"* [20:17]. Do not suppose that the Exalted Lord did not know and that Moses did know. Moses knew the staff as wood, but the Exalted Lord saw in it the secret of a serpent. If on that day He had not made that secret evident to Moses, then when the staff became a serpent on the day of war with the sorcerers, the friend would have been just as frightened as the enemy.

On the day of secret whispering the call came, "Throw down the staff!" When he threw it, it became a serpent. What a fine coffer for the wonders of power was this staff! When it became a serpent, Moses said, "I have come to know many marvelous artisanries and wonderful crafts from this staff, but this attribute is more wonderful than all."

"O Moses, take it, and fear not! We will return it to its first conduct [20:21]. Just as I brought it from being wood to being a serpent, so I will take it back from being a serpent to being wood. Transforming substances from that side to this side is the same as from this side to that side. Just as people are incapable of making wood into a serpent, so also they are incapable of making a serpent into wood. Since I can do the first, I can also do the second."

When Moses put forth his hand, it became a staff as it had been. Moses came to know that it had no business with friends, but it did have business with enemies. When the day of war arrived, everyone was gazing at the staff, but Moses was gazing on the first artisanry. They saw what they had never seen and were frightened, but Moses saw what he had already seen and was at ease.

In the same way, Muṣṭafā was taken on the *miʿrāj*. The Garden and the Blaze, the degrees of paradise and the reaches of hell, were presented to him. He saw his own station in the highest Firdaws. Tomorrow, when people come to the resurrection, they will see things they had never seen. In fear of chastisement they will say, *"my soul, my soul!"* But since he will have already seen and become carefree, he will say, *"my community, my community!"*[753]

You can also say that the wisdom was to disclose Muṣṭafā. The example of this is when Zulaykhā was afflicted by love for Joseph, she turned away from all her friends. The realizers have said that the lordly secret was to set a trap from Canaan to Egypt. The mystery of Abraham inherited by Joseph was made the decoy of the trap in order to bring a bird wandering in the sky of caprice-worship into the road.

The women of Egypt prepared a deception in order to see whether Joseph was worth all that. "We will loose the tongue of blame. If she is frightened by blame, we will know that her love is not real. If she has no fear of blame, we will know that her love is real."[754]

The great ones have said that safety in the road of love lies in blame. As long as the lover is blamed, he will be safe in his love. If this safety is cut off, there will be the danger of his destruction.

The women let loose the tongue of blame: *"The governor's wife has been trying to seduce her chevalier"* [12:30]. *When she heard their deception* [12:31]. When that blame reached Zulaykhā's ears, she said, "There is no fear. My friend is not someone for whose sake I would fear blame." Then she said, "I will disclose the friend to them so that they will know that I am not worthy of blame."

When my blamer saw my idol's face,
    he prostrated a hundred times at my door.

She prepared an invitation, as you have heard. *She said* [to Joseph], *"Come forth upon them"* [12:31]. She did not say, *"Come forth to them."* If she had said *"to them,"* they would have found safety. When she said, *"upon them,"* trial appeared. *When they saw him, they admired him greatly and they cut their hands* [12:31]. When the gaze is outward, trial comes outwardly, but when the gaze is on the secret core, trial comes to the secret core.

Another meaning: The women were not lovers, so they were owners of their own hands and acted freely with their own property. But Zulaykhā was a lover, and a lover is not an owner, but rather owned. The owned cannot act freely with the property of her lord.

Now we come to talk of Muṣṭafā. When the Exalted Lord wanted to bring Adam into existence, He said, *"I am setting in the earth a vicegerent."* The angels said, *"What, wilt Thou set therein one who will work corruption there?"* He replied, *"Surely I know what you do not know* [2:30]. I know in the midst of them what you do not know, and that is Muḥammad. Among them I have a friend, and because of the blessings of his breaths I will overlook the sins of all the sinners."

At the One's laudation the residents of heaven began to yearn for Aḥmad's beauty, for he was mentioned first but would be sent last. There was no way for them to be brought to the earth. One reason is that they had no place in the earth; another is that there was no way to evict them from their station of worship, lest they be afflicted by fear of severance and distance. This is because they saw what happened to one of them when he came to the earth in messengerhood—that is, ʿAzāzīl, upon whom be curses! Even if they were sent to the earth but not as messengers, they feared that what had happened to him would happen to them.

The Exalted Lord had mercy. He commanded that the paragon be brought to the heavens and be displayed to all. "If Zulaykhā is able to display Joseph, I am even more able to display My Muṣṭafā." Then He commanded that he pass beyond all of them so that he would put down his feet in a place where everyone was beneath his feet. By virtue of this secret He made this allusion: "My friend is such that all of you are the dust beneath his feet."

In addition, the messengers were yearning for his beauty, for a covenant had been made with each of the prophets because of Muṣṭafā: "If you happen to see him, help him and have faith in him." A verse speaks of this: *"And when God took the compact of the prophets: 'I have given you of the Book and the Wisdom. Then a messenger will come to you confirming what is with you. You shall surely have faith in him and you shall surely help him'"* [3:81]. Thus the spirits of the prophets were yearning for his beauty and had no patience left. They said, "If seeing that paragon is at the resurrection, that seeing will be for the people in general. Our specific characteristic should have some benefit." The command came, "Take him on a *miʿrāj* so that he may meet with the messengers in the heavens," just as has come in the reports of the *miʿrāj*.

You may also say that the wisdom in taking him on the *miʿrāj* was to show that his state in this world is like his state in the afterworld. The meaning of these words is that all people have a companionship and commingling with the soul. As long as the spirit has not become separate from the soul, it will not be taken to the celestial world. Muṣṭafā, however, had no companionship, commingling, and mixing with the soul. Rather, in terms of meaning, his soul had become all spirit, and his spirit was waiting for opening. In order to realize this meaning before death and demise, his soul was conveyed along with the spirit to the station of the spirit. Do you not see that Muṣṭafā, because he does not have the companionship of the soul, will not mention the soul on the Day of Resurrection?[755]

Another argument is this: In His splendorous scripture the Exalted Lord says, *"As for him who feared the station of his Lord and prohibited the soul its caprice, surely the Garden shall be the shelter"* [79:40–41]. If the soul's caprice is to be prohibited, there must first be a soul. But when He described Muṣṭafā, He said, *"Nor does he speak from caprice"* [53:3]. Had there been a soul, the soul would have had caprice. Then He would have been negating a soul that exists, but negating an existing thing is absurd.

All creatures must have death in order to be rid of the soul. Since he was rid of the soul in the state of life, his state before death was like his state after death. So before death his soul reached the station that spirits reach after death. Once death came, his state after death was just like his state before death.

If his death were like that of others, the ruling about his wives would be like the ruling about the wives of others.[756] And if his death were like that of others, affirming his messengerhood after death would be absurd, for the dead person is not a messenger. But since the command has come to say until the resurrection, *"I bear witness that Muḥammad is God's messenger,"* it is correct that his death is life. The books of the people will be presented to him in the grave, and he will be happy and give thanks for their obedience and be sad and ask pardon for their disobedience, so it is correct that his death is life.

Hence his life was death and his death life. So long as he was alive, he was aware of some people and not others. When he closed his eyes, he became aware of all the states of his community. Were his death like the death of others, it would be necessary for his knowledge to decrease, not increase.

His life was given the attribute of death because he did not have the soul, for the dead person has nothing to do with the soul; and because he did not have free choice, for the dead person has no free choice; and because he did not have opposition, for the dead person does not have opposition; and because he did not have desires, for the dead person has no desires. This is why the Real said, *"Thou didst not throw when thou threwest, but God threw"* [8:17]. Thus He negated him with *thou didst not throw*, and He affirmed him with *when thou threwest*. What a marvelous business! How can one thing be both affirmed and negated? What is the meaning? "O annihilated from your own attributes, O subsistent through My attributes!"

The Real attracted his secret core, the secret core attracted the spirit, the spirit attracted the heart, and the heart attracted the soul. His soul reached a place where it was unaware of the two worlds, his heart reached a place where it was unaware of the soul, his spirit reached a place where it was unaware of the heart, and his secret core reached a place where it was unaware of the spirit.

His being began to seek his soul, his soul began to seek his heart, his heart began to seek his spirit, his spirit began to seek his secret core, and his secret core began to seek contemplation. The being said, "I have no rest without the soul." The soul said, "I have no rest without the heart." The heart said, "I have no rest without the spirit." The spirit said, "I have no rest without the secret core." The secret core said, "I have no rest without the contemplation of the Real."

The being began to shout, "Where is the soul?" The soul began to shout, "Where is the heart?" The heart began to shout, "Where is the spirit?" The spirit began to shout, "Where is the secret core?" The secret core began to shout, "Where is contemplation?"

"Then he drew close" in his soul, "and He came down" into his heart, "so he was two-bows' length away" inside his spirit "or closer" [53:8–9] *in his secret core through contemplation.*

The soul has the station of service, the heart the station of love, the spirit the station of proximity, and the secret core the station of contemplation. If you take away the soul's capacity to serve, it will perish. If you take away the heart's capacity to love, it will cease to be. If you take away the spirit's capacity to be in proximity, it will be finished. If you take away the secret core's capacity to contemplate, it will be annihilated.

The nourishment of his soul was service, the nourishment of his heart was love, the nourishment of his spirit was proximity, and the nourishment of his secret core was contemplation. All creatures live through the spirit, but the spirit lives through the Real. *"How far apart are those who live through their hearts and those who live through their Lord!"*[757]

You may also say that the wisdom in the *miʿrāj* was that his heart was busy with the disloyalties of the community.[758] When their disloyalty was presented to him, he saw many sins and disloyalties, but he was ashamed to intercede, for when a sin is great, the interceder is ashamed to intercede. The disloyalties of the community were shown to him, and what they wanted to do with his children was told to him. Thus it has come in a report from Umm Salama that one day Muṣṭafā was in the house and Ḥusayn was next to him playing. Gabriel came and Muṣṭafā said, "O Umm Salama, take my child until I am finished with the revelation."

Gabriel said, "O Muḥammad, do you love this child?"

He said, "I do."

"As for your community, they will slaughter this child as a butcher slaughters a year-old lamb."[759]

Many disloyalties of his community were reported to him and his heart was busy with them, so he was ashamed to intercede. The Real wanted to unburden his secret core, so He commanded that he be taken on the *miʿrāj* and be shown the vastness of the world of mercy. He saw face-to-face what the Real has and what He will do. He saw that next to the Real's mercy the disloyalty of the creatures was like the part next to the whole, the mote next to the totality. The command came, "O friend, look closely at their disloyalty and look carefully at My mercy. If their disloyalty is more than My mercy, then be ashamed to intercede. If their disloyalty is less than My mercy, then do not be ashamed to intercede."

It is said that in that station the command came, "O friend, what have you brought?"

He said, "I have brought two handfuls: first my community's shortcoming in obedience, and second my community's disloyalty and disobedience. Forgive the shortcoming with Your mercy and the disloyalty with my status."

The Exalted Lord said, "I forgive. In the next world I will absolve, and in this world I will conceal."

Once the paragon knew this meaning, as a matter of course he said, *"My intercession belongs to the folk of great sins in my community."*[760] If I were to ask for a small bestowal, I would diminish both my status and Your mercy.

Disregard of the ugly-doer's disloyalty is in the measure of the tremendousness of the interceder's status. Forgiving much disloyalty for the sake of the interceder is evidence of the interceder's status.

It has come that when Gabriel took Muṣṭafā to the Lote Tree, he placed him before himself and stood still. He called to him, "Give felicitations to thy Lord!"

Muṣṭafā said, *"The felicitations, the blessings, the prayers, and the goodly things belong to God."*

The answer came from the Lord, *"The peace be upon thee, O Prophet, and God's mercy and His blessings!"*

Muṣṭafā said, *"The peace be upon us and upon God's servants, the wholesome!"*[761]

The Real made *"The peace be upon thee"* specific to him, but he himself spoke generally for the people: *"The peace be upon us."*

"O friend, there is no one with you. Why do you say '*upon us*'?"

He said, "Although they are not here in person, they are with me through solicitude."

Some have said that the wisdom of the *mi'rāj* is that before the Exalted Lord put Muṣṭafā into the oyster of dust, He kept his purified, illumined spirit in three stations: the station of proximity, the station of gentleness, and the station of awe. From proximity he found intimacy, from gentleness expansiveness, and from awe courtesy. He was caressed by proximity, his work was taken care of by gentleness, and he was melted in the crucible of fear by awe.[762]

When he was brought into the body from these stations of generous gifts, orchards of realities, gardens of approval, and palaces of light, and when he was commanded by the rulings of the Shariah, he yearned for that same station and sought that same lodging place. When you catch a little bird from the vast plain, it throws itself on the ground. Why is that? It is yearning for its homeland. When you light up a fire, it trembles and runs toward the sky. Why is that? It is yearning for its homeland.

When he yearned for that station, there was no way to take the spirit there without the body, for the moment of death had not yet come. The soul was taken along with the spirit to the spirit's station and sky so that the soul would find the same intimacy as the spirit and take on the same courtesy as the spirit. When he came back into this world, everyone who gazed upon him found hope from his station of intimacy and fear from his station of awe.

When that station, along with those generous gifts, gentle favors of union, and gifts and bestowals of advancing toward the Essence and attributes, was displayed without blight to the paragon—*Then he drew close, so He came down* [53:8]—he said, "This is a place of great ease. I will not go back."

The address came, "If you do not go back, who will invite My servants? The full moon of *today I have perfected for you your religion* [5:3] has not yet put up its head in the fourteenth night of the Shariah.

"O Muḥammad, you are like a falcon—a falcon bought for a thousand dirhams to hunt sparrows costing ten for a dirham. It is enough for the falcon that its nest be the hand of the king. In the Beginningless I issued the decree that you will be the one to invite this assembly. If you make your station here, you will not be able to bring them. But I am not incapable of bringing you to this station. Go back to the earth and invite! He who was able to bring you to this station by decree can also bring you to this station by power. As long as you can be patient with the people, be so. When you lose patience, make a *takbīr* and enter into the consecration of the prayer, for the prayer is the station of union. When you enter the prayer, I will lift the veils and show you right there, without your coming, the station to which you needed to come in order to see."

When he came back to the earth, as long as he could put up with companionship, he was a companion for the people. When he could no longer do so, he would say, *"Give us ease, O Bilāl!"*[763] Beat the drum for the falcon of mystery and release me from the people! Begin the prayer, for the lover does not have the capacity for patience. He is only able to make himself be patient with effort.

To bind the covenant of the prayer is to surrender oneself totally to the Real and to turn away from the two worlds. Do you not see that in every act of worship, there is room to mix it with the soul's desire and with seeking this world? But in the prayer, there is no seeking this world, no appetite of the soul, and no companionship with people. Adamic desires are these three things, and all three are impossible in the prayer. If you set up this world's work, the prayer is gone. If you satisfy appetite, the prayer is nullified. If you talk to people, the prayer is ruined. Thus the secret of the prayer is to declare oneself totally quit of attachments and to entrust oneself to the Friend. This is the attribute of someone whose prayer is reality, not that of someone whose prayer is habit.

This is why the paragon said, *"The delight of my eyes was put in the prayer."*[764] By God, the delight of the lovers' eyes is nothing and will be nothing other than proximity to the beloveds! In this meaning the great ones have said, *"We are negligent of the highest because of the lowest, but he was negligent of the lowest because of the highest."* The secret core of us, who are folk of the community, is occupied with something less than the prayer, so we become negligent in the prayer. But Muṣṭafā's secret core was occupied with something beyond the prayer, and that is the contemplation of the station of proximity, so he became negligent. That is why the chieftains of the Tariqah have said, "Would that our present moment was the negligence that fell upon Muṣṭafā!"

The people were aware of the *miʿrāj* of his outwardness, but in his inwardness he had a *miʿrāj* at every moment. The people were attached to him, but he was attached to the Real. The people were not at ease without him, but he was not at ease without the Real.

You can also say that the wisdom in the *miʿrāj* was for the blessing of his gaze to reach the celestial world and for that world to become exalted through his gaze. He was brought into the Garden so that the blessing of his gaze would complete the enjoyments of the Garden for his community, since a house without the gaze of the housemaster is defective. It becomes complete when the housemaster steps into it. Then He commanded that hell be presented to him so that his gaze would fall upon hell and through the blessing of his gaze the folk of his community would be delivered from chastisement.[765]

What is the good news in this allusion? It is that it has come in a report that tomorrow at the resurrection a servant named Muḥammad who had done many sins will be brought. The Exalted Lord will address him, "O My servant, your mother and father named you Muḥammad. Were you not ashamed to be so disobedient with the name of My friend? In any case, I in My generosity do not approve of chastising someone with the same name as My friend."[766]

He traveled the road of dust and clay completely, but his aspiration aimed on high. It has come in a sound report that Adam was taken to the first heaven, Jesus to the second, Joseph to the third, Idris to the fourth, Aaron to the fifth, Moses to the sixth, and Abraham to the seventh.[767] If Muṣṭafā had not traveled Adam's road completely, he would not have reached the second heaven, and so on. Then he reached Gabriel's corner at *the Lote Tree of the Final End* [53:14]. Why is it called *the Final End*? *"At it is the final end of every knower's knowledge."*[768]

Gabriel held up his days before Muṣṭafā's eyes. He said, "It is several thousand years that I act as Gabriel. I bring my several thousand years before your eyes because you are the assayer of the Presence. If tomorrow I take my register to the Exalted Threshold without the lofty signet of the paragon of paragons, it will not be accepted by the Exalted Presence."

Once Gabriel's corner had been adorned by the paragon's blessed feet, he passed beyond the Lote Tree. *When someone's goal is the Presence, how can he be content with the Lote Tree?*

"O Gabriel, will you not come along with me?"

He said, "The serving boy must stand at the edge of the carpet, and the friend must sit on the carpet of expansiveness." This is Gabriel, who had six hundred wings. If he spread one of those wings, he would bring the land and the sea beneath it.

Muṣṭafā said, "When I passed beyond the Lote Tree, I saw him *like a castaway piece of cloth.*"[769]

The sultanate is the sultanate that is run in the presence of the King.

37–38. *al-Ghafūr al-Shakūr:* the Forgiving, the Grateful

From here on I will speak briefly in fear of boring the hearts of those who love the Possessor of Majesty.

What is the Forgiving and the Grateful? The absolver of the great and the accepter of the small.

The meanings of *ghafūr*, *ghaffār*, and *ghāfir* have already been mentioned.[770] *Shakūr* is an intensive from *shākir*, just as *ghafūr* is an intensive from *ghāfir*.

Some have said that the Exalted Lord is grateful in the sense that He gives recompense for the servant's gratitude. Examples of this are many. God says, *"God will mock them"* [2:15], that is, He will give them recompense for their mockery.

Some have said that the meaning of grateful is that He praises His servants much and He rewards them for little obedience. This is because of the perfect divine bounty and kingly gentleness, for it is He who gives the success of service and it is He also who gives much praise for little service. *O generosity that has no end! "The repenters, the worshipers"* [9:112].

It is not surprising that you in your perfect deficiency praise and laud Him in the hope of *remember Me; I will remember you* [2:152]. What is surprising is that He in His perfect majesty praises and lauds you, despite the billowing ocean of His unneediness. He put the whole of this world into your work and because of its nonexistence wrote this inscription on its face: *"Say: 'The enjoyment of this world is little'"* [4:77].

Although the bride of your obedience appears from behind the veil of His success-giving, He adorns her with the curtain of gratitude and the ornaments and robes of His laudation. In the firm text of the Book He says, *"Men who remember God much and women who remember"* [33:35]. After all, how long is your life that your praise of God should be *"much"*?

"Nonetheless servant-caressing is My work. What remains that I have not done for you? And what remains that you have not done for Me? I have done for you what is done for sultans, and you have done for Me what is done for servants. O you who complain of Me to yourself though I have not complained of you! How much I complain of you secretly, but in front of people I am only grateful to you.

I complain of my friend in secret
but in public I thank him.[771]

"O you whose blame has been met with generosity and whose bad has been recompensed with good! O you whom I invited to My threshold by sending messengers despite My unneediness! O you who are detached from Me despite your neediness! O you into whose heart I fire 360 arrows of gentleness every day, though I wrote out the inscription of abandonment for all existent things! O you whose measure I conveyed beyond the measure of all beings, though you do not know your own measure! O you whom I created safe and protected from the folk of creation, though you have degraded yourself with those of no worth! O you for whose days I guaranteed the sufficient and wrote out its title deed, but you looked outside My promise with your suspicious eyes! O you whose need I attended to Myself, though you came out in confrontation! O you who in yourself were nonbeing and who came to be through My beautiful-doing! O you who had no mark in your being and who found a mark through My beautiful-doing! O you who kept no covenant with Me, though I have not trampled any covenant with you! O you who have never shown any kind favor toward My command, though I have examined all of your states with the eye of kind favor! O you whose rightful due I made incumbent on My generosity before I made anything incumbent on you!

"O you who are exalted in My eyes, do not go to the threshold of another! Do not show your need to any created thing, lest you be abased and come back in despair! The keys of heaven and earth and the openers of the treasuries of the world are in the fist of My power. Who is there in the world that will open a door if I close it? Who will close a door if I open it?"

Whatever mercy God opens up to the people, none will hold it back [35:2]. *"No one holds back what You bestow, and no one bestows what You hold back."*[772]

"When people go to the presence of this world's sultans, they look to see whose clothing is more splendid and whose respectability is greater so that they can attend to his needs. I look to see where there is a beggar so that I can attend to his needs. Where is someone penniless so that I may act according to his desire? Where is someone wearing rags so that I may decree as he requests when I decree? Where is someone helpless and driven away so that when I bestow robes of gentleness, I may place one on his shoulders?

"You see someone weak and penniless, scorned by the people. Come to My presence to see him with the awesomeness of lions and the strength of elephants! Someone else is driven away and rejected, accepted by no one—come to My threshold to see him held dear! Another is chased from every door, all skirts pulled back from him—come to the pavilion of My majesty to see his controlling power and issuing of decrees."

A dervish said, "I went to Jerusalem and saw someone saying, 'If You are going to give me back my shoes, then give them back. Otherwise I will smash the lanterns of Your house!' I said to myself, *'He is either a madman or a coquettish lover.'* All at once someone came out with shoes and placed them before him, saying, 'Stop being bilious, for we have given you back your shoes.' "

In winter when the gentle rose garden looks like a harsh thorn bed, wait until a few days pass and the hand of the hairdresser of spring puts it on display at the edge of the stream of its secrets. Tomorrow that beggar will come, *in his right hand everlastingness and in his left hand the kingdom.*

The black man who rang the bell for the Real's law was
father of night for the Arabs and *father of day* for the resurrection.
Take the blame on a poor man's name as the chamberlain of poverty;
take the ocean's bitter water as the guard of the pearl.
Wanting subsistence you should seek it from dervishes—
their being is the warp and weft of subsistence's cloak.
You will have nothing but wind in hand if you boast of anything
but the dust beneath the feet of this handful of dust-dwellers.
It is the rag-wearers who live in good fortune—
don't scorn them in pride, beware!
For the sake of a dust-dweller God took one of the exalted
and stoned him at the pavilion of harshness![773]

It is the custom among the bedouins that when someone is accepted as a neighbor and brought into their neighborhood, they say to him, *"Decree for me as an infant decrees for its mother."* If he should kill someone, they will pay the wergild; if he should dispute with someone, they will dispute along with him; if some of his property is destroyed, they will compensate for it; and if one of his animals dies, they will replace it. They say, "It is not allowed that you be sheltered by us and suffer loss, or that you be in our neighborhood and looked upon with the eyes of enmity, or that you be protected by our covenant and be deprived of something."

What harm if my neighbor
has no curtain on his door?
My fire and his are one—
I put on the pot for him before myself.[774]

The Exalted Lord is more generous than all the generous.

"There is many a disheveled, grimy possessor of two rags paid no regard by anyone who, were he to swear an oath to God, would see it answered."[775]

Abū Rayḥāna was one of the great exalted ones. One day when he was sitting on the bank of a river and sewing, his needle fell into the water. He said, "Lord God, I command You: *I enjoin You to return my needle!"* Immediately a fish came with the needle in its mouth and put it down before him.[776]

Ḥammād ibn Mūsā said, "Once I was in Mecca and wanted to go to Medina. I had a few dinars, so I said to myself that I would place them with Kahmas ibn Ḥasan.[777] I went to him and he told me to put them on a certain shelf. I put them there and went to Medina. When I came back and went to him, I asked him to return those dinars. He said that I should take them from where I left them. I stretched up my hand but did not find them. I said to him, 'I don't find them.' Kahmas stood up and searched, and he also did not find them. He put on his shoes, and I went along behind him to the Sacred Mosque. He stood before the pulpit and performed two cycles of prayer. Then he said, *'O Lord, where is Ḥammād's property?' as if he were addressing a human being.* 'Lord God, what did You do with Ḥammād's gold? I know You, but I do not know anyone else. I want You to give it back to me right now.' Then he said to me, 'Go back and take the gold.' I went back, put my hand up on the shelf, and saw that the gold was there."

I do not know who we are and who they were. This is surely the era of misfortune! This is surely the era of turning away! And we are surely the unworthy!

O chevalier, you cannot take the road along with the enemy. You claim to be burned by the Threshold, but you have set down nature's brides before you and fallen in love with their gold, ornament, color, and scent. Do you want the sultans of the Shariah and the kings of the Haqiqah to give you access to the pavilion of the secret core and the tent of piety? You wear the shirt of disloyalty and have drawn the sword of caprice, so you cannot settle down on the bench of limpidness under the dome of subsistence. *"Throwing the soul into servanthood, attaching the heart to the Lordhood, and gazing totally on the Real"*[778] must become the embroidery on the cape of your secret whispering. Then the high-aspiring falcon of the Tariqah will snatch away the colorful pheasant of your craving and appetite with the beak of asking forgiveness. Empty your skirt of this verdure of the dunghill and throw away your dear life at the banquet of the ascription of *"Say: 'O My servants!'* [39:53]."

Give up life, for it is a day to give up life;
conceal the secret, for the King is in the house.

The reality of Sufism is to elevate the aspiration beyond the communities' disputes in their fear of slipping feet and to renounce what God has permitted, not simply what He has forbidden.

Be like a man and pull back your neck from the two worlds. The garden's jasmine and roses finish quickly because they defile themselves, but the eyes gaze on cypress and pine in January because of their self-restraint, manliness, and fearlessness.

O you who have faith, if any of you turns away from your religion, God will bring a people whom He loves and who love Him, abased before the faithful [5:54]. Beware, beware, lest you wander around this envious body or circle around your helpless makeup! When the silkworm spins around itself, it stays in the prison of its own soul. If what you want is to soar in the air of bounteousness with the pinions of victory, the wings of prosperity, and the feathers of lustrousness while contemplating the beauty of the Possessor of Majesty, then come out of this dark, tenebrous midden and circumambulate the Kaabah of hope and fear. Then tomorrow He will give you a light such that the eagle of punishment, seeing your eyes on the vast plain of the resurrection, will call out, *"Pass by, O man of faith, for your light will extinguish my flames."*[779]

And beware, beware, when you aim for the Presence of Majesty, lest you take along any burden of suspicion, appetite, and wish, for it is absurd to sleep with the wide-eyed houris wearing a shirt. If tomorrow you want your eyes to be daubed with the gentle and subtle collyrium of *faces that day radiant, gazing on their Lord* [75:22–23], then today anoint the eyes of your intellect with dust from the hooves of the Burāq of the Shariah and never pull back your feet from the shackle and snare of Muḥammad God's messenger: *God, the Prophet, and the Arab religion!*

You must gamble away everything in order to pass beyond this world of generation and corruption, this place of Satan's snares and his refusal and obstinacy. Fly with one breath toward the world of holiness like a bird escaping from the cage. When you fly up, cutting yourself off from the two worlds, do not make the moon your lodging place, do not put down the cushion of your aspiration at the North Star, and do not look back at Gemini and the houris. Keep your feet with your heart, your heart with your thoughts, your thoughts with your secret core, and your secret core with the Real. Like Muṣṭafā take one step into the Sacred Mosque and the next step into the Furthest Mosque. Pass by each heaven with one stride until you step down at *the Lote Tree of the Final End* [53:14]. Then pass beyond the Lote Tree and travel into the Pure Unseen. Put aside companions, pass beyond the prophets, step above the Higher Plenum, and turn your face, alone and one, to the goal of yearning and the *seat of truthfulness* [54:55]. Once you arrive at the domicile of *then he drew close* [53:8], place your feet on the carpet of *so He came down* [53:8], rest in the proximity of *two-bows' length away* [53:9], and settle down in the station of *or closer* [53:9], you will have heard the mystery, tasted the wine, arrived at contemplation, fled from both realms of being, and come to rest with the Friend.

This is a road for runners like this, a battlefield for men like this, a vast plain for falcons like this. It is a road that wants a man whose aspiration aims high, whose goal is the highest station, whose attributes have been swallowed down by the dragon of *No* [*god*]—which is the doorkeeper of the world of *but* [*God*]—who makes his soul the precious pearl of the Shariah, who mounts his heart on the mule of seeking, who keeps his spirit waiting for opening, and who makes his secret core rejoice in God's subsistence. Then these secret lights will become the imprint on the stone of his state's seal ring: *"The hand emptied of possessions, the heart limpid of hopes, the rightful due observed in every state."*

Here you have a rare work! Here you have a marvelous story! A spirit was brought from the world of lights, the collar of *tawḥīd's* secrets bound to its neck. It was sent to you as a gift, but you do not know its worth. You have embraced the tiny soul and, by the decree of appetite, made the spirit with its angelic attributes stand on one foot in front of the pig of avaricious craving and the dog of wishful appetite.

O jailed in the prison of avarice and greed! How long will you be disloyal to the pure spirit for the sake of the soul, hostile in disposition and far from acceptance? How long will you waste and disperse your intelligence and intellect? Is it not time for you to have loyalty along with those who are sincerely truthful, those whose present moment is a seal ring imprinted with *those who are loyal to their covenant* [2:177]?

By God the Tremendous, I wonder at you! Jesus the pure had a tremendous state. The title page of his book was *the Word of God* and *the Spirit of God*. He was sat down before you and put into the grammar school of your makeup, but you in your extreme gullibility and unawareness have subjected yourself to the hooves of his donkey. But *when good fortune turns its back, what is the stratagem*?

With all this you still want to sit next to the tree of the scented garden of the Unseen, to drink the water of life from the wellspring of the meadow of gentleness, and to make the seventh sphere the dust under your feet. For a moment shut these five windows with the hand of annihilation, contemplate the hand of subsistence, and pack your bags from this world of annihilation and house of trouble.

> Water, dust, wind, and fire are enemies—
> pass beyond these four and give a turn to the five.[780]

[*As for him who feared the station of his Lord*] *and prohibited the soul its caprice, surely the Garden shall be the shelter* [79:40–41]. If you want your heart to become an oyster for the pearl of the Haqiqah's secret, be jealous in the road of recognition and become blind and deaf like an oyster to everything other than God.

Shiblī was asked, "Who are the recognizers and what is their attribute?"

He said, "They are 'deaf, dumb, blind' [2:18]."

They said to him, *"But that is the attribute of the unbelievers."*

He said, "The unbelievers are deaf to hearing the Real, dumb to speaking of the Real, blind to seeing the Real. The recognizers are deaf to hearing other than the Real, dumb to speaking of other than the Real, blind to seeing other than the Real."

What a marvelous business! A piece of chaff, trampled underfoot by the rosebushes in the garden of proximity, put a crown on its head because of avarice and greed. It made a state and moment—which is bought by the wayfarers of the Threshold for one thousand sweet lives per mithqal—into the plaything of a handful of little cutpurse Iblises. O pure spirits deposited in these piles of dust, stop listening to this handful of dust-dwelling, unintelligent, unaware dust! With the radiance of the spiritual sun shining forth from the constellation of your covenant's limpidness, turn this dust—which is the realm of the folk of missteps and the station of the folk of disloyalty—into rubies, pearls, and carnelians! When the blazing sun shines on dust for a time, it will turn it into the gold of the mines.

Here you have a rare work: A man says, "Heaven and earth cannot string the bow of my intellect and knowledge." Then like a gullible donkey he is hoodwinked by a house that, to be fair, is not worth a barleycorn.

Someone is stung by the bold scorpion of the tumult-inciting soul, then sits heedless like a snake charmer. O you who have been kept in the prison of your soul and the cavern of your nature, when will your stingy, deranged, lost soul take the road of the pure spirit? When will it, like the new moon, conceal itself from the eyes of others and depart from this place of punishing snares and falsifying traps for the nest of heaven and the balcony of the proximate, adorning the *seat of truthfulness* [54:55] with the *foot of truthfulness* [10:2]?

Once the moth-killing, loverlike candle reaches the truthfulness of love itself, its body is burned away by the spirit-burning fire that crowns it, but its heart never burns the slightest in regret for itself. When the sorrowful body is burned by the fire of tribulations and its eyes are sewn shut to observation, the spirit will spread its arms in the world of repose and see face-to-face all that was hidden from it, without the talk and chatter, the questions and answers, of the doorkeepers of the Shariah. Every fastened lock, unresolved difficulty, or strange intimation there had been will become like the sun, without obligation toward the tiny, meddling intellect or the posturing and prattling of the folk of outward meanings.

O dervish, have a high aspiration! You have not been brought into existence for a small job. Heaven and earth trembled when they heard the edict of Adam's sultanate.

> Be the companion of spirit and intellect and go to the world of holiness—
> you're no beast of burden that your world should be senses and sounds.
> Though you be obedient, don't feel secure from His presence.
> Though you've slipped, don't despair of His threshold.
> Though you're beautiful, don't look with scorn on the ugly—
> in His kingdom a fly has as much use as a peacock.[781]

When a man has been given kingship over the world of holiness, why would he allow himself to come back and watch over the world of the senses? *By God the Tremendous*, if you step forth with seriousness and striving in the world of obedient acts and practices, if you adorn yourself outwardly with the duties of the Shariah, and if you trim yourself inwardly with the subtleties of the Haqiqah, your feet will pass beyond the foremost feathers of Gabriel's wing!

Have you not seen how a mulberry leaf travels from its own makeup, passes beyond its form, and becomes an emperor's robe and king's garment because of its transformed attributes? *If you desire the stations of the Substitutes, you must transform your states.*

Before you look on from afar with regret and sorrow while the peacock of the spirit—which is Gabriel in the bodily world's *Lote Tree of the Final End*—moves on to the world of *surely unto thy Lord is the final end* [53:42], strike the pickax of struggle against the solid rock of the soul. Perhaps the wellsprings of contemplation will bubble up and you, like Jonah—or rather, like a man of destitution—may perform a full ablution there and be purified of the pollution of responding to your own soul.

39–40. *al-ʿAlī al-Kabīr:* the High, the Great

God says, "So the decree belongs to God, the High, the Great" [40:12]. The Maker's highness is not in respect of direction, nor is His greatness in respect of bulk, for both of these are attributes and traits of created things, and in the eyes of the mindful, the Lord of Lords is pure of that. His greatness and highness allude to His worthiness for the attributes of perfection, His incomparability with and hallowedness beyond descriptions of defect, and His greatness and transcendence beyond similarity with createdness. So His highness is an attribute, not a direction.[782]

It is the rightful due of anyone who believes in His highness and greatness to see all measures as nonexistent in the face of His measure and to see all majesties as evanescent in the world of His majesty, all perfections as deficiency, and all claims as loss. Along with His perfection, perfection is given over to no one, and along with His beauty, beauty is given over to no one.

Is not everything other than God unreal
and every bliss inescapably evanescent?[783]

"If you seek exaltedness, you will have no portion of it, for exaltedness is an attribute specific to Me, and abasement an attribute specific to you."

In one of the reports it has come, *"Glory be to Him who garbed Himself in splendor and was generous with it! Glory be to Him who was compassionate in exaltedness and upheld it!"*[784]

"If you seek greatness, you will not have its color, for greatness is suited for Me, and wilting, abasement, and obscurity are suited for you. If you go after exaltedness, I will cover you with the dust of abasement, and if you seek greatness, I will throw you into the pit of contempt. If you roll in the dust of My Presence with humility, I will sit you on the Burāq of exaltedness and prosperity. If you come to My Presence with your head raised high, I will strike your head with the mace of severity and destruction.

"Iblis claimed exaltedness and seized the skirt of claiming greatness. Look what I did to him: *Go forth from it; surely thou art an outcast!* [15:34]. The accursed Pharaoh displayed himself in the attribute of highness and exaltedness. Look what happened to him: *So We drowned him and those with him, all together* [17:103]. Korah boasted of his treasures. Look what I did to him: *So We made the earth engulf him and his house* [28:81]. The accursed Abū Jahl claimed exaltedness and said, 'I am exalted and obeyed among my people.' Tomorrow in hell it will be said to him, *'Taste! Surely thou art the exalted, the noble'* [44:49]. Zaqqūm and boiling water will be poured down his throat and it will be said, 'O you who claimed exaltedness in this world, drink, for the final outcome of that expansive claim is this!' "

"When someone humbles himself before God, God will lift him up, and when someone claims greatness, God will put him down."[785]

"Putting down one's face before the Real is exaltedness."[786]

When someone puts down his face before Him, He will lift up his degree.

Shiblī had tremendous nobility. Eighteen times chains were put on his hands and feet and he was put in bonds and prison. It was said to him, "What was your work with Ḥusayn Manṣūr?"

He said, "The two of us went into the same oven, but his name was 'rational.' He put down his head in the name of rationality, and I escaped with the name of madness. When a sultan comes to look at a madman, the madman says many words that the sultan would not tolerate from anyone else."

It is said that once a prince built an asylum and wanted to go and look. When he went and saw the madmen bound in chains, one of them lifted up his head and said, "O prince, you take wealth from the rational, put it to use for the mad, and then you want a reward. That is really absurd." Whenever someone's feet are put in bonds, the bonds are lifted from his tongue.

What is meant is that one day Shiblī emerged in that ecstasy of his. Someone said, "Who is Shiblī?"

He said, *"I am the point under the* b [ب]."[787]

Write out *in the name of God* [*bismi'llāh*], put the point under the *b*, and Shiblī is that point. You see the beauty, perfection, and upright stature of the *alif* [ا], while that dot is stuck in the station of being scorned and bewildered. *Alif* has an upright stature. Shiblī did not begin with the *alif* because of the demand of jealousy. He came to the beginning of the letters and saw *alif* with its upright head. He passed it by and arrived at *b*. He saw *b* humble, its face turned toward dust. He took its hand and made it the foremost of all.

Ṭāwūs Yamānī said, "I was circling in the place of circumambulation when I heard the moaning of whispered secrets. I went ahead to see who was moaning. I saw ʿAlī ibn Ḥusayn Zayn al-ʿĀbidīn, his face in the dust. I said to myself, 'This is the exalted man of the Folk of the House. Let me see what he is saying.' I listened. He was saying, *'Thy little servant is at Thy gate, Thy indigent is at Thy gate, Thy asker is at Thy gate.'* "

Ṭāwūs said, "Whenever any work became difficult for me, I made an ablution, put down my head in prostration, and said these words, and the work became easy."[788]

The Quran begins with *b*, though *alif* is first in the alphabet. This is because *alif* is standing and *b* is fallen. This shows that the fallen is more complete than the standing. The fallen are lifted up, but the standing are thrown down.

Alif has no wherewithal, but *b* has the wherewithal of the dot. Nonetheless, even though *alif* has no portion of anything else, it does have the portion of itself. The portion of the other does not do to you what the portion of yourself does to you.

The letters are twenty-eight, first *alif* and last *y* [ی]. Those who say that they are twenty-nine are mistaken, for *lām-alif* is a compound; it is not one. There is no stipulation to place a compound among those who are one and disengaged.

The *alif* at the beginning is erect in figure, straight in stature. The *y* at the end is curved in figure, bent in stature. What is this erect *alif*? The beginner on the road. What is this bent *y*? The advanced on the road, given to the wind.

The letters are twenty-eight, and the mansions of the moon are twenty-eight. *And the moon—We have determined mansions for it, till it returns like the old palm branch* [36:39]. Have you seen the moon at the end of the month—weak, wasted, and emaciated? Why is that? It traveled the road and reached the presence of the sultan, and all the traits of paragons fall apart in the presence of the sultan. In the whole month it is allowed no more than one night of perfection. For the rest it stays in its own deficiency. On the one night when it takes on perfection and beauty, the sun itself is its antagonist. It says, "As long as you do not go down, I will not come up. I will not be together with you, for two sultans will not come together in one empire. As long as you are in your own deficiency, it is all right for me to be together with you in heaven. When you claim perfection, I will not pitch the tent of my prosperity until you pack your bags."

Then, when it becomes full and walks like a houri from the palace to the vast plain of manifestation, eclipse is assigned to it. An eclipse never goes after the deficient moon. An eclipse wants a full moon in whose head is the claim of perfection; then it will show the hand of its own work and pull it from its throne of light. The crescent is already wounded by its own deficiency, and a wounded man is not struck. They break claimants and burn them, giving their ashes to the wind, but they caress the self-effaced and broken.

"When you see someone seeking Me, be his servitor."[789]

"I am with those whose hearts are broken for My sake."[790]

"I am the sitting companion of those who remember Me."[791]

"We will never combine two things in you: a burnt heart and separation." When the poor, helpless lover is weak and emaciated, broken and wounded by the arrow of love, while the Beloved is beautiful and tender, the lover does not have the wherewithal to go to the Beloved's threshold. What can the Beloved do but trample the coquetry of beauty underfoot and come forth like the merciful to the corner of the burnt lover's sorrows? He will whisper secretly in the ear of his need:

> Rise, My friend, let us put away the rebuke and war of yesterday.
> Let us confirm the covenant of love and peace today.
> Let us end yesterday's grief, stop today's sorrow,
> and prevent tomorrow's pain with happy spirit and heart.
> Stay with me and we'll celebrate peace and love;
> knocking at the door we'll mourn for war.
> We'll be lover and beloved, holding hands;
> we'll be one in heart and spirit, together in spirit and heart.
> We'll stop talking of the highway and walk with one goal;
> we'll take the way to the lovers' street singing high and low.
> We'll place the foot of aspiration high on the spheres;
> we'll bless the friends with the greatest of the oceans.
> Like Jamshid and Kawus we'll get drunk,
> sometimes from Kawus's cup, sometimes from Jamshid's jug."

There is no whispering among three, but that He is the fourth of them [58:7]. *And He is with you wherever you are* [57:4]. In the case of the common people, God's with-ness is through knowledge and power, but in the case of the elect it is through bounty and help. In any case this spirit-nurturing declaration has a tremendous effect on the hearts and spirits of the folk of recognition. By the time the work falls to the interpretation of the masters of interpretation, the lovers and possessors of bewilderment are drunk at having heard the words, with a thousand thousand paradises in hard cash.

The Companions of the Cave were in the cave of jealousy and the station of exaltedness. Although they had a high station, the Real reported about their state like this: *"They will say, 'Three; the fourth of them was their dog.' They will say, 'Five; the sixth of them was their dog'... They will say, 'Seven; the eighth of them was their dog'"* [18:22]. When the seclusion of this community arrived, He said in the firm text of His book and the established words of His address, *"There is no whispering among three, but that He is the fourth of them, nor among five, but that He is the sixth of them"* [58:7]. How far apart are those whose fourth is their dog and those whose fourth is their Lord!

"Wherever you are, I am with you. If you are in a monastery, I am with you. If you are in a tavern, I am with you. If you are in a monastery, I am with you by giving abundant blessings, but

'Come out solitary!' If you are in a tavern, I am with you by letting down the curtain of mercy, but 'Come out as hard cash!' "

Suppose you stay distant and oppose Me.
Can you keep away from My gentleness?

Even if many great sins overcome you, the Creator's love will not leave you, for the sin is your attribute, and the love His attribute. *Attributes of frail, insignificant, newly arrived things detract nothing from the attributes of the Eternal, the Gentle, the Aware.*

He—upon him be peace—said, narrating from his Lord, "My servant, if you encounter Me with offenses that nearly fill the earth, I will encounter you with the like of them in forgiveness, and I will not care."[792]

Yaḥyā ibn Muʿādh said, *"Even if the servant sins and does not care, he has a Lord who forgives and does not care."*

Tell My servants that surely I am the Forgiving, the Ever-Merciful, and that My chastisement is the painful chastisement [15:49–50]. *He threw them between fear and hope!*

"My servant, though your craft is disobedience, My attribute is forgiveness. You will not abandon your craft. Why would I abandon My attribute?

"Tell My servants: You may be disobedient, but you belong to Me. You may not obey Me, but I belong to you.

"O proximate angels, the Throne is yours! O cherubim, the Footstool is yours! O Gabriel, the Lote Tree is yours! O Riḍwān, paradise is yours! O worshipers and obedient servants, the houris, castles, rivers, and blossoms are yours! O Mālik, hell is yours! O unbelievers and hypocrites, this world is yours! O destitute and sincere, I am yours!"

At the time of sin, He called you deeply ignorant so as to pardon you, just as He says concerning Adam: *"Surely he was a great wrongdoer, deeply ignorant"* [33:72]. At the time of bearing witness, He called you a knower so as to accept you: *"God bears witness that there is no god but He, and the angels, and the possessors of knowledge"* [3:18]. At the time of obedience He called you weak—*"And man was created weak"* [4:28]—so as to pardon your shortcoming.

"Surely I am the Forgiving, the Ever-Merciful: It is I who forgive disobedience, and it is you who disobey, since everyone does what comes from himself. If you wanted not to disobey, you would not be able to do so, because you are you. If I wanted not to show mercy, indeed it would never happen that I would not show mercy, for I am I. I am the All-Merciful, the Ever-Merciful, the Forbearing, the Generous.

"When you put something into water, it becomes wet. This is not because of your command, but because of water's nature. When you throw something into fire, it burns, not because of your instruction, but because of fire's attribute. The sun and the moon give light, not out of kindness to you, but because that indeed is their work. I too—I forgive, not because of your excellence, but because that is My attribute."

Someone said to musk, "You have one defect: No matter whom you are with, you are still fragrant."

It said, "I don't look at whom I'm with, I look at who I am."

It is said that Āṣif ibn Barkhiyā sinned. The Exalted Lord revealed to Solomon, "Tell Āṣif not to do that again."

Solomon conveyed the revelation to Āṣif. He said, "I will do it again." He did it again, and revelation came. When this happened three times, Gabriel came. He said, "The Exalted Lord says, 'This work has passed the limit. I will send punishment.' "

Āṣif went out into the desert and performed two cycles of prayer. He said, *"If you do not protect me from sin, I will do it again and again."*

God said, "O Solomon, say to him, 'Since you know that protection comes from Me, I will forgive, I will forgive, and I will forgive.'"

"O Muḥammad, say, '*Surely I am the warner* [15:89]: I instill fear.' Then they will not attach their hearts to you and will come to the Threshold, for *Surely I am the Forgiving, the Ever-Merciful.*"

There is no surprise that He says to someone like Moses, *"Surely I"* [20:12]. What is surprising is that He says to the woebegone, *"Surely I."* "O Moses, '*Surely I am thy Lord.*' I am your guard and protector. When your mother threw you into the oven, I watched out for you. When she tossed you into the river, I brought you out."

There He said to Moses the speaking companion, *"Surely I, I am God"* [28:30]. And here He says to the disobedient and woebegone, *"Surely I am the Forgiving, the Ever-Merciful"*—*the Forgiving* in this world and *the Ever-Merciful* in the afterworld.

"Perhaps your Lord will have mercy on you [17:8]. *From God "perhaps" means "it is necessary that." "If you return, We will return"* [17:8]. *"If you return" to slips, "We will return to mercy." "If you return" to disloyalty, "We will return" to loyalty.* If you circumambulate nothing but taverns, I will send nothing but the wine of gentle gifts. *If you return, We will return.* Wherever you go, in the end you will come back. Whether you come or do not come, you belong to Me. The falcon has worth because it goes and it comes.

The Prophet said, "Surely God loves the tempted, the repenting."[793] *The tempted, the repenting* is the one who, every time he is forced far from the Threshold, comes back by the good fortune of repentance. The pigheaded unbeliever is like a wild crow that never departs from the alienation of distance for the intimacy of proximity. *Those are the ones whose hearts God desired not to purify* [5:41]. And the obedient, dry-brained Quran-reciter, admiring his own obedience, is like a chicken that has never come out to the vast plain and whose value is no more than two dirhams.

When someone keeps his feet firm in disobedience, his persistence damages his own makeup. When someone resides in the monastery of obedience but his eyes do not contemplate the witnessing places or look up to the covenants of the gentle divine favors and the kingly mysteries, then he is either eye-serving, or self-admiring, or associating. This is because in obedience anyone who looks at people is eye-serving, anyone who looks at himself is self-admiring, and anyone who wants compensation from other than God is associating. And anyone in the state of disobedience who wears the cloak of embarrassment and shame and goes back to the Presence with regret and asking forgiveness, as well as anyone in the state of obedience who witnesses His success-giving, sees His favors, and opens the tongue of *The praise belongs to God,* is God's beloved. God says, *"Surely God loves the repenters"* [2:222]. And He says, *"And God loves the beautiful-doers"* [2:195].

The obedient have obedience, the worshipers have worship, the renunciants have renunciation, and the knowers have knowledge. "But the disobedient have destitution, and whenever someone is destitute, My generosity and munificence are his intimate."

O dervish, if self-admiration comes and gives your obedience to the wind, if falsehood comes and gives your truthfulness to the wind, if eye-service comes and gives your sincerity to the wind, even so, the name *My servants* [15:49]—which is the signet on the edict of your existence—cannot be washed away with all the world's oceans or burned away with all its fires. Despite all their obedience, worship, and good fortune, He called the prophets *Our servants*: *"And remember Our servants Abraham and Isaac"* [38:45]. And despite all your disobedience and slips, He called you *My servants*: *"O My servants who have been immoderate against yourselves, despair not of God's mercy"* [39:53].

"The diversity of your states and the disparity of your deeds do not take you far from My Threshold. Do you not see that I called the Kaabah My house in the firm text of the Book—*'Make My house pure!'* [22:26]—so the changing states take nothing whatsoever away from its eminence. Sometimes there was prayer inside, and sometimes there were idols, but its eminence stayed the same."

It is said that in past times a renunciant worshiped in a monastery for one hundred years, but after all that, caprice overcame him and he acted with disobedience. Then he wanted to go back to his devotions. When he stepped into the niche of worship, Satan said, "O man, are you not ashamed to do something like that and then be present in the presence of the Real's majesty?" He wanted to make him despair of mercy, but then he heard a call, *"You belong to Me and I belong to you. Say to this meddler, 'What do you have?' "*

"O servant, You are mine and I am yours. Say to the meddler, *'What is this anguish? The head and the stone.' "* Here you have a head, and there you have a stone.

41. *al-Ḥafīẓ:* the Guardian

Ḥafīẓ means *ḥāfiẓ*, like *ʿalīm* in the meaning of *ʿālim*, and *ḥakīm* in the meaning of *ḥākim*.

The guardian is the preserver. The Exalted Lord is the one who preserves all existent things with His power—heaven and earth, Throne and Footstool, paradise and hell, and so on. He also preserves the hearts of His elect from paying regard to others. This is the secret of all blessings and generous gifts.

It was by the decree of this meaning that when He sent Muṣṭafā to invite the people, his relatives and tribe came out against him and tried to destroy him. This was because of the revelation that came from the Maker: "O Muḥammad, rise up and invite the people to My Threshold!" The thought passed through the Prophet's mind, *"Praise belongs to God* that this affair has come to me in the midst of my tribe, for everyone attests to my trustworthiness and purity." When this much passed through his mind and he relied on this measure, the story reversed. As much as he invited, he saw his kinsmen more repelled and further from the words. "Marvelous! As long as there was no invitation, you saw me as trustworthy. Now that the banner of messengerhood has been raised at the threshold of my good fortune, have I become a traitor?"

"O Muḥammad, We do things like this. We bring forth hope from fear itself, and We prepare fear in hope itself. You have set your heart on their becoming familiar with your invitation, but We have pitched one hundred thousand tents of separation between them and you and built a hundred thousand domes of union between you and those in whom you had no hope."

This is correct, for as they have said, *"Have more hope for that for which you do not hope than for that for which you hope."*[794]

"Were a hat to drop from heaven, it would fall only on the head of someone who had no hope for it."[795]

"We brought out his kinsmen and tribe against him so that when he saw disloyalty from the nearest of the near, he would fix his heart on the far." He brought out everyone against him with disloyalty so that he would look at the people with the eye of disloyalty and pull his secret core away from them. God wanted to cut off his secret core from the whole world and join it with Himself, *"for one is conjoined with the Real in the measure of one's disjoining from the creatures."*[796]

By God, no one who turns away from the Real and toward His creatures for the blink of an eye will find a way to Him. Everyone who is farther from the creatures is closer to the Real. When for one instant in his life someone turns away from remembering the Real and toward remembering the creatures, he will never find access to God. *This is the case of someone who turns away for one instant in his whole life. What then about someone who does not turn toward the Real for one instant in his whole life?*

"O friend, I do not approve of your reliance on any but Me in the two worlds. I will bring everyone out against you so that you will remember only Me in the two realms."

The story of Jacob was like this. He set his heart on his son and relied on that. The Exalted Lord put his near ones in charge of snatching him away from his father and throwing him into the well. Then he was sold. What were these trials and tribulations? "Yes, does My friend dare to look at his son?" Or, "Does My friend dare to rely on his tribe? All of you, come out against him! Then his secret core will be cut off from all. He will know that just as he cannot find loyalty from his kinsmen, even more so will this be the case with the distant and the strangers."

O chevalier, the Exalted Lord knew that if Muṣṭafā had given out the invitation and if his tribe had turned back to God along with him and helped him until Islam appeared, his tribe would have counted that as a favor against him, and the strangers would have counted it as an argument against him. This is because Muḥammad was from Quraysh, the Quraysh were the chieftains of the Arabs, and the Arabs were the most excellent of the world's folk. The Arabs had excellence over the whole world, and the Quraysh had excellence over all the Arabs. If his relatives had turned back to God with him, all the Arabs would have followed them and turned back along with them. Then his tribe would count that as a favor to him. They would have said, "You were a man alone. You had no retinue, servitors, soldiers, or banners. It was because of us that the people acquiesced to you." He would have remained under the burden of their favor. And the strangers would also have an argument against him. They would have said, "You took the world with the strength of the sword of Quraysh, not with the strength of prophethood, the bravery of messengerhood, and the evidence of miracles."

Hence the Exalted Lord brought all of them out against him so that they would not be his helpers, but rather his antagonists. For thirteen years he was settled in Mecca and was giving out the invitation, but they did not believe. He went off to Medina, and the Medinans came forth with love in the heart, as you have heard.

O chevalier, how blessed is turning away from the creatures, and how baneful is turning toward the creatures! Look at Adam—as long as the angels were turning toward him, he was their guest, but when a slip came into existence from him and the angels turned away, he became the vicegerent.

The paragon left his homeland for Medina, and then the secret of exile became apparent to him. "O Helpers, you must give comfort with a bit of bread!"

What a marvelous business! "You are at the head of all those who trust in God. Will you rely on creatures because of a bit of bread from Companions?"

He said, "I am not going because I am relying on creatures. I am not talking in terms of the strength of my faith, but rather in terms of the weakness of their faith. Just as it is mandatory to rely on the strength of my own faith, so also it is necessary to have mercy on the weakness of their hearts and their certainty."

Then gradually, little by little, the strength of Islam appeared and began to subjugate the world. At the Battle of Badr, there were three times as many unbelievers as faithful, with supplies, instruments, weapons, and equipment. It passed through the paragon's mind, "Oh, what will the state of my Companions be! The army of unbelief is so great, and the army of Islam is so small!"

"O Muḥammad, I will display works and mysteries from My Unseen. Did you not see what I did with your state? I assigned the Meccans to drive you out of Mecca so that the boldness and strength of your tribe and fellow townsmen would fall away from you. If today you were strong and they were weak and I were to give the hand to the strong over the weak, the people of the world would look at the strength. I want something else. I will give the hand to the weak over the strong, so that the whole world will look at the artisanry of My hand's gentleness. O you who are many and have weapons, be subjugated! O you who have no weapons, subjugate!"

On the day he entered Mecca, he struck with the sword, which is the cutting blade of chastisement and the burning brand of punishment. The Meccans said, "O Muḥammad, why have you come?"

He said, "I have come to pass everyone under the sword."

"O paragon of the two worlds! Before you went, you said that Mecca is the sanctuary."

"Yes, I have come to make the lawful forbidden and the sanctuary permitted. *'Anyone who enters the house of Abū Sufyān will be safe.'*[797] *'Kill Ibn al-Khaṭal, even if he is clinging to the curtains of the Kaabah.'*[798] From the time of Adam until now, no one has dared to draw a sword in Mecca. But today I will draw mine, for it is permitted to me."

"O Muḥammad, We have made your approval a tree whose fruit is success and faith. We have made your wrath a cloud whose flood is banishment and abandonment."

When that paragon of wondrous attributes and pure essence came into the world, the cry "Woe is me!" rose up from the throne of Chosroes, the palace of Caesar, the crown of Anushiravan, and the bench of the emperor. On the day of the conquest of Mecca the stalwarts of Quraysh and the headmen of associationism were attacking like drunken elephants, but when they saw the flash of the paragon's avenging sword, they concealed themselves like caterpillars in cocoons. The paragon had put on a black turban: Yes, today the sultan of the world is wearing black, for it is a day of harshness.

I saw you in black so I said, "A full moon
has risen in the darkness of the jet-black night."
You threw off the black, so I said, "A sun
has effaced the light of the stars with its brightness."[799]

"O Muḥammad, spilling blood in the sanctuary is forbidden, but the desire is yours. Do whatever you want, O friend, for I will make what is forbidden in Mecca permitted for the sake of your heart's desire. What do you say about My mercy, which *embraces everything* [7:156] and to which no forbiddenness has ever had access? Should I forbid it to your community?"

He struck with the sword and made the necks of his adversaries—the enemies of the religion—the sheath of his own sword.

Moreover, he was made to pass over all the stations in order to detach his secret core from all others. This is because whenever anyone has a higher station, everyone is seeking his station, but he is fleeing from the station of those beneath and below him. Every intelligent man is seeking exaltedness and fleeing from abasement.[800]

On the night of the *mi'rāj* Muṣṭafā was made to pass over all the stations so that he would be higher than everyone else. Thus they would all be seeking his station, and he would be fleeing from their stations. When he was taken through all the stations, nothing was left but stationlessness, which is the attribute of the Real. He pulled up the ropes of his secret core's tent, so he was gazing at the Real, not the station. All the creatures were gazing at the station, but he was gazing at the Real.

This is the meaning of the saying reported from Muṣṭafā: *"I seek refuge in Thy pardon from Thy punishment."*[801] The first station on the road is fear and hope. Fear arises from gazing at punishment, and hope from gazing at pardon. Pardon and punishment are two acts, and their traces are paradise and hell. He was shown that there is nothing in the hands of paradise and hell. If fire burned by its own essence, it would have burned Abraham. If paradise caressed by itself, it would have caressed Adam. "What burns is not the fire, it is My wrath. What caresses is not paradise, it is My approval. If I pour the water of approval on the fire, it will turn into a scented garden, and if I strike the fire of wrath to the scented garden, it will become hell itself."

He passed beyond this station and said, *"I seek refuge in Thy approval from Thy anger."* When he saw that paradise abides through approval, which is beneficence, and that hell abides through anger, which is punishment, he said, *"I seek refuge in Thy approval from Thy anger."*

Then he also passed beyond this station, for approval and anger are attributes, and attributes do not act. Rather, that which is described by the attributes acts. When he saw this, he put aside attachment to acts and seeking help from attributes. He said, *"I seek refuge in Thee from Thee."* I seek help in You from You, for if trial were coming from other than You, I would seek Your help. Since it is coming from You, how can I seek help from other than You?

Complaint is of three sorts: either of the Friend to other than the Friend, or of other than the Friend to the Friend, or of the Friend to the Friend Himself.

Complaining of the Friend to other than the Friend is to declare oneself quit of the Friend, for unless one is fed up with the Friend, one will not lament to other than the Friend.

Lamenting to the Friend about other than the Friend is associationism, for unless you see other than the Friend, how will you lament to the Friend? Seeing two is associationism.

Lamenting to the Friend about the Friend is *tawḥīd* itself. Outwardly it is complaint, but inwardly it is showing gratitude: "Since I have none but You, to whom should I speak?"

People fancy that the lover is complaining, but in fact these words display sincerity in love. God reported the lamentation of Job: *"Harm has touched me"* [21:83]. Despite his lamenting, He called him patient: *"Surely We found him patient. How excellent a servant he was!"* [38:44]. How could he be patient while complaining?

Here the Exalted Lord is saying this: "Complaining is to lament to other than Me. When he laments to Me, that is not complaint. Job did not say, 'O people, *harm has touched me.*' He said, 'My Lord, *harm has touched me.*' This is to take one's incapacity to His strength and to display one's lowliness to the Unneedy. It is not complaint."

Then Muṣṭafā also passed beyond this station. He said, *"I do not number Thy laudations"*: You Yourself praise Yourself, for You know.

By Thy life, surely I am the most eloquent of people,
but when I meet Thee, I become dumb.

Look at this wonder! Everybody learns how to laud the Friend from Muṣṭafā, but he admitted his own incapacity in laudation. How can that be? "Yes, when I am with the people, their knowledge next to my knowledge is ignorance. Their stipulation is to stay silent, and my stipulation is to speak. When I talk to You, next to Your knowledge my knowledge and the knowledge of all beings—and a thousand thousand times more knowledge—is ignorance. Here I remain silent."

He was also made to pass beyond this station, for saying *"I do not number"* is to admit incapacity, just as saying *"I seek refuge in Thee from Thee"* claims power. Incapacity is your attribute, just as power is His attribute. "O Muḥammad, you are still gazing on your own attributes. As long as you do not lift up your gaze to the pure attributes, you will not see Me."

He said, *"Thou art as Thou hast lauded Thyself."* Describing You is something You can do. *"I do not number"* is disengagement. *"Thou art as Thou hast lauded"* is solitariness. As long as the servant does not become disengaged from other than the Real, he will not become solitary for the Real. *Peace!*

42. *al-Muqīt:* the Nourisher

Some have said that *muqīt* means guardian, and some have said that it means the one who nourishes the creatures; it comes from *iqāta*, that is, *to give someone his nourishment.*

Every creature has a nourishment [*qūt*] from which it takes its strength. If that nourishment is taken away from it, it will perish. Outwardness has a nourishment and inwardness has a nourishment, bodies have a nourishment and spirits have a nourishment, frames have a nourishment and hearts have a nourishment. *Each people now knew their drinking place* [2:60].

The nourishment of hearts is the remembrance of Him who makes hearts fluctuate. *Are not hearts serene in the remembrance of God?* [13:28]. How strange that someone given access to the Exalted Threshold—for *"When someone remembers Me in himself, I remember him in Myself"*[802]—will then put down the bags of his aspiration in this dustbin of dread, which is the courtyard of annihilation. But it is impossible to treat stupidity. *"I treated the blind and the leper, and they all became well, but treating the stupid has thwarted me."*[803]

Kick the forms of the created things in the head and pitch the tent of your aspiration on top of the utmost end of utmost ends! *"All game is in the belly of the onager."*[804] Aim for the world of Divinity! What sort of world? A world whose majesty's throne tramples all things and whose perfection's carpet was not woven by the spheres! "Tawḥīd *belongs to the Real, and the creatures are freeloaders.*"[805]

Today your extreme ignorance makes your unworthy eyes see good fortune's bouquet of roses as a backpack of tribulation's thorns, but the jewel is in the road's dust and your moon-faced Joseph at the bottom of the well. A day will come when this curtain of suspicion will be thrown aside and the prince will be taken back from the dog-keeper and find deliverance from his hands. This is why the Prophet said, *"The first gift of the person of faith is death."*[806]

How can a donkey recognize the worth of Jesus?
How can the deaf know the song of David?[807]

Leave the straw for the donkeys and the bones for the dogs, then step forth into the world of eternity. Detach your heart completely from all others. *Devote yourself to Him devoutly* [73:8] *and let nothing remain of the others, great or small.* Then you will be given access to this dome of proximity: *"I have a moment with God embraced by no proximate angel or sent prophet."*[808]

Seize hold of the skirt of love,
trample the head of devilish appetite.

When he said, *"I spend the night at my Lord"* and *"Surely I stay with my Lord,"*[809] do you fancy that this belonged to the body? It belonged to the spiritual half. When He said, *"Say: 'I am a mortal like you'"* [18:110], that belonged to the bodily half. The bread-eaters and water-drinkers are one thing, and His men are something else.

They have said that the soul has a secret, and the spirit has a secret. The secret of the soul appeared to Pharaoh when he said, *"I am your lord the most high"* [79:24]. The secret of the spirit appeared to Muṣṭafā when he said, *"I am only a servant: I sit as servants sit and eat as servants eat."*[810] The spirit's secret was waiting to see when that paragon would step into the stirrups of existence.

There is an angel in heaven, half fire and half snow. Its glorification is this: *"Glory be to Him who combines snow and fire!"*[811] Snow is not opposed to fire as much as spirit is opposed to body. Inside the body He imprisoned an enemy with an enemy, an opposite with an opposite. Outwardly they are at peace, inwardly they are enemies.

When the state became tight for a certain exalted man, he was seen in revelry and delight. They asked, "What is this revelry?"

He said, "What is surprising about this revelry? *Union with the Friend and separation from the enemy have come near.* What a day it will be when a drink and a blow arrive suddenly at dawn! Which drink and which blow is that? It will put this unbeliever on the gallows and deliver this sultan from the dark fetters, carrying him on the Burāq of good fortune to the Presence of Majesty."

"The spirits of the martyrs are in the craws of green birds."[812] Is it not enough that the spirits of the martyrs are put into the craws of green birds, or, as has also been said, "in lamps of light" and "in meadows of paradise"? But there are groups whose love's craw is vaster than that it could enter into a bird's craw. What is their station? *The spirits of the lovers are in the grasp of exaltedness. He unveils His Essence to them and addresses them with His attributes.*

Know that in reality this is not the station of those with low aspiration. *The servant's aspiration agitates and unsettles him, so he does not become still in this world or the next,* for night-journeying is not the work of just any catamite.

Aspiration for the servant is like alchemy for the seeker of possessions.

"Most of the folk of the Garden are simpletons,"[813] *for the simpleton approves of the house instead of the neighbor and the road instead of the companion.*[814] Most of the folk of paradise are simpletons, for they are those with low aspiration.

God says, *"Surely the companions of the Garden today are in an occupation, rejoicing"* [55:36]. He ascribed the common people to paradise, but He did not ascribe the elect of His threshold to any other than Himself. He says, *"Surely the godwary will be amid gardens and a river, in a seat of truthfulness, at an Omnipotent King"* [54:54–55]. He did not say that the godwary are the companions of the Garden, *for their station is there, but their goal is something else.*

The Prophet said, "I ask Thee for the Garden, for it is the utmost end of the seekers."[815] *Beneath this is a subtle secret. The Prophet said that the Garden is the utmost end of the seekers, but concerning those who have neither seeking nor fleeing God says, "Surely unto thy Lord is the final end"* [53:42]. *"The Lote Tree of the Final End"* [53:14] *is the station of one group, and "surely unto thy Lord is the final end" is the station of another group.*

As long as the goal is still some sort of bounty or generosity, the door of response will be open and the cushion of bestowal will be thrown down. But when aspiration rises to the station of witnessing and the waystation of finding, asking will be met with rejection, going forward with blockage, and aiming with severity. When Moses asked for a few things, he was answered and it was said to him, "Thou hast been given thy request, O Moses!" [20:36]. *But when he said from the top of yearning, "Show me, that I may gaze upon Thee," it was said to him, "Thou shalt not see Me"* [7:143]. *Such is the severity of the beloveds.*[816]

As long as the aim and goal is bounty and bounteousness, bestowal and gifts, the door of response will be open and the sought object will be linked to compliance. But when a man passes beyond this station with steps of seriousness, when he raises the banner of aspiration in the world of love, when he gives a place in his heart to yearning and longing for the station of witnessing and contemplation and the waystation of unveiling and uncovering, then he will become *a sick man whom no one visits and a desirer who is not desired.*[817] Whatever he requests, whatever supplication he utters, whatever story he tells, whatever complaint he narrates—he will be presented with *"The seeking is rejected, the road blocked."*[818]

Have you not heard the story of Moses? He was granted so many of his aims and desires, but when he talked about vision, it was said to him, *"Thou shalt not see Me"* [7:143]. Yes, such is the severity of the beloveds, and upon this the work is built.

"When someone shies away from destruction, what has he to do with love?"

"The desirer is enraptured, for the desired has no likeness."

"Kings are such that there is no patience without them and no way to put up with them."

An exalted man said, *"There is no capacity to be with You and no ease in other than You, so help is sought from You against You."*[819]

He disclosed Himself to His friends in His names and His attributes until they shone with the lights of recognizing Him. Then He unveiled the glories of His face to them until they were burned away by the fire of loving Him. Then He veiled Himself from them in the core of His majesty until they wandered aimlessly in the desert of His greatness and tremendousness. Whenever they trembled while observing the core of majesty, they were confounded by what outstrips intellect and insight. Whenever they aimed to turn away in despair, they were called from the pavilions of beauty: "Have patience, O you who in ignorance and haste despair of attaining the Real!" So they stayed between rejection and acceptance, blockage and arrival, drowned in the ocean of recognizing Him and burned in the fire of loving Him.[820]

He—*majestic is His majesty!*—disclosed His names and attributes to the world so that lovers would get to work and yearners would seek for vision. By the decree of jealousy He let down the curtain of greatness and set up the banner of tremendousness. He made the attribute of exaltedness the robe on the pavilion of His majesty so that the hearts of the exalted ones would roast and the eyes of the lovers would become the source of fire and water. Whenever they become agitated and begin to seek the mysteries, the call of unity arrives from the curtains of self-sufficiency's majesty: "Away with you, away with you! O handful of dust, how dare you circle around the courtyard of solitariness!" And whenever they drink the cup of despair, put on the shirt of destitution, pull their heads into the collar of remorse, and lose hope of finding, the call of gentleness comes from the pavilions of the divine beauty: "Patience, patience! Pass some days at the threshold of Our majesty in the hope of contemplating Our beauty and be happy in the midst of fire. Though the night is dark, keep your heart strong, for sunrise is near."

He did not use the sword of His severity against the angels, but He used it against you, for in reality life belongs to you: *And that He may try the faithful with a beautiful trial* [8:17].

"O angels, it is you who fill up the treasuries of glorification and hallowing, saying, *'Glory be to God and the praise belongs to God.'* It is the Adamites who are sometimes melted by My trial and sometimes caressed by My bestowal. Sometimes I slaughter them with the sword of severity; sometimes I anoint them with the gaze of gentleness."

A dervish was made helpless by the road. Until the end of his life he dwelt in suffering and in rushing and running. In the last few days his spirit was pulled out of him, and then he was finished. The people saw that on his chest was written, *"This one was killed by God."*

"The heart I snatch from sweethearts
I never give or show to anyone."
O Spirit, with one glance You snatched my heart
as if I had lost it for a thousand years.

This is one of their sayings: *"Recognition is fire, love is fire, and this talk is fire upon fire."* It never happens that a place catches fire without tumult and burning.

At my gate how fine are the tumult and turmoil of love!
At Your gate how fine are the business and work of beauty![821]

Know that in reality as long as fire does not enter his heart, a man will not begin to seek. In the days of Abraham, all the fires were gathered inside his breast. He was so hot in the road that he saw the goal wherever he looked: *When night darkened over him, he saw a star. He said, "This is my Lord"* [6:76]. He saw the star with the eye and the Real with the heart. Because of the tumult and burning of love's fire, the heart's witnessing rushed ahead and overcame the eyes' witnessing. Abraham said, *"This is my Lord."* He reported about the heart's vision, not the eyes' vision. Do you not see that when he looked again, he saw the star and said, *"I love not those that set"* [6:76]?

In the road a man is allowed one gaze. It is this one gaze that comes pure, without the stain of share and portion. *"Do not follow the gaze with another gaze, for the first belongs to you, but the second counts against you."*[822]

Know that, in reality—and these are exalted words—the lover is not seeking his share in the first gaze, but he is seeking it in the second. All the ambushes that appear for those on the road come from seeking their own shares. This is why it is said that nothing will be set aright for him who seeks his own share.

It has also been said, *"When someone loves you for the sake of something, he will hate you when it disappears."*[823] This is why it is correct for God to have the reality of love, but no one else. When someone is helpless in his own work, he is seeking his own portion and share, but the Exalted Presence is incomparable with portion and share. When *He loves them* came in the Beginningless, it came pure of all shares. Then, since it came pure, it brought *they love Him* [5:54] under its protection. So *they love Him* was permitted under the protection of the purity of *He loves them.*

You must come into the ranks of those like Abraham who cut away attributes. In manliness you must shout out about the whole realm of being, *"They are an enemy to me"* [26:77]. Then the crown of bosom friendship will be placed on your head and the robe of love will be thrown over your shoulders. You must draw the line of dismissal across the star of gazing on others, the moon of attention to occasions, and the sun of diverting yourself with causes. Then the stars of love, the moons of recognition, and the suns of limpidness will pitch the tents of good fortune in the heaven of your heart.

The suns I saw vanished when I witnessed Your beauty,
great joy filled me when I received Your bounties.

*

O cupbearer, pour the wine, for nothing breaks abstinence but wine!
For a time let me pay no heed to this colorful wheel!
The kingdom of Adam's children has no worth—
let me serve the kingdom of Parviz.
The renunciants and wholesome belong to the Garden and Firdaws,
but this group of the carefree belongs to the love-inciting cup.
May the gardens of bliss be given to the claimants!
The early-rising drunkards want the cup time after time.
My spirit belongs to wine, my body to dust, my heart to You,
and this head full of disquiet and fancy to a sharp sword.[824]

When the night darkened over him, he saw a star [6:76]. Just as money changers pour gold on a table to determine its value, so also God's bosom friend poured the hard cash of his innate disposition on the table of thought. Next to the sunlight of bosom friendship he saw the farthings of the stars, the dirhams of the moon, and the gold coin of the sun as counterfeit and he turned away from them all. Suddenly the pure wine of *tawḥīd*, sealed with the seal of good fortune, arrived from the Exalted Presence in the cup of disengagement at the hand of the cupbearer of confirmation. Where is the allusion to this draft in the station of bosom friendship? *"Surely I have turned my face toward Him who originated the heavens and the earth, unswerving"* [6:79].

It is said that when the pain of childbirth overcame Abraham's mother and the time approached for the marvel of power to come forth to the plain of creation from the curtain of the unseen jealousy, a whole world set out searching for him to destroy him. The custom is that whenever a secret is to become apparent, a world stands up in antagonism. Nimrod commanded, "Wherever a child comes forth from its mother, cut off its head." *But the power of the Powerful suspends every contrivance.*

"He who flees from what is coming will fall into the hand of what is seeking him."[825] Yes, one cannot kill one's killer.[826] When the lion of Power strolls forth from the thicket of the Desire into the meadow of the Will, the old lame fox of the lords of deliberation does not have the gall to move.

Nimrod advised Azar to keep away from his wife, but *"When destiny comes, the eyes are blind."*[827] O painter of decree and destiny, what painting will you draw on the gold of existence?

Azar came to his house and was with his wife. Yes, *how God gifted thee!* One cannot dethrone the sultan of the beginningless. *The beginningless is not contested and the decree is not resisted.* That peerless pearl came from the oyster of Azar's loins, *"from between the feces"* *of unbelief* *"and the blood"* [16:66] *of associationism* to the jewel box of his mother's womb. *Glory be to Him who deposits the subtle in the dense and the precious in the trifling!*

"O Nimrod, now that We have conveyed the pearl from the ocean of Our gentleness to Our lodging place, you can have the oyster, and the oyster can have you."

When the time came for that sapling of good fortune to be planted in the garden of the world of manifestation, his mother was seized by pain. In the dark night she went to a cave, put

Abraham in that cave of jealousy, shut its door tightly, and came to the house. *If you fear for him, cast him into the river* [28:7]. From time to time she would come to see how he was. She would see him sucking his own finger, from which limpid milk was flowing. When a few days passed and Abraham was thriving, the sultan of intellect mounted the spy of reflection on the steed of thoughts in the world of his makeup, though he was still in the cave. *He said to his mother, "Who is my lord?"*

She said, "I am."

He said, "Who is your lord?"

She said, "Your father."

He said, "Who is my father's lord?"

She said, "Be silent!" so he became silent. But inwardly Abraham kept on making judgments.

As soon as his mother heard these words, she went to Azar and said, "O Azar, are you not aware that water has come up in the midst of your house? There is fear that you will drown. What should be done? He for the sake of whom heads are no longer on their necks has stuck up his head from your makeup, but you are not aware."

Azar came, the bazaar of Azarite torment hot, and went to Abraham. Abraham looked at him and began the story for him. *"O my father, who is my lord?"* Here you have love and patience, and here you have disgrace: *He said, "Your mother."*

He said, "Who is my mother's lord?"

He said, "I am."

He said, "Who is your lord?"

He said, "Nimrod."

He said, "Who is Nimrod's lord?" So he slapped him hard.[828]

By God, in that state Abraham made no distinction between a bite of halva and the slap of trial.

The blame of blamers circles round my distracted heart
but love for my beloved lies deep in its core.[829]

We gave Abraham his rectitude from before, and We knew him [21:51]. So he turned to his father and mother and said, "How long will you keep me in this cave? If you have given yourself over to carrion-eating and speaking out in Nimrod-worship, then I will go off into the desert of the Friend, sit on the steed of aspiration, hunt the prey of the gaze, bind it to the saddle-straps of intellect, bring it into the house of my secret core, roast it in the fire of yearning, set it on the table of pain, lift up the hands of need in contemplating the Unneedy, and place it in the mouth of acceptance. Then I will lay down the lines of the Sanctuary, build the Kaabah, and make a guest house, for there are friends who will be coming in the road." *And proclaim the hajj among the people, and they shall come to thee on foot and on every lean beast; they shall come from every deep ravine* [22:27].

43. *al-Ḥasīb:* the Reckoner/the Sufficer

And God suffices as a reckoner/sufficer [4:6]. *Ḥasīb* has two meanings. One is sufficer: He suffices for all the work of the servants and the weak. The other is reckoner: the reckoner is He who does the reckoning. In the first sense it has [the pattern] *fa ʿīl* in the meaning of *mufʿil*, like *badīʿ* [originator] in the meaning of *mubdiʿ*. In the second sense it has the meaning of *mufā ʿil*, like *nadīm* [boon companion] in the meaning of *munādim*, and so on.[830]

Know that in reality the Men have chosen poverty in fear of the reckoning. Thus they have said, *"Blessed are the poor in this world and the next. In this world they have no burdens and no taxes, and in the next they have no rebuke and no reckoning."*[831] Happy are the poor in this world and the next. In this world they have no burdens and no taxes, and in the next world they have no reckoning and no interrogation. Rather, they have the pleasure of apology, as has come in the report: *"A man will be brought on the Day of Resurrection and God will say, 'My servant, I did not hold this world back from you to scorn you. I held it back from you so that you would be wholesome and this religion and world of yours would be wholesome," or words in this meaning.*[832]

It has been said that Ibn ʿAṭāʾ preferred unneediness to poverty, and Junayd poverty to unneediness. One day the two debated. Junayd brought as proof the hadith in which the Messenger says, *"The poor of my community will enter the Garden one-half day before the unneedy among them, and that is five hundred years."*[833] He said, "Someone who goes to paradise is more excellent than someone who remains five hundred years in the reckoning."

Ibn ʿAṭāʾ said, "No, rather it is more excellent to remain in the reckoning, for the person in paradise has the pleasure of blessings, but the person in the reckoning has the pleasure of the Real's rebuke. Talking with the Friend, even if the station is the station of rebuke, is higher than being occupied with other than the Friend, even if the station is the station of blessings. This is because being in the Friend's trial with the Friend is sweeter than being in the Friend's blessings without the Friend."

Junayd answered, "Even if the rich man has the pleasure of rebuke, the poor man will have the pleasure of apology. Tomorrow the Exalted Lord will say to the poor man, 'I kept this world back from you not because of your lowliness, but because your religion's wholesomeness lay in that.' Though He rebukes the unneedy man, He apologizes to the poor man. The pleasure of apology is beyond the pleasure of rebuke, for both friend and enemy are rebuked, but apology is only for friends."[834]

The hadith of Muṣṭafā—*"The higher hand is better than the lower hand"*[835]—is not evidence of the superiority of unneediness. Rather, it is evidence of the superiority of poverty, *for the higher hand, which is the giving hand, travels the road of poverty; and the lower hand, which is the taking hand, travels the road of unneediness. God's Messenger made the seeker of poverty superior to the seeker of unneediness.* If the giver gains superiority, he does not gain it by unneediness; he gains it rather because he first chose poverty by giving and letting go of unneediness. And the taker let go of poverty and chose unneediness. Superiority is in this respect, not in the respect that the common people, *like cattle* [7:179], have understood.

Some of the great ones, when giving something to a poor man, would not place it in the poor man's hand. Rather, they would hold out their own hand before the poor man's hand so that the poor man would take it from their hand. This is because they considered poverty more excellent than unneediness, so they put their own hand beneath and the hand of the poor man above, so that the superior would be the higher hand and the inferior would be the lower hand.

It has been narrated that one of the Abbasid kings said to Ja ʿfar Ṣādiq, *"Tell us of an eminence of yours by which you exceed us so that we may attest to your superiority, for we are equal to you in every virtue."*

Ja ʿfar said, "It is a sufficient excellence for us that none of us has the wish to belong to other than us because of aversion to us, unless he is an unbeliever."

He said to Ja ʿfar, "Tell me of an eminence and an increase that you have over us so that we may acknowledge it, for we are equal to you in all the outward excellences."

Ṣādiq said, "Enough for us is this excellence: none of us wishes that he belonged to other than us by way of discounting us, unless he has become an unbeliever."

In these words of Ṣādiq, there is a secret concerning the superiority of poverty. It is that when a poor man's time becomes short and his breath reaches its end, he does not wish that he had been rich. But when death comes to the rich man, he wishes that he had been poor. Thus it is correct that poverty is better than wealth. In the same way every community wishes that it had been this community, but this community does not wish that it had been another community. Thus it is correct that this community is superior.

In the same way, the knowers do not wish for ignorance, but the ignorant wish for knowledge.

The realizers have said a good deal about the station of poverty and its explanation. One said, *"Poverty is pleasure in destitution and branding the heart with despair."*[836]

Another said, *"Poverty is to be disengaged from movement and to be solitary from possessions."*[837]

Another said, *"Poverty is intimacy with the nonexistent and dread of the known."*[838]

Another said, *"The rising of the secret cores beyond settling down with others."*[839]

Another said, *"Loyalty to covenants, then annihilation from everything customary."*[840]

Some have said, *"The poor man is he who has no lineage in the world to which he may return."*

The master Abū ʿAlī Daqqāq said, *"Companionship with a serpent is easier than companionship with poverty, for no one but a prophet or a friend can bear the realm of having no attachments."* Living disengaged and solitary in the world of attachments is the work of no one but the prophets and friends.

"The unneedy go back to what is customary for them, and the poor return to the Object of their worship."

"The unneedy aspire for provisions and the poor aspire for the Provider, for relying on the known is a cause."

It is said that once Luqmān Sarakhsī's hair had become long. It passed into his mind to wish that he had a dirham so that he could go to the bath and have his hair cut. He still had not brought this fully to mind when he saw the desert full of gold. He lifted his eyes and said to himself,

I did say something while drunk,
but why did You attach those camels to my train?

An exalted man came to the shore of the Tigris. He said, *"My Lord, I am thirsty," but he passed by and did not drink.*[841] In contemplating the Real that exalted man was detached from other than the Real. He saw neither the Tigris nor its water. When someone is busy with a work, he will not be aware even if a donkey-load is put in front of him. Also, although water is the secondary cause of the disappearance of thirst, it is not the cause. That exalted man was detached from the secondary causes while gazing at the Causer. In addition, water is given to the soul's appetite, so it was permitted for him to lament of thirst to the Friend, for he saw no refuge but the Friend in the two worlds. If he did not drink water, it was because of opposing the soul, for this group has come to know that conforming with the Real lies in opposing the soul. The more someone opposes the soul, the more he conforms with the Real. The more someone conforms with the soul, the more he opposes the Real.

Or rather, this saying is true: *"Surely your soul has a right against you."*[842] But a man gives the soul its desire when the soul is unable to serve the Friend.

Beyond this there is a secret. It is that *"I am thirsty"* does not allude to the thirst of the soul, for the soul is the enemy, and the Real is the Friend. One does not talk of enemies to the Friend. If the Friend is desired, then it is not permissible to say one word about killing the soul without the Friend's desire, whether He wants to kill it by thirst or He wants to kill it by some other means. Hence what is meant is the thirst of the secret core, and that thirst is the agitation of yearning, for love in its essence is fire, and every fire has a flame. The flame of love's fire is yearning. And what is yearning? *"The thirst of hearts to encounter the Beloved."*[843]

"Yearning is unsettledness because of distance from the place to be visited."[844]

O chevaliers, it is wine that this exalted man should have drunk, but the narrator of this story had in view the outwardness, so he took it as not having been drunk. If the world's thirsty do not find wine, they all lament. But the more lovers drink wine, the thirstier they become. If the thirst of love were to be stilled by some sort of wine, love would disappear, and love's disappearance would be worse than a Christian sash, a Jewish belt, or idol worship.

Another exalted man said, *"Poverty is not having known things." Known things are of many sorts, such as property, status, devotions, and everything for whose sake the servant is honored. But the truthful man of poverty is disengaged from all known things. God says, 'O Prophet, God suffices thee and the faithful who follow thee'* [8:64]."

As long as you fail to spend your possessions in beautiful-doing and munificence, to rub your status in the dust of the visible world, and to turn away from gazing on your devotions toward gazing on the Existent, you will not reach the secret of truthful poverty. Muṣṭafā became disengaged and solitary from everything, and then this declaration came from the Exalted Presence: *"O Prophet, God suffices thee."* O Muḥammad, We are enough for you.

When this center-point of poverty appeared, it appeared during the era of water and clay. Adam, who was the foundation of the work and the quarry of lights and secrets, was busy enjoying himself in the Garden of Eden and the highest Firdaws. When the work of the sultanate and vicegerency clapped its hands, all at once poverty charged forth from the world of jealousy and took away his crown, robe, throne, and hat. "O Adam, how can you enjoy yourself? That is a road that a son does not want for his father, nor a father for his son."

"This affair will not get done with laziness, nor with talk of this and that."

"Companionship with kings will be reached only by swallowing down cups of poison with a laughing mouth. If one pays for a transaction with shavings of the spirit and shreds of the liver, few would wish for it."

When divers go into the sea, they put aside talk of life, for they are not seeking a fish that costs a dirham—they are seeking a pearl that brightens the dark night. If a living thing dies, water will bring it to the top, and once again the precious pearl will settle down at the bottom of the sea. "If you want Us, come to Us with boots made of life."

"The poor man is unitary in essence—he accepts no one, and no one accepts him."[845] The poor man travels alone—he has nothing to do with anyone, nor does anyone take him into account. This secret of poverty became apparent in the Tariqah of Adam when the angels of the Dominion placed their hands firmly on his back as when someone is evicted.

O dervish, anyone who cannot detach his head with his own hands has never smelled a whiff of poverty's rose. Pulling back your feet and sitting in safety is the work of old women and incapable men. The man is he who, when talk of severity comes forth and a sword appears from the Unseen, takes his spirit forward in welcome.

It was said to someone, "Of whom are you the enemy in the world?"

He said, "One day when I had not yet reached puberty, I fell into a whirlpool and feared I would perish. Someone arrived, threw himself in the water, and pulled me out. I am his enemy. Why didn't he let me perish?"

O dervish, know with certitude and verification that anyone who looks at himself is held back from gazing on the Real's majesty. *Whoever says "I" has contended with the Lordhood.* Saying "I" is the secret of every unbelief. The headman of all I-sayers is Iblis.

Jābir said, "I went to the door of the Messenger's chamber and knocked. Muṣṭafā said, 'Who is it?' "

I said, "I."

The Messenger said, "O Jābir, despite God's Being, do you still affirm the being of something else?"

One day Abu'l-Ḥusayn Nūrī went to see Junayd. He said, "O Shaykh, the war has become hard."

He said, "How so?"

He said, "He is saying, *'Either Me, or you.'* "[846]

O dervishes, attach nothing to yourselves. Keep your skirts pure, for all is dust, and wash your clothes pure, for all is dirt. *"This world is a clod of which you have some dust."*[847]

When the Men saw the Real's Being with the eye of certainty, they threw away all of their own being.

O exalted ones, take whatever wherewithal you have to Him, and have no wants. *"The apportioning, the good of it and the evil of it," is from God.*[848] This is why you should throw away your wherewithal in the face of the Presence.

The day when they are dragged on their faces into the Fire: "Taste the touch of Saqar!" [54:48]. My father the Shaykh al-Islam said, "All the commentators who spoke in explanation of God's speech agree that this verse concerns the free-willers."[849] Tomorrow the free-willers will be pulled on their faces into the fire of hell. As for the Folk of the Sunnah, *faces that day radiant, gazing on their Lord* [75:22–23].

"The first thing God created was the Pen."[850] When the Maker first created, He created the Pen. When the Pen moves, it moves upside down in humility itself. When the mind thinks while the Pen is upside down in humility itself, it affirms. *Putting down one's face before the Real is exaltedness.*[851]

What is the Pen? The spokesman for mind and thought, the deputy of intellect and insight, the one whose feet are bound by talk and vision. Affirmation by all these was turned over to the Pen.

"The first thing God created was the Pen. He said to it, 'Write!'

"It said, 'What shall I write?'

"He said, 'All that will be until the Day of Resurrection.' "

Whenever someone chooses upside-downness, his negation is turned into affirmation itself and his annihilation into subsistence itself. The folk of heresy proudly hold their heads high, but the folk of the Sunnah are tainted with dust.

The man is not he who turns his face toward the formal Kaabah and talks about it. The man is he who turns his back on caprice and his heart toward the kiblah of guidance. He strikes the pickax of struggle until the water of contemplation bubbles up from the wellspring of conformity. Like Khiḍr he makes an ablution there in order to live forever. *Peace!*

44–45. *al-Jalīl al-Jamīl:* the Majestic, the Beautiful

The magnificent, the beautiful-doer.

With His majesty He melts hearts and with His beauty He caresses spirits. With His majesty He makes hearts *scattered dust* [25:23] and with His beauty He makes spirits the source of happiness and joy. With His majesty He links hearts with sorrow and grief and with His beauty He makes spirits happy and delighted.

Contemplating His majesty the recognizers breathe the sigh of *"Woe is me!"* Contemplating His beauty the lovers drink the wine of His bestowal at the hand of good fortune's cupbearer. Gazing at His majesty, livers are in the midst of blood; gazing at His beauty, sorrowful hearts are in comfort.

Oh, how many are those who were called to the road by the messenger of His beauty, and then, when their hope for union became strong, He appointed the sultan of majesty to plunder their wherewithal and give it to the wind.

What is my stratagem? Ignorant in love
I'm foolish but you're clever and seeing.

Love is built on this: At first it is all benevolence, at last all severity. At first it is all honey, at last all poison.

When they want to take a child to grammar school, they bring him and tie an amulet around his neck and give him some excuse to keep him still. When two days pass and he sees the teacher's strap, he knows that it was all a pretext. Now there is no way but patience.

In love for the pretty faces, what profits other than patience?
Keep your feet firm in love, don't turn your face from love.
O you who search for your heart here and there,
look for it where you lost it.
In truth the lovers' indigence is wealth—
the indigent win the ball in the field of love.

He clothed us in the garment of love and then offered the Trust to us. Lovers are long-suffering, so we took up the burden. Even if we did not have the strength for it, refusal was not an option. Afterward He did not shy away from rebuking us, for He said, "Surely he was a great wrongdoer, deeply ignorant" [33:72]. *And bewilderment is a pillar in the shariah of love. One of them said,*

He stood apart from me as if I were a sinner,
but I had no sin in love's decree—the sin was his.
He turned away from me when I had no recourse—
would he have been loyal had I had a heart?[852]

He clothed us in the garment of love and said, *"He loves them and they love Him* [5:54]. *Those who have faith love God more intensely* [2:165]." Then He offered the Trust to us. A lover is someone who endures, carries burdens, and is long-suffering in the road. To overburdening he comes forth with endurance, to domineering with graciousness, and to pride with self-abasement. The burning of love's fire made us lift up the burden that heaven, earth, and the mountains were unable to carry, even though we had no capacity to do so. Nonetheless, in the shariah of love bewilderment is a tremendous pillar, so we lifted up the burden and put aside refusal. Then the address came, *"Surely he was a great wrongdoer, deeply ignorant"* [33:72].

Know with certitude and verification that the perfect good fortune of Adam and the Adamites was that heaven, earth, and the mountains were not able to carry the burden and turned away. Otherwise, one of two things would have been true: Either the Adamites would have had partners or they would have been deprived. There is no pleasure in partnership and no good fortune in deprivation.

When the lovers witnessed that they were being carried by Him who always was, they did not shy away from carrying the Trust. When they carried His Trust and did not reject it, He said, "We carried them on land and sea" [17:70]. *"Is the recompense of beautiful-doing anything but beautiful-doing?"* [55:60].

Heaven and earth saw today's burden [*bār*], but Adam saw tomorrow's access [*bār*]. He came forth like a man and said, "In hope for that access I will carry a thousand burdens on the head of my aspiration without fear."

What a marvelous business! A handful of frail dust lifted up a burden that heaven and earth could not carry. Then this pure declaration came forth from the world of exaltedness: *"The praise belongs to God, the Lord of the worlds"* [1:2], *not "The praise belongs to water and clay."*

A man places an arrow in a bow and shoots at the target. They do not say *"Beautifully done"* to the arrow, they say it to the shooter. The arrow says, "It was I who was put through discipline, placed in the lathe, straightened, held to the fire, and shot. Why do you say *'Beautifully done'* to someone else?"

"O arrow, you are not on your own. *Thou didst not throw when thou threwest, but God threw* [8:17]."

A man gets up in the morning and prays. He says, "*The praise belongs to God for giving success!*" This is the secret of the Sunnah, and anything beyond this is Guebrism.

"I deposited a light in your breast so that you would accept faith. I put strength in your tongue so that you would say the Shahadah. I prepared a secret in your makeup so that you would perform wholesome deeds. You cannot come to My Presence with your own strength. A sweeper who comes from the toilet will not be put on the sultan's throne.

"Wait until I dress you in a robe of success before you come to My Presence. Then when I see you, I will see you in My robe. All your deeds without Me are unreal, but all My deeds are real. I will not make your wherewithal from the unreal. I will make it from the real, for when the real appears, the unreal vanishes. Nothing will remain in your hands. *We shall advance upon what deeds they have done and make them scattered dust* [25:23].

"We have made your wherewithal from Our success-giving, confirmation, and help. Then, when the real that is Ours appears—*That day, the kingdom, the real, shall belong to the All-Merciful* [25:26]—Our real will come to meet it. Then you will have something in the midst."

Glory be to God, how many gentle divine favors were given to this fearless handful of dust! He brought the universe into existence with His power, but there was no deficiency anywhere. The will undertook to hold back the reins, but a petitioner arose from munificence seeking power. Power looked with favor on the petitioner, so Adam appeared in the midst. The Quran gave forth this mark of this station: *"I am setting in the earth a vicegerent"* [2:30]. From clay a heart, from dried clay a conjoining, from stinking sperm a friend and a servant.

In reality the wherewithal of our finding was not our seeking, it was His giving. In the beginningless He made a contract between His bestowal and our asking, between His response and our supplication, between His forgiveness and our apology. The wherewithal in this contract was not what we did, it was His bounty. *God is the Unneedy, and you are the poor* [47:38]. A man of wealth has the wherewithal to pay in hard cash, but a poor and indigent man pays after a delay.

When people came into this world, He sent exactors to their doors: "Give what you owe! My bestowal on you is a loan, so pay back My loan by asking. My response to you is a rightful due, so pay off the rightful due by supplication. My forgiveness of you is an obligation, so come out from under the obligation by apology."

You are people with stuffed ears and closed heads. You say, "We want the exactor to be the one with whom we made the contract." So every night I Myself call out, *"Is there any asker, is there any supplicator, is there anyone asking forgiveness, is there any repenter?"*[853]

O you who passed by your lover's street,
  stopped, asked, and then turned away!
How should I be the one to apologize for your steps?
  Should I rub my eyes in the dust of your feet?

It is He who accepts repentance from His servants [42:25]. What is repentance?

"Grief over what is past."

"Constant illness in the hardship of regret."

"Removing the cloth of disloyalty and spreading the carpet of loyalty."

"A flaming fire in the heart and an unmendable hole in the liver."

"Burning linked with embarrassment and lifeblood filled with regret."

"Emaciation of the body and clinging to sorrow."

"Speedy tears because of possession by rapture."[854]

Repentance is a fire burning in the heart, water dripping on the cheeks, wind blowing in remorse, and dust pouring on a head with the attribute of the aggrieved.

O dervish, *there is nothing far-fetched about obedience from the obedient or renunciation from the renunciants. What is surprising is repentance by the disobedient and generous acceptance of the insignificant when someone has nothing else.*

It is recounted that a nomad came to a king with the aim of receiving bounty. He drew goodly water from one of the wells in the road, filled his water bag, and carried it to the king. When he entered in upon him he said, "I have come with something the like of which no one has," and he presented him with the water, which had turned because of the length of the delay.

The king said, "Fill his water bag with dinars."

His boon companions asked him about that. He said, "The nomad came to us with the only thing he had, but we have many more dinars than those we bestowed upon him. So he had the upper hand."

Is it not time for the hearts of those who have faith to be humbled to the remembrance of God? [57:16]. "Come to Our Presence! Even if you have a heavy burden of slips, We have forgiveness without measure." *It is He who accepts repentance from His servants* is good news. *And He pardons the ugly deeds* gives hope that He will be loyal to the explicit expression. *And He knows what you are doing* [42:25] is a threat by allusion.

O dervish, there is a secret here worth a thousand lives. Today in the house of annihilation the Lord does not throw you into trial without first giving you wants and hopes before warning you. Do you suppose that tomorrow in the house of bestowal and subsistence He will burn you forever and ever? What an idea! Certainly not! *He pardons the ugly deeds* [42:25] is the share of the wrongdoers. *And He responds to those who have faith* [42:26] is the share of the moderate. *And He increases them in His bounty* [42:26] is the share of the preceders.[855]

O chevalier, every repentance is accepted, except the repentance of lovers.

If someone repents of love's decree,
God will not accept his repentance.
I hoped to repent from the decree of love—
O repentance uglier than the sin![856]

Sometimes the ocean of trial begins to surge and the lover has no capacity to suffer and bear the burdens of trial. He believes that he can repent of love and be delivered from its trial. But this belief is wrong. In the shariah of love, repentance is folly, for it is seeking a reprieve and wishing for a concession. *"Sufism is force without peace"*[857] *and severity without mercy.*

O you who preach to me with good advice
and ask me to leave aside my love for Him.
On the Day of Mustering, God will gather
my ribs only while I'm loving Him.

O dervish, repentance is something you acquire, but love is neither acquired nor connected to any cause.

It sometimes happens that the beauty of the Beloved unveils the ruling properties of jealousy to the lover such that he guards his eyes against glancing and gazing, or rather against thoughts and notions. But His majesty demands that the lover abandon his own shares and desires and choose the Friend's desire over his own—in separation, severity, withholding, rejection, restraint, and repulsion. Then willingly or unwillingly the burnt lover repents of seeking his need and looking at the cause, but He assigns the assaults of yearning and the agonies of incineration to his heart and liver. The lover is unable to bear it and cannot continue with patience and self-restraint.

What a wonder is the lover in this state! What harshness he suffers, with no mercy or inclination toward him! If he preserves his repentance, He ascribes it to boredom; and if he breaks it, He accuses him of rejecting his responsibility and squandering the state. If he keeps his repentance, it is said, "*Beautifully done*—you're bored!" And if he breaks it, it is said, "Bravo, O covenant breaker!"

When I don't complain, You say, "You're bored with Me.
Why don't you weep—is your heart made of stone?"
If tears flow from my eyes, You say, "You've made Me notorious!
You've disclosed My secrets and reported My affairs!"
If I say, "Is there any way to repent of my sins?"
You say, "Yes—weep in dejection until the Mustering."

*

When I don't lament of love, O You with fairy face,
You say, "You've had enough of Me, you've left Me."
When I weep You say, "You've made Me notorious."
What can I do, tell me my heart-stealer!
My heart's burning fire has dried my eyes' water—
tell anyone with water in his eyes to come and weep for me!
I said, "O Spirit, what should I do to reap the fruit of Your love?"
He said, "You'll never succeed with love this shallow.
"You won't find your desire until you burn.
You won't see My beauty until you discard spirit and heart." [858]

No one in the world is satisfied with a scent, except a lover.

I approve though He does not,
for I'm content with false promises.[859]

He makes all lovers pleased with a scent. He makes them approve of talk, and He gives the reality to no one. There may be a waystation beyond the waystation of Moses, but he wanted to pass beyond speaking. It was said to him, "O Moses, go back to your station. Do you want to reach the station of contemplation from the station of speech?"

No one reached the standing of Moses in burning on the road of the Real, and no one reached the standing of Jacob in burning on the road of creation. "O Moses, here are some words! O Jacob, here is a scent! O Abraham, here is some color!"

He gave no one the reality of trial or the reality of bestowal. You have heard all the talk of the trials of Job. That was in the form. He did not put the trial that He placed on Job on anyone else, but every day He sent Gabriel: "Give My greetings to Job." How would trial remain there?

O dervish, lightning flashed from the Unseen and perplexed the whole world. It turned hearts upside down, placed the stamp of bewilderment on intellects, put a brand on spirits, and went back to the Unseen.

46. *al-Karīm:* the Generous

This is one of the names of the Lord. In the Arabic tongue it is applied to someone who pardons offenders and overlooks sinners. When someone does something ugly to such a person, he counters it with beautiful-doing. The Arabs call someone like this "generous."

In truth this name is a metaphor when used for created things and a reality when used for the Real. Each day His beautiful-doing is more and your disobedience more; His bestowal is greater and your missteps greater.

An exalted man said, *"I began the day with countless blessings from God despite my many disobedient acts. I do not know what to thank Him for—the beautiful things that He has outspread, or the ugly things that He has concealed."*[860]

The Real's gentleness toward His servants has no end and His generosity no limit.

"God's artisanry keeps on coming morning and evening."

"How great are God's hidden artisanry and hidden gentleness!"

"Ask of none but God, for if He bestows upon you, He will make you unneedy."

"God's artisanry brings together all good."[861]

> *God has a gentleness toward creatures*
> *beyond that of mothers and fathers.*[862]

God is gentle to His servants [42:19]. *Part of His gentleness and generosity is the servant's knowledge that He is generous and gentle. Were it not for His gentleness and generosity, the servant would not know His gentleness and generosity.*

Part of His gentleness and generosity is that He conceals the ultimate outcome. If the servant knew that he will be felicitous, he would trust in that and do few deeds. And if he knew that he will be wretched, he would despair and abandon deeds. But God desired the servant to stay between hope and fear.[863]

Part of His generosity is that He makes them forget the slips in their deeds in this world so that their joy will not be clouded in the Garden.[864]

Part of His gentleness and generosity is that He sends messengers calling to His Presence despite His perfect unneediness: "O indigent man, if you did not belong to Me, I would have no need of you. And you, O indigent man—if I did not belong to you, who would you be? If you did not belong to Me, how would that harm Me? And if I did not belong to you, who would you be and who would look after you? *Who would act beautifully toward you? Who would gaze upon you? Who would have mercy upon you? Who would be concerned about your situation?*

"Given that I disapprove that you not belong to Me, how is it that you approve that you not belong to Me? O you of little loyalty and many misdeeds, if you obey Me, I will be grateful to you. If you remember Me, I will remember you. If you take one step for My sake, I will fill the heavens and the earth with gratitude to you.

"My servant, you call upon Me once and I respond to you. It is disloyalty that I call upon you a thousand times and you do not respond to Me. 'So *let them respond to Me!'* [2:186]. Although I said to your father Adam once, *'Get out,'* I have said to you a thousand thousand times, *'Return!' 'God invites to the abode of peace'* [10:25]. Even though you are disloyal, come to My Threshold, for I have prepared many things for you *as hospitality from someone forgiving, ever-merciful* [41:32]."

The meaning of *hospitality* is bounty. He mentioned it with the expression *hospitality* to make manifest the perfection of bounty and the utmost limit of generosity. *We have heard that when kings enter a city, hospitality is offered to them. But we have not heard that when a disobedient, sinning servant enters in upon his patron, he offers him hospitality. O generosity that has no limit! O bounty that has no limit!*

He says, *"As hospitality from someone forgiving, ever-merciful."* He does not say *"from someone munificent."* This is evidence that this group needs forgiveness, and this is the mark of the disobedient. *Say: "Each acts according to his own manner"* [17:84].

O My servants who have been immoderate against yourselves, despair not of God's mercy. Surely God forgives all sins [39:53]. It has been reported that someone recited this verse before God's Messenger. When the reciter reached the words, *"Surely God forgives all sins,"* the Prophet said, *"Indeed He does, and He does not care."*[865] Then he said, *"May God curse those who make people flee," three times, that is, "those who make people despair of God's mercy."*[866]

It has come from Moses that he said, *"My God, why do You desire disobedience from the servants when You hate it?"*

God replied, "That is to set up My pardon."

Here there is a beautiful question. Someone may say, "With all the honor and eminence bestowed on the Adamites, what was the wisdom in afflicting them with disobedience?"

Know that this question has several answers. One is that you can say that the wisdom is for servants not to become self-admiring, for self-admiration calls down the veil. Have you not seen that when Balaam admired himself because of the greatest name of God, he became a dog? *So his likeness is the likeness of a dog* [7:176]. *He had been the possessor of the present moment and the heart, but through self-admiration he became more impure than a dog.*

Another answer is that the cleverness, skill, and mastery of a glassmaker appears in broken glass. Your heart is like a glass goblet, and the stone of disobedience has come and broken it. With the fire of repentance the Exalted Lord will bring it back to wholesomeness. *Surely I am all-forgiving to those who repent* [20:82]. Though He said to Moses in the majesty of His state, *"Surely I am God"* [20:14], to us He says, *"Surely I am all-forgiving."*

Another answer is this: The Real has two storehouses, one full of reward and the other full of mercy. "If you obey—rewards and generous gifts. If you disobey—mercy and forgiveness. Thereby My storehouses will not go to waste."

It has also been said that He afflicts you with disobedience so that the evil eye of Iblis will not strike you. When an orchard is beautiful, they hang a donkey's head in it so that no evil eye will strike it.

It has also been said that He decreed sin for the servants to indicate the purity of the Lord.

It has also been said that He desired only to spite Iblis—upon whom be curses! For it is much easier on the hunter if no prey falls into his trap than if prey does fall in, and then it escapes. You can also say that the lordly wisdom in afflicting His servants with acts of disobedience was to spite Iblis, for if nothing falls into a hunter's trap, he will not suffer nearly as much as if something falls in, then escapes and gets away.

Also: Wherever there is a possessor of beauty, she will not be protected from the people's gaze. Hence He set things up so that even if you were adorned with the beauty of purity and rid of the rust of disobedience, Satan would not turn his full gaze upon you. He threw you into disobedience so that you would be broken and Satan's gaze would not stay on you. After that, the mercy of the Real will descend on your broken heart, for *"I am with those whose hearts are broken."*[867]

Another answer is that if someone is pure and purified of defects, both friend and enemy will fix their eyes on him and envy him. The wisdom in afflicting you with disobedience is that everyone will reject you, and you will be singled out for Him. Have you not heard what Khiḍr said when he broke the ship? He said that the wisdom in making the ship defective was so that the wrongdoing king would not fix his eyes upon it. In the same way, Joseph placed the name of thievery on Benjamin because he wanted to hold him back and single him out for himself. The Real wanted to single the servants out for Himself, so He decreed slips for them. When they acknowledge their sins, He says, "If I make him despair, that would be a defect in My generosity, and that is not allowable."

Iblis says, *"By Thy exaltedness, I will lead them all astray"* [38:82], but the Real says, *"I will forgive them all."* He says, *"I will forgive them,"* but He does not say, *"I have forgiven them," lest the servant hold back from beseeching, weeping, fear, and hope.* The servant must stay between hope and fear, all the time beseeching, weeping, wailing, and supplicating. *Turn to God all together!* [24:31]. *Surely God forgives all sins* [39:53]: "All of you come to Me, because I am buying you all."

Part of His perfect generosity is that He rebuked the messengers because of the disobedient, such as His rebuke of Abraham at the time of his ascent to heaven, saying to him, "Hold back from My servants, O Abraham, for one of My names is the Patient."[868] *He rebuked Moses because of Korah, who asked help from him seventy times. He said, "By My exaltedness, had he asked Me for help once, I would have helped him."*[869]

The Real says, *"Say: 'O My servants!'"* [39:53].

How blessed were the days when we were in nonexistence itself,
and He [in His generosity] was saying, "O My servants!"[870]

O My servants! "If the infant in the cradle knew who was soothing him, he would melt in joy." May a thousand lives be sacrificed to the time when we were not, our hearing was not, our defiled makeup was not, and He was talking to us!

How blessed was the time of Your covenant—without it
my heart would have had no place for ardor![871]

His belonging to you before you belonged to you is part of the generosity He apportioned to you beforehand. That He belonged to you before you belonged to you is a gentleness whose least portion is not reached by the descriptions of the describers.

He said about Abraham, *"We gave Abraham his rectitude from before"* [21:51]. What did He say about us? *"I bestowed upon you before you asked from Me."*[872] *Belonging to the Beloved while one has being is generosity, before one has being is love, and after one dies is loyalty.*

O My servants! Which servants? *Not those who have obeyed, not those who have fasted, not those who have performed the prayers, not those who have made the hajj, not those who have struggled, not those who have given alms.* Which ones then? "*Those who have been immoderate* [39:53], those who have passed beyond the limits."

Joseph the sincerely truthful said, *"And He acted beautifully toward me when He brought me forth from the prison"* [12:100]. This was the utmost generosity. His brothers left no disloyalty undone. They threw him into the well, they aimed to slay him, they gave him no food, they beat him a good deal, and they sold him for a few worthless dirhams. The Exalted Lord delivered him on the day when his parents and brothers gathered together, and then he said, *"He acted beautifully toward me when He brought me forth from the prison."* He mentioned nothing of the well, or the jail, or the selling. He said, *"He acted beautifully toward me."* Then he said, *"after Satan had sowed dissension between me and my brothers"* [12:100]. He called them "brothers" even after they did what they did.

In the same way, tomorrow the books of your sins and the scrolls of your slips will be hung around the neck of that accursed one. In the story of Adam, what did He say? *"So he led the two of them on by delusion* [7:22]. *Then Satan made them slip therefrom* [2:36]."

Who have been immoderate. He did not tear the curtain. He did not say, "They committed adultery, they murdered." He mentioned the short of it—*who have been immoderate.* They were immoderate. Since He wants to, He forgives. He does not tear the curtain.

He did not say to the Throne, "O My Throne," or to the Pen, "O My Pen," or to the Tablet, "O My Tablet," or to the Garden, "O My Garden," or to the Fire, "O My Fire." He said to the disobedient, "O My servants!" That is enough for you to boast.

O My servants! This in fact pertains to this world. On the Day of Resurrection, you will say, *"my soul, my soul!"* Muṣṭafā will say, *"my community, my community!"* Paradise will say, *"my share, my share!"* Hell will say, *"my portion, my portion."* The Lord will say, *"My servant, My servant!"*

"Many thousands of glorifiers and *tawḥīd*-reciters have called out to Me in many languages, but I have never said to anyone, *'Here I am!'* You with your missteps and disloyalty turn your face to heaven and say, *'My Lord!'* and at once I say, *'Here I am, My servant!'* "

Supplicate Me; I will respond to you [40:60]. "It is many years—and how is this a place for years and months?—that I have been saying, '*My servant!*' and you have never said to Me, '*Here I am.*' Shame on you!"

Do you not see that He says, *"Let them respond to Me"* [2:186]? "My servant, when you call upon Me, I respond. Why is it that when I call upon you, you do not respond?"

Despair not of God's mercy [39:53]: "Be careful not to lose hope in My mercy or to cease wishing for My pardon. Even if your sins are without limit, your defects without excuse, and your slips without measure, it is fitting that My mercy be without bounds, My pardon be without compare, and My generosity be without measure."

In the midst of this Iblis criticized Adam by saying that he was made of clay. "O accursed one, you see the outwardness adorned with clay, but you do not see the inwardness trimmed with the heart. *And He adorned it in their hearts* [49:7]."

"O angels, you have obedience! O messengers, you have messengerhood! O renunciants, you have renunciation! O worshipers, you have worship! O disobedient ones, you have the Lord!" Do you not see that He says, "Whoever does something ugly or wrongs himself and then asks forgiveness of God, he will find God" [4:110]. *When someone finds God, what weight does anything other than God have for him?*

O chevalier, when He wants to drape you with a robe of honor, He says, *"Your Lord,"* ascribing Himself to you. When He wants to make you secure from chastisement, He ascribes you to Himself and says, *"My servants."*

"My servants, look at the Throne to see tremendousness, look at the Footstool to see embracingness, look at the Tablet to see writing, look at heaven to see elevation, look at the heart to see recognition, look at recognition to see love, and look at love to see the Beloved."

At the beginning of the verse, He says, *"O My servants!"* O My servants, O you who are Mine! At the end He says, *"Be penitent toward your Lord!"* [39:54]. O I who am yours! O I who am yours and O you who are Mine, *do not despair*! Do not lose hope in My mercy, for the servant is not without slips, and the Lord is not without mercy.

"I promised that I will forgive. I did not say, 'I have forgiven.' If I had said, 'I have forgiven,' the intercession of the Messenger would be nullified and he would not have the exaltedness of intercession. On the Day of Resurrection, Muṣṭafā will intercede and I will forgive so that he may have the exaltedness of intercession and I may have the exaltedness of divinity.

"There, where Ḥamza was killed and the antagonist was someone like Muḥammad, I pardoned.[873] Here, where intercession comes from Muḥammad and the promise of mercy from the Real, what is weighty about forgiving sins?"

Moses said, *"O God, why do you provide for the stupid and deprive the clever?"*

He said, "So that the clever will know that provision depends on apportioning, not on cleverness." On the Day of Resurrection, He will forgive the disobedient so that the creatures will know that mercy is bestowed, not earned; it derives from solicitude, not worship.

"I did not call you My servant in only one place—*Tell My servants* [15:49], *Say to My servants* [14:31], *When My servants ask thee* [2:186], *O My servants* [39:53]. I did this so that you would know that there is no way to estrangement.

"If I have called you Mine, that is no wonder. The wonder is that I have called Myself yours. *Your God is one God* [2:163]. *I am your Lord, so worship Me* [21:92]. *That is because God is the patron of those who have faith* [47:11]. *Surely your Lord is God, who created the heavens and the earth* [7:54].

"O chevalier, when kings in the world call someone their own, that person boasts in front of everyone. O friend, be happy, for I have called Myself yours.

"I called Myself the clement, the ever-merciful: '*Surely God is clement, ever-merciful toward the people*' [2:143], and I called the Messenger *clement, ever-merciful toward the faithful* [9:128]. How could someone weak be neglected between two who are ever-merciful? I am ever-merciful, My Messenger is ever-merciful, the Companions are ever-merciful—*ever-merciful among themselves* [48:29]—and the community is the object of mercy, for he said, '*My community is a community shown mercy.*'[874]

"When someone comes to the resurrection obedient, *that is the Garden that We shall give to those of Our servants who are godwary* [19:63]. And when someone comes indigent, *say: 'In the bounty of God and His mercy—in that let them rejoice'* [10:58].

"Do not despair of God's mercy, for My mercy is beginningless and your disobedience is temporal. The beginningless overcomes the temporal, not the temporal the beginningless."

It is said that Gabriel and Michael were debating. Gabriel said, "God created a creature in the most beautiful form and subjected to him heaven, earth, and everything in between. He commanded him to obey Him, but he busied himself with disobedience. If God forgives him, that will be a wonder."

Michael replied, "If He forgives him, no deficiency will appear in His kingdom."

A call came, "Michael has the upper hand."

"I called the Kaabah Mine. I said, '*My house*' [22:26], but it became a house of idols. I called the she-camel Mine: '*The she-camel of God*' [11:64], but the she-camel was killed. I called the man of faith Mine. I said, '*My servant,*' but he became estranged through disobedience. The mosque is Mine; it is not fit for selling. The she-camel is Mine; it is not fit for killing. The indigent man is Mine; he is not suited for burning.

"I called Myself the forgiving and I called Muṣṭafā the Messenger. I said, '*O Messenger, deliver what has been sent down upon thee!*' [5:67]. O Muḥammad, if you do not deliver the message, you will not be perfect in messengerhood. I will forgive so as to show the creatures the perfection of the attribute of divinity, just as I have shown the creatures the perfection of Muḥammad's messengerhood."

Someone may say: "Nothing that you say has any root, for the Exalted Lord says in His own speech, '*And none of you there is but will go down into it; that for thy Lord is a decreed decision*' [19:71]."

I would reply that the belief of the folk of the Real is that it is permissible for the faithful who commit great sins never to enter hell and for the Real to forgive all their great sins. And it is permissible for them to go to hell and for the Real to chastise them in the measure of their sins and then to bring them back out of hell and take them to paradise.

And none of you there is but will go down into it. There are two opinions concerning *it.* Mujāhid says that *it* refers to sickness. Muṣṭafā reported from the Real, *"God says: '[Sickness] is My fire to which I subject My faithful servants as an expiation for their sins.' "*[875]

The other opinion is that *it* refers to hell. If we say that hell is meant, then there are two more opinions. One is that what is meant is the unbelievers, and the other is that what is meant is both the faithful and the unbelievers.

Then concerning the quality of "going down" there are two opinions. One opinion is that what is meant by going down is entrance. This is the opinion of Ibn 'Abbās: *"Everyone, whether pious or depraved, will go down into it."* The other opinion is that what is meant by going down is reaching and passing by. God says, *"And when they went down to the water of Midian"* [28:23], that is, they reached it. Thus the believer will attain the utmost joy, because he will be saved from it after witnessing it. In the same way people commonly say, *"Buy the house from the son, not the father, because the son does not recognize its worth."*

Have you not seen that when Adam found the Garden for free, he sold it for a grain of wheat? *Thus they will go down to the Fire so that, when they are saved from it, they will know the worth of the Garden. The existence of blessing after tribulation is sweeter and more enjoyable.*

In addition, He desires to show the excellence of the tawḥīd*-voicers' elements to the unbelievers, for fire does not act on a genuine gem, nor will it corrupt it. It only corrupts crystal and the like. So the person of faith is like pure gold; fire does not harm him.* The lordly wisdom is to show the excellence of the elements and the strength of the state of the *tawḥīd*-voicers to the associators, for when the gem is genuine, the eye will not see fire in it, but fire will ruin a gem that is not genuine.

It is as if He is saying to Iblis, "At the first you said, '*Shall I prostrate myself to someone whom Thou hast created of clay?*' [17:61]. Now look—through My strength-giving, this clay has reached the place where hell cries out for help against it."[876]

O chevalier, wisdom deems it beautiful to teach courtesy. Taking the faithful into hell is to teach them courtesy, not to show wrath.

Moreover, until water and clay have been passed over fire, they do not gain value.

Again, this world is a house full of dust upon which is sitting the filth and dirt of disobedient acts. Hell was made like a bathhouse so that you may come into it and be purified of all the filth. Then you will settle down in the place of generosity and the waystation of felicity.

"Whenever We show someone tribulation, We show him blessing from the same place. Jacob's tribulation was from the shirt: *They brought his shirt with false blood on it* [12:18]. We showed him blessing from the same place: *Go with my shirt* [12:93]. We showed Moses tribulation from the river: *Cast him into the river* [28:7]. We showed him blessing from the same place: *We delivered Moses* [26:65]. The beginning of your tribulation was from fire, for Iblis said, *'I am better than he'* [38:76]. Tomorrow We will show complete blessing to the fire, for We will put the light of the recognizers' recognition in charge of the Fire so that the Fire will say, *'Pass by, O man of faith, for your light will extinguish my flames.'*[877]

"That for thy Lord is a decreed decision [19:71], *a necessary oath, a decreed obligation.* For the sake of the oath I will surely place them in the Fire. Then for the sake of showing honor to faith I will bring them out. *Thus I said to Job: 'Take in thy hand a bundle of rushes, and strike therewith, and do not fail in thy oath* [38:44]. Keep the oath and bring about the rightful due of serving it. O Job, that woman is sinless, and it is not allowed to chastise the sinless. And you are a prophet, and in prophethood it is not allowed to swear a false oath.'[878]

"I will take everyone into hell and bring them out *cleansed of sin, with immaculate breasts* and no way to be burned. So what will I do with the fire? I will make it *coolness and safety* [21:69]. Thus I will have kept the oath and I will not have punished the pure faithful."

The Master Imam—God sanctity his spirit—said this: *"They will enter it but they will not sense it. Having passed by, they will say, 'Did He not promise us hell on the path?' It will be said to them, 'You passed through it but were unaware.' "*[879]

They don't burn the burned. When a falcon aims for a pigeon, the pigeon aims for the sky. It goes so high that the heat burns away its feathers and it falls. The falcon no longer aims for it. It says, "This one is already burned. They don't burn the burned."

Someone may say, "How does this verse conform with the verse where the Maker says, *'As for those to whom the most beautiful preceded from Us, they will be far from it and will not hear a whisper of it'* [21:101–2]?"

We say that the two verses conform and correspond. What is meant here is the chieftains, the exalted, and the pure among the folk of faith, those upon the tails of whose states has sat none of the filth of sin.

"The greatest terror," which is separation, "shall not make them sorrow, and the angels shall receive them" and say to them, "This is the day that you were promised" [21:103] *as the reward. Among them will be those whom the angels receive, and among them will be those addressed by the King.*[880]

47. *al-Raqīb:* the Watcher

The watchman. When the faithful servant knows that the Real is his guard and watcher, he must put on the garment of self-watchfulness and attend to his own states, words, and deeds. He must keep the courtyard of his breast purified of the stain of heedlessness. He should make *does he not know that God sees?* [96:14] his constant litany. He should keep *there are over you guards* [82:10] before his eyes. He should inscribe *We are not heedless of creation* [23:17] on the seal ring of his own certainty.

It is said that there was a depraved woman in Mecca who said, "I will turn Ṭāwūs Yamānī away from the road." Ṭāwūs was a man of beautiful face. She came to Ṭāwūs and began talking with him in a joking way. Ṭāwūs said, "Be patient until we reach the right place." When they reached the place, he said, "If you have a goal, it can be here."

The woman said, *"Glory be to God,* all these people are looking. This is not the place for that."

Ṭāwūs said, *"Does God not see us everywhere?* O woman, do you guard against being seen by the people, who are servants, but not against being seen by the Lord of the servants?" The woman repented and became one of the sincerely truthful. There are many stories like this in the books.

O dervish, when a watcher is set over someone, he is set over someone who is beautiful. He did not say, "I am the watcher over heaven and earth; I am the watcher over the Throne and the Footstool." He said, "I am the watcher over you: *Surely God is watcher over you* [4:1]." This is because a watcher is stipulated for someone beautiful, and no existent thing has the beauty that you have: *Surely We created man in the most beautiful stature* [95:4]: "You are *the most beautiful of created things*, and I am *the most beautiful of creators. 'So blessed is God, the most beautiful of creators!'* [23:14]."

And He formed you, so He made your forms beautiful [40:64]. *"He created you" to manifest power, "then He provided for you" to manifest generosity, "then He will make you die" to manifest all-compellingness, "then He will bring you to life"* [30:40] *for the sake of reward and punishment. "So blessed is God, the most beautiful of creators," that is, form-givers. He created foreheads suited for prostration, eyes suited for taking heed, ears suited for wisdom, tongues suited for gratitude, hands suited for liberality, feet suited for service, hearts suited for recognizing, and secret cores suited for love. So "remember God's blessings upon you"* [2:231], *for He adorned your tongues with bearing witness, your hearts with recognition and felicity, and your bodies with service and worship.*

"First you were a sperm drop and I made you into a clot with My power. Then I built tissue with My will, I made bones appear with My desire, and I clothed the bones in flesh with My munificence. What is the wisdom in this? Yes, when I wanted to display you to your father and mother, first I adorned you in the oyster of the womb.

"Just as a slave trader adorns a slave girl at the time of presenting her, in the same way after turning you into dust in your grave I will adorn you for the Day of Presentation before the messengers and the Lord of the Worlds." God says, "They will be presented before thy Lord in rows" [18:48].

"I adorned the face, which is the gazing place of the creatures, with all this beauty. Look at how I adorned the heart, which I made My own gazing place!"

Whenever painters paint, they paint on something standing still, in an open place, and in brightness. The Exalted Lord paints on a moving thing *in three darknesses* [39:6] with *"Be!" so it comes to be* [2:117].

You fill a pot with water, turn it upside down, and nothing remains inside. The Exalted Lord placed the sperm drop in the womb and kept it upside down with His power. *So blessed is God, the most beautiful of creators!*

"With My power I make forms in wind, dust, water, and fire. No one else is able to do that."

Glory be to Him who compounded Adam in a composition that contains everything He created in the macrocosm! Who is able to thank God for this composition, order, arrangement, and combination?!

The Exalted Lord created some creatures in the form of prostrators, like snakes, fish, and crawling things. He created some in the form of bowers, like beasts and cattle; some in the form of standers, like trees, plants, and growing things; some in the form of sitters, like the unshakable mountains. The prostrator is compelled to prostrate, so he receives no praise for that. The stander, sitter, and bower are the same; they receive no praise, for they cannot do anything else. But He created the Adamite in a form that has the power to prostrate, the power to bow, the power to sit, and the power to stand. He also gave him choice and ability, so he is worthy of praise and laudation: *The repenters, the worshipers, the praisers, the journeyers, the bowers, the prostrators, the commanders to the honorable and prohibiters of the improper, the keepers of God's bounds—give good news to the faithful!* [9:112].

He brought together subtle air and dense earth and made apparent the fact that He is the provider: *And God is the best of providers* [62:11]. "The creatures provide, but they take the material from Me."

It is said that one day Solomon said, "O God, allow me to give Your creatures their daily portion for one day," and God allowed that. He commanded that many sorts of food be gathered. A fish came out of the water and ate all that they had gathered and then said, "Bring more!"

Solomon said, "There is nothing left."

It said, "O Solomon, today you have left me hungry." Then it said, "We are seven hundred groups, and all of them have stayed hungry, and I have found one-third of my daily portion."

He brought together the subtle spirit and the dense body and made apparent His creativity. *So blessed is God, the most beautiful of creators!* "I created with My power without instrument in the midst. I brought to life through recognition of Me without cause in the midst. I give death through My wisdom without enmity in the midst. I bring back to life without need in the midst. I take to paradise without counting it a favor in the midst. I bestow vision without form in the midst."

This prelude alludes to the beautification of outward form. As for the meanings that are connected with inwardness, they are beyond this. *Glory be to Him who "created man from an extraction of clay"* [23:12]*! Then He chose him for the noblest creed and religion and deposited in his secret core the lights of recognition and clarification. Hence the likeness of the branches of faith when they rise up from the root of certainty is "like a goodly tree, its root fixed and its branches in heaven"* [14:24].

Wāsiṭī said, "He created the spirits from the light of beauty and majesty. Had He not curtained them, every unbeliever would prostrate himself before them."[881]

These exalted ones are His storekeepers, and their breasts are His storehouses. The greatness of this storehouse is because of the Sultan. Were it not for this greatness, Iblis would show his head from your breast. Iblis says, "I dare not go after the breasts of Your men. I went after a breast once, and I was struck with a blow whose pain is still with me. I go after garbage dumps. When there is a flourishing garden, what work would I have there?"

The hearts of the exalted ones are ornamented gardens. *"The light of the Reality* [*nūr al-ḥaqīqa*] *is more beautiful than the blossom of the garden* [*nawr al-ḥadīqa*]*."*[882]

"The object of My desire is you. The marvel of My power is you. By creating you I did not make you appear—I made Myself appear."

"O hearts, what are you doing in bodies? Come to the world of My attributes' exaltedness, for your specific pack-horse is the attribute of My majesty."

"The hearts are between two fingers of the All-Merciful."[883] When He created heaven and earth, His wisdom in creating them was to create a heart. He created this world so that people would know, and He created paradise so that they would see. He adorns paradise with the friends,

He adorns the friends with the heart, and He adorns the heart with Himself. *"Neither the heavens nor the earth embraces Me, but the heart of My faithful servant does embrace Me."*[884]

Surely We offered the Trust to the heavens and the earth and the mountains, but they refused to carry it and feared it, and man carried it. Surely he was a great wrongdoer, deeply ignorant [33:72]. Many things have been said about this Trust. Some have said that the Trust consists of all the commands and prohibitions. Some have said that it is the obligations that the Real has placed upon the servants, like prayer and fasting. Some have said that the Trust is creation.[885]

It has been said, "It is tawḥīd *with belief and guarding the limits by striving."*[886]

It has been said, "The Trust is realizing tawḥīd *by the path of solitariness."*[887]

Ḥasan said, "When the Trust was offered to the heavens, the earth, and the mountains, they said, 'And what is inside it?'

"It was said to them, 'If you do the beautiful, you will be recompensed, and if you do the ugly, you will be punished.'

"They said, 'No.'"

Mujāhid said, "When God created Adam, He offered it to him. He said, 'And what is inside it?'

"It was said to him, 'Words hitting the mark.'

"He said, 'I will carry it, O my Lord!'"

Mujāhid said, "Between his carrying it and his being sent out of the Garden was no more than the measure of noon to afternoon."[888]

The offer to heaven and earth was for them to make a choice, but the offer to Adam had already been decided: *He fastened to them the word of godwariness, to which they have more right and of which they are worthy* [48:26]. *And when they carried it, they were carried.*

Adam said, "Heaven with its elevation, earth with its expanse, and the mountains with their splendor did not have the capacity for it. How will I in my weakness have the capacity?"

"O Adam, the carrying will be yours, but the guarding will be Mine."

It is said that a nomad sought and gained access to one of the caliphs. He said, "I come from the place where Muṣṭafā sleeps."

The caliph was a chevalier. He commanded that half of what was in his storehouse be given to him. The servitor said to the nomad, "On which steed will you place this gift?"

The nomad came to the caliph and said, *"Your gifts are carried by your steeds."*

This made the caliph happy, and he commanded that steeds be brought and given to him so that he could take the gift.

In the same way when Adam lifted up the burden, he lifted it with the divine success-giving, for *"No one carries His gifts but His steeds."*

When a merchant hires a porter and puts a precious burden on his back, he sends someone trustworthy along with him. Sometimes he himself goes with the porter to his house. There is no burden more valuable than recognition and *tawḥīd*. Hence He put the burden of the Trust on the back of our covenant and, by virtue of His bounty, He made 360 gazes the escort of the burden.[889]

The porter thinks and says, "I will be at ease from the hardship of the burden when I surrender it and take the wage."

The owner of the burden thinks and says to himself, "I will make a great deal of profit."

So also are the soul and the heart. The soul thinks and says to itself, "I will be at ease from the hardship of the burden when I die and am given the Garden."

The heart thinks and says, "My profit from this will be encounter, contemplation, joining, and union."

Water said to oil, "Why do you come on my head and seek to be above when I am more excellent than you?"

It said, "Because I have carried a heavy burden."

Dust is elevated above and beyond all existent things—even though dust is the most abased of things—because it has carried a heavy burden.

The hoopoe lifted up Solomon's letter and took it to the realm of Sheba, so the Real forbade killing it, *and it found silk and crown. In the same way, the person of faith carries God's Trust to find the Abode of Settledness so that God will forbid the Fire to burn his body.*

Another fine point is that when a woman dies in childbirth, she dies a martyr, for she dies while carrying. In the same way, when a person of faith dies carrying His Trust, he dies a martyr.

Also, the melon tree is weak, and carrying the melon would be a heavy burden. So it says, "I cannot carry it." They say to it, "Put it in a place that will carry it," so it puts it on the earth. In the same way, the disobedient person is not able to carry the burden of disobedience, so the Lord calls out in His gentleness, "Put it on mercy so that you will have carried it in the hope of mercy."

O dervish, the one desired by the offer to heaven and earth was Adam, but He did not address it to Adam, for Adam had slipped. In the same way, a father who is angry with his son will command a servant to do a job, but what he intends is the son. The son knows that he is intended and hurries to do the job in order to gain his father's approval. Thus heaven and earth were addressed, but Adam was quick-witted. He knew that the one intended was himself. He held out his hands, for *he was a great wrongdoer, deeply ignorant.* Perhaps He would forgive him. So He did forgive him, *and man carried it* [33:72]. He did not say that he guarded it. "The lifting is yours and the guarding is Mine: *Surely it is We who have sent down the Remembrance, and surely it is We who are its guards* [15:9]."

He offered it to heaven and earth so that if Adam and his children should fall short, heaven and earth would excuse them and come forth not with antagonism but with intercession. [*Those who carry the Throne and those around it...*] *ask forgiveness for those who have faith* [40:7].

What is meant by "heaven and earth" is the folk of heaven and earth. Some say that it is heaven and earth themselves. "After bestowing life and creating intellect, I made the offer to heaven and earth," but He unveiled Himself to them in the description of lordhood's severity and tremendousness, so they were afraid. He unveiled Himself to Adam and his offspring in the description of gentleness, so they accepted.

"In the state of the servant's encountering God, he carries heaven and earth on one of his eyelashes."[890]

Another secret: When the Real offered the Trust to creation, Adam's aspiration became attached to it and the aspiration of all the created things turned away from it.

"Your heart is the porter of recognizing Me, your tongue the porter of voicing My *tawḥīd*, your body the porter of obeying Me, and your intellect the porter of being in awe of Me."

The porter says, "When will I put down the burden and take my wage?"

The owner of the burden says, "When will I open the burden and take the profit?"

Your body is the porter of the burden, and your heart is the owner of the burden. The body says, "When will I put down the burden and take my wage?"

The heart says, "When will I reach the profit of contemplation?"

What a marvelous business! When a porter lifts up a heavy burden, they say to him, "Well done!" What is the wisdom in *Surely he was a great wrongdoer, deeply ignorant* [33:72]? Yes, here *great wrongdoer, deeply ignorant* is praise, not blame, *for he carried it with his aspiration, not his capacity.* Adam carried the burden with aspiration, not with capacity. *This is like the words of the man who says to his companion when he carries a heavy burden, "Why are you carrying that? You will hurt yourself."*

O chevalier, when the adversary admits the defects of his antagonist, the work is easy. He called him *a great wrongdoer, deeply ignorant* in the Beginningless. Then, despite His knowledge of his great wrongdoing and deep ignorance, He offered him the Trust. If he falls short, he will say, *"I have wronged myself"* [27:44]. The Exalted Lord will say, *"I forgive you and I do not care."*[891]

He said, "Surely man is a great wrongdoer, ungrateful" [14:34]. *Of Himself He said, "Surely I am all-forgiving"* [20:82]. *Peace!*

48. *al-Mujīb:* the Responder

He who answers supplications; as God says, *"And your Lord says, 'Supplicate Me; I will respond to you'"* [40:60].

The mark of response to supplication is perseverance in supplication. Even if you persevere in supplication but remain without the response that is your own share, you will not have remained without the worship that is His rightful due. The mark of response to supplication is firm fixity in supplication. If you are firmly fixed in supplication and you remain deprived of the response that is your portion, you will be given the eminence of the worship that is God's rightful due, and this step is beyond that step.

Supplication has preconditions. One is distress: *He who responds to the distressed when he supplicates Him* [27:62]. Another is seeking aid: *When you sought the aid of your Lord and He responded to you* [8:9]. Another is sincerity: *"Surely God does not respond to the supplication of a diverted heart."*[892] Another is pleading: *Supplicate your Lord in pleading and secret* [7:55]. Another is eagerness and dread: *They were supplicating Us in eagerness and dread* [21:90]. Another is eating the permitted, as Muṣṭafā said in the hadith: *"His clothing is forbidden, his food is forbidden—so how should he receive a response?"*[893]

It is recounted that one of the wrongdoers feared that good people would supplicate against him. By some stratagem he held a banquet for them so that they would eat his forbidden food and God would not respond to their supplications against him. But they kept back from eating the food, then supplicated against him, and God made the earth engulf him.

Another precondition is that the supplicator must have certainty and reliance, just as has come in the report: *"Supplicate God while being certain of response."*[894]

There was a chamber that belonged to an old woman of the Children of Israel in the neighborhood of a king. One day the old woman went out on some business. When she came back, she saw that the king had taken down her room and put it inside his castle. In her distress, the woman said, *"O God, though I was not present, where were You?" So God destroyed the king and his house.*[895]

Muḥammad ibn ʿAlī Tirmidhī said, *"When someone supplicates God without first having repaired the road of supplication with repentance, penitence, eating the permitted, following the Sunnah, and taking care of the secret core, his supplication will be rejected."*[896] When someone calls upon the Real without first repairing supplication's road with repentance, sincerity, keeping morsels and clothing pure, and guarding his inwardness against the unreal, his supplication will be rejected and the door of response will be shut.

And your Lord says, "Supplicate Me; I will respond to you" [40:60]. Several gentlenesses are placed in these words. He did not say, *"The All-Compelling says"* or *"The Severe says"* or *"God says."* If He had said that, the servant would fear and would not dare to step on the carpet of bold expansiveness. He said, *"Your Lord"*—your Nurturer—*"says, 'Supplicate Me; I will respond to you.'" It is as if He said, "I belong to you, and what I have belongs to you, so do not be shy of asking, for if you abandon asking, I will be angry with you."*

Ibrāhīm Adham was asked, "The Real says, '*Supplicate Me; I will respond to you,'* but we supplicate night and day and see no response."

He said, *"Because your hearts have died through ten things: You recognize God but do not discharge His rightful due. You recite His book but do not put it into practice. You claim to love God's Messenger but put aside his Sunnah. You claim enmity with Satan but conform with him. You claim to love the Garden but do not act accordingly. You claim to fear the Fire but pawn yourselves to it. You attest to the truth of death but do not prepare yourselves for it. You distract yourselves from your own faults with the faults of your brothers. You eat God's blessings but make ingratitude your craft. You bury your dead but do not learn any lessons."*[897]

One of the great ones said, "Someone who supplicates without deeds is like someone who shoots without a bowstring."[898]

And your Lord says, "Supplicate Me; I will respond to you." One hundred twenty-some thousand center-points of prophethood wearing the shirt of sinlessness said, *"Our Lord!"* Adam, who was the foundation and the first *alif* on the tablet of gentleness, said, *"Our Lord, we have wronged ourselves!"* [7:23]. "And We say to you, '*Supplicate Me; I will respond to you.' If you do not supplicate Me, I will supplicate you: 'The Creator of the heavens and the earth supplicates you'* [14:10]."

And your Lord says, "Supplicate Me; I will respond to you." "Supplicate Me" with apology, "I will respond to you" with forgiveness. Thus has it been said, *"The sinner's interceder is his confession, and his repentance is his apology."*[899] The sinner's confession of his sin intercedes for him, and once he confesses the sin his shelter is mercy.

"Supplicate Me" with sincerity, "I will respond to you" with deliverance. "Supplicate Me" with self-abasement, "I will respond to you" with bounteousness. "Supplicate Me" with fear and hope, "I will respond to you" with gifts and robes of honor. "Supplicate Me" without heedlessness, "I will respond to you" without delay.[900] *"Supplicate Me" by cutting off attachments, "I will respond to you"*

by bestowing realities. "Supplicate Me" without slackening, "I will respond to you" by making you attain your wishes. "Supplicate Me" on top of distress, "I will respond to you" by repelling the causes of harm and opening the doors of kindness.

Yaḥyā ibn Muʿādh said, *"I supplicate You in public as lords are supplicated, but I supplicate You in private as lovers are supplicated. In assemblies I say, 'My God,' and in private I say, 'My Beloved.'"*[901] Among the creatures I call upon You just as servants call upon their lords; I say, *"My God."* In seclusion I call upon You as friends call upon their friends; I say, *"My Beloved."*

In the splendorous scripture the Real says, *"And God supplicates to the Abode of Peace"* [10:25]. Then in the end He says, *"So let them respond to Me"* [2:186]. After that He says, *"Supplicate Me; I will respond to you."* It is as if He is saying, "I supplicate you, but you do not respond. So supplicate Me; I will respond." My servant, I call upon you but you do not respond. Call upon Me to see response upon response.

The Children of Israel said to Moses, *"Supplicate your Lord for us"* [2:68]. They themselves did not have the courage to supplicate and to step on the carpet of bold expansiveness and ask. When the turn of this community arrived, the Lord of Lords said, *"Supplicate Me; I will respond to you."* He commanded, *"Supplicate your Lord in pleading and secret"* [7:55] and *"in fear and want"* [7:56]; and He commanded *making the religion sincere for Him* [7:29]. In these verses He put down conditions and stipulations: sincerity, pleading, and fear. But in that verse He attached no condition to supplication, for He says, *"I will respond to you."*

It is the custom of people to catch birds, put them in cages, and keep them supplied with water and food so that they will sing at dawn, and also in the morning and at night. The Exalted Lord brought the recognizers into existence, made this world their cage, and prepared wholesome things and benefits for them. *Then He said in the firm text of His Book, "And in the dawns they ask for forgiveness"* [51:18]. He says, *"Those who supplicate their Lord morning and evening"* [6:52].

When will the spiritual peacock be delivered from the soulish trap and flap its wings in the space of the spirits without the intrusion of the bodies? Your body is a dense curtain. When the curtain is lifted, the lights of the secrets will glitter and gentle gifts will come one after another.

He brought the Throne into existence and said, "Tremendousness belongs to you." He brought the Footstool into existence and said, "Embracingness belongs to you." He brought Iblis into existence and said, "Curses belong to you." He brought the person of faith into existence and said, "Mercy belongs to you." He brought the recognizer into existence and said, "You belong to Me and I belong to you."

And your Lord says, "Supplicate Me" [40:60]. *Say: "What weight would my Lord give you if not for your supplication?"* [25:77]. "Why would I fear punishing you if not for your supplication?" *For you have cried lies* to My Messenger, O unbelievers, *and that will surely cling* [25:77].

Say: "What weight would my Lord give you." What would be the use of chastising you *"if not for your supplication," your worship of idols*—if you had not taken idols as the Godhood? Associating others with God is not pardoned, though bold expansiveness is. If the unbelievers are chastised for saying that He has associates, how can the faithful be chastised for saying that He is One? He says, "[*Be wary of the Fire . . .*] *prepared for the unbelievers"* [2:24], *but He does not say, "Prepared for the faithful."*

Why would God chastise you if you are grateful and have faith? [4:147]. *And every Muslim is grateful for faith.*

Say: "What weight would my Lord give you if not for your supplication?" Say to the denying unbelievers, "If these people of faith were not here, what fear would I have of chastising you?" *"For you have cried lies, and that will surely cling."* In the same way the Real says, *"The heavens are almost torn apart by it, the earth split, and the mountains falling down that they have supplicated a son belonging to the All-Merciful"* [19:90–91]. Heaven wants to be torn apart, earth wants to be split open, and the mountains want to be turned upside down and fall upon the unbelievers because they say that God has an associate. He says, "Do not hurry, for among them are the faithful: *Had it not been for certain faithful men and faithful women* [48:25]." The blessing of the faithful holds back the chastisement from the unbelievers. What do you say? Does the blessing of your faith hold back chastisement from you?

And your Lord says, "Supplicate Me." It is not the Lord of the Throne and Footstool who says this, nor the Lord of Gabriel and Michael who says it. It is the Lord of this sperm drop, blood clot, and tissue who says it.

If you had begun by saying, "My God," that would have been a claim. Moses said, *"Surely my Lord is with me"* [26:62]. Abraham said, *"My Lord is He who gives life and gives death"* [2:258]. So also were Noah, Hūd, Ṣāliḥ, Shuʿayb, and Muṣṭafā. "When your turn arrived and you rolled on the carpet of heedlessness and put on the shirt of disobedience, you did not dare to say, *'He is my Lord.'* I said it: *'And your Lord*—that is, your Nurturer, your Creator —*says.'* "

The servant of God has nothing but God, whether he be disobedient, disloyal, or loyal. When a created thing is disloyal toward a created thing, no one says that he should come and confess to it. If he does come and confess, he is put on the gallows. "I want you to come and confess to disobedience. When you do come and confess, I will overlook it."

And others who acknowledged their sins [9:102]. "When you are disloyal to someone who is created, you will bring along a thousand interceders so that perhaps he will accept. If you are outwardly disloyal to Me a thousand times and then regret it, I will overlook it. *'Regret is repentance.'*"[902]

"When kings become drunk, they appoint guards and say, 'Protect me.' You are in the midst of drunkenness and heedlessness and I will protect you. *Say: 'Who will protect you night and day?'* [21:42].

"If someone created calls his servant and he comes forth defiled, he will teach him courtesy. You have many defilements because of disobedience and then you come to My Presence. If you do not come, I call you. *So what an excellent Patron!* [22:78]. Even though you are defiled by missteps, ask your needs from Me, for I love askers. *As for the asker, do not chide* [93:10]."

According to a report, *"Give to the asker, even if he comes to you on a horse."*[903] Do not look at the horse and clothing, look at the abasement of asking.

Joseph's brothers lamented to Jacob: *"Send him forth with us tomorrow, to frolic and play"* [12:12]. Although Jacob knew their hearts were disobedient, they had the tongue of askers, so he did not keep Joseph back from them.

In the midst of a battle an unbeliever said to ʿAlī, "Give me your sword," so he gave it. He said, "O ʿAlī, you are extremely bold or tremendously naïve. Why did you give your sword to the antagonist?"

ʿAlī said, "You put forth the hand of askers to me. I did not consider it fitting for the stink of niggardliness to reach my nose. Though you have the heart of enemies, you have the tongue of askers." It is said that the unbeliever became a Muslim.

"My servant, come to My threshold, your body defiled by acts of disobedience, your frame worn down by acts of opposition! Although you have the body of the disobedient, you have the tongue of askers. Ask as is proper to your state, and I will bestow as is proper to My perfect generosity. Ask for the Garden from Me, and I will give you vision on top of that. *Those who do the beautiful shall have the most beautiful and an increase* [10:26]."

O chevalier, everything up to now has been the drinking place of the common people, who are at ease with bestowal. As for the elect and the folk of election, they take more pleasure in refusal. *"As for the disobedient among the common people, 'A single tear will extinguish the Lord's wrath.'*[904] *But if the lovers were to weep blood all life long, I would not have mercy on them."*

Love's iniquity is more beautiful than its justice,
its refusal more elegant than its giving.[905]

Love is iniquity, all of it. Wherever there is the stamp of servanthood, there is the mark of proximity and caresses, doing what is desired, providing wishes, and bestowing gifts. Wherever there is the stamp of love, there are grief and melting, burning and killing, and dying at every moment.

In the story of God's speaking companion Moses, the Exalted Lord explained these states and made them apparent to the folk of the realities: *We promised Moses thirty nights and We completed them with ten* [7:142]. He kept him waiting for thirty days and then added ten more. *When Moses came to Our appointed time and his Lord spoke to him,* he said on the carpet of bold expansiveness, " '*Show me, that I may gaze upon Thee.' Here I am before You, weak, seeking help from You in You.* The address came, *'Thou shalt not see Me'* " [7:143].

When he drank from the cup of speech and became intoxicated in that station without wine, he thought he was in the Abode of Peace, so he forgot himself—and that was it. When he found the generosity of unmediated speaking-companionship without requesting, thinking, wishing, seeking, searching, or hoping, intoxication overcame him and he could not restrain his limbs. When he saw the King's speech while intoxicated, he began to act recklessly and said, *"Show me!"* Tumult appeared in the empire because of his recklessness and bold expansiveness. The pavilion of the Real's majestic awesomeness rose up like mist surrounding a mountain and concealed the sun of the Face. "O Moses, what is this boldness you show?! Are you not the same one who said at the top of the well in Midian, *'My Lord, surely I am poor toward any good Thou sendest down upon me'* [28:24]. You were content with a loaf of bread. What is this?"

"Yes, at that time I was content with a piece of bread, for the place was Midian. Now I have heard the address, *'I chose thee for Myself'* [20:41]. If in the drunkenness of gratitude for this address the tongue should make a reckless uproar, this is the place for it."

Here you have a rare work! The Exalted Lord said, *"And your Lord says, 'Supplicate Me; I will respond to you.' "* There is no supplication beyond the supplication of Moses, no sincerity beyond his sincerity, and no yearning beyond his yearning, but he was addressed with *"Thou shalt not see Me"* [7:143]. *Such is the severity of the beloveds.*

The realizers have said that if the Real had left Moses with the words *"Thou shalt not see Me"* and had not helped and preserved him with the words *"But look at the mountain"* [7:143], he would have been effaced and destroyed instead of being thunderstruck. But He sent the sweet drink of gentleness in the cup of compassion on the hand of the cupbearer of *but*, so he came back to himself in the hope of *but*. In the same way, Muṣṭafā said, *"Surely God gazes not on your forms"*; then he aided and preserved us in *tawḥīd* with the words *"but He gazes on your hearts."*[906]

O dervish, here there is a subtle secret: If He had fulfilled the hope of Moses, who had all that discipline and struggle, then the hearts of the destitute would have been broken. "They would have fancied that gazing on Me is the recompense for deeds. To Moses with all his perfection and the merchandise of his deeds, I said, *'Thou shalt not see Me,'* so that the hearts of the destitute would not be broken. *Thou shalt not see Me* curtains the perfection of Moses's state from the eyes of the proximate."

Despite all the disobedient acts, ugly deeds, and disgraceful doings of the disobedient servant, the Maker's gaze on the heart will curtain him. He called Moses and gave him the good news of hospitality. But when he appeared in the attribute of bold expansiveness, he was refused a look. Thus when the disobedient man, in abasement and brokenness, puts his head on the doorstep of remorse and is singled out for the gaze of gentle gifts, he will be a freeloader on His generosity.

Beneath these flashing allusions and auspicious expressions is a precious pearl that cannot be brought out by anyone but a diver after the Haqiqah in the sea of the Tariqah. What was all that trouble, hardship, struggle, and adversity of Moses, and the fact that its fruit at the end was being addressed by the rejection of *thou shalt not see Me*? And what was that sudden taking of Muṣṭafā, that conversation with him, and that apology to him in the midst of those bestowals?

Yes, Moses was in Midian giving water to sheep. When he wanted something, he affirmed himself: *"Surely I am poor toward any good Thou sendest down upon me* [28:24]. I am hungry, my Lord." When he came into the desert and those things became evident, he relied on flint and stone and leaned on his staff. *"It is my staff. I lean upon it, and with it I beat down leaves to feed my sheep"* [20:18]. The Real took fire away from the stone, reliance from the staff, and hope from the bush. Then He said, *"O Moses, surely I, I am God"* [28:30]. Here you have a threat and a teaching of courtesy: "O Moses, how long will you say 'I' and 'mine'? It is I who am worthy of saying 'I.' "

As for Muṣṭafā, from the first of the work He displayed the whole of this world to him, but he paid no attention. He said, *"One day I am hungry, another I am full."*[907]

It was said, "The Lord has forgiven the slips you have made and not yet made."[908]

He did not see himself but said, *"Should I not be a grateful servant?"*[909]

Then he was made to pass beyond being, waystation, rank, place, and status and conveyed to a place where understandings and intellects are incapable of perceiving the light of his exalted shoestrings. It was said, "Speak!"

He said, *"The felicitations, the blessings, the prayers, and the goodly things belong to God,"*[910] thereby not ascribing anything to himself. Then in the banquet of ascription he was addressed like this: *"Then He revealed to His servant what He revealed"* [53:10]. Whoever takes a gift like that brings back a present like this.

"O Muḥammad, now that you have shaken the dust of all the others from the skirt of good fortune and put away all talk of yourself by saying 'belong to God,' everything belongs to you. We say, *'Thy Lord will bestow upon thee, and thou wilt approve'* [93:5]. Oh, you are all Mine and I am all yours! O Muḥammad, whatever is beneath your feet is your servitor, and your servitors are sacrifices to your feet." *And God bless Muḥammad and all his household!*

49. *al-Wāsi ʿ*: the Embracing

Some have said that the meaning of embracing is knowing, some have said unneedy, and some have said much in bestowal. In the tongue's common usage they say, *"So and so is embracing in bestowal,"* that is, much in bestowal. The Real has a bestowal with every existent thing. In His perfect generosity He does not take back His bestowal because of missteps, nor does He cut off His blessings because of disloyalty.

Dhu'l-Nūn Miṣrī recounted, "Once I went to wash clothes on the shore of the Nile. While I was busy washing clothes I suddenly saw a scorpion coming, tremendously large. I had never seen one larger. I was afraid of the scorpion, *so I sought refuge in God from its evil, and God spared me its evil."*

Dhu'l-Nūn said, "I watched the scorpion from behind until it reached the edge of the water. A big frog came out of the water and held up its back so that the scorpion could sit on its back, and it crossed the Nile. I watched in wonder and said to myself, *'The scorpion crossed the Nile on the back of a frog. Surely this is significant.'*

"I bound up my loincloth and went over to the other side of the water. The frog put down the scorpion and went back to its own place. The scorpion went forward and I was behind it. It reached a tremendous tree with many branches."

Dhu'l-Nūn said, "I looked and saw a boy, a drunk young man fallen at the tree and asleep, his intellect and awareness gone. I said, '*Surely we belong to God and to Him we will return*' [2:156]. Right now the scorpion is going to destroy that young man.' In the midst of this, I saw a serpent aiming to destroy the young man. The scorpion jumped on its back *and stung its brain, killing it. It went to the edge of the water, while I was behind it, and it crossed on the back of the frog. I returned to the young man and he was still asleep in heedlessness*. I began to sing,

O sleeper protected by the Majestic
from every evil crawling in the darkness!
How do your eyes sleep before a King
from whom beneficial blessings come to you?

The child awoke. Dhu'l-Nūn said, *"By God, the sweetness of the boy added to the sweetness of the words.* He looked at me and said, 'O shaykh, what is this state?'

"I said, 'Look at what God has turned away from you and how He has turned it away from you!' Then I told him the story. When the child heard those words, a pain and grief arose from inside his heart, *and he wept and lamented a great deal.*

"He turned his glance to heaven: 'O my Lord and Patron, this is Your act toward him who disobeyed you last night! By Your exaltedness, I will not disobey You again until I meet You! He took off the garment of foolishness and put on the garment of good and rectitude."[911]

It is said that a nomad had put his hands on the curtains of the Kaabah and was saying, *"Who is like me? I have a God such that*

"If I sin, He shows me favor,
if I repent, He gives me hope,
If I turn to Him, He brings me close,
if I turn my back, He calls to me."[912]

Surely our Lord is forgiving, grateful [35:34]. In His perfect generosity and munificence, the Exalted Lord opened four doors to you: the door of beautiful-doing, the door of blessings, the door of obedience, and the door of gentleness.

He opened the door of His beautiful-doing and kindness to you. You came forward with ugly-doing and shut the door to yourself. The Real sent the messenger of generosity with the key of overlooking and pardon: He said, *"I will curtain your ugly-doing with My mercy, for I am a gentle Lord and you are a weak servant. 'It is He who accepts repentance from His servants and pardons the ugly deeds'* [42:25]. *'As for those to whom the most beautiful preceded from Us'* [21:101]."

He opened the door of blessings to you. You came forward with ingratitude and shut the door to yourself by your shortcoming in giving thanks. *When We bless man, he turns away and pulls aside* [17:83]. The Real sent the messenger of bounty with the key of favor and said, *"Though you fall short in gratitude to Me, I will not fall short in My kindness.* Even if you allow shortcoming in gratitude for blessings, every day I will increase the blessing of My mercy. '*Say: In the bounty of God and His mercy—in that let them rejoice*'" [10:58].

He opened the door of obedience to you. You came forward with shortcoming and wanted to shut the door with disobedience, and you shut it. The Real sent the messenger of forgiveness with the key of repentance: *"When you sin and do not care, I will forgive you and I will not care.*[913] *'O My servants who have been immoderate against yourselves, despair not of God's mercy. Surely God forgives all sins'*" [39:53].

He opened the door of gentleness to you. You came forward with disloyalty and shut the door with boldness. He sent the messenger of forbearance and respite with the key of curtaining. He said, *"My servant, if you are bold toward Me with ugly practices, I will overlook it because I am your lover and I am the most merciful of the merciful."*

Wahab ibn Munabbih said, "I saw this in the Torah: *'O child of Adam, you have eaten My provisions and not shown gratitude to Me. You have come out against Me and are not ashamed before Me. My servant, though you are not ashamed before Me, I am ashamed before you.'*"

It is said that a Guebre said to Moses, "When you go to whispered prayer, tell your God that I do not need His daily provision, that I will never serve Him, and that I disdain His Godhood."

When Moses finished the whispered prayer, the Exalted Lord said, *"Deliver the message of My servant."*

Moses said, "You know it better."

He said, "Say to him, 'Though you disdain My lordhood, I do not disdain your servanthood. Though you not desire My provisions, I will provide for you despite your disdain.'"

Moses said this to the man. *He said, "It is not proper to disobey a Lord with this attribute," so he became a Muslim.*

Sometimes You caress me, sometimes You put me aside,
sometimes You mix harshness with gentleness.

It is well known that a Guebre once asked Abraham for food, but he did not give it to him. The Exalted Lord sent revelation: *"Where is your generosity?"* Abraham set off after him and accepted him so he would come back for hospitality.

The unbeliever said to him, *"Who taught you this courtesy?"*

He said, "God."

He said, "What an excellent God that He should rebuke His bosom friend because of his enemy!"

It is said that there was a woman in the era of Muṣṭafā who had an infant. It seems that one day the child went absent from her eyes. The old woman came out wailing and pouring carnelian tears on pearly cheeks. She was shouting and helping the birds of the meadow with their mourning. When she found the child, she showed it her compassion and mercy. The Prophet said, *"Surely God is more merciful to His servants than this woman is to her child."*[914] *A weak servant and a gentle Lord—mercy does not go to waste between the two!*

I have seen that one day the Companions, who were the rosebushes of the orchard of messengerhood, were sitting with the paragon and putting their hearts at ease in the beauty of prophethood. *Encountering you in the morning, I have a blessed morning.* A little bird came down from heaven and was flying above their heads. Muṣṭafā, who was the physician of their liver's pain, lifted his head and said, "Who has burned this helpless thing and separated it from its child?"

A man said, "I did that."

The paragon said, "Will you let go of that helpless thing with my intercession?"

Because of the prophetic allusion the man went and released the little bird. The bird flew happily into the desert with its child. Muṣṭafā said, *"God is gentler to His servants than this bird is to her child."* By the divine majesty, just as a tender mother keeps her suckling infant at her bosom and breast and fears that a blow will reach it from the claws of the eagle of events, so also He nurtures this handful of dust in the lap of gentleness and the bosom of secrets.

"When We bound the compact in the cradle of the covenant of *Am I not your Lord?* [7:172], We gave the milk of bestowal and bounteousness from the nipple of beautiful-doing. On that day, where were your precedents and means? If you are not wanted, have hope. If you are wanted, have no fear. Wait to see what has been written in the Unseen."

Among the Arabs one tribe was the most miserable. There was a wretched woman in that tribe who was counted among the defective in intellect. All at once a suitor came on behalf of the Messenger, without precedence or service.

> I was asleep and my friend came in the door,
> the healer of my many sorrows.

There was no introduction, no smoothing the way, no hope, no expectation. The suitor came and said that the Messenger was asking for her in marriage. The poor woman said, "I do not believe it. This wine will not fit in my cup. I cannot put up with the pain of this drunkenness."

When the contract was made and she became permissible, Muṣṭafā looked carefully and saw a white spot on the surface of her skin. *"He married a woman from Bayāḍa and saw a white spot on her waist. So he said to her, 'Rejoin your folk.'* "[915] Woe is me if he believed in two-coloredness! What is belief in two-coloredness? It is that you say, "He and I."

When the outside of a woman's skin is two-colored, the man can annul the contract, but when the color is one, he cannot annul it. Muṣṭafā annulled the contract. I have seen—*and the responsibility is on the narrator*—that Gabriel came immediately and said, "O Muḥammad, the Lord of Lords says, 'You annul the contract of union simply because of an opposing color? What will you do tomorrow when there will be a hundred thousand who have piled up haystacks of great sins? *And of the night, keep vigil!* [17:79].' "

A nomad was placed on a bier. They were bringing him on that ballista of peril, on a steed without saddle. His hands and feet were bound, his hope put to sleep, the judging tongue cut off, the spying ears deaf. A few frail children ran in his tracks and poured the dust of the scorching sand on their heads.

There was an old woman who had a little cow. A servant of the king came and took the cow by force. The old woman looked on that cow like a loving mother on her only child. The king was coming back from the hunt. He had 360 castles, 360 serving girls, and 360 viziers. Each day was the turn of one of the viziers in the house of one of the serving girls. That woman came forward with the armor of destitution on her body, the shield of not-having in hand, the sword of weeping drawn, and the tongue of courage loosed. She put forth the hand of helplessness from the veil of remorse and took hold of the king's reins. A servant wanted to push her aside and brought out a merciless whip. The king said, "Do not strike, for she has come with weeping and brought us what we do not have."

She took his reins and said, "O king, will you answer in this domicile or in that domicile?"

The king was clever. He separated his feet from the royal stirrups, sat on the dark dust, and said, "What is it?"

She said, "Your servant took my cow. Tell him to give it back lest I strike earth with heaven."

Dhu'l-Nūn Miṣrī said, "Once I saw a poor man who had not found food for several days. Then a fish came to hand. He went to the door of a house and asked for a burning brand, but they did not give it. The poor wretch turned his face to heaven and said, 'You gave no food for a long time. Then, when You put the means in my hand, You placed a brand on my liver.'

"I said to myself, 'Let's see where the blow of these words falls.'

"In the afternoon I saw that fire had fallen into the city and half of it had burned. He had the fish on the end of a stick and was roasting it. I said, 'Is this how you ask for fire?'

"He said, 'Yes. If someone does not give me fire, I strike fire into his house and family.' "

Let us come back to the story of the old woman who was sitting with the king in the dust. The servants were lined up saying, "A king before whom Jayapala of India, the khan of the Turks, the caesar of Byzantium, and the emperor of China sit in servanthood—what is it with him that he is sitting in the dust of abasement?"

Yes, *"I am with My servant's thoughts of Me, so let him think of Me what he wills."*[916]

The king commanded that the little cow be given back to her.

After a time the king passed away. The old woman heard the news. She said, "He has a right against me." When he was placed on the bier, the old woman came, stood at the end of the road, and said, "O king, since your steed was to be your bier, why did you have all those road-worthy steeds? Since in reality your palace was to be the tomb, why did you build the 360 castles? Since your bed-mate was to be crawling things, what were you doing with the heart-easing slave girls?"

When they buried him, she lifted up her hands and supplicated, asking for mercy and forgiveness for the king. Afterward, they saw him in a dream and asked him what had become of his state. He said, "Everything I wore belonged to the people and was given back to the people. I remained naked. If not for a corner of that old woman's blanket, I would have been destroyed."

What is intended is the hadith of that nomad. The bier was brought before Muṣṭafā. He asked about loans. They said, "He owes two dirhams." Then he said, *"Perform the prayer for your companion."*

I have seen—*and the responsibility is on the narrator*—that all at once the trace of revelation appeared. A hundred thousand drops like mist sat on the rose of his face and the sweet briar of his cheeks, making their color like carnelian, and then again they became like saffron. It was such that the Companions heard the beating of his heart. Gabriel said, "God says, 'Do you fancy that your existence is the cause of My mercy? Although this dead man belongs to your community, he is My servant.' "

The paragon said, "Call out, *'If anyone leaves behind property, it belongs to his heirs. If anyone leaves behind a debt, it is for me to pay it back.'* "[917]

And Dhu'l-Nūn, when he went forth wrathful and thought that We had no power over him [21:87]. He called them with gentleness and drove them away with harshness, but not one of them came forth. Because of jealousy his skin filled with anguish, so he came out from among his people with a saddened heart and set off on the ocean. All at once a wind rose up—called "the wind of trial." They said, "What is it? Perhaps there is a disobedient man among us. Let us draw lots and do it such that the lots separate truth from falsehood." They brought a box full of arrows, wrote down the names, and mixed them up. About that it is said, *"They mixed a wholesome deed with another that is ugly"* [9:102].

"When the lottery is finished we will know who will *fear not* [41:30] or *despair not* [12:87]."

When they looked, Jonah's name came forth. It was said, "Mix them up again, for you do not know the disobedient."

He said, "By the rightful due of the Real, if you put forth your hands a thousand times, only Jonah's name will come forth. If they had thrown down their staffs a thousand times, only Moses's staff would have come forth."

"And Dhu'l-Nūn"—who was Jonah the son of Mattā and was called Dhu'l-Nūn [The Owner of the Fish] *because the fish swallowed him down—"when he went forth wrathful"* [21:87].

Some have said, *"He was angry with the king when he chose him for prophethood. He said, 'Surely God teaches me. Why did you choose me?' This is because he knew that prophethood was linked with trial, so he was wrathful at him because of that.*

Some have said, *"Wrathful toward his people because they had refused faith."* And some have said, *"Wrathful toward his Lord."*[918]

The point of all this is that Jonah went forth without permission, and this was a slip on his part.

"And thought that We had no power over him" [21:87]. *Some have said, "He thought that We would not make his roads strait for him." God says, "him whose provision has power over him"* [65:7], *that is, whose provision is straitened.*

Some have said, *"He thought that We would not decree for him what We decreed."*

"Then he called out in the darknesses"—the darkness of night, the darkness of the sea, and the darkness of the fish's belly—" 'There is no god but Thou, glory be to Thee! Surely I am one of the wrongdoers' " [21:87] *against myself by leaving without permission. Nonetheless, that was not God's punishment of him, for it is not allowed for prophets to be punished. Rather, it was a teaching of courtesy, for it is allowed to teach courtesy to those who do not warrant punishment, like infants.*

"So We responded to him and delivered him from sorrow" [21:88] *for his misstep. It has also been said, "from the belly of the fish, for sorrow* [*ghamm*] *means covering* [*taghṭiya*]*."*

Concerning the period in its belly, there are three opinions: first is forty days, second is three days, and third is from noon to the end of daytime. Sha'bī said, "Four hours. Then the fish opened its mouth and Jonah saw the brightness of the sun, so he said, 'Glory be to Thee! Surely I am one of the wrongdoers,' and the fish spit him out."[919]

It is said that when it was reported to Jonah that God was going to chastise his people, he left with his family. It is said that a lion killed his wife in the road. Then a leopard took his younger son, and the ocean's waves drowned his older son. He got on the ship and the waves became disturbed. The people began to throw away their goods to lighten the ship, so Jonah said to them, "Do not throw away your goods, but toss me into it. I am the offender among you."[920]

It has reached us that he came to the side of the ship and saw a fish with its mouth open. He went to the other side and saw the same fish with open mouth. *When he had gone in every direction and knew that trial was desired for him, he threw himself into the trial. "So the fish swallowed him while he was blameworthy"* [37:142], *that is, he had come with something that is blamed.* The Exalted Lord revealed to the fish, *"Do not damage his flesh and do not break any bones.* We have made of you a jewel box and deposited within it this peerless pearl. You do not have a right to this deposit. This is My deposit, not your morsel."[921]

It has reached us that when the fish swallowed Jonah, the Exalted Lord commanded it to circle the whole ocean. In the same way, when they give someone a robe of honor, they take him around the whole city.

Somewhere I saw, *"When he went into its belly, he said, 'O Lord, You have given to me a place for a mosque that You gave to no one else.'"*[922]

What a marvelous business! Jonah was the companion of a fish for a few days, and until the resurrection people will be saying, *"The Owner of the Fish."* This ascription will never be nullified. When a truthful lover, a conforming recognizer, shows conformity in love, recognition, and service for seventy years, do you suppose that the Real will nullify that? No, never.

Jonah said, *"Glory be to Thee! Surely I am one of the wrongdoers."* Adam, who was the source of secrets and the rising place of lights, said, *"Our Lord, we have wronged ourselves"* [7:23]. Each of them shouted out from his own makeup. Wearing the armor of sinlessness Adam took one look at the unseen ambuscade and was struck in the eye by the arrow of *Adam disobeyed* [20:121].

Every time David recited the Psalms and played the instruments of intimacy in the compartments of holiness, the birds of the air came to listen. One day he got up at the time of purification, and the sunlight of the decree fell through the window of destiny. He looked and saw a slender stature with a face sculpted like the disk of the moon, and his heart inclined to her. *And thou wast concealing in thyself what God was making appear* [33:37].[923]

"The spirits are assembled troops."[924] The spirit in the body is like a bird put in a cage by the command *"Be!" so it comes to be* [2:117]. The spirit is luminous and heavenly, the soul terrestrial and dark, and the heart fluctuating and bewildered. The attribute of the spirit is all conformity, the attribute of the soul all opposition, and the heart fluctuates in the midst.

Know in verified truth that if the Adamite's wherewithal had been made only with clay, he would have been just that, and the other existent things would have been just that. But when they made his wherewithal, they made it pure of defect. From the world of nonexistence He brought the spirit by the command *"Be!" so it comes to be.* He imprisoned it in the cage of the body and gave it over to the hands of the senses.

The hunter catches the little bird and puts it in a cage with severity. It keeps on spreading the wings of hope, fancying that the door of the cage is open. It wants to fly and leave the cage behind and go back to the other birds.

In the beginning of the work the pure spirits wandered in the world of limpidness and loyalty in the gardens of approval. *"God created the spirits before the bodies."*[925] The hunter of power came and built a cage of dust and clay. Just as a cage was built for Jonah from the fish's belly, so also a cage was built for the spirit from the servant's body.

Before the spirit's opening reached Adam—the chosen, the limpid, the first wayfarer, the rising place of the sun of good fortune—he had a shirt of clay and a garment of dried clay in the shape of an *alif*, placed in the cradle of gentleness. Then the spirit was addressed, "Go down and seek proximity to the body."

It said, "O Lord, I acquiesce to the command, but I am a subtle substance and a luminous essence and I see a tenebrous prison, a dark cage, a narrow jail."

The address came, *"Enter unwillingly, and leave unwillingly!"*[926] When the lights of the spirits reached the brain, many faculties and powers became evident in keeping with the decree and destiny. A lake full of blessing appeared, within which the fish of the tongue began to speak. It said, *"The praise belongs to God."*

The Exalted Lord said, *"May your Lord have mercy upon you."*[927] *Peace!*

50. *al-Ḥakīm:* the Wise

The one who does every work fittingly and puts everything in its place.

He—*majestic is His majesty!*—is wise, not niggardly. Whatever He puts, He puts in its place. Whatever He gives, He gives to its folk. He had the power to create a world compared to which this world would be a gnat's wing, but He did not do so because of wisdom.

He is powerful so He does whatever He wants. He is wise so He does not do whatever He can do. He has a power whose reins are in the hands of wisdom, and a wisdom whose hands are around the neck of power. Thus Lordhood goes forth rightly.

He created no ant's foot or gnat's wing in this world except at the requirement of power, by the demand of wisdom, and in conformity with will. Wisdom had to take the reins of the sultan of power so that the work would go forth well ordered. If we suppose that wisdom had let go of power's reins, the world would have been thrown into turmoil.

He has attributes that are the antagonists of the existence and acts of the creatures, and He has attributes that are the interceders for the creatures' existence and states. Exaltedness, unneediness, severity, all-compellingness, magnificence, and exaltation are the creatures' antagonists. Wisdom, mercy, gentleness, clemency, munificence, and generosity are the creatures' interceders.

The interceders hold back the reins of the antagonists so that this handful of hapless creatures may live out their brief spans in the shadow of the interceders' existence. Otherwise, if the interceders let the antagonists go, in one instant everything from the Throne and Footstool down to the ant's foot and the gnat's wing would cease to be.

In the world He gave out one word about His unneediness, and it will come before the unbelievers on the Day of Separation: *"And as for those who disbelieve, surely God is unneedy toward the worlds"* [3:97]. When He wanted to make this creation appear, He put the reins of the attribute of unneediness in the hands of the attribute of munificence. Then He said to power and wisdom, "Bring a world into existence!"

Then a world appeared as a consequence of power and an effect of wisdom. In each mote of this world power had its hand around wisdom's neck and wisdom had its head resting on power's pillow. Many in the world are power-seers, but few are wisdom-seers. A hundred thousand people see the power before one of them sees the wisdom.

Once the world has been there for a while and the secret of this work and the quintessence of the command have been obtained, He will say to the attribute of munificence, "Let go of the reins of unneediness." As soon as the attribute of munificence lets go of unneediness, the resurrection will appear and the existent things will go to the attribute of nonexistence.

What is this? It is the army of the attribute of independence and unneediness charging forth from the ambuscade of exaltedness and severity. Then He will deliver the address, *"Whose is the kingdom today? God's, the One, the Severe"* [40:16]. This address will go forth from the attribute of unneediness, for the rulership will belong to severity. The first address that He gave, *"Am I not your Lord?"* [7:172], went forth from the attribute of munificence, for the rulership belonged to gentleness and munificence.

Then, after some time passes, He will once again give the reins of the attribute of unneediness into the hands of munificence. Power and wisdom along with the attributes of bounty and justice will enter the work. Then it will be said, "O folk of unbelief, go into hell with the escort of the attribute of justice in keeping with Our attributes of power and wisdom. O folk of piety, go into paradise with the escort of the attribute of bounty in keeping with Our power and wisdom." *Surely the pious will be in bliss and surely the depraved will be in hellfire* [82:13–14].

The Wise [ḥakīm] is He who decrees [ḥakama] what He wants as He wants. When someone is approaching, He drapes his breast in the waistcoat of conforming acts; when someone is withdrawing, He capes him in the shirt of opposing acts. When someone is approaching, He singles him out for acceptance; when someone is withdrawing, He decrees wilting for the branch of his covenant. When someone is felicitous, He makes the sun of His auspiciousness rise from the sphere of bounteousness; when someone is wretched, He stamps his heart with rejection such that he takes no benefit from any of His auspiciousness.

Here we have Balaam Beor. He knew the Greatest Name and drank his fill from the cups of obedient acts. It never occurred to his mind that when the suns of predetermination rise from the spheres of the apportionings, he would suffer distance and separation and be tied up with dogs. This is one of the wondrous secrets of the Unseen. He says, "So his likeness is the likeness of a dog" [7:176].

And here we have the dog of the Companions of the Cave. In the morning it was beaten and rejected, and in the evening it was accepted after rejection. In the morning no one gave a thought to it, and in the evening it became such that its story is in the book of the One, the Unique. In the morning they had no concern for its rightful due, and in the evening, as He says, "Their dog was extending its paws at the doorstep" [18:18]. *In the morning their hearts were rejecting it and in the evening, as He says, "The fourth of them was their dog"* [18:22].

By my life! In reality the form is deprived, and the lesson is hidden by the situation.

O chevalier, take no account of form. If form were of any account, what would dust have to do with the mysteries? Between the Unseen and you, between you and the Unseen, things just happen. *Love is not by choice.* What a lovely day when someone is walking down a road, and the one entrusted with this talk comes down all at once, throws the lasso of seeking around his neck, and pulls! Indeed—whether to the gallows or to the throne.

There was a distracted man in a session of the Samanids.[928] A lightning flash of this talk took up a corner of his heart and he gave out the call for plundering, but after an hour had passed, he put aside that state. Then he became regretful. He told his story to one of the pirs of the era. The pir said, "Do you still have anything of what you had before?"

He said, "The little blanket over my shoulders belongs to that."

He said, "The blanket is the veil of the orphan pearl. Throw it off."

He threw it off, and the state appeared.

When you gamble, you must gamble away everything.

Whoever is more of a master is more naked. The master of all in the Shariah and the Tariqah was the paragon who now sleeps in the dust of Medina. For several thousand years Gabriel was obedient. On the night of the *mi ʿrāj*, it was said to him, "If you want the sleeve of your covenant to have an embroidery, put that man's saddlecloth on the shoulders of your boasting."

In the morning he got up, but there was no bread in the house, and at night there was no bread. He was the master of the whole world, but more destitute than all. Look how he was stripped naked: *"Thou hast nothing of the affair"* [3:128]. A hundred thousand in the world wear patched cloaks in the hope of finding a whiff of destitution. But poverty is one thing, and beggary something else.

That He called you "poor" was so that everyone would reject you and you would belong totally to Him.

Let us come to the first talk: ʿĀʾisha said about Muṣṭafā, *"He used to seclude himself in the cave of Ḥirāʾ."*[929] He had made a place of seclusion in the cave of jealousy and the Ḥirāʾ of bewilderment so that when the bird of thought reached there, it would discard the wings of imagination. *Seclusion is one of the marks of the folk of limpidness.*[930]

Aspiration without anticipation removes the mask. *"So the Real came to him while he was in the cave of Ḥirāʾ."*[931] Suddenly the chamberlain of gentleness came from the World of the Unseen. It sprinkled the water of the secrets in the cave, spread the rug of loyalty, rolled out the carpet of limpidness, and set up the royal seat of the Seal of the Prophets at the front of the cave of jealousy. Without anything of thought or supposition this meaning came to him and seized him by the skirt.

"O Gabriel, the time has come for you to fold back your peacock wings, fasten the strap of caresses on the steed of messengerhood, and tie the rope of the pavilion of Abū Ṭālib's orphan to a branch of *the Lote Tree of the Final End* [53:14]. O Gabriel, go from the spiritual world to the corporeal world to a tribe called the Quraysh. In that tribe there is a branch called Banū Hāshim."

Muṣṭafā said, *"Surely God chose Kināna from among the children of Ishmael, He chose Quraysh from Kināna, He chose Banū Hāshim from Quraysh, and He chose me from Banū Hāshim."*[932]

"Take this crown of messengerhood and place it on the head of that man who is aspiring to heaven with Adam's chosenness, Noah's invitation, Abraham's eloquence, Ishmael's kinship, Job's patience, Elias's gratitude, Solomon's majesty, Joseph's beauty, Moses's solidity, and Jesus's renunciation."

Gabriel came, which was expressed like this: *"So the angel came and said, 'Recite!'"*[933] The angel came at the command of the King, his forehead knotted like a teacher, bringing the first fruit, *"Recite,"* from the orchard of revelation. "O Muḥammad, *recite!*" Then, tale by tale, until he said in the end, *"Recite in the name of thy Lord!"* [96:1].

O chevalier, since the master was Gabriel, he had to accept much suffering. When Gabriel was not in the midst as an intermediary, look at what the Messenger said: *"A drop fell into my mouth, so I recognized what has been and what has not been."*[934] A drop from the ocean of the Unseen fell into the oyster shell of my breast, and all the knowledge of the first folk and the last folk settled down in my inmost heart.

A man may be in a tavern when an attraction comes to him that does not come to him in the Kaabah. Once there was a man who had wine in his hand and was about to take it into his mouth. Suddenly the wine removed the mask and he saw therein the secret of the work. For the next seventy years he wandered perplexed at the scent of what he had seen in the cup.

Pharaoh's sorcerers were shown the fine point of *tawḥīd* in the midst of sorcery and unbelief. *Decree what you will decree* [20:72]. Since they had truthful solicitude and help upon help, the fact that they were sorcerers with deeds of deception and falsity was ignored. It was said, "O ropes, you who are the stuff of sorcery and illusion; and O sleight of hand, you who are nothing but deception and falsity, remove the mask from your faces and disclose yourself to them in the color of *tawḥīd*! O unbelief and sorcery, you who for so long have been the object of their love, just once lift the veil and show yourself to them without the mask of censure and the burka of embellishment! You will see wonders." They were afraid of death, and now they were passionately in love with death.

Pharaoh the unaided said to them, *"I will cut off your hands and your feet on opposite sides, then I will crucify you all together"* [7:124].

They were saying,

> *Who threatens a naked man with silk?*
> *Who menaces a starving man with stew?*

"When will this rumor become reality? When will this report become a face-to-face vision? Our enemy is our own existence. The utmost limit of our wish right now is to leave this world with the attribute of limpidness and to enter washed into that Presence, for His gaze washed us before the defilement of our own gaze could settle upon us. We will arrive at the Presence with the escort of that gaze!"

Someone in the middle of the road is suddenly taken and conveyed to the goal. Someone else finds bewilderment upon bewilderment at every moment: He comes to the edge of the Jayhun and it runs dry. He wants to go into the desert and meets the barrier of Dhu'l-Qarnayn.[935] He looks beneath his feet and sees everything withered. He wants to seek for a mark in those he meets but finds them lacking hearts. He wants to return home but does not find the road. He wants to recognize himself, but as much as he searches he loses his own name. From the Unseen a call comes, "Stay where you are, for there is no road ahead, there is no road back, and there are many in the road of Our exaltedness bewildered and perplexed like you."

> If you sprinkle your eyes' water on the field,
> sweep the sultan's threshold with your eyelashes,
> And bring a hundred lives to bribe the doorman,
> they'll say, "What weight does a life have here?"

The ocean of tremendousness began crashing and the waves of exaltedness were surging. The spirits of the seekers were taken to a place called the bazaar of the lovers and the market of the seekers. When they arrived, it was said to them, "Have you come to trade?"

They said that they had: *And man carried it* [33:72]. They exchanged their spirits for remorse and their hearts for sorrow. When they looked closely, they saw that their hands were empty. From the pavilion of exaltedness this call kept on coming: "Pitch the tent of sorrow at the top of this bazaar and then toss the dust of bewilderment on your heads with the hand of remorse, for that is just what your father did."

When he fell from paradise, which is a place of anticipating good fortune, he was seen raining down the tears of remorse and grief and throwing dust on his head. They said, "Adam, what are you doing?"

He said, "It's on me because of me."[936]

By the rightful due of the Real! If you open up the tombs of the one hundred twenty-some thousand center-points of good fortune, you will see springs of remorse flowing forth. If you go to that piece of straw on the wall and ask what has happened to the color of its face, it will say, "This is the yellow of remorse."

When Adam's turn was coming to an end and he was about to read from the slate of nonexistence—and what goes on here is the tongue of the state—Gabriel raised his voice in this station: "Adam's turn has come to an end. Of what shall we make his burial perfume?"

The call came, "There is a tree on an island in the ocean of Our exaltedness called the tree of remorse. Bring a handful of the leaves of remorse and sprinkle them on his shroud, for We will make the burial perfume of all the prophets with this."

Let us come back to the discussion. There was a handful of dust in abasement itself, fallen in the road and trampled down by the feet of the creatures. All at once the sultan of power and wisdom came and pulled back on the reins, giving forth this expression: *"I am setting in the earth a vicegerent"* [2:30]. The tongue of the Haqiqah on the pulpit of the Tariqah was saying, *"Deposited in the secret core of this vicegerent were a thousand thousand subtleties of secret realities and marvelous lights."*

They have disagreed on the meaning of setting. *Some say that its meaning is creating and some say that its meaning is doing.*[937]

As for the earth, *it is said to have been Mecca. The Prophet said, "The earth was unrolled from Mecca,"*[938] *and this is why it is called "the mother of the cities."*

A vicegerent [*khalīfa*] *is someone who stands in the station of another. This is from the saying, "So-and-so succeeded* [*khalafa*] *so-and-so." "Successors"* [*khalaf*] *are the wholesome, and "succeeders"* [*khalf*] *are the vicious. Thus in the revelation: "And they were succeeded by succeeders"* [7:169]. *And in a hadith: "Among all successors this knowledge will be transmitted by the just among them."*[939]

Concerning the vicegerency of Adam and his offspring, there are opinions. One is that the jinn were the residents of the earth, working corruption therein and shedding blood. So they were destroyed and Adam and his offspring were placed in their stead. This is the word of Ibn ʿAbbās.

Second is that He desired some among the children of Adam—those whose fathers succeeded Adam—to succeed others in putting truth into effect and making the earth flourish. This is the word of Ḥasan.

Third is that He desired a vicegerent who would "succeed Me in decreeing among the creatures," and this is Adam and those of his children who stand in his station. This is the word of Ibn Masʿūd.

"They said, 'What, wilt Thou set therein one who will work corruption there and shed blood, while we glorify Thy praise and call Thee holy?'" [2:30]. *This is the response of the angels. There is disagreement on whether it is by way of inquiry or by way of affirmation, in two respects.*

One is that the angels said it by way of inquiry and seeking news when He said, "I am setting in the earth a vicegerent." Thus they asked, "Our Lord, tell us if You are setting in the earth someone who will work corruption there and shed blood." He responded to them, "Surely I know what you do not know" [2:30].

The second is that it was a response of affirmation, even if the what *sounds like an inquiry. Thus a poet said,*

What, are you not better than all those who carry gifts,
the palms of your hands generous to the worlds?[940]

The meaning is that you are like that. Concerning their response in this respect, there are two words. One is that they said it as a conjecture, for they had seen that beforehand the jinn had worked corruption and shed blood, so they supposed that if others became their vicegerents, they would be like them. So God denied that and said, "Surely I know what you do not know." This is the word of Ibn ʿAbbās, Ibn Masʿūd, and Qatāda. Second is that they said it with certainty, for God had reported to them that He was placing a vicegerent in the earth who would work corruption there. After having known that from Him they responded to Him with their words "What, wilt Thou set therein . . . ?

In their responding to Him like this are two respects: One is that they said it to show the enormity of such activity. In other words, "How can they work corruption therein when You have blessed them and made them vicegerents?" The second is that they said it in wonder at their being made vicegerents: "How can You make them vicegerents when You know that they will work corruption therein?" So He said, "Surely I know what you do not know."

"While we glorify Thy praise." There are four opinions as to what this means. One is "We perform the prayer to Thee." God says, "Had he not been one of those who glorify" [37:143], *that is, who perform the prayer.*

Second, the meaning is "We show reverence to Thee." This is the word of Mujāhid, and the previous word is that of Ibn ʿAbbās.

Third is that this is the well-known glorification.

Fourth is that it is to lift the voice in remembering God. Mufaḍḍal said this.

"And call Thee holy." The root of calling holy is to hold pure; from this we have "the holy earth" [5:21].

Concerning what is meant by their words "and call Thee holy," there are two words. One is that this is the prayer. The second is "We hold Thee pure of defilements."

As for His words "Surely I know," there are three interpretations. One is that He means the deception, scheming, disobedience, and pride concealed by Iblis; this is the word of Ibn ʿAbbās. The second is that among Adam's offspring are the prophets and messengers who will work wholesomeness in the earth and not work corruption; this is the word of Qatāda. The third is the governing of best interests, which is specific to His knowledge.

"And when thy Lord said to the angels." The meaning is this—*and God knows better*: "O Muḥammad, remember when your Lord said to the angels, 'I will create a vicegerent in the earth.'" Concerning these words the scholars have asked, "Which angels were they to whom the Real made this address?" Some have said that they were all the angels of heaven and earth. He gathered all of them in the capital city of all-compellingness and instructed the preacher of the Will to read out to the holy spirits from the pulpit of the decree the edict declaring the covenant of dust's vicegerency. Such is the habit of sultans when they send deputies to the provinces.

What was the Maker's wisdom in speaking to them like this? It was that the Exalted Lord wanted to choose Adam and his noble children over them, He wanted to command them to prostrate themselves before Adam, and He wanted them to busy themselves with the business of the Adamites. He made them aware so that when these important things came forth, they would be ready and their hearts set. For when someone has no news of something and it comes forth, he becomes troubled.

Some have said that these words were addressed to Iblis and the group of angels who were with him in the earth.

He said, *"Surely I am setting in the earth a vicegerent."* There is also disagreement in the meaning of *vicegerent*; some have said, "God's vicegerent." There is complete wisdom in appointing a deputy in the empire, for if a sultan does everything by himself, the sultanate's awesomeness and the empire's governance will be lost. So the Real wanted to keep the empire flourishing and kingship's awesomeness in place.

Some have said this was for him to be "your vicegerent." In other words, "When I bring you [angels] back to heaven from earth, I will entrust the earth to him after you." Whenever anyone takes someone's place, he is called a vicegerent. *It is He who made night and day a* khilfa [25:62], *that is, each of them succeeds its companion until the Day of Resurrection.*

They said, "What, wilt Thou set therein . . . ?" This is not the *what* of denial, but rather the *what* of inquiry and seeking news. It means *"What, wilt Thou set therein one who will work corruption there, or one who will work wholesomeness there?"* However, they abbreviated their words.

Then they said, *"While we glorify Thy praise."* They looked at the merchandise of their own obedience and lauded themselves. This is why the great ones have said, *"No one who slips, slips in any station but that of proximity."* The evidence that this was the angels' state is that they did not dare to speak, but when the Lord spoke to them, they became bold and said what they said in boldness. The bold expansiveness of Moses at the Mount was from the same thing.

The angels said two strange things. One was praising themselves and the other was mentioning the faults of others, which is similar to backbiting. The Real's decree in the case of the backbiter is that his obedience is taken away from him and given to the one backbitten. The Exalted Lord did exactly this with the angels. He made their obedience the share of the Adamites: *"Those who carry the Throne and those around it glorify the praise of their Lord and have faith in Him and ask forgiveness for those who have faith"* [40:7]. It is as if the Exalted Lord said, "You have backbitten, so you must also apologize."

In the midst of this there is an allusion that is good news for the spirits. It is as if the Exalted Lord is saying, "My servant, I knew your faults and did not mention them, but I mentioned your virtues. I said, '*Surely the earth will be inherited by My wholesome servants*' [21:105]. We call them workers of wholesomeness. Why do you call them workers of corruption?"

As for the angels' praising themselves, that is similar to self-admiration. Whenever someone appears admiring himself, the Real afflicts him with abasement. Hence He afflicted them with prostration before Adam so that they would never admire themselves in front of any obedient person.

Another secret is that when the Real gave Adam the name *vicegerent*, He held back from him the tongues of the creatures by way of intimation and admonishment: "He is Our vicegerent, and

We do not look wrongly. We make a worthy person vicegerent, not someone unworthy." They should have been admonished—"We must not say anything about His vicegerent." Once they spoke about him, rebuke kept on coming, both in word and in act. The word: *"Surely I know what you do not know"* [2:30]. The act: *"Prostrate yourselves before Adam!"* [2:34].

The folk of recognition have said that the angels thought that the cause of being caressed is service and the cause of distance is opposition. Hence they said, "We are obedient, and they are disobedient. It is we who should receive generosity and caresses." But the Real showed them that "Our caressing is from Our bounty, not by the intermediary of obedient acts, nor by means of acts of worship." This is why He created Adam without his having a single act of obedience, while the angels had filled the seven heavens and seven earths with obedience. He commanded the rich to prostrate themselves before him who had no wherewithal.

He commanded the angels, whose faces were turned toward the Throne and who were bound by the girdle of acquiescence, to turn their backs toward the Throne. He told them to take the best of all acts of service—which is prostration, within which is the hope of proximity—to Adam. When they went forward according to the command, they turned away from the Throne and turned toward Adam, but this did not diminish the empire. The Exalted Lord showed them that, "If the whole world turns away from worshiping Me, My Presence will not be diminished in any way, and if the whole world turns their faces toward a created thing, that thing will still be a servant."

More wondrous than this is that the angels had no slips, neither in the past nor in the future. But there would be a slip on Adam's part in the future. Thus He said, *"Adam disobeyed"* [20:121]. However, beneath this is a secret, which is that the angels saw themselves as pure, and Adam saw himself as destitute. The angels were saying, *"And we call Thee holy," that is, we keep ourselves pure for Your sake.* Adam said, *"Our Lord, we have wronged ourselves"* [7:23]. The Real showed that the slip of him who sees the slip is more exalted in His eyes than the purity of him who sees the purity. That is why He gave Adam the exaltedness of being the object of prostration, and He gave the angels the attribute of prostrating. Hence no obedient person should admire himself, and no disobedient person should lose hope.

An even finer point is that when the angels lauded themselves, the Real wanted to show them the secret He has in the creatures and say to them, "Anyone pure is pure through My protection, not through his own strength." He created Adam and commanded the angels to prostrate themselves before him. But the brand of abandonment had been placed on one of them and the inscription of loss written out for him. "Since My protection was not his helper, he turned away." Thus He showed them that, "If you did not have My protection, the same thing would have come from you that came from him. Your conforming to the command I gave you was not your virtue; it was My protection. Thus no obedient person should gaze on his own obedience. Rather, he should gaze on My favor."

When the angels spoke those words, the Exalted Lord said, *"Surely I know* something about Adam that *you do not know.* He will weep for three hundred years because of one slip—whether by forgetfulness or interpretation. Weeping for slips is because of fear of separation, and fear of separation is because of the deep-rootedness of love. I knew that and you did not know it."

Even more wonderful is this: "In the oyster of Adam's loins, which is the ocean of My power, I placed a pearl that would be brought up by the diver of Will and put on the shore of the Quran's ocean. Thus the plain text of the Book says, *"You are the best community"* [3:110].

More beautiful than all is this: " '*Surely I know' among the children of this vicegerent someone who is the Chieftain of the First Folk and the Last, and 'you do not know.'* I know a man among the children of My vicegerent who is the Chieftain of the First Folk and the Last. If I were to forgive the slip of Adam and all of his offspring because of him, he has that rank and status. I will forgive these workers of corruption about whom you talk so that the exaltedness of his messengerhood and the perfect majesty of his state may become evident." *Peace!*

51. *al-Wadūd:* the Loving/the Beloved

That is: He who makes His love [*mihr*] apparent by caressing the servant; He who loves His servant despite His unneediness; He who throws love between Himself and His servant and between His servant and Himself without partnership.

He says, *"He is the Forgiving, the Loving/the Beloved"* [85:14]. And He says, *"Surely those who have faith and do wholesome deeds, to them the All-Merciful will assign love"* [19:96].

Wadūd is an intensive from *wādd* [lover]. You can also say that *wadūd* means *mawdūd* [beloved]. *The Forgiving is He who has much forgiveness, and the Loving/Beloved is He who is intense in love. In other words: He has much forgiveness toward them because He loves them and He has much forgiveness toward them because they love Him.*[941]

The master Abū ʿAlī Daqqāq said, *"He singled out Adam by creating him with His hand; He singled out Moses with His words, 'I chose thee for Myself'* [20:41]*; and He singled out us with His words, 'He loves them and they love Him'* [5:54]*."* Explaining this road of love with the tongue is easy, but undertaking love's preconditions is the work of the Men.

Ḥārith Muḥāsibī said, *"Love is your inclination toward something with your entirety; your preferring it over your soul, your spirit, and everything that belongs to you; your conformity with it secretly and openly; and your knowledge that you fall short of its rightful due."*[942] The road of love is such that you must busy yourself with the Beloved totally and give up spirit, heart, and body in His road. You must seek conformity with Him both secretly and openly, both publicly and in your secret core. You must give no priority to your own portion's evil eye over His portion. When you have done all this, you must know that you are thrown down by incapacity and recognize that you are broken by shortcoming.

Abu'l-Qāsim Naṣrābādī said, *"Love is fighting against solace in every state."*[943] Love is that whenever your heart talks of being without sorrow, you take up spear and sword and battle against your heart.

When I wanted solace from Him, an intercessor said,
"Love's promised time of solace is the grave."
Within my heart and entrails will be left for Him
love's secret "on the day the secret cores are tried" [86:9].[944]

In the two worlds, no one dared talk of love. All at once the roar of love's Kaykawusian kettledrum[945] fell into the Dominion. The proximate angels said, "What happened? Why have our many thousand years of glorifying and hallowing been given to the wind?"

It was said, "Don't look at these forms, look at the deposit of Majesty: *He loves them and they love Him* [5:54]."

Gabriel, Michael, and the other exalted ones approved of glorification and calling holy and were content. All of a sudden the footsteps of Adam came into the world. The paths changed and the foods changed: "O Gabriel, bind up your waist and be a messenger! O Michael, prepare yourself to be the keeper of the treasury! O Azrael, make your heart happy with taking away worn-out clothing! O Seraphiel, submit yourself to giving out new clothing! First, however, you must taste a draft so that the dust of your claim, *'We glorify Thy praise'* [2:30], may be washed away from you."

"What must be done?"

"Prostrate yourselves before Adam! [2:34]. You must go before that piece of clay and prostrate yourselves. That will be an increase in your road, not an increase in his, for he has already been accepted by election: *Surely God chose Adam* [3:33]. *I blew into him of My spirit* [15:29]. *Whom I created with My own two hands* [38:75]."

They all fell before Adam in prostration. When they lifted up their heads, they saw their own teacher deformed. On his forehead had appeared *"Upon thee shall be My curse until the Day of Doom"* [38:78].

"From this dust We will bring forth individuals who will be the quarry of the secrets of Our Unseen. O Adam, We placed this eminence in you and We gave you this greatness because We made your solid loins the lodging place and depository of a man, the title of the edict of whose majesty and beauty is this: *'I created what I created only for thee.'*[946] *'If not for thee, I would not have created the realm of being.'* "[947]

Moses the speaking companion was a noble paragon. Within the curtain of his secret whispering he was outwardly all listening and inwardly all togetherness. One night a thought came into his mind, and because of the greatness of his thinking the Exalted Lord clothed a thousand knowers in the garment of prophethood. On another night another thought came, and the Exalted Lord took away the lives of a thousand prophets. What fine thoughts! From their gravity a thousand people put on the clothing of prophethood and a thousand prophets drank the cup of death! He needed to have such thoughts and such aspirations so that on the peak of the Mount, on the carpet of light, in the station of presence, he could say, *"Make me one of Muḥammad's community!"*[948]

In both verification and learning the long and the short of it is that all the messengers who went before Muḥammad were laying down the foundation of his good fortune and establishing the basis of his greatness. Adam—who was the auspicious phoenix of the world of felicity, the foundation and canon of rulership, the catalog of the library of existent things, and the container of the meanings of the world—was the precursor of the rising of his good fortune's sun. Noah—who was the elder of the prophets and the second Adam—was the commander-in-chief of his creed. Abraham—who was a warrior against adversaries in the celestial orb and the terrestrial center, namely, sun, moon, stars, and idols—was the housemaster of his presence. Moses—for whom the whole of the earth was the tent of proximity—yearned for his community. Jesus—concerning whom it was said, *"And when thou createst from clay, by My leave, as the guise of a bird, and thou blowest into it, and it is a bird, by My leave"* [5:110]—gave the good news of his stepping forth. If in Solomon's era a bird went to Sheba, conveying a letter to Bilqīs, then this good-news-bringer—who reported of the stepping forth of the chieftain of the envoys and from the blessings of whose breath a clay bird began to fly—was giving the good news of his prophethood.

I mention all this verification and embellishment—with the help of success-giving—to let you know that all of them were parts, and he was the whole. Those who have passed on were the leaves, and he was the flower. O center-point of prophethood, set a sigil on this edict! *"Adam and those after him will be under my banner on the Day of Resurrection, without boasting."*[949]

It is a sound report that he was taken on the *mi'rāj*. There is no wonder in his being taken. If it is permitted for the accursed devil to go from East to West with one leap of his own power, why is it a wonder that the chieftain of chieftains, the source of exaltedness and felicities, the canon of every good fortune, the foremost of the first folk and the last, should put his foot on the head of the spheres? If intellects do not find it far-fetched that trustworthy Gabriel, the messenger of the threshold of prophethood and the servitor of the presence of messengerhood, should come in the blink of an eye from *the Lote Tree of the Final End* [53:14] to this dusty circle, how then could they find it far-fetched that he—through whose luster the spheres became the spheres and through whose secret core the angels became angels—should be escorted to the Presence of Proximity by the exalted attractions of Him *who took His servant by night* [17:1]?

When Muṣṭafā was taken to the world of limpidness, he was shown the abode of bounty and the house of justice. When a king has a friend and has built a palace, he takes the friend's hand and shows him around the palace, displaying the various sites. Muṣṭafā was shown the house of justice, the house of bounty, the encampments, the veiled virgins, and the hidden secrets so that others would speak of what they had heard and he would speak of what he had seen.

Indeed, the stipulation of your road is that you have faith in the Unseen. You must not be the servant and slave of your own eyes, for opacity is suspect. You must be the servant of Muḥammad's explication, for it is pure, clean, and sinless.

Muṣṭafā was taken on the *mi'rāj* so that he would become bold. Then tomorrow, when the awesomeness of hell's harshness becomes apparent and when Adam, Abraham, Noah, and Moses say, *"my soul, my soul,"* he will say, *"my community, my community."*[950] He will show forth this report that he had made: *"Adam and those after him will be under my banner on the Day of Resurrection, without boasting."*

"O Muḥammad, even though I said to you, *'Emulate their guidance'* [6:90], I made them all present in Jerusalem on the night of the *mi'rāj* so that they would follow and emulate your form."

As long as the paragon was on earth, everyone brought him things. Someone brought a cup of milk, another a goblet of wine. This treacherous, deluding world was sitting in the road, embellishment and delusion's rouge rubbed on her face: "If the paragon looks at me, my faults will become virtues and my venom sugar." On the pulpit of majesty the paragon answered with the tongue of his state, "O base world, what is this uncooked wish? Tonight Firdaws will not dare to come around the pavilion of my aspiration. What is this little bazaar of yours?"

O dervish, here there is a marvelous secret. On the night of the *miʿrāj* he was shown all of the Dominion and paid it no attention. But when he came to the door of Zayd's chamber and saw Zaynab, turmoil appeared. *And when thou saidst to him whom God had blessed and thou hadst blessed, "Keep thy wife to thyself and be wary of God," thou wast concealing in thyself what God was making appear. Thou didst fear the people, though God has more right for thee to fear Him* [33:37].

Qatāda, Suddī, and Sufyān Thawrī said, "That was Zayd ibn Ḥāritha, whom God had blessed with submission and whom God's Messenger had blessed with manumission. 'Keep thy wife to thyself,' that is, Zaynab bint Jaḥsh."[951]

Kalbī said, "God's Messenger came to the house of Zayd as a visitor. He saw her while she was standing and preparing bread and he admired her. He said, 'Glory be to God, the Fluctuater of hearts!'

"When Zaynab heard that from him, she sat down. When Zayd came into the house, Zaynab mentioned that to him, so he recognized that she had fallen into his soul. He came to God's Messenger and said to him, 'O Messenger of God, give me permission to divorce her, for she is proud and she torments me with her tongue.'

"God's Messenger said to him, 'Keep thy wife to thyself and be wary of God,' but in his heart there was something else."

"And thou wast concealing in thyself what God was making appear." In this they have offered three views: First, what he was concealing was that before he married her, God had let him know that she would be one of his wives; this was said by Ḥasan. Second, what he was concealing in himself was that if Zayd divorced her, he would marry her. Third, what he was concealing was his inclination toward her and his preference that she be divorced. This was said by Ibn Jurayj.

"Thou didst fear the people, though God has more right for thee to fear Him." Concerning this there are two opinions. One is that God's Messenger feared what the people would say; Qatāda said this. Second is that he feared to make it appear to the people, so God made his secret appear; Muqātil ibn Ḥayyān said this.

ʿUmar ibn Khaṭṭāb said, "Had God's Messenger hidden anything of the Quran, he would have hidden this verse."[952]

"Then when Zayd accomplished what he wanted from her, We married her to thee" [33:37]. *Here there are two readings. One is [that what he wanted means] need, the other divorce.*

Yaḥyā ibn Sallām said, "God's Messenger called Zayd and said, 'Go to Zaynab and report to her that God has married her to me.' So Zayd went off and knocked at the door. She asked who it was and he said it was Zayd. She said, 'What need have you of me? You have divorced me.'

"He said, 'God's Messenger sent me,' and she said, 'Welcome to God's messenger.' She opened the door for him. He entered, and she was weeping. He said, 'May God not let your eyes weep! For you are an excellent woman. You are quit of my portion and you obeyed my command, and God has confirmed you with better than me.'

"She said, 'Who could it be that you would not care?' "

"He said, 'God's Messenger,' and she fell down in prostration."

Anas said, "God's Messenger went to her and entered in upon her without asking permission."[953]

Qatāda said, "She used to boast to the wives of the Prophet saying, 'As for you, you were given in marriage by your fathers, but I was given in marriage by the Lord of the Throne—blessed and high indeed is He!' "[954]

The eye of prophethood, on which had been daubed the collyrium of sinlessness, fell on that covered head. He said, *"Glory be to God, the Fluctuater of hearts!"* Yes, the present moment passes over the lover such that he laments so much of love that the hell-dwellers feel mercy toward him. This is because the fire of hell burns the body, but the fire of love burns the spirit. The swords of the warriors do not do to the spirits of the Byzantines what the fire of love does to the spirits of the lovers.

When someone wears the garment of safety, tell him not to charge his horse into the field of love. Love is a severe sultan. It will take away everything you have. It will plunder your bags and furnishings, destroy your house, and set it all on fire.

The Chieftain of the Two Worlds came to the door of Zayd's house and his gaze fell on her. That gaze was the first gaze, and a man is not called to account for the first gaze.[955] But, with that first gaze the harvest of his patience was given to the wind, and that paragon turned to heaven and said, *"O Fluctuater of hearts!"* It is You who turn hearts around! This is Your work!

O chevalier, one blunder on the part of the proximate is equal to a hundred thousand years of turning away on the part of the distant. What are examples of this? At the doorstep of the kings of this world, the doormen and stablemen say a thousand foolish words and are not blamed. But if a boon companion who sits knee-to-knee with the king should gaze wrongly with a single glance, his recompense for turning away once from the king is beheading.

"O Muḥammad, one gaze of yours toward other than Me is harder than everything your community will do until the Day of Resurrection. We had the power to keep your gaze and that peril away from the courtyard and pavilion of your heart and eyes. But in that We had a divine mystery and subtlety. What is that subtlety? We wanted to make the hearts of the destitute and broken happy. We showed that Muḥammad with his majestic state, bravery of messengerhood, and strength of prophethood was not able to guard his heart. How can a handful of the helpless guard their hearts? '*Surely my heart becomes clouded.*' "[956]

Then when Zayd accomplished what he wanted from her, We married her to thee [33:37]. "The whole world seeks what I desire, but I seek what you desire. Moses said, '*I hurried to Thee, my Lord, that Thou mayest approve*' [20:84]. I said to you, '*Thy Lord will bestow upon thee, and thou wilt approve*' [93:5].

"The abodes are two: the abode of this world and the abode of the afterworld. In this world the Shariah is by your approval, and in the afterworld mercy is by your approval. Concerning this world I said, '*We will turn thee toward a kiblah that thou wilt approve*' [2:144]. Concerning the afterworld I said, '*Thy Lord will bestow upon thee, and thou wilt approve.*' In both abodes the creatures must do what I approve, but I do what you approve. When someone seeks My approval, he does so because he belongs to Me. When I seek your approval, I do so because I belong to you.

"O My friend, what worth, after all, has a woman?

"I made Jerusalem the kiblah and said, 'Turn your face there!' You aspired to the Kaabah, though you did not say that with your tongue—you thought it with your heart. I said, '*So turn thy face toward the Holy Mosque*' [2:144]. This was My service to you and your mercy to Me. My service was that I said, 'Turn your face,' because My friend wanted that. Your mercy to Me was that My friend wanted Me to give. Should I hold back? No, never!"

Know with certitude and verification that of all the existent things that came forth at the decree *"Be!"* into the vast plain of *so it comes to be* [2:117], no essence received the perfection that was received by Muḥammad's essence and no attributes received the majesty that was received by his attributes. Given that this community is *the best community* [3:110], this is evidence that the Prophet was the best prophet.

Adam was the exalted of the world, but rebuke came to him before and pardon afterward. Thus He says, *"And Adam disobeyed his Lord, so he went astray. Then his Lord chose him, so He turned toward him and guided"* [20:121–22]. But pardon came to Muṣṭafā before and rebuke afterward: *"God has pardoned thee. Why didst thou give them permission?"* [9:43].[957]

Although Idris had the generous gift of recognizing how to journey to the planets, Muṣṭafā was conveyed to a place where journey to the planets was not the road.

Noah asked for the chastisement of his people: *"My Lord, leave no disbeliever dwelling on the earth"* [71:26]. Muṣṭafā said, *"O God, guide my people, for they do not know."*[958] When someone has such tenderness toward enemies, look how he is with friends!

Abraham was addressed with the words *"Surely I am making thee a leader for the people"* [2:124], but on the night of the *miʿrāj* He made Muṣṭafā the leader of the prophets in Jerusalem. Though Abraham was given such strength of certainty that he said to Gabriel, *"Of you, no,"*[959] the strength of Muṣṭafā's certainty passed beyond that of Abraham and he said, *"I have a moment with God embraced by no proximate angel or sent prophet."*[960] The proximate angel is Gabriel and the sent prophet Abraham.

Although Solomon was given the kingdom of this world, Muṣṭafā was given the kingdom of the resurrection. Thus he said, *"The banner of praise will be in my hand, without boasting."*[961] Those beneath Solomon's banner are the jinn and the satans, but how could he be equal to someone beneath whose banner are the first creatures and the last?

Although a staff was turned into a serpent for Moses so that he could subject the sorcerers, a stick worked a miracle for Muṣṭafā so that he subjected the idols. The prostration of idols is more marvelous than the prostration of an intelligent, discerning animal.[962] Though He gave Moses the miracle of passing his people through the sea such that their skirts did not become wet, He gave Muṣṭafā the miracle of passing his community through hell such that their skirts will not be dried out by the heat.

Although Jesus was taken to the fourth sphere, Muṣṭafā was taken to *two-bows' length away, or closer* [53:9].

All these sublimities, meanings, virtues, and good qualities were gathered together in the purified essence of Muṣṭafā, though the attribute of holiness was given to no one. *Peace!*

52. *al-Majīd:* the Splendorous

The great in measure and beautiful in bestowal. The Arabs say *amjadtu'l-dābba*, meaning I fed the animal well, I gave it good fodder. But God's gifts to the servants do not come under limit and number. *"If anyone thinks that God's blessings on him consist of his drink, clothing, and sex, his knowledge has fallen short."*[963] You should not count whatever you share with the Byzantines as blessing's reality. Its reality is the religion and firm fixity in the road of certainty. *The greatest of God's blessings on His servants are two things: His teaching them His name and His making Himself recognized to them.*

The consensus of the folk of the Real and the Haqiqah is that *the evidence for God is God. "And to whomsoever God assigns no light, no light has he"* [24:40]. The one who shows the road to God is God Himself.[964]

After coming into existence the creatures are just as captive to power as they were before existence. When they were nonexistent, they were captive to power. If He wanted, He brought them into existence, and if He did not want, He did not. Now that they are existent, they are still captive to power. If He wants to keep them, He does, and if He does not want, He does not. After existence they will be exactly what they were in the state of nonexistence. And He, after bestowing existence, is exactly what He was before bestowing existence. So the existence of the creatures right now is similar to nonexistence, and their subsistence has the constitution of annihilation. It is impossible for an annihilated and nonexistent thing to find the road or to be shown the road.[965] This is why the Messenger said, *"By God, if not for God, we would not have been guided"* and so on.[966] He also said, *"I was sent as an inviter, and nothing of guidance goes back to me."*[967]

In reality, the road-shower is God, and intellect is the instrument, not the cause. If intellect were the cause of recognition, it would be impossible for a thing without intellect to recognize. But the Exalted Lord reports in the splendorous scripture that the hoopoe said, *"I found her and her people prostrating to the sun"* [27:24], and everyone agrees that birds have no intellect. And He reported about the ant, *"An ant said, 'Ants, enter your dwelling places' "* [27:18]. If that ant did not have recognition of God, how did it know who Solomon was? Yet there is consensus that ants have no intellect. So intellect is the instrument of recognition, like eyes for vision.[968]

Another secret: Intellect and evidence are secondary causes for the existence of recognition, just as male and female are secondary causes for the existence of children. Even if male and female should come together and put the perfection of their power to work, so long as the Real does not create a child, no child will come. You should know that intellect and evidence are the same.

O God, the wonder is that a vulva can be penetrated in intercourse and be under the power of creatures, but no one has the power to place a child therein without the permission of the Will. As for the heart that it is in the grasp of the Real but not under the power of creatures, how can anyone have the power to place recognition there without the signet of His desire? I have taken this allusion from the report *"The hearts are between two fingers of the All-Merciful."* The end of the hadith is this: *"He makes them fluctuate as He wants"*[969]*—if He wants, toward His justice, and if He wants, toward His bounty.*

These *"two fingers"* have the meaning of a likeness. They are not meant by way of verification. In common usage the people say about someone dominated by someone else, "So-and-so is between the two fingers of so-and-so. He does whatever he wants." By these words are meant subjugating and being subjugated or dominating and being dominated over. Evidence that hearts are not under the control of the servants is that when the Messenger's gaze fell on Zaynab, he said, *"O Fluctuater of hearts, make my heart firm!"*[970]

One of the great ones of the Tariqah said, *"No one recognizes Him unless He makes Himself recognized to him, no one voices His* tawḥīd *unless He shows him His* tawḥīd, *no one has faith in Him unless He shows him gentleness, no one describes Him unless He discloses Himself to his secret core, no one becomes purified for Him unless He attracts him to Himself, and no one becomes wholesome for Him unless He chooses him for Himself."*[971]

First he said, *"No one recognizes Him unless He makes Himself recognized to him."* No one recognizes Him unless the Real makes him familiar with Himself. If creatures could reach the Real simply by seeking, there would be no idol-worshipers in the world, for all are seeking. God says, *"We only worship them so that they will bring us nigh in proximity to God"* [39:3]. The Christian seeks Him from the Messiah.

Indeed there is something more exalted and subtle than this: When something can be found by seeking, even if it is beyond measure in the view of the creatures, no one stops seeking it. If he stops, he stops because it is of no use to him. But all creatures are in need of the Real, and felicity in both houses is tied to recognizing Him. Thus it is known that if you do not find, it is not because you do not want. Everyone wants, but unless He wants, no one will find Him.

"No one voices His tawḥīd *unless He shows him His* tawḥīd," that is, shows him that He is one. No one knows the Real as one except him to whom He shows Himself as one.

"No one has faith in Him unless He shows gentleness to him." The Exalted Lord has a gentleness toward the faithful that He does not have toward the unbelievers. If one iota of the elixir of gentleness inside the silk purse of bounty were sprinkled on the associationism of the associators and the unbelief of the unbelievers, the unbelievers' unbelief and the associators' associationism would all become *tawḥīd* itself. And if one drop of that spirit-nourishing wine that He has in the cup of the Unseen were to drip into the throat of the creatures, no denial or opposition would remain in the breast of any denier or opposer.

"No one describes Him unless He discloses Himself to his secret core." No one describes Him except someone in whose secret core He has made Himself appear. Expression is the spokesman of the secret core, and the secret core gazes on the Real. The secret core sees, and then the tongue expresses the seeing. This is what the folk of practice say. As for the folk of the Haqiqah, they say, *"He who recognizes Him does not describe Him, and he who describes Him does not recognize Him."* To express and describe is to report about something absent, but self-disclosure to the secret core is contemplation. To report in the state of face-to-face vision is associationism, and to report in the state of absence is falsehood. To report about something absent is backbiting, and to report about something present is to abandon veneration.

The heart's contemplation in this world is like eyesight's contemplation in the afterworld. If eyesight in the afterworld were to give reports in the state of contemplation, then it would be fitting for the secret core in this world to give reports in the state of contemplation. Know, however, that in reality there is no vision when there is speaking, and there is no speaking when there is vision. In the state of contemplation breathing is not guaranteed, so what about speaking?

The realizers have said, "When someone's inwardness is fixed in contemplation, he does not want to express it with the tongue lest his outwardness become aware of it."[972] If he holds it back from his own outwardness, how can he speak to others?

In the stories about Ḥallāj it is said that when they killed him, Shiblī said, "That night I whispered with the Real in prayer all night until dawn. Then I placed my head down in prostration and said, 'O Lord, he was one of Your servants, a man of faith, a *tawḥīd*-voicer, a believer, and numbered among Your friends. What was this trial that You gave him?'

"Then I slept, and the call of exaltedness reached my hearing: *'He was one of Our servants. We informed him of one of Our secrets and he disclosed it, so We sent down upon him what you saw.* It is given over to a greengrocer to call out about his vegetables, but it is absurd for a jeweler to call out about a night-brightening pearl.' "

"No one becomes purified for Him unless He attracts him to Himself." No one is pure but the one whom He pulls to Himself. Pure gold is that which has no impurity at all. God says, *"between feces and blood, pure milk"* [16:66]. "I took milk, which is your nourishment and your share, passed it over feces and blood, and preserved it from both. Hence *tawḥīd*, which is My rightful due, must pass over this world and the next and receive no trace from either. Were the trace of this world or the afterworld to sit on *tawḥīd*, it would not be worthy of Me."

"No one becomes wholesome for Him unless He chooses him for Himself." No one is worthy of Him unless He makes him His own chosen one. When the Real makes someone His chosen one, all causes and attachments are cut off from him so that he may remain disengaged and solitary.

This is explained in the story of Moses. The blood of the Egyptian was made to flow at his hand, and the people set off to kill him. He fled and fell into exile. He had to give expiation for that with ten years in the sun, putting up with the abasement of being a shepherd. He also had to have a wife. This is the portion of appetite, which must be given its rightful due. It is impossible to want this without trial upon trial, trouble upon trouble, abasement upon abasement, and severity upon severity. Once the bride came into his arms, he had no settledness anywhere. The lover has no settledness, for settledness is solace, and in love solace is associationism.

When Moses went into the midst of the desert, the night became dark, clouds gathered, and thunder and rain appeared. The pain of childbirth came to his wife, wind came up, and the sheep scattered. He lifted up the fire-steel to start a fire, but the fire-steel's nature had become niggardly. His wife was moaning and the sheep were fleeing. When no stratagem remained in Moses's hands, *he observed a fire on the side of the mountain* [28:29]—that was shown to him.

At the first of this talk there was fire upon fire. There was a great distance from Moses to where he saw the fire, but love turns distance into proximity. When Moses reached that place, he wanted to bring a brand from the fire. The tongue of love called out from the pulpit of proximity, *"This fire burns hearts and spirits, not forms and bodies."* Then the call came, "I have chosen you. How will it be if you have ease with no one but Me? When someone is worthy of Me, he is not given ease with the permitted—how could he be left with the forbidden?" Do you not see what the Exalted Lord said about him? *"And We forbade his being suckled by foster mothers"* [28:12].

Then know that in reality *He spoke to Moses in respect of Moses. Had He spoken to Moses in respect of His tremendousness, Moses would have melted.* When He spoke to Moses, He spoke in the shade of His gentleness. If He had spoken to him in the attribute of tremendousness, he would have melted at the first step such that no name or mark of him would have remained.

What a marvelous business! Mount Sinai received the self-disclosure and crumbled. Hearts receive the self-disclosure and at every moment increase in agitation, revelry, and renewal. Yes, when Mount Sinai became the locus of the gaze, it came back to itself and did not have the capacity to put up with it. When hearts become the locus of the gaze, they do not become so through themselves. They become so through His attribute: *"The hearts are between two fingers of the All-Merciful."*[973]

Another secret: His gaze on the Mount was the gaze of severity, but His gaze on hearts is the gaze of gentleness. The ruling property of severity makes things into nothing, but the ruling property of gentleness keeps things in their state. Moses asked and thereby became worthy of severity. The shadow of Moses's asking fell on the mountain and it crumbled.

"We spoke to Moses without intermediary, and after him We gave this inheritance to the hearts of the exalted ones." Wherever there is a heart, there is a Moses; and wherever there is a breast, there is a Mount Sinai. The Moses of the heart went to the station of speech on the Mount Sinai of the breast, sometimes on the packhorse of light, sometimes on the steed of shadows. *And glorify Him morning and evening* [33:42].

We are called "companions of talk," for we have talk with God, and God has talk with us. *God has sent down the most beautiful talk* [39:23]. *And who is more truthful in talk than God?* [4:87]. "We say: 'When you come to the prayer, which is the station of whispered prayer,[974] do not be silent. Talk, whether you are a follower or being followed.' "

The eyes of one imam fall on the severity of the divinity, of another imam on the perfect gentleness of all-mercifulness. Severity stamps a seal on the lips of one imam, and mercy places another imam on the carpet of bold expansiveness.

You can also say that the eyes of one imam fall on the severity of the divinity, and the eyes of another imam on the character of prophethood. The Sultan's awesomeness silences speakers, but it is not surprising that in the presence of Muḥammad's character, a stone should glorify God or a cup and a lizard should praise Him.

One imam looks at God's awesomeness. The *h* of *Allāh* has a tremendous secret, and he shuts his mouth like *Allāh's h* [ه]. The other imam looks at the gentleness of all-mercifulness and the character of messengerhood, and he opens his mouth in the shape of Muḥammad's *d* [د]. When you look at the reality, both imams take the clear water of the Sunnah from the same reservoir and fount, for if you do not combine *No god but God* with *Muḥammad is God's messenger*, your faith is not faith and your submission not submission.

> You'd say two ants put their feet in amber,
> then walked on the moon and bumped their heads.

The realizers among the folk of recognition say that speech is the mark of yearning and silence the mark of constraint and incapacity. The incapable have no way to talk. *This is why the Prophet said concerning virgins, "Their silence is their approval."*[975] When a woman is within the curtain of virginity, there is no need for her to exert herself to speak, for she is constrained by the talons of shame, so we take her not speaking as speaking. When someone is constrained by contemplating and observing majesty, why is it surprising to take his not-speaking as speaking? When someone suckles milk from the nipple of holiness and partakes of the fruit of gentleness, why is it surprising if he begins to talk and chatter because of impatience, yearning, and the need for encounter? So, with this verification, there is no disagreement between the two imams.

"Surely this prayer of ours is not wholesome when people talk."[976] At the beginning of the era of the submission, talking during the prayer was allowed. Then Muṣṭafā said that the prayer is the station of secret whispering, and in the station of secret whispering it is not permitted to talk to other than the Friend.

Also, He sent the Quran, and this Quran is His talk with you. He said, "When you speak with Us, speak with Our talk. We do not talk with outwardness—Our talk is with hearts. *Rather it is signs, clear signs, in the breasts of those who have been given knowledge* [29:49]. These outward things are the intermediaries, the means of approach, the curtains, and the drapes of the unseen meanings."

First Gabriel was sent to take a handful of dust from the earth. When Gabriel came to take it, the earth sought aid against him, for the earth was like a jewel box. Inside the jewel box of that handful of dust was the oyster for the pearl of Adam's secret core. It sought aid because its wherewithal was being plundered. Gabriel went back. Then He sent Seraphiel, and again the earth sought aid, so he went back. Then He sent Michael, and the earth shouted for help, so he went back. Finally He sent Azrael. The earth sought aid: *"I seek refuge in God from you."*

He said, *"I seek refuge in God lest I return to Him without having accomplished His command."* He took a handful of dust by force, without the approval of the earth, but he promised that he would bring the handful back.[977]

What is the wisdom in this handful? Yes, the subtleties and secrets of the Unseen must be deposited in a container. The dust was taken by severity, and the spirit was deposited within it by severity, for they were opposites. Had there been only spirit, the days would have been free of stain and the acts would have had no adulteration. But pure acts are not appropriate for this world, and from the beginning Adam was created to be the housemaster in *this* world.

The secrets were combined with dust so that they would not shine there and be found by the evil eye. The dust was put there to throw off the folk of outwardness. The army of the uncaused Will set up an ambush with Adam's dust so that Iblis would look at the dust, protest, and become accursed. "I created him of fire, but he did not know that fire is more worthy for the Fire. O accursed one, do you boast of fire? You belong to the Fire, and the Fire belongs to you. O Korah, do you boast of treasures? You belong to the treasures, and the treasures belong to you. O Pharaoh, do you boast of the river Nile? You belong to the Nile, and the Nile belongs to you! O *tawḥīd*-voicers, do you boast of Me? You belong to Me, and I belong to you."

He wanted to put a hundred thousand secrets in Adam's makeup. He gazed and saw no one in the world more trustworthy than dust, so He put the secrets in dust. He did not give them to fire, for fire burns and reduces to nothing. Deposits are not given to the treacherous; they are given to the trustworthy. The secrets were the locus of exaltation, for they were the veiled virgins of the Unseen Presence, and veiled women are kept behind the curtain. Nothing was like dust in concealing, so dust was made the curtain of the secrets. Then the privy would look at the secrets, and the non-privy would look at the dust. *Peace!*

53. *al-Bāʿith:* the Upraiser

God says, *"Surely God will raise up whosoever is in the graves"* [22:7].

He who wakes up the sleeping, brings the dead to life, and takes the hands of those who have fallen short.

Know in reality that when someone believes that a mustering and an upstirring is ahead of him, he will watch over his own states and persevere in performing the obligations and supererogations. Moment by moment he will demand from himself that he discharge what is rightfully due and, by reason of caution in the religion's road, he will take an accounting of his own soul for specks and grains.

As for the attribute that you have, having made the homeland of human nature your Kaabah, you surely know nothing of the resurrection.

Once Pir Bū ʿAlī Siyāh was walking in the bazaar. A blind man was saying, "By the rightful due of the Great Day, give me something." The pir fell down in a faint. When he came back to awareness, they said, "O Shaykh, why did you faint?"

He said, "Does anyone know anything about the Great Day? *Alas for disobedient acts and the seizing by the forelocks* [55:41] *in the plain of retaliation! Oh the sorrow at the paucity of sorrowing! Oh the grief at the paucity of grieving! Oh the remorse at the paucity of remorsefulness!"* Oh the sorrow of not being sorrowful! Oh the remorse of not being remorseful!

A whole world is busy with vestiges and traces, having left empty the presence of the Alive, the Self-Standing. One person has come down to wearing cap and tunic, never thinking about this verse: *"As for the unjust, they will be firewood for Gehenna"* [72:15]. Another has sat on a pillow, having gathered a handful of dread around himself and never thinking about the verse in which the Exalted Lord says, *"Will you command the people to piety, and forget yourselves?"* [2:44]. Another has come down to putting on robe and boots and going from door to door, making his religion the plaything of the wrongdoers. Still another has come down to inscribing black on white and drinking down the poison of shortcoming in deeds instead of the antidote. Still another has come to the point of going to his shop in the morning and selling his religion for a penny or a halfpenny.

Is it not time for the hearts of those who have faith to be humbled to the remembrance of God? [57:16]. How long this heedlessness, indolence, laxity, and conversing with wishes? The sweetbriar of intimacy has grown in the garden of holiness, and the heart-caressing roses have bloomed.

The command's gentleness keeps on addressing you: *"Are there any sinners?"*[978] The hand of exaltedness has appeared from the pavilion of love, and the tongue of the Haqiqah calls out, *"Are there any turning this way?"* The messengers of affection and the edicts of invitation have appeared with the signets and marks of the Haqiqah, while the caller of generosity says, *"Are there any Quran-reciters?"* The spirit-nurturing words and holy, purified verses come with the address, *"Are there any listeners?"* The paths of guidance have come forth with the serving boy of kind favor: *"Are there any wayfarers?"* The gems of gentleness and the pearls of generosity have come out into the open from the oysters of gentle gifts: *"Are there any gazers?"* The Kaabah of felicity has disclosed itself in the precinct of His desire: *"Are there any strivers?"* The ocean of the Unseen, replete with the pearls of faith and beautiful-doing, has boiled forth: *"Are there any divers?"* The perfect beauty of *"God is beautiful and He loves beauty"*[979] has promised union saying, *"Are there any lovers?"*

"Come to My threshold so that I may do what your father and mother never did. What did your mother do? She had her pleasure. What did your father do? He went after his appetite. The work of mothers and fathers is built on appetite and portions, but I have no appetite and no portion.

"Your mother and father pertain to now, but My work with you has no beginning. My work with you is not accidental that it should be here one day and gone the next. It is the clashing waves of the ocean of the unseen secrets, the flashing suns of the spheres of the beginningless decrees. My Godhead had no need for servants that I should say, *'Am I not your Lord?'* [7:172]. Nor was there any necessity for Me to say, *'Whose is the kingdom today?'* [40:16]. Even so, the former declaration opened the doors of the gentle gifts of the commands, and the latter declaration will be the vanguard and prelude to what was desired by the decrees."

There were a thousand thousand bowers and prostrators, a thousand thousand of the distracted and ecstatic, a thousand thousand burning at His threshold, a thousand thousand gazing on His activity, a thousand thousand bewildered by His secrets—all of them wearing the girdle of sinlessness, the shirt of service, and the waistcoat of veneration, with pious acts, with glorification and reciting *tawḥīd*, with reverence and extolling. All at once He created a fearless group and chose them over all the obedient, without any previous service or intervening intercession. He said, "O handful of dust! *Am I not your Lord?* Am I not yours?"

The folk of heaven with all their obedience and service were looking on. The Exalted Lord showed them to themselves in a handful of dust: *And when We said to the angels, "Prostrate yourselves before Adam!"* [2:34]—not because of any means of approach, virtue, merchandise, service, reverence, or worship.

"What excellence did you have? What was your instrument, your means of approach, your virtue, your merchandise, your service, your servanthood, your worship? Answer Me! You do not know. I know: *Say: 'In the bounty of God'* [10:58]. *Say: 'Surely the bounty is in God's hand'* [3:73]. *Say: 'All is from God'* [4:78]."

"All our fear and dread lie in that, without having any means of approach or stratagem, You said to us, 'Come!' What if, without sin, offense, and fault, You say, 'Go!' Where can we go?"

"O My friends, have no worry in your hearts, for We will not send away those whom We have called. We will not reject Our friends."

It is said that there was a rich man in Baghdad, eating from his inheritance. A group gathered around him and reduced his possessions to nothing. One day in sadness he wanted to throw himself into the Tigris. He went to the edge of the Tigris and argued a great deal with himself. Then he called out to a sailor. The sailor brought a skiff and sat him down in it. When they reached the middle of the Tigris, the sailor said, "Where do you want to go?"

He said, "I don't know."

He said, "Where are you coming from?"

He said, "I don't know."

The sailor was intelligent. He said to himself, "This man is destitute, or he's lost his heart, or he's under constraint." Then he said, "Tell me about your state," and the man told him. The sailor said, "I will take you to the other side. It may be that some relief will appear." He took him to the other side and he got out. On the shore of the Tigris there was a mosque. He went there and stayed for a time. The judge of the city entered with a group of notables and dignitaries and sat down. After a time an official came from the house of the caliph and said to the shaykhs, "Respond to the Commander of the Faithful." The judge and the group went, and the young man inserted himself into their midst. They all went to the house of the caliph and sat down. After a time the command came, "The Commander of the Faithful is giving so-and-so to so-and-so. Bind the contract." The judge performed the ceremony and the others acted as witnesses.

Sometime later the official came with ten trays full of gold, on top of each a bag of musk. A tray was placed before each of them, but there was no tray for the young man. The official said to the Commander of the Faithful, "A youth is left for whom there is no tray."

He said, "Weren't the names written down?"

They said, "Yes, but we invited ten and eleven came."

The Commander of the Faithful said, "Bring the youth to me." When he reached the throne, he recited a subtle supplication. The Commander of the Faithful said, "We did not invite you. Why did you come to the sanctuary of my house?"

The youth said, "O Commander of the Faithful, I did not come uninvited."

He said, "Who invited you?"

He said, "Who invited them?"

He said, "My officials."

He said, "And me, your generosity."

> Think not that I came here on my own—
> your generous traits, O king, said to me, "Come!"

The Commander of the Faithful said, *"Your inviter did well!* O serving boy, bring inkwell and pen!" They were brought, and with his own hand he wrote the edict for a province to be given to him, and he commanded that he be given a beautiful robe of honor as well as a favorite steed. Then he said, "Whenever someone is invited by an official, the robe of honor is like that. Whenever someone is invited by generosity, the robe of honor is like this."

O chevalier, there is a secret in this story. One created thing says to another by way of metaphor, "Your generosity has brought me to your court." He finds a gift like this. The Exalted Lord invites us by virtue of His own Lordhood and says, "I am yours." Are not hopes strengthened by this? *By God the Tremendous*, the hope is that He will settle us down in the abode of subsistence, seat us on the throne of approval, give us a taste of the wine of union, let us hear music without intermediary, and lift up the veil to show us vision.

The divine union, conjoining, welcoming, and gentle gift given to this handful of dust do not pertain to today. He brought us out from nonexistence into existence and enfolded this existence-giving in the attribute of love. You should believe that there is no duality in friendship and that the newly arrived does not become eternal, but you also must be fair to the gentle gifts of *He loves them and they love Him* [5:54].

Your spirit mixed with my spirit
like wine mixed with clear water.
When something touches You, it touches me,
for You are I in every state.[980]

What Ḥusayn Manṣūr Ḥallāj is saying gives voice to the secret that is the goal of the *tawḥīd* of all the *tawḥīd*-voicers and the gazing place of all the lovers. Do you fancy that this was a secret arising from a piece of clay and *molded mud* [15:26]? No, this secret was beyond that piece of clay. *"I am the Real"* alludes not to clay and *molded mud* but to the beginningless welcome extended to him. In that welcome, he was pure of the gaze of mortal nature. Otherwise, the claim *"I am the Real"* does not rise up from the wherewithal of dust. The secret of these words is *"I am permanent through the Real."*

My father said, "God's love in *'He loves them'* does not attach to dust. His love attaches to His own beginningless gaze. After all, if the cause of love were dust, there was plenty of dust in the world, but nowhere was there any love."

He drew lots with His own power and we came forth. He took an omen from His own wisdom, and we appeared.

O dervish, when He looks at you, He looks at the decree of the beginningless, not the decree of dust. If He were to look at the decree of dust, He would take back your wherewithal. If every one of your hairs turned into an 'Azāzīl, every bodily member a Pharaoh, every speck a Nimrod, and every side a hell, once He called you, no one would have a thing to say.

Abū Sulaymān Dārānī wrote a letter to Abū Yazīd: "If someone is heedless during the day and sleeps at night, will he ever reach the waystation?"

Abū Yazīd answered, *"If the wind of solicitude blows, he will reach the waystation without trouble."*

He—*majestic is His majesty!*—sees a disobedient man and knows that he will repent. What He decrees for him derives from that repentance, not from the disobedience. He sees someone sinning right now, but He knows that he will become good, so He counts him among the wholesome, not the workers of corruption. *And We wrote in the Psalms, after the Remembrance, surely the earth will be inherited by My wholesome servants* [21:105].

In wrath Moses threw the tablets on the earth, but God, *who wrote them with His own hand*, did not rebuke him. Solomon hamstrung the innocent horses: *Then he fell to slashing their shanks and necks* [38:33].[981] God did not address him, for He was not looking at the outward deed; He was looking at the beginningless precedent.

Sometimes because of justice He takes to task for a straw, and sometime because of mercy He pardons a mountain. Because of power He takes to task for a straw and less than a straw, and because of mercy He pardons a mountain and more than a mountain.

"When We affirmed friendship for you in the Beginningless, We drew the line of pardon around you. If you had to be sinless, We would have created you sinless. We created you as you had to be."

The exalted ones have said, *"Do not rely on the affection of someone who loves you only when you are sinless."*[982] Have no confidence in the friendship of someone who loves you only as sinless.

"If We had affirmed sinlessness for you, only obedience and worship would have come from you. Disloyalty, faults, and slips would not have had the gall to circle around you. Then your loyalty in deeds and acquisition would have become My associate, but I am a Lord who has no associate. Just as I have no associate in essence, I have no associate in attributes. Whenever I love someone, I take care of his work and suffice him for his adversaries. *'When someone torments a friend, he is competing with Me in battle.'*[983] If anyone comes out against one of My friends, I will be his adversary.

"First it was the angels who spoke about you. They spoke the truth, but since they spoke about you, the address came to them, 'Wait now, are you talking about My friends? You know what they have with Me, but you do not know what I have with them. You know something of their deeds with Me, but you know nothing of My secrets with them.'

"You saw what happened to Harut and Marut: upside down until the resurrection, hanging thirsty above pure water. Both of them were wounded by defaming you.[984]

"You saw that Iblis said one word about you: *'I am better than he'* [38:76]. He became accursed forever. That blow was not because of refusing to prostrate. It was a blow because of his tongue's defamation."

The exalted Noah, the shaykh of the prophets, banged the kettledrum of the invitation for 950 years. A small group became Muslims. It is said that every day those stone-hearted people beat that paragon so much that he fell unconscious. When he came back to awareness, he would say, *"The praise belongs to God."*

Yes, the stronger a building has to be, the firmer they make the foundation and the stronger the clay. Noah's heart was constricted because of his people's disloyalty. He supplicated, *"My Lord, leave no disbeliever dwelling on the earth* [71:26]. Put water in charge and bring a storm into the world." The Exalted Lord commanded, "O heaven, listen, pour water! O earth, listen, bubble up water!" Every living thing in the world was destroyed. "The pain of My friend's heart reached its rightful due. I took revenge for the suffering of the heart of one of My friends."

He destroyed Nimrod, with all his height and breadth, with half a gnat. What is this? "Retribution for the pain in the heart of My Bosom Friend."

"O dervish, you are one of My friends. Rather, you are the most exalted of friends. Know for certain that I will take care of your work with My bounty."

God has a gentleness toward creatures
beyond that of mothers and fathers.[985]

Abū Yazīd said, *"I wonder at two states: I am poor, but You love me. You are unneedy, but You have chosen me."*[986]

"When someone chosen by Me is the locus of My secrets and the quarry of My lights while his heart is adorned with My remembrance, His work is My work. *Thy Lord creates what He wants and chooses* [28:68]."

It has been narrated from ʿAlī that he said, *"Neither compulsion nor delegation."*[987] You have not been pushed aside, nor have things been left to you. You are kept in the midst of these two. This is a chain, one end of which is joined to the Beginningless, the other end attached to the Endless. As long as that end does not move, this end will not move. *And God knows better.*

54. *al-Shahīd:* the Witness

Some say that this name means knower and some say that it means present. This is presence in the sense of knowledge, vision, and power. As for the presence that is proper to mortal attributes, the Exalted Lord is incomparable with that. *Nothing is as His likeness, and He is the Hearing, the Seeing* [42:11].

When a truthful, tawḥīd*-voicing person of faith believes with certainty that the various sorts of trial that pass over him and the cups of terrible loss that he drinks down occur in the presence of his Goal and that they are witnessed by the Object of his worship, he will receive the trial with kisses and will not go back to weeping and wailing. Thus in the story of Abraham, when he was put in the ballista, he paid no attention to any others and had no concern for the punishment and the fire, for he had perfect realization and full acknowledgment.*

He gave solace to all roasted hearts when He said, "I am the Witness of whatever happens to you."

And the unbelievers have an intense chastisement [42:26]. The reason for this is that the faithful also have a chastisement [*ʿadhāb*], but it is not intense; it is sweet [*ʿadhib*], for it is on top of contemplation. They tore apart the stomachs of those who were friends and broke the teeth of those who were enemies. Then the address came: *"Be patient with thy Lord's decree, for surely thou art in Our eyes"* [52:48]. Hence the paragon said, *"This is a mountain that loves us and that we love."*[988] On the day the drink of severity was sent to me, my boon companion was Uhud.

Trial for love is like flames for gold. Love without trial is like a pot without salt. Ḥusayn ibn Manṣūr Ḥallāj said,

> *By Your rightful due, multiply the trial*
> *and turn my heart toward what You love.*
> *When You have done all that to me*
> *and left no state of hope in Your servant,*
> *Then look: Have I turned my heart*
> *from what You love to something else?*[989]

The meaning of these verses is this: By Your rightful due, multiply my trial, open up the door of the storehouse of trial, and make trial come again and again. Make my heart the ball in the polo field of trial and send it wherever You want with the mallet of severity. When you have rained down trial's arrows on me, then look at me. If a speck of my heart has turned away from friendship, decree that Ḥusayn is the apostate of the Tariqah.

> Don't think I have a friend other than You,
> that my heart is prey to any but You.
> I'll never have a Lord other than You,
> though Your servants be without number.
> I'll pass my life in talk of You
> in the measure of my days.
> O settledness of my heart, don't ever think
> I've settled down in the world without You.
> If You desire to kill me like this,
> my only desire is what You desire.

The stipulation of a man in this road is that he must open up his spirit to abasement. Wherever he sees lowliness, he should buy it with his life. Wherever he sees a slap coming, he should put forth his neck. Wherever he sees a sword drawn, he should send his own life out to welcome it.

"It is not for the person of faith to abase himself."[990] But this does not contradict the words *"Perfect exaltation is found in abasement before His gate."*

> *I've been abased—how lovely the Abaser*
> *who makes shedding my blood lawful!*
> *When He exalts Himself, I accept Him*
> *with abasement—the effort of the destitute.*[991]

What His exaltedness does to this handful of dust! Do not put down your bags with *"Whoever seeks Me shall find Me,"*[992] for beneath it lies *"Magnificence is My cloak."*[993] Do not look at *He is with you wherever you are* [57:4], for along with it comes *high indeed is God, the King, the Real!* [20:114]. Do not put down the burden because of *faces that day radiant* [75:22], for His reins have been seized by *eyesights perceive Him not* [6:103]. Whatever is given by *He is the First* is snatched away by *He is the Last.* Whatever is shown by *He is the Outward* is effaced by *He is the Inward* [57:3].

What is all this? This is so that those who have faith and certainty will circle around the realms of hope with the mysteries of fear. You cannot say that you will not find, for the Shariah disputes that. Nor can you say that you will find, for exaltedness does not approve.

"O seekers, I am the Exalted. O strivers, I am the Magnificent. O wayfarers, I am the All-Compelling. O lovers, I am the God. Go out into the desert. Wherever you look, you will see little stones piled on top of each other marking the slain in My road. *'When His friendship kills someone, his wergild is his Lord. When His love kills someone, his wergild is His vision.'*[994] Whenever I kill someone through friendship, I give him vision as wergild.

When the vanguard of the army of blessings arrives, it seeks the threshold of the estranged. When the vanguard of the army of tribulation arrives, it seeks the corner of the exalted.

"Love" [محبت] and "tribulation" [محنت] have one form in writing, but they are distinguished by the dot. When a dot-worshiping man reaches Him, he looks at the dot. When a meaning-seeker reaches Him, He looks beyond the dot and throws his spirit into the work of meaning.

Surely love [hawā] is lowliness [hawān] itself—
you encounter lowliness when you love.
You meet abasement when you love,
so be meek toward your lover, whoever it may be.[995]

"O keepers of this world, have feasts and festivals! O exalted ones, have tribulation and tumult! One group is like that, one group like this. Yes, I give that to anyone, but I do not give this trial and tribulation to everyone. I gave the unfortunate Pharaoh four hundred years of kingship and well-being and did not disturb him. But, if he had wanted the pain, burning, and hunger of Moses for one hour, I would not have given it to him.

"Look at how far the blessings of this world go! That fellow has lifted his head high with a crown—give him a thousand! Then look at how far the violence of My tribulation goes! That one has fallen down—kick him in the head!"

The strikes of the Beloved do not hurt. If all the spirits of the seekers and the lovers gathered together to thank Him for the sword of His severity, they would not be able to do so. Suppose someone had asked Zachariah what he wanted at the moment they placed the saw on the crown of his head. The cries of yearning would have come forth from his parts and motes saying, "I want them to saw me forever!"

On the day the exalted ones of the Presence claimed love, they said farewell to safety and well-being. *"Let those who love the Folk of the House put on armor for trial—trial will reach our lovers more quickly than a flood reaching its settling place."*[996]

A dervish came to a khanaqah. The servant jumped up and pulled off his boots, then said, "Are you well?"

When the dervish heard this, he put his boots back on and said, "On the day I stepped into this road, I said farewell to well-being and placed the blame of the whole world in my heart."

As long as I live I'll serve the belt of Your tunic
and put my well-being into the work of Your trial.
If I have the gall, I'll sacrifice my life to You
and make my heart, eyes, and spirit the carpet of Your house.
If You have the thought to kill Your servant,
I'll be happy and joyful in Your subsistence.

A pigeon became ill in its cage. A cat came to visit and said, "How are you?"
The pigeon said, "I was fine until I saw you."

When you twist me with love's whispering,
my whole life turns into nothing.

When the burning of love appears, do not pull back your skirt, for if they want to burn your skirt, that's better than letting it be defiled.

A mouse fell down from the ceiling and a cat was sitting there. It said, *"Get up and be healthy."* The mouse said, *"You go away and I'll be healthy."*

And that He may try the faithful with a beautiful trial [8:17].

When that bit of prophethood [Fāṭima] came together with the quarry of chivalry [ʿAlī], two pearls appeared: *From the two will come forth the pearl and the coral* [55:22]. Muṣṭafā, the grandfather, was killed by poison. Ḥasan, the older child, was killed by poison. ʿAlī, the father, was killed by the sword. Ḥusayn, the younger child, was killed by the sword. *Benevolence is for beginners, but there is no benevolence for the great.*

You must stand like a dog at this threshold for a thousand years and become nothing but anticipation, without desire and choice, and perhaps they'll open the door and throw you a bone.

We may suppose that there are people who stand at the threshold for a thousand years wishing for the answer of dogs but are not given it. What answer is given to dogs? They stand at the door of the shop from morning to night, and then at night the door is shut and a stone is thrown in their face. But a dog will not go away because of a stone.

"O deprived one, from morning to night you sit before the shop with your eyes fixed on the door. Has a day ever come when they threw you a piece of meat?"

The dog says, "No, but they have my beloved in their hands."

Shiblī was the chieftain of his age. One day they saw him rolling in the dust and shouting. Then in the midst of that he was gesturing as if to say, "Take my hand." When he came back to his own present moment, they said, "O Shaykh, why were you saying, 'Take my hand'?"

He said, "Iblis was standing in front of me. I was seeing so much of my own nobodiness in the face of perfection and beauty that I held out my hand to Iblis and said, 'Take my hand.'

"He said to me, 'With this nobodiness and misfortune that belong to me, how can I take anyone's hand? I myself am searching for someone to whose saddle-straps I can tie myself.'

"I said, 'O accursed one, with all the wherewithal of severity that you have, can't you give a little comfort? Go, for it turns out that you are weak even in satanity.' "

O dervish, there are many who envy Iblis for being addressed without intermediary. It is rare for the Sultan to talk to anyone.

A word from you, did you but know,
would pull the bees from the moringa.[997]

There was a man who did a service for a sultan. The sultan said to him, "What do you want me to give you?"

He said, "Say something in my ear during the public audience. Even if it is all curses, that will complete my work."

Benevolence is for beginners, but there is no benevolence for the great. Leniency and mildness are for children. In the road of men, there is nothing but heart-piercing arrows and liver-burning fires. *Oceans are the storehouse of pearls, heaven is the storehouse of angels, mountains are the storehouse of gold and silver, the Gardens are the storehouse of houris, and the lovers' hearts are the storehouse of sorrows.*

Junayd was whispering in prayer and saying, *"Beloved, who has tried me with You?"*

Abu'l-ʿAbbās ʿAṭā used to say, *"Would that I had never recognized Him!"* Anyone who recognizes Him wreaks havoc on his own spirit.

Another pir said it like this: "What indeed would I have done had I not been? A hundred thousand thanks that I came to be and, when I was, I belonged to You."

Love's road goes forth in severity. At every moment the lover's food is a draft of poison. *Here we have Moses, seeking vision, and he was met with rejection. The mountain, however, was provided with self-disclosure, not having sought or asked. It had no excellence over Moses, but beloveds love to burn their lovers' hearts by exalting themselves above them.*

Muṣṭafā was taken on the *miʿrāj*. There were secrets that came into words and other secrets that did not come into words but were said with disconnected letters. Then there were secrets that did not come into letters.

Gabriel's road went no farther than the letters. It was said, "O peacock of the angels and worshiper at *the Lote Tree of the Final End* [53:14]! Now that the work has reached secrets that do not enter into the container of letters, bind the belt of a stirrup-holder and place the saddlecloth on your shoulders. Then, until he reaches your station, serve the paragon, for he is the peacock in the orchard of the Haqiqah, the nightingale in the garden of the Tariqah, and the phoenix in the house of the Shariah. When he goes beyond your station, stand still in bewilderment until he reaches the Presence behind the curtain of the unseen secret, a place reached by the imagination of neither angel nor mortal, before which fall short the perception of intellects and the comprehension of minds. We will speak secrets to him that do not fit into the container of letters and do not come under words." The Eternal Speech expressed this station like this: *"So he was two-bows' length away, or closer"* [53:9].

O chevalier, *Then he drew close* was without how, and *so He came down* [53:8] was without why. *He was two-bows' length away* was beyond imagination and *or closer* was beyond understanding.

The point is that first secret: *"Beloveds love to burn their lovers' hearts by exalting themselves above them."* Why are you looking at how he was taken like an exalted man and given many stations, generosities, gifts, and rarities? Are you looking at the beauty of the taking, or at the quickness of the bringing back? Wherever there is a blessing, it is spoiled by fear of disappearance.

Despite the enviers we spent the night with talk
like the scent of musk mixed with wine.
If some of that talk was revealed to the dead,
they would come to life in the grave.
I took her in hand and made her my bedmate
and said to the night, "Stay, for the moon has slept."
Then morning dawned and we parted—
which bliss is not darkened by time?[998]

*

My beloved visited me and we embraced all night,
but my trial and affliction dawned quickly.
Would that the revolving spheres turned back!
Would that God did not create the rising sun!

Muṣṭafā was kept for several years in anticipation. A bit was shown to him, then a corner of the curtain's edge was lifted. With a hundred thousand loves and burnings he saw a flash, but again the curtain was let down. Gabriel was brought into the midst, the curtain was lifted, and the work of open hostility was given over to him. Then for seventeen days and nights it was said to Gabriel, "Hold back your steps," and the enemies and adversaries let loose their tongues and said, *"Surely Muḥammad's Lord hates him and has forsaken him."*[999]

"Undergo all these little sufferings in the state of separation and the days of anticipation and see these tribulations of the days. Now that these troubles and tribulations have been removed and eliminated, you have arrived at *two-bows' length away*. The moment you come, go back! The moment you put your foot down, lift it up! The moment you arrive, turn around!"

What is this? "This is a custom We have set down. When separation comes, it comes like the mountains, which do not travel. When union comes, it comes like the wind, which has no stopping place."

Our assignment was when night's cloak came down,
but at its longest the night was the blink of an eye.
Now she's left and my night is her sacrifice—
night with hardship, morning without anticipation.[1000]

*

I spend my nights without sleep
complaining to him and thanking him.
Ardor lengthens the night,
but the beloved shortens it.
Many are my sins,
but excess love forgives them.
I conceal love for him from the slanderers,
but my tears make it manifest.
I remember my arguments when I'm alone,
but I forget them when I see him.[1001]

When he was taken, many intermediaries were placed in the midst. First Burāq, then the *mi ʿrāj*, then the Canopy, then Gabriel's wings, then the pure Unseen. In the road he saw the prophets. When he came back, nowhere was there the *mi ʿrāj*, the Canopy, seeing the prophets, talk of Jerusalem, or mention of heaven and earth. Yes, when a man wants to go before the sultan, they hold him back in various waiting rooms, for his aim is the presence. But once he sees the sultan and comes out, they don't hold him back anywhere.

Yes, he did see Moses in coming back, but that was not to show Moses to him, but to show him to Moses. What was that showing? They sprinkled a bit of salt on the wound of *thou shalt not see Me* [7:143] so that the secret of His exalting Himself would become apparent.

The Prophet was taken with many intermediaries, but he was brought back without any intermediary. This is because when separation comes, it comes all at once, but when union comes, it comes by degrees with many intermediaries and means. When Jacob was afflicted with separation from Joseph, this was done once. They said, "A wolf destroyed your son." When the days became favorable and luck came to his aid, auspiciousness sent the breeze of good fortune and arrival as the vanguard of union. First he smelled the scent, then he saw the shirt, and then he heard the news. Then it was said, "O great pir and exalted man of the era, get on a frail donkey, travel for many farsakhs, and go to Egypt! And O young Joseph, sit in your house with a hundred thousand means and supplies, for the custom of love's road does not look at sonship and fatherhood! Wherever love arrives, it puts down the sword and looks at neither son nor father."

Then that exalted pir was coming along, sitting on a little donkey, a handful of children out in front.

"O Joseph, now rise up and bring the army. Put seventy chamberlains in front and prepare an army for each of them. And multiply the beauty of your natural disposition by means of adornment, for *beauty is one-third constitution and two-thirds adornment.*"

Jacob was coming while yearning for Joseph. He had been hoping for eighty years. Then he found the scent, then the shirt reached him, and then he was like an exile who had come from a little corner to a vast plain while the beloved showed him a hundred thousand coquetries.

O much in coquetry, rare in form,
wondrous in beauty, unique in loveliness!
I'm happy with your servant's servant as patron,
so take me as servant of your servant's servant.

Whenever he reached a chamberlain he said, "Is this my Joseph?" and it was said, "He's one of his serving boys." When they had passed seventy chamberlains, Jacob said, "Why is today a day of arranging the army? Why is it a day of presenting the troops?"

"O Jacob, it has been My custom that I do not allow the lover one glance at the Beloved's beauty until I knock on the door of his eyes with the controlling power of the watchers and the intermediating thorns of severity and spoil his days with the turbidity of companionship with others."

What a marvelous business! A hundred thousand diverse states were brought into the world, but they were not created in one guise or one attribute. If He had wanted, He would have done so, but He did not. *Had We willed, We would have given every soul its guidance* [32:13]. "Had I wanted, I would have made this work all the same. Had I wanted, I would have clothed the world in one robe. Had I wanted, I would have created these creatures from the mother of good fortune. But this business must be diverse so that hearts may be filled with tumult and burning. Then they will recognize the worth of love's road." *Peace!*

55–56. *al-Ḥaqq al-Mubīn:* the Real, the Clarifier

The Real: the existent that can never undergo annihilation. The Clarifier: He who makes the Real appear from the unreal by means of marks, without bias or caprice.

When the faithful, *tawḥīd*-voicing, believing servant with certainty knows that the existent in reality is the Possessor of Majesty, he must recognize with certainty that for him to claim existence would be absurd. An existence whose limits pull to nonexistence is a nonexistence. These words are appropriate for a man whose feet are firmly fixed.

It is said that Qāḍī Shurayḥ bought a house in Kufa. When the news reached the Commander of the Faithful, ʿAlī, he said to Shurayḥ, "I heard that you bought a house and brought a few just men as witnesses." He said that he had. ʿAlī said, *"O Shurayḥ, be wary of God, for one is coming who will not look at your document or ask about your house.* O Shurayḥ, fear God and abstain, for you will soon reach the point when no one will look at your title deed or question your witnesses. You will be taken from the house, and the house from you. O Shurayḥ, if you had reported to me at the time of buying the house and writing out the title deed, *I would have written the deed for you with this inscription.* I would have written the deed for you with an inscription such that if anyone looked at the deed at the price of two barleycorns, he would not have bought it."

Shurayḥ said, "What would you have written, O Commander of the Faithful?"

He said, "I would have written, 'In the name of God, the All-Merciful, the Ever-Merciful. This is what an abased servant bought from a dead man, who was driven away from his house by departure. A man deceived by hopes bought it from a man driven away by death. This is a house bought by someone seized by greed and wishes from someone taken from its door by the steed of annihilation and death. A man conversing with wishes bought it from a man heedless of death. *It is a house in the quarter of delusion*, on the side of annihilation, in the sector of the perishing. *It has four boundaries. The first boundary ends up at the summoners to blights, the second boundary ends up at the summoners to maladies, the third boundary ends up at the summoners to afflictions, and the fourth boundary ends up at harmful caprice and Satan who leads astray.* The first boundary opens up to the occasions of blight, the second boundary opens up to the accidents of trial, the third boundary opens up to the calamities of affliction, and the fourth boundary ends up at destructive caprice and the satan that takes from the road. *From this boundary the door of the house leads to emergence from the exaltedness of contentment and entrance into the abasement of avarice. If the buyer seeks a guarantee of indemnification, that will be upon Him who destroyed the bodies of kings and stripped away the souls of tyrants like Chosroes, Caesar, Tubbaʿ, and Jamshid. As for those who built it, raised it up, and gazed in their opinion on the house, He will bring them forth tomorrow when the two worlds are made to appear for the differentiation of the decree. Those bearing witness to this will be intellect when it is freed from the bonds of caprice and recognition when it is delivered from the fetter of wishes.* The witnesses over this title deed are intellect and recognition once delivered from the bonds of caprice and freed from the fetters of malice, the trap of pleasure, and the shackles of this person and that. *Nothing will repel death, and we await its attack on the flow of the breaths.* Even if we suppose that your life span is endless, annihilation is right behind you.' "[1002]

Muṣṭafā said to Ibn ʿUmar, *"Be in this world as if you are an exile or a passerby."*[1003] Exiles and passersby always have their heart on their native land and home.

He also said, "When light enters the heart, it becomes spacious and dilated."

It was said, "O Messenger of God, what is the mark of that?"

He said: "Withdrawal from the house of delusion."[1004]

Muṣṭafā said, "When brightness enters the heart, the heart opens up and becomes spacious." By this light he meant the light of faith, by opening he meant contemplation, and by spaciousness he meant putting up with trial, for the more spacious a container, the more it holds.

They said, "What is the mark of this?"

He said, "Going far from the house of delusion." Thus he called this world the house of deception.

Someone said, *"This would be happiness were it not delusion and it would be property were it not perishing."*[1005]

This world is people's beloved enemy. When someone is niggardly toward it, it is munificent toward him. Even if it remains for you, you do not remain for it. Fie upon its occupations when you turn toward it, and fie on its regrets when you turn away from it! He who finds it is drunk, and he who loses it is bewildered. The thing most similar to this world is the dreams of a sleeper. This world bestows upon you not to make you happy but to make you sad. When someone inclines toward this world, it attacks him, and when someone attacks it, it inclines toward him.[1006]

"This world is Satan's wine. When someone drinks of it, he does not come back to himself except among the army of the dead, failed and lost."[1007]

"It is a woman who responds to every suitor and a docile animal that carries anyone who mounts it."

In a report it has come that on the Day of Resurrection, this world will come forth adorned and say, *"O God, make me the reward for the meanest of Your servants."*

He will say, "O lowly, O nothing, I do not approve of you for him."[1008]

Shiblī said, "If the whole of this world were made a morsel and put into the mouth of a suckling infant, I would pity it, for it would still be hungry."

The great ones of the Tariqah and the foremost of the Haqiqah took nothing of this world except what should not be abandoned. Covering the private parts and a piece of bread—the servant will not be rebuked and punished for this much of this world, but rather rewarded.

It was said to Ḥasan Baṣrī, "This world has been forbidden. What should we do?"

He said, "Eat when needed and eat moderately." Take according to need and from the middle. If it is more than covering the private parts and blocking hunger, then the servant is taking it as his own portion, but portions [*naṣīb*] are mixed with hardship [*naṣab*]. In the case of that much, he will not be taking for himself but rather for what is rightfully due. If he does not cover his private parts, he will be held back from service, for the prayer is not permitted when the privates are exposed. *God says, "Put on your adornment at every place of prostration"* [7:31]. And if someone does not eat enough to stop his hunger, he will be destroyed. *God says, "And cast not yourselves with your own hands into destruction"* [2:195].

One of the exalted ones said this: "I searched my master's bag and found a piece of silver in the measure of a halfpenny. I was surprised that my master had concealed that silver from us. When the master came, I said, 'What is the story behind this?'

"He said, 'In my whole life, this is what I have been given of this world. I wanted to place it with myself in the grave, so that if I am asked for an accounting, I will say that I have brought back what You gave to me.' "[1009]

In short, the reality is that whatever the great ones of the religion and the lords of certainty do, they do for the rightful due, not for themselves. They put all their own desires off to the side and choose what the Real desires.

Beware, beware, in no way should you suppose that Solomon was looking at this lowly world! This is indicated by the fact that one day the wind took the carpet of his kingship so close to heaven that the voices of the angels reached his ears. An angel said to an angel, "How great a servant is Solomon that he has been brought to this high place!"

Another said, "If his secret core were gazing on one iota of this, he would have been taken down as far as he has been brought up."

It is said that one day the wind was taking his carpet in the air. A thought passed through his mind and a gaze came into his eyes. The thought was still in its place when the wind turned his throne around. He said, "O wind, go straight!"

It said, "As long as you keep your heart straight, I will keep the throne straight."

He said, "My Lord, forgive me and give me a kingdom that will not befit anyone after me" [38:35]. This verse was recited before Ḥajjāj and he said, *"He was envious,"*[1010] but this is wrong. As for the realizers, by means of this verse they have brought out pearls of the mind from the oceans of consciousness and put them around the neck of the folk of *tawḥīd.*

"Will not befit anyone after me." In other words, "No one will overpower me in it as Satan overpowered me."[1011] Concerning the cause of Satan's overpowering him, the scholars have said various things. Some have said, *"He fought a war against a king and was victorious. He took the king's offspring prisoner, and among them was his daughter, whom he chose for himself. She asked his permission to have a statue of her father for consolation and solace. He had fallen in love with her, so he gave her permission." They have said, "So she carved an idol and began to prostrate herself to it instead of to God. When God made that manifest to him, he came to know that he had slipped by giving her permission without consultation. So it was said to him, 'Prepare for trials.'"*

It has been narrated from Ibn ʿAbbās that he said, "Solomon was tried by the loss of his kingship for forty days because of the idol that had been worshiped in his house. So he said, 'My Lord, forgive me and give me a kingship that will not befit anyone after me.' In other words, no one will overpower me in it as Satan overpowered me."[1012]

The miracle of Solomon was his seal, but his seal was separable, and Muḥammad's seal was attached.[1013] When the seal went from his hand, no matter to whom he said, "I am Solomon," he was not believed. What a pure Lord who gives a servant exaltedness but constantly shows him his incapacity!

Solomon was working for the fishermen in the ocean because he was not finding any food. When the people accused the satan and opened the Torah before it, it threw the seal into the ocean and flew off in the air. When God desired to give Solomon's kingship back to him, a fish swallowed his seal. It fell into their nets and they gave it to Solomon as part of his wages. He split open its stomach and saw his seal. He put it on, and the sailors prostrated themselves to him. Then he went back to the throne of his kingship.[1014]

Listen to the story of Solomon! Here you have Solomon, who has lost his ring; and here you have a dervish, who has lost his heart. Your heart is like Solomon, afflicted by apprenticeship to the base and servanthood to the mean. Which day will it be when the wind of divine aid, the breeze of good fortune, and the gusts of limpidness begin to blow? Then, just as Solomon reached the throne of his kingship, the heart-Solomon will rise from the station of abasement and reach the throne of the secret core's happiness by contemplating His bounty.

There is also something more beautiful than this: *"Will not befit anyone after me," for anyone else will not stand up for the Real in it, so he will not act in obedience to God.*

There is something more exalted than this: *"Will not befit anyone after me"* who asks for the kingship; rather, he should rely upon God in what He chooses for him.

There is something higher than this: *Solomon knew that the secret core of our Prophet would have no regard for this world and its flowers. Hence he said, "Will not befit anyone after me." It is not that he was being niggardly with it in relation to our Prophet, but he knew that he would not gaze upon it.*

"So We subjected to him the wind" [38:36]. *God was grateful for his effort and subjected the wind to him in place of horses so that he would have no need to keep them with provisions.*[1015]

"O Solomon, you have made horses a path in God's road. Here you have the wind subjected to you in place of horses!" *And the wind was Solomon's, its morning course a month and its evening course a month* [34:12].

"O Jaʿfar Ṭayyār, you sacrificed your two hands. Now We have given you two wings so that you may circle around Firdaws with the pinions of victory and the wings of good fortune.[1016] O man of faith, you have put the plugs of deafness in your ears lest it hear idle talk and nonsense. You have placed the bridle of wisdom on your tongue lest it backbite. You have bound your eyes with the blindfold of veneration lest it gaze upon others. What is your recompense and gift? *'When I love him, I am for him hearing, eyesight, tongue, and hand.'* "[1017]

"So We subjected to him the wind, which ran softly at his command" [38:36]. *It is described as* soft *because the "fierce"* [1018] *is for chastisement.* The blowing wind made its top into a throne for him. It lifted up the carpet of his realm and placed the birds wing to wing: one bright yellow, another dark black, another pure white. It pulled up a shimmering pavilion like silk on top of which it rotated a parasol so that the assault of the sun's heat would not fall on Solomon's beautiful face. A soft wind came under the carpet and carried the carpet on its own head such that not one thread of the carpet moved.

[*And of the jinn some worked before him by his Lord's permission .... They were making for him whatever he wanted—places of worship, statues,*] *basins like water troughs, and anchored cauldrons* [34:12–13].

"O son of David, though We have bestowed upon you a tremendous empire, there is no reason for Me to praise Myself or call Myself its bestower: *This is Our gift, so bestow or withhold without reckoning* [38:39]."

Antimony from the gaze of subsistence was daubed on his eyes. In annihilation itself he saw subsistence. He said, "O Lord God, take it back, for it has no worth for me."

A call came, "O son of David, contradiction and disparity are not allowed in Our words. We have always spoken and will always speak. From time to time We will lift away the veil from your ears so that you may hear Our words. This is what We have bestowed. In Our generosity it is not fitting to take back what We have bestowed. If you do not want it, give it to one of your stirrup-holders. If you want it, keep it without reckoning or sin."

What a marvelous business! One person has a kingdom and empire from the moon down to the Fish. Another has a burnt heart and no power over a crust of burnt bread. He reports about the realm of Solomon and alludes to the tribulation of Job: *"And remember Our servant Job, when he called out to his Lord: 'Surely Satan has touched me with weariness and chastisement.' 'Stamp thy foot: here is a cool washing place and drink'* " [38:41–42]. About Solomon, who had the throne of kings and the kingdom of the earth under his seal, He said, *"How excellent a servant! He was penitent"* [38:30]. And about Job, whose makeup was a quarry of trial and a locus of trouble, He said, *"How excellent a servant! He was penitent"* [38:44]. *This is because trial did not distract the latter from the Trial-Giver, and gifts did not distract the former from the Gift-Giver. They were penitent toward God in blessings with gratitude and in tribulation with patience.*

It is said that Job had all sorts of property and blessings and many horses and retinue. *Iblis envied him and said, "Surely this man desires to triumph in both this world and the next world," so he desired to corrupt one of the two houses for him. In utmost envy and extreme distress the accursed one said, "Surely Your servant Job worships You because you give him abundance in this world. If it were not for that, he would not worship You."*[1019]

The skin of that one cursed in the Beginningless became full of irritation. He opened the eye of envy and said to himself, "Job wants to take a share from both this world and the next world." He said, "Job's worship is mixed with the causality of bestowal and blessing."

God said, "Surely I know from him that he would worship Me and be grateful to Me even if he did not have abundance in this world."

He said, "O Lord, give me power over him." So God gave him power over everything he had except his spirit. Iblis came to his flocks and blew into them in the guise of fire, destroying all his flocks. His tenants came and reported that to him. He praised God and said, "It is He who gave, and it is He who took, and it is He who has more right to it."

It is also said that Iblis burned his flocks and tenants and then came to him in the guise of a tenant and reported what had happened. Job said, "Were there any good in you, He would have destroyed you along with your companions, for it may be that a servant without sins is tried in order to store up reward for him."

It is said that he had seven daughters and three sons in one grammar school. Satan pulled down a column and the house collapsed on them. All these trials appeared while his tongue stayed wet with praise and laudation.

"And Job, when he called out to his Lord, 'Harm has touched me'" [21:83] by cutting me off from Your service. His words were not by way of complaint, for the Exalted Lord lauded him: *"Surely We found him patient. How excellent a servant he was! He was penitent"* [38:44].

It has also been said that God's enemy passed by him and said, "How wretched is Job's soul!" At that he said, "Harm has touched me" from the enemy's schadenfreude.

It is related that Ḥasan said, "Job stayed seven years and some months, thrown down in refuse with crawling things frequenting him." He did not ask God to remove what had come to him. There was no one on the face of the earth more honored by God than Job.

Someone said, "If Job's Lord had known any good in him, He would not have done this to him." At that point he said, "Harm has touched me."[1020]

There is also something more beautiful than this: *"Harm has touched me"* was by way of asking: *"Has harm touched me along with Thee, when 'Thou art the most merciful of the merciful'* [21:83]*?" Thus the meaning is, "Harm will not touch me so long as I recognize You."*

And there is something even more beautiful: That was the lamentation of trial because of Job's patience. *Trial was given ruling power over all, so they all sought help against trial. Then Job's patience was given ruling power over trial, so trial called out and sought help against Job's patience.*

There is something more subtle than this: *"Harm has touched me*: If I say I will have patience with trial, they will say that he is tough. If I say that I have no patience, they will say that he is wailing and protesting. If I say, 'Remove the trial,' they will say that this is taking control. But there is no way for these three. The way of deliverance is only Your mercy, *and Thou art the most merciful of the merciful."*

And there is something more exalted than this: A worm fell off of him. He took a stick and pushed it away from himself. A call came, "O Job, that is an eater of daily bread whose sustenance We have brought out from your makeup. Are you going to block the road of its daily bread?" When he heard this address, he lifted up the animal and put it back in its place. The address came, *"Are you showing manliness from yourself when We send down Our trial upon you?"* At that point Job said, " *'Harm has touched me.' There is no settledness with Thee and no escape from Thee."*

He brought Satan into war against Job and the soul against us. Satan said, "This man with all these blessings—if he did not worship You, what else would he do?" His possessions were all destroyed, as the story makes clear.

Job said, "O God, You brought the enemy into war with me and gave him the weapon of trial. What is my weapon?"

He said, "I have made patience your weapon."

Iblis struck Job with trial, and he fell into patience. With patience Job fell into ease, but with Job patience fell into trial. Patience seized Job's tongue from him and said, *"Harm has touched me."* Job himself was neither with patience nor with trial—he was with the Real.

He brought the soul into war with us. The heart battled against the soul, whose weapons are caprice and appetite. The heart said, "I too must have weapons."

It was said, "Your weapons are approval and love."

The soul struck the heart with caprice and threw it into hell. When the friend reached hell, he was at ease from hell, but hell was in trial from him. It asked for aid: "O Lord, deliver me from him!" The friend himself was in neither paradise nor hell, but *in a seat of truthfulness at an Omnipotent King* [54:55].

Virtue was mixed with fault. The virtue of Zulaykhā was friendship, and her fault was that she was ungodly. Zulaykhā was not mistaken in the root of friendship—she was mistaken in the road of friendship. "We have forgiven the mistake of the branch because of the correctness of the root. You were not mistaken in *tawḥīd's* root, you were mistaken in *tawḥīd's* road. I look at the correctness of the root, not the mistake of the graft. I lift off the garment of disobedience and put on the garment of forgiveness.

"Zulaykhā was an unbeliever. She loved My friend, and she hated Me. I did not look at her hatred of Me, I looked at her friendship for My friend and gave her the gift of faith. Bilqīs was an unbeliever. She loved Solomon and I gave her faith. Khadīja was an unbeliever. She loved Muṣṭafā and I gave her faith. O you who have faith, it is now seventy years that you beat the drum of love for Me. Will I take away your faith?"

As for "Clarifier," from the concealment of nonexistence He brings into appearance the wonders, artifacts, marvels, and curiosities that have not occurred to anyone's thoughts or been found by anyone's mind. He brings into appearance the precedent love through the subsequent blessings. This love was curtained by the concealment of nonexistence, and He made it famous by His gentleness, filling the hearts of the lovers with the light of the secrets of recognition.

57–58. *al-Wakīl al-Qawī:* the Trustee, the Strong

Wakīl means sufficient, it means guardian, and it means guarantor. Some have said that the meaning of *wakīl* is the person to whom you turn over all your work. *The Arabs say, "I entrusted the affair to so-and-so, so he is my trustee." Here the meaning of the pattern* fa'īl [*wakīl*] *is* maf'ūl [*mawkūl*, trusted].

In short, know that anyone who turns his work over to Him will reap the fruit of the *goodly life* [16:97]. *"The heart's reliance on the assurance of the Unseen"* is a tremendous pillar, *"lifting away suspicion from the precedent apportioning"* is a straight path, *"rejecting free choice through truthful poverty"* is the center-point of the compass of the Tariqah, and *"stopping with sufficiency and believing that seeking is a sin"* is the pivot of the secrets of the Haqiqah.[1021]

The Companions of the Cave delegated all to Him, and without any cause a breeze from the world of surrender blew on their dog. Then the Real gave them a place in the cave of jealousy, the shade of solicitude, the embrace of friendship, and the world of protection. *Thou wouldst have seen the sun, when it rose, turning aside from their cave to the right, and when it set, passing them by on the left, while they were in a space within it. That is among the signs of God. Whomsoever God guides, he is guided; and whomsoever He misguides, thou wilt find for him no rightly guiding friend* [18:17]. *Thou wouldst have thought them awake, but they were asleep. And We turned them now to the right, now to the left. And their dog was extending its paws at the doorstep. Hadst thou looked down upon them, surely thou wouldst have turned away from them fleeing, and thou wouldst have been filled with terror from them* [18:18].

He set up a pavilion of awesomeness over their secret cores such that the radiance of the lights of their elevated suns prevented the sun itself from having the gall to exercise its ruling authority over them. *"When it rose, turning aside," that is, inclining away from their cave toward "the right, and when it set, passing them by on the left," that is, turning aside from them while they were in a broad "space" in the cave; "thou wouldst have thought them awake, but they were asleep." It is said that their eyes were open, but they were sleeping such that the earth did not eat their flesh.*

If someone declares himself quit of free choice and contrivance, if his states are truthful in his return to God, and if he has no need for his likes and similars among those other than God, then God will shelter him in the embrace of His good fortune, suffice him in all of his occupations, and, with His perfect beauty, prepare for him a place in the shade of His bounteousness.[1022]

The shining sun had not the gall to circle around the cave of their jealousy. The lights of the manifest sun were incapable and stationary in relation to their lights and secret cores, for the lights of the sun are for the benefit of the creatures, and the lights of their secret cores were for recognizing the Real.

The light of the sun was the light of form, but the light of their hearts was the light of the secret core. When the light of the sun reached them, it was consumed by their light. In one place the sun was consumed by the inward light and in another place it was consumed by the inward fire. *When the radiance of the sun reached them, it turned aside from them and shriveled before them.*[1023] When the radiance of the sun reached them, it pulled back its skirt from the shining radiance of their love's sun.

Thou wouldst have thought them awake, but they were asleep. You would have fancied that they were awake, but they were sleeping. This is the attribute of the folk of the Tariqah. When you look at their outward selves, you see them busy in the playing fields of deeds. When you look at their secret cores, you see them detached in the scented gardens of the gentleness of the Possessor of Majesty. Outwardly busy with deeds, they gaze inwardly on the gentleness of the Beginningless. With *Thee alone we worship* [1:5] they have bound the belt of struggle, and with *Thee alone we ask for help* [1:5] they have placed the crown of contemplation on their heads. Their activity conforms to the command, and their vision conforms to the decree. On the inside they wear the shirt of surrender, and on the outside they have pulled down the robe of deeds.

"And We turned them now to the right, now to the left." This was not like the tenderness of mothers, but more complete; not like the mercy of fathers, but more exalted.[1024] How should the tenderness of mothers and the mercy of fathers become apparent in this turning and nurturing?

What a marvelous business! "I said about the Companions of the Cave, '*Surely they were chevaliers who had faith in their Lord, and We increased them in guidance*' [18:13]." He called them *chevaliers* without any service on their part. And that other one [Balaam], who knew the most tremendous name and saw everything from the Throne down to the ground, He called a dog. He showed the worldlings that "Proximity is by My caressing; it is not caused by service. Distance is by My command's disdain; it is not caused by disobedience."

The fact that He chose the dog of the Companions of the Cave is the clearest indicator and the most lucid evidence that He does not choose because of any cause, nor does He select because of any stratagem. The lowliness of the dog's measure and the impurity of its root did not hold it back from elevation, nor from coming together with the folk of proximity to Him and union with Him. "God does what He wills" [14:27] *and "He decrees what He desires"* [5:1], *no matter what rebellious Satan thinks.*

He says in the firm text of His Book, "And their dog was extending its paws at the doorstep" [18:18]. O dervish, until the resurrection people will be saying that a dog took a few steps in the tracks of the Real's friends: *"And their dog was extending its paws."* When a Muslim with burning and faith becomes the companion of the Real's friends for seventy years and takes the blackness of youth to the whiteness of old age, do you suppose that the Real will make him despair on the Day of Resurrection? *Surely He will not do that.*

The fatwa of the Shariah says about the dog's skin, *"A dog is most polluted when it is washing itself."*[1025] But when it spreads its feet on the doorstep, this spreading does not go to waste. When a truthful lover has lifted up his hands for seventy years, do you suppose that his lifting of hands will go to waste? *Surely that will not happen—by the rightful due of this world of motion and rest!*

O dervish, anyone who follows in the tracks of lions will eat the stew of onager.

> He'll keep on eating onager stew,
>   having tracked the lions on the plain.

At first they struck the dog, then they carried it on their shoulders. *Such it is when someone follows in the tracks of lovers.*[1026] In the stories it has come that the Exalted Lord brought that little thing into speech with them, and its speech caused the tie on their hearts. Thus He reports, *"And We placed a tie on their hearts"* [18:14], that is, "We guarded them in their submission." When the marks bearing witness to the Unseen flashed in their hearts, thought of doubt packed its bags.

That little thing said, "Why are you beating me?"

They said, "So that you will go back."

It said, "He who brought you has brought me. The same entrusted angel that was sent to unsettle you was sent to me."

They said, "What is the proof of this claim?"

O companions of expansive claims, meaning is sought from dogs. Won't it also be sought from you? The dog said, "It is that you flee from trial and I cling to trial. Your trial is from enemies, but my trial is from you, and you are friends."[1027]

Hadst thou looked down upon them, surely thou wouldst have turned away from them fleeing. "Looking down" is said for someone who looks from above, but when someone looks from below, it is not said that he is looking down. "O Muḥammad, if you had looked at them, you would have fled from them and your heart would have been full of fear." Here there is room for obscurity. What do you say? Was the state of the Companions of the Cave such that the Seal of the Prophets should fear them, when the title page of his glory and majesty was *"I was aided by terror"*?[1028] *No, never.* These words are addressed to Muṣṭafā, but others are meant. There are many similar instances, such as, *"O Prophet, be wary of God!"* [33:1]; *"If thou takest associates, thy deeds will surely fail"* [39:65].

There is also something more beautiful than this. Yes, Muṣṭafā is being addressed: " *'Hadst thou looked down upon them' in respect of thyself." He did not say, "Had I made thee look down upon them."* "If you had looked, O Muḥammad, you would have feared them. But when I did the showing, the whole world feared you. *'I was aided by terror at a month's journey.'* They heard Me through you." Months pass when smoke does not rise from Muṣṭafā's chambers, but in fear of him, Caesar and Chosroes have neither sleep nor settledness.

They sent terror into the enemies' hearts,
as if the battle was before the encounter.[1029]

And there is something more exalted than this. *"Hadst thou looked down upon them"*: If you had looked at them from the upper reaches of your blessings, the balcony of your eminence, and the castle of your sight, *"surely thou wouldst have turned away from them fleeing," that is, in scorn, not because their place is higher than your place.* "O Muḥammad, if you had seen them, you would have fled, not in the sense that they were greater than you, for if they were greater than you, they would have been looking down upon you, not you upon them. Rather, this is the fleeing of scorn and contempt, not the fleeing of reverence and fear. If you had looked at them from the station of your eminence and rulership, the height of your majesticness, the bravery of your messengerhood, and the strength of your prophethood, you would have been frightened and you would have said, 'What will I do if I am brought back to the station that they have?' " When a sultan is brought down to the level of beggars, he is not happy with that.

"The station of these cave-dwellers is great, but for other than you. You are greater than that anything can be great for you, for *'To revere a being derives from scorning Him who gave it being.'*

"O you who are the part of which I am the whole, and O you who are the whole of which the creatures are the part! Look at the creatures to see your wholeness! Look at Me to see your partness! Do you fear anyone? Do you flee from anyone? No, for compared with the shining face of your good fortune, all the world's shine is disgrace. You are not like Moses, who fainted when I shook the mountain; nor like Solomon, who became a fisherman when I took the kingdom from him; nor like Noah, who needed a ship to be delivered from drowning; nor like Jesus, who needed Gabriel to take him to heaven. *Glory be to Him who took His servant by night!* [17:1]."

"Be firm, Ḥirā', for none are upon you but prophet, sincerely truthful, and witness."[1030]

"The earth was brought together for me, and I was shown its eastern parts and its western parts."[1031]

You can also say that what is desired by these words is not instilling fear into Muṣṭafā but showing the greatness of their state. People often say, "So-and-so had such a trial that, had you seen it, you would have fainted." By saying this, they want to show the greatness of that work, not to declare the truth of the words. In this meaning the Exalted Lord said to Muṣṭafā, *"Hadst thou looked down upon them, surely thou wouldst have turned away from them."* By this He wanted to show the greatness of their state. But as the chieftain of the envoys, no, he would never fear them.

Their likeness is as Muṣṭafā said: *"Do not consider me more excellent than my brother Jonah son of Mattā."*[1032] He also said, *"Anyone who says that I am better than he has uttered a lie."*[1033] But there is no disagreement in the community that Muṣṭafā was more excellent than Jonah. Nonetheless, the prophetic wisdom in these words is that the Real mentioned things in the story of Jonah in the splendorous scripture such that there is fear that the servants will have a bad opinion of him. For example, He says, *"And Dhu'l-Nūn, when he went forth wrathful"* [21:87]. The Messenger said that when his community hears this verse, they should not have a bad opinion of him or look upon him with the eyes of contempt. That bad opinion would harm their religion. Even though Muṣṭafā was more excellent than he and all the messengers, he said, *"Do not consider me more excellent than Jonah."* His desire was not to scorn himself but to show reverence for Jonah, so that everyone would look upon him with the eyes of reverence.[1034] Thus He addressed His prophet with the words *"Hadst thou looked down upon them, surely thou wouldst have turned away from them,"* so that the people would look at them with the eyes of reverence and their religion would not be harmed.

And there is something higher than this: *"Hadst thou looked down upon them, surely thou wouldst have turned away from them fleeing," that is, you would have turned away from the creatures and turned toward Us. You would have been filled with terror because you were occupied with abandoning other than Us.* O fleer from creation, O seeker of Me! *"Had I taken a bosom friend, I would have taken Abū Bakr as a bosom friend; as for your companion, he is God's bosom friend."*[1035]

"Thou wouldst have turned away from them fleeing," that is, from seeing them toward seeing Us, for you cannot put up with seeing other than Us. "If I took you to heaven, I did not take you to show you heaven. I took you to show you to the heaven-dwellers. I have a great secret with you. Anyone who is unaware of that secret will be deluded by his own greatness. Earth admired itself and said, 'In me are trees, rivers, lakes, and gardens.' Heaven admired itself and said, 'In me are the pageants of the planets, the shooting stars, the sun, the moon, the angels, the *tawḥīd*-reciters,

and the glorifiers.' Paradise admired itself and said, 'In me are the chambers, marvels, gifts, houris, and palaces.' Hell admired itself and said, 'In me are many sorts of chastisement and punishment.' The Tablet admired itself and said, 'In me are so much decree and destiny.' The Pen admired itself and said, 'When the secrets appear from behind the curtains of the Unseen, I write them out.' The Footstool said, 'I am so great that it is expressed like this: *His Footstool embraces the heavens and earth* [2:255].' The Throne said, 'I am so tremendous that next to me the two worlds are like a single seed of wild rue.'

"All of them had self-admiration in their heads because of their greatness. They were unaware of your greatness, so I wanted to show your secret core's greatness to them. I sent Burāq. This world adorned itself and sat in the road of the paragon, just like a beggar sits in the road. The paragon paid no attention. 'Yes, I have a thousand thousand serving boys who, if you put the whole of this world before them, would not want it. I who am their lord would never want it.'

"O this world, have you seen his aspiration's greatness and your own nonbeing next to it? Now empty your head of the wind of arrogance, and '*serve anyone who serves Me.*'[1036]

"I brought him to heaven. All of heaven gazed upon him, and the secret of their prostration came out into the open after having been curtained. The mirrors of all their faces were behind him, and all were bewildered and perplexed by his beauty. He passed by all of them, having no reason to look to the right or the left. They said, 'Who is this with such greatness?'

"It was said to them, 'This is he whose name is paired with the formula of *tawḥīd*. The two worlds are his serving boy and the springtime of the Shariah and the Tariqah is his days. This is he whose name is there when you pass by *no god but God*. This is he than whom none is greater after Me.'

"I took him to hell and showed him hell and the various sorts of chastisement. What do you say? Is fear of those cave-dwellers more, or fear of hell? When he saw hell, he said, 'This is hell? All the people fear this? If hell knew the fire in my secret core, it would cease to be.' "

In the lover's heart is the fire of love,
hotter than the hottest fire of hell.[1037]

"We took him to the Garden. He saw the Garden with its varieties of blessings and sorts of generosities. He said, 'This is paradise? All the people hope for this? If paradise knew what blessings are inside me, it would become *scattered dust* [25:23]. The Fire will never be equal to the fire of my love, and the blessings of paradise will never be equal to the blessings of my recognition.'

"He came to the Tablet. He saw decree and destiny written in the Tablet. 'O Tablet, do you see your greatness? Now look at my greatness. You have eminence and level because the first thing written in you was my good fortune and prosperity.

"He came to the Throne. He looked at its base and saw a line written there: '*No god but God; Muḥammad is God's messenger.*' O Throne, do you fancy that your greatness is in yourself? Your greatness lies in my name.

"O Throne, you are standing in my name. O paradise, you have been caressed with my solicitude. O hell, you have melted by my turning away.

"Whenever I turn toward someone, he is yours, O paradise! And whenever I turn away from someone, he is yours, O hell!"

"O Muḥammad, whenever you turn toward something, that is My mercy, and whenever you turn away from something, that is My punishment. Lordhood is two things: bounty and justice. When you turn toward something, it becomes the rose garden of bounty. When you turn away from something, it becomes the thorn bed of severity."

All of being came under his feet. Oh, the whole world is dust under your feet! Oh, moon and sun are students of your face and thoughts! Oh, both realms of being—though you do not look at them—are there to be the gazing place of your disloyal community!

Creation became nothing beneath his feet, and he became nothing beneath the Real's Realness when gazing at His majesty, beauty, perfection, and eternity. In his aspiration all of creation is not, and in his contemplation of majesty he himself is not. *"Beautifully done,* O 'not' that 'is': 'not' in the majesty of unveiling, 'is' in the perfection of gentle gift! O friend, look at Me to see your smallness, and look at them to see your greatness!"

O dervish, there was no free man in the world like Muḥammad. He did not go to that world by putting brick upon brick, for he did not take a single thread along with him. Had he taken one, the address would have come, "Throw it away!"—as was said to Moses: *"Take off thy shoes!"* [20:12].

As for *Strong,* it means powerful. I will explain it under *Firm,* for the two have one meaning.

59. *al-Matīn:* the Firm

Strong and able. When the servant comes to know the Maker's strength and power, he will believe that He is able to do whatever He wants. He will sew up his eyes from gazing on others, burn the harvest of coveting from creatures, and sit and wait for God's gentle gifts and kindly acts, without dust in his heart or burden on his breast.

The Prophet said, *"When someone increases asking for forgiveness, God will give him relief from every concern and departure from every tightness and will provide him whence he did not reckon,"*[1038] even if he does not labor or earn.

It was said to one of the sincerely truthful, "Whence do you eat?"

He said, "From a king's stores not entered by thieves or eaten by weevils."[1039]

"Provision is apportioned, the avaricious deprived, the envious troubled, and the niggardly blamed."[1040]

Lord of the East and the West, there is no god but He, so take Him as a trustee [73:9]. "I take care of the work of East and West, but I will not take care of your dualistic work."

A hadith has come from Muṣṭafā in which he says, *"Surely God has decreed for Himself that He will guide whosoever has faith in Him, He will suffice whosoever trusts in Him, He will recompense whosoever loans to Him, He will deliver whosoever relies on Him, He will respond to whosoever supplicates Him, and He will forgive whosoever asks forgiveness from Him."*[1041]

Where is the confirmation of this hadith in the Book of God? *Whosoever has faith in God, He will guide his heart* [64:11]. *Whosoever trusts in God, He will be enough for him* [65:3]. *Whosoever holds fast to God, he will be guided to a straight path* [3:101]. *Who is it that will lend to*

God a beautiful loan? [2:245]. *And when My servants ask thee about Me, surely I am near* [2:186]. *Those who, when they do an indecency or wrong themselves, remember God and ask forgiveness for their sins* [3:135].

Sufyān Thawrī said, *"Were heaven not to rain and earth not to grow and I was a little bit concerned about my provision, I would think that I had become an unbeliever."*[1042] Had heaven become brass, earth become stone, and the thought of bread entered Sufyān's head, he would have supposed that he had become an apostate. *Refuge in God!*

One of the wanderers passed by a monk and said, "O monk, what is it that has tied you to this monastery?"

He said, "When someone walks on the earth, he stumbles."

He said, "From where do you eat?"

He said, "He who created the mill brings the flour," and pointed at his teeth.[1043]

Fatḥ Mawṣilī recounts, "Once I wanted to visit the house of God. I reached the desert and saw a child where there were no houses and no creatures, *a child to whom the rulings did not apply*—a boy not yet having the mill wheel of the Law's prescriptions turning on his head. I greeted him and he answered. I said, 'Where are you coming from?'

"He said, *'From the house of my Lord.'*

"I said, 'A child as young as you, to whom the rulings do not apply? Why did you make yourself suffer?'

"He said, 'Away with you, O shaykh. I have seen the angel of death take the spirit of those younger than me.'

"I said, 'My dear, why is it that I see no supplies or camel with you?'

"He said, 'My supplies are my certainty wherever I am, and my camel my two feet on which I walk.'" My supplies are my certainty, my camel my feet, my mount my yearning, my steed my love.

"I said, 'Surely I am not asking you about that.'

"He said, 'About what are you asking me?'

"I said, 'Water and bread.'

"He said, 'What is your name?'

"I said, 'Fatḥ.'

"He said, 'If one of your brothers or one of your bosom friends among the folk of this world invited you to his house, would you deem it beautiful to take along food to eat?'

"I said, 'No.'

"He said, 'O weak in certainty, my Patron has invited me to His house, "and He gives me to eat and drink" [26:79].'"[1044]

Ibrāhīm Khawwāṣ said, "Once I was in the road of Damascus and saw a youth with a beautiful face. I said, 'Come, let us travel the road together.' Four days passed before anyone gave us anything. I said, 'Come, let us take advantage of this.'

"He said, 'I believe in taking without intermediary.'

"I said, 'O youth, you are tremendously careful and walk a narrow road.'

"He said, *'The Assayer sees.'* Don't issue bad coin, for the Assayer sees. Then he said, *'And what do you have to do with claiming trust, O Khawwāṣ? The first of trust is that when instances of want enter in upon you, your soul looks only to God for sufficiency.'"* The first step in trust is that if the hunger and thirst of the folk of hell were to be assigned to you, your eyes would turn only to the lordly sufficiency.[1045]

One day Muʿādh Nakhshabī[1046] said to Ḥātim Aṣamm, "Why is it that your words do not find a place in our hearts?"

He said, *"Because there are curtains over your hearts,* and those curtains are the veils of the secrets."

He said, "Which curtain has remained over my heart? I have abandoned all others and become a devotee in your corner."

Ḥātim said, "You are not being fair. I speak of inwardness and you respond from outwardness. *This is because if you are praised, you become happy, so you are an eye-server. If you are reproved, you became angry, so you are proud and tyrannical. If your heart is attached to what is in your hands, you are covetous, and if you do not have something, you fear that you will not reach it, so you have an ugly opinion of your Lord."*

Muʿādh said, "Alas, curtains like mountains!"

He said, "You have heard the saying, *'When the soul has its nourishment, it becomes serene,'*[1047] but you have not come to know the soul's nourishment. The soul's nourishment is taking ease in its Lord's promise. When it finds this nourishment, it is at ease from the fear of poverty. A report says, *'Surely the most goodly of what a man eats is what his hands earn.'*[1048] But what is this earning? When night lets down the curtain of darkness, a man gets up from his soft bed, makes an ablution, and busies himself with prayer. Then he lifts up his hands and asks his needs from the Exalted Presence. This is the earning of the hands."

"How strange is the desirer who abases himself before the servants when he finds everything he desires with his Lord!"[1049]

> *If you're certain your Lord is creator*
> *and ask from a creature, you're not certain.*
> *If you doubt the provision that God*
> *has undertaken, you're not one of the faithful.*[1050]

"Do the deeds of a man who will be saved only by his deeds, and trust with the trust of a man who will reach only what has been written for him."[1051] When you step into the path of practice, practice as if you will be delivered only by practice. And when you come into the path of trust, trust as if you have no hands, feet, eyes, or ears.

The touchstone of the strides of all those who have trust is the state of Moses's mother: *So We revealed to the mother of Moses, "Suckle him, but if you fear for him, cast him into the river"* [28:7]. "O mother of Moses, when you fear the intention of the wrongdoers, put him into the ark and throw him into the sea. Well done, O cure of fear! Then We will command the sea to throw Moses into the house of Pharaoh. We will appoint the enemy, despite himself, to place Our friend at his side and nurture him at his breast."

They said to Pharaoh, "Why didn't you kill Moses?"

The tongue of his state answered from the pulpit of cutting off stratagems, *"What, should I kill my own killer?"*[1052] One cannot kill one's killer.

"We commanded all this bounty, gentleness, and beautiful-doing for the sake of Moses. We made an infant into a prophet, a shepherd into a world, the owner of a blanket into a speaking companion—without any intermediary, means, occasion, or cause. Then We held the sword of the Tariqah's jealousy over the head of his secret core so that, in the station of speech, when he looked at the staff—*'It is my staff'* [20:18]—We said, *'Cast thy staff'* [7:117]. When he paid attention to his shoes, We said, *'Take off thy shoes'* [20:12]. When he settled on his eyes, We said, *'Thou shalt not see Me'* [7:143]."

This is why the chieftain of chieftains and the source of exaltedness and felicities went from the chamber of Umm Hānī to *two-bows' length away* with the eye of free choice shut, for he had taken into account the fiery bodkin and heart-piercing arrow received by Moses.[1053]

"And what is that in thy right hand, O Moses?" He said, "It is my staff; I lean upon it and with it I beat down leaves to feed my sheep" [20:17–18]. In the station of speech it was said to Moses, the speaking companion among the prophets, *"Cast it, O Moses!" He cast it, and behold, it was a serpent, rushing* [20:19–20], so Moses was frightened. The Majestic called to him, *"Take it, and fear not"* [20:21]. *God showed him that "Though in your eyes there is nothing smaller in this world, it is a serpent and you must fear it."* He showed him that in this world there was nothing less significant in his eyes than the staff, but in fact it was a serpent. The stipulation was that he fear both the small and the great of this world.

"He cast it, and behold, it was a serpent, rushing," that is, rushing toward Moses. The serpent aimed for Moses, and the tongue of the Haqiqah began to speak from the pulpit of the Tariqah with these words: *"Everything that distracts you from the Real is your enemy, and everything with which you occupy yourself in the slightest is your adversary, like this staff."* Everything that distracts you from the Real is your enemy, and the smallest thing upon which you rely is your spirit's adversary. First it was commanded, "Throw down the staff," so that the reliance would be cut off. When the reliance was cut off, it was said, "Pick it up, for the lordly secret has appeared."

It is said that Moses had a pain in his leg and foot, and the Presence had commanded him, "Whatever you want, ask from Me." He sought the cure for the pain, and he was commanded to come to a mountain, pick a certain herb, and eat it. When he followed the decree, the infirmity disappeared. After several days had passed, the infirmity reappeared. Moses went back to the herb. He did not find healing and his pain increased. Again he supplicated. *Gabriel said to him, "You had a complaint, so you returned to God, and He healed you. But when you had a complaint and returned to the medicine, He turned you over to it."* O Moses, first you sought healing from the Presence of the Real, so you found healing. Then you sought it from the herb, so you did not find it.

It is said that when Joseph the sincerely truthful was thrown into the well, he was hanging from the top of the well by his fingernails and teeth, so his nails were wounded. When he surrendered, the Exalted Lord commanded Gabriel, "Go, spread your wing, and put Our sincerely truthful friend safely in a firm place of the well." Joseph reached the firm place of the well and his fingernails hurt. *Gabriel said to him, "If you had surrendered at the beginning of the well as you surrendered in its middle, you would have no complaint."*

It is true that in one of his books Muṣṭafā said one night, *"Who will guard us tonight?"*[1054] He said these words according to the requisite of what is molded by custom, just as Joseph the sincerely truthful said to that cupbearer, *"Remember me to your lord"* [12:42]. In the hadiths it is said that sleep pitched the tent of its ruling authority over everyone's eyes—only with the heat of the sun did they wake up—including the eyes upon which was daubed the antimony of *"My eyes sleep, but my heart does not sleep."*[1055] When those words issued from his tongue, this distinction had been curtained by jealousy. Gabriel came and said, *"Your Lord says, 'Before tonight who was guarding you, O Muḥammad?' "*

Everyone agrees that Muṣṭafā was superior to Solomon. When Solomon missed the moment for prayer, the sun was turned back, but it was not turned back for Muṣṭafā. What is the wisdom in this? Yes, it was past the moment for an obligatory act of Solomon, and the command came, "O angels entrusted with the sun, seize its horns and take it back. Give the observation of the astronomers to the wind and sprinkle dust on the calculations of the star-gazers."

When the era of the chieftain of the envoys appeared, it was said, "You have traveled the road. It is not suited for the character of the paragon to take back what has passed of the day by severity. *Surely thou hast a tremendous character* [68:4]." If his disposition does not drink the draft, then it will be right to take the reins of all the moments' steeds and give them over to the ruling power of his Shariah's intervention. It is permissible for the moment to be in bondage to Muḥammad, but not for Muḥammad's aspiration to be in bondage to the moment. He may intervene in the moment, but not the moment in him. How is this allusion expressed in the tongue of prophethood? *"When someone sleeps through a prayer and forgets it, he should pray when he remembers, for that is its moment. It has no other moment."*[1056] Exalted eyes that see only Him! Exalted ears that hear only Him! Exalted tongue that speaks only on His behalf!

It sometimes happened at the moment of the overpowering force of ecstasy that Shiblī would say, *"If the highest Firdaws were adorned for me, I would say, 'Give it to a Jew and do not let it distract me from my Lord!' "* If the highest Firdaws were brought and held before my eyes, I would say, "Give this paradise to anyone You want and do not distract me from the Presence with intermediaries."

It has also come that one day Shiblī went to the house of ʿAlī ibn ʿĪsā. ʿAlī ibn ʿĪsā turned to him and said, "O Abū Bakr, it has reached me that you tear and burn your clothes, and sometimes you pour away food and waste it. *What has this to do with learning?"* Which knowledge allows for this?

Shiblī said, *"By God, if I were given power over everything, I would burn it all."* If Shiblī had the hand, he would burn paradise and hell. *"God says in reporting about the wholesome servant, 'Then he fell to slashing their shanks and necks'* [38:33]. *What does this have to do with learning?"*

ʿAlī ibn ʿĪsā stayed silent. He said, "It was as if I had not read that in the Book."[1057]

From the era of Muṣṭafā until now they say, "Do not tear your clothing." But the pain of the lovers and the afflicted does not come under the pen of the muftis.

Sometimes I say, "I'll beat my chest,
I'll pull out my heart"—it afflicts me so much.
But I can't pull my heart from my body,
so I'll punish my shirt for its sin.

*

My heart said, "It's good to repent fully of love."
It talked bad—no, it's good for the spirit to be happy in love.
May my heart be gone from between me and You!
It's good for bad talk to be gone from both worlds.

60. *al-Walī:* the Friend

The Lord of everyone; for His familiars, the mystery linking them with love. God says, *"God is the friend of those who have faith"* [2:257].

Some have said that *walī* comes from *wālī* [protector]. Someone's friend is his protector.

Walī is an intensive. It means helper [*nāṣir*], it means caretaker [*mutawallī*], and it means friend [*dūst*].

Know that in reality your servanthood comes from His friendship, not His friendship from your servanthood. *He loves His friends without cause and does not reject them when they slip.*

It has been recounted from ʿAbd al-Raḥmān ibn Zayd ibn Aslam that he said, "God may love the servant until His love reaches the point where He says, 'Do whatever you want.' "[1058]

"Adam disobeyed" [20:121], *but disobedience did not harm him because love had already reached him. Iblis obeyed, but that did not benefit him because hate had already reached him.*

Abū Saʿīd Kharrāz or someone else said, "I was going somewhere, and Iblis appeared. I said, 'O accursed one, why did you oppose His command and step outside your own limit?"

"He said, 'O Abū Saʿīd, you too? O Abū Saʿīd, why do you say such words? If a child said these words, that would not be beautiful, much less you. You have known the straits of the road, tasted the hot and cold of the steps, and come to know the secrets of the apportionings. Then you blame me?"

O dervish, outwardly a slip came from Adam and an act of disobedience from Iblis. It was said to Adam, "Do not eat the wheat," but he did. It was said to Iblis, "Prostrate yourself to Adam," but he did not. The wherewithal of rejection and acceptance did not arise from their acts, but from the flow of the Pen and the decree of Eternity.

The Pen wrote felicity for one of them in the chronicle of the eternal will. A support was found for that in his makeup, and his sin was turned over to it by way of excuse: *He forgot, and We found in him no resoluteness* [20:115]. As for the other, the Pen had written rejection and expulsion by the decree of the eternal will, so an ambuscade was made from his makeup and his sin was turned over to himself: *He refused and was proud; and he was one of the unbelievers* [2:34]. Everything he did was turned over to the policeman of the beginningless rejection, and this was given out as the attributes of refusal, pride, self-seeing, and opposition. A collar was made from the severity of the curse and fastened to the neck of his days. His prayer-niche was given the name "idol," the belt of his struggle was given the title "Christian sash," the shirt of his practice was tied with the Jewish badge and the emblem of outsiders, and this call was given out in the world: *"He was one of the unbelievers."* Thus Iblis's deeds were made dumb, but God's knowledge was brought into words. In the hand of the assayer of His knowledge every gem that came from the crucible of Iblis's deeds was a discard. The Beginningless turned its face in enmity, knowledge declared itself quit of him, and the will disowned him. Good was given the color of bad, worship became the cause of the curse, and obedience became the occasion for being driven out. The reality of his work was expressed like this: *"No one stands up to the decree and no one contends with the Beginningless."*

Which lover of Yours do I not imitate
and which night do I not weep for You?
If You approve of nothing but my blood,
You have my permission to shed it.
Do whatever You want, but don't curtain love—
by God, don't be eager to strip it away.[1059]

In his book Ṣaḥīḥ *Muḥammad ibn Ismāʿīl Bukhārī narrates from ʿUthmān* [ibn Abī Shayba], *from Jarīr* [ibn ʿAbd al-Ḥamīd], *from Manṣūr, from Saʿd ibn ʿUbayda, from Abū ʿAbd al-Raḥmān ʿAbdallāh ibn Ḥabīb Sulamī, from ʿAlī that he said, "We were at a funeral in Baqīʿ Gharqad. The Prophet came and sat, and we sat around him. He had a stick with which he began scratching the ground. Then he said, 'No soul is born whose place has not been written in the Garden or the Fire and who has not been written as either felicitous or wretched.'*

"A man said, 'O Messenger of God, should we not rely on what is written for us and put aside deeds? Then whoever among us is of the folk of felicity will be taken to the deeds of the folk of felicity, and whoever among us is of the folk of wretchedness will be taken to the deeds of the folk of wretchedness.'

"He said, 'As for the folk of felicity, they will be eased to the deeds of the folk of felicity, and as for the folk of wretchedness, they will be eased to the deeds of the folk of wretchedness.' Then he recited His words, 'As for him who gives and is godwary, who confirms the most beautiful, We shall surely ease him to the easy, and as for him who is niggardly and deems himself without needs and cries lies to the most beautiful, We shall ease him to the hard' [92:5–10]."

The Commander of the Faithful ʿAlī said, "One day we were with the Messenger at a funeral in Baqīʿ Gharqad. The Messenger was seated, and we were all seated around him while he adorned the heaven of messengerhood with the shooting stars of companionship. The paragon said, 'Whenever it is decreed that someone will come into existence, making the journey from nonexistence to the standing place of existence and being turned over by the audience hall of power to the royal court of creativity, then, even before his existence, the story of his road and wayfaring is recorded in the scrolls of the divine decrees and written in the registers of the beginningless apportionings.' "

O dervish, the brand they placed on you was put in the fire before your existence, and the robe they draped on you was prepared for you before existence was given to you. *"God created the spirits four thousand years before the bodies."*[1060] He gave the spirits stations and waystations in which He adorned them with the jewels of generosity before creation, then He put them into these bodies. He set down the spirit next to this pharaoh and in the neighborhood of this nobody so that the soul's stink would be remedied by the spirit's purity and fragrance. Beautifully done, this preparation of the secret cores and this sewing of the robes of pious hearts before their existence by the decree of munificence!

O dervish, were it not for the assistance of the Exalted Presence, no person of faith would be able to safeguard his faith for one instant. He filled the world with assistance, He threw robes over His elect, and He placed robes on the others. The goal was the same. Yes, when a sultan brings a friend to a dwelling place and commands that a feast be held in friendship, the goal is not the dwelling place but rather the friend.

My goal in your street is your face.

*

My love's covenant is not with the dust of the earth,
but with that wherein my beloved dwells.[1061]

Know that in reality no herb subtler than the herb of love grew in the meadow of the covenant of Lordhood and servanthood. It is love that carries a man to the Beloved—all else is a thief on the road. All the *tawḥīd*-voicers' attributes fell apart in *tawḥīd*, and all the lovers' attributes came to naught in love. A *tawḥīd* remained without description, and a love remained without attribute.

All the lovers stood up and stepped forth in love. The beginningless dot in *He loves them* [5:54] came forth and welcomed them all. In their incapacity to show gratitude for that one dot they all fled. No one dared to take a breath. They knew that even if the seven heavens and the seven earths were to become their instructors, they would not know how to ask for the subtlety that He would give them without their asking.

When the lovers gazed on their own incapacity and His exaltedness, He in His gentleness placed the gift of vision on top of that. When the final end of love is not the vision of the Beloved, to speak of love is a metaphor.

Here, however, there is a rule: friendship for Him does not come together with scattered desires in the same heart. The obligation of the body is prayer and fasting, and that of the heart is friendship.

In friendship the person of faith has no escape from three states: fear, hope, and love. Fear comes from gazing at wrath, hope from gazing at generosity, and love from gazing at the divinity. Whoever finds purity finds it through His glorifiedness, and whoever finds love finds it from the divinity. Whoever sees recognizes, whoever recognizes clings, and whoever clings burns; they do not burn the burned. Those who recognize Him recognize Him through Him, and those who love Him love Him through Him.

When the turn of Adam's good fortune arrived, tumult and boiling fell into the Dominion. They said, "What happened to our many thousand years of glorifying and reciting *tawḥīd*? Why has that been given to the wind and why has Adam the dust-dweller been raised up?"

It was said, "Look not at the form of dust, look at the deposit of majesty: *He loves them and they love Him* [5:54]."

He attached the fire of love to the hearts, but He also gave out the call, *"The Real is exalted."*

Someone was afflicted by love for the son of a king. He said, "Toss him a broom so that he may sweep the doorway every day." After a time he died doing that, so he was thrown on a bier, and a shroud was pulled together for him by the passersby in the street. If you don't approve of something like this, go away like a sensible man.

O dervish, the mark of love is that when something comes from the Friend that is disliked by your nature and makeup, you place it on your very eyes. The Prophet said, *"The foul odor of the fasting person's mouth is more goodly to God than the scent of musk."*[1062] The altered smell from the mouth of the fasting person comes from the aroma of the pavilion of holiness.

If the Beloved's hand pours poison for me,
poison from His hand will be sweet.

*

The heart You burn thanks You;
the blood You shed boasts of You.

*

The blood You spill thanks You;
the heart You frighten praises You.[1063]

*

The poison I drink in remembering You is the antidote;
the madman seeing You comes back to his senses.

"Not truthful in his claim is he who takes no pleasure in his Patron's blows."[1064] Anyone who claims love and then fails to nibble the sugar of gratitude for the successive lashes of the severity of exaltedness is defiled and low in aspiration.

It has come from Ibrāhīm Adham that he said, "Once I was in Syria and went to see one of the great men of the road. I saw that he had been afflicted by many sorts of trial. He said, 'It is thirty years now that I have had this state, but I have not said, *"Harm has touched me"* [21:83]; I am so overwhelmed and drowned in the contemplation of the Friend's decree that I see no way to resist.' "

How well spoke Abū Yazīd: *"If we recognize You, You bewilder us. If we say we don't know You, You teach us good manners. If we aim for You, You throw us into hardship. If we abandon You, You pester us. So what is the path to You?"*

If I say, "I recognize You," at once I am in the depths of bewilderment. If I say, "I don't know," I am worthy of whips and blows. If I aim to come to You, I am in utter trial and punishment. If I pull my head into the sleeve of destitution, I have a hundred thousand regrets. I don't know in what my healing lies or whose hand has my pain's medicine.

Falling into the trap is not by free choice. There is no stratagem for deliverance and no way for agitation. Once you've fallen in, you must surrender.

A fish fell into a fisherman's trap. It said to the man, "I am a living being that glorifies God. Will you prevent me from glorification?"

Another fish answered him: "Are you doing God a favor by glorifying Him? What place is this for talk of glorification? Give up your sweet life and don't talk!"

He sent a whiff of this talk into the world. The whole world became distracted in the talk, but before reaching the outskirts of His majesty, they came to naught. The sword of severity was drawn, the garment of exaltedness was donned, and a hundred thousand friends and sincerely truthful were perplexed and pulled into the road. The seeker was lost in the seeking, the searcher was annihilated in the searching, ecstasy [*wajd*] reached finding [*wujūd*], ecstasy became lost in finding, and the eyes became nonexistent in seeing the Found [*mawjūd*]. The seer arrived at seeing himself, and his seeing became blind in the bewilderment of seeing. No eye is worthy of seeing Him, no heart worthy of buying this talk.

> My eyes want only Your vision;
>   my ears want only Your speech—
> Both have high aspiration,
>   but neither is worthy of You.[1065]

He created dust, He prepared recognition in the dust, and He conveyed the recognition to love. He removed the intermediaries and conveyed love to proximity. Then He removed the marks from the road and conveyed proximity to bewilderment. Bewilderment is beyond all the stations. *"O Guide of the bewildered, increase me in bewilderment!"*[1066]

Shiblī said, "These are the words of a bird in a cage. No matter where it sticks out its head, it cannot find the road."[1067]

The bewildered are those who are inside the pavilion of jealousy. If they want to come out to the creatures for a moment, they cannot. Everything outside the curtain is losing the road, and everything inside the curtain comes from the traces of the perfect divine majesty. Anyone who cannot go from creation to the Real has lost the road, and anyone who cannot go from the Real to creation is bewildered. No matter how far he goes, he comes back only to Him. This is like Moses and his people—as much as they went forth, they were at the first step.

"I had pure attributes—so there had to be a recognizer. I had unqualified beauty—so there had to be a lover. I had an Essence without how—so there had to be a seeker." There were attributes, so there had to be a recognizer. There was beauty, so there had to be a lover. There was the sought, so there had to be a seeker. There was the intended, so there had to be an intender. There was the gaze, so there had to be an object of the gaze. There was acceptance, so there had to be something accepted. There was mercy, so there had to be an object of mercy. There was forgiveness, so there had to be an object of forgiveness.

The other created things had nothing to do with love, for they did not have high aspirations. The angels' work is upright because no one talked of love with them. All this up-and-downness, this above-and-beneathness, these drafts mixed with poison, these hanging swords in the Adamites' road—all are because the talk of love was with them.

Orderly and arranged work belongs to those who know nothing of love. When a whiff of love's rose reaches the nostrils of a man's covenant, tell him to detach his heart from the rose, for *love "spares not, nor leaves alone"* [74:28].

Your love made me haunt taverns like this—
otherwise I was safe and orderly.

*

By God, I know not if I should blame my soul
for love, my ill-starred eyes, or my heart.
When I blamed my soul, she said the eyes had sinned;
when I blamed my eyes, they said, "Seize the heart for sin."[1068]

O chevalier, you hear all this talk of love, but what exactly is love? What is the servant's love for the Real? And what is the Real's love for the servant? This is a tremendous root.

The Real's love for the servant is a desire for a specific bounty and a conjoining with a specific secret and kindness. This secret is beyond speech, and only lovers know what it is, for physicians know the measure of the pain of the sick. *The lover's recompense before encounter is cruelty.* This gentleness is not brought about by any cause, nor is any stratagem its means.

As for the servant's love for the Real, it is that he finds in his heart a state whose outcome is that he conforms with the commandments. He chooses the commandments over what is chosen by the gambling, wine-drinking, commanding soul. When love is built on the body, that is the stuff of one's own shares. Anyone who seizes the belt of love detaches his heart from all shares.

Love alludes to the limpidness of the states, for its root is *ḥabab asnān*, *"the regularity of the teeth,"* when the teeth are limpid.[1069]

Love requires clinging to the gate of the Beloved. It is derived from *aḥabba'l-ba'īr*, that is, *"the camel put its knees on the ground"* such that, no matter how much you beat it, it will not move from its place.

All these words are reports and narratives, but the reality is this: *"Love is a state not expressed in words."*[1070]

At the moment the fire of love raises its banner in the lover's breast such that its sparks come out into the open along with his breath, the Exalted Presence calls out, "O angels, if any of you is using your feathers and wings, flee from the road, for whenever the brilliant, incinerating lightning of that breath touches someone, neither feathers nor wings will remain, neither position nor possession."

Tomorrow the folk of Muṣṭafā's community will reach hell and the traces of the ablution will be on their hands, the traces of prostration on their faces, the watchword of remembrance on their tongues, the fire of love in their hearts, and the brand of passion in their spirits. Mālik will say, "Are these hell-dwellers?"

When Zulaykhā wanted to put Joseph in prison, she put a crown on his head, clothed him in a robe, and bound his waist with a jewel-studded belt. The prisoners looked and said, "Is this a prisoner?"

In hell the person of faith will have a thousand times more ease than a king on the throne of his kingdom, for the king has blessings mixed with separation's stain in a world where a hundred thousand enemies have been stirred up. But in hell the person of faith will have a tribulation after which the cup of union's good fortune will overflow on the hand of the cupbearer of bestowal. How can a blessing whose disappearance is feared be equal to a tribulation along with the hope of union?

61. *al-Ḥamīd:* the Praiser/the Praised

Ḥamīd means praiser: He praises Himself and praises the faithful. It also means praised: He praised Himself and He is praised by the faithful. The first praise is God's of Himself, for He says, *"The praise belongs to God, the Lord of the worlds"* [1:2].

The Exalted Lord brought the creatures into existence, clothed them in the garment of creation, nurtured them and gave them their daily portion, preserved them from trials, accepted their obedience with all its shortcomings, and then, when they were disloyal, concealed them behind the curtain of bounty. He pardoned them for many slips and offenses when they offered one apology, He gave them the success of obedience, He bestowed on them protection from disobedience, He showed them the road of faith, He adorned their hearts with recognition, He preserved them from unbelief, He gave them the edict of the Quran, and He had them emulate the chieftain of the envoys and the Seal of the Prophets.

Since the servants were incapable of discharging gratitude for these blessings, He brought forth His bounty and generosity and made the tongue of gentleness a deputy for the broken and indigent by praising Himself. He said, *"The praise belongs to God, the Lord of the worlds."*

It is a stipulation in the road of love to act as deputy for your friend. He said, "I was beneficent toward you and thanked Myself on your behalf. Without you I gave you all the blessings I gave you, just as without you I apportioned and without you I praised."

Deputyship by virtue of friendship at first is this, and it will be the same sort at last. When no servant remains in heaven and earth, He will say, *"Whose is the kingdom today?"* [40:16]. He knows that if the friends had the tongue of speech, they would say, "God's." Since He is His friends' deputy, He will say, *"God's, the One, the Severe"* [40:16]. This is establishing the argument against the deniers and being the deputy of the friends.

There is another secret: *The praise that belongs to Me is the praise by which I praise Myself, not your praise of Me.* The praise that is worthy of Me is what I bring for Myself, not what you bring for Me. You are a creature and a newly arrived thing, and your praise is your attribute. The attribute of a creature is a metaphor, and the attribute of a newly arrived thing is a trace. Moreover, your praise is caused by requesting. How can something with a cause be worthy of Me? My majestic Presence is incomparable with causes, hallowed beyond defects, and purified of slips. The praise worthy of Me is the reality, and that is My praise, for I am the Real and My attributes are the reality. Hence I brought a real praise worthy of Myself. Now that this reality has become apparent by virtue of generosity, you also bring a praise in keeping with the utmost limit and final end of your possibility. Thus your metaphor will follow the reality, and its ruling property will become the reality's ruling property.

"O friend, if you say 'amen' and it conforms with the amen of the angels, I will forgive all your sins, for your praise will have conformed with My praise. Whose imagination can carry, whose mind can hold, and who can perceive the caress and robe of honor that I will bestow upon you?"

Let me delineate these words with a likeness and confirm them with a consideration, for hearts become mindful through likenesses.

God bears witness that there is no god but He [3:18]. "Before I commanded you to bear witness, I bore witness to Myself. You bear witness in order to request Me to keep the promise of paradise and safeguard against the threat of hell. Hence your speaking is defective through its cause, which is the request. Moreover, your bearing witness is temporal and My bearing witness is beginningless. When you bear witness, the temporal follows the beginningless. In reality you will not have an endless reward because of a temporal bearing witness, but because I make your temporal bearing witness just like My beginningless bearing witness by virtue of following. When your bearing witness becomes beginningless, your reward becomes endless."

He says, *"the Lord of the worlds"* [1:2], the nurturer of the world's folk. Nurturing is of two sorts: one outward and the other inward. Blessings are outward, and mercy inward; bounteousness is outward, and prosperity inward; worship is outward, and felicity inward.

The outward life is through blessings and the inward life through recognition and contemplation. If for one moment the lovers of the Real did not have contemplation, they would fall to pieces. What a wonder! They are not able to bear the contemplation, but they have no settledness without it. What can be done by someone helpless like this? He has no patience with separation, nor any settledness with union. He remains bewildered. When his state is like this, the Lord of Lords takes his hand, for He is the hand-taker of the bewildered.

The worlds. In this there is much disagreement. Some say that the world's folk are four groups: angels, Adamites, devils, and sprites,[1071] all of which are addressed by God. Some say the world's folk are two groups: angels and Adamites, because perfect honor belongs to these two groups. Do you not see that the messengers and prophets are from these two groups and that there are no prophets among other creatures?

The beauty of both worlds lies in two things: servanthood and love. But servanthood is the attribute of creation and love the attribute of the Real. The perfection of servanthood belongs to the angels, and the robe of friendship belongs to Adamites with faith. Among the faithful, it belongs to the elect, who are from this community.

The Exalted Lord says about the attribute of the angels, *"Nay, they are honored servants"* [21:26]. He says, *"Over them are harsh, terrible angels. They do not disobey God in what He commands them and they do as they are commanded* [66:6]. They are servants who obey Our command and put it into effect; they do not disobey Us for the blink of an eye."

About the attribute of this community He says, *"He loves them and they love Him."* He also calls this community servants, but when He calls the angels servants, He does so without attribution: *servants*. He calls this community servants with attribution: *"My servants"* [15:42].

He completed His bounty on this community in order to drive you into great boldness, audacity, sinfulness, and offense. Then when the lights of love become apparent, that will be without any precedent service or mediating obedience. This then is the attribute of love, and that is the attribute of obedience.

People whisper with friends, not servants. The servants are there for the friends, not the friends for the servants. This is the secret of the divine words, *"He subjected to you whatsoever is in the heavens and whatsoever is in the earth, all together, from Him* [45:13]. Everything We have is your servitor. Now you be the servitor of the Served One so that all the served ones may serve you."

The All-Merciful, the Ever-Merciful [1:3]. The wisdom in repeating these two names after they were mentioned at first is that He will now mention the resurrection. He mentions the names All-Merciful and Ever-Merciful before mentioning the terror of the resurrection. "O faithful, it is a tremendous day, but the king is the All-Merciful, the Ever-Merciful. On that day you will have work with someone who will have work with you—not by way of all-compellingness and severity but by way of all-mercifulness and ever-mercifulness."

The Owner of the Day of Doom [1:4], *the one who owns the enactment of the Day of Doom,* the one who can bring about the Day of Resurrection. Although in the outward expression He made this specific to the resurrection, it also lets us know that even though He is the Owner today, He has given ownership to the servants so that the owners [*mālik*] will be niggardly with their ownings [*milk*] and so that kings [*malik*] will be iniquitous with their kingdoms [*mulk*]. When the resurrection comes, He will take away all the ownings and kingdoms so that neither niggardliness nor iniquity may remain. All will be sheer bounty and unmixed justice.

Even though that day will be long, He will make it short for the faithful. Thus the report has come that when this verse came to Muṣṭafā, *"in a day whose measure is fifty thousand years"* [70:4], ʿĀʾisha began to weep. She said, "O Messenger of God, how can it be for fifty thousand years?"

The Prophet said, *"For my community God will make that day like one prescribed prayer."*[1072]

The likeness of this in the world was brought out by the Exalted Lord in the story of Ezra, who said, *"I lingered a day, or part of a day"* [2:259]; and in the story of the Companions of the Cave, who said, *"We lingered a day, or part of a day"* [18:19]. The Lord can make one hundred years one hour for Ezra and He can make 309 years one day or half a day for the Companions of the Cave. So also He can make the resurrection last one hour for the Muhammadans despite its length.

Thee alone we worship and Thee alone we ask for help [1:5]. We worship You and we ask for help from You. When someone recites this verse and makes his heart familiar with its secret, he will be quit of compulsion and free will. *"Thee alone we worship" in gratitude for Thy blessings "and Thee alone we ask for help" with patience in Thy trials.*

The reality is that the servant cannot be patient with one iota of trial unless he has the Lord's kind favor, guarding, and preservation. Thus it has come in the reports that when the Exalted Lord unveiled those trials for Job, it occurred to Job's mind one day how well he had shown patience with such severe trials. The call came, *"Did you have patience, or did We give you patience, O Job?! If We had not placed a mountain of patience under every hair of your trial, you would never have been patient."*

This view toward the kind divine favor and the kingly solicitude is not specific to the station of patience. Indeed, in all states the servant must gaze on the gentle gifts of the Lord, not upon himself, for destruction lies in seeing oneself and salvation lies in seeing God. The first to be destroyed in the world was Iblis. By virtue of seeing himself he said, *"I am better"* [38:76]. Whenever the heart of an exalted man is brought into the position of good fortune, if he ever gazes one iota on himself, the delusion of that gaze will be decapitated by the sword of jealousy, as you have heard in the story of Solomon.

In the story of Zachariah's son John it has come that when the address comes on the plain of the resurrection, *"Where is he who has not sinned or not aimed to sin?"* everyone will turn down his head except John, who will lift up his head. The call will come, *"Was it you who did not sin, or was it We who protected you from sin?"* When he hears this address, he will turn his head down in shame.[1073]

Thus *Thee alone we worship* is to carry out servanthood and *Thee alone we ask for help* is to see God. The measure and worth of discharging servanthood lies in seeing God. This is the meaning of Muṣṭafā's words in answer to Gabriel when he asked, *"What is beautiful-doing?"*

He said, "It is that you worship God as if you see Him, for if you do not see Him, surely He sees you."

They were commanded only to worship God, making the religion sincerely His, as unswerving ones, and to perform the prayer and pay the alms; that is the upright religion [98:5].

62. *al-Muḥṣī:* the Enumerator

The knower and the counter. God says, *"He has enumerated everything in numbers"* [72:28].

When the *tawḥīd*-voicing servant with faith believes on the basis of certainty, not because of instruction, that the Exalted Lord is the enumerator of breaths and the knower of sense faculties, he will not say a word without the permission of the Shariah or take a step without the leave of the Haqiqah.

It is rare for a man's steps to be straight in his own makeup. There are some whose every step is cursed by the tongue of that step's state; and there are others whose every step reports of the bosom friendship of Abraham, the generous bestowal to Moses, and the sorrow and happiness of Zachariah's son John.

No step in the world is more exalted than the step of veneration. The Messenger's companions found equanimity growing beneath the clouds of prophetic companionship; they became compliance itself in the face of the commandments and weighed their steps in the scale of veneration. They saw another fruit within themselves with every step they took. The fruit of bestowal from prosperity's tree was put next to each of their secret cores. About one of them it was said, *"The most skilled in the rules of inheritance among you is Zayd ibn Thābit."* About others: *"The most knowledgeable of the permitted and forbidden among you is Mu'ādh ibn Jabal." "The most decisive among you is 'Alī ibn Abī Ṭālib."*[1074] These paragons had become veneration itself, so the address came, *"And let not thine eyes turn away from them* [18:28]. Your eyes must not travel at all, for We did not create you for yourself."

In the morning when the Messenger came out of the house, those burnt ones would come weeping with yellow faces and dry mouths. They would say, "Has Gabriel talked of us?"

He would say, "Do not busy your hearts, for in the end the work will be done by *when those who have faith in Our signs come to thee* [6:54]."

When need is brought forth by two burnt hands, the world fills with tumult. He says, "Bring empty hands to Me, for I love empty hands. Be an asker, for I have the attribute of bestowing. Sellers want full hands, but bestowers want empty hands."

And what is that in thy right hand, O Moses? [20:17]. It was not that Moses did not know that it was his staff and needed to be reminded. Rather, He was striking fire into Moses's leaning place. First Moses's road was purified of Moses so that when he came for his need, he would come empty-handed. Then in another station a fire came that left neither Moses nor his resting place: *Then, when his Lord disclosed Himself to the mountain, He made it crumble to dust, and Moses fell down thunderstruck* [7:143]. Fire was struck into the mountain because it had given shelter to one step of Moses. Pharaoh was given to the water because Moses had busied a corner of his heart with enmity. And the woman who fixed her heart on Moses was tortured. It was said, "Moses is a man traveling by himself. It is not fitting for him to have the enmity of Pharaoh or the friendship of Āsiya."

He was kept in the desert for several years before he came to the Mount. He had a few sheep in front of him and stayed in the crucible of discipline. *And We tried thee with trials* [20:40], *that is, We cooked you well with trial.* Trial comes and demands patience. Blessing comes and demands gratitude. "You must be so patient that patience begins to lament of you."

East to West is full of sorrow and no one has the gall to say a word. Moses said a word once because of boiling, and you see what happened to him. The overpowering force of the state, the gentle gifts of exaltedness, and the various robes of honor in the Presence turned toward Moses, and he fancied that he was in the house of subsistence. It was the tongue of subsistence that requested vision in the house of annihilation. When he came back to himself, he said, *"I repent to Thee"* [7:143].

Moses's desire and felicity seized everyone from Qāf to Qāf. Shouts came forth from specks of dust: "What gall has the son of ʿImrān! He is throwing away his own holy life in the station of intimacy."

A shout came forth from Moses's makeup: "O Moses, this is not your work, whether or not the work lets you keep your life." From afar a hundred thousand reflections of Moses picked up stones and threw them at Moses's desire.[1075]

Moses was saying to Moses, "O son of ʿImrān, in danger itself you must put down your shield exactly as you put it down. If nothing comes of it, you have an excuse, for you came from Adam's dust."

These men placed the perils of the road on their own eyes. The fire of Nimrod came out into the open and pitched the tent of severity, four farsakhs by four farsakhs. A hundred thousand sinless, purified angels came into the air wanting the Bosom Friend to look at them, but the Bosom Friend was curtained by the beauty of his present moment, covered by the tranquility of his heart, sitting in seclusion with the beloved of his secret core. Gabriel was running back and forth perplexed and saying, *"Have you any need?"*[1076]

Heaven and earth were gazing on that state, and the spheres stopped short in bewilderment: "What happened?"

Today a caress went forth from the quarry of gentleness and gave Nimrod's fire its own color. Yes, do not wonder that the color of the fire changed, for its prey was the Bosom Friend and its hunter the likes of Gabriel. The world was passed through a sieve, removing the intrusion of men and jinn, so that the Bosom Friend could be given vision in Nimrod's fire.

The fire in its fireness said, "O Nimrod, beautifully done! For many years I have wanted to say a word to the Bosom Friend without intrusion. You were appointed to remove a veil embroidered with prevention and to take me to my goal."

When that commander-in-chief of the world came to the midst of the fire, he said, "What are you doing?"

The fire said, "O Bosom Friend, what a place for the appearance of the top hat of bosom friendship! I have lifted my heart away from my own fireness."

Gabriel came in this state: "O Bosom Friend, they are going to throw you into the fire!"

He said, "There's nothing to fear, for the meaning of fire is in my breast, and that is the fire of love. When meaning comes to the house of form, what can form do but come forth to serve in the guise of servitors? If fire does not come forth in the garb of a serving boy with a bouquet of herbs in hand, my meaning will wreak havoc on its form."

O dervish, you cannot strike a blow into both houses without the blow of the heart, for next to the heart's blow both houses are trivial. The paragon of the two realms struck one blow into this house saying, *"This world is accursed."*[1077] In embarrassment it fell apart until the resurrection. He struck one blow into that house saying, *"Most of the folk of the Garden are simpletons."*[1078] In shame it did not lift up its head.

It is said that Shiblī saw that paragon of the unlucky [Satan] coming along in the bazaar. He said to him, "People come and say, *'There is no power and no strength but in God,'* but you are not put to flight."

He said, "I am put to flight only by the blows of the hearts of Men."

You have heard all this talk of the greatness of the Bosom Friend and Moses. All this is a drop compared with the tremendous ocean of Muḥammad's messengerhood. "O chieftain of the world, come up to this throne, for the spectators are waiting. And beware, once you come to the throne and display yourself, keep yourself hidden from your own gaze!"

Glory be to Him who took His servant by night! [17:1]. When that paragon stepped forth from his house, he stepped forth in the manner of a paragon. When all those in the highest of the high saw the top hat of his good fortune, they burned and melted. Intellect was bewildered at the threshold of his rulership, knowledge became regret itself, and the worshipers' worship put on the garment of asking forgiveness. The majesty of his state struck fire into the worship of all the worshipers, took away the status of the kiblahs, disgraced everyone, and stripped the wherewithal from the wealthy. Then he completed the attack, and everything in the lowest of the low bound the belt of service: *"The earth was made a place of prostration for me.*[1079] From East to West they all had the garment of their own existence, but when my feet and banner appeared in the world, all were changed to the color of my affliction."

"The earth was made a place of prostration for me" alludes to the fact that they bound the belt of serving him: *"Peace be upon thee, O Prophet, and God's mercy and His blessing!* O paragon of the world, we are clods and stones and have a specific tongue that no one knows, but when the kettledrum of your messengerhood's good news was sounded, we changed our clothes and now we glorify with your tongue: *'Glory be to God, the praise belongs to God, and there is no god but*

God.'" Since the friend is alive, the traces of his life bring the dead into speech: *Your companion is not misguided, nor is he astray* [53:2]. Ask from the wood, stones, and clods so that they may tell you with eloquent tongue who this man is. *Nor does he speak from caprice. It is naught but a revelation revealed* [53:3–4].

The estranged sent the army of their scatteredness to the paragon, saying, "You say that the moon in heaven was split in half at your instruction."

He said, "If the rulership of my reign were to show itself as it is, it would leave neither the curtain of the *tawḥīd*-voicers, nor the fire of the Guebres, nor the cross and crucifix of the Byzantines." Bravo, O greatness of Muḥammad, what rank!

All at once a command came from the Presence to the one hundred thousand angels on top of the spheres behind the veil of awesomeness: "Bind your belt to hold the stirrups of the moon of moons, the full moon of full moons, the sun of suns!"

Adam and the Bosom Friend said, "What happened to us in our old age? A child with such wealth, fathers in such poverty!"

Yes, Muḥammad is an Adamite in lineage, but, in terms of created nature, Adam is a Muhammadan. Both realms of being were made the dust under his feet, and by virtue of generosity he gave churches and synagogues the same robe of honor as the Sacred House. "O crown, hang over his head, for the top of his head is too exalted to carry the burden of a crown! O robe, do not stand before his heart, for his heart is a pearl that has come to life from the limpidness of loyalty and cannot carry the burden of a robe! O Burāq, stay far away from him, for his feet have passed beyond the realm of being and do not come down to any low thing!"

If a lion approved of a dog's food,
they'd be different only in name.

The aspiration of that paragon was such that he went and came back empty-handed. He went as he came, and he came as he went. It was because one speck of that paragon's beautiful countenance had been prepared in Adam's finger that he abandoned the eight paradises, saying, "I was created wealthy; I will not lower my head to the chamber of just any beggar."

That speck kept on going. Whenever it reached someone, he would burn in remorse itself. When it reached Noah he said in wishing for that beauty, *"Leave no disbeliever dwelling on the earth"* [71:26]. They fancied that he wanted destruction, but he wanted to empty himself of intrusions so that perhaps he could see that beauty. And so it went with the other prophets and envoys.

Good fortune was the good fortune of Bilāl and Anas, for they lived in the era of the paragon. Abraham and Moses were not among the living in form. Had they been alive, the broom of service lifted by those two would have been lifted by Abraham and Moses, for *"If Moses were alive, he could do nothing but follow me."*[1080]

When Muṣṭafā spread the religion, the heads of the adversaries became strangers to their bodies. They said, "Let us see who it is with all this good fortune and greatness." They looked and saw a man hungry and naked. They said, "All this greatness belongs to him?"

It was said, "Yes. What do you know of his perfect greatness? In terms of the reality, there are two sentences in the world: *No god but God, Muḥammad is God's Messenger.* One sentence belongs to Me, the other sentence belongs to Muḥammad.

"O Muḥammad, you in your presence voice My laudation, and I in My Presence voice your laudation. O Muḥammad, you say, '*Say: "He is God, one*'" [112:1]. I say, '*Muḥammad is God's messenger*' [48:29]."

A paragon who has all this distinction, rank, perfection, and beauty says to a handful of poor beggars, *"For you I am like a father to his children."*[1081] Our tender father is that paragon.

"When violence turned bloody, we protected ourselves with God's Messenger."[1082] The Messenger's companions said, "When war became intense, we made the Messenger our shield."

It is as if I see before my eyes the weak and helpless coming along in the plain of the resurrection while their paragon is placed before them saying, "Where are you, O roaring hell?"

It almost bursts in rage [87:9]. The Exalted Lord says, "Because of its anger at My enemies, you would say that hell almost falls apart in anger."

The stipulation of tenderness is that the paragon will say on the Day of Resurrection, "Where is hell so that I may go there in place of the slave boys?" The handful of helpless ones will come under the shelter of his greatness. Then, when hell sees the paragon's beautiful countenance, the bile of its anger will settle down.

"My intercession belongs to the folk of great sins in my community.[1083] Today I look to see where the unbelief is greater so that I may invite them and lordly guidance may appear. Tomorrow at the plain of the resurrection I will look for the more tainted of the ungodly and intercede for them so that divine mercy may appear."

63–64. *al-Mubdiʾ al-Muʿīd:* the Originator, the Returner

He who begins the universe and makes the hidden appear; He who makes the old new and brings back what has gone.

Anyone who believes that he has a return ahead of him—a mustering and an upstirring, a questioning and an answering, a reckoning and a punishment—will be unsettled night and day. Moment by moment and breath by breath he will be busy with the work. *How will it be when We gather them for a day in which there is no doubt* [3:25] *and We set up the just balances for the Day of Resurrection* [21:47]*?*

Yaḥyā ibn Muʿādh said, *"Were the heavens and the earth to be struck by these three whips—death, the Reckoning, and the Fire—they would acquiesce in fear, so what about the child of Adam when struck by them?"*

This handful of dust has a tremendous work ahead of it. *"You were created for something tremendous."*[1084] There will be scales that will weigh you, a resurrection that cannot be described, and a grave that you will know. The Real says, *"God desires ease for you"* [2:185], but for certain there will be remorse. *"When someone recognizes God, his affliction will be drawn out."*

What sort of existence is this Adamic existence that all other existent things are in danger from its trial? Tomorrow at the resurrection the sun will be brought, kept outside with the whip of courtesy, and held such that it will be exposed to this harshness: "Was it you who commanded the creatures to prostrate themselves to you?" It has come that the sun in its embarrassment will fall apart, and no trace will remain of its light and splendor. *When the sun is enwrapped* [81:1] is the mask of embarrassment that will be fastened to its face. It will say, "It is several thousand years since I have felt the blow and strike of the Bosom Friend.[1085] How can I now bear this rebuke? There is no way to remain silent and no way to speak. Nothing is better for me than to put on the garment of affliction and be content with black clothing."

This harshness will still be boiling in the sun's makeup when an overflowing, poison-laced draft is sent to the purified, sinless Jesus on the hand of the cupbearer of the causeless Will: *"Didst thou say to the people, 'Take me and my mother as two gods apart from God'?"* [5:116]. He will say, "I must take a risk and gamble my life to see what happens: *'If I said it, Thou knowest it'* [5:116]. Jesus's makeup has a weak capacity, so he will not be able to bear the rebuke of the Presence: If Jesus said that, You know it, and if he did not, You also know that."

The point is that if all those at the forefront of the Presence will be addressed and rebuked like this, you should know how it will be with the rabble and retinue.

This is well known: "Three will be brought on the Day of Resurrection: a sick man, a rich man, and a slave. God will say to the rich man, 'What prevented you from worshiping Me?'

"He will say, 'My Lord, my possessions were many, so I rebelled.'

"Then Solomon will be brought with his kingship and He will say to the man, 'Were you richer, or was he?'

"He will say, 'Yes, he.'

"God will say, 'That did not prevent him from worshiping Me.'

"Then the sick man will be brought and God will say, 'What prevented you from worshiping Me?'

"He will say, 'I was distracted by my body's illness, so I was unable to worship You.'

"Then Job will be brought in his illness and God will say, 'Were you more ill, or was he?'

"He will say, 'Yes, he.'

"God will say, 'That did not prevent him from worshiping Me.'

"Then the slave will be brought and God will say, 'What prevented you from worshiping Me?'

"He will say, 'You placed over me lords who owned me, so I was unable to worship You.'

"Then Joseph will be brought in his slavehood and God will say, 'Were you more of a slave, or was he?'

"He will say, 'Yes, he.'

"God will say, 'That did not prevent him from worshiping Me.' "[1086]

Some have reported, *a poor man will be brought and addressed in the same way: "He will say, 'I was prevented by seeking my livelihood.'*

"Then Jesus son of Mary will be brought and He will say, 'Were you poorer, or was he?'

"He will say, 'Yes, he.'

"God will say, 'That did not prevent him from worshiping Me.' "

These creatures have a tremendous work ahead of them, much more than what enters supposition. The heedlessness of him who is not a chevalier will wreak havoc on him.

Woe on him whose interceders become his antagonists
when the Trumpet is blown to stir up the creatures.
Fāṭima will surely enter the resurrection,
her shirt stained with the blood of Ḥusayn.[1087]

Abū Hurayra narrated from the Prophet that he said, "When the Day of Resurrection comes, the first to be called forth will be a man who had gathered the Quran, a man who was killed in the path of God, and a man with much property. God will say to the Quran-reciter, 'Did I not teach you what I sent down upon My Messenger?'

"He will say, 'Yes, You did.'

"He will say, 'What did you do with what you knew?'

"He will say, 'I was standing with it "in the watches of the night and at the ends of the day" [20:130].*'*

"God will say, 'You lie,' and the angels will say, 'You lie.' 'Rather, you did that so that it would be said that you were a worshiper, and it was said.'

"Then the one killed in the path of God will be brought. 'Why were you killed and why did you fight?'

"He will say, 'I fought for You until I was killed for Your sake.'

"God will say, 'You lie,' and the angels will say, 'You lie.' 'Rather you desired that it would be said that you were a warrior, and it was said.'

"Then the possessor of property will be brought. God will say, 'Did I not give you ample, such that I did not leave you in need of anyone?'

"He will say, 'Yes, you did.'

"He will say, 'What did you do with what I gave you?'

"He will say, 'I was kind to my kin and I gave alms.'

"God will say, 'You lie,' and the angels will say, 'You lie.' 'Rather, you desired that it would be said that you were munificent, and it was said.'

Then Abū Hurayra said, "Then God's Messenger struck my knee and said, 'O Abū Hurayra, those three are the first of God's creatures that He will burn in the Fire on the Day of Resurrection.'"[1088]

O chevalier, *were it said to the Day of Resurrection, "What do you fear?" it would say, "The Day of Resurrection."*

The day God will gather the messengers and say, "What answer were you given?" [5:109]. When that harshness appears, all will be terrified. This verse will crash its waves against the words of those who are firmly rooted in knowledge. Some have said that this report is by way of admonition. Given that the places of limpidness, the quarries of good fortune, the wellsprings of prophecy, the keys to chivalry, and the lamps of messengerhood will have such dread and confoundedness in that station, what then will be the vengeance against the disobedient and the weak?

There is also more beautiful than this: *"The messengers know that God knows the answer they were given, so they say, 'We have no knowledge* [5:109] *of what You mean by Your question, since You already know that.'"*[1089] The messengers know that the Real knows what their communities answered when the message of the Presence was delivered. They say, *"We have no knowledge"* of the lordly wisdom in this question, given His perfect knowledge and encompassment of the community's answer.

It has also been said that the Real is making them bewildered, so they become bewildered and cut themselves off from everything but Him. This is because the Real will bring a people and say to them, "What answer were you given?" They will take pleasure in His speech and be bewildered at their pleasure in His speech. "We have no knowledge" arises from the bewilderment, bewilderment arises from the pleasure, and the pleasure arises from the address *"What answer were you given?"*

It is also said, " 'We have no knowledge' like Your knowledge, O Lord, for You know the outward and the inward, and we know only the outward."[1090]

The long and short of it is that this is an allusion to the terrors of the states at the resurrection.

Tomorrow, the people will be in two groups: One group will say, *"Where is the path to God?"* The other will say, *"Where is the escape from God?"* Where is the road of fleeing from God?

Tomorrow in the courtyards of the resurrection there will be four calls: *"my soul, my soul; my community, my community; my Lord, my Lord; and My servant, My servant."*

Adam will say, *"my soul, my soul!"* Muṣṭafā will say, *"my community, my community!"* The recognizer will say, *"my Lord, my Lord!"* The Exalted Lord will say, *"My servant, My servant!"*

What a marvelous business! How is it that a feeble sperm drop, a bit of *molded mud* [15:26], and a handful of dust are fitting for so much of severity's beating and pounding, grabbing and seizing?

O dervish, whenever He pulled something up, He pulled it up as was fitting for it. But when He pulled up the Adamites, He pulled them up as was fitting for Him. Had He pulled them up as was fitting for them and taken them down as was fitting for them, the faithful would not have reached endless caresses, and the unbelievers would not have reached everlasting punishment. For the unbelief of one hour, endless chastisement and punishment? For the obedience of one hour, everlasting reward?

He pulled up heaven as was fitting for heaven, and so also earth. But He pulled up Adam as was fitting for Him. When heaven and earth received robes of honor, they received them because of your greatness. If not for your honor and greatness, why would He have thrown this robe over the neck of heaven: *The All-Merciful sat on the Throne* [20:5]? If the workshop of your gaze was not toward heaven, how would heaven have found this eminence: *We adorned the closest heaven with the adornment of the planets* [37:6]? If earth were not the encampment of your majestic ruling authority, how would the cheek of this dusty circle have seen this caress: *And earth, We laid it out—what excellent spreaders!* [51:48]?

Those—He wrote faith in their hearts [58:22]. "Even though the Exalted Lord is not called 'scribe,' We did what scribes do because of your exaltedness. Oh, in the Beginningless, I was yours, and Oh, in the Endless, I will be yours and you Mine!"

I am setting in the earth a vicegerent [2:30]. When you give a robe of honor to those who are not close, you buy the robes from the shop of a cloth merchant. But when you want to bestow a robe on a dear friend, you take it from your own neck and put it around his neck.

"The light of the sun, the brightness of the moon, and the adornment of the stars are all for you. When you are not there, We will blind the first, blacken the second, and throw down the third. We will roll up heaven and change earth: *When the sun is enwrapped, and when the stars become opaque* [81:1–2].

"Kings make their kingdoms flourish, but We destroy the kingdom. Why do We do that? Because kings are exalted and made to flourish by their kingdoms, but We are not exalted by the kingdom—Our kingdom is exalted by Us. We destroy the universe so that the world's folk will know that everything was exalted through Us. When Our severity appears, the moon will have no status, the sun no worth and shine. We will blacken the face of the outward sun. As for the true sun that is hidden today—the sun of recognition—We will make it appear in the heart of every person with faith.

"We made earth your carpet. If you were not there, what would the carpet do? We made heaven your roof. If you were not there, what would the roof do? We made the stars your indicators. If you were not there, what would the indicators do? The sun is your cook. If you were not there, what would the cook do? The moon is your candle. If you go, of what use will be a candle?

"When a carpet is spread for a friend, it is gathered up when the friend leaves. When you leave, I will gather up this carpet. I will not create someone else. *He created for you* [2:29]. Heaven and earth, moon and sun, are go-betweens. Go-betweens are useful as long as the friend has not reached the friend. Once the friend reaches the friend, what would the go-betweens do in the midst?

"The hoopoe was the go-between. It was useful so long as the days were the days of reports. When the era of the gaze arrived, the hoopoe was of no use. As long as Muṣṭafā was in Mecca, Gabriel used to come and go. When he reached *the Lote Tree of the Final End* [53:14], Gabriel stood still. He said, 'The messenger is useful as long as the friend has not reached the friend. When the friend reaches the friend, what use is the intermediary?' "

When the sun is enwrapped, and when the stars become opaque. It is as if the Exalted Lord is saying, "Heaven and earth, moon and sun, unshakeable mountains and surging oceans, all are go-betweens and guides. Each of them has taken a torch and a flame in its hand and held it up. But tomorrow will be the time of the gaze. First We will take it all away. We will say, 'Reports have gone, the gaze has come.'

"We created heaven to be your cupbearer: *And We sent down from heaven pure water* [25:48]. Today is the day of the veil, so there must be an intermediary. Tomorrow will be the day of contemplation, so the intermediary will be of no use. Gentleness will be the cupbearer: *And their Lord will give them to drink of a pure wine* [76:21].

"We made earth an intermediary so that it would bestow upon you *grains, vines and herbs, olives and palms, gardens densely planted, fruits and pastures, and enjoyments for you and your flocks* [80:27–32]. Tomorrow We will lift the veil and say, *'Eat and drink!'* [52:19]. Of what use will be the earth?

"We created the sun to give you light, for today the light of the recognitions is hidden behind the curtains of the lovers' secret hearts because of the gentle lordly favors. Tomorrow indeed We will give you a light such that the sun will stand in service to the shoestrings of your chieftainship: *Their light running before them and on their right hands* [57:12]. *And the earth will shine with the light of its Lord* [39:69]."

Proof is needed if there is no face-to-face vision. When face-to-face vision comes, of what use will be proof? Zulaykhā used to paint pictures in her room. Wherever she looked, she saw her own pictures. When Zulaykhā reached Joseph and fell for him, she destroyed the room.

"O you with faith, when you reach Me, I will say, 'Look at Me!' When you look, of what use will any of this be? Today all of it is useful, because I have business with you and you must do what I want. Tomorrow when you come, none of it will be of any use, for I will do only what you want."

When Joseph was separated from Jacob and that old man built the House of Sorrows, Joseph sent his shirt so that he would have a reminder. It was the time of reminders, not the time of seeing. When Joseph was seen, what good was the shirt?

Moses said, *"Show me, that I may gaze upon Thee"* [7:143]. He was sent the tablets, because it was not the time of seeing: "Keep these tablets as a reminder, My friend. Today is not the day of seeing. Keep heaven and earth, the things that have come to be, the formed things, and the existent things as reminders. When the time of seeing comes, I will take them all away.

"You have done many disobedient acts in this earth, and heaven and the stars were aware of them. I will give them over to the ruling power of nonexistence so that they will be destroyed. Then I will say, 'My servant, do not fear those spies, for they are busy with themselves.' "

Yes, when a friend is dear, others are taught courtesy so that the friend will learn courtesy: *When the sun is enwrapped.* It was Abraham who asked *how Thou givest life to the dead* [2:260], and the knife was on the throats of the birds. *Peace!*

65–66. *al-Muḥyī al-Mumīt:* the Life-Giver, the Death-Giver

God says, *"It is He who gives life and gives death"* [23:80].

Rare it is for a man to die in himself from his own selfhood and come to life from the Real in the Real with the Real. In reality, life is the life that gives opening, not that which brings the spirit; and death is the death that snatches away faith, not that which takes away the spirit.

If all the spirits of all the world's folk were given to you but you did not have the spirit of faith's opening, you would be dead. And if a thousand years should pass over your dust but the fragrant herb of the All-Merciful's *tawḥīd* had grown in the garden of your spirit, you would be at the head of all the living.

Dung in the earth will give rise to pasture,
but the rancor of souls will subsist as it is.[1091]

Life is recognition, death is ignorance. *"Recognition is the heart's life with God."*[1092] Rare is the man who all at once is taken to the Water of Life and, like Khiḍr, washed therein and given endless life!

ʿUmar Khaṭṭāb was coming with a hard face, holding the whip of chastisement and the burning brand of punishment and wearing the shirt of unbelief and denial. From the Unseen the call was coming, *"O Prophet, God suffices thee, and the faithful who follow thee"* [8:64]. ʿUmar had sworn an oath to Lāt and ʿUzzā that he would not come back without bringing Muḥammad's head, and the Exalted Lord had sworn an oath by His exaltedness that He would not let him go without making him a familiar. ʿUmar had turned his face to war but the Real had sent forth the messenger of peace. "You are coming to war with Me and I am preparing to make peace with you."

O chevalier, who has the gall to speak about the decrees of the King? Here the livers of the Men are roasted and the hearts of all the exalted turn into blood, for no one is aware of the secret of the outcome and the precedent.

> Sometimes the spirit in my body turns to blood
> and its drops flow forth from my eyes.
> Were one drop to set out in the plain,
> all the desert plants would go mad.

One group sought Him, and He abandoned them; one group fled from Him, and He seized them. Nothing of enmity was left that ʿUmar had not done, and nothing of solicitude and kind favor that He had not done. ʿUmar came out of his sister's house aiming for Ḥamza's house where Muṣṭafā was. He went with enmity and in the end came back with love, he went with weapons and came back with peace, he went with denial and came back with attestation. The stalwarts of the Arabs and the unbelievers of Quraysh were waiting for him to come back with Muḥammad's head. After an hour ʿUmar came, his sword drawn, with him Muṣṭafā. When he came into the Sacred Mosque, the associators became happy and said, "Who has done what ʿUmar has done?! He has brought Muḥammad as a prisoner for all of Quraysh. Beautifully done, O Son of Khaṭṭāb!"

"Yes, I have come, having taken care of this business, but I am the slave of Aḥmad and the servant of the Unique."

They said, " 'ʿUmar too has turned away!" They all attacked ʿUmar, and ʿUmar attacked them. With one attack he took them all away from the surroundings of the Kaabah. Then the Messenger went into the Kaabah, inside of which were 360 idols. The Messenger had a stick in his hand and was striking it against the chest of the idols, saying, *"The Real has come, and the unreal has vanished away"* [17:81]. ʿUmar was saying, *"O idols, this is Aḥmad,*

> *This is the messenger of God in truth, so bear witness!*
> *If what he says is true, prostrate yourselves!"*

At once all the idols fell down in prostration.

Which day will it be when the messenger of realization along with the ʿUmar of assent enters the Kaabah of your breast at the instruction of success-giving? Then it will topple the idols that are the objects of your worship and give out this call: *"The Real has come, and the unreal has vanished away."*

"So the sorcerers were cast down in prostration [7:120]. They did not come to prostrate themselves—We brought them into prostration."

A serving boy was walking with his lord. The boy went into a mosque to say his prayers. The lord said, "Come out, boy!"

He said, "They won't let me come out."

He said, "Who won't let you come out?"

He said, "The one who won't let you come in."

So the sorcerers were cast down in prostration. It is no wonder that a hearing, speaking, knowing Adamite should prostrate himself. The wonder is that ʿUmar said to unhearing, unspeaking, unknowing idols, "If Muḥammad's religion is the truth, prostrate yourselves," and they all prostrated themselves at once.

Moses took some sticks in hand to make fire. He found prophethood and messengerhood: *Go to Pharaoh!* [20:24]. David picked up a sling to go out as a shepherd. He found victory and triumph: *And they routed them, by the leave of God, and David killed Goliath* [2:251]. ʿUmar picked up a sword to kill Muḥammad. He found recognition and bearing witness: *O Prophet, God suffices thee and the faithful who follow thee* [8:64]. What a pure Lord!

Two improper, ugly things were placed before ʿUmar: enmity toward the Messenger and wanting this world. What a beautiful state appeared from the midst! Two improper things were placed before the sorcerers: enmity toward Moses and the rulership of Pharaoh. What an exalted secret appeared from the midst! *So the sorcerers were cast down in prostration.* Two heavy tribulations were placed on Joseph: the well and the prison. Joseph's rulership and ruling authority appeared from the midst: *Thus did We establish Joseph in the earth* [12:56]. Two feeble drops were brought together in the womb. What a lovely form appeared from the midst! *And He formed you, so He made your forms beautiful* [40:64]. Two impurities were brought together: feces and blood. Limpid milk appeared from the midst: *between feces and blood, pure milk, sweet to the drinkers* [16:66]. Two distressful deeds were combined for the servant: disobedience and shortcoming in obedience. Mercy and forgiveness appeared from the midst: *He will make your deeds wholesome for you and forgive you your sins* [33:71].

In the precedent of all precedents, the beginning of all beginnings, and the beginningless before every beginningless thing, the Pen wrote the command in the Tablet that the candle of the religion's Shariah and the lamp of submission and certainty will light up in someone's breast. No matter how he may sleep, when he wakes up and sees the candle next to his pillow, he will love. When the decree of lordhood pulls and drags the servant to the Threshold, he will love. When the servant sets out running to the Threshold on the carpet of prophethood, he will love.

God separated Moses from his people and children, threw him into the dark night, and brought him into rushing and running—as you have heard in the story. Then He said, "*And what has made thee hurry from thy people, O Moses!* [20:83]. Moses, what's the rush? Why are you busy with hurry [*ʿajala*] and your people with cattle [*ʿijl*]?"

In the same way, every prophet and friend has attraction, pulling, and plundering. *So also We revealed to thee a spirit from Our command* [42:52]. Muṣṭafā had no news that he had been named in the Beginningless. Suddenly the heaven of messengerhood was adorned with the stars of knowledge and the moons of the secrets, the sapling of prophethood was planted in the garden of election and the meadow of chosenness, and the cushion of exaltedness was placed at the forefront of the majesty of messengerhood. One hundred twenty-some thousand center-points of sinlessness were made his serving boys. Then his tongue was held back from boasting that he was their paragon, but the belt of their boasting of service to him was bound to their waists. Just as God bound a covenant and made a compact between His lordhood and His servants, so also He made a compact concerning Muṣṭafā's chieftainship over the prophets and messengers and their following and accompanying him: "*And when God took the compact of the prophets: 'I have given you of a book and wisdom. When a messenger comes to you confirming what is with you, you shall surely have faith in him and you shall surely help him.' "* Then He said, *"Do you attest?* [3:81]. Have you now attested, made the covenant, and bound the compact that you will do this?"

Look at His taking Muḥammad's covenant to the limit and making it firm, and look at His leniency with His own covenant! The noble do not move for the sake of their own rightful due as much as they do for their friends' rightful due. Iblis had worshiped for several thousand years. When he did not prostrate himself to Adam once, no one looked at those several thousand years of worship; they looked at his abandonment of that one prostration. "Worship is My rightful due—though I have no need for worship—but that prostration was Adam's rightful due, and he is My friend. You are not allowed to be defective in his rightful due."

They said, "We attest." They all said, "Lord God, we attest to being serving boys of Muḥammad." *He said, "So bear witness!"* He took the angels as witnesses. *"And I am with you among those who bear witness* [3:81]. I, who am the Lord, bear witness to these words of yours."

Concerning His own rightful due, He said nothing but this: *And He had them bear witness against their own souls* [7:172]—He made them bear witness about themselves, and this is leniency itself. But when the work reached Muḥammad's compact, He took things to the limit in order to display perfect love and affection. "O center-point of sinlessness, O wellspring of honor, We have put you down in a place where the one hundred twenty-some thousand quarries of messengerhood and prophethood were pulled up so they may reach your traveling. If their being pulled up reaches your traveling, where then does your being pulled up reach?" That which others traveled by aspiration, Muḥammad traveled on foot.

The scholars say, "effort and struggle, success-giving and assistance." Effort is your traveling, and success-giving is His pulling. *"The disciple is a traveler, but the recognizer is a flier. How can the traveler reach the flier?"*[1093] The work driven by success-giving is not like the work of flapping feathers and wings. One person sits on the steed of struggle, and another sits on the Burāq of success-giving and disengagement. He says, "Let me drive my lame donkey of effort alongside the Burāq of success-giving," but it will never go forward.

Burāq goes no further than the Rock; then the *mi'rāj* appears. When the traveling is finished, the pulling appears. *He revealed to His servant what He revealed* [53:10]. One iota of pull brings about thousands of *mi'rāj*es. In this presence the intellects of the intelligent are marked by customs and branded by bewilderment. O traveling, become hidden! O pulling, come forth!

Gabriel was able to go along in some of the traveling, so he flapped the feathers and wings of holiness in some of the stations. Yes, Gabriel was on the steed of success-giving, and Muṣṭafā on the steed of struggle. Then, when the paragon mounted on the steed of success-giving, Gabriel said, *"There is none of us but has a known station"* [37:164]. O paragon, I have used my final end to pay for your beginning. *"Were I to draw closer by a finger's breadth, I would be incinerated."*[1094]

I know that the thought will occur, "If the paragon's beginnings are not reached by the final ends of others, how can it be that he was at times negligent in the station of prayer, which is the curtain of secret whispering?"

Beware, beware, do not ascribe the negligence of heedlessness to the chieftain of this world and that! That is the share of us, who are the unfortunate. After our work was examined, it was decreed that a handful of locusts from the retinue of the accursed one would come forth to chase our hearts from the presence of prayer. It was also commanded that negligence should touch upon his pure presence. Then, if this state should appear from someone weak and he is afflicted by this trial, well, he should know that he must place his head twice on the ground.[1095] But the secret of which I am speaking is not such that it comes out from any pen, nor that a pen should have the ability to bring such a fatwa to its tip.

What a marvelous business! At the beginning of the work, when Gabriel brought the surah *Recite in the name of thy Lord* [96:1], the paragon sought shelter in Gabriel, and Gabriel sheltered him with his greatness. When he had received complete discipline and when felicity had given its hand in assisting his exalted presence, Gabriel came with seventy thousand angels to bring the Surah An ʿām,[1096] but the paragon did not lift his head from the pillow. He said, "The era has passed when Gabriel's shelter was needed. Now the majesticness of my state has reached the point where the one hundred twenty-some thousand center-points of sinlessness write stories about my greatness, and I seal the back of their stories with my own lofty signet: *'Adam and those after him will be under my banner on the Day of Resurrection, without boasting.'* "[1097]

The proximate angel Gabriel had on his head the diadem of glorifying, hallowing, and reciting *tawḥīd* and was adorned with the jewels of sinlessness. When he saw the beauty at the top of the street of dust and heard the 'Make way!' that was called out by *He loves them and they love Him* [5:54], he said, "May Gabriel come in?"

He said, "This road of poverty cannot put up with all your chieftainship. If you can get rid of some of those ornaments and put on the patched cloak of human nature, I will tell you what sort of flavor this work has."

In the form of Diḥya Kalbī Gabriel said, *"What is faith?"*[1098]

O dervish, from the Throne to the ground not an iota of love is sold except in the house of the Adamites' sorrow and happiness. Many were the sinless and the pure at the Threshold, but none could carry the burden of this heart-burning, body-melting talk except this handful of dust. *And man carried it* [33:72].

Gabriel, who was the emissary of Exaltedness, did not have the capacity for this talk. Adam had to be turned around in water and dust several times before he put forth the hand of aspiration and said, "It is I who have been burned by this talk." This is because *encountering Him with the abasement of destitution is better than encountering Him with the boldness of sincerity. The sincerely truthful consider a sin through which one turns in poverty toward Him more beloved than a deed through which one becomes bold toward Him.*[1099]

When that pearl of chosenness and center-point of good fortune lifted up the sword of exaltedness, those who thought they were at the forefront saw themselves outside the Threshold. *They said, "We have no knowledge"* [2:32].

He said, "O Adam, tell them their names" [2:33]. One teacher was dismissed and another was brought to teach the names to the Dominion's angels in the grammar school of discipline. In this work Adam's makeup was saying on the pulpit of poverty, "Though I have no wherewithal with which to earn a profit, at least I have the destitution through which the adversary can be repelled."

The Exalted Lord gathered all the angels and reported that He would be creating Adam. They thought that this Adam must be an exalted somebody for him to be disclosed this way. The warmth of the ray of this declaration was still in their heads when they were addressed, *"Prostrate yourselves before Adam!"* [2:34]. One refused. What was that? The decree of the Beginningless arrived and snatched the top hat of good fortune from his head.

"What happened to me?"

"O accursed one, that paragon needed an evil eye. If everyone in Adam's service was fortunate, that would not be good. There must be both fortunate and unfortunate if the good fortune of the fortunate is to shine."

67–68. *al-Ḥayy al-Qayyūm:* the Alive, the Self-Standing

The Real is alive in reality, though He does not have a spirit.[1100] He is constant without disappearance and His existence has no beginning.

God says, *"And trust in the Alive who does not die"* [25:58]. Trust in the Alive who does not die, not in the alive who does die. It is certain that anyone who trusts in other than the Real and puts up with an iota of people's favors has placed the brand of damage on his cheek and fallen into the abyss of deprivation and loss. *"When someone makes his concerns one concern, God will spare him every concern, but when someone lets his concerns scatter him, God will not care in which streambed He destroys him."*[1101]

Hamstring the root of wanting things like yourself! Then aim for the Presence of the Alive, for *the Real and creation do not come together. "God did not make for any man two hearts in his breast"* [33:4]. Until you call down pillage on all your baggage and goods, do not turn your face to the road; as long as idol worship is in the midst, this talk will be off to the side. "Depend on Me in all your states and know that My threshold is your shelter. Then look: If I do not keep you beautiful, make your complaints."

O dervish, you should know that if the shadow of generosity were lifted from your head for one instant, all the dustmen of the world would be needed to sweep up your disgrace.

"I left the whole world open for you from cradle to grave so that you could be secluded with Me without intrusion. What is this laziness and heedlessness? This work is not a work for those nurtured in kindness. This work is the work of men. Anyone nurtured in the tents of brides is not worthy for the armor of men."

Abū Sulaymān Dārānī said, "My steps in approving of Him reached a place such that, if the call comes to the people in the courtyards of the resurrection, 'Go into hell,' all will go unwillingly, but I will go by free choice. All will go on foot, but I will go on my head. If they say, 'What is this state?' I will say, 'Though it does not accord with my desire, in any case it is not empty of the Friend's desire.' "[1102]

Bundār ibn Ḥusayn became a disciple of Shiblī. Whatever he had of worldly goods he gave away. Then he said to Shiblī, "What must I do now?"

He said, "You must wander in the bazaar and ask for bread until no one gives you anything."

He went and asked until it reached the point that no one would give him anything. He said, "What should I do now?"

He said, "You must beg."

He went from door to door asking for bread. People gave him some bread out of mercy until it reached the point that no matter which door he went to, when they knew it was Bundār, they gave him nothing. He said, "Now what must I do?"

He said, "Sit in your house and be such that weeks pass and no talk of anything but the Real enters your heart."

It wants a Bundār to have heated talk like this. If the janitor in the bathhouse gets up and says, "I want to be the commander of Khorasan," what will they say to him? There will be no gazing for you when your face has stayed so ruddy. *You will not attain piety until you expend of what you love* [3:92].

The Real placed the burden of traveling on the soul: *Surely We offered the Trust* [33:72]. If a trust-holder is not well off but rather fleeing and brazen, you will not let him go without a guarantee when you have him in hand. When the soul stood up and said, "I will discharge everything that is rightfully due," the Real asked for a guarantee. The heart is the soul's partner, and it is customary for a partner to guarantee on behalf of his partner. The heart made the guarantee. Then the Real made the intellect an exactor to knock constantly on the door of exacting. The soul was standing there saying, "I will discharge the rightful due," but it imprisoned the heart in appetite and bound the exactor's eyes with the blindfold of caprice, deceiving it with bribery.

Strive so that a corner of the heart may be emptied of intrusion, then quickly send it to the door of the Decreer. *And say, "My Lord, decree with the rightful due!"* [21:112]. Send one aggressive foot soldier to the soul—whichever of the Decreer's soldiers is harsher and stronger. Let him place a rope around the soul's neck, pulling and dragging it to the Decreer's threshold. Whether it discharges the rightful due or not, put it into the dungeon of hunger and nakedness, for this soul is an enemy such that, if all the exalted ones of the Threshold came and interceded with it, it would not bow its head. Once it is helpless in the dungeon, everything equitable can be found from it.

If you deal this way with the debtor, that is beautiful. Otherwise, the guarantor will be seized, put on the rack of trial, and beaten with the whips of severity. The least thing they do to it will be to blacken its face and take it around the empire, calling out that it has been banished.

O dervish, not just anyone can listen to this talk. It needs someone afflicted to hear talk of the afflicted. If the lords of affliction were commanded to weep, Noah's flood would never come to an end.

"We, the assemblies of prophets, do not bequeath."[1103] No one inherits gold and silver from us prophets. Whatever we have is taken by those who are burnt-hearted, afflicted, and barefoot. If the burnt-hearted are our own offspring, give them the inheritance. If the burnt-hearted are Bilāl the Abyssinian, Salmān the Persian, and Ṣuhayb the Byzantine, give it to them.

All the wealth found in the world—and I am not talking about the wealth of *this* world—holds the saddlecloth for one speck of destitution. And all the obedient, the proximate, and the spirituals hold the stirrups for a speck of the burning of a destitute man with a fevered liver and no bread in his house, with a burnt heart and work yet to be done.

In this talk you must carry the burden. You must put your spirit into the work such that giving up your spirit appears to you as nothing. Your spirit will not be the first to fall apart in this work. *They count it as a favor to thee that they have submitted* [49:17]. "I will take away the spirits of a thousand thousand disciples and make them into shoes for the exalted. I will spill the blood of a sincerely truthful man for the sake of a crow's stomach. If a meddler says something, I will say, 'The crow is My crow, and the sincerely truthful man belongs to Me.' I will place the brand of distance on one and put another on the throne of love in the garden of proximity."

ʿAbdallāh Bustī was one of the great ones and had tremendous wealth. When this talk appeared, he had title deeds against the people for a great deal of property. He gave it all back to them. Then the thought of Mecca fell to him. He consulted with a pir—a pir is the precondition for a disciple.

I have heard that Pir Bū ʿAlī Siyāh said that if a man has a loaf of bread, he must buy a pir for half a loaf. The pir must be such that, if a disciple goes ten times a day to the tavern, he will have no fear of going in after him and bringing him out.

In the era of Abū Turāb Nakhshabī there was a young man who had complete burning with tremendous discipline. The youth appeared very beautiful to Abū Turāb, who said to him, "What a shame that you have not seen Abū Yazīd!"

The youth said, "Where I am a thousand Abū Yazīds would not find access."

Again Abū Turāb said the same words, and the youth thought, "Surely Abū Turāb knows a secret in this."

They got up and left and arrived in Bastam. At the moment the youth saw the edge of Abū Yazīd's sheepskin approaching, he fell down and gave up his spirit. Abū Yazīd came forth and asked Abū Turāb about the state of that youth. Abū Turāb said, "In any case the obligation is for us to take care of his work." The two pirs washed him, put him in a shroud, said the prayers, and entrusted him to the dust. Then Abū Turāb spoke to Abū Yazīd about his state—the heat of his desire.

Abū Yazīd said, "Yes, but his spirit was seeking a corner of my sheepskin. When he looked at the trace of the sheepskin's corner, he went, letting go of the body." [1104]

The point is the account of ʿAbdallāh Bustī. When the thought of Mecca came to his heart, he told a pir. The pir said, "That's good, but do not feel secure from your soul." He went from his house as far as Kufa, and the soul wanted nothing from him. When he arrived in Kufa, the soul said, "I have come a long way and have not caused you any suffering. Now I want a bit of lawful fish. Then I will cause you no suffering until Mecca."

There was a donkey-mill, and a man was sitting there. He said to the man, "How much do you pay to rent this animal?" He said so much. ʿAbdallāh said, "Be a good man and let this animal out for a day and tie me in its place. I will give myself for the wage of one dirham." He went into the donkey-mill and did the work of animals. He took a dirham, bought fish, ate it, and went to Mecca. He said, "Whenever a wish appears for you, you must stay one day in a donkey-mill to have it."

You must put to work all the tools of your ability. When incapacity appears, all work will turn its face to you. *"The incapacity to reach perception is perception."*[1105] Abū Bakr the sincerely truthful put everything into the midst until he reached the center-point of the circle, which is the wellspring of truthfulness. He became such that the one hundred twenty-some thousand center-points of sinlessness and the angels of the Dominion bore witness that the source of truthfulness was Abū Bakr.

Suppose you then stride forth for a thousand years. If you turn your gaze slightly toward states, deeds, and works, you will have bound a thousand seven-yard belts of unbelief around your waist.

There was a young man with a tremendous desire. One day he was in that yearning and ecstasy when suddenly the call of a bird reached his ear. He looked back toward the bird's call and went beneath the tree waiting for the bird to call again. A voice spoke to him, *"You have annulled God's covenant!* You have given away the key to My covenant, for you have become intimate with another."

One of the exalted ones of the religion said, "When the report reached me of the Prophet's command, *'Marry and reproduce,'*[1106] I took someone under my decree. A child came and my heart was afflicted by it. One night when I slept I saw the resurrection in a dream. I saw banners and, in the shadow of each banner, a group. I asked what the banners were. It was said that this is the banner of the renunciants, that is the banner of the patient, and that is the banner of the truthful. I saw a banner under whose shadow was a large group. I asked, 'Whose banner is that?'

"It was said, 'That is the banner of My lovers.' I placed myself in their midst, but they took my hand and threw me out.

"I said, 'I also am one of the lovers.'

"It was said, 'You were, but now your heart has inclined toward a child. We have effaced your name from the register.'

"I said, 'Lord God, now that a child is the obstacle in the road, take away the child's spirit.' In that same hour I heard the wailing of the women. I asked what it was.

"They said, 'The child fell from the roof and gave up its spirit.' "

Take care not to be deceived by these long robes, not to be deluded by these ruddy faces, and not to look back at these flourishing bodies. When religion and certainty settle down somewhere, they strike all with fire, leaving neither robe nor turban and wreaking havoc on everything. They make ruddy faces yellow and ruin flourishing bodies.

O All-Compelling, on whomsoever You place Your brand, You wreak havoc on heart and spirit! O Severe, whosoever sees Your beauty never sees any happiness from his own heart and spirit! This talk wants a burnt Bilāl, a melted Ṣuhayb, a Salmān with his spirit at the brink of death.

Having downed this wine, Muʿādh ibn Jabal became unsettled in drunkenness. He went to the door of the chamber of this person and that saying, *"Come, so that we may have faith for an hour"*[1107]—come so that we may drink this wine for an hour.

When the Companions heard these words, they went to the presence of the paragon. "O Chieftain of the Two Worlds, Muʿādh is inviting us—despite Abū Jahl, Nimrod, and

Pharaoh—as if we have no faith, for he keeps on yelling out, *'Come, so that we may have faith for an hour.'* "

The paragon said, "O Muʿādh, are you drinking wine from the grapes of bosom friendship's garden and then stirring up a ruckus with Bilāl?"

O dervish, no existent thing had the capacity for this wine or the ability to bear this potion: *Surely We offered the Trust* [33:72]. They all gave excuses: "We do not have the capacity for this wine. If we drink this wine and put this ring on our ears, we will fall apart." If you don't believe this, recite these words from the pages of the splendorous scripture: *"If We had sent this Quran down on a mountain, thou wouldst have seen it humbled, split apart by the fear of God"* [59:21]. "But whenever anyone drinks this wine, We will sit before him like serving boys."

The pearl of prophethood stood forth from Adam's disposition and said, "Where is this wine so that I may drink it?" When he drank the wine, all the angels bound the belt of service to his moon and stood before him in service. When the flavor of the wine reached his breast, he stretched out his hand to the tree. The call was given out, "O proximate angels, lift the crown from his head and take the belt from his waist, for Adam has become drunk from this wine, and it is not the work of the drunk to have the empire!"

When Moses became drunk—*Show me, that I may gaze upon Thee* [7:143]—that too was from this wine. "O Moses, vision is not being held back from you, but you are drunk. Wait until you're sober." When he became sober, he said, *"I repent to Thee"* [7:143].

As for the paragon of the empire, the pearl of sinlessness, the sun of felicity, the center-point of chieftainship—on the night of the *miʿrāj* at the top of *two-bows' length away*, he said, *"Take us not to task if we forget or make mistakes* [2:286]." Lord God, if I say something in drunkenness, do not take me to task.[1108]

He made everyone drunk with the wine of *Am I not your Lord?* [7:172]. He created ups and downs for this world and watered them with commands and prohibitions. He sent the drunkards into the world of ups and downs and set forth His will—"Clap your hands!"—and no one had the gall to say a thing.

> You take me to the well's edge and place Your hands.
> You say, "Refuge in God!" and then You push![1109]

Yes, the perils in the road are like this, the man is drunk, there are ups and downs, and then the address comes, *"Go straight to Him, and ask forgiveness of Him* [41:6]" : Hey drunkard, walk straight!

There is a lame gnat, missing a wing, a leg, and an eye, with the other eye shut. They throw it into an ocean of fire, or an ocean of water, and then they send out the address, "Hey, don't burn your wing, don't get wet!"

> The king said to me, "Drink wine, but don't get drunk!"
> O king, everyone who drinks wine gets drunk.

As for *Self-Standing*, it is an intensive form from *standing*. Anyone who believes that the Real is self-standing will be relieved of the toil of self-governance and relax in the ease of delegation. This is one of their sayings: *"When someone's concern is bread, he has no worth with God."*[1110] *Peace!*

69. *al-Wājid:* the Finder

Some say it means knower, and some say it means unneedy.[1111] God says, *"God is the Unneedy, and you are the poor"* [47:38].

When the *tawḥīd*-voicing person of faith believes that the Exalted Lord is unneedy in reality and that others are poor, he will take shelter in nothing but God's threshold. He will not disgrace himself at the door of anyone lowly, poor, indigent, or abased, for *"A created thing seeking aid from a created thing is like a prisoner seeking aid from a prisoner."*[1112] That would stand at the head of all absurdities.

It has come in the traditions that tomorrow a man of this community will be brought forward and a hundred thousand sashes of unbelief will be removed from his waist—not outward sashes, but rather sashes of the heart. Anyone who attaches his heart to a creature has bound a sash around his heart.

There is no steed quicker that Muḥammad's mount, and no playing field vaster than Muḥammad's playing field. Heaven and earth were made the dust beneath his feet, the Spirit of God was made to sit like a chamberlain at the edge of the carpet of his good fortune, and the Spirit of Holiness carried the saddlecloth of his greatness on its shoulders.[1113] Despite all the greatness, status, and rank that were his, it was said to him, "O Muḥammad, beat the drum of your own incapacity! *Say: 'I own no benefit for myself, nor harm'* [7:188]." Say that there is nothing in the hands of Muḥammad; then the friends will know that the drink of *tawḥīd* cannot be mixed with mortal nature. *"If anyone was worshiping Muḥammad, surely Muḥammad is dead. If anyone was worshiping God, He is alive and does not die."*[1114]

God is the Unneedy, and you are the poor. "There is no one in the world who does not have business with My threshold. It is I who have no business with anyone. The banner of unneediness is raised only at the threshold of My majesty."

When He gazes at someone, he should prostrate in gratitude a hundred thousand times, for despite His unneediness, He gazed upon his need, and all his need became delight, all his delight secrets. In truth, in truth, no existent thing in the universe has the gravity to receive one exalted gaze coming from the storehouse of knowledge to the threshold of the decree. In truth, in truth—a thousand times in truth, in truth!—His gaze on you is better than your gaze on yourself. The pain and regret are that He is gazing on you, but you are gazing on other than Him.

There was a man busy with the work of one of his slave boys. When he looked at the boy, the boy saw his lord looking at him and in coquetry he looked at his own beauty. The man drew his sword and killed him. They said, "What a wonder! You destroyed the slave boy who in your view was higher than life."

He said, *"I gazed at him, and he gazed at himself.* I was looking at him. Who was he that he should look at himself? When I was gazing at him, why was he not absorbed in my gaze?"

For forty years He kept Adam between Mecca and Taif in the encampment of the subtle recognitions. Without intermediary He put the collar of His gaze on the neck of his *tawḥīd*. May a thousand thousand lives be sacrificed to that era! What pleasure can a man have beyond the wine of that gaze when his own being is not blended with it!? Unmixed wine, without self-determination, in the cup of the effacement of the Law's prescription!

When someone has put poison into the cup, how can it give pleasure? Today there is the gaze, but the gaze is mixed with your being. The true gaze is that which belonged to Adam in the era of *"He fermented Adam's clay"*[1115]—a pure gaze, without the intrusion of dust's free choice.

No wine is sweeter than the beloved's gaze
smiling on the lover's face.[1116]

Know that in reality our true life was those forty years when we were in nonexistence itself and the gaze of the Eternal was taking care of our work, without pens or steps. "O man, abandon your own gaze! Here is My gaze." No one ever abandoned anything *for God in God* without receiving something better in return.

Ibn ʿAbbās narrated that *God's Messenger was with Asmāʾ bint ʿUmays when he said, "And upon you be peace!"*

She said, "To whom were you returning the greeting?"

He said, "That was Jaʿfar ibn Abī Ṭālib. He just passed by with Gabriel and Michael."

Muṣṭafā had sent Jaʿfar to war and had made him the head of the army, so the banner of Islam was in his hand. The unbelievers had attacked and cut off his hand, so he took up the banner in the other hand. They struck him again and cut off his other hand, and they struck him seventy-three times in the breast. Jaʿfar was saying, *"God will give me two wings in place of the hands, and with them I will fly in paradise wherever I want with Gabriel and Michael."*[1117]

First a man becomes a speaker, then a knower, then a traveler, then a flier. Where is the likeness of this? The Exalted Lord says in the story of Solomon, *"Then he fell to slashing their shanks and necks"* [38:33]. Solomon had beautiful horses—wingless birds, ships on land. Each was a mountain in body, a wave in shape, adorned like an eagle, a tail like an ostrich, a face like the moon, feet striding on wind, hooves ingots, eyes like suns. When that tale of the prayer took place, he drew his sword and cut their necks.[1118] It was said to him, "Now that you have done away with the horses, We will make the wind your steed."

"O Jaʿfar, you gave your hands. Here are wings. O Solomon, you gave your horses. Here is the wind, your carrier on sea and land. O truthful lover, if you sacrifice your eyes and throw away your hearing, then here: Our gentleness will be your eyes, Our bounty will be your hearing, Our generosity will be your lamp and candle. *When I love him, I am for him hearing, eyesight, and hand.*"[1119]

May a thousand thousand hearts and eyes be sacrificed to that first gaze!

O chevalier, there was no name or mark of Adam, no trace of dust, and the lordly gaze was debating with your antagonists: *"Surely I know what you do not know"* [2:30]. When He placed the cap of chosenness on Adam's head, it concealed all of his defects. Why do you look at the fact that the child came forth ugly from its mother? Look at the mother's tenderness!

Wait a few days until this carefree handful of dust, with naked feet and head, comes out from the special chamber of dust and mounts on the steed of good fortune. What is that steed? The wings of the angels of the Dominion. Then you will see the angels' embarrassment at what they said. The answer to the blamers is given only by the beloved's beauty.

Tomorrow the exalted ones will come on noble steeds of light and horses of joy, and the drum of exaltedness will be beaten before their throne. Who will beat this drum? Gabriel and Michael?

No, no! *"Enter [the Gardens] in peace, secure* [15:46]—without the intermediary of hearing, without the intermediary of wine, without the intermediary of seeing—without intermediary!"

The greatness of dust and clay is not trivial. What was done to that accursed one was done to no one else—the door to his repentance was shut. In the perfection of His generosity, He could have pardoned a hundred thousand Iblises, but because of wisdom and the requisite of the will it was said to generosity, "Pull back on the reins." And because of Adam's greatness it was said, "Put aside the whips."

"If the angels say, *'What, wilt Thou set therein one who will work corruption there?'* [2:30], have no fear, for We have appointed the preacher of gentleness to recite the sermon of your praise and laudation from the pulpit of bounty, saying, *'The repenters, the worshipers, the praisers, the journeyers, the bowers, the prostrators'* [9:112]."

O chevalier, the angels were the proximate of the Presence, the pure ones of the Threshold, the elect of the Higher Plenum, and the worshipers at *the Lote Tree of the Final End* [53:14]. But *"Our secrets are virgin, not seized by the imagination of any imaginer."*[1120]

It is absurd for Lordhood to seek something from mortal nature, for Lordhood to come forth from the pure Unseen to the threshold of mortal nature in order to seek, or for mortal nature itself to be such that Lordhood should seek something from it. That is the form known by the folk of the outward things. The reality is that everything sought by the command derives from the will, but the pivot of all the work is based on the decree. If the command should send the sultan of the decree with the signet of caressing to Byzantium, India, and Turkistan, all would throw the shawl of submission over the shoulders of surrender. No cross or sash would remain in the abode of unbelief and no denial would remain in the breasts of the folk of misguidance.

Had they heard her speech as I heard it,
they would have fallen down before it, bowing and prostrating.[1121]

The long and the short of it is that anyone who has heard His talk has done so through Him, and anyone who has remembered Him has done so through Him. Who in the eighteen thousand worlds would have the gall to talk of Him if this lofty proclamation had not come from the Exalted Presence on the hand of the messenger of confirmation? *"So remember Me; I will remember you* [2:152]. *Supplicate Me; I will respond to you* [40:60]."

There were people in the deserts of bewilderment and the darknesses of reflective thought. All at once the lordly gentleness and divine assistance traveled into the world of dust and turned the orphan of Abū Ṭālib into the orphan pearl of every seeker. When that chieftain of the two worlds came forth, he spread the tablecloth and called out a welcome. Those who were the noblemen of Quraysh like Abū Jahl and Abū Lahab did not respond. They said, "Noblemen and paragons disdain to be present at the invitation of beggars."

The welcome of the paragon of the two worlds wandered around the regions of the world. All the burned responded. That Abyssinian man heard the paragon's welcome and set out on the road. In Byzantium Ṣuhayb heard it and came rushing and running in astonishment. Like a lover, Salmān set off from Persia for the presence. When they arrived, they all sat down at the tablecloth. Good fortune clapped its hands, and the sun of felicity reached perfection in the heaven of their desire.

The stalwarts and headstrong looked at them and saw their own ill fortune in the foreheads of their good fortune. They became envious and wanted to chase them away from the tablecloth. They said, "O Messenger of God, drive them away so that we may sit with you. It is beneath our dignity to sit with beggars." Tumult fell into the city of prophethood because of his eager desire for their submission. He wanted this work to go forward, but this address came from the Exalted Presence: "Do not torment the hearts of the burned, for it is not the habit of the generous to drive away beggars from the tablecloth. *And drive not away those who supplicate their Lord morning and evening* [6:52]. O Muḥammad, you are an exalted messenger, pulled up and chosen by Me. You are the delight of the eyes of the empire, the sultan in the royal seat of My desire. It was a dust mote shining in the sunlight of your good fortune that made Abraham come running forth in the robe of bosom friendship to hold a lamp and that made Moses son of ʿImrān aim to bind himself to your saddle-straps."

"I am the chieftain of Adam's children, without boasting":[1122] Although I cannot talk about the wingspan of my eagle, the flight of my aspiration's phoenix, and the soar of my secrets' falcon, I have been instructed to say this much to the people: *"I am the chieftain of Adam's children."* Thus they will know that I am everyone's paragon and that all must come to my threshold. But in respect of my own sorrow and happiness, this is "*without boasting*," for I am inside my own special chamber, on the door of which is written, *"Thou hast nothing of the affair"* [3:128].

O Muḥammad, there is no way to stay only in the chamber. From time to time stroll outside the chamber and make your chieftainship apparent. Let those burnt ones also take some nourishment. Say to them, *"I am the chieftain of Adam's children."* Tell them, "I cannot be with you constantly, for I have another work beyond this. The secret of my aspiration does not come down to this—*without boasting*."

How can Solomon's empire appear next to this empire? A bird was lost and Solomon said, "Where is the bird? A deficiency has appeared in my empire!"[1123]

A call came, "O Solomon, what sort of empire is perfected by the existence a bird? An empire is the empire of Muḥammad the Arab, for if a hundred thousand holy ones were to spread their wings before the pavilion of his faultless moments, his realm would not increase; and if a hundred thousand defiant rebels were to put on the garment of disloyalty, his empire would not decrease."

The point is that first statement, from which this mystery began: Muṣṭafā was the sultan of the era, and a sultan has a hat on his head and a belt on his waist. The pattern of the hat was made from the burning heart of auspicious Bilāl, and the ends of the belt were made from the pain in the breasts of Ṣuhayb and Salmān. Then this expression was given out:

From my eyes and cheeks when in union
    she plundered ruddy jewels and gold.
Wanting me to love her more
    she made them her hat's sequins and her belt's clasp.

70–71. *al-Wāḥid al-Aḥad:* the One, the Unique

Some have said that there is no difference between *one* and *unique*. Some have made them different by saying that the name *unique* is specific to Him and is not said about any created thing, but *one* is said. Also, *one* is the beginning of the numbers, but *unique* is not like that.

The One is He who has no similar or, it is said, no partner.

The Real is the One, and the servant is the *tawḥīd*-voicer. *Tawḥīd* is a drinking place pure of the filth and opacity of both compulsion and free will.

Jaʿfar Ṣādiq spoke like this about *tawḥīd*: *"Anyone who supposes that God is upon something, or in something, or from something has associated others with Him. If He were on something, He would be carried. If He were in something, He would be confined. If He were from something, He would be newly arrived."*[1124] Anyone who says that God is on something, in something, or from something is at the head of all the dualists. If He were on something, He would have been lifted. If He were in something, He would be held back. If He were from something, He would be sculpted. *High indeed is God beyond all that!*

The root of tawḥīd *is to fly in the field of disengagement, to reside with His decrees in solitariness, to cut off fear and hope for the near and the far, and to surrender the affair to God so that He may decree whatever He desires.*

Abū Yazīd said, "Travel in the field of tawḥīd *until you reach the house of solitariness, then fly in the house of solitariness until you reach the valley of everlastingness. If you are thirsty, He will pour you a cup such that you will never thirst again."*[1125]

It is said that one day Shiblī was passing someplace wearing beautiful clothes. A merchant fancied that he also was a merchant. He said to him, "Might you in kindness undertake this calculation?" He gave him a long calculation that came to more than one hundred thousand. When he reached the end, he said, "How much do you have?"

Shiblī cried out, "One."

The merchant said, "You madman, I gave you a calculation that was over one hundred thousand, and you say 'One'?"

He said, "No, rather you are the madman." It is you who are mad, for the reality is one, and the rest is metaphor.

It is said that Shiblī became extremely ill, and this was reported to the caliph. He sent the head of his own physicians to cure him, and the physician was a Christian. Among other things he said to Shiblī, "If I come to know that your healing lies in cutting off my own fingers, I will cut them off so that the caliph will approve, for his heart is tremendously attached to you."

Shiblī said, "Healing does not lie in cutting fingers, but in cutting the sash."

The physician said, "If I cut off my sash, will you be healed?"

He said, "I will."

He cut off his sash and became a Muslim. At once Shiblī got up from the bed just like the healthy, and you would think that he had never been ill. He took the hand of the physician and went to the caliph to tell the story. *The caliph said, "I reckoned that I was sending the physician to the patient, but in fact I was sending the patient to heal the physician."*[1126]

It is also told about Shiblī that he said, *"The One suffices you against all, but all will not suffice you against the One."* The Real is One. If you have a thousand antagonists and enemies but the Real is with you, He will suffice. And if we suppose that you have a thousand thousand friends and helpers but the Real is against you, you will have nothing in your hand but wind.

The second of two, when the two were in the cave, when he said to his companion, "Grieve not; surely God is with us" [9:40]. It was said to a spider that was in the area, "We have concealed the paragon of the prophets and the head of the sincerely truthful in a cave. Go, set up the corner of your incapacity and poverty at the door of the cave so that you may be their escort." Nothing in the world is more incapable than a spider, and no house is weaker than its house. *And surely the frailest of houses is the house of the spider* [29:41].

"When We want to protect a messenger like Muḥammad and a friend like Abū Bakr, We protect them with a spider. When We want to destroy an enemy like Nimrod, We destroy him with a gnat. We can protect the friend with a spider and We can destroy the enemy with a gnat. When a spider makes a house, it takes a great deal of time, but the utmost limit of its aspiration is a fly. It is We who sometimes make a fly a spider's prey and sometimes bring a messenger, who is the Seal of the Prophets and the chieftain of the envoys, into a spider's house."

There is nothing in the world more covetous and arrogant than a fly, and nothing more contented and incapable than a spider. The Real decrees that the covetous fly will fall into the trap of the contented spider so that intelligent people will know that

When the apportionings give assistance,
the incapable join with the powerful.[1127]

When the beginningless apportionings come out into the open from the curtain of the Will, the incapable reach the powerful and the poor reach the wealthy. For seven hundred thousand years the angels of the Dominion had thrown back the morning draft of glorifying and the evening draft of hallowing in the violet garden and palatial emerald dome, lifting up the call of *we glorify Thy praise and call Thee holy* [2:30]. All at once a wonder appeared from the dust and, with one step, he took priority over their seven hundred thousand years of traveling.

Iblis had piled up a thousand thousand bales of obedience and pots of worship, but in the end he came out accursed. Adam, without any rushing and running, became the prayer-niche and kiblah of a thousand thousand proximate angels: "O accursed one, you argue that *Thou hast created me of fire and Thou hast created him of clay* [38:76]. Arguments do not go forward in the road by which I came. When I was brought, I was brought from the center-point of uncaused gentleness."

The folk of the realities speak in the tongue of inanimate things so that the lords of understandings may learn a lesson from that. Thus they say that a pot began to talk with a gourd. The gourd said to the pot, "Who are you?"

The pot said, "I have done the work, and hot and cold have reached my head. But you have been nourished in the shade."

The gourd answered, "Yes, it is as you say. But you came by the door of severity, and I came by the door of gentleness. The folk of severity will never be equal to the folk of gentleness.

If you want to know, then come with me into the water. You will see that you sink and I come to the top."

A thousand thousand proximate angels had spread the prayer-carpets of obedience on this ornamented howdah in the confines of need. All at once the sultan of love drew an unhesitating blade, took dust by the hand, and pulled it into the playing field of the work: "Oh, how many there are who wanted Me, but I wanted you!"

He fastened to them the word of godwariness [48:26]. When a beggar is clothed in a robe of honor like this, no fancy will appear in his head. A beggar who does not have bread for the night is suddenly given the sultan's robe of honor. If he does not stroll around in that robe, what will he do?

To which they have more right and of which they are worthy [48:26]. It is not proper to give to the unworthy, and there is no way to hold back from the worthy. Several people asked for Fāṭima in marriage, but the paragon apologized and sent someone to ʿAlī: "Why don't you talk about Fāṭima?"

To which they have more right. This *more* is the *more* of superiority, just as when you say, *"So and so is more beautiful than so and so,"* or *"So and so is more learned than so and so."* When the dust-dwelling Adam was brought into existence, he was brought in the guise of the attribute of superiority. Hence he stepped in front of all.

All the runners ran with you until they reached
their limit—you ran on but they stood still.[1128]

Everyone had a playing field and wandered around in that playing field. Then all of a sudden the high aspiration of dust charged on the steed of the spirit into the playing field of the Men and threw dust in everyone's eyes.

He fastened to them the word of godwariness [48:26]. The *word of godwariness* is *no god but God*, and the word *no god but God* is beginningless and without origin. In the beginningless beginning this word's eyes were open, looking to see when its seeker would appear. The Throne and the Footstool were brought into existence, the Pen and the Tablet, Gabriel and Michael. This word's eyes were open and looked to the road to see when a seeker with the inscription of the Haqiqah on his clear forehead would step forth from the concealment of nonexistence into the space of the decree. Finally the turn of dust and water arrived, toward the end of Friday. *"God created Adam in the last hour of Friday."*[1129] The word's yearning came together [*jam*ʿ] with Adam's yearning and it was said, "Call this day 'Friday' [*jum*ʿ*a*], for it is the day when the yearners came together."

When two fervent lovers sit together,
the pleasure they have is not two.
They make their spirits into one
divided between two bodies.
No cup is beautiful
if not passed between two lovers.[1130]

The first wherewithal in this road is quick-wittedness and discernment of value, lest you fall flat. By means of artisanry He brought all the existent things from the concealment of nonexistence to the vast plain of manifestation. Then He made Adam's aspiration the assayer of all. Adam was sent to paradise to tell its value. The scholars disagree as to whether you can buy what you have not seen. But the intelligent do not disagree that you cannot put a value on something if you have not seen it. Among all the existent things, none was more comely and beautiful than paradise. It was said: "Assign your assayer's eyes to paradise to see its value and worth."

Given the wherewithal bestowed on him and the garb thrown on his head, how could the eight paradises have appeared there? Adam struck the eight paradises against the touchstone of his own aspiration. From the height of his aspiration he said, "O Lord, I looked with my own assaying eyes and for me these eight paradises are worth no more than a grain. O Lord, when someone fears hell, he sees paradise as worth a thousand lives. But when someone fears the awesomeness of Your majesty, he sees paradise as not worth a grain."

Adam was put on a seat whose description you may have heard. Then came the address, "O angels, lift up the seat of his good fortune, for it is you who put it there, so you must lift it up. Place his seat opposite the Throne and turn your faces away from the Throne, for Adam's beauty and majesty have dismissed the Throne and, it is feared, they will strike fire into the Footstool. It is time to sacrifice your seven hundred thousand years of worship to the cap of Adam's good fortune, for such is he who is pulled up by the Sultan."

The angels suffered a strong blow from Adam, and then they wandered around in it. All at once the paragon of the world stuck his head out from the chamber of Umm Hānī; the sun veiled itself in shame and the moon fell apart in embarrassment. The angels of the Dominion fell into tumult and turmoil and apologized for their words. The paragon said to them, "Never again say *'While we'* [2:30]." What was that? *Sprinkling salt on the wound.*

On that night Gabriel's height went down to one cubit. The paragon said, "Gabriel, why are you so tiny?"

He said, "Yes, no one sees the beggars next to the wealthy."

Surely God and His angels bless the Prophet [33:56]. For seven hundred thousand years the angels went forth glorifying and hallowing until Adam's carpet was spread. When the carpet was spread, the address came, *"Prostrate yourselves before Adam!"* [2:34]. When they finished with that they said, "What happens next?"

They and the one hundred twenty-some thousand center-points of sinlessness were commanded to busy themselves with blessing the paragon, for the Shariah stipulates that when the child is noble, the father's inheritance should be placed next to him. The greatness of the embroidery, which was the mystery of the paragon's prophethood, took the sleeve of Adam's good fortune and pulled him away from the doorstep of nonexistence. It garbed him in a robe and put a crown on his head. Then it was melted down in the crucible of desire and given out from hand to hand until the last hand. The paragon put his head outside the tent of his union and called to the one hundred twenty-some thousand center-points of good fortune, "All of you have had your turn. Now send the seal ring and signet to me, and sleep happily for a while. I still have not taken care of the rightful due of the world." When he had discharged the rightful due of the world, he called out, *"The Highest Friend!"*[1131]

It is said that on the night the veil was lifted, he saw the whole world. In the midst he saw his mother, who kept on moving her lips. He wanted to talk to her, but he was not given permission.

Beautifully done, O perfect exaltedness! A hundred thousand were stirred up to exalt the rites of Islam, lest His command fall to the ground. A thousand thousand others were stirred up to take the sash of Guebrism to heart, lest His decree go to waste. By the decree of His majesty, a group remained in deprivation, and by the decree of His beauty, a group took benefit.

In every command He gave you, He sought from you a servanthood, and in every decree He issued to you, He wanted an awareness inside your heart. In one place He struck the fire of severity to their spirits, saying, *"Do they feel secure from God's deception?"* [7:99]. In another He planted the herb of gentleness in the garden of bounty: *"Despair not of God's mercy!"* [39:53].

When a man becomes aware of this talk, he catches fire from head to toe. He gazes at the vast plain of exaltedness and does not see any dwelling place. He wanders in the bloody tears of bewilderment and pours the tears of remorse down his face.

O dervish, the sword of severity becomes sharper every day, but these hapless ones fall more and more into love. *"Kings are such that there is no way to put up with them and no patience without them."*

Forever may the ends of Your tresses be curls upon curls
    and this pain of my heart be sigh upon sigh!
You're happy in my sorrow—may I have sorrow upon sorrow!
    Whoever's not happy with You, may he be less upon less![1132]

72. *al-Ṣamad:* the Self-Sufficient

The one to whom needs are lifted even though He has already taken care of all the work before the needs.

He melts one through severity and caresses another through gentleness. He says, *"Each day He is upon some task"* [55:29]. *Its meaning is something that He makes appear, not something that He begins. So praise the Lord who, before you asked, gave you that to which you would not have been guided had you been in control.* Give thanks to the Lord who, before you asked Him, gave you a gift that, if He had left you with yourself and you had thought for a thousand thousand years under your own control, you would not have reached. *He invited you when you were heedless, He taught you when you were ignorant, and He created you when you were "not a thing remembered"* [76:1]. *From the cup of His kindness He "will give you to drink of a pure wine"* [76:21] *in the sitting place of His secret.*

O dervish, think carefully! The gentleness that requested the Presence to pull you is beyond the gentleness that requested your creation, for at first He gave you to you, and then He takes you away from yourself.

He revealed to David, *"O David, make Me beloved to My servants."* Make me a friend in the heart of My servants.

David said, "How would that be?"

He said, "Remind them of My blessings and bounties.[1133] *Did I not give you blessings when you were needy? Did I not make you unneedy when you were poor? Did I not magnify your dignity when you were lowly? Did I not open My door to you? Did I not send down upon you My book?* Did I not open the door of My kindness to you? Did I not place the cushion of revelation's secret on the bench of your heart's limpidness? *Did I not let you witness the unseen of the Dominion? Did I not scatter over you the wonders of all-compellingness? Did I not bring you near the pavilions of intimacy? Did I not give you to drink from the cup of holiness? Did I not crown you with the crown of faith? Did I not sit you on the throne of security? Did I not disclose your election to everyone near and far? Did I not let you taste the sweetness of My turning toward you? Did I not bestow upon you My felicitations and gifts? Did I not inspire you to remember Me? Did I not deposit My secret with you? Did I not lift up My curtain from you? Who has seen My like? Do I have any likeness?*

"If you suppose that your mother and father were more merciful toward you than I, that is an error. *I inspired them with tenderness toward you, I urged them to act beautifully toward you, and I adorned you in their eyes so that they would nourish you when you were small and teach you courtesy when you were big.* I stirred them up and threw it into their hearts to look upon you with tenderness. I adorned you in their eyes. Were it not for My adorning and making beautiful, no one would pay you any regard."

Fuḍayl ibn ʿIyāḍ said, *"Every night, when shadows are mixed with brightness and eyes are resting, the Majestic calls out, 'Who has more tremendous munificence than I? The creatures are disobedient, but I protect them in their beds as if they were obedient. I am munificent with bounty toward the disobedient and I am bounteous toward the ugly-doers. Who is it that asks Me and I do not give to him? Who is it that supplicates Me and I do not respond to him? Who is it that trusts in Me and I do not suffice him? Who is it that comes to My door in distress and I push him aside? I am the possessor of bounty, and bounty comes from Me. Part of My generosity and munificence is that I bestow upon him who asks Me and upon him who does not. Part of My gift is that I forgive the repenter when he repents as if he was always repentant. So where will the creatures flee away from My door?' "*[1134]

An exalted one said when an old man repents, *God says to him, "Long have I invited you, but you did not come to Me, and now only a little strength remains in you. Old man, you were slow in coming, but I am generous. I forgive you despite what you have been busy with."* Now you have come, when your strength has failed, weakness has overcome you, and people are fed up with you, calling you the onerous, miserable old man. But I am generous. I accept you as you are. For the sake of Abraham I made sand into flour, in the era of Moses I made water into blood, in the era of Jesus I made clay into a bat, for the embryo I make menstrual blood into a subtle food, and for the repenter I make ugly deeds into beautiful deeds with My generosity. *Those—God will change their ugly deeds into beautiful deeds* [25:70].

It is said that tomorrow the disobedient servant will open his book and not see disobedience anywhere. He will say, "O Lord, what happened to all those acts of disobedience?"

The address will come, "I overlooked them. You too, overlook them."

O chevalier, it may be that it will be said to you, "Though you repented, you repented only of cutting and killing. You should not have fallen short." *How will it be* if it is said, "From you a teardrop, from Me a gaze. From you some pain, from Me a 'Make way!' Today weeping, tomorrow gazing."

I have seen that hell began to talk: *"Woe on him who recognizes You and then disobeys You!"* A call came, *"Woe on him who disobeys Me and then does not repent!* My servant is not the one who does not sin. My servant is the one who, when he falls into sin, quickly comes back to My door so that disloyalty does not come together with faults."

Be not like the bad servant who breaks a one-cent glass and flees, taking away his own worth of thirty dinars.

Repentance substitutes for obedience just as dust substitutes for water [in ablution]. Though the obedient person has obedience, the disobedient person has repentance. If the compensation for obedience is the Garden, the compensation for repentance is love: *Surely God loves the repenters* [2:222].

"Love is My attribute. When there is talk of attributes, how can the eight paradises—or rather, a thousand thousand paradises—appear? If I do not forgive you, who will forgive you? *Who forgives sins but God?* [3:135]. If the prince of Khorasan does not accept you, the prince of Iraq will accept you. But if I do not accept you, who will accept you?

"Abraham, who was the father of the creed and had the robe of bosom friendship, I called a servant; Isaac and Jacob, with all their struggle and contemplation, I called servants: *And remember Our servants Abraham and Isaac and Jacob* [38:45]. Job, with all his patience, I called a servant: *And remember Our servant Job* [38:41]. Solomon, with all his gratitude, I called a servant: *How excellent a servant!* [38:30]. And you, with all your disloyalty and faults, I called a servant: *Tell My servants* [15:49]."

Say: "O My servants who have been immoderate against yourselves, despair not of God's mercy. Surely God forgives all sins" [39:53]. This is nothing but the divine solicitude and the kingly kind favor. *"Surely God wrote a writing, and it is with Him on the Throne: 'My mercy takes precedence over My wrath.'* "[1135]

Already Our word has preceded [37:171]. *As for those to whom the most beautiful preceded from Us* [21:101]. All at once the precedence of mercy charges out from the concealment of the Unseen and unsettles a man. Friendship moves in his heart, friendship becomes thought, and thought becomes aspiration. Aspiration becomes intention, intention becomes resolve, resolve becomes strength, strength becomes movement, and assistance comes continuously. Then, in seriousness and effort the man says, *"God is greater."*

In the middle of the night or at dawn, disquiet appears for the truthful lover and sleep flees from his eyes. Warm clothing, a sweet sleeping place, a beautiful spouse—but the man has no sleep. He gets up, makes an ablution, and comes in pleading to the Exalted Presence. The call comes from the Presence, "My servant, if indeed you have said farewell to sleep and ease, here is My beauty and majesty. *'Those who carry burdens for My sake are in My eyes!'* "[1136]

When will one of the attractions of the Real be taken from the quiver of the Will and shot at the target of your heart's core such that you become His prey? Once you become His prey, you will turn away from this and that.

"With one pull We turn a Guebre into a possessor of the breast and a road-robber like Fuḍayl into a road-traveler. We do not need your deeds, but you do need Our help. For the sake of your heart We bring into the midst deeds for which We have no need. Why then do you remove from the midst the help that you need?

"There is an exalted secret in your deeds. The least thing is your acquisition, and the greatest thing is My decree. By the decree of friendship We bring the least thing, which is your acquisition, into the midst. Do you approve of removing from the midst the most exalted thing, which is My success-giving?"

O dervish, when Muṣṭafā said, *"There is no* ṣalāt *without the Fātiḥa of the Book,"*[1137] it is as if he had said, "There is no prayer without God's help."

Do you fancy that obeying commands is idleness? Do you fancy that going to His threshold is a small work? You cannot go before a sultan who has the name sultan metaphorically without permission. Can you come into the Exalted Presence, the threshold of the King who always was and always will be, without the edict of permission, the signet of leave, and the sigil of acceptance?

We are the ones lifted up by His knowledge; we are the ones given eminence by His decree. No one came to the angels asking them to marry the veiled virgin of the Unseen, the daughter of nobility. They did not have the worthiness to speak to her, for they were mere servants. It would be shameful for a distinguished man to give his daughter to his own serving boy. Those worthy of being asked to marry the veiled virgin are the Adamites, for they are friends, and a man gives his noble daughter to a friend, not to a serving boy. When the angels acquired a lineage, that was from the spirit [*rūḥ*], but when the Adamite acquired a lineage, that was from opening [*futūḥ*]: *"Every tie and lineage will be cut, except my tie and my lineage."*[1138]

On the day He said, *"I blew into him of My spirit"* [15:29], the Adamites' suitability was put in place. In the beginningless He decreed that sheer servanthood would contract a marriage with utter Lordhood: *"Am I not your Lord?"* [7:172]. The contract could only be made with someone suitable. In Adam's dust He prepared a subtlety from the pure realm of the Unseen, and that subtlety was the tie of suitability, for that subtlety received a lineage from the gentleness of the Presence. *He confirmed them with a spirit from Him* [58:22] is an allusion to this subtlety.

Outwardly He said, *"Am I not your Lord?"* But He also addressed them inwardly with His words *"He loves them and they love Him"* [5:54]. He was saying, "I am your friend. *By day I am sultan, by night we are brothers."*[1139] During the day He opens up the kingdom's pavilion, sits on the cushion of kingship, and makes the elect and the common stand. But when night arrives, He comes down from the throne of kingship and sits in the midst like a brother.

We are people melted by guileless eyes,
though we ourselves melt iron.
In adversity you see us as free men
and in peace as servants to friends.[1140]

When He said, *"Am I not your Lord?"* that was the night of running the kingdom. When He said, *"He loves them and they love Him,"* that was the time of caressing. In the religion of love, both gentleness and severity come forth, both caressing and melting, both being pulled and being killed, both making do and burning. There must be caresses so that a man may know the harshness of being taken to task, and there must be taking to task so that he may recognize the value of caresses.

When His men carry the burden of caresses, they carry it while contemplating severity. When they carry the burden of severity, they carry it while seeing gentleness. Whenever anyone is nurtured in only one thing, he does not have the capacity to carry something else. If you put a dung beetle, which spends its days in stench, in the midst of roses, there is fear that it will be destroyed, for it has passed its days in stench and does not have the wherewithal to carry the burden of fragrance.

The angels were nurtured in gentleness and did have the capacity to put up with severity. But the children of Adam have the capacity to put up with both gentleness and severity. *"If You chastise me, I love You, and if You have mercy on me, I love You."*[1141] That exalted one is saying, "If you have mercy, I am your lover, and if you appoint for me a hundred thousand heart-piercing, liver-burning arrows, I am still your lover."

Sultan Maḥmūd was in the hunting place. A beggar jumped out and grabbed the reins of his mount. Maḥmūd struck him hard with a whip. The beggar lifted up his head and said, "You hit hard, but you hit sweetly. For a long time I wished that the king would strike me. *Trial for love is like flames for gold.*"

Ibrāhīm Adham was going to Mecca. The shaykhs of the sanctuary were informed and came out to welcome him, though he was coming in front of the caravan so that no one would recognize him. The servitors came forward and said to him, "Has Ibrāhīm come close? The shaykhs of the sanctuary have come to welcome him."

He said, "What do you want with that heretic?"

They did not recognize him and slapped him. They said, "The shaykhs of Mecca are coming to welcome him, and you call him a heretic?" They passed him by.

Ibrāhīm said, "Watch out, O soul, you wanted the people to come out and welcome you. Well, you took a slap in hard cash. *The praise belongs to God* that I saw your desire in you!"[1142]

It is also related about Ibrāhīm Adham that he said, "Once I was in Damascus. I was going into the city but no one would let me into a mosque. I saw a brightness. I went ahead and saw the janitor in a bathhouse taking care of the furnace. I went in and said, *'Peace be upon you.'* He looked at me but did not respond to my greeting. I said, *'The praise belongs to God* that from kingship and empire I have reached the place where a janitor will not respond to my greeting.'"

There was a world taken up by purity, a surging ocean of glorification and hallowing. He gave them all the poison of severity and brought into existence a handful of the carefree. He said, "Even though all of you keep the scrolls of your deeds safe from the black spots of disobedient acts, I am bringing into existence a group who buy blights with a thousand lives, for that is worthy of My purity."

"When I created you, I did not create you to display your servanthood. The wisdom was to display My lordhood."

The angels were at the forefront of glorification's majesty. When the Adamites came out, the angels saw their glorification next to the Adamites' blights. The call came, "O hallowers and *tawḥīd*-reciters! I have no need for your laudations. My Presence is pure of glorifying and hallowing. Hold back from glorification and offer excuses for My friends."

When the forefront was surrendered to the Adamites, it was said to the angels, "You be their supplicators in the presence of My majesty."

When the daily provisions were written out, the Tablet was next to Seraphiel. When the work reached the tablet of the heart, God did not let anyone close. Seraphiel, who is thirty-thousand-yards tall, carries the Throne on his shoulders, but with all his tallness and tremendousness, the tablet of the heart did not fit next to him.

Although He gave the pen of the provisions to Seraphiel, He kept the pen of jealousy in His own power's grasp. The hearts are behind the curtain of exaltedness. Today He is heard behind the curtain of jealousy, and tomorrow He will be seen behind the curtain of jealousy.

One of their sayings is this: *"People are jealous over souls, and the Lord is jealous over hearts."*[1143] The fact that He does not show your heart to anyone is because it is hidden behind the curtain of jealousy. Tomorrow when people go to paradise, it will be said to the hearts, "Show hospitality to the eyes." When they see Him, that will be the hearts' hospitality toward the eyes. The heart is always in the Presence. It sees the Real, and the Real looks at it. It is He who can make a public session private. *Peace!*

73–74. *al-Qādir al-Muqtadir:* the Powerful, the Potent

The lords of the principles say, *"Power is that through which the desired is established in keeping with the aim of the actor."*[1144]

When you look at the Real's power, all nonexistent things take on the color of existence. When you look at the Real's exaltedness, all existent things take on the color of nonexistence.

You should not suppose that whatever He knew, He said; whatever He could do, He did; and whatever He had, He showed. The existent things and the created things are a sample of His power. The revelations and inspirations are an iota of His knowledge. He sent you a few decrees of His knowledge, but His knowledge did not run out. He put together a few clods of earth, but His power did not reach its end. He showed you a bit of yellow and red, but His treasury did not cease to be. If He were to create a thousand thousand Thrones, Footstools, heavens, and earths, He would not have made apparent an iota of His power. "Your power is a petitioner, but My power is transcendent. Your traveling is finite, but My road is infinite."

On the night of the *mi'rāj* the Messenger went to *two-bows' length away* [53:9]. But, from the standpoint of perfection, majesty, and tremendousness, *two-bows' length away* is the same as *beneath the ground* [20:6].

When you look from the community toward Muṣṭafā, he shows you this face: *"I am the chieftain of Adam's children, without boasting."*[1145] When you look from the Real's majesty toward Muḥammad, he shows you this face: *"I am the son of a woman of Quraysh who used to eat jerky."*[1146]

In the road of the Real's bounty there is *two-bows' length away*. In the road of the Real's exaltedness there is *the lowest of the low* [95:5]. When His caress arrives, He gives *beneath the ground* the color of the highest of the high. When His majesty charges forth, He makes *two-bows' length away* just like *beneath the ground.*

He commanded the people to recognize Him, but everyone was deprived of the secret of recognition by the decree of jealousy. He said, "See Me!" and He promised, but the veil of exaltedness was in the road.

O dervish, magnificence is His mantle, exaltedness His attribute, and majesty His rightful due. Once you have taken a step, met with a cuff, and seen some suffering, will He then put aside His majesty, throw off the mantle of magnificence, and change the attribute of exaltedness? By God, He will not! Tomorrow when eyes are open, veils are lifted, and eyes see Him, by God the veil of exaltedness will not be lifted!

Abū Yaʿqūb Nahrajūrī lived in the neighborhood of the Sanctuary for thirty years and never spoke. When he was dying, they instructed him, "Say: *'I bear witness that there is no god but God.'* "

He said, "How is this the place for that talk? *Nothing remains between Him and me but the veil of exaltedness.* "[1147]

The majesty of exaltedness has blocked the road of recognition's reality. The magnificence of exaltedness has become the veil before the eyes. People will take the road of recognition, but magnificence will stay in place. People will busy themselves with vision, but the veil of exaltedness will not be lifted. Imaginations will become lost in the road of recognition because of recognition's infinity. Understandings will stay bewildered in the road of vision because of the station's greatness.

> O marvelous sign, I know not what You are—
>   You stay hidden from the keen thoughts of knowers.
> A marvelous fancy keeps falling into my heart,
>   but in no way am I able to describe it.

*

> Poets expand their words in describing You,
>   entrusting meanings to Your attributes.
> They fall short in Your description
>   and erase what is written in their hearts.

"O My unique knowledge in the beginningless beginning, give a turn to commands and prohibitions for a few days!

"One hundred and twenty-some thousand pearls of prophethood came to the vast plain, but no one discharged My rightful due. *What do water and clay have to do with talk of the Lord of the Worlds? What does the creation* [*khalīqa*] *have to do with the Reality* [*ḥaqīqa*]?

"O commands and prohibitions, give the turn back to knowledge, for My knowledge alone does the work. From East to West, whenever dust settled on a cloak, they shook the cloak. My knowledge remained pure and My decree was left for tomorrow."

He will say to His exalted ones, "In that world, you did a few little jobs. Even if outwardly you chose freely because of the Law's prescription, in reality you did it under constraint because of My decree. Behind the curtain of your freely choosing the Shariah I concealed the form of My decree. Today I will not look at the curtain of free choice. I will look at the form of the decree."

The unbelievers will be addressed by the command, and the friends will be addressed by the decree. The command will be the antagonist of the estranged, and the decree will intercede for the friends. The estranged will go forth beaten and pounded by the command's severity to the place of the command's vengeance. The friends will go forth escorted by the decree's intercession to the resting place of the decree's gentleness.

No one buys these words save the Folk of the Sunnah. Buyers appear for coarse cotton, and buyers appear for Byzantine silk.

Tell heaven and earth to stay pure and to bear witness in the Presence that this man is a tavern-goer! What we need is for the Sultan to have a beautiful opinion of us.

As for the fact that tomorrow He will allow Muṣṭafā to intercede, that is to display Muṣṭafā. Otherwise, no one will come forth to intercede for the state of the friends, because His friendship will already have interceded for them. Our work with Him will remain with our servanthood, and His work with us will remain with His Lordhood. What comes out of the house of beggars is worthy of beggars, and what comes out of the house of sultans is suited for sultans.

"Today is suited for your work with Me, and tomorrow will be suited for My work with you. Today is your never-having-been, and tomorrow will be My always-having-been. Today you are wounded by your never-having-been, and tomorrow you will be lifted up by My always-having-been."

When will they take away this mask
so we may know poison from sugar?[1148]

When the turn of His justice comes, the prophets seek a road of escape. When the turn of His bounty comes, the tavern-goers hold their heads high. David's heart became constricted and he was ashamed of what he had done. He stayed in prostration for forty days: *"O God, forgive me, though I have no excuse."*

I dare not say any more. When someone has no money for soap, why would you offer him sugar? O dervish, as long as you have not acknowledged your own destitution, nothing will come of you. A hundred thousand put on patched cloaks so that perhaps they'll find a whiff of destitution. You must not be a *tawḥīd*-voicer with your own *tawḥīd*-voicing. You must be a *tawḥīd*-voicer through His oneness.

Whoever is more of a master is more naked. The master of the whole world in the Shariah and the Tariqah was Muḥammad. It was for his sake that Gabriel was obedient for several thousand years until it was said to him on the night of the *mi'rāj*, "Hold this man's saddlecloth; that will be enough reward for your obedience." But look at how he was stripped naked: *thou hast nothing of the affair* [3:128].

The moon gambled with my heart and won,
leaving the trace of weakness in my eyes.
Ever since the moon's love sat in my heart,
there's been nothing in my heart but the moon.[1149]

By God the Tremendous, as long as you do not lift your eyes away from yourself, you will never see any brightness. Moses said, *"Show me."* He said, *"Thou shalt not see Me"* [7:143]. It was said to Muḥammad, *"Hast thou not seen thy Lord?"* [25:45]: Will you not look at Me once?

Tell anyone who wants to sniff the heart's rose to choose thorns and hold fast to them. O exalted ones of the Real, everyone who perishes, perishes in his own fancy!

An exalted man said, *"I saw seventy of the sincerely truthful who perished by imagining things."*

Revelation came to David: *"O David, give good news to the sinners, and warn the sincerely truthful!"*[1150]

It is the habit of kings that when they want to poison someone, they wait for the day he is feeling the most secure.

"When you have performed a pure hajj, done sincere prayers, and fasted without misgiving, fear Me!"

Does anyone in the world have the nerve to bring something to the All-Compelling Presence, the Severe Threshold?

It was said to that paragon, "When you go before the people, go with the flag of rulership and the banner of prophethood's elevation. When you come to My Exalted Presence, come in the shirt of servanthood and the waistcoat of effacement."

Glory be to Him who took His servant by night! [17:1]. He did not say, "His prophet."

"When there is talk of your prophethood and messengerhood, I swear an oath by your life: *'By thy life!'* [15:72]. When there is talk of My majesty and exaltedness, *thou wilt die* [39:30]."

Shaykh Abu'l-Ḥasan Kharaqānī said, "It is twenty years since my shroud was brought from heaven."[1151]

He also said, "How marvelous that when I am with the people He keeps me in the form of the living, even though He put the shroud on me from His own presence."

> Don't think about this talk, put on the shroud
> and clap your hands like a man.
> Say, "Either You or me in the city"—
> a realm with two heads is in turmoil.

When one drop of sperm [*manī*] comes out from within, outward pollution is established. When one speck of I-ness [*manī*] takes up residence inside, inward pollution comes outside. Outward pollution is lifted away with water, but inward pollution will not disappear with all the world's oceans.

All unbelief, misguidance, hypocrisy, and heresy in the world stick up their heads from the chamber of your free choice. In the eighteen thousand worlds there is no shadow more inauspicious than fancy. It is sincerity that puts fancy to flight.

Ibrāhīm Shaybān said, "I performed so may acts of discipline in the road that I slaughtered the soul with the knife of severity *until I remained without me."* I was left without me.

A poor man can take nothing to the threshold of a wealthy man other than poverty and want. The sons of Jacob took poverty and want to Joseph. They said, *"We come with scant merchandise"* [12:88]. Joseph lifted the mask from his own beauty and came forward with this tongue: *"No reproof is upon you today"* [12:92]. Rare is the eye that opens up to human incapacity and Adamic poverty and want!

God reported about the attribute of His knowledge: *"Surely God knows everything"* [29:62]. He reported about the attribute of our ignorance: *"Surely he was a great wrongdoer, deeply ignorant"* [33:72].

He reported about His attribute of power: *"Surely God is powerful over everything"* [2:109]. He reported about our attribute of incapacity: *"God strikes a likeness: a servant possessed by his master, having no power over anything"* [16:75].

He reported about His attribute of exaltation: *"Surely the exaltation, all of it, belongs to God"* [4:139]. He reported about our abasement: *"And faces are humbled to the Alive, the Self-Standing"* [20:111].

He reported about His attribute of incomparability and holiness: *"Glory be to thy Lord, the Lord of exaltedness, above what they describe"* [37:180]. He reported about our attribute of taintedness: *"Did We not create you of a feeble water?"* [77:20].

He reported about His attribute of subsistence: *"There subsists the face of thy Lord, Possessor of Majesty and Generous Giving"* [55:27]. He reported about our attribute of annihilation: *"Everything upon it undergoes annihilation"* [55:26].

He reported about His attribute of life: *"And trust in the Alive who does not die"* [25:58]. He reported about our attribute of death: *"Surely thou wilt die and surely they will die"* [39:30].

Lordhood is His attribute—*your Lord and the Lord of your fathers, the first* [26:36]—so servanthood is our attribute: *I created jinn and mankind only to serve Me* [51:56].

Unity is His attribute—*your God is one God* [16:22]—so pairedness and association are our attribute: *Of everything We created a pair* [51:49].

But when He reported about the attribute of love, He affirmed love for us just as He affirmed love for Himself: *"He loves them and they love Him"* [5:54].

Here there must be an intimation that will increase the repose of the spirit for the lovers: Knowledge, power, life, holiness, subsistence, and unity are attributes of His Essence, and His Essence is hallowed and incomparable, so those attributes are worthy of Him. *"Glory be to Him who clad Himself in exaltedness and is worthy of that!"*[1152] But when you look at the Adamic essence, it is tainted and distracted, opaque, a bit of dark water and clay. Hence many different attributes appear within it.

But the site of love is the heart, and the heart is pure gold, the pearl of the breast's ocean, the ruby of the secret core's mine. The hand of no other has touched it, nor has the eye of any non-privy fallen upon it. It has been cleansed by the contemplation of His majesty, sealed by the burnisher of the Unseen, and made bright and limpid. Since the heart's work stands on all this, the Exalted Presence has a love for it. He held the beauty of that love before the hearts of the exalted ones, and the luminous traces of the beauty of unqualified love appeared in the mirror of their hearts. So our love abides through His love, not His love through our love.

An image in a mirror subsists through the beauty of the form, not the subsistence of the mirror. If you take the form away, the image will go. If the sultan of *He loves them* put on the shirt of exaltedness and unneediness, nothing but wind would remain in the incapable hands of *they love Him*.

Bishr Ḥāfī said, "If you prostrate yourself in gratitude for the lifetime of the universe, you would not discharge what is rightfully due to Him, for in the Beginningless He included you when He talked of His friends." [1153]

There were many existent things and countless artifacts, but He had this work with no one but you. If there were any cause for this, well, He had luminous individuals in the Highest Dominion, all of whom had the garment of sinlessness, the shirt of reverence, the station of service, and the feet of obedience. But not everyone who is worthy for the edge of the carpet is worthy for the station of bold expansiveness, and not everyone who is worthy for service is worthy for love. Not everyone who is an ornament of the threshold is like the beauty of the forefront. Not everyone who was brought forth not to see is like him who was brought forth in order to see.

Someone said to Sultan Maḥmūd, "You have many Turk and Kashmiri servants more beautiful than Ayāz. Why this love for Ayāz?"

He said, "On the day the brand of love for Ayāz was placed on my heart, it was done by predetermination, not by deliberation with me."

75–76. *al-Muqaddim al-Mu'akhkhir:* the Forward-Setter, the Behind-Keeper

With His bounty He sets forward whomsoever He wants, without any cause; and with His justice He keeps behind whomsoever He wants, without any cause.

"No one sets forward what He keeps behind, and no one keeps behind what He sets forward." [1154] Once He has fixed someone's feet on the carpet of setting forward, if the world's folk want something else, they will have no portion but loss. And once He has kept someone back from the carpet of the religion with the whips of harshness, if the world's folk want to appear in opposition, their attribute will be nothing but ignorance.

They said, "Why was this Quran not sent down upon a great man from the two cities?" [43:31]. In their foolishness and recklessness the stalwarts of Quraysh said, "From the whole world the hat of prophethood and the diadem of messengerhood was placed on the head of Abū Ṭālib's orphan."

The caller of exaltedness called out, *"Is it they who divide up the mercy of thy Lord? We have divided* [43:32]. What place is this for that talk? This is the man concerning whom We addressed Moses like this in the station of whispered prayer: *'O Moses, if you desire that I be closer to you than your speech to your tongue, than your heart's thoughts to your heart, and than your spirit to your soul, then multiply blessings on Muḥammad, the unlettered prophet.'* " [1155]

Surely God and His angels bless the Prophet [33:56]. I have seen that when this verse came to Muṣṭafā, Abū Bakr said, "O paragon, this is a fine gift, but gifts are shared. What verse is coming for us?" Then this verse came: *"It is He who blesses you, and His angels"* [33:43]. [1156]

When this verse came, *"that God may forgive thee thy sins set forward and put behind"* [48:2], the Companions said, "Congratulations, O Messenger of God!" So God sent down, *"Surely God forgives all sins"* [39:53].

When this verse came, *"And that God may help thee with an exalted help"* [48:3], the Companions said, "Congratulations, O Messenger of God!" So God sent down, *"Surely We will help Our messengers and those who have faith"* [40:51].

And when this verse came, *"Did We not expand thy breast for thee?"* [94:1], the Companions said, "Congratulations, O Messenger of God!" So God sent down, *"What of him whose breast God has expanded for the submission, so he is upon a light from his Lord?"* [39:22].

What a marvelous business! They were beating the Kaykawusian kettledrum[1157] of his majestic state in the *two-bows' length away* of his messengerhood and guidance, but he was not finding any bread to eat. On silk and satin in his exalted palace the caesar of Byzantium had no settledness or rest in fear of the flashing sword of his vengeance, but he was piling one hunger on another. What was that? The exaltedness and eminence of poverty. Wherever there is a corner of poverty, that is a sanctuary of the Real's generosity, and the angels of the Dominion come to it for their hajj and umrah. The *mi'rāj* of the earth-dwellers is like the Prophet's, but the *mi'rāj* of the heaven-dwellers—in terms of meaning, not in terms of the word—is like this. Those who keep to this world delight in this world, but the poor make do with *We have divided* [43:32].

God has a gaze that pushes away, and a gaze that pulls close. Just as He said to that accursed one, *"Go out!"* [7:13], so also He said to the paragon, *"Draw near!"* [96:19]. When He turns away from someone, that is a wound that has no cure. When He turns toward someone, the dust of His house makes all the world's beggars wealthy. Whatever He does He does as He desires, and that is His rightful due. If a thousand thousand homes and families of mortal man were to sink down in black water, no dust or piece of straw would settle on the hem of the Holy Majesty.

Rare are those whose eyes witness the sites bearing witness to the majesty and beauty of unity such that they do not dispute with His unity. The Guebres were ambushed on this road of unity and said, "Yazdān and Ahrīman."

Yes, a complete man is needed to pick up a morsel from its place, put it into his mouth, and chew. When people accepted *no god but God* and aimed for the presence of *tawḥīd*, open Guebrism could not come to them, but they were ambushed by mortal nature. In ignorance they said, "If we turn all the newly arrived things over to God, He will be defective." They kept on saying, "Good is from Him and evil from us," just as that group said: "Good is from Yazdān and evil from Ahrīman." These became open Guebres, and those became secret Guebres. Both groups were ambushed in the road of unity.

"You fools, My decree has the color of My lordhood! When it turns its face toward you, it takes on your color."

In the whole world no one has the gall to move by himself without Him. *None is there in the heavens and the earth that comes not to the All-Merciful as a servant* [19:93]. We are the slaves of the All-Compelling. What is the meaning of All-Compelling? "He carried them according to His desire." He took the whole world unwillingly to what He desired. If anyone knocks on the gate of unity with anything other than the knocker of surrender, wash your hands of him.

A free-willer said to a Guebre, "Become a Muslim."

He said, "As long as He does not want it, how can I become a Muslim?"

He said, "He wants it, but Iblis does not want it."

He said, "Then I'll stay with the stronger antagonist. What would I do with the weak one?"

Let us come back to the first discussion. We were speaking about Muṣṭafā's eminence, but *"Talk has many valleys."*[1158] The truthfulness of all the world's sincerely truthful was the dust on the laces of his serving boys' shoes, but the deniers gave him the title "liar." The clamoring sound of revelation from the Unseen was in love with his exalted ears, but the estranged named him "soothsayer." The intellects of the intelligent were incapable of perceiving the light of his exaltation's shoelaces, but the unbelievers called him "madman." All the words of the world's folk were slave boys to one word from his edict's mystery, but the unworthy spoke of him as "poet."

O chevalier, whenever eyes tainted by suspicion look, they see nothing but the suspicious. *"The ugly-doer looks at people with the eye of his own nature."*[1159] They threw camel tripe at the head of a man who would be taken by night to *two-bows' length away.* The fruit on the branch of the paragon's aspiration was *then He drew close, so He came down, so he was two-bows' length away, or closer* [53:8–9], but they called him a tree without roots.

What is this? Eyes that by the decree of the beginningless gentleness did not receive the ointment of truthfulness; eyes that in the night of nonexistence were not anointed by the oculist of munificence with the antimony of welcoming his existence. Abū Bakr, ʿUmar, ʿUthmān, and ʿAlī looked with the same eyes as Abū Jahl, ʿUtba, Shayba, and ʿUqba. But Abū Jahl's eyes were dazzled by denial, and Abū Bakr's eyes were burnished by asking forgiveness. ʿUtba's eyes were veiled by the night of rejection in the Beginningless, and ʿUmar's eyes were brightened by the morning of acceptance in the Beginningless. Shayba's eyes were blindfolded because he was not wanted by the Unseen, and ʿUthmān's eyes were opened by the Unseen's welcome. ʿUqba's eyes were blinded by the Real's knowledge, and ʿAlī's eyes were anointed by the collyrium of the Real's decree.

"O Muḥammad, say to the people, 'If you want to know me, bring a heart. If you want to hear my words, search for ears. If you want to see me, seek eyes. If you want to walk with me, acquire feet.' "

"From where should we bring these bodily parts? If eyes are needed, we don't have them. If ears are needed, we don't have them—and so on to the end."

"No, no, I don't want these bodily parts, for Satan has put them to use. They are stained by the intervention of mortal nature and polluted by the being of Adamic nature. If you want to know me, bring a heart that has sought shelter in the Real's assurance of security and His sanctuary of generosity. If you want to recognize me, bring a breast that has become the dwelling place of my gaze. If you want to hear my words, bring ears washed by the pure water of the beginningless welcome. If you want to see my miracles and signs, bring eyes that have awoken from the sleep of appetites. If you want to walk my road, bring feet that have put on the shoes of my request and step forward in my desire. Otherwise, stay far away and take what is suited to what it suits: Make love to the devil's children, sleep with appetites, wake up with pleasures. If someone has not the beauty to be the sultan's boon companion, what can he do but be the comrade of the dwellers in the garbage dumps?"

I've always been a chamberlain in the taverns—
how can I be worthy of the monastery?
Though I'm a scoundrel and a rascal,
I scatter the seeds of hope and pain.

Muḥammad is not the father of any of your men [33:40]. Muḥammad is not your father. If he were your father, the testimony of a father concerning his son would not be heard. But tomorrow he will testify to the purity of his community.

But rather the messenger of God and the seal of the prophets [33:40]. "Each of the 313 envoys who came was a door in the street of explaining the Shariah. Those doors stayed open until the time of my coming. When the phoenix of revelation came to be trained at the hand of my aspiration, all the doors were shut tight so that access would be at my door and the work at my threshold; in this world are my Sunnah and congregation, and in that world will be the signet of my intercession. This world was put under the gaze of my view and that world is there for my serving boys. But why talk of this when both worlds were sacrificed to the dust under my feet? *'I created what I created only for thee.'* "[1160]

God is the light of the heavens and the earth. The likeness of his light is as a niche [24:35]. A group of the commentators, such as Muḥammad ibn Ka'b, Ḍaḥḥāk, and Ka'b said that the pronoun *his* alludes to Muṣṭafā,[1161] for his created nature was light, his children were light, his visage was light, his community was light, his practice was light, his miracles were light, his Companions were light, and he in his essence—*upon him be peace!*—was *light upon light* [24:35].

As for the explanation of the light of created nature and lineage: It has been narrated that the first thing that the Real brought forth from the concealment of nonexistence to the space of the decree was a shining, brilliant pearl, whose light cannot be justly described by any describer. *He who describes it has not done it justice.* After that *He gazed upon it with the gaze of awesomeness and it became three: a third of it was water, a third light, and a third fire. He mixed the water with the fire, so smoke shot up from it, waves became agitated by it, and the light rose high above both.* He brought earth into existence from a speck of foam and heaven from a bit of smoke. The light, whose attribute was highness, became three branches: one branch beneath, one branch in the middle, and one branch above. From the lowest branch the power of the Real brought into existence the sun, the moon, the planets, the fixed stars, and every light in the world. From the middle branch the power of the Maker brought into existence the Throne, the Footstool, and the Garden. *As for the light that rose up high, He kept it in the storehouses of His kingdom and the treasuries of His secret in order to deposit it by His wisdom in whomsoever He chose by His will. It is this light that adorns the understandings of the intelligent, the hearts of the recognizers, the secret cores of the* tawḥīd-*voicers, and the secret centers of the prophets and envoys.*

Then He commanded that the share of light concealed in the treasuries of power and belonging to the chieftain of the envoys be brought out into the open and given in trust to the proximate ones of the Presence. For a thousand years it swam in the ocean of purity. Then it swam for a thousand years in the ocean of goodliness and incomparability. Then it swam for a thousand years in the ocean of proximity and contemplation. Then the light was clothed in seventy thousand robes of honor—robes of godwariness, guidance, knowledge, sinlessness, scrupulosity, and safeguarding. Then it stood for four thousand years in the station of service and worship. When seven thousand years were completed, the Real commanded Gabriel to take a handful from the face of the earth, as you have heard.

What was this handful? It was a curtain behind which was prepared the light of Muḥammad. *Then God commanded that this light be curtained within seventy thousand veils so that it would not be seen or witnessed, lest its brightness extinguish the light of the sun and the moon. When the light was curtained, He mixed it with the soil that was the soil of Muḥammad and deposited it in the soil of Adam, so it sparkled on his forehead.*

Adam had to pack his bags from the adorned Firdaws because of the tumult and turmoil of that light. It said to Adam, "Pack your bags, for you cannot sit still if you have not traveled the road." By the decree of the Tariqah's jealousy the light in Adam's clear forehead charged forth, upsetting the eight paradises and striking against Adam like a knocker on the door. Were it not for the tugging and pulling of that light, Adam would have been happy with the paradisial houris. But the center-point of *"Our poverty is our boast"*[1162] would not give itself up to ease.

"O Adam, given how many are hungry, thirsty, and waiting on the limpid bench of your solid loins, it is not beautiful to eat alone. Leave this place and give out the call, 'Come and get it!' Then someone burnt will come from Abyssinia, someone pain-stricken from Byzantium, someone sorrowful from Persia. We will set up the House of Sorrows on the plain of the resurrection waiting for the Josephs of the community. How is this a place for gazing on houris?"

Then that light came from Adam's forehead to the brow of Seth. With the passing of time and the succession of eras it traveled until this call was given out: *"There have come to you from God a light and a clarifying book* [5:15]."

The likeness of his light is as a niche, inside the niche a lamp, the lamp inside a glass [24:35]. The *niche* is Adam, the *glass* is Noah, and the *lamp* is Muṣṭafā. Here He said *miṣbāḥ,* and elsewhere He said *sirāj* [33:46]. Both *miṣbāḥ* and *sirāj* mean lamp. When someone has a dear friend, he says to him, "O my eye and lamp!"

As for the light of his visage: The Commander of the Faithful ʿAlī narrated, *"He—God bless him—had beauty, splendor, awesomeness, and a light shining over him. Everyone who saw him up close loved him, and everyone who saw him from afar stood in awe of him."*

ʿĀʾisha the sincerely truthful narrated, "I lost a needle at night. I was searching for it but did not find it. The paragon came in from the door *and when the light of his face brightened the room I found the needle."*[1163] When I found the needle from the radiance of his beauty and the shining of his perfect face, I wept.

"Muṣṭafā said, 'Why do you weep?'

"I said, 'In fear of separation.'

"He said, 'O ʿĀʾisha, do you weep in fear of separation in this world or in fear of separation in the next world?'

"I said, 'In fear of separation in the next world.' "

As for the light of practice: On his head was the light of humility, on his forehead the light of prostration, on his eyebrows the light of humbleness, in his eyes the light of heedfulness, on his face the light of jealousy, in his ears the light of the rightful due, in his mouth the light of patience, on his tongue the light of remembrance, in his hair the light of beauty, on his neck the light of surrender, on his shoulders the light of elevation, between his shoulders the light of prophethood, on his upper arms the light of strength, on his forearms the light of struggle, on his palms the light of liberality, in his breast the light of approval, in his heart the light of recognition and limpidness, in his secret core the light of the awe of God, in his spirit the light of yearning, on his sides the light of uprightness, on his back the light of trust, in his stomach the light of contentment, in his liver the light of courage, in his private parts the light of holding in trust, on his thighs the light of shame, on his knees the light of reliance, on his calves the light of certainty, on his feet the light of service, in all of his essence the light of obedience, in his bearing witness the light of disengagement, in his disengagement the light of solitariness, in his solitariness the light of *tawḥīd,* in his *tawḥīd* the light of realization, in his realization the light of assent, in his assent the light of success-giving, in his purification the light of intention, in his intention the light of making limpid, in his making limpid the light of making blameless, in his prayer the light of conjoining, in his conjoining the light of disjoining, in his disjoining the light of union, in his alms the light of manliness, on the crown of his head the light of chivalry, in his chivalry the light of prophethood, in his fasting the light of scrupulosity, in his scrupulosity the light of abandoning wants, in his hajj the light of poverty, in his poverty the light of boasting, in his boasting the light of brokenness, in his struggle the light of jealousy, in his jealousy the light of thought, in his thought the light of heedfulness, in his heedfulness the light of the Presence, in his speech the light of wisdom, in his wisdom the light of blessings, in his blessings the light of service, in his service the light of mercy, in his mercy the light of silence, in his silence the light of reverence, and in his reverence the light of surrender.

Surely the Messenger is a light-giving lamp,
Indian steel, a burnished sword of God.
I've been told that God's Messenger threatened me,
but I hope for pardon from God's Messenger.[1164]

Tubba', the king of Himyar, said to his diviner, "Do you find any kingdom greater than my kingdom?"

The diviner said, "Yes."

He said, "Whose?"

He said, "I find it for one who is pious and blessed, aided by triumph, described in the Psalms, his community considered most excellent in the scriptures. He will dispel the darknesses with light. He is Aḥmad the prophet. Blessed will be his community when he comes!"[1165]

As for the light of birth, that is well known. Āmina, the mother of Muṣṭafā, said, "On the night when this child came from me, a light was separated from me that brightened East and West." Somewhere I saw it written that on the night when he came from his mother, he put his face on the ground at once and made a prostration. Then he looked at heaven and said with an eloquent tongue, *"I bear witness that there is no god but God, and I bear witness that Muḥammad is God's messenger."* Lest you wonder at this, Jesus, who gave the good news of his stepping forth, talked when he was in the cradle. What wonder is it if the paragon should also talk?

The light of miracles: The story of the moat is well known, and the hardness that appeared in the stone. The paragon came and struck it with a pickax, and lights jumped out, each light giving the good news of victory.[1166]

The light of the Companions: Usayd ibn Ḥuḍayr narrated, "One night I was reciting the Quran, the Surah of the Cow. I lifted up my head and saw a parasol like a sunshade, in the midst of which were lights coming from heaven. I was afraid and became silent. In the morning I went and told the paragon. He said, 'Those were angels coming to listen. *If you had continued, you would have seen wonders.*' "[1167]

The light of the community: *Their light running before them and on their right hands* [57:12].

> *If we set out at night with you in front,*
> *your face will be guide enough for our steeds.*[1168]

When the paragon was brought into the world, he was brought like a sultan. There was a world overtaken by caprice and heresy, overmastered by appetite, and commanded by desires. It was said to the Chieftain of the Two Worlds, "Go tell these ignorant people to come from the factory of caprice to the threshold of guidance" : *"None of you will have faith until you make your caprice follow what I have brought."*[1169] As long as you do not bring caprice underfoot and place what I have brought on your heads, nothing will come of you.

They had made their own dark thoughts their exemplar and turned their own inverted opinions into their leader. They considered nature their prayer-niche. The more they looked, the less they saw. The farther forward they went, the more they fell behind. As much as they sought for more, they found less. Why? Because they did not search with the Real, they searched with intellect. They did not go by a shariah, they went by nature. They spoke of the spheres, minute by minute. They knew the nature of each thing in reality, they went a hundred roads in outward treatments, and they spoke of several meanings, one by one, in the composition of each part. They spread the carpet according to their own wishes and desires and placed a hundred roads before themselves, but the Haqiqah stayed veiled by the attribute of exaltedness.

Sometimes they spoke of the intelligible as universal, sometimes they made the celestial world the goal, sometimes they described the world as eternal, sometimes they spoke of the spheres as knowing and powerful, sometimes they spoke of the stars as governors and pointers, sometimes they considered the four natures effectors and originators, and sometimes they took up a road whose end was nothing but blindness and misguidance. They made intellect their God, they made nature the messenger, and they called the spheres the determiner. They made things deemed beautiful by intellect into their shariah and spoke of things disliked by nature as prohibited. They were busy with the celestial figures and guises and wasted their days with epicycles and embellishments. Suddenly the sun of the Muhammadan Shariah's good fortune appeared from the horizon of the unitary welcome. The wind of the good fortune of the lordly guidance blew, throwing the dust of abandonment in the intellective eyes of those who were intervening in nature.

Five hundred years have now passed. They want to remove the dust of abandonment from their eyes but cannot. Beware, beware: the Shariah of Muṣṭafā, the Sunnah of the Messenger, and the words of the Prophet! *God and the Prophet, the strong religion, the open declaration of God's greatness, and the vast majority—this is the path to God, with Muḥammad ibn ʿAbdallāh.*

"We who are the Lord give assurance that We will keep Our religion far from the deception of the deceivers, the striving of the deniers, the mixing of the hypocrites, and the embellishments of the heretics. This is a work that We began with purity. We will keep it in purity and We will bring it to an end in purity. *Surely it is We who have sent down the Remembrance, and surely it is We who are its guards* [15:9]."

It is not that this talk will come to an end when this world comes to an end. Yes, the fasting and the prayer will come to an end, but love and secret whispering will not come to an end. He brought this talk into the world for subsistence, and He brought us into existence for subsistence. On the day this talk began, annihilation was dismissed. Yes, there will be annihilation, but for this world and everything subservient to it. As for us, there will be no annihilation.

It is the position of the heretics that the creatures will undergo annihilation and the world will subsist. The position of the *tawḥīd*-voicers is that this world will undergo annihilation and the creatures will subsist. *"I created you for subsistence—you will only be transferred from one house to another."*[1170]

"I will subsist, and you will subsist. I will not take you from this world to erase your names and marks. Rather, I will take you from one room to another and transfer you from one house to another."

A dervish was put under the earth. Munkar and Nakīr came and said, "Who is your Lord?"

The dervish said, "I changed my house, not my Friend."

Rather it is signs, clear signs, in the breasts of those who have been given knowledge [29:49]. Although the place of our secret core accepts annihilation, our secret core itself will not accept annihilation. Even if the essence of our secret core accepts annihilation, the secret core of our essence will not accept annihilation.

> An eye seeing You is relieved of pain;
> a spirit finding You is exempt from death.

They have said, *"This world is a bridge, the next world a bridge, and the goal is God, the Greatest." Peace!*

77–80. *al-Awwal al-Ākhir al-Ẓāhir al-Bāṭin:* the First, the Last, the Outward, the Inward

The Real is the First and the Last, the Outward and the Inward. He is the First, meaning that His existence has no beginning and His being has no outset. He is the Last, meaning that His existence has no end and His being has no limit. He is the Outward, and the meaning of outward is overpowering; He is the Inward, and the meaning of inward is knowing.

He is the First, He is the Last, He is the Outward, and He is the Inward, meaning *everything belongs to Him, everything returns to Him, everything is in Him, and everything is from Him.* Thus people say, "So-and-so is the first of this work and the last of this work, the outward of this work and the inward of this work." What they mean is that everything is in his hands.

He is "the First" through making known, "the Last" through prescribing the Law, "the Outward" through making eminent, "and the Inward" [57:3] *through alleviating; the First in that He chose you, the Last in that He guided you, the Outward in that He gave you hope, and the Inward in that He suffices you; the First through instructing, the Last through requiring, the Outward through blessing, and the Inward through honoring.*[1171]

O First who made the spirits drunk in the morning of the outset with the wine of opening: *Am I not your Lord?* [7:172]! O Last who promised the hearts the gentleness of the unseen things with the cup of familiarity! O Outward who gave the pure water of bounteousness to the lords of the Shariah with the explication of the Shari'ite applications! O Inward who struck the fire of bewilderment into the companions of the Tariqah with the intimations of the treasures of jealousy!

Whenever You caress someone with the gaze of the sultan of beauty, *his states are intimacy upon intimacy.* Whenever You drive someone distraught like a polo ball into the field of majesty, *his states are obliteration upon obliteration.* Whenever someone's eyes fall on Your majesty, he circumambulates the Kaabah of fear. Whenever someone's eyes fall on Your beauty, from the garden of felicity he begins to pick the jasmine of hope and the rose of anticipating encounter in keeping with his desire.

O dervish, His majesty displays His exaltedness, and His beauty discloses His gentleness. His majesty makes all speakers dumb, and His beauty brings all the dumb into speech. Wherever in the world there is someone dumb, he is made dumb by His majesty. Wherever in the world there is someone talking, he was brought into words by His beauty. *When someone contemplates His majesty, his sorrows are drawn out. When someone contemplates His beauty, his sorrows disappear.*

O You in whose gentleness intellects are drowned! O You in whose unveiling hearts are consumed! O exalted! *When someone recognizes Him, he recognizes that He is beyond His description.*

O brander of hearts, O healer of spirits! O wounder and healer! O bestower on hearts of the kinship of sorrow, O binder of spirits with the pact of joy! O You who make breasts mingle with love, O You who make livers familiar with pain! O You who turned away a hundred thousand of the realizing, sincerely truthful in the bloody tears of seeing Your exaltedness! O You who conveyed a hundred thousand disobedient tavern-goers to the station of proximity with Your gentleness and bounty!

No denier and no prostrator has changed except in the grasp of the King, the Exalted, the One. He prescribed the Law for them, then He exercised control over them as He willed. Among the obedient are those whom He clothed in the girdle of His beautiful-doing, and that is His bounty; among the disobedient are those whom He held down with the weight of His abandoning, and that is His justice.[1172]

Abū Bakr Wāsiṭī said—and no one in the Tariqah has spoken words of more purity—"*I would not worship a Lord who keeps distant because of disobedience and brings near because of obedience.*"[1173] I would not worship a Lord who works by means of causes.

> Many in the world seek union with You—
> the Man is he who has access to Your union.

In the end Job the patient ran out of patience and said, *"Harm has touched me"* [21:83]. In the end Noah the grateful was seized by the skirt of tenderness and said, *"Surely my son is one of my folk"* [11:45]. In the end Joseph the sincerely truthful glanced at himself and said, *"Whoever is wary of God, and is patient"* [12:90]. In the end David the generous went hunting for a little bird and netted a woman.[1174] In the end anger made Moses the speaking companion incapable and he threw the tablets of the Torah on the ground. In the end the killing of Ḥamza by the unbelievers upset the Messenger. In the end whoever enters this road is thrown down by the road.

Every day when the Messenger's Companions got up, they saw their paragon's countenance in a different color. They would say, "What is this color that wreaks havoc on our spirits?"

The Chieftain of the Two Worlds would say, "From the moment that the harsh shine of this weighty declaration—*'If thou takest associates, thy deeds will surely fail'* [39:65]—stuck up its head from the collar of my prophethood, Muḥammad's color has not stayed the same for a single hour."

I cannot look at You,
nor can I choose another.
My heart finds no ease with You,
nor can I cut myself off from You.
Sleep from my eyes, ease from my heart,
both fled the moment I saw You.
I count as a game what I've seen from You
next to what I will see one day.
Year and month I'm full without food,
day and night I'm drunk without wine.
My heart's devoted to sorrow for You,
for I've seen no road of release.

Release has not appeared and the end has not become manifest. There is no way but to give up the spirit, and if you do give up the spirit, He will say, "I have no need for your spirit."

O generous Lord,
Your love has settled down in me.
O You who take the sleep from my eyes,
You know what's happened to me.[1175]

*

You've put a brand on my heart—that's fine.
I'm the slave of a heart with Your mark.

In reality He is powerful, and in reality you are captive. Ḥusayn Manṣūr said, *"Lordhood is the implementation of power, and servanthood is acquiescence to the implementation of power."* Alas, we are all captive to Your decree. What can be done?

Happy is he who sets off for exaltedness! Happy is he who sets off for eminence! In the end he will get there. But where is this talk? *An ocean without shore, a night without morning, a pain without cure, a purity without admixture.* Where is the tower from which this beauty shines forth? Where is the coffer in which this pearl is found? A thousand thousand set off to seek this tower and coffer. They put their spirits into the work, but they found nothing.

O moon, in which heaven should I seek you?
O cypress, in which garden should I seek you?

O king, in which family should I seek you?
Mad am I to seek you from a mark.

They searched in the desert of remorse, they dove into the oceans of bewilderment, they probed the deserts of shapes. Not a speck remains from which they did not seek a mark of Him, not a caravan remains from which they did not ask news of Him, not a monastery remains that they did not enter, not a church remains into which they did not step. They sought in the monasteries, they looked in the churches, they took shelter with the shawls of the recognizers, they went under the shade of the sashes of the sash-wearers, they spoke to the scarves of the faithful, they sought His mysteries from the hats of the Guebres. At each moment they went farther away, at each instant they became more estranged. They gave whatever they had, but they found no news of this talk. *Whatsoever is in the heavens and the earth glorifies God* [57:1]. *Everyone is waiting at the gate on condition of seeking, but He is exalted.*

We call on the Friend but He doesn't answer,
we hurry to union but He's in no hurry.
We've set a trap but the plain is empty of birds,
we've thrown a hook but the water's got no fish.

Which breast has no burning for Him? Which head is not tipsy with Him? Which heart has none of the blaze of love for Him? Which spirit has none of the fire of searching for Him? Which secret core has none of the joy of His beauty?

O chevalier, there was perfect beauty, so it did not stay concealed. Beauty cannot be kept concealed, for beauty tells tales. If there is beauty, it is there for the sake of manifestation. Just as a beauty not worth seeing is defective, so also a beauty not worth showing is defective.

Joseph had complete beauty. Although he had a worthy lover, how could one lover be enough for beauty like that? Canaan did not have the capacity to tolerate Joseph's beauty, so his beauty had to be displayed to the world. Kings had to become servants of his beauty, his brothers had to be captive, the women had to sacrifice their hands, spirits had to be given to the wind, and Jacob had to build the House of Sorrows.

All these things were hidden in the treasury of the Unseen, but they cannot be limited to Canaan. The same thing happened when the Messenger was brought out of Mecca. Mecca did not have the capacity to carry his heavy burden—he was not for one city or one person. He reached *two-bows' length away* [53:9], but *two-bows' length away* also did not have the capacity, so he came back quickly. When Adam went into paradise and came out quickly, that was because paradise did not have the capacity for him. Mount Sinai tasted the same thing with Moses. O Joseph of Egypt, Canaan is an exalted place, but it does not have the capacity for your beauty.

In the end the beauty and majesty behind the veils of exaltedness will one day come out. In the end the tumult of the lovers will do something, the shouts of the seekers will bring something out into the open.

My father said, "They said to the serpent, 'Why do you come out of your hole so that they can catch you?'

"It said, 'Because of shame. Someone comes and sits at the door of my house and talks, and that catches my heart. I come out to see what he wants.' "

In the end things will not stay like this. Things will be seen with these eyes, places will be reached with these feet. You were created because a day will come when they will snatch you away and convey you to *a seat of truthfulness* [54:55].

Have you seen how a falcon or a hawk snatches something? A day will come when that subtle artisanry will appear and snatch you away. When the exalted ones go into paradise tomorrow, they will say, "Where are all those threats, the warnings of the Narrow Path and hell? In any case we haven't seen a thing."

The call will come, *"You passed over them but they were quiescent.* We made those fires cold when you reached them."

When will the tree of hope bear fruit? When will this waiting come to an end?

They said to a freeloader, "What is happiness?"

He said, "Bread, an adorned table, and a sleeping guard."

They said to a knight, "What is happiness?"

He said, "The sword bloody and the enemy dead."

They said to a traveler, "What is happiness?"

He said, "Going home and being at ease from rushing and running."

They said to a lover, "What is happiness?"

He said, *"Encountering the beloved when the watchers are heedless."*

Today the enemies are *like cattle* [7:179], and tomorrow they will be like dust under the feet. Today the friends are hurried, secret to secret, and tomorrow they will be slow, openness to openness. Today like this, tomorrow like that.

In the beginningless, the approval of *He loves them* was busy with *they love Him* [5:54] without your intervention. Today you have being, but you are far from the midst.

By the rightful due of the Real! The food of the hearts and the food of the spirits is His Being. Otherwise, they would never find subsistence. Tomorrow, when all find subsistence in that abode, they will not find it through their own being. They will find it through the food of His Being. If someone in this abode were to reach the degree where the contemplation of His Being becomes his food, death would be forbidden to him.

Since You're the soul's food, when You depart
the soul that feeds on You does not remain.[1176]

*

You are my spirit and world—were I not to see You,
good riddance to my spirit and world!

O dervish, in this road, life is bondage, the spirit a place of peril, and living a veil. Unless you come to lament of your own spirit in this road, nothing will come of you.

Come, they're selling death, so buy it—
no good's to be had in this life.

Come, let the Overseer have mercy on a free soul
whose alms are to die for his brother!
When I see a grave from afar,
I wish I were right beside it.[1177]

Your spirit is the cause of your annihilation. If you suppose that you did not have this spirit, then the angel of death would have no decree over you. Seek a life not tainted by the spirit's intermediary, a life expressed in these terms: *"Recognition is the heart's life with God."*[1178]

If a man is going to be given access to the carpet of intimacy, he must be purified of his own attributes. Where can you achieve this purification? You must go into the ocean of the Glorified and swim in the sea of glorification. *Secret cores swim in the oceans of lights. They win the pearls of* tawḥīd, *string them on the necklaces of faith, and stud them on the belts of union.*[1179] Nothing comes of a polluted man or a menstruating woman.

Let us come back to those words: In the Beginningless, *He loves them* had work with *they love Him* without you. Which day was that? There was still no garment of existence, none of this dust and clay, no universe or Adam. That proclamation was made by His bounteousness and answered by His gentleness.

O dervish, a love that appears in childhood will not disappear until old age. It is black hair that has business with a moonlike face. What is this blue and azure sky doing in the midst?

It is the custom of those who fire arrows to set up a field. On one end is a target, and on the other end is another target. There are two targets and one archer. Where does He give a mark of the words I just said? *"He is the First and the Last"* [57:3]. Even more explicit is what He said to Muṣṭafā, *"Thou didst not throw when thou threwest, but God threw"* [8:17].

O chevalier, when the scales of majestic unity and perfect divinity are brought forth, createdness does not weigh a jot, nor half a jot. Know that in reality, *no one carries the Real but the Real.* You were wanted so that you could be a spectator.

Just as He built the Kaabah and mosques with gentleness and bounty, so also He built churches and idol temples with severity and harshness. He sent out success-giving as the vanguard of the army of gentleness, and He stirred up deprivation as the vanguard of the army of justice. The hapless Adamites must pass by the armies of bounty and justice.

"When We sought faith, We sought it from Our own bounty. But We said to bounty, 'When you bring your banner out into the open, look to see where there is someone needy.' "

They say that faith comes either by acquisition or by bestowal. The acquisition is your need, and the bestowal comes from Him. Your need along with His mystery must grasp the waist of the covenant so that this secret may become apparent: *light upon light* [24:35]—*the light of bounty and the light of activity. Or, the light of beautiful-doing—"Those who do the beautiful shall have the most beautiful and an increase"* [10:26]—*and the light of the most beautiful: "As for those to whom the most beautiful preceded from Us"* [21:101].

Success-giving carries the banner of activity, and faith the banner of bounty. Bounty is His attribute. The sultan of bounty sent out the bannerman of success-giving to take the banner of faith in hand. He said, "Look to see where there is someone needy, and raise the banner of faith at the door of his breast."

Seeing various things comes by acquisition, but eyes do not come by acquisition. The heart He prepared is itself beautiful. You have no choice but to keep on reciting the edict of your own dismissal. This is a transaction between His majesty and His beauty, a contract between His knowledge and His decree. Who are you in the midst? His purity is the antagonist of all purities, His knowledge the antagonist of all knowledge, His power the antagonist of all claims, His exaltedness the antagonist of all beings. As long as you have not wreaked havoc on these abodes, you will have no benefit.

I do not know in whose eyes He wants to scatter this handful of defective dust that He has brought. How does a handful of dust have the capacity to carry His burden or taste the draft of His severity? It is His decree that lifts away His decree, His majesty that observes His beauty, and His beauty that is suited for His majesty.

When Abū Yazīd was overwhelmed, he said, *"Glory be to me, glory be to me!"* An uproar ensued. He answered, *"The Lord glorified Himself on the tongue of His servant."* Who are you to meddle when the sultan does his job in his own kingdom?

They said, "What were these words?"

He said, "It was Abū Yazīd's tongue, but His speaking. He made me speak—I did not speak." [1180]

Ḥusayn ibn Manṣūr Ḥallāj said, *"When God is someone's excuse, he has no faults."*

Ḥusayn was put into prison. Shaykh Abu'l-ʿAbbās ʿAṭāʾ sent someone to ask him what these words were.

He said, "Tell them that they should seek the excuse for whatever passed over my tongue from Him. The excuse for these words should come from Him who drove them forth, not from him who spoke them."

O chevalier, they all spoke and did some boasting. Then they came back to this dust, the furnace of the work, to see what would appear.

> There was no one to gaze on Your beauty,
>   no one to circle round Your Presence.
> They weren't shown the world from pole to pole,
>   but still they boasted with their eyes veiled.

Junayd was seen in a dream. He was asked, "What did you do with your work?"

He said, "The work was not in the measure of what I knew. The one hundred twenty-some thousand center-points of prophethood are silent. I too became silent to see what the work will be."

81. *al-Barr:* the Kind

Barr and *bārr* have the same meaning. The Persian of this word is that He is a beautiful-doer [*nīkū-kār*] toward His servants.

God is gentle to His servants [42:19]. *He guided them so that they would recognize Him, He gave them success so that they would worship Him, He instructed them so that they would ask from Him, and He illuminated their hearts so that they would love Him.* He caressed them so that they would recognize, He gave them success so that they would worship, He instructed them so that they would ask, and He made their hearts quarries of light so that they would love.

With his sword drawn, his enmity ready, and his heart turned totally away from peace, ʿUmar Khaṭṭāb was coming to take Muḥammad's head. But calculation in the house never comes out the same as calculation in the bazaar. It was said to him, "This work is not done by human contrivance, nor is it so easy. We have decreed that the tombs of Islam will be populated by the banners of your prosperity, the army of God's messenger Muḥammad will be helped by your nonhypocritical view, and the eye of faith will be illuminated by your bowing and prostrating."

It is the Real's beautiful-doing [*iḥsān*] toward the servants that made obedience temporal and rewards everlasting, *as a gift unbroken* [11:108].

Some of His beautiful-doing is that He accepts contaminated obedience and promises uncontaminated reward. He accepts a mixed obedience and promises a reward without contamination and opacity.

Some of His beautiful-doing is that He includes both the obedient and the disobedient in His invitation to repentance so that the disobedient will not be disgraced. He says, "Turn to God all together, O you with faith!" [24:31].

Some of His beautiful-doing is that He blesses in His measure and prescribes gratitude in the servant's measure.[1181] Some of the Real's beautiful-doing is that He gives blessings in His measure and asks you for gratitude in your measure.

Some of His beautiful-doing is that He gives you the success to serve, then He multiplies the praise. God says, "The repenters, the worshipers" [9:112]. *He loves without bribery, He bestows without counting it a favor, He honors without intermediary, He accepts the small and confers the great. He counts His blessings on His servants as few even if they are many, and He counts the obedience of His servants as much even if it is little.* He scatters a hundred blessings on your head and counts it as a dust mote. He accepts a straw from you and considers it a mountain.

He delivers from need anyone who is poor toward Him and exalts those who boast of Him.[1182] Whenever someone takes a need to Him, He makes him wealthy, and whenever someone exults in Him, He exalts him.

Supposing that a servant disobeys for a hundred years and then says, "I repent." What will He say? *"I accept that from you. 'It is He who accepts repentance from His servants'* [42:25]."

"Your craft is disobedience and My attribute is forgiveness. You will not abandon your craft. Will I abandon My attribute?"

A bedouin was supplicating, and it was a marvelous supplication. He said, *"O God, you will find someone other than me to chastise, but I will find no one other than You to have mercy on me!"* Lord God, You will find someone else to punish, but I will find no one else to show mercy to me.

He said to the proximate angels, "The Throne is yours!" He said to the cherubim, "The Footstool is yours!" He said to Gabriel, "The Lote Tree is yours!" He said to Riḍwān, "The Garden is yours!" He said to Mālik, "Hell is yours!" He said to the obedient, "The Gardens of Eden are yours!" The disobedient were broken and gave out sighs of remorse, standing with the feet of regret before the sanctuary of generosity. The Exalted Lord said, *"He wrote mercy against Himself* [6:54]. If you have nothing, I belong to you!"

At the time of sin, He called you ignorant so as to accept your excuse: *"a great wrongdoer, deeply ignorant"* [33:72]. At the time of bearing witness, He called you knowing so as to accept your testimony: *"except those who have borne witness to the truth while they are knowing"* [43:86]. He called you weak so your shortcomings would be effaced: *"And man was created weak"* [4:28]. He called you a wage-earner—*"They shall have a wage unfailing"* [95:6]—so that when you go to paradise you will not be ashamed to say, "I am going home."

O dervish, the worth of the falcon is that it comes and goes. *"Surely God loves the tempted, the repenting."*[1183]

The unbelievers are like wild crows—they have no value. Dry-brained Quran-reciters are like chickens—their value is one dirham. But those who are tempted and repent are like falcons that come and go. Their value is a thousand dirhams. *Surely God loves the repenters* [2:222].

"Our secret with you does not pertain to now. Our kindness to you does not pertain to today."

When there is talk of worship, speak of the heaven-dwellers. When there is talk of love, speak of the earth-dwellers.

For one act of disobedience Iblis was struck in the head so hard that he never came back to himself. And here we have a hundred thousand who never say their prayers or prostrate themselves, going instead to taverns. But He forgives them, for Iblis was a serving boy, and they are friends.

When the beloved comes with one sin,
his beautiful traits bring a thousand interceders.[1184]

How can a bit of stinking water dare claim friendship with *that which always was and will always be*? Nonetheless, the lordly light that is deposited in the secret core of the friends began to seek. The seeker is the light and the sought is the light, the gazer is the light and the object of the gaze is the light. When the light comes to the heart, it turns into love; when it comes to the secret core, it becomes unveiling; when it comes to the mind, it becomes union; when it comes to the tongue, it bears witness; when it comes to the limbs, it becomes practice; and when it comes to the intellect, it becomes recognition.

The water is one, the spring is one, the tree is one. The water reaches one place and becomes bark, it reaches another and becomes trunk, it reaches another and becomes branch, it reaches another and becomes root, it reaches another and becomes blossom, it reaches another and becomes fruit.

"The gathering of the exalted ones wants luster, and the luster of their gathering is proximity to My Presence. The friends assemble in the presence of My Presence. When two beggars come together, you should seek proximity to Me right there. When someone sighs in sorrow, put yourself beneath his sighs. When someone lets out a hot breath in pain, seek the breeze of proximity to My Presence from the breeze of his breath. It is the sultans of the world who need ten thousand cavalry before they mount up. I am a sultan whose army is My attributes and whose exaltedness is My Essence. When three beggars come together, *there is no whispering among three, but that He is the fourth of them* [58:7].

"O angels of the Higher Plenum, you have worshiped many thousand years, mentioning the purity of My Presence with the voice of your hallowing, but you have no awareness of the breeze of union with Me.

"O naked, penniless beggar, you do not have the worship of the angels, the wealth of the cherubim, or the wherewithal of the spirituals. But you do have a speck of love and burning.

Several times a day the exalted ones of My Presence cry out because of your tumult-inducing, pain-mixed burning: 'These beggars keep on striking fire into the harvest of our obedience.' I would not give away one speck of your burning for a thousand thousand years of the angels' worship. I would not sell one speck of your neediness for a thousand thousand years of the cherubim's worship. The Throne has no news of Us, the Throne-bearers no awareness of Us, the cherubim no whiff of finding Us. Our welcome, bestowal, majesty, and beauty are for you."

He has many rights against us, like obedience and worship, but in our own makeup we are destitute. He has decreed that we be destitute. When the decreer decrees that someone be destitute, the plaintiff has nothing against him.

If he is in hardship, then deferment until the time of ease [2:280]. Whenever someone is destitute, it is incumbent to give him respite so that he may acquire some wherewithal. But we will not acquire wherewithal until that world, when He will pour down the treasure of His bounty on our heads. We are not wealthy through our own being; we are wealthy through His attributes.

In this world we have the attribute of love; we are the world's paragon. In that world we will have the attribute of love; we will be that world's sultan. The parasol of exaltedness will be raised above our heads, and we will open the hands of plundering and take the wherewithal of the world's folk as plunder. Gabriel will not escape our hands, nor Michael, nor the Throne-bearers.

He has no use for treasuries and no need for anything. Whatever He has, He has for us. Tomorrow He will give the treasury of bounty to the disobedient, the treasury of mercy to the sinners, the treasury of forgiveness to the helpless. We will be able to discharge His rightful due from His treasuries, for we cannot discharge His rightful due from our own treasuries. When a sultan gives his daughter to a beggar, he does not have a dower worthy of her. From his own treasury the sultan will send the dower to the beggar so that he may give it to the princess from his treasury.

O chevalier, seek camphor from the baskets of brides or the shops of druggists, not from the bodies of the dead. You will get nothing from dead bodies, and you will be called a grave-robber.

"When We sent Muḥammad—before the brilliant Burāq of whose yearning bowed one hundred twenty-some thousand center-points of prophethood in their shirts of chivalry—it was part of Our beautiful-doing toward you that every message of the past prophets was abrogated and abolished in the face of his message. Whenever an edict was written for someone, it was followed by dismissal. Whenever someone was given a message, abrogation came as its counterpart. It was Our Messenger for whom an edict was written and a message given, and dismissal did not find its way to the edict, nor did abrogation look upon the message."

He was the last messenger and the final prophet, his road made ready by the beauty of gentleness and the perfection of severity. It is the custom of sultans that when they send messengers to their enemies, they make promises and assurances and they issue warnings and threats. Then, if none of this achieves the goal, they send the final messenger. They say: "Either peace or the sword. Make war, or come in peace."

O dervish, He created the whole world, but He did not make anyone's activity the counterpart of His activity. He created nothing more exalted than the angels, but He did not mention their activity as the counterpart of His. This is because none of them had a rank and status such that their activity could be His activity's counterpart. But when He created the Adamites,

He said to them, "You act, so that I may act!" He placed the greatness that He placed on them on no one else.

The point is that first statement: He sent one hundred twenty-some thousand pearls from the ocean of prophethood to the creatures, to some fewer and to others more. He mixed threats with robes of honor and put promises next to warnings, all to achieve the goal, which was for the creatures to wear the collar of servanthood.

Then He sent Muṣṭafā *after a gap in the messengers* [5:19]. All gentleness was in his right hand, all severity in his left hand, and behind him was the resurrection. *"I and the Hour are like these two.*[1185] It was said to us, 'O Muḥammad, you walk in front! O resurrection, you walk right behind him!'"

They sent a policeman to us from that world. Who is this policeman? The resurrection.

"The resurrection is My policeman, hell My prison, paradise My scented garden, and the Quran My nightingale. Invite these people to My road! Tell them that you are bringing good news and warning so that they may put their heads on the line of submission and their feet in the realm of faith. If you look at the policeman of severity, you will be the warner of the Presence. If you look at the robe of gentleness, you will be the good-news-bringer of the community.

"Call out to them and say, 'The work of messengerhood and the playing field of prophethood have come to an end. The period of dust and water has been drawn out and has brought the consequences of the world's natures into its own pavilion. O you who have lost the road, here is the inviter to the Threshold! O you who are perplexed by caprice, here is the guiding light! O you who are bewildered by misguidance, here is the light of guidance! This is the final book and the last messenger. If you want peace, here is a peace in which there is no war. If you aim for war, here is a war in which there is no peace.' " *You will fight them, or they will submit* [48:16]. *Slay the associators wherever you find them!* [9:5].

The greatness of this paragon is such that all existent things live under his shadow from the era of Adam to the dissolution of the world. Do you fancy that we alone have been pulled up by his greatness?

"On the plain of the resurrection, when I set up my lofty banner, noble signpost, tent of leadership, and pavilion of felicity, Adam and his offspring will seek the provisions of the Endless and the supplies of the Everlasting from the pavilion of my majesty. When Adam received the garment of chosenness, he received it from my greatness. When Idris went up to the elevated place,[1186] he went because of my good fortune. When Noah's prayer was answered and he received the title 'elder of the prophets,' he received it from my rank. When Abraham received the robe of bosom friendship and found *coolness and safety* [21:69], he found it from my degree. When Moses heard the unmediated speech at Mount Sinai and was made the foremost of the three hundred thousand children of Israel, he received it from my leadership." And so on.

Muṣṭafā came with the custom of the Turks: He tied the Throne and the Footstool to his saddle-straps, though his aspiration was detached from both.

A sultan must have a throne, a throne must have a portico, and a portico must have a courtyard. The world with all its spaciousness is the courtyard for the throne of the kingship of God's messenger Muḥammad.

That paragon is the center of the circle drawn by the compass. A man has a compass, which has two legs, and he wants to draw a circle. First he must make one leg firm. The firmer it is, the more beautifully it turns. All beauty comes from the traces of the center-point. "I placed one leg of power's compass at the Muhammadan Center, and I turned the other around the spheres."

Adam was seated on one side, Noah on another, and so also Abraham, Moses, and Jesus. But the forefront of kingship had been turned over to Muḥammad, God's messenger. At the moment the point was marked, the circle had not yet appeared. He set down the point and made the center appear, but there was no mark of the circle.

"When were you a prophet?"

He said, "I was a prophet when Adam was between water and clay."[1187]

It was said to him, "When was prophethood made necessary for you?"

He said, "Before the creation of Adam and the blowing of the spirit into him."[1188]

"Adam had still not stretched out his legs in the cradle of creation when I stretched out my hand in the cradle of prophethood's covenant and seized the teat of gentleness. On the day my prophethood came into existence, Adam's creation was not yet complete. The existence of creation was the beginning, and the existence of prophethood the end. I had drunk the wine of the end when Adam had not yet finished drinking the draft of the beginning. On the day Adam was there, Noah was not, and when Noah was, Abraham was not."

And when God took the compact of the prophets [3:81]: "Just as I made the covenant of My Lordhood, so also I made the covenant of Muḥammad. On the day I created Adam and Noah, I said to them, 'I have a secret in your existence, and that secret is Muḥammad.' "

"What was the beginning of your affair?"

He said, "The supplication of my father Abraham and the good news about me given by Jesus."[1189]

"Who was Jesus? The one who gave the good news of my auspiciousness.[1190] Who was Abraham? The intercessor for my messengerhood: *'Our Lord, and raise up in their midst a messenger from among them who will recite Thy signs to them, teach them the Book and the Wisdom, and purify them!'* [2:129].

"When they were all given something, they were given my old clothes, the remainder of my cup, and the leftover from my bowl."

Adam said, "I am God's chosen one." Abraham said, "I am God's bosom friend." Moses said, "I am God's speaking companion." Jesus said, "I am the Spirit of God." Muṣṭafā said,

Lovers drink only my leftover.[1191]

"On the day you had no existence, all these robes of honor were with me. I had them all, and then in my bounty I gave you my everyday garments. I am more beautiful in the shirt of love."

What a marvelous business! He set up all these sorts of greatness, but when He reached his paternal uncle, He said, *"Perish the hands of Abū Lahab!"* [111:1].

Yes, He pulls up the servant, but He gives Godhood to no one. He gives housemastery to the creatures, but He gives Godhood to no one.

Surely the likeness of Jesus for God is as the likeness of Adam. He created him from dust [3:59]. This talk is a sun that rose in the East and set in the West. The East was Adam and the West was Jesus. "O Muḥammad, who are you? You are neither of the East nor of the West: *kindled from a*

blessed olive tree that is neither of the East nor of the West [24:35], *rather of the Unseen Self-Sufficiency.* If you had risen in the East, at some moment you would have set in the West."

The traces, secrets, and lights of that paragon have no end. He is a lantern hung from the ceiling of a mosque, full of oil, its fire lit. As long as the ceiling is there, the lantern will be there. No, rather, as long as the lantern is there, the ceiling will be there: *"The Hour will not come as long as there is someone in the earth saying, 'God.'"*[1192] As long as there is a Muhammadan in the world, the world will stay in place.

"We made a lantern from Muḥammad's body, a glass from his heart, and a lamp from his prophethood."

The radiance of messengerhood shone outwardly. Moths charged forth from the Arabs and the non-Arabs, madmen from Byzantium and Persia. The fire itself is but one point, but the wick became all fire, the glass became all light, and the lantern became all radiance. Muḥammad became all heart, the heart became all pain, the pain became all love, the love became all truthfulness, the truthfulness became all union, the *mi'rāj* became all Canopy, the Canopy became all Lote Tree, the Lote Tree became all drawing close, and the drawing close became all *two-bows' length away.*

When heaven and earth were adorned, they were adorned with the welcome, bounteousness, sinlessness, honor, and service of Muṣṭafā. The sultanate of the two worlds was declared in his name. His name was paired with the formula of *tawḥīd.* His past and his not-yet-come were recorded in the registers of forgiveness. He was made the trusted one in the outcome and the precedent. The banner of praise, the pool of Kawthar, and the *praised station* [17:79] were made the watchwords of his pageant and the largesse of his steed. It was given to him to take care of the right and left wings for the beginningless and the endless. All this was done, but fear was not lifted from his heart for the blink of an eye. *"He would be praying while his insides were boiling like the boiling of a kettle."*[1193]

When he was finished with conveying the message, he would step into the chamber of his heart's poverty and loosen the tongue of apology, taking off the belt of sinlessness and the cap of prophethood. He would say with the tongue of incapacity, *"My sin is tremendous, and none forgives the tremendous sin but the Tremendous Lord."*[1194] When he took this painful breath, none could carry this sorrow other than the exaltedness of *no god but God.* Blossoms of grief appeared from all the trees in the world. A storm of sorrow rained down from the seven heavens. The Throne and the Footstool marveled at his pain. The proximate angels of heaven and the sincerely truthful of earth gave up hope for salvation. Every iota of the empire put on the garment of mourning. "What happened?"

It was said, "God's messenger Muḥammad is apologizing for his falling short in *no god but God* and he is seeking security for the pearl of his sinlessness from the brand of justice. This requires nothing less than that creation itself should put on the shirt of pain and remorse."

If until the resurrection Abraham the bosom friend and Moses the speaking companion should want to smell the herb that sprouted in the garden of Muṣṭafā's good fortune, they would not be able to do so without the escort of Muṣṭafā's sinlessness. Nonetheless he kept on making this supplication: *"Make me one of those You deliver, emancipate, and free from the Fire."*

"No prophet had as many tents of severity pitched in his road as I did. Trial is not that Zachariah was cut in two with a saw. Tribulation is not that John's head was lifted off by the sword of the unbelievers. Trial and tribulation are what was poured down on me, for I was given priority over the folk of heaven and earth, and the disobedience of Adam's offspring was attached to the skirt of my intercession. It was said, '*And of the night, keep vigil therein as a supererogatory act for thee* [17:79]. You must travel the road of My roadless ones, you must apologize for My sinners, you must do the work of all the lazy.'

"Sometimes a carpet is spread for me at *two-bows' length away* and sometimes I am sent to the doorstep of Abū Jahl's disloyalty. Sometimes I am not let into Mecca without a compact and sometimes the key of the world's storehouses are sent to the door of my room. Sometimes I am sent to the door of Abu'l-Shaḥma the Jew for a bit of barley,[1195] sometimes the door of Khaybar is opened at the hand of my serving boys, and sometimes my teeth are broken by the stones of the unbelievers."

O folk of the world, the road of Muṣṭafā is indeed one of trial. If you are ready for it, enter. If not, do not intrude on the road of the exalted.

82. *al-Tawwāb:* the Ever-Turning

He who gives *tawba* [turning/repentance].

Then He turned toward them so that they would turn [9:118]: "The servant's turning is through regret, and My turning is through the decree of generosity. The servant's turning is through supplication, and My turning is through bestowal. The servant's turning is through asking, and My turning is through giving. The servant's turning is through penitence, and My turning is through responding."

It is He who gives the success of turning/repentance. *Then He turned toward them so that they would turn.* When you repent through His giving success, He Himself praises you, saying, *"the turners/repenters, the worshipers"* [9:112]. He Himself wrote your name in the register of His love: *"Surely God loves the repenters, and He loves those who purify themselves"* [2:222]—*"the repenters" of disobedience, "those who purify themselves" of the blights of obedience; "the repenters" of love for this world, "those who purify themselves" of love for the next world—it is these who cling fast to love for the High, the Highest.*

So the repentance of the common people is from sins and ugly deeds, the repentance of the elect from faults and blights, and the repentance of the most elect from seeing beautiful deeds and paying attention to acts of obedience.

The exalted ones have said, *"It may happen that sin becomes the cause of reaching God. Do you not see how the hoopoe reached Solomon?"*[1196] It often happens that sin is the cause of reaching God's approval. The disobedient find regret in the heart, they weep tears from the eyes, and they sigh in remorse. It is said to them, "Today weeping, tomorrow looking; today a step, tomorrow a message; today a remorse, tomorrow a gaze; today a sigh, tomorrow a shelter; today a stride forward, tomorrow a private audience."

O Muslims, this happiness will be completed on the day they lift up the veil and give the longtime hope of the hearts to the hearts. O friends, a sound report has reached us from Muṣṭafā that when the faithful go into paradise tomorrow, there will be room left over in paradise, *"So God will configure another creation."*[1197] He will create new creatures and give them those places.

O dervish, think carefully! If it is allowable for Him in His generosity to create creatures who have never worshiped or toiled and to give them houris, palaces, servants, and children, will He send out from the door a people who have taken a little trouble, done a little work, and had a little hope, who were His longtime slave boys and first servants? In truth He will not do that.

O dervish, He sends someone to Byzantium, India, and Turkistan to bring those who have not yet come. Why would He drive away those who have already come?

What an excellent Lord—a Lord who created you, then bought you, then asked you to loan Him what He gave you! What an excellent Lord—a Lord who created you and then took you as beloved, so you are His servant and He is your beloved! What an excellent Lord—a Lord who crowned you with His guidance, gave you a necklace of His worship, clad you with His service, and mounted you on the steed of His love! What an excellent Lord—a Lord who, if you supplicate Him responds to you, if you aim for Him brings you close, and if you turn away from Him calls out to you! What an excellent Lord—a Lord who curtains you with His curtain, is gentle to you with His kindness, and gives you awareness of His secret![1198]

"You are the one to whose makeup the demand of My knowledge attached itself before the demand of your deeds attached itself to My mercy. You are the one whose heart had not yet thought of repenting when I wrote your name in the register of *the repenters.* You are the one who had not yet stepped onto the threshold of the world of existence when I recorded your name in the register of *the worshipers.*

"If I were to let you free, to whom would I give you? If I did not want you, to whom would I leave you? If you become weary of My gentleness, I will not become weary of your disobedience. If you cannot carry My burden, My great mercy will buy you along with all your offenses.

"Have patience for a few days. Today commands and prohibitions do not accord with your desire. Tomorrow everything will follow your desire. If today you see the wonders of commands and prohibitions, wait until tomorrow when you will see the marvels of knowledge and decree. If today I make you suffer by power, tomorrow I will send you ease by wisdom. If today the Law is prescribed by wisdom, tomorrow it will be lightened by bounty."

When Sultan Maḥmūd sat on the throne of kingship and held court, he would keep Ayāz standing at the edge of the carpet, his hands folded before him. At night, when they were alone together, Ayāz became Maḥmūd, Maḥmūd Ayāz.

Today the work revolves around *am I not your Lord?* [7:172]. Tomorrow the work will rest on *He loves them and they love Him* [5:54]. Today the carpet of *am I not your Lord* has been unrolled, so prayer, fasting, hajj, and struggle have come out into the open. Tomorrow you will be mustered in that world, and the carpet of *He loves them and they love Him* will be spread. There will be no fasting and no prayer—only love and joy.

"In the Beginningless all was My beautiful-doing, at the moment all is My beneficence, and in the Endless all will be My bounteousness. When My bestowal arrives, it removes differentiation from the midst.

"O intellects, be dazzled by My artisanry! When I call to account, I take to task iota by iota. But when I am lenient, I overlook mountain upon mountain."

In the end *He loves them* will take our hands. The faithful will lift their heads from the dust and He will call out, *"Welcome, may your coming be blessed!"* If He accepts you, He will not accept you because of the form of your practice. He will accept you because of the readiness that He gazed upon in His beginningless knowledge. Whatever there may be in the world follows upon that readiness.

Look closely at the subtleties of this declaration and the fine points of this expression in the firm text of the Book: "*Ḥā Mīm. The sending down of the Book is from God, the Exalted, the Knower, the forgiver of sins and the accepter of repentance, the intense in punishment, the possessor of boons. There is no god but He; to Him is the homecoming*" [40:1–3].

Ḥā Mīm: "Determined [*ḥumma*] *is what will be."*[1199] Whatever will come to be has already been decreed.

Some say that *Ḥā'* alludes to forbearance [*ḥilm*] and *Mīm* to kingship [*mulk*]: "I have a forbearance without end and a kingship without limits known by anyone. One of the wonders of My forbearance is that if you are disloyal for one hundred years and then apologize, I say, 'Do not bring any interceders lest they come to know what you have done.' "

More marvelous is this: "If disloyalty is done to you, do not call forth an interceder. On the day you want an interceder, I Myself will call forth the interceder. *Who is there to intercede with Him save by His leave?* [2:255]. And on the day I call forth an interceder, I will not enumerate your disloyalties lest he fail to intercede. It is My forbearance that will carry the burden of your disloyalty, not the interceder."

A sound report has come that on the Day of Resurrection a servant will be taken to hell. Muṣṭafā will see him and say, *"O my Lord, my community!"*

The address will come, "O Muḥammad, do you not know what he has done?" God will then enumerate his disloyalties. Muṣṭafā will say, *"Away with you, away!"*[1200] Perish, perish!

"That is what your interceder will say if I report your disloyalty to him."

" *'The sending down of the Book is from God.' Our forbearance and kingship require the sending down of the Book to you.* It is not as if I did not know what you would do with My Book when I sent it down, but I knew that your opposition would in no way diminish My kingship."

The forgiver of sins and the accepter of repentance. According to the rules of intellect, repentance should come beforehand and forgiveness afterward, but here forgiveness comes beforehand and repentance afterward: "I forgive sins and I accept repentance."

O chevalier, if He had said, "I accept repentance, then I forgive sins," people would fancy that if there were no repentance beforehand, there would be no forgiveness of sins.

"I said, 'I forgive sins and I accept repentance.' If I had said that I accept repentance and then said that I forgive sins, repentance would be the cause of My forgiveness. But I do not work by causes. Thus you will know that just as I forgive after repentance, I also forgive without repentance. The stained and tainted have no access to My threshold and no business with My presence. First I forgive. Then, when you step on My carpet, you will step in purity.

"Do you fancy that I have forgiven you because you apologized? As long as I had not purified you with the clear water of bounteousness, you would not have moved your tongue in apology. I am *forgiver* of the disobedient person who does not repent, and I am *accepter* of the one who does repent."

The evidence here that forgiveness of sins means forgiveness of those who have not repented is the *and* in the middle. This *and* is a conjunction; the thing conjoined is other than the thing to which it is conjoined, though they have the same ruling property. Thus you say, "Zayd *and* ʿAmr came to me." Zayd is one person, and ʿAmr is someone else, but the two have one ruling property in coming. If the ruling properties were opposed, the conjunction would be a mistake, and if the two were one thing, the conjunction would be an error.

How shall I make an allusion to what I desire to say? For it does not fit into my expressions.

"No one accepts the tainted and defiled but I. No one wants the defective but I. I said *forgiver* and *accepter* and thereby voiced My own attributes. Since there was talk of punishment, I said *intense in punishment.* I made *intense* the attribute of *punishment,* and I made forgiveness and acceptance My own attributes. Since My punishment is harsh, I soften it in an instant.

"Again, forgiveness and acceptance are My attributes. Punishment is a place of intervention, but My attributes do not become a place of intervention. Punishment is My kingdom, but to forgive and to accept are My attributes. If I were to reduce the kingdom to nothing, My majesty would not be decreased and My perfection would not be diminished. But there can never be any change or alteration in My attributes.

"O you whom I took as My friend even though you did not recognize Me! O you whom I wanted even though you did not know Me! O you to whom I belonged even though you did not belong to Me! O you who became My friend through the *Ḥāʾ* of My love [*maḥabbat*], not through your virtue! O you who found Me through the *Mīm* of My favor [*minnat*], not through your obedience!"

Ḥā Mīm. Ḥāʾ is an allusion to love and Mīm an allusion to favor.

"A hundred thousand were standing and supplicating, but no one paid any attention to their supplication. To you I say, '*I bestowed upon you before you asked from Me, I responded to you before you supplicated Me, and I forgave you before you asked Me to forgive you.*' "[1201]

When someone dwells in the majestic neighborhood of *no god but God,* no harm will come to him. "If I did not welcome you in the Beginningless, who would have looked at you? Like Jonah, go down so as not to see yourself. Like Muḥammad, go up so that when you see yourself, you will see through God that the surface of the earth obeys you and its stomach is full of forgiveness for you. The seven heavens are the dome of your proximity and the eight paradises are the place where you will put down the saddlebags of your journey. Do you suppose that on the night of the *miʿrāj* the Messenger went to *two-bows' length away* all alone, without Me? No, I was always with him."

If we were worthy enough for the Real to speak to us in the Beginningless—at the beginning of the work and without intermediary—why will we not be worthy enough for the Messenger to take us along with him on the night of the *miʿrāj*? It is because of the exaltedness of your movement and rest that He did not disregard anything of your movement and rest. For all of it He wrote out an inscription: rejection or acceptance, reward or punishment, approval or anger. After all, the moon and the sun move in their spheres, but no one talks about them.

O chevalier, when someone loves someone, whatever he does for him he does for himself. "If I bestow through My bounty, I will be watering the tree of friendship. If you look at heaven—your province! If you look at earth—your empire! If you look at the Throne—your name!"

What is this? "In the Beginningless I spoke words for your sake. I will finish them. From you an opinion, from Me a world. From you a step, from Me a universe. Though you have no knowledge, *'I am with My servant's thoughts of Me.'*[1202] Though you have no strength to come forward, *He is with you wherever you are* [57:4]. Turn your face against the world and draw your sword. I Myself will guard your back."

"With whom should I tangle?"

"Tangle with Iblis, for I kept him alive so that he would be killed at your hand. I will destroy the enemies at your hand until I remain, and you. Then I will kill you, and I alone will remain. You will be martyred [*shahīd*] by Him whom you witness [*shāhid*]."

May a thousand lives be sacrificed to him who breaks the idols, then dies! Going into the grave with the idols hanging around your neck will not be pleasant.

Abraham was smashing the idols, and Azar was carving the idols. The former went by his own road, and the latter went by his own road. His father was a sculptor. So also, when Abraham looked upon heaven, he saw a sculpture. *When the night darkened over him, he saw a star* [6:76], but he did not forget the Sculptor in the sculpture. *This is my Lord* [6:76] is an allusion to his breast's togetherness on the road to the goal. By God, if he had not gambled away everything, he would have been held back!

Stone is the criterion of wisdom. When a blighted hand reaches a stone, it becomes suspect. Azar carved a stone, and to the world's folk it was said, "Turn your back to it." Abraham set down a stone, and to the world's folk it was said, "Turn your face to it: *Take the station of Abraham as a place of prayer* [2:125]." Thus you will know that My choice is taken into account, not the clod or the stone.

Abraham debated Nimrod. The Bosom Friend said, *"My Lord is He who gives life and gives death."*

The accursed Nimrod said, *"I give life and I give death"* [2:258]. Half a gnat was assigned to him. "O accursed one, you claim that you give life to the dead? Give life to the half of this gnat that is dead, so that it may fly, for it does not have the strength to fly out of your nose. If you do not give life to the dead, then make the living half die so that you may be released from its hands. And if you end up incapable, what happened to the claim, *'I give life and I give death'*?"

What a marvelous business! Abraham—with all his rank, distinction, degree, elevation, and robes of honor—said, *"Make for me a tongue of truthfulness among the later folk* [26:84]: Keep my remembrance fresh on the tongue of Muḥammad's community."[1203]

"The past prophets were eager and yearning for you because I explained to them My bounteousness toward you, not your acts. If I had explained your acts, every one of them would have pulled back his skirt from you. *Surely God chose Adam and Noah and the House of Abraham* [3:33]. As long as you had not come, I chose them one by one. When your turn came, I said *generally and inclusively, 'You are the best community'* [3:110]. All of you are My chosen ones. Suppose you enter a tavern and see someone whose face is smeared with the dregs of wine—know that he too is one of you, for *We gave the inheritance of the Book to the ones We chose* [35:32]."

He brought you into this world after everyone and He will take you into that world before everyone. He brought you into this world after them so that your deeds would be a feast and a light for others. He will take you to that world before others so that your feast will be a mercy for them and they will be freeloaders at the feast of your affection and the table of your mercy.

God is the friend of those who have faith [2:257]: "I am your friend. I did not disclose an iota of the realities of My secrets before bringing you into existence. What can be disclosed to a multitude of slaves? And what can be hidden from friends?

"In the state of union friends have beauty, and in the state of separation they have the specter of imagination. Although I am pure of imagination, the waves of yearning began to clash in the state of separation, so I made a necklace of the ninety-nine names with the name *God* as its centerpiece. Then I sent it to you on the hand of the Seal of the Prophets, who is the white falcon of the world of mystery, so that it might be a sample of perfect beauty and majesty."

83. *al-Muntaqim:* the Avenger

God says, *"So We took vengeance on them"* [7:136]. The meaning of *muntaqim* is taking what is due—taking what is due from enemies and taking hearts from friends. The friends' hearts are the prey of His perfect beauty, and the lovers' spirits are tied to the falcon of His majesty's mystery.

He takes vengeance on one group and bestows blessings on another. *He is avenger toward His enemies and beneficent toward His friends.* He kills one group, *and that is justice from Him.* He pulls up another group, *and that is bounty from Him.* All the hearts were roasted and all the livers melted because the Will singled them out without cause.

He aims to snatch our hearts from us without sin;
He wants to take our lives from us for nothing.
With such a heart-taker I can't be mean with my heart;
with such a lover I can't be stingy with my life.

When the sorcerers of Pharaoh planted the tree of faith in the garden of the heart, the fruit of *We have faith in the Lord of the Worlds* [26:47] appeared on the branch of their tongue. The accursed Pharaoh became angry and said, "Who then took your heart?"

They said, "Do not cook delusions, for no one can hold the heart back from the Heart-taker."

He said, "I will cut off your hands and feet."

They said, *"No harm* [26:50]. It is better for feet that walked in service to you to be cut off, it is better for hands that took your gifts to be separated from the body, and it is better for eyes that saw you to be pulled out. We have found the good fortune of this talk and the sense organs of the Haqiqah: *'When I love him, I am for him hearing, eyesight, hand, and foot.'*[1204] In gratitude for this we will throw away the senses of nature."

O chevalier, just as He is similar to no one, so also His artisanry is not similar to anyone's. When sultans of this world caress their servitors, they give them caps and robes and bestow on them provinces. But when He caresses someone, He takes away his cap and robe and keeps him hungry and naked. This is a talk that, when it turns toward someone, does not turn away from him until it kills him.

O my blamer, O my blamer, O my blamer,
the night of the serpent-bit is not like that of the healthy!

Drowning oceans, burning fires!

Dhu'l-Nūn Miṣrī recounted, "Once I was circumambulating the Kaabah. I saw a youth with a beautiful face. He was wearing a sackcloth, strutting and laughing. He was saying to himself, *'This is the gait of him who boasts of other than You. What then will be the gait of him who has no object of worship but You and no beloved other than You?'* "

Dhu'l-Nūn said, "I went up to him and asked, *'Who is it that boasts of other than God?'*

"He said to me, 'Do you not see that young man—*the companion of servants, servitors, slave boys, and retinue?'* "

Dhu'l-Nūn said, "I looked and saw a comely youth, slave boys and servitors standing before him. He had bound a fine Egyptian shawl around his waist and thrown a mantle of the same material over his shoulders. He was strutting, and his shawl was dragging on the ground. I asked, 'Who is that?'

"He said, 'One of the slave boys of the commander of Mecca.' Then that burnt youth said, 'If he can boast about servanthood to the commander of Mecca, then it is even more appropriate that I boast about servanthood to the Lord of heaven and earth.' "

Dhu'l-Nūn said, "I went forward and said to that youth, *'How far apart are the two gaits!* You strut because you are the servant of the commander of Mecca, and he struts because he is the servant of your Lord.' "

Dhu'l-Nūn said, "When he heard what I said, the fire of my words fell into his heart. His color changed, his face turned yellow, and his elation was replaced by lassitude. Then, when he finished the circumambulation, those words went to work on him and their arrow went to its target. He went to the commander of Mecca and bought himself back from him. He gave everything he had in alms and put on a sackcloth. Three days later he came to the Kaabah, but I did not recognize him. He turned to me and said, *'O shaykh, don't you recognize me? I was boasting the other day of servanthood to the commander of Mecca. Today I am boasting of servanthood to the Lord of heaven and earth.* O Dhu'l-Nūn, what do you say? Will God accept me?' "

Dhu'l-Nūn said, *"Rejoice, for you are God's beloved. Don't you know that He calls those who have turned away from Him? How then could He not accept those who have turned toward Him?"*

"He said, 'You have made my heart happy—it was near to bursting.' Then he went."

Dhu'l-Nūn said, "On the seventh day, when I had resolved to go back, they said to me, *'May God give you a wage for that repentant youth.'* I asked about his state. They said, 'When he left you, he went to a little room, put his head on his knees, and was moaning night and day until he gave up his spirit.' "

"After they buried him," Dhu'l-Nūn said, "I saw him in a dream, in a scented garden wearing robes, with a crown on his head. When he saw me he jumped up and came to welcome me. He was strutting and saying, *'How far apart are the two gaits!'*

"I said, 'Tell me your story.'

"He said, '*Surely the godwary will be amid gardens and a river*' [54:54]."

Muḥammad ibn Sammāk and Dhu'l-Nūn went to see Rābiʿa. ʿUtba Ghulām came in, wearing a new shirt and strutting. Muḥammad Sammāk turned to him and said, "What sort of walking is this?"

He said, "Why should I not strut when I am the slave boy of the All-Compelling?" He said these words and fell. When they looked, he had given up his spirit.

A group have given up the spirit and a group go forth without the spirit.[1205] *Among them are those who fulfilled their vow, and among them are those who wait* [33:23].[1206] When it is time for spilling blood, fleeing is not the work of men. You can be a companion at the Battle of Badr because the sword-striker is Gabriel. The work is for you to be a companion at the Battle of Uhud. The Day of Badr was the day of killing enemies; the Day of Uhud was the day of killing friends.

"On the Day of Uhud I wanted to perfume the Exalted Threshold with the blood of the lovers. When a sultan sits in a private session, draws the curtain of seclusion, and gives seats to the pillars of the realm, there is no lack of scent. The sweet scent of sultans is sandalwood, musk, or ambergris. But when the Holy Palisades and the assemblies intimate with My Presence are made fragrant, they use another perfume. Which perfume is that? A hungry breath. '*The foul odor of the fasting person's mouth is more goodly to God than the scent of musk.*'[1207] Or the blood of the killed: '*Wrap them with their cuts and their blood, for surely they will be mustered on the Day of Resurrection, their wounds flowing with blood. The color will be the color of blood, but the scent will be the scent of musk.*'[1208]

"I want someone hungry, exhaling from the depth of a burnt heart, or someone killed by the sword of My severity, blood dripping from his throat. Then the mufti of the world of messengerhood will call out from the pulpit of bravery, '*Wrap them with their cuts and their blood.*' We will perfume the resurrection with the blood of the killed and we will give this world the fragrance of hungry breath.

"O hungry, let out a breath so that this world may be perfumed! O killed, lift up your heads so that the resurrection may be fragrant!

"I want someone hungry or killed. I do not want a satiated man, I do not love a living lover."

Concerning the martyrs the Real says, "*alive at their Lord*" [3:169].

Muṣṭafā was a martyr by virtue of that mouthful from Khaybar. It did not work and thereby a miracle became manifest. It left its fruit afterward and thereby he found martyrdom.[1209]

And the martyrs are at their Lord [57:19]. The sword of severity washed the stain of this world's life from them, conveying them to the wellspring of purity and the fountain of endless life. *How far apart are those who live through their souls, those who live through their hearts, and those who live through their Lord!*[1210]

Water is the cause of purity for everyone but martyrs. For them it is the cause of defilement. "O water, this man is a martyr. He gave his spirit to the point of the sword and reached the center of togetherness. Do not throw him into dispersion! The corpse-washers and prayer-sayers have no business with him, for he dwells in the wellspring of life."

One of the exalted men of the religion was fighting in God's road. He was struck by a spear in the stomach, and it was pulled out from his back. He looked down at himself and saw his blood running from his intestines and innards. He said, "*The praise belongs to God!* I have seen what You desired."

An exalted one recounted, "Once I went to Byzantium for war. A woman called from behind me: 'Stop for a moment so that I may talk to you.' I paid her no attention, but the woman kept on weeping and wailing behind me. In the end I stopped. She reached me and said, 'I need something from you. I have cut off my locks. I ask that when you reach the house of war, make it into an anklet for your horse. Perhaps some dust from God's road will settle on these locks of mine.'

"I said, 'Looking at the hair of a non-privy woman is not permitted by the Shariah.'

"She said, 'I have tied up the hair in this cloth.' Then she brought it out and gave it to me."

The exalted man said, "When I arrived near the enemy, I saw a young man from whose visage were shining the traces of burning. All at once the cry rose up that the enemy has arrived. He threw himself at them and destroyed a few. Then he attacked again and destroyed more of them. I was amazed by his courage and movement. He had a handbag with him and turned it over to me. He said, 'Take this to my mother, in such-and-such a city, in such-and-such a quarter.' Then he said, 'Give me two or three arrows.' I gave them to him. He fired one arrow and it struck down an unbeliever. He fired the second arrow and it struck down another. When he wanted to pull back the third arrow, he was struck with a blow in the middle of his forehead, and he fell on the place of prostration. We were busy with the battle. When we were finished, we lifted up the youth, dug a grave, and put him in the grave. But the dust threw him up and would not accept him, no matter the stratagem. When an hour passed, the wild animals and birds came and took him bit by bit. Yes, he will not fear that fire will be struck into the world to warm the cold."

The exalted man said, "In keeping with the testament of that youth, I went to the door of his mother with a group of warriors. I knocked on the door and a little girl came and looked at our faces. Then she went into the house and said, 'Mother, the warriors have come, and my brother is not with them.'

"The old woman came out and said, 'Have you come with condolences or congratulations?'

"I said, 'Old woman, which do you want?'

"She said, 'If my son has not died, give condolences. If he was martyred, give congratulations.' "

"I said, 'He was killed.'

"She said, '*The praise belongs to God! O Abū Quddāma, surely his being killed has a mark.*' "

The name of the exalted man who recounted this story was Abū Quddāma. "O Abū Quddāma, his being killed has a mark. If you are being truthful, what was the mark?"

He said, "The mark is that the earth would not accept him and was throwing him back out, and the wild animals and birds tore him to pieces."

She said, "The praise belongs to God, who answered his supplication!" Then she held out her hand, took the handbag, and opened it. She brought out a band, a fetter, and a sackcloth and said, "When night became dark my son had the custom to put this band on his foot and this fetter around his neck, and he would wear the sackcloth. He would go into a corner and worship God. He would supplicate, 'O God, provide me with martyrdom and muster me from the bellies of wild animals and the craws of birds!' The praise belongs to God that his supplication was answered!" [1211]

About this community this has come: *"Their sacrifices are their blood."*[1212] When they sacrifice, they sacrifice themselves. As long as the owner of a life does not lose his life with the help of his life, that life will not subsist. Dust be on the head of that life!

If there is any realizer in the world, even if the banner of his sincerity has reached Capella, he has the pain of his own existence. When will he give this existence back to the hand of nonexistence, hang this proud, impatient Guebre on the gallows, and throw out this antagonist of the decree and destiny? Then his heart will go forth on the Duldul[1213] of coquetry to gaze on the garden of *God does what He wills* [14:27].

Whenever a bird goes into water, it goes under, except the one that does not have antagonistic claws and fearful beak. They put a duck's egg under a chicken, and out comes a chick. When it reaches the edge of the water, it throws itself into the water, and the mother remains far away. Why is that? It does not have a fearful beak and antagonistic claws, so it goes into the water and does not drown.

O dervishes, being killed is a stipulation of the road. At least give your heart to an equal so that, when you are killed, it is at the hands of an equal.[1214] It would be a disgrace to give your heart to less than an equal. The whole world gave their hearts to less than equals, except these men. And if the heart had an equal in the whole world, this secret would never have come out into the open: *"The hearts are between two fingers of the All-Merciful."*[1215]

"Make your heart sound, then surrender to Me and look on from afar. The mother of Moses surrendered Moses to Me. You saw what I did. Mary's mother deposited Mary with Me. You have heard how I took care of her work.

"Moses's mother surrendered Moses to Me, and I made the enemy's lap his cradle. Seventy thousand children, noble and base, were killed in one day, and the killer nurtured him in his lap with kindness and endearment!"

"O Pharaoh, kill Moses!"

But he, with the tongue of the state, was saying, *"Should I kill my own killer?"*[1216]

"When Mary's mother surrendered Mary to Me, I did not reject her because of the defect of femaleness. What do you say about those who surrender their hearts to me? Should I reject them because of the defects and slips of mortal nature? I have an ancient work with you."

He bestows upon you as if it were an obligation and asks of you by saying that it is a loan. When He bestows, His utmost generosity makes it seem that it is obligatory for Him to give. And when He asks of you, He says that it is a loan so the blessing of your possessions will be greater. *O generosity that has no end! He thanks you for the success He gives to you.* He sends the steed of success-giving to the door of your house, appoints the emissary of confirmation, and sends the messenger of acceptance time after time. When you aim for His Presence on the steed of success-giving, He Himself voices gratitude to you for what He has given and placed. The blessing is from Him, and the gratitude is also from Him.

"A dog followed a few steps in your tracks, and I adorned its breast with the waistcoat of election, bringing it into the banquet of this ascription: *And their dog was extending its paws at the doorstep* [18:18].

"For seven hundred thousand years an angel had sung hymns of glorification like a nightingale in the garden of My approval. When he glanced at you with an evil gaze, I made him the ill-fated of the spheres so that it would be known that good fortune comes from gentle gifts, not from performing duties. Every wind is a wind, but the gentle gift of My artisanry lies in the sweet wind of Taif." That is a desire that He has for us, and He will take His desire to the end. It is not that you must join in, for He began this mystery without needs and He will take it to the end without needs.

Someone who is munificent does whatever he does by his own bounty and without any cause. Hearts are exalted by His munificence. Throw away the causes, because there are no causes in existence. The hearts of the exalted ones are pulled up by His majesty without cause. Whomever He pulls up without cause He will never put down. Whenever love has a cause, it has no root.

"I wanted to display My power, so I created you. I wanted to display My knowledge, so I deposited intellect in you. I wanted to display My speech, so I gave you hearing. I wanted to disclose My Essence, so I gave you eyesight. My Essence in My unseen was adorned with My exaltedness and majesty. I brought a hundred thousand preparations of gentleness into appearance to disclose My Essence to your eyes. When there is talk of heaven and earth, I am unseen. When there is talk of you, I am apparent.

"How long will you keep this secret in your breast? Set up the banner in the open and display your love. I will take heaven and earth into nonexistence and reduce the sun and moon to nothing. In the midst of it all, you are the one who is desired. When I spoke in the beginning, I was speaking to you. When I speak in the end, I will be speaking to you."

This is a saying of the exalted ones: *"There is nothing more splendid and no station higher than someone who stands in the place of witnessing his Beloved, bowing his head in awe while his Patron is speaking to him."*

O dervish, *bestowal may come to both the near and the far, but the beloved alone is addressed. Such is the custom of kings.* "The throne of kingship is yours and the seat of everlastingness is yours. The only attribute I approve of for you after the attribute of love is the attribute of subsistence. I plundered your spirit, I took away possessions and blessings, but I did not take away one iota of the covenant that was made in eternity."

In the reports it has come that when the angels of mercy go to lift away the spirit of the *tawḥīd*-voicer, He will call out, *"To Me, to Me!"* Like a mother He is lovingly kind. When her dear child enters the house, she says, "Spirit of your mother, come to your mother!"

O chevalier, we were born in a foreign land. In our city there were the mantle of election and the crown of chosenness. The angels were in prostration, and the shoulders of the proximate ones were our thrones. Wait until we go back to our city to see exaltation and kindness. "*'The house is your house, and I am your neighbor.'* You are My dear ones, you are My beloved children."

O dervish, even if you have a burnt liver, a sword-slashed spirit, and a heart melted by a hundred thousand remorses, paradise will compensate for pains like this. But what place is this for that talk? When they beat the drums for the pageant of our good fortune, we will tie the seven heavens and the seven earths to our saddle-straps.

There was Judge ʿAbd al-Jabbār. In the principles he believed in the creed of the Muʿtazilites.[1217] Once a dervish hosted him for dinner and prepared many sorts of blessings. When the judge sat down at the table he said, "Where is the host?"

They said to him, "He will not be present."

He said, "I will not touch the food without seeing him."

The dervish came out and said, "O Judge, in my house and at my table, you will not eat my food without seeing me. Tomorrow, in the house of bliss, how will you eat the blessings of paradise without seeing the Generous King?" *Peace!*

84. *al-ʿAfū:* the Pardoner

The overlooker and eraser of sin.

Tomorrow in that world the command will come as adversary, but bounty will offer shelter. The Shariah will seize the skirt, but mercy will intercede. Then the Real Himself will mediate between the command and the decree. Here we have a worthy mediator; here we have a just judge! The command will denounce, and the decree will intercede.

It has come in a hadith that tomorrow a book will be given into the hand of the disobedient servant. When he reaches one of his acts of disobedience, he will be ashamed to read it. The address will come, "On the day you did that, you had no shame and I did not disgrace you. Today that you are ashamed to read, would I disgrace you?"[1218]

Chosroes had prepared a tremendous feast. A chamberlain stole a gold goblet, and no one saw him but Chosroes. Though he saw, he stayed silent. As much as they looked for it they could not find it. Chosroes said, "Do not search, because the one who found it will not give it back, and the one who saw will not tell." Then one day the chamberlain was standing next to Chosroes pouring water for him and wearing beautiful clothes. Chosroes lifted his head and said, "So, is this from that?"

He replied, "This and a hundred times more are from that."

Bishr Ḥāfī was seen in a dream. It was said, "What did God do with you?"

He said, "He rebuked me: 'O Bishr, what was your fear and dread in that world all about? *Did you not know that generosity is My attribute?*' "[1219]

Tomorrow Muṣṭafā will intercede in the work of the community's sinners to the point that he will say, "O Lord, let me intercede for people who never did any good."

The address will come, *"O Muḥammad, that belongs to Me."* That is My right. Then the address will come, *"Anyone who mentioned Me once in any station or feared Me once at any moment, come out of the Fire!"*[1220]

O mercy in which asking is lost, O bounty in which wanting ceases to be, O greatness in which thought loses the road, O gentleness obeyed by the spirit!

"My servant, if you obey, acceptance is on Me; if you ask, bestowal is on Me; if you sin, pardon is on Me. Water is in My stream, comfort in My street, revelry in searching for Me, intimacy in My beauty, joy in My subsistence, happiness in My encounter. If anyone sees Me, you will see Me. If I pull anyone up, I will pull you up.

"There was a group at the beginning speaking ill of you. I said, 'My angels, if they are poor, I will give them robes of honor. If they are sinners, I will forgive them. Wait and see, then talk! You will be the first prostraters.'"

The Adamite has a marvelous power, a power beyond intellects. China is the quarry of rarities and marvels. When something is rare in China, it will not be found anywhere else. The painters in China are masters. When a form incapacitates the Chinese painters, think how rare it must be!

The final end of whatever may be in the world does not reach the beginning of the Adamites. The final end of the angels' road, which is the station of prostration, did not reach the beginning of Adam's dust. *Prostrate yourselves before Adam!* [2:34].

"O Adam, why are you leaving paradise?"

He said, "My heart is tight from being alone."

They said, "All these houris, wide-eyed maidens, slave boys, and servants—and you are alone?"

He said, "Yes."

O dervish, if impure dust had not nimbly and passionately wandered in the playing field of love's mystery, all the secrets of the Majestic Self-Sufficiency would have stayed behind the veils of the Unseen.

Wahab ibn Munabbih narrated that the Real created Adam and brought him into paradise. He dressed him in seventy robes studded with jewels, placed the crown of kingship on his head, and put anklets on his feet. Adam himself had a beautiful face; he was comely and adorned. When someone is beautiful and well adorned, what happens?

The address came, "O Adam, wander in paradise to see what is more beautiful than you."

He went everywhere and no matter where he looked, he saw himself as more beautiful. Exultation and elation appeared in him and he began to strut. The call came, *"Beautifully done,* O Adam, for none of My creation is like you! *I created you solitary for the Solitary.* You are a creation without equal. O Adam, I created you to be Mine, for I have no equal. O Adam, you will have many children, and they must have an inheritance from you. Leave this strutting for them as an inheritance. The ignorant will strut and it will be called frivolity, the wealthy will strut and it will be called pride, the lovers will strut and it will be called ecstasy."

Who is it that He—*majestic is His majesty!*—gazes upon, even the like of a fly, without the beating of drums in the seven heavens and earth for the pageant of his majestic state?

"I am the Creator and the Provider generally, but I am your Patron specifically. *That is because God is the patron of those who have faith* [47:11]."

Today is the day of our turn and the time of our good fortune. One hundred twenty-some thousand center-points of sinlessness bound the mask of dust on their faces so that they might slap down the shameless of the empire and see the days of their own good fortune.

Do you fancy that these words are foolish: *"He loves them and they love Him"* [5:54]?

One day Moses became happy and was twisting inside. He said, *"O God, I have something You do not have."* In the hut of my beggary I have something not found in the treasury of Your all-compellingness.

When the angels of the Dominion heard these words, they all stained the wings of holiness with the blood of their eyes. The address came, "O Moses, what are you saying?"—though He well knew.

> Someone asked her about me on purpose.
> She said, "Who is he? What is he to me?"[1221]

Moses said, "O Lord, I spoke the truth. You have someone like me, and there are many who have mortal nature like mine in the world. But I have someone like You, and You have no associate and no similar."

O chevalier, our interceder is our ignorance, and our leader is our negligence. Adam's greatest good fortune was that it was said about him, *"Surely he was a great wrongdoer, deeply ignorant"* [33:72].

"If I am a great wrongdoer and deeply ignorant, what is this Trust doing with me?"

They send a guard to the roof of the sultan's treasury to beat the clappers by day, but it is the sultan's greatness that protects the sultan's treasury. *It is We who have sent down the Remembrance, and it is We who are its guards* [15:9].

"When We brought you into existence, We brought tremendous works into existence. *'It was for a reason that Qaṣīr cut off his nose.'* "[1222]

It was said to Jacob, "The wolf ate Joseph."

He said, "So the dream was a lie?"

For many years now on the bench of limpidness these dervishes have been casting the lots of love and taking the omens of good fortune. All these omens come out telling of union with the beauty of the Possessor of Majesty. Will they all turn out to be lies?

"If you want endless happiness, here is the high paradise and the highest of the high. If you want endless sorrow, here is hell and the Dungeon. If you cannot tell sorrow from happiness or happiness from sorrow, here am I."

There is a secret for those who are worthy: pain and remedy, sorrow and happiness, poverty and riches—all these are attributes, waystations, and stations of the road. The man who has arrived has no station and no waystation, no spirit and no heart, no present moment and no state, no fear of separation and no hope for union.

A farmer waters the field until the expected time arrives. When the field ripens, he holds back the water. It would be a mistake to water a ripened field.

Will we ever lift up a broom and start sweeping from the top of the house? Whether it's learning or intellect, disobedience or obedience, let's sweep it all away. Perhaps we will become *tawḥīd*-voicers.

By God the Tremendous, if Muṣṭafā had had one iota of clinging from East to West, he would never have been given access to heaven. When an iota of being's burden remains for someone, can he outstrip the wind? When he went on the *miʿrāj*, his steeds were Burāq, Gabriel's wings, and the Canopy. When he returned, he never saw Gabriel's wings, Burāq, or the Canopy. "O paragon, you are the man for whom the Unseen became the seen itself! What steed can carry your burden? O secret of good fortune, you reached the exalted throne of *two-bows' length away*, but—*the praise belongs to God*—you were there for no more than an hour. You came back to us quickly."

What a marvelous business! "You heard, *'Welcome to the wholesome son, the wholesome prophet, the wholesome brother,'*[1223] but you did not make that your station. And here was the world of dust, where they called you sorcerer, poet, diviner, and madman, and you made it your station."

He said, "The wages singled out for me were given to the burnt-livered Uways Qaranī. Gabriel, the trustworthy and dependable, is the pavilion of revelation, but when he saw the groundwork of my elevation's throne, he fell down thunderstruck. Here he had been coming and going, for this is the world of my exile, but when I reached the top of my own realm, he was afraid of falling into the concealment of nonexistence."

No one in all of Qaran was further back than Uways Qaranī, but look at the exaltedness of his aspiration! A breeze from this talk's welcome blew over his burnt heart, and everything holy in the seven heavens and the earth became unsettled: "From which field of violets is this scent coming?" This secret was obscure for the folk of the seven blue domains, but they agreed that it was coming from the realm of dust. Together they said to Gabriel, "O Holy Spirit, in seven hundred thousand years we have never smelled a scent so sweet, and it has come in the era of the chieftain of *two-bows' length away.*"

When Gabriel saw the paragon, he asked him about this story. The paragon said, *"Surely I find the breath of the All-Merciful from the direction of Yemen."*[1224]

"This breeze that is the spirit's share is coming from the liver of a cameleer who is walking in the realm of my Shariah. He drank the overflowing cup that I sent to him on the hand of the courier of welcome, for '*Surely I find the breath of the All-Merciful from the direction of Yemen.*' Now he is shouting out, *'Is there any more'* [50:30]."

"O Muḥammad, you are My beloved, and the folk of your community are My beloveds. We made the seven heavens and the earth the dust beneath your feet, for We have put the hat of love on the head of your secret core. When you are present in My Presence, acknowledge your servanthood by virtue of acquiescence. But when another time comes, exercise lordhood over heaven and earth."

These words do not fit into the intellects of the sons of this era. This is an elixir that rose up in the island of the unseen gentleness and was sent as a gift to our breasts. If you place one speck of this elixir on a thousand thousand pieces of copper, all of them will turn into the red gold of the Sunnah.

The eminence of the Adamite does not derive from traveling on foot, but from the gentleness of Eternity. He is a Lord who turns a thousand years into one moment, and half a moment into a thousand years. In His beginningless knowledge He knew that if He did not disclose this talk, no one from East to West would dare talk of Him. With His bounty and generosity and without anyone's request, He put talk of Himself to the auction of *with Us there is increase* [50:35] by means of the brokerage of the one hundred twenty-some thousand center-points of prophethood: "Who will buy Our talk?"

A freeloader went to a feast. The host said, "Who invited you?"

He said, "If you didn't invite me and I didn't come, then alienation would fall between us."

He speaks to the estranged explicitly and to friends with allusions. *They refused to carry it* [33:72]. Adam stretched out the hand of need. *Surely he was a great wrongdoer, deeply ignorant* [33:72]. When He blames His men, they hear His laudation. A man allows himself to be ridiculed next to praise of his beloved. When He said, *"a great wrongdoer, deeply ignorant,"* that was prepared by His words "I am Knowing and Just." When He blames us, that is praise of Him.

If we suppose that He had not given Adam the draft mixed with poison at the beginning of the work, the Adamites would have fallen into error concerning themselves. He knew how to lay down the foundation.

They say that in India there are people who drink goblets of poison without fear. How can that be? In childhood they mix the poison with milk and pour it down the throat of nature. The prostration of the angels was milk and sugar, and the cup of great wrongdoing was poison. They were mixed together so that both the capacity for gentleness and the capacity for severity would come forth.

Moses received the harshness of *thou shalt not see Me* [7:143] as the counterpart of the robe of *his Lord spoke to him* [7:143]. Despite all this, he was given even more discipline. When he returned from the mountain it was said, *"Who is the most knowledgeable of the folk of the earth?"*

He said, "I am."

Gabriel came and said, "Now that you have made this claim, go to *the meeting place of the two seas* [18:60] in search of knowledge."

In truth, in truth, when he came back from *the meeting place of the two seas*, he was more complete than he was when he came back from the mountain. For at the mountain he heard only His words, and all the listening was his own portion. There he was given the draft of gentleness, but here he was given the draft of severity. Yes, the body is nurtured with food, but the heart is nurtured with severity.

O dervish, there is no end to His gentleness and severity toward this fearless handful of dust. *By God the Tremendous*, these seven heavens and seven earths have none of the color of this talk! If there is a place that has an inkling or scent, it belongs to this handful of dust.

When a caravan has a pot of musk, the musk is in one place and the scent everywhere. The musk bladder of passion and love belonged to God's beloved, but the scent of musk has journeyed five hundred and some years to the lovers. *"Oh, the yearning!"*[1225] comes from this.

Your hearts are under the protection of His gaze. What a heart it must be to be under the protection of His gaze! He took back His gaze from the whole world and turned it over to the heart. The core of the heart is not as much as a gnat's wing. A gaze that heaven and earth could not bear—He turned it over to a gnat's wing. He encouraged the yearners with this and said, *"But He gazes on your hearts."*[1226]

The body's heart will see the object of its desire only when its chin is bound [in the grave]. Today the tongue gives reports of the allusions of the heart, but deeds will be scattered in the dust. He will take the body to nonexistence and then make His subsistence appear. The secret cores will attest to His unity without the intrusion of that which hates diminishment.

85–89. *al-Raʾūf Mālik al-Mulk Dhu'l-Jalāl wa'l-Ikrām al-Wālī al-Mutaʿālī:* the Clement, the Owner of the Kingdom, the Possessor of Majesty and Generous Giving, the Protector, the Transcendent

The Clement is the lovingly kind and forgiving. Clemency is mercy, and it is correct that Clement means Ever-Merciful, a name about which we have already spoken.

In the same way, these other names have already been discussed: the Owner of the Kingdom, the Possessor of Majesty and Generous Giving, the Protector, and the Transcendent.

The meaning of Possessor of Majesty is Majestic, the meaning of Possessor of Generous Giving is like Generous, the meaning of Protector is like the meaning of Friend—though specifically in the sense that he undertakes affairs—and the meaning of Transcendent is the meaning of High.

The outward Persian of these names will also be given so that the common people may understand. The Owner of the Kingdom: the lord of kingship. The Possessor of Majesty: the lord of greatness. Generous Giving: to esteem the servants. The Protector: he who takes care of the work of the servants. The Transcendent: incomparable with and pure of everything that is a mark of defect.

90–91. *al-Muqsiṭ al-Jāmiʿ:* the Impartial, the Gathering

Muqsiṭ is the giver of the just due, and *qāsiṭ* is the doer of iniquity. The Real does not wrong anyone, for He is the Just; and no one can wrong Him, for He is the Exalted. The meaning of justice was mentioned earlier.

As for the Gathering, that is He who brings together. *The day He gathers you for the Day of Gathering* [64:9]. *How will it be when We gather them for a day in which there is no doubt* [3:25]. He also says, *"The day God will gather the messengers"* [5:109].

Those people today who are busy gathering and withholding have a Day of Gathering ahead of them whose attribute is this: *Were it said to the resurrection, "What do you fear?" it would say, "The resurrection."*

Tomorrow the people will be mustered in two groups. One group will say, *"Where is the path to God?"* The other will say, *"Where is the escape from God?"* One group will be clean, the other defiled.

They will say, "Alas for us! What is it with this book? It leaves aside nothing, small or large, without enumerating it" [18:49]. Ibn ʿAbbās said, *"The small is a smile, the large is laughter."*[1227]

There was an exalted man, one of the Substitutes, who said, "Once I wrote a letter to a friend. I was renting a house and wanted to put dust on the letter to dry it. It passed through my heart that I should not be so bold. But I said, 'The amount is trifling.' I scattered some dust on the letter. All at once a voice called out, *'He who thinks lightly of putting dust on writing will come to know the long accounting he will encounter tomorrow at God.'* "[1228]

In the stories they tell of a man who had a son he loved very much, so at night he would have him sleep in the same bed. One night his son was unsettled and could not sleep. The father said, "What is the cause of your sleeplessness?"

He said, "Tomorrow is Thursday, the day of presentation to the teacher. Tomorrow I must present to the teacher what I have learned during the week. My fear is from that."

That man was quick. When he heard these words, they went to work on him. He came out to the courtyard of the house, moaning and weeping. He was putting dust on his head and saying, "I am much more worthy of such fear than this child, for I have a day of presentation before me." He became one of the worshipers and Pegs.[1229]

A great man said in his whispered prayer, *"Woe on me for my long journey, woe on me for my lack of traveling supplies, woe on me for my heavy burden, woe on me for the presentation before the Majestic King!"*

Yaḥyā Muʿādh Rāzī spoke well: *"Three things will be gathered together against the sins of the servant. Were one of them to aim for the sins of all creatures and eliminate them, that would be no surprise."*

It was said, "What are they?"

*He said, "*Tawḥīd, *God's mercy, and Muḥammad's intercession."*

God's questioning the faithful on the Day of Resurrection will be like Joseph's conduct with his brothers: *"Do you know what you did to Joseph and his brother?"* [12:89]. In the same way, the Real will say to the faithful servant, *"Do you know what you did? Do you remember what you did when you were alone?"*

"Do you know what you did to Joseph and his brother?" Then because of extreme tenderness, he voiced their excuse: *"when you were ignorant"* [12:89]. Do you know what you did to Joseph in ignorance?

They said, *"What, are you indeed Joseph?"* [12:90]. For some time they had not seen his beauty. His loveliness was a garden in which fresh narcissus, red roses, and violets had increased, so they did not recognize him. His beauty threw off its mask and said to them in meaning, "Do they sell a face like this for *a paltry price* [12:20] and a few dirhams?"

O florist, how can you sell roses for silver?[1230]

Tomorrow the Real will address His servant, *"Do you know what you did?* Do you know what you did to the Joseph of the Shariah and the Benjamin of My covenant?" He will not say, *"Why did you do that?"* for heaven and earth would not have the capacity for that address, nor the gall to respond.

Then with his beautiful demeanor what did Joseph say about their conduct? *"No reproof is upon you today"* [12:92]. In the same way the Real will say, *"O My servants, no fear is upon you today"* [43:68].

Muṣṭafā with his community is like Jacob with his sons. *They said, "O our father, ask forgiveness of our sins for us"* [12:97]. *It was Jacob who asked forgiveness for them after they had burned his heart. So also tomorrow Muṣṭafā will be our intercessor with our Lord, even if we have opposed him.*

The sons made the father grieve, but the father loosed the tongue of asking forgiveness: *"I will ask my Lord to forgive you"* [12:98]. Muṣṭafā's community have done deeds of opposition, but in the vast plain of the resurrection that paragon will go to the pulpit of the Throne and loose the tongue of apology, for *it may be thy Lord will raise thee up to a praised station* [17:79]. Muṣṭafā's tenderness toward his community is beyond Jacob's tenderness toward his sons. The latter came from the loins of appetite, but the former came from the loins of the Shariah.

Spirit and body are like Zulaykhā and Joseph: *Each of them put the sin onto his companion.* Joseph said, *"It was she who tried to seduce me"* [12:26]. Zulaykhā said, *"What is the recompense of someone who desires ugliness for thy folk?"* [12:25]. Then, after their separation, when Zulaykhā confessed that Joseph was innocent of the filth of crimes, the breeze of union sprang up in the garden of proximity. In the same way, when the commanding, gambling, wine-drinking, fornicating soul confesses to its wrongdoing and treachery, the breeze of union will blow from the direction of welcome. It will take the soul's hand and put it down in the *seat of truthfulness* [54:55] of the sincerely truthful.

The owner of great sins in the Fire will be like Joseph in prison—that was the dungeon of rebuke, not the dungeon of chastisement. In the same way, for the *tawḥīd*-voicers stained by great sins, hell will be the prison of teaching courtesy, not the dungeon of chastising and punishing.

O chevalier, this talk of paradise and hell is for beginners on the road. As for the Men who adorn the playing field of love, their destination, goal, place of witnessing, and object of witnessing are something else.

In the house of the estranged there will be those who keep on calling out, "Beware, O Mālik, lest you lift up the cover! Do not give anyone access to me, for I am sitting with my heart in seclusion, contemplating the severity of majesty. I cannot put up with anyone's intrusion."

The fire of hell is for tanning uncured skin. For a thousand years they will wander in that house until the soul gains the tasting of the heart. When the soul comes to have one makeup with the heart, the two will make peace and embrace each other. Then the Fire will not be able to put up with the shine of the soul and will begin to shout. Muṣṭafā said, *"Gehenna will be crying out because of their coolness."*[1231]

O dervish, *"Gold is proven by fire."*[1232] When they want to test gold, they do so with fire. You are hard cash that has come out from the mint, but you have been put to use in the city of transaction, which is this dusty circle. The dust of gazing on others has sat upon you. A crucible has been made from the fire of hell to purify the tainted. After that the pure gold of sincerity and the precious pearls of hallowing will be deposited in the jewel box of everlastingness and the sack of existence. It will be called out, *"O folk of the Garden, everlastingness, and no death! O folk of the Fire, everlastingness, and no death!"*[1233]

Wait until this body is broken apart by death and turned into tiny specks in the dust of the grave. Perfect power will clothe it in the robe of the return. It will be put into the crucible of hell, taken from there to the River of Life and purified, and then to Firdaws where it will be perfumed. You will be clothed in seventy robes. The top one will say, "I am more excellent, for his narcissus eyes fall on me." The bottom one will say, "I am more exalted, for I touch the skin of the friend."

Power, the chief, will come and end the quarrel. Seventy times every instant the bottom robe will come to the top and the top robe will go to the bottom so that the bottom robe will have a portion of vision and the top robe a share of skin.

The robe will have one collar and seventy skirts, like a hundred-petalled rose coming forth from an emerald box. The collar will be one, the skirt one hundred. Then the exalted embroidery of endless subsistence will be pulled over the cape of your chieftainship. Sometimes the drink of *ginger* [76:17] will be given, sometimes the drink of *camphor* [76:5], sometimes the drink of *Tasnīm* [83:27]. The outward will have become the inward, and the inward the outward. The form will have become the heart, the heart the form. Just as people know the Real today without misgiving, tomorrow they will see Him without ambiguity.

And none of you there is but will go down into it [19:71]. Your heart is the incense from the ocean of munificence. Incense is thrown on the fire so that it will give off fragrance.

"And none of you there is but will go down into it," making clear to people that His kindness toward the disobedient in the Fire is greater than His kindness toward the obedient in the Garden. "My kindness to the destitute in the Fire is beyond My kindness to the obedient in paradise."

It has reached us that Muṣṭafā said, *"My community's share of the Fire is like Abraham's share of Nimrod's fire."*

The fire said to Nimrod, "You have done a good deed by showing me my being. Before Nimrod made that attempt, I did not know that I had nothing in my hands."

Abraham said, "O fire, do your work, for nothing will happen to me."

"O Bosom Friend, what place is this for that? As soon as the greatness of your bosom friendship showed its face to me, I took back my heart from myself. In any case, I am busy with a sort of service. The work is done by those who are not aware."

The call was coming, "O fire, offer your apology." From East to West, every kind of fire bound the belt of service to bosom friendship and all were left without a share of their own service. "Yes, today is the bazaar of the Bosom Friend. Today it would be disrespectful to do your work or think of your work."

What was this? It was bounty's trace in justice, and justice's trace in bounty. The wine of gentleness was sent in the cup of severity, and the Bosom Friend gratefully sent forth his spirit in welcome.

"Yes, whenever someone falls into My trap, every day he is more exalted and more subjugated."

The state of the Bosom Friend in God's Book and His messenger's Sunnah gives the *tawḥīd*-voicing man the certain knowledge that fire, unless God wills, has nothing but wind in its hands.

Here we have a lover—provided he is Moses. He was thrown into fire, but he did not burn. He was thrown into water, but he did not drown. Sometimes he was nurtured next to Pharaoh full of faults, who was saying in his ear, *"I am your lord the most high"* [79:24]. Sometimes he was nurtured in the lap of Shuʿayb, who was saying, *"He alone—He has no associate."* When he arrived at the Presence, the call came, *"Surely I, I am God"* [28:30].

"I affirmed Myself with two attributes—'O Moses, it is I who am I'—so that you will know that you are not you. You are he who came seeking fire, and when I affirmed Myself with these two attributes, you were not in the midst. As a matter of course you found the robe of elevation. When you affirmed yourself with two attributes—'S*how me, that I may gaze upon Thee*'—as a matter of course the answer came back negative: '*Thou shalt not see Me*' [7:143]."

"And none of you there is but will go down into it" so that the person of faith will be the unbeliever's guide in entering the Fire, just as Gabriel was Pharaoh's guide into the sea.

"And none of you there is but will go down into it." He who tastes the salty recognizes the worth of the sweet. Someone who has tasted salt water knows the worth of pure water. The proverb says that the house should be bought from the son, not the father.[1234]

And none of you there is but will go down into it. This is to verify the boast of the angels at the beginning of the work.

In a hadith it has come that the last person to be brought out of hell will be a man by the name of Hannād. He will remain one thousand years in hell, and in a corner of the severity of the abyss he will be calling out, *"O Ruthful, O Bestower!"*[1235] "Thus you will know that We have servants who do not turn away from Us because of punishment."

And none of you there is but will go down into it. Come into the Fire so that when you come out safely, the remorse of the unbelievers will be one hundredfold! *Perhaps the unbelievers would love that they had been submitters* [15:2]—that will be in this state.

And none of you there is but will go down into it. If you place kernels of wheat on the table, people will laugh. Intermediaries and means of approach are needed to become worthy of that place. *The wheat must be planted, reaped, ground, made into dough, and baked. Once it is tested by fire, it is placed on the table. So also is the person of faith.* Once he is bound in the oven of hell, he will become worthy of the table of the brothers.

And none of you there is but will go down into it. "The Garden is ringed around by things disliked,"[1236] *and the Fire is the greatest of the disliked things.* When the kingship of Egypt was stored away for Joseph, the road was put in the well. When paradise was perfumed for the faithful, the road was put in hell. O recognizers, paradise is a created thing and cannot be reached without putting up with hardships and much suffering. Can one reach the Exalted Presence without putting up with trial? No, no!

"And none of you there is but will go down into it," whether pious or depraved, obedient or disobedient. This is to negate schadenfreude. As long as the disobedient are in the dust of the lights of the obedient, they will not be disgraced, and the enemy will not be able to enjoy their pain.

When Zulaykhā was afflicted by the trap of passionate love, she saw the world as trial itself. The king of Egypt became aware, and she put it into his mouth that Joseph should be imprisoned. The king said, "That's good," and sent him to prison wearing a robe, a crown on his head, and servitors behind him. When the warden of the prison saw him, he ran out to meet him: "My eyes have never seen such a prisoner. Prisoners have a different attribute. This is either a noble angel or a tremendous king. I must serve him. If one day the king's rebuke comes to an end, he may cast a gaze on my work."

The person of faith comes into hell. Yes, the poor man must have help so that with its strength he may put up with the suffering. The unbelievers will be burning endlessly in their punishment. The Zabāniya will see the *tawḥīd*-voicers coming with white faces and white feet, the traces of the ablution on their hands and feet,[1237] the traces of the prostration on their foreheads, and the lights of finding in their hearts. "O Mālik, they are at the doorstep of rebuke, not in the straits of punishment."

Basṭāmī said, "If I am sent to hell tomorrow, I will say, 'What is worthy for me is this. Whenever someone unworthy like me claims Your friendship, what is worthy for him is this.' "

When the prisoners saw Joseph, they came forward to serve him. Joseph said, "I came into prison to be your servitor." He swept the prison with his own hands and served that group. One day the prisoners looked at him and said, "O chevalier, you do not resemble these Egyptians. Are you an exile?"

He said, "Yes, I am an exile, and I have pain in my heart but no physician."

They said, "How did you fall into this prison?"

He said, "By an accusation, for an exile is quickly seized by accusations."

They were talking about this when Zulaykhā's command arrived: "Beat him without kindness. Perhaps he will respond to tribulation. You must beat him such that his 'aah' reaches my ears."

The warden was at a loss. His heart would not let him strike him, for Joseph's beauty held its hand against his chest. But he also could not refuse to strike him, for the king's representative kept on coming around. The poor man was bewildered in the midst. Love gave him no fatwa to touch him, and the command's severity did not allow him to go against the governor's command. He was at a loss and went to Joseph. "O Joseph, this is the command. What should be done? O Joseph, I know that you breathe many cold signs because of the pain you have inside you. No exile is without cold sighs and painful breaths. Is there any way that you can bring out your inner sighs so that I may be excused and you also will not have to suffer?"

He said, "That is hitting the mark."

When an "aah" reached Zulaykhā's ears for the first time, she tore her veil. When she heard a second "aah," she ripped her shirt. When the heard the third "aah," she fainted. Then she shouted out, "Glory be to God! Do not beat him. I did not desire punishment. I desired that his voice would reach my ears as assistance in the days of separation."

> My ears love your sweet voice—
>   for that sweet voice I'll sell my spirit.
> Pierce both my ears, O pretty one,
>   and keep me enslaved, but don't sell me.

The command will come to the angel, *"Make the trial severe for him, for I love his voice."*[1238] When the trial becomes severe, the lover will bring up a cold sigh from his liver. The call will come, *"O Mālik, be kind to My servant, for he is an exile." Peace!*

92–93. *al-Ghanī al-Mughnī:* the Unneedy, the Need-Lifter

Without needs, and he who lifts away needs and suffices.

If you obey, you are seeking your own share, and if you disobey, you are attracting trial. The courtyards of exaltedness are too holy to be adorned by the obedience of the obedient or disfigured by the disobedience of the disobedient.

If you were to gather all the deeds of the sincerely truthful among the children of Adam from Adam's era to the dissolution of the world along with all the obedient acts of the holy ones of heaven, they would not have the weight of a dust mote in the scales of the majesty of the Possessor of Majesty. Never look at your own distracted deeds with the eye of self-admiration! The moment the human gaze falls upon you, the lordly gaze packs its bags.

O dervish, the police chief of Constantinople is not the caesar of Byzantium. The police chief of Constantinople is His unneediness: "I am the Unneedy who has no need for anyone. I am the One who has no associate or partner. I am the All-Compelling with whom none has the color of union. I am the Owner of the Kingdom—no matter what I do, no one has the gall to protest or the means to fight."

Abu'l-Ḥasan Kharaqānī said, "He cut up the hearts of the sincerely truthful and melted their livers with waiting, but He gave Himself to no one."

It came into Moses's heart, "It is I to whom He spoke."

The command came, "Strike that stone with your staff."

He looked and saw a desert within which were one hundred thousand Moseses, in the hand of each a staff, each of them saying, *"Show me"* [7:143].

There was a dervish in Nishapur who used to wander naked with his privates covered. They said to the Master Abū ʿAlī, "The air is cold and this dervish is naked." He summoned him and told him to wear a sheepskin coat, and he agreed. They sent him to the shop of a sheepskin tailor to choose one. He came to the shop, looked inside, and saw many sheepskins. He shouted out and became happy. He said, "You have so many sheepskins that I have become warm."

There was an old woman, all burned up, who set out for the House. One day the caravan dismounted, and the exhausted old woman slept. The people became frightened and the caravan left, forgetting the old woman. When she woke up, she saw in bewilderment that the caravan had gone. She lifted up her head and said, *"O God, You brought me out of my house, but You did not convey me to Your House! You abandoned me in the road. To whom will You turn me over?"* You stirred me up from my corner but did not convey me to Your House. You left me in the road. Now tell me to whom You will turn me over.[1239]

In truth, in truth, He has given us these spirits so that we may make them smaller and smaller.

O dervish, look at the abasement of the pearl-diver, and look at the exaltedness of the pearl. The diver has put on the shoes of seeking, and the oyster sits back on the throne of its exaltedness and says, "Whoever is worthy of me must come to me." A hundred thousand burnt lovers dive like pearl-divers into the ocean of majesty seeking the pearl, but moment by moment the royal pearl of the secrets becomes more curtained by the hidden affairs of the Unseen.

Whatever the scholars have said is a report and whatever the shaykhs have said is a tradition, but *the reality of the Real is beyond reports and traditions.*

He placed a field before the creatures and called out, "O folk of the world! Step into this field and walk on the road. Go forth veiled. Know not where you are going, and know not whence you have come. Set out from the threshold of Our knowledge and settle down at the threshold of Our decree!"

"Lord God, what is the wisdom?"

"Yes, if you were to know, you would be a partner in Our Lordhood."

"Then what should we do?"

"Bind your belts to serve Us, gaze upon Our will, and be prepared for Our power, either for pardon and forgiveness, or for severity and punishment. *The power of the Powerful suspends every contrivance.*

"O sword of Our decree, rise up over the world! O sultan of Our power, draw the sword of causeless desire and make the meddlesome intellect run to the crossroads of the Will!"

Do not seek Him with your own intellect. Seek Him with His bounty. *Were it not for God's bounty toward you, and His mercy, none of you would ever become pure* [24:21]. His exaltedness is His attribute, His unneediness His description. A drop from the ocean of His exaltedness smashes a hundred thousand ships of human intellect. How can knowledge, intellect, understanding, and imagination have the gall to open up before His exaltedness? If they open up before His attributes, they open up through the bounty of His attributes. If someone takes shelter in the meddlesome intellect, the attribute of exaltedness will come forth and send him back in despair. If someone takes shelter in His bounty, shouts of "Make way!" will escort him to the highest of the high. Tomorrow justice will be done to those who took shelter in intellect, and bounty will be given to those who took shelter in bounty.

The angel of the right hand is given priority over the angel of the left hand. The angel of the right is the angel of bounty, and the angel of the left is the angel of justice. "O angel of the right hand, you are the commander! O angel of the right hand, write down whatever you want! O angel of the left hand, write down nothing except what the angel of the right hand says!" [1240]

What is all this? It is the result of one decree that God issued in the Beginningless: *"My mercy takes precedence over My wrath."*[1241]

The servant sins, and the command comes to pull down the curtain. "Lord God, which curtain?" The command comes to pull down the curtain of faith so that his sin will be submerged and overwhelmed by his faith.

Then he commits so many sins so brazenly that they say, "Lord God, there are many sins. The curtain of his faith will not conceal them."

He says, "If the curtain of his faith cannot conceal them, then pull down the curtain of My generosity." Then, when he obeys, He says, "Lift the curtain and open up the road." The Throne will not veil him, nor the Footstool, nor the angels, nor the spheres, nor anything at all.

O dervish, the generous is he who gives to the undeserving, not he who gives to the deserving. This is because deservingness is a necessitating cause. Whenever there is a necessitating cause, there is a debt. One does not discharge debts with generosity.

On the day He created Adam He called out to the world, "Wherever there is someone undeserving, let him come to My Presence so that I may give him a robe of honor!"

When a sultan appoints someone as heir apparent, the least he does is to bestow robes of honor on all his deputies. "Heaven and earth, the Throne, paradise and hell, the angels, the spheres—all are your deputies."

And We made covenant with Adam before, but he forgot [20:115]. *Did I not make covenant with you, O children of Adam?* [36:60]. He made a covenant with us and He made a covenant with Himself. He made a covenant with Himself for us, and He made a covenant with us for Himself. Then He said, *"And be loyal to My covenant; I shall be loyal to your covenant"* [2:40].

When He made the covenant, Adam had not yet stepped into paradise, yet the call went out all over paradise, *"And Adam disobeyed"* [20:121]. "Lord God, disloyalty finds no room in You, and loyalty finds no room in me."

"Now that disloyalty does not come from you, *who is more loyal to his covenant than God? So rejoice* [9:111]. Even if you do not have the wherewithal to be loyal to Our covenant, you do have the wherewithal to be happy with Our loyalty. If you do not have a face of beauty, well then be happy with the beauty of Our Presence."

O dervish, at the time of largesse, anyone who is ashamed will not take a share. In some rare reports it has come, *"He contended with us, and we contended with Him. Surely God loves those who implore in supplication."*[1242]

"When someone supplicates and asks from Me while pulling down the curtain of shame over his face, I do not want him. The one I want is he who removes shame from his face and asks boldly for what he wants. He should ask with a high aspiration and not ask for something trivial. If he is not given what he wants, he should not rise up from the Threshold until he gets it."

O dervish, know for sure that whenever He gives something to someone, He gives it for free. Whenever He gives someone faith, He gives it for free. Whenever He forgives someone, He forgives him for free. The whole world is taking things from Him, and He bestows.

"Is there any asker, is there any supplicator, is there anyone asking forgiveness?"[1243] He commanded them to ask: *"Ask God of His bounty"* [4:32]. When they do not ask, He requests: *"Is there any asker?"* When He requests and they are lazy, He gives without being asked. He said, *"I responded to you before you supplicated Me, I bestowed upon you before you asked from Me."*[1244]

"I have plenty of generosity. I command you to ask. When You do not ask, I request. When you are lazy, I give unasked."

"My work with you does not pertain to today." *Each day He is upon some task* [55:29], that is, affairs He makes appear, not affairs He begins. "It is some time that I have been speaking to you, but you hear now." *Thou wast not at the side of the Mount when We called out* [28:46].

He places the collar of subjection on people's necks and ties them back with the halter of predetermination. Then He lets them roam in the vast plain. They come and they go, they travel at their fancy, they keep themselves busy. All at once He pulls the halter of power and everyone goes back to the first point. In the same way, a child has a little bird and ties a string to its foot. He releases it so that it can fly a bit. It fancies that it has been let go and it flies. All at once, he pulls back on the string.

Recognize the reality: When someone steps into this road and reaches the end, the last step that he takes will be the first step. In the beginningless beginning He made the work happen. The geometrician of the Will set up the string of the compass and established steps, pens, imaginations, and understandings as decree and destiny. Everyone reaches the end of his work by virtue of predetermination. Those who walk the road of predetermination linger through practice; a branch in the mosque with a root in the church, a root in the mosque with a branch in the church. The unbeliever arrived at unbelief because of predetermination, the person of faith arrived at faith because of the decree. Neither arrived because of practice.

Then He created this world and placed two fields out front: the field of felicity and the field of wretchedness. The final goal of the first field is approval, and the final end of the second field is anger. He brings those who walk the road of predetermination into practice so that they will walk what the Pen wrote for them. They do not take one step before or behind that is not driven by the Pen. When they reach the last step, it is the same step that they saw at first. The first step is predetermination, and the last step is practice. Who are we? Those who arrive through predetermination and linger through practice.

All these creatures you see coming and going are walking in a completed work. No one begins a new work. ʿUmar came to the Messenger and said, *"O Messenger of God! Is what we are doing today an affair that is finished, or an affair that is not yet finished?"*

He said, "It is an affair that is finished."[1245] This is a work that has already been. He conveys everyone to his domicile and makes apparent his place, then He brings him to the road of practice.

Do you fancy that the one hundred twenty-some thousand center-points of sinlessness came into this world to do new work in the world? In truth, in truth, they brought no work into the world. They placed nothing new in your breast. Rather, they put into motion what was in your breast and they called you to that which had been deposited for you. *We would not have been guided had God not guided us* [7:43]. The invitation of the one hundred twenty-some thousand pearls of sinlessness is not the cause of the salvation of one breath of yours. The books and messengers were intermediaries that He brought into the midst. All that you see came straight from the decree and predetermination.

Destiny is a tremendous secret that not every eye can see. The Commander of the Faithful ʿAlī was asked about destiny. He said, *"It is God's secret, so we do not unveil it. It is a tremendous ocean, so we do not importune it."*[1246] Human knowledge does not have the capacity to carry it.

Talk of the spirit is of this sort, and talk of destiny and the ambiguous verses is of this sort.[1247] Each of these has put on a shirt of jealousy. You see a man speaking words "so that I may tell you the reality of destiny." He strides forth "so that I may go by the road of the spirit." He intervenes "so that I may know the secret of the ambiguous verses."

Then He calls out: "Whatever I have held back will be reached by no one. The more you go forward, the more you will be bewildered. The more you intervene, the more you will fall."

> What is the spirit next to Your face but a meddler?
> What is intellect next to Your lips but a fool?[1248]

O dervish, know in reality that whoever is released is released through Him. *"No one saved will be saved except by truthfulness in taking refuge."*[1249] O Muslims, know that in reality you have found obedience through His mercy. You have not found His mercy through obeying Him. Let me make the words brief: You have not found Him by yourself. You have found yourself by Him.

The Real's attractions in the secret cores negate the opacity of bodies and spirits. If you wash your outwardness for a thousand years, your inwardness will not become pure. You will be a washer of the dead behind a wall. If your secret core is to become pure, a pull from the Real must reach it. Then your outwardness will gain the attribute of purity by following the secret core. *"A secret core safe from the frivolities of mortal nature—that is a lordly secret."*[1250] But these are not words about you.

Someone said to someone, "Does your town have saffron?"

He said, "Mostly we eat the onions with buttermilk."

He said, "So much for that—if you don't know the difference between onions and saffron!"

94–95. *al-Ḍārr al-Nāfiʿ*: the Harmer, the Benefiter

He who brings hurt and He who gives profit. The absolute owner is the Real. It is He who is able to control His possessions as He wants.

This is a sound hadith from Muṣṭafā: *"The faith of the servant will not be perfect until he has faith that if God were to throw the folk of heaven and earth into the Fire, it would be His to do so."*[1251] Muṣṭafā also said, *"Were He to chastise me and the son of Mary, He would be chastising us without wronging us."*[1252] Fear a God who does whatever He wants without anyone having the gall to protest! *"Have shame before God because of His proximity to you, and fear God because of His power over you."*[1253]

Ḥasan Baṣrī was asked, *"O Abū Saʿīd, do you doubt whether someone who says 'no god but God' is one of the faithful?"*

He said, "No, but this sentence does not dwell in the heart of any man until he melts before it in obedience to God and abandons acts of disobedience to God for its sake."

"O Abū Saʿīd, do you doubt the faith of someone who says the words *no god but God?"* He said, "No, but in reality this sentence does not descend into any breast unless acts of disobedience and indecency pack their bags."

It was also Ḥasan Baṣrī who said, *"The man of faith is a clever servant. He reflects thoughtfully, learns lessons, and sees. He betakes himself to this world and razes it, and on this he builds his afterworld. He is not someone who razes his afterworld with this world. Such is his attribute until he encounters his Lord, and His Lord approves of him and makes him approve of Him. And surely the hypocrite is an ignorant servant. He takes this world as a god. This world says, 'Woe upon you! Were you created for this? Were you commanded to do this? Do you not know that you have a Lord? You will come to know and you will regret.'"*

Muʿādh ibn Jabal narrated that Muṣṭafā said, *"O Muʿādh, surely the Quran binds back the person of faith from much of his soul's caprice and appetites. It comes between him and his perishing in the objects of his caprice. He knows that there are watchers over his hearing, his eyesight, his tongue, his feet, and his belly, even the blinks of his eyes. Godwariness is his watcher, the Quran his pointer, fear his road, yearning his steed, caution his comrade, dread his watchword, the daily prayer his cave, and fasting his vizier; and beyond all of this his 'Lord lies in wait'* [89:14]."[1254]

It has been related from Ḥasan Baṣrī that he said, *"The marks and characteristics of the submitter are strength in the religion, courage in mildness, faith with certainty, knowledge in forbearance, bestowal in the rightful due, endurance in want, obedience in counsel, patience in hardship, and kindness in spending. He keeps himself noble against the false and turns away from the ignorant."*[1255]

Abū Bakr Muḥammad ibn ʿAmr ibn Ḥazm said, *"I have met some people who, were they commanded not to drink water, would not drink it even if their livers were to expire."*[1256] What sort of era is it now? *"Lying commanders, depraved viziers, wrongdoing recognizers, and ungodly Quran-reciters, their hearts more putrid than a cadaver."*[1257]

You will see a hundred thousand thousand before you see one man who takes an accounting of his own breaths and who, when a breath comes forth in other than the sacred sanctuary of Muṣṭafā's Shariah, strikes that breath with the whip of sorrow in keeping with the punishment for drunkenness. When someone is not like this, tell him to take off the hat of claiming to be a member of the paragon's community. The paragon is he about whom Moses son of ʿImrān—for whose arrival the spirits of seventy thousand nursing infants were slaughtered like sheep—made the request, *"Make me one of Muḥammad's community!"*[1258] Keep your lying claim far from his road, for the holy spirit of Moses of ʿImrān is watching and the jealousy of John's heart is in this road.

O folk of fancy, *may God make your wage great!* O prisoners of your own caprice, *may God compensate you for your affliction!* The pure religion needs a pure man. This is not the work of the faulty.

Dāwūd Ṭāʾī was the right-hand man of the world of *no god but God.* In *"This is permitted and that is not permitted"* he was a student of Abū Ḥanīfa, but in the garden of truthfulness he was such that on the night when he left this world, a call came from the middle of heaven, *"O folk of the earth, surely Dāwūd Ṭāʾī has stepped forth to his Lord, and He approves of him."*[1259] Dāwūd has reached God, and God is pleased with him along with the beauty of his good fortune.

Abū Bakr ibn ʿAyyāsh said, "I went to Dāwūd's chamber and saw him sitting with a piece of dry bread in his hand and looking at it. I said, *'What is wrong, O Dāwūd?'*

"He said, *'I desire to eat this piece, but I do not know if it has come from the permitted or the forbidden.'* "

In truth, when someone recognizes the exaltedness of the religion, mortal nature's caprice will never reap its fruit from him. If one of the sincerely truthful were to show his head from beneath the cloak of his attributes and look down at us, he would see nothing but our worthless description.

An exalted man said, "I saw Dāwūd in the throes of death in a ruined house, intense heat, having fallen flat in the dust, his head placed on a half piece of brick, dying and reciting the Quran. I said to him, *'O Dāwūd, what would happen if you went out into the open air?'* "

"Dāwūd said, *'O so-and-so, I want to do that, but I am ashamed before my Lord—that I should step into that in which my soul finds ease.'* "[1260] He said that his soul had never had the upper hand over him, and in this state it was even more appropriate that it not have it. It was in this state, lying in the dust, that he gave up his spirit. He did not come out of the house.

God's is the praise for the fact that the straits of death are placed in the road of all creatures so that the irreligious may come to know their own worth. Of all the good fortunes in this world after *tawḥīd*, no good fortune is more exalted than death. At the gate of death the crown of the empire's magnificence will be placed on the heads of those who have the religion, those who are the felicitous of the religion. Those who reap the fruit of the Shariah will find the signet of good fortune at the door of death. Death is the sanctuary of the folk of *no god but God*, the doorstep of the kingdom of the resurrection, the walkway of the Real's visitors, the center of the recognizers' exaltedness, the steed of the spirits of the proximate, the vanguard of beginningless solicitude, and the prelude to endless kind favor. No one in the world has the ease that a godwary man has *in the grave with the One.* Having taken the banner of the submission and the kettledrum of faith into the dust, he will come to the resurrection with the banner of faith and the kettledrum of certainty in the manner of a king entering his own city. But what a waste to talk of the hungry with the full! This talk should be saved for those who are burned like they were.

Sa'īd ibn Musayyib was one of the great Followers. Shaykh Abū Nu'aym Ḥāfiẓ has narrated in *Ḥilyat al-awliyā'* that Sa'īd said, *"No muezzin has called the prayer for thirty years when I was not in the mosque.*

"I have not missed the prayer in congregation for forty years.

"I have prayed the night prayer with the ablution of darkness for fifty years.

"I have not looked at the backs of people who preceded me to the first row for forty years.

"The time of prayer has never entered in upon me unless I was prepared for it and yearning for it."[1261]

This Sa'īd was the son-in-law of Abū Hurayra and the student of Zayd ibn Thābit and Ibn 'Abbās. He said, "For thirty years the muezzin never called the prayer without seeing me sitting and waiting in the mosque. I never performed any prayer without the burn of yearning for the next prayer—when will I be released from myself?"

He had a child in the house, a girl of wholesomeness, faith, and devotion. In that era the sermon was being read in the name of 'Abd al-Malik ibn Marwān, who wanted Sa'īd's daughter for his son.[1262] He told Sa'īd, but Sa'īd refused. He implored, but to no use. 'Abd al-Malik became angry. He commanded that he be taken to the place of punishment, held down, and beaten with a hundred unkind lashes, making him black from head to foot. Then to make an example of him, he had him put on a donkey and taken around the city. In the midst of all this he was saying, *"I will not marry my daughter to someone who does not guard the prayer in the mosque of God's Messenger."* My child knows the rulings of the prayer. If I am to give her over to a man's decree, he must be sincerely truthful and his homeland must be underneath the dome of the prayer.

At the time of the afternoon prayer he was released. For forty years before that day he had never missed the congregational prayer in the Messenger's mosque. He rushed and whenever he met someone he would ask, *"Have they prayed the afternoon prayer in the mosque of God's Messenger?"* They performed the prayer in Muṣṭafā's mosque, and when that was reported to him, he fell down and was striking his head on the ground, saying, "By the rightful due of God's religion! My pain at missing this prayer is more than that of the hundred lashes with which they beat me."

We live in games and diversions, but they lived in the religion. Tomorrow every hair of the sincerely truthful will stand up to thousands of worlds, but a hundred thousand like us will not stand up to a straw.

All those awake in the religion mourn for the unaware, but you are all taken up with "What will I eat, what will I wear, what will I say to the people?" In this world you are idle, full of heedlessness, and at the resurrection you will be a porter, full of remorse. Beware, beware, do not be deluded by the succession of blessings and the raised curtain of generosity, for settling accounts and exacting dues are ahead of you!

When John the son of Zachariah was a child, the children said to him, "Come and play."

He said, *"I was not created for games."*[1263]

Ḥasan Baṣrī wrote a letter to 'Umar ibn 'Abd al-'Azīz: *"O 'Umar, be like someone medicating his wound—patient with the medicine's intensity while fearing the descent of trial."*[1264] O 'Umar, pass your days as an ill person passes his days, drinking down bitter drafts in fear of a blow from the angel of death.

O chevalier, *and forget not your portion from this world* [28:77]. Do not suppose that your portion is enjoyment and taking pleasure. *"What, did you reckon that We created you aimlessly and that you would not be returned to Us?* [23:115]. *Rather We created you for a tremendous affair: felicity or wretchedness, the kingdom or destruction, the Garden or the Fire, proximity or distance, separation or union, acceptance or rejection, generosity or penalty."*

Ḥasan Baṣrī saw a man who was laughing. He asked, *"Have you tasted death?"* Have you drunk the wine of death? He said no. He said, *"Have you become secure from the end?"* He said no. He said, *"Have you responded to Munkar and Nakīr?"* He said no. He said, "Has your obedience weighed down heavy in the Scales?" He said no. He said, "Have you left behind the Narrow Path?" He said no. He said, "Have you gone into the Garden?" He said no. *He said, "Then what is this laughter?"*[1265]

Every time the Bosom Friend remembered his slips, fire would fall into his breast and he would tremble for himself and seek. Gabriel came and said, *"The Lord greets you with peace and says, 'Have you ever seen a bosom friend afraid of his bosom friend?'"*

The Bosom Friend said, *"O Gabriel, when I remember my missteps I forget His bosom friendship."*[1266] Every time the remembrance of slips passes through my mind, my heart is torn to pieces and I do not dare to lean back on the cushion of bosom friendship.

One hundred twenty-some thousand center-points of prophethood were wandering in their livers' blood, but you wander in yearning for appetites.

Mālik Dīnār said, *"I was weeping over sins for a time, and now the sins have become my trade and I weep only for my submission."*[1267] For a long time I wept over sins. Now disobedience has become my profession. I weep because the shirt of Islam may be taken from my body and I will be naked on this side and abandoned on that side.

> For a time I ran in the wrong road
>   until the mask was torn from intellect's face.
> Now I've opened my eyes from sleep,
>   my life wasted, my book ruined.

Dhu'l-Nūn Miṣrī said, "I was walking in Basra and saw a slave girl with a beautiful face. She had bound her head in a turban on which was written, *'Whoever desires me should be afflicted for my sake.'*" Whoever is ready for me, let him prepare himself for pain, grief, and sorrow.

Manṣūr ibn ʿAmmār said, "Once I entered ruins and saw a young man saying his prayers in utter fear, fright, ecstasy, and awe. You would have thought that hell was before him and the resurrection behind him. I waited until he gave the greeting of the prayer. Then I greeted him and said, 'O youth, in hell there is a stone, under which is a valley called the Blaze. It is the prison of the disobedient and the dungeon of the disloyal.'

"When he heard these words, he shouted out and fainted. When he came to, he said, 'O master physician, can you give me another draft?'

"I recited this verse: *'Whose fuel is people and stones'* [2:24]. He let out another shout and gave up the spirit. When they put him on the washing place, I saw written on his chest *'an approved life'* [69:21]. I wanted to place my mouth between his two eyebrows. I saw a script there: *'Then repose and ease, and a Garden of Delight'* [56:89].

"The night after they put him in the ground, I saw him in a dream. He was wearing green garments in paradise and sitting on a steed of light. I said, 'What did the Real do with you?'

"He said, 'He did with me what He did with the martyrs of Badr, with an increase.'

"I said, 'Why?'

"He said, *'They were killed by the swords of the unbelievers, but I was killed by the sword of the All-Forgiving King,' by which he meant fear and fright.* "[1268]

96. *al-Nūr:* the Light

God says, *"God is the light of the heavens and the earth"* [24:35]. God is He who brightens the heavens and the earths for the gazers upon Him, the believers in Him, the lovers of Him, the fearful of Him, and the burned in His love. It is He who gives form to bodies and illuminates spirits. *All lights are from Him and through Him.*

"God is the light of the heavens." Light in reality is that which illuminates other than itself. Light in reality is that which brightens others. Anything that does not brighten others is not light, nor does it illuminate. The sun is light, the moon is light, the lamp is light—in the sense that they illuminate others, not in the sense that they are illuminated in themselves. Do you not see that mirrors, water, pearls, and the like are not called light—even though they are bright in their own essences—for they do not illuminate others? Once this reality is known, *God is the light of the heavens and the earth.* This is not an interpretation or a turning of the verse away from its outward sense. This is precisely the outward sense and reality of the words.

Some lights are outward and some inward. God says, *"What of him whose breast God has expanded for the submission, and he is upon a light from his Lord?"* [39:22]. Know that in reality nothing has as much light as the faithful person's heart. All outward lights are followers, slave boys, and servitors of the inward light. No light is more illuminating and beautiful than the sun, but in the end it becomes opaque and enwrapped: *When the sun is enwrapped* [81:1]. As for the sun that sticks up its head from the horizon of the sphere of the hearts, it has an unveiling without eclipse, a rising without setting, a radiance from the station of yearning. A poet has said,

> *The day's sun surely sets at night,*
> *but the hearts' sun will never disappear.*[1269]

All the holy ones of heaven had to let their hallowing be plundered so that this handful of defiled dust would be adorned with the robe of *What of him whose breast God has expanded for the submission, and he is upon a light from his Lord?*

There was a handful of dust remaining in the darkness of ignorance, bewildered in the darkness of its own makeup. Suddenly torrents of lights poured down from the heaven of the secrets. The dust became jasmine, the stones became gems. Once he arrived, the color of heaven and earth changed. Yes, he was dust, all darkness and gloom. He needed a makeup that is all light, limpidness, and chosenness. An unseen subtlety had to be grafted to his makeup, and the harvest of the envy of the envious had to be given to the wind. How is this subtlety expressed? *"What of him whose breast God has expanded for submission, and he is upon a light from his Lord?"*

It is well known that one of the Muslims was taken prisoner by the unbelievers and fell to the furthest limit of Byzantium, staying there for some time. One day he saw that the Byzantines were gathering in an open space and he asked the cause. They said that there was a bishop there, the leader of the bishops, the most knowing and scrupulous among them. Once every four years he would come out of the monastery, go up on the pulpit, and preach to the people. Today was the promised time of his coming out. The Muslim made himself present in that session, and it is said that thirty thousand people were present there. When the bishop came out and went to the pulpit, for a while he sat silently, with the people thirsty for him to speak. When this became drawn out, it was said to him, *"What is the matter that the bishop does not speak?"*

He said, "My tongue is tied. Is there among you an exile from the folk of Islam?"

They said, "We do not recognize any Muslim among ourselves."

The bishop said with a loud voice, "Whoever is among you from the creed and religion of Muḥammad, let him stand up!"

That Muslim said, "I was afraid to stand up."

The bishop said, "If you do not recognize the exile and he does not recognize himself, *then I will recognize him, God willing." Then he began to ponder the faces of the people.*

He said, "He looked, and I was looking at him in wonder. Then his eyes fell on me. He said quickly, 'That one, that one. Come close to me!' I found no escape. I stood up, for he kept on telling me to come closer until I was near the pulpit. Finally he commanded that I come up on the pulpit with him. *He said to me, 'Are you a Muslim?'*

"I said, 'Yes.'

"He said, 'Are you one of the knowers among the Muslims or one of the ignorant?'

"I said, 'One of the knowers of what I have learned and one of the ignorant of what I have not learned.' I said that I knew what I had learned, studied, and taken trouble for, but I did not know what I had not studied.

"He said, 'You are a knower inasmuch as you know that you are ignorant of what you do not know. The ignorant man is only he who does not know and does not know that he does not know.' Then he said to me as the people looked on in wonder, 'I will ask you three questions. *Will you respond to me?'*

"I said, 'With two conditions. One is that you tell me how you recognized me. Second is that when I have responded and you approve, I will ask three questions of you, and you will respond to me.'

"He said, 'Yes. I will tell you how I recognized you, but secretly in your ear. The questions you ask I will answer openly.'

"I said, 'That is suitable.' We agreed on this, while the folk of Byzantium were looking on and wondering what this state could be.

"Then he put his mouth next to my ear and said, *'I recognized you by the light of your faith.'*

"Then he asked me with a loud voice, 'Your messenger said to you that there is a tree in paradise that has a branch in every palace of paradise. What is the likeness of that in this world?'

"I said, 'The sun, for it is one, but in every house and every room there is a light and a shine.'

"The bishop said, '*You have spoken the truth.*' Then he said to me, 'Your Messenger reported that the folk of paradise put food and drink to work, but no excrement comes from them. Is there a likeness of this in this world?'

"I said, 'There is—*the embryo in the womb of its mother. It eats, drinks, and nourishes itself and does not urinate or defecate.*'

"The bishop said, '*You have spoken the truth.*' Then he asked the third: 'Your Messenger reported that on the Day of Resurrection, a mouthful, a mote, and a grain will be like a tremendous mountain in the Scales. Is there a likeness of this in this world?'

"I said, 'There is. In the morning when the sun comes up, or at the sunset prayer when it goes down, if you hold a one- or two-yard stick before the sun, it appears to be several yards long.'

"The bishop said, 'You have spoken the truth.'

"I said, 'Now it is time for me to ask.'

"He said, 'Ask.'

"I said, 'How many are the gates of the Gardens?'

"He said, 'Eight.'

"I said, 'How many are the gates of the Fires?'

"He said, 'Seven.'

"I said, 'You have spoken the truth.' Then I said, 'What is written on the gate of the Garden?'

"The bishop was silent, so I said, 'Answer!' But he stopped and remained silent. The people said, 'Answer, lest this foreigner say that the bishop does not know the answer to this question.'

"The bishop said, 'If this question must be answered, it will not be truthful with sash and cross.' He undid the sash and cross and said with a loud voice, '*Written on the gate of the Garden is "no god but God and Muḥammad is God's Messenger.*' "

When the Byzantines heard this answer, one cursed, another threw stones. The bishop turned to the foreigner and said, "Do you have anything memorized from the Quran?"

He said, "I do." He had a beautiful voice and he recited the verse, *"And God invites to the abode of peace"* [10:25]. For a while the bishop wept terribly. Then he went up again on the pulpit and said with a loud voice, "O people, the veil has been lifted from my eyes. Right now I see seven hundred angels coming from heaven with seven hundred ornamented litters to take the spirits of the martyrs to heaven, and I am certain that seven hundred of you agree with me in these words. Take care not to fear any antagonist. Be not afraid." Then a large group of them broke their crosses and undid their sashes, and the deniers and unbelievers were killing them and they also killed the bishop. When they counted the killed, there were seven hundred, no more and no less.

The point of this story is that the light of that *tawḥīd*-voicing man of faith was shining in the midst of a handful of deniers.

O dervish, if assistance is sent from the Unseen in your name, a warrior will not take a Byzantine prisoner as that assistance will take you prisoner, but it will not descend for any cause or travel for any reason.

Junayd was in the khanaqah with nine of the Tariqah's sincerely truthful, into whose hearts had entered the thought of war. They spoke together about that thought *from secret core to secret core and from awareness to awareness* but said nothing with the tongue. Then Junayd and those nine men got up and set out for the house of war. When they reached the field of battle, one of the enemy came out, and one of the patched cloak-wearers went out to fight him. The unbeliever was victorious, striking a blow and killing him.

Junayd said, "I saw the angels taking his spirit in a howdah to heaven. Another of the dervishes said, 'God is greater!' and threw himself into the midst. The angels were holding nine more litters in front of us. I knew that all must go. That unbeliever struck a blow and killed the dervish. His spirit was placed in the howdah of exaltedness and taken to heaven."

Junayd said, "Seven were left, and seven litters were held in front of us. I congratulated them all, and each of them bid farewell to his body and placed his spirit in the ballista of surrender. The third dervish threw himself into the midst and was also killed. The proximate ones took his spirit to the Presence. Finally the nine men who were with me were killed by that unbeliever, and the proximate ones took all their spirits to the Presence. One howdah was held before me. I detached my heart from myself and sent my spirit forth to welcome that howdah. I said to myself, 'No robe of honor is more exalted than martyrdom. This robe has been sent to me by the sword of this unbelieving warrior. This must not go to waste.' "

Junayd said, "I also threw myself into the midst of the field. Suddenly I was victorious over that unbeliever. I wanted to strike him with a blow. He said, 'O shaykh, do not strike! Before striking, offer me the formula of submission.' I offered the formula and he submitted. He turned his face to the camp of the unbelievers and undertook a tremendous battle until he was killed. The proximate of the Presence put his spirit in the last howdah and took it to heaven."

Junayd let out a miserable cry. "Alas! My bad lot still has work for me, for it has left me in this world!"

That warrior was made the close friend of the Tariqah's sincerely truthful. It was said to them, "He is the one by means of whom We have sent the robe of martyrdom to you. It would not be beautiful to separate him from you."

"I marvel at the killer with the killed in the Garden."[1270] Once Muṣṭafā was in a battle. One of the unbelievers showed great severity and killed one of the paragon's exalted Companions. After an hour, he became a Muslim and killed a group of the unbelievers. In the end he was killed. Muṣṭafā commanded that he and the man he had killed be buried in one grave. Then he said, "Tomorrow the killer and the killed will be on one throne in the Garden."

O dervish, the ocean of divinity cannot be crossed on the tiny ship of mortal intellects. *How goodly is the assistance of predetermination!* Nothing can equal a man who takes a step while a pull from eternity conforms with his step.

Abū Bakr came forth seeking the religion. He detached his heart from himself and, moaning inwardly like someone afflicted, drew the sword of attestation against his own denial. Night and day he remained unsettled, and no one knew what sort of pain he had. They asked his wife Umm Rūmān, "What happened to Abū Bakr?"

She said, "I do not know, but I have not seen a more ornate moaning and grief than his. Every night he weeps in misery and moans in pain. When morning comes, he lets out a hot sigh from which seems to come the smell of burnt liver."

Hell is a spark from my roasting heart,
the ocean a trace of my weeping eyes.

One night Abū Bakr's unsettledness reached the limit. He said to himself, "This Muḥammad is a kind man. Tomorrow I must go to him and see what he says about my work." The Greatest Law, the Green Peacock, had just come from the Exalted Presence and said to Muṣṭafā, *"Recite in the name of thy Lord who created"* [96:1].

One hundred twenty-some thousand center-points of sinlessness were strung like shining gems on the cord of wayfaring. A centerpiece was needed. The bounty of the Self-Sufficient went like a pearl-diver into the sea of faith and brought back the orphan pearl of Aḥmad, stringing it on the cord as its centerpiece. "O Muḥammad, rise up and step on the pulpit. Shout out to this world and the next. Say to the creatures that no one has any escape from God."

Muṣṭafā thought to himself, "To whom shall I tell this talk? The whole world denies it. Perhaps tomorrow I will go to the door of Abū Bakr's house, for he is a man of propriety." On the next day he stepped out of his chamber intending to see Abū Bakr. Abū Bakr came out of his house with a heart full of love intending to see Muṣṭafā. They met in the road. Muṣṭafā said, *"Where to, O Abū Bakr?"*

He said, "To you."

He said, "Why have you become so emaciated?"

He said, "O trustworthy of God, I cannot see any more of this denial. My heart is constricted. What should be done?"

He said, "O Abū Bakr, I have been sent for this work. A wine has been brought that will turn all your bewilderment into guidance, all your denial into attestation, all your pain into yearning, all your yearning into love."

My pain's from You, my cure from You,
my hardship from You, my ease from You.
Now I can't cut off from You—
obedience from me, my sweet, commands from You!

"Will you give yourself over?"

He said, "O paragon, I came to be released from this trial. This is no place for consultation."

Abū Bakr undertook truthfulness, so Muṣṭafā reported to him the talk of *no god but God.* He said, *"I never offered this affair to anyone who did not stumble except Abū Bakr, for he showed no hesitation."*[1271]

When the sun of truthfulness began to shine from the sphere of Abū Bakr's heart—*What of him whose breast God has expanded for submission, and he is upon a light from his Lord?* [39:22]—ʿUthmān, Ṭalḥa, and Saʿd pulled out their swords and came out against him: "O Abū Bakr, in the tribe of the Arabs it was you who arranged the order of the rulings. Have you now put the collar of *no god but God* on your neck so that the folk of the tribes will imitate you and put aside the creed of Lāt and ʿUzzā? Either take off the collar of submission or give us your head."

Abū Bakr put forth his head and offered his throat to their swords, saying, "Be quick about taking this meddlesome head so that I may be the first martyr in the road of these words, just as I was the first prisoner."

When they saw his seriousness, they knew that no one could be so stubborn in falsehood. They threw down their swords and said, "Give us a share of the wine you drank."

He said, *"Say: 'No god but God, Muḥammad is God's Messenger.' "* They accepted the words and he accepted their words. At once their hearts opened up. *What of him whose breast God has expanded for submission, and he is upon a light from his Lord?*

The worth of the antidote is known to the snakebitten, the worth of burning fire is known to the moth, and the worth of Joseph's shirt is known to Jacob. When someone is deluded by his own safety and is given the antidote, he will not know its worth. It needs someone whose spirit has reached his lips to know the worth and gravity of the antidote. This is why kings put the antidote in storehouses and treasuries until one day someone arrives whose spirit has reached his lips.

Don't ask a dull doctor about my heart's pain,
    don't ask a laid-back friend about my soul's torment,
Don't ask the clean and pure about the tainted.
    Look at what there is and don't ask about what's not.[1272]

My paragon used to say, "If someone seeks a moth in daytime, he will not find it. Tell him to have patience until the sun goes down and the curtain of darkness falls. He should light a candle, and the moths, wherever they may be, will come out into the open."

God's messenger Muḥammad was a candle of God's gentleness, lit on the ledge of limpidness. Moths from around the world set out for the candle. One moth came from the midst of Abyssinia, another from the core of Persia, and another from the dust of Byzantium. *"I am the chief of the Arabs, Bilāl is the chief of Abyssinia, Ṣuhayb is the chief of Byzantium, and Salmān is the chief of Persia."*[1273]

When the sun wants to lift up its head, first a light runs forth as an usher, then rays appear, and then the sun's orb sets up its tent. The folk who see the dawn are one group, the folk who see the rays are another, and the folk who see the orb are still another.

There were some who perceived the dawn of prophethood. *"The first among men to submit was Abū Bakr, the first among women Khadīja, the first among children 'Alī, and the first among slaves Bilāl."*[1274] When the dawn of prophethood had still not completely stuck up its head, there were some in whom the dawn of reconciliation stuck up its head from the midst of the spirit. When the sun of prophethood had reached the midst of chivalry's heaven, there were still some who remained in the darkness of denial.

The dawn shows, the rays burn, and the orb reduces to nothing. The likeness of this is fire. When someone says, "I need light," it says, "Keep away from me." Do you not see that Iblis came close and burned?

When someone says, "I need warmth," it says, "Come close to me."

When someone says, "I need companionship," it says, "Detach your heart from your life."

There are the folk of needs, the folk of proximity, and the folk of companionship. The folk of needs have light from afar: *He observed a fire on the side of the mountain* [28:29]. As long as Moses was one of the folk of needs, he wandered afar. When he became one of the folk of companionship, he entered the midst of the fire: *Show me, that I may gaze upon Thee* [7:143]. A candle was lit on the top of the Mount. Like a moth, Moses threw himself on the candle, and he was thunderstruck. *Moses fell down thunderstruck* [7:143]. It has been said that he was dead just like a moth that burns in a candle.

When they light a candle, the goal of the guest is one thing, the goal of the host is another thing, and the goal of the moth is something else. The lord of the house says, "The house should be bright." The guest says, "I should see the host." The moth says, "I should give up my life and be consumed in essence." The goals of the host and the guest are attributes, and the goal of the moth is the essence.

O dervish, a candle of messengerhood was lit for the sake of the splendor of the Muhammadan good fortune. The rays of that candle shone in the chamber of Abū Bakr's secret core. Like a moth he threw away everything he had. The expression of that state is this: *"God and His Messenger."*

O chevalier, there is a man in a dark house. A candle has been lit in the house, and he sees everything through its brightness. How does he see the brightness?

The night becomes dark and he sees nothing. When the sun rises, he sees everything. It would be absurd to say that he sees the sun with anything other than the sun. The man of realization is he who says, "I saw the sun with the sun."

What is the expression of this station?

> *By God, if not for God, we would not have been guided,*
> *we would not have paid alms, we would not have prayed.*[1275]

"I recognized my Lord through my Lord; if not for my Lord, I would not have recognized my Lord."[1276]

97. *al-Hādī:* the Guide

The road-shower. He says, *"He guides whomsoever He will"* [2:142]. And He says, *"Guide us on the straight path"* [1:6]: "It is I who make the beautiful rose of guidance grow in the garden of your heart with the assistance of the clear water of bounteousness. It is I who make the breeze of purity and purification blow in the meadow of your breast. It is I who make the long road simple and easy for you. It is I who caressed you in the Beginningless before the rushing and running of deeds. It is I who took care of your work without you. It is I who released your heart from the two worlds for Me." *We would not have been guided had God not guided us* [7:43].

"Despite Muḥammad's intercession, I did not give Abū Ṭālib to Muḥammad. Despite Noah's intercession, I did not give Noah's son to his father. Abraham asked for his father but I did not give him to Abraham. I have given to you without intercession. What did you do and what did they do?"

By God, can anyone ever
reap fruit from God without God?[1277]

He set up the pavilion of generosity, spread the carpet of blessings, and gave the call, *"Respond to God's inviter!* [46:31]. O beggars, come to Me! I have no need for you, but I have secrets to whisper with you."

An exalted man said, "I was walking in the desert and saw someone with one leg, hopping along with the overpowering force of his ecstasy. I said, 'Where to?'

"He said, *'The people's duty to God is to visit the House'* [3:97].

"I said, 'The hajj is no place for you. You have an excuse.'

"He said, *'We carried them on land and sea'* [17:70].

"I said, 'Surely your fervor will bring you suffering.' When I reached Mecca, I saw that he had arrived before me. I said, 'How did you arrive before me?'

"He said, 'Don't you know that you came with the exertion of acquisition, and I came with the attractions of the Unseen? How can that which comes by acquisition ever reach that which comes from the Unseen?' "[1278]

"I Myself said, *'He loves them.'* You were not able to answer this declaration, so I Myself said, *'They love Him.'* Just as I displayed My love to you, so also I displayed your love to My majesty.

"O Abraham, *'God took Abraham as a bosom friend'* [4:125]. O community of Muḥammad, *'He loves them and they love Him.'* Never have I not been God, and as long as I have been God in My Godhood, I have been your Friend.

Kharaqānī said, "He is clinging to you. You are not clinging to Him."

My friend, have you ever seen or heard tell
of a patron more generous than one who walks to a servant,
Visiting without appointment and saying,
"I kept your heart from being attached to the time"?
Between him and me the star of the cup kept on
turning in the spheres of felicity and fortune,
Sometimes kissing the narcissus of the eye,
sometimes biting the apple of the cheek.[1279]

*

Your love was with me the day I was not.
Lost to myself, Your love showed the way.
For a lifetime I was rubbish in the road of the Friend—
love's flood came and took all of me away.

It is told that an unbeliever became a Muslim. He had a small child, and the rule for the father is the rule for the child. The father became a Muslim when the child was small, but the mother did not let the father take the child, for she was an unbeliever. The father went to the judge and complained. The judge sent some people to bring the child, but the mother hid the child. The judge's people searched the whole house and at last found him. They wanted to take him, but the child shouted and yelled: "I do not want to be a Muslim. O people, help me!" Then the child grew up and the Real conveyed a secret to him. He became one of the Substitutes and Pegs, and a world was adorned by him.

In truth and in truth! If this talk had no affinity with the heart, the heart would not be the heart. If the sun of this talk did not rise from the horizon of the souls, the Adamite would be like the other existent things. At first there was this talk, in the middle this talk, and at the end there will be this talk. Today there is this talk, in the grave this talk, and tomorrow this talk.

What indeed is this talk? A mystery in an intimation, an intimation in a mystery, a gentleness in a severity, an unveiling in a veil, a light in a heart, a gaze toward a heart.

What indeed comes from this heart that would make it worthy for this gaze? The wealthy gaze on the poor, kings gaze on beggars, and beautiful ornaments are placed on the ugly. He created this world so that the heart may know, and He created the afterworld so that it may see. Today you know what you will see tomorrow, and tomorrow you will see what you know today.

"We adorn paradise with Our friends, We adorn Our friends with the heart, and We adorn the heart with Our beauty.

"You had to come into being so that the world would have light; you had to enter into existence so that Lordhood would become manifest. When the prophets became prophets, it was because of your burning; when the angels became angels, it was because of your love. When We brought the Generous Quran out from the curtain of jealousy to the open plain of exaltation, it was for the ease of your hearts. Moses at Mount Sinai was a trace of your hearts' pull. Muḥammad's *two-bows' length away* was the result of your breasts' love.

"If you bring an act of obedience, you should not look for the reward, for you are discharging the rightful due of *they love Him.* When I bestow a gift, I do not look at your acts, for I am discharging the rightful due of *He loves them.*"

O dervish, whenever He accepts someone, He does not want any wherewithal from him. And whenever He rejects someone, He does not accept any wherewithal from him. Whenever He takes someone from this world, He takes him without wherewithal. When He takes the folk of the submission to that world, He takes them without wherewithal, and when He takes the folk of unbelief, He takes them without wherewithal. Tomorrow when they lift their heads from the dust, the submission of the Muslims will not be their wherewithal and the unbelief of the unbelievers will not be their wherewithal.

The words of the angels, *"We have not worshiped Thee with the rightful due of Thy worship,"* throws the angels' wherewithal to the wind. The words of the Adamites, *"We have not recognized Thee with the rightful due of Thy recognition,"* strikes fire into the harvest of their wherewithal.[1280] The words of the Messengers, *"We have no knowledge"* [5:109], plunders what they knew.

Whatever He straightens, He straightens by His own means. Nothing of your deeds is worthy of joining with His deeds. If your obedience were the link to His mercy, He would not rightly be a God. And if your disobedience were the link to His punishment, your servanthood would be equal to His Lordhood. If He shows mercy, He does so by His own generosity, not because of your obedience. If He punishes, He does so by His own justice, not because of your disobedience.

Here all things are mixed, but there at the Exalted Threshold, all is pure without admixture. For an incurable pain, nothing benefits but the pure without admixture. From you He takes the heart, He takes the spirit, He takes your possessions and your body. You come to have no known thing and no wherewithal. All the links fall away from His acts. "O act of Mine, if you need a link, here is My desire. O decree of Mine, if you need help, here is My will." O dervish, the attribute of knowledge appears for the ignorant, the attribute of unneediness for the poor, the attribute of power for the weak, and the attribute of pardon for the sinners.

He created this universe and made the attribute of knowledge appear for the ignorant: *"Surely I know what you do not know"* [2:30]. He made the attribute of unneediness appear for the needy: *"God is the Unneedy, and you are the poor"* [47:38]. He manifested the attribute of power for the weak, He displayed the attribute of exaltedness for the abased, and He displayed the attribute of pardon for the sinners.

He created the Adamites in the midst and gave them the attribute and trait of friendship. He displayed a hundred thousand sorts of unseen gentle gifts and compassionate acts for their sake. They became bold, for their edicts were all from the court of the Sultan. They became boldly expansive and came out against the command, for they were the carefree of the empire and the shameless of creation. They defiled the world with sins and crimes. The attribute of pardon will go to work and in one instant take everything they did in seven thousand years back to nonexistence.

O chevalier, I know not what leaven they used on the day they fermented Adam's dough. It seems to me that a tree planted in dust and clay should not grow so high: *its root fixed and its branches in heaven* [14:24].

Aḥmad ibn Khiḍrūya was an exalted man. Once he went to see Abū Ḥafṣ Ḥaddād. Abū Ḥafṣ was the exalted man of the era. He had four wives. He said to them, "As much as you can, do not hold back from formality."

On the night of the invitation, they lit one hundred lamps in the house. It occurred to Aḥmad's heart that this was an extravagance. Abū Ḥafṣ was a possessor of penetrating awareness. He said to Aḥmad, "Snuff out everything lit by mortal man."

Seven thousand years went by and the radiance of this fire became sharper. Zoroaster invited people to the fire, and the Guebres worshiped it for many years. When the force of Aḥmad's realm came into the world, it took the several-thousand-year-old fire of the Guebres back to nonexistence. It showed the people that what is lit by mortal man has no root. *As often as they kindle a fire for war, God extinguishes it* [5:64].

The good fortune of dust is not something small. Sultan Maḥmūd named his son Masʿūd as heir apparent in Herat, and he himself carried Masʿūd's saddlecloth, as is well known. *We carried them on land and sea* [17:70]. "O Gabriel, you carry Muḥammad's saddlecloth as far as *the Lote Tree of the Final End* [53:14]. But when there is talk of those burned for Me, you are dismissed from carrying the saddlecloth."

What a marvelous business! He created him from dark dust. Then He chose him over everything He had created. He built the foundation of Adam and the Adamites on dust so that the creatures would know that chosenness does not come from form—it comes from attributes.

Adam—that first wayfarer, that wellspring of beginningless gentleness, that coffer of the wonders of omnipotence, that jewel box of the gentleness of the Haqiqah, that sapling in the garden of generosity—was put to bed between Mecca and Taif in the cradle of the covenant of recognitions. His precious stature was adorned and pruned with the scissors of loveliness and beauty, but the nightingale of the spirit had not yet built its nest in the garden of his brain. That possessor of ill fortune and ill eyes passed by. With the hand of envy he shook the sapling but found it empty. He said, "*This creature will not be self-possessed*; it is empty, and nothing will come forth from an empty thing." [1281]

From the top of the pulpit of loftiness and transcendence, beginningless good fortune replied: "*When good fortune turns its back, every stratagem is baneful.*"

Wait a few days until the falcon of his mystery takes flight! The first prey it hunts will be the teacher of the angels. That accursed one saw the clay but did not see the heart. He saw the form but did not see the attribute. He saw the outwardness but did not see the inwardness.

No one can put a seal on fire, but one can put a seal on dust. Dust accepts a seal, not fire. "When We brought Adam into existence from dust and clay, the wisdom was that We wanted to place the seal of the Trust on the clay of his heart, for *surely We offered the Trust to the heavens and the earth and the mountains, but they refused to carry it and feared it, and man carried it* [33:72]."

He brought a handful of dust and clay into existence, burned it with the fire of love, and placed it on the carpet of expansiveness. Then He offered the Trust to the world of form. All of them refused. Adam put out his hand. He said, "O Adam, We did not offer the Trust to you. Why do you want to receive it?"

He said, "Because I'm burned, and someone burned can only take."

Fire was deposited in stone, but a covenant was made with the stone: "Beware, don't come out into the open until someone burned appears."

Do you fancy that this fire is going to come out into the open with the strength of your hand? No, don't suppose that, for it will come out only with the intercession of someone burned.

Surely We offered the Trust: I do not know who has preserved the first covenant with the first seal.

When people leave a precious trust with someone, it is their custom to put a seal on it. On the day they want it back, they examine the seal. If the seal is in place, they praise him. *The angels will descend upon them saying, "Fear not! Grieve not!"* [41:30].

The Trust was placed with you at the covenant of lordhood—*Am I not your Lord?* Upon it was put the seal of *yes indeed* [7:172]. When the work reaches its end and you are taken to the domicile of dust, the angel will come and say, "*Who is your Lord?*" This is an examination to see whether the first seal is in place.

A seal was put on you, from your head to your feet, and that seal [*muhr*] was love [*mihr*]. A seal was placed where love appears.

A seal ring is exalted by the stone, the stone by the seal, the seal by the inscription, and the inscription by the name. Muṣṭafā was the seal of the prophets. The days of all the messengers were gathered together, and Muṣṭafā's covenant was made the seal on the prophets' days. A sultan gives everything he has to the keeper of the treasury. But he does not give the seal ring to anyone. He keeps it for himself.

"O Riḍwān, paradise is yours! O Mālik, hell is yours! O cherubim, the Throne is yours! O burnt heart with the seal of love, you are Mine, and I am yours."

What a marvelous business! He concealed a pearl in an oyster shell and stored a jewel in a box. With water and dust He prepared a citadel whose spires of eminence could not be reached by the noose of others' imagination.

Now speak of the citadel's door so that they will knock on the clay and not suspect. Make it such a clay that they will lose their nerve by looking at it.

Which pearl was it? It was the pearl of love.

What sorrow there is when someone is taken up with the work of someone and does not dare say who it is! The pain is that the spirit must be defiled by passionate love, but one does not have the nerve to say whose work it is.

I've come to ardor, but I won't say for whom.
I fear Him who fears none.
When I think about my love for him,
I feel my head's about to fly from my body.[1282]

*

When someone has a sorrow of which he can speak,
he can sweep away the heart's sorrow with talk.
Look at Your rose blooming in me:
I can't show its color or conceal its scent.[1283]

O dervishes, dervishes have no portion of love but pain—especially a dervish with high aspiration, one who will only enter the work of the Sultan. Kings have no mercy, and dervishes have no silver. Everything given to dervishes is given by way of bestowal, mercy, and charity. But the beauty of sultans is more exalted than that it should be given to dervishes by way of charity and alms tax.

O chevalier, here there is an exalted secret: When a dervish claims to love the sultan, that love will be nothing but tribulation for him. But if the sultan begins with his own generosity and caresses the dervish with his love, that love will be nothing but ease for him.

It is He who began the talk of love: *"He loves them*: O dervishes, I love you. Even if you do not reach the pavilions of My exaltedness on the carcass of your own misfortune, you will reach Me on the welcoming Burāq of My unqualified love."

O dervish, in love you must have seeing and hearing. Seeing is the food of the heart, and hearing is the portion of the spirit. In this world the eyes have no seeing—it is the heart that sees. The spirit has hearing, the heart has seeing. At the beginning of the work the spirit was given one cup of hearing with the words *"Am I not your Lord?"* Its head is still spinning in gratitude for that cup's intoxication, for no one can give reports or marks of it. But from the moment the heart came into existence, it has been receiving cup after cup of wine without cease—360 cups every day. The cups never become empty, and the thirst is never quenched.

"O coquettish heart, how boldly you disgraced the spirit and ran ahead of it!"

It said, "Yes, I am a falcon who flew from the nest of the mystery, in my beak the heaviness of dust and in my claws the opening of the spirit. I am not pure spirit, for the repair and governance of the earth is consigned to me, and that is not the work of pure spirit. Nor am I mere dust, for the *seat of truthfulness* [54:55] will be adorned by me, and that is not the mark of mere dust."

He's like the moon and the cypress, but neither moon nor cypress—
the cypress wears no tunic, the moon has no hat.[1284]

What a marvelous business! He fastened a hundred thousand ornaments and fineries on Adam and then commanded the angels to prostrate themselves before his throne. This is a secret worth a thousand holy spirits. He told you to perform the prayer, and then He turned your prayer over to a stone: "So that you may know that I have no needs."

He commanded the angels to prostrate themselves, and then He turned their prostration over to dust: "So that they may know that I have no needs."

"O Adamites, turn your faces toward a stone! O angels, turn your faces toward dust!"

The prostration of the angels was a trial, and turning your face toward a stone is a test. Their trial was by a handful of dust, and your test is by a stone: "I showed you the worth of your faces when I said, '*Turn your faces toward it*' [2:144]. Turn your faces toward a stone, for stones are worthy of clods, and clods are worthy of stones. I placed the worth of your blood in your hands when I said, 'Go to war so that the unbelievers may shed your blood!' "

The point is that first statement, that Adam's makeup was adorned with a hundred thousand ornaments, and the garden of his loveliness and beauty was pruned. Love, the original bosom friend that drank from the same cup and goblet, looked on from afar. The tree to which Adam stretched out his hand was named the tree of love. The love that was kneaded into Adam took the reins from his hands and pulled him straight to the tree.

I said to her, my eyelids wounded,
wounded by their flowing tears,
"No one's like me in rapture."
She said, "You see me as having a likeness?"[1285]

"O sorrow of Jacob, take the road of perfection, for Joseph's beauty is perfect. O beauty of Joseph, take the road of perfection, for Jacob's sorrow is perfect." Every moment Jacob's sorrow increased, and every instant Joseph's beauty advanced.

The tree of love was an exile in paradise, and at the era's beginning Adam was also an exile in paradise.

And every exile is kin to an exile.[1286]

The exile fell back on the exile. They took one hot breath. The heat of their love's fire burned the eight paradises. Now what could be done? They had to wrap their arms around each other's necks and turn their faces to the abode of the tested.

He was brought into the world of tribulation. Tribulation's rain, which is commands and prohibitions, poured down on his head from the cloud of the Law's prescription. Lowliness and tribulation make a man into a beggar. If he passes up two pieces of bread, at night he will come home and turn the house upside down. There are many houses whose décor is nothing but hunger, the carpets of pennilessness spread, the curtains of hunger hanging, the cushions of lowliness put in place.

In the whole world there was no chamber more adorned than the chamber of God's messenger Muḥammad. The Splendorous Throne wanted to become the bed of that chamber. The brocade, silk, and satin of paradise wanted to be its carpet. But it already had a bed of poverty, a cushion of hunger, a seat of want. Nonetheless, the Faithful Spirit was holding his saddlecloth at the door.

One night Muṣṭafā sent that piece of his own liver, Fāṭima Zahrā, to the house of her husband. When they took a woman to her husband's house, it was the custom to bring along a container for a fiber-filled pillow, a hand mill, and a rug. They said, "These two dear ones will be sleeping with each other. They need a bed and a couch."

Muṣṭafā said, "Let them go out into the desert and bring back some sand."

The house was low, the carpet threadbare. What was the robe of the folk of the house? *God desires only to put filth away from you, O folk of the house!* [33:33]. *Peace!*

98. *al-Badī*ʿ: the Innovating

The creator, neither in keeping with a precedent example nor for the sake of a subsequent attainment. He creates as He wants and He chooses whom He wants. In creating He is hallowed beyond associationism, and in choosing He is incomparable with suspicion. *Thy Lord creates what He wants and chooses* [28:68]: "I created, and from My creation I selected the one I wanted and I pulled him up above the other existent things."

Is it they who divide up the mercy of thy Lord? [43:32]. He gave existence at the request of power, He preserved at the request of gentleness and mercy, He took to nonexistence at the request of jealousy, and He mustered at the request of wisdom. Some He took to paradise at the request of gentleness and mercy, some He took to the abyss at the request of severity and punishment, and some He snatched away from all at the request of the divine favor: paradise for one group, hell for another group, and limpid wine for still another group. *Every people has a day, and every day a people.*

This is an affair that will not be completed with associationism. O you whose existence has thrown you into tribulation, what will you do with yourself? Quickly lose yourself in His existence, then look at His kindness and munificence to see the wonders of gentle gifts. When Jacob put his eyes into the work, Joseph's beauty gave him another eye: *He threw it on his face and he returned to seeing* [12:96]. When the traveler enters the road, he throws off his skin and attributes. Every moment another gift arrives at the hand of the messenger of confirmation. Abū Yazīd said, "I came out of Abū-Yazīd-ness like a snake from its skin." [1287] But not everyone knows the flavor of these words.

Do not fancy that He made this limpid wine so as not to give it to anyone. No, no, that supposition is absurd. The one to whom He gave it drank, wiped his lips, and took a deep breath.

Muṣṭafā summarized the story of the *mi ʿrāj* for the people; he did not tell it to anyone in detail. The sultan sends someone to summon his boon companion. The companion goes on the sultan's steed to the sultan's presence. The news falls into the city that the boon companion has gone to the sultan. The people know that he went, but they do not know what happened.

There was what there was, what I will not mention,
so think the best and ask not for news.[1288]

He passed by the heavens and saw the prophets. He went and came back. Know this summary, but beware, do not go after the details or you will be giving your head to the wind. Pure water destroys the lizard and gives life to the fish. It wants someone with a spirit like that of a fish to know the worth of pure water. In this talk the door of comparison is shut. You cannot rightly compare one leadership with another leadership. How can you rightly compare one heart with another heart?

An exalted man said, "Beware, if any sort of thorn enters your foot, do not go to the threshold of created things, for they will not look at you and will enjoy your pain. Go to God's threshold and weep to Him, just as a small child weeps to its mother."

You may have heard that on the Day of Badr, seventy unbelievers were killed and a group were taken prisoner. Muṣṭafā's paternal uncle ʿAbbās was among the prisoners. His hands and feet were bound, and at night the bonds on his hands became tight, so he was moaning. Muṣṭafā was rolling back and forth in his bed, going from right to left. Then he got up in the night and said, " 'Abbās is moaning and I have no settledness. Go and loosen his bonds."[1289]

It seems to me that when a beggar suffers deprivation one night and his moaning at his heart's grief and liver's pain goes up to heaven, then, if he is at ease the next night, the angels will be addressed, "What happened to that beggar? Why isn't he moaning tonight?"

All of you, come to the Real's Threshold, for it is a tremendous loss to let go of such a threshold and go to the door of Zayd and ʿAmr.

Muḥammad ibn ʿAlī Tirmidhī said, "Come to the threshold and knock at His door so that He Himself may say, *'Who is it?'* Who is this man? *Who is it that will lend to God a beautiful loan, that He may double and redouble it for him?* [2:245]." About this word Yaḥyā ibn Muʿādh Rāzī said, *"I wonder at someone who still has anything left when the Exalted Lord wants to borrow it."*[1290] I wonder at him who leaves a grain in his purse when the Exalted Lord asks him for a loan.

Here you have a marvelous business! "Our attribute is giving, not asking, but the penniless beggar has such worth in Our eyes that when there is talk of him, Our generosity makes a demand: 'Ask this niggardly man for something and promise to double and redouble it.' Then when the poor man takes something, he will take it from Us and not suffer the arrogance and haughtiness of the rich. And when the rich man gives something, he will give it through Us and not lay a favor on the poor man."

The Prophet said, *"Charity falls first into the hand of the All-Merciful and then into the hand of the poor."*[1291]

One day Junayd was sitting with a group of the exalted ones of the road. A man of this world entered, called for a dervish, and took him with him. After an hour the dervish came back with a basket on his head, in which were all sorts of food, the distinguished man following him.

When Junayd's eyes fell on the dervish, he said, "Brother, give the basket back to the distinguished man who needs a poor man to carry his luggage." Then he said, "Though we beggars have no comforts, we do have aspiration."

God knows and the days recognize
that we are noble though destitute.
Our dirhams are few, but our noble traits
would not be deemed few by great camels.

Who is it that will lend to God a beautiful loan, that He may double and redouble it for him? The root meaning of *qarḍ* [loan] is debt and cutting. A scissors is called *miqrāḍ* because it is an instrument for cutting. By this *loan* He means cutting off the heart. "Who is it that will cut off his heart from what he has?" Your heart is joined to this world, and this world has grasped your hand. You need scissors made of love's jealousy to separate the heart from this world. To cut "beautifully" is to cut with a deft and quick hand, such that nothing of the heart clings to this world and nothing of this world clings to the heart. When will it be that you put everything in the world into the dust and purify your heart of the stink of newly arrived things, turning your face toward the Presence, solitary and disengaged?

When a tailor cuts cloth, why does he cut it? To join it back together. If he does not cut it to join it back together, he is spoiling it. Wherever there is cutting, it is followed by joining. The farmer cuts a tree and brings a branch from somewhere else and joins it. They ask him, "Why did you cut it?"

He says, "For joining. When there is joining, fine fruit will appear."

Who is it that will lend to God a beautiful loan? You will see that some will fix their eyes on the doubling and redoubling, and there may be someone with weak aspiration who comes back from the Threshold with only the doubling and redoubling.

I want no bribe for love—
those weak in ardor want a reward.
When I reached Your love, possessions became trifles—
everything upon the dust is dust.[1292]

Friendship based on bribery comes into existence only from those mean and low in aspiration.

He gives some people ten, He gives others twenty, He gives others fifty, and He gives others *doubled and redoubled.*

Then there are other people who *stand up for God, sit down for God, love in God, and hate for the sake of God.* He said, "I have great wealth in the treasury."

They said, "What are treasuries to us?"

He said, "This world and that world belong to Me."

They said, "What are this world and that world to us?"

A man had a small child in his house. In the morning he gave him some broken little thing. That night a dervish came. He saw that the father had nothing in his hands. He said to the child, "Come, dear child, lend that broken thing to your father so that tomorrow he will give you ten times more."

What is "ten times"? Deception for children. They promise a child ten for one. To the intelligent man they say, *"Every loan that attracts profit is usury."*[1293] If you lend one dirham and you receive back one dirham and a grain, that is nothing but usury. "Ten for one" is permitted for children, but for adults, only one for one is permitted.

Who is it that will lend to God a beautiful loan, that He may double and redouble it for him? For whom is this? For those driven mad by love for this world. "As for the intelligent man, I take one and give one, and the one is I."

Did We not make for him two eyes, a tongue, and two lips? [90:8–9]. *God did not make for any man two hearts in his breast* [33:4]. The heart is one; the tongue is one. The tongue with which you assert faith in Him is one, and the heart with which you love Him is one. "And I am one. Thus 'one for one' will be known to you."

> The king of the spirits is the servant of love,
>   those born from him are the soldiers of love.
> Pure wisdom is the draft of pain,
>   the bond of intellect is the anchor of love.
> A pure gambler, free of himself,
>   our paragon was the trainee of love.
> His tears were the ink of the book of mystery,
>   his color was the explanation of the notebook of love.

This road's secret will show you its face only at the center-point of disengagement. *"Disengagement is that you become disengaged inwardly from motivations and outwardly from compensations."*[1294] Becoming disengaged inwardly is that you do not seek any compensation for what you disengage from, neither at the present moment nor in the future. This is because if someone lets go of something in the present state while seeking something else as compensation, he is a merchant, not disengaged.

It has been reported that Ibn ʿAṭāʾ said, *"When someone comes to rest in anything but the Real, his destruction lies therein."*[1295] *This is why the Prophet said, "Do not turn me over to myself for the blink of an eye!"*[1296]

When the chieftains of the Tariqah find a station in proximity such that a state is unveiled to them, they fear that the state will lead them on step-by-step, so they become so bewildered that they consider themselves less than adulterers, thieves, and tavern-goers.

O chevalier, a lioness has the tenderness of a mother, but she also has sharp claws. When ants come after a lion cub, in her tenderness she wants to remove the ants, but what will she do about the claws? If she did not have sharp claws, she would not be a lion, and if she did not have tenderness, she would not be a mother. She has the love of a mother, but she is a lion. Tenderness is born from a mother's love, but awe is born from a lion's attributes. He is the Most Generous of the Generous, but He is also the All-Compelling, the Severe.

There is an issue in jurisprudence. The Shariah's ruling is that hunting in the Sanctuary is forbidden. The security given by the Shariah is clear, but the prey itself is fearful, for it is fearful by nature. The Shariah says, "When you are ritually consecrated and in the Sanctuary, do not hunt. If you hunt, it is incumbent on you to pay a recompense."

Someone said to the prey, "Why don't you feel secure?"

It said, "There is no way for the weak to feel secure against the strong."

By the rightful due of the Real! If the one hundred twenty-some thousand center-points of sinlessness were shown to you, you would see aspirations like that of a pheasant in the claws of a falcon. *"A group from my community will enter the Garden with hearts like the hearts of birds."*[1297]

If tomorrow His bounty does not show leniency to the creatures and He displays His rightful due instead, we will not be able to say a thing. If the sultan of justice draws the sword of severity and harshness in the ranks of majesty and exaltedness, the gall bladders of the prophets and friends will burst. Look at how the strength of the mountains comes to nothing—*and the mountains crumble to dust* [56:5]—and detach your heart from your own strength. Look at the deeds of ʿAzāzīl and lift your heart away from your deeds. Look at the knowledge of Balaam and detach your heart from your knowledge. Look at the wealth of Korah and detach your heart from your wealth. Become a gambler and lose everything!

He gave Adam knowledge: *And He taught Adam the names* [2:31]. He gave Muṣṭafā strength and aid: *"I was aided by terror."*[1298] Then He said about Adam, *"Surely he was a great wrong-doer, deeply ignorant"* [33:72]. What is this? "The demand of My perfect knowledge." He said to Muṣṭafā, *"Thou hast nothing of the affair"* [3:128]. What is this? "The pointer to My never-ending power.

"Knowledge belongs to Me, power belongs to Me, the Beginningless belongs to Me, the Endless belongs to Me, this world belongs to Me, the next world belongs to Me. No one has the gall to step outside the script of My permission.

"When they bring a child to grammar school, he does not know how to write. The teacher writes a script on the tablet so that the child may follow after him. With the pen of Will I recorded the secrets of your being and nonbeing on the tablet of Desire. Then I put the pen of acquisition in your hand, but you cannot place any dots outside My knowledge and decree."

This is the secret of their words, "Tawḥīd *belongs to the Real, and the creatures are free-loaders."*[1299]

O dervishes who have no bread, and O wealthy men toward whom the world has turned its face, do not forget Him! He pardons everything except the sins and offenses of the heart. Nowhere did He say, "I love heaven," or "I love earth," or the Throne, the Footstool, the spheres, or the angels. He said, "I love the Adamites." Loyalty is the stipulation of the road.

So, what must be done? You must not let others into your heart. "If you let creatures into your heart, it will be an offender, and We will not pardon it. For if We were to pardon the heart's offense, love's jealousy would go, and if love's jealousy went, love itself would not remain."

When a heart does not carry the saddlecloth of love, kick it in the head, for it is not a heart, but an intruder in the convocation of lovers.

Tomorrow everyone will be gazing on his own heart's beloved. One will seize the skirt of paradise, another will hunt down the Garden of Eden, and still another will catch hold of the highest of the high. But the day of the friends' good fortune will be the day when they gaze on the field of unity and see it empty of the intrusion of others. *Whose is the kingdom today? God's, the One, the Severe* [40:16].

"O Seraphiel, blow into these spirits, then blow into your own spirit! *Drive them away, and you go away with them!*"

O dervish, if anyone thinks that paradise is adorned with the beauty of wide-eyed houris, then the jasmine scent of love's covenant has not yet reached his nostrils. The lords of the heart know the meaning of these words.

These hapless creatures! For seventy years in this world, newly arrived things intrude on them; then they settle down in paradise with more newly arrived things. By the decree of the Shariah, this world is the road and paradise is the sought object. But by the fatwa of the Haqiqah, paradise is both road and thief, and the Real is the only goal.

"When you see someone seeking Me, be his servitor!" O David, wherever you see one of the seekers of My presence, make your eyes the earth before him so that he may stroll upon them.

> It is forbidden for beautiful idols to walk on dust.
> I'll make my eyes the earth—stroll on my eyes!
> If one day you call me by name,
> I'll walk on top of the spheres in joy.

Gamble away desire, movement and rest, words and talk, ecstasy and states, patched cloak and pot, in the circle of unity's wine. Perhaps a draft will become your pain's share. Whenever someone takes up the road of *tawḥīd*, he will see that the Throne and the Footstool, paradise and hell, *the Lote Tree of the Final End* [53:14] and *two-bows' length away*, are the road; the object of his search is something else.

Tomorrow a group will be rebuked: "Did you have no more aspiration in that world than to perform a few cycles of prayer and say 'O Lord' a few times until you reached something to eat?" If this is what you have done, let go of it! Let it go from your sight so that it will not be a loss for you.

A man must call out on high. Aspiration is a bird that hunts only on high. Supposing Solomon's kingdom is given over to someone and he looks back at it—by God, he would be a man of mean aspiration! There is not enough wherewithal from East to West for a Guebre. Nimrod was given this world, but he was not pleased with it, so he lifted his bow and arrow and turned his face toward heaven. Why do you look at the fact that the kingdom of this world was given to Solomon? Look at the fact that he put himself among the beggars.

O dervishes, know with certitude that the sultans in their gold-embroidered tunics and jewel-studded caps seek your ease of life.

It was said to blessing, "Where will you be?"

It replied, "In Damascus."

The plague said, "I will be with you."

It was said to hunger, "Where will you be?"

It said, "In the desert."

Safety said, "I will be with you."

This talk wants a ruined corner and a burnt heart. If it needed a flourishing world, no place was more thoroughly set up than paradise. Mecca was a flourishing site, and Medina ruins.

Paradise was the site of enjoyment, and this world the site of anxieties and sorrows. At first Adam's business was getting along with exaltation, joy, and whispered secrets. After a while the dust of misery settled on his crown. He took a loving glance at destitution's beauty and became entranced by it. He threw away whatever joinings and bonds there were and entered the road of destitution like the disengaged.

This talk wants a burnt liver—someone who has lived seventy years without one thing turning out according to his desire, who has shot a thousand thousand arrows without one reaching the target, and who has lived happily and counted that as a favor.

And the moon—We have determined mansions for it [36:39]. On the eve of the fourteenth day the moon lifts away the mask from its beauty and, like a king leaning on an emerald throne, it says to you with the tongue of its state, "Why are you looking at my brightness? It is borrowed. '*The borrowed is to be answered for and given back.*'[1301] See me on the eve of the twenty-seventh—how wasted I will have become!"

"O moon, where did your brightness and splendor go?"

"Yes, I have gone through the mansions, and travelers are like this. But there is a fine point here. No sooner did I have a claim to manifestation and to light's arrogance than my antagonist, the eclipse, was in my tracks. Now that I have become so fine, the fine point is that I am protected by the courtyard of my own annihilation."

Surely My servants—thou hast no ruling power over them [15:42]. Anyone who is content with bread and water has no awareness of danger. Worshiping your own wishes is the work of dogs, but going in the tracks of aspiration is the work of lions. If the sparrow of practice flew where the phoenix of aspiration flies, its wings would burn off. When a bird is trailed by a falcon, it flies until it reaches a place where it is burned by the heat of the sun. When the falcon sees that its wings have burned, it turns back. "O falcon, why have you come back?"

It said, "Yes, that little bird with its high aspiration reached a place where it burned in the radiance of its own aspiration. My eyes no longer saw it."

Surely My servants—thou hast no ruling power over them. The accursed one and his army's troops are stragglers, and stragglers will never see the elect of the sultan. *And God knows better.*

99–100. *al-Bāqī al-Wārith:* the Subsistent, the Inheritor

The meaning of subsistent is everlasting, and the meaning of inheritor is "subsisting after the annihilation of creation."[1302] God says, *"Everything upon it undergoes annihilation"* [55:26].

The Subsistent is He who has the same description in His endlessness as in His beginninglessness. The Inheritor is He who gives the inheritance of the Book to His beloveds, as He says in the firm address: "Then We gave the inheritance of the Book to the ones We chose from among Our servants" [35:32].

The proof of the prophets' prophethood came by way of the eyes, but the proof of the Muhammadan messengerhood came by way of the hearts. The Real gave every messenger an outward miracle to be seen by the eyes. Abraham's miracle was the fire, Moses's miracle was the white hand, and Jesus's miracle was bringing the dead back to life. All of these were outward and apparent in places seen by the eyes. But Muṣṭafā's miracle was the scented garden of the limpid friends and the rose garden of those drunk with the wine of love: *Rather it is signs, clear signs, in the breasts of those who have been given knowledge* [29:49].

Yes, Muṣṭafā had many miracles in places seen by the eyes, like the splitting of the moon, the glorification by the stone, the speaking of the wolf, the submission of the lizard, and so on.[1303] The point is that Moses strove to overcome with the staff and Jesus strove to overcome with the breath, but Muṣṭafā strove to overcome with the speech of the Real: *Then bring a surah like it* [2:23]. Yes, a lordly artisanry was made ready in Moses's staff and a divine gentleness was deposited in Jesus's breath, but the staff came from the boxthorn or myrtle of paradise and the breath was deposited inside a mortal breast.

"O Muḥammad, when you go, take along no breath or stick, for sticks are appropriate for donkeys and breath is the share of the ill. Take along My eternal attribute to act as police chief. Then your miracle will be My attribute, not your attribute.

"Tomorrow a prophet will come with one person along with him, a prophet will come with two people, and a prophet will come with a larger group.[1304] But Muṣṭafā will come with followers from Qāf to Qāf. Who are they? Those tended by My eternal kind favor. *Surely it is We who have sent down the Remembrance* [15:9]. *Then We gave the inheritance of the Book* [35:32]."

Abū Hurayra narrated that Muṣṭafā said, *"God recited Ṭāhā and Yāsīn two thousand years before He created Adam. When the angels heard the recitation, they said, 'Blessed is the community upon which this descends! Blessed are the tongues that voice it! Blessed are the breasts that carry it!'* "[1305]

Muṣṭafā said that two thousand years were remaining before the creation of Adam when He recited the surahs Ṭāhā and Yāsīn. The angels listened and said, "Happy is the community to which this pure speech comes! Happy are the tongues that recite this pure speech! Happy are the breasts that are the oysters for these hidden pearls!"

Then, when the friends go into the Garden, the All-Compelling will say, "You have heard much from others. The time has come for you to hear from Me." *Then He will let them hear the surahs Fātiḥa, Ṭāhā, and Yāsīn*—a hearing without intermediary, a drinking without intermediary!

On the day we give and take the cup
from hand to hand with no remorse,
On that day our envier
will have reason for his envy.[1306]

You must take the rose from its own bush if you want to catch its scent correctly.

Hear it from him who spoke it and increase thereby
in love, for the rose in the branches is sweet.[1307]

When the poet himself is the narrator, his poetry has another taste.

O friend, what have you seen of what you will see? What have you heard of what you will hear? It is clear what realities can be unveiled in the world of metaphor. It is obvious what sort of pictures can be painted on a gnat's wing. It is clear which meanings can be disclosed to a handful of children sitting in the lap of power over being and nonbeing.

When knowledge is challenged by ignorance in the battlefield of dispute and opposition, can that be called knowledge of reality? When intellect closes its eyes like a bat in the sunlit fields of the divine majesty, can that be counted an intellect? When the heart cannot be brought to hand because of its fluctuation, wavering, and distraction, can that be named a heart? When a spirit moves beneath the fingertips of thought like an arrow shot from a bow, can that be called a spirit?

Today the gentleness of the Presence has put a quick meal before you on the dining table of this world. As for the veiled virgins of the secrets, the concealed mysteries of the work, the hidden affairs of gentleness, and the things stored away in the Unseen, they are behind the curtains of jealousy, not felt by hands, not tainted by the imaginings of others, not touched by minds, no wind having blown against them.

"Today you have become drunk with a drop and distracted by a whiff. You have thrown a world into shouting and wailing because of a scent. Wait until tomorrow, which is the world of realities. We will give you a vast capacity so that you will drink down the wine of vision cup after cup, or rather ocean after ocean, and shout out, *'Is there any more?'* [50:30]." O dervishes, be happy with Him!

Then We gave the inheritance of the Book to the ones We chose from among Our servants. His knowledge of your deeds did not hold Him back from choosing you. When by the sigil of beginningless gentleness the edict of chosenness was written for a group, the edict's first line was this: *"Among them are wrongdoers to themselves"* [35:32]. If chosenness depended on deeds, no one would ever be chosen.

It is said that one day a decorator was decorating a house, having adorned himself like a woman. In the midst of this, a work from the Unseen was disclosed to him. He fell from the top of the ladder, ran out of the house, and was shouting, *"Where is God?"* In that light and heat he went from city to city until he reached Mount Lukam in Syria, which is the place of the Substitutes and Pegs. He saw six men standing in front of a bier. They said, "Go forward and say the prayer for this dead man."

He said, "Tell me first what is going on."

They said, "First say the prayer, then ask about the story."

He performed the prayer and they did the burial. Then they said to him, "We are among the seven upon whom the world stands, and this man over whom you prayed was our head. When he was leaving this world he made this testament: 'When you have washed me, place me there and wait until someone comes from that direction. When he comes, tell him to pray over me. Instead of me he will be the Pole of the world.' "

O chevalier, a catamite is made into the Pole, and from among Pharaoh's sorcerers men are made to appear next to whom the angels of the Dominion are tiny. A handful of dust was brought into existence. Then it was said to ʿAzāzīl, "Prostrate yourself before him."

He said, *"Shall I prostrate myself to someone whom Thou hast created of clay?"* [17:61].

He said, "You will not prostrate yourself to My chosen one? *Surely upon thee shall be My curse* [38:78]."

The angels said, *"What, wilt Thou set therein one who will work corruption there?"* [2:30]. A fire from the Unseen came and burned up several thousand of them. They spoke the truth, but they spoke about the friend.

O Adam, go into this world and open up that closed oyster shell so that the one hundred twenty-some thousand pearls of prophethood and gems of sinlessness may come to the top of the ocean of power. Then the angels will be embarrassed. Yes, when someone says words he should not, he will be embarrassed more than a little.

"The angels say, *'What, wilt Thou set therein?'* I say, *'The repenters, the worshipers'* [9:112]. What do you say: Is the reproach of the angels more tremendous, or My praise and laudation? When I am your praiser, have no fear of the whole world's ridicule!"

When they bring a slave from Abyssinia, what harm is done if his lord names him Camphor? *And We wrote in the Psalms . . . , "Surely the earth will be inherited by My wholesome servants"* [21:105]. Even though by virtue of our own attributes we are depraved and made from dried potter's clay, by virtue of His generosity's robe we are the wholesome. Even though the Abyssinian is black, if you call him black, he will not give himself over to that. They say to him, "Aren't you black?"

He will say, "Yes, but what business do you have with my attributes? Why don't you call me by the name of my lord?"

The form of Bilāl had no relationship with the meaning in his heart. His meaning took its lineage from *by the bright morning* [93:1] and his form from *and by the night when it is still* [93:2]. Ungodliness and depravity are attributes of the bodily parts, but faith is the attribute and cape of the heart. The ruling property belongs to the heart, not to the bodily parts, for when He gazes, He gazes at the heart, not the bodily parts. The ruling property belongs to what is gazed upon, not what is ignored.

By God the Tremendous, the gaze of kings does not go to waste! He never looks at the heart without giving it a new gift.

One day a king looked sharply at someone. That man said, "The king is going to honor me."

The servants said, "You are talking madness."

He said, "Then he is going to punish me."

They said, "You are wrong."

He said, "Then your king is mad. A gaze is one of two: either the gaze of honor or the gaze of awesomeness."

You should not fancy that there is only one Mount Sinai and one Moses in the world. Your body is Mount Sinai and your heart Moses. The food of your heart is *surely I, I am God* [28:30]. If He was not jealous for the hearts, by God the heart would not be the heart!

A man is not jealous over a woman after he has divorced her. The marriage must be in effect for him to be jealous. If he divorces her and then falls in love with her again, what can he do but turn himself over to her. What is this? The severity of love. Kindness is shown to Quran-reciters and night-risers, but no kindness is shown to any lover.

O dervish, when will your heart go and gaze? *By God the Tremendous*, it will not go and gaze until it buries this Guebre beneath the dust and kicks it several times. They say, *"The mark of yearning is to wish for death while on the carpet of well-being."*[1308] When the work of Joseph was put in order, he said, *"Receive me as a submitter and join me with the wholesome"* [12:101].

When death comes to the door of your house, it will be the sunset prayer for those who are fasting. It is the sunset prayer that makes fasting people happy.

Abū Ḥabīb Badawī said to Sufyān Thawrī, *"Does not every good come from our Lord?"*

He said, *"Indeed it does."*

He said, *"Then why is it that we dislike death?"*

He said, "Because sins throw alienation between the servants and their Lord." When a friend becomes alienated from a friend, he cannot go boldly into his house.

No possessor of truthfulness fears death. Ḥusayn ibn ʿAlī saw his father fighting in a shirt. He said, *"This is not the dress of warriors!"*

ʿAlī said, *"Your father does not care if he falls upon death, or if death falls upon him."*[1309]

Truthfulness is the traveling supply for the journey to death. Death is the road of subsistence, and subsistence is the attribute of the elect.

When the folk of heedlessness reach the brink of death, they look at what will be taken from them. When the folk of the Haqiqah reach the brink of death, they look at what will be given to them. When a worn-out shirt is taken from your back and you are dressed in a new robe, that is a place for happiness. If a man puts on a garment and wears it for a month, he will be tired of it. When a new garment is brought for him, he will be happy. A man has had one shirt for seventy years and has worn it out. When the shirt is taken from his back and he is clothed in the shirt of the endless kingdom, is this not a place for happiness?

The life of ʿAmmār Yāsir reached ninety years. When he took a spear in hand, his hand trembled. Muṣṭafā had said to him that his last nourishment in this world would be milk. ʿAmmār was present at the Battle of Siffin, spear in hand, and he became thirsty. He asked for a little water and was given a cup of milk. He remembered the words of Muṣṭafā and said, "Today is the day of ʿAmmār's good fortune." He drank that draft and went forth saying, *"Today I will encounter the beloveds, Muḥammad and his party."*[1310]

The life of this world is a dark curtain pulled over your days. When will the hand of gentleness pull back the curtain so that you may reach the center-point of endless life? As long as this life is in place, endless subsistence will stay behind the curtain. When the curtain is lifted, endless subsistence will turn to you.

They catch a little bird from the plain and bring into the house. They clip its wings and put it in a cage. "They clipped my wings and then they put me in a narrow cage. Wasn't one punishment enough for me?"

I'm telling your story. How is this the place for birds?

"The spirits are assembled troops. Those acquainted with one another become familiar, and those not acquainted keep apart."[1311] The spirits were brought into existence several thousand years before the bodies. They were flying in that pure space. A hunter came down from Power and made a cage of water and dust. Other hunters catch with stratagems, but the hunter of the Will catches with strength. The wild bird is put in a cage, kept imprisoned, and its wings are clipped. After the bird's wings have been clipped and a few days pass, the cut feathers fall off and new wings appear beneath those wings. The lord of the house, relying on the wings having been clipped, opens the door of the cage. The wild bird returns to its nest, for a bird of the air will not gain familiarity with a cage. *O serene soul, return to thy Lord!* [89:27–28].

If the only blight of your little bit of life were that all of His works stay in the Unseen as long as you have it, that blight would be enough. A tremendous opposition was placed between this life and the secrets of the Unseen.

The prophets' lives were not their own shares, so their lives did not veil them. From the era of Adam to the dissolution of the world, no oath was sworn by anyone's life except the life of Muṣṭafā: *"By thy life"* [15:72]. Muṣṭafā had a life that was inward, a life through which he was alive. That life was the life of prophethood, while his sixty-three years of life were the life of mortal nature. When he pulled his head into the garden of dust, the life of mortal nature reached its end, not the life of prophethood.

When that paragon was pulled from the cave into the work, you should not fancy that, having come out of the cave, he said farewell to the cave's seclusion. The cave's place of seclusion rode along with the secret core in his breast: *"I spend the night at my Lord; He gives me to eat and drink."*[1312] At night he would go outwardly to ʿĀʾisha's chamber, and no one knew where his place of seclusion was. Yes, talk of ʿĀʾisha was a pretext and the story of Ḥafṣa a mark. As for the heart's secret core, it was solitary for the Real. *"Three things of this world of yours were made beloved to me."*[1313] I gazed at the whole world and saw no curtain for the house of my reality's seclusion more beautiful than the curtain of women.

When Muṣṭafā's place of seclusion was completed, it was completed by means of the women. The intrusion of people had to stay far from him, so the curtain was drawn and several of those with concealed-heads were put under his rule. Thus the concealed secret reached the core of his heart by means of several of the concealed-headed. That is why he made this declaration from the pulpit of messengerhood: *"Three things of this world of yours were made beloved to me"*: Women were made my friends, for they are a veiling mercy.

Be happy that you have such a precursor and leader. When Moses came out of Egypt, Pharaoh was coming in his tracks. The Children of Israel said that Pharaoh was coming. Moses said, *"Surely my Lord is with me; He will guide me"* [26:62]. When the musk bladder of this community's love was opened, the address came, *"Surely God is with us"* [9:40]. When the sultan of the era provides an escort for a caravan, it will stay protected. When the escort of the caravan is the sultan himself, what will that be like?

A caravan has an escort in the measure of its cargo. The more precious the cargo, the stronger the escort. The kernel of the most secret meanings is the cargo in the breasts of Muṣṭafā's community. "O community of Muḥammad, keep your hearts strong, for the hope is that you will take the entirety of the cargo to the Presence, for you have a strong escort and leader."

"We are the last, the preceders."[1314] What the philosophers say is, *"The first in thought is the last in act, and the last in act is the first in thought."*[1315] Whatever is prior in thought is posterior in act, and whatever is posterior in act is prior in thought. A man says, "I want a house to keep the cold and heat away from me." First he lays down a foundation and raises the walls. Then he puts up the roof. The roof was prior in thought but posterior in act.

The secret of the beginningless gaze was Muḥammad and Muḥammad's community. Several preliminaries and intermediaries were needed to make that beauty appear in creation. Yes, the custom is that the army goes out in front with the king in the rear. If you look at the Companions, *"My Companions are like stars."*[1316] If you look at the Folk of the House, *"God desires only to put filth away from you, O folk of the house, and to purify you"* [33:33]. If you look at the community,

"My community is like the rain; it is not known if the first of it is better or the last of it."[1317] If you look at the era, *"I was sent out in the best generation of Adam's children."*[1318]

"Whoever loves my Companions will have guidance without misguidance. Whoever loves my family will have salvation and life without cease. Whoever belongs to my community will have subsistence without annihilation."

You are the best community [3:110]. The stars, which are like gilded spikes driven into the top of this dark blue disk, are the wherewithal of guidance by virtue of brightness. Noah's ark was the wherewithal of salvation. Rain is the wherewithal of life. He attached guidance to the steps of the Companions, he attached salvation to the steps of the family, and he attached life to the steps of the community. It was the truthful nostrils of the folk of the first generation that smelled the scent of the first fruit of prophethood's garden.

And he who brought truthfulness and he who assented to it [39:33].[1319] Muṣṭafā brought the truth, and the truth sought truthfulness. Muḥammad had a truth that was searching for truthfulness, and Abū Bakr had a truthfulness that was seeking for truth. *It is He who sent His messenger with the guidance* [9:33]. Abū Bakr's heart was wounded and he was seeking a balm from the Real with truthfulness. The Messenger had a balm from the Real and was seeking someone wounded by truthfulness itself.

One day ʿUmar was talking to Abū Bakr. The Messenger came and saw them angry. The red rose of wrath bloomed in the garden of the Muhammadan cheeks. He said, *"O people, will you leave my companion to me? Surely I came with that with which I was sent, and you called me a liar, but Abū Bakr called me truthful."*[1320]

The trap of the invitation had not yet been set when Abū Bakr was caught by it, but others wandered around it. Muṣṭafā was sent from the World of the Unseen like a hunter to place the trap of the Unseen in the garden of Mecca. Whenever a trap is set, a decoy is needed. The Sincerely Truthful was made the decoy of prophethood's trap. *"Surely ʿUmar is one of the beautiful traits of Abū Bakr."*[1321] *This is why ʿUmar said, "Would that I were a hair on Abū Bakr's chest."*[1322]

Abū Bakr's breast was the jewel box and treasury for the pearls of the unseen secrets. ʿUmar is saying, "Since the treasury of pearls was placed in ʿUmar's breast, I wish that I were given to guard Abū Bakr's street so as to beat the clappers of pain on the surface of his breast. Today Abū Bakr has the cave of jealousy, and tomorrow he will have the royal court of seclusion: '*Surely God discloses Himself to the people generally and to Abū Bakr specifically.*' "[1323]

Each of the four Companions had one of the road's secrets whose meaning he then showed. Abū Bakr had a truthfulness that he showed specifically. *"Surely God discloses Himself generally to the people,"* and so on.

In ʿUmar there was the secret of a contemplation that he showed: *"Surely the Real speaks on the tongue of ʿUmar."*[1324] *"I conformed with my Lord in three things, and my Lord conformed with me in three things."*[1325] From whence did ʿUmar speak of the secrets? *"My heart spoke to me about my Lord."*[1326]

In ʿUthmān there was a shame that showed awe. *"Should I not be ashamed in front of a man before whom the angels are ashamed?"*[1327] When the sinless ones of the celestial world bow their heads in shame before someone, should I not have shame before him?

In ʿAlī there was a secret that showed love. A small child is not addressed with the words "Accept Islam!" But knowledge gave permission and made a concession, putting love constantly in charge.

> *I preceded you all to Islam*
> *as a boy not yet in puberty.*[1328]

101. *al-Rashīd:* the Director

Rashīd means *murshid,* and the Persian of *murshid* is *rāh-numāyanda* [road-shower]. The Real shows the road to whomsoever He wants.

O you who have faith, if any of you turns away from your religion, God will bring a people whom He loves and who love Him [5:54]. Whenever someone turns back from the road, We will bring others into Our road whom We love and who love Us.

Concerning Muṣṭafā He said, *"Glory be to Him who took His servant by night!"* [17:1]. Concerning us He said, *"God will bring a people."* The one who brings is the Wanter, and the one whom He brings is the wanted.

Concerning Moses He said, *"When Moses came"* [7:143]. When he came by himself, he was asked, *"And what is that in thy right hand?* [20:17]. O Moses, what do you have?" When Muṣṭafā was taken, it was said, *"Thy Lord will bestow upon thee, and thou wilt approve* [93:5]: O Muḥammad, what do you want?"

It was said to Muḥammad, *"Thy Lord will."* It was said to the community, *"God will bring a people whom He loves and who love Him."*

"When someone comes, he will come to do what I want. When I bring someone, I will bring him to do what he wants."

God will bring: "From the land of Persia I will bring lovers, from churches I will bring truthful ones, from synagogues I will bring yearners."

Whenever someone believes, it may happen that one day he turns away. But if He loves someone, it will never happen that he turns away. "I will bring people—of what sort? *Whom He loves and who love Him."*

Yaḥyā ibn Muʿādh was asked, *"Does the Beloved ever turn His face toward the lover?"*

He said, "When does the Beloved ever turn His face away from the lover?"[1329]

May a thousand lives be sacrificed to him who knows the intimations of passionate love! When the Real places the collar of love around people's necks, He nurtures them in the lap of bounty, the chamber of gentleness, the cradle of the Covenant, and the dome of proximity. Sometimes *He unveils His Essence to them,* and sometimes *He addresses them with His attributes.*

"The Throne has the attribute of elevation, and elevation is enough for it. The Footstool has the attribute of tremendousness, and tremendousness is enough for it. Heaven has the attribute of elevation and highness, and that is enough for it. Earth has the robe of expanse, and that is enough for it. The soul has the claim of fancy and egoism, and that claim is enough for it. As for the heart, it does not have the Throne's elevation, the Footstool's tremendousness, the earth's expanse, or the claim to being. It has brokenness and poverty, and I am enough for it."

Say: "In the bounty of God and His mercy—in that let them rejoice" [10:58]. *God's bounty is the Quran, and His mercy is faith.* "I gave you the Quran and I gave you faith. The Quran is My book and faith is My attribute: *the Faithful, the Overseer* [59:23]. In the Quran is My name and in faith is My mark, and you depend on My name and My mark. The first line of the Quran is My name. The first dot in the tablet of recognition and *tawḥīd* is My mark.

"Go into My playing field. At one end of the field is My name and at the other end is My mark. Wander there, sometimes from My name to My mark, sometimes from My mark to My name. Be happy with My name and My mark. This is good news worth a thousand sweet spirits.

"When the angel of death comes, he will want your spirit from you, not your faith. Spirit is a deposit, and faith a bestowal. It is permitted for the depositor to take back the deposit, but a generous man will never take back a gift. What would you do if in place of 'Give up your spirit,' it was said, 'Give up your faith'? But he will say, 'The spirit is mine, the faith is yours.' The spirit will go, and the man will stay alive through faith. The world will be surprised because the spirit has left but the man lives on."

Yes, the spirit of the form stays in place through the food of this world, but faith stays in place through the food of the lordly gaze: *God firms up those who have faith* [14:27].

"The good fortune of this handful of dust has no end. If We were to leave this work to you for you to take it to its end, you would not be able to do so."

Be the beloved! Being the lover is not your job.

"We brought whatever exists in the world of existence out from the concealment of nonexistence to the space of existence, but We did not talk about friendship with anyone. When We created you, We filled the goblets one after another with the wine of love in the session of proximity."

With opening upon opening comes cup upon cup.

He loves them and they love Him [5:54]. *I am setting in the earth a vicegerent* [2:30]: "We will bring a sultan into existence. O you who are serving boys, what do you say?"

They said, "We cannot put up with their corruption."

"Yes, if We were to send them to your threshold, you would reject them. If We offered to sell them to you, you would refuse to buy them. We will not place the broken-hearted disobedient in the hands of stuffy-headed Quran reciters. You blame them before they have sinned. Do you fear that their sinning will be greater than My mercy? Do you fear that My power will be incapable before their severity? Do you fear that their taintedness will stain My perfect holiness? My knowledge of their disobedience has not held Me back from bringing them into existence. How can their deeds hold Me back from having mercy on them?"

This is a truly exalted secret: In the beginningless beginning He made the forms of the apportionings manifest. He set up the mirror of the Endless and made the forms of the apportionings appear within it. In the mirror of the Endless the form of predetermined destruction appeared for the enemies, and in the mirror of the Endless the form of predetermined salvation appeared for the friends.

A Guebre went before one of the scholars of Muḥammad's community and said, "I have a question. I have asked many of the knowledgeable and found no answer. If you answer as stipulated, I will become a Muslim."

He said, "Ask."

He said, *"Are provisions and deeds apportioned, or are they not?"*

He said, "Yes, they are apportioned."

He said, *"What about trouble and toil?"*

He said, "They also are apportioned."

So the man submitted.

This is not as if a sultan gives a province to a slave and then the sultan's name is removed from the Friday sermon; rather, the name of the sultan is mentioned, and the slave keeps the province.

Those who enter the Unseen Presence come by the attribute of the Will, but the servant acts in servanthood. *Those—He wrote faith in their hearts* [58:22]. "This handful of dust makes up those accepted by Me by the decree of the Beginningless. I will not reject them by anyone's word."

Jacob nurtured Joseph next to himself, and the brothers were envious. They made up a stratagem and threw Joseph into the well. Go *down out of it, all of you* [2:38]: "Go down into the well of this world." Dear Joseph went out from next to his dear father and fell to the bottom of the dark well. Dear Adam went out from next to the Garden's gentleness and fell to the dust of this world.

Joseph said, "What should be done?"

"For a few days you must stay prisoner in the well until the caravan of good fortune arrives at the top of the well." *They sent down their water-drawer, who let down his bucket. He said, "Good news. Here is a boy"* [12:19].

The angels will descend upon them [41:30]. When will they send down the bucket of gentleness and pull you up from the bottom of the dark well? Then Joseph will sit with Jacob recounting stories until the end of his life.

It is not that Jacob was tried by being a lover and Joseph was not tried by being a beloved. Jacob had separation and the House of Sorrows, and Joseph had the well and the prison. Until the day when lover and beloved sat together, Jacob talked of separation and Joseph talked of prison.

It has come in the stories that one night a patrolman was passing by someplace and heard a sound. Sure enough, there was an afflicted man and he was whispering with his goal. The afflicted man was explaining his suffering and tribulation, but the goal said nothing. Then they separated.

The patrolman went up to the man and said, "What state was that? You were weeping so much, but she stayed silent."

He said, "Yes, a trial has come for me, but it has not come for her."

He said, "Wait until tomorrow and a trial will appear for her. I will command her to be given several stokes of the whip so that just as you were wailing tonight, she will wail tomorrow."

"Wait until tomorrow when I make you present. Then the meanings will come out. I will say, 'Your many disloyalties!' You will say, 'Your many trials!' "

May a thousand lives be sacrificed to the seclusion of friends!

Yaḥyā ibn Muʿādh said, *"I supplicate You in public as lords are supplicated, but I supplicate You in private as lovers are supplicated."* In the open I speak to You as a servant speaks to his lord, but in secret I speak to you as a friend speaks to a friend.

Dhu'l-Nūn Miṣrī said, "There was a time when rain did not come and the people went outside the city to pray for rain. I went along with them. I saw Sa'dūn Majnūn and said to him, 'All these people have gathered—what would it matter if you were to make an allusion?'

"He turned his face to heaven and said, *'By the rightful due of what happened last night!'* All at once the rain began."[1330] The allusion of a friend is dear to his friend.

Once Abū 'Uthmān Ḥīrī was talking about love. A youth stood up and said, *"What is the path to His love?"* What should I do to reach His friendship?

Abū 'Uthmān said, "Abandon opposition to Him."

The youth said, *"How can I claim to love Him if I have not abandoned opposition?"* How can the claim to friendship be correct if I have never pulled back my feet from the road of opposition?" Then he stood up, cried out, and wept.

Abū 'Uthmān said, *"Truthful in love for Him, falling short in His rightful due!"*[1331] Outwardly he is one of those who fall short, inwardly one of the friends.

O chevalier, if you are such that you fall short in your effort and deeds, strive not to fall short in the pain of shortcoming! *"Truthful in love for Him, falling short in His rightful due!"*

The imam, the crown of Islam,[1332] *narrated to me that Abū Ja'far Muḥammad ibn Nu'mān ibn Mūsā reported from Yaḥyā ibn Aḥmad,*[1333] *from Abu'l-Ḥusayn, from 'Abd al-Karīm ibn Abī Ḥātam, from his father Abū Ḥātam, from Sa'īd ibn Sulaymān, from Qaza'a ibn Suwayd, from Kathīr ibn Muṭṭalib, from Abū Hurayra who said, "I was with God's Messenger in the mosque when the sun was near to setting. A young man from the Helpers arrived and prayed the afternoon prayer. I said, 'He delayed that badly, and then he made up for it badly.'*

"The Messenger said, 'O Abū Hurayra, will it not make him happy that because of it he will have this world and the next?' "

Abū Hurayra said, "I left following him and reached him. I said, 'You delayed that badly and made up for it badly. Will you not sell me your prayer?'

"He said, 'For how much should I sell it?'

"I said, 'Sell it for one cycle of my prayer.'

"He said, 'I will not sell one of its cycles for the whole of this world.'

"I returned to God's Messenger and reported this to him. He said, 'Let go of those who say their prayers! Let go of those who say their prayers!' " O Abū Hurayra, do not go after those who have been seized by the Real, for they are *"truthful in love for Him, falling short in His rightful due."*

When the Adamite was created, shortcoming was made his attribute. A tree was planted in his outwardness, and a tree was planted in his inwardness. The outer tree was called "the prescription of the Law." The inner tree was called "the bestowal of recognition." The fruit of the outer tree is service, and the fruit of the tree that bestows recognition is love.

"Then I set down the custom that the tree of the Law's prescription, whose fruit is service, may be struck by blight, but the tree that bestows recognition, which is expressed in the words *'its roots fixed and its branches in heaven'* [14:24], will not be touched by any blight. Outwardly a man is in the tavern, but the reins of love are on high: *'truthful in love, falling short in His rightful due.' "*

The man afflicted with shortcoming in his deeds flees to the Threshold and cries out that the tree of the Law's prescription has not given fruit. From the Exalted Presence comes the call, *"Surely God gazes not on your forms."*[1334]

Since there is no escape from friendship, well, you might as well love Him, for whatever is killed in the Real's name is not carrion.

If a Guebre, whose tongue is dismissed from the name of the Real, slaughters an animal, they say that it is carrion. Why? Because that occurred from someone whose tongue is dismissed from the Real's name. Whatever does not die in His road is carrion.

A man came to Rābiʿa and said, "I love you for the sake of God."

She said, "If that is so, I advise you to strive to remove the intermediary from the midst, for I do not want to intrude in the road of lovers."[1335]

O chevalier, truthfulness in love makes up for shortcoming in deeds, but fully performing deeds does not make up for shortcoming in love.

God said to the angels, *"Surely I know"* [2:30], and He said to Iblis, *"What prevented thee?"* [38:75]. "O angels, do not look at the disloyalty of their deeds, look at the limpidness of My knowledge! O Iblis, do not look at the *molded mud* [15:33], look at the robe of My attributes! Though My friends slip and adulterate the coin of their practice with disobedience, I hold before them the crucible of repentance—*the repenters, the worshipers* [9:112]. The wisdom of the slip is that when they look at themselves in that slip, they will bring forth poverty, but if they were to look at Us in obedience, they would bring forth boasting."

It is told that David said, "O Lord, why have You thrown me into sin?"

He answered, "Because before you sinned you used to enter in upon Me as kings enter in upon their servants, but now you enter in upon Me as servants enter in upon their king."

Self-admiration went to the head of that accursed one: *"Shall I prostrate myself to someone whom Thou hast created of clay?"* [17:61]. "O accursed one, do you know what you are saying? You see the clay, but you do not see My intervention in the clay!"

The accursed one said, *"I am better than he: Thou hast created me of fire and Thou hast created him of clay* [38:76]. What is the wisdom that You tell light to prostrate itself before darkness?" Through these words he became an unbeliever.

"Do you think that We make mistakes? Dust is better than fire. Dust sets things right, but fire corrupts. If a father has two sons, he will give each of them some wherewithal. If one of them spends the wherewithal in the tavern and the other preserves it, what do you say? Which is more to be praised and accepted?"

Also: dust in itself has no need for fire. But fire has need for trees, and trees are the result of dust.

Again: Fire tells tales, but dust curtains the mystery. If you want to know how dust keeps secrets, go to the cemetery and look at the tombs. You will see that they are all the same, but under the dust there are great differences. One is being caressed, and another melted in fire. One is dreaming of *lovely maidens*, the other of *emaciated men*.

Again: Fire is for putting burdens on top, not for carrying them. When you put a burden on fire, it burns it, but when you put a burden on dust, it carries it and keeps silent.

Again: Fire has force, but dust has good fortune. *"Good fortune belongs to the Real, and force to the unreal."* The unreal shows itself, but it does not last.

"O accursed one, when they kill fire, they kill it with two things: dust or water. *He created you from dust, then from a sperm drop* [40:67].

"O accursed one, if you boast and have greatness because of fire, I give you to the fire. Here is the fire, and here you are.

"O Pharaoh, do you boast of your rivers? Here is water, and here are you: *They were drowned, and made to enter a fire* [71:25].

"O Korah, do you boast of your treasures? Here are the possessions, and here you are: *So We made the earth engulf him and his house* [28:81].

"O you who have faith, what do you boast of?"

"Of *God, the One, the Severe* [12:39]."

"Here am I, and here are you: *Faces that day radiant, gazing on their Lord* [75:22–23]."

It is said that when Adam's body was placed between Mecca and Taif, the accursed one passed by. He looked at it carefully, and awe entered his heart. He was afraid and said to himself, "I read in the Guarded Tablet that the Real's Threshold has an enemy whose name is Iblis. Perhaps this is that enemy."

You poor wretch! How would you know what is happening in the world?

Then he said, "O angels, what will come of this? It does not have a heart. I entered into it and looked at it from the top of its head to its feet. When someone does not have a heart, what will come of him?" O dervish, why would He show your heart to the enemy?

"My mercy takes precedence over My wrath."[1336] *My mercy toward Adam takes precedence over My wrath toward Iblis.* The newly arrived will never reach the Eternal. The servant's gratitude will never reach the Real's blessing. Obedience will never reach *tawḥīd.* Wrath will never reach mercy.

When Adam was addressed with the words *"May your Lord have mercy on you,"*[1337] he put his hand on his head and said, "What sin have I done that the Real says, 'May God have mercy on you'?"

He was addressed with the words "O Adam, which of My blessings have you enjoyed that you should say, *'The praise belongs to God'*? You are a created thing. You are giving thanks for blessings not enjoyed. I am the Most Generous of the generous. Why is it surprising that I forgive someone who has not slipped?"

When the spirit of that precious pearl settled down in its lodging place at the command of the Faithful Spirit, the Real dressed Adam in the robe of knowledge, placed the crown of recognition on his head, put the bracelet of the secrets on his wrist, and fastened the anklet of good fortune to his foot: *And He taught Adam the names, all of them* [2:31]. *Surely God chose Adam* [3:33].

This is how Adam had to be displayed to the adversary. Zulaykhā first adorned Joseph, then presented him to the women of Egypt. Zulaykhā adorned Joseph with clothing and jewelry, and God adorned Adam with pure knowledge. Like an adversary He then said [to the angels], *"Tell Me the names of these if you are truthful"* [2:31]. He did not say, "Tell Adam." He said, "Tell Me." They fell apart in awe at that address. Then He said to Adam, *"Tell them their names"* [2:33]. He said, "Tell them." He did not say, "Tell Me," for you learned from Me.

"Yes, as angels your boast lies in your deeds, and deeds are your attribute. Adam's boast lies in knowledge, and knowledge is My attribute."

He called Himself knower: *"The knower of the Unseen"* [34:3]. He also called us knowers: *"The possessors of knowledge"* [3:18].

"When I apportioned bearing witness, I said, 'It must not be done without the beautiful friends: *God bears witness that there is no god but He* [3:18].' When I apportioned exaltedness, I said, 'The friends should have a portion: *To God belongs the exaltation, and to the Messenger, and to the faithful* [63:8].' When I apportioned the prayers of blessing, I said, 'The friends should have a share: *It is He who blesses you, and His angels* [33:43].'

"O Muḥammad, on the day We praised your community and called you knowers, We saw those with long lives and all that obedience. On the day We created the bee and gave it honey, We saw those strong falcons. On the day We gave silk to that little worm, We saw those awesome serpents. On the day We gave ambergris to the sea cow, We saw the tremendous elephants. On the day We gave pearls to the oyster, We saw those powerful crocodiles. On the day We gave sweet songs to the nightingale, We saw those decorated peacocks. On the day We praised and lauded Muḥammad's community, We saw those long-lived obedient ones. On the day We praised this handful of dust, We saw the angels lined up in rows of service."

Before you wanted I wanted you;
all the world I adorned for you.
Thousands in the city are in love with Me.
Live in joy—I wanted you.

Moses looked over all the Children of Israel and singled out Aaron: *"Make him a partner in my affair* [20:32]. Make Aaron my partner in prophethood."

"Moses looked at all of the Children of Israel and chose Aaron. I looked from the Throne to the earth and chose you. Moses made Aaron a partner in prophethood. I made you a partner in bearing witness: *God bears witness that there is no god but He, and the angels, and the possessors of knowledge* [3:18]. O you who have faith, I say about Myself 'God.' You also say about Me 'God.' "

Tell them their names [2:33]. When someone has a best friend and a new infant arrives, he says to him, "What name should I give this child?"

God said, "Let's wait until that friend comes and see what he says. We will give it the name he says."

He brought the existent things into existence, from the tip of the Pleiades to the end of the earth. "Lord God, what are the names of these created things?"

The answer came, "I have a friend in the concealment of nonexistence. Wait until I bring that friend into the confines of existence. I will present all these existent things to the friend to see what names he gives them. O Adam, whatever name you give, I have given."

What a pure Lord! He creates an individual like this from a handful of dust and chooses him above all existent things. Then, in the banquet of ascription, He makes the declaration, *"whom I created with My own two hands"* [38:75].

The Real gave Adam superiority over the angels with this address: *"I created with My own two hands."* Those who interpret this to mean the hand of blessing and the hand of power nullify its specific characteristic and give Iblis an excuse for not prostrating himself. Those who talk of fingers and palms are declaring similarity and giving God parts and pieces. Whoever has faith in the hand and does not interpret or declare similarity has been released from both denial and unbelief. He raises the banner of the Sunnah, affirms the specific characteristic of Adam, and establishes the argument against the accursed one. He accepts the words of God and the Messenger and follows the leaders of the past. *So which of the two groups has a greater right to security?* [6:81].

102. *al-Ṣabūr:* the Patient

The forbearing who has no hurry to punish. *"He grants respite, but He does not disregard."*[1338]

The literal meaning of patience is restraint. *When the Lord is described as patient, the meaning is that He restrains from punishing those who deserve it by lengthening their respite.*

When the *tawḥīd*-voicing servant believes that the Real is the Patient, then conformity is a stipulation of love. He must make patience his own holdfast and support. He must be so patient that patience no longer has patience with him. Then he must command patience to be patient.

He vied patiently with patience, so patience asked him for help.
The lover said to patience, "Patience!"[1339]

What then is the very reality of patience? The great ones have said, *"Patience is swallowing down trial without claiming anything."*[1340] Patience is to taste the poison of trial without voicing any claims.

"Patience is keeping tribulation secret and making favor manifest."[1341] Patience is to keep tribulation hidden and to make blessings apparent.

In the jewel box of the spirits of those jealous for You, how many
secretly wail without redress in the pain of Your love!
You set down a firm base for beauty on which
nothing is written but *there subsists the face of thy Lord* [55:27].[1342]

What other than patience profits the lower millstone? The burden that heaven and earth were not able to carry was placed on your head by your choice. How can you now cry out for help?

Someone entered in upon a sick man who said, "Āh!"
He said, "About whom are you moaning?"
He became silent.
Then he said, "With whom are you being patient?"
He said, "What should I do then?"
He said, "Silence, but not with toughness; words, but not with complaint." Silence, but not because of manliness, and speech, but not by way of alienation.

Surely Abraham was forbearing, always sighing [11:75]. In the reports it has come that the Real sent three of His names to Abraham. One of them was *Āh*, for Abraham was constantly saying *"Āh,"* so He called him *awwāh* [always sighing]. If the safe and healthy must have ninety-nine names, the folk of affliction must have one name. The ninety-nine names come forth from the tongue, but *Āh* comes forth from the midst of the spirit. Pleasure has no access to *Āh*.

O chevalier, when the tree of pain and sorrow sticks up its head, it does so from the garden of dust's covenant. There were those who had been worshiping for seven hundred thousand years, reciting the beads of holiness on the string of intimacy, but that was a simple stew, without the salt of pain. Adam was the source of pain. Because of pain he put forth his hands: *And man carried it* [33:72].

What would have happened if he had been patient for an hour? *"Ask not for commandership. For, if you are given it after asking for it, you will be turned over to it. But if you are given it without asking for it, you will be given help with it."*[1343] If a hat falls on your head without your asking for it, help will come along with it. But if you put the hat on your head by your own intervention, loss will come along with it and seize your reins.

Heaven and earth were put to flight, but Adam put out his hands. What would have happened if he had not put out his hands for an hour and said that he would not buy it? However, He did not want to sell it to anyone else. The pearl that was brought out into the open from the treasury of the Unseen was for the oyster of Adam's love alone. The pearl was worthy for him, and he was worthy for the pearl. Then the sultan of love came along and struck fire into the harvest of his patience.

In the morning Jacob was saying, *"Beautiful patience!"* [12:18]. Evening had not yet arrived when he was shouting, *"Oh my grief for Joseph!"* [12:84].

Surely We offered the Trust to the heavens and the earth [33:72]. Adam was drunk with love. A heavy burden was put on his head. Though he was weak, his love was hot.

For seven hundred thousand years the pure ones of the Empire had put down the prayer carpets of obedient acts in the station of generous gifts. In the khanaqah of sinlessness and the prayer grounds of reverence they had been leaning on their service: *We are those in rows, we are the glorifiers* [37:165–66]. They did not know that there is a world beyond createdness. Suddenly water and dust were mixed and their clay was kneaded. It was the head of Adam's aspiration that passed beyond createdness. The cure of all pains was put inside him, but he was given a pain without cure.

The four paragons among them—Gabriel, Michael, Seraphiel, and Azrael—set out in the tracks of Adam's pain, hoping to find the road, but none of them found the road to that pain.

"O Michael, now that you are burning for this pain, sit at the gate of their provisions so that when the nourishment of the pain is sent from the Presence and the scent of it reaches your nose, that will keep your nose moist."

To Gabriel it was said, "Take care of coming and going and convey the nourishment to their breasts. When you are standing at the top of the table, they will not refuse to give you a bite.

"O Azrael, sit at the gate of death and take away the patched cloak they were wearing during their journey.

"O Seraphiel, put the trumpet to your mouth. When they lift up their heads from the dust, they will put on new clothes. Take away their old patched cloaks. Paragons should have someone special like that—called 'the wardrobe-keeper.' O Seraphiel, you be their wardrobe-keeper."

Adam's makeup was an all-comprehensive tree within which was the wherewithal of both delicious fruit and bitter colocynth. The makeup given to him was not small, and the names thrown to him were not lowly.

What do you know of yourself? You know nothing of intellect, spirit, and heart other than the names. They will not expose their faces to you today—they will show you their faces in the city of Byzantium.

The tree of Adam's makeup had many sorts of irrigation, so many sorts of fruit appeared from it. Each leaf had a different pattern. The one hundred twenty-some thousand protected sinless ones appeared from this tree. If you want roses, come to this tree, and if you want thorns, come also to this tree. The eight paradises are adorned with this tree, and the seven depths of hell are kindled from this tree.

Here you have an exalted seed! On the day they planted the seed, a whole world was perplexed: "What is this seed?" He who planted the seed knows it, not the spectator. The spectator knows the greenness of the leaves. How should he know the taste of the fruit?

The date tree has an ugly form with sprouting thorns. "But," they say, "have patience, for it has an exalted fruit. Wait and a spathe will appear, from the spathe a blossom, from the blossom a cluster, and from the cluster unripe dates. Several days will be needed for them to gain flavor. Then they will become healing for the ill and food for the hungry."

O dervish, there is a tree that drinks water from a stream, a tree that drinks water from a spring, and a tree that drinks water from heaven. Then there is a tree whose roots are watered such that, if He had turned over the watering of this tree to creatures, no one would know where to find the water. He plants it, He takes care of it, and He waters it. He placed several thousand capacities in this tree. In every era a new secret has become apparent. In Adam's era one secret, in Noah's era another secret, in Abraham's era another secret, in Moses's era another secret, in Muḥammad's era still another secret. *"Do you wonder that bosom friendship belongs to Abraham, speech to Moses, and vision to Muḥammad?"*[1344]

Dust was the depository of Adam's makeup, and Adam's makeup was the depository of the unseen secrets. A precious pearl must be placed in an unknown site. The angels were the good and the pious who prayed while standing, supplicating, bowing, and prostrating. They had subtle makeups adorned with sinlessness and pruned of slips. But a nest for birds is one thing, and an oyster for the night-brightening pearl something else.

"O universe, become an oyster, for Adam is the night-brightening pearl! O makeup of Adam, become an oyster, for the heart is the pearl! O heart, become an oyster, for the secret core is the pearl! O secret core, become an oyster, for Our gaze is the pearl!"

All animals in the ocean move, but the oyster with the pearl does not move. In his makeup Adam was given a settledness. Everyone who came, came to Adam, but he did not go to anyone.

When a man makes a mill, the mill has a fixed spindle. Whatever instruments the mill may have, they all rotate around the spindle. Why? Because if it were to move, everything would be turned upside down. *When the sun is enwrapped* [81:1]: That is the time when the spindle will start to move. When the sultan intends to sleep, the chamberlain must snuff out the candles.

He created an individual, placed the noose of subjection around the neck of everything in heaven and earth, and put it in his hand. The sun holds the torch and cooks, the moon dyes and calculates, the stars guide, the mountains take care of the treasuries. When the dust of a slip sits on the skirt of a disobedient person's days, the Shariah sends a proclamation to the spirit of the animals that this man must purify the stain of his sin: "An edict has been written to your spirits that you must sacrifice your lives to his good fortune."

"Venerate your sacrificial animals, for they are your steeds on the Path."[1345]

He created an individual, He created all things for him, and He did not turn him over to anything. He sat him on a throne, but He did not turn him over to it. He made this world his empire, but He did not turn him over to this world. At first he was in the garment of nonexistence, but He did not turn him over to nonexistence. He brought him into existence, but He did not turn him over to existence. He gave him a name, but He did not turn him over to the name. He gave him attributes, but He did not turn him over to the attributes. He gave him beauty and presented him to the world's folk; a hundred thousand seekers stood up, but He did not turn him over to anyone. "If You did not want to sell, what was the wisdom in giving him to the broker?"

The pure ones knew that a work would appear from one of them. Gabriel was going before ʿAzāzīl, who today is Iblis, and saying, "If such a state appears, put your hands on my head."

He was saying, "That is not your work."

The chieftains among the angels were coming and making requests like this. To each of them he made the guarantee, "Have a carefree heart, for I will stand up for you."

Then the sun of the command shone forth: *Prostrate yourselves before Adam!* [2:34]. As long as the carpet of Adam's existence had not been unrolled, no command had come from the Unseen. Before his existence, the angels had not seen the beauty of the command. When that paragon was given a robe of honor, his retinue was also given robes along with him. The command *prostrate yourselves* had a tremendous awesomeness, but the accursed one did not pull back the reins of chieftainship. He puffed out his chest and came forth in chieftainship. He held himself like a tree before the command. The screaming wind of the command tore him up from the roots.

What a marvelous business! A command came for Iblis, *"Prostrate yourselves!"* and a prohibition came for Adam, *"Do not go near this tree!"* [2:35]. The prohibition pulled back on the reins, but the decree struck the whip of severity.

Surely it is thine not to be hungry therein, nor to go naked [20:118]. Adam did not know the flavor of hunger, though he had heard its name. A physician must know a thing's flavor. He aimed for the tree and the address came, "Don't do it, for it is poison! Wait until it becomes the antidote. You will have traveled your road, and it also will have traveled its road. As long as you are cooked and it is raw, things will not be set right. *Do not go near this tree!* Do not eat it, for as long as it is in its own homeland, it is poison. When it travels with you, it will become the antidote."

Jujube is like this. If you eat it in its homeland, it increases the blood; once it is exiled, it decreases the blood.

When they tasted the tree, their shameful parts were shown to them [7:22]. The address came, *"And Adam disobeyed"* [20:121]. Adam ruined his stomach.

What is meant by these words is that the tree was sent to this house along with him. Then Adam's traveling was shown by its traveling. Adam became hungry and he wanted to eat it. He was addressed with the words "It has not yet traveled its road. If you eat it, it will still be poison. Put it in the dust so that it may cease to be."

When it stuck its head up from the earth, he tried to eat it. He was addressed with the words "Do not eat it, for it is still raw and has its own being. Wait until it becomes nothing in the road. Put it between two stones until it becomes tiny specks."

He did what he was commanded and then he wanted to eat it. The address came, "Be patient until it is kneaded." When it was kneaded, he wanted to eat it. The address came, "Don't touch it until it rises." When it rose, he aimed for it. The address came, "Now you must cook it. Your hand must go and come with it. The fire will do its own work. *'Act, for everyone will be eased to that for which he was created.'* "[1346]

When it was cooked, it was said, "Now is the time for eating." The wheat fancied that it had traveled its road completely, but now it had reached the road's beginning. Adam put out his hand, put a morsel in his mouth, and chewed. This was just like Adam's being brought from paradise into this world.

The wheat said, "This indeed is another work. This mill cannot be compared to the previous mill. That mill ground the flour, but then water had to be brought from someplace for kneading. This mill itself has a spring of flowing water."

Then when it falls into the oven of the stomach, the bodily members and parts gather around it, eating at the heart's gate. The members and parts take what is limpid in their own measure and then carry the heavy leftover back to its origin, the earth. Thus beginners are given strength.

O dervish, the sultan of sultans was Muṣṭafā, and every sultan has a physician. Muṣṭafā's physician was Adam. Adam said, "I tasted the poison, bore the suffering, picked up the burden of blame, and was beaten by the whip. This was done so that when the paragon leaned back on the throne of prophethood, the table would be put before him."

And God bless Muḥammad and his family, all of them!

Notes

1. In place of this prayer the printed edition begins with a short introduction, found only in one manuscript and clearly written by a copyist: *"The praise belongs to God, possessor of majesty and generous bestowal; and blessings be upon Muḥammad, the best of mankind, and upon his Companions, the pious, the generous. Thus said the shaykh, the most majestic, most exalted, most glorious, most excellent, and great leader; the shooting star of the Real and the religion, the pride of the submission and the submitters, the propagator of the Shariah, the unveiler of the Haqiqah, the reviver of the Sunnah, the restrainer of heresy, the leader of the two denominations, the king of the Kalam, the pride of the people, the mufti of East and West, the people's guide to the Real, Abu'l-Qāsim Aḥmad ibn Abi'l-Muẓaffar Manṣūr al-Sam'ānī."*

2. The anecdote is from Qushayrī, *Sharḥ* 72.

3. Ascribed to Anṣārī, *Munājāt* 19.

4. Perhaps a version of the saying by Abū Yazīd that Ibn al-ʿArabī (*Fuṣūṣ* 88) cites in this form: *"Were the Throne and all that surrounds it to be one hundred thousand thousand times in a corner of the recognizer's heart, he would not sense it."*

5. Bayhaqī, *Iʿtiqād* 49; Qushayrī, *Sharḥ* 65–66.

6. Thaʿālibī (*Tamthīl* 8) cites this as a word of wisdom.

7. A sound hadith (that is, one that is found in Bukhārī or Muslim or both). It begins with a sentence that is translated at the beginning of the paragraph, namely, *"Death will be brought in the guise of a salt-colored ram."*

8. Cited anonymously by Qushayrī in *Sharḥ* 69.

9. Qushayrī, *Risāla* (*Epistle* 24); hereafter, RQ.

10. Bayhaqī, *Iʿtiqād* 49.

11. Largely translated from Qushayrī's remarks on the *basmalah* of surah 5 (*Laṭāʾif* 1:396).

12. This seems to be a version of a saying sometimes attributed to the Prophet (e.g., by Aflākī, *Manāqib al-ʿārifīn* 351). Shi'ite authors typically ascribe it to ʿAlī (e.g., Āmulī, *Jāmiʿ al-asrār* 205, 363, 381). For a translation of the usual version of the saying, see Shahkazemi, *Justice* 167–68.

13. In his commentary on 41:2, Ḥaqqī ascribes this saying to "one of the recognizers." Ḥaqqī took it from Maybudī's commentary on the same verse, who in turn took it from this passage in Samʿānī.

14. Bayhaqī, *Iʿtiqād* 49; Qushayrī, *Sharḥ* 73.

15. Various sources also ascribe the sentence to a conversation between God and David or between God and Abū Yazīd.

16. A sound hadith.

17. Mutanabbī (*Dīwān* 443).

18. Qushayrī provides a different version of this saying in *Sharḥ* 75.

19. In the printed edition of the text, this paragraph is followed by three lines from a ghazal of Saʿdī (fl. 150 years after Samʿānī).

20. Ibn Munawwar ascribes the verse to Abū Saʿīd (*Asrār* 148; *Secrets* 245).

21. Saying sometimes ascribed to an anonymous philosopher.

22. Ascribed to Anwarī (1126–89), but his dates make this unlikely (Sahi, "Poems of Anvari" 34).

23. Thaʿālibī (*Iʿjāz* 100) ascribes this proverbial saying to Muḥammad ibn Yazdād Marwazī (d. 844–45), a vizier of the caliph Maʾmūn.

24. The anonymous lines are quoted by Ghazālī in *Iḥyāʾ* 1:102 (with *al-simāk al-aʿzal*, "Spica Virginis," in place of *al-samāʾ al-awwal*, "the first heaven").

25. This translation of the two lines is given a frame story and put into the mouth of Abū Saʿīd by Ibn Munawwar in *Asrār* 185 (*Secrets* 289).

26. Qushayrī, *Sharḥ* 79.

27. Ghazālī ascribes this divine saying both to the Prophet (*Iḥyāʾ* 3:9) and—more in agreement with the Hadith experts—to the Torah by way of the Companion Abu'l-Dardā, as recounted by the Follower Kaʿb al-Aḥbār (*Iḥyāʾ* 4:324; *Love* 91).

28. Niftawayh (Ibn ʿAsākir, *Taʾrīkh* 51:6).
29. Fāris ibn ʿĪsā Dīnawarī (RQ on *shawq*; *Epistle* 338).
30. RQ on *shawq*; *Epistle* 338.
31. Abū Firās Ḥamdānī (Thaʿālibī, *Yatīma* 1:81).
32. RQ on *shawq* (*Epistle* 338–39).
33. Abū ʿAlī Daqqāq (RQ on *shawq*; *Epistle* 337).
34. Abū ʿUthmān Ḥīrī (RQ on *shawq*; *Epistle* 336).
35. The paragraph is translated from RQ on *shawq* (*Epistle* 337).
36. Quoted from RQ on *shawq* (*Epistle* 337), the poem is by Hārūn Rashīd, addressing his wife Khayzurān (Ibn ʿAsākir, *Taʾrīkh* 73:317–18).
37. Abū Nuwās (Ibn ʿAsākir, *Taʾrīkh* 56:225).
38. Ḥasan Baṣrī (Ibn Abī Shayba, *Īmān* 38, no. 93).
39. "Substitute" (*badal*) is used in Sufism to designate a high-ranking friend of God.
40. Muslim and other sources.
41. Ibn al-Muqriʾ, *Muʿjam* 51 (no. 63).
42. Muḥammad ibn Sarī Sarrāj (Tanūkhī, *Taʾrīkh* 1:41).
43. Sanāʾī, *Dīwān* 855.
44. Cited by RQ on *shawq* (*Epistle* 336). The poem is by Abū Nuwās (ʿAskarī, *Dīwān* 1:215).
45. Bayhaqī, *Iʿtiqād* 49–50; Qushayrī, *Sharḥ* 82.
46. Translation of *Iʿtiqād* 50; Qushayrī, *Sharḥ* 82.
47. Translation of Qushayrī, *Sharḥ* 82.
48. Qushayrī gives a version of this story in *Sharḥ* 180–81.
49. Qushayrī cites the verse in both RQ on *ṣabr* (*Epistle* 200) and *Sharḥ* 263.
50. From a *qaṣīda* by Abū Tammām in praise of the caliph Maʾmūn (Tabrīzī, *Sharḥ* 2:73). Qushayrī cites it anonymously in his commentary on 3:147 (*Laṭāʾif* 1:283).
51. Translation of a saying found in RQ on *khawf* (*Epistle* 147).
52. RQ on *khawf* (*Epistle* 145).
53. Muʿizzī (Dihkhudā, *Lughat-nāma*, under *bīgāna*).
54. Balaam was a diviner whose prayers were always answered until he was asked by the king to pray against Moses and the Israelites (cf. Numbers 22–24). His story is told by commentators on this Quranic verse.
55. Specifically Abraham, the son of Azar; and Canaan, the son of Noah (the story of the latter is told on p. 50).
56. This sentence, mentioned later on in two more instances, is also found in Ibn Munawwar, *Asrār* 162 (*Secrets* 262).
57. Maybudī cites this anonymous verse in *Kashf al-asrār*, the commentary on 3:117.
58. In *Muḥāḍarāt* 1:770 Rāghib says that the caliph Maʾmūn composed these lines about a drunken companion.
59. Ascribed to ʿUmar Khayyām (Mīr-Afḍalī, *Rubāʿiyyāt*).
60. Shiblī (Abū Nuʿaym, *Ḥilya* 10:252).
61. ʿĀmilī (*Kashkūl* 364) cites this anonymously with an additional line.
62. Qays (Anṭākī, *Tazyīn* 54).

63. Buḥturī (Thaʿālibī, *Laṭāʾif* 92).

64. Samʿānī quotes the whole quatrain on p. 34.

65. Qushayrī, *Sharḥ* 88.

66. Qushayrī provides two versions of this poem (RQ on *qurb wa buʿd*; *Epistle* 104; *Sharḥ* 86), neither of which is exactly the same as that given here.

67. Abū Sulaymān Dārānī (RQ on *ḥayāʾ*; *Epistle* 227).

68. RQ on *ḥayāʾ* (*Epistle* 228).

69. The classification is based partly on a briefer account in RQ (*Epistle* 228).

70. From a hadith cited on the authority of Ibn ʿAsākir (Ibn Kathīr, *Bidāya* 1:184).

71. The poem is not found in some manuscripts; the first two lines are ascribed to Muʿawwaj Riqqī (ʿAmīdī, *Ibāna* 45). A slightly different version is given on p. 104.

72. Bukhārī provides a hadith to this effect in his chapter on *ghusl al-madhy*.

73. Ibn Rajab, *Jāmiʿ* 662.

74. Hadith found in Tirmidhī and Aḥmad.

75. The hadith literature says that God has shame, but it typically ascribes "forbidding indecencies" to His jealousy.

76. RQ on *ḥayāʾ* (*Epistle* 228).

77. RQ on *ḥayāʾ* (*Epistle* 229).

78. The line is by Abū Ṣakhr Hudhalī, typically cited with ʿUlayya instead of Buthayna. See Ibn Manẓūr, *Lisān*, under *r.m.th*.

79. Sanāʾī, *Dīwān* 499.

80. Bayhaqī (*Shuʿab* 1:372, no. 428) quotes this as part of a saying of Fuḍayl ibn ʿIyāḍ, who in turn quotes it from "one of the sages." Its first part reads, *"I am ashamed before my Lord to worship Him merely hoping for the Garden, lest I be like an odious wage-earner. Then if He gave, I would work, and if He did not give, I would not work."*

81. This may be a version of Wāsiṭī's saying, *"Beware of seeking the sweetness of obedient acts, for that is a fatal poison"* (RQ on *riḍā*; *Epistle* 208).

82. Wāmiq was the lover of ʿAdhrā, "the virgin"; the two were celebrated in an early Persian romance, mostly lost, by ʿUnṣurī.

83. Jarīr ibn ʿAṭiyya (Ibn Kathīr, *Bidāya* 13:50).

84. The hadith is mentioned by Aḥmad.

85. In the Arabic original of this saying, Shiblī adds, *"Would that I were one of them!"* (Sarrāj, *Lumaʿ* 406).

86. Abū Dhuʾayb Hudhalī (Ibn Ḥamdūn, *Tadhkira* 6:121).

87. Ascribed to ʿAbbās ibn Aḥnaf (Sarī, *Muḥibb* 2:51).

88. This paragraph is summarized and translated from Qushayrī, *Sharḥ* 87.

89. Jaʿfar Ṣādiq (Sulamī, *Ḥaqāʾiq*, commentary on 57:1).

90. Qushayrī, *Sharḥ* 88.

91. In *Sharḥ* 88 Qushayrī cites the first line of this poem anonymously and then cites the hadith in the paragraph that follows.

92. The hadith is found in Muslim.

93. The first of these lines is ascribed to Di'bil (Ibn 'Abd Rabbih, *'Iqd* 8:104), the second and third to 'Alī ibn Jahm (Khaṭīb, *Ta'rīkh* 13:291).

94. A similar saying, well known in later texts, reads as follows: *"O son of Adam, I created the things for you, and I created you for Me."* Ibn 'Arabī says that it is from the Torah; he cites it seven times in *al-Futūḥāt al-makkiyya* and incorporates it into the title of chapter 333.

95. Though often attributed to the Prophet, the saying is not found in the standard books of Hadith.

96. Maybudī quotes a slightly different version of the poem (*Kashf al-asrār* on 3:169).

97. Sanā'ī, *Dīwān* 933.

98. Although Fakhr al-Dīn Rāzī (d. 1209) ascribes the same passage to himself at the very end of his commentary on surah 16 (*Mafātīḥ* 20:290), he must be quoting it from somewhere.

99. Ibn al-Mu'tazz (Rāghib, *Muḥāḍarāt* 2:136).

100. RQ on *qurb* (*Epistle* 105).

101. 'Abbās ibn Aḥnaf, *Dīwān* 19. Qushayrī says that Daqqāq often used to cite the first line (RQ on *qurb*; *Epistle* 104–5).

102. Ibn Lankak (Tha'ālibī, *Khāṣṣ* 189).

103. Uqayshir Asadī (Iṣfahānī, *Aghānī* 11:175). Qushayrī cites the lines anonymously in his commentary on 9:60 (*Laṭā'if* 2:40).

104. Abū Firās (Tha'ālibī, *Yatīma* 1:79).

105. Ibn 'Abd al-Barr (*Bahja* 1:22) cites the verse anonymously.

106. Qushayrī, *Sharḥ* 91.

107. The first two sentences of this passage are based on Qushayrī, *Sharḥ* 91–92.

108. The sayings in these two sentences are frequently cited together (as also later on pp. 215 and 466). The first comes in a long hadith about the angels (Bayhaqī, *Shu'ab* 1:183); the second is sometimes called a hadith but does not seem to have an early source.

109. Sanā'ī, *Dīwān* 1134. The quatrain has been wrongly ascribed to Rūmī (Furūzānfar no. 660, Gamard no. 1421).

110. Aḥmad Rifā'ī (*Ḥāla* 86–87) quotes almost identical words as part of a saying of "one of the folk of recognition."

111. Junayd heard a different version of these lines being sung by a slave girl ('Umarī, *Masālik* 8:109).

112. The first of these two lines is by 'Abbās ibn Aḥnaf (*Dīwān* 97), but the second is not in his divan.

113. Sulamī mentions the two lines, which are generally ascribed to Majnūn Laylā, in his account of Abu'l-'Abbās ibn Masrūq (*Ṭabaqāt* 193).

114. Sulamī quotes the saying in his Quran commentary (*Ḥaqā'iq* 1:1) but with "God" in place of "No god but God."

115. Abu'l-Ḥasan Ḥuṣrī (Hujwīrī, *Kashf* 243).

116. Tha'ālibī, *Tamthīl* 1:44.

117. Mutanabbī, *Dīwān* 198.

118. *Ḥadīth qudsī* found in Muslim.

119. Part of a long *ḥadīth qudsī* found in Muslim.
120. Nasāʾī and other sources.
121. Sanāʾī, *Dīwān* 816.
122. Translation of Qushayrī, *Sharḥ* 94.
123. Sound hadiths mention that God's shawl is tremendousness and His cloak pride.
124. Aḥnaf ibn Qays (Dīnawarī, *Mujālasa* 5:301, no. 2163).
125. Tirmidhī. Ibn ʿAsākir provides the text in *Taʾrīkh* 79:4. Qurayẓa and Naḍīr were two Jewish tribes of Medina, defeated at the Battle of Khaybar in 628.
126. Ghazālī, *Iḥyāʾ* 3:356–57.
127. Buḥturī (Nuwayrī, *Nihāya* 3:231).
128. The hadith is well known, with differences of opinion as to the degree of its reliability.
129. Translation of an anecdote from Qushayrī, *Sharḥ* 94.
130. Hadith found in Tirmidhī, Aḥmad, and other sources.
131. Ghazālī cites this as a hadith in *Iḥyāʾ* 4:277.
132. The hadith is well known and has many versions, though it is not considered sound.
133. The hadith is well known though weak.
134. Dhahabī mentions this story as a spurious hadith in *Talkhīṣ* 1:322.
135. Summary of Qushayrī, *Sharḥ* 96.
136. Rābiʿa (Ibn al-Muqriʾ, *Muʿjam* 54, no. 73).
137. Abū Sahl Ṣuʿlūkī gives this as a definition of Sufism rather than of servanthood (RQ on *taṣawwuf*; *Epistle* 292).
138. Mutanabbī, *Dīwān* 321.
139. Anonymous (RQ on *ʿubūdiyya*; *Epistle* 211).
140. Anonymous (RQ on *ʿubūdiyya*; *Epistle* 211).
141. Dhu'l-Nūn Miṣrī (RQ on *ʿubūdiyya*; *Epistle* 211).
142. Anonymous (RQ on *ʿubūdiyya*; *Epistle* 211).
143. Ibn ʿAṭāʾ (RQ on *ʿubūdiyya*; *Epistle* 212).
144. Naṣrābādī (RQ on *ʿubūdiyya*; *Epistle* 213).
145. Jurayrī (RQ on *ʿubūdiyya*; *Epistle* 213).
146. Qushayrī, *Manthūr* 62.
147. Qushayrī, *Manthūr* 62.
148. RQ on *samṭ* (*Epistle* 139). Sarrāj (*Lumaʿ* 27) says the line is by ʿAlī ibn ʿAbd al-Raḥīm Qannād.
149. Samnūn Muḥibb (RQ on Samnūn; *Epistle* 50).
150. His father Manṣūr.
151. Kulaynī provides a similar saying of Jaʿfar in *Kāfī* 1:159, no. 9.
152. Acquisition (*kasb*) is a much-discussed technical term in Ash'arite theology. It is generally understood to mean that people are both predestined and free; they *acquire* responsibility for the acts that they choose to do, even though God is the creator of those acts.
153. Daqqāq (RQ on *istiqāma*; *Epistle* 220); the addition in brackets is from RQ; judging from the partial Persian translation in the next sentence, it was dropped by a copyist.
154. Translation of a story from RQ on *qurb* (*Epistle* 104).

155. RQ on *qurb* (*Epistle* 104).
156. RQ on *qurb* (*Epistle* 104).
157. The quatrain is ascribed to Anṣārī, *Munājāt* 23.
158. Shiblī (Iṣfahānī, *Kharīda* 4/2:512).
159. Version of a saying by Daqqāq (RQ on *taṣawwuf*; *Epistle* 292).
160. This also seems to be a version of a saying by Daqqāq cited by RQ: *"If the poor man had only a spirit and it were presented to the dogs at the door, no dog would look at it"* (*Epistle* 292).
161. RQ on *khushū'* (*Epistle* 165).
162. RQ on *khushū'* (*Epistle* 165).
163. RQ on *khushū'* (*Epistle* 165).
164. The "standing place" (*mawqif*) refers to the plain of Arafat, where the people gather as part of the hajj. Maybudī ascribes the original of this saying to a "chevalier of the Tariqah" (commentary on 28:83). In *Shu'ab* (6:302, no. 8253) Bayhaqī ascribes it to the father of 'Abdallāh ibn Bakr.
165. Sanā'ī, *Dīwān* 888.
166. Ibn 'Asākir (*Ta'rīkh*, 73:316–17) says that Hārūn Rashīd composed this line for a slave girl.
167. *Alif* (١) has "nothing" in contrast to the remaining letters, each of which has distinguishing marks or shapes. *Alif* commonly symbolizes the One, the "Unseen Unity," as Sam'ānī suggests in the next sentence, not least because the number one (١) is written almost the same way.
168. The notion that the lifetime of this world is seven thousand years is fairly common, supported by a number of weak hadiths.
169. From a ghazal by Mu'izzī. The "son of the Magi" refers to wine. The verses are also cited by Aḥmad Ghazālī (*Sawāniḥ* 9). Rakhsh is the name of the great hero Rostam's horse.
170. The quatrain has been wrongly ascribed to Rūmī (Furūzānfar no. 310, Gamard no. 1366).
171. Ibn al-Kharrāṭ (*'Āqiba* 1:177) cites Qushayrī as saying that Daqqāq used to recite this verse.
172. Khayyām, *Rubā'iyyāt* no. 55.
173. Proverb (Ābī, *Nathr* 6:326).
174. This paragraph seems to be inspired by Mustamlī, *Sharḥ* 756–57.
175. Sanā'ī, *Dīwān* 548.
176. Anonymous (Rāghib, *Muḥāḍarāt* 1:361).
177. Proverbial (Tha'ālibī, *Rasā'il* 44).
178. Abū Nuwās, *Dīwān* 49. Sam'ānī has taken the lines from Qushayrī's commentary on 2:30 (*Laṭā'if* 1:75).
179. The paragraph is partly based on Qushayrī's commentary on 2:30 (*Laṭā'if* 1:76).
180. Sa'īd ibn Ḥamīd (Tha'ālibī, *Muntaḥil* 96).
181. The entire line is given on p. 229.
182. Bukhārī, Muslim, and other standard sources give versions of this *ḥadīth qudsī*.
183. The hadith is well known but generally considered weak.
184. The hadith has many versions, usually with "created" or "planted" instead of "built."
185. A sound hadith that has come in several versions.
186. A sound hadith.
187. Shiblī (Sulamī, *Ṭabaqāt* 265).

188. Ibn Būqa (Rāghib, *Muḥāḍarāt* 1:481). Qushayrī cites the verse anonymously in his commentary on 7:172 (*Laṭāʾif* 1:585).

189. Thaʿālibī tells the anecdote in *Tamthīl* 136–37.

190. Abū Tammām (Thaʿālibī, *Iʿjāz* 169).

191. Muslim.

192. Rāghib, *Muḥāḍarāt* 2:484.

193. Ṭabarī and others cite the hadith in commenting on this verse.

194. ʿAṭṭār provides this saying, though with significantly different wording, in his account of Kharaqānī (*Tadhkira* 672).

195. Khaṭīb, *Taʾrīkh* 16:307 (no. 7449).

196. Khaṭīb, *Muntakhab* 123 (no. 101).

197. Imruʾ al-Qays (Dīnawarī, *Mujālasa* 5:56–57, no. 1860).

198. According to Rāghib (*Muḥāḍarāt* 2:646) the lines were heard from the Abbasid vizier Qāsim ibn ʿUbaydallāh.

199. Abū Sulaymān Khaṭṭābī (Thaʿālibī, *Yatīma* 4:383).

200. When Muḥammad entered Medina on his camel, he refused to accept the hospitality of any of those who offered it and let his camel wander. It finally knelt down near the house of Abū Ayyūb Khālid ibn Zayd, who took its saddle into his house. It was there that Muḥammad lived until he built a house and mosque where his camel had knelt. Abū Ayyūb participated in most of the early battles of the Muslim community and died in the year 672 on the outskirts of Constantinople. His tomb in Istanbul is an important site of pilgrimage.

201. This clause is from Ibn Hishām's description of the conquest of Mecca (*Sīra* 4:45; Guillaume, *Life* 548).

202. Mutanabbī, *Dīwān* 475.

203. Ibn ʿAsākir ascribes the lines to Qāḍī ʿAbd al-Ḥamīd ibn ʿAbd al-ʿAzīz (d. 292/905; *Taʾrīkh* 34:83). According to Thaʿālibī, they are by Abu'l-Ḥasan ibn Muqla (*Yatīma* 3:133).

204. The story is translated from Qushayrī, *Sharḥ* 107–8.

205. Hadith from Bukhārī. The basic understanding of the evil eye (Persian, *chashm-i bad*) is that looking at someone's beauty with envy, or even with simple admiration, may have a harmful effect.

206. Talisman translates *chashm-zakhm* (literally, "eye-wound"), which here has the meaning of something used to ward off the effects of the evil eye, as in the verse of Sanāʾī: "Man is more broken when sinful; the peacock's [ugly] feet are the *chashm-zakhm* of its head" (Dihkhudā, *Lughat-nāma*). On the peacock's feet, see p. 227.

207. Mutanabbī, *Dīwān* 319.

208. The second hemistich of an anonymous verse; the first hemistich reads, *"The country where my amulets* [protecting me as a child] *were cut off by young manhood"* (Ibn ʿAbd al-Barr, *Bahja* 1:169).

209. According to Thaʿālibī (*Thimār* 285, no. 528), the sentence is by Badīʿ al-Zamān Hamadhānī.

210. Anṭākī (*Tazyīn* 1:194) cites the verse anonymously.

211. This sentence is found in some later versions of the hadith of the Pen.

212. Words of Gabriel when he could not keep up with the Prophet during the *mi ʿrāj*. The saying is often found in accounts of the Prophet's *mi ʿrāj* (e.g., Qushayrī, *Mi ʿrāj* 79).

213. According to Qushayrī these words were received by Nibājī in a dream (RQ on *ru ʾya*; *Epistle* 398).

214. Qushayrī, *Sharḥ* 75.

215. Qushayrī, *Sharḥ* 89 (commentary on the name *ʿazīz*).

216. Qushayrī, *Sharḥ* 89.

217. Qushayrī, *Sharḥ* 89.

218. Translation of an explanation given by Daqqāq, Qushayrī, *Sharḥ* 89.

219. Ḥamdūn Qaṣṣār (Sulamī, *Ḥaqā ʾiq*, commentary on 21:66).

220. The poem (without the anecdote) is found in Ibn Khallikān's *Wafayāt al-a ʿyān* 3:404 under Sayf al-Dawla [ʿAlī ibn ʿAbdallāh] ibn Ḥamdān.

221. The account is loosely translated from Bukhārī's *Ṣaḥīḥ* (*Kitāb aḥādīth al-anbiyāʾ*).

222. A well-known hadith, considered sound by some scholars.

223. The lines are by Abū Tammām in praise of the caliph Muʿtaṣim Billāh (Nuwayrī, *Nihāya* 3:174). Abū Nuʿaym (*Ḥilya* 10:373) tells of an occasion when Shiblī recited the poem.

224. Proverb (Rāghib, *Muḥāḍarāt* 1:239).

225. Zamakhsharī (*Rabīʿ* 3:422) tells the story.

226. The quatrain is ascribed plausibly to Masʿūd Saʿd Salmān and wrongly to Rūmī (Furūzānfar no. 1493, Gamard no. 251).

227. The lines are also found in Aḥmad Ghazālī, *Sawāniḥ*, chapter 16.

228. A well-known *ḥadīth qudsī*, though not considered sound.

229. Hadith found in Aḥmad.

230. According to Abū Nuʿaym (*Ḥilya* 8:351), "agitation without stillness" is part of a description of trust (*tawakkul*) by Bishr Ḥāfī.

231. Thaʿālibī, *Tamthīl* 256.

232. Abū Nuʿaym tells the Junayd anecdote in *Ḥilya* 10:271.

233. Famous lines by Rūdakī.

234. Anonymous (Ibn al-Jawzī, *Yāqūta* 69).

235. Translated from Qushayrī, *Sharḥ* 111.

236. Qushayrī, *Sharḥ* 111.

237. Qushayrī, *Sharḥ* 111–12.

238. Ābī, *Nathr* 2:143.

239. ʿAbd al-Karīm Samʿānī (*Ansāb* 2:389–90) attributes these answers to Jaʿfar Khuldī, one of Junayd's disciples.

240. Translation of a story from RQ on *tawakkul* (*Epistle* 184–85).

241. RQ on *tawakkul* (*Epistle* 186)

242. RQ on *yaqīn* (*Epistle* 196).

243. Translated from RQ on *yaqīn* (*Epistle* 195).

244. Tawḥīdī (*Baṣā ʾir* 9:158) ascribes the saying to Luqmān the sage.

245. RQ on *yaqīn* (*Epistle* 194).
246. Nahrajūrī (RQ; *Epistle* 196).
247. Qushayrī, commentary on 21:83 (*Laṭā'if* 2:517).
248. Ruwaym (RQ on *riḍā*; *Epistle* 209).
249. Muṣʿab ibn Zubayr, killed at the Battle of Dayr al-Jathaliq (691).
250. For an Arabic version of this account, see Ibn ʿAsākir, *Ta'rīkh* 58:452.
251. Dhu'l-Nūn Miṣrī (Sarrāj, *Maṣāriʿ* 1:90).
252. Perhaps this is a version of a saying by Abū ʿUthmān Ḥīrī (d. 910): *"No man"—or "no man's faith"—"becomes perfect until four things are equal in his heart: withholding, bestowal, exaltedness, and abasement"* (RQ on Ḥīrī; *Epistle* 45).
253. The saying is ascribed to both Abū Dharr and Abū Dardā (Ibn al-Mubārak, *Zuhd* 88–89, no. 262). When Samʿānī quotes it again, he attributes it to the latter.
254. Ruwaym (Hujwīrī, *Kashf* 293).
255. The words addressed to Khadīja are taken from Bukhārī's account of the beginning of the revelation.
256. Maybudī (*Kashf* 2:196) ascribes the verse to Sanā'ī; the style is his, but the verse is not found in his printed divan.
257. ʿAlī ibn Ḥasan Bākharzī (Bākharzī, *Dumya* 2:804).
258. Ibn Abi'l-Dunyā, *Ṣifa* 221 (no. 340).
259. The paragraph is based on Qushayrī, *Sharḥ* 115.
260. Dhu'l-Nūn Miṣrī (*Ḥilya* 9:371).
261. Allusion to Quran 67:5: *"And We adorned the lower heaven with lamps, and We made them the stonings of the satans."*
262. The sentence combines two proverbs. The first was voiced by ʿUmar right after the death of the Prophet (Ibn Qutayba, *Imāma* 7). The second is mentioned by Thaʿālibī (*Khāṣṣ* 35).
263. Second verse of a quatrain attributed to Abū Saʿīd. The first reads, "I became such that I could not be seen / when I was put down before You, O Beloved" (Ibn Munawwar, *Asrār* 313; *Secrets* 486).
264. Proverbial (Hāshimī, *Amthāl* 71, no. 337).
265. The second verse of this quatrain is ascribed to Abū Saʿīd (Ibn Munawwar, *Asrār* 47; *Secrets* 120).
266. Ibn Munawwar tells a gambling story with the same punchline (*Asrār* 216; *Secrets* 330).
267. *Labbayk Allāhumma labbayk—"Here I am, O God, here I am"*—is chanted by pilgrims to Mecca.
268. Majlisī, *Biḥār* 6:109.
269. A standard definition of faith.
270. Tawḥīdī (*Baṣā'ir* 1:151) attributes another version of this saying to Junayd.
271. Version of a saying quoted by Daqqāq (RQ on *maʿrifa*; *Epistle* 324).
272. Daqqāq. For a longer version, see p. 170.
273. A sound *ḥadīth qudsī* narrated by Muslim and others. The text continues: *"When he says, 'The All-Merciful, the Ever-Merciful,' God says, 'My servant is lauding Me.' When he says, 'The owner of the Day of Doom,' God says, 'My servant is magnifying Me,' and sometimes He says, 'My servant is*

delegating to Me.' When he says, 'Thee alone we worship, and from Thee alone we ask for help,' God says, 'This is between Me and My servant, and My servant shall have what he asks for.' When he says, 'Guide us on the straight path, the Path of those whom Thou hast blessed, not of those who incur wrath, nor of the misguided,' God says, 'This belongs to My servant, and My servant shall have what he asks for.' "

274. The more famous form of this saying is *"The prayer is the* miʿrāj *of the person of faith."* Although typically attributed to the Prophet, it is not found in the earliest sources.

275. Daqqāq (Qushayrī, *Sharḥ* 174; also *Laṭāʾif* on 18:18).

276. Sanāʾī, *Dīwān* 570.

277. Often cited, but not found in the earliest sources.

278. Aḥmad ibn Ḥanbal, *Kitāb al-Zuhd* 1:302 (no. 2186).

279. Ibn Hishām, *Sīra* 4:18 (Guillaume, *Life* 534).

280. Wakīʿ, *Zuhd* 396 (no. 163).

281. The first two lines of a ghazal attributed to Anwarī (no. 293). Given that he seems to have died some decades after Samʿānī, Anwarī may have added lines to an earlier quatrain.

282. Qushayrī gives a brief version of this anecdote in *Shawāhid* 25.

283. Version of a line by Shiblī (Ibn ʿAsākir, *Taʾrīkh* 66:73).

284. See note 575.

285. Words famously attributed to Abū Yazīd Basṭāmī. Samʿānī is probably alluding to accounts of Basṭāmī's *miʿrāj*; he may also have in mind his saying, *"I have no attributes"* (see Chittick, *Sufi Path of Knowledge* 376).

286. Sanāʾī, *Dīwān* 888 (though the second line is not in the printed edition).

287. Bashār ibn Bard (Iṣfahānī, *Aghānī* 3:158).

288. Tangarī is a Turkish word for God. ʿAṭṭār gives an account of these and other sayings of Abū Yazīd on his deathbed in *Tadhkira* 208–9 (*Memorial* 241–42).

289. This anonymous verse is often cited as an example of the word *abūqalamūn* meaning a satin fabric that appears in shifting colors (Thaʿālibī, *Thimār* 206).

290. Proverbial; cited by RQ on *waṣiyya* (*Epistle* 409).

291. According to Abshīhī (*Mustaṭraf* 397), the verses were part of an exchange of lines by singing girls in the house of Abū ʿĪsā, the son of the caliph Mutawakkil.

292. Zamakhsharī, commentary on 41:9–12 (*Kashshāf* 4:189).

293. Ghazālī cites this anonymous line along with two others in *Iḥyāʾ* 1:178. Subkī (*Ṭabaqāt* 5:34) says that Aḥmad's father Manṣūr was heard reciting it in someone's dream vision shortly before his conversion to the Shafi'i school.

294. Words of God to David (RQ on *dhikr*; *Epistle* 236).

295. Dhu'l-Nūn Miṣrī (Ibn al-Jawzī, *Muthīr* 80).

296. Famous words of Ḥallāj.

297. Sanāʾī, *Dīwān* 89.

298. See note 253.

299. ʿAlī ibn Ḥasan Quhistānī (Bākharzī, *Dumya* 2:779).

300. RQ on *aḥwāluhum* (*Epistle* 315) says that Abu'l-Ḥusayn Nūrī died as a result of hearing this line.

301. These Arabic sentences are from the very beginning of Ghazālī's chapter on *tafakkur* (*Iḥyā*ʾ 4:423).

302. An expression found in various divine sayings, such as this *ḥadīth qudsī* from Tirmidhī: *"O child of Adam, if you supplicate Me and hope for Me, I will forgive you despite what is within you and I do not care. O child of Adam, if your sins reach the high heavens and then you ask forgiveness of Me, I will forgive you and I do not care."*

303. Cited anonymously by Ghazālī in the chapter on love (*Iḥyā*ʾ 4:337; *Love* 127).

304. ʿAbbās ibn Aḥnaf, *Dīwān* 221.

305. *Ḥadīth qudsī* (see note 119).

306. A sound hadith, usually without "then the friends," though Ghazālī, among others, cites it so.

307. Ṣāḥib ibn ʿAbbād (*Dīwān* 166).

308. ʿIshraqa (Qālī, *Amālī* 1:29).

309. Ibn ʿAbbās (Dāraquṭnī, *Ruʾya* 1:190, no. 66).

310. Ismāʿīl Qarāṭīsī (Sarī, *Muḥibb* 2:40).

311. Anonymous (ʿUmarī, *Masālik* 10:641). Hujwīrī quotes the line in *Kashf* 12.

312. Qushayrī cites the line in his commentary on Quran 2:43 (*Laṭāʾif* 1:86)

313. Qushayrī cites the saying anonymously (RQ on *hayba*; *Epistle* 81); ʿUmarī (*Masālik* 8:119) says it is by Ruwaym.

314. See note 105.

315. Sanāʾī, *Dīwān* 792.

316. Thaʿlabī, *ʿArāʾis*/*Lives* 334.

317. Ascribed to Abū Saʿīd (Ibn Munawwar, *Asrār* 131; *Secrets* 223).

318. ʿAbbās ibn Aḥnaf. See note 101.

319. Qushayrī attributes the last two verses to himself in his commentary on 34:16 (*Laṭāʾif* 3:181).

320. Zamakhsharī (*Rabīʿ* 1:457) provides a frame story for these anonymous lines.

321. RQ on *maḥabba* (*Epistle* 330).

322. RQ on *ghayra* (*Epistle* 265).

323. See note 71.

324. Mutanabbī, *Dīwān* 333.

325. A slave girl (Masʿūdī, *Murūj* 4:83); RQ on *maḥabba* (*Epistle* 333).

326. This hadith is frequently quoted in the literature on love, though its authenticity is debated.

327. ʿAbbās ibn Aḥnaf, *Dīwān* 116.

328. That is, his son was left to drown.

329. When Nimrod threw Abraham into the fire, Gabriel came and asked, *"Have you any need of me?"* and this was his reply (Ibn ʿAsākir, *Taʾrīkh* 6:182–83).

330. The paragraph is translated from Qushayrī, *Sharḥ* 121.

331. Ruwaym (RQ on *riḍā*ʾ; *Epistle* 209).

332. Anonymous (Abū Tammām, *Dīwān* 240).

333. Anonymous (Abū Tammām, *Dīwān* 254).

334. Fluctuater of Hearts (*muqallib al-qulūb*) is a divine name found in the hadith literature. Here there is an allusion to Quran 24:37, which speaks of men not distracted in their worship because they fear the Day of Resurrection, *"when hearts and eyes will fluctuate."*

335. ʿAbbās ibn Aḥnaf, *Dīwān* 255.

336. ʿAbbās ibn Aḥnaf, *Dīwān* 84–85.

337. Sanāʾī, *Dīwān* 931.

338. Qushayrī cites the poem anonymously in his commentary on 9:111 (*Laṭāʾif* 2:64).

339. Attributed to Abū Nuwās (Jurjānī, *Dalāʾil* 320n3).

340. See note 37.

341. Sufyān Thawrī (Ibn ʿAsākir, *Taʾrīkh* 10:204).

342. Reference to the hadith *"Every night God descends to the nearest heaven"* (no. 16, n. 11).

343. *"When his Lord disclosed Himself to the mountain . . ."* (7:143).

344. Kuthayyir (Ibn Kathīr, *Bidāya* 13:32).

345. Bashār ibn Burd (Bayhaqī, *Shuʿab* 6:326, no. 8360).

346. Almost a quote from Ghazālī, *Iḥyāʾ* 1:112.

347. Muslim.

348. See note 95.

349. This seems to be a paraphrase of this sound hadith: *"Hospitality is for three days; anything after that is charity. It is not permitted to dwell with him so long as to cause hardship for him."*

350. See note 7.

351. In his commentary on 24:61 (*Laṭāʾif* 5:623), Qushayrī says that he composed these verses to explain the meaning of true friendship (*ṣadāqa*).

352. ʿAlī ibn Aḥmad Nuʿaymī (Samʿānī, *Ansāb* 5:511); also cited later, with a second line (p. 212). Qushayrī adds two more lines in *Sharḥ* 127.

353. Probably an allusion to a hadith cited by Ghazālī (*Iḥyāʾ* 4:81) in which the Prophet says that *"those who praise much"* (*ḥammādūn*) will be called forth on the Day of Resurrection; the hadith adds that they are those *"who thank God in every state."*

354. Words of God to David (RQ on *dhikr*; *Epistle* 236).

355. Bayhaqī, *Shuʿab* 1:451, no. 680.

356. Bukhārī and Muslim.

357. The meditations here on Quran 1:5 may have been inspired by this saying of Daqqāq: " *'Thee alone we worship' is to guard the Shariah, and 'Thee alone we ask for help' is to attest to the Haqiqah"* (RQ on *sharīʿa*; *Epistle* 105).

358. Part of a hadith found in Aḥmad beginning like this: *"If the son of Adam had a valley full of possessions, he would wish for two valleys. If he had two valleys, he would wish for three valleys."*

359. For the full text of the hadith (in a slightly different version), see p. 247.

360. A more common form of this weak hadith is this: *"Poverty is my boast, and through it I boast over the other prophets"* (Sakhāwī, *Maqāṣid* 480, no. 745).

361. Ibrāhīm Mawṣilī. The line is given a frame story by Ibn ʿAbd Rabbih in *ʿIqd* 7:35.

362. Jaḥẓa Barmakī (Thaʿālibī, *Khāṣṣ* 186).

363. Ṭabarī gives four short versions of this saying as a *ḥadīth qudsī* in his commentary on 28:46.

364. Sulamī, *Ṭabaqāt* 265; Ibn ʿAsākir, *Taʾrīkh* 66:64.

365. ʿAbd al-Wahhāb Mālikī (Ibn al-Bassām, *Dhakhīra* 8:523).

366. See note 94.

367. Abū Nuʿaym (*Ḥilya* 7:303) mentions these sentences as words of God recited by someone, perhaps Khiḍr, who was seen at the Kaabah by Sufyān ibn ʿUyayna.

368. Bukhārī.

369. This seems to be a truncated version of a saying by Wāsiṭī cited by RQ on *firāsa* (*Epistle* 242–43).

370. Ṭabarī among others cites this saying in the commentary on 55:29. Some sources make it part of the Prophet's own commentary on the verse.

371. See note 53.

372. Bayhaqī, *Iʿtiqād* 192.

373. Proverb (Rāghib, *Muḥāḍarāt* 2:703).

374. Sanāʾī, *Dīwān* 110.

375. See note 346.

376. See note 109.

377. Hadith found in Aḥmad and other sources.

378. Well-known hadith (e.g., Bayhaqī, *Qaḍāʾ* 183, no. 167).

379. Qushayrī cites this anonymous verse in his commentary on 2:30 (*Laṭāʾif* 1:75).

380. Shiblī (Rāghib, *Muḥāḍarāt* 1:531).

381. Faḍl Lahabī (Tawḥīdī, *Ṣadāqa* 127).

382. Bukhārī and Muslim.

383. Ghazālī cites the saying (*Iḥyāʾ* 4:328; *Love* 101–2) and then explains: *"Abū Saʿīd means that He is the All, and nothing else exists. When someone loves only himself, his acts, and his compositions, his love does not transgress his essence and the concomitants of his essence inasmuch as they are connected to his essence. Thus God loves only Himself."*

384. Commentary on 20:14 (*Laṭāʾif* 2:449).

385. Given the direction of the discussion that follows, this sentence could be based on a passage by Tawḥīdī in *Imtāʿ* (1:144), where he is explaining the inaccessibility of the Divine Reality. Having pointed out the difficulty of grasping matters pertaining to the created realm of spirits, he writes, *"What then would be our state in investigating the confines of the Divinity and the very hub of the lordhood, where there is no being, nor anything that has any relationship with being? The most we have in our hands is keeping ourselves busy with existence."*

386. Sanāʾī, *Dīwān* 384–85.

387. Manṣūr Samʿānī and others mention ʿUmar's saying in their commentaries on this verse.

388. Hadith found in Tirmidhī.

389. Part of a formula, beginning with *"There is no god but God,"* whose invocation is encouraged by hadiths found in Bukhārī, Muslim, and other standard sources.

390. Abu'l-Faḍl ibn ʿAmīd (Zawzanī, *Ḥamāsa* 1:20)

391. Ascribed to Abū Saʿīd (*Rubāʿiyyāt* no. 372).

392. Reference to the angels inasmuch as they say, *"There is none of us but has a known station"* (37:164).

393. See note 379.

394. Abū Nuʿaym, *Ḥilya* 10:34.

395. A different version of this quatrain is attributed to Anṣārī (*Munājāt* 46).

396. Ghazālī gives the Arabic text of this account in *Iḥyāʾ* 4:295.

397. Ghazālī traces this saying of David back to Shiblī (*Iḥyāʾ* 4:361; *Love* 192).

398. Perhaps based on the account of Mamshād's death in RQ on *khurūj* (*Epistle* 317).

399. Some of the manuscripts provide truncated versions of this *isnād*. As noted in the introduction, practically nothing is known of Abu'l-Faḍl ʿAbdallāh ibn Aḥmad, other than that he transmitted Hadith in Merv. In chapter 31 of *Taʿarruf* (*Doctrine* 76), Kalābādhī gives a different version of this saying.

400. RQ on *sirr* (*Epistle* 110).

401. Dhu'l-Nūn Miṣrī (Abū Nuʿaym, *Ḥilya* 9:377).

402. Anonymous; RQ, the chapter on *mujāhada* (*Epistle* 121).

403. Cited anonymously by Qushayrī in his commentary on 18:20 (*Laṭāʾif* 2:388), but with *abrār* (pious) instead of *aḥrār* (free).

404. Labīd ibn Rabīʿa (p. xxii).

405. Qushayrī cites the two lines in *Shawāhid* 26.

406. See note 131.

407. Ibn al-Jawzī says that this is a hadith (*Mudhish* 524).

408. Reference to the sound hadith, *"My community will be the bright-faced and white-cuffed on the Day of Resurrection because of the trace of the ablution."*

409. In commenting on 20:131 Manṣūr Samʿānī and others ascribe the saying to Ubayy ibn Kaʿb.

410. The proverb, which refers to a stratagem of the pre-Islamic vizier Qaṣīr ibn Saʿd Zahrānī, suggests human ignorance of the truth of affairs.

411. Sanāʾī, *Dīwān* 696. The poetic conceit is that the beloved's wink sends forth eyelashes like arrows. This eight-line ghazal ends with the line, "Like others I have made my spirit a target in the hope / that when Your wink becomes an arrow, You'll shoot it at Sanāʾī."

412. This paragraph is based on Ghazālī, *Kīmiyā* 21.

413. There are several hadiths to this effect.

414. This and the following paragraph seem to be based on Ghazālī, *Kīmiyā* 19–21.

415. The saying is well known and sometimes attributed to the Prophet.

416. Muḥammad ibn al-Faḍl (RQ, the chapter on *maʿrifa*; *Epistle* 325).

417. Life is generally considered the first attribute of spirit. As Samʿānī's father Manṣūr remarks in his commentary on 15:29, *"The spirit is a subtle body [jism laṭīf] through which the human being comes to life."* In his commentary on 42:52 he says, *"Here* spirit *is the Quran. He named it a spirit because hearts come to life through it, just as souls come to life through the spirit."*

418. Ghazālī, *Iḥyāʾ* 3:10.

419. A well-known general rule (*qāʿida*) in jurisprudence.

420. These two paragraphs are based on Ghazālī, *Kīmiyā* 26.

421. This and the following five paragraphs are based on and sometimes directly translated from Ikhwān, *Rasāʾil* 2:462–67.

422. The Quranic word "form" (*ṣūra*) is understood here in the Aristotelian sense as the complement of "matter" (*mādda*). This is clear from a part of the passage that Samʿānī has dropped: *"The world of the soul is the form of human nature* [*ṣūrat al-insāniyya*], *because the Maker created man in* the most beautiful stature [95:4], *formed him in the most perfect form, and made his form the mirror of Himself"* (*Rasāʾil* 2:462).

423. Hadith found in Bukhārī (but not cited in the Ikhwān passage).

424. Ikhwān, *Rasāʾil* 2:475

425. Ikhwān, *Rasāʾil* 2:474–75.

426. Ikhwān, *Rasāʾil* 2:378–79.

427. As noted earlier, this sentence is from a sound *ḥadīth qudsī.*

428. Sanāʾī, *Dīwān* 968–69.

429. A sound hadith found in Muslim and other sources.

430. Bukhārī and Muslim.

431. Shiblī (Kalābādhī, *Taʿarruf*, chap. 49; not found in Arberry's translation).

432. Some manuscripts lack the second couplet; the whole quatrain has been ascribed to two later authors, Afḍal al-Dīn Kāshānī and Fakhr al-Dīn ʿIrāqī.

433. See note 131.

434. Part of a conversation of David with God, a version of which is given by Tustarī in his commentary on 6:54.

435. The second hemistich reads, "I am the slave of Your Khorasani wonders!" Abū Saʿīd recited the verse upon being asked whether poverty is more complete or wealth. He then explained that talk of "more complete" and "more perfect" is the language of the Shariah. When God turns His gaze on someone, his poverty turns into wealth, and his wealth into poverty (Ibn Munawwar, *Asrār* 313; *Secrets* 487).

436. A sound hadith.

437. Bukhārī and Muslim. The rest of the hadith reads, *"So every man shall have what he intended. When someone's emigration is for God and the Messenger, then his emigration is for God and the Messenger. But when someone's emigration is for a share of this world or a woman to marry, his emigration is to that for which he emigrated."*

438. See note 423.

439. This sentence and the four paragraphs that follow this paragraph are based on Ikhwān 2:380–82 (the treatise *Fī tarkīb al-jasad*).

440. This paragraph is based on Ikhwan 2:458 (the treatise *Fī qawl al-ḥukamāʾ inna al-insān ʿālam ṣaghīr*).

441. In this discussion Samʿānī mostly uses the Quranic term *qalb* (Persian *dil*), though the Ikhwān al-Ṣafāʾ use the philosophers' preferred term, namely *nafs*, soul.

442. This paragraph is based on Ikhwān 2:386.

443. These two paragraphs up to here are based on Ikhwān 2:458.

444. Hadith (Ṭabarānī, *Kabīr* 2:305, no. 2271).
445. Part of a sound hadith about the Day of Resurrection.
446. These two paragraphs up to here are based on Ikhwān 2:458.
447. These two paragraphs are based on Ikhwān 2:414–15 (the treatise *Fī tahdhīb al-nafs wa iṣlāḥ al-akhlāq*).
448. Allusion to the hadith *"I have a moment with God embraced by no proximate angel, nor any sent prophet"* (Sakhāwī, *Maqāṣid* 565, no. 926).
449. This sentence and the story about the king in the rest of the paragraph are translated from Ikhwān 2:460–61.
450. This saying is often quoted by critics of Sufism, such as Ibn al-Jawzī (*Talbīs* 1:304).
451. Qushayrī gives a brief version of this story in *Shawāhid* 13.
452. The quatrain is wrongly ascribed to Rūmī (Furūzānfar no. 932, Gamard no. 1348)
453. Ibn al-Jawzī, *Ṣifa* 2:294.
454. ʿUmar ibn ʿAbd al-ʿAzīz (Abū Nuʿaym, *Ḥilya* 5:319).
455. Mustamlī cites the saying anonymously in *Sharḥ-i taʿarruf* 1085. Rūzbihān considers it a hadith (*Maknūn* no. 139).
456. This may be Abu'l-Qāsim Ḥasan ibn Muḥammad ibn Ḥabīb (d. 1015), homilist and author of *ʿUqalāʾ al-majānīn* (Dhahabī, *Siyar* 1446, no. 1632)
457. Jaḥẓa (Thaʿālibī, *Luṭf* 14).
458. Junayd (RQ intro.; *Epistle* 4).
459. The full Quranic verse reads, *"Those are unbelievers who say that God is the third of three."*
460. Ibn ʿAsākir cites a different version of this saying, by ʿAlī Jarjarāʾī, as advice given to Bishr Ḥāfī (*Taʾrīkh* 43:294)
461. Hadith (Ibn ʿAsākir, *Taʾrīkh* 51:133).
462. See note 302.
463. Abu'l-Ḥasan Ḥuṣrī (Khaṭīb, *Muntakhab* 90).
464. For an Arabic version of this saying, see Maybudī's commentary on 2:34 (*Kashf* 1:159–60). Samʿānī provides a longer translation on p. 440.
465. First line of a *qaṣīda* by ʿAbdallāh ibn Dumayna (Marzūqī, *Sharḥ* 1:909).
466. Qushayrī cites a slightly expanded version of this saying in his commentary on 8:23 (*Laṭāʾif* 1:614).
467. Abū Nuʿaym (*Ḥilya* 10:367) says that Shiblī often used to recite this verse.
468. Yaḥyā ibn Muʿādh (Ḥaqqī, commentary on 17:111).
469. Muslim ibn Yasār (Ibn al-Jawzī, *Mudhish* 455).
470. Description of the heart of a person of faith from a hadith that mentions four sorts of heart (Abū Nuʿaym, *Ḥilya* 1:276).
471. Shiblī (RQ, the chapter on *ghayra*; *Epistle* 266).
472. Hadith found in Aḥmad.
473. Hadith found in Abū Dāwūd and Tirmidhī (Sakhāwī, *Maqāṣid* 600, no. 1013).
474. ʿAbbās ibn Aḥnaf, *Dīwān* 10; Qushayrī cites the verse in his commentary on 3:110 (*Laṭāʾif* 1:270).

475. ʿAṭṭār ascribes the second of these two lines to Junayd (*Tadhkira* 422; *Memorial* 332).
476. See note 366.
477. Ḥallāj, *Dīwān* 30.
478. See note 131.
479. Qushayrī, commentary on 6:2 (*Laṭāʾif* 1:460).
480. ʿAlī ibn Muḥammad Tihāmī, *Dīwān* 314.
481. Proverb (Thaʿālibī, *Tamthīl* 38).
482. RQ on Yūsuf ibn Ḥusayn (*Epistle* 52).
483. Allusion to the words of Adam and Eve after eating the forbidden fruit: *"Our Lord, we have wronged ourselves, and if Thou dost not forgive us, and have mercy upon us, we shall surely be among the losers"* (7:23).
484. See note 347.
485. These two sentences, included among the formulae of the ritual prayer, are said to be part of the Prophet's conversation with God during the *miʿrāj*. For a more detailed reference to this exchange, see p. 256.
486. Ghazālī cites this and a second anonymous line in *Iḥyāʾ* 4:97.
487. Sanāʾī, *Dīwān* 181.
488. Cited anonymously by RQ on *ṣaḥw* (*Epistle* 94).
489. Beginning with this paragraph, the next five pages leading up to the explanation of the verse *"Then he drew close . . ."* (53:8–9) on page 163, are mostly an abridgement of Mustamlī, *Sharḥ* 571–89 (chapter 12).
490. A sound hadith.
491. The account is found in many sources, such as Abū Yaʿlā, *Muʿjam* 42–43 (no. 10).
492. A sound hadith.
493. Qushayrī, commentary on 7:178 (*Laṭāʾif* 1:589).
494. See note 171.
495. As Mustamlī explains in the source of this passage (*Sharḥ* 578), "The Quran came by installments, and whenever something comes by installments, the Arabs call the installments 'stars.' "
496. Hadith found in Tirmidhī and Aḥmad.
497. Abū Nuʿaym, *Ḥilya* 1:276.
498. Bukhārī and others provide the text of the hadith on which this paragraph is based.
499. I could not find the source of this paragraph. Given that the first three clauses are found almost verbatim in the commentary of Naysābūrī (d. 1327) on 53:8, he must have used the same source.
500. Sulamī, *Ḥaqāʾiq*, commentary on 53:10.
501. See note 401.
502. Ḥusayn ibn ʿUbaydallāh (Ibn Ḥibbān, *Rawḍa* 191).
503. Ibn al-Muʿtazz (Thaʿālibī, *Rasāʾil* 67).
504. Shaʿrānī, *Ṭabaqāt* 1:155.
505. According to the standard account, God told Muhammad during the *miʿrāj* that

his community should perform the ritual prayer fifty times a day, but at Moses's insistence, Muhammad kept on asking God to reduce the number until it became five.

506. A sound hadith.

507. This and three other lines are found in the story "the various singing girls" (*al-jawārī al-mukhtalifa*) in *1,001 Nights.*

508. The quatrain is ascribed to Abū Saʿīd, with the two hemistiches of the first line reversed (*Asrār* 35; *Secrets* 103).

509. Majlisī, *Biḥār* 26:336.

510. See note 329.

511. See note 448.

512. See note 212.

513. See note 371.

514. This "Kullabite" formula in Kalam asserts that the divine attributes are neither God nor other than God. If they were the same as God, they would be identical with the Essence and no different from one another; if they were other than God, they would necessitate a multiplicity of eternal beings.

515. Labīd (p. xxii).

516. As ʿAṭṭār tells this story, the old man was Shiblī (*Tadhkira* 627–28).

517. The two sentences are commonly found in popular supplications, especially those relevant to surah 36 Yāsīn.

518. Sanāʾī, *Dīwān* 206, 208.

519. Abū Nuwās (Sarī, *Muḥibb* 1:97, no. 154).

520. Anonymous (Ibn al-ʿArabī, *Muḥāḍara* 2:437).

521. This famous divine saying, not found in the early hadith literature, goes on to say, *"so I created the creatures that I might be recognized."*

522. Mutanabbī, *Dīwān* 332.

523. A slave girl (Kharāʾiṭī, *Iʿtilāl* 2:308, no. 602).

524. Abu'l-Fatḥ Kushājim (Thaʿālibī, *Yatīma* 5:139).

525. See note 434.

526. A brief version of this story is told by Qushayrī (*Shawāhid* 80–81).

527. See note 325.

528. From a *ḥadīth qudsī* often mentioned in Sufi sources; Shi'ite sources sometimes trace it back to ʿAlī.

529. See note 23.

530. Qushayrī on 2:30 (*Laṭāʾif* 1:76).

531. Hadith found in Muslim.

532. See note 178.

533. This paragraph is based on Qushayrī's commentary on 2:30 (*Laṭāʾif* 1:75).

534. Qushayrī cites the verse anonymously in his commentary on 20:39 (*Laṭāʾif* 2:456).

535. Qushayrī on 2:30 (*Laṭāʾif* 1:76). The rest of the paragraph is partly based on Qushayrī's discussion of this verse.

536. In his commentary on this verse, Māwardī says that this view of Mujāhid is one of four basic interpretations.

537. A sound hadith that has several versions.

538. In traditional Islamic medicine, foods are graded from 0 to 5 on the basis of four qualities (hot, cold, wet, and dry), with 0 being neutral and 5 being poisonous. Both walnuts and dates are considered hot in the second or third degree.

539. See note 167.

540. Umm Ḥakīm bint Yaḥyā (Ibn ʿAsākir, *Taʾrīkh* 70:230).

541. Ḥuṣrī (*Nūr* 10) quotes a similar saying from the poet Kulthūm ibn ʿAmr.

542. Abū Nuʿaym cites the hadith in *Arbaʿūn* (no. 45).

543. Sanāʾī, *Dīwān* 878.

544. A slightly different version of this quatrain is ascribed to Rūmī (Furūzānfar no. 1444, Gamard no. 1724).

545. See note 379.

546. Words of Abū Ḥafṣ Ḥaddād addressed to Abū ʿUthmān Ḥīrī (Tawḥīdī, *Ṣadāqa* 55). Qushayrī ascribes an almost identical saying to Abū ʿUthmān himself (RQ on *tawba*; *Epistle* 113).

547. A saying of the litterateur Abū Bakr Muḥammad ibn ʿAbbās Khwārazmī (Thaʿālibī, *Yatīma* 4:226).

548. This paragraph and the verse that follows are taken from Qushayrī on 2:35 (*Laṭāʾif* 1:81).

549. Wrongly ascribed to Rūmī (Furūzānfar no. 523, Gamard no. 1033).

550. Buḥturī (Ẓāhirī, *Zahra* 63).

551. Thaʿālibī (*Yatīma* 4:302) says that this is a saying of the *ḥukamāʾ*, the men of wisdom or philosophers.

552. See note 316.

553. RQ on *khushūʿ* (*Epistle* 165).

554. RQ on *khushūʿ* (*Epistle* 163).

555. On p. 108 Samʿānī ascribes this saying to his father.

556. Abū Muḥammad Ṭāhir ibn Ḥusayn Makhzūmī (Thaʿālibī, *Yatīma* 2:141).

557. Bassām ibn ʿAbdallāh (Qurṭubī, *Jāmiʿ*, commentary on 53:43).

558. Samawʾal ibn ʿĀdiyā (Samuel bin ʿAdiya) (Qālī, *Amālī* 1:269).

559. See note 448.

560. See note 410.

561. Qushayrī cites this verse in his commentary on 32:7 (*Laṭāʾif* 3:140); it is by Muḥammad ibn Wuhayb (Nuwayrī, *Nihāya* 2:92).

562. Reference to the stories of the Companions of the Cave and Balaam Beor.

563. A sound *ḥadīth qudsī*.

564. The hadith, found in Tirmidhī, is cited on p. 325.

565. Hadith found in Ibn Māja and other sources.

566. Maybudī (*Kashf al-asrār* 10:272) mentions this as the second couplet of a quatrain. The first is this: "Many creatures are seeking your road, / a world has been killed in awe of your army!"

567. Typically ascribed to the Prophet, the saying is not considered authentic by the Hadith experts.

568. Cf. the similar passages on pp. 191 and 379.
569. Hadith found in Aḥmad and Dārimī.
570. Both Bayhaqī (*I'tiqād* 51) and Qushayrī (*Sharḥ* 137) mention both meanings, though Bayhaqī takes the word as a synonym of *barr* rather than *muḥsin*. Qushayrī adds that *laṭīf* in the meaning of "subtle" or "fine" (as opposed to *kathīf*, "dense" or "coarse") does not apply to God. Gentleness (*luṭf*) is typically understood as the complement of severity (*qahr*).
571. Qurṭubī ascribes a version of this saying to Junayd in his commentary on 3:19.
572. By the Companion Ḥassān ibn Thābit.
573. The first of these two hemistiches is from a *qaṣīda* by Mutanabbī, *Dīwān* 252.
574. The verse is ascribed to a number of poets, most commonly Yazīd ibn al-Ṭathariyya.
575. Words heard from the Unseen by one of the Prophet's Companions before the beginning of his mission (Bayhaqī, *Dalā'il* 2:110).
576. Allusion to Quran 15:17–18: *"And guarded them from every outcast satan, except him who listens by stealth, and then a clear flaming star follows him."*
577. Part of the hadith quoted on p. 42 (note 120).
578. Hadith found in Aḥmad and other sources.
579. Hadith (Aḥmad).
580. See note 274.
581. See the account of the *mi'rāj* on p. 256.
582. See p. 163 (note 498).
583. Reference to a hadith found in Ibn Māja beginning with the words *"I am the chieftain of Adam's children, without boasting"* and going on to say that, on the Day of Resurrection, *"the banner of praise will be in my hand."*
584. Variant of a hadith found in Bukhārī.
585. Part of the hadith cited on p. 153 (note 472).
586. Hadith (Ibn Māja and Tirmidhī).
587. Compare the well-known line of Ibn al-Fāriḍ (d. 1234), also put into the mouth of the Prophet: *"Though in form I am Adam's son, / a meaning within him bears witness that I am his father"* (Cf. Homerin, *'Umar*, v. 631).
588. The reference is to this hadith found in Muslim: *"I was given five things that were given to no one before me: I was aided by terror at a month's journey; the earth was made a place of prostration and purity for me, so let a man of my community pray wherever he may be when prayer time reaches him; spoils were made lawful to me, and they were made lawful to no one before me; I was given intercession; and the prophet before me was sent specifically to his people, but I was sent to all people."* Sam'ānī cites a shorter version of the hadith later on in this chapter (p. 200).
589. Hadith (Aḥmad).
590. Mutanabbī, *Dīwān* 392.
591. Perhaps a loose translation of a hadith in Aḥmad saying that when he was born, his mother had a vision of a light emerging from her and illuminating the castles of Syria.
592. Ibn 'Asākir, *Ta'rīkh* 4:82.

593. This *ḥadīth qudsī* has come in a number of versions, though it is not found in the earliest sources.

594. See note 445.

595. This sentence is taken from a long conversation between Moses and God. Ṭabarī cites it in his commentary on 7:150 (and traces it back to Qatāda).

596. A sound hadith.

597. See note 589.

598. During the Battle of Uhud, some of the Companions asked the Prophet to supplicate against the enemy, but he responded instead with this prayer (Bayhaqī, *Shu ʿab* 2:164).

599. Version of a sound hadith concerning the resurrection.

600. The hadith is found in Bukhārī.

601. Allusion to the miracle of splitting the moon (discussed in commentaries on 54:1).

602. The hadith is found in Majlisī, *Biḥār* 16:408, but not in the standard Sunni sources.

603. A sound hadith about Dajjāl, found in Muslim and other sources, includes the sentence *"God is my vicegerent over every Muslim."*

604. According to Kutubī (*Fawāt* 1:43) the lines are by Ibrāhīm ibn Kayghalagh.

605. Abu'l-Qāsim ʿAlī ibn Mūsā (Bākharzī, *Dumya* 2:737).

606. Ibn Māja.

607. See note 212.

608. Muslim and other sources.

609. Jaʿfar Ṣādiq (Rāghib, *Muḥāḍarāt* 2:411).

610. A sound hadith.

611. See note 578.

612. A sound *ḥadīth qudsī.*

613. See note 448.

614. This seems to be a loose translation of a saying of Jaʿfar given by Bayhaqī (*Shu ʿab* 2:184, no. 1492).

615. A standard interpretation of the meaning of the verse, sometimes attributed to Ibn ʿAbbās.

616. Hubal was the most prominent of the gods worshiped by the Quraysh.

617. Two cities said to exist at the two ends of the earth.

618. Reference to one of several interpretations of the two letters *ṭāhā*, according to which they are a form of *ṭa ʾa*, which is the imperative of *waṭa ʾ*, meaning to step. See Qushayrī on 20:1–2 (*Laṭā ʾif* 2:445).

619. That is, the author's eldest brother.

620. ʿAbd al-Karīm provides a brief account of him under the name Zāhirī in *Ansāb* 3:126. He says that both his father and grandfather heard Hadith from him and that he himself had heard from him by the intermediary of several scholars including his uncle Ḥasan.

621. The hadith is found in Tirmidhī with the same early narrators.

622. A sound hadith found in many variants.

623. *Kakh-kakh* is a sound used in Persian to warn children not to do something. Bukhārī provides the text of the hadith to which Samʿānī is referring (while noting that the word is Persian):

"*Ḥasan the son of ʿAlī took a date from the charitable gifts and put it in his mouth. God's Messenger said,* 'Kakh-kakh, *take it out! Do you not know that we do not eat the charitable gifts?*' "

624. Both Bukhārī and Muslim provide the text of the hadith. The Prophet said the words when Jābir prepared food for those working on the dike to protect Medina.

625. The hadith comes in various sources, though it is generally considered weak.

626. See note 160.

627. In the old orthography, one dot was used to indicate both *b* and *p*, so nothing specified the *p* but the context (*p* later came to be differentiated from *b* by using three dots instead of one).

628. ʿAṭṭār gives a rather different version of this saying in *Tadhkira* 792.

629. The saying is attributed to the Prophet, for instance, by Abshīhī (*Mustaṭraf* 307).

630. Version of a divine saying traced back to Abū Yazīd (Abū Nuʿaym, *Ḥilya* 10:40).

631. This is part of a well-known hadith, usually considered weak, that begins, "*The first thing God created was the Intellect.*" Ṭabarānī gives the text in *Awsaṭ* 2:235–36, no. 1845; 7:190–91, no. 7241.

632. Sanāʾī, *Dīwān* 902.

633. Būshanjī (Ibn ʿAsākir, *Taʾrīkh* 41:216).

634. Ḥuṣrī (Hujwīrī, *Kashf* 243).

635. "One of them" (RQ on *ḥasad*; *Epistle* 171).

636. Labīd ibn ʿUṭārud (Ibn ʿAbd al-Barr, *Bahja* 90).

637. From a hadith (Ibn Kathīr, *Bidāya* 1:184).

638. Translation of Quran 7:15: "*Said He, 'Thou art among the ones reprieved.'* "

639. Ibn al-Jawzī, *Ṣifa* 2:292.

640. From a poem by Ibn al-Muʿtazz (Thaʿālibī, *Rasāʾil* 1:22).

641. His misstep was to look at a woman and become entranced by her, as Samʿānī explains on p. 314. The story of David and Bathsheba is told by commentators like Ṭabarī on Quran 38:24.

642. Retelling of a hadith about a youth named Buhlūl; for an eloquent version of the Arabic text, see Ibn Bābawayh, *Amālī* 97–100.

643. Part of a divine saying that Ghazālī traces back to Kaʿb al-Aḥbār, who quotes it from the "Torah" (*Iḥyāʾ* 4:324; *Love* 91).

644. See note 92.

645. Abū ʿAṭāʾ Sindī (Marzūqī, *Sharḥ* 44–45).

646. Qushayrī tells the story in *Shawāhid* 124.

647. See note 352.

648. Sanāʾī, *Dīwān* 485, 488.

649. Bukhārī and Muslim.

650. The anecdote is from Mustamlī, *Sharḥ* 595.

651. A *ḥadīth qudsī* going back to Jaʿfar Ṣādiq (*Ḥilya* 3:194).

652. The Arabic of the story is found in RQ on *karāmāt* (*Epistle* 376).

653. RQ on *karāmāt* (*Epistle* 378).

654. Sanāʾī, *Dīwān* 1136.

655. Sanāʾī, *Dīwān* 1148.

656. Qushayrī has a version of this anecdote in *Shawāhid* 96.
657. Qushayrī, commentary on 18:31 (*Laṭāʾif* 2:394–95).
658. Qushayrī (Ṣafadī, *Wāfī* 19:64).
659. Sanāʾī, *Sayr* 214–16. For the two sayings in the last couplet, see note 108.
660. Sanāʾī, *Sayr* 216
661. Qushayrī, commentary on 2:33 and 2:34 (*Laṭāʾif* 1:78–79).
662. Sanāʾī, *Dīwān* 482–84.
663. Qushayrī, *Sharḥ* 142; Bayhaqī, *Iʿtiqād* 51.
664. According to a *ḥadīth qudsī*, these are God's words to Gabriel when the latter wanted to punish Pharaoh at once for saying, *"And what is the Lord of the worlds?"* (26:23). Ibn Abi'l-Dunyā, *ʿUqūbāt* 164 (no. 244).
665. For the Arabic of this story, see Qushayrī, *Sharḥ* 143.
666. For an Arabic version of this story, see Ibn al-Jawzī, *Tabṣira* 264–66.
667. The saying is found without ascription in Ṭāʾī, *Arbaʿīn* 179.
668. A version of this saying of Rāzī: *"Glory be to Him who abases the servant through sin and abases the sin through forgiveness! My God, if You pardon, You are the best of the merciful; and if You chastise, You are not a wrongdoer"* (Ṭarṭūshī, *Sirāj* 77).
669. Ibn al-Jawzī, *Ṣifa* 2:293.
670. Qushayrī on 2:35 (*Laṭāʾif* 1:81).
671. Reference to ʿUmar's setting out to kill Muḥammad. For more on this well-known story, see pp. 380–82.
672. Sanāʾī, *Dīwān* 1006.
673. Another version of this quatrain is found in Rūmī's *Dīwān* (Furūzānfar no. 1001, Gamard no. 1951).
674. In Firdawsī's *Shāhnāma* Fereydun killed the tyrant Ḍaḥḥāk with the aid of Kaveh the blacksmith and then ruled in peace for five hundred years.
675. Sanāʾī, *Dīwān* 704–7.
676. Anonymous (Thaʿālibī, *Tamthīl* 325).
677. Hadith found in Aḥmad.
678. Ṭabarānī cites the hadith (*Kabīr* 8:257, no. 7868).
679. Hadith found in Aḥmad and Tirmidhī.
680. Ibn Abi'l-Dunyā, *Mutamannīn* 26–27, no. 12.
681. The usual version of the saying is: *"Would that I were ashes scattered by the winds"* (Dhahabī, *Siyar* 2935, no. 4305).
682. These three clauses—"all is He, all is in Him, and all is from Him"—became prominent in later discussions of the notion of *waḥdat al-wujūd*, which was famously criticized by Shaykh Aḥmad Sirhindī (d. 1624), who defined it as meaning "All is He." He held up the other two clauses as correct theological positions. Maybudī speaks of these three assertions as ascending levels of *tawḥīd* (see Maybudī, *Kashf* 176, 358; Chittick, *Divine* 221).
683. Shiblī. See note 158.
684. Abu'l-ʿAtāhiya (Ẓāhirī, *Zahra* 118).

685. Commentators on Quran 11:42–43 generally say that the name of Noah's son who drowned was Kanʿān (Canaan); some, like Fakhr al-Dīn Rāzī, add that his name is also said to have been Yām.

686. That is, Pharaoh's wife Āsiya, mentioned, though not by name, in Quran 66:11; in a hadith narrated by both Bukhārī and Muslim she and Mary are said to have been two women who achieved perfection (*kamāl*), along with "many men."

687. Cf. Quran 12:9–10.

688. Probably based on a saying by Mālik ibn Dīnār (Abū Nuʿaym, *Ḥilya* 2:377). The first sentence is the same, but the second reads, "*Wherever* [the pearl] *may be, its beauty goes along with it.*"

689. A sound hadith.

690. In his commentary on 78:40, Ṭabarī cites this hadith: On the Day of Resurrection "*God will muster all the creatures—all crawling things, flyers, and men. To the beasts and the birds He will say, 'Be dust!' At that point the unbeliever will say, 'Oh, would that I were dust'* [78:40]."

691. Proverb (Ābī, *Nathr* 6:315).

692. Sharīf Raḍī, *Dīwān* 315.

693. Khayyām (note 172).

694. Sanāʾī, *Dīwān* 586.

695. See note 567.

696. Ṣanawbarī (Thaʿālibī, *Tamthīl* 108).

697. See note 604.

698. ʿIzz al-Dawla (Thaʿālibī, *Yatīma* 2:260).

699. See note 121.

700. Hadith (note 461).

701. The mythic salamander walks through fire without being burned.

702. Hadith found in Aḥmad and Ibn Māja.

703. Proverbial (Thaʿālibī, *Yatīma* 1:140).

704. Mutanabbī, *Dīwān* 102.

705. This is the last hemstitch of a quatrain ascribed to Rūmī (Furūzānfar no. 921, Gamard no. 1580).

706. Mutanabbī, *Dīwān* 571.

707. ʿAbbās ibn Mirdās (Baṣrī, *Ḥamāsa* 1:13, no. 28).

708. Translated from Qushayrī, *Sharḥ* 145–46.

709. Words of God to David (RQ on *dhikr*; *Epistle* 236).

710. Qushayrī says that the saying (with *abrār*, "pious," instead of *aḥrār*, "free") is well known (*Miʿrāj* 77).

711. ʿAṭṭār gives a somewhat different version of this saying in his account of Kharaqānī in *Tadhkira* 687.

712. Proverb; in other words, waiting is like being tortured to death.

713. Aḥmad and Tirmidhī.

714. Nasāʾī and other sources.

715. Abū Dāwūd.

716. See note 211.
717. Bukhārī and Muslim.
718. Bayhaqī, *Shu ʿab* 2:164 (no. 1445).
719. Ābī, *Nathr* 4:40.
720. See note 465.
721. Jaḥẓa (Irbilī, *Ṭayf* 13).
722. ʿAyn al-Quḍāt Hamadānī also mentions the line (*Nāma-hā* 2:174).
723. Qushayrī tells this anecdote about Zulaykhā instead of Jacob (*Shawāhid* 4).
724. The anonymous saying usually has *"malady of the hearts of the noble."*
725. Rāghib (*Muḥāḍarāt* 2:43) ascribes this saying from Plato's *Phaedrus* to "one of the philosophers."
726. "*Love is the Real's net*" is a saying attributed to Abū Saʿīd (*Asrār* 310; *Secrets* 481). As cited here the saying is attributed to Aḥmad Rifāʿī (d. 1182), though he must have been quoting it.
727. Muslim.
728. Hadith (Samarqandī, *Tanbīh* 87, no. 77).
729. Bahdalī (Thaʿālibī, *Yatīma* 5:28).
730. Reference to Noah's call to his son to join him on the ark (Quran 11:42).
731. Hadith (Ibn Shāhīn, *Faḍāʾil* 37).
732. Versions of this hadith are found in Aḥmad, Tirmidhī, and other sources.
733. Manṣūr ibn Ismāʿīl Tamīmī (Khaṭṭābī, *ʿUzla* 79).
734. Version of a hadith found in Bukhārī and Muslim.
735. Bukhārī and other sources.
736. See note 326.
737. Ibn Māja and others.
738. Ibn Māja.
739. Bukhārī.
740. Abū ʿAlī Raqqī (Ājurrī, *Ghurabāʾ* 27).
741. Another reference to the story of Bathsheba (note 641). As Thaʿlabī tells it (*Lives* 468ff.), Satan took the form of a golden dove and interrupted David's devotions. When the dove flew to a window, David went after it, but it flew away. He looked to see where it went and his eyes fell on Bathsheba, bathing in a neighborhood garden.
742. The hadith is well known, though usually considered weak.
743. Bukhārī and other sources.
744. Muslim.
745. The hadith is found in Muslim and other standard sources. For several versions, see Ibn Kathīr, *Bidāya* 1:191–99.
746. Kharāʾiṭī, *Iʿtilāl* 257 (no. 520).
747. The unnamed scholars in question seem to be those from whom Mustamlī (*Sharḥ* 592–94) draws in a discussion that is summarized in the following paragraphs (down to the poem by Sanāʾī).
748. See note 492.
749. Sanāʾī, *Dīwān* 163. Kayqubad, Bahman, and Parviz are ancient Persian kings. Ḥajjāj ibn Yūsuf (d. 714) was an Umayyad commander of legendary cruelty; he famously conquered Mecca in 692.

750. Mustamlī, *Sharḥ* 595.
751. See note 492.
752. These three paragraphs are from Mustamlī, *Sharḥ* 591.
753. These five paragraphs are from Mustamlī, *Sharḥ* 595–96.
754. This and the next eight paragraphs, though not the verse, are derived from Mustamlī, *Sharḥ* 600–4.
755. That is, everyone else will say, *"My soul, my soul"* (see p. 252). This and the next eleven paragraphs (up to the quote from Qushayrī) are derived from Mustamlī, *Sharḥ* 627–31.
756. The Prophet prohibited his wives from remarrying after his death, though widows are generally encouraged to remarry.
757. Qushayrī (RQ on *maʿrifa*; *Epistle* 321).
758. This and the next sixteen paragraphs (up to "Some have said") are based on Mustamlī, *Sharḥ* 608–11.
759. For another version of this hadith, see Ibn ʿAbd Rabbih, *ʿIqd* 5:132.
760. See note 717.
761. The three sentences in this dialogue (beginning with *"The felicitations"*) are recited during the seated portion of the ritual prayer.
762. This and the next nine paragraphs (up to "You can also say") are based mainly on Mustamlī, *Sharḥ* 614–15.
763. The Prophet's words to Bilāl when he wanted him to give the call to prayer (Aḥmad, Abū Dāwūd).
764. See note 120.
765. This and the following paragraph are from Mustamlī, *Sharḥ* 599.
766. A weak *ḥadīth qudsī* says, *"By My exaltedness and majesty, I will not chastise in the Fire anyone named by your name, O Muḥammad!"* Mustamlī concludes with a sentence that clarifies the relevance of the second paragraph to the first: "If a name given by a mother and father can be the cause of deliverance, then with even more reason Muḥammad's gaze can be the cause of deliverance."
767. Bukhārī, the chapter on the *miʿrāj*.
768. In his commentary 53:14 Ṭabarī ascribes this explanation to *"one of the folk of knowledge among the folk of interpretation."*
769. Hadith found in Ṭabarānī (*Awsaṭ* 5:64, no. 4679) and other sources.
770. No. 17, the All-Forgiving.
771. Abū Firās (Thaʿālibī, *Yatīma* 1:75).
772. Part of a supplication recited by the Prophet after each prescribed prayer (Bukhārī and Muslim).
773. Sanāʾī, *Dīwān* 186, 185. The first verse alludes to Bilāl, the last to Adam and Iblis.
774. Ḥātim Ṭāʾī (Kharāʾiṭī, *Makārim* 96, no. 253).
775. Muslim and other sources.
776. Lālkāʾī, *Karāmāt* 228. Abū Rayḥāna was a Companion.
777. Kahmas (d. 766) was a transmitter of Hadith.
778. The phrases are said to be part of a description of Sufism by Abū Yazīd (Maḥmūd, *Sulṭān* 110).

779. Words ascribed to hell in a well-known hadith, though it is considered weak.

780. Sanā'ī, *Dīwān* 496. The five daily prayers are being contrasted with the four elements of this world.

781. Sanā'ī, *Dīwān* 307–8.

782. A summary translation of Qushayrī's remarks in *Sharḥ* 150.

783. Labīd (p. xxii).

784. Tirmidhī.

785. A sound hadith.

786. Inscription on the ring of the sixth-century Himyarite king, Sayf ibn Dhī Yazan (Abshīhī, *Mustaṭraf* 257).

787. Qushayrī explains these words of Shiblī in *Shawāhid* 108.

788. For the Arabic of this account, see Ibn ʿAsākir, *Ta'rīkh* 41:380–81. ʿAlī ibn Ḥusayn was the Prophet's great-grandson and the revered author of *al-Ṣaḥīfat al-sajjādiyya*.

789. Words of God addressed to David (Ibn ʿAsākir, *Ta'rīkh* 36:335).

790. See note 434.

791. Part of a conversation between Moses and God cited by Bayhaqī and others (Sakhāwī, *Maqāṣid* 167–68).

792. This seems to be a conflation of two hadiths, nos. 4 and 12 among the thirteen that Ibn Kathīr cites in his commentary on 4:48.

793. Hadith found in Aḥmad.

794. Ibn ʿĀ'isha (Zamakhsharī, *Rabīʿ* 3:278).

795. Proverb (RQ on *zuhd*; *Epistle* 135).

796. Called a hadith in some late sources, this is more likely a Sufi saying.

797. A sound hadith, uttered when the Prophet was negotiating with Abū Sufyān for the surrender of Mecca.

798. The hadith is in Bukhārī. ʿAbdallāh ibn al-Khaṭal was one of four men who were executed after the conquest of Mecca.

799. Aḥmad ibn Abī Fanan (Sarī, *Muḥibb* 1:296).

800. Beginning with this paragraph and continuing to the end of this chapter, the text is abridged from Mustamlī, *Sharḥ* 618–20.

801. The hadith, including the portions cited later, is found in many sources, such as the *Ṣaḥīḥ* of Ibn Ḥibbān.

802. *Ḥadīth qudsī*, Bukhārī and Muslim.

803. The saying is ascribed to Jesus (Zamakhsharī, *Rabīʿ* 2:39).

804. The proverb, which is said to have been uttered by the Prophet (ʿAskarī, *Jamhara* 2:162–63), alludes to someone who has surpassed all others.

805. RQ on *tawḥīd* (*Epistle* 311) cites this saying anonymously.

806. The hadith is well known though considered weak.

807. Sanā'ī, *Sayr* 189.

808. See note 448.

809. The two hadiths are found in Bukhārī, Aḥmad, and other sources.

810. Bayhaqī and others give the hadith.
811. From accounts of the *miʿrāj* (e.g., Khargūshī, *Sharaf* 2:177).
812. See note 689.
813. Hadith (Bayhaqī, *Shuʿab* 2:125).
814. Allusion to this hadith, given by Ṭabarānī and others: *"Seek out the neighbor before the house and the companion before the road."*
815. *"I ask Thee for the Garden"* is found in the hadith literature (Abū Dāwūd), but apparently not the second clause.
816. Some of the phrasing in this paragraph, including the last sentence, seems to be drawn from Qushayrī on 7:143 (*Laṭāʾif* 1:565–66).
817. The Arabic here is from RQ on *ghayra* (*Epistle* 265.)
818. See note 56.
819. See note 110.
820. This paragraph is derived from the very beginning of Ghazālī's chapter on love (*Iḥyāʾ* 4:293–94; *Love* 1).
821. Sanāʾī, *Dīwān* 883.
822. The hadith, found in Tirmidhī, is addressed to ʿAlī and refers to an occasion when a beautiful woman walked by.
823. Ābī (*Nathr* 4:165) gives a different version of this saying as a proverb.
824. Sanāʾī, *Dīwān* 26. Chosroes Parviz (d. 628), here a symbol for God as King, was the last great monarch of the Sassanid empire.
825. In his commentary on 38:21 (*Laṭāʾif* 3:250) Qushayrī ascribes this saying to "the sages."
826. The sentence alludes to a saying of ʿAlī cited on p. 359: *"What, should I kill my own killer?"* ʿAlī uttered the words after he told someone that he would be killed by ʿAbd al-Raḥmān ibn Muljam and was asked why he did not kill him first (Majlisī, *Biḥār* 42:196).
827. Hadith found in Tirmidhī.
828. This story is told in commentaries on 6:76, such as Ṭabarī and Manṣūr Samʿānī.
829. Mutanabbī, *Dīwān* 352.
830. Summary of Qushayrī, *Sharḥ* 156.
831. Version of a saying by Abū Bakr Warrāq (RQ on *faqr*; *Epistle* 289)
832. Ghazālī cites the hadith in *Iḥyāʾ* 4:196.
833. The hadith has come in various versions in Muslim, Tirmidhī, and other sources.
834. Hujwīrī gives a brief version of this anecdote in *Kashf* 34.
835. Muslim.
836. Qushayrī, *Manthūr* 66.
837. Qushayrī, *Manthūr* 66.
838. Qushayrī, *Manthūr* 65–66.
839. In Qushayrī, *Manthūr* 69, this is a definition of aspiration (*himma*).
840. In Qushayrī, *Manthūr* 68, this is a definition of *taṣawwuf.*
841. Kalābādhī tells an anecdote to this effect about ʿAbdallāh Qashshāʿ (*Doctrine* 151); some of the explanation in this paragraph is inspired by Mustamlī, *Sharḥ* 1751.

842. A sound hadith with many variants.
843. Qushayrī, *Manthūr* 68.
844. Qushayrī, *Manthūr* 68.
845. The saying is by Ḥallāj, though with "Sufi" instead of "poor man" (RQ on *taṣawwuf*; *Epistle* 289).
846. Qushayrī provides a version of this saying in *Shawāhid* 96.
847. In his commentary on 12:26, Sulamī ascribes this saying to Wāsiṭī; Qushayrī ascribes it to Shiblī (*Sharḥ* 218).
848. From the well-known Hadith of Gabriel (Muslim).
849. See, for example, Ṭabarī's commentary on the verse, in which he cites a number of hadiths to this effect. In his commentary Samʿānī's father Manṣūr cites one hadith in this meaning.
850. A sound hadith.
851. See note 786.
852. Version of a poem by Sayf al-Dawla Ḥamdānī (Thaʿālibī, *Yatīma* 1:55).
853. Part of the already cited hadith that begins *"Every night God descends"* (note 182).
854. Except for the first, these definitions are from Qushayrī, *Mukhtaṣar* 22–23.
855. The division into these three types—the wrongdoers, the moderate, and the preceders—is derived from Quran 35:32 and is much discussed by commentators. See, for example, Maybudī's remarks in *Kashf al-asrār* (*Unveiling* 409–11).
856. This and the following two poems are quoted from Qushayrī (*Mukhtaṣar* 27–28); the prose passages in between are mostly translated or quoted from the same place.
857. This saying of Junayd (RQ on *taṣawwuf*; *Epistle* 290) is not from *Mukhtaṣar*.
858. The editor has removed this ghazal from his working revised edition, though it is found in some of the manuscripts. Its style conforms with other ghazals that seem to be by the author (see the list on p. lxxv n. 142).
859. See note 87.
860. Dhu'l-Nūn Miṣrī (Bayhaqī, *Zuhd* 225, no. 585).
861. All four sayings are cited as anonymous aphorisms by Thaʿālibī (*Tamthīl* 8–9).
862. Ibn al-Rūmī (Thaʿālibī, *Khāṣṣ* 179).
863. These two paragraphs are from Qushayrī on 42:19 (*Laṭāʾif* 3:349).
864. Ṭabarsī says almost the same thing in his commentary on 47:15.
865. Abū Dāwūd and Tirmidhī.
866. Fattanī says that this saying is wrongly ascribed to the Prophet (*Mawḍūʿāt* 228).
867. See note 434.
868. This may be a reference to a hadith according to which Abraham used to supplicate against everyone he saw disobeying God. Then God revealed to him, *"O Abraham, let My servants be. Any servant of Mine who falls short is one of three: Either he will turn back toward Me and I will turn toward him; or he will ask forgiveness of Me and I will forgive him; or there will emerge from his loins someone who will worship Me"* (Ibn al-Wazīr, *Īthār* 201).
869. The rebuke of Moses is mentioned by Ghazālī (*Iḥyāʾ* 4:545).
870. The phrase in brackets seems to have been dropped (see p. 61).

871. Shiblī (note 187).
872. See note 363.
873. The reference is to Waḥshī ibn Ḥarb, an Abyssinian slave who killed the Prophet's uncle Ḥamza at the Battle of Uhud and was later accepted into Islam by the Prophet.
874. See note 715.
875. This and the next two paragraphs are translated and quoted from Māwardī's commentary on 19:71.
876. Reference to the hadith cited four paragraphs later.
877. See note 779.
878. For reasons about which there is a good deal of discussion in the commentaries, Job swore an oath during his illness to beat his wife with one hundred lashes, and this verse is telling him to fulfill his oath without harming his wife.
879. Qushayrī on 19:71 (*Laṭāʾif* 2:438), quoting a hadith that is also found in Bayḍāwī's commentary on this verse.
880. Qushayrī on 21:103 (*Laṭāʾif* 2:525).
881. Rāzī cites this saying in his commentary on 17:85 (*Mafātīḥ* 21:404).
882. Shiblī (Thaʿālibī, *Iʿjāz* 123).
883. See note 429.
884. See note 228.
885. These views may be translations of some of Māwardī's comments on the verse.
886. Qushayrī on 33:72 (*Laṭāʾif* 3:173).
887. Ibn ʿAṭāʾ (Sulamī, *Ḥaqāʾiq* 33:72).
888. The quotes from Ḥasan Baṣrī and Mujāhid are from Māwardī on 33:72.
889. This may be an allusion to a saying of Ibn ʿAbbās according to which God gazes on the Guarded Tablet 360 times a day (Thaʿlabī, *Kashf* 55:29).
890. Perhaps inspired by the saying of Shiblī, *"Where are the heavens and the earths that I may carry them on one of my eyelashes?"* (Maybudī, *Kashf* on 29:19).
891. See note 302.
892. Hadith found in Tirmidhī and Aḥmad.
893. Muslim.
894. Tirmidhī.
895. Dhahabī (*Kabāʾir* 107) ascribes an Arabic version of this story to Wahab ibn Munabbih.
896. Ḥaqqī gives a longer version of this saying in his commentary on 40:60.
897. Abū Nuʿaym, *Ḥilya* 8:15–16.
898. Wahab ibn Munabbih (Ibn al-Mubārak, *Zuhd* 109, no. 322).
899. Jaʿfar Ṣādiq (Ibn Ḥamdūn, *Tadhkira* 4:105).
900. This sentence is from Qushayrī's commentary on the verse (*Laṭāʾif* 3:313).
901. Bayhaqī, *Shuʿab* 1:457, no. 705.
902. Hadith (Aḥmad and Ibn Māja).
903. Hadith (Aḥmad and Abū Dāwūd).
904. A weak hadith.

905. Qushayrī cites the verse in his commentary on 7:143 (*Laṭā ʾif* 1:566).
906. Muslim.
907. Tirmidhī.
908. Translation of the verse, *"So that God may forgive thee thy sins set forward and put behind"* (48:2).
909. A sound hadith, typically mentioned as the Prophet's response to God's revelation of 48:2 and explained as meaning that forgiveness does not take away religious obligations.
910. Part of the conversation with God during the *mi ʿrāj* (see p. 256).
911. For the Arabic of the story, see Abshīhī, *Mustaṭraf* 365.
912. In Abū Nu ʿaym (*Ḥilya* 10:62) these two lines are given as part of a nine-line poem recited by Yaḥyā ibn Mu ʿādh Rāzī.
913. See note 302.
914. Bukhārī and Muslim.
915. Ibn ʿAsākir, *Ta ʾrīkh* 3:234 (the woman from Banū Ghifār).
916. *Ḥadīth qudsī* from Dārimī, Aḥmad, and other sources.
917. Muslim. According to one explanation of this hadith, when a Companion died, the Prophet would ask if he had any debts. If not, he would perform the funeral prayer over him, and if so, he would tell his Companions to perform it. After wealth began to come by way of conquest, he changed this policy (ʿAsqalānī, *Fatḥ* 12:10).
918. These two paragraphs are partly from Qushayrī on 21:87 (*Laṭā ʾif* 2:518). Qushayrī also writes that when Jonah asked the king why he had chosen him, he answered, *"God revealed to my prophet, 'Tell your king to choose someone to be sent to Nineveh with the message.' So it weighed down on Jonah that the king had chosen him."*
919. The five paragraphs to here are from Māwardī's commentary on 21:87.
920. This paragraph is from Qushayrī on 21:87 (*Laṭā ʾif* 2:519).
921. This paragraph is partly quoted and partly paraphrased from Qushayrī (*Laṭā ʾif* 2:519).
922. For a different version of this saying, see commentaries on 37:141, such as Ṭabarī or Ibn Kathīr.
923. The verse refers to the Prophet's falling in love with the wife of Zayd, an event about which Sam ʿānī talks on pp. 326—27.
924. Hadith found in Muslim.
925. Hadiths to this effect are well known but considered weak. Ibn Qayyim (*Rūḥ* 453–510) reviews scholarly opinions for and against the precreation of spirits and concludes in effect that it all depends on definitions.
926. Ibn Qayyim (*Rūḥ* 535) mentions that traditions about the creation of Adam say that the spirit "*entered unwillingly and will leave unwillingly.*"
927. According to a hadith recorded by Tirmidhī, when God blew the spirit into Adam's clay, he sneezed. Adam said, *"The praise belongs to God,"* and God responded by saying, *"May God have mercy on you."*
928. The Samanid dynasty ruled much of Khorasan in the ninth and tenth centuries.
929. Bukhārī.
930. Qushayrī says almost the same thing toward the beginning of RQ on *khalwa* (*Epistle* 122).

931. Bukhārī.

932. Muslim.

933. Bukhārī.

934. This may be a reference to a hadith found in several standard sources according to which God asked the Prophet if he knew why the angels were disputing among themselves (as mentioned in Quran 38:69). He replied that he did not. God then placed His hand on his breast, and, he said, *"I came to know everything in the heavens and everything in the earth."*

935. Reference to Quran 18:94.

936. This sentence—*az māst ka bar māst*—is proverbial, signifying that people receive their just deserts. Its oldest mention may be in a poem by Nāṣir Khusraw (*Dīwān*, no. 260), which puts it into the mouth of an eagle shot from the sky after it had delighted in its exalted status.

937. This along with the following eighteen paragraphs (until the discussion comes back to *And when thy Lord said to the angels*) is taken almost verbatim from Māwardī's commentary on 2:30.

938. Weak hadiths to this effect are cited by commentators.

939. Bayhaqī, *Sunan* 10:209 (no. 20700).

940. Jarīr, *Dīwān* 77.

941. The paragraph is partly translated and partly quoted from Qushayrī on 85:14 (*Laṭā'if* 3:712).

942. RQ on *maḥabba* (*Epistle* 330).

943. The text of this saying in RQ (*Epistle* 330) and other sources has *mujānaba* (avoiding) in place of *muḥāraba* (fighting against).

944. Aḥwaṣ (Itlīdī, *Nawādir* 1:293).

945. Kaykawus was a legendary Persian emperor celebrated in Firdawsī's *Shāhnāma*. Samʿānī mentions his name to highlight love's kingly status (and because the name rhymes with *kūs*, "kettle-drum").

946. See note 94.

947. See note 593.

948. See note 595.

949. Tirmidhī.

950. See note 498.

951. The text from this paragraph through the next twelve paragraphs as far as the saying of Anas is taken from Māwardī's commentary on the verse.

952. In his commentary on this verse Samʿānī's father Manṣūr ascribes this saying to ʿĀʾisha, as do most sources other than Māwardī.

953. Muslim, Nasāʾī; Manṣūr Samʿānī, commentary on 33:37.

954. Hadiths to this effect are found in Bukhārī and Muslim.

955. On the permissibility of the first gaze, see p. 278.

956. Hadith from Muslim. The second half reads, *"and surely I ask forgiveness from God one hundred times a day."*

957. Beginning with this paragraph, the comparison of Muḥammad with other prophets is drawn from Mustamlī, *Sharḥ* 878–81.

958. See note 598.
959. See note 329.
960. See note 448.
961. See note 583.
962. Samʿānī tells the story of the stick on p. 381.
963. See note 409.
964. This paragraph, minus the Quran quote, is from Mustamlī's commentary on the beginning of Kalabādhī's chapter on *maʿrifa* (*Sharḥ* 703).
965. The paragraph to here is from Mustamlī, *Sharḥ* 715.
966. This is the first hemistich of a poem by the Companion ʿAbdallāh ibn Rawāḥa, recited by the Prophet on the day of the Trench (and cited by Mustamlī, *Sharḥ* 711). The poem goes on, *"We would not have paid alms, nor would we have prayed. // So send down tranquility upon us and fix our feet when we meet // the associators who defied us. When they desired discord, we refused."*
967. See note 378.
968. This paragraph is based mostly on Mustamlī, *Sharḥ* 703.
969. Tirmidhī, Ibn Māja.
970. These three paragraphs are a summary of Mustamlī, *Sharḥ* 720–21.
971. Kalābādhī, *Taʿarruf*, chapter 21 (*Doctrine* 47). The explanation of this saying in the next fourteen paragraphs as far as the verse *"And We forbade his being suckled"* is abridged from Mustamlī, *Sharḥ* 734–45.
972. This saying is ascribed by Mustamlī to "the great ones."
973. See note 429.
974. Reference to the hadith cited on pp. 189–90.
975. Aḥmad.
976. Muslim and other standard sources.
977. For an English translation of an early version of this story, see Ṭabarī, *History* 1:258–59.
978. The questions in this paragraph allude to the *ḥadīth qudsī "Every night God descends..."* (p. 61, note 182).
979. Hadith found in Muslim and other standard sources.
980. Ḥallāj (Khaṭīb, *Taʾrīkh* 8:693).
981. See note 1118.
982. See note 546.
983. Part of the hadith in Bukhārī that includes the words *"When I love him, I am for him hearing..."*
984. Harut and Marut are two angels mentioned in Quran 2:102. According to commentators, they protested at Adam's creation, were embodied and sent to earth, and sinned. They were punished by being hung upside down in a well until the Day of Resurrection.
985. See note 862.
986. This may be a version of the saying cited on p. 127 (note 394).
987. The saying is usually attributed to Jaʿfar Ṣādiq (e.g., Kulaynī, *Kāfī* 1:160, no. 13).
988. Bukhārī and Muslim.

989. Khaṭīb Baghdādī (*Ta'rīkh* 10:325) ascribes a version of this poem to Samnūn Muḥibb.
990. Hadith (Ibn Abi'l-Dunyā, *Amr* 79, no. 38).
991. See note 203.
992. See note 643.
993. See note 118.
994. This may be a (somewhat corrupted) version of a saying ascribed to Dhu'l-Nūn Miṣrī (Bayhaqī, *Shu'ab* 1:373, no. 431).
995. Anonymous. Qurṭubī gives a somewhat different version of the poem in his commentary on 45:23. The first hemstitch appears in a poem cited by Washshā' (*Muwashshā* 88).
996. Shi'ite sources cite this as a saying of the Prophet (Mufīd, *Ikhtiṣāṣ* 311).
997. Abū Dhu'ayb (Mawṣilī, *Khaṣā'iṣ* 1:220).
998. Ḥusayn ibn 'Abdallāh Ghanādūstī (Sam'ānī, *Ansāb* 4:311). The last hemistich is found in an anonymous line cited by Tha'ālibī (*Yatīma* 3:383).
999. That Gabriel did not come to the Prophet for a time is recounted in commentaries on 93:3 (Nasr, *Study Quran* 1526).
1000. Ibn al-Mu'tazz (Sarī, *Muḥibb* 2:237).
1001. Kushājim (Sarī, *Muḥibb* 2:237).
1002. Another version of this text is found as the second letter (*kitāb*) of 'Alī's *Nahj al-balāgha* (3:4–5).
1003. Bukhārī and other sources.
1004. The hadith is often quoted by commentators on 6:125, such as Ṭabarī, though experts consider it weak.
1005. Mazdak (Māwardī, *Adab* 111–12).
1006. These sentences are found among others in Tha'ālibī's chapter on this world in *Tamthīl* 249–50.
1007. Yaḥyā ibn Mu'ādh Rāzī (Ibn al-Jawzī, *Ṣifa* 2:297).
1008. Fuḍayl ibn 'Iyāḍ (Zamakhsharī, *Rabī'* 1:43).
1009. Abu'l-Ḥusayn Darrāj (d. ca. 932). Kalābādhī gives a version of this anecdote in *Ta'arruf*, the chapter on poverty (Mustamlī, *Sharḥ* 1249).
1010. Ṭabarī, commentary on 38:36.
1011. Words of Ibn 'Abbās, as indicated shortly.
1012. Ibn 'Asākir provides some of this account (*Ta'rīkh* 22:260–61).
1013. Reference to a birthmark on the Prophet's left shoulder that was recognized as the "seal" or mark of his being chosen as a prophet; several sound hadiths mention it. As for Quran 33:40, *"the messenger of God and the seal of the prophets,"* commentators agree that this means that there will be no prophet after him.
1014. This paragraph is derived largely from Qushayrī on 38:34 (*Laṭā'if* 3:255–56).
1015. The three paragraphs to here are derived from Qushayrī on 38:35–36 (*Laṭā'if* 3:256–57).
1016. On the wings of Ja'far Ṭayyār, an elder brother of 'Alī ibn Abī Ṭālib, see p. 391.
1017. *Ḥadīth qudsī* from Bukhārī.
1018. Reference to Quran 21:81: *"And Solomon's is the wind, fierce, running at his command."*

1019. This and most of the next four paragraphs are from Samarqandī's commentary on 21:83.
1020. These two paragraphs are found in Ṭabarī's commentary on the verse.
1021. The four quotes are from Qushayrī, *Manthūr* 61–62. The first and second are definitions of trust (*tawakkul*), the third of servanthood (*ʿubūdiyya*), and the fourth of contentment (*qanaʿa*).
1022. This paragraph is from Qushayrī on 18:16 (*Laṭāʾif* 2:382).
1023. Qushayrī on 18:17 (*Laṭāʾif* 2:383).
1024. Qushayrī on 18:18 (*Laṭāʾif* 2:384).
1025. See note 373.
1026. Qushayrī on 18:18 (*Laṭāʾif* 2:385).
1027. The remarks on *their dog was stretching its paws* are loosely translated from Qushayrī on 18:18 (*Laṭāʾif* 2:384–85).
1028. See note 588.
1029. Mutanabbī, *Dīwān* 237.
1030. The hadith is found in Muslim and other sources. The Prophet was climbing Mount Hira (Mount Uhud in some versions of the hadith) along with a few Companions, including Abū Bakr the sincerely truthful, when the mountain shook, so he said this and it stopped shaking.
1031. See note 492.
1032. Aḥmad and Abū Dāwūd.
1033. Bukhārī.
1034. The discussion of Jonah in this paragraph seems to be derived from Mustamlī, *Sharḥ* 872–73.
1035. "Your companion," that is, the speaker, Muḥammad. The hadith is found in Muslim.
1036. See note 651.
1037. Mutanabbī, *Dīwān* 8.
1038. The hadith is found in Aḥmad and other sources.
1039. Qushayrī, *Sharḥ* 111.
1040. Words inscribed in gold inside a book belonging to Jaʿfar ibn Yaḥyā Barmakī (Tawḥīdī, *Baṣāʾir* 4:171).
1041. Abū Nuʿaym (*Ḥilya* 2:221–22) ascribes this saying (interspersed with the Quranic verses in the next paragraph) to the Follower Abu'l-ʿĀliya.
1042. Abū Nuʿaym, *Ḥilya* 7:65.
1043. The "wanderer" was ʿAbd al-Wāḥid ibn Zayd, a disciple of Ḥasan Baṣrī. For the text of his long discussion with a monk from which this is taken, see Khaṭīb, *Muntakhab* 1:94–96.
1044. For a slightly different version of the story, see Abshīhī, *Mustaṭraf* 150–51.
1045. Quoted and translated from RQ on *tawakkul* (*Epistle* 183).
1046. This must be the same as Muʿādh Nasafī, an almost unknown teacher quoted once in RQ, the chapter on *faqr* (*Epistle* 281).
1047. Salmān Fārisī (Ibn Abi'l-Dunyā, *Iṣlāḥ* 44, no. 92).
1048. A hadith found in Aḥmad, Ibn Māja, Dārimī, and other sources.
1049. Nibājī (RQ on *ruʾya*; *Epistle* 398).
1050. Aḥmad ibn Masrūq (Khaṭīb, *Muntakhab* 63).
1051. Muslim ibn Yasār (Abū Nuʿaym, *Ḥilya* 2:292).

1052. See note 826.
1053. The Prophet was sleeping in the house of his cousin Umm Hānī when Gabriel came and took him on the *mi ʿrāj*.
1054. The hadith is found in Aḥmad and other standard sources.
1055. A sound hadith.
1056. Bukhārī, Muslim.
1057. ʿAlī ibn ʿĪsā (d. 946) was a vizier of the caliph. Abū Nuʿaym gives the text in *Ḥilya* 10:373–74.
1058. Khuttalī, *Maḥabba* 28, no. 41.
1059. Makhzūmī (Sarī, *Muḥibb* 2:169).
1060. The well-known version of this hadith has "two" rather than "four" (note 925).
1061. Abu'l-Naṣr Asadī (Jāḥiẓ, *Rasā ʾil* 2:399).
1062. Bukhārī, Muslim.
1063. Sayf al-Dawla Ḥamdānī (Thaʿālibī, *Yatīma* 1:39).
1064. Mālik Dīnār (ʿAṭṭār, *Tadhkira* 86; *Memorial* 112).
1065. See note 157.
1066. Mustamlī ascribes the saying to Abū Yazīd (*Sharḥ* 765). As for the notion that bewilderment is beyond all the stations, Ibn ʿArabī explains that it is the human correlative of the all-comprehensive name *God*, which is the coincidence of opposites (*jam ʿ al-aḍdād*) and thereby bewilders rational thought (see Chittick, *Sufi Path of Knowledge* 380).
1067. ʿAṭṭār, *Tadhkira* 633.
1068. Anonymous (Ibn Qayyim, *Rawḍa* 110).
1069. The text of this and the following paragraph is corrupted in the edition; my translation is based on Qushayrī's discussion of love's etymology in his chapter on *maḥabba* (RQ, *Epistle* 356) and manuscript MJ.
1070. Munāwī begins his explanation of the word with this sentence (*Tawqīf* 299).
1071. By devils (*dīwān*) and sprites (*pariyān*) Samʿānī presumably means the two basic sorts of jinn: followers of Iblis and followers of the prophets.
1072. The hadith is often cited in commentaries on the verse, though without reference to ʿĀʾisha (e.g., Ṭabarī, Manṣūr Samʿānī).
1073. Various hadiths say that every child of Adam has sinned or aimed to sin except for John (e.g., Ibn ʿAsākir, *Ta ʾrīkh* 64:193).
1074. These three hadiths are well known and come in various early sources.
1075. Samʿānī provides a bit more detail on the story of the many thousands of Moseses on p. 450. The point is that God showed Moses that he was one of countless individuals of equal rank, so he came to understand his audacity in desiring to see God.
1076. See note 329.
1077. Tirmidhī and Ibn Māja.
1078. See note 813.
1079. Part of the hadith of the six things given specifically to the Prophet (p. 200).
1080. Hadith found in Aḥmad.
1081. Aḥmad, Ibn Māja.

1082. A saying of ʿAlī found in Aḥmad.
1083. See note 717.
1084. From a hadith about the creation of Adam found in Tirmidhī and other sources.
1085. Reference to Abraham's words about the sun: *"I am quit of what you associate"*(6:78).
1086. The account comes from Mujāhid (Abū Nuʿaym, *Ḥilya* 3:288).
1087. The lines are ascribed to Masʿūd ibn ʿAbdallāh Qāʾinī, about whom nothing is known save that he must have lived before the tenth century (Shubbar, *Adab* 3:259–60).
1088. Muslim, Tirmidhī, Nasāʾī.
1089. Sahl Tustarī (Sulamī, *Ḥaqāʾiq* on 5:109).
1090. Short version of a saying by Abū ʿAmr Muḥammad ibn al-Ashʿath (Sulamī, *Ḥaqāʾiq* on 5:109).
1091. Ẓufar ibn Ḥārith (Ibn ʿAsākir, *Taʾrīkh* 19:37).
1092. See note 416.
1093. Perhaps inspired by Abū Yazīd's saying *"The recognizer is a flyer, the renunciant a traveler"* (RQ on *maʿrifa*; *Epistle* 322).
1094. See note 448.
1095. On the basis of various hadiths, including some that refer to examples from the Prophet's own performance of the prayer, the Shariah holds that negligence (*sahw*) needs to be followed by two prostrations.
1096. According to a hadith cited by Ṭabarānī (*Kabīr* 12:215), *"The Surah al-Anʿām descended at night all at once in Mecca, and around it seventy thousand angels were busy glorifying God."*
1097. See note 564.
1098. Reference to the famous Hadith of Gabriel, found in Muslim and other collections, according to which the angel came in human form (some say in the form of the Companion Diḥya Kalbī) and asked the Prophet several questions.
1099. Version of an already quoted saying of Yaḥyā ibn Muʿādh (p. 206).
1100. A standard definition of spirit is "that through which something is alive" (see note 417).
1101. Hadith in Ibn Māja.
1102. ʿAṭṭār gives a different translation of this saying (*Tadhkira* 280).
1103. Aḥmad and other standard sources.
1104. ʿAṭṭār also tells this story (*Tadhkira* 169; *Memorial* 197–98).
1105. The saying is typically ascribed to Abū Bakr and sometimes to ʿAlī.
1106. Abū Dāwūd, Nasāʾī.
1107. The hadith literature ascribes this saying both to Muʿādh and to ʿAbdallāh ibn Rawāḥa.
1108. For an account of how this verse was revealed during the *miʿrāj*, see Maybudī, *Kashf* 2:285–86.
1109. Ascribed to Abū Saʿīd (Munawwar, *Asrār* 301; *Secrets* 460–61).
1110. Sahl ibn ʿAbdallāh (Abū Nuʿaym, *Ḥilya* 10:208). Qushayrī quotes the saying without mentioning a source in his commentary on this name in *Sharḥ* 210.
1111. So say both Qushayrī (*Sharḥ* 212) and Bayhaqī (*Iʿtiqād* 54). The latter adds that it may also be derived from the word finding (*wujūd*) in the sense of *"not weighed down by seeking nor kept separate from the sought."*
1112. See note 219.

1113. The Spirit of God (*rūḥ allāh*) is a title of Jesus (Quran 4:171), and the Spirit of Holiness (*rūḥ al-qudus*) a title of Gabriel (Quran 16:102). In three verses the Quran says that God confirmed Jesus with the Spirit of Holiness (2:87, 2:253, 5:110).
1114. A famous saying of Abū Bakr shortly after the death of the Prophet, recorded, for example in the *Ṣaḥīḥ* of Bukhārī.
1115. See p. 46 (note 131).
1116. Abū Nuwās (Sarī, *Muḥibb* 4:213).
1117. Dhahabī, *Siyar* 1300.
1118. According to one well-known interpretation of 38:33, Solomon was so engrossed with inspecting his horses that he missed the time for prayer, so he sacrificed them as expiation (Nasr, *Study Quran* 1108–9).
1119. See note 983.
1120. See note 400.
1121. Shiblī recited this verse in explanation of his falling into ecstasy at a singer's words, though the words had no effect on anyone else (Ibn ʿAsākir, *Taʾrīkh* 66:71).
1122. See note 583
1123. Reference to Solomon's words, *"How is it that I do not see the hoopoe?"* (27:20).
1124. Cited in RQ, intro. (*Epistle* 12).
1125. Abū Nuʿaym, *Ḥilya* 10:35.
1126. Ibn ʿAsākir (*Taʾrīkh* 66:58).
1127. Anonymous (Rāghib, *Muḥāḍarāt*, 1:530).
1128. Mutanabbī (see note 590).
1129. Muslim.
1130. A singing girl by the name of Sundus (Tawḥīdī, *Imtāʿ* 275).
1131. Last words of the Prophet on his deathbed (Bukhārī).
1132. Sanāʾī, *Dīwān* 1126.
1133. Ghazālī (*Iḥyāʾ* 4:145) gives a version of this revelation to David ending with this sentence; the rest may be Samʿānī's embellishment.
1134. Abū Nuʿaym (*Ḥilya* 8:92–93) provides a slightly different version of this saying.
1135. See note 563.
1136. *Ḥadīth qudsī* (Ibn Abi'l-Dunyā, *Ḥusn* 97, no. 90).
1137. Abū Dawūd, Ibn Māja.
1138. Abū Dawūd, Ibn Māja. Maybudī (commentary on 49:10) explains: "What is meant is the lineage of the religion and godwariness, not the lineage of water and clay. If it were the lineage of water and clay, Abū Lahab and Abū Jahl would have a portion of it. It is this to which He alludes with the words, '*Surely the noblest of you with God is the most godwary*' [49:13]."
1139. Ṣāḥib ibn ʿAbbād (Thaʿālibī, *Yatīma* 3:233).
1140. Abū Dulaf (Ibn ʿAsākir, *Taʾrīkh* 49:146). Ibn ʿAsākir reads *ghawānī* (fair ladies) instead of *mawālī* (friends).
1141. ʿUtba Ghulām (Abū Nuʿaym, *Ḥilya* 6:235).
1142. For ʿAṭṭār's version of this story, which may well be based on this passage, see *Tadhkira* 106–7 (*Memorial* 132).

1143. Version of a saying by Shiblī (RQ, the chapter on *ghayra*; *Epistle* 266).
1144. Qushayrī, *Sharḥ* 220.
1145. See note 583.
1146. See note 128.
1147. RQ, the chapter on their states at departing this world (*Epistle* 318).
1148. Sanāʾī, *Dīwān* 154.
1149. Aḥmad ibn Ḥātim Munqarī (Zawzanī, *Ḥamāsa* 13).
1150. Samarqandī (*Tanbīh* 77) cites this as part of a hadith. The text goes on to say that David asked God what He meant, and God replied, *"Give the sinners the good news that there is no sin too great for Me to forgive, and warn the sincerely truthful not to admire* [*ʿujb*] *their own deeds, for I will not set My justice and reckoning upon someone without destroying him."*
1151. ʿAṭṭār gives a longer version of the saying in *Tadhkira* 677.
1152. Part of a long supplication of the Prophet found in Tirmidhī.
1153. ʿAṭṭār gives a different translation of the saying in *Tadhkira* 135 (*Memorial* 162).
1154. The sentence is part of a saying of ʿAlī (Kulaynī, *Kāfī* 7:78).
1155. Part of a long conversation of Moses with God going back to Kaʿb al-Aḥbār (Abū Nuʿaym, *Ḥilya* 6:33).
1156. Wāḥidī, *Asbāb* on 33:43.
1157. See note 945.
1158. Proverb (Dīnawarī, *Mujālasa* 2:367).
1159. Thaʿālibī (*Iʿjāz* 57) ascribes a version of this saying to Porus, the king of India (d. ca. 315 BC).
1160. See note 94.
1161. Ṭabarī and Baghawī attribute this interpretation of the verse to Kaʿb al-Aḥbār, Ḍahhāk, and Saʿīd ibn Jubayr.
1162. See note 360.
1163. Up to here the story of the needle is well known (e.g., Ibn ʿAsākir, *Taʾrīkh* 3:310), but not the rest of this account.
1164. The two verses are from the *Qaṣīdat al-burda* by the Prophet's Companion, Kaʿb ibn Zuhayr (Abū Nuʿaym, *Maʿrifa* 1:425).
1165. Ṭabarī, *Taʾrīkh* 2:111.
1166. Aḥmad, Nasāʾī.
1167. Muslim, Aḥmad.
1168. ʿAmr ibn Sha's (Jubūrī, *Shiʿr* 84).
1169. Well-known hadith, though often considered weak.
1170. Version of a saying by Bilāl ibn Saʿd (Ibn al-Mubārak, *Zuhd* 167, nos. 485–6).
1171. Qushayrī on 57:3 (*Laṭāʾif* 3:532).
1172. Paraphrase of Qushayrī on 57:1 (*Laṭāʾif* 3:531).
1173. ʿAṭṭār (*Tadhkira* 744) translates what seems to be a longer version of this saying like this: "I disown a lord who would be pleased with my obedience and angry at my disobedience. He would then be tied to seeing what I do. No, rather, the friends are friends in the Beginningless, and the enemies are enemies in the Beginningless."

1174. See note 641.
1175. Shiblī (RQ on *maḥabba*; *Epistle* 331).
1176. Junayd (Abū Nuʿaym, *Ḥilya* 10:276).
1177. Abū Muḥammad Muhallabī (Tanūkhī, *Nishwār* 7:253).
1178. See note 416.
1179. Qushayrī on 57:1 (*Laṭāʾif* 3:530).
1180. For another version of this story, see ʿAṭṭār, *Tadhkira* 166–67 (*Memorial* 194–95).
1181. Based on a saying by Sulaymān Taymī (Ibn Abi'l-Dunyā, *Shukr* 7, no. 8).
1182. Ṭabarsī offers this sentence as one of the meanings of *laṭīf* in his commentary on 2:103.
1183. See note 793.
1184. See note 379.
1185. Bukhārī, Muslim.
1186. Allusion to Quran 19:57: *"We elevated him to a high place."*
1187. Tirmidhī gives this version of the hadith: " *'O Messenger of God, when were you a prophet?' He said, 'When Adam was between spirit and body.'* " See also p. 192 (note 589).
1188. Hadith found in Aḥmad.
1189. From a hadith found in Aḥmad.
1190. The reference is to Quran 61:6: *"And when Jesus son of Mary said, 'Children of Israel, I am indeed the Messenger of God to you . . . giving good news of a messenger coming after me, whose name is Aḥmad.'"*
1191. Sharīf Raḍī (p. 231, note 692).
1192. Muslim, Aḥmad.
1193. Aḥmad, Abū Dāwūd, Nasāʾī.
1194. Hadith (Ibn ʿAsākir, *Taʾrīkh* 54:238).
1195. Accounts are given by Bukhārī and Muslim; the name Abu'l-Shaḥma is given by Bayhaqī (*Maʿrifa* 8:187) and Qushayrī (commentary on 2:245; *Laṭāʾif* 1:189).
1196. Reference to Quran 27:19ff.
1197. Hadith mentioned in Aḥmad.
1198. This Arabic paragraph, not in the printed edition, is from manuscript MJ. Nāgawrī quotes it from *Rawḥ al-arwāḥ* in his commentary on this name in *Ṭawāliʿ al-shumūs*.
1199. Qushayrī, commentary on 40:1 (*Laṭāʾif* 3:294). The letters *ḥāʾ* and *mīm* in this verse are typically read as disconnected; if they are read as connected, *ḥumma* is a likely pronunciation.
1200. Bukhārī and Muslim.
1201. See note 363.
1202. See note 356.
1203. In his commentary on this verse Ṭabarī writes that it means: *"Appoint for me a beautiful remembrance and a lovely laudation among the people, one that will remain in the generations coming after me."* He remarks that this supplication explains why Abraham alone—in contrast to Moses, Jesus, and Muḥammad—is praised by all three communities: Jewish, Christian, and Muslim.
1204. See note 1017.
1205. As becomes clear from the following passages, "without the spirit" (*bī-jān*) and later "without life" (*bī-ḥayāt*) refer to dying to oneself in the path of God. In this discussion Rūmī and many others cite a purported hadith, *"Die before you die!"*

1206. Commentators take the verse as a reference to those who were killed (*"fulfilled their vow"*) at the Battle of Uhud and others who, despite the defeat there, waited patiently for God's help.
1207. Bukhārī and Muslim.
1208. Words of the Prophet concerning those killed at Uhud (Aḥmad, Nasāʾī).
1209. See p. 196 (note 600).
1210. Variation of a sentence by Qushayrī (see p. 255; note 757).
1211. An Arabic and much longer version of these two stories, beginning with the trip to Byzantium, identifies the "exalted man" as Abū Quddāma Shāmī, a contemporary of some of the Prophet's Companions (Ibn al-Naḥḥās, *Mashāri*ʿ 285–92).
1212. According to Ibn Kathīr (*Bidāya* 9:109), this sentence is part of a long passage found in the scrolls of Isaiah predicting the coming of the Prophet.
1213. The name of the Prophet's mule.
1214. The allusion is to the juridical principle of "equality" (*kafāʾa*) in marriage. In discussing it jurists list various factors that should be taken into account to assure compatibility between spouses.
1215. See note 429.
1216. See note 826.
1217. Qāḍī ʿAbd al-Jabbār was a famous Muʿtazilite theologian who held that God cannot be seen, whether in this world or the next.
1218. This seems to be a paraphrase of the passage from Qushayrī cited earlier, *"You did what you did..."* (p. 76).
1219. ʿAṭṭār provides this account in almost identical words (*Tadhkira* 136; *Memorial* 162–63).
1220. This sentence is given as a *ḥadīth qudsī* by Tirmidhī.
1221. Second line of an anonymous quatrain. The first line reads, "Night and day, early and late, that moon of heaven / was not separate from my embrace for one moment" (Maybudī, *Kashf* 2:229).
1222. See note 410.
1223. This is Adam's greeting to the Prophet during the *miʿrāj*, as mentioned in Bukhārī and other standard sources.
1224. The hadith (Aḥmad) is often interpreted as a reference to Uways, whom the Prophet never met in the flesh. For ʿAṭṭār's account of him, see *Memorial* 53–63.
1225. The reference is to a hadith in which the Prophet says, *"Oh, the yearning to encounter my brothers!"* For the version to which Samʿānī is referring, see Makkī, *Qūt* 1:247.
1226. Muslim (note 906).
1227. Baghawī cites this saying of Ibn ʿAbbās in his commentary on the verse.
1228. RQ on *waraʿ* provides the Arabic text (*Epistle* 132).
1229. "Peg" (*watad*), like Substitute, is used to designate an outstanding friend of God, one whose existence serves to keep the universe in place. The term is derived from Quran 78:7, which refers to mountains as "pegs" that stabilize the earth.
1230. Kisāʾī (*Dīwān*: *gul*). The second hemstitch reads, "What can silver buy more precious than roses?"

1231. Aḥmad.
1232. Luqmān (Ghazālī, *Iḥyāʾ* 4:133).
1233. See note 7.
1234. For the proverb, see p. 296.
1235. This "hadith" goes back to Ḥasan Baṣrī (Ghazālī, *Minhāj* 270).
1236. Bukhārī and Muslim.
1237. Reference to the hadith mentioned in note 408.
1238. Ṭabarānī (*Kabīr* 8:195) cites a hadith to this effect.
1239. Ibn ʿAbd Rabbih (*ʿIqd* 4:72) gives a brief version of this anecdote.
1240. In his commentary on 13:11 Ṭabarī provides a long hadith about angels to this effect.
1241. See note 563.
1242. The second sentence is a well-known hadith, though usually considered weak. Bayhaqī gives the text in *Shuʿab* 2:38, no. 1108.
1243. From the *ḥadīth qudsī*, *"Every night God descends"* (note 182).
1244. See note 363.
1245. Tirmidhī.
1246. The first of these two sentences is commonly ascribed to ʿAlī in later texts.
1247. Reference to a Quranic verse about the spirit (*"Of knowledge you are given but little,"* 17:85), the saying of ʿAlī just quoted, and a verse about Quranic ambiguity (*"None knows its interpretation but God,"* 3:7).
1248. Sanāʾī, *Dīwān* 902.
1249. Junayd (RQ on *khalwa*; *Epistle* 128).
1250. Sulamī (*Ṭabaqāt* 364) ascribes the saying to Abu'l-Qāsim Naṣrābādī.
1251. A similar hadith is found in Muslim.
1252. Abū Nuʿaym among others mentions the hadith (*Ḥilya* 8:132).
1253. A version of a saying by Wuhayb ibn Ward (Ibn Rajab, *Jāmiʿ* 478–79).
1254. Tustarī gives a longer version of this saying in his commentary on 23:1.
1255. A different version of what appears to be the same saying is given by Ibn Abi'l-Dunyā (*Yaqīn* 47, no. 32).
1256. Zamakhsharī (*Rabīʿ* 3:99) cites this saying of this Companion.
1257. Abū Nuʿaym (*Ḥilya* 3:358) traces a version of a hadith from which these phrases are drawn back to Ḥudhayfa Yamān.
1258. See note 595.
1259. Qushayrī says this about Ḥasan Baṣrī (RQ on *ruʾya*; *Epistle* 397).
1260. Zamakhsharī, *Rabīʿ* 5:6.
1261. *Ḥilya* 2:162–63 (each sentence with a different *isnād*).
1262. ʿAbd al-Malik was the fifth Umayyad caliph (r. 685–705). Abū Nuʿaym's version of this story is much shorter (*Ḥilya* 2:168–69).
1263. Commentators on Quran 19:12 provide this anecdote (e.g., Māwardī).
1264. Qālī, *Amālī* 2:44.
1265. For the Arabic text, see Ibn al-Jazarī, *Zahr* 66.

1266. Zamakhsharī, *Rabīʿ* 1:386.
1267. Ghazālī ascribes a shorter version of this saying to Sufyān Thawrī (*Iḥyāʾ* 4:178).
1268. An Arabic version of this story is given by Thaʿlabī in *Qatlā* 54–55.
1269. Qushayrī (*Sharḥ* 83) attributes the line to Daqqāq.
1270. Reference to the sound hadith *"God wonders* (or in other versions *"laughs"*) *at two men, one of whom kills his companion."*
1271. The hadith is well known but generally considered weak.
1272. Sanāʾī, *Dīwān* 1144.
1273. Part of a long hadith about who or what deserves the name *sayyid* (Shajarī, *Tartīb* 2:4, no. 1392).
1274. This is a conflation of several well-known reports.
1275. See note 966.
1276. Dhu'l-Nūn Miṣrī (RQ on *maʿrifa*; *Epistle* 323).
1277. Sanāʾī, *Dīwān* 201.
1278. Nāgawrī (*Lawāʾiḥ* 8) gives a different translation of this anecdote, ascribing it to Dhu'l-Nūn Miṣrī.
1279. Khubzaʾarzī (Thaʿālibī, *Yatīma* 2:429–30).
1280. See note 108.
1281. Words of Iblis from a hadith found in Muslim.
1282. Abū Nuwās (Mahzimī, *Akhbār* 19, no. 51).
1283. Another version of this quatrain is found in Rūmī's *Dīwān* (Furūzānfar no. 420, Gamard no. 1942).
1284. Farrukhī (*Dīwān*, no. 178), from a poem in praise of Sultan Maḥmūd.
1285. Aḥmad ibn Kayghalagh or Dīk al-Jinn (Thaʿālibī, *Yatīma*, 122).
1286. Imruʾ al-Qays (note 197).
1287. ʿAṭṭār gives a longer version of the saying (*Tadhkira* 189; *Memorial* 218).
1288. Ibn al-Muʿtazz (note 503).
1289. For the Arabic, see Bayhaqī, *Sunan* 9:151, no. 18145.
1290. Bayhaqī, *Shuʿab* 3:263, no. 3493.
1291. The hadith is found in commentaries on 9:104 (e.g., Ṭabarī).
1292. Abū Firās Ḥamdānī (Thaʿālibī, *Yatīma* 1:95).
1293. As a hadith this saying is weak, but jurists consider the meaning sound.
1294. Kalābādhī, *Taʿarruf* 111; *Doctrine* 104; Mustamlī, *Sharḥ* 1421.
1295. Mustamlī, *Sharḥ* 161.
1296. Nasāʾī and other sources.
1297. Muslim.
1298. See note 588.
1299. See note 805.
1300. See note 789.
1301. A conflation of two short hadiths found in Abū Dāwūd and other sources.
1302. Qushayrī, *Sharḥ* 260.

1303. The Prophet's miracles (*muʿjiza*) are described in traditional accounts of his life. Ghazālī lists forty-five in book 20 of the *Iḥyāʾ* (translated by Zolondek).
1304. Reference to a hadith found in Bukhārī and other sources concerning the prophets and their communities on thc Day of Resurrection.
1305. The hadith is well known, though considered weak.
1306. Ḥusayn ibn Ḍaḥḥāk (Iṣfahānī, *Aghānī* 7:147).
1307. Abu'l-Qāsim Zaʿfarānī (Thaʿālibī, *Yatīma* 3:227).
1308. See note 33.
1309. Zamakhsharī, commentary on 2:94 (*Kashshāf* 1:166).
1310. Abū Nuʿaym, *Ḥilya* 1:141.
1311. See note 924.
1312. See note 809.
1313. See note 120.
1314. See note 445.
1315. Ibn Qutayba (*Adab* 8) attributes the saying to al-Ḥakīm, "the Sage," that is, Aristotle.
1316. Well known but considered weak.
1317. Tirmidhī.
1318. Bukhārī.
1319. Commentators (e.g., Ṭabarī) offer two basic interpretations for this verse: either that both clauses refer to the Prophet, or that the second clause refers rather to Abū Bakr, as here.
1320. Bukhārī.
1321. Ṭabarānī (*Awsaṭ* 2:159) gives the text, though it is usually considered weak.
1322. Ibn Abi'l-Dunyā (*Mutamannīn* 58).
1323. Ibn al-Jawzī (*Mawḍūʿāt* 1:304–7) says that the hadith is likely fabricated.
1324. Similar hadiths are found in Abū Dāwūd and Ibn Māja.
1325. The first half of the saying is found in Muslim. See Suyūṭī, *Taʾrīkh* 224–26.
1326. Usually attributed to Abū Yazīd Basṭāmī.
1327. Muslim.
1328. From a poem by ʿAlī (Ibn ʿAsākir, *Taʾrīkh* 42:521).
1329. Sirjānī, *Bayāḍ* 320.
1330. Ibn al-Jawzī tells a long version of this story in *Ṣifa* 1:570–71.
1331. Bayhaqī gives the Arabic in *Shuʿab* 1:387, no. 496.
1332. This may be Aḥmad's brother Muḥammad. The printed edition, but not all manuscripts, adds "Imām al-Ḥaramayn." If this is part of the text, it cannot refer to the famous Imām al-Ḥaramayn Juwaynī, since he died ten years before Aḥmad's birth.
1333. There are discrepancies in the manuscripts, but the full names of the transmitters seem to be as follows: Abu'l-Qāsim Yaḥyā ibn Aḥmad ibn Aḥmad al-Sībī (d. 490/1097; *Ansāb* 3:355); Abu'l-Ḥusayn Muḥammad ibn al-Ḥusayn al-Qattān (d. 415/1024); Abū Muḥammad ʿAbd al-Raḥmān ibn Muḥammad, known as Ibn Abī Ḥātim (d. 327/938), and his father Abū Ḥātim Muḥammad ibn Idrīs Rāzī (d. 277/890); Abū ʿUthmān Saʿīd ibn Sulaymān (d. 225/840); Abū Muḥammad Qazaʿa ibn Suwayd al-Bāhilī (d. ca. 172/789); Kathīr ibn al-Muṭṭalib ibn Abī Widāʿa al-Qurashī.

1334. See note 906.

1335. In what may be the original Arabic of this saying, Rābiʿa responds, *"Then do not disobey Him for whose sake you love me"* (Ibn Khallikān, *Wafayāt* 2:286).

1336. See note 563.

1337. See note 927.

1338. See note 6.

1339. See note 49.

1340. Qushayrī, *Manthūr* 61.

1341. Qushayrī, *Manthūr* 61.

1342. Sanāʾī, *Dīwān* 996.

1343. Bukhārī, Muslim.

1344. Ibn ʿAbbās (Ibn Manda, *Tawḥīd* 3:146–47, no. 581).

1345. Hadith, though considered weak (Sakhāwī, *Maqāṣid* 114, no. 108).

1346. Version of the hadith cited on p. 363.

WORKS CITED

Primary Sources

ʿAbbās ibn al-Aḥnaf, al- (d. ca. 192/808). *Dīwān*. Edited by ʿĀtikat al-Khazrajī. Cairo: Dār al-Kutub al-Miṣriyya, 1954. https://archive.org/details/Deiwan_Ela7naf.

Ābī, Abū Saʿd Manṣūr al- (d. 421/1029). *Nathr al-durr*. Edited by Khālid ʿAbd al-Ghanī Maḥfūẓ. 7 vols. Beirut: Dār al-Kutub al-ʿIlmiyya, 2003. http://shamela.ws/index.php/book/7853.

Abshīhī, Aḥmad al- (d. 852/1448). *al-Mustaṭraf fī kull fann mustaẓraf*. Beirut: ʿĀlam al-Kutub, 1998. http://shamela.ws/index.php/book/23802.

Abū Dāwūd (d. 275/889). *al-Sunan*. Edited by Aḥmad Saʿd ʿAlī. 2 vols. Cairo: Muṣṭafā al-Bābī al-Ḥalabī, 1952.

Abū Nuʿaym al-Iṣfahānī (d. 430/1038). *al-Arbaʿūn ʿalā madhhab al-mutaḥaqqiqīn min al-ṣūfiyya*. Edited by Badr ibn ʿAbdallāh al-Badr. Beirut: Dār Ibn Ḥazm, 1993. http://shamela.ws/index.php/book/8246.

———. *Ḥilyat al-awliyāʾ*. Cairo: Dār al-Fikr, 1996. https://archive.org/details/waq54172.

———. *Maʿrifat al-ṣaḥāba*. Edited by ʿĀdil ibn Yūsuf al-ʿAzzāzī. 8 vols. Riyadh: Dār al-Waṭan li'l-Nashr, 1998. http://shamela.ws/index.php/book/10490.

Abū Nuwās al-Ḥasan ibn Hānī (d. 199/813). *Dīwān*. http://al-hakawati.net/arabic/civilizations/diwanindex4a43.pdf.

Abū Rawḥ Luṭfallāh ibn Abī Saʿd (d. 541/1147). *Ḥālāt wa sukhanān Abū Saʿīd Abu'l-Khayr*. Edited by Muḥammad-Riḍā Shafīʿī Kadkanī. Tehran: Sukhan, 2005.

Abū Saʿīd ibn Abi'l-Khayr (d. 440/1049). *Rubāʿiyyāt*. http://ganjoor.net/abusaeed. *See also* Abū Rawḥ and Ibn Munawwar.

Abū Tammām (d. ca. 231/845). *Dīwān al-ḥamāsa* Edited by Aḥmad Ḥasan Basaj. Beirut: Dār al-Kutub al-ʿIlmiyya, 1998. https://archive.org/details/waq66437.

Abū Yaʿlā al-Mawṣilī (d. 307/919). *al-Muʿjam*. Edited by Irshād al-Ḥaqq Atharī. Faisalabad: Idārat al-ʿUlūm al-Athariyya, 1987. http://shamela.ws/index.php/book/13175.

Aflākī, Shams al-Dīn Aḥmad (d. 761/1360). *Manāqib al-ʿārifīn*. Edited by T. Yazıcı. Ankara: Türk Tarih Kurumu Basimevi, 1959–61.

Aḥmad ibn Ḥanbal (d. 241/855). *Kitāb al-Zuhd*. Beirut: Dār al-Kutub al-ʿIlmiyya, 1999. http://shamela.ws/index.php/book/8494.

———. *al-Musnad*. 6 vols. Beirut: Dār Ṣādir, n.d.

Aḥmad al-Rifāʿī (d. 578/1182). *Ḥāla ahl al-ḥaqīqat maʿ Allāh*. http://www.gamei-rifai.com/IMG/pdf/halet-ahl-al-haqiqah.pdf.

Ājurrī, Abū Bakr Muḥammad al- (d. 360/970). *al-Ghurabā'*. Edited by Badr al-Badr. Kuwait: Dār al-Khulafā', 1983. http://shamela.ws/index.php/book/13045.
ʿAlī ibn Abī Ṭālib. *Nahj al-balāgha*. Edited by Muḥammad ʿAbduh. 3 vols. Cairo: Maṭbaʿat al-Istiqāma, n.d.
ʿAlī ibn al-Ḥusayn (d. ca. 95/713). *al-Ṣaḥīfat al-sajjādiyya*. Text with translation by William C. Chittick. London: Muḥammadi Trust, 1988.
ʿAlī ibn Muḥammad al-Tihāmī, Abu'l-Ḥasan (d. 416/1025). *Dīwān*. Edited by Muḥammad ibn ʿAbd al-Raḥmān al-Rabīʿ. Riyadh: Maktabat al-Maʿārif, 1982. https://archive.org/details/WAQ120352WAQ.
ʿAmīdī, Abū Saʿd Muḥammad al- (d. 433/1041). *al-Ibāna ʿan sariqāt al-Mutanabbī*. Edited by Ibrāhīm al-Dassūqī al-Bisāṭī. Cairo: Dār al-Maʿārif, 1961. https://archive.org/details/ebana_motanabee.
ʿĀmilī, Bahā' al-Dīn al- (d. 1030/1621). *al-Kashkūl*. http://islamport.com/w/adb/Web/555/1.htm.
Āmulī, Sayyid Ḥaydar (d. 787/1385). *Jāmiʿ al-asrār wa manbaʿ al-anwār*. Edited by Henry Corbin and Othman Yahya. Paris: Librairie d'Amérique et d'Orient, 1969.
Anṣārī, ʿAbdallāh (d. 467/1088). *Munājāt*. http://www.sufi.ir/books/download/farsi/khajeh-abdollah/monajat-abdullah.pdf.
Anṭākī, Dāwūd al- (d. 1008/1599). *Tazyīn al-aswāq fī akhbār al-ʿushshāq*. http://shamela.ws/index.php/book/630.
Anwarī, Awḥad al-Dīn Muḥammad (d. ca. 583/1187). *Dīwān*. http://ganjoor.net/anvari/divan-anvari/.
ʿAskarī, Abū Hilāl al- (d. ca. 395/1005). *Dīwān al-maʿānī*. Edited by Aḥmad Ḥasan Basaj. Beirut: Dār al-Kutub al-ʿIlmiyya, 1994. https://archive.org/details/waq72929.
——. *Jamharat al-amthāl*. 2 vols. Beirut: Dār al-Fikr, 1988. http://shamela.ws/index.php/book/6897.
ʿAsqalānī, Ibn Ḥajar al- (d. 852/1449). *Fatḥ al-bārī fī sharḥ Ṣaḥīḥ al-Bukhārī*. Edited by Muḥibb al-Dīn al-Khaṭīb. Beirut: Dār al-Maʿrifa, 1959. http://shamela.ws/index.php/book/1673.
ʿAṭṭār, Farīd al-Dīn (d. ca. 618/1221). *Tadhkirat al-awliyā'*. Edited by Muḥammad Istiʿlāmī. Tehran: Zuwwār, 1346/1967.
——. *Farid al-Din ʿAttār's Memorial of God's Friends*. Translated by Paul Losensky. New York: Paulist Press, 2009.
Awliyā', Niẓām al-Dīn. *See* Sijzī.
ʿAyn al-Quḍāt Hamadānī (d. 525/1131). *Nāma-hā*. Edited by ʿAlīnaqī Munzawī and ʿAfīf ʿUsayrān. 3 vols. Tehran: Bunyād-i Farhang, 1969–1972; Asāṭīr, 1998.
Baghawī, al-Ḥusayn ibn Masʿūd al- (d. 516/1122). *Maʿālim al-tanzīl*. altafsir.com.
Bākharzī, Abu'l-Ḥasan ʿAlī ibn al-Ḥasan al- (d. 467/1075). *Dumyat al-qaṣr*. 3 vols. Beirut: Dār al-Jabal, 1993. http://shamela.ws/index.php/book/10665.
Baṣrī, Ṣadr al-Dīn ʿAlī al- (d. 606/1209–10). *al-Ḥamāsat al-Baṣriyya*. Edited by Mukhtār al-Dīn Aḥmad. Beirut: ʿĀlam al-Kutub, n.d. http://shamela.ws/index.php/book/6901.
Bayḍāwī, Naṣīr al-Dīn al- (d. 685/1286). *Anwār al-tanzīl wa asrār al-ta'wīl*. altafsir.com.

Bayhaqī, Abū Bakr Aḥmad al- (d. 458/1066). *al-Asmāʾ waʾl-ṣifāt*. Edited by ʿAbdallāh ibn Muḥammad al-Ḥāshidī. 2 vols. Cairo: Maktabat al-Suwādī, 1991. https://archive.org/details/asmaosifaatbehqi.

———. *Dalāʾil al-nubuwwa*. Edited by ʿAbd al-Muʿṭī Qalʿajī. 7 vols. Beirut: Dār al-Kutub al-ʿIlmiyya, 1988. https://archive.org/details/FPdlnbbidlnbbi.

———. *al-Iʿtiqād waʾl-hidāya ilā sabīl al-rashād*. Edited by Aḥmad ibn Ibrāhīm Abuʾl-ʿAynayn. Riyadh: Dār al-Faḍīla, 1999. http://shamela.ws/rep.php/book/5334.

———. *Maʿrifat al-sunan waʾl-āthār*. Edited by ʿAbd al-Muʿṭī Amīn Qalʿajī. 15 vols. Damascus: Dār Qutayba, 1991. http://shamela.ws/index.php/book/2863.

———. *al-Qaḍāʾ waʾl-qadar*. Edited by Muḥammad ibn ʿAbdallāh Āl ʿĀmir. Riyadh: Maktabat al-ʿUbaykān, 2000. http://shamela.ws/index.php/book/13053.

———. *Shuʿab al-īmān*. Edited by Muḥammad al-Saʿīd ibn Basyūnī Zaghlūl. 9 vols. Beirut: Dār al-Kutub al-ʿIlmiyya, 2000. https://archive.org/details/shoab_elmeya.

———. *al-Sunan al-kubrā*. Edited by Muḥammad ʿAbd al-Qādir ʿAṭā. 11 vols. Beirut: Dār al-Kutub al-ʿIlmiyya, 2003. http://shamela.ws/index.php/book/7861.

———. *al-Zuhd al-kabīr*. Edited by ʿĀmir Aḥmad Ḥaydar. Beirut: Muʾassasat al-Kutub al-Thaqāfiyya, 1996. http://shamela.ws/index.php/book/13025.

Bukhārī, Muḥammad ibn Ismāʿīl al- (d. 256/870). *al-Ṣaḥīḥ*. 9 vols. N.p.: Maṭābiʿ al-Shuʿab, 1378/1958–59.

Damīrī, Muḥammad ibn Mūsā al- (d. 808/1405). *Ḥayāt al-ḥayawān al-kubrā*. Beirut: Dār al-Kutub al-ʿIlmiyya, 2003. http://shamela.ws/index.php/book/10664.

Dāraquṭnī, ʿAlī ibn ʿUmar al- (d. 385/995). *Ruʾyat Allāh*. Jordan: Maktabat al-Manār, 1991. http://shamela.ws/index.php/book/21794.

Dārimī, Abū Muḥammad ʿAbd Allāh al- (d. 255/869). *al-Sunan*. 2 vols. N.p.: Dār Iḥyāʾ al-Sunnat al-Nabawiyya, n.d.

Dhahabī, Shams al-Dīn Muḥammad al- (d. 748/1348). *al-Kabāʾir*. Beirut: Dār al-Nadwat al-Jadīda. http://shamela.ws/index.php/book/6848.

———. *Siyar aʿlām al-nubalāʾ*. Edited by Ḥassān ʿAbd al-Mannān. Amman: Bayt al-Afkār al-Duwaliyya, 2004. https://archive.org/details/saanz.

———. *Talkhīṣ kitāb al-mawḍūʿāt li Ibn al-Jawzī*. Edited by Yāsir ibn Ibrāhīm. Riyadh: Maktabat al-Rushd, 1998. http://shamela.ws/index.php/book/6068.

Dīnawarī, Aḥmad ibn Marwān al- (d. 333/941). *al-Mujālasa wa jawāhir al-ʿilm*. Edited by Mashhūr ibn Ḥasan Āl Salmān. 10 vols. Beirut: Dār Ibn Ḥazm, 1998. http://shamela.ws/index.php/book/9948.

Fārisī, ʿAbd al-Ghāfir al- (d. 529/1135). *al-Muntakhab min al-Siyāq li taʾrīkh Naysābūr*. Edited by Muḥammad Aḥmad ʿAbd al-ʿAzīz. Beirut: Dār al-Kutub al-ʿIlmiyya, 1989. https://archive.org/details/WAQ19286.

Farrukhī Sīstānī (d. 429/1037–38). *Dīwān*. http://ganjoor.net/farrokhi/.

Fattanī, Muḥammad Ṭāhir al-Hindī al- (d. 986/1578). *Tadhkirat al-mawḍūʿāt*. Cairo: Idārat al-Ṭibāʿat al-Munīriyya, 1924–25. http://shamela.ws/index.php/book/12738.

Ghazālī, Abū Ḥāmid Muḥammad al- (d. 505/1111). *Iḥyā ʾ ʿulūm al-dīn*. Beirut: Dār al-Maʿrifa. http://shamela.ws/index.php/book/9472.
——. *Book XX of al-Ghazālī's Iḥyā ʾ*. Translated by Leon Zolondek. Leiden: Brill, 1963.
——. *Kīmiyā-yi saʿādat*. Edited by Ḥusayn Khadīw-Jam. Tehran: Jībī, 2001.
——. *Love, Longing, Intimacy and Contentment. Book XXXVI of the Revival of the Religious Sciences*. Translated by Eric Ormsby. Cambridge: The Islamic Texts Society, 2011.
——. *al-Maqṣad al-asnā*. Edited by Fadlou Shehadi. Beirut: Dār al-Mashriq, 1971.
——. *Minhāj al-ʿābidīn*. Edited by Maḥmūd Muṣṭafā Ḥalāwī. Beirut: Muʾassasat al-Risāla, 1989. https://archive.org/details/Minhaj_al_3abidine.
——. *The Ninety-Nine Beautiful Names of God: al-Maqṣad al-asnā*. Translated by David Burrell and Nazih Daher. Cambridge: The Islamic Texts Society, 1992.
Ghazālī, Aḥmad (d. 520/1126). *Sawāniḥ*. Edited by N. Pourjavady. Tehran: Intishārāt-i Bunyād-i Farhang-i Īrān, 1980.
Ḥallāj, Ḥusayn Manṣūr al- (d. 309/922). *Dīwān*. http://al-hakawati.net/arabic/civilizations/diwanindex4a53.pdf.
Ḥaqqī, Ismāʿīl (d. 1137/1725). *Rūḥ al-bayān*. altafsir.com.
Hāshimī, Zayd ibn ʿAbdallāh al- (d. after 401/1010). *al-Amthāl*. Damascus: Dār Saʿd al-Dīn, 2002. http://shamela.ws/index.php/book/10533.
Ḥudūd al-ʿālam min al-mashriq ila'l-maghrib. Edited by Manūchihr Sutūda. Tehran: Ṭahūrī, 1983.
——. Translated by V. Minorsky. *Ḥudūd al-ʿālam: 'The Regions of the World.' A Persian Geography 372 A.H.–982 A.D.* Oxford: Oxford University Press, 1937. https://archive.org/details/in.ernet.dli.2015.281514.
Hujwīrī, ʿAlī ibn ʿUthmān (d. 465/1073). *Kashf al-maḥjūb*. Edited by Maḥmūd ʿĀbidī. Tehran: Surūsh, 2004.
——. Translated by R. A. Nicholson. *The Kashf al-Maḥjūb: The Oldest Persian Treatise on Ṣūfiism*. Leyden: Brill, 1911.
Ḥuṣrī, Ibrāhīm ibn ʿAlī al- (d. 453/1061). *Nūr al-ṭarf wa nawr al-ẓarf*. http://shamela.ws/index.php/book/5351.
Ibn ʿAbd al-Barr (d. 463/1071). *Bahjat al-majālis*. http://shamela.ws/index.php/book/558.
Ibn ʿAbd Rabbih al-Andalūsī (d. 328/940). *al-ʿIqd al-farīd*. 8 vols. Beirut: Dār al-Kutub al-ʿIlmiyya. http://shamela.ws/index.php/book/23789.
Ibn Abi'l-Dunyā (d. 281/894). *al-Amr bi'l-maʿrūf wa'l-nahy ʿan al-munkar*. Maktabat al-Ghurabāʾ al-Suʿūdiyya, 1997. http://shamela.ws/index.php/book/8207.
——. *Ḥusn al-ẓann bi'llāh*. Edited by Mukhliṣ Muḥammad. Riyadh: Dār Ṭayyiba, 1988. http://shamela.ws/index.php/book/13113.
——. *Iṣlāḥ al-māl*. Edited by Muḥammad ʿAbd al-Qādir ʿAṭā. Beirut: Muʾassasat al-Kutub al-Thaqāfiyya, 1993. http://shamela.ws/index.php/book/13187.
——. *al-Mutamannīn*. Beirut: Dār Ibn Hazm, 1997. http://shamela.ws/index.php/book/13057.
——. *al-Shukr*. Kuwait: al-Maktab al-Islāmī, 1980. http://shamela.ws/index.php/book/13036.
——. *Ṣifat al-janna*. Edited by Najm ʿAbd al-Raḥmān Khalaf. Beirut: al-Risāla, 1997. http://ia601402.us.archive.org/0/items/waq35693/35693.pdf.
——. *al-ʿUqūbāt*. Beirut: Dār Ibn al-Ḥazm, 1996. http://shamela.ws/index.php/book/8266.

——. *al-Yaqīn*. Beirut: Dār al-Bashā'ir al-Islāmiyya. http://shamela.ws/index.php/book/8220.

Ibn Abī Shayba (d. 328/849). *Kitāb al-īmān*. Edited by Muḥammad Nāṣir al-Dīn al-Albānī. Beirut: al-Maktab al-Islāmī, 1983. http://shamela.ws/index.php/book/7767.

Ibn al-ʿArabī, Muḥyi'l-Dīn (d. 638/1240). *Fuṣūṣ al-ḥikam*. Edited by Abu'l-ʿAlā ʿAfīfī. Beirut: Dār al-Kitāb al-ʿArabī, 1946. https://archive.org/details/Taswuf_20170107.

——. *al-Futūḥāt al-makkiyya*. 4 vols. Cairo: 1911.

——. *Muḥāḍarat al-abrār wa musāmarat al-akhyār*. Beirut: Dār Ṣādir, n.d. https://archive.org/details/mohadaratabrar.

Ibn ʿAsākir, ʿAlī ibn al-Ḥasan (d. 571/1175). *Muʿjam al-shuyūkh*. Edited by Wafāʾ Taqī al-Dīn. Damascus: Dār al-Bashā'ir, 2000. http://shamela.ws/index.php/book/12750.

——. *Ta'rīkh Madīna Dimashq*. Beirut: Dār al-Fikr, 1995. https://archive.org/details/FP24037.

Ibn Bābawayh, al-Shaykh al-Ṣadūq (d. 329/991). *al-Amālī*. Qum: Mu'assasat al-Baʿtha, 1996. http://lfile.ir/hadith-library/25.pdf.

Ibn al-Bassām al-Shantarīnī (d. 542/1147). *al-Dhakhīra fī maḥāsin ahl al-jazīra*. Tunis: al-Dār al-ʿArabiyya li'l-Kitāb, 1978–81. http://shamela.ws/index.php/book/1035.

Ibn Ḥabīb al-Naysābūrī, al-Ḥasan ibn Muḥammad (d. 406/1015–16). *ʿUqalā' al-majānīn*. Edited by Muḥammad al-Saʿīd ibn Basyūnī Zaghlūl. Beirut: Dār al-Kutub al-ʿIlmiyya, 1985. http://shamela.ws/index.php/book/1593.

Ibn Ḥamdūn, Muḥammad ibn al-Ḥasan (d. 562/1166–67). *al-Tadhkira*. Edited by Iḥsān ʿAbbās and Bakr ʿAbbās. 10 vols. Beirut: Dār Ṣādir, 1996. http://shamela.ws/index.php/book/10646.

Ibn Ḥibbān al-Bustī, Muḥammad (d. 354/965). *Rawḍat al-ʿuqalā' wa nuzhat al-fuḍalā'*. Beirut: Dār al-Kutub al-ʿIlmiyya, 2010. http://shamela.ws/index.php/book/6944.

——. *al-Ṣaḥīḥ*. Edited by Aḥmad Muḥammad Shākir. Cairo: Dār al-Maʿārif, 1952. https://archive.org/stream/waq96504/96504#page/n0/mode/2up.

Ibn Hishām (d. 218/833). *al-Sīrat al-nabawiyya*. Edited by 'Umar 'Abd al-Salām Tadmurī. 4 vols. Beirut: Dār al-Kutub al-ʿArabī, 1990. https://archive.org/details/FP94563.

——. *The Life of Muḥammad*. Translated by A. Guillaume. Karachi: Oxford University Press, 1967.

Ibn al-Jawzī (d. 597/1201). *al-Mawḍūʿāt*. Edited by ʿAbd al-Raḥmān Muḥammad ʿUthmān. 3 vols. Medina: al-Maktab al-Salafiyya, 1966–68. http://shamela.ws/index.php/book/882.

——. *al-Mudhish*. Beirut: Dār al-Kutub al-ʿIlmiyya, 1985. http://shamela.ws/index.php/book/6940.

——. *al-Muntaẓam fī ta'rīkh al-mulūk wa'l-umam*. Edited by Muḥammad and Muṣṭafā ʿAbd al-Qādir ʿAṭā. 19 vols. Beirut: Dār al-Kutub al-ʿIlmiyya, 1995. https://archive.org/details/FP76981.

——. *Muthīr al-gharām al-sākin ilā ashraf al-amākin*. Edited by Muṣṭafā Muḥammad Ḥusayn al-Dhahabī. Cairo: Dār al-Ḥadīth, 1995. http://shamela.ws/index.php/book/10437.

——. *Rawḥ al-arwāḥ*. Beirut: Dār al-Kutub al-ʿIlmiyya, 1990. https://archive.org/details/waq82947

——. *Ṣifat al-ṣafwa*. Beirut: Dār al-Maʿrifa, 1979. http://shamela.ws/index.php/book/12031.

——. *al-Tabṣira*. Beirut: Dār al-Kutub al-ʿIlmiyya, 1986. http://shamela.ws/index.php/book/26351.
——. *Talbīs Iblīs*. Beirut: Dār al-Fikr, 2001. http://shamela.ws/index.php/book/11438.
——. *al-Yāqūta*. http://shamela.ws/index.php/book/8160.
Ibn al-Jazarī, Shams al-Dīn Muḥammad (d. 833/1429). *al-Zahr al-fāʾiḥ fī dhikr man tanazzah ʿan al-dhunūb waʾl-qabāʾiḥ*. Edited by Muḥammad ʿAbd al-Qādir ʿAṭā. Beirut: Dār al-Kutub al-ʿIlmiyya, 1986. http://shamela.ws/index.php/book/9102.
Ibn Kathīr, Ismāʿīl (d. 774/1373). *al-Bidāya waʾl-nihāya*. Edited by ʿAbdallāh ibn ʿAbd al-Muḥsin al-Turkī. 25 vols. Giza: Hajr, 2003. https://archive.org/details/alhelawy07.
——. *Tafsīr*. altafsir.com.
Ibn Khallikān, Aḥmad ibn Muḥammad (d. 681/1282). *Wafayāt al-aʿyān*. Edited by Iḥsān ʿAbbās. Beirut: Dār Ṣādir, 1977–78. https://archive.org/details/WAQ17074.
——. *Ibn Khallikan's Biographical Dictionary*. Translated by W. M. Slane. Paris: Oriental Translation Fund, 1843. https://archive.org/details/ibnkhallikansbi00slangoog.
Ibn al-Kharrāṭ, ʿAbd al-Ḥaqq al-Ishbīlī (d. 581/1186). *al-ʿĀqiba fī dhikr al-mawt*. Kuwait: Dār al-Aqṣā, 1986. http://shamela.ws/index.php/book/6862.
Ibn Māja, Muḥammad ibn Yazīd (d. 273/887). *al-Sunan*. 2 vols. Edited by M. F. ʿAbd al-Bāqī. Cairo: Dār Iḥyāʾ al-Kutub al-ʿArabiyya, 1952.
Ibn Manda, Muḥammad ibn Isḥāq (d. 395/1004–5). *al-Tawḥīd wa maʿrifat asmāʾ Allāh*. 3 vols. Medina: Maktabat al-ʿUlūm waʾl-Ḥikam, 2002. https://archive.org/details/WAQ2060.
Ibn Manẓūr, Muḥammad ibn Mukarram (d. 711/1312). *Lisān al-ʿArab*. https://archive.org/details/waq10576.
Ibn al-Mubārak, ʿAbdallāh (d. 181/797). *al-Zuhd waʾl-raqāʾiq*. Edited by Ḥabīb al-Raḥmān al-Aʿẓamī. Beirut: Dār al-Kutub al-ʿIlmiyya. http://shamela.ws/index.php/book/13028.
Ibn Munawwar, Muḥammad (d. after 574/1178). *Asrār al-tawḥīd fī maqāmāt al-Shaykh Abī Saʿīd*. Edited by Muḥammad-Riḍā Shafīʿī Kadkanī. Tehran: Intishārāt-i Āgāh, 1987.
——. *The Secrets of God's Mystical Oneness*. Translated by John O'Kane. Costa Mesa, CA: Mazda, 1992.
Ibn al-Muqriʾ, Abū Bakr Muḥammad (d. 381/991). *al-Muʿjam*. http://shamela.ws/index.php/book/8244.
Ibn al-Naḥḥās al-Dimashqī, Aḥmad ibn Ibrāhīm (d. 814/1411). *Mashāriʿ al-ashwāq ilā maṣāriʿ al-ʿushshāq*. Edited by Idrīs Muḥammad ʿAlī and Muḥammad Khālid Istanbūlī. Beirut: Dār al-Bashāʾir al-Islāmiyya, 2002. https://archive.org/details/MAAEMAO.
Ibn Qayyim al-Jawziyya (d. 750/1350). *Rawḍat al-muḥibbīn wa nuzhat al-mushtāqīn*. Beirut: Dār al-Kutub al-ʿIlmiyya, 1983. http://shamela.ws/index.php/book/11229.
——. *Kitāb al-rūḥ*. Edited by Muḥammad Ajmal Ayyūb al-Iṣlāḥī and Kamāl ibn Muḥammad al-Qālimī. Mecca: Dār ʿĀlam al-Fawāʾid, 2011. https://archive.org/details/WAQ118630s.
Ibn Qutayba al-Dīnawarī (d. 276/889). *Adab al-Kātib*. Edited by Muḥammad al-Dālī. Beirut: Muʾassasat al-Risāla, n.d. https://archive.org/details/tanmawia.com_15789.
——. *al-Imāma waʾl-siyāsa*. http://arab-unity.net/up/uploads/files/unity-a43100d385.pdf.
Ibn Rajab al-Ḥanbalī, Zayn al-Dīn (d. 795/1392–93). *Jāmiʿ al-ʿulūm waʾl-ḥikam*. Cairo: Dār al-Salām, 2004. https://archive.org/details/gamolohikgamolohik.

Ibn Shāhīn (d. 385/996). *Faḍā ʾil Fāṭima*. Edited by Badr al-Badr. Kuwait: Dār Ibn al-Athīr, 1994. http://shamela.ws/index.php/book/9434.

Ibn al-Wazīr, Muḥammad ibn Ibrāhīm (d. 840/1436). *Īthār al-ḥaqq ʿalaʾl-khalq fī radd al-khilāfāt ilā madhhab al-ḥaqq min uṣūl al-tawḥīd*. Beirut: Dār al-Kutub al-ʿIlmiyya, 1987. http://shamela.ws/index.php/book/5937.

Ikhwān al-Ṣafāʾ (ca. 3rd/9th c.). *Rasā ʾil*. 4 vols. Beirut: Dār Ṣādir, 1957. http://www.tasavof.ir/books/download/arabic/ekhvan-asafa/ikhwan-as-safa-2.pdf.

Irbilī, Bahāʾ al-Dīn (d. 692/1293). *Risālat al-ṭayf*. http://shamela.ws/index.php/book/764.

Iṣfahānī, Abu'l-Faraj (d. 356/976). *Kitāb al-aghānī*. Edited by Iḥsān ʿAbbās et al. Beirut: Dār Ṣādir, 2002. https://archive.org/details/Al-Aghani.

Iṣfahānī, ʿImād al-Dīn (d. 597/1201). *Kharīdat al-qaṣr wa jarīdat al-ʿaṣr*. 17 vols. Baghdad: al-Majmaʿ al-ʿIlmī al-ʿIrāqī, 1955ff. https://archive.org/details/Kharidatqasr.

Itlīdī, Muḥammad Diyāb (12th/18th c.). *Nawādir al-khulafāʾ* (= *Iʿlām al-nās bi-mā waqaʿa liʾl-Barāmika maʿa Baniʾl-ʿAbbās*). Beirut: Dār al-Kutub al-ʿIlmiyya, 2004. http://shamela.ws/index.php/book/408.

Jāḥiẓ, al- (d. 255/868). *al-Rasā ʾil*. Edited by ʿAbd al-Salām Muḥammad Hārūn. Cairo: Maktabat al-Khānjī, 1964. http://shamela.ws/index.php/book/10428.

Jarīr ibn ʿAṭiyya (d. ca. 114/732). *Dīwān*. Beirut: Dār Bayrūt, 1986. https://archive.org/details/waq83149.

Jurjānī, ʿAbd al-Qāhir al- (d. 471/1078). *Dalā ʾil al-iʿjāz*. Beirut: Dār al-Kutub al-ʿIlmiyya, 2001. http://shamela.ws/index.php/book/37697.

Kalābādhī, Abū Bakr (d. ca. 384/994). *Baḥr al-fawā ʾid al-musammā bi-maʿānī al-akhbār*. Edited by M. Ismāʿīl and Aḥmad al-Mazīdī. Beirut: Dār al-Kutub al-ʿIlmiyya, 1999.

———. *al-Taʿarruf li-madhhab al-taṣawwuf*. Edited by A. J. Arberry. Cairo: Maktabat al-Khānjī, 1933. https://archive.org/details/123boukrika44_maktoob_20140203_2202.

———. *The Doctrine of the Sufis*. Translated by A. J. Arberry. Cambridge: Cambridge University Press, 1935. http://www.ghazali.org/books/kalabadhi.pdf.

Kāshifī, ʿAlī ibn al-Ḥusayn Wāʿiẓ (d. ca. 939/1532). *Rashaḥāt ʿayn al-ḥayāt*. Edited by ʿAlī Aṣghar Muʿīniyān. 2 vols. Tehran: Bunyād-i Nīkūkārī-yi Nūriyānī, 1977.

Khalīfa, Ḥājjī (d. 1068/1657). *Kashf al-ẓunūn ʿan asāmī al-kutub waʾl-funūn*. Istanbul: Maarif Matbaasi, 1941. https://archive.org/details/WAQkzkz.

Kharāʾiṭī, Muḥammad ibn Jaʿfar al- (d. 327/938). *Iʿtilāl al-qulūb*. Mecca: Nizār Muṣṭafā al-Bāz, 2000. http://shamela.ws/index.php/book/1304.

———. *Makārim al-akhlāq*. Edited by Ayman ʿAbd al-Jābir al-Buḥayrī. Cairo: Dār al-Āfāq al-ʿArabiyya, 1999. http://shamela.ws/index.php/book/9595.

Khargūshī, ʿAbd al-Malik ibn Muḥammad (d. 407/1017). *Sharaf al-Muṣṭafā*. 6 vols. Mecca: Dār al-Bashāʾir al-Islāmiyya, 2004. http://shamela.ws/index.php/book/23644.

Khaṭīb al-Baghdādī, Aḥmad ibn ʿAlī al- (d. 463/1071). *al-Muntakhab min kitāb al-zuhd waʾl-raqāʾiq*. Edited by ʿĀmir Ḥasan Ṣabrī. Beirut: Dār al-Bashāʾir al-Islāmiyya, 2000. https://archive.org/details/zohd_khateeb.

———. *Taʾrīkh madīnat al-salām*. Edited by Bashār ʿAwwād Maʿrūf. 17 vols. Beirut: Dār al-Gharb al-Islāmī, 2000–1. https://archive.org/details/WAQtaba.

Khaṭṭābī, Abū Sulaymān al- (d. 388/998). *al-ʿUzla*. Cairo: al-Maṭbaʿat al-Salafiyya, 1979. http://shamela.ws/index.php/book/13042.

Khayyām, ʿUmar (d. ca. 517/1124). *Rubāʿiyyāt*. http://ganjoor.net/khayyam/robaee/.

Khumrakī, Muʾammal ibn Masrūr (d. ca. 516 or 517/1123–24). *Rawḍat al-fariqayn*. Edited by ʿAbd al-Ḥayy Ḥabībī. Tehran: Dānishgāh, 1980.

Khuttalī, Abū Isḥāq ibn ʿAbdallāh al- (d. ca. 270/884). *al-Maḥabba lillāh*. Edited by ʿĀdil ibn ʿAbd al-Shakūr al-Zarqī. Riyadh: Dār al-Ḥiḍāra li'l-Nashr wa'l-Tawzīʿ, 2003. http://shamela.ws/index.php/book/26872.

Kisāʾī Marwazī, Majd al-Dīn (d. after 390/1000). *Dīwān*. http://ganjoor.net/kesayee/.

Kulaynī, Muḥammad ibn Yaʿqūb (d. 329/941). *al-Kāfī*. Edited by ʿAlī Akbar al-Ghaffārī. Tehran: Dār al-Kutub al-Islāmiyya, 1968. http://lib.eshia.ir/11005/1/1.

Kutubī, Muḥammad ibn Shākir al- (d. 764/1363). *Fawāt al-wafayāt*. Edited by Iḥsān ʿAbbās. Beirut: Dār Ṣādir, 1973–74. http://shamela.ws/index.php/book/1003.

Lālkāʾī, Hibatallāh ibn al-Ḥasan al-Ṭabarī al- (d. 418/1027). *Karāmāt al-awliyāʾ*. Edited by Aḥmad ibn Saʿd al-Ghāmidī. Riyadh: Dār Ṭayyiba, 1992. http://shamela.ws/index.php/book/13150.

Lisān al-ʿArab. *See* Ibn Manẓūr.

Majlisī, Muḥammad Bāqir (d. 1110/1698). *Biḥār al-anwār*. 110 vols. Beirut: Muʾassasat al-Wafāʾ, 1983. http://books.rafed.net.

Makkī, Abū Ṭālib (d. 386/996). *Qūt al-qulūb*. Edited by ʿĀṣim Ibrāhīm al-Kiyālī. 2 vols. Beirut: Dār al-Kutub al-ʿIlmiyya, 2005. http://shamela.ws/index.php/book/482.

Marzūqī, Aḥmad ibn Muḥammad al- (d. 421/1030). *Sharḥ dīwān al-ḥamāsa*. Beirut: Dār al-Kutub al-ʿIlmiyya, 2003. http://shamela.ws/index.php/book/26536.

Masʿūdī, ʿAlī ibn al-Ḥusayn (d. 345/956). *Murūj al-dhahab*. Beirut: al-Maktab al-ʿAṣriyya, 2005. https://archive.org/details/Meroujzahab.

Māwardī, ʿAlī ibn Muḥammad al- (d. 450/1058). *Adab al-dunyā wa'l-dīn*. Dār Maktabat al-Ḥayāt, 1986. http://shamela.ws/index.php/book/765.

———. *al-Nukat wa'l-ʿuyūn*. altafsir.com.

Mawṣilī, Abu'l-Fatḥ (d. 392/1002). *al-Khaṣāʾiṣ*. 3 vols. Cairo: al-Hayʾat al-Miṣriyya al-ʿĀmma li'l-Kitāb. http://shamela.ws/index.php/book/9986.

Maybudī, Rashīd al-Dīn (middle 6th/12th c). *Kashf al-asrār wa ʿuddat al-abrār*. Edited by ʿAlī Aṣghar Ḥikmat. 10 vols. Tehran: Danishgah, 1331–39/1952–60.

———. *Kashf al-asrār: The Unveiling of the Mysteries*. Partial translation by William C. Chittick. http://www.altafsir.com/Books/kashf.pdf.

Mihzamī, Abū Haffān ʿAbdallāh ibn Aḥmad al- (d. 257/871). *Akhbār Abī Nuwās*. http://shamela.ws/index.php/book/5369.

Mufīd, Muḥammad, al-Shaykh al- (d. 413/1022). *al-Ikhtiṣāṣ*. http://ar.lib.eshia.ir/11001/1/1.

Munāwī, ʿAbd al-Raʾūf al- (d. 1031/1621). *al-Tawqīf ʿalā muhimmāt al-taʿārīf*. Cairo: 1990. http://shamela.ws/index.php/book/10640.

Muslim ibn al-Ḥajjāj (d. 261/875). *al-Ṣaḥīḥ*. 8 vols. Cairo: Maṭbaʿa Muḥammad ʿAlī Ṣabīḥ, 1334/1915–16.

Mustamlī, Ismāʿīl (d. 434/1042). *Sharḥ-i taʿarruf.* 4 vols. Lucknow: Munshi Naval Kishore, 1328–30/1910–12.
——. *Sharḥ al-taʿarruf.* Edited by Muḥammad Rawshan. 5 vols. Tehran: Asāṭīr, 1363–66/1984–87.
Mutanabbī, Abū Ṭayyib Aḥmad ibn Ḥusayn al- (d. 354/965). *Dīwān.* Beirut: Dār Bayrūt li'l-Ṭibāʿa, 1983. https://archive.org/details/waq78396.
Nāgawrī, Ḥamīd al-Dīn (d. 643/1246). *ʿIshqiyya.* Dehli: Maṭbaʿ Qayṣariyya, 1332/1914.
——. *Lawāʾiḥ.* Ascribed to ʿAyn al-Quḍāt Hamadānī and edited by Raḥīm Farmanish. Tehran: Hunar, 1337/1958.
——. *Ṭawāliʿ al-shumūs.* Manuscript, Kitābkhāna-yi Āyatallāh al-ʿUẓmā Burūjirdī, Qum.
Nasāʾī, Aḥmad ibn Shuʿayb (d. 303/915). *al-Sunan,* bi sharḥ al-Suyūṭī. Edited by Ḥasan Muḥammad al-Masʿūdī. 8 vols. Beirut: Iḥyāʾ al-Turāth al-ʿArabī, 1930.
Nāṣir Khusraw (d. 481/1088). *Dīwān.* Edited by Mujtabā Mīnuwī and Mehdi Mohaghegh. Tehran: Dānishgāh, 1974.
Naysābūrī, Niẓām al-Dīn Ḥasan al- (d. 728/1327). *Gharāʾib al-qurʾān.* altafsir.com.
Nuwayrī, Aḥmad ibn ʿAbd al-Wahhāb (d. 733/1333). *Nihāyat al-arab fī funūn al-adab.* Beirut: Dār al-Kutub al-ʿIlmiyya, 2004. https://archive.org/details/nihayat-al-arab.
Qālī, Abū ʿAlī Ismāʿīl al- (d. 356/967). *Kitāb al-amālī.* Edited by Muḥammad ʿAbd al-Jawād al-Aṣmaʿī. 2 vols. Cairo: Dār al-Kutub al-Miṣriyya, 1926. http://shamela.ws/index.php/book/9160.
Qurṭubī, Abū ʿAbdallāh Muḥammad ibn Aḥmad al- (d. 670/1273). *al-Jāmiʿ li-aḥkām al-qurʾān.* altafsir.com.
Qushayrī, Abu'l-Qāsim (d. 465/1072). *Arbaʿ rasāʾil fī'l-taṣawwuf.* Edited by Qāsim Sāmarāʾī. Baghdad: al-Majmaʿ al-ʿIlmī, 1969. https://archive.org/stream/quchairi/4rasael#page/n0/mode/2up.
——. *Laṭāʾif al-ishārāt.* Edited by Ibrāhīm Basyūnī. 3 vols. Cairo: al-Hayʾat al-Miṣriyyat al-ʿĀmma li'l-Kitāb, 2000. http://shamela.ws/index.php/book/23629.
——. *Manthūr al-khiṭāb fī mashhūr al-abwāb.* In Qushayrī, *Arbaʿ rasāʾil,* 60–70.
——. *Kitāb al-miʿrāj.* Edited by ʿAlī Ḥasan ʿAbd al-Qādir. Cairo, 1964. https://archive.org/stream/quchairi/mi3raj#page/n0/mode/2up.
——. *al-Mukhtaṣar fī'l-tawba.* In Qushayrī, *Arbaʿ rasāʾil.*
——. *Risāla al-Qushayriyya.* Edited by ʿAbd al-Ḥalīm Maḥmūd and Maḥmūd ibn al-Sharīf. 2 vols. Cairo: Dār al-Maʿārif. http://shamela.ws/index.php/book/9953.
——. *al-Qushayri's Epistle on Sufism.* Translated by Alexander Knysh. Reading: Garnet, 2007. http://privat.bahnhof.se/wb449823/00_DATA/Kutub/English/Qushayri_Risala.pdf.
——. *Sharḥ asmāʾillāh al-ḥusnā* (= *al-Taḥbīr fī ʿilm al-tadhkīr*). Edited by Aḥmad ʿAbd al-Munʿim ʿAbd al-Salām. Beirut: Dār al-Āzāl, 1986.
——. *al-Shawāhid wa'l-amthāl.* Compiled by ʿAbd al-Raḥīm Qushayrī (d. 1120). Edited by Mujtabā Shahsawārī. Pre-publication PDF.
Raḍī, Muḥammad ibn al-Ḥusayn al-Sharīf al- (d. 406/1015). *Dīwān.* http://al-hakawati.net/arabic/civilizations/diwanindex4a2.pdf.

Rāghib al-Iṣfahānī, al- (d. 502/1109). *Muḥāḍarāt al-udabāʾ wa muḥāwarāt al-shuʿarāʾ*. 2 vols. Beirut: Dār al-Arqam, 1999. http://shamela.ws/index.php/book/9078.

Rāzī, Fakhr al-Dīn (d. 606/1209). *Mafātīḥ al-ghayb* (*al-Tafsīr al-kabīr*). Beirut: Dār Iḥyāʾ al-Turāth al-ʿArabī, 1999. http://shamela.ws/index.php/book/23635.

RQ. See Qushayrī, *Risāla*.

Rūmī, Jalāl al-Dīn (d. 672/1273). *Dīwān* (*Kulliyyāt-i Shams*). Edited by Badīʿ al-Zamān Furūzānfar. Tehran: Dānishgāh, 1957–67.

———. *Mathnawī*. Edited and translated by R. A. Nicholson. 8 vols. London: Luzac, 1925–40.

———. *The Quatrains of Rūmī*. Text and translation by Ibrahim Gamard and A. G. Ravan Farhadi. San Rafael, CA: Sufi Dari Books, 2008.

———. *Rubāʿiyyāt*. Vol. 8 of the *Dīwān*. Tehran: Dānishgāh, 1964.

Rūzbihān Baqlī (d. 606/1209). *al-Maknūn*. Edited by ʿAlī Ṣadrāʾī Khūyī. http://ar.lib.eshia.ir/27484/1/255.

Sabziwārī, Mullā Hādī (d. 1313/1873). *Sharḥ al-asmāʾ al-ḥusnā*. Edited by Najaf-ʿAlī Ḥabībī. Tehran: Dānishgāh, 1373/1994.

Ṣafadī, Ṣalāḥ al-Dīn Khalīl al- (d. 764/1363). *al-Wāfī biʾl-wafayāt*. 29 vols. Beirut: Dār Iḥyāʾ al-Turāth, 2000. https://archive.org/details/FP49931.

Ṣāḥib ibn ʿAbbād, al- (d. 385/925). *al-Dīwān*. Edited by Ibrāhīm Shams al-Dīn. Beirut: al-Muʾassasat al-Aʿlamī liʾl-Maṭbūʿāt, 2001. http://alfeker.org/library.php?id=2797.

Sakhāwī, Shams al-Dīn Muḥammad al- (d. 902/1497). *al-Maqāṣid al-ḥasana fī bayān kathīr min al-aḥādīth al-mushtahara ʿalaʾl-alsina*. Edited by Muḥammad ʿUthmān al-Khist. Beirut: Dār al-Kutub al-ʿArabī, 1985. http://shamela.ws/index.php/book/23177.

Samʿānī, Abū Manṣūr Muḥammad ibn ʿAbd al-Jabbār al- (d. 450/1058). *Majmūʿ gharāʾib aḥādīth al-nabī*. 4 vols. Edited by Muḥammad ibn Saʿd ibn ʿAbd al-Raḥmān Āl Suʿūd. Taif: Nādī Makkat al-Thaqāfī al-Adabī 1428/2007, and Mecca: Maṭābiʿ al-Ṣafā, 1431/2010.

Samʿānī, Abuʾl-Muẓaffar Manṣūr ibn Muḥammad al- (d. 489/1096). *al-Iṣṭilām fīʾl-khilāf bayn imāmayn al-Shāfiʿī wa Abī Ḥanīfa*. Edited by Nāʾif ibn Nāfiʿ al-ʿAmrī. 4 vols. Cairo: Dār al-Manār, 1992. https://archive.org/details/FP130577.

———. *Qawāṭiʿ al-adilla fī ʿilm al-uṣūl*. Edited by ʿAlī al-Ḥakamī. 5 vols. Riyadh: Maktabat al-Tawba, 1418/1998. https://archive.org/details/WAQ36914.

———. *Tafsīr al-Qurʾān*. Edited by Abū Tamīm Yāsir ibn Ibrāhīm and Abū Bilāl Ghunaym ibn ʿAbbās ibn Ghunaym. 6 vols. Riyadh: Dār al-Waṭan, 1418/1997.

Samʿānī, Abuʾl-Qāsim Aḥmad ibn Manṣūr (d. 534/1140). *Rawḥ al-arwāḥ fī sharḥ asmāʾ al-malik al-fattāḥ*. Edited by Najib Mayel Heravi. Tehran: Intishārāt-i ʿIlmī wa Farhangī, 1989.

Samʿānī, Abū Saʿd ʿAbd al-Karīm ibn Muḥammad ibn Manṣūr al- (d. 562/1166). *Adab al-imlāʾ waʾl-istimlāʾ*. Edited by Aḥmad Muḥammad ʿAbd al-Raḥmān. Mecca: Jāmiʿa Umm al-Qurā, 1993. https://archive.org/details/FP7541.

———. *al-Ansāb*. 5 vols. Edited by ʿAbdallāh ʿUmar al-Bārūdī. Beirut: Dār al-Jinān, 1988. https://archive.org/details/ansab_smani.

———. *Faḍāʾil al-shām*. Edited by ʿAmr ʿAlī ʿUmar. Damascus: Dār al-Thaqāfat al-ʿArabiyya, 1992. https://archive.org/details/waq23691.

——. *al-Muntakhab min Muʿjam shuyūkh al-Samʿānī.* Edited by Muwaffaq ibn ʿAbdallāh ibn ʿAbd al-Qādir. Riyadh: Dār ʿĀlam al-Kutub, 1996. http://shamela.ws/index.php/book/21556.

——. *al-Taḥbīr fiʾl-Muʿjam al-kabīr.* Edited by Munīra Nājī Sālim. 2 vols. Baghdad: Dīwān al-Awqāf, 1975. http://shamela.ws/index.php/book/1694.

Samarqandī, Abu'l-Layth Naṣr ibn Muḥammad al- (d. 373/983). *Baḥr al-ʿulūm.* altafsir.com.

——. *Tanbīh al-ghāfilīn bi-aḥādīth sayyid al-anbiyāʾ waʾl-mursalīn.* Beirut: Dār Ibn Kathīr, 2000. http://shamela.ws/index.php/book/10488.

Sanāʾī Ghaznawī, Abu'l-Majd Majdūd (d. ca. 535/1140). *Dīwān.* Edited by Mudarris Raḍawī. Tehran: Ibn Sīnā, 1962.

——. *Sayr al-ʿibād ilaʾl-maʿād.* In *Mathnawī-hāyi Ḥakīm Sanāʾī,* edited by M. T. Mudarris Raḍawī, 181–233. Tehran: Dānishgāh, 1348/1969.

Sarī ibn Aḥmad al-Raffāʾ, al- (d. ca. 362/972). *al-Muḥibb waʾl-maḥbūb waʾl-mashmūm waʾl-mashrūb.* Edited by Miṣbāḥ Ghalāwunjī. Damascus: Majmaʿ al-Lughat al-ʿArabiyya, 1986. https://archive.org/details/almhb.

Sarrāj, Abū Naṣr al- (d. 378/988). *Kitāb al-lumaʿ.* Edited by R. A. Nicholson. Leyden: Brill, 1914. https://archive.org/details/kitaballuma00sarruoft.

Sarrāj, Jaʿfar ibn Aḥmad al- (d. 500/1106). *Maṣāriʿ al-ʿushshāq.* http://shamela.ws/index.php/book/26549.

Shajarī, Yaḥyā ibn al-Ḥusayn al- (d. 499/1105). *Tartīb al-amālī al-khamīsa.* Beirut: Dār al-Kutub al-ʿIlmiyya, 2001. http://shamela.ws/index.php/book/9392.

Shaʿrānī, ʿAbd al-Wahhāb al- (d. 973/1565–66). *al-Ṭabaqāt al-kubrā.* Cairo: Maktabat al-Thaqāfat al-Dīniyya, 2005. https://archive.org/details/attabaqat_alkobra.

Shahrazūrī, Ibn al-Ṣalāḥ (d. 643/1245). *An Introduction to the Science of Hadith.* Translated by E. Dickinson. Reading, UK: Garnet, 2006.

Sijzī, Amīr Ḥasan (d. 737/1337). *Fawāʾid al-fuʾād.* Edited by Muḥammad Laṭīf Malik. Tehran: Rawzana, 1377/1998.

——. *Morals for the Heart.* Translated by Bruce Lawrence. New York: Paulist Press, 1992.

Sirjānī, Abu'l-Ḥasan (d. ca. 470/1077). *Kitāb al-bayāḍ waʾl-sawād: Sufism, Black and White.* Edited by Bilal Orfali and Nada Saab. Leyden: Brill, 2012.

Subkī, Tāj al-Dīn ʿAbd al-Wahhāb ibn ʿAlī al- (d. 771/1370). *Ṭabaqāt al-shāfiʿiyya al-kubrā.* https://archive.org/details/WAQ5093.

Sulamī, Abū ʿAbd al-Raḥmān al- (d. 412/1021). *Ḥaqāʾiq al-tafsīr.* altafsir.com.

——. *Kitāb al-Arbaʿīn fiʾl-taṣawwuf.* Edited by A. J. Arberry. Hyderabad, 1951.

——. *Ṭabaqāt al-ṣūfiyya.* Edited by Muṣṭafā ʿAbd al-Qādir ʿAṭā. Beirut: Dār al-Kutub al-ʿIlmiyya, 1998. http://shamela.ws/index.php/book/6686.

Ṣūlī, Abū Bakr Muḥammad ibn Yaḥyā al- (d. ca. 335/946). *Ashʿār awlād al-khulafāʾ wa akhbāruhum.* Edited by J. Heworth-Dunnej. Cairo: Maṭbaʿat al-Ṣāwī, 1936. http://shamela.ws/index.php/book/7822.

Suyūṭī, Jalāl al-Dīn al- (d. 911/1505). *Taʾrīkh al-khulafāʾ.* Qatar: Wizārat al-Awqāf, 2004. https://archive.org/details/FP145257.

Ṭabarānī, Sulaymān ibn Aḥmad al- (d. 360/971). *al-Muʿjam al-awsaṭ*. 10 vols. Cairo: Dār al-Ḥaramayn, 1995. https://archive.org/details/WAQmat.

——. *al-Muʿjam al-kabīr*. 25 vols. Cairo: Maktaba Ibn Taymiyya, 1994. https://archive.org/details/WAQ15954.

Ṭabarī, Abū Jaʿfar al- (d. 310/923). *Tafsīr*. altafsir.com.

——. *The History of al-Ṭabarī*, vol. 1. Translated by Franz Rosenthal. Albany: State University of New York Press, 1989.

——. *Taʾrīkh al-rusul wa'l-mulūk*. 11 vols. Beirut: Dār al-Turāb, 1967. http://shamela.ws/index.php/book/9783.

Ṭabarsī, Abū ʿAlī Faḍl al- (d. 548/1153). *Majmaʿ al-bayān fī tafsīr al-Qurʾān*. altafsir.com.

Tabrīzī, al-Khaṭīb Yaḥyā ibn ʿAlī al- (d. 502/1109). *Sharḥ Dīwān Abī Tammām*. Edited by Rājī al-Asmar. 2 vols. Beirut: Dār al-Kutub al-ʿArabī, 1994. https://archive.org/details/waq59940.

Ṭāʾī, Abu'l-Futūḥ Muḥammad al- (d. 555/1160). *al-Arbaʿīn*. Beirut: Dār al-Bashāʾir al-Islāmiyya, 1999. http://shamela.ws/index.php/book/26842.

Tanūkhī, Abu'l-Maḥāsin al-Mufaḍḍal al- (d. 442/1050). *Taʾrīkh al-ʿulamāʾ al-naḥwiyyīn*. Edited by ʿAbd al-Fattāḥ Muḥammad al-Ḥulw. Cairo: Hajr li'l-Ṭibāʿa wa'l-Nashr, 1992. http://shamela.ws/index.php/book/1386.

Tanūkhī, al-Qāḍī al-Muḥsin ibn ʿAlī al- (d. 384/994). *Nishwār al-muḥāḍara wa akhbār al-mudhākara*. Edited by ʿAbūd al-Shālijī al-Maḥāmī. 8 vols. Beirut: 1971–73. http://shamela.ws/index.php/book/10275.

Ṭarṭūshī, Muḥammad ibn Muḥammad al- (d. 520/1126). *Sirāj al-mulūk*. Cairo, 1872. http://shamela.ws/index.php/book/1585.

Tawḥīdī, Abū Ḥayyān ʿAlī ibn Muḥammad al- (d. ca. 400/1010). *al-Baṣāʾir wa'l-dhakhāʾir*. Edited by Wadād al-Qāḍī. 10 vols. Beirut: Dār Ṣādir, 1988. http://shamela.ws/index.php/book/26423.

——. *al-Imtāʿ wa'l-muʾānasa*. Beirut: al-Maktab al-ʿUnṣuriyya, 2011. shamela.ws/index.php/book/10521.

——. *al-Ṣadāqa wa'l-ṣadīq*. Edited by Ibrāhīm al-Kīlānī. Beirut: Dār al-Fikr al-Muʿāṣir, 1998. http://shamela.ws/index.php/book/11485.

Thaʿālibī, Abū Manṣūr al- (d. 429/1038). *al-Iʿjāz wa'l-ījāz*. Cairo: Maktab al-Qurʾān. http://shamela.ws/index.php/book/23741.

——. *Khāṣṣ al-khāṣṣ*. Edited by Maḥmūd ibn Yaḥyā Muḥyi'l-Dīn al-Jinān. Beirut: Dār al-Kutub al-ʿIlmiyya, 1994. http://ia600304.us.archive.org/30/items/waq66916/66916.pdf.

——. *al-Laṭāʾif wa'l-ẓarāʾif*. http://shamela.ws/index.php/book/10509.

——. *al-Luṭf wa'l-laṭāʾif*. http://shamela.ws/index.php/book/595.

——. *al-Muntaḥil*. Edited by Aḥmad Abū ʿAlī. Alexandria: al-Tijāriyya, 1901. http://ia902602.us.archive.org/5/items/montahlmontahl/montahl.pdf.

——. *Rasāʾil*. http://shamela.ws/index.php/book/623.

——. *al-Tamthīl wa'l-muḥādara*. Edited by ʿAbd al-Fattāḥ Muḥammad al-Ḥuluw. Tunis: al-Dār al-ʿArabiyya li'l-Kitāb, 1981. http://shamela.ws/index.php/book/5683.

——. *Thimār al-qulūb fi'l-muḍāf wa'l-mansūb*. Edited by Muḥammad Abu'l-Faḍl Ibrāhīm. Beirut: Maktabat al-ʿAṣriyya, 2003. https://archive.org/details/waq63658.

——. *Yatīmat al-dahr*. Edited by Mufīd Muḥammad Qamīḥa. Beirut: Dār al-Kutub al-ʿIlmiyya, 1983. https://archive.org/details/waq4387.

Thaʿlabī, Abū Isḥāq Aḥmad ibn Muḥammad al- (d. 427/1035–36). *ʿArāʾis al-majālis fī qiṣaṣ al-anbiyāʾ or Lives of the Prophets*. Translated by William M. Brinner. Leiden: Brill, 2002.

——. *al-Kashf waʾl-bayān*. altafsir.com.

——. *Qatlaʾl-Qurʾān*. Edited by Nāṣir ibn Muḥammad al-Manīʿ. Riyadh: Obeikan, 2008. http://mlffat.tafsir.net/files/310.pdf.

Tilimsānī, ʿAfīf al-Dīn al- (d. 690/1291). *Sharḥ asmāʾ al-ḥusnā*. ms.

Tirmidhī, Muḥammad ibn ʿĪsā al- (d. 279/892). *al-Jāmiʿ al-ṣaḥīḥ, wa huwa Sunan al-Tirmidhī*. 5 vols. Edited by A. M. Shākir. Cairo: al-Maktab al-Islāmiyya, 1938.

Tustarī, Sahl al- (d. ca. 283/896). *al-Tafsīr*. altafsir.com.

ʿUmarī, Ibn Faḍlallāh al- (d. 749/1349). *Masālik al-abṣār fī mamālik al-amṣār*. Abu Dhabi: al-Majmaʿ al-Thaqāfī, 2002. http://shamela.ws/index.php/book/11790.

Wāḥidī, ʿAlī ibn Aḥmad al- (d. 468/1075). *Asbāb al-nuzūl*. Edited by ʿIṣām ibn ʿAbd al-Muḥsin al-Ḥamīdān. Dammam: Dār al-Iṣlāḥ, 1992. http://shamela.ws/index.php/book/11314.

——. *Asbāb al-nuzūl*. Translated by Mokrane Guezzou. Amman: Royal Aal al-Bayt Institute for Islamic Thought, 2008.

Wakīʿ ibn al-Jarrāḥ, al- (d. 197/812–13). *al-Zuhd*. Edited by ʿAbd al-Raḥmān ʿAbd al-Jabbār al-Farīwāʾī. Medina: Maktabat al-Dār, 1984. https://archive.org/details/waq16875.

Washshāʾ, Abuʾl-Ṭayyib Muḥammad al- (d. 325/936–37). *al-Muwashshā* (= *al-Ẓarf waʾl-ẓurafāʾ*). Edited by Kamāl Muṣṭafā. Cairo: Maṭbaʿat al-Iʿtimād, 1953. http://shamela.ws/index.php/book/26102.

Yāqūt al-Ḥamawī (d. 626/1229). *Muʿjam al-buldān*. Beirut: Dār Ṣādir, 1977. https://archive.org/details/waq0093.

Ẓāhirī, Muḥammad ibn Dāwūd al- (d. ca. 296/909). *al-Zahra*. http://shamela.ws/index.php/book/738.

Zamakhsharī, Abuʾl-Qāsim Maḥmūd al- (d. 538/1144). *al-Kashshāf ʿan ḥaqāʾiq ghawāmiḍ al-tanzīl*. Beirut: Dār al-Kutub al-ʿArabī, 1987. http://shamela.ws/index.php/book/23627.

——. *Rabīʿ al-abrār wa nuṣūṣ al-akhbār*. Edited by ʿAbd al-Amīr Muhannā. 5 vols. Beirut: Muʾassasat al-Aʿlamī, 1992. http://shamela.ws/index.php/book/10668.

Zawzanī, ʿAbdallāh ibn Muḥammad al- (d. 431/1039). *Ḥamāsat al-ẓurafāʾ*. http://shamela.ws/index.php/book/752.

Secondary Sources

Bulliet, Richard. *The Patricians of Nishapur: A Study in Medieval Social History*. Cambridge, MA: Harvard University Press, 1972.

Chiabotti, Francesco. "ʿAbd al-Karīm al-Qushayrī (d. 465/1072): Family Ties and Transmission in Nishapur's Sufi Milieu." In *Family Portraits with Saints*, edited by C. Mayeur-Jaoun and A. Papas, 255–307. Berlin: Klaus Schwarz Verlag, 2014.

Chittick, William C. *Divine Love: Islamic Literature and the Path to God*. New Haven: Yale University Press, 2013.

———. "The Myth of Adam's Fall in Aḥmad Sam'ānī's Rawḥ al-arwāḥ." In *Classical Persian Sufism: From Its Origins to Rūmī*, edited by L. Lewisohn, 337–59. London: Khaniqahi Nimatullahi Publications, 1993. Also in Chittick, *Sufism*, 111–36.

———. "Rūmī and Waḥdat al-Wujūd." In *Poetry and Mysticism in Islam: The Heritage of Rūmī*, edited by A. Banani, R. Hovannisian, and G. Sabbagh, 70–111. Cambridge: Cambridge University Press, 1994. Revised version in Chittick, *In Search of the Lost Heart*, chaps. 8–9. Albany: State University of New York Press, 2012.

———. *The Sufi Path of Knowledge: Ibn al-'Arabī's Metaphysics of Imagination*. Albany: State University of New York Press, 1989.

———. *The Sufi Path of Love: The Spiritual Teachings of Rūmī*. Albany: State University of New York Press, 1983.

———. *Sufism: A Short Introduction*. Oxford: Oneworld, 2000.

Dānishpazhūh, Muḥammad-Taqī. "Rawḥ al-arwāḥ-i Sam'ānī." *Majalla-yi Dānishkada-yi Adabiyyāt wa 'Ulūm-i Insānī* 15 (1346–47/1967–68): 300–15, 407–18.

Dihkhudā. *Lughat-nāma*. http://www.vajehyab.com/.

Ernst, Carl. "Shaykh 'Alī Hujwīrī." Foreword to the Nicholson translation of Hujwīrī, *Revealing the Mystery* (*Kashf al-mahjūb*). New York: Pir Press, 1999.

Faryāmanish, Mas'ūd. "Rawḥ al-arwāḥ-i Sam'ānī wa Dīwān-i Ḥāfiz: Barkhī mushābahat-hā." *Wīzha-nāma-yi hamāyish-i bayn al-milalī-yi Ḥāfiz-i Shīrāzī*. Tehran: Dānishgāh-i Āzād, 1:371–403.

Furūzānfar, Badī' al-Zamān. *Sharḥ-i Mathnawī-yi sharīf*. Tehran: Dānishgāh, 1348/1969.

Gimaret, Daniel. *Les noms divins en Islam: Exégèse lexicographique et théologique*. Paris: Les Éditions du Cerf, 1988.

Griffel, Frank. *al-Ghazālī's Philosophical Theology*. Oxford: Oxford University Press, 2009.

Homerin, Th. Emil. *'Umar ibn al-Fāriḍ: Sufi Verse, Saintly Life*. Mahwah, NJ: Paulist Press, 2001.

de Jong, Fred, and Radtke, Bernd. *Islamic Mysticism Contested: Thirteen Centuries of Controversies and Polemics*. Leiden: Brill, 1999.

Jubūrī, Yaḥyā al-. *Shi'r 'Amr ibn Sha's al-Asadī*. Kuwait: Dār al-Qalam, 1983. https://archive.org/details/ShaaS.

Karamustafa. *Sufism: The Formative Period*. Edinburgh: Edinburgh University Press, 2007.

Knysh, Alexander. *Islamic Mysticism: A Short History*. Leiden: Brill, 2000.

———. *Sufism: A New History of Islamic Mysticism*. Princeton: Princeton University Press, 2017.

Lawrence, Bruce. "The Lawa'ih of Qazi Hamid ud-Din Nagauri." *Indo-Iranica* 28 (1975): 34–53.

Lumbard, Joseph E. B. *Ahmad al-Ghazali, Remembrance, and the Metaphysics of Love*. Albany: State University of New York Press, 2017.

Maḥmūd, 'Abd al-Ḥalīm. *Sulṭān al-'Ārifīn Abū Yazīd al-Basṭāmī*. Cairo: al-Maktab al-Miṣrī li'l-Ṭibā'a wa'l-Nashr, n.d.

Mīr-Afḍalī, Sayyid 'Alī. *Rubā'iyyāt-i Khayyām dar manābi'-i kuhan*. Tehran: Markaz-i Nashr-i Dānishgāhī, 1390/2011.

Murata, Sachiko. *The Tao of Islam: A Sourcebook on Gender Relationships in Islamic Thought*. Albany: State University of New York Press, 1992.

———, and William C. Chittick. *The Vision of Islam*. New York: Paragon House, 1994.

Nasr, Seyyed Hossein, Caner K. Dagli, Maria Massi Dakake, and Joseph E. B. Lumbard, eds. *The Study Quran*. HarperOne, 2015.

Nguyen, Martin. *Sufi Master and Quran Scholar: Abū'l-Qāsim Qushayrī and the Laṭā'if al-ishārāt*. Oxford: Oxford University Press, 2012.

Ridgeon, Lloyd, ed. *The Cambridge Companion to Sufism*. Cambridge: Cambridge University Press, 2014.

———. *Morals and Mysticism in Persian Sufism: A History of Sufi-Futuwwat in Iran*. Abingdon and New York: Routledge, 2010.

Sahi, M. Sharifi. "Newly-Found Poems of Anvari in an Old Manuscript." https://www.academia.edu/4163756, p. 34.

Shahkazemi, Reza. *Justice and Remembrance: Introducing the Spirituality of Imam Ali*. London: I. B. Tauris, 2006.

Shubbar, Jawād. *Adab al-Ṭaff aw shuʿarā' al-Ḥusayn*. 10 vols. Beirut: Dār al-Murtaḍā, 1988. https://archive.org/details/adabtof.

Yazigi, Maya. "A Claim for Tajdīd in the Sixth/Twelfth Century? al-Samʿānī, His Kitāb al-Ansāb and a Legacy Contested." *Oriens* 39 (2011): 165–98.

Zargar, Cyrus Ali. *The Polished Mirror: Storytelling and the Pursuit of Virtue in Islamic Philosophy and Sufism*. Oxford: Oneworld Academic, 2017.

INDEX OF QURANIC VERSES

1:1 In the name of God.... 71, 164
1:2 The praise belongs to God.... lxiii, 90–92, 157, 183, 269, 270, 286, 368–69, 373
1:3 The All-Merciful, the Ever-Merciful. 370, 504–5n273
1:5 Thee alone we worship, and Thee alone.... 116–17, 353, 370–71, 504–5n273
1:6 Guide us on the straight path. 464, 504–5n273
2:3 who have faith in the Unseen. xlviii, 76
2:15 God will mock them. 25
2:18 deaf, dumb, blind. 263
2:23 Then bring a surah like it. 478
2:24 Whose fuel is people and stones. 447; prepared for the unbelievers. 304
2:29 He created for you. 379
2:30 When thy Lord said to the angels. 320; I am setting in the earth a vicegerent. 14, 46, 65, 191, 217, 236, 287, 319–22, 378, 485; What, wilt Thou set therein one who will work corruption there, and shed blood. 59, 143, 157, 172–74, 217, 319–21, 392, 479–80; While we glorify Thy praise and call Thee holy? 13, 53, 86, 173, 183, 202, 218, 232, 238, 319–20, 322, 324, 395, 397, 483; He said, "Surely I know what you do not know." 59–60, 91, 127, 141, 153, 157, 173, 176–77, 217, 226, 253, 320, 322–23, 391, 467, 488
2:31 And He taught Adam the names.... xlix, 172, 226, 475, 489; Tell Me the names of these.... xlix, 14, 172, 489
2:33 O Adam, tell them their names. 98, 145, 184, 384, 489–90
2:34 And when We said to the angels, "Prostrate yourselves before Adam".... 14, 46, 53, 145, 177, 184, 185, 217, 233, 322, 324, 335, 385, 397, 440, 494; He refused and was proud.... 362
2:35 O Adam, dwell thou and thy spouse in the Garden. 86; Eat thereof easefully. 65; But do not go near this tree! 143, 150, 494
2:36 Then Satan made them slip. 293; Go down! 103, 157, 205
2:38 Go down out of it. 110, 143, 486; If guidance comes to you from Me.... 123, 158
2:40 And be loyal to My covenant; I shall be loyal.... 451
2:44 Will you command the people to piety...? 334
2:60 Each people now knew their drinking place. 275
2:74 Then your hearts became hardened.... 203
2:89 And from before they had been seeking victory.... 192
2:109 Surely God is powerful over everything. 407
2:117 And when He decrees an affair, He says to it only "Be!"... 34, 168, 183, 298, 314, 328
2:124 Surely I am making thee a leader for the people. 328
2:125 a place of visitation for the people. 88. Take the station of Abraham.... 432
2:129 Our Lord, and raise up in their midst a messenger.... 426
2:142 He guides whomsoever He will. 464
2:143 Surely God is clement.... 295
2:144 We have seen thy face turning.... 199; We will turn thee toward a kiblah.... 162, 327; So turn thy face toward the Holy Mosque. 327; Turn your faces toward it. 470

2:152 So remember Me; I will remember you. 168, 258, 392
2:156 Surely we belong to God.... 172, 308
2:158 Surely Safa and Marwa are among the rites of God. 55
2:163 Your God is one God. 295
2:165 Those who have faith love God more intensely. 286
2:177 Those who are loyal to their covenant.... 115, 155, 262
2:179 Surely you have life in retaliation. 5
2:185 God desires ease for you. 375
2:186 And when My servants ask thee about Me....156, 295, 358; So let them respond to Me! 291, 294, 304
2:189 They ask thee about the new moons....192
2:195 And cast not yourselves with your own hands.... 347; God loves the beautiful-doers. 269
2:200 So remember God, as you remember your fathers.... 153
2:222 Surely God loves the repenters and He loves those.... 186, 269, 400, 423, 428
2:231 Remember God's blessings upon you. 298
2:245 Who is it that will lend to God a beautiful loan...? 358, 472–74
2:255 Who is there to intercede with Him...? 41, 219, 430; His Footstool embraces.... 181, 356
2:256 Whoever disbelieves in idols and has faith in God has laid hold of the firmest handle. 20, 131
2:257 God is the friend of those who have faith. lxii, 58, 60, 111, 362, 433
2:258 My Lord is He who gives life and gives death. 305; I give life and I give death. 432
2:259 I lingered a day, or part of a day. 370
2:260 Show me how Thou givest life to the dead. 96, 380
2:261 in every ear a hundred grains. 131
2:280 If he is in hardship, then deferment.... 424
2:286 Take us not to task if we forget.... 389
3:18 God bears witness that there is no god but He...and the possessors of knowledge. 89, 268, 369, 490
3:25 How will it be when We gather them...? 375, 444
3:30 God warns you of Himself. And God is clement toward the servants. 164
3:31 Say: "If you love God, follow me; God will love you." 198
3:33 Surely God chose Adam and Noah.... 60, 97, 112, 143, 155, 182, 186, 191, 324, 432, 489
3:59 Surely the likeness of Jesus for God.... 426
3:73 Say: "Surely the bounty is in God's hand." 335
3:81 And when God took the compact of the prophets.... 253, 382–83, 426
3:92 You will not attain piety until you expend of what you love. 386
3:97 signs, clear signs. 88; The people's duty to God.... 465; God is unneedy toward the worlds. 315
3:101 Whosoever holds fast to God, he will be guided to a straight path. 357
3:110 You are the best community. 200, 323, 328, 432, 483
3:119 Die in your rage! 120
3:128 Thou hast nothing of the affair. 317, 393, 405, 475
3:135 And those who, when they do an indecency.... and who forgives sins but God?...208, 358, 400
3:140 If a wound touches you.... 93
3:169 alive at their Lord. 435
4:1 Surely God is watcher over you. 298
4:6 God suffices as a reckoner/sufficer. 281
4:28 And man was created weak. 268, 423
4:32 Ask God of His bounty. 452
4:77 Say: "The enjoyment of this world is little." 258
4:78 Say: "All is from God." 335
4:87 And who is more truthful in talk than God? 332
4:110 Whoever does something ugly...will find God. 294
4:113 He taught thee what thou didst not know. 162
4:125 God took Abraham as a bosom friend. 60, 155, 187, 198, 465
4:139 Surely the exaltation, all of it, belongs to God. 41, 407
4:147 Why would God chastise you if you are grateful and have faith? 305

4:153 Show us God openly. 167
4:164 God spoke. 100, 101
4:165 messengers bringing good news and warning. 181
5:1 He decrees what He desires. 113, 159, 169, 353
5:3 Today I have perfected for you your religion. 256
5:15 There have come to you from God a light.... 199, 412
5:18 To Him is the homecoming. 42
5:19 after a gap in the messengers. 425
5:20 And He made you kings. 120
5:21 the holy earth. 320
5:41 Those are the ones whose hearts God desired not to purify. 269
5:54 God will bring a people whom He loves.... 21, 261, 484; He loves them and they love Him. lxvi, 58, 60, 111, 118, 123, 128, 131, 147, 155–56, 181, 186, 232–33, 239, 278, 286, 323–24, 337, 364, 369, 384, 401, 407, 419, 429, 440, 485
5:64 As often as they kindle a fire for war, God extinguishes it. 467
5:67 O Messenger, deliver what has been sent down upon thee! 295
5:73 the third of three. 150
5:109 The day God will gather the messengers.... "We have no knowledge...." 39, 140, 377–78, 444, 466
5:110 And when thou createst from clay.... 325
5:116 Didst thou say to the people, "Take me and my mother as two gods...?" 211, 376
5:119 God approves of them.... 115
6:18 And He is the Severe.... 67
6:52 And drive not away those who supplicate.... 304, 393; desiring His face. 231
6:54 When those who have faith in Our signs...372; Your Lord wrote mercy.... 173, 182, 422
6:75 So also We were showing Abraham the dominion.... 195
6:76 When the night darkened over him, he saw a star. He said, "This is my Lord." 278, 279, 432; I love not those that set. 278
6:78 I am quit of what you associate. 532n1085
6:79 Surely I have turned my face toward Him.... 279
6:81 So which of the two groups has a greater right...? 491
6:90 Emulate their guidance. 325
6:91 They measure not God with the rightful due.... xxxiii, 41, 140; Say "God," then leave them. 153, 216
6:96 the Splitter of the dawn. 132; That is the predetermination.... 135
6:103 Eyesights perceive Him not, and He perceives the eyesights.... 41, 140, 340
6:115 Complete is the word of your Lord.... 226
7:11 We created you.... "Prostrate yourselves before Adam." 153
7:12. *See* 38:76
7:13 Go out! 409
7:15 Said He, 'Thou art among the ones reprieved.' 517n638
7:22 So he led the two of them on.... 293. When they tasted the tree.... 495
7:23 Our Lord, we have wronged ourselves. 65, 66, 97, 98, 117–18, 177, 203, 233, 303, 314, 322, 518n483
7:29 making the religion sincere for Him. 304
7:31 Put on your adornment at every place of prostration. 347
7:33 He forbade indecencies. 28, 153
7:43 We would not have been guided had God.... 453, 464
7:54 Your Lord is God.... 295; He sat upon the Throne. 111
7:55 Supplicate your Lord in pleading.... 302, 304
7:56 Supplicate Him in fear and want. 304
7:99 Do they feel secure from God's deception? 398
7:117 Cast thy staff. 360
7:120 So the sorcerers were cast down.... 381
7:124 I will cut off your hands and your feet.... 318
7:136 So We took vengeance on them. 433
7:143 When Moses came to Our appointed time and his Lord spoke to him. 101, 159, 443, 484; Show me, that I may gaze upon Thee! Thou shalt not see Me. 10, 17, 96, 100–2, 139, 159, 165, 166, 178, 197, 218, 235, 276, 277, 306–7, 344, 360, 380, 389, 405, 443, 447, 450, 464; But look at the mountain. 54, 102, 180, 307;

7:143 (*cont'd*)
Then, when his Lord disclosed Himself. . .Moses fell down thunderstruck. 159, 181, 197, 372, 464, 507n343; I repent to Thee. 165, 372, 389
7:144 I have chosen thee. . . . 100; Take what I have given thee. . . . 194
7:150 he threw down the tablets. 34
7:155 And Moses chose his people. . . . 167
7:156 embraces everything. 273
7:172. When thy Lord took from the children of Adam. . . . "Am I not your Lord?" They said, "Yes indeed, we bear witness." 62, 96, 113–15, 118, 130, 135, 142, 310, 316, 335, 383, 389, 401, 416, 429, 468
7:176 So his likeness is the likeness of a dog. 23, 135, 291, 316
7:179 They are like cattle. No, they are further astray. 134, 281, 419
7:180 To God belong the most beautiful names. lx
7:185 Have they not gazed on the dominion of the heavens and the earth? 55, 133
7:188 Say: "I own no benefit for myself, nor harm." 390
7:204 And when the Quran is recited, listen to it. 153
8:9 When you sought the aid of your Lord. . . . 302
8:17 Thou didst not throw. . . . 254, 287, 420;. . .with a beautiful trial. 106, 277, 342
8:37 So that God may distinguish the vile. . . . 151
8:64 O Prophet, God suffices thee. . . . 283, 380, 382
9:5 Slay the associators wherever you find them! 425
9:23 That He may make it prevail over every religion. 192
9:32 They desire to extinguish God's light with their mouths. 192
9:33 It is He who sent His messenger with the guidance. 483
9:40 The second of two. . . . "Surely God is with us." 191, 395, 482
9:43 God has pardoned thee. . . . 328
9:61 Say: "An ear of good for you." 199
9:102 And others who acknowledged. . . . 305; They mixed a wholesome deed. . . . 312
9:111 Surely God has bought. . . . 75; Who is more loyal to his covenant than God? So rejoice. . .! 120, 451
9:112 The repenters, the worshipers. 237, 258, 299, 422, 428–29, 480, 488; the praisers, the journeyers, the bowers. . . . 299, 392
9:118 Then He turned toward them. . . . liv, 428
9:128 clement, ever-merciful toward the faithful. 295
10:2 foot of truthfulness. 130, 263
10:14 Then We made you vicegerents. 120
10:25 And God invites/supplicates to the abode of peace. 11, 291, 304, 460
10:26 Those who do the beautiful shall have the most beautiful and an increase. 8, 18, 306, 420
10:58 Say: "In the bounty of God and His mercy. . . ." 89, 295, 309, 335, 485
11:37 Make the ship before Our eyes. 132
11:43 And the waves came between the two. 50
11:44 O earth, swallow thy water. . .! 50
11:45 Surely my son is one of my folk. 50, 416
11:46 Surely he is not of thy folk. 106, 139
11:64 The she-camel of God. 29
11:75 Surely Abraham was forbearing. . . . 492
11:107 Doer of what He desires. 93, 141
11:108 as a gift unbroken. 422
11:118–19 Except those on whom your Lord has mercy. . . . 173
11:120 All that We recount to thee of the tidings. . . . 189
12:3 the most beautiful of stories. 246
12:18 They brought his shirt with false blood. 296; Beautiful patience! 492
12:19 They sent down their water-drawer. . . . 486
12:20 a paltry price. . . . they had been renouncing him. 106, 445
12:25 What is the recompense of someone who desires ugliness. . .? 446
12:26 It was she who tried to seduce me. 446
12:30 The governor's wife has been trying to seduce. . . . 252
12:31 When she heard their deception. . . . they cut their hands. 252–53; This is no mortal. . . . 135
12:39 God, the One, the Severe. 67, 489
12:42 Remember me to your lord. 361

12:47 leave in its ear. 198
12:53 I do not absolve my soul. 246; Surely the soul commands to ugliness. 145
12:56 Thus did We establish Joseph in the earth. 382
12:63 Father, the measure was denied to us. 243
12:70 You are thieves. 243
12:76 Above every possessor of knowledge.... 144
12:84 Oh my grief for Joseph! 492
12:87 Despair not of the repose of God.... xliv, 312
12:88 We come with scant merchandise. 217, 406
12:89 Do you know what you did to Joseph...? 142, 445
12:90 "What, are you indeed Joseph?" He said, "I am Joseph." 142, 445; Whoever is wary of God, and is patient. 416
12:92 No reproof is upon you today. 406, 445
12:93 Go with my shirt. 296
12:94..."Surely I find the fragrance of Joseph." 77, 241–42
12:96 He threw it on his face and he returned to seeing. 471
12:97 O our father, ask forgiveness of our sins for us. 445
12:98 I will ask my Lord to forgive you. 445
12:100 And He acted beautifully toward me.... after Satan had sowed dissension. 293
12:101 Receive me as a submitter and join me with the wholesome. 16, 480
12:108 upon insight, I and whosoever follows me. 46
13:2 without pillars. 189
13:11 When God desires ugliness for a people.... 138
13:28 Are not hearts serene in the remembrance of God? 275
14:4 We sent no messenger save in the tongue of his people. 201
14:10 The Creator of the heavens and the earth supplicates you. 303
14:19 If He wants He will take you away.... 23
14:22 And Satan will say, once the affair is decided. 205
14:24 A goodly word is like a goodly tree.... 88, 131, 151, 299, 467, 487
14:25 It gives its fruit every season by the leave of its Lord. 131
14:27 God firms up those who have faith. 485; God does what He wills. 113, 159, 169, 216, 353, 437
14:31 Say to My servants. 295
14:34 Surely man is a great wrongdoer, ungrateful. 302
14:36 Then whosoever follows me is of me. 198
14:37 in a valley without crops. 87
15:2 Perhaps the unbelievers would love.... 448
15:9 Surely it is We who have sent down the Remembrance.... 189, 301, 415, 441, 478
15:17–18.... except him who listens by stealth.... 515n576
15:26 Surely We created man of dried clay.... 13, 34, 61, 156, 174, 175, 182, 217, 219, 337, 378
15:29 And I blew into him of My spirit. 46, 134, 144, 180, 324, 401. Fall before him in prostration! 123
15:30 the angels, all of them, prostrated themselves. 173
15:34 Go forth from it; surely thou art an outcast. 205, 265
15:39–40 I shall adorn for them...except Thy sincere servants among them. 206, 225
15:42 Surely My servants—thou hast no ruling power over them. 369, 477
15:49–50 Tell My servants. 268, 270, 295, 400. Surely I am the Forgiving.... 268
15:72 By thy life! 93, 155, 193, 200, 234, 406, 482
15:88 stretch not thine eyes. 165
15:89 Surely I am the warner. 269
16:22 Your God is one God. 407
16:66 between feces and blood, pure milk.... 279, 331, 382
16:68 Thy Lord revealed to the bee. 47
16:75 God strikes a likeness: a servant.... 407
16:97 goodly life. 84, 352
17:1 Glory be to Him who took His servant by night. 158–60, 195, 210, 325, 355, 373, 406, 484
17:7 If you do the beautiful..., and if you do the ugly.... 11, 217
17:8 Perhaps your Lord...We will return. 269

17:29 Make not thy hand. 199
17:44 There is nothing that does not glorify Him. 155
17:46 And when thou rememberest thy Lord.... 89
17:61 Shall I prostrate myself to someone...created of clay? 296, 479, 488
17:70 We honored the children Adam. 131, 237; We carried them.... 156, 286, 465, 467
17:74 Had We not made thee firm. 93
17:79 And of the night, keep vigil.... 311, 428; It may be...a praised station. 183, 191, 427, 445
17:81 The Real has come, and the unreal.... lv, 188, 381
17:84 Say: "Each acts according to his own manner." 291
17:85 the spirit is of the command of my Lord. 123; Of knowledge you are given but little. 537n1247
17:86 If We willed, We would take away that which We revealed to thee. 194
17:103 So We drowned him and those with him, all together. 265
18:13 Surely they were chevaliers who had faith in their Lord.... 215, 353
18:14 And We placed a tie on their hearts. 354
18:17 Thou wouldst have seen the sun, when it rose.... 352
18:18 Thou wouldst have thought them awake.... 215, 352–53; And We turned them now to the right...352–53; And their dog was extending its paws.... 23, 91, 121, 202, 316, 352–53, 437; Hadst thou looked down upon them...thou wouldst have been filled with terror from them. 352, 354–55
18:19 We lingered a day, or part of a day. 370
18:22 They will say, 'Three; the fourth of them was their dog.'.... 70, 267, 316
18:28 Desiring His face. And let not thine eyes turn away from them. 215, 371
18:48 They will be presented before thy Lord in rows. 298
18:49 They will say, "Alas for us! What is it with this book?..." 444
18:60 the meeting place of the two seas. 443
18:67 Surely you will not be able to bear patiently with me. 51
18:71 You have done a terrible thing. 51
18:77 Had you wanted, you could have taken a wage for it. 51
18:78 This is separation between me and you. 51
18:110 Say: "I am a mortal like you." 93, 136, 275
19:25 Shake to thyself the trunk of the palm tree. 132
19:30 Surely I am the servant of God. 158, 159
19:52 We called to him from the right side of the mountain. 198
19:57 We elevated him to a high place. 535n1186
19:63 that is the Garden that We shall give.... 295
19:64 We descend not save by the command of thy Lord. 160
19:71 And none of you there is but will go down...a decreed decision. 295, 297, 447–48
19:90–91 The heavens are almost torn apart.... 305
19:93 None is there...that comes not to the All-Merciful as a servant. 409
19:96 Surely those who have faith...assign love. 323
19:97 For We have made it easy on thy tongue. 199
20:1–2 Ṭāhā. We did not send down the Quran upon thee.... 161, 199
20:5 The All-Merciful sat on the Throne. 24, 26, 61, 378
20:6 beneath the ground. 201, 204, 403
20:7 He knows the secret and the most hidden. 42
20:12 Surely I am thy Lord, so take off thy shoes.... holy valley. 153, 164, 269, 357, 360
20:14 Surely I am God. 153, 292
20:17 And what is that in thy right hand, O Moses? 50, 251, 360, 372, 484
20:18 He said, "It is my staff; I lean upon it...." 50, 153, 307, 360
20:19–20 "Cast it, O Moses!" He cast it.... 360
20:21 O Moses, take it, and fear not!...252, 360
20:24 Go to Pharaoh! 382
20:27 Unloose the knot from my tongue. 102
20:32 Make him a partner in my affair. 490
20:36 Thou hast been given thy request, O Moses! 102, 276

20:39 I cast upon thee love from Me. 100, 101
20:40 You killed a soul. 246; We tried thee with trials. 372
20:41 I chose thee for Myself. 60, 100, 155, 188, 306, 323
20:44 Speak to him with soft words. 220
20:70 We have faith. 80
20:71 I will surely cut off your hands and your feet.... 80
20:72 So decree what you decree! 80, 318
20:82 Surely I am all-forgiving to those who repent. 292, 302
20:83 And what has made thee hurry from thy people, O Moses! 382
20:84 I hurried to Thee, my Lord, that Thou mayest approve. 327
20:110 They encompass Him not in knowledge. xxxiii, 140
20:111 And faces are humbled to the Alive.... 407
20:114 High indeed is God, the King, the Real! 340
20:115 We made covenant with Adam before, but he forgot...no resoluteness. 41, 63, 98, 111, 144, 204–5, 216, 362, 451
20:118 Surely it is thine not to be hungry therein.... 494
20:121 Adam disobeyed his Lord, so went astray. 97, 110, 112, 122–23, 131, 143, 151, 177–78, 182–84, 216, 218, 223, 314, 322, 328, 362, 451, 495
20:122 Then his Lord chose him, so He turned toward him and guided. 112, 113, 122, 182, 186, 191, 219, 229, 328
20:130 in the watches of the night.... 377
21:23 He will not be asked about what He does.... 42, 93, 107, 141, 169
21:26 Nay, they are honored servants. 118, 177, 181, 237, 369
21:32 We made heaven a guarded roof. 191
21:47 And We set up the just balances.... 375
21:51 We gave Abraham his rectitude from before.... 280, 293
21:63 No, it was the large one of them that did it. 245
21:69 coolness and safety. 195, 297, 425
21:81 And Solomon's is the wind, fierce.... 529n1018
21:83 And Job, when he called out to his Lord, "Harm has touched me...." 80, 246, 274, 350–51, 365, 416
21:87 And Dhu'l-Nūn.... he called out in the darknesses, "There is no god but Thou..." 312–13, 355
21:88 So We responded to him and delivered him from sorrow. 313
21:90 They were supplicating Us in eagerness and dread. 302
21:92 I am your Lord, so worship Me. 295
21:101–2 As for those to whom the most beautiful preceded from us.... 297, 319, 400, 420
21:103 The greatest terror shall not make them sorrow.... 297
21:105 And We wrote..."Surely the earth will be inherited...." 321, 337, 480
21:107 We sent thee only as a mercy to the worlds. 205
21:112 And say, "My Lord, decree with the rightful due!" 386
22:7 Surely God will raise up whosoever is in the graves. 334
22:24 Go to Pharaoh! 102
22:26 Make My house pure! 87, 270, 295
22:27 And proclaim the hajj among the people.... 280
22:29 Circumambulate the Ancient House. 55
22:47 Surely a day with your Lord is like a thousand years.... 173
22:73 If a fly steals something.... Feeble are the seeker and the sought! 56, 68
22:78 And struggle in God.... 212; the creed of your father Abraham. 48; So what an excellent Patron! 305
23:12 We created man from an extraction of clay. 144, 156, 299
23:13 Then We placed him as a sperm-drop.... 156
23:14 Then We configured him.... 189; So blessed is God, the most beautiful of creators! 47, 57, 145, 156, 298–99
23:17 We are not heedless of creation. 297
23:60 Those who give what they give, their hearts quaking. 63
23:80 It is He who gives life and gives death. 380
23:107 bring us forth out of it. 31

23:108 Slink you into it, and do not talk to Me. 31
23:115 What, did you reckon that We created you aimlessly...? 457
24:2 Let a group of the faithful witness their chastisement. 231
24:21 Were it not for God's bounty toward you.... 450
24:31 Turn to God all together...! 292, 422
24:35 God is the light of the heavens and the earth.... 411, 412, 420, 458; kindled from a blessed olive tree.... 131, 427
24:37 ...when hearts and eyes will fluctuate. 507n334
24:39 like a mirage in a spacious plain. 37
24:40 And to whomsoever God assigns no light.... 138, 329
25:23 We shall advance upon what deeds they have done...scattered dust. 9, 37, 39, 41, 285, 287, 356
25:26 That day, the kingdom, the real, shall belong to the All-Merciful. 287
25:45 Hast thou not seen thy Lord? 159, 195, 197, 405
25:48 And We sent down from heaven pure water. 379
25:51 If We willed, We would send out a warner in every city. 194
25:58 And trust in the Alive who does not die. 388, 410
25:62 It is He who made night and day a *khilfa*. 321
25:63 and the servants of the All-Merciful. 159
25:70 Those—God will change their ugly deeds into beautiful deeds. 172, 399
25:77 Say: "What weight would my Lord give you...For you have cried lies...." 304–5
26:23 And what is the Lord of the worlds? 518n664
26:36 your Lord and the Lord of your fathers, the first. 407
26:47 We have faith in the Lord of the Worlds. 433
26:50 No harm. 433
26:62 Surely my Lord is with me; He will guide me. 305, 482
26:65 We delivered Moses. 296
26:77 They are an enemy to me. 278
26:79 and He gives me to eat and drink. 358
26:84 Make for me a tongue of truthfulness among the later folk. 195, 432
26:193–94 Brought down upon thy heart by the Faithful Spirit.... 199
27:18 An ant said, "Ants, enter your dwelling places!..." 202, 329
27:20 How is it that I do not see the hoopoe? 533n1123
27:24 I found her and her people prostrating to the sun. 329
27:30 It is from Solomon, and it is in the name of God.... 126
27:34 Kings, when they enter a town, work corruption there. 58
27:44 I have wronged myself. 302
27:62 He who responds to the distressed when he supplicates Him. 302
27:88 Thou shalt see the mountains...passing by like clouds. 77
28:7 Suckle him, but if you fear for him, cast him into the river. 51, 280, 296, 359
28:12 And We forbade his being suckled by foster mothers. 331
28:23 And when they went down to the water of Midian. 296
28:24 My Lord, surely I am poor toward any good Thou sendest down upon me. 17, 306, 307
28:25 walking with shame. 28
28:29 He observed a fire on the side of the mountain. 120, 331, 464
28:30 ...he was called from the right bank of the watercourse.... 132; O Moses, surely I, I am God. 100, 101, 269, 307, 447, 480
28:46 Thou wast not at the side of the Mount when We called out. 452
28:68 Thy Lord creates what He wants and chooses. 339, 471; They have no choice.... 101
28:70 He is God. 124
28:77 And forget not your portion from this world. 457
28:81 So We made the earth engulf him and his house. 265, 489
28:88 Everything is perishing but His face. lv, lxiii
29:41 And surely the frailest of houses is the house of the spider. 395
29:49 Rather it is signs, clear signs, in the breasts.... 156, 333, 415, 477

29:62 Surely God knows everything. 407
30:4 To God belongs the command before and after. 248
30:40 He created you, . . .then He will make you die 298
32:4 in six days. 142
32:13 Had We willed, We would have given every soul its guidance. 345
32:16 Their sides shun their couches as they supplicate 91
32:17 No soul knows what delight of the eyes is hidden away for them 146, 213
33:1 O Prophet, be wary of God. 354
33:4 God did not make for any man two hearts in his breast. 385, 474
33:23 Among them are those who fulfilled their vow 435
33:33 Flaunt not your charms . . . . 225; God desires only to put filth away from you 471, 482
33:35 Men who remember God much and women who remember. 259
33:37 . . ."Keep thy wife to thyself and be wary of God." . . . . We married her to thee. 314, 326–27
33:40 Muḥammad is not the father of any of your men, but . . .the seal of the prophets. 193, 411, 529n1013
33:42 And glorify Him morning and evening. 42, 332
33:43 It is He who blesses you, and His angels. 408, 490
33:44 Their greeting on the day that they encounter Him 14
33:46 a light-giving lamp. 161, 412
33:53 not lingering for talk. 27
33:56 God and His angels bless the Prophet. 397, 408
33:71 He will make your deeds wholesome for you 382
33:72 We offered the Trust to the heavens and the earth and the mountains. 85, 142, 181, 300, 386, 389, 468, 492; But they refused to carry it and feared it. 85, 142, 443, 468; And man carried it. 219, 300, 301, 318, 384, 468, 492; Surely he was a great wrongdoer, deeply ignorant. 13, 97, 123, 142, 157, 219, 229, 233, 237, 268, 286, 300–2, 407, 422, 441, 443, 475
34:3 The knower of the Unseen. 490
34:12 And the wind was Solomon's 197, 349
34:13 basins like water-troughs, and anchored cauldrons. 349
35:1 having wings two, three, and four. 236
35:2 Whatever mercy God opens up to the people 259
35:32 We gave the inheritance of the Book . . . . 432, 477–79; Among them are wrongdoers to themselves. 479
36:39 And the moon—We have determined mansions for it 266, 477
36:60 Did I not make covenant with you, O children of Adam? 96, 451
36:82 His only command when He desires a thing is to say to it 'Be!'. . . xlix
37:6 We adorned the closest heaven 378
37:11 clinging clay. 174
37:90 Surely I am sick. 245
37:99 Surely I am going to my Lord. 195
37:142 So the fish swallowed him while he was blameworthy. 313
37:143 Had he not been one of those who glorify. 320
37:164 There is none of us but has a known station. 250, 383, 509n392
37:165–66 We are those in rows, we are the glorifiers. 131, 492
37:171 Already Our word has preceded. 400
37:180 Glory be to thy Lord, the Lord of exaltedness 407
38:26 O David, surely We made thee a vicegerent 196
38:30 How excellent a servant! . . .350, 400
38:33 Then he fell to slashing their shanks and necks. 338, 361, 391
38:35 My Lord, forgive me and give me a kingdom 197, 250, 348–49
38:36 We subjected to him the wind, which ran softly 349
38:39 This is Our gift, so bestow or withhold without reckoning. 349
38:41–42 And remember Our servant Job . . . . here is a cool washing place 349
38:44 Take in thy hand a bundle of rushes . . . . 298; We found him patient. How excellent a servant! . . .274, 350

38:45 And remember Our servants Abraham and Isaac and Jacob. 270, 400
38:71 Surely I am creating a mortal of clay. 157
38:75 What prevented thee from prostrating thyself...? 52, 174, 324, 488, 490
38:76 I am better than he. Thou hast created me of fire...65, 157, 296, 371, 338, 395, 488
38:78 Upon thee shall be My curse.... 46, 52, 324, 479
38:82 By Thy exaltedness, I will lead them all astray. 292
39:3 We only worship them so that they will bring us nigh in proximity to God. 330
39:6 three darknesses. 298
39:22 What of him whose breast God has expanded...? 138, 216, 409, 458–59, 462–63
39:23 God has sent down the most beautiful talk. 332
39:30 Surely thou wilt die.... 193, 234, 406, 407
39:47 there appeared to them from God.... 20
39:53 Say: "O My servants who have been immoderate.... God forgives all sins." 61, 261, 270, 291–95, 309, 398, 400, 408
39:54 Be penitent toward your Lord! 294
39:65 If thou takest associates, thy deeds will surely fail. 41, 93, 354, 417
39:69 And the earth will shine with the light of its Lord. 379
40:1–3 Ḥā Mīm. The sending down of the Book.... to Him is the homecoming. 430–31
40:7 Those who carry the Throne...ask forgiveness.... 236, 301, 321
40:12 So the decree belongs to God.... 216, 264
40:16 Whose is the kingdom today? God's.... 10, 114–15, 130, 315, 335, 368, 475
40:39 Abode of Settlement. 20
40:51 Surely We will help Our messengers and those who have faith. 408
40:60 And your Lord says, "Supplicate Me; I will respond to you." 294, 302–5, 392
40:64...And He formed you, so He made your forms beautiful. li, 57, 298, 382
40:67 He created you from dust, then from a sperm drop. 489
41:6 Go straight to Him.... 389
41:30 The angels will descend upon them.... 312, 468, 486
41:31 Therein you shall have whatsoever your souls hunger for. 152
41:32 As hospitality from someone forgiving, ever-merciful. 291
41:37 Do not prostrate yourselves to the sun and the moon.... 153
42:7 A group in the Garden and a group in the Blaze. 146
42:11 Nothing is as His likeness.... liv, 41, 60, 339
42:19 God is gentle to His servants. 89, 186, 290, 421
42:25 It is He who accepts repentance.... 222, 288, 309, 422. He knows what you are doing. 288
42:26 He responds to those who have faith.... He increases them.... 288;...an intense chastisement. 339
42:48 unthankful. 237
42:52 So also We revealed to thee a spirit.... 134, 180, 382; Thou knewest not what the Book was.... 193
42:53 in the signs on the horizons and your souls. lxiii
43:31 Why was this Quran not sent down upon a great man...? 408
43:32 Is it they who divide up the mercy of thy Lord?...168, 408, 471
43:51 And these rivers, flowing beneath me. 250
43:68 O My servants, no fear is upon you today. 445
43:71 and pleases the eyes. 152
43:77 You will surely tarry. 31
43:86 except those who have borne witness to the truth.... 423
44:32 We chose them, out of knowledge, above the worlds. 131, 167
44:49 Taste! Surely thou art the exalted, the noble. 265
45:13 He subjected to you whatsoever is in the heavens.... 155, 370
47:11 That is because God is the patron.... 295, 440
47:38 God is the Unneedy, and you are the poor. xxxi, 124, 215, 287, 390, 467

48:1 We have opened up for thee a clear opening. 193
48:2 that God may forgive thee thy sins 408, 526n908
48:3 And that God may help thee 408
48:4 He it is who sent down the tranquility 132
48:16 You will fight them, or they will submit. 425
48:18 When they swore allegiance to thee 132
48:25 Had it not been for certain faithful men 305
48:26 He fastened to them the word of godwariness 60, 168, 174, 300, 396
48:29 Muḥammad is God's messenger. 193, 375; ever-merciful 295
49:7 And He adorned it in their hearts. 294
49:13 Surely the noblest of you with God 533n1138
49:17 They count it as a favor to thee that they have submitted. 387
50:16 And We are nearer to him than the jugular vein. 172
50:18 He utters not a word but by him is a ready watcher. 41
50:29 With Me the word does not change 167
50:30 Is there any more? 19, 86, 442, 479
50:35 with Us there is increase. 442
51:18 And in the dawns they ask for forgiveness. 304
51:21 And in your souls; what, do you not see? 133
51:48 And earth, We laid it out—what excellent spreaders! 378
51:49 Of everything We created a pair. 407
51:56 I created jinn and mankind only to serve Me. 407
52:4 the Inhabited House. 201
52:19 Eat and drink! 379
52:48 Be patient with thy Lord's decree 339
53:1 By the star when it fell! 161
53:2 Your companion is not misguided, nor is he astray. 161–62, 374
53:3 nor does he speak from caprice. 161–62, 189, 254, 374
53:4 It is naught but a revelation revealed. 161–62, 189, 374
53:5 taught to him by one intensely strong. 161–62
53:6 Possessor of power, he stood up straight. 161–64
53:7 while he was on the highest horizon. 161–64, 195
53:8 Then he drew close, so He came down. 161, 163, 164, 180, 195, 255, 256, 262, 343, 410
53:9 So he was two-bows' length away. 45, 55, 112, 163, 164, 180, 190–91, 193, 195, 197, 209, 213, 215, 242, 249, 255, 262, 328, 343–44, 360, 389, 403, 409, 410, 418, 427, 428, 431, 441, 442, 466, 476; or closer. 163, 164, 180, 195, 255, 262, 328, 343, 410
53:10 Then He revealed to His servant what He revealed. 164–65, 198, 210, 308, 383
53:11 His heart did not lie about what it saw. 199
53:13 Indeed he saw Him another time. 165
53:14 at the Lote Tree of the Final End. 165, 250, 258, 262, 276, 317, 325, 343, 379, 392, 467, 476
53:17 The eyesight did not swerve, nor did it trespass. 164, 165, 180, 183, 189, 199, 249–50
53:42 Surely unto thy Lord is the final end. 71, 165, 182, 264, 276
54:20 as if they were uprooted palm trunks. 186
54:48 The day when they are dragged . . . . "Taste the touch of Saqar!" 284
54:54 Surely the godwary will be amid gardens and a river. 147, 276, 435
54:55 in a seat of truthfulness at an Omnipotent King. 83, 144, 147, 148, 262, 263, 276, 351, 419, 446, 470
55:14 Dried clay, like pottery. 61
55:22 From the two will come forth the pearl and the coral. 342
55:26 Everything upon it undergoes annihilation. 407, 477
55:27 There subsists the face of thy Lord 407, 491
55:29 Each day He is upon some task. 120, 240, 398, 452
55:36 Surely the companions of the Garden today 276
55:41 seizing by the forelocks. 334
55:60 Is the recompense of beautiful doing . . . ? 156, 286

56:5 and the mountains crumble to dust. 475
56:88 But if he should be of those brought near.... xliv
56:89 Then repose and ease.... xliv, 458
57:1 Whatsoever is in the heavens and the earth glorifies God. 418
57:3 He is the First and the Last.... 41, 340, 415–16, 420
57:4 And He is with you wherever you are. liv, 36, 70, 116, 267, 340, 432
57:12 Their light running before them.... 230, 379, 414
57:16 Has the time not come...humbled to the remembrance of God? 288, 334
57:19 And the martyrs are at their Lord. 435
58:7 There is no whispering among three...but that He is the sixth of them. 70, 267, 423
58:22 He wrote faith in their hearts and confirmed them.... 116, 131, 378, 401, 486
59:2 So take heed, O you who have eyes! 7, 153, 238
59:21 If We had sent this Quran down on a mountain, thou wouldst have seen it humbled, split apart by the fear of God. 155, 389
59:22 He is God; there is no god but He.... lvi
59:23 the Faithful, the Overseer. lvi, 485
61:6 And when Jesus son of Mary said, "... whose name is Aḥmad." 535n1190
62:4 That is God's bounty. 89
62:11 And God is the best of providers. 299
63:8 To God belongs the exaltation.... 44, 490
64:9 The day He gathers you.... 444
64:11 Whosoever has faith in God, He will guide his heart. 357
65:3 Whosoever trusts in God, He will be enough for him. 357
65:7 him whose provision has power over him. 313
66:6 Over them are harsh, terrible angels...as they are commanded. 59, 181, 369
67:5 And We adorned...and We made them the stonings of the satans. 504n261
68:4 Surely thou hast a tremendous character. lvi, 189, 200, 361
69:21 an approved life. 458
70:4 in a day whose measure is fifty thousand years. 370
70:19–21 Surely man was created grasping... impatient..., grudging. 117, 237
71:16 And He made the sun a lamp. 161
71:19 God made earth a carpet for you. 191
71:25 They were drowned, and made to enter a fire. 489
71:26 My Lord, leave no disbeliever dwelling on the earth! 195, 328, 338, 374
72:8 Surely we touched heaven.... 189
72:15 As for the unjust, they will be firewood.... 334
72:19 and when the servant of God stood. 159
72:28 He has enumerated everything in numbers. 371
73:1 O thou enwrapped one! 82
73:5 Surely We shall cast upon thee a heavy word. 82
73:8 And devote yourselves to Him devoutly. 153, 275
73:9 Lord of the east and the west..., so take Him as a trustee. 153, 357
74:28 spares not, nor leaves alone. 366
75:22–23 Faces that day radiant, gazing on their Lord. 116, 167, 239, 262, 285, 340, 489
76:1 There came upon man a time when he was not.... 124, 187, 398
76:5 camphor. 447
76:17 ginger. 447
76:20 And when you see, you will see bliss.... 239
76:21 And their Lord will give them to drink.... 58, 60, 118, 134, 187, 379, 398
77:20 Did We not create you of a feeble water? 34, 407
78:12 seven firmaments. 166
78:40 Oh, would that I were dust. 513n523
79:24 I am your lord the most high. 51, 55, 68, 250, 275, 447
79:40–41 As for him who...prohibited the soul...the Garden. 116, 254, 263
80:27–32 grains, vines and herbs...for you and your flocks. 379
81:1 When the sun is enwrapped. 375, 378, 458, 494
81:2 and when the stars become opaque. 378
82:10 There are over you guards. 297
82:13–14 Surely the pious... and surely the depraved.... 316

83:15 No indeed, but on that day they shall be veiled.... 6
83:27 *Tasnīm*. 447
85:1 By heaven, possessor of the constellations! 135
85:12 Surely thy Lord's assault is terrible. 41
85:14 He is the Forgiving, the Loving/the Beloved. 323
87:9 It almost bursts in rage. 375
89:14 Thy Lord lies in wait. 454
89:21 crumbling to dust. 10
89:27–28 O serene soul, return to thy Lord...! xliv, 67, 136, 145, 481
90:8–9 Did We not make for him two eyes...? 474
92:5–10 As for him who gives and is godwary...and as for him who is niggardly.... 363
93:1–2 by the bright morning and by the night.... 480
93:5 Thy Lord will bestow upon thee, and thou wilt approve. 162, 241, 308, 327, 484
93:6–8 Did He not find thee an orphan and... free thee of need? 193
94:1 Did We not expand thy breast for thee? 199, 409
94:2–3 Did We not lift from thee thy burden...? 199–200
94:4 Did We not raise up thy mention for thee? 195, 199
95:4 Surely We created man in the most beautiful stature. 46, 57, 298, 510n422
95:5 the lowest of the low. 135, 403
95:6 They shall have a wage unfailing. 423
96:1 Recite in the name of thy Lord who created. 317, 384, 462
96:3–5 Recite, and thy Lord is the most generous.... 146
96:14 Does he not know that God sees? 297
96:19 Draw near! 409
98:5 They were commanded only to worship God.... the upright religion. 41, 371
100:6 ungrateful. 237
101:4 scattered moths. 202
105:3–5 And He sent against them birds in swarms.... 68
110:3 So glorify the praise of thy Lord! 162
111:1 Perish the hands of Abū Lahab! 426
112:1 Say: "He is God, one." 375
112:3 He begets not, nor was He begotten. 156

INDEX OF HADITHS AND ARABIC SAYINGS

H. hadith
HQ. *ḥadīth qudsī* (loosely defined, i.e., non-Quranic words of God)
HP. hadith translated into Persian
S. Arabic sayings, aphorisms, proverbs

ʿAbbās is moaning, and I have no settledness. HP. 472
Abraham uttered three lies about God. H. 245
Accept me, though I'm adulterated.... S. 176
Act, for everyone will be eased to that for which he was created. H. 495
Adam and those after him will be under my banner.... H. 182, 191, 325, 384
Adam said, "No, but I am ashamed before You...". H. 27
The affair has three states: abandoning blights,...S. 212
ʿAlī was ashamed to ask Muṣṭafā.... HP. 27
All game is in the belly of the onager. S. 275
The All-Compelling will place His foot in the Fire.... H. 174
Among all successors this knowledge will be transmitted.... H. 319
The angel came and said, "Recite!" H. 317
The angel of the right hand is given priority.... H. 451
Anyone who enters the house of Abū Sufyān will be safe. H. 272
Anyone who mentioned Me once in any station.... HQ. 439
Anyone who says that I am better than he has uttered a lie. H. 355
Anyone who sees worth in himself.... S. 54, 179
Apology, even if a little, is the price of sin.... S. 206
The apportioning, the good of it and the evil of it. H. 284
Approval is to welcome the decrees with joy. S. 81, 107
Approve of me as a lover!...S. 31, 91
Are you hungry that I may feed you...? HQ. 186
As for the folk of felicity, they will be eased.... H. 363
As for the secrets.... S. 129
As long as love remains.... S. 19
Ask not for commandership.... H. 492
Ask of Me—even the salt for your dough.... HQ. 27
Ask of none but God.... S. 290
Aspiration for the servant is like alchemy.... S. 276
At first love is being duped, and at last it is being killed.... S. 104
At it is the final end of every knower's knowledge. S. 258
At the beginning [God's friends] were [the dog's] trials.... S. 91
Away with you, away! H. 430
The banner of praise will be in my hand.... H. 328, 515n583
Be at ease, for I am the son of a woman of Quraysh.... H. 45, 193, 403
Be dust! HQ. 230
Be firm, Ḥirāʾ.... H. 355

Be in this world as if you are an exile or a passerby. H. 346
Be the neighbor of an ocean or a king. S. 75
Beautiful-doing...is that you worship God as if you see Him.... H. lxii, 371
Beauty is one-third constitution and two-thirds adornment. S. 345
Before the Unseen are curtains.... S. 33
Before you sinned, you used to enter in upon Me.... HQ. 488
The beginningless is not contested.... S. 279
Beloveds love to burn their lovers' hearts.... S. 343
Benevolence is for beginners.... S. 178, 342
The best fragrance...is the fragrance of the person you love.... S. 241
Bestowal may come to both the near and the far.... S. 438
Between the favors appear the shadows of the teeth. S. 151
Beware of kings!...S. 178
Beware of seeking the sweetness.... S. 498n81
Blessed are the poor in this world and the next.... S. 281
The borrowed is to be answered for and given back. H. 477
The breasts of the free.... S. 129, 164
Buy the house from the son.... S. 296
By day I am sultan, by night we are brothers. S. 401
By God, if not for God, we would not have been guided.... H. 329, 464
By My exaltedness, had he asked Me for help once.... HQ. 292
By My exaltedness and majesty, I will not chastise.... HQ. 521n766
Charity falls first into the hand of the All-Merciful.... H. 472
Children are a cause of niggardliness.... H. 244
Come quickly to the Exalted Presence.... S. 124
Come, so that we may have faith for an hour. H. 388–89
Command them to the prayer when they are children.... H. 154
Companionship with a serpent is easier than.... S. 292
Companionship with kings.... S. 284
A created thing seeking aid from a created thing.... S. 72, 390
Curse not the aeon, for God is the aeon. H. 10, 61
Death will be brought in the guise.... H. 596n7
The decrees of majesty are far too majestic.... S. 112, 121
Deeds are [judged] by intentions. H. 144
The delight of my eyes was put in the prayer. H. 42, 189, 257
The desirer is enraptured.... S. 277
Die before you die! H. 535n1205
The disciple is a traveler, but the recognizer.... S. 383
Disregard of the ugly-doer's disloyalty.... S. 255
Do not consider me more excellent.... H. 355
Do not delude me with your forbearance.... S. 75
Do not follow the gaze with another gaze.... H. 278
Do not give the child one.... S. 17
Do not lavish praise on me.... H. 247
Do not let the limpidness of the present moments delude you.... S. 151
Do not rely on the affection of someone who loves you only.... S. 177, 338
Do not turn me over to myself.... H. 474
Do the deeds of a man who will be saved.... S. 359
Do you wonder that bosom friendship belongs to Abraham...? H. 101
A dog is most polluted when.... S. 121, 353
Don't become proud, lest you be disowned. S. 96, 103
A drop fell into my mouth, so I recognized.... H. 317
Each of you is a shepherd.... H. 120
The earth was brought together for me.... H. 160, 249, 251, 355
The earth was made a place of prostration for me. H. 200, 373, 515n588
The earth was unrolled from Mecca. H. 319
Either Me or you. S. 28, 284
Embrace poverty, make patience your pillow.... S. 150
Encountering Him.... *See* If you encounter Him
Encountering the beloved when the watchers are heedless. S. 419

Encountering you in the morning.... S. 310
Enter unwillingly, and leave unwillingly. HQ. 314
The envier is a refuser.... S. 204
Even if the servant sins and does not care.... S. 268
Every loan that attracts profit is usury. H. 473
Every night God descends.... HQ. 61, 287, 452, 507n342, 524n853, 528n978, 537n1243
Every people has a day.... S. 471
Every place has its words.... S. 17
Every tie and lineage will be cut, except.... H. 401
Everyone is waiting at the gate.... S. 417
Everything that distracts you from the Real.... S. 360
The Exalted is He who is not grasped.... S. 32
An existence between two nonexistences.... S. 124
Expecting compensation for obedient acts.... S. 29
Extend your feet in the measure of your cloak. S. 7
The eye is real. H. 69
Faith is belief in the heart.... S. 89
The faith of the servant will not be perfect.... H. 454
Fāṭima is part of me. H. 244
Fear is masculine and hope is feminine.... S. 62
Fear is to expect punishment.... S. 22
The felicitations, the blessings, the prayers.... H. 158, 256, 308
The felicitous person is he who has an outwardness.... S. 201
The first among men to submit was Abū Bakr.... H. 463
The first gift of the person of faith is death. H. 275
The first in thought is the last in act.... S. 482
The first thing God created was the Intellect. H. 46–47, 203, 517n631
The first thing God created was the Pen.... H. 285
For my community God will make that day.... H. 370
For you I am like a father to his children. H. 375
The forbidden is enticing. S. 117, 151
The foul odor of the fasting person's mouth.... H. 365, 435
The free-willers are the Magi of this community. H. 122
From the moment that the harsh shine of this weighty declaration.... HP. 417
Gabriel, why are you so tiny? HP. 397
The Garden has no business with me.... S. 29
The Garden is ringed around by things disliked. H. 448
Gehenna will be crying out.... H. 446
Give to the asker, even if.... H. 305
Give us ease, O Bilāl! H. 257
Glory be to God, the Fluctuater of hearts! H. 326, 327
Glory be to Him, the Exalted.... S. 33
Glory be to Him who abases the servant.... S. 518n668
Glory be to Him who after seventy years admonished me with a eunuch.... S. 147
Glory be to Him who clad Himself in exaltedness.... H. 407
Glory be to Him who combines snow and fire! H. 275
Glory be to Him who compounded Adam in a composition.... S. 298
Glory be to Him who deposits the subtle in the dense.... S. 279
Glory be to Him who garbed Himself in splendor.... H. 265
Glory be to Him who is severe to His servants.... S. 68
Glory be to Him who placed His treasuries.... S. 168
Glory be to Him who was compassionate.... H. 265
Glory be to me!...S. 93, 94, 96, 421
Go to Zaynab and report to her.... HP. 326
God chose Kināna.... H. 317
God created Adam from a handful of dust.... H. 46
God created Adam in the last hour of Friday. H. 396
God created the spirits before the bodies. H. 314, 363
God discloses Himself to the people generally.... H. 483
God does not respond to the supplication of a diverted heart. H. 302

God gazes not on your forms.... H. 307, 443, 488
God grants respite, but He does not disregard. S. 5, 491
God has decreed for Himself that He will guide.... H. 357
God has lifted away from my community.... H. 246
God has ninety-nine names.... H. lii
God has shame and is generous.... H. 28
God hates the healthy and carefree. H. 202
God is beautiful, and He loves beauty. H. li
God is gentler to His servants than this bird.... H. 310
God is more merciful to His servants than this woman.... H. 310
God is my vicegerent over you. H. 196
God loves the tempted, the repenting. H. 269, 423
God loves those who implore in supplication. H. 452
God may love the servant until His love.... S. 362
God recited Ṭāhā and Yāsīn two thousand years.... H. 478
God was, and there was nothing with Him. H. 191
God will configure another creation. H. 429
God will defend His faithful servant.... H. 162
God will give me two wings.... S. 491
God will muster all the creatures.... H. 519n690
God wonders at two men.... H. 538n1270
God's artisanry brings together all good. S. 290
God's artisanry keeps on coming.... S. 290
God's Messenger did not give permission to lie except.... H. 245
God's Messenger would visit the ill, escort caskets.... H. 44
God's shawl is.... HQ. 43–44
Gold is proven by fire. S. 446
Good fortune belongs to the Real.... S. 489
Good from us is a slip, and evil is our attribute. S. 204
The greatest of God's blessings.... S. lxii, 329
A group from my community will enter the Garden with hearts.... H. 475
Had God's Messenger hidden anything of the Quran.... H. 326
Had I taken a bosom friend.... H. 355
The hand emptied of possessions.... S. 262
Have mercy on the rich.... S. 80
Have shame before God as is the rightful due.... H. 28
Have shame before God because of His proximity to you.... S. 454
Have you fled from Us, O Adam? HQ. 205
He alone—no associate has He. H. 125, 211
He bestowed upon you before you asked. *See* I bestowed
He built the Garden of Eden with His hand. H. 61
He contended with us, and we.... H. 452
He created Adam in His form. H. 123
He created us so that we would benefit from Him.... S. 11
He disengaged love from every cause. S. 155
He fermented Adam's clay in His hand.... H. 46, 131, 142, 156, 391
He gazes on your hearts. H. 307, 443
He guided them so that they would recognize Him.... S. 421
He had beauty, splendor, awesomeness.... H. 412
He has made for us a *sūr*. H. 201
He lifts up a group and He puts down a group. H. 120
He loved you before you loved Him.... H. 118
He loves His friends without cause.... S. 362
He married a woman from Bayāḍa.... H. 311
He mentioned you, then He named you, then.... S. 172
He planted the tree of Ṭūbā with His hand. H. 61
He singled out Adam by creating him.... S. 323
He spoke to Moses in respect of Moses.... S. 19, 332
He threw them into sin to make them recognize.... S. 222
He unveils His Essence to them.... S. 276, 484
He used to feed the camels, sweep the house, repair shoes.... H. 44
He used to seclude himself in the cave of Ḥirā'. H. 317
He was more comely, but I am more lovely. H. 196
He who does not put up with perils will not reach the goal. S. 16
He who flees from what is coming.... S. 279

He who has no secret.... S. 129
He who loves, stays chaste, conceals, and dies, dies a martyr. H. 105, 245
He who recognizes God will not put up.... S. 10
He who recognizes Him does not describe Him.... S. 330
He who seeks nearness to the King by sitting in the corner.... S. 12
He who thinks lightly of putting dust.... S. 444
He will unveil one group through His Essence.... S. 152
He would be praying while his insides.... H. 427
The heart is like a feather in the desert.... H. 237
The heart was named *qalb* because of its fluctuation. H. 76
The hearts are between two fingers.... H. 138, 299, 329, 332, 437
The hearts of the folk of recognition...incline toward.... S. 119
The hearts of the free do not tolerate waiting. S. 241
The hearts of the seekers are enraptured.... S. 98
The hearts of the yearners are illumined by God's light.... S. 15
The heart's reliance on the assurance of the Unseen.... S. 352
Here I am.... H. 96, 175, 222, 294, 306, 504n267
The higher hand is better than the lower hand. H. 281
The Highest Friend! H. 397
His character was the Quran. H. lvi, 159
His clothing is forbidden, his food is forbidden.... H. 304
His love came and burned away everything else. S. 153
Hold back from My servants, O Abraham.... HQ. 292
Hospitality is for three days; anything after that is charity.... H. 507n349
The house is your house, and I am your neighbor. S. 438
How beautiful it is for the rich to show compassion to the poor.... S. 72
How beloved are the three disliked things.... S. 82, 97
How can I enjoy myself when Seraphiel.... H. 125
How close you are to the Fire! H. 208
How could He destroy a community.... H. 241
How far apart are the two gaits! S. 434
How far apart are those who live through their hearts.... S. 255, 435
How goodly is the assistance of predetermination! S. 461
How great are God's hidden artisanry.... S. 290
How is your state in the precinct of holiness?...HP. 22
How strange is the desirer who abases himself.... S. 359
I am ashamed before my Lord to worship Him.... S. 498n80
I am hidden in the heart of the person of faith. HQ. 215
I am jealous and Sa'd is jealous, and God is more jealous.... H. 153, 191
I am only a servant.... H. 275
I am the chief of the Arabs, Bilāl is the chief.... H. 463
I am the chieftain of Adam's children.... H. 393, 403, 515n583
I am the King and invite you to become kings!...HQ. 120
I am the most eloquent of the Arabs. H. 34, 112
I am the point under the *b*.... S. 266
I am the Real. S. 96, 337
I am the sitting companion of those who remember Me. HQ. 267
I am the son of the Beginningless. S. 156
I am with My servant's thoughts of Me.... HQ. 116, 313, 432
I am with those whose hearts are broken.... HQ. 142, 171, 267, 292
I am yours, whether you wish it or refuse.... S. 13, 23, 167
I and the Hour are like these two. H. 425
I ask forgiveness from God for my lack of sincerity.... S. 63
I ask forgiveness from God one hundred times a day. H. 63, 157, 527n956
I ask Thee for the Garden.... H. 276
I began the day with countless blessings.... S. 290
I bestowed upon you before you asked from Me.... HQ. 118, 293, 431, 452

I came to know everything in the heavens.... H. 527n934
I cling to you inescapably, so cling to the inescapable. HQ. 9
I conformed with my Lord in three things.... H. 483
I created the hearts of the servants from My approval. HQ. 155
I created the whole world for you, and I created you for Me. HQ. 119, 155
I created what I created only for thee. HQ. 34, 324, 411
I created you for subsistence—you will only be transferred.... HQ. 415
I created you solitary for the Solitary. HQ. 151, 440
I do not care. HQ. 99, 151, 268, 291, 302, 309
I do not number Thy laudations.... H. 33, 112, 157, 210, 274
I find the breath of the All-Merciful.... H. 442
I forgive you and I do not care. HQ. 302, 309
I have a moment with God.... H. 166, 180, 198, 275, 328, 511n448
I have created no creature more honored by Me than you. HQ. 203
I have divided the prayer between Me and My servant.... HQ. 90, 513n509
I have met some people who, were they commanded.... S. 454
I looked at this affair and saw no path nearer to God than.... S. 65
I marvel at the killer with the killed in the Garden. H. 461
I never offered this affair to anyone who did not stumble.... H. 462
I prayed the last prayer of the night with you.... H. 160
I recognized my Lord through my Lord.... S. 464
I responded to you before you supplicated Me.... HQ. 118, 431, 452
I saw seventy of the sincerely truthful.... S. 406
I seek refuge in Thy pardon from Thy punishment.... H. 273
I sent you to try you and to try by means of you. HQ. 42, 99, 137
I sit with him who remembers Me. HQ. 116
I spend the night at my Lord.... H. 275, 482
I supplicate You in public as lords are supplicated, but.... S. 304, 486
I stay with my Lord. H. 275
I treated the blind and the leper.... S. 275
I was a hidden treasure.... HQ. 170
I was a prophet when Adam.... H. 192, 194, 426
I was aided by terror at a month's journey. H. 192, 200, 354, 475, 515n588
I was given excellence over the prophets with six things.... H. 200
I was given five things that were given to no one before me.... H. 515n588
I was sent as an inviter.... H. 122, 329
I was sent out in the best generation.... H. 483
I was sent with the easy, easygoing, primordial way. H. 226
I was the Seal of the Prophets.... H. 192
I was weeping over sins for a time.... S. 457
I went to the Throne and found it thirstier.... S. 24
I will not approve for any of my community to be in the Fire. H. 241
I will not be mentioned unless you are mentioned.... HQ 199
I wonder at anyone who still has anything left when.... S. 472
I wonder at two states: I am poor.... S. 339
If anyone leaves behind property, it belongs to his heirs.... H. 312
If anyone supposes that Muḥammad saw his Lord.... H. 165
If anyone thinks that God's blessings toward him lie in his drink.... S. 132, 328–29
If anyone was worshiping Muḥammad, surely Muḥammad is dead.... H. 390
If Hagar had not done that.... HP. 74
If He forgives, He is the best of the merciful.... S. 222
If I were given power over everything, I would burn it all.... S. 361
If Moses were alive.... H. 374
If not for thee, I would not have created.... HQ. 193, 324
If someone humbles himself before a wealthy man.... H. 72
If someone lies about me intentionally.... H. xix
If the highest Firdaws were adorned for me.... S. 361

If the infant in the cradle knew.... S. 293
If the poor man had only a spirit.... S. 501n160
If the praying person knew.... H. 190
If the wind of solicitude blows.... S. 337
If You chastise me, I love You.... S. 402
If you desire the stations of the Substitutes.... S. 17, 147, 264
If you did not sin, God would bring a people.... H. lxvii, 172, 244
If you encounter Him with the abasement.... S. 206, 384
If you encounter Me with.... HQ. 268
If you had continued, you would have seen wonders. H. 414
If you suppose that this season has witnessed anyone worse.... S. 54
If we recognize You, You bewilder us.... S. 365
I'll backbite my brother.... S. 157
In earth they are ascribed to heaven and in heaven.... S. 130
In the body there is a lump of flesh.... H. 135, 144
In the Garden are what no eye has seen.... H. 213
In the state of the servant's encountering God.... S. 301
In what we are busy with the nearest nearness.... S. 36
In your view you have no escape from your daily provision.... S. 74, 210
The incapacity to reach perception is perception. S. 388
Increase me in my trial! S. 125
Indeed He does, and He does not care. H. 291
The intelligent man is... the clever man who.... S. 18
Is not everything other than God unreal...? H. xxii, lv, 130, 168, 265
Is there any asker.... *See* Every night God descends
It is a knowledge between God and His friends.... H. 129
It is an affair that is finished. H. 453
It is forbidden for a heart to catch a whiff of certainty.... S. 80
It is God's secret, so we do not unveil it.... S. 453
It is not beautiful for the desiring, free man to abase himself.... S. 72
It is not for the person of faith to abase himself. H. 340
It may happen that sin becomes the cause of reaching God.... S. 428
It was for a reason that Qaṣīr cut off his nose. S. 132, 181, 441
Jealousy is two.... S. 153
Jesus walked on water.... HP. 80
Kakh kakh. H. 201
Kill Ibn al-Khaṭal.... H. 272
Kings are such that there is no patience.... S. 277, 398
Knowledge is a light.... S. 134
Let go of those who say their prayers! H. 487
Let me live in indigence.... H. 197
Let them go out into the desert.... HP. 471
Let those who love the Folk of the House put on armor.... H. 341
Lifted away from my community are mistakes.... H. 246
Light has become manifest, falsehood.... S. 93, 188
The light of the Reality is more beautiful.... S. 299
Light upon light, joy upon joy, delight upon delight. S. 53, 133, 164
The likeness of this religion is a fixed tree.... H. 89
Long have I invited you, but you.... HQ. 398
Look at this man, whose heart God has illuminated.... H. 176
Lordhood is the implementation of power.... S. 417
Love for my Lord extracts from me.... S. 29
Love for the ugly is abandonment.... S. 215
Love is.... S. 104, 243, 278, 306, 316, 323, 367
The lover's recompense before encounter.... S. 367
[Lovers' sins] are sins of constraint, not free will. S. 246
Lying commanders, depraved viziers.... H. 454
Magnificence is My cloak.... HQ. 41, 340
Make me one of those You deliver.... H. 427
Make the trial severe for him, for I love his voice. HQ. 449
A man may do the deeds of the folk of the Garden.... H. 138
The man of faith is a clever servant.... S. 454

A man will be brought on the Day of Resurrection.... HQ. 281
The mark of yearning.... S. 16, 480
The marks and characteristics of the submitter.... S. 454
Marry and reproduce! H. 388
May God alienate you from your own proximity! S. 53
May God curse those who make people flee! H. 291
May God disgrace a man who approves of.... S. 176
May God give you no taste of your own self.... S. 157
May God have mercy on the man who recognizes his own worth. S. 46
May God have mercy on you. HQ. 526n927
May your Lord have mercy upon you. HQ. 315, 489
The metaphor is the bridge.... S. lxiii
[Moses said to Adam,] "You are the one who made us wretched...." H. 117
The most astute of words are those spoken by Labīd.... H. xxii, lv
The most decisive among you.... H. 371
The most goodly of what a man eats.... H. 359
The most knowledgeable of the permitted and forbidden.... H. 371
Most of the folk of the Garden are simpletons. H. 276, 373
The most skilled in the rules of inheritance.... H. 371
Muʿādh ibn Jabal entered into the presence.... HP. 206–9
Muḥammad's Lord hates him.... H. 344
My abasement has suspended.... S. 54, 179
My beloved, who has tried me with You?... S. 125, 342
My community is a community shown mercy. H. 241, 295
My community is like the rain.... H. 241, 483
My community, my community! H. 163, 191, 252, 293, 325, 378
My community will be the bright-faced.... H. 132, 509n408
My community's share of the Fire.... H. 447
My companions are like stars. H. 482
My eyes sleep, but my heart does not sleep. H. 361
My heart becomes clouded. H. 327
My heart spoke to me about my Lord. S. 483
My intercession belongs to the folk of great sins.... H. 241, 255, 375
My mercy takes precedence over My wrath. HQ. 181–82, 400, 451, 489
My proof is my need.... S. 65
My servant, if you encounter Me with offenses.... HQ. 268
My sin is tremendous.... H. 427
My soul, my soul. H. 163, 252, 293, 325, 378, 521n755
A naked heart, within it a shining lamp. H. 153
Near not through adherence.... S. 165
Neither compulsion nor delegation. S. 339
Neither He nor other than He. S. 168
Neither the heavens nor the earth embraces Me.... HQ. 76, 300
The night is long—do not shorten it with sleep.... S. 149
The night is more concealed for wailing. S. 208
No man becomes a recognizer until withholding.... S. 81
No one carries His gifts but His steeds. S. 300
No one carries the loads of kings but the steeds of kings. S. 56
No one carries the Real but the Real.... S. lxvii, 56, 420
No one holds back what You bestow.... H. 259
No one hurries to punish unless he fears escape. HQ. 220
No one is truthful in love for Him.... S. 81
No one reaches the All save him who.... S. 213
No one recognizes Him unless.... S. 330–31
No one saved will be saved except.... S. 453
No one says, "No god but God," for whoever says it.... S. 40
No one sets forward what He keeps behind.... S. 408
No one stands up to the decree.... S. 363
No one who slips, slips in any station but that of proximity. S. 321
No one who turns away from the Real.... S. 271
No recognizer's recognition perceives the Real.... S. 139–40
No soul is born whose place has not been written.... H. 363

None are suited for this Tariqah but those.... S. 54
None of you will have faith until.... H. 414
Not truthful in his claim is he who takes no pleasure.... S. 365
Nothing is worthy of the heart's attention but He. S. 4
Nothing remains between Him and me but.... S. 403
Nothing will fill up the stomach of Adam's child but dust. H. 117
A people's cupbearer is the last to drink. S. 184
O Abraham, let My servants be.... HQ. 524n868
O Abū Hurayra, what is it with you?...HP. 201
O Abū Hurayra, will it not make him happy...H. 487
O child of Adam, if you supplicate Me.... HQ. 506n302
O child of Adam, you have eaten My provisions.... HQ. 309
O David, be like a cautious bird.... HQ. 136
O David, give good news to the sinners.... HQ. 406
O David, make Me beloved.... HQ. 398
O David, My remembrance is for the rememberers.... HQ. 129
O Fluctuater of hearts, make my heart firm! H. 327, 330
O folk of the Garden, everlastingness.... HQ. 5, 113, 446
O generosity that has no end!...S. 70, 258, 291, 437
O God, approve of me as a lover!...S. 31, 91
O God, guide my people, for they do not know. H. 195, 328
O God, however You chastise me.... S. 5
O God, make me one of Muḥammad's community! S. 194, 324, 455
O God, show gratitude to You through me.... S. 19
O God, You will find other than me.... S. 422
O Guide of the bewildered.... S. 366
O Jābir, despite God's Being, do you still affirm.... HP. 284
O Lord, in Thee I am. H. 249
O Moses, if you desire that I be closer to you.... HQ. 408
O Muʿādh, are you drinking wine from the grapes...? HP. 389
O Muʿādh, surely the Quran binds back the person of faith.... H. 454
O my Lord, my community.... Away with you.... H. 430
O people, will you leave my companion to me...? H. 483
O Ruthful, O Bestower! H. 448
O this world, serve whosoever serves Me.... HQ. 213, 356, 530n1036
O Ubayy, the Lord of Lords said to me.... HP. 31
O Umm Salama, take my child.... HP. 255
An ocean without shore.... S. 106, 417
The ocean's water is pure, its carrion permitted. H. 75
Oceans are the storehouse of pearls.... S. 342
The occupied are not put to work. S. 134
Oh my head! H. 246
Oh, the yearning to encounter my brothers! H. 443
Oil and water do not mix. S. 184
On the day you did that, you had no shame.... HQP. 443
Once the caravan has been waylaid, it is secure. S. 175
One day I am hungry, another I am full. H. 307
One does not have recourse to kings when they are wrathful. S. 108
One group sought Him, and He abandoned them.... S. 23, 167, 226, 381
One is conjoined with the Real in the measure.... S. 271
One mark of the hypocrite is that he loves praise...S. 91
One of the characteristics of the free.... S. 130
One sigh of the lovers would burn up the two worlds.... S. 110
Our secrets are virgin.... S. 130, 392
Our treasuries are full of acts of obedience, so you must have.... HQ. 202
The paragon struck it with a pickax.... HP. 414
Part of this world's trouble.... S. 41
Pass by, O man of faith, for your light.... H. 261, 296
Patched cloaks are the curtains of pearls. S. 131
Patience is.... S. 491

Pay no regard, for if you pay regard, you will fall. S. 213
Peace be upon us. H. 191, 256
People are jealous over souls.... S. 403
The people most severely tried are the prophets.... H. 99
Perfect exaltation is found in abasement.... S. 340
The person of faith is like a pearl.... S. 230
The poor man is.... S. 282, 284
The poor of my community will enter the Garden.... H. 281
Poverty is.... S. 214, 282, 283
Poverty is blackness of face.... H. 184, 233
Poverty is our boast. H. 118, 412
The power of the Powerful suspends.... S. 279, 450
The praise belongs to God in every state. H. 48
The prayer is the *miʿrāj* of hearts. H. 90, 190
The praying person is whispering with his Lord. H. 190, 197
Provision is apportioned, the avaricious deprived.... S.357
Putting down one's face before the Real.... S. 265, 285
The Real came to him while he was in the cave.... H. 317
The Real is exalted, the path long.... S. 35
The Real is solitary in His majesty.... S. 55
The Real speaks on the tongue of ʿUmar. H. 483
The Real's attractions in the secret cores.... S. 453
The reality of Sufism...S. 261
The reality of the Real is beyond reports.... S. 450
Recognition is fire, love is fire.... S. 278
Recognition is the heart's life with God. S. xlii, 134, 380, 420
Recognition is the radiance of lights.... S. 120
Recognition is to scorn all measures.... S. 72
Recognition is waves that fall.... S. 89
The recognizers are... "deaf, dumb, blind."...S. 263
Regret is repentance. H. 305
Rejoice in Me...! HQ. 96, 116, 241
The religion is not gained with wishfulness and self-adornment. S. 17
The renunciant is the Real's prey in this world.... S. 152
Repentance is.... S. 288
The resting place of the worshipers.... H. 131
The root of *tawḥīd* is to fly in the field of disengagement.... S. 394
Say to the young men of Israel.... HQ. 15
The scholars point you to the Garden.... S. 241
Seclusion is one of the marks of the folk of limpidness. S. 317
A secret core safe from the frivolities.... H. 453
Seeing proximity is a veil of proximity.... S. 53
Seek out the neighbor before the house.... H. 523n814
The seeking is rejected, the road blocked. S. 23, 167, 277
Seraphiel would cover his head with his wings.... S. 27
The servant is bewildered, the served one proud. S. 23
The servant of God has nothing but God.... S. 305
The servant will not find the sweetness of faith until trial.... S. 110
The servant's aspiration agitates and unsettles him.... S. 276
Servanthood is.... S. 49, 56
Should I kill my own killer? S. 359, 437, 523n826
Should I not be a grateful servant? H. 307
Should I not be ashamed in front of a man...? H. 483
A sick man whom no one visits...S. 277
[Sickness] is My fire.... HQ. 296
A sin through which I turn in poverty toward Him.... S. 206, 384
Sincerity is to be wary of glancing.... S. 53
A sinful community and a forgiving Lord! H. 71, 241
A single breath of the yearners.... S. 232
A single tear will extinguish the Lord's wrath. H. 306
The sinner's interceder is his confession.... S. 303
Slips do not intrude upon the Endless. S. 59
The snakebitten does not sleep. S. 149
Solicitude comes before water and clay. S. 47, 232
Solicitude destroys sins. S. 187
The solicitude of the judge.... S. 57
Someone who has twice traveled the urinary canal.... S. 44

Someone who supplicates without deeds.... S. 303
Sometimes I pray two cycles for God.... S. 28
The soul is the greatest idol. H. 149
The spirit entered unwillingly and will leave unwillingly. H. 526n926
The spirits are assembled troops.... H. 314, 481
The spirits of the lovers are in the grasp.... S. 276
The spirits of the martyrs.... H. 230, 276
The spirits of this group were presented to the dogs.... S. 54, 201
Stand on the carpet and beware of expansiveness.... S. 101
Stand up and declare My splendor.... HQ. 83
The strikes of the Beloved do not hurt. S. 341
Such is the custom of kings. S. 438
Such is the severity of the beloveds. S. 276, 307
Sufism is.... S. 77, 261
The supplication of my father Abraham.... H. 426
Supplicate God while being certain of response. H. 302
The Surah al-An'ām descended at night.... H. 532n1096
Swallow the bitters without frowning. S. 154
Take from the bad debtor, even if only a brick. S. 176
Talk has many valleys. S. 409
Tawḥīd belongs to the Real.... S. 275, 475
Tawḥīd is disengagement from the world of the others.... S. 89
Tawḥīd is to isolate the Eternal from the newly arrived. S. 150
That was Ja'far ibn Abī Ṭālib.... H. 391
"Thee alone we worship" is to guard the Shariah.... S. 507n357
Their sacrifices are their blood. S. 437
Their silence is their approval. H. 333
There is many a disheveled, grimy.... H. 197, 260
There is no alienation with God.... S. 5
There is no artifice against rejection.... S. 160
There is no capacity to be with You.... S. 39, 277
There is no consultation in love. S. 12, 172
There is no good in a love whose torment cannot be borne.... S. 177
There is no inhabitant in the house. S. 140
There is no morsel more appetizing than the morsel of *tawḥīd*...S. 115
There is no *ṣalāt* without the Fātiḥa of the Book. H. 401
There is no settledness with Thee and no escape.... S. 351
There is no sin too great for God to forgive. H. 244, 514n538
There is none of you to whom your Lord will not speak.... H. 197
There is none of you who has not been entrusted.... H. 194
There is nothing more beautiful for servitors.... S. 44
There is nothing more splendid and no station higher.... S. 438
They are the ones who pray, fast, give alms.... H. 63
Think about the creatures, but do not think about the Creator. H. 133
This affair will not get done with laziness.... S. 284
This creature will not be self-possessed.... H. 468
This is a mountain that loves us and that we love. H. 339
This is an affair that will be not completed with associationism. S. 28, 140, 471
This is nothing but throwing away the spirit.... S. 82
This prayer of ours is not wholesome when.... H. 333
This world is.... S. 347, 384, 415
This world is accursed. H. 373
This would be happiness were it not delusion.... S. 347
Those who carry burdens for My sake are in My eyes! HQ. 400
Those who praise God much in every state. H. 116
Thou art as Thou hast lauded Thyself. *See* I do not number
Three things of this world of yours were made beloved to me.... H. 42, 482
Three things will be gathered together against the sins.... S. 445
Three will be brought on the Day of Resurrection.... H. 376
Throwing the soul into servitude.... S. 261

Thy little servant is at Thy gate.... S. 266
To Me, to Me! HQ. 438
To revere a being derives from scorning Him.... S. 355
Today I will encounter the beloveds.... S. 481
The toil of your right hand.... S. 96
Tomorrow a prophet will come with one person.... HP. 478
Travel in the field of *tawḥīd* until.... S. 394
Trial for love is like flames for gold. S. 169, 339, 402
Trials are in keeping with the heights. S. 178
The Trust is.... S. 300
Truthful in love for Him, falling short.... S. 487
Two swords do not come together in one scabbard.... S. 85
The ugly-doer looks at people with the eye of his own nature. S. 410
ʿUmar is one of the beautiful traits of Abū Bakr. H. 483
The unbeliever is like a pine tree.... H. 186
The unbeliever will be brought.... H. 196
The unbelievers are deaf to.... S. 263
The unneedy aspire for provisions and the poor aspire.... S. 282
The unneedy go back to what is customary for them, and the poor.... S. 282
Unveiling upon unveiling.... *See* Light upon light
Venerate your sacrificial animals.... H. 494
Waiting is the red death. S. 241
We are negligent of the highest because.... S. 257
We are the last, the preceders. H. 146, 194, 482
We have not recognized Thee.... S. 39, 215, 466
We have not worshiped Thee.... H. 39, 215, 466
We, the assemblies of the prophets, do not bequeath. H. 386
A weak servant and a gentle Lord—mercy does not go to waste...! S. 310
The weaker someone is, the gentler to him is the Lord. S. 90–91
Welcome to the wholesome son.... H. 195, 442
Were a hat to drop from heaven.... S. 271
Were He to chastise me and the son of Mary.... H. 454
Were heaven not to rain and earth.... S. 358
Were I to draw closer by a finger's breath.... H. 71, 166, (197), 383
Were it not that He loves to pardon you, He would not have.... S. 222
Were it not that pardon is one of His attributes.... S. 222
Were it said to the Day of Resurrection, "What do you fear?"...S. 377, 444
Were pardon not one of the things most beloved.... S. 223
Were the heavens and the earth to be struck.... S. 375
Were the religion suspended from the Pleiades.... H. 200
Were the Throne and all that surrounds it.... S. 496n4
Were there a prophet after me.... H. 227
What an excellent Lord.... H. 429
What do water and clay have to do with talk of the Lord?...S. xxxiii, 140, 404
What happens to the back of the person being flogged.... S. 230
What have I to do with this world?.... H. 162
What I ate at Khaybar keeps coming back to me.... H. 196
What I want and what the horse wants are different. S. 236
What is faith? H. 384
When destiny comes, the eyes are blind. H. 279
When does the Beloved ever turn His face away.... S. 484
When God created the intellect, He said to it, 'Stand,'...H. 46–47, 203
When God is someone's excuse, he has no faults. S. 421
When good fortune turns its back.... S. 263, 468
When He loves someone in the beginningless.... S. 229
When He loves you, He conceals you.... S. 197
When His love kills someone.... S. 340
When I kill someone, I am his wergild. HQ. 172
When I love him, I am for him hearing.... HQ. 349, 391, 433, 528n983
When I passed beyond the Lote Tree.... HP. 258
When it is time both for the prayer and for dinner.... H. 226
When light enters the heart, it becomes spacious.... H. 346
When my mother became pregnant with me.... HP. 193

When remembrance of Me busies someone.... HQ. 198
When someone approves of his station, he is veiled.... S. 250
When someone comes to rest in anything but the Real.... S. 474
When someone contemplates His majesty.... S. 416
When someone has been taken far by the precedents.... S. 152
When someone humbles himself before God.... H. 265
When someone increases asking for forgiveness.... H. 357
When someone loves you for the sake of something.... S. 278
When someone makes his concerns one concern.... H. 385
When someone puts down his face before Him.... S. 265
When someone recognizes God/Him.... S. 89, 108, 149, 170, 375, 416
When someone remembers Me in himself.... HQ. 275
When someone seeks this world.... S. 251
When someone shies away from destruction.... S. 277
When someone sleeps through a prayer.... H. 361
When someone stores up provisions in this world.... H. 146
When someone supplicates God without.... S. 302
When someone torments a friend, he is competing with Me.... HQ. 338
When someone's concern is bread, he has no worth with God. S. 389
When the Day of Resurrection comes, the first to be called forth.... H. 377
When the first of the jug is dregs.... S. 41, 204
When the folk of the Garden enter the Garden.... H. 18
When the light of his face brightened the room.... H. 412
When the Lord is tremendous in the heart.... S. 72
When the ocean of mercy bubbles up.... S. 9
When the Real whispers to you.... S. 140
When the self-disclosure is sound.... S. 166
When the servant reaches the realities of certainty, trial.... S. 80
When the soul has its nourishment.... S. 359
When they drink, they seek; when they seek.... S. 8
When violence turned bloody.... H. 375
When was prophethood made necessary for you?...426
When water lingers for a time.... S. 77
When you see someone seeking Me.... HQ. 267, 476
When you sin and do not care, I will forgive you.... HQ. 309
Whenever I consider opposing Him.... S. 26
Where are the heavens and the earth that I may carry them...? S. 525n890
Where is the path to God?...Where is the escape.... S. 378, 444
Who has more tremendous munificence than I...? HQ. 398
Who will guard us tonight?...H. 360
Whoever loves Me becomes indigent.... HQ. 89
Whoever says "I" has contended.... S. 284
Whoever seeks Me shall find Me. HQ. 209, 340
Whosoever hates Bilāl hates God. H. 241
Why do You desire disobedience from the servants...? HQ. 291
Why do you provide for the stupid and deprive...? HQ. 293
Why don't you talk about Fāṭima? HP. 396
Will you part from me in a place like this? H. 166
Without boasting. H. 183, 325, 328, 384, 393, 403
Woe on me for my long journey.... S. 445
Women are Satan's snares. H. 247
The wonder is not that anyone fails to recognize Him.... S. 139
The wonder is not that I love You.... S. 127
The worst of men is he who eats alone.... H. 151, 235
Would that I had never recognized Him! S. 342
Would that I were a furnace-stoker.... S. 95
Would that I were one of them. S. 498n85
Would that the Lord of Muḥammad had not created Muḥammad! H. 91
Would that when I die I would not be raised up again! S. 92

Wrap me up!...H. 82
Wrap them with their cuts and their blood.... H. 435
Yearning is.... S. 283
The yearning of the pious to encounter Me.... HQ. 15
You did what you did, and I am ashamed.... HQ. 28
You should partake of the two healings.... H. 47
You were created for something tremendous. H. 375
You were gentle to Your friends, so they recognized You.... S. 187
Your beauty lies far beyond the gaze of my likes. H. 104
Your soul has a right against you. H. 283

INDEX AND GLOSSARY OF TERMS

Entries without page numbers are for words that occur repeatedly throughout the text but have no technical significance. They are mentioned to provide readers with the original Persian and Arabic terms.

Aaron, 220, 258, 490
abandoning (*tark*), by servants, 29, 49, 69, 79, 84, 87, 147, 212, 268, 289, 290, 303, 330, 347, 355, 365, 374, 383, 391, 422, 454, 487; abandonment (*khidhlān, mahjūrī*), by God, 6, 23, 46, 109, 167, 184, 215, 226, 259, 272, 322, 381, 383, 414, 416, 457
abasement (*dhull*), 5–6, 54, 85, 120, 179, 235, 321; and exaltedness, 9, 12–13, 43–45, 59, 65, 68, 84, 138, 178, 187, 216, 259, 265, 273, 340–41, 407, 450, 467; self-abasement (*tadhallul*), 286, 303
ʿAbbās (ibn ʿAbd al-Muṭṭalib, d. 32/653), 472
ʿAbbās ibn al-Aḥnaf (d. ca. 192/808), 498n87, 499n101, 499n112, 506n304, 506n318, 506n327, 507n335, 507n336, 511n474, 524n859
ʿAbbās ibn Mirdās al-Sulamī (1st/7th c.), 519n707
Abbasid, xiii, xiv, 68, 282
ʿAbd al-Ḥamīd ibn ʿAbd al-ʿAzīz (d. 292/905), 502n203
ʿAbd al-Jabbār (ibn Aḥmad, Qāḍī, d. 415/1025), 439
ʿAbd al-Malik ibn Marwān (d. 86/705), 114, 456, 537n1262
ʿAbd al-Muṭṭalib (d. 578), 188, 189
ʿAbd al-Raḥmān ibn Muljam (40/661), 523n826
ʿAbd al-Raḥmān ibn Zayd ibn Aslam (d. 182/798–99), 362
ʿAbd al-Wahhāb al-Mālikī (d. 422/1031), 508n365
ʿAbd al-Wāḥid ibn Zayd (d. after 150/767), 129, 213, 530n1043
ʿ*abdallāh*, 50
ʿAbdallāh al-Bustī (Abu'l-ʿAbbās ibn Muḥammad, d. 384/994), 387–88
ʿAbdallāh ibn Bakr (d. 208/823), 501n164
ʿAbdallāh ibn Dumayna (d. 130/747), 511n465
ʿAbdallāh ibn Masʿūd, 92, 319, 320
ʿAbdallāh ibn Rawāḥa (d. 8/629), 92, 528n966, 532n1107
ʿAbdallāh ibn Ubayy ibn Salūl (d. 9/631), 67
ʿAbdallāh Qashshāʿ, 523n841
ability (*istiṭāʿat, tawān, yāragī*)
ablution (*wuḍūʾ*), 99, 190, 266, 285, 359, 367, 400, 448, 456; full ablution (*ghusl*), 87, 264
Abraha (sixth c.), 68
Abraham (the bosom friend), 48, 101, 187, 252, 258, 290, 292, 305, 310, 317, 399, 400, 457, 492; and Ishmael, 50, 187, 196; and the Kaabah, 73, 87, 88, 193; lies of, 245; and Muḥammad, 166, 195–96, 198–99, 324, 325, 328, 374, 393, 425–27, 432, 464; and Nimrod (and the fire), 102, 114, 139, 166, 195, 248, 273, 279–80, 339, 372–73, 432, 447, 477; vision of, 195, 278, 376, 432, 497n55, 506n329, 524n868, 532n1085, 535n1203
abrār, 519n710
abrogation (*naskh*), 56, 198, 424
absence (*ghaybat*), 7, 8, 178, 330; and presence, 16, 119, 159
absolute (*muṭlaq*), 9, 454
absurd (*muḥāl*)
Abu'l-ʿAbbās ʿAṭāʾ. *See* Ibn ʿAṭāʾ Ādamī
Abū ʿAlī, the master. *See* Daqqāq
Abū ʿAlī al-Raqqī (d. 297/909), 520n740

Abu'l-ʿĀliya, Rufayʿ ibn Mihrān (d. ca. 90/709), 530n1041
Abū ʿAmr Muḥammad ibn al-Ashʿath, 532n1090
Abū ʿĀṣim Baṣrī (al-Ḍaḥḥāk ibn Mukhallad, d. 212/828), 213
Abū ʿAṭāʾ Sindī (early 2nd/8th c), 517n645
Abu'l-ʿAtāhiya (d. 213/826), 518n684
Abū Ayyūb al-Anṣārī (d. ca. 52/673), 67, 69, 71, 502n200
Abū Bakr (al-Ṣiddīq, d. 13/634), 68–71, 204, 358, 391, 398, 412, 413, 465–66, 467, 468, 487, 530n1030, 532n1105, 533n1114, 539n1319
Abū Bakr ibn ʿAyyāsh, 459
Abū Bakr Muḥammad ibn al-ʿAbbās al-Khwārazmī (d. 383/993), 514n547
Abū Bakr Muḥammad ibn ʿAmr ibn Ḥazm (d. 120/737), 454
Abū Bakr Warrāq (d. ca. 280/893), 28, 523n831
Abū Dardāʾ (d. 32/652), 97, 496n27
Abū Dāwūd (d. 275/889), *Sunan*, notes, passim
Abū Dharr Ghifārī (d. 32/652), 82, 504n253
Abū Dhuʾayb al-Hudhalī (d. ca. 30/650), 498n86, 529n997
Abū Dulaf (al-Qāsim ibn ʿĪsā al-ʿIjlī, d. ca. 226/840), 533n1140
Abu'l-Faḍl ʿAbdallāh ibn Aḥmad, xiv, 129
Abu'l-Faḍl ibn ʿAmīd (d. 360/970), 508n390
Abu'l-Fayḍ Aḥmad ibn Muḥammad ibn Isḥāq, 200
Abū Firās al-Ḥamdānī (d. 357/968), 497n31, 499n104, 521n771, 538n1292
Abū Ḥabīb Badawī (2nd/8th c.), 480
Abū Ḥafṣ Ḥaddād (d. ca. 260/873), 467, 514n546
Abū Ḥanīfa (d. 150/767), xvi, 455
Abu'l-Ḥasan ibn Muqla (4th/10th c.), 502n203
Abū Hurayra, lvi-lx, 200, 201, 377, 456, 478, 487
Abu'l-Ḥusayn Darrāj (d. ca. 320/932), 529n1009
Abū ʿĪsā (ibn al-Mutawakkil), 505n291
Abū Jahl, lxvi, 51, 82, 114, 265, 388, 392, 410, 428, 533n1138
Abū Lahab, lxvi, 22, 51, 121, 168, 392, 426, 533n1138
Abū Makīs Dīnār, xxv, lxxiin71
Abū Muḥammad Muhallabī (d. 352/963), 535n1177
Abū Muḥammad Ṭāhir ibn Ḥusayn Makhzūmī, 514n556
Abū Mūsā (al-Ashʿarī, d. ca. 45/665), xxvii
Abu'l-Naṣr Asadī (Muḥammad ibn Qays, 2nd/8th c.), 531n1061
Abū Nuʿaym (Aḥmad ibn ʿAbdallāh al-Iṣfahānī, d. 430/1038), xxvi, xxix, xxxiv, 456; *Arbaʿūn*, 514n542; *Ḥilyat al-awliyāʾ*, xxxiv, 456; 497n60, 503n223, 503n230, 503n232, 508n367, 509n394, 509n401, 511n454, 511n467, 511n470, 512n497, 517n630, 518n688, 525n897, 526n912, 530n1041, 530n1042, 531n1051, 531n1057, 532n1086, 532n1110, 533n1125, 533n1134, 533n1141, 523n1155, 535n1176, 537n1252, 537n1257, 537n1262, 539n1310; *Maʿrifa*, 534n1164
Abū Nuwās (al-Ḥasan ibn Hānī, d. 198/813), xxxii, 497n37, 497n44, 501n178, 507n339, 513n519, 533n1116, 538n1282
Abu'l-Qāsim ʿAlī ibn Mūsā al-Mūsawī (5th/11th c.), 516n605
Abu'l-Qāsim Ismāʿīl ibn Muḥammad ibn Aḥmad, 200
Abu'l-Qāsim Mudhakkir, 150
Abu'l-Qāsim al-Zaʿfarānī (ʿUmar ibn Ibrāhīm, 4th/10th c.), 539n1307
Abū Qays, 522n799
Abū Quddāma Shāmī (1st/7th c.), 436, 536n1211
Abū Rayḥāna (Shamʿūn al-Anṣārī), 260
Abū Sahl Ṣuʿlūkī (d. 369/979), 500n137
Abū Saʿīd ibn Abi'l-Khayr (Faḍl ibn Aḥmad Mīhanī, d. 440/1049), xxi, xxxvi, xlvii, 17, 87, 123, 187, 508n383, 508n391, 520n726. *See* Ibn Munawwar
Abū Saʿīd ibn Khalīfa (Muḥammad ibn Muḥammad, d. 544/1149), xxxi-xxxii, xxxv
Abū Saʿīd Kharrāz (d. 277/890–1), 362
Abū Saʿīd Khudrī, 44
Abū Ṣakhr al-Hudhalī (d. ca. 80/700), 498n78
Abu'l-Shaḥma, 428
Abū Sufyān (ibn Ḥarb, d. ca. 32/654), 272
Abū Sulaymān Khaṭṭābī (d. 388/998), 502n199
Abū Ṭālib (ibn ʿAbd al-Muṭṭalib, d. ca. 619), 464; orphan of, 317, 392, 408
Abū Tammām (d. 231/845), 497n50, 502n190, 503n223, 506n332, 506n333
Abū Turāb Nakhshabī (d. 345/859), 387
Abū Yaʿqūb Aqṭaʿ Baṣrī, 79
Abū Yazīd. *See* Basṭāmī
abūqalamūn, 505n289

Abyssinia, 22, 121, 168, 235, 241, 386, 392, 412, 463, 480, 525n873
acceptance (*qabūl, padhīruftan*), 14, 29, 88, 104, 107, 112, 119, 195, 218, 222, 248, 268, 288, 324, 366, 368, 399–401, 422, 430–31, 439; and rejection, 23, 31, 38, 59, 121, 167, 226, 259, 277, 316, 362, 410, 431, 437, 457, 486
accident (*ʿaraḍ*), 61, 174, 335
accounting, calling to account (*ḥisāb, muṭālabat*), 27, 38, 93, 146, 203, 327, 334, 347, 430, 444, 454
accursed (*malʿūn*). *See* Iblis
accusation (*tuhmat*), 24, 36, 129, 157, 243, 246, 449
acknowledgment (*iʿtirāf*)
acquiescence (*inqiyād*), 6, 49, 85, 172, 271, 314, 322, 375, 417, 442
acquisition (*kasb*), 52–53, 74, 338, 400–1, 420–21, 465, 475, 500n152
act, activity (*fiʿl*), 482; God's, 4, 10, 17, 190, 273, 322, 335, 424, 467; man's, 12, 52, 60, 63, 85, 90, 94, 106, 201, 217, 315, 320, 333, 353, 362, 420, 432, 466
Adam (the chosen, *ṣafī*), xliv, xlv, xlix, lii, liv, lxiv, lxv; and the angels, 13, 53–54, 58–59, 86, 91, 97–98, 103, 123, 127, 131, 142, 144, 157, 170, 172–73, 176–77, 181–84, 202, 207, 217–18, 226, 232–33, 235–38, 253, 272, 284, 319–22, 324, 335, 364, 384–85, 389, 391, 395–97, 402, 440, 470, 479–80, 489–94; all-comprehensiveness of, 135, 493–95; aspiration, need, and poverty of, 65–66, 86, 117–18, 141, 144, 176, 183, 216, 233–33, 235, 248, 249, 284, 301–2, 384; chosenness of, 111–13, 120–22, 131, 155, 172, 186, 204, 206, 217, 226, 229, 378, 391, 440, 451, 467–68, 492; creation of, 46–47, 137, 144–47, 172–74, 182–83, 191, 233–34, 247, 295, 314, 322–24, 333, 391–92, 396–97, 426, 451, 466–68, 478, 494; heart of, 76–77, 123, 144, 173, 237; ignorance of, 475; knowledge of, 184, 490; and love, lxv-lxvi, 86–87, 103–5, 111–13, 118, 127, 150–51, 169–70, 172–73, 176, 178, 181–82, 185, 215–16, 219, 223, 229, 232–33, 248–49, 470, 492; and Muḥammad, 158, 183–84, 191–92, 194, 324, 374, 397, 425–26, 495; and paradise, 65–67, 83, 86–87, 93, 95, 97, 112–13, 117–18, 122, 128, 139, 141–43, 150–52, 157, 174–76, 183–84, 204, 213, 215, 218, 232–33, 235, 248–49, 273, 283, 318–19, 374, 389, 397, 412, 418, 440, 451, 470, 476–77, 495; slip/disobedience of, 41, 63, 97–98, 111–13, 117, 122–23, 127, 142, 143, 157–58, 173–75, 178, 184, 186, 194, 204, 297, 217, 219, 223, 226, 235, 236–38, 244, 247–49, 272, 293, 314, 322–23, 443; spirit of, xliv, 137; suffering of, 76, 83, 103–6, 110, 169–70, 178, 186, 194, 319, 492; traveling of, 118, 158, 494–95; vicegerency of, 319–23, 378. *See also* Iblis, makeup, remorse, Trust, sultanate, wheat
Adamic, Adamite (*ādamī*), xlix, li-lii, 5, 8, 16, 40, 46, 47, 54, 55, 58, 59, 66, 74, 76, 86, 117, 118, 134–36, 147, 155, 157, 170, 172, 174–75, 179, 180, 184, 195, 202, 204, 216, 230, 235–37, 244, 257, 277, 286, 291, 299, 314, 321, 366, 369, 374, 375, 378, 381, 384, 401–2, 406, 407, 420, 424, 440, 442, 443, 466, 467, 470, 475, 487; Adamic nature (*ādamiyyat*), 6, 65, 84, 410. *See also* human, makeup, mortal
address (*khiṭāb*)
ʿ*adhāb*, 339; ʿ*adhib*, 339
ʿAdhrā, 100, 498n82
ʿ*ādil*, 167
admonition (*iʿtibār, waʿẓ*)
adornment (*ḥilya, ārāyish, zīnat*)
adversary (*khaṣm*), 80, 118, 127, 133, 176, 248, 273, 302, 324, 338, 360, 374, 385, 489
adversity (*shiddat, ʿanāʾ*)
advice (*pand*)
aeon (*dahr*), 10, 45, 55, 61, 188; aeonist (*dahrī*), 10, 230
affection (*mawaddat*), 10, 86, 127, 131, 132, 138, 177, 178, 235, 335, 338, 383. *See also* love
affinity (*mujānasat*), 66, 466
affirmation (*ithbāt*), and effacement, 20, 239; and negation, 114, 124, 125, 254, 285
affliction (*muṣībat, ibtilāʾ*), 5, 12, 25, 28, 43, 67, 76, 80, 108, 125, 202, 215, 222–23, 227–28, 235, 245, 252, 253, 291–92, 321, 346, 348, 361, 365, 373, 375, 386, 448, 457, 486, 488, 492
afterworld (ʿ*ubqā*), and this world, 132, 145, 163,

191, 225, 250, 251, 253, 269, 327, 330, 331, 454, 466
Āh, 492
aḥad, 69
Aḥmad, 188–89. *See* Muḥammad
Aḥmad (ibn Ḥanbal; d. 241/855), 213; *Musnad*, 498n74, 498n84, 500n130, 503n229, notes, passim; *Zuhd*, 505n278
Aḥmad ibn Ghassān al-Baṣrī, 129
Aḥmad ibn Ḥātim Munqarī, 537n1149
Aḥmad ibn Ismāʿīl Jawharī (Abū Bakr, d. 514/1121), xxxiv
Aḥmad ibn Jaʿfar Rādhakī Ṭūsī, 129
Aḥmad ibn Kayghalagh (d. after 324/936), 538n1285
Aḥmad ibn Khiḍrūya (d. 240/855), 467
Aḥmad ibn Masrūq (d. ca. 298/911), 530n1050
Aḥmad ibn Muḥammad Rūdhbārī (Abū ʿAlī, d. 322/933), xxii
Aḥmad al-Ṣūfī (Aḥmad ibn ʿAbdallāh al-Fāzī), xx
Aḥnaf ibn Qays (d. 72/691), 124
aḥrār, 519n710
Ahrīman, 409
aḥwāl, xxxviii
Aḥwaṣ al-Anṣārī (d. ca. 100/718), 527n944
ʿĀʾisha, lvi, 42, 63, 159, 165, 246, 317, 370, 412, 482, 527n952, 531n1072
akhlāq, lv
ʿAlāʾ ibn ʿAbd al-Raḥmān, 200
Alast ("Am I not?"), Covenant of, 113–15
Aleppo, 72
ʿAlī (ibn Abī Ṭālib, d. 40/661), 27, 134, 149, 306, 339, 342, 346, 363, 366, 373, 396, 410, 412, 453, 463, 481, 484, 496n12, 513n528, 516n623, 523n822, 523n826, 529n1002, 529n1016, 532n1082, 532n1105, 534n1154, 537n1246, 537n1247, 539n1328
ʿAlī Filakī (Abu'l-Ḥasan ibn Muḥammad al-Iṣbahānī, d. 550/1155), xxxiv
ʿAlī ibn ʿAbd al-Raḥīm Qannād (3rd/9th c.), 500n148
ʿAlī ibn Aḥmad Nuʿaymī (d. 423/1032), 507n352
ʿAlī ibn Ḥajar, 200
ʿAlī ibn Ḥasan Bākharzī, 504n257
ʿAlī ibn Ḥasan Quhistānī (d. after 435/1043), 505n299
ʿAlī ibn al-Ḥusayn Zayn al-ʿĀbidīn (d. ca. 95/713), 266, 522n788
ʿAlī ibn ʿĪsā (d. 335/946), 361
ʿAlī ibn al-Jahm (d. 249/863), 499n93
ʿAlī ibn Muḥammad al-Tihāmī (d. 416/1025), 512n480
ʿAlī ibn Mūsā Riḍā (d. 202/818), xiv, xl
ʿAlī Jarjarāʾī, 511n460
alienation (*waḥshat*), 5, 29, 53, 269, 443, 481, 491
alif, 56, 130, 175, 202, 266, 303, 314, 501n167
All-Compelling (*jabbār*). *See* compulsion
all-comprehensive (*jāmiʿ*), 135, 200, 493, 513n531, 531n1066
Allāh, xvii, 4, 332
allusion (*ishāra*), 3, 8, 32, 60, 135, 137, 144, 146, 147, 225, 253, 257, 279, 310, 321, 329, 378, 401, 432, 443, 487; and expression, 47, 240, 288, 307, 361, 431
alms (*ṣadaqa*), 11, 63, 79, 107, 293, 377, 413, 420, 434, 464; alms tax (*zakāt*), 89, 101, 190, 371, 469
ambiguity (*shubhat*), 41, 447; ambiguous verses (*mutashābihāt*), 453
ambush (*kamīn*)
ʿAmīdiyya Madrasa, xiii, xxxix
Āmina (d. 577), 413
ʿāmm, xviii
ʿAmmār ibn Yāsir (d. 37/657), 481
amr, lxvi
ʿAmr and Zayd (i.e., this person and that), 15, 431, 472
ʿAmr ibn Maʿdī Karib (d. 21/642), 219
ʿAmr ibn Shaʾs (al-Asadī, d. ca. 20/641), 534n1168
amulet (*taʿwīdh*), 93, 234, 245, 286, 502n208
anāfat, 130
Anʿām, Surah, 387, 532n1096
Anas ibn Mālik (d. ca. 90/710), xxv, 44, 69, 89, 326, 374
Andāqī, Ḥasan (Abū ʿAbdallāh ibn al-Ḥusayn, d. 552/1157), xxxix
angel (*malak*, *firishta*), 13, 22, 27, 120, 133, 253, 275, 297, 325, 384, 414, 449, 451, 460–61, 466, 468, 478–79; of death, 210, 368, 420, 457, 485; of the microcosm, 120, 133, 135, 145; proximate, 15, 58, 60, 65, 91, 95, 100, 138, 144, 146, 166, 175, 191, 198, 201, 210, 217, 238, 249, 268, 275, 324, 328, 384, 387, 389, 392, 395, 396, 411, 422,

427, 438, 461. *See also* Adam, Dominion, human being, worship
anger (*sakhṭ, khashm*), 205, 231, 244, 245, 375, 416. *See also* approval
animals (*ḥayawān, jānwar*), li, 14, 68, 69, 134, 136, 230, 260, 328, 347, 351, 387, 488, 493; wild (*wuḥūsh*), 113, 208, 436–37; in man, 64, 135–36; ant, 35, 69, 122, 202–3, 315, 329, 332, 474; bat, 13, 123, 399, 478; bear, 136; bee, 31, 47–48, 136, 342, 490; bird, 53, 68, 70, 113, 148, 171, 207, 224, 230, 236, 276, 310, 314, 329, 349, 380, 391, 436–37, 475, 493; (and cage/snare), 8, 136–38, 225, 262, 304, 314, 341, 366, 418, 452, 481; camel, 23, 31, 37, 44, 69, 70, 79, 93, 98, 103, 128, 135, 136, 156, 160–61, 162, 193, 214, 238, 282, 295, 358, 367, 442, 473; cat, 135, 214, 341, 342; caterpillar, 273; cattle, 134, 281, 298, 382, 419; chameleon, 14, 237; chicken, 151, 230, 269, 423, 437; cow, 95, 311–12; crawling things (*ḥasharāt*), 298, 312, 350; crocodile (*nahang*), 7, 35, 56, 133, 145, 202, 490; crow, 12, 17, 169, 269, 387, 423; dog, 23, 25, 31–32, 54, 64, 69, 70, 91, 92, 94, 121, 134–37, 181, 201–3, 237, 262, 267, 275, 291, 316, 342, 352–54, 374, 437, 477; donkey, 44, 105, 124, 134, 263, 275, 292, 345, 383, 387, 457, 478; dragon (*azhdahā*), 37, 69, 130, 262; duck, 118, 437; dung beetle, 402; eagle, 261, 310, 391, 393; elephant, 56, 136, 156, 230, 259, 273, 490; falcon, 10, 12, 13, 26, 34, 80, 114, 120, 127, 140, 147–48, 198, 217, 218, 223, 230, 247, 256, 257, 261, 262, 269, 297, 393, 419, 423, 433, 468, 470, 475, 477, 490; finch, 80; fish, 19, 74–76, 136, 140, 238, 260, 284, 298, 299, 311–12, 313–14, 348, 365–66, 387, 418, 472; fly, 56, 68, 69, 264, 395, 440; fox, 44, 102, 135, 136, 279; gazelle, 17, 83, 104, 110, 127, 136, 208, 223; gnat, 68, 69, 106, 250, 315, 338, 389, 395, 432, 443, 478; grouse, 136; hawk, 171, 419; hoopoe, 68, 126, 203, 301, 329, 379, 428; horse, 9, 68, 83, 90, 134, 139, 166, 171–72, 190, 194, 217, 224, 236, 305, 327, 337, 349, 350, 391; leopard, 136, 313; lion, 44, 82, 85, 121, 127, 136, 223, 230, 259, 279, 313, 353, 374, 474, 477; lizard, 14, 69, 76, 332, 472, 478; locust, 384; moth (and candle), 11, 34, 88, 125, 137, 202, 214, 229, 263, 427, 463, 464; mouse, 342; nightingale (*bulbul, hazār-dastān*), 6, 8, 10, 107, 114, 136–37, 177, 208, 216, 343, 425, 438, 468, 490; onager, 275, 353; ostrich, 136, 391; owl, 136; oyster and pearl, 13, 34, 45, 47, 75, 90, 131, 182, 188, 199, 223, 230, 232, 256, 263, 279, 298, 317, 323, 333, 335, 450, 469, 478, 479, 490, 492, 493; packhorse (*bāragī*), 90, 183, 192, 332; parakeet, 136; partridge, 127, 223; peacock, 10, 86, 120, 136, 225, 227, 264, 304, 343, 490, 502n206; (=Gabriel), 71, 111, 317, 343, 462; pheasant, 475; pig, 64, 94, 134–36, 262; phoenix (*ʿanqāʾ, humā*), 98, 120, 123, 136, 170, 215, 324, 343, 393, 411, 477; pigeon, 69, 136, 297, 341; quail, 247; rabbit, 136; rat, 68, 136; rooster, 230; salamander, 236; scorpion, 263, 308–9; sea cow, 490; serpent, 36, 60, 64, 67, 152, 214, 251–52, 282, 308–9, 360, 418, 490; sheep, 27, 37, 44, 50, 77, 106, 120, 136, 139, 196, 307, 331, 360, 372, 455; silkworm, 261, 490; snake, 263, 298, 471; sparrow, 13, 56, 148, 156, 250, 256, 477; spider, 68, 69, 71, 395; vulture, 238; weevil, 357; wolf, 36, 69, 136, 143, 345, 441, 478. *See also* beast
annihilation (*fanāʾ*), and subsistence, 7, 29, 42, 84, 96, 115, 130, 131, 140, 159, 162–63, 230, 244, 251, 254, 263, 285, 329, 349, 372, 407, 415, 447
Anṣārī, ʿAbd al-Bāqī (Abu'l-Majd ibn ʿĀmir, d. 525/1131), xxxvii
Anṣārī, ʿAbdallāh (d. 481/1088), xii, xxxvi-xxxvii, 496n3, 501n157, 513n513
Anṣārī, ʿAbdallāh ibn Jābir (Abū Ismāʿīl, d. 561/1166), xxxvii
Anṣārī, Jābir ibn ʿAbdallāh (Abū ʿAṭiyya, d. 520/1126), xxxvi-xxxvii
antagonist (*khaṣm*), 266, 272, 301, 315, 376, 391, 395, 404, 409, 421, 437, 477
anticipation (*intiẓār*), 14, 24, 84, 85, 90, 217, 240, 317, 342, 344, 416
antidote (*tiryāq*), 123, 129, 334, 365, 463, 494
antimony (*uthmud*), 122, 245, 349, 361, 410
Anushiravan (d. 579), 272

Anwarī (d. ca. 583/1187), 496n22, 505n281
apology (*'udhr*), 206, 208–10, 281, 287, 303, 307, 321, 368, 397, 427–28, 430–31, 445
apostasy (*irtidād*), 76, 340, 358
apparent (*āshkārā, paydā*)
appetite (*shahwat*), 17, 20, 85, 87, 130, 133–35, 137, 145, 147, 150, 178, 188, 238, 247, 257, 261, 262, 275, 283, 331, 335, 410, 446, 457. *See also* caprice
apportioning (*qisma, qadar*; pl. *maqādīr*), lxvii, 49–50, 55, 57, 84, 98, 104, 113, 122, 140, 154, 159, 161, 284, 293, 294, 316, 352, 357, 362, 363, 368, 395, 485–86, 490
apprehension (*ishfāq*), 85, 218
approach, means of (*wasīlat*), 118, 152, 232, 333, 335, 448
approval (*riḍā'*), 6, 31–32, 38, 49, 67, 81, 89, 90, 91, 93, 105, 107, 115, 118, 137, 155, 179, 204, 212, 216, 260, 271, 273, 289–91, 333, 351, 363, 365, 385, 419, 428, 438, 454; and anger, 40, 67, 101, 235, 251, 273, 431, 452. *See also* Muḥammad
'Āqib, 188
'aqīda, xvi
Aqṣā (the Furthest) Mosque, 210, 262
Arabs, 34, 113, 200–1, 219, 260, 262, 271, 311, 381, 427, 462, 463; Arabic, xv, xviii, 14, 32, 38, 63, 84, 290, 328, 352, 512n495
Arafat, 88, 501n164
Arberry, A. J., xlvi, 510n431
argument (*ḥujjat*), 41, 52, 58, 109, 117–18, 125, 226, 254, 271, 344, 368, 395, 491
Aristotle, 539n1315
armor (*zirih*)
arrangement (*niẓām*), 127, 144, 176, 298
arrival (*wurūd, wuṣūl, rasīdan*). *See* new arrival
arrogance (*nakhwat*), 32, 44, 85, 106, 151, 225, 232, 356, 472, 477
artifacts (*ṣanā'i'*), 130, 181, 182, 235, 351, 408; artisan (*ṣāni'*), 130, 145; artisanry (*ṣun'*), 4, 46, 47, 57, 98, 128, 158, 172, 181, 182, 231, 252, 272, 290, 396, 419, 430, 433, 438, 478; faculty of, 146
ascription (*iḍāfa, nisbat*), 87, 149, 219, 314; banquet of, 187, 261, 308, 437, 490
Ash'arite, xliii, lvi, 500n152
Ash'ath, 149
'Āṣif ibn Barkhiyā, 269
Āsiya, 372, 519n686
asking (*su'āl*), 117, 303, 305–6, 332
asmā' al-ḥusnā, al-, xlviii
Asmā' bint 'Umays, 391
aspiration (*himmat*), 3, 7, 10, 17, 20, 30, 34, 44, 45, 47, 48, 54, 65, 70, 71, 74–75, 86, 93, 96, 115, 117, 119, 120, 122, 128, 130, 132, 133, 136, 141, 144, 148, 153, 156, 158, 163, 166, 176, 194, 195, 199, 206, 208-10, 212-15, 217, 225, 236, 246, 249–50, 257, 261, 262, 264, 267, 275, 276, 280, 282, 286, 301, 302, 317, 324, 325, 327, 356-58, 361, 365, 366, 374, 383, 384, 393, 395–97, 400, 410, 411, 425, 442, 452, 469, 473, 475–77, 492, 523n839
asrār al-'ibādāt, xli
assayer (*naqqād*), 38–39, 233, 258, 358, 363, 397
assistance (*madad*), 90, 116, 136, 167, 180, 364, 383, 392, 395, 400, 460, 461, 464
association(ism) (*shirk*), lxvi, 11, 16, 28, 41, 62, 93, 140, 180–81, 187, 222, 269, 273–74, 279, 296, 304–5, 330–31, 338, 381, 394, 417, 441, 449, 471
assurance (*ḍamān*), 72, 352, 410, 415, 424
astronomer (*munajjim*), 140, 361
at-ness (*'indiyya*), 144
attachment (*'alāqa, ta'alluq*), 96, 129, 257, 273, 282, 303, 331
'Aṭṭār, Farīd al-Dīn (d. ca. 1221), xi, xiv, xxxvi, 502n194, 505n288, 502n475, 513n516, 517n628, 519n711, 531n1064, 532n1102, 532n1104, 533n1142, 534n1151, 534n1153, 534n1173, 535n1180, 536n1219, 536n1124, 538n1287
attestation (*iqrār*), 11, 20, 52, 89, 115, 270, 303, 383, 443, 507n357; and denial (*inkār*), 41, 381, 461, 462
attraction (*jadhba*), 6, 209, 242, 254, 317, 326, 331, 382, 400, 453, 465; faculty of, 145
attribute (*ṣifat*), and act, 17, 273; divine, 4, 56, 92, 140, 159–60, 162, 167, 174, 182, 222, 231, 235, 240, 248, 254, 264, 265, 268, 273, 274, 295, 299, 310, 328, 332, 337, 368–69, 372, 400, 404, 407–8, 414, 420, 422, 424, 431, 439, 447, 467–68, 472, 478, 485, 486, 488, 490; complementarity of divine, lxiii-lxviii, 11, 41, 52, 55, 67, 76–77, 103–4, 125, 138, 168, 174, 181, 213, 277,

315–16, 332, 451, 474; of the created, 5, 7, 20, 23, 38, 40, 41, 44, 62, 64, 65, 75–76, 86, 90, 93, 94, 96–97, 102, 115, 120, 121, 138, 143, 159–60, 162, 174, 178, 179, 182, 185, 189, 190, 204, 219, 224, 229, 234, 236, 252, 278, 288, 307, 314, 318, 322, 334, 339, 345, 353, 362, 364, 368–69, 396, 407–8, 411, 420, 438, 441, 444, 447, 448, 453–55, 454, 471, 480, 481, 484, 487, 494; and names, l-lv, lxiii, 277; of the Prophet, 44, 66, 67, 159–60, 162, 254, 257, 262–65, 268, 272, 274, 328, 478. *See also* essence
audacity (*bī-bākī*), 120, 369
avarice (*ḥirṣ*), 117, 135, 136, 145, 206, 229, 262, 263, 346, 357
Avicenna (Ibn Sīnā, d. 416/1037), xlviii
awareness (*āgāhī, bā-khabarī, iṭṭilā*ʿ, *hūsh*), 26, 35, 38, 39, 47, 59, 124, 133, 141, 166, 174, 189, 201, 203, 216, 242, 247, 254, 283, 308, 321, 331, 334, 338, 380, 398, 423, 429, 461, 467, 477
awe, awesomeness (*haybat*), 6, 7, 27, 163–64, 332, 474; and intimacy, 166, 256
Awliyāʾ, Niẓām al-Dīn (d. 725/1325), xii
awwāh, 492
āyāt, xxxix, xlviii
Ayāz (Abu'l-Najm, d. 449/1057), 408, 429
Ayyūb Sakhtiyānī (d. 131/748), 221
Azar, 149, 187, 279–80, 432, 512n501
ʿAzāzīl, 120, 144, 185, 204, 229, 253, 337, 475, 479, 494. *See* Iblis
Azrael (the angel of death), 55, 211, 324, 333, 492
ʿAzza, 114

backbiting (*ghībat*), 59, 157, 173, 321, 330, 349
badal, 497n39
Badr, 42, 69, 93, 238, 272, 435, 458, 472
Baghawī, Ḥusayn (Abū Muḥammad ibn Masʿūd, d. 516/1122), xxvi
Baghdad, xiii, xiv, xvi, xx, xxii, xxv, xxvii, xxxv, xxxviii, xli, lxxiin82, 21, 336
Bahāʾ al-Dīn Naqshband (d. 791/1389), xxxviii
Bahdalī (Abu'l-Qāsim ʿAlī ibn Muḥammad), 520n729
Bahman, 251
Bākharzī, ʿAlī ibn al-Ḥasan (d. 467/1075), 504n257
balāʾ, 115, 183
Balaam Beor, lii, 23, 64, 121, 291, 316, 353, 475, 497n54, 514n562
ballista (*manjanīq*), 106, 139, 166, 311, 339, 461
banishment (*tabʿīd*), 5, 23, 229, 272, 386
banquet (*ḍiyāfat*)
Banū Hāshim, 188, 317
Banū Manda, xxxv
Banū Tamīm, xv
Banū ʿUdhrā, 88
Baqīʿ Gharqad, 363
Bāqillānī, Abū Ghālib Muḥammad (d. 500/1106), xx
bār, 142, 286
barāʾat, 130
baraka, xxxix
Bārnābādhī, ʿAbd al-Raḥmān (Abū Muḥammad ibn ʿAlī al-Naʿīmī, d. 542/1147), xxvi
barr, 515n570
Bashār ibn Burd (d. 168/783), 505n287, 507n345
basmala, lxiii
Basra, 457
Bassām ibn ʿAbdallāh (al-Ṣayrafī), 514n557
Basṭāmī, Abū Yazīd, 24, 59–60, (94, 96), 127, 147, 212, 337, 339, 365, 387, 394, 421, 448, 471, 496n4, 496n15, 505n285, 505n288, 517n630, 521n778, 531n1066, 532n1093, 539n1326
Basṭāmī, ʿUmar (ibn Abi'l-Ḥasan), xxv
Bathsheba, 517n641, 520n741
bāṭil, lv
battlefield (*maʿraka*), 34, 133, 212, 238, 262, 478
Bayāḍa, 311
bayʿat al-riḍwān, xxx
Bayhaqī, Abū Bakr (Aḥmad ibn al-Ḥusayn, d. 458/1066), xliii; *Asmāʾ*, xliii, lvi, lx, lxi; *Dalāʾil*, 515n575; *Iʿtiqād*, xliii; 496n5, 496n10, 496n14, 497n45, 508n372, 515n570, 518n663, 532n1111; *Maʿrifa*, 535n1195; *Qaḍāʾ*, 508n378; *Shuʿab*, 498n80, 499n108, 501n164, 507n345, 507n355, 516n598, 516n614, 520n718, 523n813, 525n901, 529n994, 537n1242, 538n1290, 539n1331; *Sunan*, 527n939, 538n1289; *Zuhd*, 524n860
Bayhaqī, Ismāʿīl (Abū ʿAlī ibn Aḥmad, d. 507/1113), xliii
beast (*bahīma*), 64, 113, 120, 134–35, 200, 202, 298; of burden (*sutūr*), 44, 264

beauty (*ḥusn, jamāl, nīkū'ī*), 245; of Adam/Adamites, 46, 58, 98, 178, 183, 185, 217, 229, 231, 233–35, 239, 298, 324, 468, 470, 494; of Joseph, 196, 200, 230, 241–43, 245, 317, 345, 406, 418, 445, 449; and majesty, lxiv, 8, 10, 11, 13, 15, 19, 23, 26, 33–34, 38, 43, 55, 56, 58, 85, 93, 96–100, 102, 104, 107, 126, 128, 130, 141, 145, 152, 154, 158, 165, 167, 178, 182, 217, 233–35, 261, 277, 285, 289, 299, 324, 357, 397, 398, 400, 402–7, 409, 416, 418, 421, 424, 433; of Moses, 100, 188, 246; of Muḥammad, 199, 253, 310, 356, 375, 384, 412, 470, 471, 482; perfection of, 11, 12, 17, 56, 104, 196, 246, 266; and ugliness, 121, 192, 215, 236, 264, 290, 382, 456; beautiful deeds (*ḥasanāt*), 22, 64; and ugly deeds, 40, 54, 172, 312, 399, 428; beautiful-doing (*iḥsān, nīkūkārī*), xxix, lxii, lxvi,18, 20, 46, 57, 62, 90, 100, 113, 122, 153, 156, 175, 186–87, 191, 216, 259, 269, 283, 285, 286, 293, 298, 310, 335, 360, 371, 416, 420–22, 424, 428, 429; and ugly-doing, 11, 217, 290, 300, 309, 399. *See also* love

bedouin. *See* nomad

beggar (*gadā*)

beginning (*bidāyat, ibtidā'*), 51, 96–98, 109, 120, 132–33, 137, 160, 173, 174, 181, 191, 204, 314, 382, 384, 396, 431, 443, 448, 469, 495; and end, 9, 12, 77, 86, 91, 103, 114, 195, 206, 383, 415, 426, 438, 440, 470, 495; beginner (*mubtadī*), 184, 209, 342, 446, 495; and advanced (*muntahī*), 114, 178, 233, 266

Beginningless, the (*azal*), 6, 8, 10, 46, 56, 120, 156, 232, 256, 278, 302, 338, 350, 353, 362, 363, 382, 385, 401, 408, 410, 419, 420, 431–32, 451, 464, 486, 534n1173; and the Endless, 182, 240, 339, 427, 429, 475, 477; beginningless and endless, 14, 59, 70, 124, 139, 141, 209, 214, 369; beginningless beginning, 173, 396, 404, 452, 485. *See also* gentleness, knowledge, love, solicitude

being (*hastī, būd, kawn*), 5, 9, 13, 62, 64, 71, 74, 91, 96, 123, 133, 150, 153, 185, 193, 227, 235, 254, 260, 274, 293, 307, 355, 357, 390–91, 410, 419, 421, 424, 441, 447, 466, 484, 495; of God, 215, 240, 284, 415, 419; and nonbeing, 48, 76, 91–92, 114, 124–25, 215, 240, 259, 285, 475, 478; realm of (*kawn*), 4, 7, 45, 57, 70, 122, 131, 152, 184, 232, 250, 262, 278, 324, 357, 374; (engendered) beings (*akwān, kā'ināt, mukawwanāt*), 55, 69, 194, 240, 259; Being-Bestower (*mukawwin*), 74, 250, 355; bringing to be (takwīn), 46, 60, 236. *See also* existence

belief (*i'tiqād*), 10, 20, 33, 44, 48, 52, 56, 62, 72, 74, 89, 112, 155, 173, 211, 213, 215, 288, 295, 300, 311, 337, 352, 439, 458, 484

beloved (*maḥbūb, ma'shūq, ḥabīb, jānān*)

beneficence (*in'ām*), 131, 175, 193, 368, 429, 433; and punishment, 170, 273

benevolence (*rifq*), 179, 285, 342

Benjamin, 243, 292, 445

bestial (*bahīmī*), 120

bestowal (*'aṭā', nawāl, bakhshāyish, hadiyya*), 5, 54, 90, 93, 107, 111–13, 116, 131, 163, 164, 215, 225, 240, 244, 276, 277, 285, 287, 288, 290, 308, 310, 328, 350, 420, 428, 429, 438, 439, 469, 485; and refusal, 81, 306. *See also* generosity

betrayal, treachery (*khiyānat*), 219, 226, 334, 446

bewilderment (*ḥayrat*), 21, 23–24, 33, 34, 37, 40, 41, 56, 62, 70, 84–85, 96, 98, 100, 103, 106, 123, 125, 126, 139–41, 178, 215, 223, 239, 245, 267, 286, 290, 314, 317, 318, 343, 347, 356, 365–66, 369, 377–78, 383, 392, 398, 404, 416, 453, 458, 474, 531n1066

bias (*mayl*). *See* iniquity

bida', xlvii

Bilāl (d. 19/640), 22, 121, 127, 168, 241, 257, 374, 386, 388–89, 392–93, 463, 480, 521n763, 521n773

Bilāl ibn Sa'd (1st/6th c.), 534n1170

Bilqīs, 68, 126, 325, 351

birr, 130

Bishr Ḥāfī (d. 227/842), 72, 149, 408, 439, 503n230, 511n460

Black Stone (*ḥajar aswad*), 88

blame (*malāmat, dhamm*), 117, 147, 174, 177, 247, 252, 260, 341, 485, 495; and love, 21, 49, 143, 170, 215, 226, 228, 246, 280, 367, 391. *See also* praise

Blaze (*sa'īr*), 146, 252, 457

blessing (*ni'mat*), 8–9, 16, 19, 33, 66, 89, 90,

113, 132, 174, 184, 231, 236, 249, 267, 270, 281, 290, 308–9, 328–29, 343, 351–52, 356, 398, 422, 438, 465, 489, 491; and tribulation, 41, 80, 228, 296, 340–41, 350, 367–68, 369, 416, 438, 456, 465, 476, 489, 491; (*barakat*), 81, 158, 253, 256, 257, 305, 308, 314, 325, 437; (*ṣalāt*), 59, 373, 397, 408, 490
blight (*āfat*), 14, 43, 50, 58, 63, 86, 94, 96, 114, 135, 151, 154, 180, 192, 212, 238, 256, 346, 402, 428, 432, 481, 487
bliss (*na'īm*), 37, 71, 102, 168, 265, 343; of paradise, 6, 117, 152, 157, 208, 239, 279, 316, 439
blockage (*sadd*)
boasting (*fakhr, iftikhār*), 11, 68, 91, 94, 118, 122, 183, 195, 202, 206, 225, 250, 260, 265, 293, 295, 317, 325, 326, 328, 333, 365, 382, 384, 393, 403, 412, 413, 421, 422, 434, 448, 488, 489–90
body (*tan, kālbud, qālab, jism, shabaḥ, jasad*), 25, 89, 112, 116, 135–37, 145–46, 156, 165, 261, 301, 304, 306, 388, 424 (*see also* heart, soul, spirit); bodily (*jismānī*), 16, 236, 264; bodily member/part (*'uḍw, jāriḥa*), 59, 125, 133, 135, 145, 174, 199, 337, 410, 480, 495
boldness (*dilīrī, dalāl, gustākhī*), 114, 206, 216, 245, 309, 321, 325, 369, 384, 467; bold expansiveness (*inbisāṭ*), 12, 17, 166, 303, 304, 306–7, 321, 332, 408
boon companion (*nadīm*), 71, 202, 213, 219, 223, 224, 288, 327, 339, 410, 472
Bosom Friend (*khalīl*). *See* Abraham
bounteousness (*ifḍāl*), 53, 58, 72, 93, 112, 119, 120, 132, 178, 183, 199, 216, 261, 276, 303, 310, 316, 352, 369, 399, 416, 420, 427, 429, 430, 432, 464
bounty (*faḍl*), 11, 89, 322, 335, 485; and justice, 10, 11, 38, 52, 138, 152, 224, 251, 316, 325, 329, 357, 370, 405, 408, 416, 420, 433, 447, 450–51, 475
bowing (*rukū'*)
brain (*dimāgh*), 120, 133, 145, 314, 468
brand (*dāgh*)
brazenness (*bī-bākī*), 66, 177, 386, 451
breast (*sīna, ṣadr*), 3, 6, 7, 10, 19, 21, 26, 29, 69, 72, 74, 126, 128, 129, 133, 138, 141, 144, 148, 149, 156, 164, 167, 188, 194, 199, 209, 212, 215, 232–33, 278, 287, 297, 299, 310, 317, 332, 333, 367, 373, 381, 382, 385, 407, 409, 410, 415, 432, 458–59, 462–63, 474, 477, 478, 483; burning of, 47, 188, 216, 418; possessor of, 167, 400
breath (*dam, nafas*)
bribery (*rushwat*), 318, 386, 422, 473
bride (*'arūs*), 66, 70, 96, 129, 186, 214, 258, 261, 331, 385, 424
brightness (*rawshanā'ī, ḍiyā'*)
brilliance (*sanā'*)
brokenness (*inkisār, shikastagī*), 85, 90–92, 137, 142, 171, 173, 238, 266, 267, 292, 307, 323, 327, 368, 413, 422, 484, 485
Bū 'Alī. *See* Siyāh
Buhlūl, 517n642
Buḥturī (d. 248/897), 498n63
Bukhara, xiv, xxvi, xxxix, xl, xlvi, lxxiiin102
Bukhārī (Muḥammad ibn Ismā'īl, d. 256/870), xiv; *Ṣaḥīḥ* of, xxii, xxvi, lii, 73, 363, 496n7, 503n221, 516–17n623, notes, passim
Bulliett, Richard, xxxii, xxxvi
Bundār ibn Ḥusayn (d. 353/964), 386
Būqubays, 87, 213
Burāq, 44, 71, 81, 124, 160, 190, 242, 262, 265, 276, 344, 356, 374, 383, 424, 441, 469
burning (*sūz, ḥurqa*), 19, 62, 73, 76, 77, 138, 141, 143, 151, 154, 169, 180, 181, 186, 212, 216, 243, 261, 263, 267, 288–90, 297, 335, 341, 353, 365, 386–87, 392–93, 418, 436, 456, 464, 466–67, 476–77; not burning the burned, 297, 364. *See* love
Būshanjī (Abu'l-Ḥasan 'Alī, d. 348/959), 517n633
Bust, 66
Buthayna, 29
Byzantium (*rūm*), Byzantine (*rūmī*), 113, 125, 167, 239, 241, 312, 327, 329, 374, 386, 392, 405, 409, 412, 427, 429, 436, 449, 459–60, 463, 493, 500n121

Caesar (*qayṣar*), 45, 188, 191, 272, 312, 346, 354, 409, 449
cage (*qafaṣ*). *See* bird (*under* animal)
caliph (*khalīfa*), tales of, 68, 220, 251, 282, 300, 336–37, 394
Canaan (Kan'ān, son of Noah), 497n55, 519n685
Canaan (place), 242, 252, 418
candle (*sham'*). *See* moth (*under* animal)

capacity (*ṭāqat, wus'*, *ḥawṣala*)
Capella, 437
caprice (*hawā*), 3, 7, 20, 116, 130, 145, 162, 189, 207–8, 212, 225, 243, 245, 248, 252, 254, 261, 263, 270, 285, 345, 346, 374, 425, 455; and appetite, 175, 208, 351, 386, 414, 454
carefree (*fārigh, lā-ubālī*), 111, 169, 188, 202, 242, 248, 252, 279, 391, 402, 467, 494
caress (*nawākhtan*)
carpet (*bisāṭ, farsh*)
carrion (*murdār, mayta*)
cash, hard (*naqd*), 14, 33, 116, 130, 138, 150, 152, 204, 241, 244, 267, 268, 279, 287, 402, 446
castigation (*nakāl*), 5, 11, 120, 234, 236
catamite (*mukhannath*), 225, 276, 479
cause (*'illat, sabab*), 7, 29, 74, 107, 163, 195, 196, 229, 329, 337, 363, 369, 420, 428, 435, 451; First, 140; God's lack of, 4, 22, 56–57, 100–1, 114, 119, 121, 131, 151, 155, 167–68, 170, 173, 181, 220, 231, 234, 239, 251, 289, 299, 312, 322, 333, 352–53, 360, 362, 367–68, 395, 408, 430, 433, 438, 460; secondary cause (*sabab*), 283, 329
celestial (*'ulwī*), 112, 122, 225; figures, 13, 58, 181, 414; world, 84, 120, 136, 253, 257, 414, 483; and terrestrial, 45, 48, 93, 136, 144, 199, 267, 324, 414. *See also* sphere
center (*markaz*), 84, 133, 142, 183, 435, 455; Muhammadan, 426; terrestrial, 45, 93, 199, 204, 324; center-point (*nuqṭa*), 20, 76, 177, 201, 216, 352, 388, 474, 481; Adam as, 106, 111, 120, 142, 156, 172, 184, 283, 384, 395, 412; Muḥammad as, 325, 383, 389, 426; prophets as, 44, 66, 99, 153, 188, 197, 200, 303, 319, 382, 384, 388, 397, 421, 424, 440, 442, 453, 457, 462, 475
certainty (*yaqīn*), 20, 41, 79–80, 94, 125, 132, 134, 139, 272, 299, 302, 328, 329, 347, 358, 382, 388, 454; knowledge/eye of, 3, 10, 80, 219, 284
certitude (*qaṭ'*)
chamber (*ḥujra*)
character, character trait (*khulq*), lv-lvi, lx, lxv, 82, 89, 115, 130, 159, 189, 200, 221, 332, 361
characteristic (specific, *khāṣṣiyyat*), 134, 136, 144, 155, 253, 454, 491
charity (*ṣadaqa*), 89, 204, 469, 472
chashm-i bad, 502n205; *chashm-zakhm*, 502n206
chastisement (*'adhāb*), 5, 55, 132, 231, 251, 252, 257, 268, 294, 305, 328, 339, 349, 356, 378, 446
cherubim (*karrūbiyyūn*), 210, 268, 422–24, 469
chevalier (*jawānmard, fatā*), xxiii, xliii, 179, 215, 235, 300, 353, 376
chief, chieftain (*sayyid*). chieftainship (*siyādat, khwājagī*)
Chigil, 164
China, 312, 440
Chishtī, Mu'īn al-Dīn (d. 633/1235), xii
chivalry (*jawān-mardī, futuwwat*), lxxin51, 200, 207, 342, 377, 413, 424, 463
choice, free choice (*ikhtiyār*), 40, 49–50, 69, 70, 84, 101, 125, 140, 147, 154, 167, 176, 234, 248, 254, 299, 300, 316, 339, 342, 352, 360, 365, 385, 391, 404, 406, 432, 491
chosenness (*ijtibā', iṣṭinā'*), 126, 188, 331, 432, 479; of Adam, 46, 52, 62, 66, 98, 112, 121–22, 131, 184, 186, 204, 206, 213, 229, 236, 317, 384, 391, 425, 426, 438, 458, 467; of Moses, 100, 331; of Muḥammad, 382, 393
Chosroes, 272, 346, 354, 439
Christian, 21, 26, 126, 158, 179, 211, 226, 247, 283, 330, 362, 394, 535n1203
church (*kalīsiyā*), 26, 41, 69, 114, 129, 204, 211, 223-24, 241, 374, 418, 420, 452, 484
circle (*dā'ira*), 38, 218, 388, 426; of being, 60, 236; dusty, 34, 57, 110, 325, 378, 446; (*dawr, ḥalqa*), 94, 476; circling (*ṭawf, gird gashtan*)
circumambulation (*ṭawāf*), 54, 55, 74, 77, 79, 88, 125, 171, 183, 198, 202, 249, 261, 266, 269, 416, 434
claim, making claims (*da'wā, iddi'ā'*), 9, 15, 20, 50, 51, 54, 55, 64–65, 68–69, 85, 94, 144, 173, 174, 225, 247, 261, 265–66, 274, 279, 305, 324, 337, 341, 345, 354, 365, 421, 423, 432, 443, 448, 455, 477, 484, 491; to love, 12, 229, 303, 469, 487
clay (*ṭīnat, gil*)
clemency (*ra'fat*), 164, 295, 315, 444
cloak, tattered (*khirqa*), xxx, 96, 154, 179, 216; patched cloak (*muraqqa'*), 97–98, 122–23, 131, 211, 215, 247, 317, 384, 405, 461, 476, 492, 493

clod (*kulūkh*)
coffer (*durj*)
collyrium (*tūtiyā, kuḥl*), 6, 20, 45, 46, 55, 91, 121, 122, 158, 165, 208, 217, 218, 262, 327, 410
color (*rang, ṣibgha, lawn*), 154, 212, 224, 239, 261, 311, 403, 417, 458; God's, 96, 99, 318, 409; world of, 133
command, commandment (*amr, farmān*), 6, 13, 47–48, 53–54, 56, 76, 117, 122–26, 128, 134, 140, 153–54, 160, 180, 185–86, 189, 216, 240, 248, 259, 315, 321–22, 362, 367, 371, 382, 401, 449, 467, 494; vs. decree, lxvi-lxvii, 34, 38–39, 49, 51–52, 86, 125, 151, 182, 186, 335, 353, 392, 398, 403–5, 439, 494; and prohibition, 51, 90, 162, 202, 223, 299, 300, 389, 404, 429, 470, 494; and rightful due, 38–39, 70; commanding (*ammāra*; *see* soul)
common (people, *ʿāmma*). *See* elect
community (*ummat*). *See* Islam
compact (*mīthāq*), 107, 125, 132, 235, 253, 310, 382–83, 426
companionship, company (*ṣuḥbat, hamrāhī*). Companions of the Cave (*aṣḥāb-i kahf*), 352–54, 370; the dog of, 23, 69, 70, 91, 121, 181, 202, 203, 267, 316, 352–54, 437, 514n562
compass (*pargār*), 142, 174, 185, 352, 426, 452
compassion (*ʿaṭf*), 58, 60, 72, 265, 307, 310, 467
compensation (*ʿiwaḍ, tāwān*), 29, 31, 32, 260, 269, 400, 438, 455, 474
complaint (*shakāwat, gila, nālīdan*), 25, 30, 78, 107–9, 259, 274, 277, 289, 344, 350, 360, 385, 491
completion (*tamām*)
compliance (*imtithāl*), 124, 177, 276, 371
composition, compound (*tarkīb, taʾlīf*), 35, 46, 47, 58, 60, 122, 135–36, 138, 144, 145–47, 154, 236, 266, 298, 414
compulsion (*jabr*), 298, 339; and free will, lxvii, 52, 117, 154, 370, 394. All-Compelling (*jabbār*), 5, 7, 22, 38, 50, 61, 169, 174, 217, 220, 303, 340, 388, 409, 435, 449, 474, 478; all-compellingness (*jabbāriyyat*), 38, 55, 68, 298, 315, 320, 370, 399, 440
concealment (*katm*), 34, 98, 400. *See also* nonexistence
conclusion (*khātimat*)
condition, precondition (*sharṭ*), 133, 157, 216, 302, 304, 323, 387, 418
confessing (*iqrār*), 52, 85, 303, 305, 446
configuring (*inshāʾ*), 4, 9, 189, 429
confirmation (*taʾyīd*), 88, 116, 131, 251, 253, 279, 287, 363, 383, 392, 401, 437, 471
conformity (*muwāfaqat*), 113, 154, 163, 201, 285, 353; of love, 21–22, 70, 105, 367, 491; and opposition, 59, 112, 217, 251, 283, 314, 316
confounded (*madhūsh*), 8, 96, 100, 124, 125, 138, 197, 213, 277, 377
Confucius, liv
congregation (*jamāʿat*), 51, 411, 456
conjoining, conjunction (*ittiṣāl*), 163, 173, 271, 287, 337, 367, 413; and disjoining, 36, 271, 413
conquest (*fatḥ*)
consecration (ritual, *iḥrām*), 190, 256
consensus (*ijmāʿ*), 179, 329
consignment (*ḥawāla*), 76, 122, 168, 175, 203, 470
Constantinople, 449, 502n200
constellation (*burj*), 10, 13, 45, 58, 85, 135–36, 182, 198, 203, 263
constitution (*mizāj*), 135
constraint (*iḍṭirār*), 248–49, 332–33, 404
consultation (*mushāwarat*), 12, 172, 387, 462
consumed (*mustahlak*), 8, 84, 352, 416, 464
contemplation (*mushāhadat*), lx, 5, 10, 13, 16, 19, 48, 49, 56, 76, 87, 92, 94, 96, 109, 116, 124, 130, 133, 254–55, 257, 261–64, 277, 280, 283, 285, 290, 301–2, 330–31, 333, 339, 346, 353, 357, 365, 369, 379, 407, 411, 416, 419, 483. *See also* unveiling
contempt (*ḥaqārat, hawān*), 12, 35, 120, 144, 225, 231, 265, 354, 355
contentment (*qanāʿat, khursandī*), 346, 413, 530n1021
contract (*ʿaqd*), 174, 214, 287, 311, 336, 401, 421
contraction (*qabḍ*), and expansion, 20, 107, 178
contradiction (*tanāquḍ*), 112, 340, 349
contrivance (*ḥīlat, tadbīr*), 4, 279, 352, 422, 450
control (*taṣarruf, taḥakkum*), 61, 145, 146, 155, 259, 330, 345, 351, 398, 416, 454
convocation (*anjuman*), 96, 133, 224, 475
coquetry (*dalāl*), 10, 104, 166, 179, 181, 223, 267, 345, 390, 437, 469

core (*kunh*, *ṣamīm*). heart's core (*suwaydā*). *See* secret core
corporeal (*jismānī*), and spiritual, 158, 213, 237, 317
corruption (*fasād*), 58, 59, 80, 135, 143, 144, 157, 172, 173, 175, 217, 220, 222, 226, 241, 253, 262, 296, 319–21, 323, 337, 350, 392, 479, 488, 488
cosmos (*ʿālam*), xlviii-l, 47, 135, 183. *See also* universe, world
counterfeit (*nufāya*), 38–39, 150, 179, 204, 232, 279
courage (*shajāʿat*, *yārā*), 19, 83, 205, 218, 311, 436, 454
courier (*barīd*)
court (*bārgāh*)
courtesy (*adab*), 108, 134, 147–48, 237, 248, 256, 296, 305, 307, 310, 313, 375, 380, 399, 446
covenant (*ʿahd*), 115–116; of Alast, 115, 310, 468; of Lordhood, 115, 116, 364, 426, 468
craving (*nahmat*), 202, 261, 262
creation (*khalq*, *āfarīnish*), 4–5, 8–9, 11, 23, 34, 41, 46–49, 52–53, 55, 57–58, 60, 119, 138, 144, 151–53, 155–57, 181, 185, 189, 193, 203, 228, 240, 248, 285, 298–301, 315, 319, 338, 345, 363, 368, 375, 379, 398, 402, 424–25, 427, 429, 438, 452, 456–57, 471, 477, 485, 487, 488, 490–91; creature, created thing (*khalq*, *makhlūq*), 7, 23, 45, 124, 133, 216–17, 230, 233, 305, 359, 390, 399, 403, 411, 453; and the Real, 4, 10–11, 29, 35, 72, 82, 84, 88, 140, 182, 247, 255, 271–73, 275, 290, 329–30, 357, 366, 369, 385, 404, 475–76; created nature (*khilqat*), 225, 374, 411; createdness (*khalqiyyat*), 125, 162, 264, 420, 492; creativity (*fiṭrat*), 96, 104, 151, 165, 237, 299, 363. *See also* Adam, disposition
credit (*nasya*), 226; and hard cash, 116, 241
critique of Muslims/readers, 28, 149, 175, 198, 202–4, 261–63, 334, 385, 454–56, 476
cross (*ṣalīb*), 114, 139, 374, 392, 460
crown (*tāj*)
cruelty (*jafāʾ*, *jawr*, *sitam*), 35, 40, 108, 178, 228, 367
cupbearer (*sāqī*), 20, 96, 140, 158, 178, 184, 213, 215, 216, 241, 279, 285, 307, 361, 368, 376; of gentleness, 90, 128, 172, 379
cure (*ʿilāj*), 51, 106, 228, 360, 409, 417
curse (*laʿnat*), 94, 139, 291, 359, 371, 373. *See also* Iblis
curtain (*sitr*, *parda*), 5, 33, 63, 67, 71, 127, 129, 133, 153, 192, 193, 197, 229, 246, 293, 304, 307, 344, 359, 404, 412, 429, 451, 481, 482; curtaining (*pūshīdan*, *satr*), 63, 225, 309. *See also* jealousy, unseen, veil
custom (*ʿādat*, *rasm*)
cutting (*burīdan*, *qaṭʿ*)

Dabbūsī, Maḥmūd (Abu'l-Qāsim ibn Maymūn, d. 535/1141), xxiv, xxxviii
Ḍaḥḥāk (ibn Muzāḥim, d. ca. 105/723), 411, 534n1161
Ḍaḥḥāk (the tyrant), 518n674
Dajjāl, 516n603
Damascus, xxvii, xli, 358, 402, 476
dancing (*raqṣ*, *dast-afshānī*), 13, 35, 54
danger (*khaṭar*), 64, 79, 102, 142, 150, 223, 252, 372, 375, 477
Daniel, 200
Dānishpazhūh, Muḥammad-Taqī (d. 1996), xiii
Daqqāq, Abū ʿAlī (Ḥasan ibn ʿAlī, d. 405/1015), xxxvi, xlvi, 29, 60, 74, 80, 155, 170, 187, 210, 241, 282, 323, 450, 497n33, 499n101, 500n153, 501n159, 501n160, 501n171, 503n218, 504n271, 504n272, 505n275, 507n357, 538n1269
Daqqāq, Muḥammad (Abū ʿAbdallāh ibn ʿAbd al-Wāḥid al-Iṣbahānī, d. 516/1122), xxiv, lxxiiin102
Dārānī, Abū Sulaymān (d. 215/830), xxv, 54, 337, 385, 498n67
darkness (*ẓulmat*, *tārīkī*), 175, 187, 191, 199, 230, 238, 298, 313, 392, 413, 458, 463, 488
darwīsh, xxxi
David, 126, 196, 200, 203, 382; and Bathsheba, 207, 247, 314, 405, 416, 488; revelation to, 15, 129, 136, 186, 398, 406, 476; singing of, 83, 275, 314; 496n15, 505n294, 507n354, 509n397, 510n434, 513n521, 519n709, 520n741, 522n789, 526n923, 533n1133, 534n1150
Dāwūd Ṭāʾī (d. ca. 165/780), 455

death (*mawt, marg*), 5, 27, 75, 82, 97, 104, 107, 113, 129, 135, 136, 145, 146, 221–22, 238, 239, 241, 253–54, 256, 275–76, 282, 299, 303, 324, 346, 375, 380, 388, 407, 415, 419, 432, 446, 455, 457, 481, 492; before death, 225; and love, 23, 28, 81, 104, 105, 171, 243, 318; to self, 225, 254; wishing for death, 16, 37, 318, 419, 480. *See also* angel (of death), Azrael
deception (*makr, farīb*), 50, 53, 91, 104, 106, 137, 243, 252, 318, 320, 347, 398, 415, 473
decoy (*milwāḥ*), 136–37, 252, 483
decrease (*nuqṣān, kāstan*)
decree (*ḥukm, qaḍā'*), God's, lxvi-lxvii, 5, 9, 35, 40, 49–50, 61, 63, 65, 70, 74, 81, 85, 90, 92, 93, 98, 107, 108, 112, 115, 120–22, 124, 127, 159, 167–69, 176, 189, 197, 204, 216, 217, 224, 229, 230, 238, 246, 249, 256, 259, 292, 316, 320, 321, 335, 337, 362–64, 381, 382, 384–86, 394–96, 398, 400, 405, 409–12, 417, 420, 424, 428, 430, 451, 467, 476, 486. *See also* command, destiny, knowledge
deed (*'amal, kard*), 38–39, 54, 64, 144, 146, 157, 225, 237, 338, 353, 359, 363, 382, 400, 449, 466, 475, 479, 487–88, 490. *See also* beautiful, wholesome
defect (*khalal, naqṣ*), 13, 16, 20, 94, 166, 175, 198, 237, 257, 268, 369, 383, 391, 409, 418, 421, 431, 437; pure of, 11, 14, 212, 264, 292, 294, 302, 314, 368, 444
deficiency (*nuqṣān*), 8, 40, 146, 258, 265, 266, 295, 393
defilement (*ālāyish, tar-dāmanī, lawth, ḥadath*), 20, 40, 59–60, 133, 168, 202, 222, 244, 261, 293, 305, 306, 318, 320, 341, 365, 431, 435, 444, 458, 467, 469
delegation (*tafwīḍ*), 339, 352, 389, 504–5n273
deliberation (*tadbīr, rawiyyat*), 98, 142, 172, 279, 408
delight (*ḥubūr, irtiyāḥ, nāz, qurrat al-'ayn*)
deliverance (*khalāṣ, rastagārī, najāt*), 52, 79, 136, 157, 257, 275, 276, 288, 293, 296, 303, 304, 313, 346, 351, 355, 357, 359, 365, 422, 427
delusion (*ghurūr, sawdā*), 9, 37, 39, 52, 64, 75, 91, 92, 106, 125, 149, 151, 179, 202, 221, 225, 293, 325, 326, 346–47, 355, 371, 388, 433, 456, 463
denial (*inkār, juḥūd*), 38, 41, 43, 55, 68, 158, 159, 187, 305, 321, 330, 368, 380, 381, 392, 409, 410, 415, 416, 460–63, 491
dense (*kathīf*), 304. *See* subtle
deposit (*wadī'at*), 47, 123, 132, 137, 145, 146, 155, 182, 189, 199, 223, 234, 235, 263, 279, 287, 299, 313, 319, 324, 333–34, 364, 399, 411, 412, 423, 437, 438, 446, 453, 468, 478, 485; depository (*mustawda'*), 132, 229, 324, 493
depraved (*fājir*), 139, 220, 296, 297, 316, 448, 454, 480
deprivation (*khidhlān, salb, fāqat*), 20, 21, 24, 30, 98, 157, 218, 227, 286, 294, 385, 398, 403, 420
deputy (*nā'ib*), 114, 218, 231, 240, 285, 320–21, 368, 451, 454
dervish (*darwīsh*), xxiii, xxx, xxxi, 3, 74, 108, 122, 156, 171, 179, 229, 233, 260, 277, 341, 348, 415, 439, 441, 450, 469, 472, 473. *See* poverty
descent (*nuzūl*), 61, 78, 84, 111, 160, 161, 192, 292, 454, 460, 468, 478, 486
description (*waṣf, na't*)
desire, object of desire (*irāda, murād*), 16–17, 28, 36, 37, 44, 47, 50, 72, 81–83, 84, 86, 94, 96, 106, 109, 125, 147–48, 162, 181, 198, 209, 212, 216, 250, 254, 257, 342, 347, 364, 367, 372, 377, 388, 397, 414, 429, 443, 476; causeless, 22, 120, 170, 450; God's, 7, 9, 16, 23, 40, 53, 68, 76, 81–83, 86, 93, 110, 113, 118, 127, 140, 141, 159, 162, 168–70, 172, 173, 176, 178, 181, 279, 283, 289, 291, 298–99, 301, 327, 329, 340, 385, 393, 394, 409, 438, 467, 475; not reaching, 97, 103, 106, 111, 218, 277, 385, 477; desirer (*murīd*), 159, 359; and desired (*murād*), 14, 81–83, 159, 277. *See also* disciple
despair (*qunūṭ, ya's, nawmīdī*), 31, 40, 62, 94, 98, 187, 222, 259, 264, 270, 277, 282, 290–92, 294–95, 309, 312, 363, 398, 400, 451
destination (*maqṣad*)
destiny (*qadar*), 314, 453; and decree (*qaḍā'*), 52, 279, 314, 356, 437, 452

destitution (*iflās*), 32, 34, 39, 85, 113, 143, 191, 270, 277, 282, 307, 317, 322, 327, 384–85, 387, 405, 424, 477
destruction (*halāk, maḥq, talaf, bar ham zadan*), 5, 23, 88, 100, 150, 162, 169, 187, 205, 219, 241, 252, 265, 270, 277, 279, 303, 307, 312, 319, 327, 338, 347, 350–51, 370–71, 374, 378, 380, 385, 395, 402, 432, 457, 472, 474, 485
detachment (*farāgha, bar dāshtan, bar giriftan*), 49, 283, 284, 425; of the secret core, 273, 353. *See also* heart
devising (*ikhtirāʿ*), 4, 48, 55
devotee (*muʿtakif*), 84, 88, 167, 216, 359
devil (*dīw*), 188, 194, 197, 275, 325, 369, 410, 531n1071
Dhahabī (Abū ʿAbdallāh Muḥammad ibn Aḥmad, d. 748/1348), xli
dhāt, xlviii
dhikr, xvii, lx
Dhu'l-Nūn (Jonah), 312–13, 355
Dhu'l-Nūn Miṣrī (d. 245/860), 308–9, 311, 434–35, 457, 487, 500n141, 504n251, 504n260, 505n295, 509n401, 524n860, 529n994, 538n1276, 538n1278
Dhu'l-Qarnayn, 318
Diʿbil (ibn ʿAlī Khuzāʿī, d. 220/835), 499n93
Diḥya Kalbī (d. ca. 45/665), 384
Dīk al-Jinn (d. ca. 236/850), 538n1285
dil, 510n441
dīnī, lxvi
disagreement (*ikhtilāf*), 78, 241, 319, 321, 333, 355, 369, 397
disappointment (*nākāmī*), 13, 43, 64, 105, 109, 229
disciple (*murīd*), 53, 194, 209, 211, 383, 386, 387. *See also* desirer
discipline (*riyāḍat*), 30, 116, 133, 147, 148, 153, 167, 205, 212, 287, 307, 372, 384, 387, 406, 443
disclosing (*jilwa dādan*). *See* self-disclosure
disdain (*tadallul, anafat*), 10, 32, 43, 87, 130, 149, 153, 179, 181, 310, 353, 392
disengagement (*tajrīd*), 82, 155, 197, 225, 279, 383, 474, 477; and solitariness (*tafrīd*), 6, 7, 20, 29, 70, 74, 86–87, 89, 90, 119, 184, 216, 274, 282–83, 331, 394, 413, 473
disjoining (*infiṣāl*), 36, 271, 413
disloyalty (*jafāʾ*), 15, 204, 255, 271, 291, 293–94, 309, 430. *See* loyalty
disobedience, disobedient act (*maʿṣiyat*). *See* Adam, obedience
dispersion (*tafriqa*), 150, 435
disposition (*sirisht, ṭīnat, khūy, mizāj*), 94, 128, 236, 262, 279, 345, 361, 389; innate/created disposition (*fiṭrat*), 144, 156, 279
disquiet (*waswās, qalaq*), 89, 400; of Satan, 194, 207, 247, 279
disregard (*ihmāl*), 5, 52, 255, 431, 491
dissolution (*inqirāḍ*), 56; of the world, 189, 226, 425, 449, 482
distance (*buʿd*). *See* proximity
distinction (*manqabat*), 93, 123, 361, 375, 432
distracted (*sarāsīma, shūrīda*)
divesting (attributes from God, *taʿṭīl*), lv, 92, 174
diving (*ghawṣ*)
divinity (*ilāhiyyat*), 4, 39, 40, 59, 124, 217, 276, 294, 296, 332, 364, 420, 461; divine (*ilāhī*), 8, 12, 14, 15, 37, 59, 84–86, 90, 123, 124, 136, passim; beauty, 12, 85, 124, 277; decree, lxvii, 86, 107, 122, 363; gentleness, 80, 96, 192, 244, 478; power, 135, 159, 231; wisdom, 85, 135, 146
dīwān, 531n1071
doing (*kard*)
dome (*qubba*)
domination (*ghalaba*), 32, 37, 53, 62, 88, 175, 329
Dominion (*malakūt*), 55, 120, 133, 195, 326, 364, 399; angels of, 22, 39, 47, 48, 53, 58, 67, 85, passim
doubt (*shakk, gumān*), 20, 41, 464
dream (*khwāb, nawm*), 72, 152, 158, 193, 220, 221, 249, 312, 347, 388, 421, 434, 439, 441, 458, 503n213, 505n293
dregs (*durdī*), 20, 41, 96, 111, 129, 204, 432
drunkenness (*mastī*), 6, 17, 20, 26, 36–37, 41, 43, 64, 96, 99–101, 111, 116, 124, 126, 130, 138, 141, 144, 153, 177, 178, 193, 215, 229, 234, 267, 279, 305, 306, 347, 388–89, 416, 417, 455, 479, 492. *See also* intoxication
duality (*dawʾī*), xxviii, 85, 337
due, just (*dād*), 20, 30, 66, 71, 113, 444. *See also* rightful due

Duldul, 437
dust (*khāk, ghubār*), 5, 12, 17, 41, 45–47, 64–65, 86, 113, 136, 156, 173–76, 181–82, 187, 219, 228–32, 234, 236–37, 263, 284, 301, 333–34, 337, 391–92, 421, 440, 458, 467–70, 488–89, 493; dustbin (*khākhdān*). dust-dwelling (*khāk-bāsh, khākī*). dust mote (*dharra*), 4, 90, 201, 422; and sun, 13, 29, 84–85, 96, 393
dūst, 362

earth (*arḍ, zamīn*). *See* heaven
ease (*rāḥat, ārām, āsāyish*)
eclipse (*kusūf*), 69, 199, 266, 458, 477
ecstasy (*wajd*), 10, 18, 19, 26, 37, 119, 130, 151, 265, 361, 366, 388, 440, 457, 465, 476
Eden, 6, 61, 121, 152, 191, 283, 422, 475
edict (*manshūr*)
effacement (*maḥw*), 7, 20, 27, 72, 102, 114, 123, 168, 209, 215, 251, 307, 340, 388, 390, 406, 423; of attributes, 93, 96–97; self-effacement (*sar-afkandagī*), 203, 266
effort (*jahd, sa'y*), 17, 30, 56, 61, 68, 74, 117, 340, 383, 400, 487
egoism (*anāniyyat*), 9, 484
Egypt, Egyptian, 16, 79, 106, 196, 235, 242, 246, 252, 331, 345, 418, 434, 448, 482, 489
elation (*nishāṭ*)
elder (*pīr*)
elect (*khawāṣṣ*), 65, 96, 107, 129, 166, 189, 270, 364, 392, 481; and common, xvii-xviii, 3, 54, 72, 80, 98, 118, 163, 267, 276, 306, 401, 428; election (*ikhtiṣāṣ, iṣṭinā'*), 66, 96, 109, 121, 178, 188, 204, 369, 399, 438
electuary (*ma'jūn, iṭrīfal*), 62, 142, 156, 172
element (*'unṣur*), 144, 296, 522n780; the four, 58, 263, 298
elevation (*raf'at*), 43, 48, 135, 138, 174, 181, 188, 195, 203, 231, 301, 425, 432, 442, 447; of Adam, 97, 123, 177; of heaven, 86, 111, 170, 294, 300, 484
Elias, 200, 317
elixir (*kīmiyā'*), 122, 182, 198, 442
eloquence (*faṣāḥat*)
embarrassment (*khijlat*), 17, 28, 37, 140, 157, 269, 288, 373, 375, 391, 397, 480
embroidery (*ṭirāz*)
emigration (*hijrat*), 67, 69–72, 510n437; Emigrants (*muhājirūn*), 45
eminence (*sharaf*), 10, 57, 59–60, 66, 70, 91, 112, 134, 172, 181, 184, 190, 196, 226, 270, 282, 291, 302, 324, 356, 378, 401, 409, 417, 442, 469; of the Prophet, 34, 45, 165, 191, 193, 198–99, 354, 409
emissary (*safīr*)
empire (*mamlakat*)
emulation (*iqtidā'*), 199, 325, 368
encompassment (*iḥāṭat*), 10, 39, 75, 89, 90, 140, 201, 220, 240, 377
encounter (*liqā'*), 14, 15, 33, 89, 90, 116, 119, 132, 178, 206, 268, 283, 301, 333, 367, 384, 416, 419, 439, 454, 481
end (*nihāyat*), 5, 56, 67, 106, 165; final end (*muntahā*), 71, 152, 165, 182, 195, 250, 258, 262, 264, 276, 317, 325, 343, 364, 368, 379, 383, 392, 440, 452, 467. *See also* beginning
endless (*abad*), 5, 14, 16, 19, 143, 378, 380, 435, 441, 446, 455, 481. *See also* beginningless
enemy (*dushman, 'adū*). *See* friend
enjoyment (*'aysh, tamattu', tana''um*)
enraptured (*wālih*), 19, 98, 277
entrusting (*muwakkal kardan, sipurdan*), 194, 231, 257, 316, 321; entrusted angel, 354, 361
envoy (*mursal*), 374; chieftain of, 69, 132, 183, 194, 205, 325, 355, 361, 368, 395, 411
envy (*ḥasad*), 94, 111, 139, 167, 204, 206, 212, 227, 261, 292, 342, 348, 350, 357, 393, 459, 468, 478, 486
equipment (*uhbat*)
era (*'ahd*)
escape (*budd, chāra, farār*)
escort (*badraqa*)
essence (*dhāt*), divine, xlviii, lxiii, 39, 240; and attributes, 36, 40, 43, 152, 168, 231, 256, 276, 338, 366, 407, 423, 438, 464, 484, 513n514; human, 123, 135, 144, 172, 177, 184, 237, 314, 407, 415
estranged, stranger (*bīgāna, gharīb*), 22, 23, 26, 47, 121, 126, 140, 168, 211, 271, 295, 340, 374, 404–5, 410, 418, 443, 446
eternity (*qidam*), 12, 40, 124; and new arrival, 150, 168, 240, 268, 337, 489
Eve, 247, 512n483

everlasting (*jāwdān, sarmad*), 5, 16, 148, 378, 422, 425, 477; everlastingness (*khuld*), 5, 66, 86, 90, 113, 260, 394, 438, 446; uppermost, 19, 132, 191
evidence (*dalīl*), 6, 91, 240, 251, 255, 281, 329
evident (*āshkārā*)
evil (*sharr, badī*), 20, 50, 96, 308, 438. *See also* eye, good
exaltation, exaltedness (*ʿizz, ʿizzat*). *See* abasement
excellence (*faḍl, hunar*), 49, 63, 158, 268, 271, 282, 296, 335
excuse (*ʿudhr*), 125, 184, 205, 211, 230, 238, 244–47, 286, 294, 301, 362, 372, 405, 421, 422, 445, 465, 491
exertion (*jidd, ijtihād*), 23, 30, 61, 215, 465
exile (*ghurba*), 25, 56, 66–67, 69, 103, 107, 143, 166, 235, 246, 272, 331, 345, 346, 442, 448–49, 459, 470, 494
existence (*wujūd*), world of, 4, 57, 177, 192, 429, 485; and nonexistence, 10, 23, 54–55, 64, 84, 94, 124–25, 140, 192, 227–28, 230, 238, 240, 329, 337, 346, 363, 403, 410, 437, 471, 494; existence-giving (*ījād*), 4, 5, 172, 337. *See also* being, nonexistence
expansion (*basṭ*), 20, 107, 178, 234; (of the breast, *inshirāḥ*), 69, 138, 199, 215, 409, 458–59, 462–63; (bold) expansiveness (*inbisāṭ*), 17, 96, 101, 181, 256, 304, 306–7, 321, 408, 467; carpet (*bisāṭ*) of, 12, 17, 45, 93, 96, 101, 153, 166, 176, 258, 303, 306, 332, 468; joyful expansiveness (*mubāsaṭat*), 137, 163
experienced (*kār-uftāda*), 37, 203
expiation (*kaffāra*), 296, 331
expression (*ʿibārat*), 39, 46, 47, 120, 130, 152, 330–31, 367, 370. *See also* allusion
extolling (*madḥ*)
extraction (*nazʿ*)
exultation (*faraḥ*)
eye (*chashm, ʿayn*). evil eye (*chashm-i bad, chashm-zakhm*), 57, 69, 155, 204, 219, 227, 234, 237, 292, 323, 333, 385, 502n205–6
eye-service (*riyāʾ*), 52–53, 187, 269–70
Ezra, 105, 370

face (*wajh, rūy*)
faculty (*quwwat*), 98, 133, 135, 145–46, 314, 371
Faḍl Lahabī (ibn al-ʿAbbās, d. ca. 95/714), 508n381
faith (*īmān*), xxix, 19–20, 52, 62–63, 76, 89–90, 110, 138, 143, 272, 305, 351, 380, 420, 451–52, 454, 480, 485; and submission, 332, 425, 455; and beautiful-doing, 20, 335; faithful, person of faith (*muʾmin*)
Fakhr al-Dīn Rāzī (d. 606/1209), 499n98, 519n685
Fakhrāwar Rāzī (Abu'l-Majd ibn Shahfūr), xxvi
falsehood (*kidhb*)
familiarity (*āshnāʾī, ulfat*), 16, 22–23, 25–26, 51, 91, 108, 121, 130, 149, 154, 163, 168, 172, 177, 187, 209, 222, 271, 330, 362, 370, 380, 416, 481
fancy (*pindār*)
faqīr, xxxi
Fāris ibn ʿĪsā al-Dīnawarī (c. ca. 340/951), 497n29
Fārisī, ʿAbd al-Ghāfir (d. 529/1135), xvii-xviii, xxiv
Fārmadī, ʿAbd al-Wāḥid (Abū Bakr ibn al-Faḍl, d. 530/1135), xxxvi, xxxix
Fārmadī, Abū ʿAlī (Faḍl ibn Muḥammad, d. 477/1084), xvii, xxxi, xxxv-xxxvi, xxxviii, xxxix
farness (*buʿd, dūrī*), 36, 165. *See* proximity
Farrukhī (Sīstānī, ca. 429/1037), 538n1284
fasting (*rūza, ṣawm*), 56, 89, 116, 190, 300, 364, 365, 413, 415, 429, 435, 454, 480
fatā, xxiii
fatḥ, 69, 84
Fatḥ Mawṣilī (d. 220/835), 358
Fātiḥa, xlv, lxiii, 401, 478
Fāṭima bint Abū ʿAlī Daqqāq (d. 480/1088), xxxvi, xxxvii
Fāṭima Zahrā (bint Muḥammad, d. 10/632), 27, 244, 342, 376, 396, 471
fattāḥ, xlv
fault (*ʿayb*)
favor (*minnat, imtinān*), divine, 89, 90, 110, 114, 146, 231, 299, 309, 322, 379, 431, 471; counting as by people, 12, 29, 64, 271, 385–87, 422, 472, 477; kind favor (*riʿāyat*), 90, 142, 182, 187, 259, 335, 478. *See also* solicitude
fear (*khawf, tars, bīm*). *See* hope

fearless (*bī-bāk*),
felicitations (*taḥiyyāt*), 88, 256, 308, 399
felicity (*sa'ādat*), 6, 28, 44, 90, 96, 107, 119, 123, 132, 135, 187–89, 201, 215, 236, 296, 298, 324, 330, 369, 416, 425, 455, 465; source/sun of felicities (Muḥammad), 45, 69, 206, 213, 325, 360, 389, 393; and wretchedness, 5, 23, 121, 167, 172, 173, 290, 316, 362–63, 452, 457
femininity (*unūthat*), 62
Fereydun, 224
fermentation (*takhmīr*), 46, 131, 142, 156, 172, 391, 467
fervor, mad (*sawdā*), 34, 36
festival (*'īd*), 205, 245, 341
field, playing (*maydān*)
figure (*haykal*), 37, 47, 136, 155; celestial, 13, 58, 181, 414
finding (*wujūd, yāft*), xlviii, li, 10, 13, 48, 92, 130, 172, 225, 276, 277, 294, 366, 448, 532n1111; and seeking, 74, 84, 179, 210, 287
finger (*angusht, unmūla*), 33, 71, 146, 166, 196, 239, 280, 374, 383, 394, 491; two, 138, 299, 329, 332, 447; of wonder, 85, 193, 123, 171
Firdaws, 88, 143, 252, 279, 283, 325, 349, 361, 412, 446. *See also* paradise
Firdawsī (d. ca. 400/1010), 518n674, 527n945
fire (*ātish, nār*), 62–63, 86, 195, 233, 238–39, 248, 256, 268, 273, 275, 296, 331, 353, 446, 447, 463, 467, 495; vs. dust, 131, 134, 157, 173–74, 219, 234, 296, 333–34, 395, 468, 488–89; and water, 51, 183, 224, 270, 277, 289, 296, 389, 411, 434, 447. *See also* Abraham, hell, love
fire-temple (*ātish-kada*), 26, 203
First (*awwal*), and Last, 41, 125, 340, 415–16, 420
Fīrūzābād, xxxii
Fish (*māhī*, under the earth), 349. *See also under* animal
fiṭra, lii
fleeing (*farār, gurīkhtan, harb*)
flirting (*'ishwa*), 143, 223, 228
fluctuation (*taqallub*), 76, 275, 314, 329, 479, 507n334
folk (*ahl*)
following (*mutāba'at, ittibā'*), 46, 123, 158, 198, 201, 209, 210, 283, 303, 325, 369, 374, 380, 382, 453, 491
folly (*hawas*), 9, 42, 80, 140, 188, 198, 201, 288
foot (*pā, qadam*), 47, 80, 183; of God, 61, 174
footstool (*kursī*), in the soul, 120. *See* Throne
forbearance (*ḥilm, burdbārī*), 39, 75, 87, 92, 220, 226, 268, 309, 430, 454, 491–92
forbidden (*ḥarām*). *See* permitted
forerunner (*muqaddam*)
forgetfulness (*nisyān, farāmūshī*), xliv, lxiv, lxviii, 8, 27, 46, 184, 191, 227, 246, 291, 322, 334, 361, 389, 432, 457, 475
forgiveness (*maghfirat, āmurzish*), 63, 157, 207–9, 222, 244, 255, 268–69, 287, 291, 296, 301–2, 323; asking, 247, 294
form (*ṣūrat*), l-li, 6, 36, 55, 77, 131, 149, 162, 211, 213, 223, 245, 275, 331, 382, 384, 404, 407, 430, 440, 447, 485; of Adam, l, lv, lxiv, 46, 57–58, 123, 134, 151, 243, 295, 298–99; and meaning/reality, xxix, 69, 121, 144, 146, 147, 155, 170, 184, 191, 200, 241, 264, 290, 299, 307, 316, 324, 352, 364, 373, 392, 467–68, 480; world of, 74, 136, 153, 468; form-giving (*taṣwīr*), l, 48, 57–58, 298, 458
fortune, good (*dawlat, iqbāl*), 5, 7, 10, 13–16, 23, 30, 45, 46, 58–59, 66–67, 83, 90, 91, 93, 95, 97, 98, 100, passim
foundation (*qā'ida*), 65, 80, 93, 144, 174, 184, 193, 218, 219, 324, 338, 443, 467, 482
freedom (*ḥurriyyat, āzādagī*), 41, 72, 87, 129–30, 164, 197, 241, 357, 401, 429, 474; free choice (*ikhtiyār*), lxvii, 40, 49–50, 69, 70, 84, 101, 140, 147, 154, 167, 248, 254, 352, 360, 365, 385, 391, 404, 406; free will (*qadar*), xvi, 52, 117, 122, 174, 285, 409; for free (*rāygān*), 124, 166, 296, 452
freeloader (*ṭufayl*), 61, 275, 307, 419, 433, 442, 475
friendship (*walāyat, dūstī*), 5–8, 14–18, 47, 55, 61, 80, 90, 91, 96, 105, 108, 112–13, 121, 127, 132, 142, 151, 155, 157, 162, 183, 187, 198–99, 221, 226, 277, 299–300, 337–38, 340, 351–53, 362, 364, 368–69, 379, 383, 400, 404–5, 423, 431–33, 448, 466, 467, 473, 479, 481, 485, 487–88;

friendship (*cont'd*)
the Friend (*dūst, walī*), 5, 7, 14, 21, 28, 29, 58, 60, 71, 74, 111, 116, 120, 172, 242, 274, 281, 283, 362, 444, 465; and enemy, 114, 122, 151, 187, 204, 252, 276, 281, 292, 328, 339, 354, 359, 435, 486; and servanthood, 113, 119, 128, 177, 190, 216–17, 237, 258, 304, 369–70, 401–2, 423, 486, 490; bosom friendship (*khullat*), 101, 106, 187, 195, 199, 245, 248, 278, 279, 371, 373, 389, 393, 400, 447, 457, 493. *See also* love
frivolity (*ruʿūnat*), 16, 239, 240, 440, 453
Fuḍayl ibn ʿIyāḍ (d. 187/803), 54, 179, 399, 400, 498n80, 529n1008
Furāwī, Muḥammad (Abū ʿAbdallāh ibn al-Faḍl, d. 530/1136), xxiv-xxv, xxxviii, xxxix
Furāwī, Sharīfa (Umm al-Kirām bint Muḥammad, d. 536/1141–42), xxv
Furthest Mosque (*masjid-i aqṣā*), 262
Furūzānfar, Badīʿ al-Zamān (d. 1970), xiii
futūḥ, xlv, 69
futuwwa, lxxin51

gabrī, lxvi
Gabriel, 22, 55, 58, 193, 242, 268, 295, 319, 391, 422, 435, 447; and Abraham, 372–73, 457; of the body, 264; hadith of, xxix, lxii, 371, 384; and humans, 58, 111, 114, 123, 134, 143–44, 185, 186, 324, 333, 384, 391, 396, 411, 424, 492, 494; and the *miʿrāj*, 71, 160–62, 166, 197, 224, 250, 256, 258, 317, 325, 328, 343, 344, 355, 379, 383, 397, 405, 441–442, 467; and revelation, 82, 255, 269, 290, 311, 312, 317, 344, 360, 361, 372, 384, 443; wings of, 73, 218, 232, 239, 264, 441; 503n212, 506n329, 518n664, 524n848, 529n999, 531n1053, 532n1098, 533n1113
gall (*zahra*)
gambling (*qumār, dar bākhtan*), 87, 111, 175, 205, 262, 316, 376, 405, 432, 474, 475
Garden (*jannat*), 5, 6, 17–18, 19, 86, 92, 116, 128, 129, 152, 165, 213, 230, 235, 241, 247, 249, 254, 257, 263, 276, 279, 281, 291, 295, 300–1, 306, 342, 373, 392, 400, 411, 458, 461, 475, 478, 486; and Fire/Blaze, 29, 113, 138, 146, 161, 252, 293, 296, 303, 356, 363, 422, 446, 447, 448, 457, 460. *See also* Eden, paradise
gathering (*jamʿ*), 444–45
gaze (*naẓar*), beginningless, 337, 482; divine, 28, 47, 62, 76, 80, 108, 123, 138, 153, 160, 167, 219–20, 230, 234, 237, 239, 277, 307, 318, 332, 337, 366, 379, 390–91, 399, 409, 411, 416, 443, 466, 480, 485, 493; human, 41, 53, 66, 122, 133, 158, 196, 225, 243–45, 257, 274, 278, 327, 337, 349, 353, 370–71, 378, 388, 428, 449, 475; of Satan, 292, 438
Gehenna, 241, 334, 446
Gemini, 262
generation (*kawn*) and corruption, 262
generosity, generous bestowal (*karam, karāmat*), 27, 146, 310; of God, 8, 12, 38, 47, 50, 58, 63, 67, 85, 90, 94, 100, 120, 156, 173, 184, 186, 193, 210, 212, 215, 222–23, 226, 243, 270, 276, 290–94, 296, 298, 306–9, 315, 322, 335–36, 349, 363, 364, 368, 371, 385, 392, 399, 409, 422, 428, 429, 437, 439, 442, 444, 451–52, 457, 465, 466, 472, 480
Genghis Khan, xiii
gentleness (*luṭf*), 186–87, 240–41, 310; beginningless, 8, 59, 62, 111, 112, 116, 156, 214, 410, 468, 479; and severity, lxiv-lxv, 11, 22, 52, 55, 63, 66, 76–77, 93, 103, 120, 125, 151, 168, 183, 194, 204, 224, 226, 230–31, 277, 285, 288, 315–16, 332–33, 395, 398, 401–2, 405, 420, 424–25, 443; gentle gift (*alṭāf, mulāṭafat*), 58, 59, 61, 62, 84, 88, 155, 157, 162, 178, 187, 212, 230, 269, 304, 307, 335, 337, 357, 370, 372, 438, 467, 471
ghamm, 313
ghayr, 6; *ghayra*, 6
Ghazālī, Abū Ḥāmid Muḥammad (d. 505/1111), xiv, xv, xvii, xxvi, xxxi, xxxii, xxxv-xxxvi, xxxviii, xlvi, li, liii, liv; *Iḥyāʾ ʿulūm al-dīn*, xxxv, xlii, xlvi, 496n24, 496n27, 505n293, 506n301, 506n303, 507n346, 508n383, 509n396, 512n486, 523n820; *Kīmiyā-yi saʿādat*, xlii, xlvi, 509n412, 509n414, 510n420; *al-Maqṣad al-asnā*, lvi, lx-lxi, lxvii, lxxn6
Ghazālī, Aḥmad (d. 520/1126), xv, xxxi; *Sawāniḥ*, xxxv, xlvii, 501n169, 503n227

Ghazna, xiv, xxxiii, xxxiv
Ghuzz, xiii, xx
gift (*tuḥfa*)
Gimaret, Daniel, liii, lv, lvi
glorification (*tasbīḥ*), 69, 137, 155, 162, 172, 173, 202, 203, 205, 218, 230, 238, 275, 332, 335, 356, 365–66, 373, 418, 420, 421, 438, 478, 492; and hallowing/reciting *tawḥīd*, 11, 13, 20, 39, 46, 53, 55, 58, 85, 127, 131, 170, 176–77, 183, 184, 210, 214, 217, 230–32, 277, 294, 319–21, 324, 335, 355–56, 364, 384, 395, 397, 402; glories (*subuḥāt*), 98, 277; glorifiedness (*subbūḥī*), 10, 364
goal (*maqṣūd*), 4, 14, 37, 40, 98, 216, 218, 230, 236, 258, 262, 267, 276, 278, 318, 337, 414, 415, 432, 446, 464, 476; God's, 16, 59, 67, 192, 364, 425
God (*khudā, allāh*), 4, 466–67; Godhood (*khudā'ī*), 47, 68, 169, 304, 310, 426, 465
godwariness (*taqwā*), 60, 63, 130, 133, 147, 148, 151, 168, 174, 208, 276, 295, 300, 363, 396, 411, 435, 454, 455, 533n1138
Goliath, 382
good (*khayr, nīkī*), and evil, 84, 204, 284, 409. good news (*bashārat*), 13, 60, 80, 97, 120, 193, 207, 209, 257, 299, 307, 321, 325, 373, 413–14, 426, 485, 486; and warning, 181, 189, 288, 406, 425
goodly (*ṭayyib*), 18, 84, 88–89, 131–32, 151, 158, 180, 212, 256, 299, 308, 352, 359, 365, 435, 461
gold (*zar*)
Gospel, 193
governance, self-governance (*tadbīr*), 49, 50, 135, 320, 389, 414; (*imārat*), 470; (*siyāsat*), 321
grammar school (*maktab*), xxiv, 23, 56, 110, 146, 175, 178, 204–5, 262, 286, 350, 384, 475
gratitude (*shukr*), 19, 80, 89, 94, 215, 240, 258, 274, 291, 298, 306, 309, 350, 364, 365, 368, 370, 372, 390, 408, 422, 433, 437, 469, 489. *See also* thanks
greatness (*kibriyā', ḥishmat*)
Greeks, 235
grief (*ghamm, andūh, ghuṣṣa*)
Guebre (*gabr*), Guebrism (*gabrī*), lxvi-lxvii, 26, 64, 94, 122, 139, 149, 167, 179, 188, 201, 202, 203, 225, 287, 310, 374, 398, 400, 409, 418, 437, 467, 476, 480, 485, 488
guidance (*hidāyat*), 3, 11, 12, 20, 62, 89, 90, 132, 160, 218, 286, 329, 345, 357, 375, 453, 464; and misguidance, 122, 352, 414, 426, 483

habit (*'ādat*), 41, 251, 257, 320, 393, 406
ḥadath, 168
Ḥaddād, Ḥasan (Abū 'Alī ibn Aḥmad ibn al-Ḥasan, d. 515/1122), xxvi, xxxiv
ḥadīqa, 299
hadith (*ḥadīth*), xiv-xv, xxxi-xxxii, 61, 201, 211, 247, 281, 302, 312, 319, 329, 357, 361, 439, 448, 454; *ḥadīth qudsī*, 499n118, 500n119, 501n182, 503n228, 504–5n273, 506n302, 506n305, 508n363, 510n427, 513n528, 514n563, 516n593, 516n612, 517n651, 518n664, 521n766, 522n802, 526n916, 528n978, 529n1017, 530n1036, 533n1136, 535n1201, 536n1220, 537n1243. *See also* report
hafiz, xxvii
Ḥāfiẓ (d. 792/1390), xi
Ḥafṣa (bint 'Umar, d. 45/665), 482
Hagar, 73–74
hajj, 23, 56, 73, 87, 88, 190, 192, 202, 280, 293, 406, 409, 413, 429, 465, 501n164
Ḥajjāj ibn Yūsuf (d. 95/714), 213, 251, 348, 520n749
Ḥājjī Khalīfa, xi
ḥakīm, 168, 316–17; *ḥākim*, 167
Ḥallāj, Ḥusayn ibn Manṣūr (d. 309/922), xlv, 96, 252, 266, 323, 339–41, 421, 425, 505n296, 512n477, 524n845, 528n980
hallowing, calling holy (*taqdīs*), 20, 39, 402. *See* glorification, incomparability
Hamadānī, 'Ayn al-Quḍāt (d. 525/1131), xii, 520n722
Hamadānī, Badī' al-Zamān (d. 398/1007), 502n209
Hamadānī, Ḥamza (Abū 'Imāra ibn Muḥammad, d. 575/1179), xxxv
Hamadānī, Yūsuf (Abū Ya'qūb ibn Ayyūb, d. 535/1140), xxiv, xxxviii-xxxix
Haman, 168
Ḥamdūn Qaṣṣār (d. 271/884–85), 503n219
Ḥammād ibn Mūsā, 260–61
ḥammādūn, 507n353
Ḥammāmī, Abū 'Abdallāh Muḥammad, xxvii

Ḥamza (ibn ʿAbd al-Muṭṭalib, d. 3/625), 294, 381, 417, 525n873
Ḥamza ibn Ḥusayn (Abū Saʿd ibn ʿAlī al-Qāʾinī, b. ca. 430), xxxiii
Hanafi jurisprudence, xvi, xviii
hand (*yad, dast*), 47, 80, 145, 148, 183, 281–82, 298, 359, 372; of God, 52, 61, 174, 323, 324, 490–91; of severity, 5, 7, 76, 235. *See also* right
handful (*musht, qabḍa*)
hapless (*bīchāra*)
happiness (*shādī*). *See* sorrow
Haqiqah (*ḥaqīqat*) xvii, lxi, lxiii, 53, 74, 129, 148, 212, 224, 263, 299, 329, 330, 335, 396, 404, 414, 433, 468, 481. *See* Shariah, Tariqah
ḥaqq, lv
ḥarb, 190
hardship (*ḥaraj, mashaqqat*)
Ḥārith Muḥāsibī, 323
harshness (*siyāsat*), 68, 154, 246, 260, 273, 289, 310, 312, 325, 375–77, 401, 408, 420, 443, 475
Hārūn al-Rashīd (d. 193/809), xiv, 497n36, 501n166
Harut and Marut, 338
Ḥasan (ibn ʿAlī, d. 50/670), 201, 342, 516–17n623
Ḥasan Baṣrī (d. 110/728), 43, 129, 221–22, 300, 319, 326, 347, 350, 454, 456–57, 497n38, 525n888, 530n1043, 537n1235, 537n1259
Ḥasan ibn Aḥmad Marwazī, xvi
Ḥasan ibn Muḥammad, Abu'l-Qāsim (d. 405/1015), 511n456
Ḥasan ibn Sahl, 62
Ḥāshir, 188
Ḥassān ibn Thābit (d. ca. 54/674), 515n572
hate, hatred (*dushmanī, bughḍ*)
Ḥātim Aṣamm (d. 237/851–52), 78, 359
Ḥātim Ṭāʾī, 521n774
hawā, 341
ḥayawān nāṭiq, li
ḥayy, liv
ḥaẓẓ, lx
headman (*raʾīs*)
headstrong (*sarkash*)
healing (*shifāʾ*), 34, 47–48, 106, 360, 365
hearing (*samāʿ, shanīdan*)
heart (*qalb, dil*), 123, 133–35, 138, 144–47, 153, 275, 285, 294, 299–300, 303, 306, 318, 330, 332–34, 338–43, 345, 346, 348, 352, 354, 356, 359, 361–62, 365, 368, 371, 373, 374, 379, 388, 398–99, 402–3, 433, 466, 475–76, 489; and body/soul, 49, 72, 116, 130, 133, 141, 144–47, 155–56, 162–65, 169, 179, 212, 227, 241, 254–56, 262–63, 298, 299, 301–2, 304, 307, 323, 331, 351, 352, 361, 364, 367, 386, 403, 427, 435, 443, 446, 480, 484, 489; betweenness/fluctuation of, 76–77, 108, 237, 245, 275, 314, 326–27, 329–30, 332, 469–70, 479, 507n334; detachment of, 50, 75, 79, 83, 92, 124, 136, 142, 169, 179, 275, 366, 367, 385, 390, 461, 463, 473, 475; losing, 348
heartache (*ghamm*)
heaven (*samāʾ, āsmān*), 71, 161, 170–71, 257–58, 342, 355–56; and earth, 50, 55, 61, 74, 76, 78, 117, 120, 130, 132–33, 135, 142, 154–56, 158, 185, 188–89, 191–92, 195, 203–4, 234, 237, 253, 270, 295, 299–301, 305, 321, 378–80, 427–28, 432, 438, 451, 458, 475, 491, 494; seven, 123, 142, 158, 205, 257–58, 427, 431, 440, 442; and seven earths, 48, 322, 364, 438, 443; heavenly (*samāʾī, āsmānī*), 120, 136, 314; heaven-dwellers (*āsmāniyān*), 355, 409, 423. *See also* Trust
heedfulness, taking heed (*ʿibrat*)
heedlessness (*ghaflat*), 23, 130, 145, 149, 297, 305, 334, 376, 384, 385, 456
hell (*dūzakh, jahannam*), 30, 31, 195–96, 218, 285, 327, 328, 337, 359, 367, 375, 385, 399, 419, 430, 457; and mercy, 195, 296–97, 446–48. *See also* paradise
Helpers (*anṣār*), 45, 272, 487
helplessness (*bīchāragī, darmāndagī*)
Herat, xiv, xxxii, xxxvi, xxxvii, 467
Heravi, Najib Mayel, ix, lxviii, lxxn8, lxxvn142
heresy (*zandaqa, bidʿat*), 41, 151, 159, 194, 285, 402, 406, 414
hidden (*pinhān, nahān*)
highness, height (*ʿulūw*)
Hijaz, 160, 176, 188, 199
ḥilm, 430
himma, 523n839
Himyar, 413, 522n786
Ḥirāʾ, 82, 317, 355, 530n1030

Ḥīrī, Abū Bakr (Aḥmad ibn al-Ḥasan, d. 421/1030), xxvii
Ḥīrī, Abū ʿUthmān (d. 298/920), 48, 497n34, 504n252, 514n546
holiness (*quds, quddūsī*), 10, 153, 237, 247, 328, 333, 383, 399, 407, 441, 485, 492; place of, 13, 22, 46, 83, 98, 147, 233, 262, 264, 314, 334, 365; Spirit of, 390, 533n1113. *See also* hallowing, incomparability
homeland (*waṭan*), 66–70, 113, 256, 272, 456, 494; of nature, 84, 113, 334
honor (*ḥurmat, karāmat, ābrūy*). robe of honor (*khalʿat*)
honorable (*maʿrūf*), 89, 299
hope (*rajāʾ, umīd*), 24, 44, 73, 101, 168, 178, 234, 244, 277, 285, 288, 294, 301, 307, 322, 337, 428–29; and fear, 62–63, 74, 84, 89, 91, 256, 261, 268, 271, 273, 286, 290, 292, 303, 310, 340, 356, 364, 368, 394, 441
hopelessness (*nawmīdī*)
host (*mīzbān*)
houris (*ḥūr*), 6, 19, 70, 129, 159, 211, 261–62, 266, 268, 342, 356, 412, 429, 440, 476
housemastery (*kad-khudāʾī*), 47, 70, 145, 169, 257, 324, 333, 426
how, without (*bī-kayf, bī-chūn*), 18, 40, 126, 132, 140, 343, 366
Hubal, 167, 199, 516n616
Hūd, 305
Ḥudhayfa ibn al-Yamān (d. 36/656), 129, 537n1257
Hujwīrī, ʿAlī ibn ʿUthmān (d. 465/1073), *Kashf al-maḥjūb*, xlvii, 499n115, 504n254, 506n311, 517n634, 523n834
ḥukamāʾ, 513n551
ḥukm, lxvi
human being (*insān*), and the angels, 14, 39, 46–47, 53–55, 58–60, 65, 85, 97, 112, 118, 138, 155–57, 170, 172–73, 177, 183–85, 201, 216, 230, 236–38, 253, 277, 324, 338, 366–67, 369, 392, 401–2, 409, 423–24, 438, 440, 443, 458–59, 466, 488; rank of, 46–47, 57–61, 134–35, 144–45, 190, 216–17, 230; incapacity/affliction of, 56, 204, 228, 258–59; human nature (*insāniyyat*), 6, 84, 147, 209, 334, 384, 510n422. *See also* Adam, Adamic, mortal
humbleness (*khushūʿ, tawāḍuʿ*), 20, 45, 72, 179, 196–97, 265–66, 288, 334, 389, 407, 412; humility (*khuḍūʿ, tawāḍuʿ*), 20, 38, 44–45, 90, 173–74, 179, 203, 265, 285, 412
hunger (*gurusnagī, jūʿ*), 30, 41, 90, 101, 136, 144, 148, 249, 307, 341, 347, 359, 374, 386, 409, 412, 434, 435, 456, 471, 476, 493–95
hunting (*ṣayd*)
Ḥusayn (ibn ʿAlī, d. 61/680), 255, 342, 376, 481
Ḥusayn ibn ʿAbdallāh al-Ghanādūstī, 529n998
Ḥusayn ibn al-Ḍaḥḥāk (d. 250/864), 539n1306
Ḥusayn ibn Ḥasan Ṣūfī, xvi
Ḥusayn ibn ʿUbaydallāh, 512n502
Ḥuṣrī, Abu'l-Ḥasan (d. 371/981), 152, 499n115, 511n463, 517n634
hypocrisy (*nifāq*), 41, 67, 69, 91, 268, 406, 415, 422, 454

I-ness (*manī*), saying I, 9, 284, 406
ʿibāda, xxxix, xli
Iblis, the accursed one, teacher of the angels, 22, 49, 145, 154, 175, 229, 237, 238, 263, 292, 296, 299, 304, 320, 325, 384, 409, 432, 463, 466, 477; and Adam, 13, 46, 53, 58, 63, 65–67, 113, 120–23, 157, 174, 184–86, 194, 204–6, 219, 225–26, 229, 233, 234–35, 247–48, 260, 293, 294, 321, 333, 362, 383, 385, 392, 395, 468, 488–89, 491, 494; as an angel, 113, 194, 438; claims and egoism of, 65, 265, 284, 296, 338, 371, 488; and curses, 46, 52, 59, 122, 205–6, 231, 235, 248, 304, 324, 342, 362–63; and Job, 350–51; predetermined fate of, 23, 52, 59, 63, 121, 122, 206, 226, 362–63, 423; visions of, 342, 362, 373; worship of, 59, 67, 113, 174; 521n773, 531n1071, 5385n1281. *See also* ʿAzāzīl, Satan
Ibn ʿAbbās, ʿAbdallāh (d. ca. 66/687), 73, 200, 238, 249, 296, 319, 320, 348, 391, 444, 456, 506n309, 516n615, 525n889, 529n1011, 536n1227, 540n1344
Ibn Abi'l-Ṣalt (d. ca. 3/625), xxii
Ibn ʿĀʾisha (ʿUbaydallāh ibn Muḥammad al-Taymī, d. 228/843), 522n794
Ibn ʿArabī, Muḥyi'l-Dīn (d. 638/1240), xi, xii, xlviii, xlix, liv, lxii, lxvii, lxix n. 1, lxxv n. 149, 531n1066; *Fuṣūṣ*, lxv, 496n4; *Futūḥāt*, xlv, liii, lxxvn153, 499n94

Ibn ʿAsākir (Abu'l-Qāsim ʿAlī ibn al-Ḥasan ibn Hibatallāh, d. 571/1175), xxvii, xli-lxii, lxxiin80, lxxiiin102, 498n70; *Ta'rīkh*, 497n28, 497n36, 497n37, 500n125, 501n166, 502n203, 504n250, 505n283, 506n329, 507n341, 508n364, 511n460, 511n461, 514n540, 515n592, 517n633, 522n788, 522n789, 526n915, 529n1012, 531n1073, 532n1091, 533n1121, 533n1126, 533n1140, 534n1163, 535n1194, 538n1300, 539n1328
Ibn ʿAṭā' Ādamī, Abu'l-ʿAbbās Aḥmad (d. 309/922), 281, 342, 421, 474
Ibn ʿAṭā' Rūdhbārī, Aḥmad (369/980), xxii, 129, 500n143, 525n887
Ibn Būqa, 502n188
Ibn al-Dumayna, ʿAbdallāh al-Khathʿamī (2nd/8th c.), 511n465
Ibn al-Fāriḍ (d. 632/1234), 515n587
Ibn Hishām (d. 218/833), 502n201, 505n279
Ibn al-Jawzī (ʿAbd al-Raḥmān ibn ʿAlī, d. 597/1201), lxxiin81, lxxivn137, 503n234, 505n295, 509n407, 511n450, 511n453, 511n469, 517n639, 518n666, 518n669, 529n1007, 539n1323, 539n1330
Ibn Jurayj (d. 150/768), 328
Ibn Khallikān (d. 681/1282), xx, xxi, lxxn14, 540n1335
Ibn al-Khaṭal, ʿAbdallāh (d. 8/629), 272
Ibn Khuzayma (Muḥammad ibn Isḥāq, d. 311/923), xxiv
Ibn Lankak (d. ca. 360/970), 499n102
Ibn Māja, Muḥammad (d. 273/887), *Sunan*, notes, passim
Ibn Masʿūd. *See* ʿAbdallāh ibn Masʿūd
Ibn Munawwar (d. after 574/1178), *Asrār al-tawḥīd*, xxxvi, 496n20, 496n25, 497n56, 504n263, 504n265, 504n266, 506n317, 510n435, 513n508, 513n520, 532n1109
Ibn al-Muʿtazz (ʿAbdallāh, d. 296/908), lxxiiin106, 499n99, 512n503, 517n640, 529n1000, 538n1288
Ibn al-Najjār al Baghdādī (d. 643/1245), xiv
Ibn al-Rūmī (d. 283/896), 524n862
Ibn ʿUmar, ʿAbdallāh (d. 73/693), 346
Ibrāhīm Adham (d. ca. 165/780), 127, 249, 303, 365, 402
Ibrāhīm ʿAṭā'ī (Abū Isḥāq ibn Aḥmad ibn Muḥammad, d. 536/1141), xxiv, xxv, xxxiii
Ibrāhīm ibn Kayghalagh (d. 303/916), 516n604
Ibrāhīm ibn Shaybān (d. ca. 310/912), 406
Ibrāhīm Khawwāṣ (d. 291/904), 79, 358
Ibrāhim al-Mawṣilī (d. 188/804), 507n361
idol (*but, ṣanam*), 22, 23, 64, 71, 149, 167, 187, 203, 204, 228, 241, 245, 270, 283, 295, 324, 328, 330, 362, 381–82, 385, 420, 432; (= beloved), 42, 97, 140, 172, 252, 476; idol-worship (*but-parastī*), 71, 203, 283, 304, 330, 348, 385
Idris, 258, 328, 425
ignorance (*jahl*), 18, 34, 41, 134, 137, 184, 199, 225, 274, 275, 277, 282, 407, 408, 409, 441, 445, 478; (*nakarat*), 380, 458; deep ignorance (*jahūlī*; *see* wrongdoing)
iḥrām, 87
iḥsān, xxix, lxii, 422
iḥṣā', lii
ijāza, xx
ikhtirāʿ, 48
ikhtiyār, lxvii
Ikhwān al-Ṣafā', xlvi, li, 510n421–26, 510n439–43, 511n446, 511n447, 511n449
Īlāqī, Muḥammad (Abū ʿAbdallāh ibn Dāwūd, d. 539/1144), xxxviii-xxxix
ʿilm, xxxii; *ʿālim*, xxxii
image (*khayāl*), 3, 27, 78, 104, 122, 407
imagination (*khayāl, wahm*), lxii-lxiii, 23, 37, 38, 40, 85, 94, 98, 119, 120, 122, 123, 129, 130, 164, 172, 213, 217, 317, 343, 369, 392, 404, 406, 433, 451, 452, 469, 479; faculty of, 133, 141, 146; specter of, 104, 119, 433
imam (*imām*), lxiv-lxv, 190, 216, 332
īmān, xxix
imkān, lxiv
impurity (*najāsat, ghashsh*), 12, 14, 75, 112, 168, 175, 190, 222, 227, 232–33, 291, 331, 353, 382, 440
ʿImrān, 188. *See* Moses
ʿImrān ibn Ḥusayn (d. 52/673), 228
Imru' al-Qays (d. ca. 500 A.D.), 502n197, 538n1286
inaccessibility (*taʿazzuz*), 32, 43
inanimate (*jamād*), 128, 395
incapacity (*ʿajz, quṣūr, bī-ṭāqatī*)

inclination (*mayl, girāʾīdan*), 10, 103, 119, 237, 245, 289, 314, 323, 326, 347, 352, 388
incomparability, assertion of (*tanzīh*), liv-lv, lxiii-iv; incomparable (*munazzah*), 24, 36, 168, 220, 239, 278, 339, 411, 444; and hallowed/holy, 11, 38, 43, 237, 264, 368, 407, 471
increase (*ziyādat, mazīd*)
incumbent (*wājib*), 11, 173, 186, 259, 424, 474
indecency (*fāḥisha*), 28, 153, 208, 220, 234, 358, 454
India, 34, 312, 392, 413, 429, 443, 534n1159
indigence (*maskanat, fāqat*), 28, 34, 64, 65, 70, 85, 89, 90, 118, 125, 127, 197, 209, 219, 232, 266, 286, 287, 291, 295, 368, 390
individual (*shakhṣ*), 41, 46–47, 177, 185, 235, 236, 324, 490, 494; luminous, 58, 181, 408
Inhabited House (*al-bayt al-maʿmūr*), 201
iniquity (*jawr*), 11, 126, 306, 370, 444; without iniquity and bias, 120, 138, 167, 226
innate (*jibillī*), 135, 173, 174; innate nature (*jibillat*), 100. *See* disposition
innovation (*bidʿa, ibdāʿ*), 4, 7, 9, 54, 471
insān al-kāmil, al-, xlviii; *insāniyyat*, 510n422
insight (*baṣīrat*), 33, 46, 65, 122, 145, 153, 217, 277, 285
inspiration (*ilhām*), 399, 403
instrument (*āla*), 4, 68, 147, 272, 299, 329, 335, 473, 493
intellect, intelligence (*ʿaql, khirad*), xv, lxi, 8, 18, 33, 46, 47, 98, 103, 120, 133–36, 145, 169, 192, 203, 227, 262, 264, 273, 280, 285, 301, 308, 325, 328, 386, 396, 397, 411, 430, 438, 441, 457, 473–74, 493; defective, 140, 154, 217, 311; meddlesome, 7, 203, 204, 450–51, 453; and recognition, 140, 329, 346, 423; shortcoming of, 23–24, 33, 38–39, 54, 96, 98, 114, 121–23, 126, 141, 158–59, 164, 196, 203, 224, 239, 263, 277, 290, 307, 311, 343, 373, 383, 410, 414, 416, 440, 442, 450–51, 453, 461, 478
intensity (*shiddat*)
intention (*niyyat, qaṣd*), 144, 190, 225, 245, 359, 400, 413
intercession (*shafāʿat*), 41, 122, 177, 186, 202, 205–6, 246, 248, 255, 301, 303, 305, 310, 335, 386, 423, 426, 441, 468; by the Prophet, 45, 163, 184, 197, 207, 220, 241, 294, 375, 405, 411, 428, 445, 464, 515n588; by God, 63, 219–20, 315, 404–5, 430, 439
intermediary (*wāsiṭa*), 317, 333, 344–45, 361, 379, 420, 448, 453, 482; without (unmediated), 8, 14, 17, 47, 70, 96, 100, 114, 159, 173, 188, 197, 206, 306, 332, 337, 342, 344, 358, 360, 366, 390, 392, 422, 425, 431, 478, 488
interpretation (*taʾwīl*), 267, 322, 458
intimacy (*uns*), 8, 13, 33, 48, 70, 83, 84, 88, 97, 100, 119, 123–24, 130, 132, 138, 147, 154, 163, 165, 166, 177, 187, 191, 208, 215, 256, 269, 270, 282, 314, 334, 372, 399, 416, 420, 492; gardens of, 46, 233, 238
intimation (*ramz*), 96, 137, 213, 264, 321, 407, 416, 466, 484
intoxication (*sukr*), 96, 100, 104, 306, 469; and sobriety, 20, 130, 158, 215, 389
intrusion (*zaḥmat*)
invitation (*daʿwat*)
inward, inwardness (*bāṭin*), 3, 4, 117, 188, 212, 216, 299, 303, 352, 482; and outward(ness), 41, 47–48, 51, 59, 69–71, 74, 87, 88, 94, 120, 125, 126, 128–29, 148–49, 157, 163, 173, 176, 179–80, 196, 201, 209, 222, 223, 257, 264, 274–76, 294, 324, 331, 333, 338, 340, 353, 359, 369, 378–79, 390, 401, 406, 415–16, 447, 453, 458, 468, 474, 477, 487
iota (*dharra*)
Iraq, xxviii, xxxi, xxxviii, 81, 95, 96, 400
ʿIrāqī, Fakhr al-Dīn (d. 688/1289), 510n432
Isaac, 200, 270, 400
Isaiah, 536n1212
ishāra, xxix
Ishmael, 50, 73–74, 87, 196, 317
ʿishq, lxi
ʿIshraqa al-Muḥārabiyya (pre-Islamic), 506n308
Islam (*islām*), xxix, 21, 22, 118, 143, 187, 272, 391, 398, 422, 459, 484; (*musalmānī*), 204, 212, 271, 457; and other communities, 37, 70, 71, 90, 166–67, 190, 195–97, 200, 241, 267, 282, 304, 324, 328, 432, 453, 482–83. *See also* critique, submission
Ismāʿīl ibn ʿAlī (ibn Sahl al-Ṣūfī, d. 518/1124), xxxiii
Ismāʿīl ibn ʿAlī ibn Muḥammad (Abu'l-Futūḥ), xxxiii
Ismāʿīl Qarāṭīsī (2nd/8th c.), 506n310

isnād, xiv-xv, xviii, xix, xxii, xxv, xxvii, lxi
Israel, 243; Children of, 15, 79, 303, 304, 425, 482, 490, 512n501, 535n1190
ittiṣāf, lxi
ʿIzz al-Dawla (ibn Muʿizz al-Dawla, d. 367/978), 519n698

Jābir. *See* Anṣārī
Jābir (ibn ʿAbdallāh, d. 78/697), 201, 284
Jabulqa and Jabulsa, 199
Jacob, 43, 106, 200, 400; and House of Sorrows, 106, 139, 242, 380, 412, 418, 486; and Joseph, 77, 139, 142, 241–43, 245, 271, 290, 296, 305, 344–45, 380, 400, 418, 441, 445, 463, 470, 471, 486, 492, 520n723
Jaʿfar ibn Muḥammad, Abu'l-Faḍl, 129
Jaʿfar ibn Yaḥyā Barmakī (d. 187/803), 530n1040
Jaʿfar al-Khuldī (d. 348/959), 503n239
Jaʿfar Ṣādiq (d. 148/765), 52, 163, 198–99, 206, 282, 394, 498n89, 516n609, 517n651, 525n899, 528n987
Jaʿfar Ṭayyār (ibn Abī Ṭālib, d. 8/629), 349, 391
Jāgharq, xxvi
Jaḥẓa Barmakī (d. 326/937–38), 507n362, 511n457, 520n721
jalīl, lxiv
jamʿ, 396; *jamʿ al-aḍdād*, 531n1066
jamīl, lxiv
Jamshid, 13, 268, 348
Jarīr ibn ʿAbd al-Ḥamīd (1st/7th c.), 363
Jarīr ibn ʿAṭiyya (d. ca. 114/732), 498n83, 527n940
jawānmard, xxiii
Jayapala, 312
Jayhun, 77, 318
jealousy (*ghayrat*), 5, 6, 17–18, 29, 43, 65, 68–70, 80, 99, 100, 102, 107, 109–10, 119, 124–25, 127, 129, 142, 143, 152–54, 164–6, 176, 185, 191, 209, 213, 215, 217, 218, 243, 249, 263, 266, 277, 279, 283, 289, 312, 360, 361, 366, 371, 412, 413, 416, 453, 455, 471, 480, 491; cave of, 69–70, 143, 267, 280, 317, 352, 483; curtain of, 133, 164, 179, 277, 279, 361, 366, 403, 466, 479; of love, 60, 473, 475; and the others, 17, 69, 119, 142, 152–53, 164, 479
Jerusalem (*bayt al-muqaddas*), 22, 55, 74, 159, 160, 199, 260, 325, 327, 328, 344
Jesus, 22, 55, 101, 168, 200, 211, 241, 257, 275, 317, 330, 355, 376, 399; claims about, 247, 376; in the human makeup, 262; and Muḥammad, 80, 159, 193, 198, 325, 328, 413, 426–27, 477–78; revelations to, 27; sayings of, 128–29, 202, 522n803, 533n1113, 535n1190, 535n1203
Jew, Jewish, 26, 54, 92, 126, 158, 179, 202, 283, 361, 362, 428, 500n125, 535n1203
jihad (*jihād*), 190
jinn (*jinn*), 145
jism laṭīf, 509n416
journey (*safar*)
Job, 80, 139, 200, 246, 274, 290, 297, 317, 349–51, 370, 376, 400, 416, 525n878
John, 22, 43, 83, 106, 139, 200, 207, 371, 427, 455, 456, 531n1073
Jonah, 200, 264, 312–14, 355, 431, 526n918
Joseph, 257, 416; beauty of, 100, 127, 196, 200, 230, 234, 235, 242–43, 245, 317, 418, 449, 470, 471; brothers of, 23, 142, 229, 293, 305, 406, 445, 486; hardships of, 16, 43, 106, 139, 293, 360, 376, 382, 446, 448–49, 486; kingship of, 16, 345, 382, 448; and Muḥammad, 196, 198; shirt of, 241–43, 296, 380, 463; sinlessness of, 234, 246; symbolism of, 235, 241, 275, 412, 445–46; yearning of, 16, 480. *See also* Benjamin, Jacob, Zulaykhā
Joshua, 200
joy (*nāz, surūr, shādī*)
Judah, 229
judge (*qāḍī*), 57, 84, 171, 182, 336, 439, 465
judging (*qiyās, dāwarī*)
judiciousness (*ḥazm*), 111, 133
jumʿa, 396
Junayd (Abu'l-Qāsim Muḥammad, d. 297/910), xxii, 22, 77, 78, 92–93, 125, 165, 251, 281, 284, 342, 421, 460–61, 472, 499n111, 503n239, 504n270, 511n458, 512n475, 515n571, 524n857, 535n1176, 537n1249
Junayd Qāʾinī (Abu'l-Qāsim ibn Muḥammad ibn ʿAlī, d. 547/1152), xxxii
Jupiter, 45, 69, 198
Jurayrī (Abū Muḥammad, d. 311/923–24), 500n145
jurisprudence (*fiqh*), xvi, xxiii, xxvii, xxx-xli, 474, 509n419, 514n536

justice (*ʿadl, dād*). *See* bounty
Juwaynī, Fakhr (Abu'l-Qāsim ʿAbd al-Malik ibn Muḥammad ibn Hibatallāh, d. 533/1138–39), xl
Juwaynī, Imām al-Ḥaramayn (Abu'l-Maʿālī ʿAbd al-Malik ibn ʿAbdallāh, d. 478/1085), xiv, xvi, xvii, xxi, xxv, xl, lxxiiin107, 539n1332
Juwaynī, Muḥammad (Abū ʿAbdallāh ibn Ḥammūya, d. 530/1135), xxxix
juzʾiyyāt, xlix

Kaabah, 22, 28, 55, 64, 74, 87–88, 149, 183, 204, 209, 251, 261, 270, 272, 280, 285, 295, 309, 317, 327, 335, 381, 416, 420, 434, 508n367
kaʾanna, lxii
Kaʿb (al-Aḥbār, d. ca. 35/655), 411, 496n27, 517n643, 534n1155, 534n1161
Kaʿb ibn Zuhayr (d. 26/646), 534n1164
kafāʾa, 536n1214
Kahmas ibn Ḥasan (d. 149/766), 260–61
Kākūʾī, Faḍl (Abū ʿAmr ibn Aḥmad, d. 506/1113), xxiii
Kākūʾī, Khalaf (Abū Bakr ibn Aḥmad, d. after 506/1113), xxiii, xxxiii
Kalābādhī, Abū Bakr (Muḥammad ibn Abī Isḥāq, d. ca. 384/994), xlvi-xlvii; *Taʿarruf*, xlvi-xlvii, 509n399, 510n431, 523n841, 528n964, 528n971, 529n1009, 538n1294
Kalam, xi, xxv, xxxv, xlvi, xlvii, lii, liii, lvi, lxi, lxv, 140, 495n1, 513n514
Kalbī (Hishām ibn al-, d. 204/819), 326
kamāl, 519n686
Kāmkār (Abū Muḥammad ibn ʿAbd al-Razzāq), xxiii, xxiv
karāmāt, xxxix
Karamustafa, Ahmet, xxix
Karīma Kūfānī (Umm al-Ḥasan bint Aḥmad, d. 555/1160), xxxviii
kasb, 500n152
Kāshānī, Afḍal al-Dīn (d. ca. 610/1213), 510n432
Kāshifī, ʿAlī (Fakhr al-Dīn ibn Ḥusayn al-Wāʿiẓ, d. ca. 939/1532), xxxix
Kashmiri, 408
kathīf, 515n570
Kātip Çelebi, xi
Kaveh, 224
kawn, lxvi
Kawthar, 427
Kaykawus, 324, 409; Kawus, 267
Kayqubad, 251
khabīr, xxx
Khadīja (d. 619), 82, 188, 354, 467, 504n255
khalīfa, xxxix, xlix, 321
khalīqa, 404
khalqī, lxvi
Khān al-Barāzīn, xxv
khanaqah (*khānaqāh*), xxxi
Kharaqānī, Abu'l-Ḥasan (d. 425/1033), 64, 241, 406, 450, 465, 502n194, 519n711
khāṣṣ, xviii
khaṭīb, xxi, xxxviii; *khuṭba*, xxi
Khaṭīb Baghdādī (Aḥmad ibn ʿAlī, d. 463/1071), xiv
khayāl, lxii
Khaybar, 69, 196, 428, 435, 500n125
Khayr Nassāj (d. 322/934), 211
Khayyām, ʿUmar (d. 526/1131), xlvii, 497n59, 501n172, 519n693
Khayzurān, 497n36
Khiḍr, 50–51, 285, 292, 380, 508n367
khirqa, xxx
Khorasan, xiii-xiv, xxviii, xxxvi, 142, 386, 400, 526n928
Khubzaʾarzī (Naṣr ibn Aḥmad, d. ca. 317/929), 538n1279
khudāy, 6; *khudāʾī*, 169
khuluq, lv
Khumrakī, Muʾammal (Abu'l-Rajāʾ ibn Masrūr, d. ca. 517/1123), xl-xli
Khwāfī (Aḥmad ibn Muḥammad, d. ca. 500/1105), lxxiiin107
khwājagān, xxxviii
Khwarazm, xxii, xxv, xxviii
Khwārazmī, Maḥmūd (Abū Muḥammad ibn Muḥammad, d. 1173), xxviii
kiblah (*qibla*), 23, 88, 119, 162, 177, 181, 183, 199, 212, 327, 373, 395; of heart, 4, 285
killing (*kushtan, qatl*), 83, 96, 127, 176, 198, 246, 260, 272, 279, 342, 359, 433, 436, 437, 460–61; by love, 6, 25, 31, 34, 43, 49, 75, 104–5, 118, 154, 171–72, 229, 242, 263, 277, 283, 306, 340–41, 390, 401, 432, 434, 435, 437, 458, 488
Kināna, 188, 317

kindness (*birr, muḥābā, nāz*), 62, 81, 82, 109, 110, 130, 166, 223, 241, 268, 304, 309, 367, 385, 394, 398, 399, 423, 429, 437, 438, 447, 454, 471, 480; kind favor (*riʿāyat*), 62, 90, 132, 142, 182, 187, 259, 335, 370, 381, 400, 455
king (*malik, pādshāh*), 14, 17, 25, 31, 44, 54, 56, 58, 66, 68, 75, 101, 108, 113, 120, 133, 145, 170–72, 178, 182, 184, 189, 197, 200, 202, 218, 224, 227–29, 237, 251, 256, 277, 282, 284, 291, 295, 303, 305, 311–12, 325, 327, 346, 350, 365, 367, 370, 378, 389, 398, 402, 406, 418, 438, 448, 456, 463, 466, 469, 474, 480, 482, 488; God as, 5, 9–10, 12, 92, 111, 120, 135, 144, 146, 147, 217, 220, 258, 261, 276, 297, 308, 317, 340, 351, 381, 401, 416, 439, 445, 458; spirit-king, 46, 144. *See also* sultan
kingdom (*mulk*), 6, 185, 191, 197, 250, 328, 348–50, 355, 370, 413, 421, 455, 457, 476; God's, 9–10, 46, 114–15, 120, 130, 168, 264, 279, 287, 295, 315, 335, 368, 378, 401, 411, 431, 444, 450, 475; everlasting, 5, 16, 239, 260, 481. kingship (*pādshāhī, mulk*), 9, 38, 65, 66, 86, 112, 120, 217, 220, 264, 321, 341, 347–49, 376, 401, 402, 425–26, 429, 430, 438, 440, 444, 448
Kisāʾī (Majd al-Dīn Marwazī, d. ca. 390/1000), 536n1230
Kiyāʾ Harāsī (ʿAlī ibn Muḥammad, d. 504/1110), lxxiiin107
knowledge (*ʿilm*), beginningless/divine, xlix, 14, 19, 23, 52, 61, 63, 90, 121, 127, 131, 139, 176–77, 181–82, 184, 201, 226, 229, 234, 240, 267, 302, 320, 339, 362-63, 390, 401, 403, 404, 407, 410, 430, 438, 467, 475, 479, 485, 488; and decree, lxvii, 14, 23, 139, 182, 363, 390, 401, 403, 404, 410, 421, 429, 450, 475; human, 18, 39, 41, 45, 46, 54, 80, 94, 112, 120, 129, 132–35, 140, 146–47, 151, 157, 165, 172, 181, 184, 258, 263, 274, 282, 290, 317, 373, 377–78, 411, 432, 451, 453, 475, 478, 489–90
Knysh, Alexander, xvii, lxxn25
Korah, 265, 292, 333, 475, 489
Kufa, 346, 387
kulliyyāt, xlix
Kulthūm ibn ʿAmr (al-ʿAttābī, d. 220/835), 514n541
kun, lxvi
Kushājim, Abu'l-Fatḥ (d. ca. 360/970), 513n524, 529n1001
Kuthayyir (d. ca. 105/723), 114, 507n344

labbayk, 87
Labīd ibn Rābiʿa (d. ca. 41/660), xxii, lv, 509n404, 513n515, 522n783
Labīd ibn ʿUṭārud (al-Tamīmī, 1st/7th c.), 517n636
lamentation (*faryād, nālīdan*)
Lāmishī, Ḥusayn (Abū ʿAlī ibn ʿAlī, d. 522/1128), xxv
lamp (*charāgh, miṣbāḥ*)
Lāt, 167, 380, 462
laṭīf, lxiv, 187, 509n417, 515n570, 535n1182
laudation (*thanāʾ*), 33–34, 89, 90, 92, 112, 157, 210, 253, 274, 321–22, 375, 392, 402, 443
Law. *See* prescription
Lawrence, Bruce, xii
Laylā, 130
laziness (*kāhilī*)
leadership (*sarwarī*)
learning (*taḥṣīl, ʿilm*). learning lessons (*iʿtibār*)
leniency (*musāmaḥat*), 27, 176, 226, 342, 383, 430, 475
letters (*ḥurūf*), 47, 130, 146, 161, 266, 343, 501n167, 516n618, 535n1199
lexicology (*lughat*), liii, lv, 32, 38, 84
life (*ḥayāt, zindagī, jān*), 40, 74–76, 82–83, 115, 125, 128, 132, 134, 180, 212, 214, 224, 224, 229, 277, 318, 340, 369, 374, 391, 407, 419–20, 433, 435, 437, 472, 476, 481–83; and death, 27, 104, 136, 216, 254, 298–99, 334, 343, 380, 432, 477; detachment from, 83, 92, 261, 284, 366, 463–64; fountain of, 74, 84, 435; River of, 446; water of, 74–75, 180, 212, 224, 263, 380
light (*nūr*), 15, 84–85, 88, 120, 128, 134, 136, 138, 161, 166, 179, 181, 182, 192, 197–99, 227, 230, 231, 239, 256, 261, 262, 268, 277, 287, 296, 304, 307, 329, 332, 339, 346, 352–53, 369, 375, 378–79, 409, 420, 422, 423, 425, 427, 433, 448, 458–60, 462–64, 466, 477, 479; of Adam, 13, 46, 47, 61, 98, 180, 183, 234, 283, 299, 314, 319; and darkness, 191, 488; of intellect, 39; of Muḥammad, 165, 199, 410–414, 427

lightness (*khiffat*), 236
likeness (*mithl, mathal*), 32, 89, 134, 135, 136, 157, 166, 299, 329, 355, 369, 370, 391; lack of, liv, 41, 60, 111, 277, 339, 399, 411, 412, 426, 459–60, 463, 470; declaring likeness (*tamthīl*), 61, 123
limbs (*jawāriḥ*)
limit (*ḥadd*)
limpidness (*ṣafā'*), 10, 66, 84, 89, 94, 96, 116, 121, 132, 148, 173, 190, 229, 237, 248, 314, 317, 318, 367, 458, 488; bench of, 217, 224, 261, 412, 441; of the heart, 3, 122, 237, 262, 399, 407, 413; of knowledge, 181, 182, 488; of wine, 112, 172, 216, 471; world of, 314, 325. *See also* loyalty
listening (*samā'*)
liver (*jigar*), blood of, 21, 31, 81, 82, 93, 106, 126, 183, 207, 285, 457; burning of, 43, 138, 150, 289, 342, 381, 387, 402, 433, 438, 442, 450, 461, 477; of a lion, 58, 142; in millstone, 43, 109, 139, 186
loan (*qarḍ, wām*), 72, 287, 312, 357–58, 429, 437, 472–74
location (*makān*)
locks, tresses (*zulf*), 23, 35, 43, 57, 71, 98–99, 102–3, 105, 109, 119, 126, 130, 139, 141, 169, 235, 398
Lordhood (*rubūbiyyat*), 8, 74, 248–49, 284, 315, 357, 392, 409; covenant of, 115, 116, 364, 426, 468; and servanthood, 10, 38, 49–50, 52, 115–16, 152, 168, 261, 303, 310, 364, 382, 401–2, 406, 407, 417, 442, 450, 466
lot (*bakht*)
Lote Tree of the Final End (*sidrat al-muntahā*), 165, 166, 250, 256, 258, 262, 264, 268, 276, 317, 325, 343, 379, 382, 422, 427, 467, 476
lotus (*nīlūfar*), 179–80
love (*'ishq, maḥabbat, mawaddat, mihr*), 10, 12–13, 16, 19, 21, 25–26, 29, 40, 47, 56, 60, 86, 88, 96–97, 100–1, 104–6, 111–13, 115–16, 118–32, 143–44, 153, 162, 172–73, 177–78, 182, 191, 194, 197–99, 200, 209, 215–16, 218–19, 223–24, 226, 228–33, 235, 239, 242–45, 248–49, 251–53, 255, 263, 267–69, 274, 278, 285–86, 323–24, 327, 335, 351–52, 362–69, 383–84, 388, 400–1, 407, 415, 424, 428–30, 438, 440, 443, 446, 466, 468–70, 473–76, 484–88, 491–92; and beauty, 11, 12, 21, 25, 32, 76, 104, 107, 127, 170–71, 204, 218, 245, 285, 289, 335, 345, 366, 391, 407, 418, 433, 466; beginningless, lxvi, 111, 156, 172, 186, 242, 338, 419–20, 431–32; and blame, 252; burning/fire of, 3, 22, 24, 26, 31, 33, 34, 37, 43, 47, 86, 88, 95, 99, 104–6, 108, 110–11, 122, 128, 130, 138, 139, 150, 153, 170–71, 183, 188, 199, 203, 207, 218, 224, 231–33, 238–39, 245–46, 263, 277–78, 283, 286, 289, 306, 327, 331, 339, 341–45, 356, 364, 367, 373, 384, 401, 418, 423–24, 434, 450, 458, 468–70; causeless, 56, 155, 173, 316, 337, 362, 438; and creation, 172, 233–35, 337; and killing, 31, 33, 43, 81, 104–5, 154, 169, 171–72, 243, 340, 435, 488; and obedience, 177, 181, 238, 369–70, 396, 408, 423–24, 429; path of, 16, 29, 37, 40, 66, 130, 244, 245, 252, 286, 323, 343, 345, 351, 364, 366, 368, 487, 488; and recognition, 277, 294, 352, 364, 366, 379, 423, 487; repentance from, 288–89; rightful due of, 226; shariah of, 286, 288; severity/suffering of, 32, 36–37, 42–43, 66, 76, 82, 92, 95, 98–99, 102–10, 169–71, 176, 178, 211, 227–29, 231–32, 243–44, 267, 276–77, 285, 289–90, 306–7, 327, 331, 339, 341–45, 361, 365, 398, 402, 449, 469, 480; unconditional, lxviii (*see* unqualified); world of, 29, 53, 124, 128, 276. *See also* conformity, friendship, passion, secret, sultan, wine
lowliness (*dhull, khwārī, khāksārī*)
loyalty (*wafā'*), 27, 35, 76, 475; to the covenant, 48, 49, 115, 148, 155, 262, 282, 451; and disloyalty, 11, 59, 80, 210, 269, 288, 305, 338; and limpidness, 6, 8, 9, 74, 90, 116, 156, 189, 216, 229, 261, 263, 314, 317, 374, 488
Lukam, Mount, 479
luminous (*nūrānī*)
Luqmān (al-Ḥakīm), 503n244, 537n1232
Luqmān Sarakhsī (5th/11th c.), 282
luster (*rawnaq, farr*)
luṭf, 515n570
lying (*durūgh, kidhb*), 91, 117, 151, 160, 222, 244–45, 377, 409, 441, 455

macrocosm (*ʿālam-i akbar*). *See* microcosm
mad (*majnūn, dīwāna*), 12, 38, 41, 96, 125, 229, 260, 265, 365, 381, 394, 410, 418, 427, 442, 474, 480; mad fervor (*sawdā*), 34, 36
mādda, 510n422
madhhab, xvi
Magi(an), 56, 94, 118, 122, 149
magnification (*tamjīd*), 137, 217
magnificence (*kibriyāʾ*, *buzurgwārī*), 25, 33, 41, 43, 98, 183, 217, 239, 285, 315, 340, 404, 455
maḥabbat, 170, 341, 431
Māhānī, Muḥammad (Abū Naṣr ibn Muḥammad), xxiii, xxiv
Māḥī, 188
maḥmūd, 189
Maḥmūd, Sultan (d. 421/1030), 402, 408, 429, 467, 538n1284
Maḥmūd ibn ʿAbd al-Raḥmān (Abu'l-Majd, d. 525/1131), xxxvii
majāz, lxiii
majbūr, lxvii
majesty, majesticness (*jalāl*), 5, 17, 25, 27, 35, 37, 39–43, 54–56, 55, 71, 72, 76, 84, 94, 99, 105, 112–15, 117, 121, 122, 124–25, 127, 140–41, 154, 166, 177–78, 217, 237–40, 243, 258, 259, 265, 275, 284, 324, 333, 364, 366, 390, 397, 431, 438, 444, 446, 449–50, 465, 475, 478; of humans, 39, 45, 58–59, 103, 112, 123, 143–44, 158, 177, 181, 193, 197, 217, 231, 249, 323, 327–28, 354; of Muḥammad, 45, 183, 188, 193, 197, 249–50, 323, 325, 327–28, 354, 373, 382, 384, 425. *See also* beauty
Majnūn (Laylā, Qays ibn al-Mulawwah, d. 68/688), 130, 497n62, 499n113
makeup (*nihād*), 7, 10, 12, 17, 27, 35, 53, 86; of Adam(ite), 45, 46, 51, 65–66, 97, 120, 133, 144, 147, 178, 184, 212, 228, 235–38, 261, 262, 264, 269, 280, 287, 293, 314, 334, 362, 365, 371, 385, 424, 429, 446, 458, 470, 493
Makhzūmī (Maḥmūd), 531n1059
Makkī, Abū Ṭālib (d. 386/996), xii
maktab, xxiv
malik, xlv, 9, 370; *mālik*, 9, 370; *mulk*, 9, 370, 430
Mālik (angel of hell), 31, 55, 138, 211, 230, 231, 235, 248, 268, 367, 422, 446, 448, 449, 468
Mālik ibn Anas (d. ca. 92/710), lxxiin71
Mālik ibn Dīnār (d. ca. 131/748), 220, 221, 457, 519n688, 531n1064
Mamshād Dīnawarī (d. 299/911), 129
Maʾmūn (d. 218/833), 62, 496n23, 497n50, 497n58
man, male (*mard, rajul*), xxiii, 85, 202, 236, 284; manliness (*rujūliyyat, mardānagī*), 7, 20, 70, 86, 115, 218, 261, 278, 351, 413, 491
manī, 406
manifestation (*ẓuhūr*), making manifest (*iẓhār*), 85, 93, 109, 111, 122, 163, 173, 182, 188, 200, 217, 218, 225, 237, 249, 251, 279, 291, 298, 344, 348, 417, 418, 466, 467, 477, 485, 491; plain of, 84, 127, 143, 154, 176, 192, 217, 266, 397. *See also* outwardness
mansion (*manzil*), 47, 80, 266, 477
Manṣūr ibn ʿAmmār (d. 225/839), 457
Manṣūr ibn Ismāʿīl al-Tamīmī (d. 306/918), 520n733
maqāmāt, xxxviii
maʿrifa, xxx, xlii, lx
mark (*nishān*)
marriage, 207, 214, 311, 326–27, 388, 396, 401, 424, 456, 480, 510n437, 521n756, 536n1214
martyrdom (*shahādat*), 33, 105, 132, 196, 225, 230, 238, 245, 276, 301, 432, 435–36, 458, 460–61, 463
marvels (*badāyiʿ*, *ʿajāyib*, *ṭuraf*)
Marwah, 20, 55, 73–74, 88
Mary, 132, 188, 211, 437, 519n686
Mashhad, xiv, xl, lxviii
Masjid al-Khayf, 88
Masjidī, Aḥmad (Abū Bakr ibn Sahl, d. 539/1144), xxvi
Masjidī, Sahl (Abu'l-Qāsim ibn Ibrāhīm, d. after 523/1129), xxvii, lxxiin76
masmūʿāt, xxxiii
Masʿūd (ibn Maḥmūd of Ghazna, d. 431/1040), 467
Masʿūd ibn ʿAbdallāh al-Qāʾinī, 532n1087
Masʿūd Saʿd Salmān (d. 515/1121–22), 503n226
Mattā, 313, 355
Māwardī, ʿAlī ibn Muḥammad (d. 450/1058), xlv; *Adab*, 529n1005; *Tafsīr (Nukat)*, 500n133, 514n536, 525n875, 525n885,

525n888, 526n919, 527n937, 527n951, 527n952, 537n1263
mawqif, 501n164
Maybudī, Rashīd al-Dīn (6th/12th c.), *Kashf al-asrār*, xi-xii, xliii, xlviii, 496n13, 497n57, 499n96, 501n164, 504n256, 511n464, 514n566, 518n682, 524n855, 5254n890, 532n1108, 533n1138, 536n1221
Mazdak (d. ca. 525), 529n1005
meaning (*ma'nā*). *See* form
measure (*qadr, andāza*)
Mecca, xiv, xvi, xxxi, 45, 66, 67, 69, 70, 73, 74, 79, 161, 183, 191, 193, 197, 199, 209, 234, 260, 272–73, 297, 319, 379, 387, 390, 402, 418, 428, 434, 465, 468, 476, 483, 489, 502n201, 504n267, 520n749, 522n797, 522n798, 532n1096
Medina, 67, 69, 71–72, 191, 199, 209, 260–61, 272, 316, 476, 500n125, 502n200, 517n624
meddling (*fuḍūl*), 155, 169, 211, 212, 244, 270, 387, 421, 463. *See also* intellect
meditation (*fikrat*), 98, 146, 17
melt (*gudākhtan*)
memory (*ḥifẓ*), 133, 146
mention (*dhikr, yād*)
merchandise (*biḍā'at*), 95, 132, 145, 175, 177, 217, 232, 307, 321, 335, 406
Mercury, 198
mercy (*raḥmat*), 6–9, 44, 52, 55, 59, 67, 80, 83, 88, 90, 101, 129, 164, 168, 172, 173, 197, 200, 205, 208, 222, 226, 231–32, 238, 241, 251, 253, 255, 268–70, 273, 288, 289, 291–92, 294–96, 301, 303, 304, 306, 309–10, 312, 315, 327, 332, 338, 351, 353, 357, 366, 369, 375, 382, 386, 398, 400, 402, 422, 424, 429, 433, 438, 439, 444, 445, 450, 453, 466, 469, 471, 482, 485; in hell, 245, 296; of the Prophet, 205, 207, 272, 295, 327, 357, 413; and wrath, 181–82, 400, 451, 489; All-Merciful (*raḥmān*), 7–9, 24, 128, 133, 164, 268, 370, 378, all-mercifulness (*raḥmāniyyat*), 332, 370; ever-merciful (*raḥīm*), 7–9, 45, 50, 164, 269, 291, 295, 370
Merv, xiii-xvii, xx-xxii, xxiv-xxvi, xxxii, xxxv-xxxviii, xl, xliii, xiv, 150, 509n399
messenger (*rasūl*)
Messiah, 330
metaphor (*majāz*), 12, 181, 336, 364, 401; and reality, xx, lxiii-lxiv, lxvi, 41, 124, 290, 368, 394, 478
Michael, 55, 58, 114, 123, 134, 185, 193, 224, 295, 305, 324, 333, 391, 396, 424, 492
microcosm (*'ālam-i aṣghar*), and macrocosm, 135–38, 144–47
Midian, 296, 306–7
mihr, 323, 468
miḥrāb, 190
mildness (*musāhalat*), 27, 342, 454
Mina, 74, 88
mind (*ḍamīr, khāṭir, lubb*), 4, 29, 33, 40, 98, 99, 119, 158, 164, 212, 216, 217, 270, 272, 282, 285, 324, 343, 348, 351, 369, 370, 423, 457, 479
minna, 431
Miqdād ibn Aswad (d. 33/653–54), 27
miracles (*mu'jiza*), 271, 328, 348, 410, 411, 414, 435, 477–78, 516n601, 539n1303; (*karāmāt*), xxxix-xl
mi'rāj, of believer, 209–10, 251, 262–63, 383, 409; and the prayer, 90, 189–90; of the Prophet, 45, 71–72, 80, 158–61, 165, 195, 199, 213, 224, 249, 251–53, 255–57, 273, 325–26, 343–44, 403, 405, 427, 431, 441, 472, 503n212, 505n285, 512n485, 512–513n505, 523n811, 526n910, 531n1053, 532n1108, 536n1223
mirror (*āyīna, mir'āt*)
miṣbāḥ, 412
misery (*idbār, istikānat*)
misfortune (*idbār, badbakhtī*), 12, 76, 135, 140, 143, 187, 207, 261, 342, 469
misguidance (*ḍalāl*), 122, 199, 352, 392, 406, 414, 426, 483
misstep, mistake (*khaṭā'*)
mole (*khāl*), 97, 130, 177, 218; and beauty, l, 44, 109, 234
moment, present moment (*waqt, ḥāl*), xxx, 3, 54, 74, 115, 130, 133, 151, 166, 180, 182, 210, 247, 251, 257, 262, 263, 275, 291, 327, 328, 342, 361, 372, 393, 441, 511n448
monastery (*ṣawma'a*), 23, 30, 31, 41, 46, 216, 228, 267, 269, 270, 358, 410, 418, 459
Mongols, xiii, xxii, xxvii, xxviii
monk (*rāhib*), 358

moon (*māh, qamar*), 161, 192–93, 196, 203, 216, 266, 477; (= beloved) 43, 49, 55, 57, 62, 234, 314, 374, 382, 389, 405, 411–12, 417, 470; full moon (*badr*), 18, 49, 181, 198, 273, 374; to the Fish, 349. *See also* sun
mortal, mortal man (*bashar*), 17, 38, 40, 47, 50, 70, 85, 93, 124, 135, 136, 144, 157, 181, 198, 213, 229, 241, 275, 339, 343, 409, 461, 467, 478; mortal nature (*bashariyyat*), 6, 7, 48, 84, 111, 122, 126, 135, 138, 157, 167, 178, 189, 203, 207, 219, 225, 337, 390, 392, 409, 410, 437, 441, 453, 455, 482
Moses (the speaking companion, *kalīm*), 27–28, 120, 132, 141, 164, 193, 258, 292, 296, 317, 323, 337, 366, 382, 416, 440–41, 447, 450, 490, 516n595, 522n791, 534n1155, 535n1203; and Adam, 117, 247; boldness of, 17, 101, 306, 321, 389; of the heart, 10, 153, 332, 466, 480; and Khiḍr, 50–51; mistake of, 246; mother of, 51, 359, 437; at the mountain, 50, 54, 90, 100–3, 178, 180, 188, 236, 242, 276–77, 306–7, 331–32, 343, 360, 372, 405, 418, 443, 464; and Muḥammad, 159–60, 165–67, 194, 197–98, 304, 305, 324–25, 344, 357, 360, 373, 374, 380, 389, 393, 408, 425–27, 455, 482, 484; need of, 17, 464; and Pharaoh, 51, 139, 168, 220, 246, 341, 359, 479, 482; and revelation/speech, 9, 17, 19, 43–44, 100, 101, 269, 290, 291, 292, 294, 306, 310, 332, 360, 408, 426; and sorcerers, 80, 187, 252, 318, 328, 381–82, 433, 479; staff of, 251–52, 313, 328, 478; and vision, 17, 100, 103, 104, 165, 235, 277, 343, 372, 389; and whispered prayer, 27, 43, 132, 165, 197, 251, 310, 408
mote (*dharra*)
mother (*mādar, umm*), 51, 54, 60, 63, 94, 193, 211, 221–22, 234, 260, 269, 310, 311, 319, 331, 345, 359, 376, 391, 397, 413, 436, 437–38, 460, 472, 474; of the Book, 27, 192; and father, 82, 236, 257, 279–80, 290, 298, 335, 338, 353, 399, 465
movement, motion (*ḥarakat*), 47, 134, 145, 216, 282, 400; and rest/stillness, 77, 90, 125, 201, 353, 431, 476
Muʿādh ibn Jabal (d. 18/639), 81, 206–7, 371, 388–89, 454, 532n1107
Muʿādh Nakhshabī (Nasafī), 359, 530n1046
Muʿawwaj al-Riqqī (d. 307/919–20), 498n71
Mufaḍḍal (ibn Muḥammad al-Ḍabbī, d. after 163/780), 320
mufassir, xxiii, xlii
mufti (*muftī*), xxiii, 361, 435
Muḥammad (Muṣṭafā, the Prophet, the paragon), approval of, 162, 199, 241, 272, 308, 327, 484; ascent of, 93, 158–167, 209–10, 224, 249–58, 262, 273–275, 307–8, 325, 343–44, 355–57, 373–74, 379, 383, 403, 431, 441–42; accounts of, 33–34, 44–46, 187–200, 270–71, 317, 414, 461–63, 471, 482–83; eloquence of, 33–34, 112, 274; emigration of, 66–67, 69–70, 272; eminence of, 323, 328, 354, 361, 374–75, 408–9, 424–28; exaltedness and abasement of, 67, 93, 405–9, 428; and Iblis, 59, 194; intercession of, 220, 294, 325, 375, 405, 430, 439, 445, 464; light of, 411–14; and the Meccans, 271–72, 381, 392–93, 410; poverty and need of, 33–34, 91, 209, 283, 390, 406; and the prophets, 100–1, 187–88, 194–200, 304–5, 324–25, 328, 355, 382–83, 424–28, 468, 477–78; suffering and trial of, 42, 82, 99, 139, 342–44, 427–28; Muhammadan, 184, 189, 192, 206, 207, 250, 370, 374, 414, 426, 427, 464, 477, 483. *See also* Adam, Moses
Muḥammad Ashhabī (Abu'l-Makārim ibn ʿUmar ibn Amīrja, d. 532/1138), xxxvii
Muḥammad ibn al-Faḍl (Balkhī, d. 319/931), xlii, 509n416
Muḥammad ibn Kaʿb (al-Qurẓī, d. 117/735), 411
Muḥammad ibn Nuʿmān ibn Mūsā, 487, 539n1333
Muḥammad ibn Sammāk (d. 183/799), 435
Muḥammad ibn Sarī al-Sarrāj (d. 322/934), 497n42
Muḥammad ibn Wuhayb al-Ḥimyarī (early 3rd/9th c.), 514n561
Muḥammad ibn Yazdād Marwazī (d. 230/844–45), 496n23
Muḥammad Kurāʿī (Abū Manṣūr ibn ʿAlī ibn Maḥmūd, d. 525/1131), xxi
Muḥammad Kushmīhanī (Abu'l-Fatḥ ibn ʿAbd al-Raḥmān, d. 548/1153), xxxvii
muḥaqqiq, xxiii

muḥdath, lxiv, 168
muhr, 468
muḥsin, 515n570
Muʿizzī, Amīr (d. ca. 520/1126), xlvii, 497n53, 501n169
Mujāhid (ibn Jabr, d. 104/722), 296, 300, 320, 514n536, 525n888, 532n1086
muʿjiza, 539n1303
mukāshafa, lx
mukhtaṣṣ, xxxvii
Muliyan River, 77
mulk, 9, 370, 430
munāẓir, xxiii
munificence (*jūd*), 17, 47, 85, 96, 117, 124, 131, 144, 287, 291, 315–16, 399, 438
Munkar and Nakīr, 231, 415, 457
muqaddam, xxx
muqallib al-qulūb, 507n334
Muqātil ibn Ḥayyān (d. 150/767), 326
murāqaba, xxx
Murata, Sachiko, lxiv
murīd, xxx, xxxvii, xxxix
murshid, 484
Muṣʿab ibn ʿUmayr (d. 3/625), 176
Muṣʿab ibn Zubayr (d. 72/691), 81
muṣawwir, li, 57
mushāhada, lx
Muslim (ibn al-Ḥajjāj, d. 261/875), *Ṣaḥīḥ* of, xxii, xxiv, lii; notes, passim
Muslim ibn Yasār (d. 100/718), 511n469, 531n1051
Mustamlī, Ismāʿīl (d. 434/1043), xlvi-xlvii; *Sharḥ al-taʿarruf*, 501n174, 511n455, 512n489, 512n495, 517n650, 520n747, 521n750, 521n752–55, 521n758, 521n762, 521n765, 521n766, 522n800, 523n841, 527n957, 528n964–66, 528n968, 528n970–72, 529n1009, 530n1034, 531n1066, 538n1294, 538n1295
mustering (*ḥashr*), 197, 230, 334, 375, 429, 435, 444, 471
Muʾta, Battle of, 92
Mutanabbī (d. 354/965), 496n17, 499n117, 500n138, 502n202, 502n207, 506n324, 513n522, 515n573, 515n590, 519n704, 519n706, 523n829, 530n1029, 530n1037, 533n1128
Muʿtaṣim Billāh (d. 227/842), 503n223
Mu'tazilite, xvi, 112, 121, 439, 536n1217
Muzdalifa, 88
mystery (*rāz*, *sirr*), 67, 113, 148, 164, 228, 234, 240, 262, 316, 327, 420, 438, 479; falcon of, 10, 13, 80, 140, 148, 218, 257, 433, 468, 470; of love, 70, 142, 362, 440, 466. *See also* secret

Naḍīr, 44, 500n125
nafs, xliv, 510n441
Nāgawrī, Ḥamīd al-Dīn (Muḥammad ibn ʿAṭāʾ, d. 643/1246), xii, lxxn6, 535n1198, 538n1278
Nahrajūrī, Abū Yaʿqūb (d. 330/941–42), 404, 504n246
Najd, 152, 242
Nakhshabī, ʿAbd al-ʿAzīz (Abū Muḥammad ibn Muḥammad, d. ca. 456/1064), xlvii
name (*ism*, *nām*), 4, 29, 46; and attributes, l-lv, lxiii, 277; greatest, lii, 64, 121, 291, 316; ninety-nine, 433, 492; taught to Adam, 46, 98, 145, 172, 184, 384, 475, 489–90, 493
Nāqidī, ʿAbd al-Jabbār al- (Abū Muḥammad ibn ʿAbd al-Wahhāb, d. 507/1114), xxiii-xxiv
Nāqidī, Ismāʿīl al- (Abū Ibrāhīm ibn ʿAbd al-Wahhāb, d. ca. 493/1100), xxiii-xxiv
naql, lxi
Naqshbandī, xxxviii, xxxix
naṣab, *naṣīb*, 347
Nasāʾī, Aḥmad (d. 303/915), *Sunan*, notes, passim
Nāṣir Khusraw (d. 481/1088), 527n936
Naṣr ibn ʿAlī Maqdisī, 129
Naṣr Ṣaffār (Abu'l-Fatḥ ibn Manṣūr, d. 532/1138), xxxv
Naṣrābādī, Abu'l-Qāsim (d. 367/977), 92, 202, 323, 500n144, 537n1250
nature (*ṭabʿ*, *ṭabīʿat*), 48, 94, 103, 120, 144, 261, 263, 268, 331, 365, 410, 414, 425, 433, 443, 474. *See also* Adamic, created, human, mortal
Nawqan, xiv, xliv
Nawqānī, ʿUmar, lxxiiin107
Nawqānī, ʿUthmān (Abu'l-Qāsim ibn ʿAlī ibn Muḥammad, d. 539/1145), xxxix-xl
nawr, 299
Naysābūrī (Niẓām al-Dīn Ḥasan, d. 728/1327), 512n499
nearness (*qurb*, *nazdīkī*), liii, lx, 7, 12, 88, 99, 107, 156, 163, 165, 215; and distance, 24, 32, 36, 40, 103, 271. *See also* proximity

necessary (*wājib*), 38–39, 269, 272, 297, 426, 451
need (*niyāz, ḥāja, iftiqār*), 65–66, 72, 82, 85, 87, 90, 94, 98, 103, 106, 116, 117, 118, 130, 141, 150, 156, 166, 176, 190, 191, 202, 209–10, 216, 223, 232–33, 247–48, 251, 259, 267, 280, 289, 330, 372, 390, 396, 398, 420, 422, 424, 443, 464
negation (*nafy*), 52, 448, 453. *See also* affirmation
neglect, negligence (*sahw*), 149, 257, 384, 441, 532n1095
neighborhood (*jiwār*)
new arrival (*ḥudūth*), 37, 43, 174, 217, 368, 394, 409, 473, 476. *See also* eternity
Nibājī (Abū ʿAbdallāh Saʿīd, 3rd/9th c.), 503n213, 530n1049
Nicholson, R. A., xlvii, lxixn1
Nifṭawayh, Ibrāhīm ibn Muḥammad (d. 323/935), 497n28
niggardliness (*bukhl*), 222, 244, 306, 315, 331, 347, 349, 357, 363, 370, 472
Nile, 308, 333
Nimrod, lxvi, 51, 68, 106, 114, 168, 195, 245, 248, 279–80, 337, 338, 372–73, 388, 395, 432, 447, 476, 506n329
Nineveh, 526n918
Nishapur, xiv, xvi, xvii, xx, xxi, xxiv-xxvii, xxxii, xxxvi, xxxviii, xl, xli, 150, 450
Niẓām al-Mulk (Ḥasan ibn ʿAlī al-Ṭūsī, d. 485/1092), xvi, xvii, xxii, xxxii
Niẓāmiyya madrasa, xiii, xvi, xx, xxiii, xxvi, xxvii, xliii
No Place (*lā makān*), 80
Noah, lxv, 16, 43, 60, 101, 106, 131, 139, 200, 305, 317, 324, 325, 338, 374, 386, 412, 432, 483, 493; and Canaan, 50, 229, 244, 416, 464; and the Prophet, 195, 328, 355, 425–26, 497n55, 519n685, 520n730
nobility (*karāmat, khwājagī*)
nomad/bedouin (*aʿrābī*), 88, 311–12; anecdotes, 72–73, 75, 260, 288, 300, 309, 422
nonbeing (*nīstī*), 84, 356. *See* being
nonexistence (*ʿadam*), 5, 9, 124, 315, 380, 397, 438, 443, 467; blessing of, 61, 293, 391; concealment of, lxvi, 57, 65, 102, 114, 124, 177, 186, 216, 233, 351–52, 396, 411, 442, 485, 490; creation from, 48, 172–73, 314, 337; taking to (*iʿdām*). *See also* existence
notebook (*daftar*)
nourishment (*qūt*), 46, 48, 69, 75, 95, 131, 143, 150, 167, 213, 255, 274–75, 331, 359, 393, 481, 492
nūr, 299
Nūrī, Abu'l-Ḥusayn (d. 295/907), 36, 141, 284, 505n300
nurture (*tarbiyat, parwarish*), 9, 51, 75, 76, 85, 131, 153, 157, 175, 176, 187, 226, 230, 267, 310, 335, 353, 359, 368, 369, 385, 401–2, 437, 443, 447, 484, 486; (*pay-mūdan*), of delusions, 37, 106, 125; Nurturer (*parwardagār*), 62, 303, 305

oath (*qasam, sawgand*), 80, 161, 197, 229, 243, 260, 297, 380, 406, 482
obedience, obedient act (*ṭāʿat*), and/or disobedience, 11, 12, 29, 38, 54, 58–59, 63–64, 71, 92, 113, 122, 137, 172, 174–75, 177, 183, 206, 207–8, 212, 222, 232, 238, 248, 264, 268–70, 290–96, 305–7, 309, 316, 322, 334, 353, 380, 399–400, 402, 416, 422, 428, 439, 448, 449, 454, 466, 486, 492
obligatory (*farḍ*), 187, 210, 334, 361, 364, 437
obstinacy (*muʿānada*), 43, 55, 68, 217, 262
ocean (*baḥr, daryā*)
occupation (*shughl*), 49, 127, 134, 257, 276, 281, 347, 352, 355, 360
offense (*jurm, jināyat*)
offer (*ʿarḍ*)
offspring (*dhurriyyat*), of Adam, 67, 96, 118, 172, 226, 245, 301, 319, 320, 323, 428
oil (*rawghan*), 62–63, 301, 427
opacity (*kudūrat*), 9, 59, 177, 182, 238, 247, 325, 378–79, 394, 407, 422, 453, 458; and limpidness, 104, 172, 189
opening (*futūḥ*), xlv, 21, 69, 84, 180, 188, 253, 262, 304, 314, 346, 380, 401, 416, 470, 485
opinion (*ẓann, qawl*)
opposite (*ḍidd*), 89, 275–76, 333
opposition (*mukhālafat*), 26, 32, 91, 113, 149, 151, 172, 206, 245, 254, 268, 306, 322, 330, 362, 408, 430, 445, 478, 481, 487. *See also* conformity
orb (*haykal*), celestial, 144, 199, 324
other (*ghayr*), than God, 5–7, 10, 11, 14, 15, 17–18, 26, 29, 33, 39, 50, 72, 74, 78–80, 84, 87, 89, 122–24, 129–30, 134, 157, 165, 168, 173, 176, 189, 197, 234, 251, 263,

265, 269, 270, 273–78, 281–83, 294, 308, 327, 331, 333, 339, 340, 345, 349, 352, 355, 357, 385, 390, 407, 422, 434, 446, 475. *See also* jealousy
outcome (*'āqibat*)
outward, outwardness (*ẓāhir*), 36, 96, 133–34, 153, 170, 237, 245, 253, 370, 414; folk of, 51, 122, 130, 264, 333, 392. *See also* inwardness
overpowering (force; *ghalaba*), 18, 37, 348, 361, 372, 415, 465
overmastery (*istīlā'*), 178, 208, 245, 414

pain (*dard, alam*), 21, 24–26, 31, 48, 66, 73, 87, 98, 105–7, 110, 111, 122, 129, 139, 169, 181, 191, 200, 202–3, 209, 212, 222, 225, 235, 280, 341, 360, 365, 390, 393, 399, 415, 423, 427, 438, 441, 456, 457, 461–63, 467, 472, 474, 476, 483, 487, 492; of existence, 91, 227–28, 437; of heart, 31, 73, 116, 141–42, 150, 164, 169, 208, 338, 398, 449; of love and separation, 76, 170, 176, 211, 227, 230–31, 233, 244, 361, 367, 416, 417, 427, 469, 491
painting (*naqsh kardan, nigāshtan, ṣūrat-garī*), 57–58, 64, 211, 215, 279, 298, 379, 440, 478
palisade (*ḥaẓīra*)
paradise (*bihisht, firdaws*), 18, 19, 44, 50, 55, 56, 71, 88, 116, 140, 165, 208, 228, 230–32, 241, 281, 299, 391, 403, 423, 429, 438, 439, 458, 459–60, 466, 475–76; eight, 16, 19, 65, 86, 95, 97, 117, 128, 129, 143, 150, 175, 189, 215, 267, 276, 374, 397, 400, 412, 431, 470, 493; and hell, 6, 16, 22, 29, 61, 74, 93, 128, 130, 138, 150, 152, 158, 159, 170, 209, 211, 231, 248–49, 251–52, 257, 265, 268, 270, 273, 293, 295–97, 316, 351, 356, 361, 369, 397, 422, 425, 441, 446, 448, 451, 469, 471, 476, 493. *See also* Adam
paragon (*mihtar*)
pardon (*'afw*), 12, 38, 59, 63, 92, 112, 129, 172, 175, 177, 206, 208, 222–23, 226, 244, 247, 254, 268, 273, 288, 290–91, 294, 304, 309, 328, 338, 368, 392, 413, 439, 450, 467, 475
pariyān, 531n1071
partnership (*anbāzī, shirkat*), 28, 60, 286, 323, 386, 449, 490
Parviz, Chosroes (d. 628), 252, 280, 523n824
passion, passionate love (*'ishq, hawā*), 10, 20, 56, 105, 128, 131, 134, 138, 170, 177, 186, 218, 245, 367, 443, 448, 469, 484; passionate lover (*'āshiq*), 40, 69, 88, 104, 116, 215. *See* love
Path, Narrow (*ṣirāṭ*), 28, 64, 101, 231, 419, 457; straight path (*ṣirāṭ mustaqīm*), 20, 133, 352, 357, 464. *See* road
patience (*ṣabr*), 3, 15, 21, 39, 49, 51, 75, 80–82, 88–90, 92, 98, 101, 128, 137, 148, 150, 200, 220, 243, 246–48, 253, 256–57, 274, 277, 280, 286, 289, 292, 317, 327, 333, 339, 350–51, 369, 370, 372, 388, 398, 400, 412, 416, 429, 437, 454, 456, 491–93, 495
patron (*mawlā*), 72, 171, 229, 250, 251, 291, 295, 305, 309, 345, 358, 365, 438, 440, 464
peace (*salām*), 11, 14–15, 143, 177, 256, 291, 304, 306, 392, 460; (*ṣulḥ, āshtī*), 15, 69, 103, 238, 276, 288, 446; and war, 32, 36, 64, 245, 267, 380–81, 422, 424–25
pearl (*gawhar, durr*), 10, 13, 17, 22, 33, 34, 36, 38, 60, 67, 91, 110, 114, 119, 120, 122, passim. *See also* oyster (*under* animal)
peer (*naẓīr, nidd, hamtā*), 9, 32, 60, 279, 313
Peg (*watad*), 445, 466, 479, 536n1229
pen (*qalam*), 21, 44, 48, 111, 116, 122, 128, 141, 146, 209, 361, 384, 391, 403, 452; of eternal gentleness, 46, 116, 162; and tablet, 46, 146, 475; Pen (and Tablet), 61, 70–71, 144, 159, 285, 293, 356, 362, 382, 396, 452
penitence (*inābat*), 20, 48, 75, 90, 294, 303, 350, 428
perception (*idrāk, dar yāft*), 13, 33, 38, 40, 41, 85, 139–40, 146, 217, 240, 340, 343, 369, 388, 463
perfection (*kamāl*), 112, 145, 183, 231, 307, 342, 369, 470, 519n686; of God 16, 23, 39, 40, 43, 55, 93, 124, 199, 216, 224, 238, 264–65, 275, 295, 357, 403, 431; of Muḥammad, 44, 45, 71, 191, 251, 295, 328, 375. *See also* beauty
perfume (*'aṭr*)
peril (*khaṭar*)
permanence (*dawām*)
permitted (*ḥalāl*), and forbidden, 37, 75, 78, 148, 261, 272–73, 302, 331, 371, 465

perplexed (*sar-gardān, sar-gashta*)
perseverance (*muwāẓabat*)
Persia, Persians (*ʿajam*), 79, 200–1; (language, *fārsī*), xi-xiii, xviii, xxviii, xxxi, xxxv, xxxvi, xli, xlii, xliii, xlvi-xlvii, 3, 6, 9, 14, 57, 79, 120, 202, 421, 444, 484, 498n82
Pharaoh, lxvi, 51, 52, 55, 68, 80, 102, 114, 139, 168, 179, 186, 187, 197, 230, 247, 250, 266, 276, 319, 335, 339, 343, 362, 366, 375, 385, 392, 437, 441, 451, 483, 486, 493, 518n664, 518n686
piety (*birr*), 261, 316, 334, 386; pious (*bārr*), 15, 33, 108, 147, 335, 364, 413, 493; and depraved, 296, 316, 448
pillar (*rukn*), of the Shariah, 73, 190, 286, 352
pir (*pīr* = shaykh), 53, 77, 94, 96, 121, 128, 147, 211, 214, 222, 316, 343, 345, 387
plain, open/vast (*ṣaḥrā*)
planet (*sayyāra, kawkab*), 34, 68, 135–37, 328, 355, 378, 411; chief/emperor of, 21, 45, 84, 163, 192, 198
Plato, 520n725
pleading (*taḍarruʿ*)
pleasure (*ladhdhat, kām*), 10, 28, 66, 81, 87, 107, 126, 127, 281, 282, 286, 306, 365, 377–78, 390–91, 410, 457; and pain, 18, 83, 105
Pleiades, 68, 112, 115, 132, 161, 200, 212, 490
Plenum, Higher (*malaʾ-i aʿlā*), 118, 123, 144, 183, 210, 262, 392, 423
point, subtle (*laṭīfa*). *See also* center
poison (*zahr, samm*), 5, 29, 42, 49, 52, 55, 69, 92, 98, 105, 107, 109, 110, 123, 139, 162, 178, 193, 196, 211, 225, 284, 285, 334, 342, 343, 365, 366, 376, 391, 405, 406, 443, 491, 494, 495; of severity, 7, 122, 125, 206, 402
policeman (*shiḥna*), 6, 68, 96, 114, 115, 155, 157, 210, 243, 246, 362, 425
pollution (*janābat*), 53, 130, 264, 406
polo (*chawgān*), 30, 112, 141, 171, 340, 416
pondering (*taʾammul*)
portion (*naṣīb, sahm, ḥaẓẓ*). *See* share
possible (*mumkin*)
poverty (*faqr, darwīshī*), xxiii, xxx-xxxii, 10–12, 17, 20, 25, 64–65, 69, 70, 82, 85, 90, 94, 97, 117–18, 150, 171, 177, 184, 202, 206, 208–9, 214–16, 232–33, 235, 241, 259–60, 281–84, 306–7, 311, 317, 352, 359, 384–85, 395, 409, 412, 427, 440, 471, 484, 488; and riches/unneediness, 11, 44, 45, 72, 80, 84, 107, 124, 232–33, 281–82, 287, 322, 339, 374, 376, 390, 395, 398, 406, 422, 441, 466–67, 472–73
power (*qudrat*), divine, 7, 8–10, 46, 52, 54–55, 107, 114, 123, 137, 140, 151, 168, 174, 182–83, 191, 217, 230, 231, 237, 239–40, 252, 259, 267, 270, 274, 279, 298, 299, 314, 327, 329, 338, 339, 357, 363, 373, 403, 407, 411, 417, 421, 426, 438, 446, 452, 454, 467, 478, 485, 491; human, 122, 180, 299, 314, 329, 395, 440; and jealousy, 60, 124, 403; and knowledge, 122, 471, 475; ocean/world of, 4, 9, 60, 144, 200, 230, 323, 480; and will, 200, 279, 287, 298, 450, 481; and wisdom, 4–5, 135, 159, 234, 315–16, 319, 337, 429
practice (*muʿāmalat*), 53, 89, 93, 116, 146, 148, 173, 175, 177, 228, 264, 309, 330, 359, 362, 411, 412, 423, 430, 452–53, 477, 488
praise (*ḥamd, madḥ, sitāyish*), 90–92, 115–16, 131, 157, 258–59, 274, 286–87, 298–99, 320–21, 359, 368, 422, 480, 490; and blame, 38, 91, 237, 302, 443; praised station, 183, 191, 427, 445
prayer (*ṣalāt, namāz*), 12, 28, 42, 50, 56, 64, 89, 90, 99, 110, 116, 154, 158, 160, 165, 189–90, 192, 202, 203, 226, 256–57, 261, 269, 270, 293, 300, 308, 312, 320, 332, 333, 347, 359, 361, 364, 370, 371, 381, 383–84, 387, 391, 401, 406, 413, 415, 423, 429, 432, 435, 454, 456, 457, 470, 476, 479, 480, 487, 490; whispered prayer (*munājāt*), 125, 131, 192, 206, 222, 331, 332, 342, 383, 445 (*see also* Moses); prayer-niche (*miḥrāb*), 84, 362, 395, 414
preacher (*wāʿiẓ, khaṭīb*), 5, 26, 123, 140, 172, 320, 392
precedence (*sabq*), 122, 181, 297, 309, 400, 420, 451, 484, 489; preceder (*sābiq*), 28, 91, 146, 194, 288, 482, 524n855; precedent (*sābiq*), 23, 61, 114, 152, 310, 338, 351, 352, 369, 382; and outcome, 138, 381, 427; and subsequent, 186, 351, 471
predator (*sabʿ*), 120, 208
predetermination (*taqdīr*), lxvii, 49, 50, 107, 113, 118, 126, 135, 181, 207, 217, 238,

316, 408, 452–53, 461, 485; predetermined things (*maqdūrāt*), 27, 55, 240
prescription (of the Law, *taklīf*), 39, 136, 155, 240, 358, 370, 390, 404, 415, 416, 422, 429, 470, 487–88
presence (with God, *ḥuḍūr*), 7, 53, 54, 88, 133, 165, 270, 324, 339, 423; (*ḥaḍrat*), of God (Exalted, Majestic, My), passim; of Muhammad, 193, 206, 207, 250, 324, 325, 332, 375, 384, 392
present moment (*waqt*). *See* moment
preserving (*ḥifẓ, nigah dāshtan*)
pretext (*bahāna*), 57, 157, 224, 231, 233, 286, 482
prey (*ṣayd*)
pride (*kibr, takabbur*), 9, 23, 32, 43–44, 51, 68, 72, 85, 96, 100, 103, 126, 139, 151, 157, 173–74, 193, 206, 226, 227, 286, 320, 359, 362, 437, 440
principle (*aṣl*), 33, 78, 82, 403, 439
priority (*taqaddum*), 44, 46, 53, 58, 98, 113, 323, 395, 428, 451
privy (*maḥram*), 53, 96, 334, 407, 436
proclamation (*tawqīʿ*)
prohibition (*nahy*), 113, 116, 121, 254, 263, 414. *See* command
promise (*waʿda*), 18, 20, 32, 86, 110, 116, 125, 130, 202, 205, 259, 289, 294, 297, 306, 323, 333, 335, 359, 369, 403, 416, 422, 424, 425, 472, 473
proof (*burhān, ḥujjat, dalīl*), 4, 65, 98, 133, 175, 240, 281, 354, 379, 477
prophets (*nabī, payghāmbar*), and friends, 38, 80, 99, 190, 209, 227, 248, 282, 382, 475; mission of, 153–55; slips of, 244–47; prophethood (*nubuwwat*), 194–95
propriety (*sadād*), 45, 462
prosperity (*iqbāl*), 5, 10, 12, 14, 44, 53, 58, 65, 89, 100, 112, 119, 120, 128, 131, 132, passim
prostration (*sujūd*), 190, 328, 373, 381; of the angels, 13, 53, 58, 65, 112, 177, 217, 229, 321–22, 324, 356, 383, 438, 440, 443, 470
protest (*iʿtirāḍ*), 49–51, 107, 151, 169, 173, 217, 333, 351, 450, 454
provision (*rizq, rūzī, ʿuddat*), 55, 65, 68, 74, 78–79, 84, 105, 107, 142, 146, 210, 231, 282, 294, 299, 309–10, 313, 349, 357–59, 402–3, 425, 486, 492
proximity (*qurb*), 19, 36, 45, 104, 159, 165, 215, 219, 224, 225, 255–57, 321, 366, 423, 454, 474, 484; and distance, 35, 53, 187, 223, 250, 322, 327, 331, 353, 387, 457 (*see also* nearness); proximate (*muqarrab*), 87, 129, 140, 263, 307, 327, 455. *See also* angels
Psalms, 314, 337, 413, 480
punishment (*ʿuqūbat*), 5, 22, 52, 118, 120, 144, 154, 159, 170, 174, 209, 220, 231, 238, 244, 261, 269, 272, 273, 297, 300, 304, 313, 339, 356, 357, 365, 375, 380, 422, 430–31, 446, 448–50, 455, 466, 471, 481, 491. *See also* reward
pure (*pāk, ṭāhir, khāliṣ*)

Qadarī, xvi
Qāf, 372, 478
qahr, 515n570; *qahhār*, lxiv, 67
qāʿida, 509n419
qalb, 77, 510n441
qanāʿa, 530n1021
qarḍ, 473
Qāsim ibn ʿUbaydallāh (d. 291/904), 502n198
Qaṣīr (ibn Saʿd), 132, 181, 441, 509n410
Qatāda (ibn Diʿāma al-Sadūsī, d. 117/735), 320, 326, 516n595
Qays. *See* Majnūn
quarry (*maʿdan*)
quintessence (*khulāṣa*), 172, 315
Quran-reciter (*qāriʾ*), 64, 110, 269, 335, 377, 423, 454, 480
Quraysh, 45, 67, 68, 160, 188, 193, 271, 273, 317, 381, 392, 403, 408, 516n616
Qurayẓa, 44, 500n125
Qushayrī, ʿAbd al-Munʿim (Abu'l-Muẓaffar ibn Abi'l-Qāsim, d. 532/1138), xxiv, xxxviii
Qushayrī, ʿAbd al-Wāḥid (Abū Saʿīd ibn Abi'l-Qāsim, d. 494/1101), xxi, xxii
Qushayrī, Abu'l-Qāsim (ʿAbd al-Karīm ibn Hawāzin, d. 465/1072), xvii, xxi, xxix, xxxi, xxxiii, xxxv, xxxvi, xxxvii, xxxix, xlvi, 123, (297), 518n658; *Laṭāʾif al-ishārāt*, xliii, 496n11, 497n50, 499n103, 501n178, 501n179, 502n188, 504n247, 505n275, 506n312, 506n319, 507n338, 507n351, 508n379, 508n384, 509n403, 511n466, 511n474, 512n479, 512n493, 513n530, 513n533–35, 514n548, 514n561, 516n618,

Qushayrī, Abu'l-Qāsim: *Laṭā'if al-ishārāt (cont'd)* 518n657, 518n661, 518n670, 523n816, 523n825, 524n863, 525n879, 525n880, 525n886, 525n900, 526n905, 526n918, 526n920, 526n921, 527n941, 529n1014, 529n1015, 530n1022–24, 530n1026, 530n1027, 534n1171, 534n1172, 535n1179, 535n1195, 535n1199; *Manthūr al-khiṭāb*, xlvi, 500n146, 500n147, 523n836–40, 524n843, 524n844, 530n1021, 540n1340, 540n1341; *Mi'rāj*, 519n710; *Mukhtaṣar fi'l-tawba*, xlvi, 524n854, 524n856; *Risāla* (*Treatise, RQ*), xxx, xxxiv, xxxviii, xlii, xlvii, lxix, 496n9, 497n29, 497n30, 497n32–36, 497n44, 497n49, 497n51, 497n52, 498n66–69, 498n76, 498n77, 498n81, 499n100, 499n101, 500n137, 500n139–45, 500n148, 500n149, 500–1n153–56, 501n159–63, 503n213, 503n240–43, 504n245, 504n246, 504n248, 504n252, 504n271, 505n290, 505n294, 505n300, 506n313, 506n321, 506n322, 506n325, 506n331, 507n354, 507n357, 508n369, 509n398, 509n400, 509n402, 509n416, 511n458, 511n471, 512n482, 512n488, 514n546, 514n553, 514n554, 517n635, 517n652, 517n653, 519n709, 521n757, 522n795, 522n805, 823n817, 523n831, 524n845, 524n857, 526n930, 527n942, 527n943, 530n1045, 530n1046, 530n1049, 531n1069, 532n1093, 533n1124, 534n1143, 534n1147, 535n1175, 536n1228, 537n1249, 537n1259, 538n1276; *Sharḥ asmā' Allāh al-ḥusnā* (*al-Taḥbīr*), xliii, lvi-lxi, 496n2, 496n5, 496n8, 496n14, 496n18, 496n26, 497n45–49, 498n65, 498n66, 498n88, 498n90, 498n91, 499n106, 499n107, 500n122, 500n129, 500n135, 502n204, 503n214–18, 503n235–37, 504n259, 505n275, 506n330, 507n352, 508n570, 518n663, 518n665, 519n708, 522n782, 523n830, 524n847, 530n1039, 532n1110, 532n1111, 534n1144, 538n1269, 538n1302; *Shawāhid*, 505n282, 509n405, 511n451, 513n526, 517n646, 518n656, 520n723, 522n787, 524n846

Qushayrī, Hibat al-Raḥmān (Abu'l-As'ad ibn 'Abd al-Wāḥid, d. 546/1152), xxxvi

Qushayrī, 'Ubayd (Abu'l-'Alā' ibn Muḥammad ibn 'Ubayd, d. 512/1118), xxi, xxiv

Rābi'a 'Adawiyya (d. 185/801), 63, 435, 488, 500n136, 540n1335

radiance (*ḍiyā'*, *shu'ā'*)

ra'īs, xx

Rakhsh, 56

rancor (*ḥiqd*)

rank (*manzilat*)

rapture (*walah*), 171, 216, 288, 470. enraptured (*wālih*), 19, 98, 277

raqīb, 26, 47

rascal (*qallāsh*), 12, 218, 410

rational (*'āqil*), and mad, 38, 265

raw (*khām*), 51, 494, 495

rawḥ, xliv

Rāzī, Yaḥyā ibn Mu'ādh (d. 258/872), 65, 149, 187, 206, 212, 222, 248, 268, 304, 375, 445, 472, 484, 486, 511n468, 518n668, 526n912, 529n1007, 532n1099

real (*ḥaqq*), (=God), passim; and creatures (*see* creation); and unreal, lv, 130, 168, 265, 287, 303, 346, 381, 489

reality (*ḥaqīqat*), 40, 41, 257, 290, 299, 318, 329, 332, 363, 367, 368, 374, 404, 450, 452, 458, 478; and form, 146, 184, 241; world of, 479. *See also* metaphor, Haqiqah

realization (*taḥqīq*), lxi, 4, 20, 48, 64, 70, 122, 339, 381, 413, 464; realizer (*muḥaqqiq*), xxxiii, 29, 80, 222, 252, 282, 307, 331, 332, 348, 437

realm of being (*kawn*). *See* being

rebuke (*'itāb*), 6, 249, 281, 310, 322, 328, 337, 376, 446, 448

reckless (*'ayyār*), 177, 306

reckoning (*ḥisāb*), 6, 7, 231, 281, 349, 375

recognition (*ma'rifat*, *shinākht*), xxx, xlii, lx-lxii, 10, 15, 20, 26, 38–39, 41, 47, 54, 56, 61, 72, 89, 108, 119, 120, 126, 134, 139–41, 149, 170, 183, 187, 277–78, 294, 298, 299–301, 303, 304, 329–30, 342, 346, 352, 356, 364–66, 368, 369, 375, 379, 380, 382, 390, 399, 403–4, 413, 416, 420, 421–23, 464, 466, 468, 485, 487, 489, 496n4, 513n521,

532n1093; of self, 46, 136, 318. recognizer (*ʿārif*), folk of recognition (*ahl-i maʿrifat*), 39, 60, 81, 119, 152, 222, 263, 267, 285, 296, 304, 314, 322, 332, 366, 378, 382, 411, 418, 448, 454, 455
recompense (*jazāʾ*), 90, 156, 231, 258, 307, 327, 349, 367, 474
reconciliation (*ṣulḥ*), 21, 463
refractory (*gardan-kash, ḥarūn*)
refusal (*juḥūd, ibāʾ*)
regard (*iltifāt*)
register (*jarīda*)
regret (*nadāmat, pashīmānī*), 5, 81, 208, 263–64, 269, 288, 305, 390, 422, 428
reins (*ʿinān*)
rejection (*radd*), 5, 6, 22, 31, 46, 92, 121, 179, 229, 245, 276, 289, 292, 303, 307, 317, 335, 343. *See also* acceptance
release (*rahāʾī*), 130, 196, 257, 417, 432, 452, 453, 456, 462, 464, 491
reliance (*iʿtimād*)
religion (*dīn*), xlii, lxvi, 3, 20, 21, 34, 41, 48, 64, 72, 81, 89, 132, 134, 192, 199, 200, 205–6, 212, 256, 261, 262, 273, 281, 299, 304, 329, 334, 355, 371, 374, 382, 388, 408, 414, 415, 454–56, 461, 484; (*madhhab*), of love, xxviii, 401
remembrance (*dhikr, yād*), xvi-xvii, lx, 72, 89, 96, 99, 105, 107, 116, 118, 119, 124, 126, 129, 153, 155, 159, 163, 165, 168, 181, 187, 189, 191, 198, 205–8, 217, 240, 243, 258–59, 267, 271, 275, 288, 291, 298, 301, 320, 334, 337, 339, 358, 361, 365, 367, 392, 398, 399, 412, 415, 432, 441, 457, 478; formulae of (*adhkār*), 132
remorse (*ḥasrat*), 28, 66–67, 85, 225, 277, 288, 307, 334, 374–75, 398, 427–28, 456; of Adam, 13, 43, 66, 106, 183, 232, 318–19
renunciation (*zuhd*), xvii, xxi, xxii, xxxv, xxxix, 26, 59, 90, 129, 152, 200, 261, 270, 279, 288, 294, 317, 388
repentance (*tawbat*), liv, 20, 52, 186, 222, 269, 287–89, 292, 303, 305, 309, 337, 392, 399–400, 422–23, 428–31, 488
report (*khabar*), 33, 140, 146, 156, 197, 319, 377; vs. vision, 318, 330, 379–80, 450; (=hadith), 72, 160, 197, 200, 244, 245, 247, 255, 257, 281, 302, 305, 329, 347, 359, 370, 388; sound, 17, 117, 257, 325, 428, 430. *See also* hadith
repose (*rawḥ*), xliv, 40, 153, 215, 458; of the spirit, 45, 67, 119, 122, 212, 160, 229, 264, 407
resident (*sākin*)
resolve, resoluteness (*ʿazm*), 41, 63, 98, 111, 133, 147, 153, 204–5, 216, 224, 362, 400
respite (*muhlat*), 5, 183, 226, 309, 424, 491
response (*ijābat, jawāb*), 5, 10, 31, 61, 163, 264, 276, 287, 288, 307, 313, 392, 428, 445, 457, 465. *See also* supplication
responsibility (*ḥaqq ʿalayh, ʿuhda*), 128, 289
rest (*ārām, qarār, sukūn*), 7, 17, 39, 76, 83, 97, 131, 146, 218, 238, 254, 262, 409, 474. *See also* movement
resurrection (*qiyāmat*), 27, 59, 64, 146, 148, 150, 161, 163, 178, 183–84, 197, 205, 230, 231, 241, 248, 249, 252–54, 257, 260, 261, 281, 285, 293–95, 314, 315, 321, 325, 327, 328, 334, 338, 347, 353, 370–71, 373, 375–78, 384, 385, 388, 412, 425, 427, 430, 435, 444–47, 455–57, 460
retaliation (*qaṣāṣ*), 5, 334
return (*maʿād, rujūʿ*), 67, 136, 137, 143, 148, 269, 282, 291, 308, 352, 360, 375, 415, 446, 457, 481
revelation (*waḥy, tanzīl*), 9, 15, 27, 30, 47, 51, 80, 105, 119, 128, 129, 134, 136, 155, 156, 159, 161, 162, 164, 166, 180, 189, 194, 198, 209–10, 213, 219, 255, 269, 270, 308, 310, 312, 313, 317, 319, 343, 359, 374, 382, 383, 398, 399, 403, 406, 410, 411, 442
revelry (*ṭarab*)
reverence (*taʿẓīm, ḥurmat*), 44, 90, 181, 335, 354, 355, 408, 413, 492
reward (*thawāb*), 12, 72, 92, 171, 258, 292, 297, 347, 350, 369, 405, 422, 466, 473; and punishment, xvi, lxvii, 47, 178, 298, 347, 378, 431
rich (*tawāngar, ghanī*), 28, 281–82, 336, 376. *See also* poverty, unneedy
ribat (*ribāṭ*), xxxi; Ribāṭ al-Sulṭān, xxv
ridicule (*hajw*)
Riḍwān (angel in charge of paradise), 6, 55, 138, 142, 143, 218, 230, 231, 235, 268, 422, 469

Rifāʿī, Aḥmad (d. 578/1182), 499n110, 520n726
right (*yamīn, rāst*), and left (*shimāl, chap*), 75, 131, 135, 136, 145, 163, 260, 352–53, 356, 425, 427, 451; right hand, 92, 95, 226, 249, 251, 360, 372, 379, 414, 484
rightful due, right (*ḥaqq*), 8, 19, 28, 38–39, 50, 51, 56, 60, 65, 70, 104, 123, 130, 140, 151, 175, 186, 212, 218, 226, 259, 262, 264, 283, 287, 297, 300, 302, 303, 312, 313, 316, 323, 326, 331, 334, 338, 339, 347, 350, 353, 383, 386, 396, 397, 404, 408, 409, 424, 439, 454, 456, 466, 475, 487
rīḥ, 70
rijāl, in Hadith, xiv; in Sufism, xxiii
rite (*shāʿira*), 55, 88, 398
riyāḍ, 147; *riyāḍa*, 147
road, path (*rāh, sabīl, ṭarīq*), xxix-xxx, xlii, 10, 19, 23–24, 29–30, 34, 35, 38, 43, 48, 54, 56, 64, 65, 75, 81–82, 85–87, 91, 95–96, 98, 100, 102, 109, 113–15, 121–22, 125, 126, 130, 133, 134, 137, 139–42, 145, 148, 150, 154, 159, 163, 167, 169, 172, 176, 178–79, 183, 184, 187, 191, 194–95, 197, 201, 202, 204, 209–10, 212–13, 218, 225–26, 228, 229, 231–33, 236, 249, 257–58, 261–63, 266, 273, 275, 277–78, 280, 281, 285, 290, 297, 300, 316, 318, 324, 325, 329, 334, 335, 340, 341, 342, 359, 362–66, 372, 378, 384, 385, 388, 389, 396, 403–4, 406, 410, 412, 414, 417, 419, 425, 428, 432, 435, 437, 441, 444, 446, 448, 450, 452–53, 464, 471, 472, 474–77, 481, 483, 484, 488, 492, 494–95. *See also* love
Rostam, 56, 133, 218
Rūdakī (d. 329/940), xlvii, 503n233
Rūdhbārī, Abū ʿAlī Aḥmad ibn Muḥammad (d. 322/933), xxii
Rūdhbārī, Aḥmad ibn ʿAṭāʾ (d. 369/980), xxii
rūḥ, xliv, 70; *rūḥ allāh*, 533n1113; *rūḥ al-qudus*, 533n1113; *arwāḥ*, xliv
rule (*ḥukm, rasm*)
rulership (*wilāyat*), 45, 90, 94, 144, 182, 191, 193, 197, 245, 315–16, 324, 354, 373, 374, 382, 406
ruling (*ḥukm*), 35, 40, 167, 182, 225, 254, 256, 358, 456, 462, 474; ruling authority (*salṭanat*), 169, 241, 361, 378, 382; ruling power (*sulṭān*), 12, 22, 53, 54, 70, 76–77, 99, 106, 107, 150, 156, 203, 350, 361, 380, 477 (*see also* sultan); ruling property (*ḥukm*), 289, 332, 368, 431, 480
Rūmī, Jalāl al-Dīn (d. 672/1273), xi, xii, xiii, xiv, xlvii, l, lxiii, lxvi, lxixn1, 499n109, 501n170, 503n226, 511n452, 514n544, 514n549, 518n673, 519n705, 535n1205, 538n1283
Ruwaym (ibn Aḥmad, d. 303/915), 92, 504n248, 504n254, 506n313, 506n331
Rūzbihān (Baqlī, d. 606/1209), 511n455

Sabziwārī, Mullā Hādī (d. 1873), liii
Sacred Mosque (*masjid-i ḥarām*), 88, 221, 261, 262, 381
sacrifice (*fidāʾ, qurbān*), 61, 62, 74, 81, 107, 150, 185, 187, 196, 211, 216, 293, 308, 341, 344, 349, 390, 391, 397, 411, 418, 432, 437, 484, 486, 494
Saʿd (ibn Abī Waqqāṣ, d. 55/674), 153, 462
Saʿd ibn ʿUbayda, 363
ṣadāqa, 507n351
Saʿdī Shīrāzī (d. 690/1292), xi, 496n19
Saʿdūn Majnūn, 487
Safa, 20, 55, 73–74, 88
safety (*ʿāfiyat, salāmat*)
safina, 195
Ṣāḥib ibn ʿAbbād (d. 385/925), 506n307, 533n1139
Sahl ibn ʿAbdallāh Tustarī, 19, 62, 65, 80, 532n1089, 532n1110
Sahl Kammūnī (Abu'l-Qāsim ibn Muḥammad, d. 557/1162), xxxviii
sahw, 532n1095
Saʿīd ibn Ḥamīd (d. ca. 250/864), 501n180
Saʿīd ibn Jubayr (d. 95/714), 534n1161
Saʿīd ibn Musayyib (d. 94/712), 456
Ṣakhr the jinni, 197
sakīna, 195
salāma, 14
ṣalāt, 401
ṣāliḥ, xxxiii
Ṣāliḥ (the prophet), 200, 305
Ṣāliḥ Murrī (d. ca. 172/788), 221
Salmān (Fārisī, d. ca. 35/655), 69, 386, 388, 392, 393, 463, 530n1047
salvation (*najāt*), 132, 163, 195, 370, 427, 453, 483, 485
samāʿ, xiv, xxi, 77

Sam'ān, xv
Samanids, 316
Sam'ānī, 'Abd al-Karīm (Abū Sa'd ibn Muḥammad ibn Manṣūr al-Sam'ānī, d. 562/1166), xiv-xv, xx-xxvii, xxxi-xliii, xlvi-xlvii, lvi, 516n620; *Adab al-imlā'*, xxxi; *Ansāb (Ascriptions)*, xiv-xv, 503n239, 507n352, 516n620, 529n998, 539n1333; *Muntakhab (Abridgement)*, xiv-xv
Sam'ānī, 'Abd al-Raḥīm (Abu'l-Muẓaffar ibn 'Abd al-Karīm), xxii
Sam'ānī, 'Abd al-Wahhāb (Abu'l-Muẓaffar ibn Muḥammad ibn Manṣūr, d. 517/1123), xx, xxiii, xxv
Sam'ānī, 'Alī (Abu'l-Qāsim ibn Muḥammad ibn 'Abd al-Jabbār), xv-xvi, lxxn16
Sam'ānī, 'Alī ibn 'Alī (Abu'l-'Alā'), xvi
Sam'ānī, Aḥmad ibn Manṣūr (Abu'l-Qāsim, d. 534/1140), xi-xiii, xxi, xxiii-xxviii, 495n1
Sam'ānī, Ḥasan ibn Manṣūr, xxii-xxiii
Sam'ānī, Ḥurra (Amatallāh), xx, xxiii
Sam'ānī, Manṣūr (Abu'l-Muẓaffar ibn Muḥammad ibn 'Abd al-Jabbār, d. 489/1096), xv-xix, xxii, xxiv, xxvi, xxxi-xxxv, xxxvii, xxxviii, xl, xlvi, lxxn16; (Shaykh al-Islām/my paragon/my father), 50, 51, 58, 108, 134, 180, 188, 228, 236, 284, 337, 418, 463, 500n150, 505n293, 508n387, 509n409, 509n417, 514n555, 523n828, 524n849, 527n952, 527n953, 531n1072
Sam'ānī, Muḥammad ibn 'Abd al-Jabbār (Abū Manṣūr, d. 450/1058), xiv, xv
Sam'ānī, Muḥammad ibn 'Abd al-Karīm (Abū Zayd), xxii
Sam'ānī, Muḥammad ibn Aḥmad (Tāj al-Islām Abū Bakr), xxviii
Sam'ānī, Muḥammad ibn Ḥasan (Abū Manṣūr, d. 533/1139), xxiii
Sam'ānī, Muḥammad ibn Manṣūr (Abū Bakr, d. 510/1116), xviii-xxiv, xxvii, xxxiv, xxxvii, xlv, lxxin36, lxxiin76, lxxivn134, 201
Samarqandī, Abu'l-Layth (Naṣr ibn Muḥammad, d. 373/983), xlvi; *Baḥr*, 530n1019; *Tanbīh*, 520n728, 534n1150
Samaw'al ibn 'Ādiyā (6th c.), 514n558
Samnūn al-Muḥibb (d. ca. 300/912), 500n149, 529n989
Sanā'ī (Abu'l-Majd Majdūd, d. 535/1140), xiv, xlvii; *Dīwān*, 497n43, 498n79, 499n97, 499n109, 500n121, 501n165, 501n175, 502n206, 504n256, 505n276, 505n286, 505n297, 506n315, 507n337, 508n374, 508n386, 509n411, 510n428, 512n487, 513n518, 514n543, 517n632, 517n648, 517n654, 517n655, 518n662, 518n672, 518n675, 519n694, 519n699, 520n749, 521n773, 522n780, 522n781, 523n821, 523n824, 533n1132, 534n1148, 537n1248, 538n1272, 538n1277, 540n1342; *Sayr*, 518n659, 518n660, 522n807
Ṣanawbarī, Abū Bakr (d. 334/945), 519n696
sanctuary (*ḥaram*), 74, 79, 88, 130, 190, 272–73, 280, 336, 402, 404, 409, 410, 422, 454, 455, 474
Sarah, 245
Sarakhs, xx, xxiv, xxxviii
Sarakhsī, Nāṣir ibn Aḥmad (Abu'l-Fatḥ, d. 514/1120), xxxiv
Sarī Saqaṭī (d. ca. 252/865), 5, 22, 213
Sarrāj (Abu'l-Naṣr, d. 378/988), *Luma'*, 498n85, 500n148
sash (*zunnār*), 16, 21, 41, 76, 94, 126, 167, 225, 283, 362, 390, 392, 394, 398, 418, 460
Sassanid Empire, xiii, 523n824
Satan (*shayṭān*), lii, 20, 64, 106, 122, 135, 194, 202, 205, 207, 231, 247, 262, 270, 292, 293, 303, 346, 347, 348–51, 353, 373, 410, 515n576, 520n741; satans, 22, 85, 145, 189, 202, 328, 504n261; satanity, 6, 342. *See also* Iblis
Saturn, 218
Sawsaqānī, Muḥammad (Abū Bakr ibn Aḥmad ibn al-Ḥasan, d. ca. 510/1116), xxiii
Sayf al-Dawla ('Alī ibn 'Abdallāh al-Ḥamdānī, d. 356/967), 72–73, 503n220, 524n852, 531n1063
Sayf ibn Dhī Yazan (d. 578), 522n786
Sayyidī, Hibatallāh (Abū Muḥammad ibn Sahl, d. 533/1138), xxiv, xxv, xxxix, xl
scales (*tarāzū, mīzān*), 35, 54, 65, 112, 121, 201, 204, 231, 375, 420, 449, 457, 460
scent (*bū, rīḥ*), 241–42
scissors (*miqrāḍ, gāz*), 247, 468, 473
scorn (*ḥaqārat*)
scoundrel (*qalandar*), 111, 410
script (*raqam, khaṭṭ*)

scrupulosity (*wara'*), xvii, xxii, xxxviii, 411, 413, 469
seal (*khātam, muhr*), 39, 41, 121, 146, 152, 192–94, 200, 209, 216, 227, 262, 279, 297, 332, 348, 350, 384, 397, 468–69, 529n1013
seclusion (*khalwat*), xxxviii, 24, 29, 48, 61, 82, 93, 126, 191, 267, 304, 317, 372, 435, 446, 482, 483, 486
secret (*sirr*), 7, 11, 14, 17, 33, 35, 41, 44, 55, 59, 70–71, 84, 88–89, 100, 111–12, 121–23, 126, 129–31, 133, 141, 146, 148, 153, 156, 164, 188–89, 209, 223, 231, 241, 262, 263, 275, 279, 317, 335, 337–39, 343, 392, 393, 433, 440, 450, 453, 479, 483, 488, 493; of Adam, 47, 76, 97–98, 123, 129, 142–44, 168, 170, 176, 177, 187, 216–17, 231, 233, 234, 235, 237, 241, 249, 283, 310, 314, 324, 333–34, 356, 399, 423, 426, 459, 489; of love, 86, 113, 120, 175, 177, 218, 242, 248, 251, 323, 367; secret core (*sirr*), 4, 6–7, 10, 11, 33, 47, 48, 61, 74, 76, 77, 80, 88–89, 90, 92, 120, 122, 123, 125, 147, 149, 153, 157, 180–82, 201, 212–13, 216, 250, 261–62, 282, 283, 298, 299, 319, 323, 330, 348, 352–53, 364, 371, 407, 411, 415, 418, 420, 423, 443, 453, 493; secret core of Muhammad, 146, 162–63, 166, 193, 199, 253–55, 257, 271, 273, 325, 349, 356, 413, 427, 442, 482; secret whispering (*rāz*), 10, 106, 138, 189–90, 216, 232, 233, 252, 261, 266, 333, 415, 476
security (*amn*)
seeking (*ṭalab, justan*), 7, 8, 11, 23–24, 37, 54, 56–57, 74, 98–99, 108, 140, 167, 176, 179, 182, 204, 209–12, 216, 232–33, 235, 240, 242–43, 250, 262, 273, 277, 278, 316, 330, 352, 418, 450, 483; and finding, 24, 74, 141, 209–12, 287, 330, 366
self (*khwud, khwīsh, nafs*), xlviii, 37, 201–2, 205; obstacle of, 91, 157, 201, 223, 225; levels of, 4, 153, 162, 163, 212, 253–56, 262–64. *See also* soul, spirit
self-admiration (*'ujb*), 16, 52–53, 97, 158, 206, 222, 225, 269–70, 291, 321–22, 355–56, 449, 488
self-determination (*taṣarruf*), 124, 390
self-disclosure (*tajallī*), lii, lv, 8, 102, 111, 128, 159, 166, 181, 197, 277, 330, 332, 343, 372, 483
self-goverance. *See* governance
self-made (*khwīshtan-sākhta*), 202, 238
self-restraint (*khwīshtan-dārī*), 206, 261, 289
self-seeing (*khwīshtan-bīnī*), 64, 68, 85, 239, 248, 362
Self-Standing (*qayyūm*), 146, 334, 385, 389, 407
self-sufficiency (*ṣamadiyyat*), 10, 11, 38, 79, 85, 130, 193, 277, 398, 427, 440, 462
senses, sense faculties (*ḥawāss*), 46, 120, 132–35, 145–46, 213, 263–64, 297, 314, 371, 433; senseless (*bīhūsh*), 125, 138
separation (*firāq, judā'ī*), 5–6, 40, 67, 75–76, 152, 245, 267, 276, 289, 297, 322; and union, 14–15, 22, 34–36, 95, 103, 119, 121, 132, 138, 152, 176, 183, 187, 271, 344–45, 367–68, 369, 433, 441, 446, 457
Seraphiel (Isrāfīl), 5, 27, 35, 55, 123, 125, 231, 324, 333, 402–3, 476, 492, 493
serene (*muṭma'inn*), 238; soul, 67, 92, 145, 359, 481
seriousness (*jidd*)
sermon (*khuṭba*)
servanthood (*'ubūdiyyat, bandagī*), 56. *See* Lordhood
service (*khidmat*), 54, 112, 117, 149, 154, 160, 163, 181, 200, 205, 256, 258, 298, 311, 314, 322, 327, 335, 347, 353, 369, 373, 374, 379, 382, 389, 408, 411, 429, 447, 487, 490, 492
session (*majlis*)
Seth, 200, 412
settledness (*qarār*)
severance (*inqiṭā'*)
severity (*qahr*), 5–7, 98–99, 105, 110, 174, 178, 181, 218, 235, 276–77, 357, 378. *See also* gentleness
Sha'bī ('Āmir ibn Sharāḥīl, d. ca. 105/723), 313
Shādhān ibn 'Abdallāh, 129
Shāfi'ī, Muḥammad ibn Idrīs (d. 204/820), xlv, 18, 121, 175
Shafi'i jurisprudence, xvi, xviii, xxii, xxiii, xxiv, xxvii, xli, 505n293
Shahadah, liv, lxiv, lxvi, 131, 287
shahīd, xxvi, 26, 432; *shāhid*, 432
shame (*ḥayā', sharm, nang*), 12, 26–28, 44, 71, 85, 89, 90, 92, 148, 207, 237, 245, 255,

269, 270, 333, 373, 397, 406, 413, 419, 423, 439, 452, 454, 483; of God, 28, 309
shape (*shakl*), 35, 84, 87, 123, 135, 144–46, 218, 227, 418
share (*ḥaẓẓ, naṣīb*), 8, 11, 40, 61, 76, 186, 229, 293, 302, 321, 323, 331, 335, 347, 367, 443; seeking one's own, 84, 278, 367, 449, 474
sharḥ, lii
Shariah (*sharī'at*), 37, 56, 73, 112, 134, 185, 189, 191, 192, 198, 206, 256, 262, 264, 327, 340, 353, 361, 382, 397, 404, 411, 414, 436, 439, 442, 445–46, 454, 455, 474, 494; of love, 286, 288, 510n435; and Tariqah (and/or Haqiqah), xvii, xxx, xxxiii, 17, 51, 114, 125–27, 132, 140, 143, 176, 201, 225, 261, 264, 316, 343, 356, 371, 405, 416, 476, 495n1, 507n357
Sharīf al-Raḍī, al- (d. 406/1015), 519n692, 535n1191
Sharīfa Furāwī (Umm al-Kirām bint Muḥammad, d. 536/1141–42), xxv
shawq, lxi
Shayba (ibn Rabī'a, d. 2/624), 410
shaykh, xx-xxi, xxx-xxxiv, 53, 81, 202, 239, 336, 338, 402, 450
Sheba, 301, 325
Shiblī (Abū Bakr, d. 334/946), 18, 31, 40, 54, 78, 81, 92–93, 95, 119, 150, 152, 179, 251, 263, 265–66, 331, 342, 347, 361, 366, 373, 386, 394–95, 498n69, 498n85, 501n158, 501n187, 503n223, 505n283, 508n380, 509n397, 510n431, 511n467, 511n471, 513n516, 518n683, 522n787, 524n847, 525n871, 525n882, 525n890, 533n1121, 534n1143, 535n1175
shirk, lxvi
Shīruwī, 'Abd al-Ghaffār al- (Abū Bakr ibn Muḥammad, d. 510/1117), xxi, xxiv, xxvii, xli, lxxiin80
shortcoming (*taqṣīr*), 84, 163, 255, 268, 309, 323, 334, 368, 382, 423, 487–88
Shu'ayb, 17, 27, 54, 305, 447
Shu'ayb ibn Ḥarb, 54
Shurayḥ (ibn Ḥārith), Qāḍī (d. ca. 90/710), 346
showing (*numūdan*)
sieve (*ghirbāl*)
Siffin, Battle of, 481
sight (*baṣar*)
signet (*tawqī'*)
Sijzī, Amīr Ḥasan (d. 738/1337), xii
similarity (*mushābahat*), 264. assertion/declaration of similarity (*tashbīh*), liv-lv, 61, 111, 123, 167, 174, 491
simpleton (*salīm-dil, ablah*), 64, 80, 276, 373
sin (*gunāh, dhanb, ithm, jināya*), 16, 18, 22, 27, 28, 40, 60, 63–64, 68, 71, 118, 122, 127, 149, 169, 172, 175, 177, 185, 187, 197, 206–9, 219–20, 222–23, 232, 241, 244, 245, 248, 249, 253, 255, 257, 268–69, 286, 288, 289, 291–94, 296, 297, 303, 305, 309, 335, 344, 349, 350, 352, 358, 361, 362, 367, 368, 371, 382, 384, 400, 408, 422, 423, 427, 428, 430–31, 433, 439, 445, 446, 451, 457, 467, 475, 481, 488, 489, 494; great sins (*kabā'ir*), 112, 241, 255, 268, 295, 311, 375, 446
Sinai, Mount, 10, 17, 100, 111, 139, 153, 180, 181, 193, 197, 242, 332, 418, 425, 466, 480
sincerity (*ikhlāṣ*), 41, 53, 206, 212, 270, 274, 302, 384, 406. *See also* truthfulness
singling out (*takhṣīṣ*)
Sinjidhān, xxi, xxxviii
sinlessness (*'iṣma*), 177, 244, 297, 338, 411; of angels, 58–59, 127, 173, 181, 217, 238, 335, 372, 384, 408, 483, 492, 493; of Muḥammad, 207, 325, 327, 383, 389, 397; of prophets, 38, 99, 106, 139, 190, 197, 200, 206, 216, 245, 246, 303, 314, 376, 382–84, 388, 397, 440, 453, 462, 475, 479, 493
sīra, xxxix
sirāj, 412
Sirhindī, Aḥmad (d. 1034/1624), 518n682
Siyāh, Bū 'Alī (d. 434/1033), 50, 334, 387
skirt (*dāman*)
slip (*zallat*), 9, 185, 204, 313, 362, 488, 494. *See also* Adam
snare (*dām*)
snatching (*rubūdan*)
sobriety (*ṣaḥw*), 96, 114. *See* intoxication
solace (*salwat, qurra*), 323, 331, 339, 348
solicitude (*'ināyat*), lxiii, 10, 22, 47, 57, 90, 215, 232, 237, 294, 337, 352, 356; beginningless, 61, 62, 111, 167, 229, 248, 456; and kind favor, 62, 132, 187, 370, 381, 400, 455

solitary (*fard, mufrad*), God as, 4, 55, 95, 151, 214, 240, 440; man as, 96, 100, 115, 137, 151, 176, 214, 240, 268, 274, 440. solitariness (*fardiyyat, fardāniyyat, tafrīd*), 39, 84, 87, 94, 137, 152, 277, 300. *See also* disengagement
Solomon, 101, 205, 269, 299, 317, 325, 361, 371, 400; and the ants, 202–3, 329; and Bilqīs, 126, 301, 325, 351, 428; of the heart, 348; and the horses, 337, 349, 391; kingdom of, 197, 250, 328, 347–50, 355, 376, 393, 476; 529n1018, 533n1118, 533n1123
sorcery (*siḥr, jādū*), 103, 211, 442. *See also* Moses
sorrow (*ḥuzn, andūh, ghamm*), 19, 26, 40, 67, 72, 91, 102, 108, 151, 170–71, 184, 244, 264, 267, 313, 318, 323, 342, 372, 398, 416, 423, 427, 454, 457, 469, 470, 476, 492; and happiness, 91, 96, 107, 109, 231, 285, 288, 371, 384, 393, 441; house of sorrows (*bayt al-aḥzān*), 12, 128. *See also* Jacob
soul (*nafs*), xliv-xlv, 10, 64, 67, 91, 136, 176, 185, 213, 225, 257, 261, 334, 419, 455, 466, 513n510; animal, 145; appetitive, 145; blaming, 145; and body, 116, 135, 137, 163, 212; prison of, 109, 245, 261, 263; commanding/deceiving, 91, 106, 145, 149, 246, 367, 446; opposition to, 74, 92, 120, 130, 212, 254, 264, 283, 351, 386–87, 406; lack of, 254; serene, 67, 145, 359, 481; sorts of, 245; tumult-inciting, 67, 69, 263; soulish (*nafsānī*), 304. *See also* heart, self, spirit
soundness (*ṣiḥḥat*)
space, open space (*faḍā'*), 41, 53, 58, 74, 124, 304, 459, 481; of the decree (*qaḍā'*), 5, 65, 396, 411; of existence, 216, 233, 485
specter (*ṭayf*), 104, 119, 433
speech (*sukhan, qawl, kalām, guftār*), of animals and objects, 354, 372–73, 395; of God, xlviii, 54, 174, 178, 189, 240, 366, 377–78, 392, 438, 478, 491, 493; human, 52, 111, 112, 129, 135–36, 146, 189, 332, 366, 368, 408, 416. *See also* Moses
spend (*infāq*)
sperm (*manī*), 406; sperm drop (*nuṭfa*), 61, 90, 92, 156, 189, 209, 287, 298, 305, 378
sphere, celestial sphere (*falak*), 13, 14, 18, 35, 45, 47, 57, 69, 86, 104, 110, 112, 120, 121, 130, 135–36, 140, 144, 147, 158, 178, 182, 184, 187, 191, 192, 202, 204, 207, 237, 239, 263, 267, 275, 316, 325, 328, 335, 343, 372, 374, 414, 426, 431, 438, 451, 458, 462, 465, 475, 476
spirit (*rūḥ, jān*), 136, 180, 299, 469, 476, 485, 509n417, 533n1113; and body/soul, 25–26, 36, 107, 116, 132, 137, 145, 165, 169, 211, 225, 236–37, 253–56, 262–64, 275–76, 279, 299, 304, 314, 323, 327, 331, 363–64, 396, 408, 446, 453, 458, 467, 481; Faithful, 199, 471, 489. spiritual (*rūḥānī*), 58, 136, 146, 213, 263, 304, 387, 423; and bodily/corporeal, 158, 237, 275, 317
splendor (*majd, bahā'*)
spoils (*ghanīmat*)
spokesman (*tarjumān*)
spring (*bahār*)
sprite (*parī*), 369
spy (*jāsūs*), 96, 133, 280, 311, 380
stability (*tamkīn*), 107, 113, 165
staff (*'aṣā'*)
stage (*marḥala*)
stain (*lawth, shayn*)
stalwarts (*ṣanādīd*), 67, 68, 272, 381, 393, 408
star (*sitāra, najm*), 45, 47, 84–85, 138, 161, 183, 189, 193, 195, 198, 202, 233, 273, 278–79, 324, 361, 378–80, 382, 411, 414, 432, 465, 482, 483, 494; north star (*farqadayn*), 193, 199, 262
state (*ḥāl*), 119, 316, 476. *See* station
station (*maqām*), 273–74; and states, xxxviii, xlvi, 41, 215, 441
stationlessness (*bī-maqāmī*), 273, 441
status (*jāh*)
steed (*markab, maṭiyya*)
stillness, rest (*sukūn*), 22, 36, 75, 112, 474. *See also* movement
stipulation (*sharṭ*)
stone (*sang, ḥajar*)
storehouse (*khizāna*), 78, 232, 292, 299, 342, 390, 411, 428
straight (*rāst*)
stranger. *See* estranged
stratagem (*ḥīlat*), 57, 74, 79, 161, 229, 240, 263, 285, 302, 331, 335, 353, 359, 365, 367, 468, 481, 486
strength (*quwwat*)
striving (*jahd*)

struggle (*mujāhadat*), xl, 10, 39, 53, 56, 89, 116, 120, 132, 144, 146, 153, 162, 167, 172, 190, 212, 215, 264, 285, 293, 307, 353, 362, 383, 400, 413, 429
subjection (*taskhīr*), 133, 155, 185, 197, 202, 213, 230, 263, 295, 296, 328, 349, 370, 452, 494
subjugated (*maqhūr*), 33, 96, 164, 245, 272, 329, 447
Subkī, Tāj al-Dīn (d. 771/1370), xv, xvi, xix, xxi, xxii, xxiv-xxv, xxviii, 505n293
submission (*islām*), xxix, 48, 138, 333, 354, 382, 392, 393, 409, 457–59, 461, 462–63, 466, 478; and faith, 332, 425, 455
subsequent (*lāḥiq*). *See* precedent
subsistence (*baqāʾ*), 5, 8, 16, 29, 39, 62–63, 66, 86, 90, 119, 125, 127, 132, 148, 149, 164, 182, 193, 250, 260–63, 337, 341, 419, 438, 439, 443, 446, 477, 481. *See also* annihilation
substance (*gawhar, jawhar*), 128, 134, 136, 157, 209, 228, 234, 236, 252, 314; and accident, 61
Substitutes (*abdāl*), 17, 147, 264, 444, 466, 479, 496n13, 536n1229
subtle (*laṭīf*), subtlety (*laṭāfa*), 13, 20, 67, 89, 98, 120, 123, 137, 146, 155, 182, 183, 187, 223, 228, 235, 236, 264, 319, 327, 364, 390, 399, 401, 419, 509n417; and dense, 137, 229, 234, 236–37, 279, 299, 314, 333, 458–59, 493, 515n570
success, success-giving (*tawfīq*), 62, 122, 136, 157, 258, 269, 287, 300, 368, 381, 383, 401, 420, 421–22, 428, 437
Suʿdā, 35
Suddī (Ismāʿīl ibn ʿAbd al-Raḥmān, d. 127/745), 326
suffering (*ranj*)
sufficiency (*kifāyat*), 72, 89, 90, 132, 352, 359
Sufism (*taṣawwuf*), xvii, xxviii-xli, xlvi, liii, 77, 124, 179, 261, 288, 500n137, 521n778; Sufi (*ṣūfī*), xxxvii, 51, 82, 103
Sufyān ibn ʿUyayna (d. 198/814), 508n367
Sufyān Thawrī (d. 161/777–78), 28, 326, 358, 480, 507n341, 538n1267
Ṣuhayb ibn Sinān (d. 38/659), 17, 386, 388, 392, 393, 463
Sulamī, Abū ʿAbd al-Raḥmān (Muḥammad ibn al-Ḥusayn al-Nīshābūrī, d. 412/1021), xxv, xxxiv, xxxvi; *Ḥaqāʾiq al-tafsīr*, 498n89, 499n114, 503n219, 512n500, 524n847, 525n887, 532n1089, 532n1090; *Ṭabaqāt al-ṣūfiyya*, 499n113, 501n187, 508n364, 537n1250
Sulaymān Taymī (d. 143/760), 535n1181
sultan (*sulṭān*), 5–7, 9, 14, 23, 25, 34, 41, 44, 47, 56, 65, 70, 81, 85, 86, 89–90, 96, 107, 118, 120, 124, 127, 133, 140, 141, 151, 152, 166, 167, 172, 178, 182, 235, 238, 239, 249, 259, 261, 265, 266, 273, 276, 279, 280, 287, 299, 318, 320, 321, 332, 342, 344, 364, 392, 393, 397, 401, 405, 410, 414, 416, 420, 421, 423–25, 433, 435, 441, 451, 467, 468, 469, 472, 475, 476, 477, 482, 485, 486, 494, 495; of knowledge, 41, 127, 176, 182, 185, 189, 192, 193, 196, 202, 217, 219, 220, 224, 228; of love, 122, 143, 155, 178, 218, 327, 396, 407, 492; of majesty, 124, 140, 285; of power, 46, 315, 319, 450; and slaves/beggars, 12–13, 45, 46, 96, 111, 170–72, 213, 223–24, 228–29, 233, 259, 311–12, 354, 396, 424, 469.
sultanate (*salṭanat*), 203, 209, 258, 427; of Adam, 46, 59, 97, 113, 158, 184, 216, 249, 264, 283, 321
sun (*shams, khurshīd*), and moon, 34, 57, 120, 153, 183, 185, 187, 190, 191, 195, 198, 239, 268, 273, 278–79, 357, 378, 379, 397, 431, 438, 458, 494
Sundus, 533n1130
Sunnah (*sunnat*), xxxi, 124, 129–30, 303, 332, 411, 414, 442, 447, 491; folk of, 9, 51–52, 158, 174, 230, 285, 290, 405; secret of, 287
supererogatory (*nāfila*), 334, 428
superiority (*faḍīlat*)
supplication (*duʿāʾ*), 38, 61, 89, 91, 94, 116, 129, 171, 181, 205–6, 250, 277, 292, 312, 336, 392, 393, 399, 402, 422, 426–29, 431, 436–37, 452, 486, 493; and response, 118, 220, 222, 287, 291, 294, 302–7, 357, 392, 399, 429, 431, 452
supposition (*gumān*)
ṣūra, li, 510n422
surrender (*taslīm*), 9, 20, 49, 89, 96, 116, 186, 203, 241, 257, 352, 353, 360, 365, 392, 394, 409, 412, 413, 437

suspicion (*tuhmat*), 24, 26, 275, 352, 410, 471
sweetness (*ḥalāwat*)
synagogue (*kunasht*), 26, 69, 114, 374, 484
Syria, 160, 188, 365, 479, 515n591

tablecloth (*sufra*)
tablet (*lawḥ*). Guarded Tablet (*lawḥ-i maḥfūẓ*), 27, 51, 117, 120, 147, 489
tadhkīr, xvii-xviii, lxv
Ṭāhā, 161, 199, 478, 516n618
taḥqīq, lxi
Taif, 183, 234, 390, 438, 468, 489
tainted (*ālūda*), 17, 84, 127, 168, 285, 375, 407, 410, 420, 430, 431, 479, 485; and pure, 22, 229, 446, 463
takbīr, 256
takhalluq bi-akhlāq Allāh, lv, lx
taklīfī, lxvi
talāwat, 130
Ṭalḥa (d. 36/656), 462
talisman (*chashm-zakhm*), 69, 234, 244–46, 502n206
talk (*ḥadīth*), 332–33; this talk, 29, 56, 66, 85, 95, 106, 108, 118, 125–26, 129–30, 142, 149, 155, 180, 203–5, 229, 241, 278, 316, 331, 366, 384–88, 398, 406, 415, 417, 418, 426, 433, 442, 443, 456, 462, 476–77; and Adamites, 157, 170, 194, 231, 384, 466
Tangarī, 94
tanzīh, liv-lv, lxii, lxiv
taqallub, 77
taqdīr, lxvii
taqlīd, lxi
taqwā, 130
tarbiya, xxx, xxxix, 131
Tariqah (*ṭarīqat*), xvii, 7, 54, 92, 109, 138, 179, 203, 220, 239, 241, 257, 284, 330, 340, 412, 460–61, 474; and Haqiqah, 91, 94, 98, 234, 307, 319, 347, 352, 353, 360. *See also* Shariah
taṣawwuf, xvii, xli, 523n840; *mutaṣawwif*, xli
tashbīh, liv-lv, lxii, lxiv
taṣwīr, li
ta'ṭīl, lv
tavern (*kharābāt, maṣṭaba*), tavern-goer (*kharābātī*), 20, 22, 26, 37, 39, 41, 64, 95–97, 110–11, 121, 133, 149, 170, 175, 196, 210, 232, 251, 267–69, 317, 367, 387, 405, 410, 416, 423, 432, 474, 487, 488
tawakkul, 503n230, 530n1021
tawba, liv, 428
tawḥīd, liv-lv, lxiii, lxv-lxvii, 11, 18, 20, 28, 41, 70, 74, 89, 115, 119, 140, 149–52, 155, 198, 202, 207, 212, 274, 279, 300, 301, 307, 318, 330–31, 337, 348, 351, 364, 380, 390, 394, 409, 413, 420, 438, 455, 476, 485, 489, 518n682; formula (*kalima*) of, 199, 356, 427; *tawḥīd*-voicer (*muwaḥḥid*), 7, 33, 39, 52, 63, 72, 296, 333, 374, 405, 438, 441, 446–48; *tawḥīd*-reciting (*tahlīl, muhallil*), 13, 42, 85, 176. *See also* glorification
Tawḥīdī, Abū Ḥayyān 'Alī (d. ca. 400/1010), 503n244, 504n270, 508n381, 508n385, 514n546, 530n1040, 533n1130
Ṭāwūs ibn Kaysān al-Yamānī (d. 106/723), 266, 297
teacher (*mu'allim*)
temporal (*zamānī*), 136, 295, 369, 422
tenderness (*shafaqat, riqqat*), 60, 72, 88, 134, 144, 204, 267; of Muḥammad, 45, 241, 328, 375, 445; of parents, 82, 83, 244, 310, 353, 375, 391, 399, 416, 445, 474
tenebrous (*ẓulmānī*), 136, 261, 314
terrestrial (*suflī*), 84, 314. *See also* celestial
text, firm (*muḥkam*), 128, 199, 213, 219, 259, 267, 270, 304, 353, 430
thanks (*shukr*), 49, 88, 94, 105, 118, 141, 194, 204, 254, 259, 290, 298, 309, 341, 343, 344, 365, 368, 398, 437, 489. *See also* gratitude
thirst (*'atash, tashnagī*)
thought (*andīsha, fikr, khāṭir, ẓann*), 14, 22, 26, 33, 40, 47, 48, 70, 71, 85, 98, 116, 125, 126, 134, 138, 143, 146, 151, 153, 160, 162, 172–73, 212, 246, 262, 279–80, 285, 289, 312, 317, 324, 348, 351, 357, 358, 383, 398, 400, 408, 413, 414, 432, 439, 460, 479, 482; reflective thought (*tafakkur*), 392, 454
threat (*tahdīd, wa'īd*), 16, 80, 110, 130, 187, 245, 288, 307, 318, 369, 413, 419, 424, 425
threshold (*dargāh*)
Throne (*'arsh*), and Footstool, 3, 15, 24, 36, 47, 61, 74, 76, 93, 117, 144, 155, 170, 181, 192, 204, 209, 231, 234, 268, 270, 294, 298, 304, 305, 315, 356, 396, 397, 403, 411, 422, 425, 427, 451, 475, 475,

484; throne (*takht*), 6, 13, 16, 46, 65, 66, 68, 88, passim
Tigris, 283, 336
Tihama, 188
Tilimsānī, ʿAfīf al-Dīn (d. 690/1291), liii
tipsiness (*khumār*), 13, 99, 100, 154, 418; of eyes, 26, 43, 234
Tirmidhī (d. 279/892), lvi; notes, passim
Tirmidhī, Muḥammad ibn ʿAlī (al-Ḥakīm, d. ca. 300/912), 303, 472
togetherness (*jamʿ*, *jamʿiyyat*), 70, 74, 84, 150, 324, 432, 435
toleration (*taḥammul*), 127, 241, 265, 418
tongue (*zabān*, *lisān*), 395; of the state, 4, 68, 71, 105, 166, 203, 239, 319, 326, 359, 437, 477
Torah, 15, 51, 117, 193, 247, 309, 348, 417, 496n27, 499n94, 517n643
trace (*athar*)
tradition (*athar*), 390, 450
tranquility (*sakīna*), 69, 132, 195, 372
transaction (*muʿāmalat*), 157, 205, 219, 232, 284, 421, 446
transcendence (*taʿālī*), 151, 231, 264, 403, 444, 468
transmission (*naql*), xviii, xlii, lxi; and intellectual, 33
trap (*dām*)
traveling (*rawish*, *sayr*, *sulūk*), xxix, 50, 54, 57, 63, 80, 83, 118, 125, 130, 133, 135, 137, 157, 167, 175, 183, 189, 209, 213, 228, 231, 247, 257–258, 262, 264, 266, 281, 284, 361, 372, 383, 386, 391, 394, 395, 400, 403, 428, 442, 452, 471, 494–95; of Adam, 118, 158, 412, 494–95
treasure (*ganj*, *khizāna*)
tree (*shajara*, *dirakht*), 88–90, 131–32, 180, 185–86
tremendousness (*ʿaẓamat*), God's, 19, 33, 41, 44, 52, 54–55, 72, 238–40, 277, 301, 318, 332, 403, 427, 484; human, 120, 246, 375–76, 441, 457; of Muḥammad, 41, 189, 194, 200, 361, 373; of the Throne, 170, 181, 231, 294, 304, 356
tresses (*zulf*). *See* locks
trial (*balāʾ*), lxvi, 14, 28, 41–42, 76, 80, 83, 95, 99, 104, 106, 108–10, 115, 118, 125–27, 137, 150, 166, 169, 178, 182, 183, 215, 218, 223, 235, 244–46, 253–53, 277, 288, 290, 312–13, 331, 339–42, 350–51, 354, 365, 370, 372, 427–28, 448–49, 470, 486, 491
tribulation (*miḥnat*), 66, 154, 170, 228, 275, 341, 344, 382, 470–71; and blessing, 41, 80, 296, 340, 368, 491
trickery (*ḥīlat*), 20, 21, 108, 115, 157
Trumpet (*ṣūr*), 5, 55, 125, 231, 376, 493
trust (*tawakkul*), 20, 48, 78–79, 89, 272, 290, 357–59, 385, 399, 407, 413, 512n503, 530n1021; trustee (*wakīl*), 4, 153, 352, 357; the Trust (*amānat*), 22, 85–86, 142, 156–57, 181, 218–19, 251, 286, 300–3, 386, 389, 441, 468, 491–92; trustworthy (*amīn*), 189, 217, 300, 334; (= Gabriel), 123, 143, 189, 197, 325, 334, 442; (= Muḥammad), 209, 270, 462
truth (*ḥaqq*, *rāstī*), 78, 80, 143, 303, 312, 338, 355, 382, 390, 423, 441, 460, 479, 483 (*see also* verification); truth-confirming (*muṣaddiq*), 19–20
truthfulness (*ṣidq*), 10, 15, 18–20, 30, 48, 53, 87, 93, 117, 120, 122, 130, 150, 155, 158, 194, 215, 226, 227, 245, 247, 250, 270, 388, 409, 410, 427, 453, 455, 462, 481, 483; foot of, 130, 263; seat of, 83, 144, 147, 148, 262, 263, 276, 351, 419, 446, 470; tongue of, 195, 432; truthful (*ṣādiq*), 14, 16, 19, 81, 91, 99, 100, 105, 110, 125, 131, 162, 170, 182, 209, 212, 231, 283, 332, 352, 365, 460, 484, 489; lover, 41, 314, 353, 391, 487–88, 400; sincerely truthful (*ṣiddīq*), 25, 41, 48, 55, 63, 82, 92, 96, 109, 124, 131, 139, 149, 152, 169, 194, 202, 205–6, 262, 298, 355, 357, 366, 384, 387, 406, 409, 416, 427, 446, 449–50, 455, 456, 460–61
Ṭūbā, 61
Tubbaʿ, 346, 413
tumult (*shūr*, *ghawghā*)
turbat, 131
Turk, xiii, xxii, 94, 312, 408, 425; Turkistan, 392, 429
turmoil (*āshūb*, *shūr*)
turning away (*iʿrāḍ*), and turning toward (*iqbāl*)
Ṭūsī, Qāḍī Ḥassān (Abū Badr ibn Kāmil, b. ca. 460/1068), xxvi

Ubayy ibn Kaʿb (d. ca. 30/649), 31, 509n409
ʿubūdiyya, 530n1021

ugliness (*sū'*, *zishtī*, *qubḥ*), 104, 119, 138, 145, 225, 359, 391, 446, 493; ugly deeds (*sayy-i'āt*), 54, 222, 244, 288, 307; ugly-doing (*isā'at*), 256, 290, 294, 309, 410. *See also* beauty, beautiful deeds

Uhud, 42, 69, 93, 238, 339, 435, 516n598, 525n873, 530n1030, 536n1206, 536n1208

'ulamā', xv

'Ulayya, 498n78

ulfat, 130

'Umar (ibn al-Khaṭṭāb, d. 23/644), 23, 124, 203, 224, 227, 238, 326, 380–82, 410, 422, 453, 483, 504n262, 508n387, 518n671

'Umar ibn 'Abd al-'Azīz (d. 101/720), 46, 456, 511n454

Umm 'Amr, 15

Umm Ḥakīm bint Yaḥyā (early 2nd/8th c.), 514n540

Umm Hānī (Fākhita bint Abī Ṭālib, d. after 40/661), 360, 397, 531n1053

Umm Rūmān (d. 6/628), 461

Umm Salama (d. 64/683), 255

unaware (*bī-khabar*)

unbelief (*kufr*), 55, 57, 62, 76, 118, 159, 174, 186, 196, 200, 201, 225, 233, 263, 276, 269, 284, 296, 304–5, 316, 330, 361, 375, 378, 388, 390, 392, 404, 406, 423, 452, 488, 491; and Islam, 187, 272, 448, 466

understanding (*fahm*), 23, 38, 72, 98, 126, 130, 137, 140, 141, 147, 207, 217, 237, 307, 343, 395, 404, 411, 451, 452

ungodly (*fāsiq*), 38, 41, 162, 208, 220, 222, 351, 375, 454

union (*wiṣāl*). *See* separation

unique (*aḥad*), 316, 381, 394

unity (*aḥadiyyat*, *waḥdāniyyat*), 4–5, 10, 20, 33, 38, 56, 64, 74, 87, 94, 130, 277, 407, 409, 420, 443, 475, 501n167. *See also tawḥīd*

universe (*'ālam*, *gītī*), xlviii-xlix, 47, 142, 216, 287, 375, 378, 390, 408, 420, 432, 467, 493. *See also* world

unmediated (*bī-wāsiṭa*), speech, 100, 306, 425. *See* intermediary

unneediness (*ghinā*, *bī-niyāzī*), divine, 9, 11, 13, 16, 43, 54, 82, 99, 194, 217, 259, 274, 291, 308, 315–16, 323, 407, 438, 449–51, 465, 470; and need/poverty, 11, 124, 166, 216, 280–82, 287, 339, 390, 398, 467; fire/ocean/wind of, 22, 34, 36, 39, 64, 86, 125, 139, 258; world of, 54, 76

unqualified (*bī-kayfiyyat*), 366; love, 23, 60, 103, 116, 228, 407, 469

unreal (*bāṭil*). *See* real

unseen (*ghayb*), xlviii, lxiii, 6, 22, 316–18, 440–42; curtain of, 22, 154, 174, 199, 333–34, 343, 356; pure, 47, 195, 197, 217, 232, 262, 344, 392; secrets of, 33, 35, 108, 123, 188, 316, 324, 333, 335, 343, 481, 493; world of, 56, 65, 70, 71, 100, 133, 217, 249, 317, 483

unsettledness (*bī-qarārī*)

'Unṣurī (d. 431/1040), 498n82

unveiling (*kashf*, *mukāshafa*), 8, 10, 51, 69, 152, 153, 165, 218, 250, 276, 289, 301, 357, 416, 423, 458, 466, 474, 478, 484; and contemplation, lx-lxi, 53, 84, 132, 162, 277

unworthy (*nā-ahl*)

upright (*rāst*)

upstirring (*nashr*), 334, 375

Uqayshir al-Asadī, al- (1st/7th c.), 499n103

'Uqba (ibn Abī Mu'ayṭ, d. 2/624), 410

Usayd ibn Ḥuḍayr (d. 20/640), 414

ustādh, xxx

uṣūl, xlviii

'Utba (ibn Rabī'a, d. 2/624), 410

'Utba Ghulām (late 2nd/8th c.), 435, 533n1141

'Uthmān (ibn 'Affān, d. 35/656), 410, 462, 483

'Uthmān ibn Abī Shayba (d. 239/853), 363

utmost (*ghāyat*)

Uways Qaranī (d. 37/657), 442, 536n1224

'Uzza, 380, 462

vat (*khum*), 37, 41, 99, 111, 201

veil (*ḥijāb*), 3, 5, 6, 18, 52–53, 56, 63, 65, 67, 85, 96, 101, 113, 129, 132, 147, 148, 154, 161, 166, 180, 183, 215, 222, 224–25, 258, 291, 257, 318, 337, 349, 359, 374, 379, 397, 412, 419, 428, 440, 451, 460, 466, 482; of exaltedness, 133, 403, 404, 418. *See also* curtain

veneration (*ḥurmat*, *ijlāl*, *ta'ẓīm*), 27, 52, 53, 104, 330, 335, 349, 371

vengeance (*intiqām*), 138, 212, 377, 405, 409, 433

Venus, 198

verification (*taḥqīq*), 146, 324, 325, 329, 333; verified truth, 4, 10, 16, 50, 63, 90, 112, 122, 128, 136, 146, 210, 284, 286, 152, 157, 219, 314

vicegerency (*khilāfat*), xlix, 14, 34, 46, 47,

65–66, 86, 103, 120, 172, 184, 185, 191, 196, 217, 236, 249, 253, 272, 283, 287, 319–23, 378, 485
victory (*ẓafar*)
vile (*khabīth, la ʾīm*)
virginity (*bakārat*), 333; veiled virgin (*mukhaddara*), 14, 61, 148, 325, 334, 401, 479
vision (*ru ʾya, dīdār*), 54, 77, 285, 329, 339; of God, 17–19, 54, 74, 89, 101, 132, 195, 277–78, 299, 306, 330, 337, 340, 353, 364, 366, 373, 404, 446, 447, 493 (*see also* Moses). face-to-face vision (*ʿiyān*), 318, 330, 379

Wahab (Wahb) ibn Munabbih (d. ca. 112/730), 91, 151, 309, 440, 525n895, 525n898
waḥdat al-wujūd, liii
Waḥshī ibn Ḥarb (d. ca. 45/665), 525n873
waʿiẓ, xxiii
wakefulness (*bīdārī*)
walā ʾ, 183
Wāmiq, 30, 100
want (*khwāst, ṭamaʿ*)
waqt, xxx
war (*jang, ḥarb*)
waraʿ, xvii
warning (*nadhīr, waʿīd*), 16, 181, 189, 194, 199, 269, 288, 406, 419, 424, 425
warrior (*ghāzī*)
Wāsiṭī, Abū Bakr (d. ca. 320/932), xxxvii, 399, 416, 498n81, 508n369, 524n847
watad, 536n1229
watcher (*raqīb*), 26, 41, 47, 345, 419, 454; (self-) watchfulness (*murāqabat*), 26, 53, 84, 148–49, 201, 216, 297–98, 334
watchword (*shiʿār*), 90, 367, 427, 454
wayfarer (*sālik*), 53, 91, 93, 96, 99, 106, 133, 201, 224, 243, 247, 263, 314, 335, 340, 363, 462, 468
waystation (*manzil*), 61, 84, 88, 98, 130, 144, 164, 191, 209, 219, 224, 276–77, 290, 296, 307, 337, 363, 441
we-ness (*naḥniyyat*), 13, 144, 232
weakness (*ḍaʿf*)
wealth (*ghinā ʾ, tawāngarī*)
welcome (*iqbāl, istiqbāl*), 13, 76, 81, 90, 107, 191, 284, 337, 340, 364, 410, 414, 424, 427, 431, 442, 446, 447, 469
well-being (*ʿāfiyat, salāmat*), 16, 44, 108, 141, 341, 480
wergild (*diya*), 172, 206, 260, 340
wheat (the forbidden fruit; *gandum, ḥinṭa*), 27, 65–66, 93, 95, 98, 104, 110, 112, 117, 121, 122, 128, 131, 137, 141–43, 150–51, 156–57, 175, 183, 186, 204, 214, 229, 233, 249, 296, 362, 397, 448, 494–95
wherewithal (*sarmāya*), 37, 40, 41, 48, 52, 54, 84, 125, 131, 157, 173, 174–76, 217, 219, 225, 232–33, 236, 266, 267, 284, 285, 287, 314, 322, 333, 337, 342, 362, 373, 385, 396–97, 402, 423, 424, 451, 466–67, 476, 483, 488, 493
whispering, secret (*rāz*)
whole (*kull*), and part (*juz ʾ*), 255, 325, 355
wholesomeness (*ṣalāḥ*), xxiii, xxxviii, 38, 135, 144, 195, 256, 279, 281, 304, 330, 331, 333, 442, 480; and corrupt, 222, 321, 337, 361; wholesome deeds (*ṣāliḥāt*), 137, 145, 287, 312, 319, 323, 382
why, without (*bī-chūn, bī-chagūna*), 126, 343
will (*mashī ʾat*), 99; causeless, 176, 185, 186, 376; and power, 287
wine (*khamr, sharāb*), 36–37, 283; of love, 20, 26, 97, 111, 130, 134, 215, 477, 485
wisdom (*ḥikmat*), divine, 4–5, 47, 52, 135, 146, 147, 159, 181, 234, 299, 315–16, 319, 337, 377, 392, 411, 429, 432, 471; human, 33, 60, 133–34, 184, 190, 225, 298, 349, 413, 474; the wisdom in, 45, 85, 101, 119, 135, 151, 161, 165, 166, 175, 189, 198, 237, 249, 251–53, 255–57, 291–92, 296, 298, 299, 302, 321, 333, 355, 361, 370, 402, 450, 468, 488, 494
wishes, wishing (*amal, umniyya, ārzū*)
with-ness (*maʿiyyat*), 267–68
withholding (*manʿ*)
witness (*shāhid*), 124, 182, 336, 339, 346, 432; witnessing (*shuhūd*), 10, 26, 48, 49, 123, 176, 177, 231, 276, 278, 286, 339, 399; bearing/giving witness (*shahādat, guwāhī*), 15, 27, 132, 135, 298, 346, 369, 382, 383, 388, 409, 413, 422–23, 490; marks bearing witness (*shawāhid*), 19, 240, 268, 354; object of witnessing (*mashhūd*), 4, 26, 446; place of witnessing (*mashhad*), 145, 269, 446; World of Witnessing (*ʿālam-i shahādat*), 249

witr, 160
woman (*zan*, *nisā ʾ*), 42, 88, 188, 225, 247, 301, 310–12, 327, 333, 347, 420, 436, 471, 479, 480, 482
word (*kalima*, *guftār*)
work (*kār*)
world (*ʿālam*, *jahān*), 4, 5, 9, 11, 13, 23, 24, 34, 40, 41, 61, 76, 84, 119, 125, 127, 133, 140, 142, 154–55, 176, 186, 189, 193, 194, 199, 216–17, 228, 233, 238, 315, 322, 324, 328, 345–47, 349, 357, 366, 369, 385, 387, 390, 397, 409, 414, 425, 427, 430, 440, 452, 455–56, 492; eighteen thousand, 118, 392, 406; two (*kawnayn*, *ʿālamayn*), 8–10, 44, 45, 85, 108, 110, 115, 120, 122, 128, 130, 153, 164, 183, 184, 185, 193, 213, 214, 218, 233, 234, 254, 257, 324, 346, 356, 427, 464; chieftain/paragon of, 69, 237, 246, 327, 388, 392, 414, 417; this world (*dunyā*, *īn ʿālam*), 15, 39, 41, 42, 55, 125, 151, 152, 162, 165, 175, 191, 195, 204, 213, 219, 221, 224, 225, 230, 235, 236, 241, 248, 249, 256–58, 265, 268, 284, 287, 291, 293, 296, 299, 304, 307, 318, 325, 341, 356, 360, 373, 382, 389, 409, 415, 435, 452, 453, 457, 459–60, 469, 479, 481, 482, 485, 486, 494–95; and/or the next world (*ākhirat*)/that world (*ān ʿālam*), 18, 56, 66, 97, 114–15, 130, 132, 143, 146, 150, 196, 236, 245–47, 255, 256, 276, 281, 331, 323, 350, 411, 412, 415, 424–25, 428–29, 433, 439, 445–46, 466, 473–76, 487. *See also* afterworld
worship (*ʿibādat*, *parastish*), 8, 12, 22, 30, 41, 64, 116–18, 131, 149, 155, 167, 187, 211, 215, 222, 237, 243, 257, 258, 268, 270, 294, 298–99, 302, 330, 335, 338, 341, 350–51, 353, 369–71, 373, 376–77, 390, 392, 411, 416, 421–22, 428, 429, 445, 467, 477, 480, 488; by angels, 39, 58, 59, 98, 170, 176–77, 183, 233, 238, 253, 322, 397, 423–24, 466, 492; by Iblis, 64, 113, 174, 229, 363, 383, 395; object of worship (*maʿbūd*), 4, 14, 48–50, 108, 179, 282, 339, 381, 434
worth (*qadr*, *qīmat*)
wounded (*khasta*, *zakhm*)
wrath (*ghaḍab*), 75, 272, 313, 337, 355, 364, 483; God's, 30, 177, 195, 205, 235, 273, 296, 306; and mercy, 181–82, 400, 451, 489; and appetite, 133–34
wretchedness (*shaqāwat*), 68, 108, 117, 151, 161, 199, 206, 221, 350. *See also* felicity
wrongdoing (*ẓulm*), 22, 77, 199, 207, 223, 288, 292, 302, 313–14, 334, 359, 446, 454, 479; great wrongdoing (*ẓalūmī*), and deep ignorance, 13, 97, 123, 131, 142, 157, 204, 216, 219, 227, 229, 233, 237, 268, 286, 300–2, 407, 422, 441, 443, 475
Wuhayb ibn al-Ward (d. ca. 153/770), 537n1253
wujūd, xlviii-li, 366, 532n1111; *wajd*, 366; *wājid*, xlviii; *mawjūd*, xlviii, 366

Yaḥyā ibn Sallām (d. 200/815), 326
Yām, 519n685
Yāqūt Ḥamawī (d. 626/1229), xiii
Yāsīn, 478; 513n517
Yazdān, 409
Yazīd ibn al-Ṭathariyya (d. 126/744), 515n574
yearning (*shawq*), lxi, 5, 8, 15–16, 19, 37, 47, 56, 106, 236, 242, 253, 256, 276, 283, 289, 307, 332–33, 396, 433, 454, 458, 462, 480; God's, 15, 443, 536n1225
Yemen, 212, 442; Yemen Pillar, 88

Zabāniya (angels of hell), 231, 248, 448
Zachariah, 43, 83, 106, 132, 139, 188, 341, 371, 427, 456
Zamzam, 73–74, 88, 130, 131
Zandakhānī, Fāṭima bint al-Ḥasan (d. 533/1138), xx
Zandakhānī, Muḥammad (Abū Bakr ibn al-Ḥasan, d. 549/1154), xx
Zanjānī, Saʿd ibn ʿAlī al- (d. 471/1078), xvi
Zaqqūm, 265
Zayd (ibn Ḥāritha, d. 8/629), 326–27, 526n923
Zayd and ʿAmr (i.e., this person and that), 15, 431, 472
Zayd ibn al-Khaṭṭāb (d. 12/632), 238
Zayd ibn Thābit (d. ca. 40/660), 371, 456
Zaynab (bint Jaḥsh, d. 21/641), 326, 330
Zoroaster, 471; Zoroastrianism, lxvi
Ẓufar ibn al-Ḥārith (al-Kilābī, d. ca. 75/695), 532n1091
zuhd, xxvi, lxxn25
Zulaykhā, 246, 252–53, 351, 367, 379, 446, 448–49, 489, 520n723